Visit classzone.com and get connected

MW00676549

Online resources for students and parents

ClassZone resources are linked together and provide instruction, practice, and learning support.

eEdition Plus ONLINE

This interactive version of the text encourages students to explore mathematics.

eWorkbook Plus ONLINE

Interactive practice, correlated to the text, provides support for key concepts and skills.

eTutorial Plus ONLINE

This interactive tutorial reinforces key skills and helps students prepare for tests.

Chapter-Based Support

Examples, state test practice, quizzes, vocabulary support, and activities help students succeed.

McDougal Littell

INDIANA EDITION

McDougal Littell Middle School

COURSE 3

Math

$V = Bh$

$3n + 11 = -7$

Larson Boswell Kanold Stiff

McDougal Littell
A HOUGHTON MIFFLIN COMPANY
Evanston, Illinois • Boston • Dallas

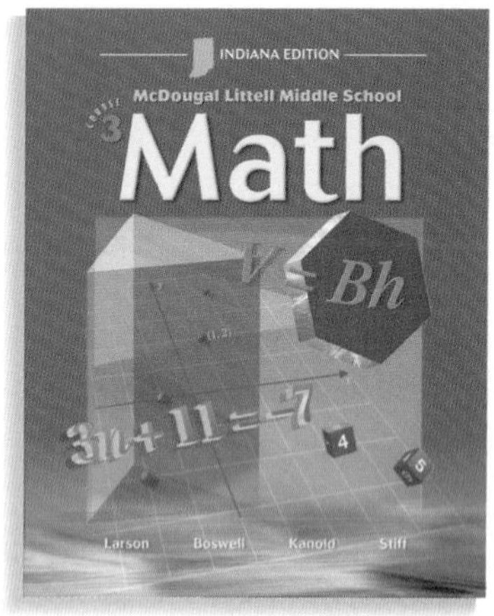

About Middle School Math: Course 3

McDougal Littell Middle School Math, Indiana Edition will help you be successful in this course. The clearly written lessons with frequent step-by-step examples make even difficult math concepts and methods easier to understand. The number and variety of problems, ranging from basic to challenging, give you the practice you need to develop your math skills. This book will also help you develop your notetaking and problem-solving skills. Look for notetaking strategies and Help Notes that support problem solving, vocabulary, reading, homework, technology, and review. Enjoy the Brain Games — they will challenge your thinking skills!

In writing this Indiana Edition, the authors paid special attention to the Indiana Academic Standards for mathematics. To help you check your progress in learning this Indiana content, there are margin notes indicating the standards you will study.

ISBN: 0-618-29144-X 23456789–DWO–08 07 06 05 04

Internet Web Site: http://www.classzone.com

ABOUT THE AUTHORS

Ron Larson

Ron Larson is a professor of mathematics at Penn State University at Erie, where he has taught since receiving his Ph.D. in mathematics from the University of Colorado. Dr. Larson is well known as the author of a comprehensive program for mathematics that spans middle school, high school, and college courses. Dr. Larson's numerous professional activities keep him in constant touch with the needs of teachers and supervisors. He closely follows developments in mathematics standards and assessment.

Laurie Boswell

Laurie Boswell is the mathematics department chair at Profile Junior-Senior High School in Bethlehem, New Hampshire. A recipient of the Presidential Award for Excellence in Mathematics Teaching, she has also been a Tandy Technology Scholar. She serves on the National Council of Teachers of Mathematics Board of Directors. She speaks frequently on topics related to instructional strategies and course content.

Timothy Kanold

Timothy Kanold is the superintendent of Adlai E. Stevenson High School District 125, where he served as a teacher and the Director of Mathematics for 16 years. He recently received his Ph.D. from Loyola University Chicago. Dr. Kanold is a recipient of the Presidential Award for Excellence in Mathematics and Science Teaching and served on The Academy Services Committee for NCTM. He is a frequent speaker at mathematics meetings where he shares his in-depth knowledge of mathematics teaching and curriculum.

Lee Stiff

Lee Stiff is a professor of mathematics education in the College of Education of North Carolina State University at Raleigh. His extensive experience in mathematics education includes teaching at the middle school and high school levels. He has received the W. W. Rankin Award for Excellence in Mathematics Education, and was Fulbright Scholar to the Department of Mathematics of the University of Ghana. He served as President of the National Council of Teachers of Mathematics (2000–2002).

Advisers and Reviewers

Curriculum Advisers and Reviewers

Donna Foley
Curriculum Specialist for Math
Chelmsford Middle School
Chelmsford, MA

Wendy Loeb
Mathematics Teacher
Twin Groves Junior High School
Buffalo Grove, IL

Barbara Nunn
Secondary Mathematics Specialist
Broward County Schools
Fort Lauderdale, FL

Tom Scott
Resource Teacher
Duval County Public Schools
Jacksonville, FL

Teacher Panels

Florida Panel

Kathy Adams
Mathematics Teacher
Allapattah Middle School
Miami, FL

Sue Carrico-Beddow
Mathematics Teacher
Bayonet Point Middle School
New Port Richey, FL

Melissa Grabowski
Mathematics Teacher
Stone Middle School
Melbourne, FL

Micki Hawn
Mathematics Teacher
Pompano Beach Middle School
Pompano Beach, FL

Pat Powell
Mathematics Department Chair
Stewart Middle School
Tampa, FL

Barbara Schober
Mathematics Department Chair
Okeeheelee Middle School
West Palm Beach, FL

Laurie St. Julien
Mathematics Teacher
Oak Grove Middle School
Clearwater, FL

Kansas and Missouri Panel

Linda Cordes
Department Chair
Paul Robeson Middle School
Kansas City, MO

Linda Dodd
Mathematics Department Chair
Argentine Middle School
Kansas City, KS

Melanie Dowell
Mathematics Teacher
Raytown South Middle School
Raytown, MO

Rhonda Foote
Mathematics Department Chair
Maple Park Middle School
North Kansas City, MO

Cas Kyle
District Math Curriculum Coordinator
Richard A. Warren Middle School
Leavenworth, KS

Jan Rase
Mathematics Teacher
Moreland Ridge Middle School
Blue Springs, MO

Dan Schoenemann
Mathematics Teacher
Raytown Middle School
Kansas City, MO

Texas Panel

Judy Carlin
Mathematics Teacher
Brown Middle School
McAllen, TX

Judith Cody
Mathematics Teacher
Deady Middle School
Houston, TX

Lisa Hiracheta
Mathematics Teacher
Irons Junior High School
Lubbock, TX

Kay Neuse
Mathematics Teacher
Wilson Middle School
Plano, TX

Louise Nutzman
Mathematics Teacher
Sugar Land Middle School
Sugar Land, TX

Clarice Orise
Mathematics Teacher
Tafolla Middle School
San Antonio, TX

Wonda Webb
Mathematics Teacher
William H. Atwell Middle School
and Law Academy
Dallas, TX

Karen Young
Mathematics Teacher
Murchison Elementary School
Pflugerville, TX

Field Test Teachers

Kathryn Chamberlain
McCarthy Middle School
Chelmsford, MA

Sheree Daily
Canal Winchester Middle School
Canal Winchester, OH

Deborah Kebe
Canal Winchester Middle School
Canal Winchester, OH

Jill Leone
Twin Groves Junior High School
Buffalo Grove, IL

Wendy Loeb
Twin Groves Junior High School
Buffalo Grove, IL

Melissa McCarty
Canal Winchester Middle School
Canal Winchester, OH

Deb Mueth
St. Aloysius School
Springfield, IL

Gail Sigmund
Charles A. Mooney Middle School
Cleveland, OH

Teacher Reviewers

Susanne Artiñano
Bryn Mawr School
Baltimore, MD

Lisa Barnes
Bishop Spaugh Academy
Charlotte, NC

Beth Bryan
Sequoyah Middle School
Oklahoma City, OK

Jennifer Clark
Mayfield Middle School
Oklahoma City, OK

Lois Cole
Pickering Middle School
Lynn, MA

Louis Corbosiero
Pollard Middle School
Needham, MA

James Cussen
Candlewood Middle School
Dix Hills, NY

Kristen Dailey
Boardman Center Middle School
Boardman, OH

Shannon Galamore
Clay-Chalkville Middle School
Pinson, AL

Tricia Highland
Moon Area Middle School
Moon Township, PA

Myrna McNaboe
Immaculate Conception
East Aurora, NY

Angela Richardson
Sedgefield Middle School
Charlotte, NC

James Richardson
Booker T. Washington Middle School
Mobile, AL

Dianne Walker
Traverse City Central High School
Traverse City, MI

Stacey Wood
Cochrane Middle School
Charlotte, NC

CHAPTER 1

Variables and Equations

Exercise 29, p. 31

Internet Resources

- eEdition Plus Online
- eWorkbook Plus Online
- eTutorial Plus Online
- State Test Practice
- More Examples

Pre-Course Assessment

Integer Operations

Notetaking and Student Help

- eEdition Plus Online
- eWorkbook Plus Online
- eTutorial Plus Online
- State Test Practice
- More Examples

EXPLORING MATH IN SCIENCE

Exercise 44, p. 89

Solving Equations and Inequalities

Example 3, p. 110

Notetaking and Student Help

- eEdition Plus Online
- eWorkbook Plus Online
- eTutorial Plus Online
- State Test Practice
- More Examples

Unit 1 Assessment

Factors, Fractions, and Exponents

Notetaking and Student Help

- eEdition Plus Online
- eWorkbook Plus Online
- eTutorial Plus Online
- State Test Practice
- More Examples

Exercise 10, p. 194

Rational Number Operations

Assessment

Notetaking and Student Help

- eEdition Plus Online
- eWorkbook Plus Online
- eTutorial Plus Online
- State Test Practice
- More Examples

Exercise 20, p. 226

Multi-Step Equations and Inequalities

Exercise 23, p. 298

Ratio, Proportion, and Percent

Example 1, p. 327

Notetaking and Student Help

- eEdition Plus Online
- eWorkbook Plus Online
- eTutorial Plus Online
- State Test Practice
- More Examples

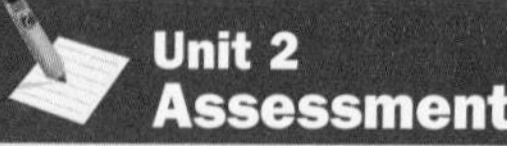

Polygons and Transformations

Notetaking and Student Help

- eEdition Plus Online
- eWorkbook Plus Online
- eTutorial Plus Online
- State Test Practice
- More Examples

Example 1, p. 416

Real Numbers and Right Triangles

Example 5, p. 465

Notetaking and Student Help

- eEdition Plus Online
- eWorkbook Plus Online
- eTutorial Plus Online
- State Test Practice
- More Examples

EXPLORING MATH IN SCIENCE

Earth Science

Measurement, Area, and Volume

Example 1, p. 519

Notetaking and Student Help

- eEdition Plus Online
- eWorkbook Plus Online
- eTutorial Plus Online
- State Test Practice
- More Examples

Unit 3 Assessment

Linear Equations and Graphs

Notetaking and Student Help

Notetaking, 540, 558, 562, 564, 565, 570, 572, 577, 584, 588
Vocabulary, 570, 584
Solving, 542, 550, 557, 582, 583, 584, 585
Review, 571, 577
Watch Out, 541, 558, 571

Sidewalk Scramble, 538
Plot the Picture, 539
Late Night Show, 553

- eEdition Plus Online
- eWorkbook Plus Online
- eTutorial Plus Online
- State Test Practice
- More Examples

Exercise 32, p. 586

Data Analysis and Probability

Example 1, p. 627

Notetaking and Student Help

- eEdition Plus Online
- eWorkbook Plus Online
- eTutorial Plus Online
- State Test Practice
- More Examples

EXPLORING MATH IN SCIENCE

Polynomials and Functions

Notetaking and Student Help

- eEdition Plus Online
- eWorkbook Plus Online
- eTutorial Plus Online
- State Test Practice
- More Examples

Example 3, p. 658

Contents of Student Resources

Help with Taking Notes

One of the most important tools for success in mathematics is organizing what you have learned. Writing down important information in a notebook helps you remember key concepts and skills. You can use your notebook as a reference when you do your homework or when you study for a test.

Taking Notes
Your textbook displays important ideas and definitions on a notebook. You'll want to include this information in your notes.

Notetaking Strategies
You'll find a different notetaking strategy at the beginning of each chapter. Within the chapter, you'll find helpful hints about taking notes.

Notebook Review
Your textbook includes frequent notebook reviews. These reviews help you use your notebook to check your understanding of important skills and concepts.

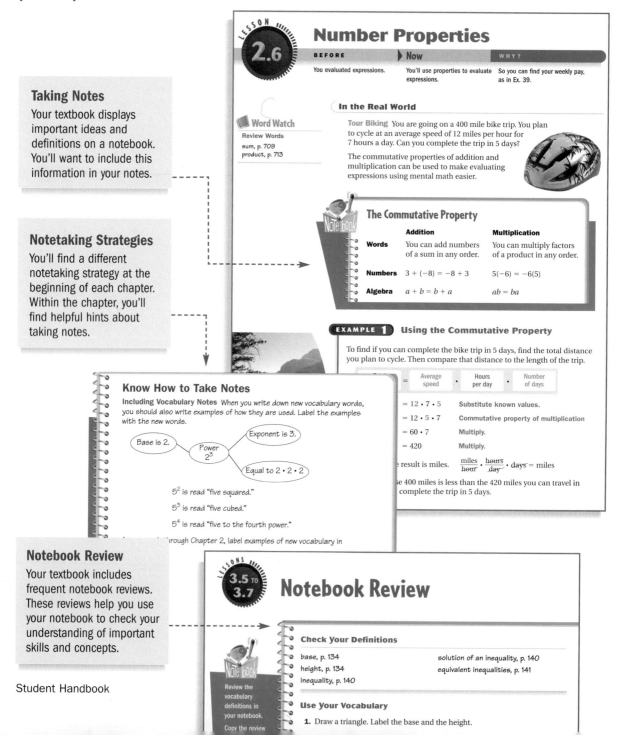

LESSON 2.6 **Number Properties**

BEFORE	Now	WHY?
You evaluated expressions.	You'll use properties to evaluate expressions.	So you can find your weekly pay, as in Ex. 39.

In the Real World

Word Watch
Review Words
sum, p. 709
product, p. 713

Tour Biking You are going on a 400 mile bike trip. You plan to cycle at an average speed of 12 miles per hour for 7 hours a day. Can you complete the trip in 5 days?

The commutative properties of addition and multiplication can be used to make evaluating expressions using mental math easier.

The Commutative Property

	Addition	Multiplication
Words	You can add numbers of a sum in any order.	You can multiply factors of a product in any order.
Numbers	$3 + (-8) = -8 + 3$	$5(-6) = -6(5)$
Algebra	$a + b = b + a$	$ab = ba$

EXAMPLE 1 Using the Commutative Property

To find if you can complete the bike trip in 5 days, find the total distance you plan to cycle. Then compare that distance to the length of the trip.

= Average speed • Hours per day • Number of days

$= 12 \cdot 7 \cdot 5$ Substitute known values.
$= 12 \cdot 5 \cdot 7$ Commutative property of multiplication
$= 60 \cdot 7$ Multiply.
$= 420$ Multiply.

result is miles. $\frac{\text{miles}}{\text{hour}} \cdot \frac{\text{hours}}{\text{day}} \cdot \text{days} = \text{miles}$

e 400 miles is less than the 420 miles you can travel in complete the trip in 5 days.

Know How to Take Notes

Including Vocabulary Notes When you write down new vocabulary words, you should also write examples of how they are used. Label the examples with the new words.

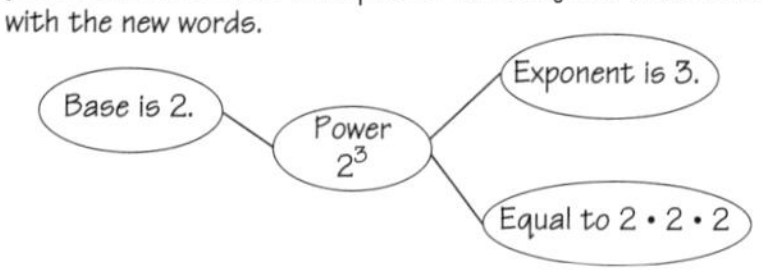

Base is 2. — Power 2^3 — Exponent is 3. — Equal to 2 • 2 • 2

5^2 is read "five squared."

5^3 is read "five cubed."

5^4 is read "five to the fourth power."

...rough Chapter 2, label examples of new vocabulary in

LESSONS 3.5 TO 3.7 **Notebook Review**

Review the vocabulary definitions in your notebook.

Copy the review

Check Your Definitions

base, p. 134
height, p. 134
inequality, p. 140
solution of an inequality, p. 140
equivalent inequalities, p. 141

Use Your Vocabulary

1. Draw a triangle. Label the base and the height.

Help with Learning Mathematics

Your textbook helps you succeed in mathematics. Keep your eye out for notes that help you with reading mathematics, learning vocabulary terms, solving problems, using technology, and doing your homework. Some examples of the types of notes you'll see are shown below.

Help Notes

These notes help you understand and apply what you've learned.

HELP with Solving

Another way to undo operations is to add the opposite to undo addition or subtraction. Then multiply by the reciprocal to undo multiplication or division.

EXAMPLE 2 Solving with a Variable in the Numerator

$\frac{x}{2} - 14 = 8$	Original equation
$+14 \quad +14$	Add 14 to each side to undo subtraction.
$\frac{x}{2} = 22$	Simplify.
$\frac{x}{2} \cdot 2 = 22 \cdot 2$	Multiply each side by 2 to undo division.
$x = 44$	Simplify.

✓ **Check** $\frac{44}{2} - 14 \stackrel{?}{=} 8$ Substitute 44 for x in original equation.

$22 - 14 = 8$ ✓

HELP with Review

Remember that you can solve an equation vertically or horizontally. See p. 110.

EXAMPLE 3 Solving with a Negative Coefficient

$8 = 12 - 2x$	Original equation
$8 - 12 = 12 - 2x - 12$	Subtract 12 from each side to undo addition.
$-4 = -2x$	Simplify.
$\frac{-4}{-2} = \frac{-2x}{-2}$	Divide each side by -2 to undo multiplication.
$2 = x$	Simplify.

$6 = 16 - a$

Watch Out!

These notes help you avoid common errors.

Watch Out!

In part (b) of Example 2, notice that $\frac{40 + 7y}{8y} \neq \frac{47y}{8y}$ because 40 and $7y$ are not like terms. The expression is already in simplest form.

EXAMPLE 2 Simplifying Variable Expressions

Algebra **Simplify the expression.**

a. $\frac{2x}{5} - \frac{x}{6} = \frac{12x}{30} - \frac{5x}{30}$ Rewrite fractions using LCD of 30.

$= \frac{12x - 5x}{30}$ Write difference over LCD.

$= \frac{7x}{30}$ Combine like terms.

b. $\frac{5}{y} + \frac{7}{8} = \left(\frac{5}{y} \cdot \frac{8}{8}\right) + \left(\frac{7}{8} \cdot \frac{y}{y}\right)$ Multiply $\frac{5}{y}$ by $\frac{8}{8}$ and $\frac{7}{8}$ by $\frac{y}{y}$ for LCD of $8y$.

$= \frac{40}{8y} + \frac{7y}{8y}$ Multiply inside parentheses.

$= \frac{40 + 7y}{8y}$ Write sum over LCD.

Help with Homework

These notes tell you which textbook examples may help you with homework exercises, and let you know where to find extra help on the Internet.

HELP with Homework

Example	Exercises
1	12-15, 32
2	16-19, 28-31
3	20-27
4	33-34

Online Resources CLASSZONE.COM
- More Examples
- eTutorial Plus

Practice and Problem Solving

Find the quotient.

12. $\frac{4}{9} \div \frac{4}{7}$ **13.** $-\frac{3}{8} \div \frac{7}{12}$ **14.** $\frac{9}{14} \div \left(-\frac{3}{26}\right)$ **15.** $-\frac{21}{22} \div \frac{-7}{11}$

16. $\frac{8}{11} \div 4$ **17.** $\frac{9}{10} \div (-12)$ **18.** $-\frac{5}{12} \div 10$ **19.** $\frac{63}{8} \div (-9)$

Find the quotient.

20. $5\frac{1}{4} \div 2\frac{1}{3}$ **21.** $7\frac{7}{8} \div \left(-2\frac{1}{4}\right)$ **22.** $12\frac{1}{7} \div 5\frac{5}{6}$ **23.** $-22\frac{2}{3} \div 3\frac{1}{5}$

24. $-9\frac{3}{5} \div (-8)$ **25.** $1\frac{5}{7} \div (-6)$ **26.** $8\frac{4}{13} \div 6\frac{3}{4}$ **27.** $9\frac{9}{14} \div 4\frac{1}{6}$

28. Writing Are the numbers $\frac{1}{9}$ and -9 reciprocals? Explain.

Use mental math to find the quotient.

29. $\frac{1}{2} \div 3$ **30.** $4 \div \frac{1}{2}$ **31.** $1 \div \frac{4}{7}$ **32.** $\frac{2}{3} \div \frac{3}{2}$

33. Dog Food Your dog Bodie eats about $\frac{3}{5}$ of a pound of dog food per day.

Reading Your Textbook

You need special skills to read a math textbook. These skills include *identifying the main idea, learning new vocabulary,* and *focusing on the important concepts* in a lesson. Most important, you need to *be an active reader.* You need to practice and apply the ideas you read about.

Identify the Main Idea

Even before you begin reading a lesson, check to see what the lesson is about. Then you'll know what to focus on in the lesson. You can also assess how well you understand the lesson content when you've finished reading the lesson.

Lesson Opener Look at the lesson opener for information about the main idea of the lesson.

Example Heads Use other clues, such as the heads that appear above examples, to identify the main idea.

Understand the Vocabulary

Reading mathematics involves learning and using new vocabulary terms. Refer to diagrams and worked-out examples to clarify your understanding of new terms. If you forget what a term you've already learned means, look back at previous lessons or use the Glossary, which starts on page 747.

Vocabulary New vocabulary terms are highlighted within a lesson. In addition, the *Word Watch* at the beginning of the lesson lists the important vocabulary terms in the lesson.

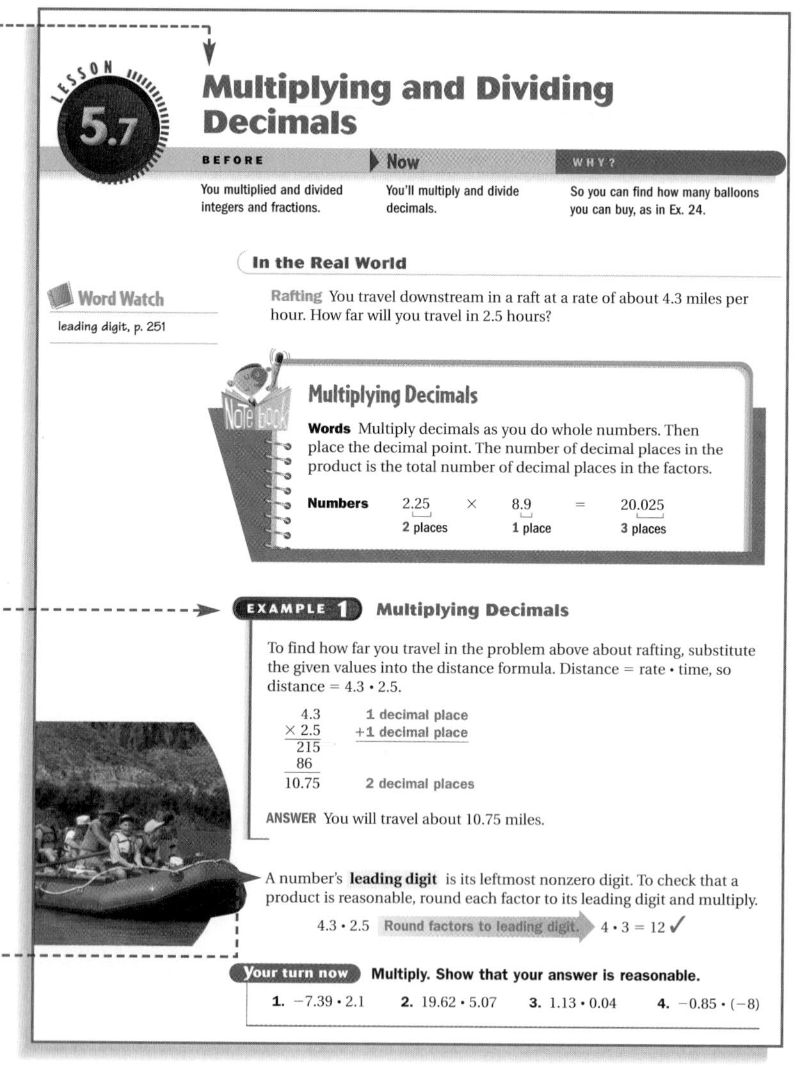

LESSON 5.7

Multiplying and Dividing Decimals

BEFORE	Now	WHY?
You multiplied and divided integers and fractions.	You'll multiply and divide decimals.	So you can find how many balloons you can buy, as in Ex. 24.

Word Watch

leading digit, p. 251

In the Real World

Rafting You travel downstream in a raft at a rate of about 4.3 miles per hour. How far will you travel in 2.5 hours?

Note Book

Multiplying Decimals

Words Multiply decimals as you do whole numbers. Then place the decimal point. The number of decimal places in the product is the total number of decimal places in the factors.

Numbers 2.25 (2 places) × 8.9 (1 place) = 20.025 (3 places)

EXAMPLE 1 **Multiplying Decimals**

To find how far you travel in the problem above about rafting, substitute the given values into the distance formula. Distance = rate • time, so distance = 4.3 • 2.5.

4.3	1 decimal place
× 2.5	+1 decimal place
215	
86	
10.75	2 decimal places

ANSWER You will travel about 10.75 miles.

A number's **leading digit** is its leftmost nonzero digit. To check that a product is reasonable, round each factor to its leading digit and multiply.

4.3 • 2.5 Round factors to leading digit. 4 • 3 = 12 ✓

Your turn now **Multiply. Show that your answer is reasonable.**

1. −7.39 • 2.1 **2.** 19.62 • 5.07 **3.** 1.13 • 0.04 **4.** −0.85 • (−8)

Know What's Important

Focus in on the important information in a lesson. Pay attention to highlighted vocabulary terms and definitions. Be on the lookout for definitions, properties, formulas, and other information displayed on a notebook. Make sure that you understand the worked-out examples.

Notebook Focus in on key ideas that are displayed on a notebook.

Worked-Out Examples Do the worked-out examples to make sure you know how to apply new concepts.

Be an Active Reader

As you read, keep a pencil in your hand and your notebook ready so that you can write down important information, practice new skills, and jot down questions to ask in class.

Your Turn Now Solve the *Your turn now* exercises to check your understanding.

Use Your Notebook As you solve the examples yourself, you may find it helpful to describe the steps you follow. Write down any questions you have so you can ask them in class.

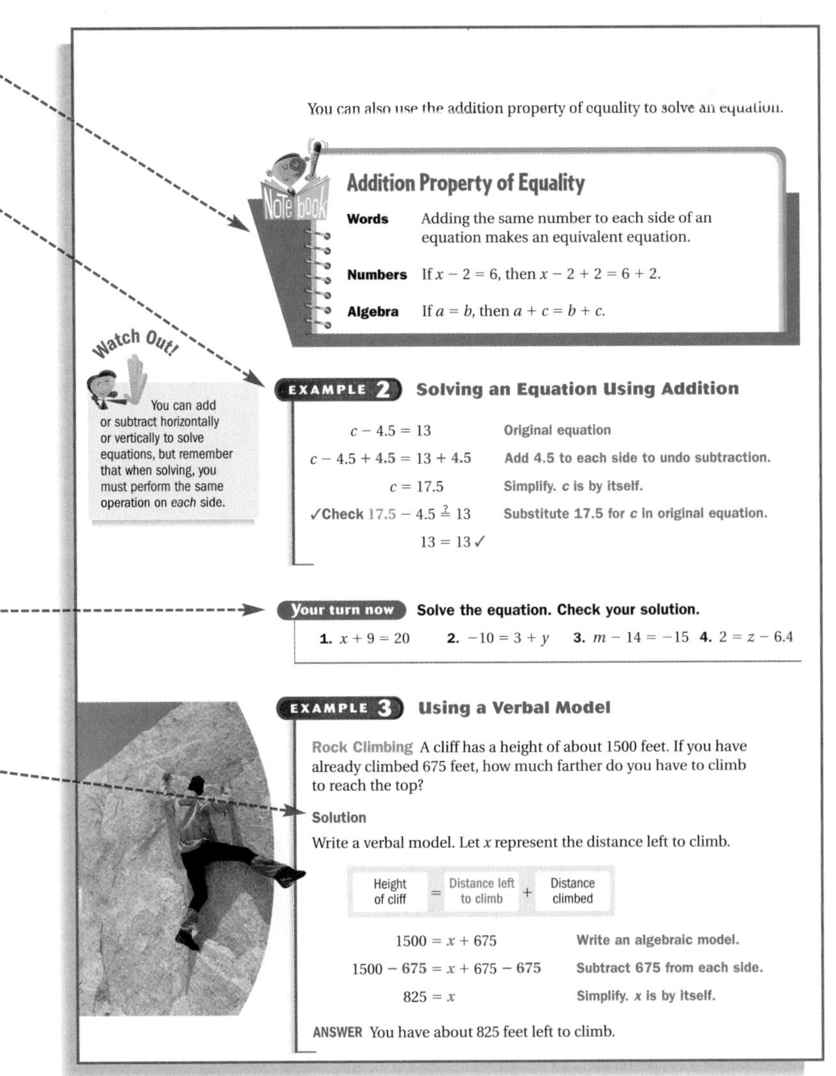

You can also use the addition property of equality to solve an equation.
Notebook
Addition Property of Equality
Words Adding the same number to each side of an equation makes an equivalent equation.
Numbers If x − 2 = 6, then x − 2 + 2 = 6 + 2.
Algebra If a = b, then a + c = b + c.
Watch Out!
You can add or subtract horizontally or vertically to solve equations, but remember that when solving, you must perform the same operation on each side.
EXAMPLE 2 Solving an Equation Using Addition
c − 4.5 = 13 Original equation
c − 4.5 + 4.5 = 13 + 4.5 Add 4.5 to each side to undo subtraction.
c = 17.5 Simplify. c is by itself.
✓Check 17.5 − 4.5 ≟ 13 Substitute 17.5 for c in original equation.
13 = 13 ✓
Your turn now Solve the equation. Check your solution.
1. x + 9 = 20 2. −10 = 3 + y 3. m − 14 = −15 4. 2 = z − 6.4
EXAMPLE 3 Using a Verbal Model
Rock Climbing A cliff has a height of about 1500 feet. If you have already climbed 675 feet, how much farther do you have to climb to reach the top?
Solution
Write a verbal model. Let x represent the distance left to climb.
Height of cliff = Distance left to climb + Distance climbed
1500 = x + 675 Write an algebraic model.
1500 − 675 = x + 675 − 675 Subtract 675 from each side.
825 = x Simplify. x is by itself.
ANSWER You have about 825 feet left to climb.

Reading and Problem Solving

The language in your math textbook is precise. When you do your homework, be sure to read carefully. For example, the direction line below asks you to do three different things for each of the exercises: sketch, measure, and compare.

> Estimation **Sketch a line segment of the given length without using a ruler. Then use a ruler to check your estimate. How close was your estimate?**
>
> **21.** 6.5 cm **22.** 45 mm **23.** 0.01 m **24.** 0.15 m

Reading Word Problems

Before you can solve a word problem, you need to read and understand it. You may find it useful to copy a word problem into your notebook. Then you can highlight important information, cross out unnecessary information, and organize your thinking.

You have a recipe that makes 24 cookies. The ingredients include 2 eggs, 1 cup of sugar, 1.5 cups of flour, ~~1 teaspoon of vanilla, and 1 teaspoon of baking soda~~. What is the greatest number of cookies you can make if you have 12 eggs, 4 cups of sugar, and 9 cups of flour?

	Needed (one batch)	Already have
Number of eggs	2	12
Cups of sugar	1	4
Cups of flour	1.5	9

Make sure that you've solved a word problem completely. For example, to solve the word problem at the right, you need to calculate how many more points you need for Levels 5, 6, and 7. But to answer the question, you must determine how many total points you need.

In a certain video game, when you reach 50 points, you reach Level 2. You need 70 more points to reach Level 3, and then you need 90 more points to reach Level 4. Suppose the pattern continues. How many points do you need to reach Level 7?

Level 5: 110 more, Level 6: 130 more, Level 7: 150 more

Total points:
$50 + 70 + 90 + 110 + 130 + 150 = 600$

Additional Resources in Your Textbook

Your textbook contains many resources that you can use for reference when you are studying or doing your homework.

Skills Review Handbook Use the Skills Review Handbook on pages 704–726 to review material learned in previous courses.

Tables Refer to the tables on pages 740–746 if you need information about mathematical symbols, measures, formulas, and properties.

Glossary Use the Glossary on pages 747–772 to look up the meanings of math vocabulary terms. Each glossary entry also tells where in your book a term is covered in more detail.

Index Use the Index on pages 773–795 as a quick guide for finding out where a particular math topic is covered in the book.

Selected Answers Use the Selected Answers starting on page SA1 to check your work or to see whether you are on the right track in solving a problem.

Textbook Scavenger Hunt

Get some practice using your textbook. Use the additional resources described above to answer each question. Give page numbers to show where you found the answer to the question.

1. What is a biased sample?
2. Tell what each of these symbols means: $\stackrel{?}{=}$, $\sim$, $\pm$.
3. How many square inches are there in one square foot?
4. On what page or pages of the book is the distributive property first discussed?
5. What is the normal body temperature in degrees Fahrenheit? in degrees Celsius?
6. What is a variable?
7. On what page can you review the skill of adding and subtracting decimals?
8. On what page of the book can you find selected answers for Lesson 1.1?
9. What formula can you use to find the volume of a cylinder?

Pre-Course Test

Number Sense and Operations

Place Value and Rounding *(Skills Review, pp. 704–705)*

Write the number in expanded form.

1. 34,777 **2.** 837.4 **3.** 5459 **4.** 1002.003

Round the number to the place value of the red digit.

5. 3465 **6.** 44,656 **7.** 66,789 **8.** 55.677

Operations with Decimals and Fractions *(Skills Review, pp. 707–715)*

Write the mixed number as an improper fraction or the improper fraction as a mixed number.

9. $4\frac{2}{3}$ **10.** $12\frac{1}{2}$ **11.** $\frac{13}{6}$ **12.** $\frac{24}{5}$

Find the sum, difference, product, or quotient. Simplify if possible.

13. $6.77 + 5.66$ **14.** $77.555 - 34.55$ **15.** $\frac{4}{12} - \frac{3}{12}$ **16.** $\frac{4}{5} + \frac{3}{5}$

17. 3.4×45 **18.** $10\frac{2}{3} \times 5\frac{1}{4}$ **19.** $14.49 \div 7$ **20.** $2.1 \div 84$

21. $\frac{3}{4} \times \frac{1}{4}$ **22.** 3.89×16 **23.** $1\frac{2}{3} \times 1\frac{4}{5}$ **24.** $3 \times 4\frac{1}{2}$

Problem Solving *(Skills Review, pp. 712, 717)*

25. The computer club has already raised \$120.95 for new software. A math program costs \$39.50, a game costs \$24.75, and a reading program costs \$66.29. How much more money does the club need to raise to pay for the software?

26. The soccer team had a car wash to raise money. They charged \$3 for each car. If they washed 23 cars, how much money did they earn?

Estimation *(Skills Review, pp. 711, 716)*

Estimate the sum or difference.

27. $666 + 453 + 123$ **28.** $45,768 - 23,409$ **29.** $7666 + 4555 + 994$

Find a low and high estimate for the product or quotient.

30. 54×19 **31.** $788 \div 9$ **32.** 560×236 **33.** $8557 \div 29$

Geometry

Points, Lines, and Planes *(Skills Review, p. 718)*

In Exercises 34–36, use the diagram.

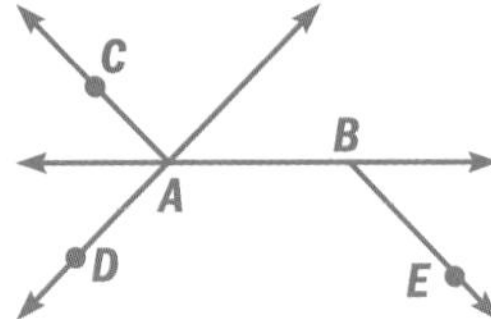

34. Name three points.

35. Name two rays.

36. Name two lines.

Using a Protractor *(Skills Review, p. 721)*

Use a protractor to measure the angle.

37.

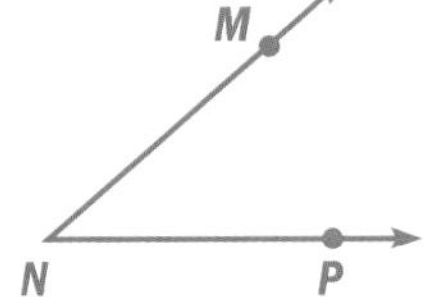

38.

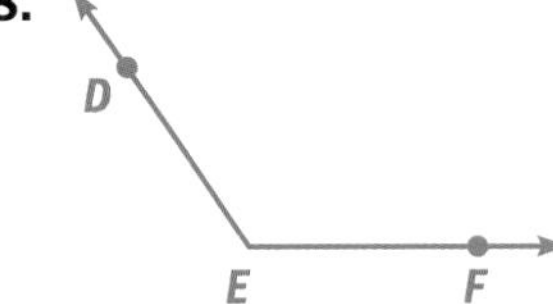

Use a protractor to draw an angle that has the given measure.

39. 125° **40.** 34° **41.** 90°

Data Analysis

Reading Bar Graphs and Line Graphs *(Skills Review, pp. 724–725)*

In Exercises 42 and 43, use the bar graph.

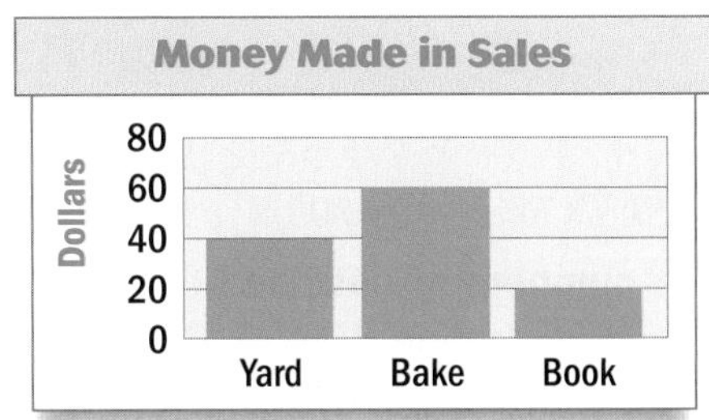

42. Which sale made the least money?

43. How much more money was made from the bake sale than the yard sale?

In Exercises 44 and 45, use the line graph.

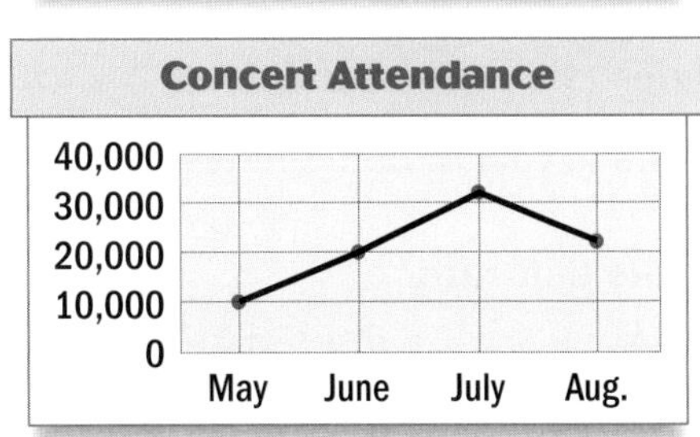

44. Which month had the greatest concert attendance?

45. What was the difference in concert attendance between June and May?

Pre-Course Practice

Number Sense and Operations

Place Value and Rounding *(Skills Review, pp. 704–705)*

Write the number in expanded form.

1. 45,708
2. 4.056
3. 1003.04
4. 405.305

Write the number in standard form.

5. $4 \times 100{,}000 + 7 \times 10 + 8 \times 1 + 8 \times 0.001$
6. $5 \times 100 + 8 \times 1 + 3 \times 0.1 + 4 \times 0.01$

Round the number to the place value of the red digit.

7. 2234
8. 48,139
9. 4.566
10. 33.86
11. 13.444
12. 556.78
13. 73.845
14. 546,888

Divisibility *(Skills Review, p. 706)*

Test the number for divisibility by 2, 3, 4, 5, 6, 8, 9, and 10.

15. 44
16. 88
17. 385
18. 870

Mixed Numbers and Improper Fractions *(Skills Review, p. 707)*

Write the mixed number as an improper fraction.

19. $4\frac{1}{2}$
20. $2\frac{4}{5}$
21. $8\frac{4}{9}$
22. $9\frac{4}{7}$

Write the improper fraction as a mixed number.

23. $\frac{12}{7}$
24. $\frac{18}{4}$
25. $\frac{21}{5}$
26. $\frac{33}{7}$

Ratio and Rate *(Skills Review, p. 708)*

The table shows the numbers of cats and dogs owned by the students in the seventh and eighth grades. Use the table to write the ratio.

27. Cats of 8th graders to cats of 7th graders
28. Dogs of 7th graders to dogs of 8th graders
29. Cats of 7th graders to cats of both grades

	Cats	Dogs
8th Grade	12	14
7th Grade	11	15

Write the rate and the unit rate.

30. \$3.90 for 30 ounces
31. 250 miles in 4 hours
32. \$4.50 for 30 minutes long distance
33. 329 miles on 14 gallons of gas

Operations with Decimals and Fractions *(Skills Review, pp. 709–714)*

Find the sum or difference.

34. $8.4 - 3.3$ **35.** $23.8 + 84.9$ **36.** $38.6 + 4.7$ **37.** $5.44 - 2.33$

38. $4.67 + 3.85$ **39.** $49.55 - 18.23$ **40.** $66.77 + 3.45$ **41.** $34.56 - 30.89$

42. $5.329 + 8.455$ **43.** $14.86 - 6.656$ **44.** $888.66 - 56.88$ **45.** $475.67 + 89.44$

Find the sum or difference.

46. $\frac{1}{7} + \frac{4}{7}$ **47.** $\frac{14}{17} - \frac{11}{17}$ **48.** $\frac{7}{9} - \frac{5}{9}$ **49.** $\frac{9}{13} + \frac{8}{13}$

50. $\frac{5}{12} + \frac{2}{12}$ **51.** $\frac{3}{9} + \frac{4}{9}$ **52.** $\frac{12}{13} - \frac{4}{13}$ **53.** $\frac{5}{8} - \frac{4}{8}$

54. $\frac{1}{4} + \frac{2}{4}$ **55.** $\frac{12}{14} - \frac{9}{14}$ **56.** $\frac{7}{8} - \frac{4}{8}$ **57.** $\frac{5}{11} + \frac{3}{11}$

Find the product. Simplify if possible.

58. $\frac{2}{9} \times \frac{1}{7}$ **59.** $\frac{1}{5} \times \frac{2}{3}$ **60.** $\frac{3}{4} \times \frac{1}{8}$ **61.** $\frac{1}{4} \times \frac{3}{7}$

62. $\frac{1}{4} \times \frac{3}{4}$ **63.** $\frac{4}{5} \times \frac{7}{8}$ **64.** $\frac{1}{8} \times \frac{4}{5}$ **65.** $3 \times 1\frac{1}{5}$

66. $5\frac{1}{2} \times 6$ **67.** $2 \times 3\frac{1}{7}$ **68.** $4\frac{2}{3} \times 1\frac{3}{4}$ **69.** $1\frac{3}{8} \times 4\frac{2}{3}$

Find the product or quotient.

70. 2.3×67 **71.** $3.42 \div 3$ **72.** $367.5 \div 5$ **73.** 0.55×88

74. 7.54×88 **75.** 8.44×77 **76.** $2.934 \div 9$ **77.** $584.85 \div 7$

78. 555×34.3 **79.** 788×66.4 **80.** $0.48 \div 6$ **81.** 45.905×78

82. $16.68 \div 2$ **83.** $12.32 \div 4$ **84.** 345.88×55 **85.** $401.1 \div 7$

Problem Solving *(Skills Review, pp. 712, 717)*

86. A middle school has three grades and 667 students total. The eighth grade has 216 students. The seventh grade has 229 students. How many students are in the sixth grade?

87. Maria bought a hamburger for \$1.59 and juice for \$.68. She paid with a \$5 bill. How much change should Maria receive?

88. Lee spent \$7.89 for a hammer, \$2.26 for nails, and \$3.55 for a stapler. What was the total cost of Lee's purchase?

89. A sweater costs \$28, and a pair of boots costs \$56. What is the total cost of the sweater and the boots?

90. You bought 98 trading cards and gave 45 to your brother. How many cards do you have left?

91. Sue has 12 CDs, and Kate has 28 CDs. How many CDs do Sue and Kate have all together?

92. The recycling committee collected 2575 newspapers and tied them in bundles. Each bundle contained 25 newspapers. How many bundles of newspapers did they make?

93. Your school cafeteria has enough seats for 540 students. Each table seats 12 students. How many tables are in the cafeteria?

94. A youth organization sold 132 books of carnival ride coupons. Each book contained 18 ride coupons. How many ride coupons were sold?

95. Basketball tickets cost \$35 each. The team sold 12,383 tickets to their first game. How much money did the team make for the first game?

Estimation *(Skills Review, pp. 711, 716)*

Estimate the sum or difference.

96. $6845 + 2687$ **97.** $7356 - 4699$ **98.** $8999 + 3456$ **99.** $4567 - 3499$

100. $1867 + 5409$ **101.** $7865 - 5433$ **102.** $6577 - 3444$ **103.** $6999 + 5987$

Find a low and high estimate for the product or quotient.

104. 44×18 **105.** 555×34 **106.** $333 \div 8$ **107.** $6566 \div 8$

108. 434×56 **109.** $344 \div 23$ **110.** $7656 \div 19$ **111.** 808×66

Geometry

Points, Lines, and Planes *(Skills Review, p. 718)*

In Exercises 112–115, use the diagram.

B C A E D

112. Name three points.

113. Name two rays.

114. Give two different names for the line.

115. Name a segment that has D as an endpoint.

Using a Protractor *(Skills Review, p. 721)*

Use a protractor to measure the angle.

116. 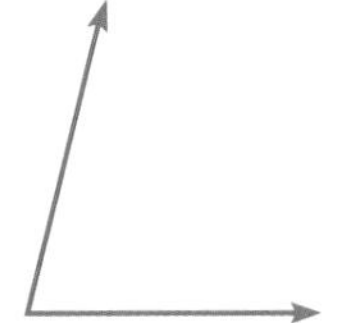

117. 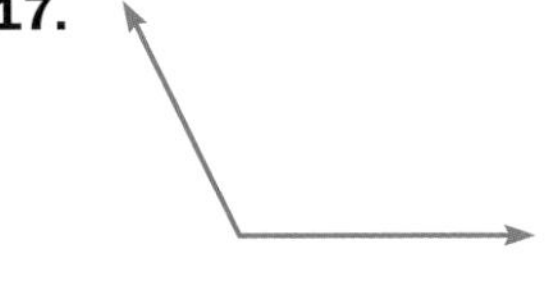

118. 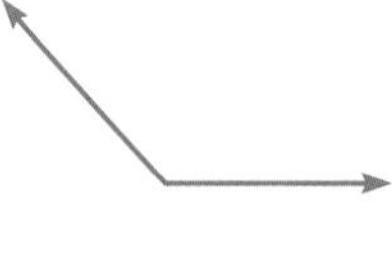

Use a protractor to draw an angle that has the given measure.

119. 56°   **120.** 125°   **121.** 140°   **122.** 15°

Data Analysis

Reading Bar Graphs and Line Graphs *(Skills Review, pp. 724–725)*

In Exercises 123–125, use the line graph. It shows the numbers of books sold on five different days.

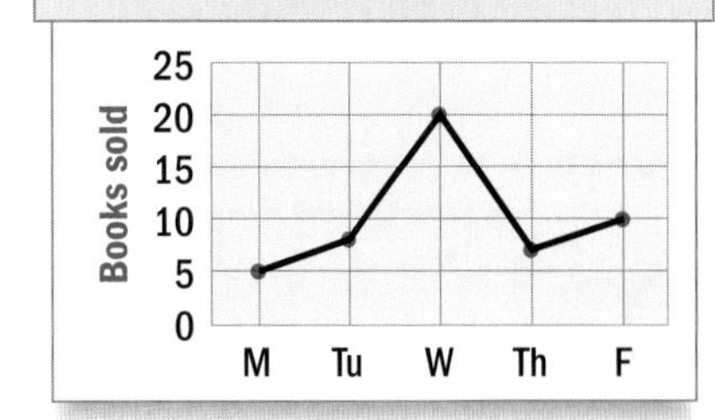

123. On what day were the fewest number of books sold?

124. On what day were 8 books sold?

125. How many more books were sold on Wednesday than on Monday?

In Exercises 126–128, use the bar graph. It shows the numbers of students that participate in school activities.

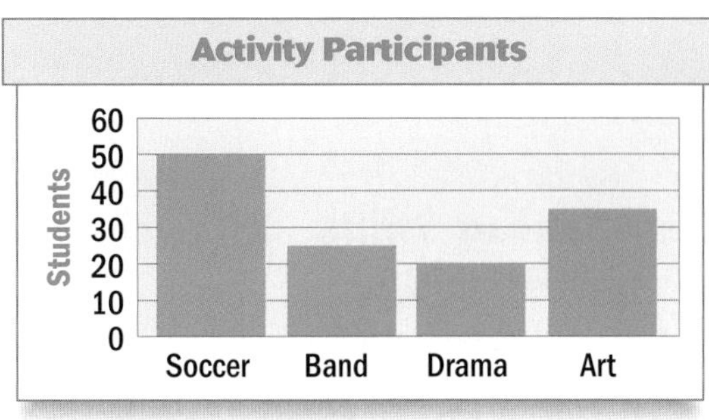

126. How many more students participate in the band than in drama?

127. In what activity do the greatest number of students participate?

128. In what activity do 35 students participate?

Venn Diagrams and Logical Reasoning *(Skills Review, p. 726)*

Draw a Venn diagram of the set described.

129. Of the whole numbers less than 14, set A consists of numbers that are greater than 9, and set B consists of even numbers.

130. Of the whole numbers less than 12, set C consists of multiples of 2, and set D consists of odd numbers.

Content and Assessment

Course Content

The authors have developed a sequence of lessons that include all the concepts and skills you need in this course. What you learn is connected to prior knowledge and to your daily life.

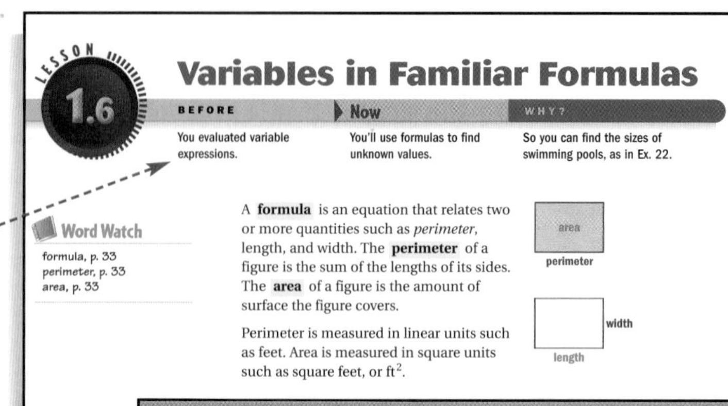

LESSON 1.6

Variables in Familiar Formulas

BEFORE	Now	WHY?
You evaluated variable expressions.	You'll use formulas to find unknown values.	So you can find the sizes of swimming pools, as in Ex. 22.

Word Watch

formula, p. 33
perimeter, p. 33
area, p. 33

A **formula** is an equation that relates two or more quantities such as *perimeter*, length, and width. The **perimeter** of a figure is the sum of the lengths of its sides. The **area** of a figure is the amount of surface the figure covers.

Perimeter is measured in linear units such as feet. Area is measured in square units such as square feet, or ft^2.

Test-Taking Practice

Each lesson includes test-taking practice that helps you become comfortable with different formats of test questions. Additional practice is provided on the Internet. There is also a chapter standardized test for each chapter.

Chapter Standardized Test

Test-Taking Strategy **Avoid spending too much time on one question. Skip questions you have trouble with, and return to them after you have finished.**

Multiple Choice

1. Which ratio is *not* equivalent to $\frac{3}{7}$?

   A. $\frac{9}{21}$ B. $\frac{1.5}{3.5}$ C. $\frac{300}{700}$ D. $\frac{18}{39}$

2. Susan types at a speed of 54 words per minute. What is her typing speed in words per second?

   F. 5400 words per second
   G. 3240 words per second
   ...per second
   ...er second

... shows $\frac{10 \text{ feet}}{4 \text{ seconds}}$ correctly ...nit rate?

... $\frac{5 \text{ ft}}{\text{sec}}$ C. $\frac{2.5 \text{ ft}}{\text{sec}}$ D. $\frac{2 \text{ ft}}{5 \text{ sec}}$

...l of a school building is ...g and 3 inches high. The actual building is 231 feet long. How tall is the actual building?

F. 21 ft G. 33 ft

7. An item with a wholesale price of \$8.40 is marked up 60%. What is the retail price?

   A. \$3.36 B. \$5.04 C. \$13.44 D. \$14.40

8. You and your friend are leaving a tip after eating dinner. The cost of the dinner is \$15.35. You want to leave *about* an 18% tip. How much should you leave as a tip?

   F. \$1.25 G. \$2.75 H. \$8.50 I. \$18.00

9. You randomly draw a marble from a bag of 3 red, 8 yellow, and 13 blue marbles. What is the probability that the marble is yellow?

   A. $\frac{13}{24}$ B. $\frac{1}{2}$ C. $\frac{1}{3}$ D. $\frac{1}{8}$

Short Response

10. You deposit \$1350 into a savings account that pays a simple annual interest rate of 2.8%. How much interest will you earn in 15 months? Compare this to the interest you would earn for the same amount of time in an account with a simple annual interest rate of 4%.

Extended Response

...random from a bag ...d yellow marbles ...ou record its color and ...ag of 75 marbles. The ...he table below. How ...arble do you predict ...n.

...	Green	Yellow
...	5	9

Test-Taking Practice

INTERNET
State Test Practice
CLASSZONE.COM

48. Multiple Choice What is the prime factorization of 72?

    A. $2^2 \cdot 3 \cdot 6$ B. $2 \cdot 6^2$ C. $2^3 \cdot 3^2$ D. $2^2 \cdot 3^2 \cdot 6$

49. Short Response A teacher can arrange a class into groups of 2, 5, or 6 students with no one left out. What is the least number of students that the teacher can have in class to do this? Explain how you found your answer.

Test-Taking Skills and Strategies

At the end of each unit, you'll find pages that help you build and practice test-taking skills and strategies.

UNIT 2
Chapters 4–7

BUILDING **Test-Taking Skills**

Strategies for Answering

Short Response Questions

Scoring Rubric

Full credit
- answer is correct, *and*
- work and reasoning are included

Partial credit
- answer is correct, but reasoning is incorrect, *or*
- answer is incorrect, but reasoning is correct

No credit
- no answer is given *or*
- answer makes no sense

Problem

You work for your uncle this summer. He pays you \$20 on your first day. Each day after that, you will get a raise. You can choose from 2 payment plans. With Plan A, you earn a \$5 raise each day. With Plan B, you earn a 20% raise each day. Which plan is a better deal?

Full credit solution

Plan B is a better deal if you work more than 5 days.

Day	1	2	3	4	5	6
Plan A pay	20.00	25.00	30.00	35.00	40.00	45.00
Plan A total	20.00	45.00	75.00	110.00	150.00	195.00
Plan B pay	20.00	24.00	28.80	34.56	41.47	49.76
Plan B total	20.00	44.00	72.80	107.36	148.83	198.59

Data is used to justify the solution.

Plan A is better if you work 5 days or less, but Plan B is better if you work more than 5 days. By day 6, the pay with a 20% increase is more than the pay with a \$5 raise, so it will continue to be the better plan.

The question is answered clearly and in complete sentences.

Partial credit solution

UNIT 1

Algebra, Integers, and Equation Solving

Chapter 1 Variables and Equations

- Write and evaluate numerical and variable expressions.
- Use a variety of strategies to predict, find, and check results.
- Find lengths, perimeters, and areas in real-world situations.

Chapter 2 Integer Operations

- Use integers in numerical and variable expressions.
- Use number properties to solve problems.
- Plot points in a coordinate plane.

Chapter 3 Solving Equations and Inequalities

- Write and solve one- and two-step equations.
- Write and solve one-step inequalities.
- Model real-world situations with equations and inequalities.

From Chapter 3, p. 136
How fast can a polar bear swim?

Variables and Equations

BEFORE

In previous courses you've...

- Compared quantities
- Performed operations on numbers

Now

In Chapter 1 you'll study...

- Using graphs to analyze data
- Evaluating and writing numerical and variable expressions
- Solving equations using mental math
- A four-step problem solving plan

WHY?

So you can solve real-world problems about...

- volcanoes, p. 5
- cliff diving, p. 23
- tiger beetles, p. 35
- parachuting, p. 37

Internet Preview
CLASSZONE.COM

- eEdition Plus Online
- eWorkbook Plus Online
- eTutorial Plus Online
- State Test Practice
- More Examples

Chapter Warm-Up Games

Review skills you need for this chapter in these quick games.

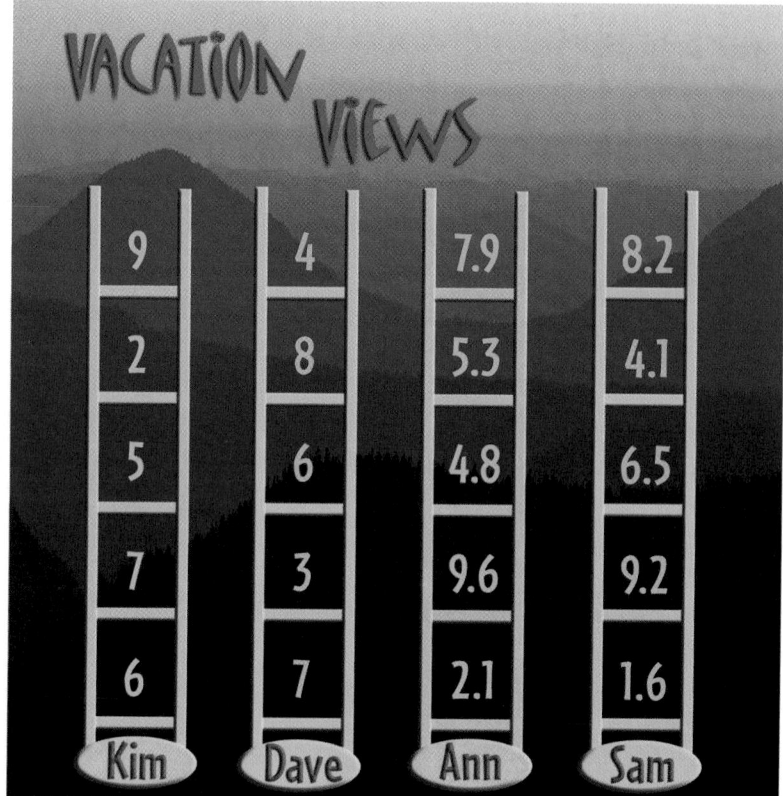

BRAIN GAME

Key Skill:
- Finding the sums of whole numbers and decimals

On a family vacation trip the first stop is a mountain lookout tower. The four ladders lead to the top of the tower. Which child gets to the top first?

- Find the sum of the numbers on the rungs of each ladder.
- The ladder with the least sum is where the fastest person climbs.

NEXT STOP

415.79	410 M	420 U	430 E	Tens ?
19.45	17 D	18 A	19 N	Ones ?
8.178	8.16 A	8.17 T	8.18 H	Hundredths ?
589.63	589.6 C	589.7 R	589.8 S	Tenths ?
627.4	600 L	700 E	899 N	Hundreds ?

Key Skills:
- Rounding
- Identifying place value

Help the kids figure out what the next stop is on the family trip by solving the puzzle.

- Each number has been rounded to one of its digits. Select the answer that shows the number rounded correctly.
- On the right, write each letter below the place value it was rounded to.
- Put letters in correct place value order to figure out the next stop.

Stop and Think

1. **Critical Thinking** Order the names in *Vacation Views* from who gets to the top first to who gets there last (the least sum to the greatest).
2. **Writing** In *Next Stop*, a student thinks that the result of rounding 8.178 is 8.17 because the last digit is removed. What is wrong with the student's reasoning?

Getting Ready to Learn

Review What You Need to Know 

Using Vocabulary **Copy and complete using a review word.**

1. When you add two numbers, the result is called the _?_.
2. When you multiply two numbers, the result is called the _?_.

Write the place value of the red digit. *(p. 704)*

3. 26.10 **4.** 45.901 **5.** 139.07 **6.** 6.394

Find the sum, difference, product, or quotient. *(p. 709)*

7. 29 + 45 **8.** 103 + 8 **9.** 25 − 12 **10.** 72 − 56

11. 13 × 3 **12.** 27 × 8 **13.** 96 ÷ 6 **14.** 60 ÷ 12

15. 12.7 − 9.4 **16.** 17.8 + 26.3 **17.** 9.64 + 6.36 **18.** 20.24 − 16.5

19. You are shopping for new clothes for school. If you have $75.00 and buy a pair of jeans for $37.75, how much money do you have left? *(p. 709)*

Word Watch

Review Words

whole number, p. 704
sum, p. 709
difference, p. 709
product, p. 713
quotient, p. 715

You should include material that appears on a notebook like this in your own notes.

Know How to Take Notes

Keeping a Notebook Your math notebook is an important tool for learning and reviewing the topics of this course. Here are some tips for organizing your notes. Organize your notes in the same way for each lesson.

Start with the date and topic.

September 7 Decimals

To add decimals, line up the decimal points.

Example: Adding Decimals

Copy examples shown in class.

$$\begin{array}{r} 23.40 \\ +\ 36.15 \\ \hline 59.55 \end{array}$$

In Lesson 1.4, you should organize your notes by labeling the examples that you copy.

Interpreting Graphs

BEFORE	Now	WHY?
You compared quantities.	You'll use graphs to analyze data.	So you can make conclusions about mall businesses, as in Exs. 6–8.

In the Real World

bar graph, p. 5
data, p. 5
frequency table, p. 6
histogram, p. 6

INDIANA
Academic Standards

- Data Analysis and Probability (8.6.4)

Volcanoes The *bar graph* at the right shows the number of historically active volcanoes in four countries. Which country has the most historically active volcanoes?

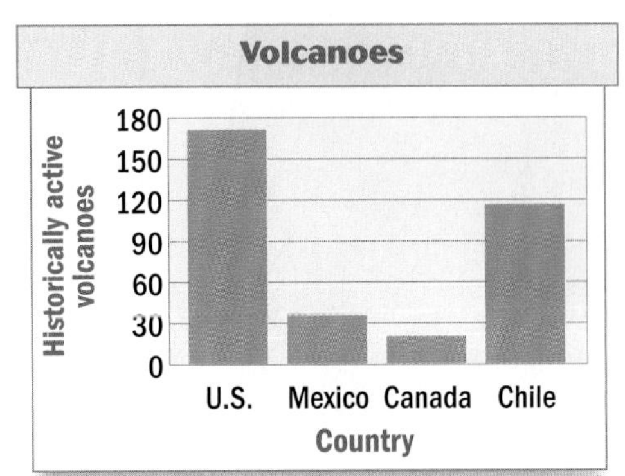

A **bar graph** is a type of graph in which the lengths of bars are used to represent and compare *data* in categories. **Data** are information, facts, or numbers that describe something.

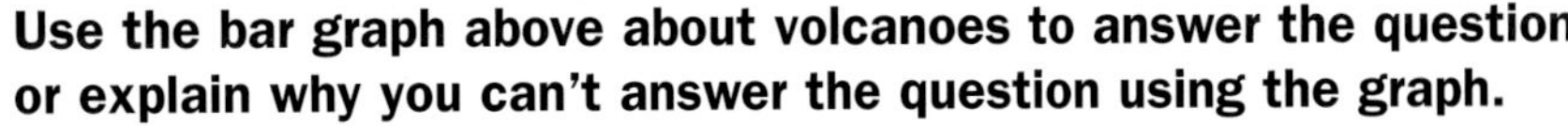

EXAMPLE 1 Interpreting a Bar Graph

Use the bar graph above about volcanoes to answer the question or explain why you can't answer the question using the graph.

a. Which country has the most historically active volcanoes?

b. Which country has the most volcanic eruptions in a given year?

Solution

a. The vertical axis in the bar graph is labeled *Historically active volcanoes*, so the tallest bar represents the country with the most historically active volcanoes. Because the United States has the tallest bar, it has the most historically active volcanoes.

b. Having more historically active volcanoes doesn't necessarily mean having more eruptions, so you can't answer this question from the bar graph.

Your turn now **Use the bar graph about historically active volcanoes.**

1. About how many more historically active volcanoes does Chile have than Mexico?

2. Which country has the least number of historically active volcanoes?

Histograms When you have a large set of data to organize, you may be able to use a **frequency table** to group the data into *intervals*. The frequency of an interval is the number of values in the interval. You can graph data organized into equal intervals in a **histogram**. The height of each bar in a histogram indicates the frequency of an interval.

EXAMPLE 2 Making a Frequency Table

Roller Coasters The data show the heights, in meters, of the tallest roller coasters in the world. Make a frequency table of the data.

66.4, 94.5, 68.3, 115, 62.5, 97, 66.4, 126.5, 63.4, 74.7, 63.4, 70.1, 66.4, 64.9, 63.7, 79, 63.4, 63.1, 62.5, 61.9, 71.6

(1) Choose intervals of equal size for the data.

(2) Tally the data in each interval. Use tally marks to record each occurrence of a height in its interval.

(3) Write the frequency for each interval by totaling the tally marks.

Height (m)	Tally	Frequency
60–69.9	𝍸 𝍸 III	13
70–79.9	IIII	4
80–89.9		0
90–99.9	II	2
100–109.9		0
110–119.9	I	1
120–129.9	I	1

For help with data displays, see p. 724.

EXAMPLE 3 Making a Histogram

Make a histogram of the data shown in the frequency table in Example 2.

(1) Draw and label the horizontal and vertical axes. Start the vertical scale at 0 and end at 15. Use increments of 3.

(2) Draw a bar to represent the frequency of each interval. The bars of neighboring intervals should touch.

(3) Write a title.

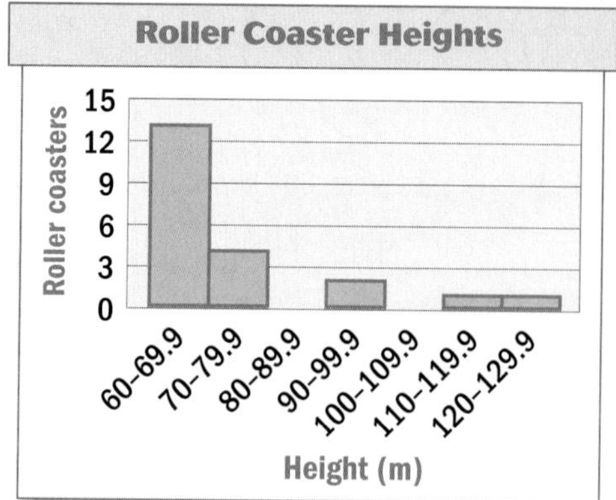

Your turn now

3. Which interval has the greatest number of roller coasters?

4. When the next roller coaster between 60 and 130 meters tall is built, in what interval do you think it will be? Explain.

1.1 Exercises

More Practice, p. 727

Getting Ready to Practice

1. **Vocabulary** Copy and complete: A histogram is a graph that shows data that are divided equally into ? .

In Exercises 2–4, use the graph at the right. It displays the number of times each country has won the World Cup in soccer.

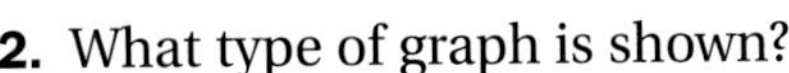

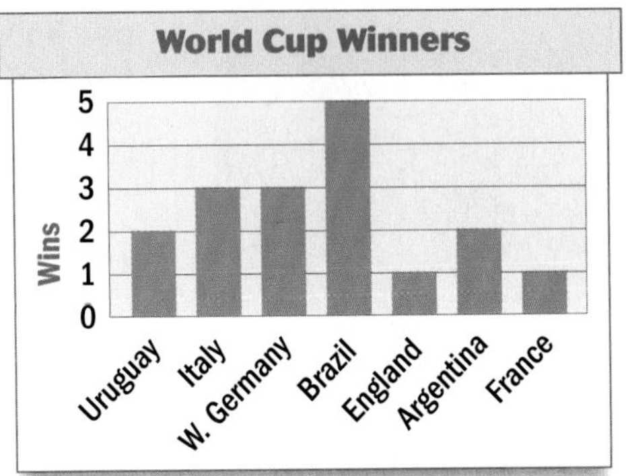

2. What type of graph is shown?
3. How many times has Italy won?
4. How many more times has Argentina won than France?
5. **Guided Problem Solving** The frequency table shows when new states were added to the United States. Use the frequency table to make a graph.
   1. Decide what kind of graph to use.
   2. Draw and label horizontal and vertical axes.
   3. Draw bars. Write a title.

Years	States
1787–1836	25
1837–1886	13
1887–1936	10
1937–1986	2

Practice and Problem Solving

HELP with Homework

Example	Exercises
1	6–10, 15–17
2	12, 18–19
3	12–14, 18–20

- More Examples
- eTutorial Plus

Use the bar graph at the right. It shows the number of businesses at a mall in each category.

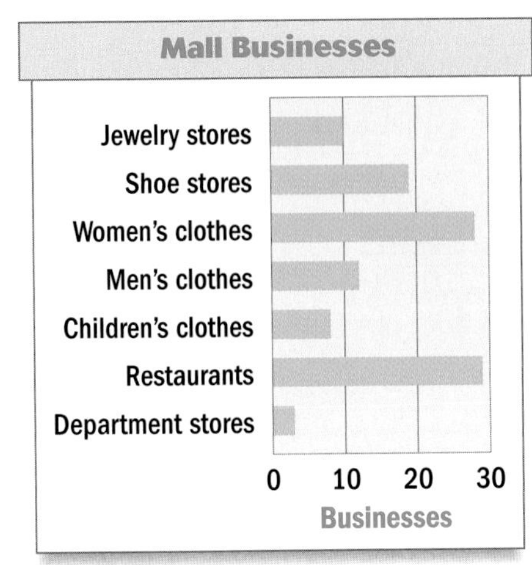

6. Which category has the greatest number of businesses?
7. Which category has the least number of businesses?
8. About how many more shoe stores are there than jewelry stores?
9. **Writing** Can you tell from the graph which category of businesses uses the most floor space in the mall? Explain.

10. **Movies** The table shows the numbers of movies released in the United States from 1995 through 2000. Make a bar graph of the data.

Year	1995	1996	1997	1998	1999	2000
Movies	411	471	510	509	461	478

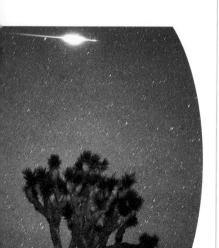

11. **Critical Thinking** If you need to know an exact amount, is it easier to find this information from a table or a bar graph? Explain.

Meteors The data show the average numbers of meteors that fall per hour during 39 annual meteor showers. For example, in the first meteor shower, an average of 60 meteors fall each hour.

60, 4, 1, 5, 5, 1, 40, 4, 5, 20, 2, 15, 8, 6, 21, 15, 20, 30, 3, 15, 10, 62, 25, 26, 50, 12, 20, 12, 15, 30, 10, 10, 20, 12, 12, 60, 10, 12, 20

12. Make a frequency table to organize the data using intervals of 10, starting with 0–9.
13. Make a histogram of the data displayed in the frequency table.
14. Which display would you use to find the number of meteor showers that average 20 to 29 meteors falling per hour? Explain.

Hurricanes The histogram shows the numbers of hurricanes in the Atlantic Ocean from 1950 through 1999.

15. About how many hurricanes were there in the Atlantic Ocean from 1980–1989?
16. Can you determine the number of hurricanes there were in the Atlantic Ocean in 1965? Explain.
17. Can you use the histogram to predict the number of hurricanes in 2000–2009? Why or why not?

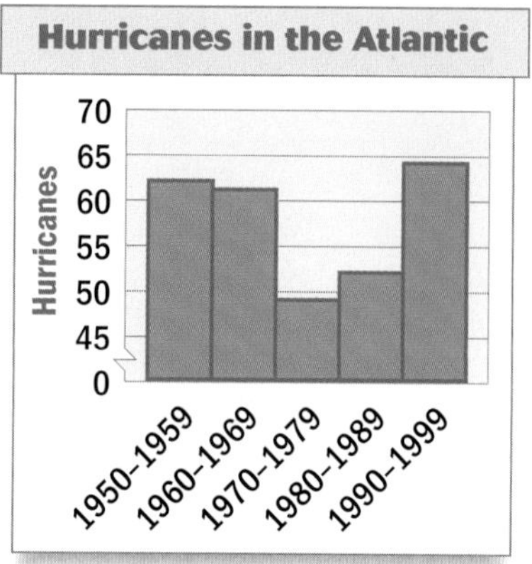

Extended Problem Solving The data show the numbers of hours 30 students in a class spent on the Internet in a week.

4, 2.5, 5.7, 1.8, 3.7, 5.4, 5.5, 11.6, 3.7, 6.5, 2, 10, 0.5, 4.5, 5, 9.5, 2.1, 4.5, 7.5, 2.5, 8, 1, 9, 4.2, 8, 7, 3, 7, 5, 6

18. **Graph** Make a histogram of the data using the intervals 0–1.9, 2–3.9, 4–5.9, 6–7.9, 8–9.9, and 10–11.9.
19. **Graph** Make a histogram of the data using the intervals 0–2.9, 3–5.9, 6–8.9, and 9–11.9.
20. **Compare** Does the histogram in Exercise 18 or in Exercise 19 give a clearer representation of the data? Explain your reasoning.

Media **In Exercises 21 and 22, use the *double bar graph.* It shows the numbers of U.S. high schools with media activities in 1991 and 1998.**

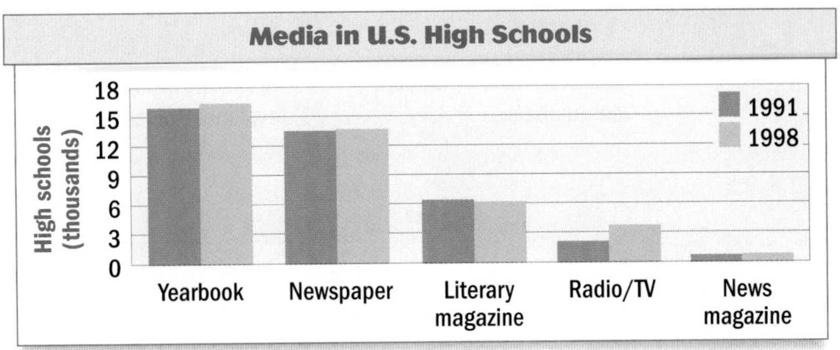

21. About how many of the schools offered radio or TV in 1998?

22. Describe the trends in media at the schools from 1991 to 1998.

23. Challenge What trend do you notice in the number of DVD players sold in the United States shown in the graph at the right? Do you think that this trend continued? Explain your reasoning.

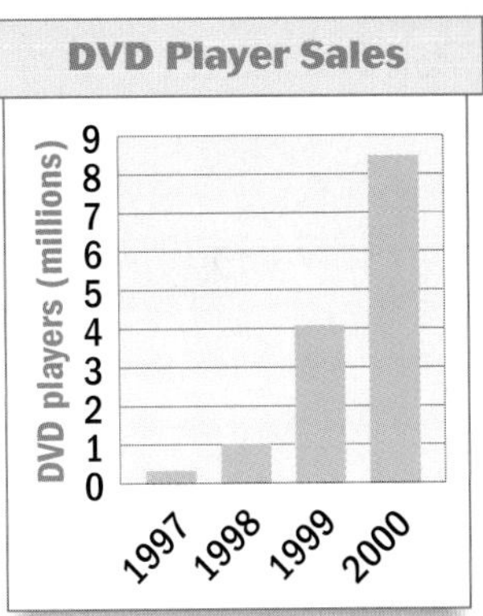

24. Critical Thinking You want to collect data about the pets students in your class have. What data would you collect to make a histogram? What data would you collect to make a bar graph?

Find the product or quotient. *(p. 713)*

25. 34×4 **26.** 6×15 **27.** $140 \div 20$ **28.** $84 \div 7$

Basic Skills **Find the sum or difference.**

29. $25.8 + 19.64$ **30.** $106.58 - 56.33$ **31.** $88.7 - 29.92$

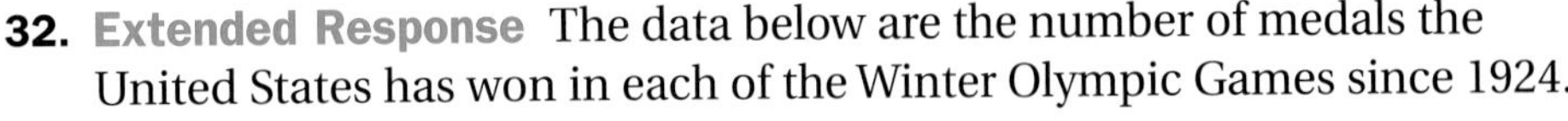

32. Extended Response The data below are the number of medals the United States has won in each of the Winter Olympic Games since 1924.

4, 7, 12, 4, 9, 11, 7, 10, 6, 7, 8, 10, 12, 8, 6, 11, 13, 13, 34

Create a histogram of the data with intervals of 5 starting with 0–4 and a second histogram with intervals of 10 starting with 0–9. Tell which histogram you would use to predict how many medals the United States will win in the future and why.

Order of Operations

BEFORE	Now	WHY?
You performed operations on numbers.	You'll use order of operations to evaluate numerical expressions.	So you can find how much money to raise for a team, as in Ex. 19.

numerical expression, p. 10
evaluate, p. 10
order of operations, p. 10
verbal model, p. 11

INDIANA Academic Standards
- Computation (8.2.1)

In the Real World

Visiting an Aquarium You and four friends visit an aquarium, but only three of you go to the movie at the aquarium. What is the total cost of the visit? You will find the total cost of the visit in Example 3.

Aquarium Prices	
Admission	$13.50
Sea Lion show	Free
Movie	$8.00

Order of Operations A **numerical expression** consists of numbers and operations. To **evaluate** a numerical expression is to find its value. When a numerical expression has more than one operation, you must use a set of rules called the **order of operations**.

Order of Operations

To evaluate an expression that has more than one operation:

1. Evaluate expressions inside grouping symbols.
2. Multiply and divide from left to right.
3. Add and subtract from left to right.

You can express multiplication by using parentheses or the symbols • or ×.
$3(4) = 12$
$3 \cdot 4 = 12$
$3 \times 4 = 12$

EXAMPLE 1 Using the Order of Operations

Evaluate the expression $7 + 16 \cdot 3 \div 6$.

$7 + 16 \cdot 3 \div 6 = 7 + 48 \div 6$ Multiply 16 by 3.

$= 7 + 8$ Divide 48 by 6.

$= 15$ Add 7 and 8.

Watch Out! You can express division using either the symbol ÷ or a fraction bar. To evaluate an expression with a fraction bar, evaluate the numerator and the denominator before you divide.

Grouping Symbols The most common grouping symbols are parentheses ( ), brackets [ ], and fraction bars.

EXAMPLE 2 Using Grouping Symbols

a. $(14 + 6) \cdot 8 = 20 \cdot 8$ Add inside parentheses first.

$= 160$ Then multiply.

b. $\frac{9 \times 8}{4 + 8} = \frac{72}{4 + 8}$ Evaluate numerator.

$= \frac{72}{12}$ Evaluate denominator.

$= 6$ Divide.

c. $45 \div [63 \div (56 \div 8)] = 45 \div [63 \div 7]$ Divide inside the innermost set of grouping symbols.

$= 45 \div 9$ Divide inside brackets.

$= 5$ Divide.

Your turn now Evaluate the expression.

1. $14 + 6 \div 2$ **2.** $20 - 7 \times 2 + 1$ **3.** $5 \cdot 7 - 2 \cdot 13$

4. $35 \div (9 - 4)$ **5.** $3 \cdot [(11 - 1) \div 5]$ **6.** $\frac{45 + 19}{2 \times 8}$

When you solve a problem, it may help to write a **verbal model** using symbols for operations and words to label necessary information.

EXAMPLE 3 Using a Verbal Model

To find the total cost of the visit to the aquarium described on the previous page, you can use a verbal model to write and evaluate an expression.

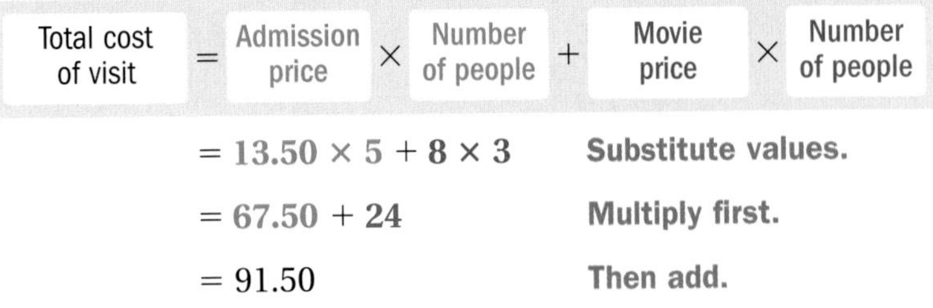

Total cost of visit
=
Admission price
×
Number of people
+
Movie price
×
Number of people

$= 13.50 \times 5 + 8 \times 3$ Substitute values.

$= 67.50 + 24$ Multiply first.

$= 91.50$ Then add.

ANSWER The total cost of the visit is $91.50.

Getting Ready to Practice

1. **Vocabulary** Use the order of operations to list in order the steps needed to evaluate the following expression: $8 + 2 \times 5 - 4$.

State the first step in evaluating the expression. Then evaluate.

2. $10 \cdot 6 - 20$
3. $5 \times 15 \div 3$
4. $4 + 8 \div 2$
5. $2 \times 5 + (15 - 7)$
6. $6 + 14 - 10 \div 2$
7. $10 \cdot [9 \div (5 - 2)]$
8. **Fundraising Walk** Your friend pledges \$10 to you for a fundraising walk and \$.25 for each mile you walk. You walk 6 miles. How much money will your friend contribute? Use the expression $10 + 0.25(6)$.
9. **Find the Error** Describe and correct the error in the solution.

$$\begin{aligned} \times\quad 3 \times 3 + 63 \div 9 &= 9 + 63 \div 9 \\ &= 72 \div 9 \\ &= 8 \end{aligned}$$

Practice and Problem Solving

Example	Exercises
1	10–29, 33
2	10–18, 21–29
3	34

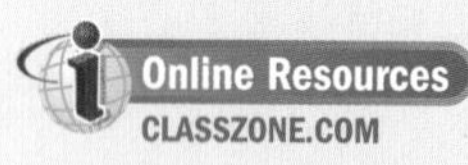

· More Examples
· eTutorial Plus

Evaluate the expression.

10. $12 + 10 - 4$
11. $7 \cdot 3 + 2 \cdot 4$
12. $\dfrac{16}{7 - 3}$
13. $9 \times 3 + 2 - 5$
14. $16 - 6 + 2 \times 4$
15. $26 - 15 + 8 \div 2$
16. $8 + 2 \times (4 - 3)$
17. $120 \div [(6 + 2) \cdot 3]$
18. $18 \div (8 + 4 - 9)$
19. **Softball Uniforms** Your school softball team has 25 members. The school contributes \$30 toward each \$40 uniform. To find how much money the team needs to raise, evaluate the expression $40 \cdot 25 - 30 \cdot 25$.
20. **Supplies** You buy 3 notebooks at \$2 each and 4 pens at \$1.50 each. What is the total cost? Use the expression $3 \times 2 + 4 \times 1.50$.

Evaluate the expression.

21. $\frac{7}{4} - \frac{5}{4} + \frac{1}{4}$
22. $9 \div \left[3 \cdot \left(\frac{5}{3} + \frac{4}{3}\right)\right]$
23. $3 \cdot \left(\frac{7}{2} + \frac{1}{2}\right)$
24. $(1.5 - 0.5) \times 2$
25. $9.4 + 4.2 \div 6$
26. $6 \times (2.4 - 0.4 + 3)$
27. $7.8 \times (5 + 2)$
28. $8.4 \div (21 - 14)$
29. $4 + 3.9 \div 1.3$

Critical Thinking **Add parentheses to make the statement true.**

30. $5 \cdot 2 + 3 - 8 = 17$

31. $12 \div 6 + 4 - 7 = 4$

Extended Problem Solving **In Exercises 32–34, suppose Liz and Ty are making cookies for a school bake sale. Liz makes 5 batches of 36 cookies, and Ty makes 4 batches of 48 cookies.**

32. Translate Translate *5 batches of 36 cookies plus 4 batches of 48 cookies* into an expression.

33. Evaluate Evaluate the expression.

34. Extend Liz and Ty decide to make packages of three cookies. Write and evaluate an expression to find the number of packages they can make.

35. Number Sense Complete the statement 12 _?_ 4 + 2 using each of the operations +, −, ×, and ÷. Which operation symbol gives the expression the greatest value? Find the greatest possible value if you add one set of parentheses to the four expressions.

36. Challenge Your cousin is 14 years old. Your brother is 10 years less than twice your cousin's age. Write and evaluate an expression to find your brother's age.

Mixed Review 

The bar graph shows the numbers of students on teams. *(Lesson 1.1)*

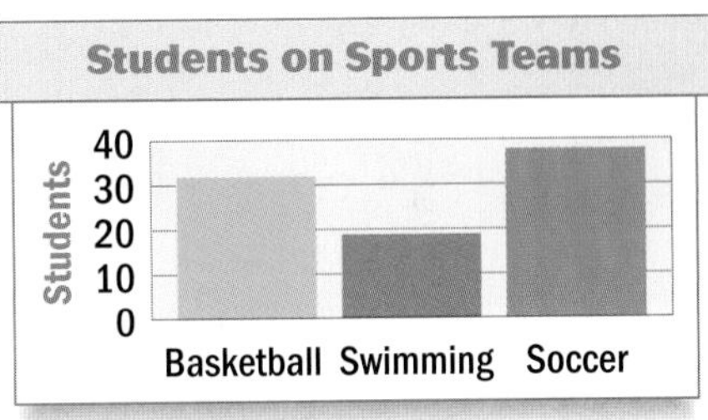

37. About how many students are on the basketball team?

38. Which team has the most students?

Basic Skills **Find the missing number.**

39. 11 − _?_ = 7

40. _?_ ÷ 4 = 8

41. 9 • _?_ = 54

Test-Taking Practice 

INTERNET
State Test Practice
CLASSZONE.COM

42. Multiple Choice In what order should the operations be performed in the expression $2 \times 4 - 6 \div 3 + 1$?

A. ×, ÷, −, + **B.** ×, −, ÷, + **C.** ×, ÷, +, − **D.** ×, +, −, ÷

43. Multiple Choice Which operation should be performed first when finding *the difference of twenty and the quotient of eighteen and six*?

F. 20 − 18 **G.** 18 ÷ 6 **H.** 20 − 6 **I.** 20 ÷ 6

CALCULATOR

1.2 Technology Activity

INDIANA: Academic Standards
- Problem Solving (8.7.4)

Using Order of Operations

GOAL Use a calculator to evaluate numerical expressions with decimals.

Example **You and three friends are ordering a pizza. The cost of the pizza is $15.90, but you have a coupon for $1.50 off. How much should each of you pay if you want to divide the total cost equally?**

Solution

Cost per person $= \dfrac{\text{Price of a pizza} - \text{Coupon}}{\text{Number of friends} + \text{Yourself}}$ **Write a verbal model.**

$= \dfrac{15.90 - 1.50}{3 + 1}$ **Substitute.**

To find the cost per person, use the order of operations.

Keystrokes	**Display**
(15.90 − 1.50) ÷ (3 + 1) =	3.6

ANSWER Each person should pay $3.60 for the pizza.

HELP with Technology

The keystrokes shown here may not be the same as on your calculator. See your calculator's instruction manual for the appropriate keystrokes.

Your turn now **Use a calculator to evaluate the expression.**

1. $62 + 7 \times 6.4$

2. $8.32 - 9 \div 2$

3. $6.8 \div 4 + 15.9 \div 3$

4. $36.2 - 4.3 \cdot 5$

5. $\dfrac{14 + 11}{4 + 1}$

6. $\dfrac{20 - 3.5}{10.3 - 7}$

7. $\dfrac{10}{3.8 + 1.2}$

8. $\dfrac{17.7 - 13.7}{0.2 + 4.8}$

9. **Snacks** You buy 3 bags of snack mix for $1.49 each, 2 boxes of raisins for $1.79 each, and lemonade for $2.39. Find the total cost using the expression $3 \cdot 1.49 + 2 \cdot 1.79 + 2.39$.

10. **Clothing** You buy 3 T-shirts at $9.99 each, a pair of sneakers for $44.89, a hat for $10.59, and a pair of socks at a cost of 4 pairs for $8.60. Find the total cost.

11. **Music** You pick out 2 CDs for $12.99 each, 3 CDs for $9.49 each, and a CD for $15.97. At the register you find out that when you buy 5 CDs you get the sixth CD for half off. Find the total cost if you get the most expensive CD for half off. Round to the nearest cent.

Variables and Expressions

BEFORE	Now	WHY?
You evaluated numerical expressions.	You'll write and evaluate variable expressions.	So you can find how far you travel on a bike, as in Exs. 23–24.

Word Watch

variable, p. 15
variable expression, p. 15

INDIANA
Academic Standards

- Algebra and Functions (8.3.1)

In the Real World

Hot Air Balloons You are riding in a hot air balloon. After traveling 5 miles, the balloon speed changes to 6 miles per hour. What is the total distance you travel if the balloon stays at this speed for 1 hour? for 2 hours? You will find the answer in Example 1.

Variable Expressions A **variable** is a symbol, usually a letter, that represents one or more numbers. A **variable expression** consists of numbers, variables, and operations. To evaluate a variable expression, substitute a number for each variable. Then find the value of the numerical expression.

You can write the product of a number and a variable by writing the number next to that variable. For example, you can write $5 \cdot n$ as $5n$.

EXAMPLE 1 Using a Variable Expression

To answer the questions above about distance traveled, let t represent the time in hours that the balloon travels at 6 miles per hour. So, the total distance traveled is *original distance* + *speed* • *time*, which is $5 + 6t$.

1 Write hours traveled t.	2 Substitute for t in the expression $5 + 6t$.	3 Evaluate to find total distance.
1	$5 + 6(1)$	11
2	$5 + 6(2)$	17

ANSWER If the balloon travels at 6 miles per hour for 1 hour, you travel a total of 11 miles. After 2 hours you travel a total of 17 miles.

Your turn now **Use the information above about hot air balloons.**

1. If you travel for 3 hours more, what is the total distance?
2. If you travel for $\frac{1}{2}$ hour more, what is the total distance?

EXAMPLE 2 Evaluating Variable Expressions

Evaluate the expression when $x = 8$ and $y = 2$.

a. $7x + 15 = 7(8) + 15$ — Substitute 8 for x.

$= 56 + 15$ — Multiply.

$= 71$ — Add.

b. $3x - 5y = 3(8) - 5(2)$ — Substitute 8 for x and 2 for y.

$= 24 - 10$ — Multiply.

$= 14$ — Subtract.

Writing Expressions Many words and phrases suggest mathematical operations. The following common words and phrases indicate addition, subtraction, multiplication, and division.

Addition	Subtraction	Multiplication	Division
plus the sum of increased by total more than added to	minus the difference of decreased by fewer than less than subtracted from	times the product of multiplied by of	divided by the quotient of per

Order is important when translating verbal expressions that suggest subtraction and division. *The difference of a number and 6* means $n - 6$, not $6 - n$. *The quotient of a number and 10* means $n \div 10$, not $10 \div n$.

EXAMPLE 3 Translating Verbal Phrases

Verbal Phrase	**Variable Expression**
The sum of a number and 9	$n + 9$
The difference of a number and 21	$n - 21$
The product of 6 and a number	$6n$
The quotient of 48 and a number	$\frac{48}{n}$
One third of a number	$\frac{1}{3}n$

Your turn now **Evaluate the expression when $a = 12$ and $b = 3$.**

3. $9a$ **4.** ab **5.** $b(a - 6)$ **6.** $\frac{6a}{a - b}$

Write the phrase as a variable expression using x.

7. a number increased by 15 **8.** 8 times a number

Heart Rate

To find a reasonable target heart rate during exercise, subtract your age from 220, then multiply that number by 0.7. What is your target heart rate?

EXAMPLE 4 Writing and Evaluating an Expression

Heart Rate To measure your heart rate in beats per minute, count the number of heartbeats n in 15 seconds. Then multiply by 4 to find your heart rate in beats per minute.

a. Use n to write an expression for heart rate in beats per minute.

b. You count 18 beats in 15 seconds. Find your heart rate.

Solution

a. The phrase *multiply by* suggests multiplication. So, the variable expression for heart rate in beats per minute is $4n$.

b. Substitute 18 for n in the expression $4n$ to find your heart rate.

$$4n = 4(18)$$
$$= 72$$

ANSWER Your heart rate is 72 beats per minute.

1.3 Exercises

More Practice, p. 727

Getting Ready to Practice

1. **Vocabulary** Copy and complete: $3t - 4$ is a(n) _?_ expression and $5 + 13$ is a(n) _?_ expression.

Match the phrase with the correct variable expression.

2. 8 times a number	**A.** $n + 8$
3. 8 fewer than a number	**B.** $8n$
4. a number increased by 8	**C.** $n - 8$
5. the quotient of 8 and a number	**D.** $8 \div n$

Evaluate the expression when $p = 6$ and $s = 5$.

6. $11p$ **7.** $7s + 9$ **8.** $6s + 4p$ **9.** $\frac{50 - s}{p + 3}$

10. **Guided Problem Solving** You buy a hat for \$8 and rent 5 videos for \$2.50 each. How much do you spend?

(1) Write a variable expression for the cost to rent m videos.

(2) Add the cost of the hat to this expression.

(3) Evaluate the expression for $m = 5$.

Practice and Problem Solving

Example Exercises

Example	Exercises
1	23–24
2	11–18, 29–36
3	19–22
4	26–28

- More Examples
- eTutorial Plus

Evaluate the expression for the given value(s) of the variable(s).

11. $4x - 5, x = 7$

12. $10n + 115, n = 9$

13. $11c + 34, c = 0.5$

14. $2s - t, s = 8, t = 4$

15. $p + 2q, p = 3, q = 1$

16. $8a - 3b, a = 3, b = 8$

17. $\frac{3}{4}x + y, x = 4, y = 3$

18. $\frac{d + 10}{c - d}, c = 14, d = 8$

Translate **Write the phrase as a variable expression. Let *x* represent the variable.**

19. two fifths of a number

20. a number subtracted from 10

21. 12 increased by a number

22. the quotient of a number and 7

Bicycling **Evaluate the expression 9*t* to find how many miles you go if you ride your bike for *t* hours at 9 miles per hour.**

23. How far do you go if you ride your bike for 2 hours?

24. How far do you go if you ride your bike for $3\frac{1}{2}$ hours?

25. Writing Write a real world situation that can be modeled by $2 + 8d$.

26. Television You watch x thirty-minute TV shows and y sixty-minute TV shows in one week. Write a variable expression representing the total number of minutes you spend watching television that week.

27. CD Club You are purchasing CDs from a music club. You pay $4 for shipping any number n of CDs, plus $17 for each CD. Write a variable expression for the cost of n CDs. Then find the cost of 6 CDs.

28. Estimation A 17 inch vine grows 3 inches per week. Write a variable expression for the length of the vine after w weeks. Then estimate the vine's length after 19 weeks.

Evaluate the expression when $x = 2.4$ and $y = 8$.

29. $7x + 2y$

30. $y - 2x$

31. $5xy$

32. $\frac{y}{x - 0.4}$

33. $4x - y$

34. $7.2y \div x$

35. $\frac{3y}{x}$

36. $1.6xy$

37. Writing Write a variable expression that requires the use of the order of operations to evaluate correctly. Explain the correct order to use.

38. Nutrition Rice has 13 grams of protein per serving, beans have 15 grams per serving, and an orange has 2 grams per serving. Write a variable expression for the total grams of protein in x servings of rice, y servings of beans, and z oranges.

39. **Movies** At the movies, popcorn costs \$2.75 and drinks cost \$1.25. Write an expression to find the total cost of p popcorns and d drinks. Find the total cost for snacks if 3 people buy popcorn and 4 people buy drinks.

40. **Challenge** Evaluate the expression $\frac{5(3x + 2z + 0.5425)}{x + y + z}$ when $x = 1.05$, $y = 1.3$, and $z = 0.9$.

Mixed Review

Evaluate the expression. *(Lesson 1.2)*

41. $12 \cdot 3 + 14$ **42.** $93 - 74 \div 2$ **43.** $16 + 6 \cdot 3 \div 2 - 7$

Basic Skills **Find the product or quotient.**

44. $17 \cdot 52$ **45.** $91 \cdot 45$ **46.** $123 \div 3$ **47.** $252 \div 6$

Test-Taking Practice

48. **Short Response** A personal CD player costs \$35 and CDs cost \$15 each. Write an expression to represent the total cost for the CD player and CDs. You buy a personal CD player and 4 CDs. Evaluate your expression to determine the total amount of money you spend.

49. **Multiple Choice** You are saving money to buy a bike that costs \$126. You want to buy the bike in 6 weeks by saving the same amount of money each day. How much money should you save each day?

A. \$1 **B.** \$2 **C.** \$3 **D.** \$21

Brain Game

Find the Key

A key will unlock a door if the variable expressions on the door have the same value when the number on the key is substituted for the variable.

Which key opens each door?

Powers and Exponents

BEFORE	Now	WHY?
You evaluated numerical and variable expressions.	You'll evaluate expressions with powers.	So you can find the height of a cliff, as in Example 3.

power, p. 20
exponent, p. 20
base, p. 20

INDIANA Academic Standards

- Algebra and Functions (8.3.3, 8.3.4)

In the Real World

Waterfall A stone falls over the edge of a cliff next to a waterfall. The stone hits the water 5 seconds later. How tall is the cliff?

To find the height of the cliff, you will use an expression with a *power* in Example 3. A **power** is a product with a repeated factor. The **exponent** tells how many times the **base** is used as a factor.

Base — Exponent

$$b^8 = \underbrace{b \cdot b \cdot b \cdot b \cdot b \cdot b \cdot b \cdot b}_{b \text{ is a factor } 8 \text{ times.}}$$

Power

Taughannock Falls State Park, New York

EXAMPLE 1 Reading Powers

Power	Repeated Multiplication	Description in Words
4^2	$4 \cdot 4$	4 to the *second power,* or 4 *squared*
9^3	$9 \cdot 9 \cdot 9$	9 to the *third power,* or 9 *cubed*
y^5	$y \cdot y \cdot y \cdot y \cdot y$	y to the *fifth power*

EXAMPLE 2 Evaluating a Power

Evaluate five cubed.

$5^3 = 5 \cdot 5 \cdot 5$ Write 5 as a factor 3 times.

$= 125$ Multiply.

Your turn now **Write the product as a power.**

1. $7 \times 7 \times 7 \times 7 \times 7 \times 7$ **2.** $10 \cdot 10 \cdot 10 \cdot 10$ **3.** $w \cdot w$

Describe the power in words and then evaluate.

4. 6^3 **5.** 2^5 **6.** 13^2 **7.** 3^1

Order of Operations When you evaluate expressions with powers, evaluate any powers before multiplying or dividing.

Order of Operations

1. Evaluate expressions inside grouping symbols.
2. Evaluate powers.
3. Multiply and divide from left to right.
4. Add and subtract from left to right.

EXAMPLE 3 Using a Power

To find the height of the cliff from the previous page, use the expression $16t^2$. This expression gives the distance in feet that an object has fallen t seconds after it begins to fall.

$16t^2 = 16(5)^2$ Substitute 5 for t.

$= 16(25)$ Evaluate the power.

$= 400$ Multiply.

ANSWER The height of the cliff is 400 feet.

HELP with Notetaking

In your notes, you may want to label the different examples that you copy.

EXAMPLE 4 Using the Order of Operations

Evaluate the expression.

a. $(6 - 4)^3 + 5 - 3^2 = 2^3 + 5 - 3^2$ Evaluate inside grouping symbols.

$= 8 + 5 - 9$ Evaluate powers.

$= 4$ Add and subtract from left to right.

b. $2 \cdot (7 + 1)^2 \div 4^2 = 2 \cdot 8^2 \div 4^2$ Evaluate inside grouping symbols.

$= 2 \cdot 64 \div 16$ Evaluate powers.

$= 8$ Multiply and divide from left to right.

Your turn now **Evaluate the expression.**

8. $(5 - 2)^3 - 7 + 4^3$ **9.** $12 + (4 + 2)^2 - 2^4$ **10.** $7^3 + 24 \div (7 - 6)^4$

11. Use the expression in Example 3 to find the height of a cliff if a stone hits the water 8 seconds after falling over the edge.

1.4 Exercises

More Practice, p. 727

Getting Ready to Practice

1. **Vocabulary** Write a power and label the base and the exponent.

Evaluate the power.

2. three squared
3. eleven cubed
4. one to the ninth
5. 2^6
6. 5^5
7. 0^7

Evaluate the expression.

8. $(2 + 1)^4 \div 9 - 4$
9. $48 \div (9 - 7)^3$
10. $(5 \times 3)^2 - 4$

11. **Find the Error** Describe and correct the error in the solution.

$$7^2 = 7 \times 2$$
$$= 14$$

Practice and Problem Solving

HELP with Homework

Example	Exercises
1	12-14
2	15-20
3	27-29, 35-37
4	21-29

· More Examples
· eTutorial Plus

Write the product as a power and describe the power in words.

12. $9 \cdot 9 \cdot 9 \cdot 9 \cdot 9$
13. $3 \cdot 3 \cdot 3$
14. $n \cdot n \cdot n \cdot n \cdot n \cdot n$

Evaluate the power.

15. 6^1
16. 11^2
17. 2^7
18. 10^3
19. 1^8
20. 20^2

Evaluate the expression.

21. $(2 \times 5)^2 + 9$
22. $500 \div (12 - 7)^1$
23. $6 \times 18 \div 3^2$
24. $(9 - 7)^5 + 17$
25. $108 \div (5 + 1)^2$
26. $9^2 - 3^3$

Evaluate the expression when $g = 4$.

27. $g^4 \div 16$
28. $(3 + g)^3$
29. $(3g)^2 - 25$

30. **Critical Thinking** If $x^2 = x^3$, give the two possible values for x.

31. **Football** The season attendance at your school's football games is 1000 people one year. The attendance doubles each year for the next 3 years. Write an expression with a power that shows the season attendance at the football games after 3 years.

Copy and complete the statement using <, >, or =.

32. 3^2 ? 2^3 **33.** 5^4 ? 4^5 **34.** 10^1 ? 1^{10}

Evaluate the expression when $x = 4.2$, $y = 5.9$, and $z = 11.8$.

35. $y^2 - x^2$ **36.** $10z^2 \div y$ **37.** $(x + y)^3$

38. Writing Describe how to find the value of 3^9 using the fact that $3^8 = 6561$.

39. Cliff Diving At Kaunolo in Hawaii, divers jump from a platform on top of a cliff 82 feet above the water. At time t seconds, a diver has fallen $16t^2$ feet. Do the divers reach the surface of the water in 2 seconds? Explain your reasoning.

Evaluate the expression when $a = 3$, $b = 7$, and $c = 11$.

40. a^3b^2 **41.** $(c - a)^3 - 210$ **42.** $2 \cdot (b + 2)^2 \div a$

43. Challenge The personal computers of the early 1980s had 64 kilobytes of memory. Computers today often have more than one gigabyte of memory. Use the table to find how much memory personal computers of the early 1980s had in bytes.

Name	Bytes
Kilobyte	2^{10}
Megabyte	2^{20}
Gigabyte	2^{30}

Mixed Review

Evaluate the expression when $x = 3$ and $y = 9$. *(Lesson 1.3)*

44. $5x - 12$ **45.** $6x - y$ **46.** $\frac{y}{x} + 20$

Choose a Strategy **Use a strategy from the list to solve the following problem. Explain your choice of strategy.**

47. You have 3 shirts and 2 pairs of pants that you are packing for a trip. You can wear each shirt with each pair of pants. How many different outfits are possible?

Problem Solving Strategies
- Look for a Pattern
- Draw a Diagram
- Make a List

Test-Taking Practice

INTERNET
State Test Practice
CLASSZONE.COM

48. Multiple Choice What is the value of the expression $5^3 - 3^4$?

A. 3 **B.** 19 **C.** 44 **D.** 128

49. Multiple Choice The *volume* of a cube is s^3, where s is the length of one side of the cube. A cube has a side length of 14 centimeters. What is the volume of the cube in cubic centimeters?

F. 42 **G.** 196 **H.** 1400 **I.** 2744

Notebook Review

Review the vocabulary definitions in your notebook.

Copy the review examples in your notebook. Then complete the exercises.

Check Your Definitions

bar graph, p. 5
data, p. 5
frequency table, p. 6
histogram, p. 6
numerical expression, p. 10
evaluate, p. 10
order of operations, p. 10
verbal model, p. 11
variable, p. 15
variable expression, p. 15
power, p. 20
exponent, base, p. 20

Use Your Vocabulary

1. What is the first step in the order of operations?

1.1 Can you analyze data displays?

EXAMPLE The bar graph shows the average depths of the Great Lakes. Which of the lakes has the greatest average depth?

ANSWER Lake Superior has the longest bar, so it has the greatest average depth.

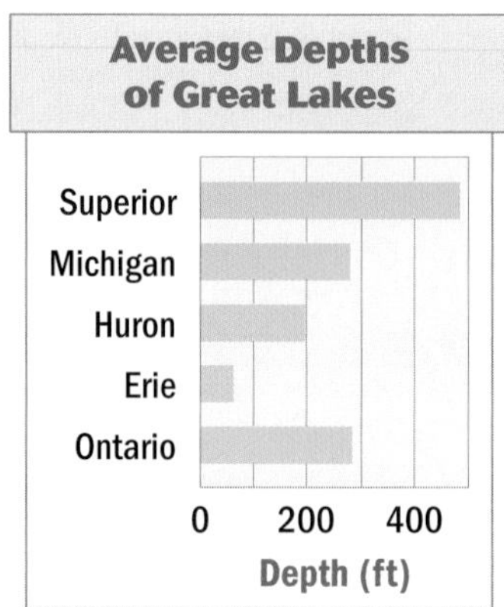

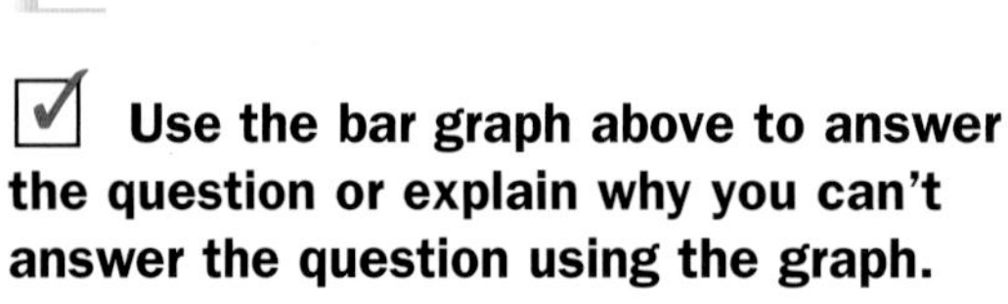

Use the bar graph above to answer the question or explain why you can't answer the question using the graph.

2. Which of the Great Lakes is the largest in area?

3. Which Great Lake is the shallowest on average?

1.2–1.3 Can you evaluate variable expressions?

EXAMPLE Evaluate the expression $4x - y + 12$ when $x = 7$ and $y = 10$.

$4x - y + 12 = 4(7) - 10 + 12$ **Substitute 7 for *x* and 10 for *y*.**

$= 28 - 10 + 12$ **Multiply.**

$= 30$ **Add and subtract from left to right.**

Evaluate the expression when $x = 3$ and $y = 6$.

4. $(x + 3) \cdot x$ **5.** $\frac{3y - 9}{x}$ **6.** $5 + y \div x$

1.4 Can you evaluate expressions with powers?

EXAMPLE Evaluate the expression $4^3 \div (2 \times 2)^2$.

$4^3 \div (2 \times 2)^2 = 4^3 \div 4^2$	**Multiply inside parentheses.**
$= 64 \div 16$	**Evaluate powers.**
$= 4$	**Divide.**

Evaluate.

7. $9 \times 2^3 - 15$ **8.** $(2^5 + 8) \cdot 5^2$ **9.** $(18 \div 6)^3 + (11 - 4)^3$

Stop *and* Think about Lessons 1.1–1.4

10. **Critical Thinking** The numbers 100 and 1000 can be written as 10^2 and 10^3. How does the number of zeros relate to the exponents of these powers of 10?

Review Quiz 1

1. **Home Runs** The table shows the record number of home runs hit in a single season by position. Make a bar graph that displays the data.

2. How many more home runs is the record for outfield than for pitcher?

Position	Home Runs
Catcher	41
1st base	69
Pitcher	9
2nd base	42
Shortstop	52
3rd base	48
Outfield	73

Evaluate the expression.

3. $21 - 2 \cdot 7$ **4.** $8 \times 10 - 40 + 25$ **5.** $24 - (9 + 7) \div 4$

6. $(3 + 1)^2 - 1^5$ **7.** $10^4 \div 5^3$ **8.** $3^4 + 7 \cdot 5$

9. **Plants** A plant is 14 inches tall and grows 4 inches each year. Another plant is 8 inches tall and grows 6 inches each year. Write variable expressions for the plants' heights. Then evaluate the expressions to find the heights in 5 years.

Evaluate the expression for the given value of the variable.

10. $5a - 3 + 7$ when $a = 4$ **11.** $8 + b + 4 \cdot 11$ when $b = 3$

12. $2 \cdot z^4 \div 8$ when $z = 4$ **13.** $(9 - x)^5 \cdot 3 - 16$ when $x = 7$

1.5 Problem Solving Strategies

INDIANA: Academic Standards
• Problem Solving (8.7.1, 8.7.5)

Guess, Check, and Revise

- Look for a Pattern
- Draw a Diagram
- Act It Out
- Work Backward
- Guess, Check, and Revise
- Make a Table
- Solve a Simpler Problem

Problem Consecutive numbers are numbers that follow one after another. The numbers 1, 2, and 3 are consecutive numbers. The sum of three consecutive numbers is 66. What are these numbers?

1 Read and Understand

Read the problem carefully.

The problem asks for the three consecutive numbers that add up to 66.

2 Make a Plan

Decide on a strategy to use.

One way to solve the problem is to use the guess, check, and revise strategy. Guess the answer and check it to see if you are correct. If not, revise your guess and try again.

3 Solve the Problem

Reread the problem. Then make a guess, check the answer, and revise, if necessary.

Reasoning	Guess	Check
Because 22 is one third of 66, you might choose 22, 23, and 24 for the first guess.	22, 23, 24	$22 + 23 + 24 = 69$ ✗
Because the first guess was too high, revise your guess using smaller numbers.	20, 21, 22	$20 + 21 + 22 = 63$ ✗
Second guess is too low. Try again.	21, 22, 23	$21 + 22 + 23 = 66$ ✓

So, the consecutive numbers that add up to 66 are 21, 22, and 23.

4 Look Back

Check your answer by adding the numbers again to see if their sum is 66.

$$21 + 22 + 23 \stackrel{?}{=} 66$$
$$66 = 66 \checkmark$$

Practice the Strategy

Use the strategy *guess, check, and revise.*

1. **Consecutive Numbers** The sum of two consecutive numbers divided by 3 is 71. What are the numbers?

2. **Money** There are some nickels, dimes, and quarters in your pocket. You know you have exactly 15 coins, exactly 5 of them are nickels, and the total amount is $2.30. How many dimes do you have? How many quarters?

3. **Game** You are playing a game where you collect blue chips and green chips. For every blue chip you get one point. For every green chip you lose a point. If you have a total of 20 chips and a total of 14 points, how many blue chips do you have? How many green chips do you have?

4. **Video Game** Damon has saved $33 to buy a new video game that costs $52. His mother offers to contribute $5. How much more does he need to save?

5. **Triangle** Copy the triangle below. Fill in the circles using each of the numbers 1, 2, 3, 4, 5, 6, and 7 exactly once so that the sum of each side and the sum of the middle column is 10.

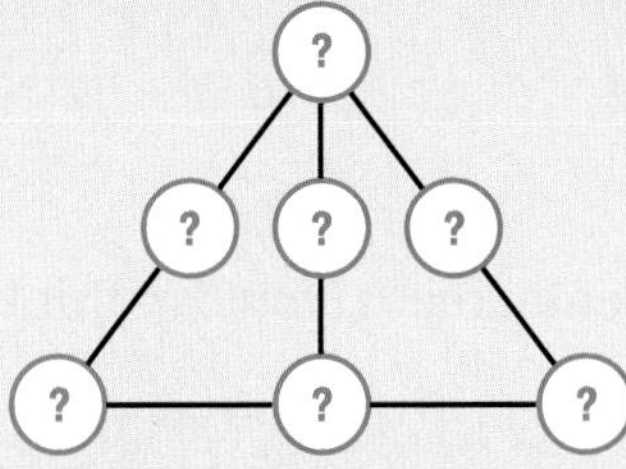

6. **Fundraising** You sell 14 items for a school fundraiser and make a total of $142. A T-shirt costs $11 and a hat costs $9. How many T-shirts did you sell? How many hats did you sell?

Mixed Problem Solving

Use any strategy to solve the problem.

7. **Ice Cream** An ice cream shop offers week-long special deals when you purchase a large ice cream cake. They offer a free small ice cream cake every fifth week, a free pint of ice cream every sixth week, and a free ice cream cone every third week. How many times in one year will they offer all three deals in the same week if they offer all three the first week of the year?

8. **Flowers** Hannah is in charge of buying carnations to give away at a school dance. The flower shop sells carnations at a discount in groups of 12. Hannah needs 170 carnations for the dance. How many groups of 12 carnations should she buy?

9. **Height** Justin, Bob, Kelly, Michelle, and Tim are all different heights. Kelly is taller than Michelle and Justin. Tim is shorter than Justin but taller than Michelle. Bob is the tallest of the group. Put the students in order from tallest to shortest.

10. **Talent Show** Your school talent show allows people to sign up for 3 or 5 minute acts. There is one minute between acts. The talent show has 15 acts and lasts for 79 minutes. How many 3 minute acts are there?

Equations and Solutions

BEFORE

You wrote and evaluated variable expressions.

Now

You'll write and solve equations using mental math.

WHY?

So you can find the weight of a baby elephant, as in Ex. 29.

Word Watch

equation, p. 28
solution, p. 28
solving an equation, p. 28

INDIANA Academic Standards

- Computation (8.2.4)
- Algebra and Functions (8.3.1)
- Problem Solving (8.7.11)

Activity **You can use algebra tiles to solve equations.**

In an *equation*, the quantities on each side of the equal sign have the same value. The algebra tile model below represents the equation $x + 2 = 6$.

(1) With how many 1-tiles should you replace the x-tile so that the quantities on both sides of the equal sign have the same value? Explain.

(2) What value of x makes the equation $x + 2 = 6$ a true statement?

Make a model to represent the equation. Then tell what value of x makes the equation a true statement.

1. $x + 3 = 8$ **2.** $x + 4 = 5$ **3.** $6 + x = 10$

An **equation** is a mathematical sentence formed by placing an equal sign (=) between two expressions.

A **solution** of a variable equation is a number that you can substitute for a variable to make the equation true. Finding all the solutions of an equation is called **solving an equation**.

EXAMPLE 1 Using Mental Math to Solve Equations

Solve the equation using mental math.

a. $15 - n = 4$ **b.** $8x = 32$ **c.** $r \div 12 = 4$

Solution

To solve simple equations using mental math, you can think of the equation as a question.

a. 15 minus **what number** equals 4? $15 - 11 = 4$, so $n = 11$.

b. 8 times **what number** equals 32? $8(4) = 32$, so $x = 4$.

c. **What number** divided by 12 equals 4? $48 \div 12 = 4$, so $r = 48$.

EXAMPLE 2 Checking Solutions of Equations

Tell whether the value of the variable is a solution of $n - 8 = 20$.

a. $n = 12$ **b.** $n = 28$

Solution

Substitute for n and then simplify.

a. $n - 8 = 20$

$12 - 8 \stackrel{?}{=} 20$

$4 \neq 20$

b. $n - 8 = 20$

$\mathbf{28} - 8 \stackrel{?}{=} 20$

$20 = 20$

ANSWER 12 is not a solution of $n - 8 = 20$, and 28 is a solution.

HELP with Reading

The $\stackrel{?}{=}$ symbol means *are these values equal?*
The $\neq$ symbol means *is not equal to.*

Your turn now **Solve the equation using mental math.**

1. $5x = 45$
2. $16 + n = 21$
3. $t \div 6 = 9$

Tell whether the value of the variable is a solution of the equation.

4. $a + 9 = 16$; $a = 7$
5. $88 \div y = 8$; $y = 8$
6. $7n = 13$; $n = 2$

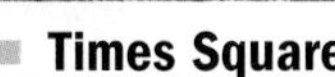

Times Square

The Times Square New Year's Eve Ball in New York City has a total of 696 lights. Of these, 168 are on the exterior and 432 are on the interior. The remaining lights are strobe lights. How many strobe lights are there?

EXAMPLE 3 Writing an Equation

Times Square The Times Square New Year's Eve Ball drops a total of 77 feet in 60 seconds. After 54 seconds the ball has dropped 69 feet. How many more feet will the ball drop?

Solution

You can use a verbal model to write an equation. Let d represent the distance left to drop.

Total distance ball drops	=	Distance ball has dropped	+	Distance left to drop	**Write a verbal model.**
77	=	69	+	d	**Substitute.**
77	=	69	+	**8**	**Use mental math.**

ANSWER Because $d = 8$, the ball will drop 8 more feet.

✓ **Check** You can check your answer by finding the sum of 8 and 69.

$8 + 69 \stackrel{?}{=} 77$

$77 = 77$ ✓

More Practice, p. 727

Getting Ready to Practice

1. **Vocabulary** Give an example of an equation with a variable. Explain how to find the solution of the equation.

Solve the equation using mental math.

2. $9 + p = 21$
3. $y - 10 = 34$
4. $7x = 77$
5. $56 \div k = 8$

Tell whether the value of the variable is a solution of the equation.

6. $35 - x = 21; x = 16$
7. $75 \div x = 5; x = 15$
8. $x + 29 = 42; x = 13$
9. $7x = 84; x = 14$

10. **Fireworks** Your town's fireworks show cost \$1000 per minute. The total cost was \$25,000. Use a verbal model to write and solve an equation to find how many minutes the fireworks show lasted.

Practice and Problem Solving

HELP with Homework

Example	Exercises
1	11-14, 19-26
2	15-18
3	27

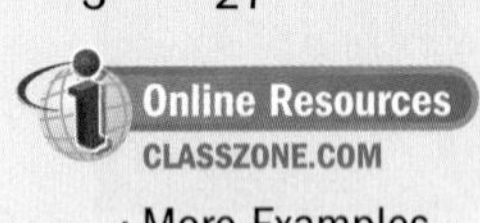

- More Examples
- eTutorial Plus

Match the equation with the corresponding question.

11. $24 \div t = 8$
12. $t + 8 = 24$
13. $24t = 8$
14. $\frac{t}{24} = 8$

A. What number divided by 24 equals 8?
B. 24 divided by what number equals 8?
C. What number plus 8 equals 24?
D. 24 times what number equals 8?

Tell whether the value of the variable is a solution of the equation.

15. $15 + b = 28; b = 13$
16. $37 - d = 14; d = 21$
17. $6w = 72; w = 14$
18. $9c = 108; c = 12$

Solve the equation using mental math.

19. $z + 8 = 19$
20. $6m = 48$
21. $c - 16 = 13$
22. $51 \div k = 3$
23. $\frac{32}{n} = 16$
24. $26 - r = 17$
25. $10y = 150$
26. $7 + x = 31$

27. **Rainfall** The highest recorded rainfall in the United States in a 24 hour period is 43 inches. Write an equation to find how much more rain needs to fall in the remaining time to equal the record, if 14 inches has already fallen in less than 24 hours. Then solve the equation.

28. **Writing** Explain how you would tell whether 5 is a solution of the equation $4x = 20$.

29. **Elephants** A baby elephant at the Bronx Zoo would get on a scale only with its mother. The zoo weighed the mother as 5033 pounds. They weighed the mother and the baby together as 5396 pounds. Write and solve an equation to find the weight of the baby elephant.

30. **Measurement** Describe how you could use mental math to find the number of feet in 3600 inches.

31. **Invitations** You are writing invitations to a party. It takes you four minutes to complete each invitation. Write and solve an equation to find how many invitations you can complete in one hour.

32. **Guess, Check, and Revise** Find the value of x that makes the equation below true.

$$[(x + 3) \cdot 4 - 7] \div 3 = 3$$

Challenge Tell which of the given values is a solution of the equation.

33. $3x + 6 = x + 12$; $x = 1, 2, 3$

34. $2x - 7 = x + 1$; $x = 8, 9, 10$

35. $8 - 4x = 4x$; $x = 0, 1, 2$

36. $2x - 4.5 = x \div 2$; $x = 3, 4, 5$

37. **Marathon** To qualify for the Boston Marathon, Hillary has to run a qualifying time of 3 hours 40 minutes or less. Her best time so far is 4 hours 5 minutes. Write and solve an equation to find by how many minutes Hillary must improve her time to qualify.

Mixed Review

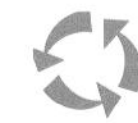

Evaluate the expression when $y = 8$. *(Lesson 1.3)*

38. $7y + 17$

39. $(36 - 24) \cdot y$

40. $y \cdot 4 + 20 \cdot y$

Basic Skills Estimate the sum or difference.

41. $8748 - 3109$

42. $876 + 622$

43. $147 + 89 + 791$

Test-Taking Practice

INTERNET
State Test Practice
CLASSZONE.COM

44. **Multiple Choice** Which of the following is a solution of $63 \div x = 9$?

A. 6 **B.** 7 **C.** 9 **D.** 54

45. **Short Response** You and your friend volunteer at a zoo during the summer. One week you volunteer 12 hours. The sum of the hours you and your friend work that week is 23. Write an equation that can be used to determine how many hours your friend worked. Then solve the equation.

1.6 Hands-on Activity

INDIANA: Academic Standards
- Measurement (8.5.4)

GOAL
Develop formulas for finding the areas of rectangles and squares.

MATERIALS
- square tiles

Modeling Area

You can use square tiles to find the *areas* of rectangles and squares.

Explore

Find the area of a 5 unit by 3 unit rectangle.

1. Use square tiles to make a rectangle with side lengths of 5 units and 3 units.

2. The area of the rectangle is equal to the number of square unit tiles that cover it. Count the square tiles to find the area of the rectangle.

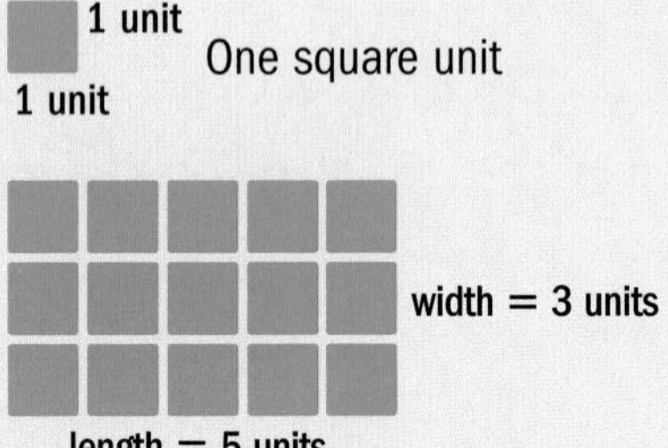

Your turn now

1. Use square tiles to make a rectangle that is the size given in the table. Copy and complete the table.

Dimensions	Length	Width	Number of square tiles	Area of rectangle
3 by 4	?	?	?	?
4 by 4	?	?	?	?
5 by 6	?	?	?	?
3 by 3	?	?	?	?

2. Write a variable equation to find the area of a rectangle and explain what each variable represents.

3. Write a different equation to find the area of a square and explain what each variable represents.

Stop *and* Think

4. **Critical Thinking** Area is measured in square units. Perimeter is the distance around a shape. Is perimeter measured in square units? Why or why not?

Variables in Familiar Formulas

BEFORE	Now	WHY?
You evaluated variable expressions.	You'll use formulas to find unknown values.	So you can find the sizes of swimming pools, as in Ex. 22.

Word Watch

formula, p. 33
perimeter, p. 33
area, p. 33

INDIANA
Academic Standards

- Measurement (8.5.2, 8.5.4)

A **formula** is an equation that relates two or more quantities such as *perimeter*, length, and width. The **perimeter** of a figure is the sum of the lengths of its sides. The **area** of a figure is the amount of surface the figure covers.

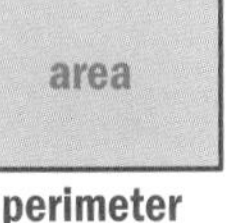

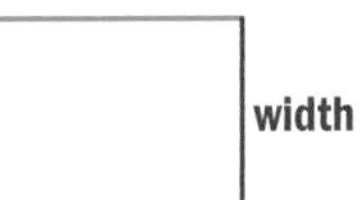

Perimeter is measured in linear units such as feet. Area is measured in square units such as square feet, or ft^2.

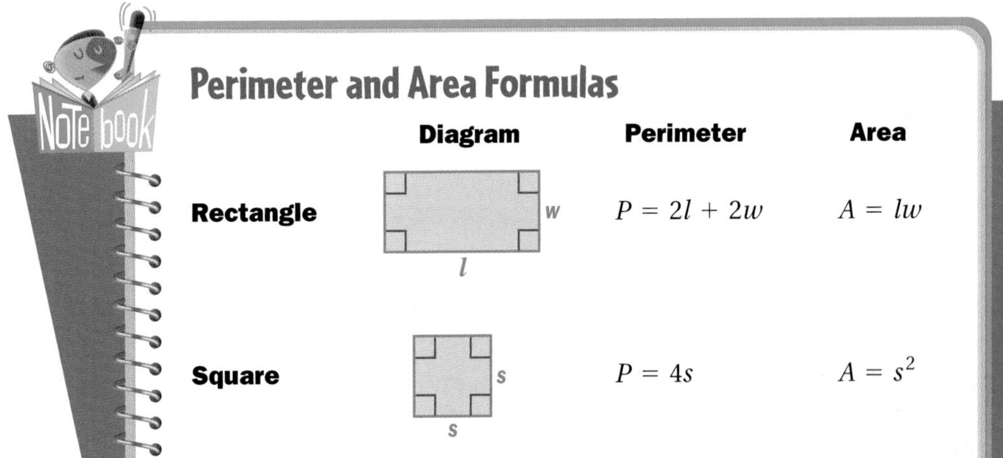

Perimeter and Area Formulas

	Diagram	Perimeter	Area
Rectangle	l, w	$P = 2l + 2w$	$A = lw$
Square	s, s	$P = 4s$	$A = s^2$

EXAMPLE 1 Finding Perimeter and Area

Find the perimeter and area of the rectangle.

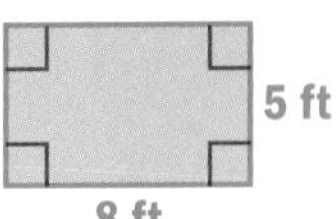

Solution

Find the perimeter.

$P = 2l + 2w$	Write formula.
$= 2(8) + 2(5)$	Substitute.
$= 26$	Multiply, then add.

Find the area.

$A = lw$	Write formula.
$= (8)(5)$	Substitute.
$= 40$	Multiply.

ANSWER The perimeter is 26 feet, and the area is 40 square feet.

HELP with Reading

The mark ⌉ tells you that an angle measures 90°.

EXAMPLE 2 Finding Side Length

Find the side length of a square with an area of 81 square feet.

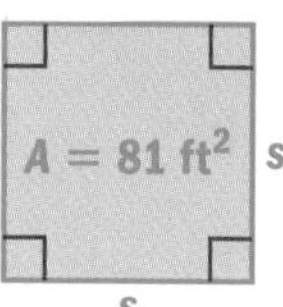

$A = s^2$	Write formula for area of a square.
$81 = s^2$	Substitute 81 for A.
$9 = s$	Use mental math: $9^2 = 81$.

ANSWER The side length of the square is 9 feet.

Distance Formula Another useful formula is the distance formula. You can use the distance formula to find distance traveled.

Distance Formula

Words The distance traveled d is the product of the rate r and the time t.

Algebra $d = r \cdot t$ or $d = rt$

Numbers $d = 45 \frac{\text{miles}}{\cancel{\text{hour}}} \cdot 3 \cancel{\text{hours}} = 135 \text{ miles}$

In the formula $d = rt$, rate is the speed of travel.

EXAMPLE 3 Using the Distance Formula

Rabbits A rabbit is running at a rate of 26.4 feet per second. How far does the rabbit travel in 5 seconds?

Solution

$d = r \cdot t$	Write distance formula.
$= 26.4 \cdot 5$	Substitute 26.4 for r and 5 for t.
$= 132$	Multiply.

ANSWER The rabbit travels 132 feet in 5 seconds.

Your turn now **Solve.**

1. Find the perimeter and area of a square with a 7 inch side length.
2. Find the side length of a square that has an area of 100 square yards.
3. How far does a car travel in 2 hours at a rate of 40 miles per hour?

You can write the distance formula in different forms to find rate or time. Use $t = \frac{d}{r}$ to find the time and $r = \frac{d}{t}$ to find the rate.

EXAMPLE 4 Using the Distance Formula to Find Time

How long will it take a rabbit to travel 264 feet at a rate of 22 feet per second?

Solution

$t = \frac{d}{r}$ Write distance formula.

$= \frac{264}{22}$ Substitute 264 for *d* and 22 for *r*.

$= 12$ Divide.

ANSWER It will take a rabbit 12 seconds to travel 264 feet.

1.6 Exercises

More Practice, p. 727

Getting Ready to Practice

1. **Vocabulary** Describe the difference between area and perimeter.

Find the perimeter and area of the rectangle or square.

2. 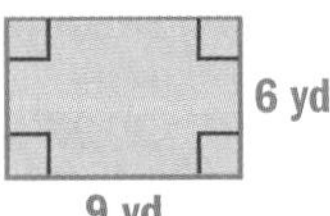

3. 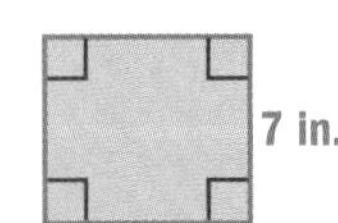

4. 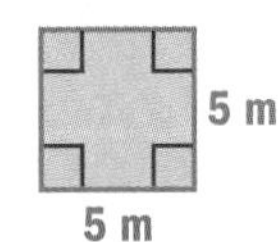

5. **Tiger Beetles** A tiger beetle runs at a rate of 53 centimeters per second for 3 seconds. How far does the beetle run?

6. **Find the Error** Describe and correct the error in the solution.

X $A = s^2$
$= 4^2$
$= 16$ meters

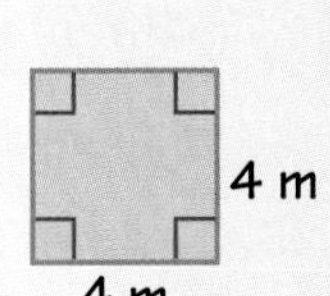

Practice and Problem Solving

HELP with Homework

Example	Exercises
1	7–13, 22
2	14–15, 22
3	17–21, 27
4	17–20, 23

Online Resources
CLASSZONE.COM
- More Examples
- eTutorial Plus

Find the perimeter and area of the rectangle or square.

7. 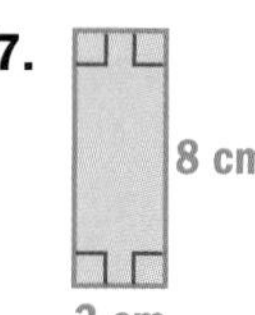

8. 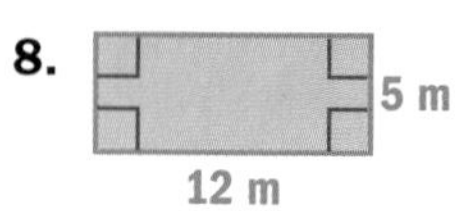

9. 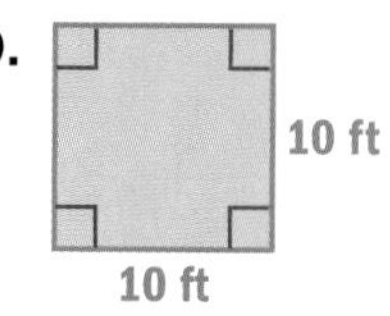

In Exercises 10–13, find the perimeter and area of the rectangle or square.

10. length = 17 m, width = 9 m

11. side length = 18 in.

12. length = 11 ft, width = 2 ft

13. length = 14 cm, width = 13 cm

14. Find the side length of a square that has an area of 36 square yards.

15. Find the side length of a square that has a perimeter of 24 meters.

16. **Mental Math** The area of a rectangle is 88 square inches. The width is 8 inches. Use mental math to find the length of the rectangle.

Use the distance formula to find the unknown value.

17. $d = 36$ km, $r = ?$, $t = 4$ h

18. $d = ?$, $r = 0.5$ mi/min, $t = 10$ min

19. $d = ?$, $r = 7$ mi/h, $t = 1.5$ h

20. $d = 40$ ft, $r = 5$ ft/sec, $t = ?$

21. **Arizona** The speed limit on rural interstates in Arizona is 75 miles per hour. A car travels at this rate for 3 hours. How far does it travel?

22. **Swimming Pools** The table shows information about two swimming pools. Copy and complete the table.

	Length	Width	Area	Perimeter
Pool A	60 ft	22 ft	?	?
Pool B	?	30 ft	1800 ft^2	?

23. **Train** A train travels 226 miles from Washington, D.C., to New York City in about 2 hours 30 minutes. What is the average speed of the train in miles per hour? Round to the nearest mile per hour.

24. **Temperature Formula** To convert from degrees Celsius to degrees Fahrenheit, you can use the formula $F = \frac{9}{5}C + 32$. Convert 20°C to degrees Fahrenheit.

25. **Estimation** The driving distance between Houston and Dallas is 224 miles. Suppose a car travels at an average rate of 52 miles per hour. Estimate how long the trip from Houston to Dallas takes.

26. **Measurement** Write a formula for converting meters to centimeters.

What do you think? **Travel**

Arizona

U.S. Highway 66, often called Route 66, was commissioned in 1926. It connected Illinois to California traveling through eight states, including Arizona. Route 66 ceased to exist as an official highway in 1984. How many years was it an official highway?

27. **Parachutist** A parachutist falls for 2 minutes at a speed of 13 feet per second. How far does the parachutist fall during this time?

Yard Fencing **In Exercises 28 and 29, your rectangular yard has a length of 50 feet and a width of 45 feet.**

28. You want to fence in your yard. How much fencing do you need?

29. You want to fertilize your yard. Each bag of fertilizer covers 2000 square feet. How many bags should you buy?

Challenge **Find the perimeter and area of the figure.**

30.

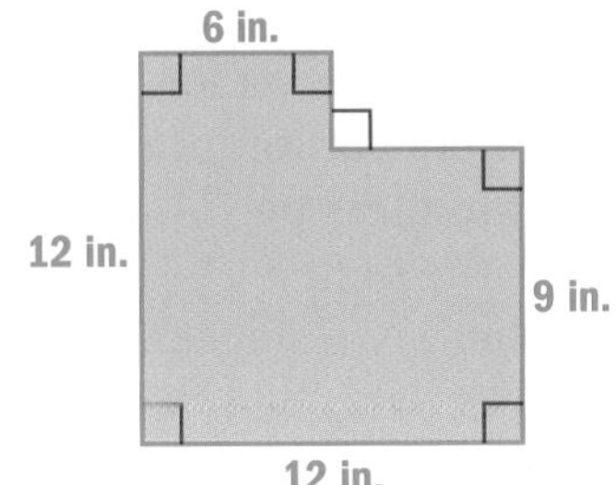

31.

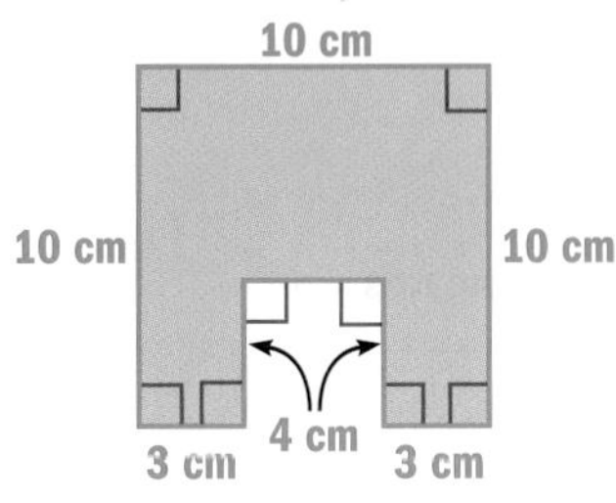

32. **Critical Thinking** Find the perimeter and area of a rectangle with a length of 6 inches and a width of 5 inches. Then find the perimeter and area of a rectangle with a length of 12 inches and a width of 10 inches. How does the perimeter of a rectangle change if length and width are doubled? How does the area of a rectangle change if the length and width are doubled?

Mixed Review 

Solve the equation using mental math. *(Lesson 1.5)*

33. $8x = 72$ **34.** $g - 19 = 37$ **35.** $\frac{y}{3} = 10$

Basic Skills **Round the number to the place value of the red digit.**

36. 7.528 **37.** 15.538 **38.** 13.974

Test-Taking Practice 

INTERNET
State Test Practice
CLASSZONE.COM

39. **Multiple Choice** You drive 50 miles per hour for 1 hour 30 minutes. Which expression can be used to find how many miles you travel?

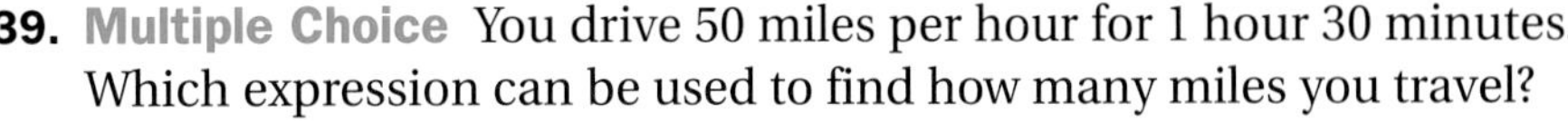

A. 50×130 **B.** 50×90 **C.** 50×1.5 **D.** $50 \div 90$

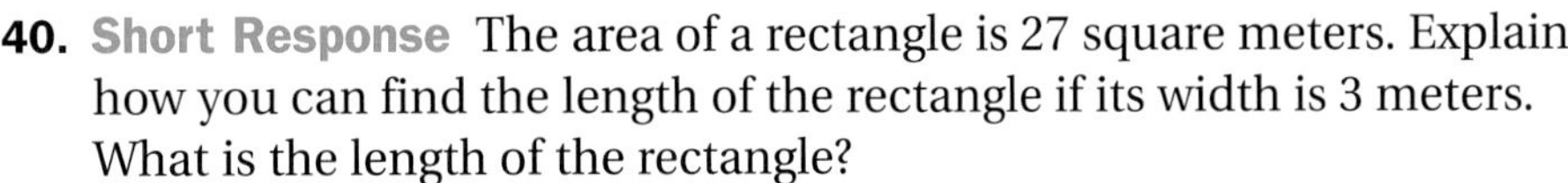

40. **Short Response** The area of a rectangle is 27 square meters. Explain how you can find the length of the rectangle if its width is 3 meters. What is the length of the rectangle?

A Problem Solving Plan

BEFORE	Now	WHY?
You used problem solving strategies to solve problems.	You'll use a problem solving plan to solve problems.	To find how much cheese you need for lasagna, as in Ex. 9.

Review Word

formula, p. 33

INDIANA Academic Standards

- Measurement (8.5.2)
- Problem Solving (8.7.1)

In the Real World

Triathlon You and a friend decide to compete in a triathlon. You both swim 200 meters, bike 10 kilometers, and then run 2 kilometers.

The table shows your speeds for swimming, in meters per minute, and biking, in kilometers per minute. Who has the better total time after these two stages?

	Swimming (m/min)	Biking (km/min)
You	76.9	0.43
Friend	82.6	0.41

EXAMPLE 1 Understanding and Planning

To solve the triathlon problem, you need to make sure you understand the problem. Then make a plan for solving the problem.

Read and Understand

What do you know?

The table tells you each of your speeds for each stage.

You both swim 200 meters and bike 10 kilometers.

What do you want to find out?

Who has the better total time for swimming and biking

Make a Plan

How can you relate what you know to what you want to find out?

Find each of your swimming and biking times.

Find each of your total times and then compare these times.

You will solve the problem in Example 2.

 **Use the information at the top of the page.**

1. Which formula would you use to find swimming and running times? Explain your reasoning.

A. $distance = rate \cdot time$ **B.** $time = \dfrac{distance}{rate}$ **C.** $rate = \dfrac{distance}{time}$

EXAMPLE 2 Solving and Looking Back

To solve the triathlon problem from the previous page, you need to carry out the plan from Example 1 and then check the answer.

Solve the Problem

To find each of your times, use the formula *time* = $\frac{distance}{rate}$.

	You	Friend
Swimming	$t = \frac{d}{r}$ $= \frac{200}{76.9}$ $\approx$ 2.6 min	$t = \frac{d}{r}$ $= \frac{200}{82.6}$ $\approx$ 2.4 min
Biking	$t = \frac{d}{r}$ $= \frac{10}{0.43}$ $\approx$ 23.26 min	$t = \frac{d}{r}$ $= \frac{10}{0.41}$ $\approx$ 24.39 min

HELP with Reading

The $\approx$ symbol means *is approximately equal to.*

Add to find the total time for each of you.

You 2.6 + 23.26 = 25.86 min
Friend 2.4 + 24.39 = 26.79 min

ANSWER You have the better total time after the two stages.

Look Back

Does your answer make sense?

Notice that you swim at a slower rate than your friend, so it makes sense that your swimming time is greater. You bike at a faster rate than your friend, so it makes sense that your biking time is less. So the calculations appear reasonable.

Problem Solving Plan

1. **Read and Understand** Read the problem carefully. Identify the question and any important information.
2. **Make a Plan** Decide on a problem solving strategy.
3. **Solve the Problem** Use the problem solving strategy to answer the question.
4. **Look Back** Check that your answer is reasonable.

Unit Analysis You can use *unit analysis* to evaluate expressions with units of measure and to check that your answer uses the correct units.

For example, when you find the product of rate and time using the units below, the units for distance will be miles.

$$\frac{\text{miles}}{\cancel{\text{hour}}} \cdot \cancel{\text{hour}} = \text{miles}$$

EXAMPLE 3 Using a Problem Solving Plan

New York City In parts of New York City, the blocks between avenues are called *long blocks*. There are 4 long blocks per mile. Blocks between streets are called *short blocks*. There are 20 short blocks per mile. You walk 40 short blocks and 6 long blocks. How many miles do you walk?

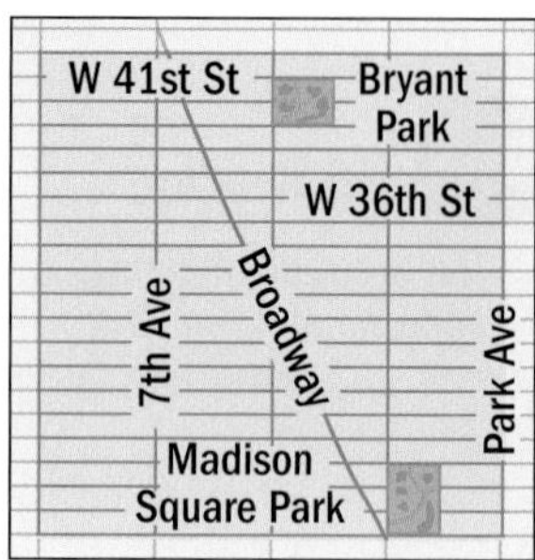

Solution

Read and Understand You walk 40 short blocks and 6 long blocks. There are 20 short blocks per mile and 4 long blocks per mile. You are asked to find how many miles you walk.

Make a Plan Convert short blocks to miles and long blocks to miles using unit analysis. Then add to find the total miles.

Solve the Problem

Because there are 20 short blocks in one mile, you can multiply the number of short blocks you walk by $\frac{1 \text{ mile}}{20 \text{ short blocks}}$ to convert short blocks to miles.

$$40 \cancel{\text{ short blocks}} \times \frac{1 \text{ mile}}{20 \cancel{\text{ short blocks}}} = 2 \text{ miles}$$

Multiply the number of long blocks you walk by $\frac{1 \text{ mile}}{4 \text{ long blocks}}$ to convert long blocks to miles.

$$6 \cancel{\text{ long blocks}} \times \frac{1 \text{ mile}}{4 \cancel{\text{ long blocks}}} = 1.5 \text{ miles}$$

ANSWER You walk a total of $2 + 1.5 = 3.5$ miles.

Look Back Check your answer by drawing a diagram.

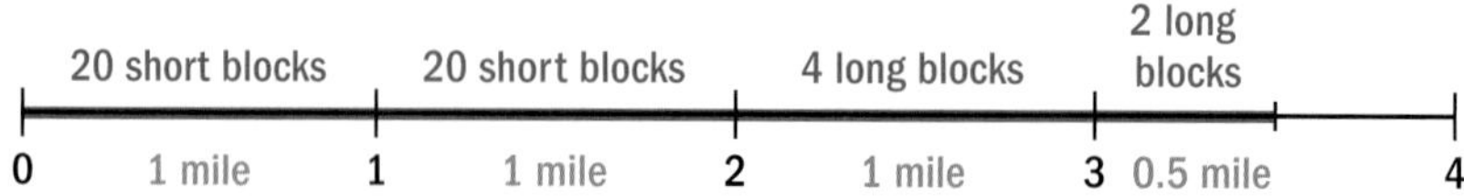

From the diagram you can see that 40 short blocks are 2 miles and 6 long blocks are 1.5 miles, which totals 3.5 miles. So, your answer checks. ✓

1.7 Exercises

More Practice, p. 727

Getting Ready to Practice

1. **Vocabulary** List the four steps of the problem solving plan.

2. **Tickets** You pay $15 a ticket for 4 tickets and a service charge of $2 for every ticket after the second one. You are charged $64 for this order. Describe a way to check that this is the correct price.

3. **Guided Problem Solving** A monorail ride at an amusement park has 5 cars per trainload, and each car can hold 4 passengers. In one hour, 900 people can ride the monorail. How many trainloads run in one hour?

   (1) Write a verbal model of the problem.

   (2) Use the model to find the number of trainloads in one hour.

   (3) Check your answer.

Practice and Problem Solving

Example	Exercises
1	4-9
2	4-9
3	4-9

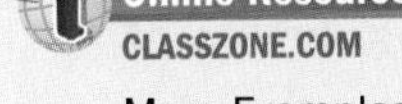

· More Examples
· eTutorial Plus

4. **Find the Error** Daniel has enough film to take 96 pictures on a 5 day trip. He takes 45 pictures the first 2 days. He wants to take an equal number of pictures each day for the last 3 days. Describe and correct the error in the solution.

   X $\frac{96}{3} = 32$

   So, I can take 32 pictures each day.

5. **Saving** Fran is saving money for a color printer that costs $210. She makes $6 an hour baby-sitting, and her parents will contribute $120. Use the problem solving plan to find how many hours she needs to baby-sit to earn enough money for the printer.

6. **Look for a Pattern** Draw the next two shapes in the pattern below.

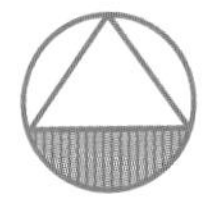 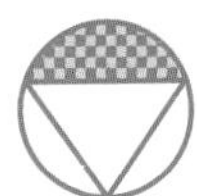 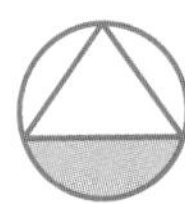 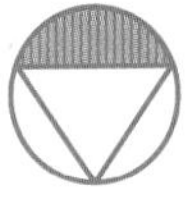 

7. **Music** You practice for 2 hours each weekday and for 3 hours on each weekend day. How many hours per week do you practice?

8. **Bicycle Race** A Tour de France bicycle race covered 3462 kilometers in 21 days. Riders traveled 3152 kilometers during the first 19 racing days and then traveled 160 kilometers the next day. How long was the ride on the last day?

9. **Community Service** You are making lasagna for 30 people at a homeless shelter. It takes 8 ounces of mozzarella cheese to make enough to serve 10 people. You have 12 ounces of mozzarella cheese. How much more do you need?

Critical Thinking In Exercises 10–13, complete the pattern.

10. 2, 7, 12, _?_, _?_

11. 9, 7, 5, _?_, _?_

12. 3, 12, 48, _?_

13. 21, 17, 13, _?_, _?_

14. **Writing** Is there enough information to answer the following question? Explain how to solve the problem, or tell what information is needed.

    Amanda has sold magazine subscriptions worth $330 for a school fundraiser. If she reaches a total of $500, she wins a gift certificate. How many more subscriptions does she need to sell to reach $500?

15. **Sales** During a 4 week period, a salesperson at a photography studio wants to sell photography packages worth a total of $16,000. Sales for the first 3 weeks are $1240, $3720, and $5980. What does the sales amount need to be in week 4 to reach the $16,000 goal?

16. **Number Sense** The product of two numbers is 48. Their sum is 16. Find the two numbers.

Critical Thinking In Exercises 17–20, complete the pattern.

17. $2x, 4x, 6x$, _?_, _?_

18. $65x, 52x, 39x$, _?_, _?_

19. $7x^2, 15x^2, 23x^2$, _?_, _?_

20. $81x, 78x^2, 75x^3, 72x^4$, _?_, _?_

21. **Garden** You have 28 feet of fencing and want to construct a rectangular garden with the largest possible area with whole number dimensions. Find the side lengths of the largest possible garden. What is its area?

Guess, Check, and Revise In Exercises 22–25, find the solution of the equation.

22. $4x = 2x + 14$

23. $6x = 9x - 15$

24. $2x + 3 = 5x - 9$

25. $9 - 3x = 2x - 11$

26. **Basketball** The table shows the numbers of people who attended Women's National Basketball Association (WNBA) games from 1997 through 2001. Describe how you could predict the attendance for WNBA games in 2002. What is your prediction? How can you check your prediction?

Year	1997	1998	1999	2000	2001
Attendance	1,082,093	1,630,315	1,959,733	2,322,429	2,323,164

27. **Challenge** Bill's house is third in a row of 12 houses. There are 5 houses between Chris's house and Audrey's house, and 2 between Chris's house and Bill's house. How many houses are between Audrey's house and the first house? Explain how you got your answer.

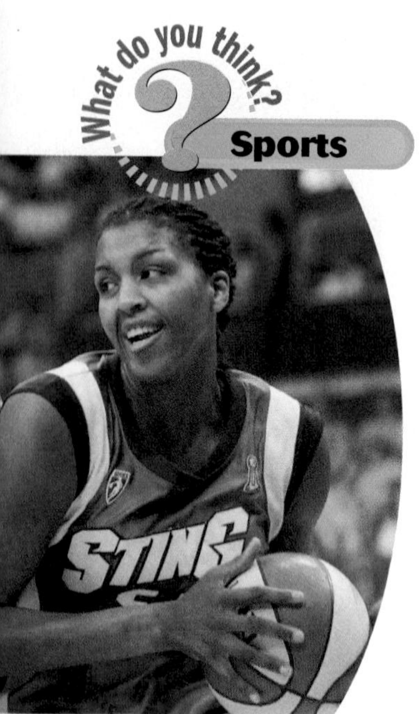

Basketball

In 1997, the WNBA had eight teams. Two teams were added in 1998. In 1999, two more teams were added. Four teams were added in 2000. How many teams were in the WNBA in 2000?

Mixed Review

Evaluate the expression. *(Lesson 1.2)*

28. $7 + 4 \times 3 - 6$ **29.** $24 \div (2 \times 4) - 3$ **30.** $70 \div [14 - 2 \times 2]$

Find the perimeter and area of the figure. *(Lesson 1.6)*

31. a 16 in. by 3 in. rectangle **32.** a square with a 237 ft side

Basic Skills **Complete the statement using $<$ or $>$.**

33. 23.2 _?_ 23 **34.** 0.5 _?_ 5 **35.** 0.1 _?_ 0.01 **36.** 1.4 _?_ 4.1

Test-Taking Practice

INTERNET
State Test Practice
CLASSZONE.COM

37. Multiple Choice You are trying to earn 400 points in a game. In the first round you get 154 points. The next round you get 78 points. How many more points do you need?

A. 76 **B.** 168 **C.** 176 **D.** 268

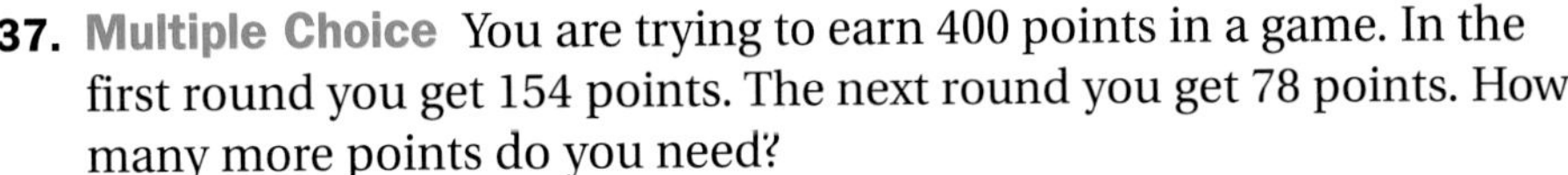

38. Multiple Choice Which picture represents the next arrow in the pattern?

F. **G.** **H.** **I.** 

What's Happening?

Scott, John, Annie, and Rebecca are each doing a different activity. Who is doing what?

- Scott and John are not at the debate.
- Scott can't go to the student council meeting.
- Annie is not going to student council or to art club.
- Rebecca is not a member of the student council.
- Annie and Rebecca do not tutor.

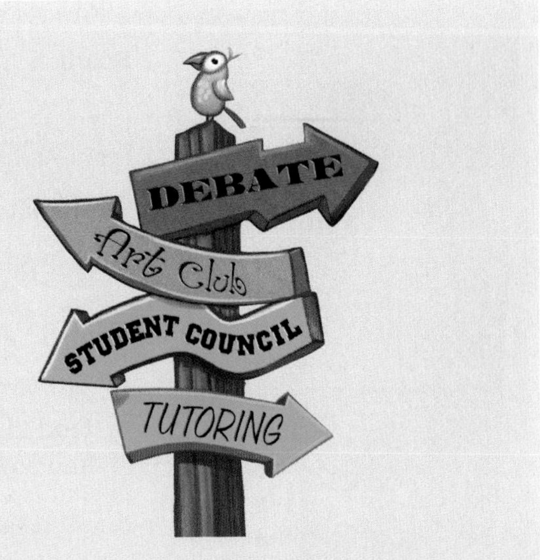

Notebook Review

Review the vocabulary definitions in your notebook.

Copy the review examples in your notebook. Then complete the exercises.

Check Your Definitions

equation, p. 28
solution, p. 28
solving an equation, p. 28
formula, p. 33
perimeter, p. 33
area, p. 33

Use Your Vocabulary

1. What is the formula for the perimeter of a rectangle?

1.5 Can you solve equations using mental math?

EXAMPLE Solve $32 \div n = 8$.

$32 \div n = 8$	Write original equation.
$32 \div 4 = 8$, so $n = 4$.	Solve equation using mental math.

Use mental math to solve the equation.

2. $5 + m = 18$ **3.** $t - 9 = 3$ **4.** $7h = 21$ **5.** $\frac{d}{3} = 6$

1.6 Can you use formulas to find unknown values?

EXAMPLE In 1990, Arie Luyendyk set a record at the Indianapolis 500 race with an average speed of about 186 miles per hour. About how long did it take him to complete the 500 mile race?

Solution

$t = \frac{d}{r}$	Write distance formula.
$= \frac{500}{186}$	Substitute 500 for *d* and 186 for *r*.
≈ 2.69	Divide. Round to the nearest hundredth.

ANSWER Arie Luyendyk completed the race in about 2.69 hours.

6. Find the perimeter and area of a rectangle with a length of 7 meters and a width of 4 meters.

1.7 Can you use a problem solving plan?

EXAMPLE You are filling a 55 gallon aquarium with water using a pitcher from your kitchen. It takes 3 trips with the pitcher to fill a 5 gallon aquarium. How many trips with the pitcher will you need to fill the 55 gallon aquarium?

Read and Understand and Make a Plan Find how many times 5 gallons goes into 55 gallons. Multiply that number by 3, because it takes 3 pitchers to make 5 gallons.

Solve the Problem $\frac{55 \text{ gallons}}{5 \text{ gallons}} = 11$

$11 \cdot 3 \text{ trips} = 33 \text{ trips}$

ANSWER It will take 33 trips with the pitcher to fill the aquarium.

7. If you like 2 teaspoons of sugar in an 8 ounce glass of iced tea, how much sugar should you add to a 36 ounce thermos of iced tea?

Stop *and* Think about Lessons 1.5–1.7

8. **Critical Thinking** Can you tell whether area or perimeter is being measured if you know only the unit of measurement? Explain.

Review Quiz 2

Solve the equation using mental math.

1. $h + 12 = 21$ **2.** $22 - y = 8$ **3.** $54 = 6x$ **4.** $\frac{108}{r} = 9$

5. **Video Games** You have $24 to spend on video game rentals. Each rental costs $3. How many video games can you rent?

6. **Geometry** Find the perimeter and area of a rectangle with a length of 14 feet and a width of 11 feet.

7. **Driving** On the highway you drive at a speed of 55 miles per hour for 3 hours. How far do you drive?

8. **Exercise** You plan to exercise 200 minutes over 5 days. The first four days you exercise 45 minutes, 30 minutes, 20 minutes, and 1 hour. Use the problem solving plan to find the number of minutes you need to exercise on the fifth day to meet your goal.

Chapter Review

Vocabulary

bar graph, p. 5
data, p. 5
frequency table, p. 6
histogram, p. 6
numerical expression, p. 10
evaluate, p. 10
order of operations, p. 10
verbal model, p. 11
variable, p. 15
variable expression, p. 15
power, p. 20
exponent, p. 20
base, p. 20
equation, p. 28
solution, p. 28
solving an equation, p. 28
formula, p. 33
perimeter, p. 33
area, p. 33

Vocabulary Review

Copy and complete the statement.

1. You can graph data organized in a frequency table using a(n) _?_.

2. _?_ is the amount of surface covered by a figure.

3. To evaluate an expression that has more than one operation, use the _?_.

4. A(n) _?_ is a symbol, usually a letter, that represents one or more numbers.

5. A power has an exponent and a(n) _?_.

Tell whether the statement is *true* or *false*.

6. A variable expression is a mathematical sentence that is formed by placing an equal sign between two expressions.

7. A formula is an equation that has only one variable.

8. The perimeter of a figure is the sum of the lengths of its sides.

9. A solution of an equation is a number that, when substituted for a variable, makes the equation true.

Review Questions

In Exercises 10 and 11, use the table at the right. It shows the numbers of volunteers at a local animal shelter. *(Lesson 1.1)*

Age group	Volunteers
15–24	24
25–34	30
35–44	31
45–54	30
55–64	27
65–74	12
75–84	11

10. Which age group has the most volunteers? Which age group has the fewest volunteers?

11. Can you determine the number of volunteers who are teenagers? Explain.

Evaluate the expression. *(Lesson 1.2)*

12. $16 + 5 \times 3 + 8$

13. $40 \div [(14 + 6) \cdot 2)]$

14. $10 + \frac{60}{31 - 26}$

Review Questions

15. Clothes You are saving money to buy two sweaters that each cost \$28.50. You have already saved \$20. To find out how much more money you need to save, translate *2 times 28.5 minus 20* into an expression and then evaluate. *(Lesson 1.2)*

Evaluate the expression when $x = 4$ and $y = 9$. *(Lesson 1.3)*

16. $\frac{xy}{3x}$

17. $\frac{y + 19}{x + 3}$

18. $5y - 6x$

19. $3xy - xy$

20. Dolphins After swimming 22 miles, a dolphin changes direction and swims at a rate of 18 miles per hour. Use the expression $22 + 18t$ to find the total distance traveled by the dolphin after 2 more hours. *(Lesson 1.3)*

Evaluate the power. *(Lesson 1.4)*

21. 15^2

22. 4^5

23. 10^4

24. 9^3

Evaluate the expression. *(Lesson 1.4)*

25. $(5 + 4)^2 \div 3$

26. $5 \cdot (6 - 3)^5 + 45$

27. $[10 + (4 \times 2)^3] \div 2$

Solve the equation using mental math. *(Lesson 1.5)*

28. $7b = 56$

29. $\frac{84}{x} = 12$

30. $98 - t = 35$

Find the perimeter and area of the rectangle or square. *(Lesson 1.6)*

31.

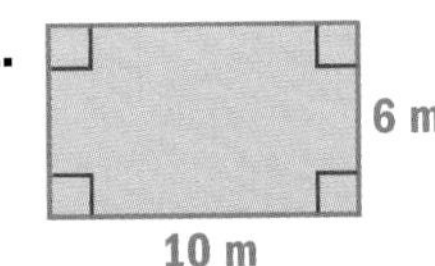

32.

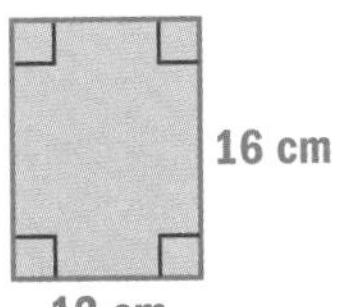

33.

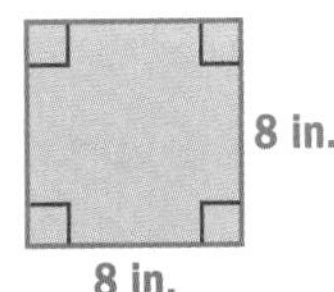

34. Cars A car travels at an average rate of 50 miles per hour for 3 hours. How far does it travel? *(Lesson 1.6)*

35. Radio You are the disc jockey for a 15 minute radio show at your school. You must leave 3 minutes open for announcements, and you want to play 3 songs. Use the table at the right to determine the 3 songs you can play. *(Lesson 1.7)*

Song	A	B	C	D	E
Length (minutes)	6	4	3	5	6

CHAPTER 1

Chapter Test

Sports In a survey, 3000 people in Japan were asked about their participation in ten sports. The results for four sports are in the table.

Sport	Participants
Gymnastics	1002
Bowling	996
Jogging	807
Swimming	717

1. Make a bar graph of the data.
2. Is it possible to make a histogram of the data? Explain.

Evaluate the expression.

3. $20 + 12 \div 4$
4. $6 \times 5 - 20 \div 2$
5. $(3 + 7) \div 5 + 10$

6. Plumbing A plumber charges a flat rate of \$25 plus an additional \$55 for each hour of work. To find how much money the plumber makes in 5 hours at one location, evaluate the expression $25 + 55 \cdot 5$.

7. Fruit You are buying 3 apples and 4 oranges for a fruit salad. The cost of one apple is x dollars. The cost of one orange is y dollars. Write a variable expression to represent the cost of 3 apples and 4 oranges. If one apple costs \$.75 and one orange costs \$.50, what is the total cost?

Evaluate the expression.

8. $(2 + 3)^4 \div 5$
9. $10^2 - 3^4 + 22$
10. $(11 - 5)^4 - 300 \div 12$

Solve the equation using mental math.

11. $17 - t = 5$
12. $9n = 72$
13. $49 \div b = 7$
14. $21 + a = 27$

Tell whether the value of the variable is a solution of the equation.

15. $z + 2 = 15; z = 13$
16. $65 \div y = 16; y = 4$
17. $11x = 45; x = 4$

18. Court Area The lengths and widths of three different types of courts are listed in the table. Find the area of each court. Which court has the largest area? Which court has the smallest area?

Court	Length	Width
Squash	32 feet	21 feet
Tennis	78 feet	27 feet
Racquetball	40 feet	20 feet

19. Horses A horse travels at a rate of 60 feet per second. How far does the horse travel in 4 seconds?

20. Park A rectangular park that is 90 feet long and 60 feet wide needs to be planted with sod. A roll of sod covers 1 square yard. Use the problem solving plan to find how many rolls of sod are needed to cover the park.

Chapter Standardized Test

Test-Taking Strategy **Most standardized tests are based on concepts and skills taught in school. The best way to prepare is to keep up with your daily studies.**

Multiple Choice

1. The histogram shows the times 25 people arrived at a party. How many people arrived between 9 and 10:59?

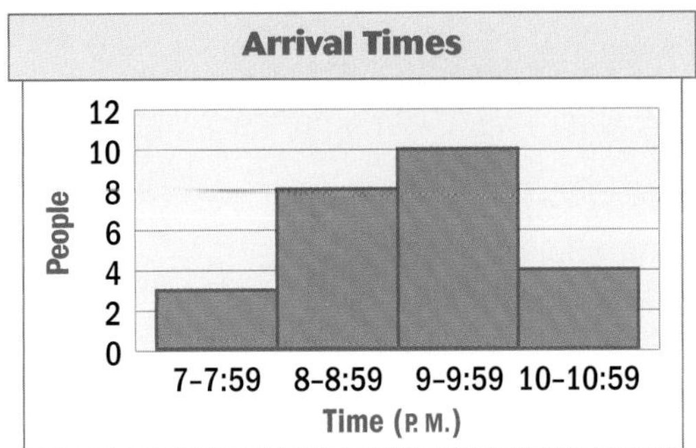

A. 4 **B.** 14 **C.** 21 **D.** 25

2. In what order should the operations be performed in the expression $3 + 7 \times 4 \div 2 - 6$?

F. $\times, -, \div, +$ **G.** $+, \times, \div, -$

H. $\times, \div, +, -$ **I.** $+, -, \times, \div$

3. Which expression has a value of 20?

A. $15 + 5 \times 4 \div 2 - 1$

B. $(15 + 5) \times (4 \div 2 - 1)$

C. $(15 + 5) \times 4 \div 2 - 1$

D. $(15 + 5) \times 4 \div (2 - 1)$

4. What is the correct value of the expression $(11 - 9)^4 + 6 \times 3$?

F. 26 **G.** 34 **H.** 42 **I.** 66

5. Which statement is true?

A. $2^6 < 6^2$ **B.** $4^7 < 7^4$

C. $1^9 > 9^1$ **D.** $3^5 > 5^3$

6. Which equation represents this statement: *The quotient of twenty and a number is five?*

F. $20 \div r = 5$ **G.** $t \div 20 = 5$

H. $5 \div p = 20$ **I.** $20g = 5$

7. What is the solution of the equation in Exercise 6?

A. $\frac{1}{4}$ **B.** 2 **C.** 4 **D.** 100

8. If $a = 4$ and $b = 9$, which equation is true?

F. $a = 5 + b$ **G.** $ab = 13$

H. $b \div 3 = a$ **I.** $2a + b = 17$

Short Response

9. The area of the rectangle is 120 square centimeters. Write an equation you can use to find the width w. Then solve the equation for w.

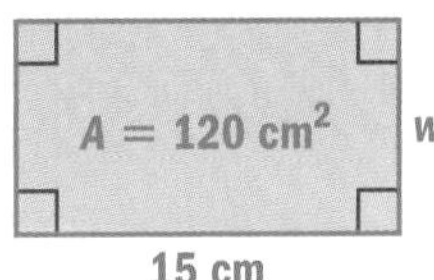

Extended Response

10. Your car's fuel gauge is broken. The car can go 22 miles on one gallon of gasoline. You start a trip with 13 gallons of gasoline. If you want to always have at least a gallon in the tank, what is the farthest you should drive before stopping for more gasoline? Explain.

Integer Operations

BEFORE

In previous chapters you've...

- Performed operations on whole numbers
- Evaluated expressions

Now

In Chapter 2 you'll study...

- Operations on integers
- Using properties to evaluate expressions
- Identifying and plotting points in the coordinate plane

WHY?

So you can solve real-world problems about...

- space shuttles, p. 56
- dinosaurs, p. 66
- diving, p. 70
- murals, p. 89

Internet Preview
CLASSZONE.COM

- eEdition Plus Online
- eWorkbook Plus Online
- eTutorial Plus Online
- State Test Practice
- More Examples

Chapter Warm-Up Game

Review skills you need for this chapter in this quick game. Work with a partner.

Key Skill:
Multiplying whole numbers

FOUR IN A ROW

MATERIALS

- 2 Answer Cards
- 24 Expression Cards
- 24 Markers

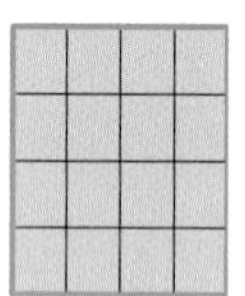

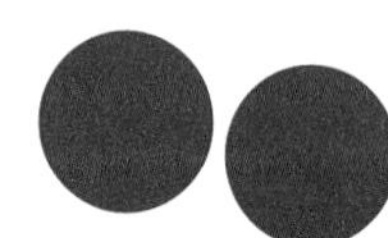

PREPARE Fill in your Answer Card with 16 of the 24 answers given below. Place the Expression Cards face down in a pile. On each turn follow the steps on the next page.

168	196	240	315	338	342
352	361	405	414	418	441
516	522	529	595	720	792
832	851	918	961	975	1020

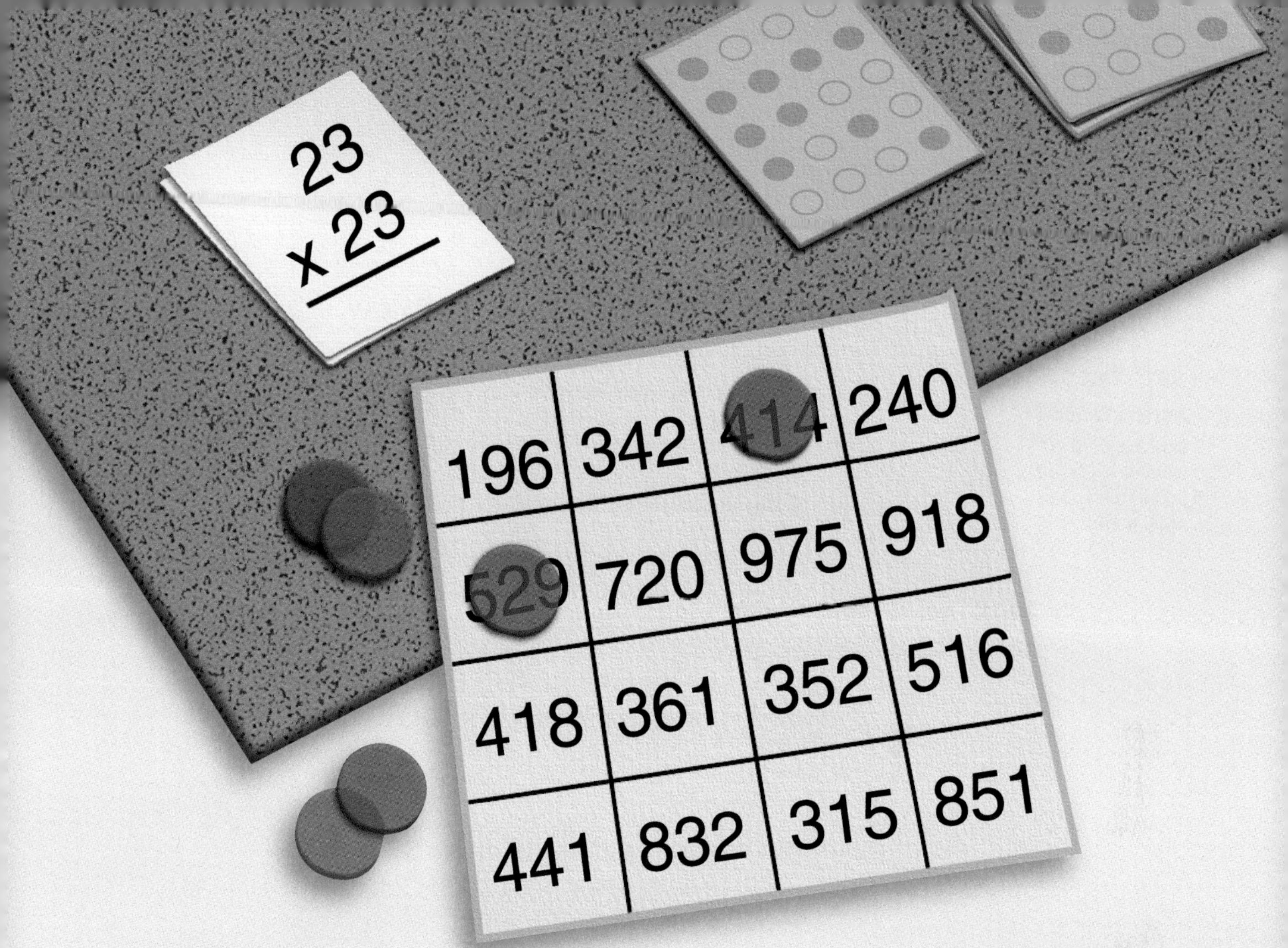

23
x 23

196	342	414	240
529	720	975	918
418	361	352	516
441	832	315	851

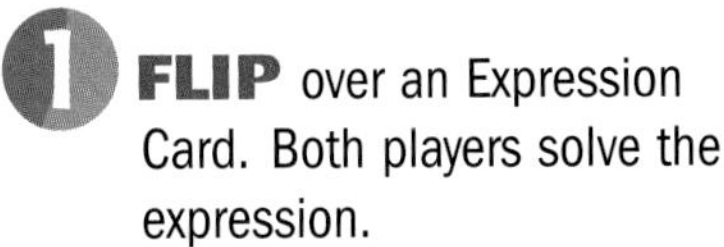

1 FLIP over an Expression Card. Both players solve the expression.

2 LOOK for the answer on your Answer Card. If you find it, place a marker over the answer.

HOW TO WIN Mark 4 answers in a row across, up and down, or diagonally.

Stop *and* Think

1. How many ways can you get 4 answers in a row on your card?
2. **Critical Thinking** How many squares can you mark without winning?

Getting Ready to Learn

Word Watch

Review Words

variable, p. 15
variable expression, p. 15
perimeter, p. 33
area, p. 33

Review What You Need to Know

Using Vocabulary Copy and complete using a review word.

1. A symbol that represents one or more numbers is called a(n) _?_.
2. The surface covered by a figure is called the _?_.

Round the decimal to the nearest whole number. *(p. 705)*

3. 10.61
4. 134.7
5. 0.25
6. 12.86

Evaluate the expression. *(p. 10)*

7. $32 - 27 + 14$
8. $4 \cdot 12 \div 6$
9. $6 + 34 \div 2$

Evaluate the expression when $s = 4$ and $t = 16$. *(p. 15)*

10. $(t - 9) + s$
11. $s(t - 5)$
12. $\frac{1}{4}t - 4$

Solve the equation using mental math. *(p. 28)*

13. $3x = 39$
14. $x - 6 = 12$
15. $x + 13 = 17$

You should include material that appears on a notebook like this in your own notes.

Know How to Take Notes

Including Vocabulary Notes When you write down new vocabulary words, you should also write examples of how they are used. Label the examples with the new words.

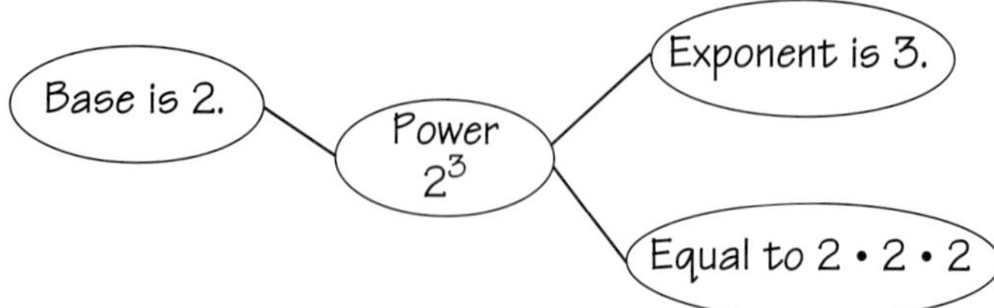

5^2 is read "five squared."

5^3 is read "five cubed."

5^4 is read "five to the fourth power."

As you work through Chapter 2, label examples of new vocabulary in your notes.

Integers and Absolute Value

BEFORE	Now	WHY?
You studied whole numbers.	You'll study integers.	So you can order lake elevations, as in Ex. 24.

In the Real World

integer, p. 53
negative integer, p. 53
positive integer, p. 53
absolute value, p. 54
opposite, p. 54

Geography The Global Positioning System (GPS) can be used to determine elevations. The table shows the minimum elevations of several countries. Which country in the table has the lowest elevation?

Minimum Elevations	
Country	**Elevation (m)**
United States	-86
Canada	0
China	-154
Bolivia	90
Czech Republic	115

Each number in the table is an *integer*. The following numbers are **integers**.

$$\ldots, -5, -4, -3, -2, -1, 0, 1, 2, 3, 4, 5, \ldots$$

Negative integers are less than 0. They lie *to the left* of 0 on a number line. **Positive integers** are greater than 0. They lie *to the right* of 0 on a number line. Zero is neither positive nor negative. When you use a number line to compare numbers, numbers increase as you move to the right.

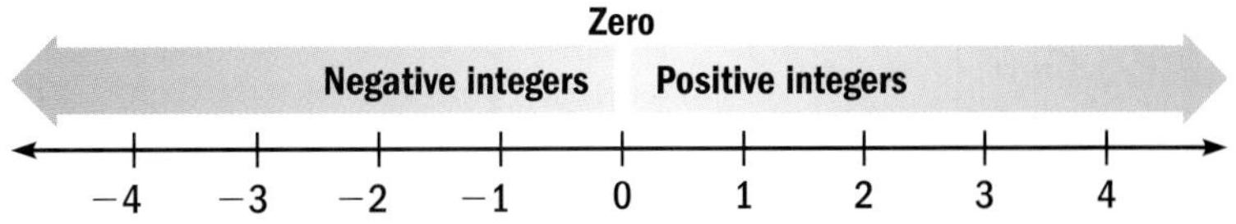

Global Positioning System (GPS) satellite

EXAMPLE 1 Graphing and Ordering Integers

To find which country in the table above has the lowest elevation, graph each integer on a number line.

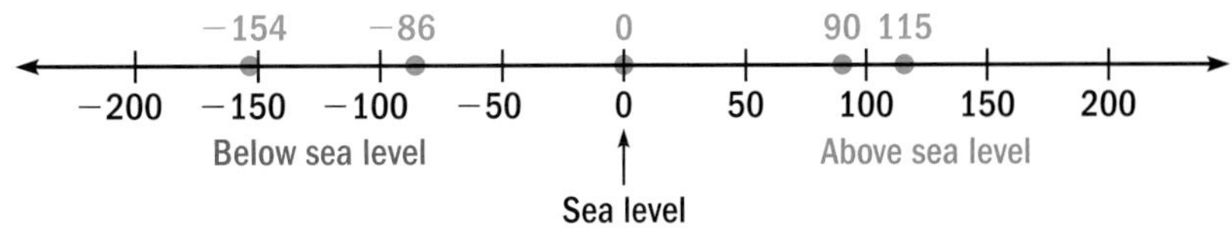

ANSWER China has the lowest elevation, at -154 meters.

Your turn now **Order the integers from least to greatest.**

1. $-7, 2, -1, 0, -2$ **2.** $9, -4, 12, -11, -1$ **3.** $0, -99, 44, -60, 16$

The **absolute value** of a number is the distance between the number and zero on a number line. The absolute value of a number n is written as $|n|$. The absolute value of 0 is 0.

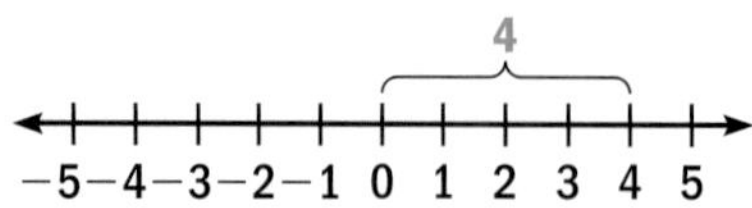

The distance between 4 and 0 is 4. So, $|4| = 4$.

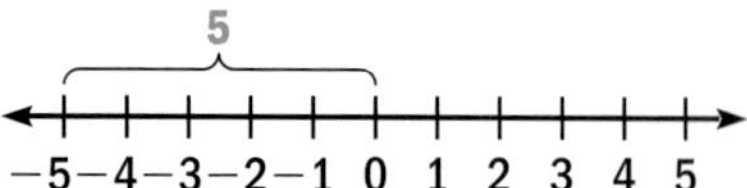

The distance between -5 and 0 is 5. So, $|-5| = 5$.

EXAMPLE 2 Finding Absolute Value

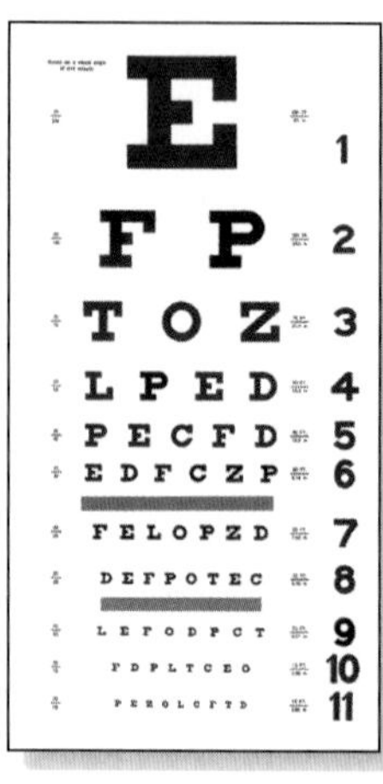

Eyeglasses An eyeglass prescription is given as a positive or negative number. A prescription of a person who is farsighted is positive. A prescription of a person who is nearsighted is negative. The greater the absolute value, the stronger the prescription. Which prescription is stronger, -3 or 2?

Solution

$|-3| = 3$ and $|2| = 2$.

ANSWER The prescription of -3 is stronger because $3 > 2$.

HELP with Reading

The integer "-2" can be read "negative 2" or "the opposite of 2."

Two numbers are **opposites** if they have the same absolute value but different signs. Opposites are the same distance from 0 on a number line and are on opposite sides of 0. The opposite of 0 is 0.

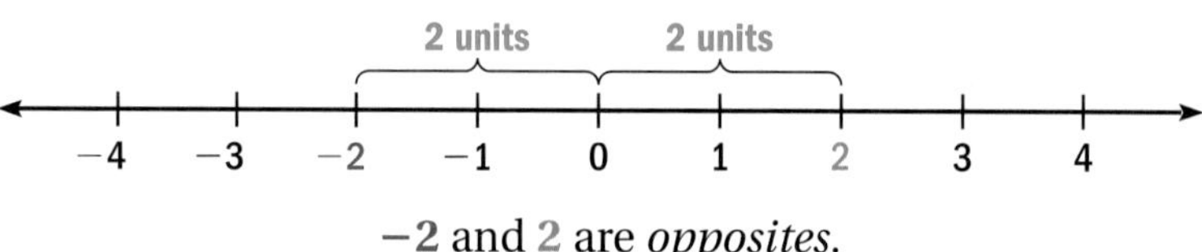

-2 and 2 are *opposites.*

EXAMPLE 3 Finding Opposites

Write the opposite of the integer.

a. 5 The opposite of 5 is -5.

b. -12 The opposite of -12 is 12.

c. $|-9|$ Because $|-9| = 9$, the opposite of $|-9|$ is -9.

Your turn now **Write the opposite and the absolute value of the integer.**

4. -16 **5.** 140 **6.** 1 **7.** $|-55|$

2.1 Exercises

More Practice, p. 728

Getting Ready to Practice

1. Vocabulary Copy and complete: Two integers are _?_ if they have the same absolute value but different signs.

Use a number line to order the integers from least to greatest.

2. 5, −10, 15, 27, −20, 13

3. 120, 62, 0, −56, 74, −130

Write the opposite and the absolute value of the integer.

4. 19

5. −8

6. −740

7. 1327

8. Find the Error A student was asked to order the integers 3, 1, 0, −9, −2, and 5 from least to greatest. Describe and correct the error in the solution.

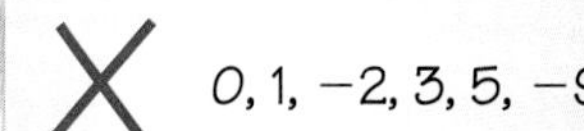

Practice and Problem Solving

Example	Exercises
1	9–18
2	19–22
3	19–22

- More Examples
- eTutorial Plus

Copy and complete the statement with $<$ or $>$.

9. 4 _?_ −6

10. −12 _?_ 1

11. −9 _?_ −2

12. 0 _?_ −5

13. 5 _?_ −5

14. −17 _?_ 2

15. 34 _?_ −29

16. −20 _?_ −14

Use a number line to order the integers from least to greatest.

17. 64, −12, 18, 59, −20, 44

18. 278, 121, −301, 262, −155

Match the integer expression with the verbal expression.

19. $-|7|$

20. $|-7|$

21. $-|-7|$

22. $-(-7)$

A. the opposite of negative seven

B. the opposite of the absolute value of seven

C. the absolute value of negative seven

D. the opposite of the absolute value of negative seven

In Exercises 23 and 24, use the table showing elevations of lakes.

Name	Elevation (ft)
Jones Lake	−30
Silver Lake	90
Gieselmann Lake	−162
Seneca Lake	445
Craigs Pond	0

23. Compare Which lake is at a lower elevation, Gieselmann Lake or Silver Lake?

24. Arrange the lake elevations in order from least to greatest.

HELP with Solving

The opposite of an opposite is the original number. For example, $-(-16) = 16$.

Simplify the expression.

25. $|-32|$ **26.** $-|9|$ **27.** $-|29|$ **28.** $-(-5)$

29. $-(-81)$ **30.** $-|-17|$ **31.** $-|-3|$ **32.** $-(-(-4))$

Copy and complete the statement with <, >, or =.

33. $|4| \underline{?} |-4|$ **34.** $|-6| \underline{?} -|6|$ **35.** $-|-9| \underline{?} -(-9)$

36. Critical Thinking What numbers have opposites that are the same as their absolute values? What numbers have opposites that are different from their absolute values?

37. Launch Countdown Put the following activities for a shuttle launch in the order that they occur. "T−5 minutes" means 5 minutes before liftoff.

T−5 minutes	Pilot starts auxiliary power units.
T+7 seconds	Shuttle clears launch tower, and control switches to the Mission Control Center.
T−2 hours, 55 minutes	Flight crew departs for launch pad.
T−6 seconds	Main engine starts.
T−0	Liftoff.

Challenge Order the numbers from least to greatest.

38. $-28, -(-73), |-65|, |95|, -|47|$

39. $|-19|, -74, -|12|, -(-56), -|-58|$

Mixed Review

Evaluate the expression when *a* = 8 and *b* = 2. *(Lesson 1.3)*

40. $5ab$ **41.** $\frac{a}{b} + 15$ **42.** $4a - 3b$

43. Patty needs to read a 238 page book in 6 days. By the end of the first day she has read 68 pages. How many pages does she need to read each day to finish the book on time? *(Lesson 1.7)*

Test-Taking Practice

INTERNET
State Test Practice
CLASSZONE.COM

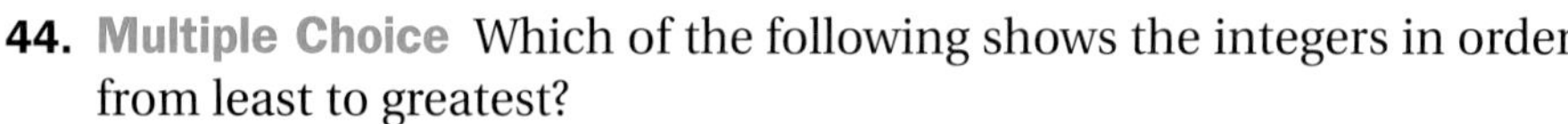

44. Multiple Choice Which of the following shows the integers in order from least to greatest?

A. $-1, -6, -12, -34$ **B.** $-1, -12, -34, -6$

C. $-34, -12, -6, -1$ **D.** $-34, -6, -12, -1$

45. Multiple Choice The Java Trench in the Indian Ocean lies 7258 meters below sea level. Which number represents this elevation in meters?

F. -7258 **G.** $-(-7258)$ **H.** $|-7258|$ **I.** $|7258|$

2.2 Hands-on Activity

INDIANA: Academic Standards
- Computation (8.2.1)

GOAL
Model integer addition on a number line.

MATERIALS
- pencil
- paper

Adding Integers

You can model addition of integers by using a number line.

Explore **Find the sum −15 + 11.**

1. Draw a number line, place a pencil at 0, and move 15 units to the left to show −15.
2. Move 11 units to the right to show the addition of 11.

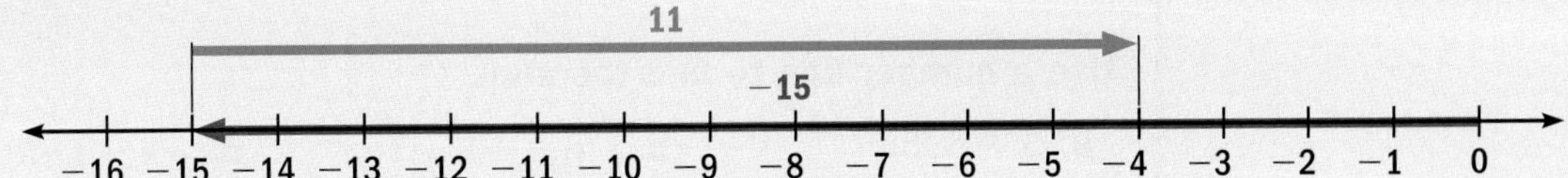

3. The final position is −4. So, −15 + 11 = −4.

Your turn now **Write an addition expression to represent the figure. Then evaluate the expression.**

1.

2.

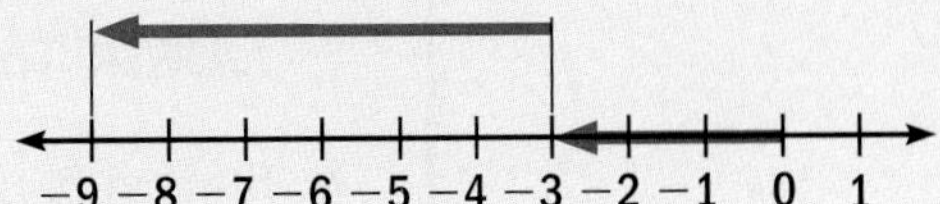

Use a number line to find the sum.

3. $-7 + (-14)$ **4.** $20 + (-50)$ **5.** $-10 + 65$ **6.** $-7 + (-33)$

7. $41 + (-25)$ **8.** $-23 + 52$ **9.** $-18 + (-34)$ **10.** $35 + (-37)$

Stop and Think

11. The sum of two positive integers is always positive. What is the sign of the sum of two negative integers? Use a number line to explain.

12. Critical Thinking How can you predict the sign of the sum of a positive and a negative integer before you add the numbers?

13. Writing Write the steps you use to evaluate $25 + (-13) + 5 + (-20)$. Then evaluate the expression.

Adding Integers

BEFORE	Now	WHY?
You added whole numbers.	You'll add integers.	So you can find a miniature golf score, as in Ex. 43.

Review Words

integer, p. 53
absolute value, p. 54
sum, p. 709

INDIANA
Academic Standards

- Computation (8.2.1)
- Problem Solving (8.7.4)

You can use a number line to add integers.

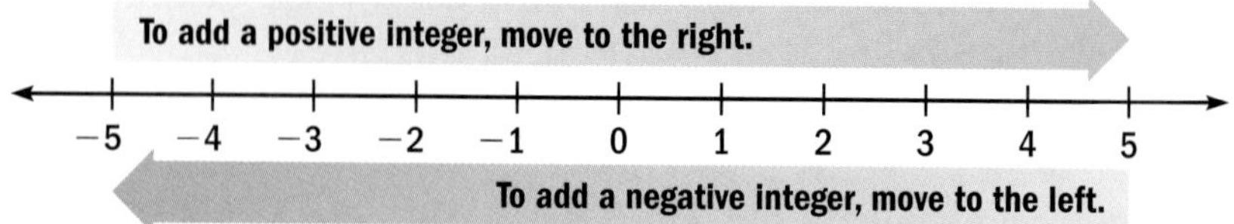

EXAMPLE 1 Adding Integers Using a Number Line

Use a number line to find the sum.

a. $5 + (-8)$ **b.** $-6 + 10$ **c.** $-4 + (-3)$

Solution

a. Start at 0, move **5** units to the right. Then move **8** units to the left.

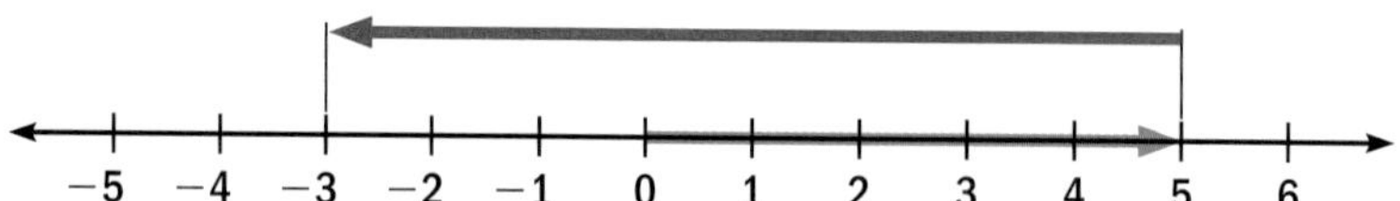

ANSWER The final position is -3. So, $5 + (-8) = -3$.

b. Start at 0, move **6** units to the left. Then move **10** units to the right.

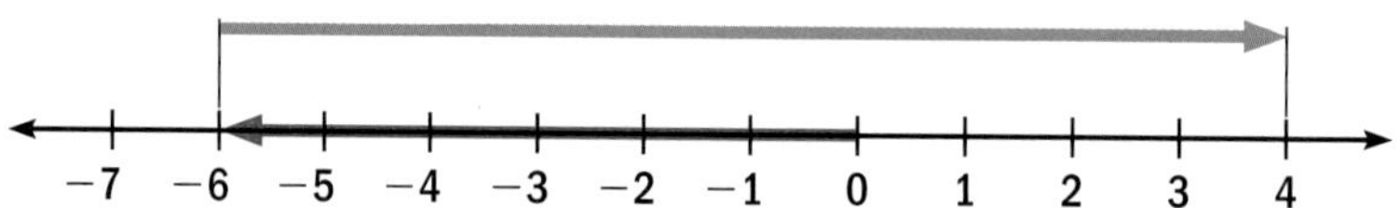

ANSWER The final position is 4. So, $-6 + 10 = 4$.

c. Start at 0, move **4** units to the left. Then move **3** units to the left.

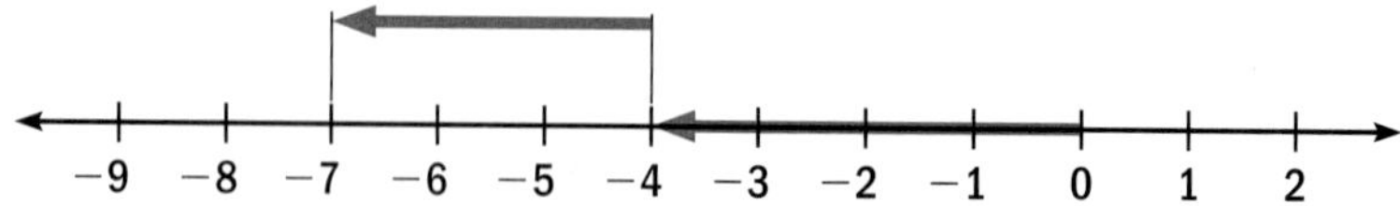

ANSWER The final position is -7. So, $-4 + (-3) = -7$.

Your turn now **Use a number line to find the sum.**

1. $12 + (-5)$ **2.** $-8 + 4$ **3.** $-1 + (-6)$ **4.** $2 + (-2)$

Using a Rule You can add integers without using a number line by following these rules.

Same sign Add the absolute values and use the common sign.

Different signs Subtract the lesser absolute value from the greater absolute value. Use the sign of the number with the greater absolute value.

EXAMPLE 2 Adding Integers

Find the sum $-12 + 4$.

$-12 + 4 = -8$

Different signs, so subtract $|4|$ from $|-12|$.

Use sign of number with greater absolute value.

✓**Check** Use a number line to find the sum.

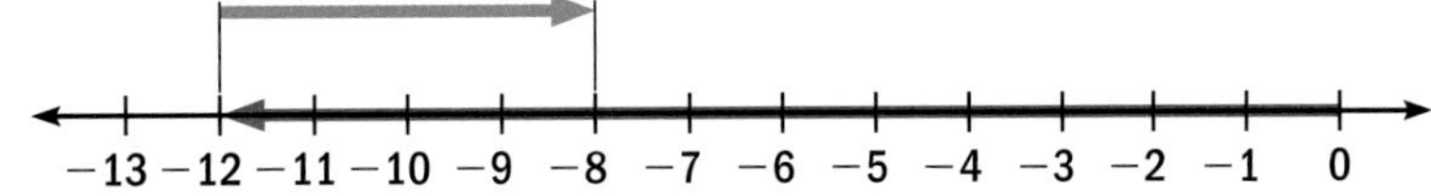

Additive Identity Property

Words The sum of an integer and zero is the integer.

Numbers $5 + 0 = 5$
$-3 + 0 = -3$

Algebra $a + 0 = a$

EXAMPLE 3 Adding More Than Two Integers

a. Use the left to right rule of order of operations to find the sum.

$-84 + 0 + (-124) = -84 + (-124)$ Additive identity property

$= -208$ Same sign, so sum has common sign.

b. Use the left to right rule of order of operations to find the sum.

$-46 + (-53) + 63 = -99 + 63$ Same sign, so sum has common sign.

$= -36$ Use sign of number with greater absolute value.

EXAMPLE 4 Adding More Than Two Integers

School Fair Your class has a fair to raise money for a field trip. The table shows the incomes and expenses for the fair. How much money was raised?

Games	$750
Display tables	$625
Donations	$36
Advertising	−$16
Decorations	−$60
Game rentals	−$500

Solution

First, add the positive integers, and then add the **negative integers**.

$$750 + 625 + 36 + (-16) + (-60) + (-500) = 1411 + (-576)$$
$$= 835$$

ANSWER Your class raised $835.

Your turn now **Find the sum.**

5. $-20 + (-15)$

6. $18 + 0 + (-54)$

7. $300 + 111 + (-44) + (-256)$

8. $-230 + (-512) + 178 + 94$

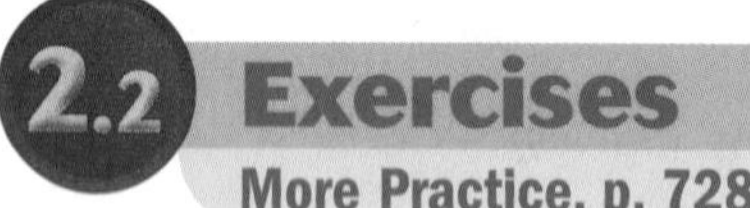

2.2 Exercises

More Practice, p. 728

Getting Ready to Practice

1. **Vocabulary** Copy and complete: To add two integers with the same sign, add the _?_ and use the common sign.

Use a number line to find the sum.

2. $-6 + 8$ **3.** $-3 + (-9)$ **4.** $5 + (-7)$ **5.** $-4 + 4$

Find the sum.

6. $42 + (-23)$ **7.** $-32 + 0$ **8.** $-51 + (-67)$

9. $19 + 19 + (-34)$ **10.** $-12 + 9 + (-5)$ **11.** $20 + (-15) + (-22)$

12. **Checking** You record withdrawals and deposits in your checkbook. The starting balance is $125. The first withdrawal is $25. The second withdrawal is $13. The first deposit is $35. The second deposit is $50. The third withdrawal is $68. What is the final balance?

HELP with Homework

Example	Exercises
1	13-16
2	17-26
3	18-26, 34-37
4	34-37

Online Resources
CLASSZONE.COM
- More Examples
- eTutorial Plus

Practice and Problem Solving

Use a number line to find the sum.

13. $-2 + (-1)$ **14.** $-10 + (-9)$ **15.** $-3 + 7$ **16.** $7 + (-5)$

17. Find the Error Describe and correct the error in the solution.

Find the sum of -8 and 5.
$-8 + 5 = -13$ X

Find the sum.

18. $-63 + (-49)$ **19.** $-93 + (-16)$ **20.** $0 + (-25)$

21. $-82 + 0$ **22.** $98 + (-128)$ **23.** $-57 + 31 + 27 + 11$

24. $-42 + (-65) + 78$ **25.** $-87 + 48 + 36$ **26.** $-81 + (-75) + (-65)$

Critical Thinking Copy and complete the statement using *always*, *sometimes*, or *never*.

27. The sum of two negative integers is _?_ negative.

28. The sum of two positive integers is _?_ negative.

29. The sum of a positive integer and a negative integer is _?_ negative.

30. The sum of an integer and zero is _?_ zero.

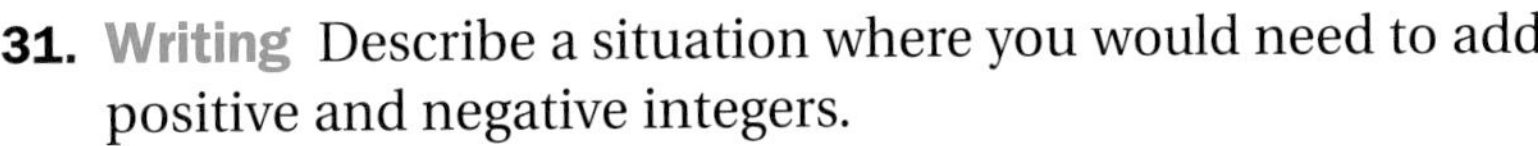

31. Writing Describe a situation where you would need to add positive and negative integers.

In Exercises 32 and 33, use the information to write an expression. Then use a number line to find the sum.

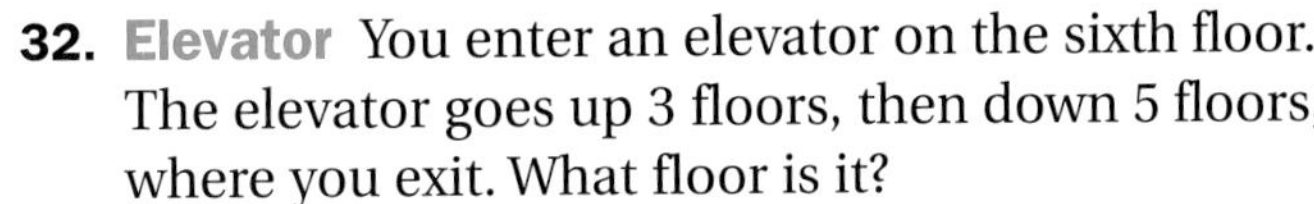

32. Elevator You enter an elevator on the sixth floor. The elevator goes up 3 floors, then down 5 floors, where you exit. What floor is it?

33. Mexico The influential period of the *Olmec* culture in Mexico lasted approximately 800 years. It started about 1200 B.C. About what year did this period end?

Jade sculpture from the Olmec culture in Veracruz, Mexico

Find the sum.

34. $42 + 36 + (-16) + 0 + (-84)$ **35.** $(-17) + (-63) + 91 + 79$

36. $174 + (-196) + 245 + (-210)$ **37.** $-182 + 307 + 163 + (-142)$

Algebra Evaluate $x + (-478)$ for the value of x.

38. $x = 806$ **39.** $x = -729$ **40.** $x = |-349|$ **41.** $x = -|-521|$

42. Making Connections The sum of a number and its *additive inverse* is 0. For example, $5 + (-5) = 0$, so 5 and -5 are additive inverses. Give another example of additive inverses. What vocabulary word from this chapter is another name for additive inverses?

43. **Miniature Golf** In miniature golf, *par* is the number of strokes considered necessary to get a ball in the hole. The score for each hole is the number of strokes above or below par. Find the total score by adding the scores for each hole. Is Jill's score *above* par, *under* par, or *at* par?

HOLE	1	2	3	4	5	6	7	8	9	OUT
PAR	4	5	3	3	5	4	3	5	3	35
Jill	0	+1	−2	−1	0	+1	+2	0	−1	

Chemistry In Exercises 44–46, use the information below. Find the sum of the charges. Tell whether the atom is an ion.

- A proton has a charge of $+1$.
- An electron has a charge of -1.
- An atom is an ion if it has a positive or negative charge.

44. Sodium: 11 protons, 10 electrons

45. Chlorine: 17 protons, 17 electrons

46. Oxide: 8 protons, 10 electrons

Mental Math Solve the equation using mental math.

47. $-3 + k = 2$ 48. $-6 = x + (-9)$ 49. $-7 = 12 + j$

50. **Challenge** Does $|x + y| = |x| + |y|$ if x and y are both positive? What if x and y are both negative? What if x is positive and y is negative? Explain.

Mixed Review 

Evaluate the expression. *(Lesson 1.4)*

51. $5^3 + 21 \div 7 - 6$ 52. $6^2 \cdot (2 + 4) \div 18$ 53. $(12 - 4) \cdot (9 - 1)^2$

Order the integers from least to greatest. *(Lesson 2.1)*

54. $-2479, 1802, 2479, -1802$ 55. $-346, -125, -921, 724, 128$

Test-Taking Practice 

56. **Multiple Choice** Evaluate $-83 + 34$.

A. -117 **B.** -49 **C.** 49 **D.** 117

57. **Multiple Choice** Evaluate $-498 + (-512) + 573 + (-645)$.

F. -1232 **G.** -1082 **H.** 1082 **I.** 1232

Subtracting Integers

BEFORE

You added integers.

Now

You'll subtract integers.

WHY?

So you can find the length of dinosaur periods, as in Ex. 41.

Review Words

integer, p. 53
opposite, p. 54
difference, p. 709

INDIANA
Academic Standards

- Computation (8.2.1)
- Problem Solving (8.7.4)

Activity **You can use patterns and mental math to discover a rule for subtracting integers.**

1. Copy the table. In the second column, write the answer to the subtraction problem. Use a pattern to find the differences involving negative integers.

2. In the third column, complete the addition problem so the sum is equal to the number in the difference column.

Subtraction problem	Difference	Addition problem
$3 - 3$	0	$3 + -3$
$3 - 2$	?	$3 +$?
$3 - 1$	?	$3 +$?
$3 - 0$	?	$3 +$?
$3 - (-1)$	?	$3 +$?
$3 - (-2)$	?	$3 +$?
$3 - (-3)$	?	$3 +$?

3. How is the second number in the addition problems related to the second number in the subtraction problems?

4. Describe how to use addition to subtract integers.

In the activity above, you saw that when you subtract integers you can write the expression as an addition expression and then use the rules for adding integers.

Subtracting Integers

Words To subtract an integer, add its opposite.

Numbers $3 - 7 = 3 + (-7) = -4$
$2 - (-6) = 2 + 6 = 8$

Algebra $a - b = a + (-b)$
$a - (-b) = a + b$

EXAMPLE 1 Subtracting Integers

a. $-56 - (-9) = -56 + 9$ Add the opposite of -9.

$= -47$ Add.

b. $-14 - 21 = -14 + (-21)$ Add the opposite of 21.

$= -35$ Add.

Your turn now Find the difference.

1. $15 - 41$ **2.** $-16 - 8$ **3.** $38 - (-27)$ **4.** $-76 - (-109)$

EXAMPLE 2 Evaluating a Variable Expression

Evaluate $15 - a - b$ when $a = 24$ and $b = -36$.

Solution

$15 - a - b = 15 - 24 - (-36)$ Substitute 24 for a and -36 for b.

$= 15 + (-24) - (-36)$ Add the opposite of 24.

$= -9 - (-36)$ Add 15 and -24.

$= -9 + 36$ Add the opposite of -36.

$= 27$ Add.

What do you think? **Science**

SOFAR

Humpback whales use the SOFAR channel to communicate with other whales. The speed of sound in water at 68°F is 1482 meters per second. The speed of sound in air at 68°F is 344 meters per second. How much faster does sound travel in water?

EXAMPLE 3 Using Integer Subtraction

SOFAR The SOFAR (*SO*und *F*ixing *A*nd *R*anging) channel is a layer of water in the oceans that allows sounds to travel extremely long distances. Use the diagram to find the vertical height of the SOFAR channel.

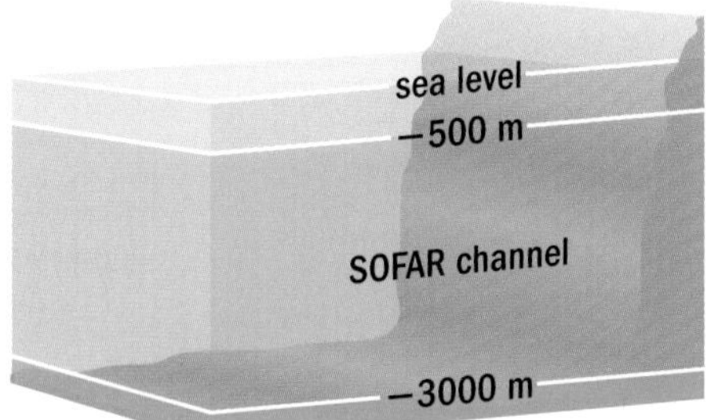

Solution

The vertical height is the difference of the upper and lower elevations.

Vertical height $= -500 - (-3000)$ Write subtraction statement.

$= -500 + 3000$ Add the opposite of -3000.

$= 2500$ Add.

ANSWER The vertical height of the SOFAR channel is 2500 meters.

2.3 Exercises

More Practice, p. 728

INTERNET
eWorkbook Plus
CLASSZONE.COM

Getting Ready to Practice

Vocabulary **Translate the verbal phrase into a numerical expression.**

1. The difference of negative two and six
2. The difference of the opposite of five and the opposite of three

Find the difference.

3. $5 - 12$
4. $6 - (-16)$
5. $-11 - (-7)$
6. $-9 - 10$

Evaluate the expression when $x = 15$ and $y = -8$.

7. $5 - x$
8. $-9 - y$
9. $y - x$
10. $x - y$

11. Guided Problem Solving Use the diagram to find the distances between the bird and the boat, the boat and the reef, and the bird and the reef.

(1 Identify which elevation is greater for each situation.

(2 Subtract the lower elevation from the greater elevation.

(3 Answer the original question by completing each statement.

The bird is __?__ feet above the boat.

The boat is __?__ feet above the reef.

The bird is __?__ feet above the reef.

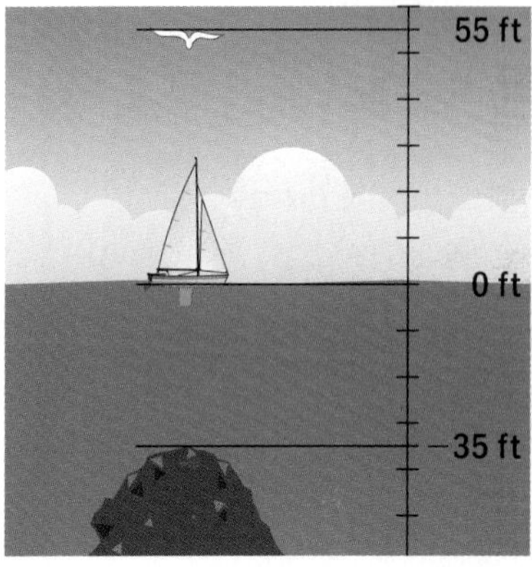

Practice and Problem Solving

HELP with Homework

Example	Exercises
1	12-20
2	22-24
3	21, 26-28

Online Resources
CLASSZONE.COM
· More Examples
· eTutorial Plus

Find the difference.

12. $-13 - 12$
13. $-14 - (-14)$
14. $11 - (-6)$
15. $9 - 17$
16. $-18 - (-12)$
17. $-20 - 7$
18. $32 - 40$
19. $28 - (-16)$
20. $-39 - (-13)$

21. Game Show A game show contestant has -400 points. He answers a question incorrectly and loses 600 points. What is his total score?

Evaluate the expression when $c = -5$ and $d = 10$.

22. $c - 6 - d$
23. $10 - c - d$
24. $c - d - 8 - 4$

25. Critical Thinking Explain how you can find the distance between the points on the number line using subtraction.

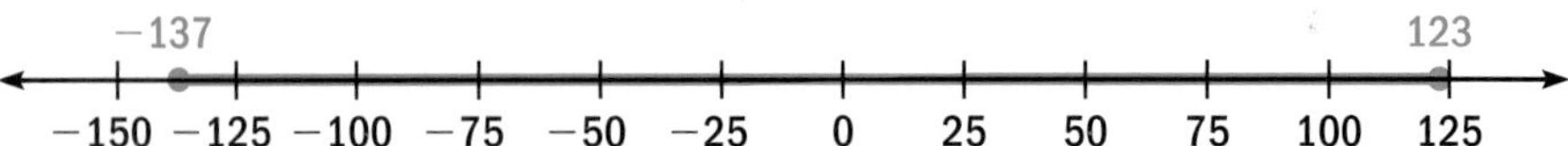

Temperatures In Exercises 26–28, use the table. It shows the coldest temperatures ever recorded for four states.

Coldest Recorded Temperatures	
State	**Temperature**
Alaska	−80°F
Colorado	−61°F
Kentucky	−37°F
Mississippi	−19°F

26. How much colder is Alaska's coldest temperature than Kentucky's?

27. How much colder is Colorado's coldest temperature than Mississippi's?

28. Which two states have the greatest difference of coldest temperatures? Which two states have the least difference of coldest temperatures?

Evaluate the expression.

29. $41 - 300$ **30.** $144 - 612$ **31.** $-309 - (-2111)$

32. $-5 - (-5) - (-5)$ **33.** $8 - 2 - 6 - 10$ **34.** $-4 - 7 + (-9) - 1$

35. $-1 + (-8) - 9$ **36.** $6 - (-4) - 10$ **37.** $3 - (-7) - (-2)$

38. $15 + (-29) - (-72)$ **39.** $-52 - (-18) - 37$ **40.** $91 + (-40) - 34$

41. Dinosaurs The table shows the ranges of three dinosaur periods during the Mesozoic Era. Calculate how long each of the periods lasted.

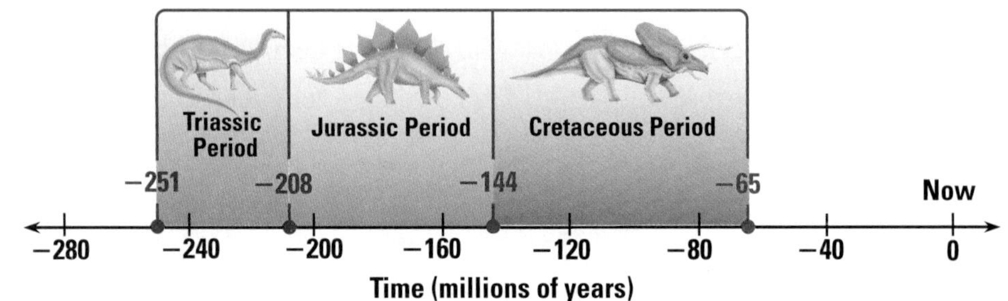

Evaluate the expression when $a = -9$, $b = 18$, and $c = -4$.

42. $a + c - 10$ **43.** $14 - a - b$ **44.** $a - b - c$ **45.** $c + a - b$

Challenge Copy and complete the statement using *always*, *sometimes*, or *never*.

46. A negative number minus a positive number is _?_ negative.

47. A positive number minus a negative number is _?_ negative.

What do you think? **Science**

Dinosaurs

Scientists believe that if a Tyrannosaurus Rex was able to run more than 25 miles per hour it would have to have had more than 80% of its body mass in its legs. If a Tyrannosaurus Rex weighed 13,000 pounds, this would mean the legs weighed 10,400 pounds. How much would the rest of its body have weighed?

48. **Weather** To collect data on winter storms developing in the north Pacific Ocean, a cylinder that measures wind speed, humidity, and temperature at different elevations is dropped from a plane. If the plane is 40,000 feet above sea level and the cylinder drops to the bottom of the Pacific Ocean, 13,000 feet below sea level, how far does the cylinder fall?

Mixed Review 

Solve the equation using mental math. *(Lesson 1.5)*

49. $v + 5 = 13$ **50.** $7w = 42$ **51.** $12 - x = 9$

Find the sum. *(Lesson 2.2)*

52. $-8 + 17$ **53.** $11 + (-9)$ **54.** $-22 + (-6)$

Basic Skills **Find the difference.**

55. $257 - 89$ **56.** $500 - 166$ **57.** $6641 - 992$ **58.** $8250 - 98$

Test-Taking Practice 

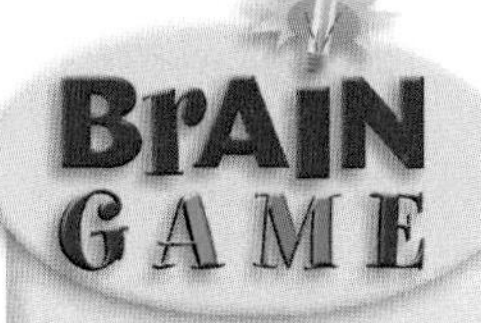

59. **Multiple Choice** What is the value of $-5 - (-7) - (-1) - 10$?

A. -23 **B.** -13 **C.** -7 **D.** 13

60. **Multiple Choice** Evaluate the expression $-c + 2a - b$ when $a = 5$, $b = -9$, and $c = 3$.

F. -2 **G.** 4 **H.** 16 **I.** 22

BRAIN GAME

Argyle Arithmetic

Each number in a purple diamond is the sum of the two numbers below it. Each number in a green diamond is the difference of the two numbers above it. Copy and complete the argyle arithmetic.

2.4 Problem Solving Strategies

INDIANA: Academic Standards
- Problem Solving (8.7.1, 8.7.5)

Look for a Pattern

- Guess, Check, and Revise
- Draw a Diagram
- Act It Out
- Work Backward
- Look for a Pattern
- Make a Table
- Solve a Simpler Problem

Problem Greg is setting up for a craft fair and is stacking gift boxes for a display. He knows a pyramid with a height of 2 boxes contains 5 boxes, a pyramid with a height of 3 boxes contains 14 boxes, and a pyramid with a height of 4 boxes contains 30 boxes. How many boxes will he need to make a pyramid with a height of 6 boxes?

1 Read and Understand

Read the problem carefully.

You need to find how many boxes Greg needs to make a pyramid with a height of 6 boxes.

2 Make a Plan

Decide on a strategy to use.

Sketch or model a pyramid with 5 boxes and a pyramid with 14 boxes. Look for a pattern. You can follow the pattern to determine how many boxes Greg will need.

3 Solve the Problem

Reread the problem and look for a pattern.

Sketch or model several rectangular pyramids and count how many boxes are at each level. Make a table that shows the number of boxes in each level.

Level n	Boxes in level n	Boxes in n-level pyramid
1	1^2	$1^2 = 1$
2	2^2	$1^2 + 2^2 = 5$
3	3^2	$1^2 + 2^2 + 3^2 = 14$

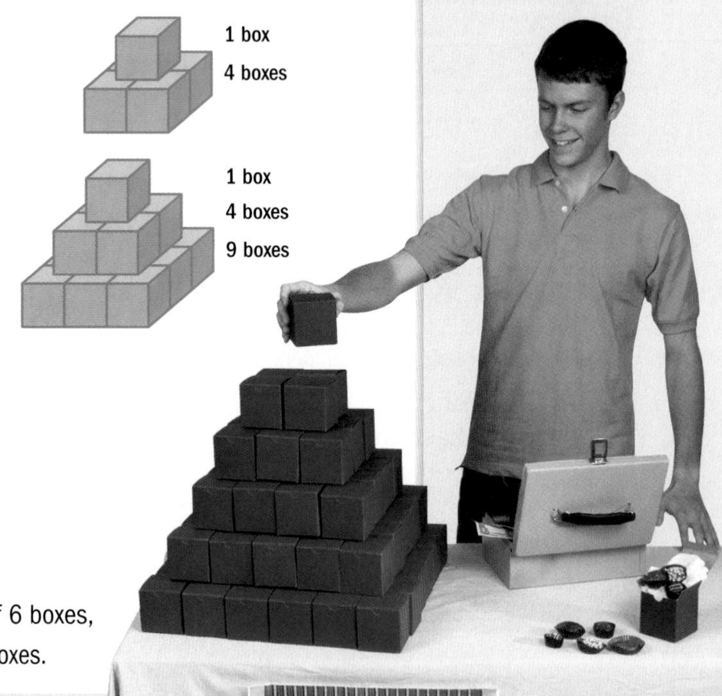

The number of boxes in each level is the square of the number of the level. The number of boxes in a pyramid is the sum of the squares.

ANSWER To make a rectangular pyramid with a height of 6 boxes, Greg will need $1^2 + 2^2 + 3^2 + 4^2 + 5^2 + 6^2 = 91$ boxes.

4 Look Back

Sketch a top view of each level to check your answer.

Practice the Strategy

Use the strategy *look for a pattern.*

1. **Geometry** Make a table showing the number of dots in each triangle. Determine the number of dots in the ninth triangle in this sequence.

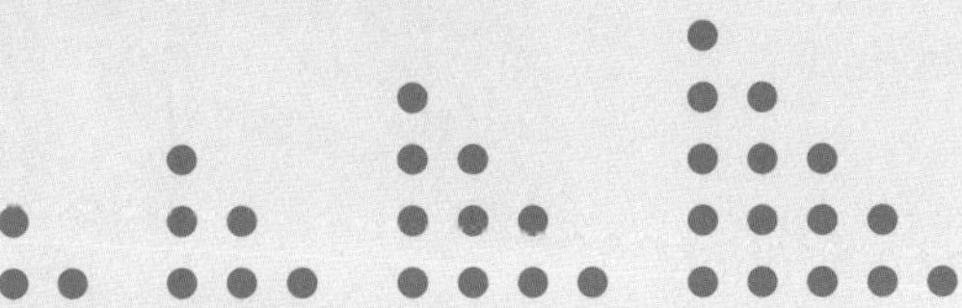

2. **Track** Your track coach tells you to do a running drill in which you run 16 feet and run back. Then you run 32 feet and run back. Next you run 48 feet and run back. How far would you expect to run next?

3. **Tiling** Jason and Emily are laying tiles in the kitchen of a restaurant that measures 36 feet by 24 feet. Each tile measures 1 foot by 1 foot. If they follow the pattern shown below, how many blue tiles will they need to fill the entire kitchen with this pattern?

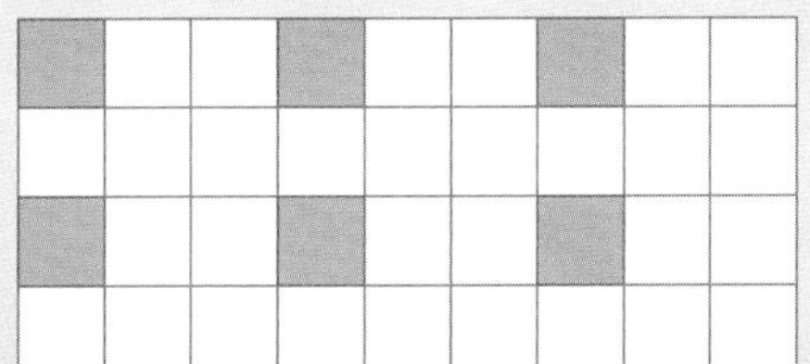

4. **Number Sense** Copy and complete the table below. Look for a pattern so you can evaluate 11 • 97 using mental math.

11 • 12	132	12 + 120
11 • 13	143	13 + ?
11 • 14	154	14 + ?
11 • 15	165	15 + ?
11 • 16	176	16 + ?

Mixed Problem Solving

Use any strategy to solve the problem.

5. **Who's Oldest?** Scott is two years older than Anne, and Kelly is three years younger than Scott. Ben is nine years less than twice Scott's age, and Anne is 10 years old. Determine the ages of Scott, Ben, and Kelly.

6. **Baking** You have a recipe that makes 24 cookies. The ingredients include 2 eggs, 1 cup of sugar, 1.5 cups of flour, 1 teaspoon of vanilla, and 1 teaspoon of baking soda. What is the greatest number of cookies you can make if you have 12 eggs, 4 cups of sugar, and 9 cups of flour?

7. **Stock Prices** A newspaper reports these changes in the price of a stock during a 5-day period: -1, -8, $+2$, -4, and $+6$. The stock price ended at \$35 on the fifth day. How much was the price of a stock before the 5-day period started?

8. **Cereal** You are stacking boxes of cereal for a display. You use a total of 78 boxes, and each row has one fewer box than the row below it. How many rows make up the display if the top row has one box?

9. **Basketball** In a basketball game, there are 1 point free throws, 2 point field goals and 3 point field goals. How many ways can you score 12 points?

Multiplying Integers

BEFORE	Now	WHY?
You added and subtracted integers.	You'll multiply integers.	So you can find the worth of a coin in a game, as in Ex. 32.

Review Words

integer, p 53
product, p. 713

INDIANA Academic Standards

- Computation (8.2.1)

In the Real World

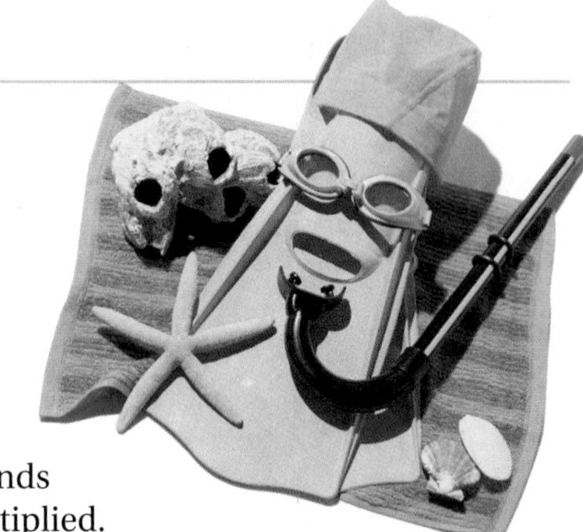

Diving A diver is exploring a coral reef. The diver's depth is changing by −6 feet per second. If the diver started at sea level, what is the diver's position after 10 seconds?

To find the position, you can multiply integers. When you multiply integers, the sign of the product depends on the signs of the integers being multiplied.

Multiplying Integers

Words	Numbers
The product of two integers with the same sign is positive.	$4 \cdot 2 = 8$ $-3 \cdot (-7) = 21$
The product of two integers with different signs is negative.	$4 \cdot (-2) = -8$ $-3 \cdot 7 = -21$

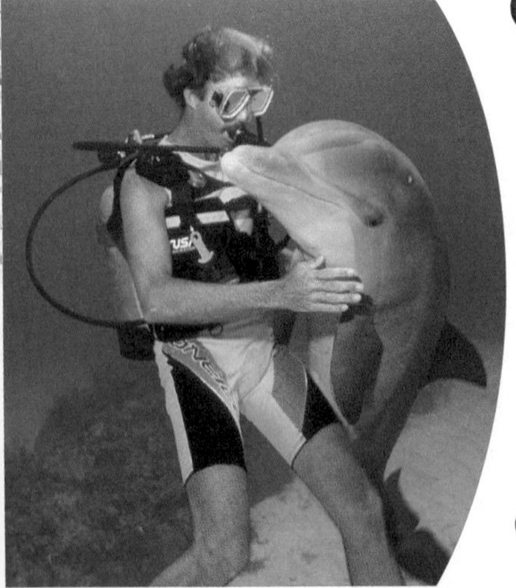

Multiplying Integers

To find the diver's position relative to sea level after 10 seconds, use the distance formula $d = rt$.

$d = rt$ Write the distance formula.

$d = \mathbf{-6}(\mathbf{10})$ Substitute −6 for r and 10 for t.

$d = -60$ Different signs, so product is negative.

The diver's position relative to sea level is −60 feet.

Use the information above.

1. Find the diver's position relative to sea level after 13 seconds.

Multiplication Properties

Multiplication Property of Zero

Words The product of an integer and 0 is 0.

Numbers $-4 \cdot 0 = 0$ **Algebra** For any value of a, $a \cdot 0 = 0$.

Identity Property of Multiplication

Words The product of an integer and 1 is the integer.

Numbers $4(1) = 4$ **Algebra** For any value of a, $a(1) = a$.

When you multiply a number by -1, the product is the *opposite* of the original number.

HELP with Solving

When you multiply more than two positive or negative integers:

- If there is an *even* number of negative factors then the product is *positive*.
- If there is an *odd* number of negative factors then the product is *negative*.

EXAMPLE 2 Multiplying Two or More Integers

a. $-1(6) = -6$ Different signs, so product is negative.

b. $-8(-2) = 16$ Same sign, so product is positive.

c. $-15(0) = 0$ Product of an integer and 0 is 0.

d. $4(-10)(-12) = -40(-12)$ Multiply from left to right.

$= 480$ Multiply.

EXAMPLE 3 Evaluating an Expression with Integers

Evaluate $a^2 + 3b$ when $a = -5$ and $b = -11$.

$a^2 + 3b = (-5)^2 + 3(-11)$ Substitute -5 for a and -11 for b.

$= 25 + 3(-11)$ Evaluate the power.

$= 25 + (-33)$ Multiply.

$= -8$ Add.

Your turn now **Find the product.**

2. $-1(4)$ **3.** $7(0)$ **4.** $-6(-11)$ **5.** $-1(-12)(-9)$

Evaluate the expression when $a = 3$, $b = -4$ and $c = -8$.

6. $ac - b$ **7.** $ac + b$ **8.** $a^2 + bc$ **9.** $ab - c^2$

2.4 Exercises

More Practice, p. 728

Getting Ready to Practice

1. **Vocabulary** Copy and complete: The product of a positive integer and a negative integer is a _?_ integer.

Find the product.

2. $-4(-7)$
3. $0(-9)$
4. $-3(6)$
5. $-1(-2)(-3)$
6. $2(-4)(5)$
7. $10(-9)(-3)$

8. **Banking** You have $500 in a savings account. Over a 2 month period, you make 9 withdrawals of $30 each. What is your new balance?

9. **Find the Error** Describe and correct the error in the solution.

✗ $-8(-12) = -96$

Practice and Problem Solving

HELP with Homework

Example	Exercises
1	10–21
2	10–21
3	22–25

- More Examples
- eTutorial Plus

Find the product.

10. $-6(7)$
11. $-1(-17)$
12. $0(-13)$
13. $-4(-11)$
14. $9(-2)$
15. $3(-5)$
16. $-15(-12)$
17. $-1(-32)$
18. $-2(5)(-6)$
19. $6(-4)(12)$
20. $-8(-7)(-5)$
21. $12(0)(-45)$

Evaluate the expression when $x = -9$, $y = -7$, and $z = -4$.

22. $xy + z$
23. $xy - y$
24. $2xyz$
25. $-3xy + 2yz$

Find the product.

26. $|-2| \cdot 5$
27. $-12 \cdot |11|$
28. $-7(-8) \cdot |-4|$

Mental Math **Use mental math to solve the equation.**

29. $2x = -8$
30. $-21y = 63$
31. $-5(-4)z = -80$

32. **Video Game** David is playing a video game. If he falls into a pit, he loses 125 points. If he collects coins, he will gain points. He has 400 points before he falls into 3 pits. After he collects a coin in each pit, his score is 175 points. How many points is each coin worth?

33. **Look for a Pattern** Evaluate $(-10)^1$, $(-10)^2$, $(-10)^3$, $(-10)^4$, and $(-10)^5$. How is the exponent related to the sign of the power?

34. **Critical Thinking** Does $(-3)^2$ equal -3^2? Explain your reasoning.

Evaluate the expression when $a = -8$ and $b = -11$.

35. $-a(-a)$
36. $a(-b^2)b$
37. $[a + (-a)b]^2$

38. **Check for Reasonableness** A coconut falls 100 feet from a palm tree. The equation $h = -16t^2 + 100$ gives the height h, in feet, of the coconut after falling for t seconds. Evaluate the equation when t equals 2, 2.5, and 3 seconds. When does the coconut hit the ground? What is the actual height of the coconut after 3 seconds?

39. **Stock Market** Your uncle owns 25 shares of stock A, 45 shares of stock B, and 60 shares of stock C. In one day, the price per share changed by +$.56 for stock A, −$1.46 for stock B, and −$.50 for stock C. Find the total change in value of your uncle's stock.

Evaluate the expression when $w = -31$, $y = 52$, and $z = -63$.

40. wyz
41. $yz - wyz$
42. $3yz - wy$
43. $-2wy - 2wz$

44. **Challenge** The product of a number and its *multiplicative inverse* is 1. For example, $4 \cdot \frac{1}{4} = 1$, so 4 and $\frac{1}{4}$ are multiplicative inverses. Give an example of a negative number and its multiplicative inverse.

Mixed Review

45. Find the side length of a square with a perimeter of 68 feet. *(Lesson 1.6)*

Find the difference. *(Lesson 2.3)*

46. $5 - 7$
47. $-9 - 14$
48. $-23 - (-12)$

Basic Skills **Find the quotient.**

49. $75 \div 5$
50. $0 \div 12$
51. $34 \div 17$
52. $63 \div 7$

Test-Taking Practice

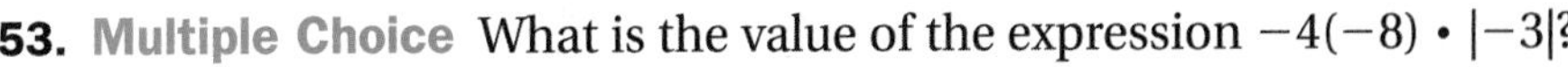

INTERNET
State Test Practice
CLASSZONE.COM

53. **Multiple Choice** What is the value of the expression $-4(-8) \cdot |-3|$?

A. −96 **B.** −36 **C.** 12 **D.** 96

54. **Multiple Choice** When you multiply an integer less than 1 and an integer less than −1, the product is which of the following?

F. less than zero
G. greater than zero
H. less than or equal to zero
I. greater than or equal to zero

Dividing Integers

BEFORE	Now	WHY?
You added, subtracted, and multiplied integers.	You'll divide integers.	So you can convert temperatures, as in Ex. 31.

In the Real World

mean, p. 75

INDIANA Academic Standards
- Computation (8.2.1)
- Problem Solving (8.7.4)

Temperatures One of the coldest places on Earth is the Russian town of Verkhoyansk, located near the Arctic Circle. The table shows the average high temperatures in Verkhoyansk. What is the average of these temperatures?

Winter Temperatures

Month	Average High
December	−44°F
January	−48°F
February	−38°F
March	−7°F

You will use the rules for dividing integers to find an average temperature in Example 2. These rules are similar to the rules for multiplying integers.

Dividing Integers

Words	Numbers	
The quotient of two integers with the same sign is positive.	$\frac{12}{6} = 2$	$\frac{-12}{-6} = 2$
The quotient of two integers with different signs is negative.	$\frac{12}{-6} = -2$	$\frac{-12}{6} = -2$
The quotient of zero and any nonzero integer is 0.	$\frac{0}{12} = 0$	$\frac{0}{-12} = 0$

Watch Out! You cannot divide a number by 0. Any number divided by 0 is *undefined*.

EXAMPLE 1 Dividing Integers

a. $\frac{-40}{-8} = 5$ **Same sign, so quotient is positive.**

b. $\frac{-14}{2} = -7$ **Different signs, so quotient is negative.**

c. $\frac{36}{-9} = -4$ **Different signs, so quotient is negative.**

Temperatures

One of the lowest temperatures on Earth, -90°F, was recorded in Verkhoyansk, Russia, on February 7, 1892. How much colder is this than today's temperature where you live?

The **mean** of a data set is the sum of the values divided by the number of values.

$$\text{mean} = \frac{\text{sum of values}}{\text{number of values}}$$

EXAMPLE 2 Finding a Mean

Temperatures To find the mean of the monthly average high temperatures in Verkhoyansk, Russia, given on page 74, first find the sum of the temperatures.

$-44 + (-48) + (-38) + (-7) = -137$

Then, divide the sum by the number of temperatures.

$\frac{-137}{4} = -34.25$

ANSWER The mean of the temperatures is about -34°F.

Your turn now **Find the quotient.**

1. $\frac{-33}{11}$
2. $\frac{-25}{-5}$
3. $\frac{0}{-4}$
4. $\frac{72}{-9}$

Find the mean of the data.

5. $-16, 17, 8, -23, -31$
6. $0, -4, -10, 4, 11\ -9, -13$
7. $-9, 26, -78, -40, -34$
8. $-7, -2, -12, 15, -8, -25, -17$

EXAMPLE 3 Evaluating Expressions

Evaluate the expression when $a = -24$, $b = 8$, and $c = -4$.

a. $\frac{a}{b}$

b. $\frac{ab}{c}$

Solution

a. $\frac{a}{b} = \frac{-24}{8}$ **Substitute values.**

$= -3$ **Different signs, so quotient is negative.**

b. $\frac{ab}{c} = \frac{-24 \cdot 8}{-4}$ **Substitute values.**

$= \frac{-192}{-4}$ **Multiply.**

$= 48$ **Same sign, so quotient is positive.**

Exercises

More Practice, p. 728

Getting Ready to Practice

1. **Vocabulary** Copy and complete: To find the _?_ of three numbers, add them and divide the sum by three.

Find the quotient.

2. $\frac{-44}{4}$ 3. $\frac{0}{-7}$ 4. $\frac{-81}{-9}$ 5. $\frac{50}{-10}$

Evaluate the expression when $x = 18$, $y = -12$, and $z = -6$.

6. $\frac{y}{z}$ 7. $\frac{x}{z}$ 8. $\frac{xz}{y}$ 9. $\frac{z^2}{y}$

10. **Guided Problem Solving** Will opened a used musical instrument shop. The table shows his profits for the first three months. Find his mean profit for these months.

Month	Profit
October	−\$172
November	−\$203
December	\$157

(1 Add the profits.

(2 Count the number of months given.

(3 Divide the sum in Step 1 by the number in Step 2. Should you give an exact or approximate answer?

Practice and Problem Solving

Find the quotient.

11. $\frac{-42}{-6}$ 12. $\frac{-28}{2}$ 13. $\frac{36}{-4}$ 14. $\frac{-19}{-1}$

15. $\frac{-49}{-7}$ 16. $\frac{-66}{-11}$ 17. $\frac{0}{-18}$ 18. $\frac{-27}{0}$

Find the mean of the data.

19. −12, 5, −9, 10, 16, −8, −2, 8 20. 4, −3, −8, 7, −1, 4, −2, −9, −1

21. **Writing** Is the mean of a set of negative numbers *always, sometimes,* or *never* negative? Give an example to support your reasoning.

Evaluate the expression when $m = 16$, $n = -8$, and $p = -32$.

22. $\frac{m}{n}$ 23. $\frac{p}{n}$ 24. $\frac{n^2}{m}$ 25. $\frac{p}{n+m}$

Example	Exercises
1	11-18, 27-30
2	19-20, 26
3	22-25

· More Examples
· eTutorial Plus

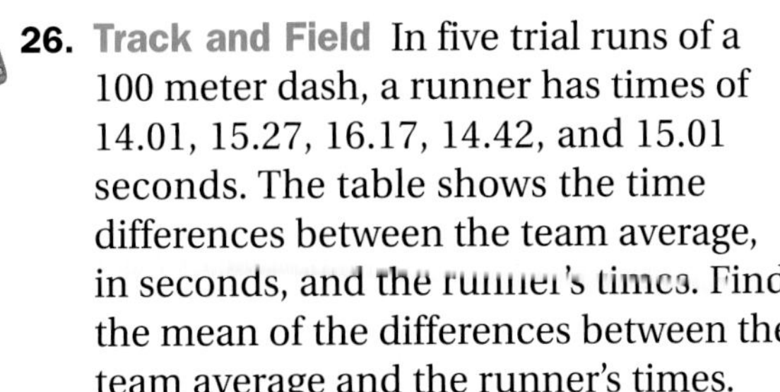

26. **Track and Field** In five trial runs of a 100 meter dash, a runner has times of 14.01, 15.27, 16.17, 14.42, and 15.01 seconds. The table shows the time differences between the team average, in seconds, and the runner's times. Find the mean of the differences between the team average and the runner's times.

Trial	Difference
1	−1.51
2	−0.25
3	0.65
4	−1.1
5	−0.51

Find the quotient.

27. $\frac{-9}{6}$ **28.** $\frac{15}{-12}$ **29.** $\frac{-8}{-10}$ **30.** $\frac{-6}{-30}$

31. **Reindeer** The natural habitat of a reindeer is the Arctic tundra. The average temperature during the winter in the Arctic tundra is −34°C. You can convert degrees Celsius C to degrees Fahrenheit F by using the formula $F = \frac{9}{5}C + 32$. What is the average winter Arctic tundra temperature in degrees Fahrenheit?

Challenge **Evaluate the expression when $a = -15$, $b = 50$, and $c = 20$.**

32. $\frac{b^2 + c}{c^2 a}$ **33.** $\frac{-2(a^2 + c^2)}{b}$ **34.** $\frac{(b + c)^2}{a}$

Mixed Review 

Write the product as a power. *(Lesson 1.4)*

35. $5 \cdot 5 \cdot 5 \cdot 5 \cdot 5$ **36.** $8 \cdot 8 \cdot 8 \cdot 8 \cdot 8 \cdot 8$ **37.** $b \cdot b \cdot b \cdot b$

Find the product. *(Lesson 2.4)*

38. $-11(-8)$ **39.** $12(-6)$ **40.** $6(-8)(-2)$

Test-Taking Practice 

INTERNET
State Test Practice
CLASSZONE.COM

41. **Multiple Choice** When you multiply the quotient of a negative integer and a positive integer by −1, what is the sign of the product?

A. negative **B.** positive **C.** zero **D.** cannot be determined

42. **Short Response** The table shows the temperatures in Fairbanks, Alaska. Calculate the mean temperature. Show your work or explain in words how you determined the mean. Should you give an exact or approximate answer?

Day	Temperature
Monday	−8°F
Tuesday	−1°F
Wednesday	−6°F
Thursday	−21°F
Friday	−31°F
Saturday	−34°F

Notebook Review

Review the vocabulary definitions in your notebook.

Copy the review examples in your notebook. Then complete the exercises.

Check Your Definitions

integer, p. 53	positive integer, p. 53	opposite, p. 54
negative integer, p. 53	absolute value, p. 54	mean, p. 75

Use Your Vocabulary

1. Draw a number line. Label three positive integers and three negative integers. Graph the two integers that have an absolute value of 3.

2.1 Can you graph and order integers?

EXAMPLE Order the integers from least to greatest: 24, −6, −45, 0, 12, −20, −32.

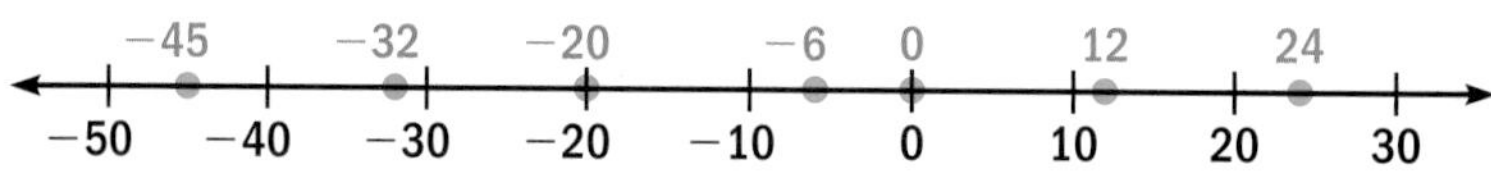

In order from least to greatest: −45, −32, −20, −6, 0, 12, 24

Use a number line to order the integers from least to greatest.

2. −15, 16, 1, −5, 4, 8 **3.** 40, −60, 98, −85, −6, 42

2.2–2.3 Can you add and subtract integers?

EXAMPLE Find the sum or difference.

a. $-22 + (-18) = -40$ Same sign, so sum has common sign.

b. $19 - 34 = 19 + (-34)$ Add the opposite of 34.

$= -15$ Add.

☑ **Find the sum or difference.**

4. $-26 + 64$ **5.** $37 + (-92)$ **6.** $-41 + (-78)$

7. $16 - 82$ **8.** $-51 - 14$ **9.** $-44 - (-29)$

2.4–2.5 Can you multiply and divide integers?

EXAMPLE Find the product or quotient.

a. $-7 \cdot 6 = -42$ **Different signs, so product is negative.**

b. $\frac{-56}{-7} = 8$ **Same sign, so quotient is positive.**

☑ **Find the product or quotient.**

10. $(-52)(-6)$ **11.** $31(-2)$ **12.** $\frac{-90}{15}$ **13.** $\frac{-52}{-13}$

Stop *and* **Think** about Lessons 2.1–2.5

14. Critical Thinking Is the opposite of the sum of two numbers equal to the sum of the opposites of the numbers? Explain.

Review Quiz 1

Copy and complete the statement with < or >.

1. $-8 \ \underline{?}\ 8$ **2.** $0 \ \underline{?}\ -14$ **3.** $-20 \ \underline{?}\ -30$ **4.** $-7 \ \underline{?}\ 5$

Evaluate the expression.

5. $-6 + 1$ **6.** $-20 + (-10)$ **7.** $-4 - (-3)$

8. $-6(-8)$ **9.** $-12(4)$ **10.** $\frac{-48}{-8}$

Find the mean of the data.

11. $-9, -15, 16, 4, 2, -10, 8, 20$ **12.** $-10, 6, -11, -6, -7, 3, -4, 1, 1$

13. $8, -9, -13, 5, -4, -3, -5$ **14.** $5, -6, -10, -15, 7, 9, -1, -3, 4$

Evaluate the expression when $a = -2$, $b = 10$, and $c = -3$.

15. $b - a$ **16.** $a - c - b$ **17.** abc **18.** $\frac{b}{a}$

19. Gravity You drop a ball out of a window that is 144 feet above the ground. The equation $h = -16t^2 + 144$ gives the height h, in feet, of the ball after falling for t seconds. Find the height of the ball after 1, 2, 3, and 4 seconds. When does the ball hit the ground?

Number Properties

BEFORE	Now	WHY?
You evaluated expressions.	You'll use properties to evaluate expressions.	So you can find your weekly pay, as in Ex. 39.

In the Real World

Review Words
sum, p. 709
product, p. 713

INDIANA Academic Standards
- Computation (8.2.1)
- Problem Solving (8.7.1)

Tour Biking You are going on a 400 mile bike trip. You plan to cycle at an average speed of 12 miles per hour for 7 hours a day. Can you complete the trip in 5 days?

The commutative properties of addition and multiplication can be used to make evaluating expressions using mental math easier.

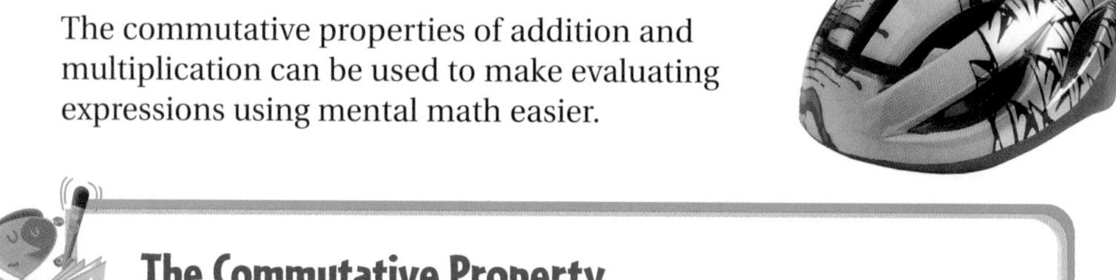

The Commutative Property

	Addition	Multiplication
Words	You can add numbers of a sum in any order.	You can multiply factors of a product in any order.
Numbers	$3 + (-8) = -8 + 3$	$5(-6) = -6(5)$
Algebra	$a + b = b + a$	$ab = ba$

EXAMPLE 1 Using the Commutative Property

To find if you can complete the bike trip in 5 days, find the total distance you plan to cycle. Then compare that distance to the length of the trip.

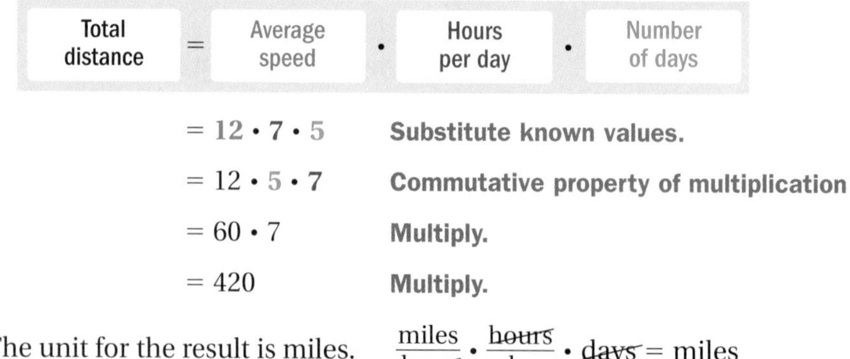

Total distance = Average speed • Hours per day • Number of days

$= 12 \cdot 7 \cdot 5$ **Substitute known values.**

$= 12 \cdot 5 \cdot 7$ **Commutative property of multiplication**

$= 60 \cdot 7$ **Multiply.**

$= 420$ **Multiply.**

The unit for the result is miles. $\frac{\text{miles}}{\cancel{\text{hour}}} \cdot \frac{\cancel{\text{hours}}}{\cancel{\text{day}}} \cdot \cancel{\text{days}} = \text{miles}$

ANSWER Because 400 miles is less than the 420 miles you can travel in 5 days, you can complete the trip in 5 days.

with Solving

When deciding what numbers to add or multiply first, look for pairs whose sum or product ends in zero, because multiples of 10 are easier to work with.

Subtracting a number is the same as adding the opposite, so you can write expressions to use the commutative property of addition.

EXAMPLE 2 Using the Commutative Property

$-54 + 35 - 16 = -54 + \mathbf{35} + (\mathbf{-16})$ **Change subtraction to addition**

$= -54 + (\mathbf{-16}) + \mathbf{35}$ **Commutative property of addition**

$= -70 + 35$ **Add −54 and −16.**

$= -35$ **Add −70 and −35.**

Your turn now **Use the commutative property to evaluate.**

1. $2 \cdot (-9) \cdot 5$ **2.** $47 + (-99) - (-53)$ **3.** $94 - 56 - 44$

The associative properties of addition and multiplication can also be used to make evaluating expressions using mental math easier.

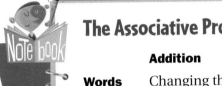

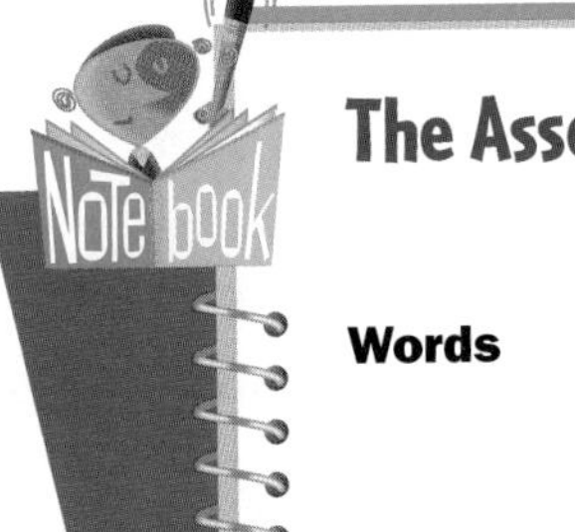

The Associative Property

	Addition	**Multiplication**
Words	Changing the grouping of numbers will not change their sum.	Changing the grouping of factors will not change their product.
Numbers	$(2 + 3) + 4 = 2 + (3 + 4)$	$(7 \cdot 4) \cdot 5 = 7 \cdot (4 \cdot 5)$
Algebra	$(a + b) + c = a + (b + c)$	$(ab)c = a(bc)$

EXAMPLE 3 Using the Associative Property

with Review

Grouping fractions and adding them makes mental math easier. For help adding fractions with common denominators, see p. 710.

$\frac{-3}{5} + \left(\frac{-2}{5} + 3\right) = \left(\frac{-3}{5} + \frac{-2}{5}\right) + 3$ **Associative property of addition**

$= \frac{-5}{5} + 3$ **Add fractions.**

$= -1 + 3$ **Write $\frac{-5}{5}$ as −1.**

$= 2$ **Add.**

with Vocabulary

Commute means change locations. You can use the *commutative properties* to change the order of numbers.
Associate means group together. You can use the *associative properties* to group numbers differently.

EXAMPLE 4 Using the Associative Property

$5 \cdot (11 \cdot 2) = 5 \cdot (2 \cdot 11)$ Commutative property of multiplication

$= (5 \cdot 2) \cdot 11$ Associative property of multiplication

$= 10 \cdot 11$ Multiply inside grouping symbols.

$= 110$ Multiply.

Your turn now **Evaluate the expression using mental math.**

4. $18 + (-34 + 12)$ **5.** $46 + (-63 - 46)$ **6.** $-2(46 \cdot 50)$

7. $4\left(\frac{1}{4} \cdot 23\right)$ **8.** $\frac{3}{7} + \left(8 + \frac{4}{7}\right)$ **9.** $[-21 \cdot (-29)] \cdot 0$

2.6 Exercises

More Practice, p. 728

Getting Ready to Practice

Vocabulary **Match the equation with the property it illustrates.**

1. $(x + 9) + 1 = x + (9 + 1)$ **A.** Identity property of addition

2. $12(1) = 12$ **B.** Commutative property of multiplication

3. $8a = a \cdot 8$ **C.** Commutative property of addition

4. $-16 + 0 = -16$ **D.** Associative property of multiplication

5. $(5 \cdot 7)y = 5(7y)$ **E.** Associative property of addition

6. $-24 + a = a + (-24)$ **F.** Identity property of multiplication

Mental Math **Evaluate the expression using mental math. Name the property or properties you used.**

7. $17 + 15 + 13$ **8.** $43 + (-27) - 13$ **9.** $5 \cdot (-29) \cdot 2$

10. $-2(-9 \cdot 50)$ **11.** $-53 + (-27 + 44)$ **12.** $[-4 \cdot (-7)](-5)$

13. Juice Box You have a juice box that is 2.5 inches long, 1.5 inches wide, and 4 inches high. The formula for the *volume* of a box is $V = lwh$. How much juice is in the box, in cubic inches?

Practice and Problem Solving

Example	Exercises
1	14–29, 32
2	14–26
3	14–26
4	14–26

- More Examples
- eTutorial Plus

Use the properties of addition and multiplication to find the missing number. Name the property.

14. $28 + \underline{?} = 65 + 28$

15. $54 \cdot 16 = 16 \cdot \underline{?}$

16. $(7 \cdot 3)3 = \underline{?}\,(3 \cdot 3)$

17. $4 + (\underline{?} + 2) = (4 + 9) + 2$

Evaluate the expression. Justify each step.

18. $-86 + 29 + (-34)$

19. $45 - (-68) - 44$

20. $-57 - 38 - (-57)$

21. $12 + (-39 + 48)$

22. $(-26 + 33) + (-4)$

23. $[25 \cdot (-7)]4$

24. $-40\left(\frac{1}{2} \cdot 45\right)$

25. $(-20 \cdot 9) \cdot 5$

26. $(3.2 \cdot 4.5)(10)$

Algebra **Simplify the expression.**

27. $7 \cdot x \cdot 10$

28. $-67 + [x + (-13)]$

29. $(52 + x) + 18$

30. Writing You need to find the sum of 52, 99, 65, 38, and 11. Explain how the commutative and associative properties of addition can help you find the sum using mental math.

31. Critical Thinking Is division commutative? Justify your answer with an example.

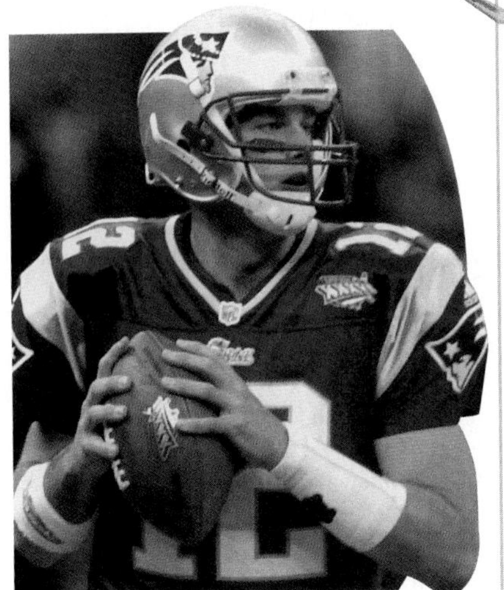

32. Super Bowl During Super Bowl XXXVI, six New England Patriots rushed the football for 92 yards, 22 yards, 15 yards, 5 yards, 3 yards, and −4 yards. What was the total number of their rushing yards?

Evaluate the expression. Show each step.

33. $3.6 + 5.7 + (-3.6)$

34. $\frac{1}{2} \cdot 17 \cdot 20$

35. $5(7 \cdot 4)(0.25)$

36. $\left(-\frac{2}{7} + 5\right) + \frac{3}{7}$

37. $12 \cdot (7 \cdot 1 \cdot 5)$

38. $\left(\frac{2}{3} \cdot 7\right) \cdot 21$

39. Paycheck The table shows the hours you worked during one week. Your hourly wage is \$6 per hour. Use the commutative property of multiplication to find the amount you earned for the week.

Time Card

Day	Time in	Time out
Monday	4 P.M.	6 P.M.
Tuesday	4 P.M.	6 P.M.
Wednesday	—	—
Thursday	3 P.M.	5 P.M.
Friday	3 P.M.	5 P.M.
Saturday	11 A.M.	1 P.M.

40. Compare Is the expression $-15 + 34 - 44 - 19 + 51$ equivalent to the expression $34 - 19 + 15 - 44 + 51$? Explain your reasoning.

41. **Critical Thinking** Explain how the student used the commutative property of addition to go from the first expression to the second expression. Use the same method to find the sum of the numbers from 1 to 19.

$$1 + 2 + 3 + 4 + 5 + 6 + 7 + 8 + 9 = 10 + 10 + 10 + 10 + 5$$
$$= 45$$

42. **Sale Price** You are buying 8 yards of fabric that costs \$5.25 per yard. You have a coupon for half off the original price. What is the price of your purchase after the discount?

43. **Challenge** Use the commutative properties of addition and multiplication to write three expressions equivalent to $4 \cdot 8 + 5$.

Mixed Review

44. **Temperature** During the first 10 days of January, 2002, the daily low temperatures in Alaska, in degrees Fahrenheit, were $-29°$, $-24°$, $-18°$, $-42°$, $-42°$, $-42°$, $-40°$, $-44°$, $-26°$ and $-19°$. Find the mean daily low temperature for these 10 days. *(Lesson 2.5)*

Choose a Strategy **Use a strategy from the list to solve the following problem. Explain your choice of strategy.**

45. You have two stacking bookcases that are 60 inches tall when stacked on top of each other. If you place them side by side, the difference of their heights is 8 inches. How tall is each bookcase?

Problem Solving Strategies
- Guess, Check, and Revise
- Look for a Pattern
- Work Backward

Basic Skills **Use a number line to compare the numbers.**

46. 1.2 and 0.8   47. 1.35 and 1.53   48. 0.24 and 0.25

Test-Taking Practice

INTERNET
State Test Practice
CLASSZONE.COM

49. **Multiple Choice** Which of the following is equivalent to $7 - 5 - (-4) + 6$?

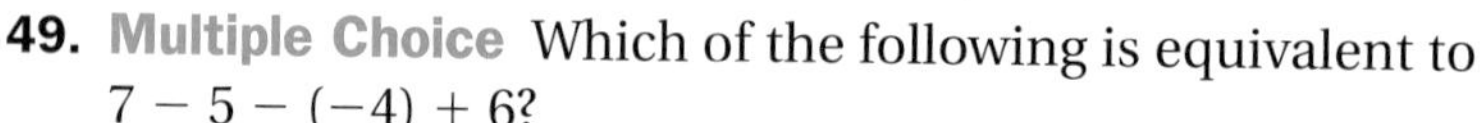

A. $7 - 6 - (-4) + 5$ **B.** $5 - 7 - (-4) + 6$

C. $7 - 5 + 2$ **D.** $7 + (-5) + 4 + 6$

50. **Short Response** You need to find the product of 25, 6, 4, and 7. Explain how the commutative and associative properties of multiplication can help you find the product using mental math.

The Distributive Property

BEFORE	Now	WHY?
You used addition and multiplication properties.	You'll use the distributive property.	So you can find the cost of souvenirs, as in Ex. 25.

distributive property, p. 85
terms, p. 86
like terms, p. 86
coefficient, p. 86
constant term, p. 86

INDIANA
Academic Standards

- Computation (8.2.1)
- Measurement (8.5.4)

In the Real World

Architecture A replica of the Parthenon, an ancient temple in Greece, was built in Nashville, Tennessee, in 1897. The diagram below shows the approximate dimensions of two adjacent rooms inside the replica. How can you find the total area of the two rooms?

EXAMPLE 1 Finding a Combined Area

Two methods can be used to find the total area of the two rooms.

Method 1 Find the area of each room, then find the total area.

$$\text{Area} = 63(44) + 63(93)$$
$$= 2772 + 5859$$
$$= 8631 \text{ square feet}$$

63 ft
93 ft
44 ft

Method 2 Find the total length, then multiply by the common width.

$$\text{Area} = 63(44 + 93)$$
$$= 63(137)$$
$$= 8631 \text{ square feet}$$

ANSWER The total area of the two rooms is 8631 square feet.

Example 1 demonstrates the distributive property.

The Distributive Property

Algebra $a(b + c) = ab + ac$ **Numbers** $6(4 + 3) = 6(4) + 6(3)$

$a(b - c) = ab - ac$ $7(8 - 5) = 7(8) - 7(5)$

The distributive property can be applied to expressions involving a sum or difference of two or more numbers or variable expressions.

EXAMPLE 2 Using the Distributive Property

a. $-5(x + 10) = -5x + (-5)(10)$ Distributive property

$= -5x + (-50)$ Multiply.

b. $3[1 - 20 + (-5)] = 3(1) - 3(20) + 3(-5)$ Distributive property

$= 3 - 60 + (-15)$ Multiply.

$= 3 + (-60) + (-15)$ Add the opposite of 60.

$= -72$ Add.

Your turn now **Write two expressions for the total area of the two rectangles. Find the total area.**

1.

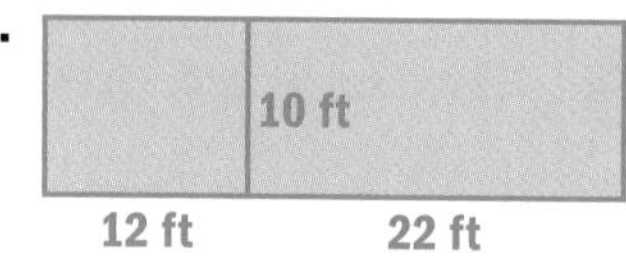

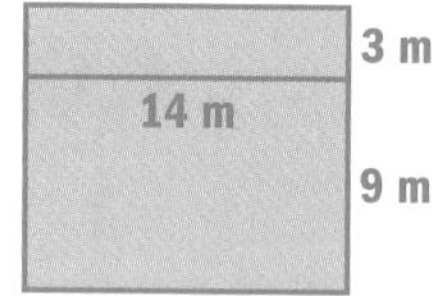

Use the distributive property to evaluate or simplify the expression.

3. $-2(5 + 12)$ **4.** $-4(-7 - 10)$ **5.** $2(w - 8)$ **6.** $-8(z + 25)$

HELP with Notetaking

When you add new vocabulary words to your notebook be sure to include examples of how they are used.

Combining Like Terms In a sum the parts that are added together are the **terms** of the expression. You can use the distributive property to combine *like terms.* **Like terms** have identical variable parts raised to the same power. In a term the number multiplied by the variable is the **coefficient** of the variable. A term that has no variable is a **constant term** .

Coefficients are 4 and 8.   Constant term is 1.

$4x + 8x + 1$

$4x$ and $8x$ are like terms.

EXAMPLE 3 Combining Like Terms

a. $3x + 4x = (3 + 4)x$ Distributive property

$= 7x$ Add inside grouping symbols.

b. $-9y + 7y + 5z = (-9 + 7)y + 5z$ Distributive property

$= -2y + 5z$ Add inside grouping symbols.

You may need to use the distributive property before you can combine like terms.

HELP with Solving

Remember that $x = 1 \cdot x$, so x has a coefficient of 1.

EXAMPLE 4 **Simplifying an Expression**

a. $2(4 + x) + x = 8 + 2x + x$ Distributive property

$= 8 + 3x$ Combine like terms.

b. $-5(3x - 6) + 7x = -15x + 30 + 7x$ Distributive property

$= -8x + 30$ Combine like terms.

Your turn now **Simplify the expression by combining like terms.**

7. $4x - 7x$ **8.** $5y + 9z - 7 - 3y$ **9.** $5(x - 6) + 3x + 4$

2.7 Exercises

More Practice, p. 728

INTERNET
eWorkbook Plus
CLASSZONE.COM

Getting Ready to Practice

1. Vocabulary Identify any *like terms* and *coefficients* in the expression $7x - 3y - 6y + x + 2$.

Use the distributive property to write an equivalent expression.

2. $4(7 + 8)$ **3.** $-7(3 + 2)$ **4.** $3(5 + 6)$

Simplify the expression by combining like terms.

5. $3y + 6y$ **6.** $9a - 4b + a$ **7.** $8m + n - 2m - 4b$

8. Guided Problem Solving You are buying three pairs of flip-flops that cost \$12.90 each. Use mental math and the distributive property to find the total cost of the flip-flops.

(1) Write 3(12.90) as 3(13 − 0.10).

(2) Find the products 3(13) and 3(0.10).

(3) Find the difference of the products.

Example	Exercises
1	33, 44
2	9-18, 27-32
3	19-24, 27-32
4	19-24, 27-32

- More Examples
- eTutorial Plus

Practice and Problem Solving

Match the expression with its simplified expression.

9. $3(x + 4)$ **10.** $4(x + 3)$ **11.** $2(2x - 6)$ **12.** $x(4 + 9)$

A. $4x - 12$ **B.** $3x + 12$ **C.** $13x$ **D.** $4x + 12$

Use the distributive property to evaluate or simplify the expression.

13. $9(x - 3)$ **14.** $-12(4 + 5 + y)$ **15.** $8(5 + 2)$

16. $19[7 + w + (-2)]$ **17.** $-34(z - 21 - 5)$ **18.** $-13(-12 + 9)$

Simplify the expression by combining like terms.

19. $r + 2s + 3r$ **20.** $11w + 9z + 3z + 5w$

21. $7a - 2a + 8b - 2b$ **22.** $3x + 2x + y + 2y - 3$

23. $-3x + 2x - 9y - 2x$ **24.** $r + 2s - (-3r) - s$

25. Souvenirs You are on vacation in Massachusetts and want to buy souvenirs for 6 friends at home. You decide to buy a trading pin that costs \$2.35 and a pen that costs \$.65 for each friend. Explain how to use mental math to find how much money you will need.

26. Find the Error Describe and correct the error in the solution.

$$4x + 2y - 7y - 2x = 4x - 2x + 2y - 7y$$
$$= 2x - 5y$$
$$= -3xy$$

Simplify the expression.

27. $7(y - 2)$ **28.** $9x(4 - 2 + 6)$ **29.** $3x + 2 - 5x + 4x$

30. $5(z + 2z) - 4z$ **31.** $8d - 2(3d - 5d)$ **32.** $4(3c - 4) + 2 - 4c$

33. Area A floor plan of a house is shown. You want to carpet the family room and the living room. The carpeting you want to use in these two rooms sells for \$3.12 per square foot. How much will the carpet cost?

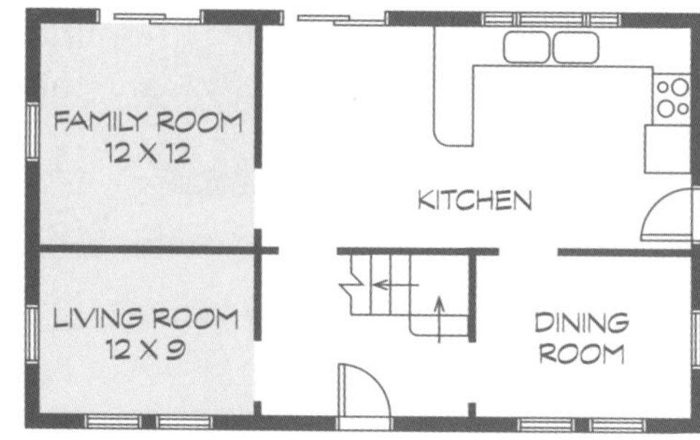

Simplify the expression by combining like terms.

34. $3a + 4b - 5 - a + 7b + 3 - b$

35. $5(x + 2) - 5(y + 3) - 2x + 5y$

36. $3.2(2z - 3x) + 4(1.1y + x) - 2z$

37. $7(y - 1.3) + 2.4 - 5.3y$

38. **Writing** Explain what you should consider when deciding which expression is easier to evaluate, $8(1000 - 2)$ or $8 \cdot 1000 - 8 \cdot 2$. Give an example of a problem you think is easier to solve using the distributive property and an example you think is not easier to solve using the distributive property.

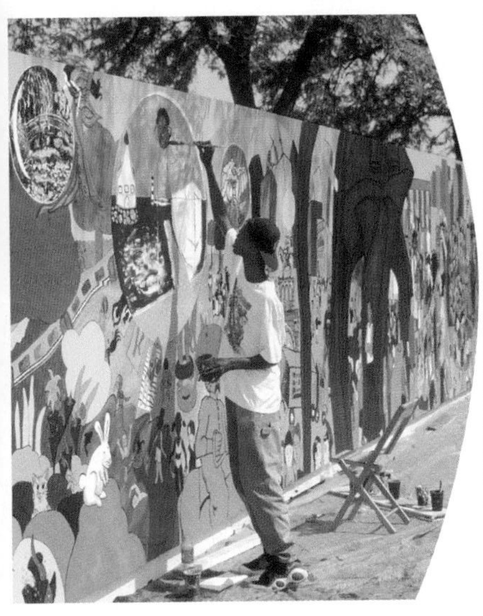

Mental Math **Use mental math to find the product using a method like the one in Exercise 8 on page 87. Explain your reasoning.**

39. 4(34)

40. 9(19)

41. 24(12)

42. 65(24)

43. **Critical Thinking** Are $3xy$ and $4yx$ like terms? Explain your reasoning.

44. **Mural** Some students have been given permission to paint murals on 5 walls at your school. The walls are all 8 feet tall. The mural widths are 21.5 feet, 35 feet, 27.5 feet, 33.5 feet, and 22.5 feet. Write two expressions to find the total area of the murals. Then find the total area.

45. **Challenge** You are ordering T-shirts with your school logo. Each T-shirt costs $7.25. There is a $25 setup fee for silk-screening, and a screening charge of $1.85 per shirt. Write an expression to find the total cost for x T-shirts. What is the total cost for 75 T-shirts? for 170 T-shirts?

Mixed Review

Order the integers from least to greatest. *(Lesson 2.1)*

46. $-90, 35, 19, -35, 80$

47. $70, -20, -90, 0, -100$

Evaluate the expression. *(Lesson 2.6)*

48. $-5(4 \cdot 17)$

49. $(-23 + 14) - 12$

50. $17 + (3 - 12) + 24(0)$

51. $(-4 \cdot 7) \cdot 25$

Test-Taking Practice

INTERNET
State Test Practice
CLASSZONE.COM

52. **Extended Response** The perimeter of the entire stage is 200 feet. Find the value of x. Show your work. Explain two different ways to find the area of the stage. Use either method to find the area.

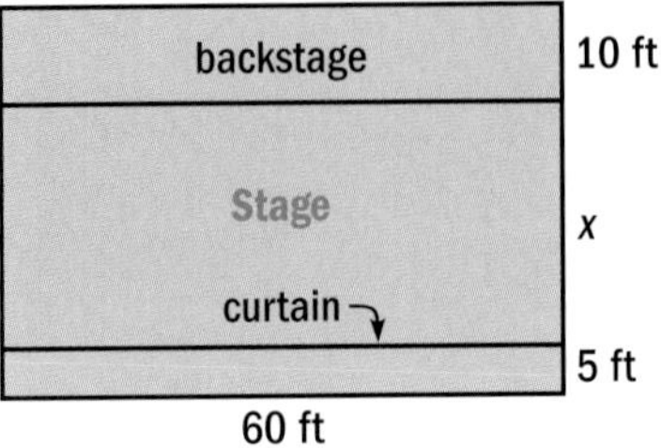

2.7 Technology Activity

CALCULATOR

INDIANA: Academic Standards
• Computation (8.2.1)

Using Integer Operations

GOAL Use a calculator to evaluate expressions.

Example **Use a calculator to evaluate the expression.**

a. $-900{,}018 + (-805{,}560)$ **b.** $\frac{-278 \cdot (-640)}{-139}$

Solution

Use the following keystrokes to find your answer.

	Keystrokes	Display
a.	(−) 900018 + (−) 805560 =	−1705578

ANSWER $-900{,}018 + (-805{,}560) = -1{,}705{,}578$

	Keystrokes	Display
b.	(−) 278 × (−) 640 ÷ (−) 139 =	−1280

ANSWER $\frac{-278 \cdot (-640)}{-139} = -1280$

Watch Out!

The − button performs subtraction. Use the (−) button to enter a negative number.

Your turn now **Use a calculator to evaluate the expression.**

1. $18{,}432 + (-46{,}978)$ **2.** $-50{,}215 + 1315$ **3.** $7010 - (-3999)$

4. $-14{,}300 - (-500)$ **5.** $-751 \cdot 2804$ **6.** $-1940 \cdot (-689)$

7. $3336(-198 \cdot 398)$ **8.** $\frac{-105{,}638}{-221}$ **9.** $\frac{-67{,}771}{671}$

10. **Moon** The distance of the moon's orbit around Earth is about 2,415,000 kilometers. The moon travels at an average speed of 3700 kilometers per hour. How long will it take the moon to complete one orbit?

11. **Earth** The diameter of Earth is about 4 times the diameter of the moon. The diameter of the moon is 3476 kilometers. What is the diameter of Earth? Find the difference of the diameter of Earth and the diameter of the moon.

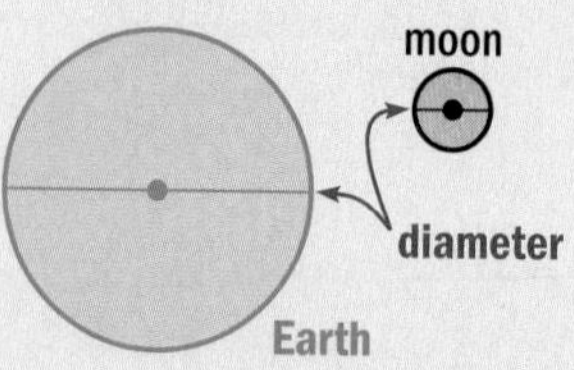

The Coordinate Plane

BEFORE	Now	WHY?
You used number lines.	You'll identify and plot points in a coordinate plane.	So you can predict the price of a phone call, as in Ex. 29.

Word Watch

coordinate plane, p. 91
x-axis, y-axis, p. 91
origin, p. 91
quadrant, p. 91
ordered pair, p. 91
x-coordinate, p. 91
y-coordinate, p. 91

INDIANA
Academic Standards

- Data Analysis and Probability (8.6.5)
- Measurement (8.5.4)

A **coordinate plane** is formed by the intersection of a horizontal number line called the **x-axis** and a vertical number line called the **y-axis**. The axes meet at a point called the **origin** and divide the coordinate plane into four **quadrants**.

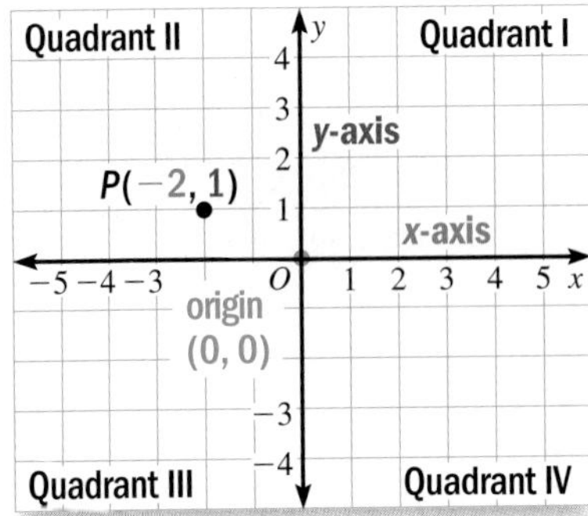

Points in a coordinate plane are represented by **ordered pairs**. The first number is the **x-coordinate**. The second number is the **y-coordinate**. Point P above is represented by the ordered pair $(-2, 1)$.

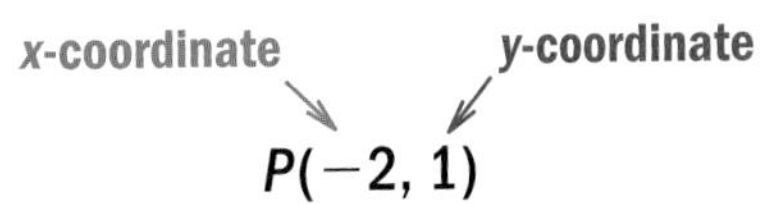

EXAMPLE 1 Naming Points in a Coordinate Plane

Give the coordinates of the point.

a. A **b.** B **c.** C

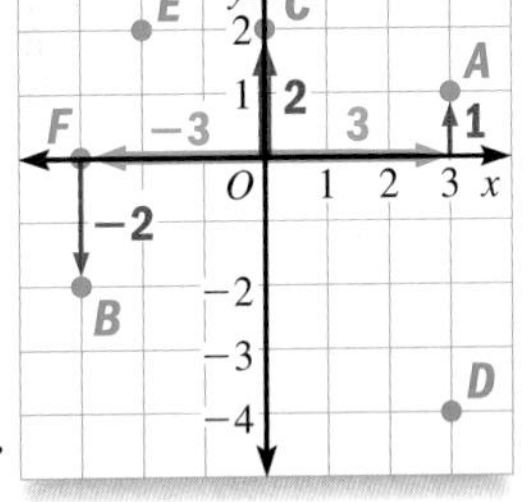

Solution

a. Point A is 3 units to the right of the origin and 1 unit up. So, the x-coordinate is 3 and the y-coordinate is 1. The coordinates of A are $(3, 1)$.

b. Point B is 3 units to the left of the origin and 2 units down. So, the x-coordinate is -3 and the y-coordinate is -2. The coordinates of B are$(-3, -2)$.

c. Point C is 2 units up from the origin. So, the x-coordinate is 0 and the y-coordinate is 2. The coordinates of C are $(0, 2)$.

Your turn now **Give the coordinates of the point.**

1. D **2.** E **3.** F

EXAMPLE 2 Graphing Points in a Coordinate Plane

Plot the point and describe its location.

a. $A(4, -2)$ **b.** $B(-1, 2)$ **c.** $C(0, -3)$

Solution

a. Begin at the origin, move 4 units to the right, then 2 units down. Point A lies in Quadrant IV.

b. Begin at the origin, move 1 unit to the left, then 2 units up. Point B lies in Quadrant II.

c. Begin at the origin, move 3 units down. Point C lies on the y-axis.

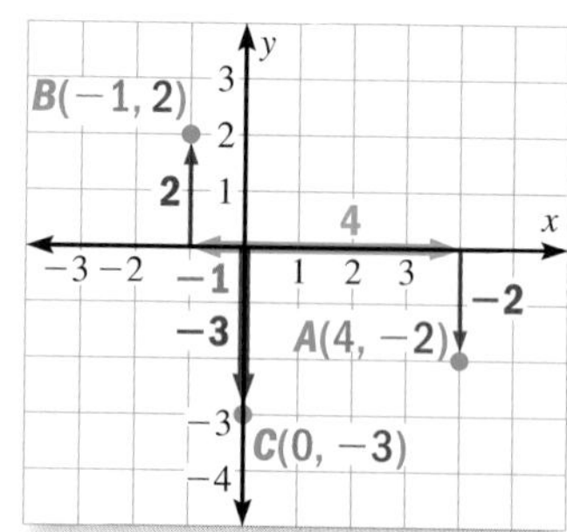

HELP with Solving

Points on the x-axis or y-axis do not lie in any quadrant.

EXAMPLE 3 Finding Perimeter

Identify the figure and find its perimeter.

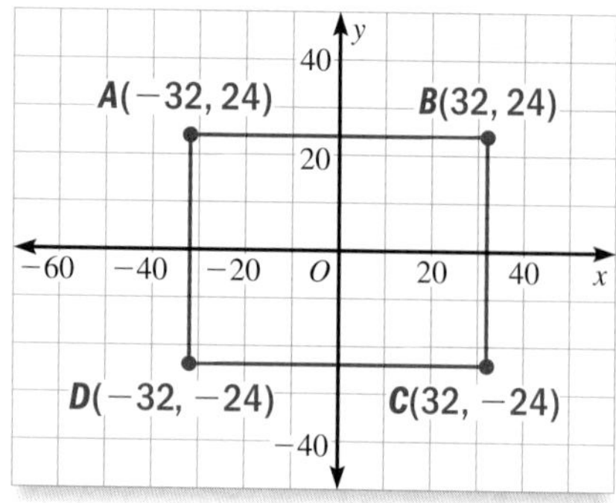

Solution

Points A, B, C, and D form a rectangle.

To find the length l, find the *horizontal* distance from A to B.

$$l = |x\text{-coordinate of } A - x\text{-coordinate of } B|$$
$$= |-32 - 32| = |-64| = 64$$

To find the width w, find the *vertical* distance from A to D.

$$w = |y\text{-coordinate of } A - y\text{-coordinate of } D|$$
$$= |24 - (-24)| = |48| = 48$$

$$\text{Perimeter} = 2l + 2w = 2(64) + 2(48) = 224$$

ANSWER The rectangle has a perimeter of 224 units.

HELP with Solving

You need to use absolute value signs because length and width are always positive.

Your turn now **Plot the point and describe its location.**

4. $R(-3, 4)$ **5.** $S(1, 2)$ **6.** $T(0, 3)$ **7.** $U(-4, 0)$

8. Plot and connect points $A(-20, 25)$, $B(25, 25)$, $C(25, -20)$, and $D(-20, -20)$. Identify the resulting figure and find its perimeter.

2.8 Exercises

More Practice, p. 728

Getting Ready to Practice

1. **Vocabulary** Draw a coordinate plane and label the x-axis, y-axis, each quadrant, and the origin.

Give the coordinates of the point.

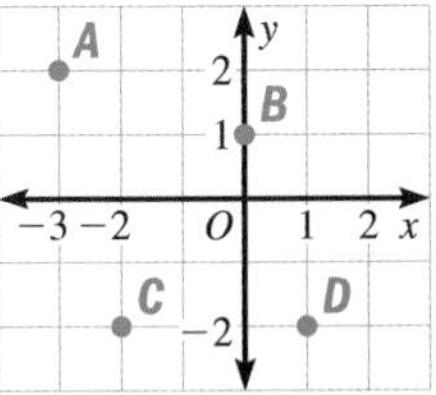

2. A **3.** B

4. C **5.** D

Plot the point in a coordinate plane.

6. (4, 1) **7.** (2, −3) **8.** (−3, 0) **9.** (−2, −1)

10. **City Park** The rectangle with corners A, B, C, and D represents a city park. Find the distance around the city park if the length and width of each small square on the coordinate grid represents 100 feet.

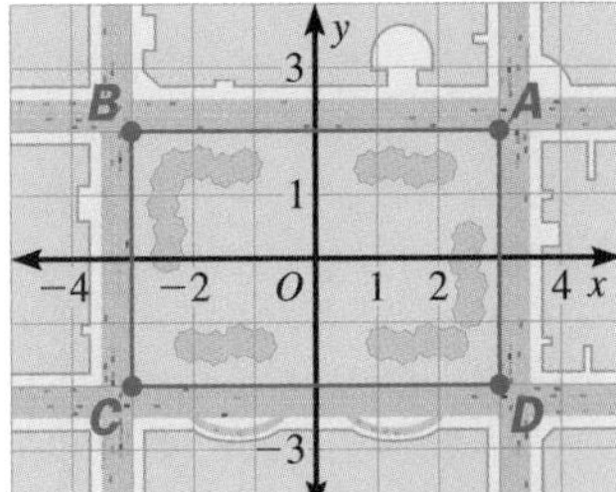

Practice and Problem Solving

Example	Exercises
1	11–16
2	17–20
3	21–22, 24–26

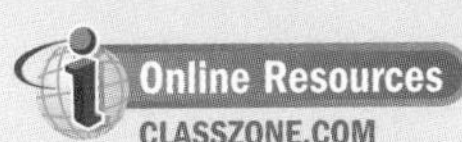

- More Examples
- eTutorial Plus

Give the coordinates of the point.

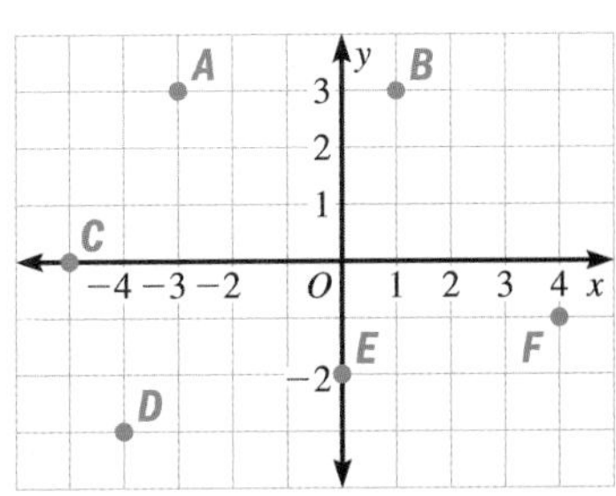

11. A **12.** B

13. C **14.** D

15. E **16.** F

Plot the point in a coordinate plane and describe its location.

17. (−2, 3) **18.** (3, −1) **19.** (0, −5) **20.** (−3, −4)

Plot and connect the given points. Then identify the resulting figure and find its perimeter.

21. $A(-2, 6)$, $B(2, 6)$, $C(2, -6)$, $D(-2, -6)$

22. $J(5, 4)$, $K(5, -2)$, $L(-1, -2)$, $M(-1, 4)$

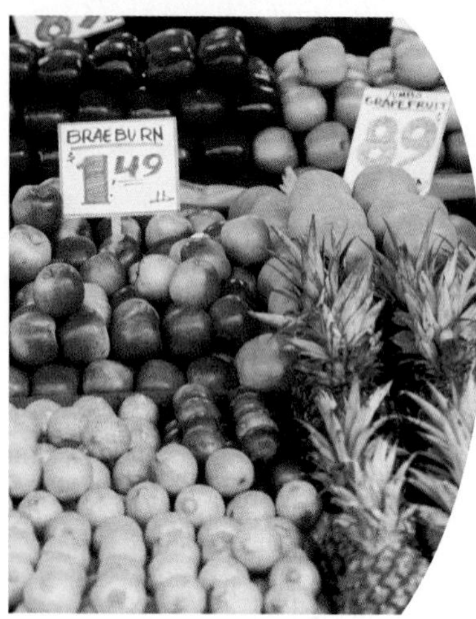

23. **Fruit** The following ordered pairs represent the cost of buying several weights of pineapple from a fruit stand. The x-coordinate represents the number of pounds and the y-coordinate represents the cost.

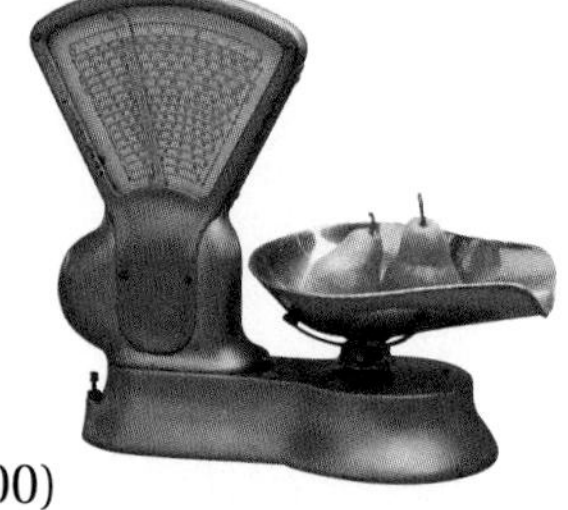

(1, \$3.50), (2, \$7.00), (3, \$10.50), (4, \$14.00)

Plot the points in a coordinate plane. Identify the pattern.

Use the pattern to estimate the cost of $2\frac{1}{2}$ pounds of pineapple.

Plot and connect the points. Find the perimeter and area of the rectangle formed.

24. $Q(5, 2)$, $R(5, -5)$, $S(-3, -5)$, $T(-3, 2)$
25. $K(0, -5)$, $L(-5, -5)$, $M(-5, 0)$, $N(0, 0)$
26. $W(-1, -7)$, $X(-1, 3)$, $Y(2, 3)$, $Z(2, -7)$

Extended Problem Solving In Exercises 27–29, suppose your phone card charges 7 cents per minute for a phone call.

27. **Calculate** Find the cost of a 10 minute call, a 20 minute call, and a 30 minute call.

28. **Graph** Plot the costs you found in Exercise 27 in a coordinate plane, where the x-coordinate represents the length (in minutes) of the call and the y-coordinate represents the total cost of the call, in dollars.
29. **Estimate** Draw a line through the points. Use the line to estimate the cost of an hour-long call.
30. **Challenge** Draw a rectangle that has points in all four quadrants. Multiply each coordinate by 2 and draw this rectangle. Compare this rectangle with the original one and compare their perimeters. What do you find?
31. **Slide** Copy the figure. Move the figure 2 units to the left and 3 units up. Give the new coordinates of A, B, C, D, and E.

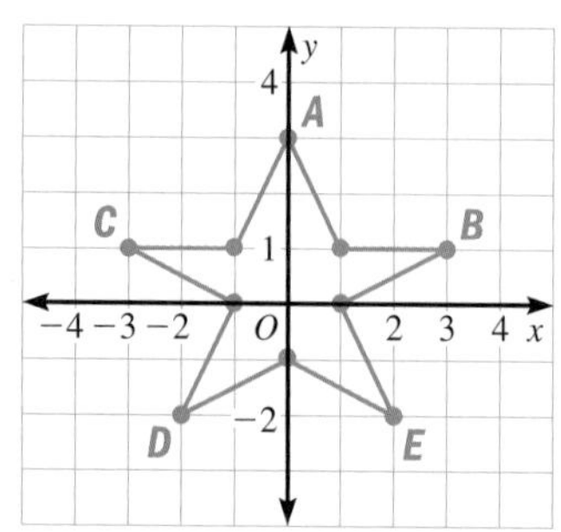

Mixed Review

Find the sum. *(Lesson 2.2)*

32. $24 + (-9) + (-12)$ **33.** $-14 + 30 + (-17)$ **34.** $-40 + 8 + 12$

Simplify the expression. *(Lesson 2.7)*

35. $4(x + 9)$ **36.** $6y(8 - 6)$ **37.** $-9(z - 2)$

38. **Basic Skills** You are selling T-shirts as a fundraiser for your school's soccer team. You need to sell 35 shirts to reach your goal, and you have sold 18 shirts. How many more T-shirts do you need to sell?

Test-Taking Practice 

INTERNET
State Test Practice
CLASSZONE.COM

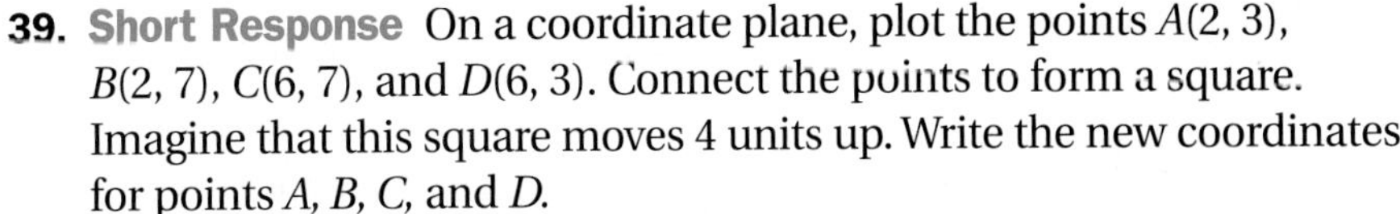

39. **Short Response** On a coordinate plane, plot the points $A(2, 3)$, $B(2, 7)$, $C(6, 7)$, and $D(6, 3)$. Connect the points to form a square. Imagine that this square moves 4 units up. Write the new coordinates for points A, B, C, and D.

40. **Multiple Choice** Which labeled point shown has an x-coordinate of 2?

A. M **B.** N

C. P **D.** R

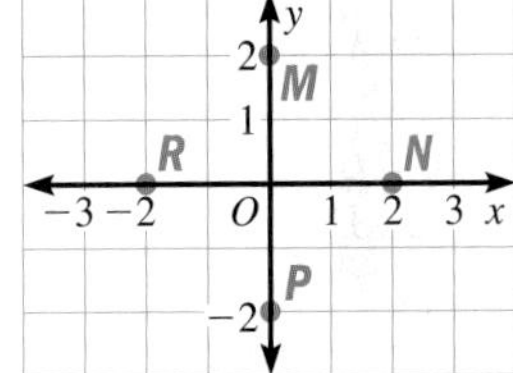

Spatial Delivery

Jack delivers balloons in a city. Below is a grid of Jack's city and a list of the deliveries he made today. Copy the diagram on graph paper and plot each stop. How many blocks did Jack travel?

Delivery Stops

Began at Main and State Street

1. E 3rd St. and Main
2. E 3rd St. and N 2nd Ave.
3. E 1st St. and N 2nd Ave.
4. E 1st St. and S 2nd Ave.
5. W 2nd St. and S 3rd Ave.
6. W 3rd St. and S 1st Ave
7. W 3rd St. and N 2nd Ave.
8. W 1st St. and N 2nd Ave.

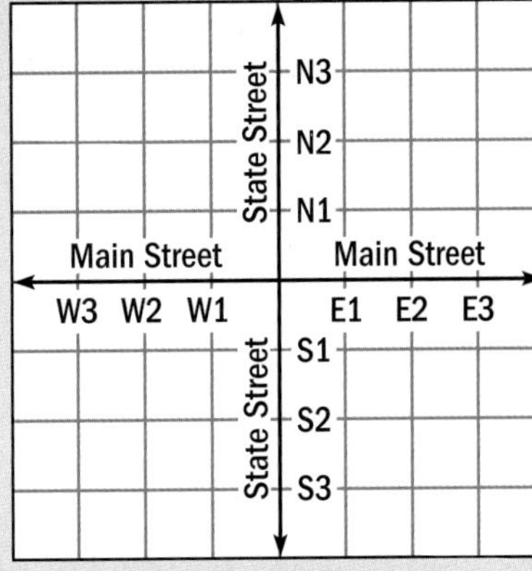

Notebook Review

Review the vocabulary definitions in your notebook.

Copy the review examples in your notebook. Then complete the exercises.

Check Your Definitions

distributive property, p. 85
terms, like terms, p. 86
coefficient, p. 86
constant term, p. 86
coordinate plane, p. 91
x-axis, y-axis, p. 91
origin, p. 91
quadrant, p. 91
ordered pair, p. 91
x-coordinate, p. 91
y-coordinate, p. 91

Use Your Vocabulary

1. What is the y-coordinate of the point $(5, -5)$?

2.6 Can you use commutative and associative properties?

EXAMPLE Evaluate the expression.

$(-3 + 5) - 7 = (-3 + 5) + (-7)$	Change subtraction to addition.
$= [5 + (-3)] + (-7)$	Commutative property of addition
$= 5 + [-3 + (-7)]$	Associative property of addition
$= 5 + (-10)$	Add inside grouping symbols.
$= -5$	Add.

Use mental math to evaluate the expression. Justify.

2. $-5(19 \cdot 2)$ **3.** $-25 \cdot 13 \cdot 4$ **4.** $-42 + (-18 - 23)$

2.7 Can you use the distributive property?

EXAMPLE Simplify the expression.

$6(2x + 7) - 9x = 12x + 42 - 9x$	Distributive property
$= 12x + 42 + (-9x)$	Change subtraction to addition.
$= 12x + (-9x) + 42$	Commutative property of addition
$= 3x + 42$	Combine like terms.

Use the distributive property to simplify the expression.

5. $9(3a + 11) - 4$ **6.** $-8b + 12(7b + 3)$ **7.** $2c - 8(9c - 5)$

2.8 Can you identify and plot points?

EXAMPLE Plot the point and describe its location.

a. $A(-1, 1)$ **b.** $B(4, -3)$

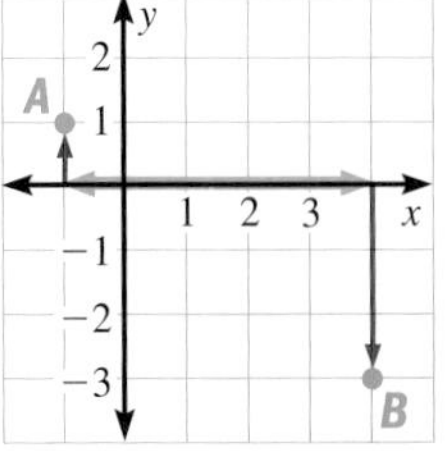

Solution

a. Begin at the origin, move 1 unit to the left and 1 unit up. Point A lies in Quadrant II.

b. Begin at the origin, move 4 units to the right and 3 units down. Point B lies in Quadrant IV.

☑ **Plot the point and describe its location.**

8. $L(3, -5)$ **9.** $M(0, -1)$ **10.** $N(6, 0)$ **11.** $P(-4, 2)$

Stop and Think about Lessons 2.6–2.8

12. Writing Explain how you can use the distributive property and mental math to evaluate the expression $4 \cdot 6.11$.

Review Quiz 2

Evaluate the expression. Justify each step.

1. $(19 + 33) + 11$ **2.** $15(23)(-4)$ **3.** $3(-4 \cdot 9)$

Simplify the expression.

4. $9x + 22x$ **5.** $3a - 2b + 6 - a$ **6.** $8(y + 2) - 4y$

In Exercises 7–9, use the coordinate plane.

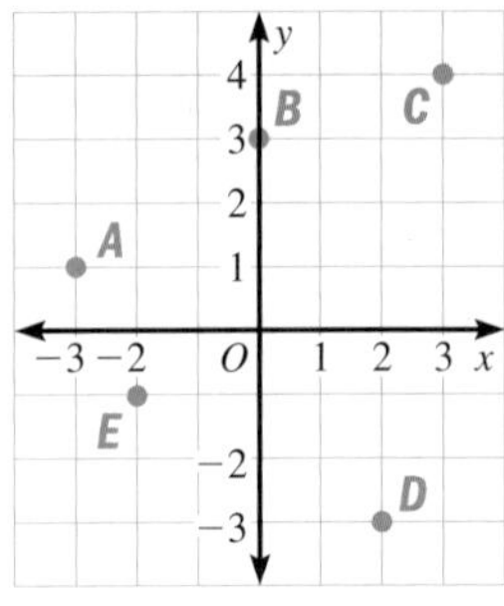

7. Write the coordinates of points $A, B, C, D,$ and E.

8. Which point lies on the y-axis?

9. Which point lies in Quadrant II?

10. Basketball In a basketball game Joe scored 13 points in the first quarter, 6 points in the second quarter, 7 points in the third quarter, and 14 points in the fourth quarter. How many points did Joe score?

CHAPTER 2

Chapter Review

Vocabulary

integer, p. 53
negative integer, p. 53
positive integer, p. 53
absolute value, p. 54
opposite, p. 54
mean, p. 75
distributive property, p. 85
terms, p. 86
like terms, p. 86
coefficient, p. 86
constant term, p. 86
coordinate plane, p. 91
x-axis, p. 91
y-axis, p. 91
origin, p. 91
quadrant, p. 91
ordered pair, p. 91
x-coordinate, p. 91
y-coordinate, p. 91

Vocabulary Review

1. How many numbers have an absolute value of 15? List them.
2. Copy the expression. List any like terms and coefficients.

$$-6y + 8 - 7x + 17x - 21y$$

3. How many quadrants are in a coordinate plane? Draw a coordinate plane and label each quadrant.

Copy and complete the statement.

4. A point in a coordinate plane is represented by a(n) _?_.
5. A(n) _?_ is formed by the intersection of a horizontal number line and a vertical number line.
6. The _?_ is the sum of the values divided by the number of values.

Review Questions

Order the integers from least to greatest. *(Lesson 2.1)*

7. −42, 53, 8, −31, −5, 11
8. −56, −102, 98, −58, 114

Write the opposite and the absolute value of the integer. *(Lesson 2.1)*

9. 22
10. −13
11. −512
12. 102

Find the sum or difference. *(Lessons 2.2, 2.3)*

13. $-81 + (-91)$
14. $32 + (-79)$
15. $-324 + 500$
16. $-468 + (-196)$
17. $-29 - 57$
18. $62 - (-58)$
19. $-43 - (-122)$
20. $31 - 108$

Find the product. *(Lesson 2.4)*

21. $-6(9)$
22. $31(-4)$
23. $-9(-23)(0)$
24. $-2(-3)(6)(-12)$

Review Questions

Evaluate the expression when $x = -6$, $y = -4$, and $z = -8$. *(Lesson 2.4)*

25. xyz **26.** $9z - 2x$ **27.** $11y - 2xz$ **28.** $2x + 3yz$

29. Hot Air Balloon A hot air balloon at a height of 110 feet rises for 6 minutes at a rate of 18 feet per minute, then drops 22 feet per minute for 3 minutes. What is the height of the balloon? *(Lesson 2.4)*

Find the quotient. *(Lesson 2.5)*

30. $\frac{-26}{2}$ **31.** $\frac{-98}{-7}$ **32.** $\frac{-120}{-15}$ **33.** $\frac{63}{-7}$

Find the mean of the data. *(Lesson 2.5)*

34. 5, 7, −9, −2, −6, 8, −9, 6

35. 15, −9, 6, −14, −18, 12, 7, 5, −2, 8

Evaluate the expression using mental math. Name the property or properties used. *(Lesson 2.6)*

36. $19 - (-58 - 81)$ **37.** $(-45 + 97) - (-45)$ **38.** $(-28 - 95 + 85) + (-62)$

39. $4(19 \cdot 25)$ **40.** $(-15 \cdot 5) \cdot (-20)$ **41.** $[-54 \cdot (-56)] \cdot 0 \cdot (-17)$

Use the distributive property to simplify the expression. *(Lesson 2.7)*

42. $5(12x - 20)$ **43.** $7(9 + 11y)$ **44.** $4(25z - 30)$

Simplify the expression by combining like terms. *(Lesson 2.7)*

45. $14x - 3y - 7x + y$

46. $4x - 11y + 2(1 - x)$

47. Baseball Caps Use mental math and the distributive property to find the total price of 3 baseball caps that cost \$12.90 each. *(Lesson 2.7)*

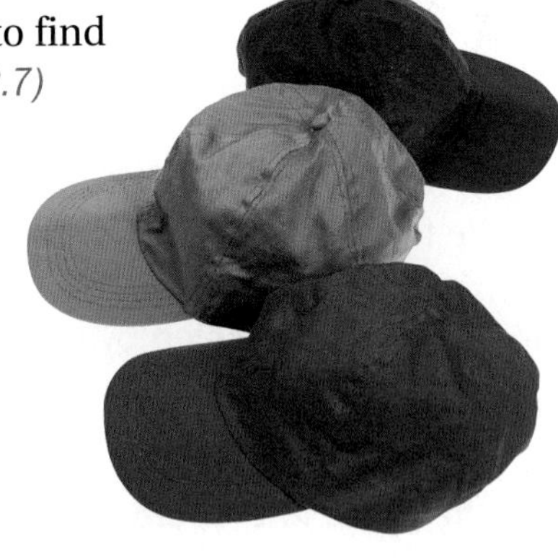

Give the coordinates of the point. *(Lesson 2.8)*

48. A **49.** B

50. C **51.** D

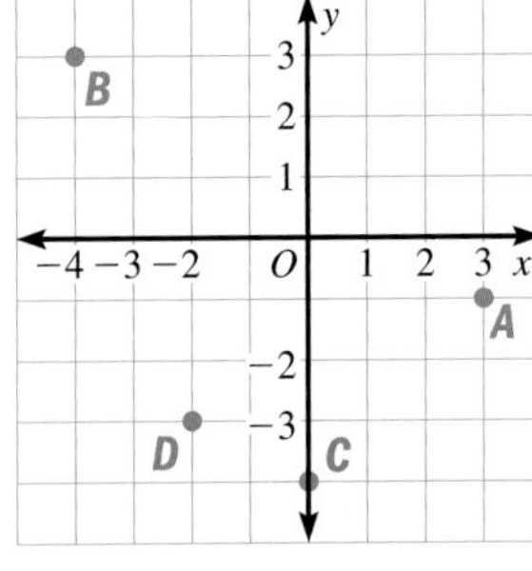

52. Geometry Plot, label, and connect in order the following points in a coordinate plane. Find the perimeter of the figure. *(Lesson 2.8)*

$A(0, 7)$, $B(4, 7)$, $C(4, 4)$, $D(8, 4)$, $E(8, 0)$, $F(0, 0)$

CHAPTER 2

Chapter Test

Order the integers from least to greatest.

1. $-9, 8, 14, -11, 0, -1$

2. $123, 87, -59, -12, -111, 22$

Find the number.

3. Find $|x|$ when x is 2 and when x is -4.

4. Find $-(-x)$ when x is -1 and when x is 7.

Find the sum or difference.

5. $17 + (-9)$

6. $-8 + (-14)$

7. $-2 + (-21)$

8. $-33 + 26$

9. $1 - 19$

10. $-4 - 17$

11. $10 - (-15)$

12. $-7 - (-18)$

Find the product or the quotient.

13. $-5(14)$

14. $-12(-20)$

15. $\frac{-152}{-19}$

16. $\frac{-132}{6}$

17. **Temperature** The following temperatures were taken during a week in December in Nome, Alaska. What is the mean temperature to the nearest degree?
$-5°F, -8°F, -13°F, -16°F, -8°F, 11°F, 0°F$

Evaluate the expression when $a = 3$, $b = -15$, and $c = 15$.

18. $\frac{c}{-a}$

19. $\frac{6b}{2c}$

20. $\frac{c}{-5a}$

21. $\frac{b^2}{a^2}$

22. **Groceries** You are purchasing a loaf of bread for $2.16, a box of cereal for $3.25, and 2 cans of soup for $.42 each. Write an expression to find the total cost. Then evaluate your expression.

Simplify the expression by combining like terms.

23. $3x + 4 - x + 1$

24. $2x - 3y + 5x - (-9y)$

25. $2(9x - 22y) + 4x$

Plot the point in a coordinate plane and describe its location.

26. $(-3, 3)$

27. $(6, 0)$

28. $(-4, -8)$

29. $(5, -2)$

30. **Critical Thinking** Fill in the table for the equation $y = |x|$. Then plot the points on a coordinate plane. Describe the shape of the graph.

x	−3	−2	−1	0	1	2	3
y	?	?	?	?	?	?	?

Chapter Standardized Test

Test-Taking Strategy **If you are unsure of an answer, try to eliminate answers that you know are wrong.**

1. Which of the following shows the integers in order from least to greatest?

A. $-7, 11, 5, -6, 0$ **B.** $0, -7, -6, 5, 11$

C. $-7, -6, 0, 5, 11$ **D.** $0, -6, 5, -7, 11$

2. Which of the following is equal to -10?

F. $-|-10|$ **G.** $-(-10)$

H. $|10|$ **I.** $|-10|$

3. Which numerical expression represents the verbal expression "the absolute value of the opposite of negative 6"?

A. $-(-|6|)$ **B.** $-(-6)$

C. $|-(-6)|$ **D.** $-|-6|$

4. What is the value of $-21 + (-15) - 32$?

F. -68 **G.** -24

H. -4 **I.** 39

5. If the temperature is $-6°$ Fahrenheit and it changes by $-12°$ Fahrenheit, what is the new temperature?

A. $-18°F$ **B.** $-6°F$

C. $6°F$ **D.** $18°F$

6. What is the value of $20 - x - (-y)$ when $x = 9$ and $y = -6$?

F. -23 **G.** 5

H. 17 **I.** 35

7. Which product is *not* equal to -336?

A. $7(-8)(2)(-3)$ **B.** $56(-2)(3)$

C. $3(-7)(8)(2)$ **D.** $-8(-7)(-3)(2)$

8. Evaluate $-4ac + bc - 2a$ when $a = 6$, $b = -2$, and $c = -3$.

F. -66 **G.** -54

H. 66 **I.** 90

9. What is the mean of the following set of data?

$-7, 6, -1, 11, -8, -9, 0, -8$

A. -4 **B.** -2

C. 2 **D.** 6

10. Which ordered pair represents point S in the coordinate plane?

F. $(3, -4)$

G. $(-3, 4)$

H. $(-4, -3)$

I. $(4, -3)$

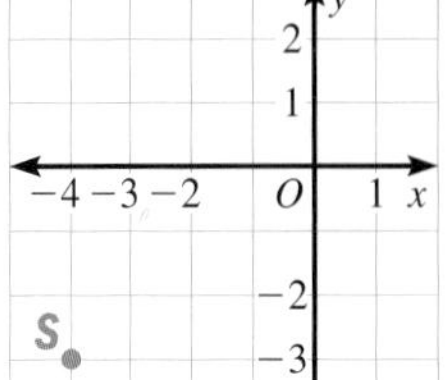

Short Response

11. Explain how the commutative and associative properties of addition can help you find the sum using mental math.

$$(57 + 24) + (36 + 83)$$

Extended Response

12. You are planning a field trip to a museum. The bus ride will cost \$250. Admission is \$8 and lunch is \$5 for each person. Write two expressions to find the total cost for x students. What would the cost be if 20 students went on the trip? 25 students? Did you use the distributive property to find your answer? Explain why or why not.

Supercool Squirrels

Hibernating in the Arctic

Animals living in very cold climates may hibernate to survive during winter. Hibernating animals have a decreased heart rate and decreased respiratory rate. The body temperature of a hibernating animal also drops significantly, often to just a few degrees higher than the surrounding temperature.

The arctic ground squirrel's body temperature drops below 0°C during hibernation. The graph below shows the body temperature of an arctic ground squirrel during the last few months of its hibernation.

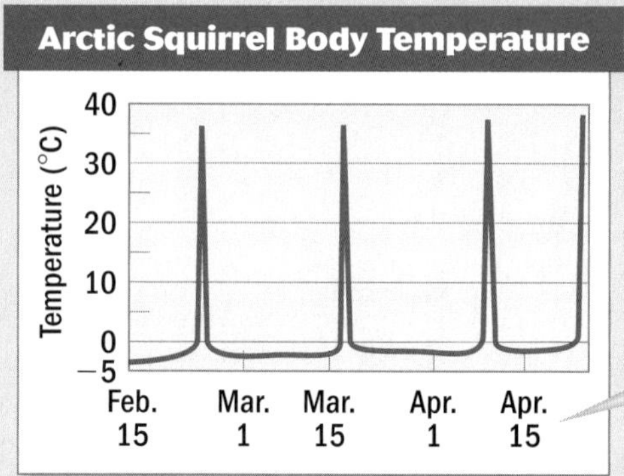

The squirrel hibernates from early September until late April.

The peaks in the graph represent short periods of time during which the squirrel wakes up from hibernation and warms itself up.

1. Estimate the difference of the squirrel's highest and lowest body temperatures for the period shown on the graph.
2. Which is the best estimate for the longest period during which the squirrel's body temperature was above zero? below zero?

   A. 1 hour **B.** 1 day **C.** 5 days **D.** 20 days
3. A squirrel's approximate body temperatures for several days in March were –3°C, –1°C, 36°C, 6°C, –2°C, and –3°C. What is the mean of the temperatures?
4. **Critical Thinking** Do you think your answer from Exercise 3 is a good representation of the squirrel's usual body temperature during the period of time shown by the graph? Explain your reasoning.

Soil Temperature

The graph below displays the squirrel body temperature data for March and April. It has a smaller temperature range, so waking periods are not fully displayed in the graph.

It also shows the soil temperature at 1 meter below ground, the depth at which the squirrel usually digs its burrow.

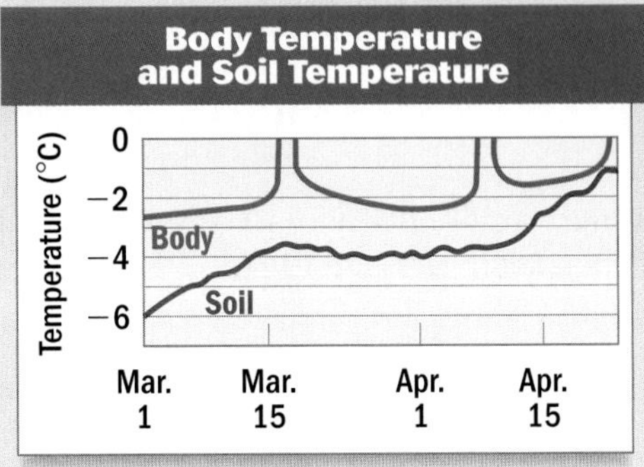

5. What is the difference of body temperature and soil temperature on March 1? What is the difference of these two temperatures on April 15th?

6. **Critical Thinking** A scientist claims that a hibernating animal's body temperature is always within 1 or 2 degrees of the surrounding temperature. Discuss whether this claim seems reasonable for the arctic ground squirrel, based on the data given.

Project IDEAS

- **Report** Find out more about the arctic ground squirrel. In what areas does it live? What foods does it eat? What are its predators? Present your findings to the class.
- **Research** Some reptiles and amphibians, such as the painted turtle and the wood frog, can survive subzero temperatures. Find out more about one of these animals. How low can its body temperature go? What mechanisms does it use to avoid freezing? Present your findings to the class.
- **Career** Find out more about the work that biologists do. What are some topics or areas in which a biologist might specialize? Present your findings to the class.

INTERNET
Project Support
CLASSZONE.COM

Solving Equations and Inequalities

BEFORE

In previous chapters you've...

- Evaluated expressions
- Solved word problems

Now

In Chapter 3 you'll study...

- Solving one-step equations
- Solving two-step equations
- Writing equations
- Formulas for area and perimeter
- Writing and solving inequalities
- Real life modeling

WHY?

So you can solve real-world problems about...

- sea lions, p. 112
- cartoonists, p. 121
- biplane rides, p. 143
- DJs, p. 149

Internet Preview
CLASSZONE.COM

- eEdition Plus Online
- eWorkbook Plus Online
- eTutorial Plus Online
- State Test Practice
- More Examples

Chapter Warm-Up Games

Review Skills you need for this chapter in these quick games. Work with a partner.

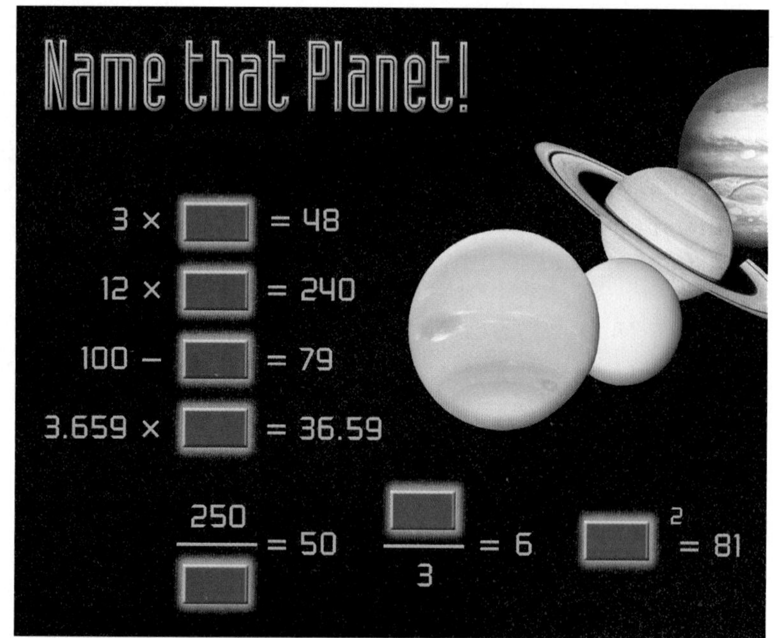

Key Skill:
Solving mental math equations

- Use mental math to find the missing number.
- Match each answer with the corresponding letter of the alphabet. (1 = A, 2 = B, etc.)
- Rearrange the letters to find the name of a planet.

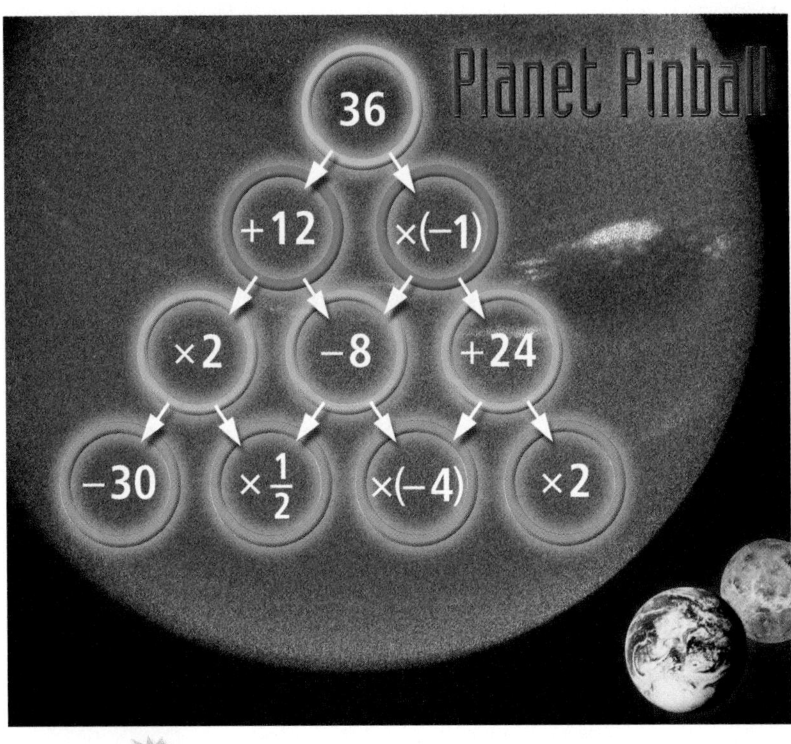

Key Skill:
Operations with integers

Materials:
penny

- Both players start at the top planet with 36 points.
- On your turn, toss a coin. If you get heads, go to the planet on the left. If you get tails, go to the planet on the right.
- Perform the operation written on the planet. The result is your current score.
- Take turns moving until both players reach the bottom row.
- The player with the higher score wins.

Stop *and* Think

1. **Writing** Without tossing the coin, work with your partner to find the route through the planets in the *Planet Pinball* that gives the highest score. Explain how you know you have found the best route.
2. **Extension** Choose another planet name. Write a puzzle like *Name that Planet!* with that name as the solution.

Getting Ready to Learn

Review What You Need to Know 

Word Watch

Review Words

variable, p. 15
equation, p. 28
solution, p. 28
opposite, p. 54
like terms, p. 86
coefficient, p. 86

Using Vocabulary **Copy and complete using a review word.**

1. 5 is the _?_ of -5.
2. 6 is the _?_ in the expression $6x$.
3. A(n) _?_ shows that two expressions are equal.

Solve the equation using mental math. *(p. 28)*

4. $x - 1 = 5$
5. $x - 2 = 9$
6. $4 + x = 12$
7. $10 = x + 3$
8. $5 - x = 2$
9. $x - 3 = 1$
10. $x + 3 = 4$
11. $8 + x = 8$

In Exercises 12–15, evaluate the expression. *(pp. 58, 63, 70)*

12. $-3 - 2 + 8$
13. $3 - 7 + 2 - 1$
14. $-2(3 + 1) + 2$
15. $8(1 - 4) - 9$
16. A tsunami wave caused by an underwater earthquake travels across the ocean at 500 miles per hour. Write and solve an equation to find how far it travels in 15 minutes. *(p. 33)*

You should include material that appears on a notebook like this in your own notes.

Know How to Take Notes

Organizing Information Sometimes you can organize complicated information in a table to make it easier to understand.

Multiplying Integers

x	Positive	Negative
Positive	+	−
Negative	−	+

In Lesson 3.7, you may want to make a table to help you organize information about solving inequalities.

3.1 Hands-on Activity

INDIANA: Academic Standards
- Algebra and Functions (8.3.1)

GOAL
Solve addition and subtraction equations using algebra tiles.

MATERIALS
- algebra tiles

Modeling One-Step Equations

You can use algebra tiles to model and solve one-step addition equations and one-step subtraction equations.

Represents the variable x	Represents a positive unit, or 1	Represents a negative unit, or -1
+	+	−
x-tile	1-tile	-1-tile

When you combine a 1-tile and a -1-tile, the result is zero. This pair of tiles is called a *zero pair* and may be removed from the model.

Explore 1 Model and solve $x + 3 = 8$.

1. Model $x + 3 = 8$ using algebra tiles.

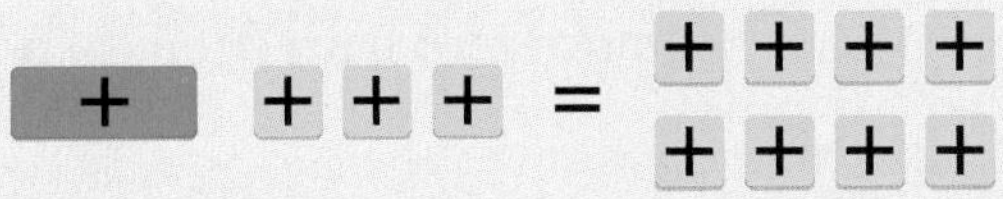

2. Remove three 1-tiles from each side so the x-tile is by itself.

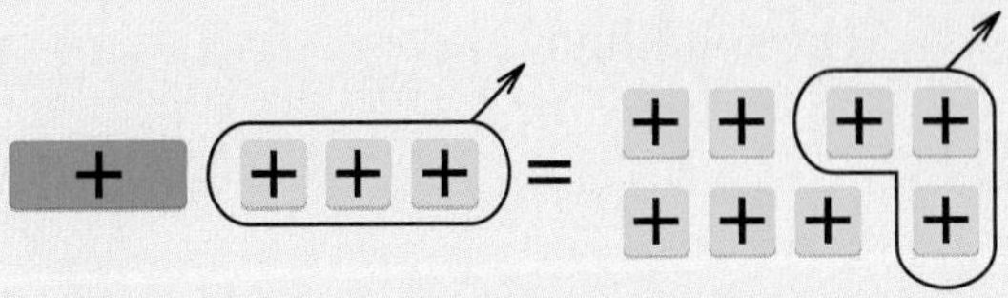

3. The solution of the equation is 5.

Your turn now

1. Use algebra tiles to model each step below. Draw a picture of each step.

(1) Model the equation $x + 5 = 7$.

(2) Remove five 1-tiles from each side.

(3) Find the solution.

Use algebra tiles to model and solve the equation.

2. $x + 4 = 9$ **3.** $5 + x = 7$ **4.** $6 = x + 2$ **5.** $7 + x = 9$

Explore 2 **Model and solve $x - 5 = -3$. Write the equation at each step.**

	Tile Model	Algebra
1	 To get the x-tile by itself, you can add the same number of 1-tiles to each side to create zero pairs. So, add five 1-tiles to each side.	$x - 5 = -3$
2	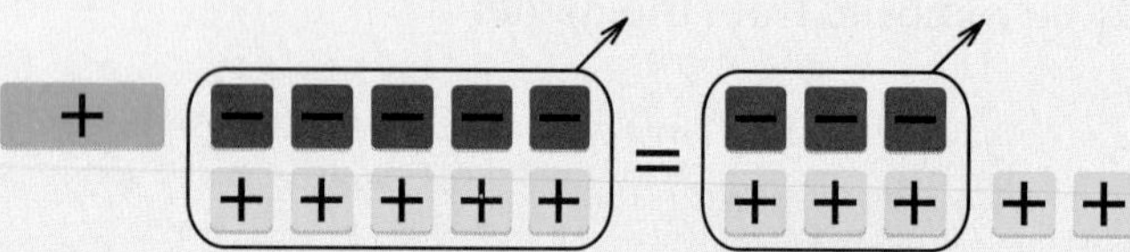 You can remove zero pairs from each side.	$x - 5 + 5 = -3 + 5$
3	+ = + + The solution is 2.	$x = 2$

Your turn now **Use algebra tiles to model and solve the equation. Write the equation at each step.**

6. $x - 3 = 6$ **7.** $x - 5 = 5$ **8.** $x + 6 = 2$ **9.** $8 + x = 1$

10. $x - 4 = -2$ **11.** $x - 7 = -3$ **12.** $x + 8 = 4$ **13.** $x - 3 = -6$

Stop and Think

14. **Writing** Give an example of an equation that requires you to make zero pairs to solve. How do you know that zero pairs are required?

15. **Critical Thinking** Can you model the equation $x + \frac{3}{2} = 5$ using x-tiles and 1-tiles? Explain.

Solving Equations Using Addition or Subtraction

BEFORE	Now	WHY?
You solved equations using mental math.	You'll solve equations using addition or subtraction.	So you can find the amount that a sea lion grows, as in Ex. 36.

equivalent equations, p. 109
inverse operation, p. 109

INDIANA
Academic Standards

- Algebra and Functions (8.3.1)

You can model and solve an equation by using a scale as shown.

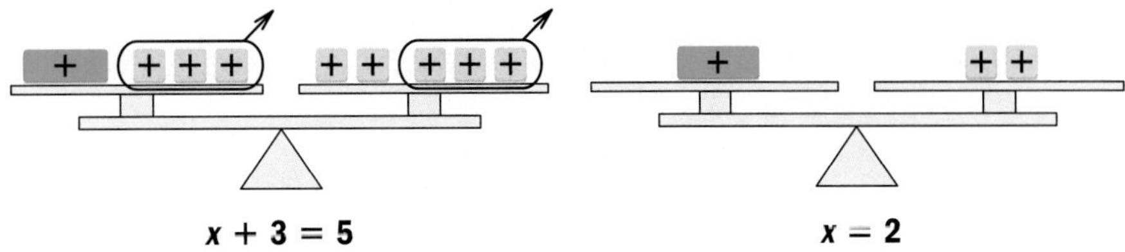

In the model above, removing three 1-tiles from each side of the scale keeps the scale in balance.

When you perform the same operation on each side of an equation, the result is a new equation that has the same solution. Equations that have the same solution(s) are **equivalent equations**.

You can solve an equation by using *inverse operations* to write equivalent equations. An **inverse operation** is an operation that "undoes" another operation. Addition and subtraction are inverse operations.

Subtraction Property of Equality

Words Subtracting the same number from each side of an equation makes an equivalent equation.

Numbers If $x + 5 = 7$, then $x + 5 - 5 = 7 - 5$.

Algebra If $a = b$, then $a - c = b - c$.

EXAMPLE 1 Solving an Equation Using Subtraction

$x + 8 = -15$	Original equation
$\underline{-8 \quad\; -8}$	Subtract 8 from each side to undo addition.
$x = -23$	Simplify. x is by itself.

ANSWER The solution is -23.

You can also use the addition property of equality to solve an equation.

Addition Property of Equality

Words Adding the same number to each side of an equation makes an equivalent equation.

Numbers If $x - 2 = 6$, then $x - 2 + 2 = 6 + 2$.

Algebra If $a = b$, then $a + c = b + c$.

You can add or subtract horizontally or vertically to solve equations, but remember that when solving, you must perform the same operation on *each* side.

EXAMPLE 2 Solving an Equation Using Addition

$c - 4.5 = 13$	Original equation
$c - 4.5 + 4.5 = 13 + 4.5$	Add 4.5 to each side to undo subtraction.
$c = 17.5$	Simplify. c is by itself.
✓Check $17.5 - 4.5 \stackrel{?}{=} 13$	Substitute 17.5 for c in original equation.
$13 = 13$ ✓	

Your turn now Solve the equation. Check your solution.

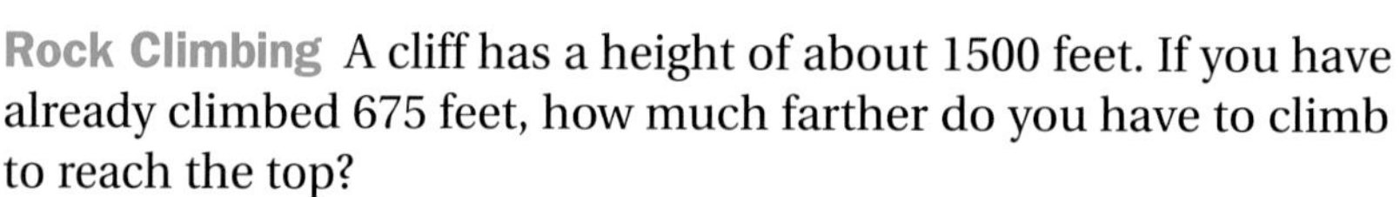

1. $x + 9 = 20$ **2.** $-10 = 3 + y$ **3.** $m - 14 = -15$ **4.** $2 = z - 6.4$

EXAMPLE 3 Using a Verbal Model

Rock Climbing A cliff has a height of about 1500 feet. If you have already climbed 675 feet, how much farther do you have to climb to reach the top?

Solution

Write a verbal model. Let x represent the distance left to climb.

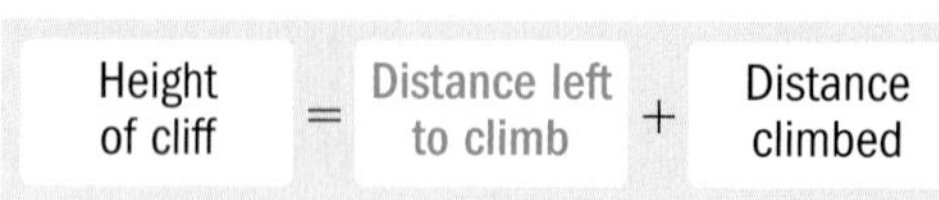

$1500 = x + 675$	Write an algebraic model.
$1500 - 675 = x + 675 - 675$	Subtract 675 from each side.
$825 = x$	Simplify. x is by itself.

ANSWER You have about 825 feet left to climb.

3.1 Exercises

More Practice, p. 729

Getting Ready to Practice

1. **Vocabulary** Copy and complete: Addition and subtraction are _?_ operations.

Solve the equation. Check your solution.

2. $x + 10 = 16$
3. $12 = x - 8$
4. $x + 1.3 = 2.5$
5. **Guided Problem Solving** You buy new school supplies. The price of the items is \$54.99, but after sales tax is added, they cost \$58.29. How much is the sales tax?

(1) Copy and complete the verbal model.

Price + _?_ = Total cost

(2) Substitute numbers and variables in the verbal model to write an algebraic model.

(3) Solve the algebraic model. Check your solution.

Practice and Problem Solving

with Homework

Example	Exercises
1	9-20
2	9-20
3	21-24

· More Examples
· eTutorial Plus

Describe an inverse operation that will undo the given operation.

6. Adding 4
7. Adding 4.5
8. Subtracting 35

Solve the equation.

9. $r + 2 = 7$
10. $t - 5 = 2$
11. $9 = p - 4$
12. $6 + x = 8$
13. $z + 9 = 11$
14. $23 = 6 + s$
15. $y - 15 = 9$
16. $13 = d - 27$
17. $24 = 52 + n$
18. $204 = m - 41$
19. $43 = a - 21$
20. $11 = c + 48$

Tell whether the equation correctly represents the real-life problem. If not, correct the equation.

21. At 62 inches tall, you are 5 inches taller than your sister. How tall is your sister? Equation: $62 = s + 5$.
22. There are 540 freshmen this year. This is 29 more than last year. How many freshmen were there last year? Equation: $f - 29 = 540$.
23. The mean temperature for February 4 in Chicago is 3°F below the mean temperature of 29°F for all of February in Chicago. What is the mean temperature for February 4? Equation: $t - 3 = 29$.
24. An item that usually costs \$2.29 will cost \$1.79 with a coupon. How much is the coupon worth? Equation: $2.29 - c = 1.79$.

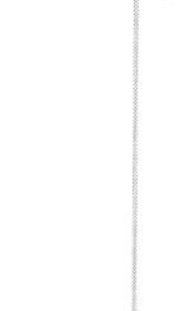

25. **Writing** Write a word problem that can be represented by the equation $s + 13 = 55$.

26. **Critical Thinking** What inverse operation undoes adding -5 to a number?

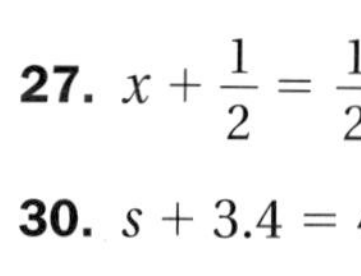

Sea lions

Solve the equation.

27. $x + \frac{1}{2} = \frac{1}{2}$ 28. $\frac{2}{3} = d + \frac{1}{3}$ 29. $y - \frac{3}{4} = \frac{1}{4}$

30. $s + 3.4 = 4.4$ 31. $1.76 = a - 2.94$ 32. $3.777 + c = 3.977$

33. $m + (-20) = -12$ 34. $-2 = b + (-4)$ 35. $r - (-36) = 5$

36. **Sea Lions** The length of a Steller sea lion at birth is about 45 inches. The average adult female Steller sea lion is 104 inches long. About how many inches do female sea lions grow between birth and adulthood? Write a verbal model. Then write and solve an algebraic model for the problem.

Challenge **Solve the equation.**

37. $3x - 2x + 8 - 10 = 7$ 38. $0.2x + 3.4 + 0.8x - 2.1 = 4.2$

39. **Cost** You spent a total of $11.09 at the store. You bought two bottles of water for $1.29 each, a magazine for $3.50, trail mix for $1.49, and some markers. How much did the markers cost? (Assume there is no sales tax.)

Mixed Review 

Plot the point in a coordinate plane and describe its location. *(Lesson 2.8)*

40. $(-2, 5)$ 41. $(5, -2)$ 42. $(-2, -5)$ 43. $(5, 5)$

Basic Skills **Find a low and high estimate for the product.**

44. 15×19 45. 11×13 46. 42×7 47. 42×71

Test-Taking Practice 

INTERNET
State Test Practice
CLASSZONE.COM

48. **Multiple Choice** Five less than the total number of students is twenty-four. Which equation represents this sentence?

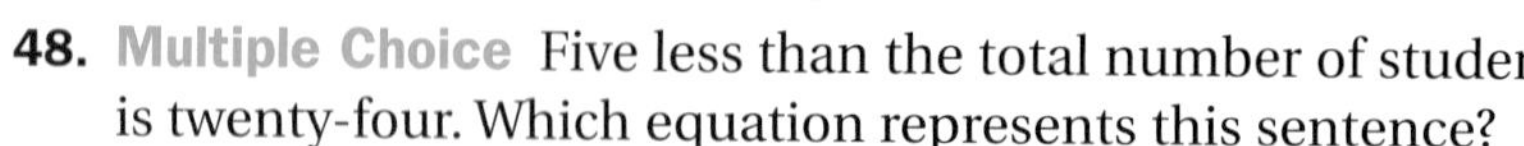

A. $5 - x = 24$ **B.** $24 - 5 = x$ **C.** $x + 24 = 5$ **D.** $x - 5 = 24$

49. **Multiple Choice** Solve $-4 + x = 8$.

F. -12 **G.** -4 **H.** 4 **I.** 12

Solving Equations Using Multiplication or Division

BEFORE	Now	WHY?
You solved equations using addition or subtraction.	You'll solve equations using multiplication or division.	So you can find how much a whole pizza costs, as in Ex. 17.

Word Watch

Review Words

equivalent equations, p. 109
inverse operation, p. 109

INDIANA
Academic Standards

- Algebra and Functions (8.3.1)

Activity You can use multiplication to solve equations.

$\frac{x}{2} = 5$ → Multiply each side by 2. → $\frac{x}{2} \cdot 2 = 5 \cdot 2$ → Simplify. → $x = 10$

Solve the equations.

1. $\frac{y}{5} = 4$
2. $\frac{h}{6} = 9$
3. $\frac{m}{6} = -3$
4. What operation did you use to solve each division equation? How did you use that operation? Write a rule for solving division equations.

In the activity, you used multiplication to solve equations involving division. Multiplication and division are inverse operations.

Multiplication Property of Equality

Words Multiplying each side of an equation by the same nonzero number makes an equivalent equation.

Numbers If $\frac{x}{3} = 4$, then $\frac{x}{3} \cdot 3 = 4 \cdot 3$.

Algebra If $a = b$ and $c \neq 0$, then $ac = bc$.

EXAMPLE 1 Solving an Equation Using Multiplication

	$\frac{y}{3} = 5$	Original equation
	$\frac{y}{3} \cdot 3 = 5 \cdot 3$	Multiply each side by 3 to undo division.
	$y = 15$	Simplify. *y* is by itself.
✓ Check	$\frac{15}{3} = 5$ ✓	Substitute 15 for *y* in original equation.

Remember to check your answer by substituting it in the original equation.

You can use division to solve equations involving multiplication.

Division Property of Equality

Words Dividing each side of an equation by the same nonzero number makes an equivalent equation.

Numbers If $2x = 24$, then $\frac{2x}{2} = \frac{24}{2}$.

Algebra If $a = b$ and $c \neq 0$, then $\frac{a}{c} = \frac{b}{c}$.

Watch Out! When solving an equation, remember to perform the same operation on each side.

EXAMPLE 2 Solving an Equation Using Division

$-2.5x = 20$ Original equation

$\frac{-2.5x}{-2.5} = \frac{20}{-2.5}$ Divide each side by -2.5 to undo multiplication.

$x = -8$ Simplify. x is by itself.

Your turn now Solve the equation. Check your solution.

1. $21 = \frac{x}{9}$ **2.** $\frac{x}{3.5} = 14$ **3.** $9x = 54$ **4.** $45 = -9x$

EXAMPLE 3 Writing and Solving an Equation

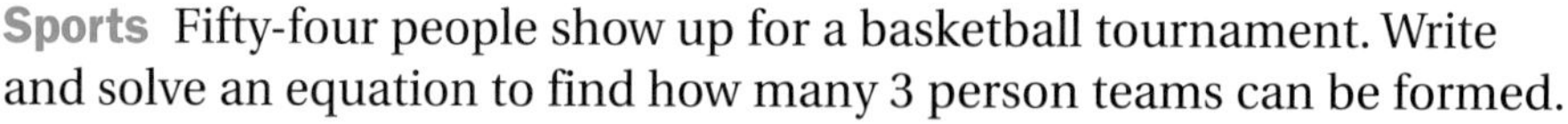

Sports Fifty-four people show up for a basketball tournament. Write and solve an equation to find how many 3 person teams can be formed.

Solution

Let t be the number of 3 person teams that can be formed.

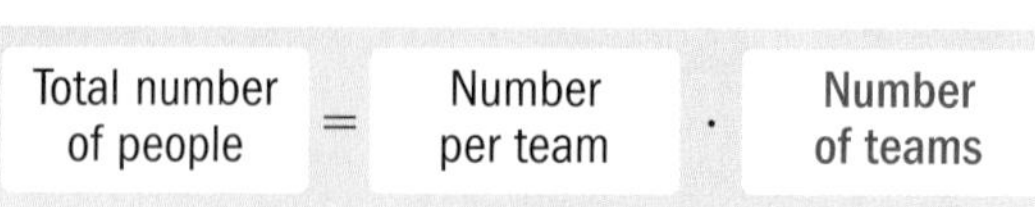

$54 = 3t$ Write an algebraic model.

$\frac{54}{3} = \frac{3t}{3}$ Divide each side by 3.

$18 = t$ Simplify.

ANSWER Eighteen 3 person teams can be formed.

3.2 Exercises

More Practice, p. 729

INTERNET eWorkbook Plus CLASSZONE.COM

Getting Ready to Practice

1. **Vocabulary** Copy and complete: To solve $6x = 36$, _?_ each side of the equation by 6.

Copy and complete the solution. Justify each step.

2. $6x = 72$

$\frac{6x}{?} = \frac{72}{?}$

$x = ?$

3. $\frac{y}{9} = -3$

$\frac{y}{9} \cdot ? = -3 \cdot ?$

$y = ?$

4. **Concert** You are at a sold-out concert. There are 1950 people at the concert, and the arena has 30 seats in each row.

People at concert = Seats per row · Number of rows

Write and solve an equation to find how many rows of seats there are.

Practice and Problem Solving

HELP with Homework

Example	Exercises
1	5-16
2	5-16
3	17-18

Online Resources CLASSZONE.COM
- More Examples
- eTutorial Plus

Solve the equation. Check your solution.

5. $\frac{p}{2} = 9$

6. $\frac{t}{8} = 6$

7. $14 = \frac{x}{5}$

8. $4x = 32$

9. $18 = 6g$

10. $3b = 39$

11. $7 = \frac{k}{15}$

12. $25 = \frac{h}{14}$

13. $\frac{r}{18} = 12$

14. $17y = 51$

15. $14h = 35$

16. $48 = 96z$

17. **Pizza** A pizza shop cuts a pizza into 8 slices. One slice costs \$1.10. Which equation can you use to find the cost of the whole pizza?

A. $1.10x = 8$ **B.** $8x = 1.10$ **C.** $\frac{x}{8} = 1.10$ **D.** $x = \frac{1.10}{8}$

18. **Mowing Lawns** You charged your neighbors \$56 for mowing their lawn 7 times. How much do you charge for mowing the lawn once?

Describe an inverse operation that will undo the given operation.

19. Multiplying by 5

20. Dividing by -9

21. Adding -6

Solve the equation. Check your solution.

22. $12 = -2z$ **23.** $\frac{h}{6} = -36$ **24.** $-3x = -57$

25. $44 = 4.4p$ **26.** $\frac{z}{1.8} = 5$ **27.** $13 = \frac{w}{2.3}$

28. $-2.4k = 48$ **29.** $-21 = -0.7p$ **30.** $\frac{y}{-1.5} = 21$

31. $1368 = 456x$ **32.** $8 = \frac{-b}{5.5}$ **33.** $12m = -25.2$

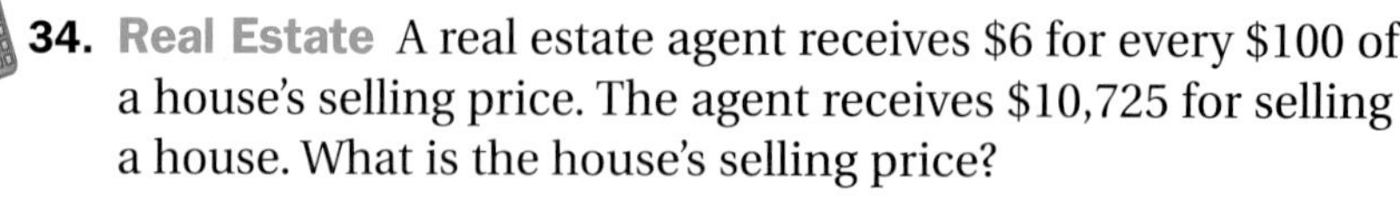

34. **Real Estate** A real estate agent receives \$6 for every \$100 of a house's selling price. The agent receives \$10,725 for selling a house. What is the house's selling price?

35. **Critical Thinking** Write a multiplication equation and a division equation that have the same solution.

36. **Challenge** Solve the equation.

$$3(6n) + 5(3n) - 2^2n = 261$$

37. **Hens** About 240 million laying hens produce about 50 billion eggs each year in the United States. About how many eggs does each hen lay in a month? in a week?

Mixed Review

Copy and complete the statement with < or >. *(Lesson 2.1)*

38. $3 \underline{?} -6$ **39.** $-21 \underline{?} -17$ **40.** $-12 \underline{?} -5$ **41.** $0 \underline{?} -3$

Basic Skills **Write the number in words.**

42. 12,448 **43.** 16.02 **44.** 5.107 **45.** 7,540,688

Test-Taking Practice

INTERNET
State Test Practice
CLASSZONE.COM

46. **Multiple Choice** Which operation should you perform to solve the equation represented by the verbal sentence?

The quotient of a number and four is the opposite of two.

A. Divide each side by 4. **B.** Multiply each side by 4.

C. Divide each side by −4. **D.** Multiply each side by −4.

47. **Short Response** Joanne drove for three hours traveling at a constant speed throughout her trip. She traveled a total of 204 miles. Write an equation that represents the situation. Let *r* represent Joanne's speed. Solve the equation to find her speed. Show all the steps you used to solve the equation.

3.3 Hands-on Activity

INDIANA: Academic Standards
- Algebra and Functions (8.3.1)

GOAL
Use algebra tiles to solve two-step equations.

MATERIALS
- algebra tiles

Modeling Two-Step Equations

A *two-step equation* is an equation you solve using two operations. You can use algebra tiles to model and solve two-step equations.

Explore 1 **Model and solve $2x + 3 = 7$.**

1. Model the equation $2x + 3 = 7$.

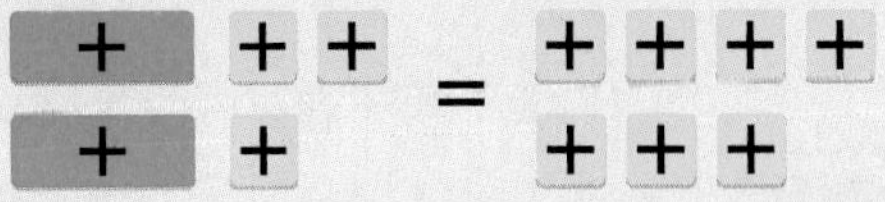

2. Remove three 1-tiles from each side.

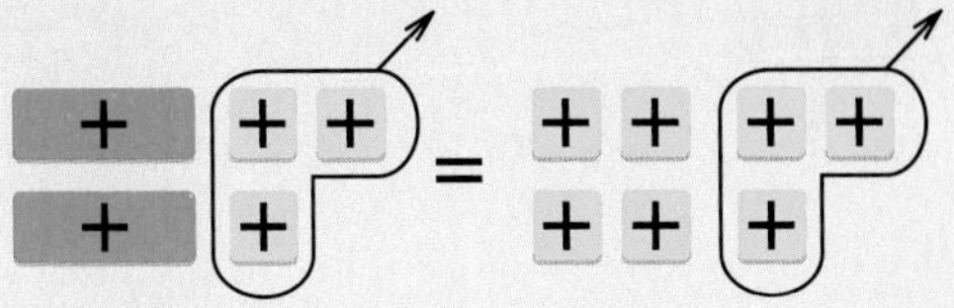

3. The coefficient of x is 2, so divide the remaining tiles on each side into 2 identical groups.

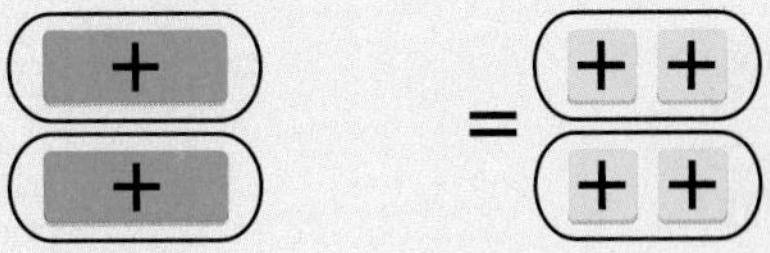

4. Keep one of these groups. One x-tile is equal to two 1-tiles. So, the solution is 2.

Your turn now **Use algebra tiles to model and solve the equation.**

1. Model each step described below. Draw a picture of each step.

(1) Use algebra tiles to model the equation $3x + 1 = 10$.

(2) Remove one 1-tile from each side.

(3) Divide the remaining tiles into three identical groups.

(4) Solve the equation. Then check your solution by substituting in the original equation.

Explore 2 **Model and solve $3x - 4 = 5$. Write the equation at each step.**

Tile Model	Algebra
1	$3x - 4 = 5$
2 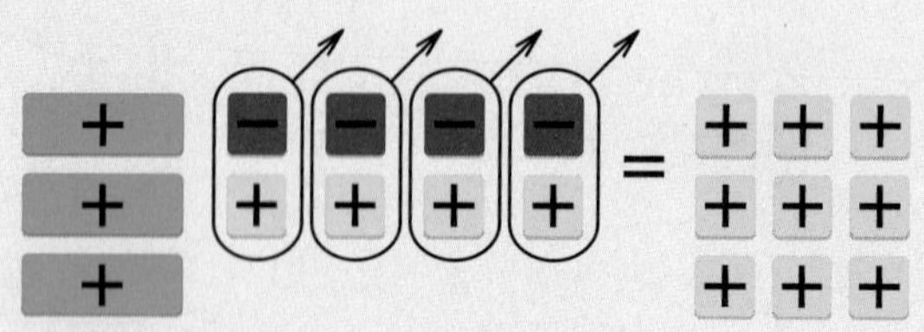 Remove zero pairs.	$3x - 4 + 4 = 5 + 4$
3	$\frac{3x}{3} = \frac{9}{3}$
4	$x = 3$

Your turn now **Use algebra tiles to model and solve the equation. Write the equation at each step.**

2. $3x + 1 = 7$ **3.** $2x - 3 = 7$ **4.** $4x + 2 = -10$ **5.** $2x - 5 = -9$

Stop and Think

6. **Writing** Explain what kinds of equations are difficult or impossible to solve using algebra tiles. Give an example.

7. **Work Backward** Use algebra tiles to write a two-step equation whose solution is 1.

Solving Two-Step Equations

BEFORE	Now	WHY?
You solved one-step equations.	You'll solve two-step equations.	So you can make a plan to earn money, as in Ex. 36.

In the Real World

Word Watch

Review Words

equation, p. 28
solution, p. 28

INDIANA Academic Standards

- Algebra and Functions (8.3.1)
- Problem Solving (8.7.1)

Music Club You pay \$7 to join an Internet music club. You pay \$2 for each song that you download. Your cost for joining and downloading some songs is \$23. How many songs did you download?

JAZZ | CLASSICAL | BLUES | WORLD
ONLINE music
$2
download songs by your favorite artist!

In Example 1, you will answer this question by solving the two-step equation $7 + 2x = 23$. The value of x is the number of songs you downloaded.

EXAMPLE 1 Solving a Real-World Problem

Cost to join + Cost per song • Number of songs = Total Cost

$$7 + 2x = 23$$ Write an algebraic model.

$$-7 \qquad -7$$ Subtract 7 from each side to undo addition.

$$2x = 16$$ Simplify.

$$\frac{2x}{2} = \frac{16}{2}$$ Divide each side by 2 to undo multiplication.

$$x = 8$$ Simplify. x is by itself.

ANSWER You downloaded 8 songs.

Your turn now Use the equation in Example 1.

1. Substitute 8 for x in the original equation in Example 1 to check the solution.
2. What is the cost to join the club and download 5 songs?
3. Suppose the cost to join and download songs is \$27. How does this change the equation you solve to find the number of songs?

Solving a Two-Step Equation

Some equations require two inverse operations to solve.

$2x + 1 = 5$	**Original equation**
$2x + 1 - 1 = 5 - 1$	**Undo addition or subtraction.**
$2x = 4$	**Simplify.**
$\frac{2x}{2} = \frac{4}{2}$	**Undo multiplication or division.**
$x = 2$	**Simplify.**

HELP with Solving

Another way to undo operations is to add the opposite to undo addition or subtraction. Then multiply by the reciprocal to undo multiplication or division.

EXAMPLE 2 Solving with a Variable in the Numerator

$\frac{x}{2} - 14 = 8$	**Original equation**
$\underline{+14} \quad \underline{+\ 14}$	**Add 14 to each side to undo subtraction.**
$\frac{x}{2} = 22$	**Simplify.**
$\frac{x}{2} \cdot 2 = 22 \cdot 2$	**Multiply each side by 2 to undo division.**
$x = 44$	**Simplify.**

✓ **Check** $\frac{44}{2} - 14 \stackrel{?}{=} 8$ **Substitute 44 for x in original equation.**

$22 - 14 = 8$ ✓

HELP with Review

Remember that you can solve an equation vertically or horizontally. See p. 110.

EXAMPLE 3 Solving with a Negative Coefficient

$8 = 12 - 2x$	**Original equation**
$8 - 12 = 12 - 2x - 12$	**Subtract 12 from each side to undo addition.**
$-4 = -2x$	**Simplify.**
$\frac{-4}{-2} = \frac{-2x}{-2}$	**Divide each side by −2 to undo multiplication.**
$2 = x$	**Simplify.**

Your turn now **Solve the equation. Check your answer.**

4. $13 = 11 + \frac{y}{3}$ **5.** $\frac{z}{5} - 3 = 4$ **6.** $-6x + 5 = 23$ **7.** $6 = 16 - a$

3.3 Exercises

More Practice, p. 729

Getting Ready to Practice

1. Write the two operations, in order, that you would use to solve the equation $3w - 2 = 7$. Then solve the equation.

2. **Find the Error** Describe and correct the error in the solution.

X
$3x - 9 = 18$
$3x = 9$
$x = 3$

Solve the equation. Check your answer.

3. $2x + 1 = 7$
4. $3y - 4 = 2$
5. $10 - 7z = 3$
6. $15 = 4p + 7$
7. $1 = 2k + 9$
8. $11 = \frac{h}{6} + 8$

9. **Guided Problem Solving** You draw illustrations. You charge \$50 per illustration and \$12 per hour to make changes. You get a check for \$198 to pay for 3 illustrations and changes. How many hours did you spend making changes to the illustrations?

(1 Read the problem. What is the main idea? What do you know and what do you need to find?

(2 You can use the equation $3(50) + 12n = 198$ to find the number of hours you spent making changes to the illustrations. Why is the value of n the number of hours you spent making changes?

(3 Solve the equation and check your answer.

Practice and Problem Solving

HELP with Homework

Example	Exercises
1	10-23
2	24-35
3	10-21, 24-35

Online Resources
CLASSZONE.COM
- More Examples
- eTutorial Plus

Solve the equation. Check your answer.

10. $4z + 8 = 12$
11. $18 = 4h + 2$
12. $29 = 5a + 4$
13. $40 = 8p - 16$
14. $100 - 7r = 44$
15. $8q - 9 = -7$
16. $6 + 2c = 15$
17. $3g + 4 = 13$
18. $-9 + 2k = -25$
19. $-36 = 18 - 6x$
20. $7 + 5b = -23$
21. $10 = 2d + 11$

22. **Measurement** To find the number of inches in 5 feet 4 inches, you can evaluate the expression $5(12) + 4$. The diameter of the largest cookie ever made was 81 feet 8 inches. Write and evaluate an expression that will give the diameter of the cookie in inches.

23. **Hiking Trails** Students are cleaning up 11 miles of trails in a local park. After an hour, they have cleaned about 3 miles of trails. Solve the two-step equation $3h + 3 = 11$. Explain why the value of h is an estimate of the number of hours it will take to finish.

Solve the equation. Check your answer.

24. $3 = 12 - 3x$
25. $-7 = 7 - 2r$
26. $20 - 6w = 14$
27. $9p + 8 = -7$
28. $\frac{x}{9} - 4 = 5$
29. $-7 + \frac{z}{4} = 3$
30. $8 = 5 + \frac{m}{2}$
31. $3 + \frac{t}{5} = 14$
32. $32 = 17 + \frac{d}{2}$
33. $2 - z = 9$
34. $11 - b = 34$
35. $\frac{c}{3} - 7 = 1$

36. **Walking Dogs** You earn money by walking dogs in your neighborhood. One neighbor pays you \$20 each week, and other neighbors pay you \$5 per walk. If your goal is to earn \$50 per week, how many walks do you need to do at \$5 each? To answer this question, solve the equation $20 + 5w = 50$.

37. **Phone Card** You have \$2.10 remaining on your phone card. You pay 7 cents for each minute of a call and a 75 cent charge for using a pay phone. If you make a call from a pay phone, what is the maximum whole number of minutes that you can talk? (*Hint:* The cost is the sum of the pay phone charge and 7 cents per minute for your call.)

Compare and Contrast **In Exercises 38 and 39, a method for solving the equation $2(m + 3) = 18$ is shown. Explain each step of the solution.**

38.

$$2(m + 3) = 18$$
$$2m + 6 = 18$$
$$2m + 6 - 6 = 18 - 6$$
$$2m = 12$$
$$\frac{2m}{2} = \frac{12}{2}$$
$$m = 6$$

39.

$$2(m + 3) = 18$$
$$\frac{2(m + 3)}{2} = \frac{18}{2}$$
$$m + 3 = 9$$
$$m + 3 - 3 = 9 - 3$$
$$m = 6$$

Choose a Method **In Exercises 40–42, use one of the methods in Exercises 38 and 39 to solve the equation.**

40. $3(r + 1) = 9$
41. $4 = -1(z + 11)$
42. $6\left(\frac{1}{3} + h\right) = 20$

Challenge **Solve the equation.**

43. $2(10 + x) + 4(12 - x) = 34$
44. $-5(3 - z) + 1(z - 9) = 0$

Extended Problem Solving In Exercises 45–47, use the given information about the cost of using the city pool.

CITY POOL RATES
SUMMER PASS $100
unlimited visits – including registration
DAY PASS $3
additional $12 registration

45. **Evaluate and Explain** Evaluate the expression $3(40) + 12$. What does the answer tell you about the payment plans?

46. **Interpret** Solve the two-step equation $3x + 12 = 100$. What does the answer tell you about the payment plans?

47. **Compare and Contrast** For each payment plan, give one reason why you might choose it.

Swimming

About 8% of adults in the United States say that swimming is one of their three favorite leisure activities. About how many students would be 8% of your class? of your school?

Mixed Review

Solve the equation. Check your answer. *(Lessons 3.1, 3.2)*

48. $p + 9 = 19$ 49. $13 = n - 6$ 50. $-20 = 4x$ 51. $\frac{1}{2}y = 24$

Choose a Strategy Use a strategy from the list to solve the following problem. Explain your choice of strategy.

52. A running club has six members. The instructor wants each member to race one-on-one against every other member. How many times will each member race? How many races will there be altogether?

Problem Solving Strategies
- Guess, Check, and Revise
- Draw a Diagram
- Look for a Pattern

Basic Skills Write the number as a percent.

53. $\frac{1}{2}$ 54. 0.75 55. $\frac{20}{100}$ 56. 0.35

Test-Taking Practice

INTERNET
State Test Practice
CLASSZONE.COM

57. **Multiple Choice** Solve the equation $21 = 3x + 9$.

A. -2 **B.** 4 **C.** 10 **D.** 16

58. **Short Response** Jamie is a certified youth soccer referee. After completing a course that cost \$24, she earned \$16 per game. Her profit in the first season was \$280. Which equation should you use to find g, the number of games Jamie refereed? Explain.

A. $16g + 24 = 280$ **B.** $16g - 24 = 280$

Writing Two-Step Equations

BEFORE	Now	WHY?
You solved two-step equations.	You'll solve problems by writing two-step equations.	So you can calculate sandwich sales, as in Ex. 9.

In the Real World

Review Words

equation, p. 28
solution, p. 28

INDIANA
Academic Standards

- Algebra and Functions (8.3.1)

American Flamingos This year, a zoo spent \$1580 to feed its American flamingos. Next year, its budget for feeding the flamingos is \$2370. Next year it will cost \$395 to feed each additional flamingo. How many additional flamingos can the zoo buy? You can use a verbal model to help you write a two-step equation.

EXAMPLE 1 Writing and Solving a Two-Step Equation

You can write and solve a two-step equation to find how many additional flamingos the zoo can buy. Write a verbal model. Let n be the number of additional flamingos.

Budget available	=	Cost of each new flamingo	•	Number of new flamingos	+	Cost of existing flamingos

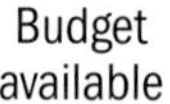

$2370 = 395n + 1580$ **Write an algebraic model.**

$2370 - 1580 = 395n + 1580 - 1580$ **Subtract 1580 from each side.**

$790 = 395n$ **Simplify.**

$\frac{790}{395} = \frac{395n}{395}$ **Divide each side by 395.**

$2 = n$ **Simplify.**

ANSWER The zoo can buy 2 additional flamingos next year.

✓ **Check** $2370 \stackrel{?}{=} 395(2) + 1580$ **Substitute 2 for *n* in original equation.**

$2370 \stackrel{?}{=} 790 + 1580$

$2370 = 2370$ ✓

Your turn now **Write a two-step equation to solve the problem.**

1. It costs a zoo \$1150 per year to feed its Aldabra tortoises. Each additional tortoise will cost \$575 per year to feed. The zoo's budget for the tortoises' food next year is \$2875. Write and solve an equation to find how many new tortoises the zoo can buy next year.

EXAMPLE 2 Writing and Solving a Two-Step Equation

The sum of 4 times a number and −6 is 14. What is the number?

Solution

4 times **a number** and −6 is 14.	**Write a verbal model.**
$4 \cdot n + (-6) = 14$	**Translate.**
$4n - 6 = 14$	**Write equation.**
$4n - 6 + 6 = 14 + 6$	**Add 6 to each side.**
$4n = 20$	**Simplify.**
$\frac{4n}{4} = \frac{20}{4}$	**Divide each side by 4.**
$n = 5$	**Simplify.**

HELP with Solving

Remember that adding -6 is the same as subtracting 6.

Your turn now **Write a two-step equation to find the number.**

2. The difference of six times a number and 9 is −3. What is the number?
3. The sum of a number divided by 6 and −5 is −2. What is the number?

EXAMPLE 3 Writing and Solving a Two-Step Equation

Reading You have to read several books for a class. You want to find how many pages you need to read per week in order to finish by the time the term is over. There are a total of 1244 pages. You have already read 500 pages. If there are six weeks left in the term, how many pages do you have to read per week?

Solution

Let p be the number of pages to read per week.

Total pages	=	Weeks left	•	Pages per week	+	Pages I've read

$1244 = 6p + 500$	**Write an algebraic model.**
$1244 - 500 = 6p + 500 - 500$	**Subtract 500 from each side.**
$744 = 6p$	**Simplify.**
$\frac{744}{6} = \frac{6p}{6}$	**Divide each side by 6.**
$124 = p$	**Simplify.**

ANSWER You have to read 124 pages per week.

Getting Ready to Practice

Match the statement with the correct equation.

1. The sum of 3 and a number is 16. **A.** $3n - 2 = 16$
2. The product of 3 and a number is 16. **B.** $3(2n) = 16$
3. The difference of three times a number and 2 is 16. **C.** $3n = 16$
4. The product of 3 and twice a number is 16. **D.** $3 + n = 16$
5. **Bicycle Rental** A bicycle rental shop charges $5 per hour plus a fee of $10 each time you rent a bicycle. Which equation can you use to find the number of hours you can rent a bicycle if you have $45?

   A. $5h + 10 = 45$ **B.** $10h + 5 = 45$ **C.** $5 + h + 10 = 45$

6. **Guided Problem Solving** You and your friends decide to have a car wash as a fundraiser. You spend $15 on supplies and charge $6 per car. At the end of the day your profit is $93. How many cars did you and your friends wash?

   1. Write a verbal model.
   2. Translate your verbal model into an algebraic model.
   3. Solve the equation.
   4. Check that your answer is reasonable.

Practice and Problem Solving

Example	Exercises
1	9-13
2	7-8
3	9-13

· More Examples
· eTutorial Plus

In Exercises 7 and 8, translate the statement into an equation. Then solve the equation.

7. The sum of 5 times a number and 4 is 9.
8. Seven subtracted from the quotient of a number and 2 is -6.
9. **Restaurant** At a restaurant one day, 60 sandwiches are sold in total, some on rye bread and some on white bread. The number of sandwiches sold on rye bread is twice the number sold the day before. The number of sandwiches on white bread is 28. How many sandwiches on rye bread were sold yesterday?
10. **Hourly Wage** You had $20 at the beginning of the week. You worked 10 hours during the week and ended the week having $70. How much do you earn each hour?

11. **Writing** Write a word problem that can be modeled by the equation $5x - 6 = 9$.

12. **Party Supplies** You need 124 plastic forks for a party. At one store you buy 5 boxes that contain 8 forks each. At another store you find boxes that contain 12 forks each. How many of these boxes do you need to buy?

13. **Magazine Subscription** You subscribe to a magazine that costs \$26 yearly. You make an initial payment of \$5 and then make three equal payments. How much is each payment?

14. **Critical Thinking** Write a one-step equation and a two-step equation that both have 8 as a solution.

In Exercises 15–18, translate the statement into an equation. Then solve the equation.

15. The sum of 2 times a number and 5 is 12.

16. The difference of the product of 3 and a number and $-\frac{1}{2}$ is $-\frac{5}{2}$.

17. The sum of -2 times a number and 3.5 is 7.5.

18. Three less than the quotient of a number and 2 is 8.

19. **School Fair** The senior class at your school made a \$300 profit at the school fair by having a dunk tank. The dunk tank cost \$125 to rent, and the senior class charged \$5 for each person to play. How many people played?

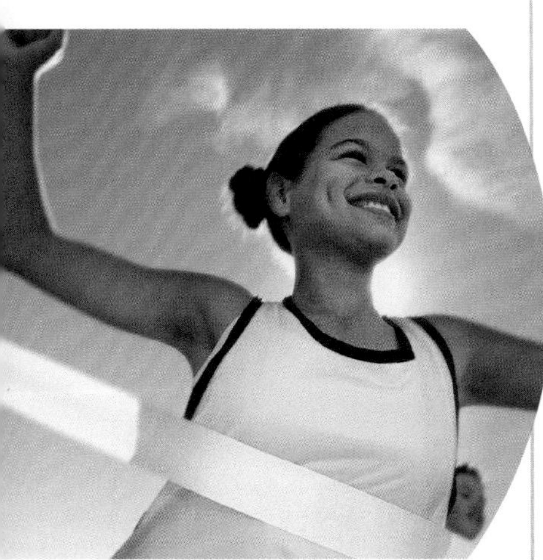

20. **Taxicab** A taxicab charges a \$2 fee plus an additional \$1.50 for every mile driven. Your cab ride cost \$17. How many miles did you travel?

Critical Thinking Exercises 21 and 22 are missing information. Tell what information is needed in order to solve the problem.

21. You have a job in which you make \$6 per hour plus tips. You made a total of \$34 yesterday. How much did you make in tips?

22. To train for a race, you jog for 5 minutes and then you run for 20 minutes. For each week after, you jog for 5 minutes, but increase the time that you run. After how many weeks will you be training for a total of 85 minutes?

Challenge Translate the statement into an equation. Then solve the equation.

23. The product of a number divided by 5 and 2 is 1.

24. The sum of 2 and 3, plus 3 times a number, is -4.

25. The quotient of -36 and 9, subtracted from 4 times a number, is -8.

26. The product of 8 squared divided by 16 and a number is 24.

Mixed Review 

Find the perimeter and area of the rectangle or square. *(Lesson 1.6)*

27. 

28. 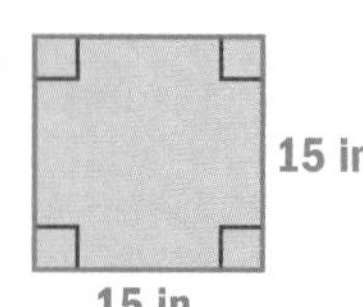

29. 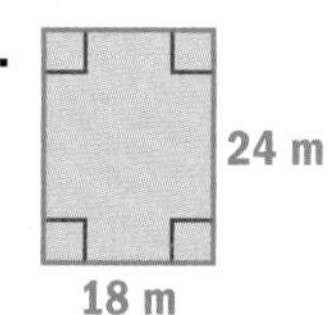

Solve the equation. *(Lessons 2.7, 3.3)*

30. $2(x + 5) = 30$ **31.** $2x + 8(-2) = 54$ **32.** $3(t - 6) = 9$

Test-Taking Practice 

33. **Multiple Choice** Which equation has the solution -2?

A. $2x + 7 = 11$ **B.** $2x - 7 = -3$ **C.** $2x + 7 = 8$ **D.** $2x - 7 = -11$

34. **Extended Response** Mr. Andreas has a video rental business. The table shows how much he charges to rent videos. Write an equation that could be used to find the cost of renting x videos. Explain how you found your equation. Use your equation to find the cost of renting 10 videos.

Videos	Price
1	\$4.00
2	\$6.00
3	\$8.00
4	\$10.00
5	\$12.00
6	\$14.00

BRAIN GAME

Behind the Magic

- Choose any number.
- Multiply the number by 2.
- Add 14. Divide by 2.
- Subtract the number you started with.
- Multiply by 3. Your answer is 21.

To figure out why the answer is always 21, let x be the number you choose and write an algebraic expression that shows all of the steps. Then simplify the expression. What is your answer?

Technology Activity

INTERNET

INDIANA: Academic Standards
- Algebra and Functions (8.3.1)

Searching for Information

GOAL Use the Internet to search for information necessary to write an equation.

Example A class is planning a trip to the Naismith Memorial Basketball Hall of Fame in Springfield, Massachusetts. The class has $190 to spend on admission. There are 35 students in the class. How many adults can they afford to bring?

Solution

Follow these steps to perform a search on the Internet:

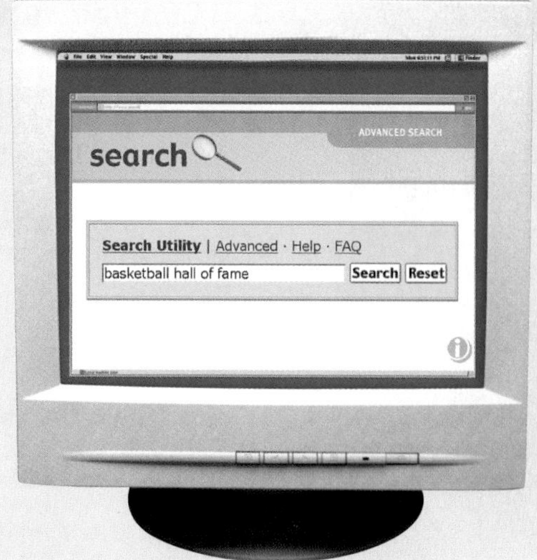

1. Pick a search engine.
2. Type keywords that cover the topic you would like to search. Then select Search.
3. Of the results the search engine finds, pick a site that is likely to have the information you need.

Use the steps described above to find the prices for students and adults. (*Hint:* There are over 35 people going, so the group rates would apply.)

Amount to spend = Number of students • Price per student + Number of adults • Price per adult

Your turn now **Use the results of your search.**

1. Write and solve an equation to solve the problem in the example.
2. Your class is planning a trip to a museum. Use the Internet to research prices for student and adult tickets at a nearby museum. If your class has $200 to spend on admission, how many adults can you afford to bring?

Notebook Review

Review the vocabulary definitions in your notebook.

Copy the review examples in your notebook. Then complete the exercises.

Check Your Definitions

equivalent equations, p. 109 inverse operation, p. 109

Use Your Vocabulary

1. Name two pairs of inverse operations.

3.1 Can you solve addition and subtraction equations?

EXAMPLE Solve the equation.

$x - 23 = 9$	**Original equation**
$+23 \quad +23$	**Add 23 to each side.**
$x = 32$	**Simplify.**

$y + 17.3 = 68.8$	**Original equation**
$-17.3 \quad -17.3$	**Subtract 17.3 from each side.**
$y = 51.5$	**Simplify.**

Solve the equation.

2. $c + 14 = 3$ **3.** $y - 31 = 11$ **4.** $7.7 = s - 4.3$

5. $2 = r - 45$ **6.** $29 = 40 + p$ **7.** $b + 3.09 = -5.91$

3.2 Can you solve multiplication and division equations?

EXAMPLE Solve the equation.

$\frac{y}{4} = -8$	**Original equation**
$\frac{y}{4} \cdot 4 = -8 \cdot 4$	**Multiply each side by 4.**
$y = -32$	**Simplify.**

$-7x = -56$	**Original equation**
$\frac{-7x}{-7} = \frac{-56}{-7}$	**Divide each side by −7.**
$x = 8$	**Simplify.**

Solve the equation.

8. $\frac{m}{3} = 9$ **9.** $\frac{h}{5} = -8$ **10.** $-5 = \frac{w}{-11}$

11. $-15n = 60$ **12.** $-25x = 0$ **13.** $7 = 3.5t$

3.3–3.4 Can you write and solve two-step equations?

EXAMPLE A catering company charges \$100 for setup plus \$15 per guest. How many guests can be served within a \$1000 budget?

Solution

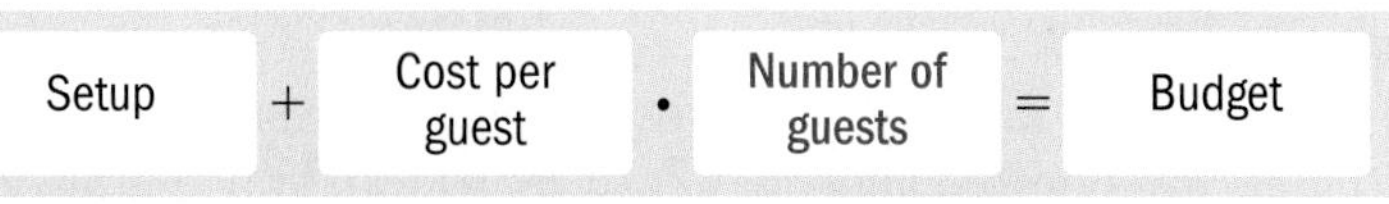

$100 + 15n = 1000$	**Write an algebraic model.**
$15n = 900$	**Subtract 100 from each side.**
$n = 60$	**Divide each side by 15.**

ANSWER Sixty guests can be served within a \$1000 budget.

14. You are stuffing 560 envelopes for a school event. By 1:00 P.M., you have stuffed 140 envelopes. How many envelopes an hour do you need to stuff to finish by 5:00 P.M.?

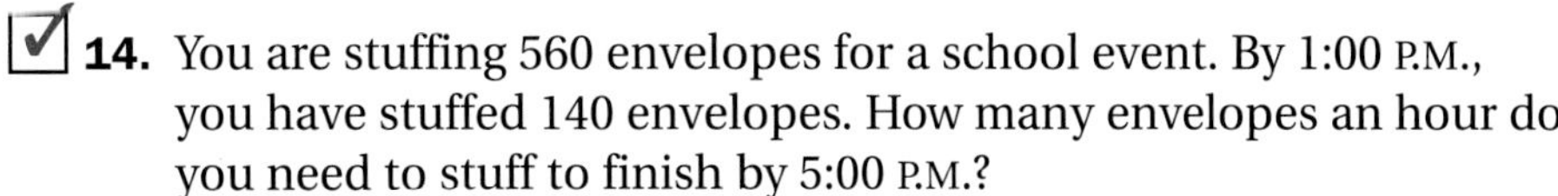

15. **Critical Thinking** How is the order of the steps you use to solve a two-step equation related to the order of operations for evaluating expressions?

Review Quiz 1

Solve the equation.

1. $x - 16 = 8$ **2.** $-330 = -10x$ **3.** $42 = \frac{1}{6}x$ **4.** $5x - 12 = 23$

5. **Field Trip** Your class is going to a museum. Your teacher buys 32 tickets that are all the same price. The total charge for all the tickets is \$256. Write and solve an equation to find the price of one museum ticket.

Translate the statement into an equation. Then solve.

6. The sum of 10 times a number and 5 is -15.

7. The difference of 4 times a number and -7 is 39.

8. **Bicycle** Mary wants to buy a bicycle that costs \$280. Her parents agree to pay half. Mary will save \$20 a week. Write and solve an equation to find how long it will take her to save enough money.

3.5 Problem Solving Strategies

INDIANA: Academic Standards
• Algebra and Functions (8.3.1) • Measurement (8.5.4)

Draw a Diagram

- Guess, Check, and Revise
- Look for a Pattern
- Act It Out
- Work Backward
- **Draw a Diagram**
- Solve a Simpler Problem
- Draw a Graph

Problem Your class is hosting a science fair. Your classroom is 30 feet by 20 feet. You need to keep a 10 foot by 10 foot space empty for a demonstration. How much space do you have left for exhibits?

1 Read and Understand

Read the problem carefully.

- You need to find the area of the room after the demonstration space is identified.

2 Make a Plan

Decide on a strategy to use.

One way to see the situation is to draw a diagram. To solve this problem, you can draw a diagram of the classroom.

3 Solve the Problem

Reread the problem and draw a diagram.

First, draw and label a diagram of the classroom.

30 ft
20 ft
10 ft
10 ft

Next, draw a space to save for the demonstration. The problem doesn't specify where the space needs to be, so you might choose to put it in one corner.

The space available for exhibits is the total area of the classroom minus the area kept for the demonstration.

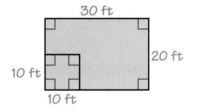

Total Area $= 30 \times 20$ **Demonstration Area** $= 10 \times 10$

Area for Exhibits = Total Area − Demonstration Area

$= 30 \times 20 - 10 \times 10$ **Write an algebraic model.**

$= 600 - 100$ **Multiply.**

$= 500$ **Subtract.**

Area is measured in square units, so the area for exhibits is 500 square feet.

4 Look Back

When the question involves measurements, check to be sure your answer includes the appropriate units.

Practice the Strategy

Use the strategy *draw a diagram.*

1. **Restaurant Space** Your favorite pizza place has a new addition. The original building was 30 feet by 16 feet. The addition is 12 feet by 16 feet. What is the total area of the building with the addition?

2. **Cafeteria** Mark, Kristine, Todd, and Alia are in line for lunch at the cafeteria in that order. Kristine lets Alia cut in front of her. Mark lets Todd cut in back of him. Todd then lets Kristine cut in front of him. In what order are they now?

3. **Mall Stores** Stores rent space in a mall. If the cost to rent Store 58 is $35 per square foot, what is the total rent for the store?

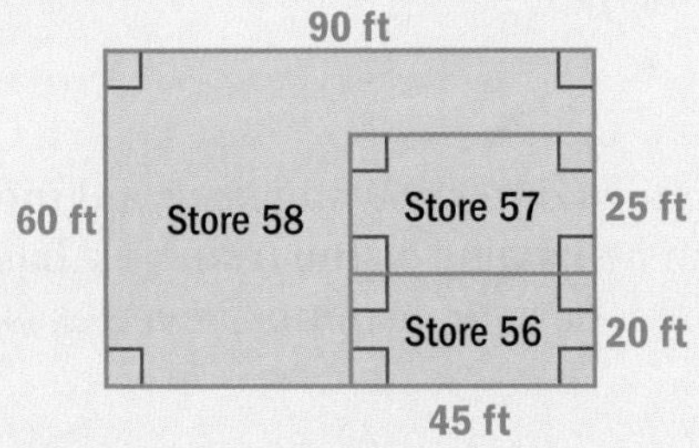

4. **School Gym** A gym is 100 feet by 70 feet. Bleachers are along both 100 foot sides of the gym. The bleachers are 4 feet deep when closed. When open, they are 9 feet deep. Compare the available area in the gym when the bleachers are closed to when they are open.

5. **Classrooms** Two classrooms are the same size. Each has seating for 28 students. In one room, each student has a desk and chair that take up 9 square feet. In the other room, each group of 4 students shares a table and chairs that take up 35 square feet. Each room also has one large table that takes up 15 square feet. Which room has more walking space?

Mixed Problem Solving

Use any strategy to solve the problem.

6. **Internet Sales** In May 2001, spending on online auctions was $556 million, about $\frac{2}{3}$ of which was through one auction site. What was the total spending on auctions at that site in May 2001?

7. **Survey** A group of 1238 students in grades 7–12 were asked to name the reasons for community involvement. How do you know that some students gave more than one answer? Graph the data.

Reason	Number
Makes me feel good	842
Fun to do	829
Right thing to do	805

8. **Video Games** In a video game, when you reach 50 points, you reach Level 2. You need 70 more points to reach Level 3, and then you need 90 more points to reach Level 4. How many points do you need to reach Level 7 without skipping any levels?

9. **Creating a Maze** You are painting a 10 foot by 10 foot maze at your school. Inside the maze will be a 2 foot by 2 foot area that is the goal. What is the longest path you can create if the path, including lines, is one foot wide? Draw one solution. Explain how you know you have found the longest path.

Applying Geometric Formulas

BEFORE	Now	WHY?
You measured rectangles.	You'll use formulas for perimeter and area.	So you can evaluate advertising claims, as in Ex. 26.

base, p. 134
height, p. 134

INDIANA Academic Standards

- Measurement (8.5.4)

Activity **You can use a model to find the area of a triangle.**

1. Copy the diagram on graph paper.
2. Cut out the three pieces.
3. Arrange the pieces to make two equal-sized triangles.

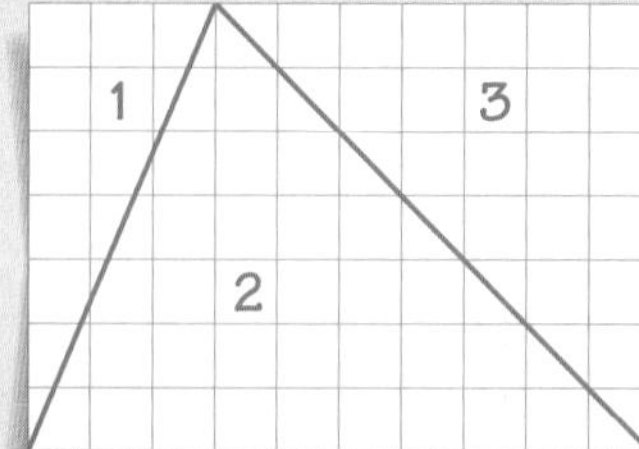

4. Compare the height of triangle 2 to the height of the original rectangle. What is the area of the rectangle? of triangle 2?
5. Draw your own triangle on graph paper so that its longest side is a side of the rectangle and the vertex touches the opposite side. Find its area by following the steps above.
6. Write a formula for the area of a triangle.

To find the area of a triangle, you need to know the *base* and the *height*. Any side of a triangle can be labeled as the triangle's **base**. The perpendicular distance from a base to its opposite vertex is the **height** of a triangle.

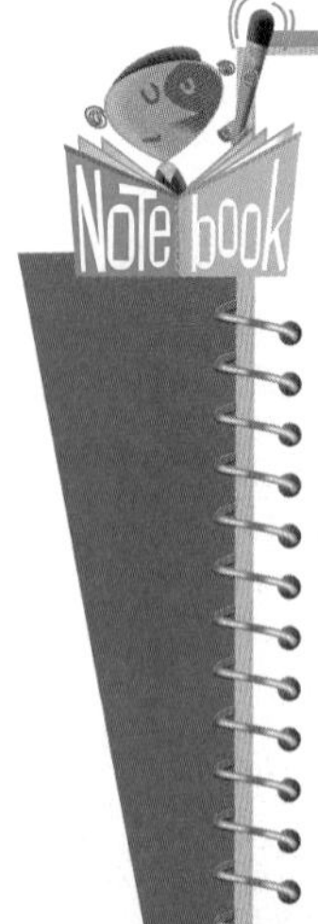

Area and Perimeter of a Triangle

Words The *area* of a triangle is one half the product of its base b and height h.

The *perimeter* of a triangle is the sum of the lengths of all three sides a, b, and c.

Algebra $A = \frac{1}{2}bh$

$P = a + b + c$

Diagram

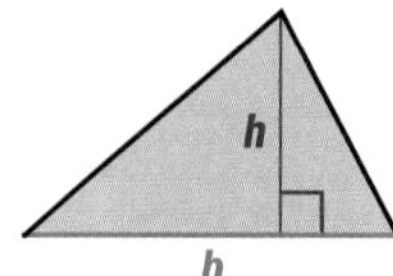

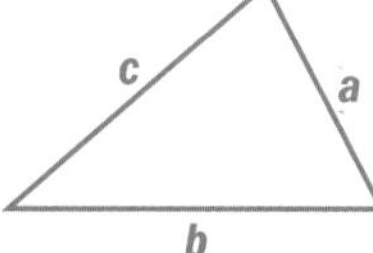

EXAMPLE 1 Finding Area and Perimeter of a Triangle

Find the area and perimeter of the triangle.

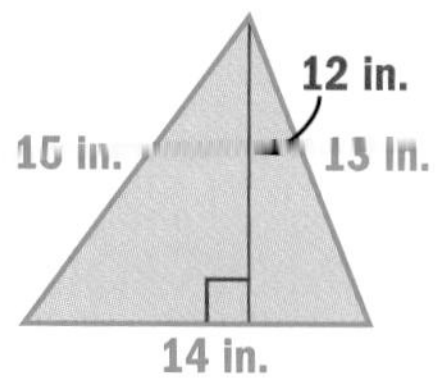

$$A = \frac{1}{2}bh \qquad P = a + b + c$$

$$= \frac{1}{2}(14)(12) \qquad = 13 + 14 + 15$$

$$= 84 \text{ in.}^2 \qquad = 42 \text{ in.}$$

EXAMPLE 2 Finding the Area of a Triangle

Sailboats Find the area of the sail.

Solution

$A = \frac{1}{2}bh$ **Write area formula.**

$= \frac{1}{2}(171)(134)$ **Substitute values.**

$= 11{,}457$ **Multiply.**

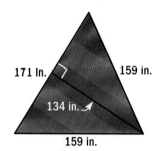

ANSWER The area of the sail is 11,457 square inches.

Your turn now **Use the given information about the triangle.**

1. Its height is 9 inches and its base is 10 inches. Find its area.
2. Its side lengths are 4 feet, 6 feet, and 2.5 feet. Find its perimeter.

Now that you can solve equations, you can use area and perimeter formulas to find missing dimensions of geometric shapes.

EXAMPLE 3 Finding a Missing Width

Find the width of the rectangle shown if the area is 63 square feet.

HELP with Review
If you need help with area and perimeter of squares and rectangles, see p. 33.

$A = lw$ **Write area formula.**

$63 = 9w$ **Substitute values.**

$\frac{63}{9} = \frac{9w}{9}$ **Divide each side by 9.**

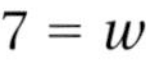

$7 = w$ **Simplify.**

ANSWER The width of the rectangle is 7 feet.

EXAMPLE 4 Finding a Missing Length

The rectangle has a perimeter of 20 inches. Find the length of the rectangle.

4 in.

l

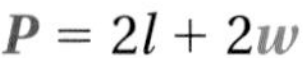

$P = 2l + 2w$	Write perimeter formula.
$20 = 2l + 2(4)$	Substitute 20 for P and 4 for w.
$20 = 2l + 8$	Multiply.
$20 - 8 = 2l + 8 - 8$	Subtract 8 from each side.
$12 = 2l$	Simplify.
$\frac{12}{2} = \frac{2l}{2}$	Divide each side by 2.
$6 = l$	Simplify.

ANSWER The length of the rectangle is 6 inches.

Your turn now Find the unknown dimension.

3. Perimeter = 36 ft

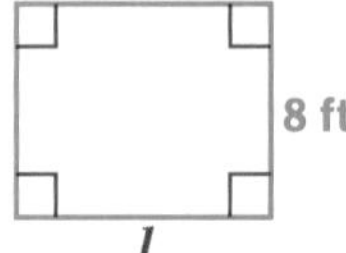

4. Area = 32 mm^2

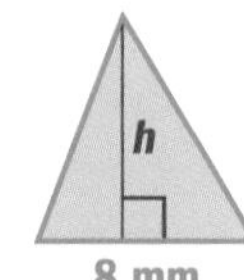

5. Area = 6 $in.^2$

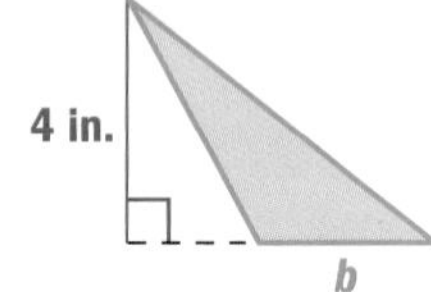

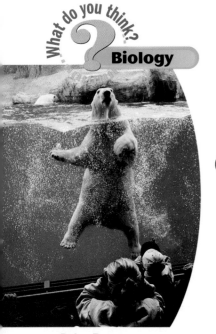

What do you think? Biology

Polar Bears

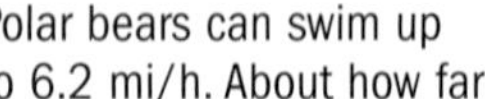

Polar bears can swim up to 6.2 mi/h. About how far can a polar bear swim in 6 minutes?

EXAMPLE 5 Using an Area Formula

Zoo A polar bear exhibit includes a pool and a region with rocks for climbing. Find the area of the region with rocks.

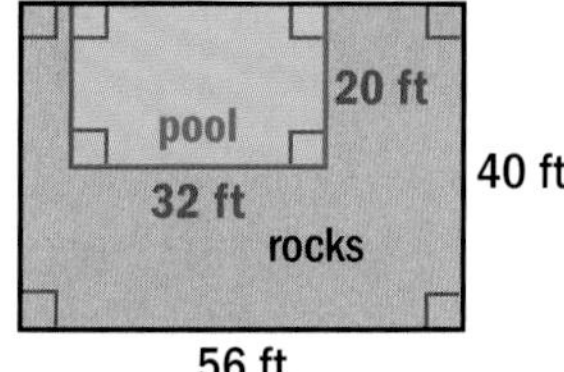

Solution

Let r be the area of the region with rocks.

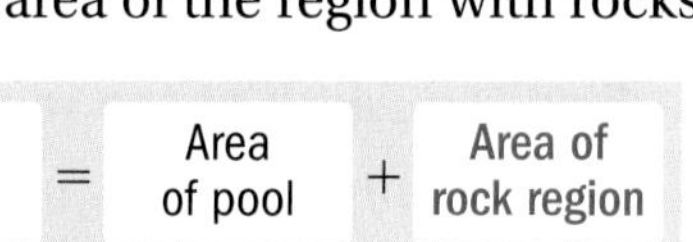

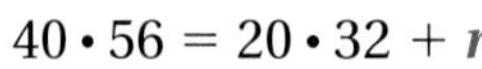

$40 \cdot 56 = 20 \cdot 32 + r$	
$2240 = 640 + r$	Write an algebraic model.
$2240 - 640 = 640 - 640 + r$	Subtract 640 from each side.
$1600 = r$	Simplify.

ANSWER The area of the region with rocks is 1600 square feet.

Getting Ready to Practice

1. **Vocabulary** Copy and complete: In order to find the area of a triangle, you need to know the length of a(n) _?_ and the _?_.

Find the area and perimeter of the figure.

2. 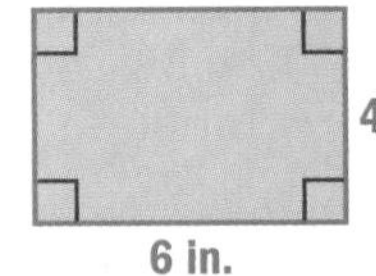

3. 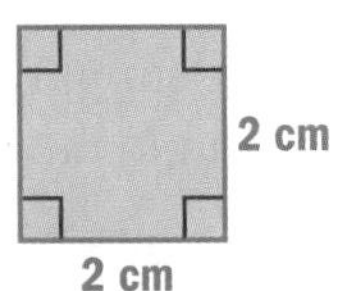

4. 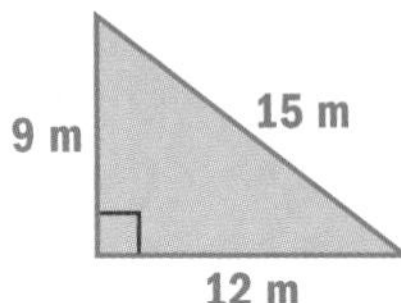

5. **Guided Problem Solving** Find the area of the patio shown at the right.
   (1 Find the area of the rectangle.
   (2 Find the area of the square.
   (3 Add the two areas.

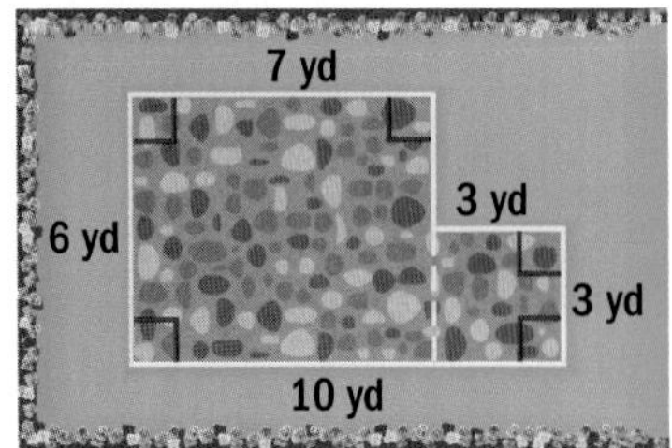

Practice and Problem Solving

HELP with Homework

Example	Exercises
1	6-8
2	6-8
3	9-11
4	12-14, 17
5	21-23

· More Examples
· eTutorial Plus

Find the area and perimeter of the triangle.

6. 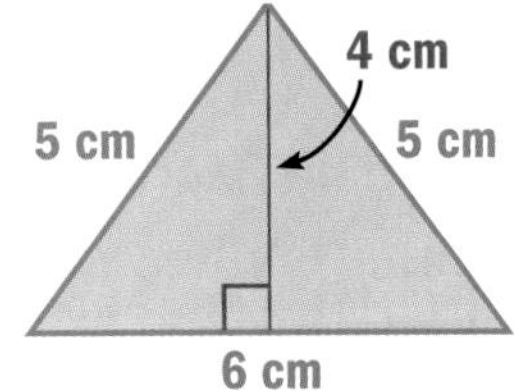

7. 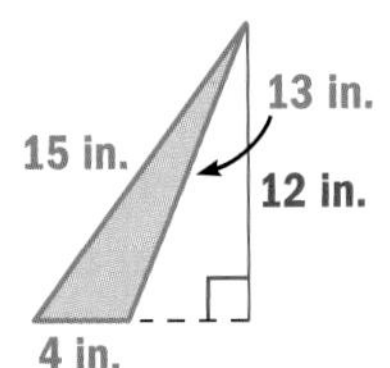

8. 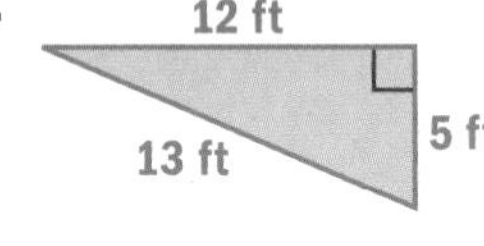

Find the unknown dimension.

9. $A = 18 \text{ ft}^2$

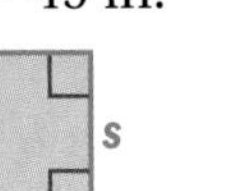

10. $A = 49 \text{ in.}^2$

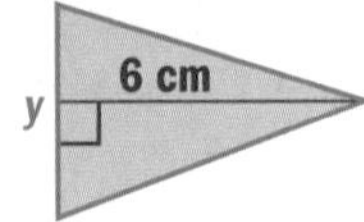

11. $A = 12 \text{ cm}^2$

Find the unknown dimension.

12. $P = 44$ in.

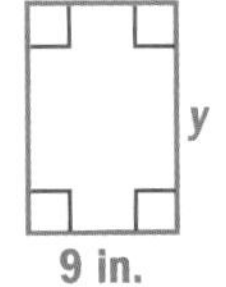

13. $P = 60$ m

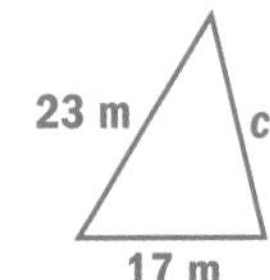

14. $P = 24$ ft

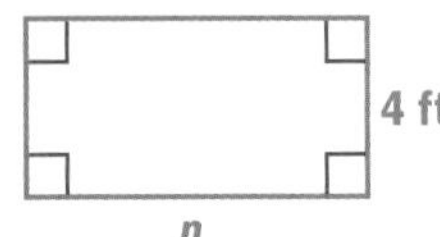

15. Find the Error Describe and correct the error in the solution.

$$A = \frac{1}{2}(5 \text{ in.})(4 \text{ in.})$$
$$A = \frac{1}{2}(20 \text{ in.})$$
$$A = 10 \text{ in.}$$

16. Critical Thinking Explain how the formulas for the perimeter and area of a rectangle can be used to find the perimeter and area of a square.

Find the dimension.

17. A rectangle has a perimeter of 146 inches and a length of 49 inches. What is the width of the rectangle?

18. A triangle has an area of 36 square meters and a height of 8 meters. What is the length of its base?

19. A triangle has an area of 5 square meters and a base of $2x$. What is the height of the triangle in terms of x?

20. A rectangle has an area of 70 square inches and a width of $3.5w$. What is the length of the rectangle in terms of w?

Find the area of the shaded region in the figure.

21. 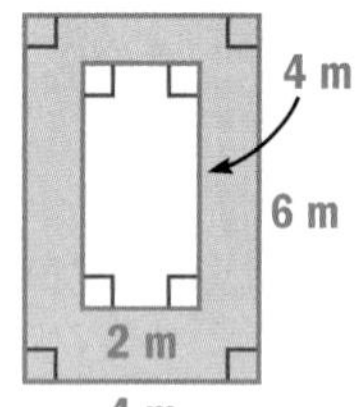

22. 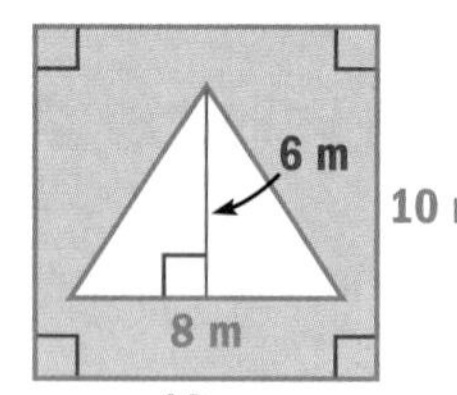

23. 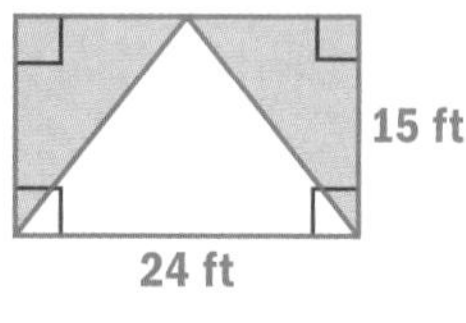

Extended Problem Solving **In Exercises 24–26, use the tent advertisement shown.**

EXTREME
Measures 9 feet by 9 feet with 5 foot 10 inch peak height
COMFORTABLY FITS FOUR

24. Calculate Find the area of the tent floor.

25. Estimate Estimate the dimensions of a rectangular sleeping bag and find its area.

26. Critical Thinking Do you think this tent will comfortably fit four sleeping bags? Draw a diagram and explain your answer.

Critical Thinking **Explain how the area of a triangle changes if you change the triangle as described.**

27. Double the height.

28. Double the base.

29. Double both the height and the base.

30. Change its shape, but not its base or height.

31. Sharing Space Michelle and her sister Kate share a bedroom that is 18 feet by 14 feet. They want to divide the room so that each sister has half the area. Kate marks out her space. It is a square with sides 11 feet long in the center of the room. Does Kate have half the area of the room? Explain.

Find the area of the figure.

32.

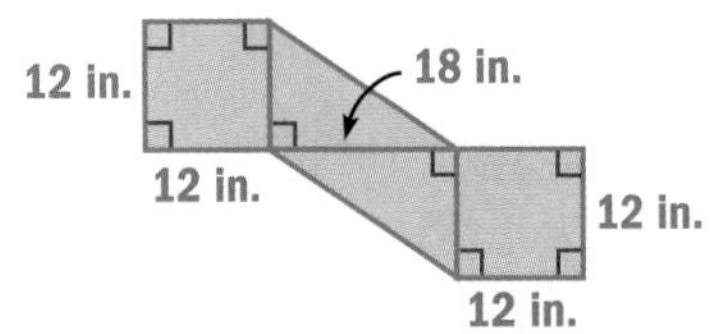

33.

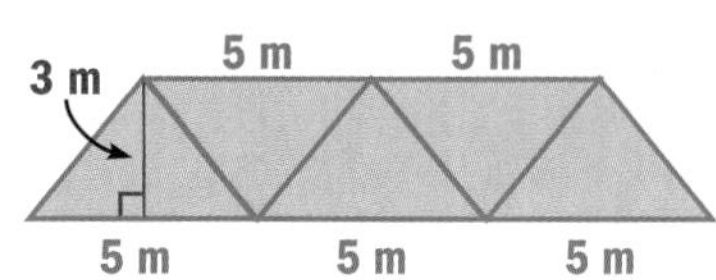

34. Challenge A roll of weather stripping for windows is about 6 feet long. How many rolls are needed to go around three square windows that measure 3 feet on each side, and one rectangular window that measures 3 feet by 5 feet?

Mixed Review 

Find the sum or difference. *(Lessons 2.2, 2.3)*

35. $-18 - 42$ **36.** $-21 - (-14)$ **37.** $8 - (-10) - (-3)$

38. $15 + (-10)$ **39.** $-20 + (-12)$ **40.** $11 + (-5) + (-8)$

In Exercises 41–43, evaluate the expression when $a = 2$, $b = -5$, and $c = -7$. *(Lessons 2.3, 2.4)*

41. $a - b$ **42.** $c + b^2$ **43.** $abc - bc$

44. You have \$80 today. If you save \$40 a week, how many weeks will it take to save enough to buy a camera that costs \$320? How many weeks will it take if you save \$35 a week? *(Lesson 3.4)*

Basic Skills **Copy and complete the statement with <, >, or =.**

45. $3 \underline{?} -3$ **46.** $-5 \underline{?} -6$ **47.** $-17 \underline{?} -13$ **48.** $13 \underline{?} |13|$

Test-Taking Practice 

INTERNET
State Test Practice
CLASSZONE.COM

49. Multiple Choice A rectangular garden has an area of 64 square feet. Its length is 16 feet. Which equation can you use to find the width?

A. $64 - x = 16$ **B.** $x + 16 = 32$ **C.** $64x = 16$ **D.** $16x = 64$

50. Multiple Choice What is the length of a rectangular room that is 22 feet wide with a perimeter of 114 feet?

F. 20 feet **G.** 25 feet **H.** 30 feet **I.** 35 feet

LESSON 3.6

Solving Inequalities Using Addition or Subtraction

BEFORE	Now	WHY?
You solved equations using addition or subtraction.	You'll solve inequalities using addition or subtraction.	So you can find how much to improve your distance, as in Ex. 40.

Word Watch

inequality, p. 140
solution of an inequality, p. 140
equivalent inequalities, p. 141

INDIANA
Academic Standards

- Algebra and Functions (8.3.1)

In the Real World

Disc Golf In a game of disc golf, the target is beyond a pond the far end of which is 300 feet away. Your first throw travels 134 feet. How far does your second throw have to go in order to clear the pond? You will use an inequality to answer this question in Example 3.

Inequalities An **inequality** is a statement formed by placing an inequality symbol between two expressions, such as $x \le 6$. The **solution of an inequality** is the set of numbers that you can substitute for the variable to make the inequality true.

You can graph the solution of an inequality using a number line. When graphing inequalities with > or <, use an open circle. When graphing inequalities with ≥ or ≤, use a closed circle.

EXAMPLE 1 Graphing Inequalities

Inequality	Graph	Verbal Phrase
a. $y < 7$		All numbers less than 7
b. $q \le 3$		All numbers less than or equal to 3
c. $x > -5$		All numbers greater than −5
d. $h \ge 2\frac{1}{2}$	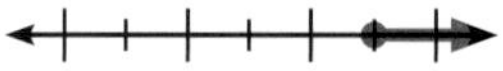	All numbers greater than or equal to $2\frac{1}{2}$

Your turn now Graph the inequality.

1. $z \ge -1$
2. $4 > p$
3. $k \le -3.5$
4. $m > \frac{1}{2}$

When you solve an inequality, you find all solutions of the inequality. Inequalities that have the same solutions are **equivalent inequalities**.

Addition and Subtraction Properties of Inequality

Words Adding or subtracting the same number on each side of an inequality produces an equivalent inequality.

Algebra If $a > b$, then $a + c > b + c$.

If $a > b$, then $a - c > b - c$.

with Solving

Remember that the inequality symbols can be read as follows.
> "greater than"
< "less than"
≥ "greater than or equal to"
≤ "less than or equal to"

EXAMPLE 2 Solving Inequalities

Solve the inequality. Then graph its solution.

a. $x - 5 < 8$ Original inequality

$x - 5 + 5 < 8 + 5$ Add 5 to each side.

$x < 13$ Simplify.

9 10 11 12 13 14 15

b. $y - 7 \geq -10$ Original inequality

$y - 7 + 7 \geq -10 + 7$ Add 7 to each side.

$y \geq -3$ Simplify.

−5 −4 −3 −2 −1 0 1

c. $8 + m > 15$ Original inequality

$8 - 8 + m > 15 - 8$ Subtract 8 from each side.

$m > 7$ Simplify.

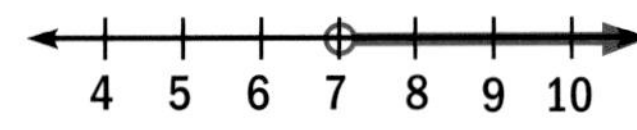

4 5 6 7 8 9 10

Your turn now **Solve the inequality. Then graph its solution.**

5. $x - 3 > -2$ **6.** $6 > t - 1$ **7.** $12 \geq p + 14$

EXAMPLE 3 Writing and Solving an Inequality

Disc Golf Using an inequality, you can find the distance needed to clear the pond described on page 140.

Let d be the distance needed to clear the pond on your second throw.

Distance of 2nd throw	+	Distance of 1st throw	>	Distance to far end of pond

$d + 134 > 300$	**Write an algebraic model.**
$d + 134 - 134 > 300 - 134$	**Subtract 134 from each side.**
$d > 166$	**Simplify.**

ANSWER Your second throw needs to travel more than 166 feet.

3.6 Exercises

More Practice, p. 729

Getting Ready to Practice

1. **Vocabulary** Copy and complete: $-4 + x < -6$ and $x < -2$ are _?_.

Matching Match the inequality with its graph.

2. $x < -1$

3. $x \leq 1$

4. $x \geq 1$

5. $x > -1$

A. −2 −1 0 1 2

B. −2 −1 0 1 2

C. −2 −1 0 1 2

D. −2 −1 0 1 2

Solve the inequality. Then graph its solution.

6. $x - 5 < 5$

7. $8 > t + 10$

8. $12 + p > 7$

9. **Guided Problem Solving** On four tests you scored 90, 85, 98, and 87. To earn a B in math class, you need at least 425 points on 5 tests. Write and solve an inequality that represents the possible test scores you could get on your fifth test and still get at least a B in the class.

   (1) Add your current scores.

   (2) Let x represent the fifth score. Write and solve the inequality.

   (3) Graph the possible test scores.

Practice and Problem Solving

HELP with Homework

Example	Exercises
1	10–21
2	22–30
3	31, 33

Online Resources
CLASSZONE.COM
· More Examples
· eTutorial Plus

Write the inequality represented by the graph.

10. 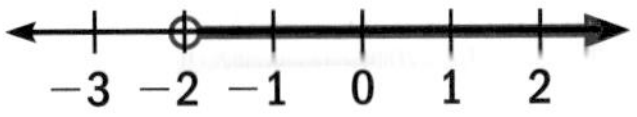

11. 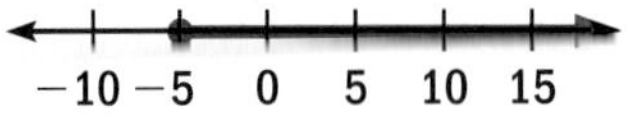

12. 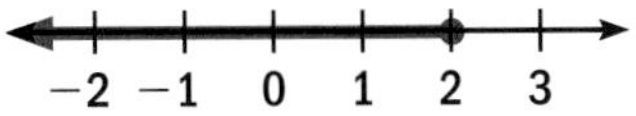

13. 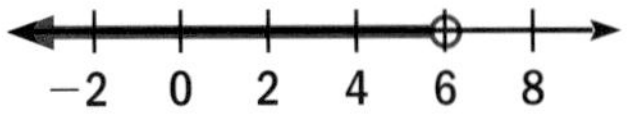

In Exercises 14–17, tell whether the number is a solution of the inequality graphed below.

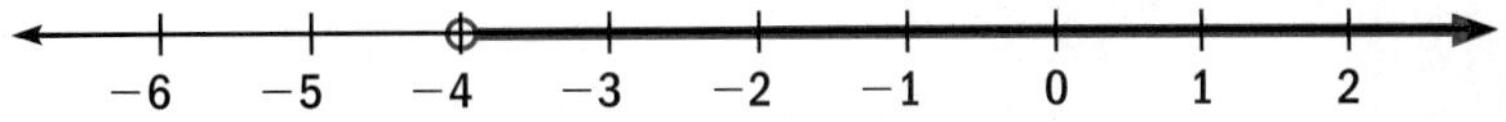

14. -4.5 **15.** -4 **16.** $2\frac{1}{2}$ **17.** 0

Write a verbal phrase to describe the inequality.

18. $z \le 8$ **19.** $j > -4$ **20.** $w \ge -15$ **21.** $n < 0$

Solve the inequality. Then graph its solution.

22. $k + 4 \le 11$ **23.** $5 < 8 + t$ **24.** $n - 6 > 3$

25. $17 + r \ge 25$ **26.** $m + 6 \ge -10$ **27.** $p - 12 > -5$

28. $-9 < d - 21$ **29.** $-8 \ge m - 19$ **30.** $-42 + x > -59$

31. **Banking** You have \$33.96 in a savings account. At your bank, you must have a minimum balance of \$50 in your account to avoid a fee. Write and solve an inequality to represent the amount of money you must deposit in order to reach or exceed the minimum balance.

32. **Critical Thinking** Write an equivalent inequality that you would use addition to solve and whose solution is $p < 6$.

33. **Biplane Ride** Your family bought your grandmother a biplane ride for her 80th birthday. The flight can last up to one hour and 15 minutes. If she does 10 minutes of corkscrew rolls, 15 minutes of hammerheads, and 30 minutes of over-water flying, how much time can she use for scenic low-altitude flying without going over the time limit?

Solve the inequality. Then graph its solution.

34. $5.45 + b < -3.55$ **35.** $r - 3.1 < 4.4$ **36.** $-3.5 < w - 9$

37. $\frac{2}{3} \le p - 2\frac{1}{3}$ **38.** $-\frac{1}{2} \le k + 2$ **39.** $t + \frac{1}{4} > 5$

40. **Ski Jumping** In a ski jumping competition, the top four jumpers perform as shown. How much farther does the fourth place jumper need to jump in order to place first? Write and solve an inequality that describes the situation.

Name	Distance
Cara	238.2 m
Jason	233.6 m
Marisa	250.2 m
Mitchell	236.3 m

41. **Writing** Explain why $x - 3 \geq 10$ and $x \geq 13$ are equivalent inequalities.

Tell whether −6 is a solution of the inequality.

42. $8 + x \geq -2$

43. $x - 15 > -20$

44. $-10 - x \leq -4$

45. **Vocal Range** The frequency range of the human singing voice is between about 81 hertz and about 1100 hertz. Write two inequalities that describe this range.

46. **Careers** You are investigating a job that pays a maximum of \$34,000 and a minimum of \$25,000. Write two inequalities that describe this range.

Vocal Range

In an octave, the frequency doubles from the lowest to the highest note. Aretha Franklin's voice can range over about 3 octaves, but she is an exception. A typical person's singing voice can range over about 2 octaves. If your vocal range is 2 octaves and begins at 220 hertz, predict your full vocal range.

EXAMPLE

Write a compound inequality that represents the set of all numbers greater than or equal to 0 and less than 4.

The set can be represented by two inequalities.

$0 \leq x$ and $x < 4$

The two inequalities can then be combined in a single inequality:

$0 \leq x < 4$

The compound inequality may be read in these two ways:

x is greater than or equal to 0 and x is less than 4.

x is greater than or equal to 0 and less than 4.

In Exercises 47–49, refer to the above example. Write a verbal sentence that describes the *compound inequality*.

47. $-2 < y < 1$

48. $7 \leq t < 9$

49. $4 \leq m \leq 11$

50. **Tigers** Until 1900, the tiger population in India was approximately 40,000. Beginning in 1960, the population dropped dramatically until 1972, when the population fell below 2000. Now the tiger population is rising again. The current population can be described by the inequality $2000 \leq x \leq 4556$. Explain what this says about the current population.

51. **Challenge** Find the values of x that will make the following statement true: $4x - 10 < 8x + 4 - 3x$.

52. **Advertising** During the first Super Bowl in 1967, a 30 second television commercial cost about \$42,000. In 2001, advertisers paid about \$2.4 million for a 30 second commercial. Assuming those were the least and greatest costs during that period, write an inequality that describes the cost c of 30 seconds of commercial time during the Super Bowl from 1967 through 2001.

Mixed Review 

Evaluate the expression. *(Lessons 2.2–2.5)*

53. $(-24) \div 3 + 5 \times (-9)$

54. $(-12) \div (-33 + 45) - 19$

55. $(-13 - 44) + 100 \div 2$

56. $(-3) \times (15 - 7) \div 2 + 4$

Basic Skills **Write the number in standard form.**

57. Nine and fifty-three thousandths

58. Sixty-four and seven tenths

Test-Taking Practice

59. **Multiple Choice** What value of x makes $x - 3 \geq 20$ true?

A. 17 **B.** 20 **C.** 22 **D.** 24

60. **Short Response** Lauren can spend at most \$60 at the mall. She buys a birthday gift that costs \$35. She also wants to buy a backpack for herself. Let x represent the cost of a backpack. Write and solve an inequality to find how much Lauren can spend on the backpack. Explain what the solution of the inequality means.

BRAIN GAME

Prized Positions

The student council is holding a raffle to raise money. The officers must decide how many prizes to award, but each officer has a different opinion.

- The president thinks there should be more than 1 prize.
- The vice president wants to give no more than 10 prizes.
- The treasurer believes at least 4 prizes should be awarded.
- The secretary says there should be fewer than 5.

How many prizes should the student council award? Find a number that will make everyone happy.

Solving Inequalities Using Multiplication or Division

BEFORE	Now	WHY?
You solved equations using multiplication or division.	You'll solve inequalities using multiplication or division.	So you can find how many students must attend a dance, as in Ex. 26.

Word Watch

Review Words

inequality, p. 140
solution of an inequality, p. 140
equivalent inequalities, p. 141

INDIANA
Academic Standards

- Algebra and Functions (8.3.1)
- Problem Solving (8.7.1)

In the Real World

Bats About 15,000 fruit-eating bats live on Panama's Barro Colorado Island. Every year they consume up to 61,440,000 grams of fruit. About how many grams of fruit does each bat consume in a year? You will use an inequality to solve this in Example 3.

There is one important difference between solving inequalities and solving equations. When multiplying or dividing each side of an inequality by a negative number, you must *reverse the direction of the inequality symbol.*

You might want to use a table to organize this information about reversing the inequality symbol.

Multiplication Property of Inequality

Words	Algebra
Multiplying each side of an inequality by a *positive* number makes an equivalent inequality.	If $4x < 10$, then $\left(\frac{1}{4}\right)(4x) < \left(\frac{1}{4}\right)(10)$.
Multiplying each side of an inequality by a *negative* number and *reversing the direction of the inequality symbol* makes an equivalent inequality.	If $-5x < 10$, then $\left(-\frac{1}{5}\right)(-5x) > \left(-\frac{1}{5}\right)(10)$.

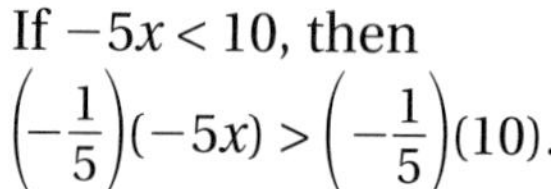

EXAMPLE 1 Solving an Inequality Using Multiplication

$-\frac{1}{8}n \geq 2$ **Original inequality**

$-8 \cdot \left(-\frac{1}{8}\right)n \leq -8 \cdot 2$ **Multiply each side by −8. Reverse inequality symbol.**

$n \leq -16$ **Simplify.**

Division Property of Inequality

Words	Algebra
Dividing each side of an inequality by a *positive* number makes an equivalent inequality.	If $2x < 10$, then $\frac{2x}{2} < \frac{10}{2}$.
Dividing each side of an inequality by a *negative* number and *reversing the direction of the inequality symbol* makes an equivalent inequality.	If $-5x < 15$, then $\frac{-5x}{-5} > \frac{15}{-5}$.

EXAMPLE 2 Solving an Inequality Using Division

$15 > -3m$ — Original inequality

$\frac{15}{-3} < \frac{-3m}{-3}$ — Divide each side by -3. Reverse inequality symbol.

$-5 < m$ — Simplify.

What do you think? **Bats**

Your turn now Solve the inequality.

1. $\frac{t}{6} > 4$
2. $-\frac{1}{2}x \le 10$
3. $27 > -3t$
4. $9n < 63$

EXAMPLE 3 Using the Division Property of Inequality

Bats You can find how much each fruit-eating bat eats annually as described on the previous page as follows.

Solution

Write a verbal model. Let *g* represent the number of grams one bat eats in a year.

Number of bats • Grams each bat eats ≤ Maximum amount eaten annually

$15{,}000g \le 61{,}440{,}000$ — Write an algebraic model.

$\frac{15{,}000g}{15{,}000} \le \frac{61{,}440{,}000}{15{,}000}$ — Divide each side by 15,000.

$g \le 4096$ — Simplify.

ANSWER Each bat eats as much as 4096 grams of fruit in a year.

Fruit Bats

Fruit bats help forests regrow by spreading the seeds from the figs that they eat each night. One kind of fruit bat is about 25 grams and can eat 2.5 times its body mass in figs in one night. How many grams of figs can one of these bats eat?

3.7 Exercises

More Practice, p. 729

Getting Ready to Practice

1. **Vocabulary** Copy and complete: When you multiply both sides of an inequality by a negative number, you need to _?_ the inequality symbol.

Decide whether the solution strategy will require reversing the inequality symbol.

2. $\frac{1}{3}x < 18$ Multiply each side by 3.

3. $-6x \geq 24$ Divide each side by -6.

Solve the inequality. Then graph its solution.

4. $\frac{1}{2}x < 4$ **5.** $\frac{m}{-7} \geq 6$ **6.** $9 \leq -3z$ **7.** $30 > -6p$

8. **Fundraising** The diving club is selling lessons to raise money. The profit is \$15 per lesson. The diving club wants to raise at least \$300. How many lessons must be sold?

Practice and Problem Solving

Solve the inequality. Match the inequality with the graph of its solution.

9. $\frac{1}{4}x \leq 8$ **10.** $-4x \geq 8$ **11.** $4x \geq -8$ **12.** $-\frac{1}{4}x \leq 8$

A. −8 −6 −4 −2 0 2

B. −40 −32 −24 −16 −8 0

C. −8 −6 −4 −2 0 2

D. 0 8 16 24 32 40

Solve the inequality. Then graph its solution.

13. $\frac{1}{4}x > 1$ **14.** $-\frac{1}{7}t \geq 3$ **15.** $-\frac{1}{5}b \geq 72$ **16.** $\frac{1}{3}d < -33$

17. $4g < 24$ **18.** $12 \geq -3s$ **19.** $-9c \leq 54$ **20.** $5z < -15$

21. $7 > -\frac{1}{8}r$ **22.** $-6t \geq 36$ **23.** $-39 \leq -13k$ **24.** $-\frac{1}{7}a < 54$

25. **Critical Thinking** Is it possible to list every number in the solution set of an inequality? Explain your answer.

HELP with Homework

Example	Exercises
1	9-24
2	9-24
3	26

Online Resources
CLASSZONE.COM
- More Examples
- eTutorial Plus

26. Dance The student council must pay a DJ $275 to work at a dance. A ticket to the dance costs $5.50. The amount of money received from ticket sales must at least cover the cost of the DJ. Write and solve an inequality that gives the number of students that must attend the dance in order to pay the $275 for the DJ.

Solve the inequality. Then graph its solution.

27. $12 > 6 - 2x$ 28. $3y - 4 < 2y + 5$ 29. $4p - 9 \geq -1$

30. $5(1 - t) \leq 4(3 - t)$ 31. $4d < -2(33 + d)$ 32. $7z + 3 \leq 5z - 1$

33. Writing How is solving an inequality like solving an equation? How is solving an inequality different from solving an equation?

34. Borrowing Money You borrow $200 from your aunt to buy a new surfboard. If you pay her back at a rate of $12 per week, when will you owe her less than $60?

Solve the inequality.

35. $5(x - 20) \geq 3x + 60$ 36. $4(12 - 5x) \geq -4$ 37. $2(3 - x) \leq 10x$

Challenge **Solve the compound inequality.**

38. $-6 < 2x < 10$ 39. $-35 \leq 7x \leq -14$ 40. $10 < 5x < 100$

41. Monitor The height of a rectangular computer screen is 20 centimeters less than twice the width. The perimeter is at least 53 centimeters. Find the minimum dimensions of the screen if each dimension is an integer.

Mixed Review 

Use mental math to solve the equation. *(Lessons 2.2, 2.4)*

42. $-4x = 0$ 43. $11a = 11$ 44. $z + (-12) = -12$

Solve the inequality. Then graph its solution. *(Lesson 3.6)*

45. $c + 7 \leq 11$ 46. $3 < 12 + s$ 47. $x - 12 > 17$

Basic Skills **Find the missing number.**

48. 7 hours = _?_ minutes 49. 3 days = _?_ hours

Test-Taking Practice 

INTERNET
State Test Practice
CLASSZONE.COM

50. Short Response An elevator can hold a maximum of 2000 pounds. Using 150 pounds as the average weight per person, write an inequality that models the situation. What does the variable represent? If you solve the inequality, what does the answer tell you in terms of the number of people who can ride in the elevator?

Notebook Review

Review the vocabulary definitions in your notebook.

Copy the review examples in your notebook. Then complete the exercises.

Check Your Definitions

base, p. 134
height, p. 134
inequality, p. 140
solution of an inequality, p. 140
equivalent inequalities, p. 141

Use Your Vocabulary

1. Draw a triangle. Label the base and the height.

3.5 Can you use formulas for perimeter and area?

EXAMPLE Find the height of the triangle. Its area is 21 square inches.

$A = \frac{1}{2}bh$	**Write area formula.**
$21 = \frac{1}{2}(6)(h)$	**Substitute known values.**
$21 = 3h$	**Multiply.**
$7 = h$	**Divide each side by 3.**

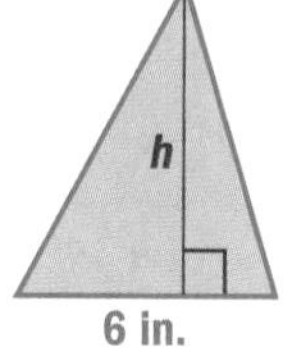

ANSWER The height of the triangle is 7 inches.

Find the unknown dimension of the triangle.

2. $A = 50\text{ cm}^2$, $b = 10$ cm, $h = \underline{?}$ **3.** $A = 45\text{ ft}^2$, $h = 10$ ft, $b = \underline{?}$

3.6 Can you solve addition or subtraction inequalities?

EXAMPLE Solve $x - 9 < -4$.

$x - 9 < -4$	**Write original inequality.**
$x - 9 + 9 < -4 + 9$	**Add 9 to each side.**
$x < 5$	**Simplify.**

Solve the inequality. Then graph its solution.

4. $h - 12 > 12$ **5.** $-4 + k \le 6$ **6.** $7 < 15 + p$ **7.** $d + 11 \ge 5$

3.7 Can you solve multiplication or division inequalities?

EXAMPLE

$\frac{t}{7} > 2$	Original inequality	$-12k \le 60$	Original inequality
$7 \cdot \frac{t}{7} > 7 \cdot 2$	Multiply each side by 7.	$\frac{-12k}{-12} \ge \frac{60}{-12}$	Divide each side by −12. Reverse inequality symbol.
$t > 14$	Simplify.	$k \ge -5$	Simplify.

Solve the inequality.

8. $\frac{d}{6} \le 34$ **9.** $-\frac{1}{5}x \ge 20$ **10.** $5c > 25$ **11.** $-15b < 60$

Stop *and* **Think** about Lessons 3.5–3.7

12. Writing Mary claims that she has at least 50 CDs at home and she just got 4 more for her birthday. Write an inequality for the number of CDs she has now.

13. Critical Thinking What is the greatest integer solution of $-7x > -56$? Justify your answer.

Review Quiz 2

Find the length of each side.

1. A rectangle has a perimeter of 30 millimeters and a width of 6 millimeters. Find the length.
2. A triangle has an area of 26 square yards and a height of 4 yards. Find the base.

Solve the inequality. Then graph its solution.

3. $a + 9 \ge -1$ **4.** $-16 > y - 12$ **5.** $\frac{x}{3} < -3$ **6.** $-x > 5$

7. Apples An empty basket weighs 2 pounds. When filled with apples, the basket weighs more than 13 pounds. Write and solve an inequality that represents this situation. What does the variable stand for?

8. Calling Card You have \$9.50 with which to recharge your phone card. Write and solve an inequality to find how many minutes you can add to your phone card if each minute costs \$.10.

CHAPTER 3

Chapter Review

Vocabulary

equivalent equations, p. 109
inverse operations, p. 109
base, height, p. 134
inequality, p. 140
solution of an inequality, p. 140
equivalent inequalities, p. 141

Vocabulary Review

1. List 2 pairs of inverse operations. Explain why these are called inverse operations.
2. How can two inequalities be equivalent? Give an example of equivalent inequalities.

Copy and complete the statement.

3. Two equations that have the same solution are _?_.
4. A(n) _?_ is a statement formed by placing an inequality symbol between two expressions.

Review Questions

Solve the equation. *(Lessons 3.1, 3.2)*

5. $r - 11 = 21$
6. $v + 13 = 29$
7. $34 = g + 19$
8. $12p = 108$
9. $\frac{h}{5} = 8$
10. $\frac{z}{-7} = 23$
11. $-46 = \frac{w}{-28}$
12. $t - \frac{3}{7} = \frac{1}{7}$
13. $x + (-5) = -8$
14. $3.9 + y = 10.9$
15. $-9.5m = -22.8$
16. $-72 = -6n$

17. **ATVs** You rent an all-terrain vehicle that has $\frac{5}{8}$ of a tank of fuel. When you are done riding, there is $\frac{3}{8}$ of a tank left. Write a verbal model to represent the fraction of a tank of fuel you used. Then write and solve an algebraic model. *(Lesson 3.1)*

18. **Intramurals** A college brochure states that 215 students participate in intramural sports. This is one third of the students. How many students attend the college? *(Lesson 3.2)*

Solve the equation. *(Lesson 3.3)*

19. $2p - 5 = 13$
20. $19 + 8v = 43$
21. $9g + 16 = -29$
22. $-10c + 6 = 46$
23. $-82 = 53 - 5t$
24. $-33 = -15t - 12$

Review Questions

Solve the equation. *(Lesson 3.3)*

25. $\frac{d}{5} + 13 = -10$ **26.** $17 = \frac{x}{12} - 31$ **27.** $-21 - \frac{t}{3} = -6$ **28.** $-57 = -9 + \frac{w}{-7}$

29. Fruit Baskets Your class is making fruit baskets and selling them to raise money for a charity. The supplies cost \$26 and the baskets sell for \$7 each. Your class makes a profit of \$100. How many baskets did your class sell? *(Lesson 3.4)*

Find the unknown dimension. *(Lesson 3.5)*

30. Perimeter = 11 in.

c
2 in.
5 in.

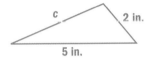

31. Perimeter = 28 m

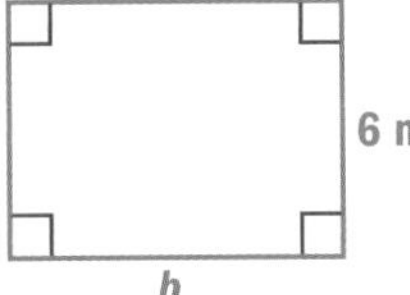

32. Perimeter = 26 cm

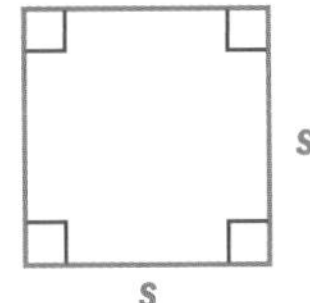

Find the area of the triangle. *(Lesson 3.5)*

33.

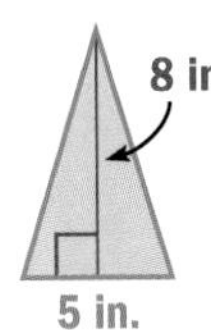

34.

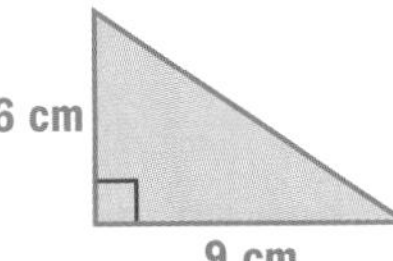

35.

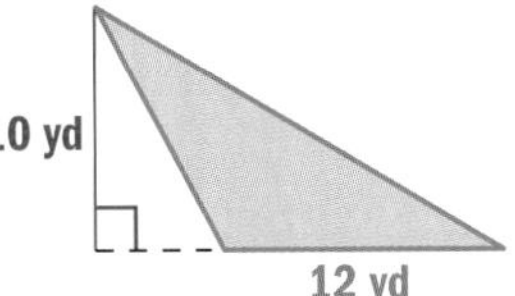

36. Ticket Line You are standing in line for concert tickets. The ticket window is at street level at the middle of one side of a building that is 30 feet long and 20 feet wide. The line extends from the ticket window, around the corner of the building, and all the way to the next corner of the building. How long is the line? Explain why there are two possible answers. *(Lesson 3.5)*

Solve and graph the inequality. *(Lessons 3.6, 3.7)*

37. $96 \geq -12 + c$ **38.** $-\frac{1}{3}x > 4$ **39.** $-96 < 24h$ **40.** $78 - k \leq 21$

Find the Error Describe and correct the error in the solution.
(Lessons 3.6, 3.7)

41.

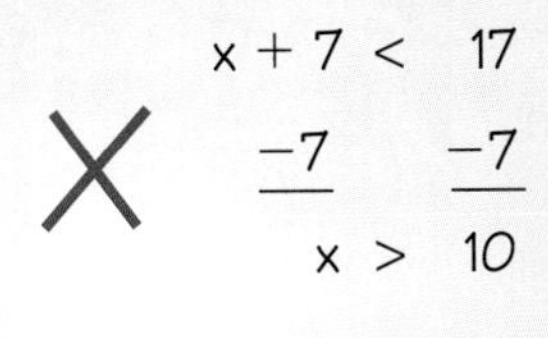

42.

$-6c < 18$

$\frac{-6c}{-6} < \frac{18}{-6}$

$c < -3$

Chapter Test

Solve the equation.

1. $s - 6 = 39$

2. $x + 12 = -2$

3. $14.6 = \frac{k}{2.5}$

4. $24v = 288$

5. $\frac{1}{9} = t + \frac{1}{9}$

6. $-9.8 = \frac{y}{-4.7}$

7. $5b - 7 = 120$

8. $-236 = 29 - 5g$

9. Hiking You go on a 20 mile hike. In the morning you hike 8.2 miles, and by 2:00 P.M., you have covered 7.5 more miles. Write and solve an equation to find how many miles you have left to go.

In Exercises 10 and 11, write and solve an equation.

10. A bookstore offers three books in a set for \$21.75. Each book costs the same amount. How much does each book cost?

11. A calf weighs 90 pounds. The calf gains 65 pounds a month. In how many months will the calf weigh 1000 pounds?

Translate the verbal phrase into an equation. Then solve the equation.

12. A number times 3 subtracted from 20 is -4.

13. The sum of 5 times a number and 14 is 9.

In Exercises 14 and 15, use the formula $P = 2l + 2w$. Solve the equation to find the unknown measure of the rectangle.

14. $P = 28$ in., $l = 13$ in. Find the width.

15. $P = 62$ cm, $w = 10$ cm. Find the length.

16. Find the height of a triangle with a base of 25 centimeters and an area of 200 square centimeters.

Solve the inequality.

17. $y + 78 < -124$

18. $-8.56 + k \geq 5.32$

19. $-8x < 64$

20. Lunch You and a friend are having lunch together. You can spend no more than \$30 on both meals. The total cost of your friend's meal is \$14.78. Write and solve an inequality to determine how much you can spend on your meal.

21. Figure Skating You are taking figure skating lessons. You can rent skates for \$5 per lesson. You can buy skates for \$75. What inequality expresses the number of lessons for which it is cheaper to buy skates?

Chapter Standardized Test

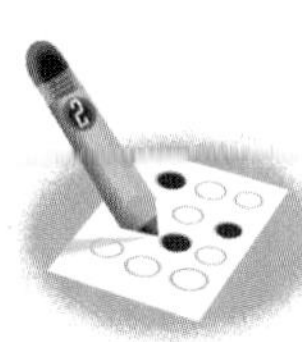

Test-Taking Strategy **Start to work as soon as the testing time begins. Keep working and stay focused on the test.**

Multiple Choice

1. Which is an inverse operation for the operation of adding -7?

A. Subtracting -7 **B.** Adding -7

C. Subtracting 7 **D.** Dividing by 7

2. Which equation does *not* have a solution of 8?

F. $x - 4 = 4$ **G.** $7 + x = 15$

H. $x - 4.4 = 3.6$ **I.** $x + 6.2 = 1.8$

3. Which equations are equivalent?

I. $\frac{3}{5}x = 3$ **II.** $\frac{x}{5} = 3$

III. $3x = 15$ **IV.** $-x = 15$

A. I and III **B.** II and IV

C. I, II, and IV **D.** I, III, and IV

4. The bill for the repair of a car is \$560. The cost of parts is \$440. The cost of labor is \$40 per hour. Which equation can you use to find the number of hours of labor?

F. $40 + 440x = 560$

G. $40x + 440 = 560$

H. $40(x + 440) = 560$

I. $40 + x + 440 = 560$

5. A rectangle has a perimeter of 54 inches and a width of 8 inches. What is the length of the rectangle?

A. 19 inches **B.** 26 inches

C. 38 inches **D.** 46 inches

6. A triangle has an area of 8 square feet. Which measurements *cannot* be the base length b and height h of the triangle?

F. $h = 4$ ft, $b = 8$ ft

G. $h = 8$ ft, $b = 2$ ft

H. $h = 1$ ft, $b = 16$ ft

I. $h = 4$ ft, $b - 4$ ft

7. Which statement about the inequality $x - 8 \geq -5$ is true?

A. The arrow on the graph of its solution set points to the left.

B. -5 is a solution.

C. 3 is not a solution.

D. The circle on the graph of the solution set is closed.

Short Response

8. Write and solve an equation for this sentence: The quotient of a number and -14 is 7.

Extended Response

9. The Uniform Building Code requires at least 20 square feet of space for each person in a classroom. A classroom is 28 feet long and 18 feet wide. Write and solve an inequality that models the number of people that can be in the classroom legally. Explain how to use the solution to find the maximum number of people allowed in the classroom.

Strategies for Answering

Multiple Choice Questions

You can use the problem solving plan on page 39 to solve any problem. The strategies below can help you answer a multiple choice question. You can also use these strategies to check whether your answer to a multiple choice question is reasonable.

Strategy: Estimate the Answer

Problem 1

You will use powers and exponents to solve this problem.

The table shows how many pennies you save each day. If the pattern continues, what is the first day you will save more than ten dollars worth of pennies?

Day	1	2	3
Pennies	$2^1 = 2$	$2^2 = 4$	$2^3 = 8$

A. **Day 8**

B. **Day 9**

C. **Day 10**

D. **Day 11**

Estimate: 2^8 is a little more than 250, so $2^9 > 500$ and $2^{10} > 1000$. The correct answer is C.

Strategy: Use Visual Clues

Problem 2

The garden's area is 900 square feet. Use the Guess, Check, and Revise strategy to find the length of one side of the garden. Each side of the garden is 30 feet long.

How many feet of fencing do you need to enclose the square garden shown?

900 ft^2

F. **30 ft**

G. **60 ft**

H. **90 ft**

I. **120 ft**

Multiply the side length by 4 to find the total amount of fencing needed. To enclose the garden, you need 120 feet of fencing. The correct answer is I.

Strategy: Use Number Sense

Problem 3

The problem involves integers, not fractions or decimals.

When multiplying a positive integer by a negative integer, the product is ? .

A. greater than the positive integer

B. greater than the negative integer

C. less than or equal to the negative integer

D. less than the negative integer

The sign is negative and the absolute value of the product is greater than or equal to either factor. C is the correct answer.

Eliminating Unreasonable Choices The strategies used to find the correct answers for Problems 1–3 are the same strategies you can use to eliminate answer choices that are unreasonable or obviously incorrect.

Problem 4

Read the problem carefully. Degrees Fahrenheit are 32° more than almost twice the temperature in degrees Celsius.

The average body temperature of a polar bear is 37°C. Use the formula $F = 1.8C + 32$ to find the temperature in degrees Fahrenheit.

F. 34°F — *Not* correct. A temperature of about 1°C is 34°F.

G. 69°F

H. 74.95°F

I. 98.6°F — $1.8(37) + 32 = 98.6$, so the correct answer is I.

Watch Out! Some answers that appear correct at first glance may be incorrect. Be aware of common errors.

Your turn now

Explain why the selected answer choice is unreasonable.

1. Two times a number plus 7 is −21. What is the number?

   A. −14 **B.** −7 ~~**C.** 7~~ **D.** 14

2. Your school earns $1.50 for every T-shirt sold. Find the minimum number of T-shirts you must sell in order to raise $500.

   F. 333 **G.** 334 **H.** 500 ~~**I.** 750~~

GO ON

PRACTICING Test-Taking Skills

Multiple Choice

1. Ryan rode his bike 15 miles in 2 hours 30 minutes. What is his average speed in miles per hour?

   A. 6 **B.** 6.5 **C.** 34.5 **D.** 37.5

2. Bob's exam of 21 questions takes 50 minutes. He needs at least 10 minutes for the extended response question. He uses an equal amount of time on all of the 20 multiple choice problems. What is the greatest number of minutes Bob can spend on one multiple choice problem?

   F. 1 **G.** 2 **H.** 3 **I.** 4

3. The graph shows the inches of rainfall in Topeka, Kansas. What is the best estimate of rainfall in April?

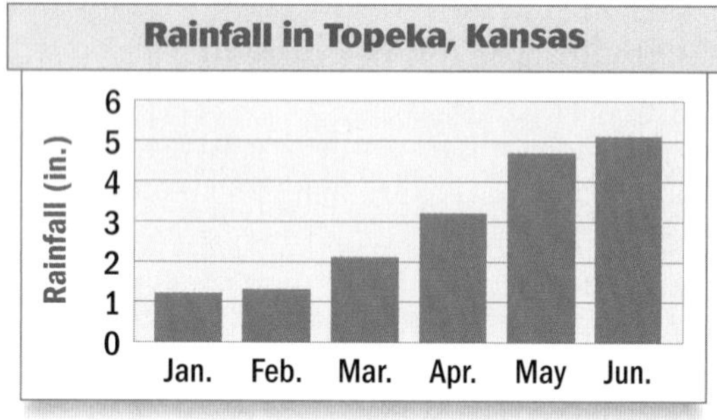

   A. 2.5 in. **B.** 3.0 in. **C.** 3.2 in. **D.** 3.5 in.

4. The height of a triangle is 12 inches, and its base is 5 inches long. What is its area?

   F. 17 in. **G.** 30 in.^{2} **H.** 60 in. **I.** 60 in.^{2}

5. The student council made $130 at a school dance. Now they have $50. How much money did they spend?

   A. $70 **B.** $80 **C.** $180 **D.** $190

6. A bank statement for the month of January is shown below. What is the sum of the transactions in this month?

January 5	+$25
January 6	−$15
January 15	−$30

   F. −$20 **G.** $20 **H.** $40 **I.** $70

7. Meg is scuba diving. She ascends to the surface at a rate of 30 feet per minute. After 2 minutes, her elevation is −15 feet. What was Meg's elevation when she began her ascent?

   A. −75 ft **B.** −45 ft **C.** 45 ft **D.** 75 ft

8. A lacrosse field is 110 yards long and 60 yards wide. Which of the following is true about a lacrosse field?

   F. Its length is more than twice its width.

   G. Its perimeter is 170 yards.

   H. Its perimeter is 6600 yards.

   I. Its area is 6600 square yards.

9. Sara leaves at 8:30 A.M. and drives at an average speed of 55 miles per hour. She reaches her destination at 11:30 A.M. How many miles does Sara travel?

   A. 18.3 **B.** 160 **C.** 165 **D.** 260

10. Each week Annie makes $40 babysitting, spends $25 at the mall, and spends $8 at the movies. Annie saves the rest of her money. Which expression tells how much money Annie saves after 5 weeks?

   F. $40 - 25 - 8 + 5$ **G.** $40 - (25 + 8) \cdot 5$

   H. $5 \cdot (40 - 25 + 8)$ **I.** $(40 - 25 - 8) \cdot 5$

Short Response

11. A package of 8 erasers costs $.64, and a package of 12 costs $.88. Ms. Maddox needs at least 44 erasers for her class. How many of each kind of package should she buy in order to pay the least amount of money? Explain your answer.

12. The perimeter of a rectangular field is 500 feet. The field is 100 feet wide. How long is the field? Draw a diagram and explain how you found your answer.

13. A person must be at least 16 years old to have a driver's license in North Carolina. Tracy got her license 6 years ago. Write an inequality that expresses Tracy's age. Graph the solution of the inequality on a number line. Explain your inequality and your graph.

14. Caleb and Peter hiked for 2 hours, took a break, then hiked some more. They traveled 10.5 miles at an average speed of 3 miles per hour. For how many hours did Caleb and Peter hike after their break? Write and solve an equation to find your answer. Explain your steps.

15. Rachel has $60 in savings. If she saves $5 each week, in how many weeks will she have $100 in savings? Write and solve an equation to find your answer.

16. Rob and Angela shared a roll of tickets at an amusement park. Angela took half of the tickets and used 15 of them. Now she has 30 tickets. How many tickets were on the original roll? Explain how you found your answer.

Extended Response

17. Alice bought carpet for two rooms in her house. The floor plan of the rooms is shown here. Find the area of the room with red carpet and the area of the room with blue carpet.

Alice spent $444 total on carpet. The red carpet cost $14 per square yard. Find the cost of the blue carpet per square yard.

How much would it cost for Alice to carpet both rooms in blue? Explain how you found your answer.

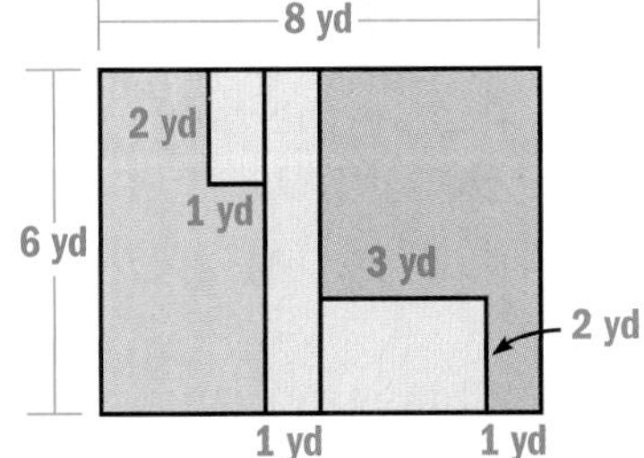

18. The results of a poll are shown at the right. Use the data to make a frequency table using the following 4 intervals: *0–1 day, 2–3 days, 4–5 days,* and *6–7 days.*

Use your frequency table to create a histogram of the data.

How many people polled use a computer more than once a week? Which data display is more helpful when answering that question? Explain.

How many days a week do you use a computer at home?

6	4	2	1	7	3
5	3	0	1	2	2
5	7	6	4	2	3
1	3	2	3	2	

GO ON

Cumulative Practice for Chapters 1–3

Chapter 1

Multiple Choice In Exercises 1–8, choose the letter of the correct answer.

1. How many more mums than tulips are in the garden? Refer to the graph. *(Lesson 1.1)*

   A. 10 **B.** 20 **C.** 30 **D.** 40

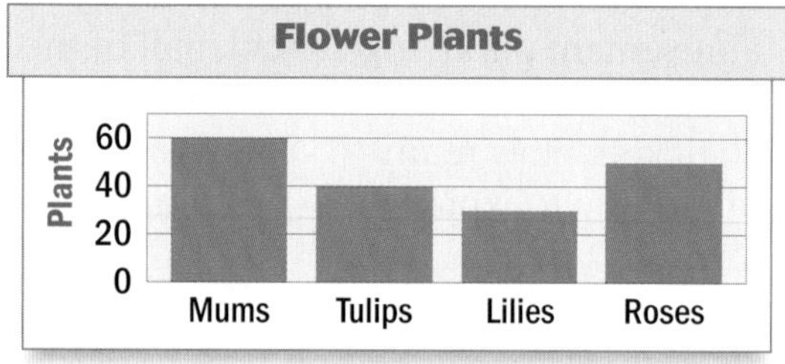

2. Which operation is performed first when evaluating the expression $9 + 3(4 - 2) \cdot 6 \div 3$? *(Lesson 1.2)*

   F. $+$ **G.** $-$ **H.** $\cdot$ **I.** $\div$

3. What is the value of $2 \cdot 6 - 10 \div 2$? *(Lesson 1.2)*

   A. 1 **B.** 6 **C.** 7 **D.** 17

4. What is the value of the expression $8x - 4y$ when $x = 4$ and $y = 6$? *(Lesson 1.3)*

   F. 8 **G.** 16 **H.** 32 **I.** 38

5. What is the value of the expression $(6 - 2)^2 - 8 + 3^3$? *(Lesson 1.4)*

   A. 9 **B.** 17 **C.** 27 **D.** 35

6. What is the value of w in the equation $w + 18 = 36$? *(Lesson 1.5)*

   F. $\frac{1}{2}$ **G.** 2 **H.** 18 **I.** 54

7. Nicki is driving at a rate of 50 miles per hour. How many hours will it take her to travel 275 miles? *(Lesson 1.6)*

   A. 5 **B.** 5.5 **C.** 22 **D.** 22.5

8. A package of 8 computer disks costs $10, and a package of 15 disks costs $16.50. How much money will you save per disk if you buy a package of 15 instead of a package of 8? *(Lesson 1.7)*

   F. $.15 **G.** $1.25 **H.** $1.50 **I.** $6.50

9. **Short Response** A store has 10 pairs of black shoes and three times as many pairs of brown shoes as black. There are 10 more pairs of sandals than black shoes. What is the total number of sandals and shoes? *(Lesson 1.7)*

10. **Extended Response** You are planting a rectangular garden and want to separate the garden area from the rest of your yard with a wooden border. You have 32 pieces of wood that are each one foot long. You want to build the border without cutting any of the wood. *(Lesson 1.6)*

    a. List all the possible dimensions (length and width) of the garden border that you can build with your 32 pieces of wood.

    b. Find the area of each of the rectangles in your list.

    c. Which of the dimensions in your list would give the garden the largest area?

    d. Describe the difference in appearance between the rectangles with the largest area and the smallest area.

Chapter 2

Multiple Choice In Exercises 11–20, choose the letter of the correct answer.

11. Which set of integers is listed in order from least to greatest? *(Lesson 2.1)*

A. $-3, -10, -5, -1, 0$

B. $0, -1, -3, -5, -10$

C. $0, -3, -1, -5, -10$

D. $-10, -5, -3, -1, 0$

12. What is the value of the expression $-39 + (-61) + 74 + (-24)$? *(Lesson 2.2)*

F. -50 **G.** 28 **H.** 50 **I.** 150

13. A seal dove 120 meters beneath the surface of the sea, then ascended 90 meters. What is the elevation of the seal? *(Lesson 2.3)*

A. -210 m **B.** -30 m

C. 30 m **D.** 210 m

14. Find the value of the expression $3c + 3a - b$ when $a = -4$, $b = 8$, and $c = -6$. *(Lesson 2.4)*

F. -38 **G.** -32 **H.** -22 **I.** 18

15. What is the value of $\frac{147}{-7}$? *(Lesson 2.5)*

A. -140 **B.** -21 **C.** 21 **D.** 140

16. Which expression is equivalent to $-3 + 5 - (-2) - 7$? *(Lesson 2.6)*

F. $-3 - (-2) - 7 + 5$

G. $-3 + (-2) - 7 + 5$

H. $-3 - 7 - 2 + 5$

I. $-3 - (-2) + 7 - 5$

17. Which expression is equivalent to $5 - 3x + 4 - 2y - x$? *(Lesson 2.7)*

A. $2x + 2y - x$ **B.** $9 - 4x - 2y$

C. $2x + y$ **D.** $9 - 2x - 2y$

18. Which expression is equivalent to $-3(2x + 4)$? *(Lesson 2.7)*

F. $-6x + 4$ **G.** $-6x + 12$

H. $-6x - 12$ **I.** $-6x - 3$

19. Which points have a y-coordinate of -2 in the coordinate plane? *(Lesson 2.8)*

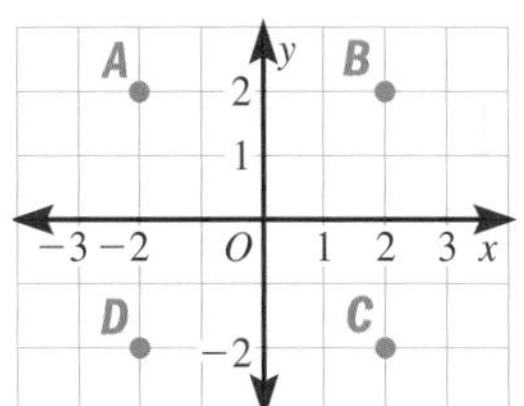

A. A and B **B.** B and C

C. A and D **D.** C and D

20. The point $(-3, 6)$ is in which quadrant? *(Lesson 2.8)*

F. I **G.** II **H.** III **I.** IV

21. Short Response Find the mean elevation of the locations listed in the table below.

Location	Elevation
Salinas Chicas, Argentina	−40 m
Lake Eyre, Australia	−15 m
Baltic Sea	0 m
Laguna Salada, Mexico	−10 m
Caspian Sea	−20 m
Lake Maggiore, Switzerland	195 m
Death Valley, United States	−86 m

Which locations have an elevation below the mean? *(Lesson 2.5)*

GO ON

Cumulative Practice continued

22. **Extended Response** In a coordinate plane, plot the points $A(-1, 3)$, $B(4, 3)$, $C(4, -4)$, and $D(-1, -4)$. Connect the points to form a rectangle. *(Lesson 2.8)*

a. Find the length, width, and area of the rectangle.

b. Draw a new rectangle that has twice the length and twice the width of the original rectangle. Find the area of the new rectangle.

c. Does the new rectangle have twice the area of the original rectangle? Explain.

Chapter 3

Multiple Choice In Exercises 23–29, choose the letter of the correct answer.

23. What is the value of n in the equation $n - 34 = -17$? *(Lesson 3.1)*

A. -51 **B.** -17 **C.** 17 **D.** 51

24. Laura ran at a rate of 3.6 miles per hour. She ran 3 miles total. Which equation could you use to find how many hours Laura ran? *(Lesson 3.2)*

F. $3.6x = 3$ **G.** $x \div 3.6 = 3$

H. $3x = 3.6$ **I.** $3.6 - 3 = x$

25. What is the value of x in the equation $20 = 3x + 2$? *(Lesson 3.3)*

A. 6 **B.** 7 **C.** 8.5 **D.** 16

26. On each weekday that she worked in July, Kate worked 6 hours. She also worked 9 hours on one Saturday. Kate worked 117 hours total in July. How many weekdays did Kate work in July? *(Lesson 3.4)*

F. 7 **G.** 9 **H.** 12 **I.** 18

27. What is the area of the triangle? *(Lesson 3.5)*

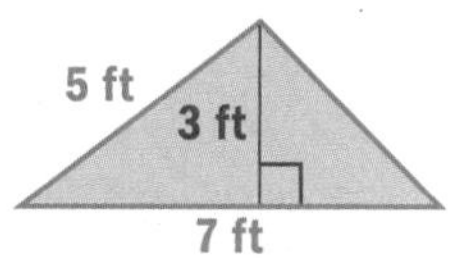

A. 7.5 ft^2 **B.** 10.5 ft^2 **C.** 17.5 ft^2 **D.** 21 ft^2

28. Which inequality is represented by the graph? *(Lesson 3.6)*

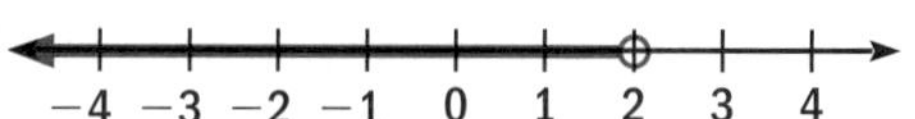

F. $x \le 2$ **G.** $x > 2$ **H.** $x < 2$ **I.** $x \ge 2$

29. Solve the inequality $x - 4 \le -12$. *(Lesson 3.6)*

A. $x \le -16$ **B.** $x \ge -16$

C. $x \le -8$ **D.** $x \ge -8$

30. **Short Response** Kaila traveled from her house to the city library by bus. She took one bus 2 miles. Then she changed buses. The second bus traveled at an average speed of 55 miles per hour. Kaila's entire trip covered 18 miles. How much time did she spend on the second bus? Write and solve an equation to answer the question. *(Lesson 3.4)*

31. **Extended Response** Gabe, Frank, and Sam are playing a game. The player with the most points at the end is the winner. Gabe has four more than twice as many points as Frank. Frank has three less than half as many points as Sam. Sam has 60 points. *(Lessons 3.4, 3.6)*

a. Write equations that you can use to find each player's total number of points.

b. Which player is in first place? second place? third place?

c. Write and solve an inequality to show how many more points Frank needs to win.

UNIT 2 Algebra and Rational Numbers

Chapter 4 Factors, Fractions, and Exponents

- Find greatest common factors and least common multiples.
- Identify equivalent fractions and write fractions in simplest form.
- Use rules of exponents and scientific notation.

Chapter 5 Rational Number Operations

- Perform operations with fractions, mixed numbers, and decimals.
- Compare and convert between fractions, mixed numbers, and decimals.
- Find the mean, median, and mode(s) of a data set.

Chapter 6 Multi-Step Equations and Inequalities

- Write and solve multi-step equations and inequalities.
- Find circumferences of circles.

Chapter 7 Ratio, Proportion, and Percent

- Write and identify ratios and rates.
- Write and solve proportions.
- Use proportions and the percent equation to solve percent problems.

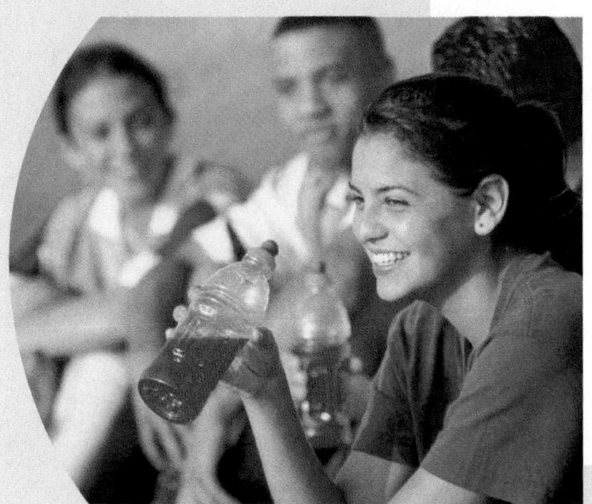

From Chapter 5, p. 223
Which fruit juice blend do the most students prefer?

CHAPTER

4 Factors, Fractions, and Exponents

BEFORE

In previous chapters you've...

- Multiplied and divided numbers
- Compared and ordered integers

Now

In Chapter 4 you'll study...

- Factoring numbers
- Simplifying fractions
- Multiplying and dividing expressions with exponents
- Reading and writing numbers using scientific notation

WHY?

So you can solve real-world problems about...

- geography, p. 182
- orangutans, p. 193
- computer memory, p. 199
- bubbles, p. 205

Internet Preview
CLASSZONE.COM

- eEdition Plus Online
- eWorkbook Plus Online
- eTutorial Plus Online
- State Test Practice
- More Examples

Chapter Warm-Up Game

Review skills you need for this chapter in this quick game.

Key Skill:
Whole number division

BICYCLE MATH

HOW TO PLAY

1. **PICK** the number with each letter that divides evenly into the bold number in the matching fact.

   A. 4, 8, 42
   B. 7, 13, 23
   C. 15, 17, 21

2. **USE** the answer for each letter to evaluate the expression below. The value of the expression is the world record bicycle speed in miles per hour, set by Fred Rompelberg in 1995.

   A (B + C) + 30.9

A. In 1884, the "safety bicycle," a bicycle resembling the ones we use today, was invented.

B. In 2001, 39,000,000 people in the United States rode a bicycle more than once.

C. In 2002, 189 cyclists competed in the Tour de France.

Stop and Think

1. **Writing** A student thinks that 42 divides evenly into 1884 because 42 divides evenly into 84. Explain what is wrong with the student's reasoning.
2. **Critical Thinking** What number will divide evenly into any even number? Explain.

Getting Ready to Learn

Word Watch

Review Words

power, p. 20
base, p. 20
exponent, p. 20
fraction, p. 707

Review What You Need to Know

Using Vocabulary Copy and complete using a review word.

1. In the expression 2^6, 2 is called the _?_.
2. The expression 3^7 is a(n) _?_ of 3.
3. In the expression 5^4, 4 is called the _?_.

Evaluate the expression. *(p. 20)*

4. $3^2 \cdot 3$
5. $(2 + 3)^2$
6. $4^2 \div 4^2$
7. $(6 - 5)^7$
8. $3^2 + 4 \cdot 5$
9. $12 - 8 \div 2^2$
10. $7^2 - 3^3$
11. $6^2 \div 2^2$

Simplify the expression by combining like terms. *(p. 85)*

12. $7x + 4 - 3x$
13. $-2x + 5x - x$
14. $x + 4 - 12x$
15. $6x - 5 + x$

Solve the equation. Check your answer. *(p. 119)*

16. $2a + 6 = 14$
17. $8 - 4m = 20$
18. $-7 + 5c = -32$

You should include material that appears on a notebook like this in your own notes.

Know How to Take Notes

Preview the Chapter Skim the content of the chapter you are about to study. If you already know something about the topic, outline what you know in your notes.

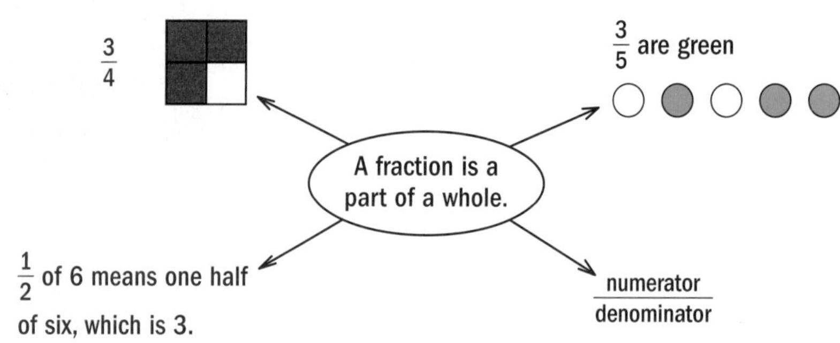

In Chapter 4, you will learn more things about fractions that you can add to your outline.

4.1 Hands-on Activity

GOAL

Introduce prime and composite numbers.

MATERIALS

- paper
- colored pencils

Investigating Factors

A *prime* number is a whole number that has exactly two factors: 1 and itself. A *composite* number has more than two factors. In this activity, you will look at a number pattern attributed to Eratosthenes, a mathematician who lived in Alexandria, Egypt, around 230 B.C.

Explore **Create the Sieve of Eratosthenes with the integers 1 to 60.**

1 Write the whole numbers 1 to 60 in a rectangular array as shown at the right.

1	2	3	4	5	6	7	8	9	10
11	12	13	14	15	16	17	18	19	20
21	22	23	24	25	26	27	28	29	30
31	32	33	34	35	36	37	38	39	40
41	42	43	44	45	46	47	48	49	50
51	52	53	54	55	56	57	58	59	60

2 Start with the number 2. Circle it and cross out every multiple of 2 after 2.

3 Move to the next number that is not crossed out, 3. Circle it and cross out every multiple of 3 after 3.

4 Move to the next number that is not crossed out. Circle it and cross out all other multiples of that number.

1	(2)	(3)	~~4~~	5	~~6~~	7	~~8~~	~~9~~	~~10~~
11	~~12~~	13	~~14~~	~~15~~	~~16~~	17	~~18~~	19	~~20~~
~~21~~	~~22~~	23	~~24~~	25	~~26~~	~~27~~	~~28~~	29	~~30~~
31	~~32~~	~~33~~	~~34~~	35	~~36~~	37	~~38~~	~~39~~	~~40~~
41	~~42~~	43	~~44~~	~~45~~	~~46~~	47	~~48~~	49	~~50~~
~~51~~	~~52~~	53	~~54~~	55	~~56~~	~~57~~	~~58~~	59	~~60~~

Skip the numbers that have already been crossed out.

5 Repeat Step 4 until every number except 1 is either crossed out or circled.

Your turn now

1. What type of numbers are circled in your array?
2. What type of numbers are crossed out in your array?

Stop and Think

3. **Writing** If you continued this process with the numbers 61 to 100, what type of numbers would you expect to be circled? Why?

Factors and Prime Factorization

BEFORE	Now	WHY?
You multiplied and divided numbers.	You'll write the prime factorization of numbers.	So you can design a quilt with square patches, as in Ex. 10.

In the Real World

Word Watch

prime number, p. 169
composite number, p. 169
prime factorization, p. 169
factor tree, p. 169
monomial, p. 170

INDIANA Academic Standards

- Computation (8.2.1)

Lettering Members of the art club are designing their own lettering style, as part of their school arts program. Their first project is to make posters to display their new lettering style. Each poster will display the alphabet and the digits 0 through 9.

They want each row on the poster to have the same number of letters or digits. How many ways can they arrange the rectangular display?

You can use factors to determine how many arrangements are possible.

EXAMPLE 1 Writing Factors

Each arrangement will contain a total of 36 letters and digits (26 letters and the digits 0 through 9). To find the number of possible rectangular arrangements, first find the factors of 36.

(1) Write 36 as a product of two numbers in all possible ways.

1×36 $\quad 2 \times 18$ $\quad 3 \times 12$ $\quad 4 \times 9$ $\quad 6 \times 6$

The factors of 36 are 1, 2, 3, 4, 6, 9, 12, 18, and 36.

(2) Using these factors, find all the possible rectangular arrangements.

1×36 $\quad 2 \times 18$ $\quad 3 \times 12$ $\quad 4 \times 9$ $\quad 6 \times 6$

36×1 $\quad 18 \times 2$ $\quad 12 \times 3$ $\quad 9 \times 4$

ANSWER There are nine possible rectangular arrangements.

Your turn now **Write all the factors of the number.**

1. 20 **2.** 29 **3.** 42 **4.** 57

A **prime number** is a whole number greater than 1 whose only positive factors are 1 and itself. A **composite number** is a whole number greater than 1 that has positive factors other than 1 and itself.

HELP with Review

You can use divisibility tests to help find all the factors of a composite number. For help with divisibility tests, see p. 706.

EXAMPLE 2 Identifying Prime and Composite Numbers

Write all the factors of the number and tell whether it is *prime* or *composite*.

Number	Factors	Prime or Composite?
a. 32	1, 2, 4, 8, 16, 32	Composite
b. 39	1, 3, 13, 39	Composite
c. 43	1, 43	Prime
d. 76	1, 2, 4, 19, 38, 76	Composite
e. 149	1, 149	Prime
f. 189	1, 3, 7, 9, 21, 27, 63, 189	Composite

Prime Factorization When you write a number as the product of prime numbers, you are writing its **prime factorization**. One way to write the prime factorization of a number is to use a **factor tree**.

EXAMPLE 3 Writing Prime Factorization

Write the prime factorization of 450.

Three factor trees are shown. Notice that each factor tree produces the same prime factorization, differing only in the order of the factors.

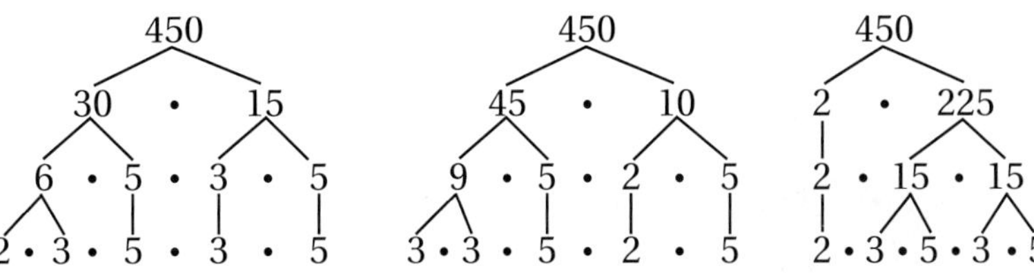

So, $450 = 2 \cdot 3 \cdot 3 \cdot 5 \cdot 5$.

ANSWER Using exponents, the prime factorization of 450 is $2 \cdot 3^2 \cdot 5^2$.

Your turn now **Tell whether the number is *prime* or *composite*. If it is composite, write its prime factorization using exponents.**

5. 24 **6.** 51 **7.** 73 **8.** 560

Factoring Monomials A **monomial** is a number, a variable, or a product of a number and one or more variables. To factor a monomial means to write the monomial as a product of its factors.

EXAMPLE 4 Factoring a Monomial

Factor the monomial $12x^2y$.

Solution

$12x^2y = 2 \cdot 2 \cdot 3 \cdot x^2 \cdot y$ Factor 12.

$= 2 \cdot 2 \cdot 3 \cdot x \cdot x \cdot y$ Write x^2 as $x \cdot x$.

Your turn now **Factor the monomial.**

9. $3mn$ **10.** $18t^2$ **11.** $14x^2y^3$ **12.** $54w^3z^4$

4.1 Exercises

More Practice, p. 730

Getting Ready to Practice

1. Vocabulary Copy and complete: The only positive factors of a _?_ number are the number itself and one.

Write all the factors of the number.

2. 18 **3.** 27 **4.** 41 **5.** 66

Write the prime factorization of the number.

6. 28 **7.** 55 **8.** 82 **9.** 96

10. Guided Problem Solving You are making a quilt out of 120 square patches. What are the two most reasonable rectangular arrangements of the patches for the quilt?

(1) List all of the factors of 120.

(2) List all the pairs of factors from Step 1 that have a product of 120. These are the possible arrangements of the patches.

(3) List the two most reasonable arrangements of the patches. Then explain why the other arrangements are not reasonable.

Practice and Problem Solving

HELP with Homework

Example	Exercises
1	11-14, 31-38
2	15-18
3	19-25
4	27-30

· More Examples
· eTutorial Plus

Write all the factors of the number.

11. 34 **12.** 64 **13.** 108 **14.** 175

Tell whether the number is *prime* or *composite*.

15. 21 **16.** 45 **17.** 59 **18.** 91

Write the prime factorization of the number.

19. 56 **20.** 97 **21.** 102 **22.** 135

Copy and complete the factor tree. Then write the prime factorization of the number.

23.

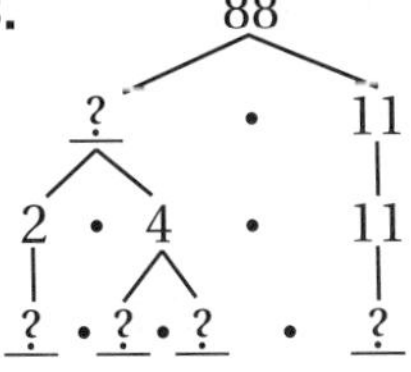

24.

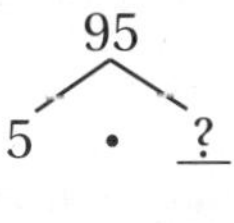

25.

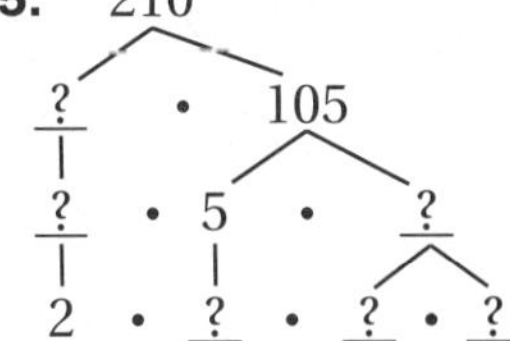

26. Writing Explain how you can create two different factor trees for 540. Do both factor trees result in the same prime factorization?

Algebra **Factor the monomial.**

27. $15cd$ **28.** $40pq$ **29.** $9a^2b^4$ **30.** $48n^3m^3$

Flags of the United States **Each star on the U.S. flag represents a state. Some U.S. flags had a number of stars that could have been arranged in rows and columns evenly. Describe how to do this for the number of stars indicated.**

31. 15 **32.** 28 **33.** 30 **34.** 49

Write all the factors of the number.

35. 299 **36.** 336 **37.** 400 **38.** 512

Write the prime factorization of the number using exponents.

39. 280 **40.** 396 **41.** 1125 **42.** 2000

Critical Thinking **Many even numbers can be expressed as the sum of two primes. For example, 8 can be expressed as 3 + 5. Write the number as the sum of two primes.**

43. 10 **44.** 16 **45.** 28 **46.** 30

What do you think? History

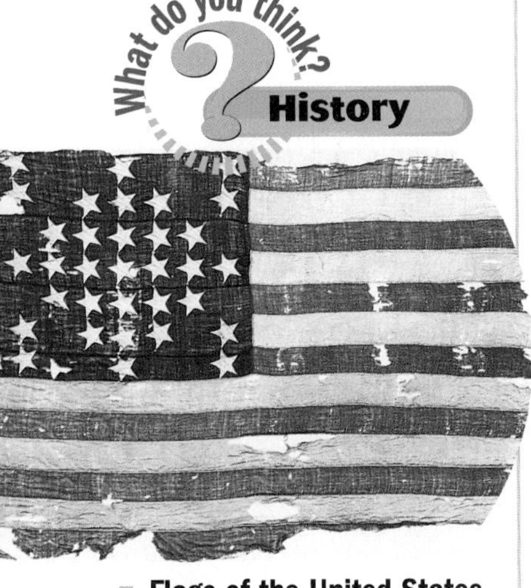

Flags of the United States

The flag shown above was displayed over Fort Sumter in 1861. The flag has 33 stars. What rectangular arrangement could have been used to display the stars?

47. **Ring Toss Game** You are in charge of a ring toss game at a school fair. In this game, players try to throw a small ring over a bottle that is in a rectangular display. You have 140 bottles, and you want to arrange them in equal rows. Can you have 40 equal rows? Explain.

48. **Field Day** There are 180 students participating in field day activities. The students must be divided into teams of equal size. How many students will be on each team? List all the possibilities.

49. **Critical Thinking** Name two prime numbers that have a difference of 1.

50. **Challenge** Twin primes are prime numbers that have a difference of 2. For example, 5 and 7 are twin primes. List five pairs of twin primes other than 5 and 7.

51. **Volume** The volume of a box can be found by using the formula *Volume* = *length* × *width* × *height.* A box has a volume of 200 cubic inches. Find all possible whole number dimensions of the box.

Mixed Review 

Simplify the expression by combining like terms. *(Lesson 2.7)*

52. $4x - 5y + 3x - 4 + y$ **53.** $a - 2b - 5a + 2 + 6b$

Solve the inequality. *(Lesson 3.7)*

54. $5x \leq -20$ **55.** $\frac{1}{8}y \geq 5$ **56.** $-9z > 108$

Choose a Strategy **Use a strategy from the list to solve the following problem. Explain your choice of strategy.**

Problem Solving Strategies
- Guess, Check, and Revise
- Look for a Pattern
- Draw a Diagram

57. The bookstore at your favorite mall is expanding to include the space adjacent to it. The original store was 20 feet by 25 feet. The space adjacent to it is 14 feet by 25 feet. What is the total area of the store with the additional space?

Basic Skills **Find low and high estimates for the product or quotient.**

58. 37×21 **59.** 143×58 **60.** $700 \div 14$ **61.** $1330 \div 87$

Test-Taking Practice 

62. **Extended Response** The area of a rectangle is 24 square inches. Its length and width are measured in whole inches. Find all possible dimensions of the rectangle. Show your work and explain how you found all of the possibilities.

Greatest Common Factor

BEFORE	Now	WHY?
You found the factors of a number.	You'll find the greatest common factor of two or more numbers.	So you can decide how many food baskets you can make, as in Ex. 21.

Word Watch

common factor, p. 173
greatest common factor (GCF), p. 173
relatively prime, p. 174

INDIANA Academic Standards

- Computation (8.2.1)
- Problem Solving (8.7.4)

Activity The lists below show the factors of the given numbers.

Number	Factors
36	1, 2, 3, 4, 6, 9, 12, 18, 36
24	1, 2, 3, 4, 6, 8, 12, 24
20	1, 2, 4, 5, 10, 20

1. Which number(s) are factors of 20 and 36?
2. Which number(s) are factors of 24 and 36?
3. Which number(s) are factors of 20, 24, and 36?
4. What is the greatest factor that is in all three lists?

HELP with Vocabulary

The GCF is sometimes called the greatest common divisor (GCD) because it is the largest common factor that can be divided evenly into the given numbers.

A **common factor** is a whole number that is a factor of two or more nonzero whole numbers. The greatest of the common factors is the **greatest common factor (GCF)**.

One method for finding the GCF of two or more numbers is to use the prime factorization of each number. The GCF is the product of all the factors that the numbers have in common.

EXAMPLE 1 Finding the Greatest Common Factor

Find the greatest common factor of 42 and 70.

Begin by writing the prime factorization of each number. Find the product of the common prime factors.

$42 = 2 \times 3 \times 7 \qquad 70 = 2 \times 5 \times 7$

The common prime factors are 2 and 7. The GCF of 42 and 70 is the product of these factors.

ANSWER The GCF of 42 and 70 is $2 \cdot 7$, or 14.

Two numbers are **relatively prime** if their greatest common factor is 1. For example, 8 and 15 are relatively prime.

EXAMPLE 2 Identifying Relatively Prime Numbers

Decide whether the numbers 112 and 45 are relatively prime. If they are not relatively prime, find the greatest common factor.

Begin by writing the prime factorization of each number. Then find the product of the common prime factors.

$112 = 2^4 \cdot 7 \qquad 45 = 3^2 \cdot 5$

There are no common prime factors. However, two numbers always have 1 as a common factor. So, the GCF is 1.

ANSWER The numbers 112 and 45 are relatively prime.

Your turn now **Find the greatest common factor of the numbers.**

1. 12, 18 **2.** 24, 60 **3.** 36, 90 **4.** 96, 120

Decide whether the numbers are relatively prime. If they are not relatively prime, find the GCF.

5. 48, 72 **6.** 124, 128 **7.** 39, 44 **8.** 200, 63

You can find the greatest common factor of two monomials by factoring the monomials.

EXAMPLE 3 Finding the GCF of Monomials

Find the greatest common factor of $12a^3$ and $9a^2$.

First factor each expression.

$12a^3 = 2 \cdot 2 \cdot \mathbf{3} \cdot \boldsymbol{a} \cdot \boldsymbol{a} \cdot a \qquad 9a^2 = 3 \cdot \mathbf{3} \cdot \boldsymbol{a} \cdot \boldsymbol{a}$

The common factors are 3 and a^2. The GCF is the product of the common factors.

ANSWER The GCF is $3a^2$.

Your turn now **Find the greatest common factor of the monomials.**

9. $6x$, $18x$ **10.** $6xy$, $4xy^2$ **11.** $15y$, $9x^2y^2$ **12.** $5xy^3$, $10x^2y^2$

EXAMPLE 4 Using the Greatest Common Factor

Pep Rally Packs Students at your school are planning to hand out pep rally packs to support your school's athletic program. The students have 240 bumper stickers, 360 pennants, and 720 pencils. Every pack must have the same contents, and there should be no leftover items. What is the greatest number of pep rally packs that can be made?

Solution

You can find the greatest number of pep rally packs by finding the GCF.

$240 = 2^4 \cdot 3 \cdot 5 \qquad 360 = 2^3 \cdot 3^2 \cdot 5 \qquad 720 = 2^4 \cdot 3^2 \cdot 5$

The common prime factors are 2^3, 3, and 5. The GCF is $2^3 \cdot 3 \cdot 5$, or 120.

ANSWER The greatest number of pep rally packs is 120. Each pack will contain 2 bumper stickers, 3 pennants, and 6 pencils.

4.2 Exercises

More Practice, p. 730

Getting Ready to Practice

1. **Vocabulary** Copy and complete: Six is the _?_ of 12 and 18.

Matching **Match the pair of numbers with its GCF.**

2. 6, 9	3. 4, 10	4. 5, 15	5. 14, 21
A. 5	B. 3	C. 7	D. 2

6. **Find the Error** Describe and correct the error in the solution.

$210 = 2 \cdot 3 \cdot 5 \cdot 7$

$495 = 3 \cdot 3 \cdot 5 \cdot 11$

The GCF is 5. ✗

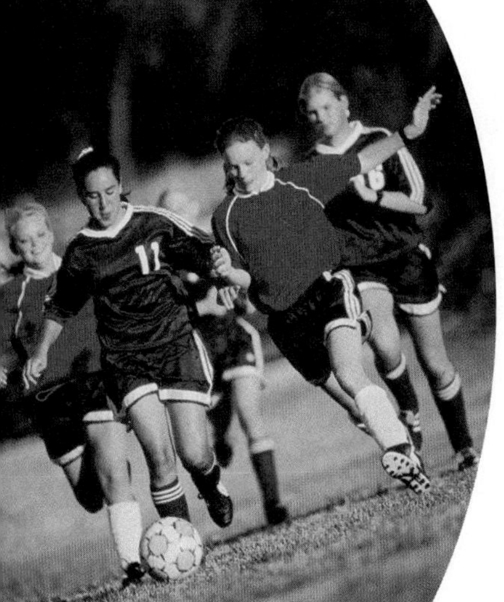

7. **Guided Problem Solving** There are 56 girls and 68 boys in a youth sports league. Each student will be placed on a team. Each team will have an equal number of players and will have the same number of girls. What is the greatest number of teams that can be formed?
   1. Write the prime factorizations of the numbers 56 and 68.
   2. What are the common prime factors of the two numbers?
   3. Multiply the common prime factors to get the GCF. What meaning does the GCF have in the situation?

Practice and Problem Solving

with Homework

Example	Exercises
1	8–11
2	12–20
3	22–27
4	21, 33

Online Resources
CLASSZONE.COM

- More Examples
- eTutorial Plus

Find the greatest common factor of the numbers.

8. 3, 9, 27 **9.** 21, 28, 56 **10.** 17, 18, 20 **11.** 24, 36, 180

Decide whether the numbers are relatively prime. If not, find the greatest common factor.

12. 5, 18 **13.** 10, 25 **14.** 28, 42 **15.** 55, 72

16. 21, 66 **17.** 18, 216 **18.** 212, 312 **19.** 268, 515

20. Writing Can two even numbers be relatively prime? Explain why or why not.

21. Food Baskets Your class is making Thanksgiving baskets to be distributed by a food bank. You have collected 60 cans of cranberry sauce, 120 cans of canned fruit, 90 cans of corn, and 60 boxes of muffin mixes. You want every basket to be the same with no leftover items. What is the greatest number of baskets you can assemble? What will each basket contain?

Algebra **Find the GCF of the monomials.**

22. $3x^2, 9x$ **23.** $4z^3, 2z^2$ **24.** $5t^4, 15t^5$

25. $12x^2y^2, 16xy^3$ **26.** $18rs^2, 30st^2$ **27.** $15bc^3, 75b^3c$

Critical Thinking **Copy and complete the statement using *always*, *sometimes*, or *never*.**

28. The greatest common factor of two numbers is _?_ equal to one of the two numbers.

29. The number 1 is _?_ the greatest common factor of relatively prime numbers.

30. The greatest common factor of two numbers is _?_ greater than both of the numbers.

31. Critical Thinking Name two composite numbers that are relatively prime.

32. Carpentry You must cut four pieces of wood that measure 36 inches, 45 inches, 108 inches, and 81 inches, into smaller, equally sized pieces. What is the longest each piece can be so that each piece is the same length?

33. Bouquets A florist must make a batch of identical bouquets. The florist has 360 tulips, 270 roses, and 180 lilies. There cannot be any flowers left over. What is the greatest number of bouquets that the florist can make?

Jacob sheep can have two, four, and occasionally six horns.

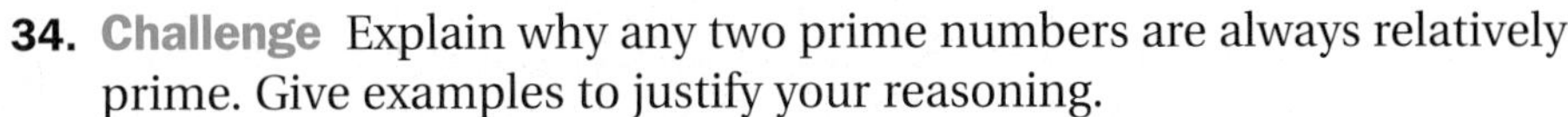

34. **Challenge** Explain why any two prime numbers are always relatively prime. Give examples to justify your reasoning.

35. **Sheep** A farmer needs to build two adjacent rectangular pens for his sheep. He wants one pen to have an area of 204 square feet, and the other to have an area of 144 square feet. Fence lengths are available in one-foot increments. What is the greatest length the farmer can make the fence that is shared by the two pens?

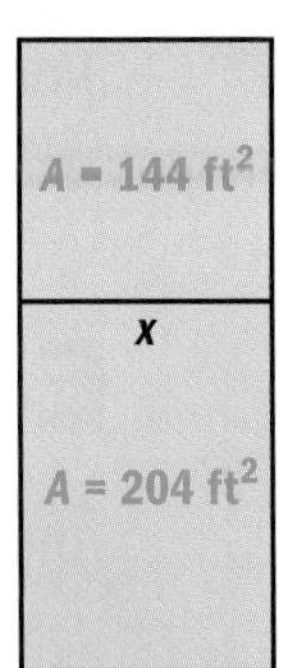

Mixed Review

In Exercises 36–38, solve the equation. *(Lesson 3.1)*

36. $-6 + n = 4$ 37. $n + 13 = 5$ 38. $n + 2.7 = 5.7$

39. Write the prime factorization of 84. *(Lesson 4.1)*

Basic Skills Use a metric ruler to draw a segment with the given length.

40. 7 cm 41. 15 cm 42. 145 mm 43. 84 mm

Test-Taking Practice

44. **Multiple Choice** What is the greatest common factor of $4x^2$ and $6x$?

A. x **B.** $2x$ **C.** $4x$ **D.** $2x^2$

45. **Multiple Choice** What is the greatest common factor of 144, 300, and 240?

F. 4 **G.** 6 **H.** 12 **I.** 60

BRAIN GAME

Marble Mystery

You have a bucket full of marbles. If the marbles in the bucket are counted by twos, threes, fives, and sevens, there is exactly one left over each time. What is the fewest number of marbles that could be in the bucket?

4.3 Hands-on Activity

INDIANA: Academic Standards
- Computation (8.2.1)

GOAL
Use area models to find equivalent fractions.

MATERIALS
- graph paper
- colored pencils

Equivalent Fractions

You can use area models to find equivalent fractions.

Explore **Find two fractions equivalent to $\frac{6}{8}$.**

1 Draw a rectangle on a piece of graph paper. Divide the rectangle into 8 equal parts and shade 6 of the parts.

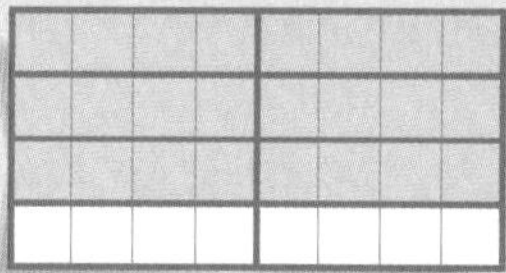

2 Look for other ways of dividing the rectangle into equal parts.

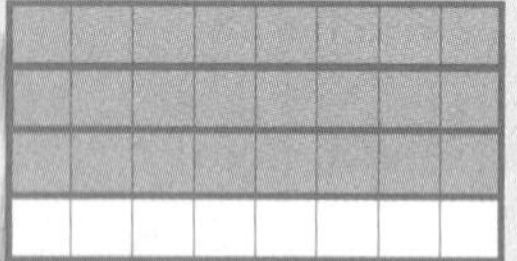

There are 4 parts and 3 are shaded.

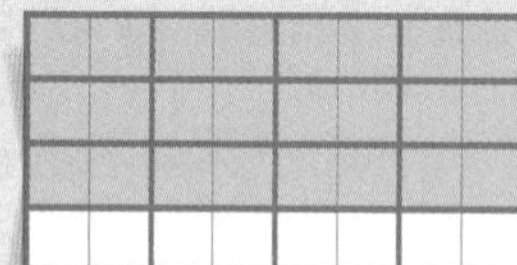

There are 16 parts and 12 are shaded.

3 Write the equivalent fractions.

The fractions $\frac{3}{4}$ and $\frac{12}{16}$ are equivalent to $\frac{6}{8}$.

Your turn now **Draw a model of the given fraction. Then find two equivalent fractions.**

1. $\frac{4}{6}$ **2.** $\frac{10}{12}$ **3.** $\frac{4}{16}$ **4.** $\frac{10}{16}$

Stop and Think

5. Writing How can factoring both the numerator and denominator of a fraction help to write an equivalent fraction?

Simplifying Fractions

BEFORE	Now	WHY?
You evaluated numerical expressions.	You'll simplify fractions.	So you can find the fractions of threatened species, as in Ex. 39.

In the Real World

History One of the Czech Republic's royal coronation jewels is the St. Wenceslas crown. It was made around 1345 and is decorated with 44 spinels, 30 emeralds, 22 pearls, 19 sapphires, and 1 ruby. What fraction of jewels in the crown are emeralds? You will see how to solve this problem in Example 1.

Fractions A *fraction* is a number of the form $\frac{a}{b}$ $(b \neq 0)$ where a is called the numerator and b is called the denominator. A fraction is in **simplest form** if its numerator and denominator have 1 as their GCF. **Equivalent fractions** represent the same number. They have the same simplest form.

Word Watch

simplest form, p. 179
equivalent fractions, p. 179

INDIANA Academic Standards

- Computation (8.2.1)

EXAMPLE 1 Writing a Fraction in Simplest Form

Write the fraction of jewels in the crown that are emeralds. Then simplify.

$$\frac{\text{Number of emeralds}}{\text{Total number of jewels in the crown}} = \frac{30}{116}$$

Method 1: Write the prime factorization of each number.

$30 = 2 \cdot 3 \cdot 5 \qquad 116 = 2^2 \cdot 29$

The GCF of 30 and 116 is 2.

$\frac{30}{116} = \frac{30 \div 2}{116 \div 2}$ **Divide numerator and denominator by GCF.**

$= \frac{15}{58}$ **Simplify.**

Method 2:

$\frac{30}{116} = \frac{2 \cdot 3 \cdot 5}{2 \cdot 2 \cdot 29}$ **Write prime factorizations.**

$= \frac{\cancel{2}^1 \cdot 3 \cdot 5}{\cancel{2}_1 \cdot 2 \cdot 29}$ **Divide out common factor.**

$= \frac{15}{58}$ **Simplify.**

ANSWER The fraction of jewels that are emeralds is $\frac{15}{58}$.

Emerald

Ruby

Sapphire

Pearl

EXAMPLE 2 Identifying Equivalent Fractions

Tell whether the fractions $\frac{3}{8}$ and $\frac{18}{48}$ are equivalent.

Write each fraction in simplest form.

$\frac{3}{8}$ is in simplest form. $\quad \frac{18}{48} = \frac{18 \div 6}{48 \div 6} = \frac{3}{8}$

ANSWER The fractions are equivalent.

EXAMPLE 3 Writing Equivalent Fractions

HELP with Solving

A fraction has many equivalent fractions. There are other correct answers to Example 3.

Write two fractions that are equivalent to $\frac{4}{10}$.

Multiply or divide the numerator and denominator by the same nonzero number.

$\frac{4}{10} = \frac{4 \times 3}{10 \times 3} = \frac{12}{30}$ Multiply numerator and denominator by 3.

$\frac{4}{10} = \frac{4 \div 2}{10 \div 2} = \frac{2}{5}$ Divide numerator and denominator by 2, a common factor of 4 and 10.

ANSWER The fractions $\frac{12}{30}$ and $\frac{2}{5}$ are equivalent to $\frac{4}{10}$.

Spinel

Sapphire

Your turn now **Use the information on page 179. Write the fraction of jewels in the crown that are the given jewel. Simplify if possible.**

1. pearls **2.** sapphires **3.** spinels

Write two fractions that are equivalent to the given fraction.

4. $\frac{8}{16}$ **5.** $\frac{9}{15}$ **6.** $\frac{10}{12}$ **7.** $\frac{21}{24}$

You can use Method 2 of Example 1 to simplify fractions that contain variable expressions.

EXAMPLE 4 Simplifying a Variable Expression

$\frac{14x}{7xy} = \frac{2 \cdot 7 \cdot x}{7 \cdot x \cdot y}$ Factor numerator and denominator.

$= \frac{2 \cdot \cancel{7}^{1} \cdot \cancel{x}^{1}}{\cancel{7}_{1} \cdot \cancel{x}_{1} \cdot y}$ Divide out common factors.

$= \frac{2}{y}$ Simplify.

with Notetaking

You may want to add information on simplifying fractions with variable expressions to the outline that you started on p. 166.

EXAMPLE 5 Evaluating a Variable Expression

Evaluate the expression $\frac{-4x^3}{2x}$ when $x = 5$.

$\frac{-4x^3}{2x} = \frac{-1 \cdot 2 \cdot 2 \cdot x \cdot x \cdot x}{2 \cdot x}$ — Factor numerator and denominator.

$= \frac{-1 \cdot 2 \cdot \overset{1}{\cancel{2}} \cdot \overset{1}{\cancel{x}} \cdot x \cdot x}{\underset{1}{\cancel{2}} \cdot \underset{1}{\cancel{x}}}$ — Divide out common factors.

$= -2x^2$ — Simplify.

$= -2(5)^2$ — Substitute 5 for x.

$= -50$ — Evaluate powers and simplify.

Your turn now **Simplify the variable expression.**

8. $\frac{4xy}{6x}$ **9.** $\frac{32a}{8ab}$ **10.** $\frac{2m^3}{6m}$ **11.** $\frac{5r^2s}{10rs}$

12. Evaluate the expression $\frac{35a^4}{-5a^2}$ when $a = 3$.

4.3 Exercises

More Practice, p. 730

Getting Ready to Practice

Vocabulary Tell whether the fractions are equivalent.

1. $\frac{2}{3}, \frac{4}{6}$ **2.** $\frac{15}{25}, \frac{3}{4}$ **3.** $\frac{15}{18}, \frac{5}{6}$ **4.** $\frac{21}{49}, \frac{3}{7}$

Write the fraction in simplest form.

5. $\frac{10}{15}$ **6.** $\frac{16}{20}$ **7.** $\frac{25}{40}$ **8.** $\frac{36}{72}$

9. Write two fractions that are equivalent to $\frac{1}{5}$.

10. Write two fractions that are equivalent to $\frac{12}{15}$.

11. Evaluate the expression $\frac{8x^3}{2x}$ when $x = 4$.

12. **Eggs** In a carton of one dozen eggs, 2 eggs are broken. What fraction of the eggs are broken? What fraction of the eggs are unbroken? Write your answers in simplest form.

Practice and Problem Solving

Example	Exercises
1	13-16, 33-39
2	21-24
3	25-28
4	17-20
5	29-32

- More Examples
- eTutorial Plus

Write the fraction in simplest form.

13. $\frac{39}{52}$ **14.** $\frac{18}{27}$ **15.** $\frac{-9}{72}$ **16.** $\frac{-49}{56}$

17. $\frac{4ab}{8a}$ **18.** $\frac{6c}{18cd}$ **19.** $\frac{-9rst}{30rs}$ **20.** $\frac{25xy}{35xyz}$

Tell whether the fractions are equivalent.

21. $\frac{4}{5}, \frac{20}{25}$ **22.** $\frac{21}{28}, \frac{1}{3}$ **23.** $\frac{7}{35}, \frac{2}{10}$ **24.** $\frac{32}{72}, \frac{4}{9}$

Write two fractions that are equivalent to the given fraction.

25. $\frac{45}{90}$ **26.** $\frac{36}{81}$ **27.** $\frac{24}{60}$ **28.** $\frac{48}{140}$

Evaluate the expression when $x = 3$ and $y = 5$.

29. $\frac{3x}{x^3}$ **30.** $\frac{2y^2}{-5y}$ **31.** $\frac{5y}{y^2}$ **32.** $\frac{4x^4}{24x^3}$

Geography **Write the number of states in the region as a fraction of all of the states. Write your answer in simplest form.**

33. Northeast: 9

34. Midwest: 12

35. South: 16

36. West: 13

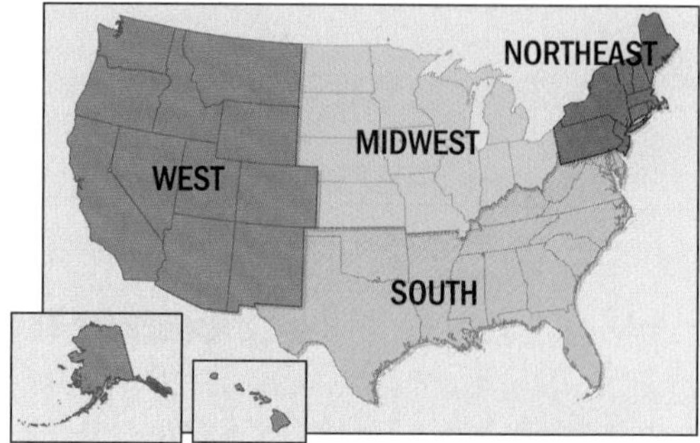

The U.S. Census Bureau divides the 50 states into 4 regions.

Extended Problem Solving **In Exercises 37–39, use the table. It gives information about animals in Peru. Write your answer in simplest form.**

37. What fraction of mammal species are threatened?

38. What fraction of reptile species are threatened?

39. Number Sense Use rounding to compare the fractions of threatened mammal and bird species. Then write the fractions of threatened species in each group (mammals, birds, and reptiles) in order from least to greatest.

Peruvian Animal Species

	Known	Threatened
Mammals	460	46
Birds	1541	64
Reptiles	360	9

Yellow-faced Parrot

Write the fractions in simplest form. Tell whether they are equivalent.

40. $\frac{30}{60}, \frac{27}{54}$ **41.** $\frac{24}{40}, \frac{30}{50}$ **42.** $\frac{15}{18}, \frac{36}{48}$ **43.** $\frac{24}{32}, \frac{15}{24}$

44. $\frac{30}{75}, \frac{75}{105}$ **45.** $\frac{45}{54}, \frac{90}{108}$ **46.** $\frac{54}{96}, \frac{144}{256}$ **47.** $\frac{84}{112}, \frac{168}{192}$

Write the fraction in simplest form.

48. $\frac{-2x^3y}{xy}$ **49.** $\frac{5xy^2z}{5xz}$ **50.** $\frac{2x^3y}{-3xyz}$ **51.** $\frac{-8^2z^2}{16x^2yz}$

52. Critical Thinking If you divide the numerator and denominator of a fraction by a common factor, will the resulting fraction always be in simplest form? Give an example to justify your answer.

Tell whether the fractions are equivalent.

53. $\frac{4abc}{5ab}, \frac{4c}{5a}$ **54.** $\frac{3a}{5}, \frac{6a^2}{10a}$ **55.** $\frac{2a}{3b}, \frac{10a^2b}{15ab^2}$

56. Challenge Jason believes that if the numerator or the denominator of a fraction is prime, then the fraction is in simplest form. Explain why this is not always true.

Mixed Review 

In Exercises 57–59, evaluate the expression. Justify each step. *(Lesson 2.6)*

57. $-12 + 46 - 18$ **58.** $10 \cdot (-25) \cdot 0$ **59.** $\frac{1}{3} \cdot (20 \cdot 15)$

60. Find the greatest common factor of $3x^3y$ and $6x^2y^2$. *(Lesson 4.2)*

Basic Skills Use a protractor to draw an angle with the given measure.

61. 53° **62.** 97° **63.** 145°

Test-Taking Practice 

INTERNET
State Test Practice
CLASSZONE.COM

64. Multiple Choice Mr. Wilkens has attended 18 of his son's 24 basketball games. What fraction of the games has he attended?

A. $\frac{3}{8}$ **B.** $\frac{2}{3}$ **C.** $\frac{3}{4}$ **D.** $\frac{4}{3}$

65. Multiple Choice Which pair of fractions are equivalent?

F. $\frac{6}{10}, \frac{9}{25}$ **G.** $\frac{3}{8}, \frac{15}{35}$ **H.** $\frac{14}{21}, \frac{24}{36}$ **I.** $\frac{2}{5}, \frac{5}{20}$

4.4 Problem Solving Strategies

INDIANA: Academic Standards
• Problem Solving (8.7.1)

Make a List

Problem Mia is trying to remember Jasmine's phone number. She knows the first three digits are 889, but she is confused about the last four numbers. Mia knows the last four digits are a 3, 4, 5, and 6, but she cannot recall their correct order. How many possibilities are there for Jasmine's phone number?

1 Read and Understand

Read the problem carefully.

You know the last four digits of a phone number, but not their order. You need to find how many ways these numbers can be arranged.

2 Make a Plan

Decide on a strategy to use.

One way to solve the problem is to make a list of all the possible four-digit numbers. Then you can use the list to count the number of possibilities for a phone number.

3 Solve the Problem

Reread the problem and make a list.

First, list all of the four-digit numbers that begin with the number **3**.

3456 **3**465 **3**546 **3**564 **3**645 **3**654

Similarly, list all of the four-digit numbers that begin with the numbers 4, 5, and **6**.

4356 4365 4536 4563 4635 4653

5346 5364 5436 5463 5634 5643

6345 **6**354 **6**435 **6**453 **6**534 **6**543

Now count all of the four-digit numbers in the list.

ANSWER There are 24 possibilities for Jasmine's phone number.

4 Look Back

Double-check your list to make sure you didn't repeat any numbers or forget a number.

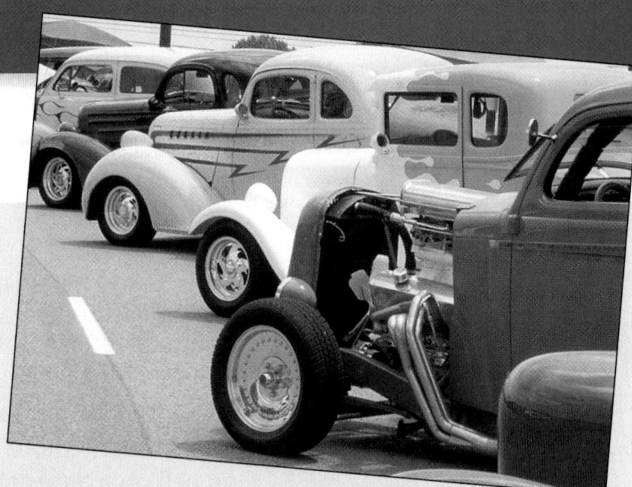

Practice the Strategy

Use the strategy *make a list*.

1. **Baseball** The first team to win 3 out of 5 possible games will be the winner of a baseball tournament. In how many ways can a team win 3 out of 5 games?
2. **Telephone Prefixes** A certain town can use the digits 0, 1, 2, 6, 7, and 8 for its telephone prefixes. How many three-digit telephone prefixes are possible for this town if each digit can be used only once in a prefix and the first digit cannot be a 1 or a 0?
3. **Number Cube** Derek rolled 2 number cubes and added the two numbers on the top of each cube. List all the possible sums. In how many different ways can he roll a sum of 7?
4. **Tennis** Three boys and three girls sign up for a mixed doubles tennis tournament. In mixed doubles a team consists of one boy and one girl. How many mixed doubles teams can be made?
5. **Checkbook Covers** A bank has checkbook covers that are either pocket or desk size. The covers can be white, black, red, or tan. The customer's name will be stamped on the cover in gold or silver. How many different choices are available for checkbook covers?
6. **Summer Job** A student was hired by a city's maintenance department to paint parking space numbers in a city parking lot. Each digit had to be painted separately, and the student earned 20 cents per digit. The student painted parking space numbers from 1 to 225. How much did the student earn?

Mixed Problem Solving

Use any strategy to solve the problem.

7. **Car Show** The manager of a mall is asked to rope off a rectangular section of the parking lot for a car show. The area roped off is 250 feet by 300 feet. Posts are to be placed every 25 feet around the lot. How many posts are needed?
8. **Consultant Fees** Two consultants were hired by a company. The total consultant fees were $12,500. If one consultant had earned $500 less, each consultant would have been paid the same. How much did each consultant earn?
9. **Gardening** Joyce has planted a kudzu vine in her yard. The kudzu vine is a fast growing Japanese plant that was brought to the United States in 1876. Use the information in the table below to predict how long Joyce's vine will be after 2 weeks.

Days	1	2	3	4
Length of kudzu vine (inches)	12	24	36	48

10. **Video Games** Chris buys a video game and two T-shirts for $44 at the mall. One week later he buys two more video games and a T-shirt for $52. Each video game has the same price, and each T-shirt has the same price. How much does one video game cost?

Least Common Multiple

BEFORE

You found the greatest common factor of two numbers.

Now

You'll find the least common multiple of two numbers.

WHY?

So you can plan your weekly schedule, as in Ex. 26.

Word Watch

multiple, p. 186
common multiple, p. 186
least common multiple (LCM), p. 186

INDIANA
Academic Standards

- Computation (8.2.1)

In the Real World

Animal Clinic A veterinarian at an animal clinic is on call every four days. Today is Saturday, and the vet is on call. In how many more days will the vet be on call on a Saturday again? You will see how to solve this problem in Example 1.

JUNE

S	M	T	W	T	F	S
						1
2	3	4	5	6	7	8
9	10	11	12	13	14	15
16	17	18	19	20	21	22
23	24	25	26	27	28	29
30						

A **multiple** of a number is the product of the number and any nonzero whole number. A multiple that is shared by two or more numbers is a **common multiple**. The least of the common multiples of two or more whole numbers is the **least common multiple (LCM)**.

EXAMPLE 1 Finding the Least Common Multiple

The veterinarian described above is on call every 4 days. A Saturday occurs every 7 days. To determine the next Saturday the vet will be on call, find the least common multiple of 4 and 7.

Method 1: Make a list.

List the multiples of each number.

Multiples of 4: 4, 8, 12, 16, 20, 24, **28**, 32, 36, 40, 44, ...

Multiples of 7: 7, 14, 21, **28**, 35, 42, 49, 56, ...

The LCM of 4 and 7 is 28.

Method 2: Use prime factorization.

Write the prime factorization of each number.

$4 = 2^2$ $\qquad 7 = 7$

Write the product of the highest power of each prime number in the prime factorizations.

$2^2 \cdot 7 = 28$

The LCM of 4 and 7 is 28.

ANSWER In 28 days, the veterinarian will be on call on a Saturday.

EXAMPLE 2 Finding the Least Common Multiple

Find the LCM of 32, 96, and 120 using prime factorization.

Solution

Write the prime factorization of each number.

$32 = 2^5$ $\qquad 96 = 2^5 \cdot 3$ $\qquad 120 = 2^3 \cdot 3 \cdot 5$

Write the product of the highest power of each prime number in the prime factorizations.

$2^5 \cdot 3 \cdot 5 = 480$

ANSWER The LCM of 32, 96, and 120 is 480.

Your turn now **Find the least common multiple of the numbers.**

1. 6, 15 **2.** 4, 20 **3.** 12, 28 **4.** 24, 36, and 72

Method 2 of Example 1 is also useful for finding the least common multiples of monomials.

EXAMPLE 3 Finding the LCM of Monomials

Find the LCM of $6x^2y$ and $9x^4z$.

Solution

Factor each expression using exponents.

$6x^2y = 2 \cdot 3 \cdot x^2 \cdot y$

$9x^4z = 3^2 \cdot x^4 \cdot z$

Find the product of the highest power of each factor, including the variables.

$2 \cdot 3^2 \cdot x^4 \cdot y \cdot z = 18x^4yz$

ANSWER The LCM of $6x^2y$ and $9x^4z$ is $18x^4yz$.

Your turn now **Find the least common multiple of the monomials.**

5. $8x^3, 20x^7$ **6.** $12y^4, 36y^8$

7. $4ab^2, 10a^2b$ **8.** $6m^3np^2, 8mp^3$

4.4 Exercises

More Practice, p. 730

Getting Ready to Practice

Vocabulary **Copy and complete the statement.**

1. A(n) _?_ of 6 and 9 is 54.

2. The _?_ of 6 and 9 is 18.

Matching **Match the pair of numbers with its LCM.**

3. 36, 18 **4.** 45, 75 **5.** 6, 18 **6.** 42, 105

A. 18 **B.** 36 **C.** 210 **D.** 225

7. Find the Error Describe and correct the error in the solution.

Find the LCM of 12 and 24.

$12 = 2 \cdot 2 \cdot 3$ $24 = 2 \cdot 2 \cdot 2 \cdot 3$

The LCM is $2 \cdot 2$, or 4. ✗

Practice and Problem Solving

Example	Exercises
1	8–11, 25, 26
2	12–19
3	20–23

- More Examples
- eTutorial Plus

List the first few multiples of each number. Then use the lists to find the LCM of the numbers.

8. 4, 6 **9.** 6, 21 **10.** 8, 10 **11.** 10, 15

Write the prime factorization of the numbers. Then find their LCM.

12. 36, 90 **13.** 17, 57 **14.** 90, 108 **15.** 125, 500

16. 6, 8, 12 **17.** 8, 16, 32 **18.** 6, 15, 45 **19.** 20, 24, 60

Find the LCM of the monomials.

20. $5ab, 7ab^2$

21. $7s^3t, 49st^2$

22. $4x^3y^3, 18xy^5$

23. $24c^2d^3, 60c^2d^6$

24. Writing Could you find the *greatest* common multiple of two numbers? Explain your reasoning.

25. Traffic Lights One traffic light turns red every 45 seconds. Another traffic light turns red every 60 seconds. Both traffic lights just turned red. In how many seconds will they turn red at the same time again?

26. Schedule Your class schedule changes on a three-day rotation. Every three days you have math class during the last class period of the day. This week, you have math class the last period on Friday. In how many more school days will you have math class the last period on Friday?

Find the LCM of the numbers using prime factorization.

27. 160, 432 **28.** 144, 576 **29.** 21, 36, 57 **30.** 18, 54, 84

31. 30, 75, 100 **32.** 36, 54, 72 **33.** 10, 12, 30, 60 **34.** 21, 42, 63, 105

Find the LCM of the monomials.

35. $24x^4y, 30y^7$ **36.** $17m^3n^3, 9m^2n^6$ **37.** $45gh^5k^3, 33g^4hk^3$

38. **Lasagna** Zoe is making lasagna for a family reunion. Her recipe calls for twelve noodles for each batch of lasagna. One box of lasagna noodles contains 14 noodles. What is the least number of batches of lasagna that Zoe can make without having any noodles left over?

39. **Swimming** Will swims one lap in 160 seconds, while Martin swims one lap in 180 seconds. The boys start their laps at the same time from the same side of the pool and maintain their pace. When will they both be at their starting place at the same time again? Write your answer in minutes and seconds.

40. **Writing** You are asked to find the LCM of two numbers. One of the numbers is a factor of the other number. Is there a shortcut to finding their LCM? Explain.

41. **Challenge** Could the GCF of two different numbers also be the LCM of those numbers? Explain.

Mixed Review

42. Rebecca ran on her treadmill at 5.6 miles per hour for one half hour. How many miles did Rebecca run? *(Lesson 1.6)*

43. Simplify the expression $7x + 9 + 12x + 11 + 2y$ by combining like terms. *(Lesson 2.7)*

44. Find the greatest common factor of 121 and 187. *(Lesson 4.2)*

Basic Skills **Find the sum.**

45. 24.63 + 49.07 **46.** 14.125 + 16.8 **47.** 33.87 + 100.9

Test-Taking Practice

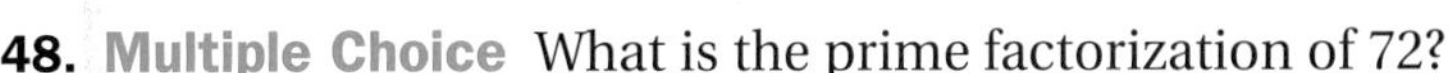

48. **Multiple Choice** What is the prime factorization of 72?

A. $2^2 \cdot 3 \cdot 6$ **B.** $2 \cdot 6^2$ **C.** $2^3 \cdot 3^2$ **D.** $2^2 \cdot 3^2 \cdot 6$

49. **Short Response** A teacher can arrange a class into groups of 2, 5, or 6 students with no one left out. What is the least number of students that the teacher can have in class to do this? Explain how you found your answer.

Notebook Review

Review the vocabulary definitions in your notebook.

Copy the review examples in your notebook. Then complete the exercises.

Check Your Definitions

prime number, p. 169
composite number, p. 169
prime factorization, p. 169
factor tree, p. 169
monomial, p. 170
common factor, p. 173
greatest common factor (GCF), p. 173
relatively prime, p. 174
simplest form, p. 179
equivalent fractions, p. 179
multiple, p. 186
common multiple, p. 186
least common multiple (LCM), p. 186

Use Your Vocabulary

1. Copy and complete: A factor tree can be used to find the _?_ of a number.

4.1 Can you write a prime factorization?

EXAMPLE Write the prime factorization of 504.

$504 = 2 \cdot 2 \cdot 2 \cdot 3 \cdot 3 \cdot 7$, or $2^3 \cdot 3^2 \cdot 7$

ANSWER The prime factorization of 504 is $2^3 \cdot 3^2 \cdot 7$.

Write the prime factorization of the number.

2. 40 **3.** 7 **4.** 85 **5.** 120

4.2 Can you find the GCF of two numbers?

EXAMPLE Find the GCF of 36 and 60.

$36 = 2^2 \cdot 3^2$ $60 = 2^2 \cdot 3 \cdot 5$

The common factors are 2^2 and 3. So, the GCF is $2^2 \cdot 3$, or 12.

ANSWER The GCF of 36 and 60 is 12.

Find the GCF of the numbers or monomials.

6. 48, 80 **7.** 60, 100 **8.** $14a^3, 21a$ **9.** $20y^4, 60y^5$

4.3 Can you write a fraction in simplest form?

EXAMPLE Write $\frac{48}{72}$ in simplest form.

$$\frac{48}{72} = \frac{48 \div 24}{72 \div 24} = \frac{2}{3}$$

Write the fraction in simplest form.

10. $\frac{15}{45}$ **11.** $\frac{12}{80}$ **12.** $\frac{9ab}{27a}$ **13.** $\frac{18n^3}{54n}$

4.4 Can you find the LCM of two numbers?

EXAMPLE Find the LCM of 20 and 48.

$20 = 2^2 \cdot 5$ $48 = 2^4 \cdot 3$

ANSWER The LCM of 20 and 48 is $2^4 \cdot 3 \cdot 5$, or 240.

Find the LCM of the numbers or monomials.

14. 28, 42 **15.** 54, 90 **16.** $10cd$, $25c^2$ **17.** $9n^3$, $12n^2$

Stop and Think about Lessons 4.1–4.4

18. **Writing** Explain the difference between listing the factors of a number and finding the prime factorization of a number.

Review Quiz 1

Find the GCF of the numbers or monomials.

1. 24, 90 **2.** 36, 72, 108 **3.** $20c^3$, $48c^2$ **4.** $64m^2$, $80m^5$

Find the LCM of the numbers or monomials.

5. 88, 99 **6.** 36, 96 **7.** $7xy$, $21y^3$ **8.** $6ab^2$, $30ab$

Tell whether the fractions are equivalent.

9. $\frac{9}{27}, \frac{60}{180}$ **10.** $\frac{39}{91}, \frac{42}{56}$ **11.** $\frac{40}{48}, \frac{70}{84}$ **12.** $\frac{108}{120}, \frac{189}{210}$

13. **Supermarket** A supermarket gives every tenth customer a coupon and every twenty-fifth customer a gift. Which of the first 200 customers receive both a coupon and a gift?

Comparing Fractions and Mixed Numbers

BEFORE	Now	WHY?
You compared and ordered integers.	You'll compare and order fractions and mixed numbers.	So you can determine the greater fraction of games won, as in Ex. 28.

least common denominator (LCD), p. 192

INDIANA Academic Standards

- Computation (8.2.1)

You can use models to compare the fractions $\frac{2}{3}$ and $\frac{3}{4}$.

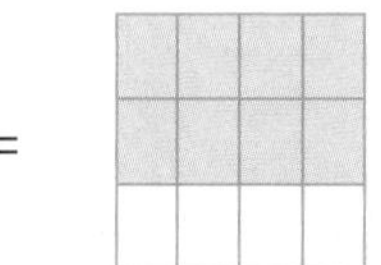

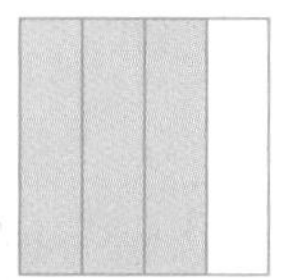

$$\frac{2}{3} = \frac{2 \cdot 4}{3 \cdot 4} = \frac{8}{12} \qquad \frac{3}{4} = \frac{3 \cdot 3}{4 \cdot 3} = \frac{9}{12}$$

In the diagram above, $\frac{8}{12} < \frac{9}{12}$, so $\frac{2}{3} < \frac{3}{4}$.

The **least common denominator (LCD)** of two or more fractions is the least common multiple of the denominators. You can compare fractions by using the least common denominator to write equivalent fractions.

EXAMPLE 1 Comparing Fractions Using the LCD

Compare $\frac{3}{8}$ and $\frac{5}{12}$.

(1) Find the least common denominator of the fractions.
The LCM of 8 and 12 is 24, so the least common denominator is 24.

(2) Use the least common denominator to write equivalent fractions.

$$\frac{3}{8} = \frac{3 \cdot 3}{8 \cdot 3} = \frac{9}{24} \qquad \frac{5}{12} = \frac{5 \cdot 2}{12 \cdot 2} = \frac{10}{24}$$

(3) Compare the numerators: $9 < 10$, so $\frac{9}{24} < \frac{10}{24}$.

ANSWER Because $\frac{9}{24} < \frac{10}{24}$, you can write $\frac{3}{8} < \frac{5}{12}$.

with Solving

You can write equivalent fractions by multiplying or dividing the numerator and denominator by the same nonzero number.

Your turn now **Copy and complete the statement with <, >, or =.**

1. $\frac{2}{3} \ \underline{?}\ \frac{5}{8}$ 2. $\frac{2}{4} \ \underline{?}\ \frac{15}{20}$ 3. $\frac{3}{10} \ \underline{?}\ \frac{2}{4}$ 4. $\frac{9}{16} \ \underline{?}\ \frac{11}{18}$

To compare or order improper fractions and mixed numbers, first write any mixed numbers as improper fractions.

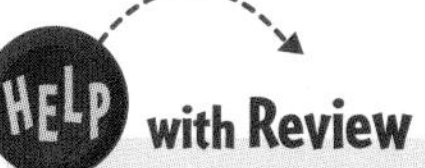

HELP with Review

For help with writing mixed numbers as improper fractions, see p.707.

EXAMPLE 2 Ordering Fractions and Mixed Numbers

Order the numbers $4\frac{7}{16}$, $\frac{19}{4}$, and $\frac{35}{8}$ from least to greatest.

(1 Find the least common denominator of the fractions.

The LCM of 16, 4, and 8 is 16, so the LCD is 16.

(2 Use the least common denominator to write equivalent fractions.

$$4\frac{7}{16} = \frac{4 \cdot 16 + 7}{16} = \frac{71}{16} \qquad \frac{19}{4} = \frac{19 \cdot 4}{4 \cdot 4} = \frac{76}{16} \qquad \frac{35}{8} = \frac{35 \cdot 2}{8 \cdot 2} = \frac{70}{16}$$

(3 Compare the numerators: $70 < 71$, and $71 < 76$, so $\frac{70}{16} < \frac{71}{16}$ and $\frac{71}{16} < \frac{76}{16}$.

ANSWER From least to greatest, the numbers are $\frac{35}{8}$, $4\frac{7}{16}$, and $\frac{19}{4}$.

EXAMPLE 3 Comparing Mixed Numbers

Orangutans A female orangutan is about $3\frac{1}{2}$ feet tall. A male orangutan is about $3\frac{2}{5}$ feet tall. Which of the two orangutans is taller?

Solution

The LCM of 2 and 5 is 10, so the least common denominator is 10.

Use the least common denominator to write equivalent fractions.

$$3\frac{1}{2} = \frac{3 \cdot 2 + 1}{2} = \frac{7}{2} \qquad 3\frac{2}{5} = \frac{3 \cdot 5 + 2}{5} = \frac{17}{5}$$

$$\frac{7}{2} = \frac{7 \cdot 5}{2 \cdot 5} = \frac{35}{10} \qquad \frac{17}{5} = \frac{17 \cdot 2}{5 \cdot 2} = \frac{34}{10}$$

Because $35 > 34$, you can write $\frac{35}{10} > \frac{34}{10}$.

ANSWER The female orangutan is taller.

What do you think? Zoology

Orangutans

An orangutan's arms are about two thirds as long as its height. How long would the arms of a 3 foot orangutan be?

Your turn now **Copy and complete the statement with <, >, or =.**

5. $\frac{16}{5}$? $3\frac{1}{3}$

6. $1\frac{4}{5}$? $\frac{21}{12}$

7. $-2\frac{2}{3}$? $-4\frac{5}{6}$

8. Order the numbers $2\frac{7}{9}$, $2\frac{5}{12}$, and $\frac{11}{4}$ from least to greatest.

More Practice, p. 730

Getting Ready to Practice

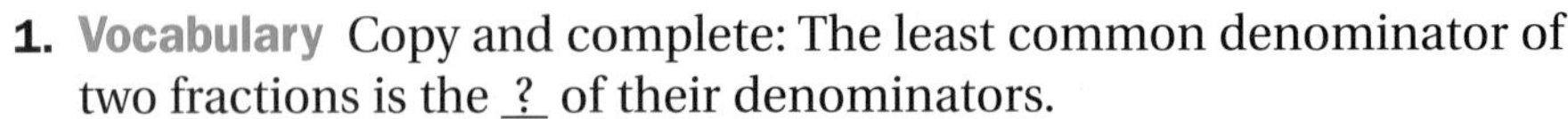

1. **Vocabulary** Copy and complete: The least common denominator of two fractions is the _?_ of their denominators.

Find the least common denominator of the fractions.

2. $\frac{1}{2}, \frac{2}{3}$
3. $\frac{3}{4}, \frac{7}{20}$
4. $\frac{11}{24}, \frac{5}{6}$
5. $\frac{5}{12}, \frac{7}{18}$

Copy and complete the statement with <, >, or =.

6. $\frac{3}{5}$ _?_ $\frac{7}{10}$
7. $\frac{7}{18}$ _?_ $\frac{5}{9}$
8. $\frac{24}{32}$ _?_ $\frac{3}{4}$
9. $\frac{5}{8}$ _?_ $\frac{7}{12}$

10. **Guided Problem Solving** Sarah walks two thirds of a mile to school every day. Amy walks five eighths of a mile to school. Whose walk to school is longer?
    (1 Find the least common denominator.
    (2 Rewrite both fractions using the LCD.
    (3 Use your answer to find whose walk is longer.

Practice and Problem Solving

Copy and complete the statement with <, >, or =.

11. $3\frac{1}{4}$ _?_ $\frac{13}{12}$
12. $\frac{31}{6}$ _?_ $5\frac{1}{6}$
13. $\frac{5}{11}$ _?_ $\frac{42}{55}$
14. $2\frac{4}{5}$ _?_ $\frac{7}{3}$
15. $\frac{165}{36}$ _?_ $4\frac{5}{12}$
16. $\frac{11}{18}$ _?_ $\frac{9}{14}$

Order the numbers from least to greatest.

17. $\frac{1}{2}, \frac{1}{8}, \frac{3}{4}, \frac{5}{16}$
18. $1\frac{1}{2}, \frac{5}{4}, \frac{11}{6}$
19. $\frac{5}{3}, \frac{35}{15}, 2\frac{2}{5}, \frac{15}{16}$

20. **Commercials** During a 30 minute TV show, there are 8 minutes of commercials. During a 2 hour movie, there are 31 minutes of commercials. Write each commercial time as a fraction of the total time. Which TV program has a greater fraction of commercial time?

21. **Writing** Explain how comparing fractions with like denominators differs from comparing fractions with unlike denominators.

HELP with Homework

Example	Exercises
1	11-16
2	17-19, 22, 23
3	11-16, 20

Online Resources
CLASSZONE.COM
· More Examples
· eTutorial Plus

HELP with Solving

A negative fraction can be written in various ways. For example,

$-\frac{a}{b} = \frac{a}{-b} = \frac{-a}{b}$.

Write the numbers in order from least to greatest.

22. $7\frac{1}{4}, \frac{31}{4}, \frac{63}{8}, \frac{47}{6}, 7\frac{19}{24}$

23. $\frac{-34}{3}, -11\frac{7}{12}, -11\frac{17}{48}, \frac{-23}{2}, \frac{-47}{4}$

Copy and complete the statement with <, >, or = by first comparing each fraction to $\frac{1}{2}$.

24. $\frac{25}{50} \ \underline{?} \ \frac{37}{74}$

25. $\frac{17}{30} \ \underline{?} \ \frac{10}{33}$

26. $\frac{23}{100} \ \underline{?} \ \frac{19}{36}$

27. **Critical Thinking** In Exercises 24–26, does it help to compare each number to $\frac{1}{2}$ first? Will this step always work? If not, could you use another fraction to help make comparisons?

28. **Little League** Teams from California have played in the Little League World Series 19 times and won the championship 5 times. Texas teams have appeared in 7 Little League World Series and won twice. Which state has won a greater fraction of their World Series games?

29. **Challenge** Consider the fractions $\frac{1}{2x}$ and $\frac{1}{x}$. What is their LCD? Write each fraction using the LCD.

Mixed Review

30. Find the area of the figure at the right. *(Lesson 3.5)*

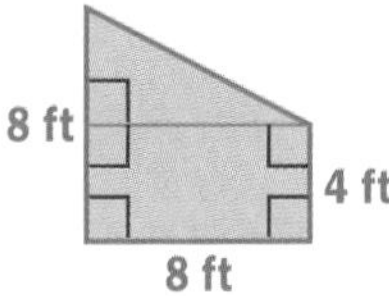

31. Write the prime factorization of 336. *(Lesson 4.1)*

32. **Basic Skills** Find the quotient of 1998 and 42. Round your answer to the nearest thousandth.

Test-Taking Practice

INTERNET
State Test Practice
CLASSZONE.COM

33. **Multiple Choice** Which list of fractions is written correctly in order from least to greatest?

A. $\frac{12}{18}, \frac{13}{30}, \frac{8}{15}$ **B.** $\frac{4}{18}, \frac{9}{15}, \frac{18}{27}$ **C.** $\frac{6}{10}, \frac{4}{18}, \frac{16}{24}$ **D.** $\frac{7}{11}, \frac{7}{8}, \frac{15}{25}$

34. **Multiple Choice** In a class of 32 people, 28 were at school, so $\frac{28}{32}$ of the class was present. What is another way to express this number?

F. $\frac{4}{8}$ **G.** $\frac{24}{28}$ **H.** $\frac{7}{8}$ **I.** $\frac{15}{16}$

Rules of Exponents

BEFORE

You multiplied and divided numerical expressions.

Now

You'll multiply and divide expressions with exponents.

WHY?

So you can compare the memory in two computers, as in Exs. 49–50.

Review Words

exponent, p. 20
power, p. 20

INDIANA Academic Standards

- Number Sense (8.1.5)

Activity **Using patterns to discover rules for multiplying powers.**

1 Copy and complete the table.

Expression	Expanded Expression	Number of Factors	Product as a Power
$2^2 \cdot 2^4$	$(2 \cdot 2) \cdot (2 \cdot 2 \cdot 2 \cdot 2)$	6	2^6
$3^3 \cdot 3^1$	$(3 \cdot 3 \cdot 3) \cdot 3$	?	$3^?$
$7^2 \cdot 7^3$	?	?	?

2 How are the exponents in the first and last columns related?

3 Write the product $6^5 \cdot 6^{11}$ as a single power.

As you saw in the activity, you can expand expressions to find their product. The following equation suggests a rule for multiplying powers with the same base when the exponents are integers.

$$a^4 \cdot a^2 = \underbrace{\overbrace{(a \cdot a \cdot a \cdot a)}^{\text{4 factors}} \cdot \overbrace{(a \cdot a)}^{\text{2 factors}}}_{\text{6 factors}} = a^{4+2} = a^6$$

Product of Powers Property

Words To multiply powers with the same base, add their exponents.

Algebra $a^m \cdot a^n = a^{m+n}$ **Numbers** $5^6 \cdot 5^3 = 5^{6+3} = 5^9$

EXAMPLE 1 Using the Product of Powers Property

$x^4 \cdot x^7 = x^{4+7}$ **Product of powers property**

$= x^{11}$ **Add exponents.**

Watch Out!

Remember that numbers raised to the first power are usually written without an exponent. For example, $3 = 3^1$.

EXAMPLE 2 Using the Product of Powers Property

$3^2x^2 \cdot 3x^3 = (3^2 \cdot 3) \cdot (x^2 \cdot x^3)$	Commutative property of multiplication
$= 3^{2+1} \cdot x^{2+3}$	Product of powers property
$= 3^3x^5$	Add exponents.
$= 27x^5$	Evaluate the power.

The following equation suggests a rule for dividing powers with the same base when the exponents are integers.

$$\frac{a^5}{a^3} = \frac{\overbrace{a \cdot a \cdot a \cdot a \cdot a}^{\text{5 factors}}}{\underbrace{a \cdot a \cdot a}_{\text{3 factors}}} = \frac{a \cdot a \cdot \cancel{a}^1 \cdot \cancel{a}^1 \cdot \cancel{a}^1}{\cancel{a}_1 \cdot \cancel{a}_1 \cdot \cancel{a}_1} = \overbrace{a \cdot a}^{\text{2 factors}} = a^{5-3} = a^2$$

Quotient of Powers Property

Words To divide two powers with the same nonzero base, subtract the exponent of the denominator from the exponent of the numerator.

Algebra $\frac{a^m}{a^n} = a^{m-n}$ **Numbers** $\frac{4^7}{4^4} = 4^{7-4} = 4^3$

EXAMPLE 3 Using the Quotient of Powers Property

Simplify the expression. Write your answer as a power.

a. $\frac{x^{12}}{x^7} = x^{12-7}$ Quotient of powers property

$= x^5$ Subtract exponents.

b. $\frac{9^7}{9^3} = 9^{7-3}$ Quotient of powers property

$= 9^4$ Subtract exponents.

Your turn now **Simplify the expression. Write your answer as a power.**

1. $a^6 \cdot a^4$ **2.** $2^3 \cdot 2^4$ **3.** $\frac{a^6}{a^4}$ **4.** $\frac{10^9}{10^6}$

Watch Out!

The bases of the powers must be the same to use the product or quotient property. In part (b) of Example 4, you cannot simplify the numerator any further because the bases, x and y, are different.

EXAMPLE 4 **Simplifying Fractions with Powers**

a. $\frac{y^4 \cdot y}{y^3} = \frac{y^5}{y^3}$ Simplify numerator using product of powers property.

$= y^{5-3}$ Quotient of powers property

$= y^2$ Subtract exponents.

b. $\frac{xy^4}{y^3} = xy^{4-3}$ Quotient of powers property

$= xy$ Subtract exponents.

Your turn now Simplify the expression. Write your answer as a power.

5. $\frac{q^3 \cdot q^5}{q^4}$ **6.** $\frac{4^3 \cdot 4^{12}}{4^5}$ **7.** $\frac{a^2b^8}{b^2}$ **8.** $\frac{x^5y^{11}}{y^5}$

4.6 Exercises

More Practice, p. 730

Getting Ready to Practice

Vocabulary **Copy and complete the statement.**

1. Three is the _?_ of the expression 3^4.
2. Seven is the _?_ of the expression 4^7.

Tell whether the product of powers property can be used to simplify the expression.

3. $9^3 \cdot 9^4$ **4.** $7^2 \cdot 2^7$ **5.** $r^6 \cdot s^6$ **6.** $n^5 \cdot n^8$

Simplify the expression. Write your answer as a power.

7. $4^2 \cdot 4^4$ **8.** $8 \cdot 8^3$ **9.** $a^5 \cdot a^7$ **10.** $b^9 \cdot b^9$

11. $\frac{c^6}{c^5}$ **12.** $\frac{5^8}{5^4}$ **13.** $\frac{8^7}{8^2}$ **14.** $\frac{d^8}{d}$

15. Find the Error Describe and correct the error in the solution.

X $2^2 \cdot 2^4 = (2 \cdot 2)^{2+4}$
$= 4^6$

Example	Exercises
1	16-19, 24-27, 32, 33
2	36-39
3	20-23, 28-31, 34, 35
4	40-43

CLASSZONE.COM

- More Examples
- eTutorial Plus

Practice and Problem Solving

Simplify the expression.

16. $u^7 \cdot u^8$ **17.** $v^2 \cdot v^{10}$ **18.** $b^9 \cdot b^6$ **19.** $m^{11} \cdot m^8$

20. $\frac{a^4}{a}$ **21.** $\frac{x^{10}}{x^6}$ **22.** $\frac{w^{15}}{w^9}$ **23.** $\frac{y^{20}}{y^{18}}$

Simplify the expression. Write your answer as a power.

24. $3^2 \cdot 3^4$ **25.** $(-4)^2 \cdot (-4)^3$ **26.** $5^4 \cdot 5$ **27.** $7^2 \cdot 7^2$

28. $\frac{(-7)^7}{(-7)^4}$ **29.** $\frac{2^{13}}{2^3}$ **30.** $\frac{6^{11}}{6^8}$ **31.** $\frac{9^8}{9^4}$

Determine the number that correctly completes the equation.

32. $2^3 \cdot 2^? = 2^{11}$ **33.** $5^4 \cdot ?^5 = 5^9$ **34.** $\frac{8^7}{8^?} = 8^3$ **35.** $\frac{12^?}{12^5} = 12^4$

Simplify the expression.

36. $3a^3 \cdot 3a^2$ **37.** $2y^3 \cdot 2y^2$ **38.** $3^2x^5 \cdot 3^3x^4$ **39.** $4a^3b^4 \cdot 4^2a^4b^6$

40. $\frac{p^5q^9}{pq^5}$ **41.** $\frac{z^6 \cdot z^3}{z^4}$ **42.** $\frac{3^3m^9}{3^2m^5}$ **43.** $\frac{5^5n^{15}}{5^3n^{12}}$

44. **Critical Thinking** Write a quotient that simplifies to x^4y^4.

Measurement In Exercises 45–48, use the table. It shows the number of meters in some metric measures written as powers of ten.

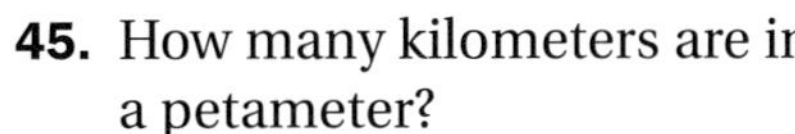

45. How many kilometers are in a petameter?

46. How many gigameters are in a zettameter?

47. How many terameters are in a yottameter?

48. How many megameters are in an exameter?

Metric Units

Unit	Meters
Yottameter	10^{24}
Zettameter	10^{21}
Exameter	10^{18}
Petameter	10^{15}
Terameter	10^{12}
Gigameter	10^9
Megameter	10^6
Kilometer	10^3
Decameter	10^1

Computers In the 1970s and early 1980s, computer random access memory was measured in kilobytes (KB) and could be added only in quantities equal to a power of 2. In Exercises 49 and 50, how many times more memory did the newer computer have?

49. 1979: 2^3 KB; 1980: 2^5 KB **50.** 1982: 2^6 KB; 1987: 2^9 KB

Measurement

The distance to the Andromeda Galaxy is 21 quintillion kilometers, which is 21 followed by 18 zeros. How many exameters are in 21 quintillion kilometers?

Challenge **Evaluate the expression.**

51. $(3^2 \cdot 3)^2$ **52.** $(2^0 \cdot 2^2)^3$ **53.** $\left(\frac{4^7}{4^5}\right)^2$ **54.** $\left(\frac{5^8}{5^7}\right)^4$

Mixed Review

Evaluate the expression. *(Lesson 1.4)*

55. $(4 \times 3)^2 + 13$ **56.** $405 \div (14 - 11)^4$ **57.** $96 \div 2^5 \times 6$

Copy and complete the statement with <, >, or =. *(Lesson 4.5)*

58. $\frac{5}{2} \underline{?} \frac{15}{6}$ **59.** $\frac{9}{24} \underline{?} \frac{5}{16}$ **60.** $\frac{5}{8} \underline{?} \frac{7}{11}$

Test-Taking Practice

61. **Multiple Choice** What is the value of $3^2 \cdot 3^2 - 4^3$?

A. -46 **B.** -17 **C.** 17 **D.** 46

62. **Multiple Choice** What is another expression for $\frac{a^9 \cdot a^4}{a^5}$?

F. a^4 **G.** a^5 **H.** a^8 **I.** a^{13}

Brain Game

Mix and Match

Materials: cards marked from 1 to 6

Number of Players: 2 or 3 players

Winning Strategy: Make the largest number possible in each round.

Mix the cards and place them face down on a flat surface. Each player takes two cards. Then using only the two cards, make the largest number possible. For example, if you picked the cards 2 and 6, you could make the following numbers:

26 62 2^6 6^2

The largest number you can make is 2^6, or 64. So, you would score 64 points for that round. After each round, reshuffle the cards to play another round.

The player with the highest score after three rounds wins.

Negative and Zero Exponents

BEFORE	Now	WHY?
You simplified expressions with positive exponents.	You'll simplify expressions with negative exponents.	So you can describe very small objects, as in Ex. 31.

In the Real World

Review Words

exponent, p. 20
common factor, p. 173

INDIANA Academic Standards

- Number Sense (8.1.4)

Strobes The picture at the right was taken using a strobe light. The flash of the strobe light lasted about 1 microsecond. How can you write this time in seconds as a power of ten? You will see how to solve this problem in Example 1.

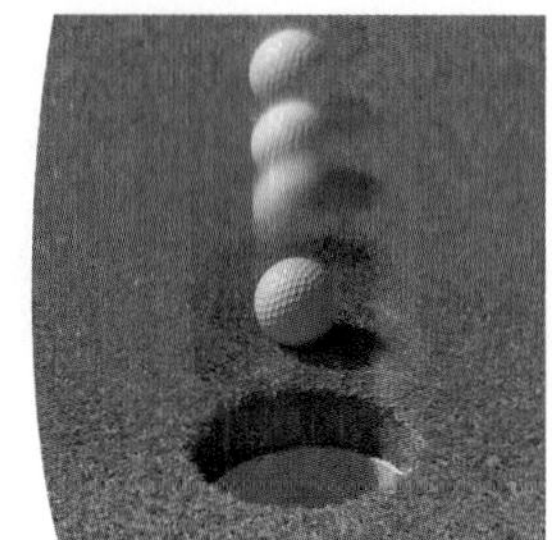

You have seen two methods for evaluating expressions involving division of powers.

Divide out common factors.

$$\frac{x^5}{x^7} = \frac{\overset{1}{\cancel{x}} \cdot \overset{1}{\cancel{x}} \cdot \overset{1}{\cancel{x}} \cdot \overset{1}{\cancel{x}} \cdot \overset{1}{\cancel{x}}}{\underset{1}{\cancel{x}} \cdot \underset{1}{\cancel{x}} \cdot \underset{1}{\cancel{x}} \cdot \underset{1}{\cancel{x}} \cdot \underset{1}{\cancel{x}} \cdot x \cdot x} = \frac{1}{x^2}$$

Quotient of powers property

$$\frac{x^5}{x^7} = x^{5-7} = x^{-2}$$

So $\frac{1}{x^2} = x^{-2}$, which suggests the definition for negative exponents.

Negative Exponents

Words For any integer n and any number $a \neq 0$, a^{-n} is equal to $\frac{1}{a^n}$.

Algebra $a^{-n} = \frac{1}{a^n}$

Numbers $2^{-3} = \frac{1}{2^3}$

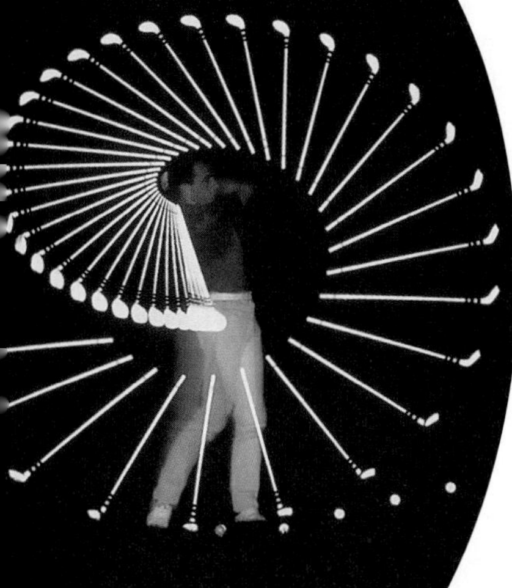

EXAMPLE 1 Using a Negative Exponent

The flash above lasts 1 microsecond, or $\frac{1}{1,000,000}$ second.

$\frac{1}{1,000,000} = \frac{1}{10^6}$ **Write 1,000,000 as 10^6.**

$= 10^{-6}$ **Definition of negative exponent**

ANSWER One flash of a strobe light lasts about 10^{-6} second.

EXAMPLE 2 Evaluating a Numerical Expression

$5^2 \cdot 5^{-5} = 5^{2+(-5)}$ Product of powers property

$= 5^{-3}$ Simplify.

$= \frac{1}{5^3} = \frac{1}{125}$ Use definition of negative exponent and evaluate power.

Zero Exponents

Algebra If a is a nonzero number, then $a^0 = 1$.

Numbers $2^0 = 1$

Watch Out!

In an expression such as $-2n^0$ and $4n^{-5}$, the exponent is applied only to the variable, not to the coefficient.

EXAMPLE 3 Simplifying Variable Expressions

Simplify. Write the expression using only positive exponents.

a. $-2n^0 = -2 \cdot n^0$ Zero exponent applies only to n.

$= -2 \cdot 1$ Definition of zero exponent

$= -2$ Multiply.

b. $4n^{-5} = 4 \cdot n^{-5}$ Exponent applies only to n.

$= 4 \cdot \frac{1}{n^5}$ Definition of negative exponent

$= \frac{4}{n^5}$ Multiply.

c. $\frac{8x^{-3}}{x} = \frac{8 \cdot x^{-3}}{x^1}$ Exponent applies only to x.

$= 8 \cdot x^{-3-1}$ Quotient of powers property

$= 8 \cdot x^{-4}$ Simplify.

$= \frac{8}{x^4}$ Definition of negative exponent

Your turn now Evaluate the expression.

1. 7^{-2} **2.** $(-2)^{-5}$ **3.** $6 \cdot 6^{-3}$ **4.** $10^{-5} \cdot 10^7$

Simplify. Write the expression using only positive exponents.

5. $-6m^{-1}$ **6.** $b^2 \cdot b^{-2}$ **7.** $\frac{5x^4}{x^7}$ **8.** $\frac{10a^{-3}}{a^4}$

INTERNET eWorkbook Plus CLASSZONE.COM

Getting Ready to Practice

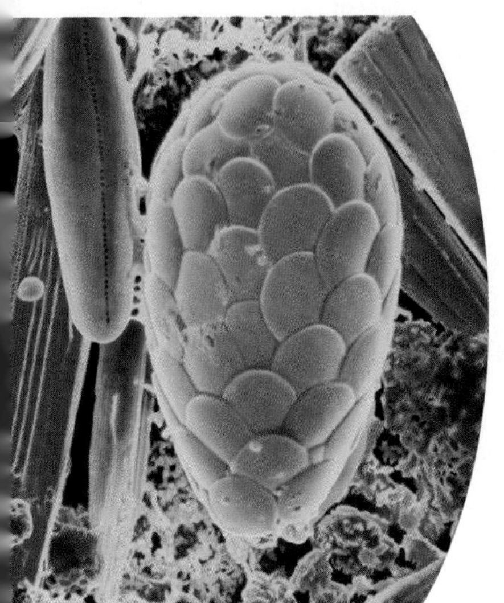

Single-celled alga

Vocabulary Determine whether the statement is *true* or *false*.

1. The base of the expression 2^{-5} is 2.
2. The exponent of the expression 2^{-5} is 5.

Evaluate the expression.

3. 3^{-4} 4. $(-4)^{-3}$ 5. $2^{-10} \cdot 2^{6}$ 6. 12^{0}

7. **Find the Error** Describe and correct the error in the solution.

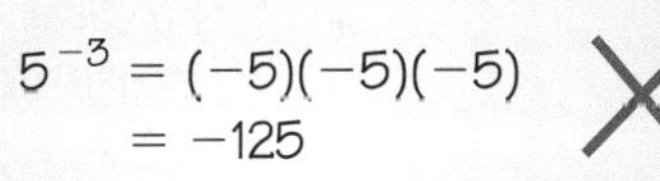

$$5^{-3} = (-5)(-5)(-5)$$
$$= -125$$

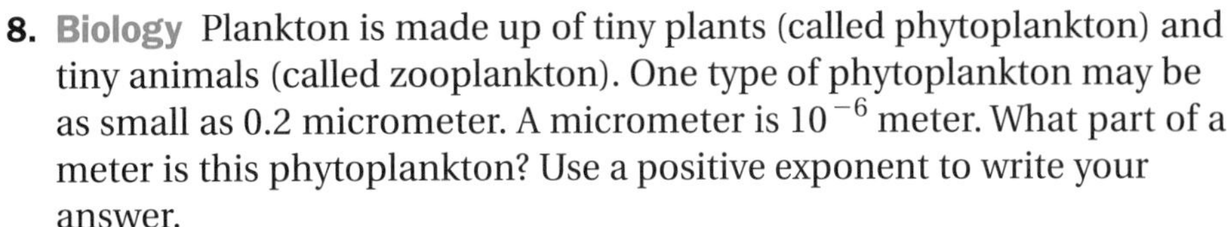

8. **Biology** Plankton is made up of tiny plants (called phytoplankton) and tiny animals (called zooplankton). One type of phytoplankton may be as small as 0.2 micrometer. A micrometer is 10^{-6} meter. What part of a meter is this phytoplankton? Use a positive exponent to write your answer.

Practice and Problem Solving

HELP with Homework

Example	Exercises
1	21, 31
2	9-12
3	13-20

Online Resources CLASSZONE.COM
· More Examples
· eTutorial Plus

Evaluate the expression.

9. $(-6)^{-2}$ 10. $2 \cdot 2^{-6}$ 11. $5^{4} \cdot 5^{-8}$ 12. 9^{0}

Simplify. Write the expression using only positive exponents.

13. $m^{-9} \cdot m^{5}$ 14. $x^{5} \cdot x^{-5}$ 15. $9n^{-3}$ 16. $c^{-1} \cdot c^{-2} \cdot c^{-4}$

17. $b^{3} \cdot b^{-4} \cdot b^{-5}$ 18. $\frac{4z^{-2}}{z^{4}}$ 19. $\frac{a^{-5}}{a^{8}}$ 20. $\frac{18r^{-6}}{3r^{3}}$

21. **Physics** Pressure is measured in units called *pascals*. This unit can be expressed as $\text{kg} \cdot \text{m}^{-1} \cdot \text{s}^{-2}$. Write the unit without negative exponents.

Find the missing exponent.

22. $(4x^{5})^{?} = 1$ 23. $15a^{?} = \frac{15}{a^{8}}$ 24. $y^{?} \cdot y^{4} = \frac{1}{y}$ 25. $\frac{x^{-3}}{x^{?}} = \frac{1}{x^{13}}$

26. **Writing** Your friend missed today's class. Write a note to show your friend how to simplify the expression $\frac{6a^{-3}}{a^{3}}$.

Measurement In Exercises 27–30, use the table. It shows the number of meters in some metric measures written as powers of ten.

Metric Units	
Unit	Meter
Decimeter	10^{-1}
Centimeter	10^{-2}
Millimeter	10^{-3}
Micrometer	10^{-6}
Nanometer	10^{-9}
Picometer	10^{-12}
Attometer	10^{-18}
Yoctometer	10^{-24}

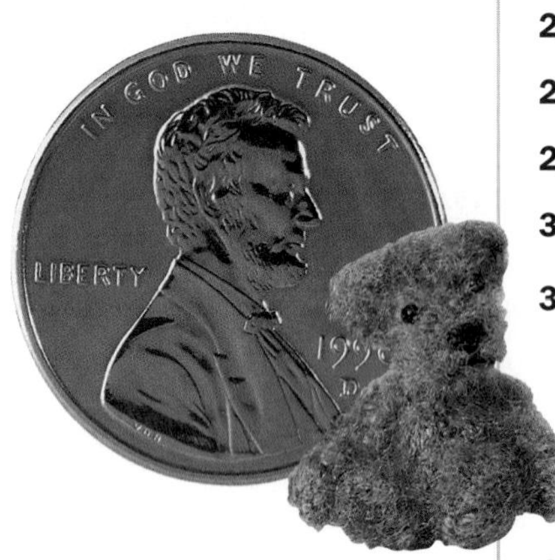

27. How many picometers are in a decimeter?
28. How many yoctometers are in a micrometer?
29. How many nanometers are in a decimeter?
30. How many attometers are in a centimeter?
31. **Teddy Bear** In 1997, German teddy bear specialist Hanne Schramm made the smallest teddy bear in the world. It measures 0.47 inch or about 10 millimeters. How many nanometers are in 10 millimeters?

Critical Thinking In Exercises 32–33, copy and complete the statement using *always, sometimes,* or *never.*

32. A power with a negative exponent can _?_ be written as a fraction.
33. A power with a positive base and a negative exponent is _?_ negative.
34. **Challenge** Use the product of powers property to explain why $a^0 = 1$, where a is a nonzero number, makes sense.

Mixed Review 

Simplify the expression. *(Lessons 2.2–2.5)*

35. $-18 + (-7)$
36. $-46 + 0$
37. $34 - (-18)$
38. $16 - 30$
39. $-6 \cdot (-15)$
40. $0(-8)$
41. $51 \div (-3)$
42. $-18 \div (-9)$

Basic Skills Find the unknown number.

43. _?_ $+ 8 = 7$
44. $9 \times$ _?_ $= 108$
45. _?_ $\div 12 = 6$

Test-Taking Practice 

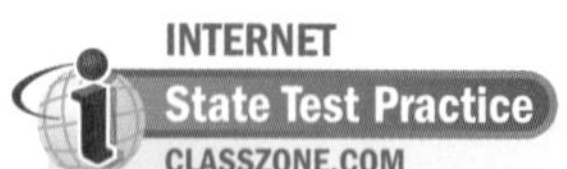

46. **Multiple Choice** Simplify the expression $\left(\frac{8^{-2}}{8}\right)^0$.

A. $\frac{1}{512}$ B. $\frac{1}{8}$ C. 1 D. 8

47. **Multiple Choice** Simplify the expression $\frac{-3x^{-4}}{x^2}$.

F. $\frac{-3}{x^6}$ G. $-3x^6$ H. $\frac{-3}{x^{-6}}$ I. $\frac{-3x}{x^6}$

Scientific Notation

BEFORE	Now	WHY?
You multiplied numbers by powers of 10.	You'll read and write numbers using scientific notation.	So you can find the number of new \$1 bills printed, as in Ex. 39.

In the Real World

scientific notation, p. 205

INDIANA
Academic Standards
- Number Sense (8.1.1)

Bubbles The brilliant colors observed in soap bubbles occur as a result of light reflecting from the inner and outer surfaces of the bubble. The thickness of a soap bubble is about 0.000004 meter. How can you use the powers of 10 to write 0.000004? You will see how to solve this problem in Example 1, part (a).

One way to write very small or very large numbers is to use *scientific notation.*

Using Scientific Notation

A number is written in **scientific notation** if it has the form $c \times 10^n$ where $1 \le c < 10$ and n is an integer.

Standard form	Product form	Scientific notation
325,000	$3.25 \times 100{,}000$	3.25×10^5
0.0005	5×0.0001	5×10^{-4}

Powers of ten
$10^5 = 100{,}000$
$10^4 = 10{,}000$
$10^3 = 1000$
$10^2 = 100$
$10^1 = 10$
$10^0 = 1$
$10^{-1} = 0.1$
$10^{-2} = 0.01$
$10^{-3} = 0.001$
$10^{-4} = 0.0001$
$10^{-5} = 0.00001$

EXAMPLE 1 Writing Numbers in Scientific Notation

a. The thickness of a soap bubble is about 0.0000004 meter.

Standard form	Product form	Scientific notation
0.000004	4×0.000001	4×10^{-6}
Move decimal point 6 places to the right.		Exponent is −6.

b. There are over 300,000,000,000 stars in the Andromeda Galaxy.

Standard form	Product form	Scientific notation
300,000,000,000	$3 \times 100{,}000{,}000{,}000$	3×10^{11}
Move decimal point 11 places to the left.		Exponent is 11.

EXAMPLE 2 Writing Numbers in Standard Form

	Scientific notation	Product form	Standard form
a.	7.2×10^5	$7.2 \times 100{,}000$	720,000
	Exponent is 5.		Move decimal point 5 places to the right.
b.	4.65×10^{-7}	4.65×0.0000001	0.000000465
	Exponent is −7.		Move decimal point 7 places to the left.

Your turn now **Write the number in scientific notation.**

1. 4000 **2.** 7,300,000 **3.** 63,000,000,000

4. 0.00475 **5.** 0.00000526 **6.** 0.0000000082

Write the number in standard form.

7. 3.5×10^3 **8.** 2.48×10^6 **9.** 6×10^{11}

10. 5.1×10^{-4} **11.** 9.16×10^{-2} **12.** 1.02×10^{-8}

You can use the product of powers property to multiply two numbers written in scientific notation.

Watch Out!

When a number is in scientific notation, the factor c must be greater than or equal to 1 and less than 10. The number 28.35×10^{10} is not written in scientific notation because $28.35 > 10$.

EXAMPLE 3 Multiplying Numbers in Scientific Notation

Find the product $(4.5 \times 10^3) \times (6.3 \times 10^7)$.

Solution

$(4.5 \times 10^3) \times (6.3 \times 10^7)$

$= 4.5 \times 6.3 \times 10^3 \times 10^7$ Commutative property of multiplication

$= (4.5 \times 6.3) \times (10^3 \times 10^7)$ Associative property of multiplication

$= 28.35 \times 10^{10}$ Product of powers property

$= 2.835 \times 10^1 \times 10^{10}$ Write 28.35 in scientific notation.

$= 2.835 \times 10^{11}$ Product of powers property

Your turn now **Write the product in scientific notation.**

13. $(1.25 \times 10^6) \times (7.6 \times 10^{12})$ **14.** $(8 \times 10^5) \times (5.65 \times 10^4)$

4.8 Exercises

More Practice, p. 730

Getting Ready to Practice

Vocabulary Tell whether the number is expressed in scientific notation.

1. 9.32×10^5 **2.** 56.8×10^2 **3.** 7×10^{-4}

Write the number in scientific notation.

4. 89,200,000,000 **5.** 0.468 **6.** 0.0000671

Write the number in standard form.

7. 4.35×10^6 **8.** 5.72×10^{-3} **9.** 9.62×10^7

10. **Guided Problem Solving** The mass of Earth is about 1.3×10^{25} pounds. The mass of Jupiter is about 4.2×10^{27} pounds. About how many times greater is Jupiter's mass than Earth's mass?

(1 Write the quotient of 4.2 and 1.3 as a decimal.

(2 Write the quotient of the powers of 10.

(3 Write the product of the quotients in scientific notation.

Practice and Problem Solving

HELP with Homework

Example	Exercises
1	11–16, 27
2	17–22, 28
3	23–26

· More Examples
· eTutorial Plus

Write the number in scientific notation.

11. 7900 **12.** 8,100,000,000 **13.** 2,130,000

14. 0.0312 **15.** 0.000000415 **16.** 0.0000000342

Write the number in standard form.

17. 8.71×10^{-2} **18.** 6.35×10^{-6} **19.** 1.76×10^{-9}

20. 4.13×10^9 **21.** 2.83×10^{12} **22.** 3.61×10^7

Write the product in scientific notation.

23. $(3 \times 10^3) \times (2 \times 10^5)$ **24.** $(8 \times 10^6) \times (7 \times 10^4)$

25. $(7.8 \times 10^6) \times (8.4 \times 10^7)$ **26.** $(3.6 \times 10^8) \times (5.2 \times 10^5)$

27. **Well Water** In the United States, 15,000,000 households use private wells for their water supply. Write this number in scientific notation.

28. **State Parks** The United States has a total of 1.2916×10^7 acres of land reserved for state parks. Write this number in standard form.

29. **Number Sense** Explain how you can tell whether a number is very small or very large when the number is written in scientific notation.

Copy and complete the statement with <, >, or =.

30. 6.92×10^{11} _?_ 6.92×10^{12}

31. 3.67×10^{-3} _?_ 3.76×10^{-4}

Find the product or quotient. Write your answer in scientific notation.

32. $(6.8 \times 10^{-2}) \times (3.9 \times 10^{-5})$

33. $(2.6 \times 10^{7}) \times (4.1 \times 10^{-3})$

34. $(7.6 \times 10^{-8}) \times (4.8 \times 10^{-6})$

35. $(5.4 \times 10^{-5}) \times (3.6 \times 10^{-9})$

36. $\dfrac{4.08 \times 10^{6}}{3.4 \times 10^{2}}$

37. $\dfrac{2.765 \times 10^{21}}{7.9 \times 10^{9}}$

38. $\dfrac{5.46 \times 10^{28}}{6.5 \times 10^{24}}$

39. **U.S. Currency** The United States Bureau of Engraving and Printing prints about 17 million new $1 bills each day. About how many bills are printed in one week? in one year? Write your answers in scientific notation.

40. **Critical Thinking** Order the numbers from least to greatest.

3.75×10^{8} 37,500,000 3.57×10^{9} 5.37×10^{7}

41. **Science** The radius of a proton is about 1.2 Fermis. One Fermi is equal to 10^{-15} meter. How many centimeters is the radius of a proton? Write your answer in scientific notation.

42. **Challenge** Light travels 1.86×10^{5} miles in 1 second. How far does light travel in one year?

U.S. Currency

The United States Bureau of Engraving and Printing prints about 4,440,000 new $5 bills each day. What is the dollar value of these bills?

Mixed Review

In Exercises 43–44, evaluate the expression. *(Lessons 2.2, 2.3)*

43. $-8 + 12 + (-16) + 18$

44. $34 - (-43) - (3 - 6)$

45. Simplify $\dfrac{6n}{9mn}$. *(Lesson 4.3)*

46. **Basic Skills** Find the amount of time that has elapsed from 10:46 A.M. to 3:13 P.M.

Test-Taking Practice

INTERNET
State Test Practice
CLASSZONE.COM

47. **Multiple Choice** In 2000, there were approximately 281,000,000 people in the United States. Which of the following is *not* another way of expressing the number 281,000,000?

A. 28.1 million **B.** 0.281 billion **C.** 28.1×10^{7} **D.** 2.81×10^{8}

48. **Short Response** A space probe travels about 1.5×10^{6} miles per day to its destination 21 million miles away. It has already traveled 9 million miles. About how many days of travel does it have left?

CALCULATOR

4.8 Technology Activity

INDIANA: Academic Standards
- Number Sense (8.1.1)

Using Scientific Notation

GOAL Use a calculator to perform operations on numbers written in scientific notation.

Example **The Sun is about 1.5×10^8 kilometers from Earth, and Proxima Centauri is about 2.5×10^5 times farther from Earth than the Sun. How far is Proxima Centauri from Earth?**

Solution

To find how far Proxima Centauri is from Earth, multiply the distance between the Sun and Earth by 2.5×10^5.

HELP with Technology

The EE key on a calculator means "times 10 raised to the power of."

Keystrokes	**Display**
1.5 EE 8 × 2.5 EE 5 =	3.75 x10 13

ANSWER Proxima Centauri is approximately 3.75×10^{13} kilometers from Earth.

Your turn now **Use a calculator to evaluate the expression. Write your answer in scientific notation.**

1. $(3.19 \times 10^7) \times (8.5 \times 10^6)$
2. $(6.7 \times 10^{-3}) \times (1.12 \times 10^{15})$
3. $(3.3 \times 10^{-3}) \times (4.8 \times 10^{-9})$
4. $(7.1 \times 10^{-9}) \times (2.05 \times 10^6)$
5. $\dfrac{8.1 \times 10^{10}}{3.02 \times 10^3}$
6. $\dfrac{1.44 \times 10^{-15}}{1.6 \times 10}$
7. $\dfrac{2.8 \times 10^{-11}}{2.05 \times 10^{-4}}$
8. **Water** About 110 billion gallons of water flow through Lake Erie each day. How many gallons of water flow through Lake Erie in a week? in a year?
9. **Biology** The nucleus of a human cell is about 7×10^{-6} meter in diameter. A ribosome, another part of a cell, is about 3×10^{-8} meter in diameter. How many times larger is a nucleus than a ribosome?

Notebook Review

Review the vocabulary definitions in your notebook.

Copy the review examples in your notebook. Then complete the exercises.

Check Your Definitions

least common denominator (LCD), p. 192 scientific notation, p. 205

Use Your Vocabulary

1. Copy and complete: A number is written in _?_ if it has the form $c \times 10^n$ where $1 \le c < 10$ and n is an integer.

4.5 Can you compare and order fractions?

EXAMPLE Compare $\frac{11}{18}$ and $\frac{3}{4}$.

The LCM of 18 and 4 is 36, so the least common denominator is 36.

$\frac{11}{18} = \frac{11 \cdot 2}{18 \cdot 2} = \frac{22}{36}$ $\frac{3}{4} = \frac{3 \cdot 9}{4 \cdot 9} = \frac{27}{36}$

ANSWER Because $\frac{22}{36} < \frac{27}{36}$, you can write $\frac{11}{18} < \frac{3}{4}$.

☑ **Copy and complete the statement with <, >, or =.**

2. $\frac{2}{3}$ _?_ $\frac{5}{9}$ **3.** $\frac{5}{12}$ _?_ $\frac{1}{3}$ **4.** $\frac{4}{5}$ _?_ $\frac{6}{7}$ **5.** $\frac{16}{24}$ _?_ $\frac{20}{30}$

4.6 Can you use the rules of exponents?

EXAMPLE Multiply or divide. Write your answer as a power.

a. $x^7 \cdot x^8 = x^{7+8}$

$= x^{15}$

b. $\frac{a^6}{a^3} = a^{6-3}$

$= a^3$

☑ **Simplify. Write your answer as a power.**

6. $n^4 \cdot n^9$ **7.** $y^6 \cdot y^{10}$ **8.** $\frac{x^7}{x^5}$ **9.** $\frac{c^{12}}{c^8}$

4.7 Can you use negative exponents?

EXAMPLE Write $x^{-4} \cdot x^{-3}$ using only positive exponents.

$$x^{-4} \cdot x^{-3} = x^{-4 + (-3)} = x^{-7} = \frac{1}{x^7}$$

☑ **Simplify. Write the expression using only positive exponents.**

10. $12a^{-5}$ **11.** $n^7 \cdot n^{-10}$ **12.** $\frac{m^{-6}}{m^5}$ **13.** $\frac{c^{-9}}{c^4}$

4.8 Can you write a number in scientific notation?

EXAMPLE Write the number in scientific notation.

a. $980{,}000{,}000 = 9.8 \times 10^8$ **b.** $0.000012 = 1.2 \times 10^{-5}$

☑ **Write the number in scientific notation.**

14. 34,600,000,000 **15.** 0.0000009 **16.** 0.000000000502

Stop and Think about Lessons 4.5–4.8

17. Writing Explain how to find the product $(5 \times 10^9) \times (4 \times 10^{15})$ without using a calculator.

Review Quiz 2

Copy and complete the statement with <, >, or =.

1. $\frac{2}{5} \underline{?} \frac{6}{15}$ **2.** $\frac{5}{6} \underline{?} \frac{4}{9}$ **3.** $\frac{9}{15} \underline{?} \frac{5}{9}$ **4.** $\frac{35}{40} \underline{?} \frac{21}{24}$

Order the numbers from least to greatest.

5. $\frac{2}{3}, \frac{5}{6}, \frac{1}{2}, \frac{5}{12}$ **6.** $1\frac{4}{7}, 1\frac{5}{14}, \frac{5}{4}, 1\frac{5}{8}$

Multiple or divide. Write your answer as a power using only positive exponents.

7. $b^2 \cdot b^4$ **8.** $c^5 \cdot c^{-2}$ **9.** $\frac{a^7}{a^2}$ **10.** $\frac{n^{-2}}{n^3}$

11. Popcorn People in the United States eat 1,120,000,000 pounds of popcorn a year. Write this number in scientific notation.

CHAPTER 4

Chapter Review

Vocabulary

prime number, p. 169
composite number, p. 169
prime factorization, p. 169
factor tree, p. 169
monomial, p. 170
common factor, p. 173
greatest common factor (GCF), p. 173
relatively prime, p. 174
simplest form, p. 179
equivalent fractions, p. 179
multiple, p. 186
common multiple, p. 186
least common multiple (LCM), p. 186
least common denominator (LCD), p. 192
scientific notation, p. 205

Vocabulary Review

1. Describe the difference between the *greatest common factor* and the *least common multiple* of two numbers.
2. Give three examples of prime numbers greater than 20.
3. Give three examples of monomials.
4. Describe what it means for two numbers to be relatively prime.

Copy and complete the statement.

5. A fraction is in _?_ if its numerator and denominator have 1 as their GCF.
6. A(n) _?_ is a whole number that has positive factors other than 1 and itself.
7. When you write a number as the product of prime numbers, you are writing its _?_.
8. Two fractions are _?_ if they represent the same number.

Review Questions

Write the prime factorization of the number. *(Lesson 4.1)*

9. 54 **10.** 70 **11.** 150 **12.** 184

Factor the monomial. *(Lesson 4.1)*

13. $19a^2b$ **14.** $28xy^3$ **15.** $56u^2v^2$ **16.** $80p^4q^3$

Find the greatest common factor of the numbers or monomials. *(Lesson 4.2)*

17. 20, 40, 90 **18.** 56, 84, 196 **19.** 48, 60, 165

20. $2x, x^2, x^3$ **21.** $18xy^2, 81xy$ **22.** $54s^4t^4, 164st^3$

Review Questions

Write the fraction in simplest form. *(Lesson 4.3)*

23. $\frac{16}{48}$ **24.** $-\frac{38}{95}$ **25.** $-\frac{32}{102}$ **26.** $\frac{104}{39}$

27. $\frac{3bc}{9b}$ **28.** $-\frac{9abc}{12a}$ **29.** $\frac{20m}{5mn}$ **30.** $\frac{21bcd}{7bc}$

Find the least common multiple of the numbers or monomials. *(Lesson 4.4)*

31. 15, 35 **32.** 180, 240 **33.** $5m^2n^4, 25mn^3$ **34.** $6p^2q^3r^4, 14pq^2r^3$

35. **Fountain** A fountain in an amusement park has special-effect devices called *shooters*. They shoot columns of water at different time intervals. One shooter goes off every 8 seconds while another goes off every 12 seconds. How long after the fountain is turned on will both shooters go off at the same time? *(Lesson 4.4)*

Copy and complete the statement with <, >, or =. *(Lesson 4.5)*

36. $\frac{79}{16} \underline{\ ?\ } \frac{35}{8}$ **37.** $6\frac{2}{3} \underline{\ ?\ } \frac{81}{12}$ **38.** $\frac{161}{9} \underline{\ ?\ } 17\frac{8}{9}$ **39.** $\frac{223}{15} \underline{\ ?\ } 14\frac{4}{5}$

40. **Calories** One serving of rice pilaf has 220 calories, including 35 calories from fat. One serving of soup has 70 calories, including 15 calories from fat. Write the calories from fat as a fraction of the total calories for each food. Which food has a greater fraction of calories from fat? *(Lesson 4.5)*

Simplify the expression. Write your answer as a power. *(Lesson 4.6)*

41. $8 \cdot 8^3$ **42.** $2^2 \cdot 2^5$ **43.** $7^9 \div 7^7$ **44.** $\frac{5^{10}}{5^7}$

Simplify. Write the expression using only positive exponents. *(Lesson 4.7)*

45. $7x^{-4}$ **46.** $a^{-6} \cdot a^4$ **47.** $\frac{8w^{-6}}{24w^2}$ **48.** $\frac{16r^{-2}}{4r^3}$

49. Write 6.58×10^{-4} in standard form. *(Lesson 4.8)*

50. Write 78,900,000,000 in scientific notation. *(Lesson 4.8)*

51. **Niagara Falls** In tourist season, the water at Niagara Falls flows at 100,000 cubic feet per second during the day. How fast does it flow per minute? per hour? Write your answers in scientific notation. *(Lesson 4.8)*

Chapter Test

Write the prime factorization of the number.

1. 49 **2.** 68 **3.** 95 **4.** 112

Find the greatest common factor of the monomials.

5. $3pq, 12pq$ **6.** $12a^2, 18ab$ **7.** $2z^3, 3z^2$ **8.** $14r^2, 42r$

Find the least common multiple of the numbers or monomials.

9. 4, 16, 32 **10.** 18, 24, 36 **11.** $5x^2y, 21xy^3$ **12.** $54pq^2, 63p^3q^3$

Copy and complete the statement with <, >, or =.

13. $\frac{11}{12} \underline{?} \frac{41}{48}$ **14.** $4\frac{3}{6} \underline{?} \frac{9}{2}$ **15.** $8\frac{7}{16} \underline{?} \frac{17}{2}$

16. **Cake** Three equal-sized round layer cakes were served at a party. Each cake was cut into a different number of equal-sized slices. After the guests left, $\frac{1}{8}$ of the yellow cake, $\frac{3}{16}$ of the chocolate cake, and $\frac{1}{6}$ of the carrot cake remained. Which type of cake had the least amount left over? Which had the most? Explain your reasoning.

Simplify the expression. Write your answer as a power.

17. $m^8 \cdot m^3$ **18.** $6^2 \cdot 6^6$ **19.** $\frac{n^{16}}{n^{10}}$

Simplify. Write the expression using only positive exponents.

20. $5x^{-3}$ **21.** $c^{-1} \cdot c^{-7}$ **22.** $\frac{-4u^{-9}}{u^3}$ **23.** $\frac{16a^2b^5}{8a^4b}$

24. **Science** Scientists have created a microfabric using molded plastic. Its narrowest links are $\frac{1}{1,000,000}$ meter. Write this fraction as a power of ten.

Write the product in scientific notation.

25. $(6 \times 10^5) \times (5 \times 10^7)$ **26.** $(8.1 \times 10^4) \times (9.2 \times 10^8)$ **27.** $(4.2 \times 10^{-5}) \times (6 \times 10^{-2})$

Chapter Standardized Test

Test-Taking Strategy Be careful about choosing an answer that seems obvious. Carefully read the problem and all the choices before answering.

Multiple Choice

1. Which number is a prime number?

A. 51 **B.** 67 **C.** 82 **D.** 93

2. What is the greatest common factor of 420 and 385?

F. 5 **G.** 15 **H.** 35 **I.** 4620

3. Which fraction is written in simplest form?

A. $\frac{3}{16}$ **B.** $\frac{4}{10}$ **C.** $\frac{9}{21}$ **D.** $\frac{15}{33}$

4. Two toy cars begin at the starting line of a circular track at the same time. Car A goes around the track every 20 seconds. Car B goes around the track every 8 seconds. In how many seconds will the two cars reach the starting line at the same time?

F. 4 seconds **G.** 24 seconds

H. 40 seconds **I.** 60 seconds

5. Which list is *not* in order from least to greatest?

A. $\frac{1}{4}, \frac{3}{8}, \frac{7}{12}, \frac{2}{3}$

B. $\frac{1}{2}, \frac{3}{4}, \frac{13}{16}, \frac{7}{8}$

C. $1\frac{5}{18}, 1\frac{7}{9}, \frac{17}{12}, \frac{11}{6}$

D. $2\frac{4}{21}, 2\frac{5}{14}, \frac{18}{7}, \frac{17}{6}$

6. Which expression is *not* equal to 5^4?

F. $5^3 \cdot 5$ **G.** $5^2 \cdot 5^2$

H. $\frac{5^8}{5^4}$ **I.** $\frac{5^8}{5^2}$

7. Which number is equal to $\frac{2^9}{2^3}$?

A. 8 **B.** 64 **C.** 520 **D.** 4096

8. Write $\frac{-5x^{-6}}{x^3}$ using only positive exponents.

F. $\frac{-5}{x^9}$ **G.** $\frac{1}{5x^9}$ **H.** $-5x^6$ **I.** $30x^3$

9. Simplify $(5 \times 10^{-7}) \times (3.6 \times 10^4)$.

A. 1.8×10^{-4} **B.** 1.8×10^{-3}

C. 1.8×10^{-2} **D.** 18×10^{-4}

Short Response

10. **Planting Trees** A conservation group wants to plant 48 trees in a rectangular arrangement so that each row has the same number of trees. How many trees can be planted in each row? List all possibilities. Of the possible arrangements, which one is closest to having a length three times its width?

Extended Response

11. **History** The Orb of 1661 is a gold sphere set with 365 diamonds, 363 pearls, 18 rubies, 9 emeralds, 9 sapphires, and 1 amethyst. What is the total number of jewels? What fraction of jewels are rubies? What fraction are emeralds? Write each fraction in simplest form. Jane estimates that about half of the jewels in the Orb are diamonds. Do you agree with this estimate? Explain.

Rational Number Operations

BEFORE

In previous chapters you've...

- Added, subtracted, multiplied, and divided integers
- Interpreted tables and graphs

Now

In Chapter 5 you'll study...

- Performing operations on fractions, mixed numbers, and decimals
- Rewriting fractions and decimals
- Describing data sets using mean, median, mode, and range

WHY?

So you can solve real-world problems about...

- snakes, p. 220
- sledding, p. 226
- rafting, p. 251
- deep sea jellies, p. 257

Internet Preview
CLASSZONE.COM

- eEdition Plus Online
- eWorkbook Plus Online
- eTutorial Plus Online
- State Test Practice
- More Examples

Chapter Warm-Up Games

Review skills you need for this chapter in these quick games.

Scale the Cliff

$\frac{7}{32}$	$\frac{1}{3}$	$\frac{2}{7}$	$\frac{3}{11}$
$\frac{7}{17}$	$\frac{4}{9}$	$\frac{4}{15}$	$\frac{11}{25}$
$\frac{6}{11}$	$\frac{13}{21}$	$\frac{4}{7}$	$\frac{3}{8}$
$\frac{1}{2}$	$\frac{5}{8}$	$\frac{7}{11}$	$\frac{9}{14}$
$\frac{3}{4}$	$\frac{5}{6}$	$\frac{3}{5}$	$\frac{5}{7}$
	$\frac{2}{3}$		

Key Skill:
Comparing fractions

Find the handholds you can use to scale the cliff.

- Start at $\frac{2}{3}$ and move up, selecting a handhold in each row.
- The value of each handhold must be less than the value of the handhold below it.

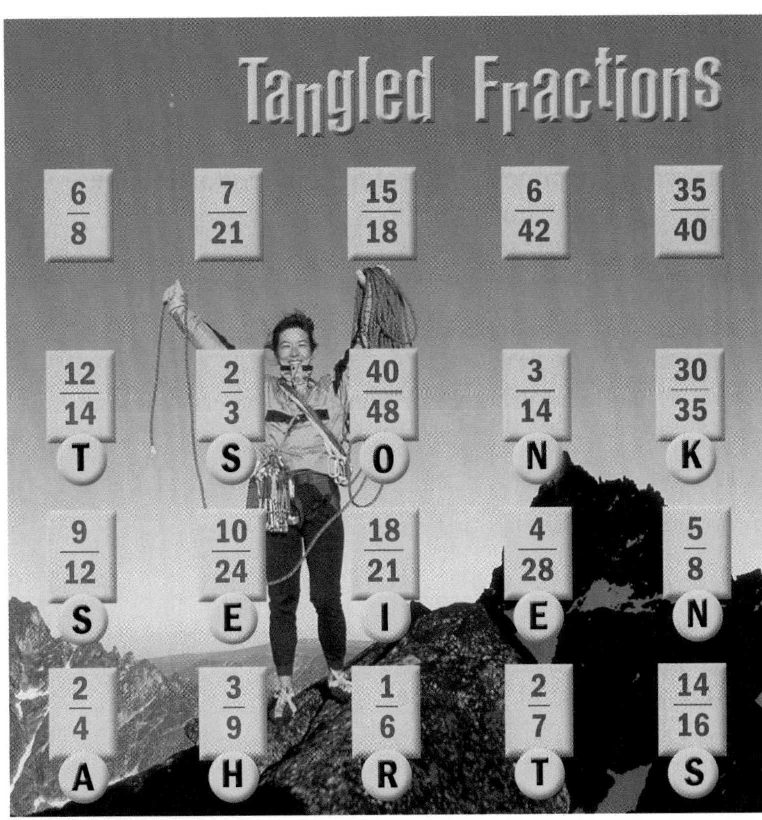

Key Skill:
Identifying equivalent fractions

Susan is going rock climbing. Help her figure out what equipment she is missing.

- In each column, find a fraction equivalent to the top one to decode the name of the equipment Susan is missing.

Stop and Think

1. **Critical Thinking** A student thinks that a fraction cannot be smaller than another fraction if the first fraction's denominator is greater than the second fraction's denominator. Explain why the student is wrong.
2. **Writing** Explain how to tell whether fractions with different denominators are equivalent.

Getting Ready to Learn

Word Watch

Review Words

simplest form, p. 179
least common denominator (LCD), p. 192
improper fraction, p. 707
mixed number, p. 707

Review What You Need to Know 

Using Vocabulary **Copy and complete using a review word.**

1. If 1 is the greatest common factor of the numerator and the denominator, then the fraction is in _?_.

2. A number like $3\frac{4}{7}$, whose value is the sum of a whole number part and a fraction part, is called a(n) _?_.

In Exercises 3–6, find the product or quotient. *(pp. 70, 74)*

3. $-125 \cdot 2$ 4. $-4 \cdot (-23)$ 5. $-39 \div 3$ 6. $-136 \div (-17)$

Write the fraction in simplest form. *(p. 179)*

7. $\frac{4}{12}$ 8. $\frac{35}{50}$ 9. $\frac{12}{32}$ 10. $\frac{24}{52}$ 11. $\frac{14}{49}$

12. You bought a sweater for \$15.65 and a pair of jeans for \$23.95. What was the total cost of your purchase? *(p. 709)*

You should include material that appears on a notebook like this in your own notes.

Know How to Take Notes

Writing Helpful Hints In your notebook, write down any helpful hints your teacher or your textbook gives you for solving problems.

Equivalent Fractions

Write equivalent fractions by multiplying by a fraction that is equal to one.

$$\frac{3}{5} \times \frac{4}{4} = \frac{12}{20} \qquad \frac{3}{5} \times \frac{9}{9} = \frac{27}{45} \qquad \frac{3}{5} \times \frac{100}{100} = \frac{300}{500}$$

← **A fraction has many equivalent forms.**

You can rename a mixed number as an equivalent improper fraction.

$$3\frac{5}{6} = \frac{6 \cdot 3 + 5}{6} = \frac{23}{6}$$

In Lesson 5.1, you should write down helpful hints about subtracting with mixed numbers.

Fractions with Common Denominators

BEFORE	Now	WHY?
You added and subtracted whole numbers and integers.	You'll add and subtract fractions with common denominators.	So you can compare coin sizes, as in Ex. 28.

Review words

order of operations, p. 10
numerator, p. 707
denominator, p. 707

INDIANA
Academic Standards

- Computation (8.2.1)

One way to add or subtract fractions with common denominators is to use a model.

$$\frac{2}{5} + \frac{1}{5} = \frac{3}{5}$$

The model suggests the following rule.

Adding and Subtracting Fractions

Words To add fractions or subtract fractions with a common denominator, write the sum or difference of the numerators over the denominator.

Numbers $\frac{3}{9} + \frac{5}{9} = \frac{8}{9}$ **Algebra** $\frac{a}{c} + \frac{b}{c} = \frac{a+b}{c}$ $(c \neq 0)$

$\frac{3}{5} - \frac{2}{5} = \frac{1}{5}$ $\frac{a}{c} - \frac{b}{c} = \frac{a-b}{c}$ $(c \neq 0)$

To add or subtract mixed numbers, find the sum or difference of the whole numbers and the sum or difference of the fractions. Then combine these quantities.

EXAMPLE 1 **Fractions and Mixed Numbers**

a. $-\frac{11}{13} + \frac{8}{13} = \frac{-11+8}{13}$

$= -\frac{3}{13}$

b. $-5\frac{6}{7} + 3\frac{2}{7} = -5 - \frac{6}{7} + 3 + \frac{2}{7}$

$= -5 + 3 - \frac{6}{7} + \frac{2}{7}$

$= -2\frac{4}{7}$

HELP with Notetaking

Part (b) of Example 1 shows how to operate with negative mixed numbers. You may wish to copy this into your notebook.

EXAMPLE 2 Simplifying Fractions with Variables

a. $-\frac{a}{9} + \frac{7a}{9} = \frac{-a + 7a}{9}$ — Write sum over common denominator.

$= \frac{6a}{9}$ — Combine like terms.

$= \frac{\overset{2}{\cancel{6}}a}{\underset{3}{\cancel{9}}}$ — Divide out common factor.

$= \frac{2a}{3}$ — Simplify.

b. $\frac{6x}{11y} - \frac{10x}{11y} = \frac{6x - 10x}{11y}$ — Write difference over common denominator.

$= \frac{-4x}{11y}$, or $-\frac{4x}{11y}$ — Combine like terms.

HELP with Solving

Remember that the following fractions are equivalent.

$\frac{-a}{b} = \frac{a}{-b} = -\frac{a}{b}$

Your turn now Find the sum or difference. Then simplify if possible.

1. $\frac{1}{12} + \frac{5}{12}$ **2.** $\frac{3}{8} - 2\frac{1}{8}$ **3.** $-\frac{t}{3} - \frac{2t}{3}$ **4.** $\frac{y}{8a} + \frac{-5y}{8a}$

EXAMPLE 3 Solving an Equation with Mixed Numbers

Biology A corn snake that is $14\frac{3}{4}$ inches long grows g inches to a length of $27\frac{1}{4}$ inches. To find the amount of growth, subtract the original length from the current length.

$g = 27\frac{1}{4} - 14\frac{3}{4}$

$= 26\frac{5}{4} - 14\frac{3}{4}$ ← $\frac{1}{4} < \frac{3}{4}$, so rename $27\frac{1}{4}$ so its fraction part is greater than $\frac{3}{4}$.

$= \left(26 + \frac{5}{4}\right) - \left(14 + \frac{3}{4}\right)$

$= 26 + \frac{5}{4} - 14 - \frac{3}{4}$ ← Remember to distribute the subtraction.

$= (26 - 14) + \left(\frac{5}{4} - \frac{3}{4}\right)$

$= 12 + \frac{2}{4}$

$= 12\frac{1}{2}$ ← $\frac{2}{4} = \frac{1}{2}$

ANSWER The snake grows $12\frac{1}{2}$ inches.

Order of Operations The rules for adding and subtracting fractions can be applied to longer expressions. Remember to use the order of operations.

EXAMPLE 4 **Evaluating Longer Expressions**

a. $\frac{2}{11} - \frac{5}{11} + \frac{9}{11} = \frac{2 - 5 + 9}{11}$ Write 2 − 5 + 9 over common denominator.

$= \frac{6}{11}$ Evaluate numerator from left to right.

b. $3\frac{6}{7} - 2\frac{3}{7} + 4\frac{5}{7} = (3 - 2 + 4) + \left(\frac{6}{7} - \frac{3}{7} + \frac{5}{7}\right)$ Group whole numbers and fractions.

$= 5\frac{8}{7}$ Evaluate inside parentheses.

$= 6\frac{1}{7}$ Rename.

Your turn now **Evaluate. Then simplify if possible.**

5. $\frac{3}{4} + \frac{7}{4} + \frac{5}{4}$ **6.** $\frac{15}{8} - \frac{7}{8} + \frac{3}{8}$ **7.** $2\frac{1}{3} - \frac{2}{3} + 3\frac{2}{3}$

5.1 Exercises

More Practice, p. 731

INTERNET
eWorkbook Plus
CLASSZONE.COM

Getting Ready to Practice

1. Vocabulary Copy and complete: In the fraction $\frac{4}{9}$, 9 is the __?__ and 4 is the __?__.

2. Find the Error Describe and correct the error.

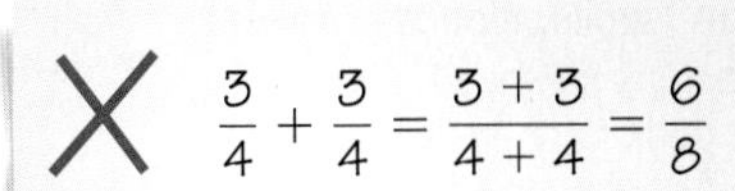
$\frac{3}{4} + \frac{3}{4} = \frac{3+3}{4+4} = \frac{6}{8}$

Find the sum or difference. Then simplify if possible.

3. $\frac{5}{18} + \frac{7}{18}$ **4.** $\frac{3}{10} - \frac{7}{10}$ **5.** $\frac{4}{15} - \frac{1}{15}$ **6.** $1\frac{5}{9} + \frac{2}{9}$

7. $3\frac{1}{7} - 1\frac{5}{7}$ **8.** $2\frac{7}{9} + \frac{8}{9}$ **9.** $\frac{c}{6} + \frac{5c}{6}$ **10.** $\frac{3d}{5} - \frac{2d}{5}$

11. Knitting When the scarf you are knitting is $21\frac{3}{8}$ inches long, you find a mistake and have to pull out $2\frac{5}{8}$ inches. How much scarf is left?

Practice and Problem Solving

Example	Exercises
1	12-23
2	24-27
3	28-30, 40
4	31-39

· More Examples
· eTutorial Plus

Find the sum or difference.

12. $\frac{4}{17} + \frac{8}{17}$ **13.** $\frac{7}{18} - \frac{5}{18}$ **14.** $\frac{9}{14} - \frac{5}{14}$ **15.** $\frac{-13}{24} + \frac{-9}{24}$

16. $\frac{5}{21} + \frac{2}{21}$ **17.** $\frac{12}{25} + \frac{-7}{25}$ **18.** $\frac{1}{6} - \frac{11}{6}$ **19.** $-\frac{3}{4} - \left(-\frac{1}{4}\right)$

20. $-2\frac{5}{12} + 1\frac{11}{12}$ **21.** $1\frac{4}{15} + \left(-\frac{11}{15}\right)$ **22.** $-4\frac{2}{7} - 4\frac{2}{7}$ **23.** $-7\frac{3}{5} - \frac{4}{5}$

Algebra **Simplify the expression.**

24. $\frac{h}{13} + \frac{6h}{13}$ **25.** $-\frac{8n}{21} + \frac{5n}{21}$ **26.** $\frac{9a}{20b} - \frac{7a}{20b}$ **27.** $-\frac{5q}{18p} - \frac{13q}{18p}$

28. Euros A 2-euro coin is $25\frac{3}{4}$ millimeters at its widest. A 1-euro coin is $23\frac{1}{4}$ millimeters at its widest. How much wider is a 2-euro coin?

29. Volunteering You did volunteer work for $6\frac{1}{6}$ hours last week and $8\frac{5}{6}$ hours this week. For how many total hours have you volunteered? How many more hours did you volunteer this week than last week?

30. Auto Racing Some cars in a recent race were allowed to reduce the height of their rear spoilers by one fourth inch. After the change, one car's spoiler was $6\frac{1}{4}$ inches tall. How tall was the spoiler before the change in height?

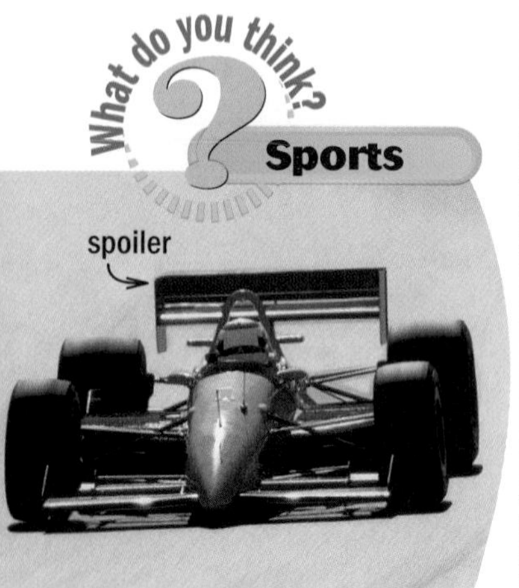

Auto Racing

Decreasing the height of a race car's spoiler reduces *drag*, increasing speed. What do you think happens when the spoiler's height is increased?

Evaluate.

31. $\frac{13}{18} + \frac{5}{18} + \frac{11}{18}$ **32.** $-\frac{4}{5} - \frac{1}{5} - \frac{2}{5}$ **33.** $-\frac{4}{25} + \frac{3}{25} + \frac{9}{25}$

34. $\frac{5}{7} - 1\frac{3}{7} + \frac{4}{7}$ **35.** $-\frac{3}{16} + 2\frac{1}{16} - \frac{15}{16}$ **36.** $1\frac{3}{8} + \frac{5}{8} - 1\frac{7}{8}$

37. $-5\frac{4}{15} - 3\frac{7}{15} + \frac{8}{15}$ **38.** $-\frac{9}{20} + \frac{19}{20} - 1\frac{1}{20}$ **39.** $4\frac{5}{12} - \left(1\frac{11}{12} - \frac{7}{12}\right)$

40. Long Jump You want to match your school's long jump record of 17 feet $8\frac{1}{4}$ inches. Your best long jump so far is 15 feet $11\frac{3}{4}$ inches. How much farther do you need to jump to match the school record?

Algebra **Solve the equation.**

41. $x + \frac{5}{8} = \frac{7}{8}$ **42.** $\frac{10}{11} - y = \frac{2}{11}$ **43.** $z - \frac{9}{15} = \frac{11}{15}$

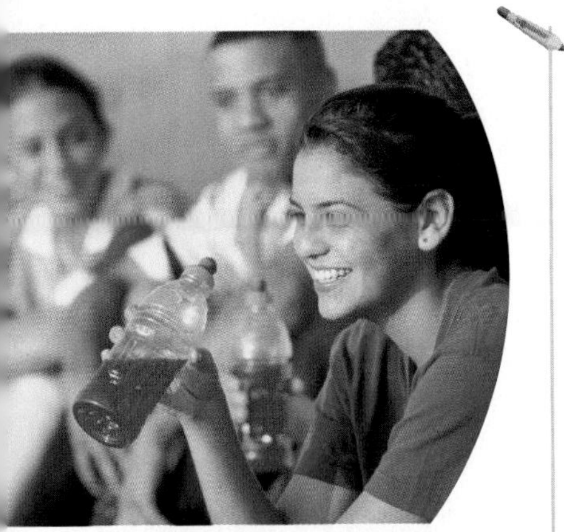

44. **Writing** One hundred students try three new fruit juice blends, and each picks a favorite, as shown at the right.

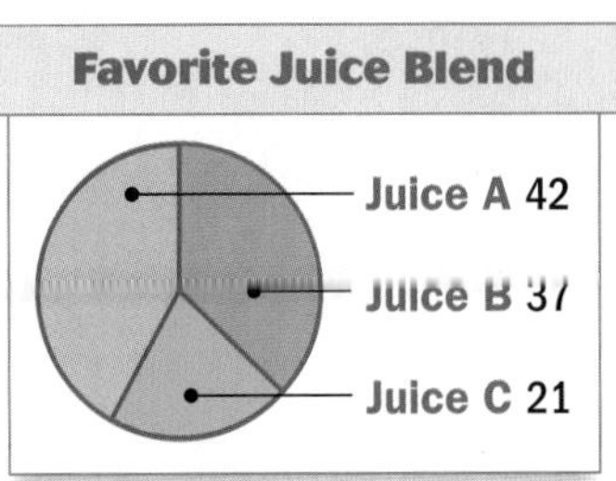

Your friend says that if you make each number the numerator in a fraction with a denominator of 100, the sum of these fractions must be 1. Is your friend right? Explain.

Challenge **Find the value that makes the equation true.**

45. $\frac{5}{11} + \frac{9}{11} - \underline{?} = -\frac{2}{11}$

46. $\frac{7}{16} + \frac{9}{16} - \underline{?} = \frac{5}{16}$

Mixed Review

Find the sum or difference. *(Lessons 2.2, 2.3)*

47. $22 + (-17)$ 48. $-14 - 9$ 49. $-7 + (-35)$ 50. $16 - (-13)$

Find the least common multiple of the numbers. *(Lesson 4.4)*

51. 15, 35 52. 19, 76 53. 37, 50 54. 27, 81

Find the least common denominator of the fractions. *(Lesson 4.5)*

55. $\frac{2}{3}, \frac{4}{9}$ 56. $\frac{1}{5}, \frac{9}{20}$ 57. $\frac{3}{8}, \frac{7}{12}$ 58. $\frac{1}{6}, \frac{4}{15}$

Basic Skills **Find the quotient.**

59. $32 \div 2$ 60. $60 \div 5$ 61. $10 \div 8$ 62. $50 \div 4$

Test-Taking Practice

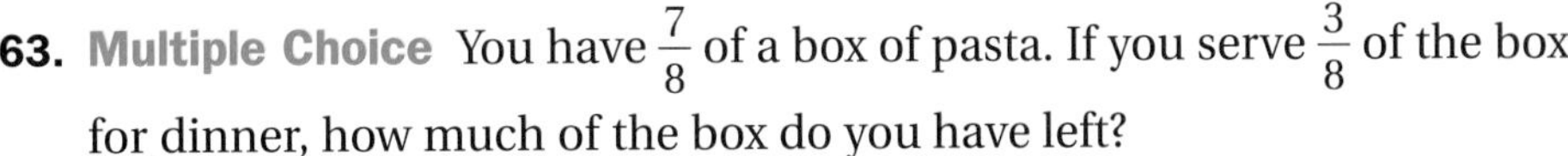

INTERNET
State Test Practice
CLASSZONE.COM

63. **Multiple Choice** You have $\frac{7}{8}$ of a box of pasta. If you serve $\frac{3}{8}$ of the box for dinner, how much of the box do you have left?

A. $\frac{1}{4}$ **B.** $\frac{1}{2}$ **C.** $\frac{5}{8}$ **D.** $\frac{3}{4}$

64. **Multiple Choice** You are fencing a rectangular plot of land. The plot and its dimensions are shown. How many feet of fencing do you need?

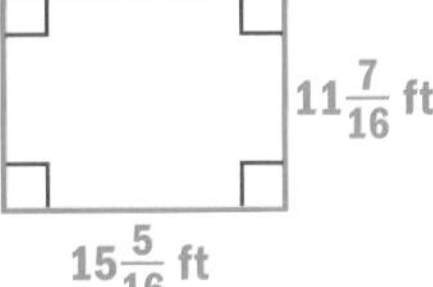

F. $26\frac{3}{4}$ feet **G.** $52\frac{1}{2}$ feet

H. $53\frac{1}{4}$ feet **I.** $53\frac{1}{2}$ feet

Fractions with Different Denominators

BEFORE	Now	WHY?
You added and subtracted with common denominators.	You'll add and subtract with different denominators.	So you can find a sled length, as in Ex. 20.

In the Real World

Review Words

least common denominator (LCD), p. 192

INDIANA Academic Standards

- Computation (8.2.1)

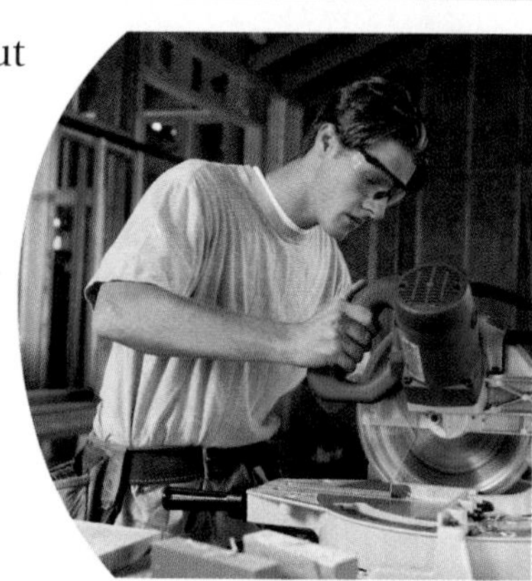

Carpentry A board is $36\frac{5}{8}$ inches long. You cut off a piece $12\frac{3}{4}$ inches long. The saw blade destroys an additional $\frac{1}{16}$ inch of wood. You will find the length of the remaining piece of wood in Example 3 on page 225.

Rewriting Fractions To add or subtract fractions with different denominators, first rewrite the fractions so the denominators are the same.

HELP with Review

For help with rewriting fractions with common denominators, see p. 192.

EXAMPLE 1 Adding and Subtracting Fractions

a. $\frac{7}{8} + \frac{-2}{5} = \frac{35}{40} + \frac{-16}{40}$ Rewrite fractions using LCD of 40.

$= \frac{35 + (-16)}{40}$ Write sum over LCD.

$= \frac{19}{40}$ Evaluate numerator.

b. $\frac{3}{10} - \frac{5}{6} = \frac{9}{30} - \frac{25}{30}$ Rewrite fractions using LCD of 30.

$= \frac{9 - 25}{30}$ Write difference over LCD.

$= \frac{-16}{30}$ Evaluate numerator.

$= -\frac{8}{15}$ Simplify.

Your turn now Find the sum or difference. Then simplify if possible.

1. $\frac{1}{3} + \frac{3}{8}$ **2.** $\frac{3}{4} - \frac{9}{10}$ **3.** $\frac{5}{12} + \frac{-7}{9}$ **4.** $\frac{1}{6} - \frac{11}{15}$

EXAMPLE 2 Simplifying Variable Expressions

Algebra **Simplify the expression.**

a. $\frac{2x}{5} - \frac{x}{6} = \frac{12x}{30} - \frac{5x}{30}$ **Rewrite fractions using LCD of 30.**

$= \frac{12x - 5x}{30}$ **Write difference over LCD.**

$= \frac{7x}{30}$ **Combine like terms.**

b. $\frac{5}{y} + \frac{7}{8} = \left(\frac{5}{y} \cdot \frac{8}{8}\right) + \left(\frac{7}{8} \cdot \frac{y}{y}\right)$ **Multiply $\frac{5}{y}$ by $\frac{8}{8}$ and $\frac{7}{8}$ by $\frac{y}{y}$ for LCD of $8y$.**

$= \frac{40}{8y} + \frac{7y}{8y}$ **Multiply inside parentheses.**

$= \frac{40 + 7y}{8y}$ **Write sum over LCD.**

Watch Out!

In part (b) of Example 2, notice that

$\frac{40 + 7y}{8y} \neq \frac{47y}{8y}$

because 40 and $7y$ are not like terms. The expression is already in simplest form.

EXAMPLE 3 Modeling with Mixed Numbers

Carpentry To find the length of the remaining piece of wood from the problem at the top of page 224, write a verbal model.

Remaining length L = Original length − (Length cut off + Blade width)

$L = 36\frac{5}{8} - \left(12\frac{3}{4} + \frac{1}{16}\right)$ **Write an algebraic model.**

$= 36\frac{10}{16} - \left(12\frac{12}{16} + \frac{1}{16}\right)$ **Rewrite fractions using LCD of 16.**

$= 36\frac{10}{16} - 12\frac{13}{16}$ **Add inside parentheses.**

$= 35\frac{26}{16} - 12\frac{13}{16}$ **Rename $36\frac{10}{16}$ as $35\frac{26}{16}$.**

$= (35 - 12) + \left(\frac{26}{16} - \frac{13}{16}\right)$ **Group whole numbers and fractions.**

$= 23\frac{13}{16}$ **Subtract whole numbers and fractions.**

ANSWER The remaining piece of wood is $23\frac{13}{16}$ inches long.

Your turn now **Find the sum or difference. Then simplify if possible.**

5. $\frac{w}{3} + \frac{w}{12}$ **6.** $\frac{2}{5} - \frac{2}{z}$ **7.** $5\frac{3}{4} + 2\frac{3}{5}$ **8.** $7\frac{5}{6} - 3\frac{8}{9}$

5.2 Exercises

More Practice, p. 731

Getting Ready to Practice

1. **Vocabulary** Copy and complete: To add two fractions with different denominators, rewrite the fractions using the _?_ of the fractions.

Find the sum or difference. Then simplify if possible.

2. $\frac{1}{2} + \frac{1}{3}$
3. $4\frac{5}{8} - 2\frac{2}{3}$
4. $\frac{2x}{7} - \frac{x}{2}$
5. $\frac{4}{x} + \frac{1}{9}$

6. **Guided Problem Solving** You are building a stone wall 13 feet long. You build $4\frac{1}{3}$ feet of wall on Monday and $5\frac{3}{4}$ feet on Tuesday. How much wall do you have left to build?
   (1) Write a verbal model to describe the problem.
   (2) Substitute the given values into the model.
   (3) Solve the equation to find the length left to build.

Practice and Problem Solving

HELP with Homework

Example	Exercises
1	7-13, 21-22
2	24-27
3	14-20, 23

· More Examples
· eTutorial Plus

Find the sum or difference.

7. $\frac{7}{8} - \frac{1}{4}$
8. $\frac{3}{7} + \frac{9}{14}$
9. $\frac{5}{9} + \frac{1}{6}$
10. $\frac{2}{3} - \frac{3}{10}$
11. $\frac{1}{8} - \frac{5}{32}$
12. $-\frac{7}{12} + \frac{4}{15}$
13. $\frac{-3}{8} + \frac{-9}{20}$
14. $5\frac{1}{2} - \frac{7}{10}$
15. $12\frac{5}{18} - \frac{3}{4}$
16. $-7\frac{3}{11} - (-8)$
17. $7\frac{4}{5} + 5\frac{3}{7}$
18. $12\frac{2}{9} - 16\frac{3}{7}$

19. **Tree Removal** A dead tree $25\frac{1}{2}$ feet tall is being cut down. On the first cut, $9\frac{1}{3}$ feet are cut off. On the next cut, $7\frac{5}{6}$ feet are cut off. How much of the tree remains to be cut down?

20. **Olympic Sledding** Olympic skeleton sleds range from $31\frac{1}{2}$ inches to $47\frac{1}{4}$ inches long. What is the difference in length of the longest and shortest sleds?

Tell whether the statement is *true* or *false*.

21. $\frac{1}{4} - \frac{6}{7} + \frac{3}{14} = -\frac{11}{28}$
22. $\frac{4}{5} + \frac{5}{8} - \frac{7}{10} = \frac{57}{80}$
23. $1\frac{1}{3} - \frac{2}{9} - \frac{5}{6} = \frac{7}{18}$

Algebra Simplify the expression.

24. $\frac{6t}{13} - \frac{6t}{7}$ **25.** $\frac{9s}{4} - \frac{7s}{5}$ **26.** $\frac{18}{7a} + \frac{11}{21}$ **27.** $\frac{16}{25n} + \frac{9}{10n}$

Equator In Exercises 28 and 29, use the following information.

Traveling east from the Galapagos Islands to Nairobi, Kenya, you go about $\frac{9}{25}$ of the way around Earth's equator. It is then about $\frac{9}{50}$ of the way around the equator from Nairobi traveling east to Singapore.

28. What fraction of the equator do you cover if you travel east from the Galapagos Islands to Singapore?

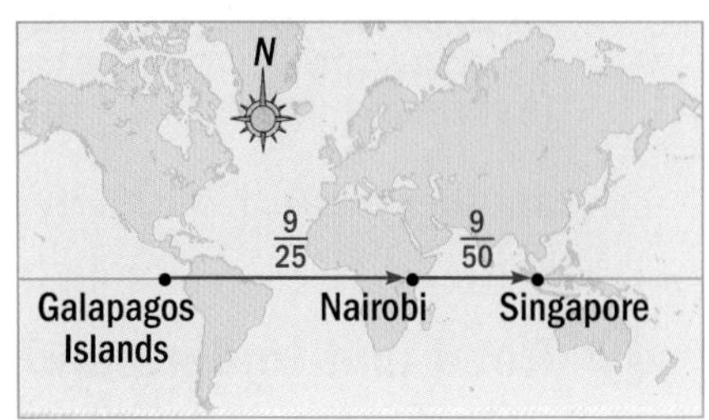

29. **Writing** Is traveling from the Galapagos Islands to Singapore a shorter trip if you travel *east* or *west*? Explain.

Algebra Solve the equation.

30. $6\frac{3}{8} + 2\frac{5}{12} - x = 4\frac{3}{4}$ **31.** $7\frac{7}{8} - 6\frac{5}{9} - y = \frac{1}{6}$ **32.** $z + 3\frac{4}{7} - 5\frac{2}{5} = 1\frac{1}{2}$

33. **Challenge** To evaluate $3\frac{1}{4} + 5\frac{3}{8}$, Cal groups the whole numbers and the fractions, and then rewrites the fractions with a common denominator. May rewrites the fractions with a common denominator first, and then groups the whole numbers and the fractions. Do Cal and May get the same sum? Explain.

Mixed Review

Find the product. *(Lesson 2.4)*

34. $-9(7)$ **35.** $0(-5)$ **36.** $7(-3)(13)$ **37.** $-9(-7)(-2)$

Copy and complete the statement with <, >, or =. *(Lesson 4.5)*

38. $\frac{1}{7} \underline{?} \frac{1}{8}$ **39.** $\frac{3}{8} \underline{?} \frac{4}{9}$ **40.** $\frac{5}{12} \underline{?} \frac{7}{16}$ **41.** $\frac{7}{10} \underline{?} \frac{18}{25}$

Test-Taking Practice

INTERNET
State Test Practice
CLASSZONE.COM

42. **Multiple Choice** What is the value of $\frac{5}{6} + \frac{1}{9} - \frac{2}{3}$?

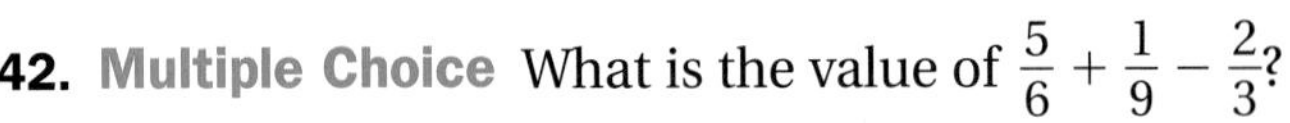

A. $\frac{1}{6}$ **B.** $\frac{2}{9}$ **C.** $\frac{5}{18}$ **D.** $\frac{1}{3}$

43. **Short Response** You are getting ready for a backpacking trip. You pack $4\frac{2}{3}$ pounds of food and $5\frac{1}{8}$ pounds of equipment into a $2\frac{1}{4}$ pound backpack. What is the total weight you will carry?

5.3 Problem Solving Strategies

INDIANA: Academic Standards
- Computation (8.2.1)
- Problem Solving (8.7.1)

Act It Out

- Guess, Check, and Revise
- Look for a Pattern
- Draw a Diagram
- Make a Model
- Act It Out
- Make a Table
- Solve a Simpler Problem

Problem You are hiking a trail that is $7\frac{1}{2}$ miles long. Before your first break, you hike $2\frac{3}{4}$ miles. Then you hike $2\frac{1}{2}$ miles and take another break. How many miles do you have left to hike?

1 Read and Understand

Read the problem carefully.

- You know that you are hiking a total distance of $7\frac{1}{2}$ miles, and that you have already hiked $2\frac{3}{4}$ miles and $2\frac{1}{2}$ miles.
- You want to find the remaining distance that you have left to hike.

2 Make a Plan

Decide on a strategy to use.

One way to solve this problem is to use the act it out strategy. You can act out the hike by using a common item like floor tiles to represent distance traveled.

3 Solve the Problem

Reread the problem and act it out.

The fractions have an LCD of 4, so let each floor tile represent $\frac{1}{4}$ of a mile. Use masking tape to mark off 30 tiles for $7\frac{1}{2}$ miles. Walk across 11 tiles to represent $2\frac{3}{4}$ miles hiked and 10 more tiles to represent $2\frac{1}{2}$ miles hiked. Notice that 9 tiles remain, which represent $2\frac{1}{4}$ miles left to hike.

ANSWER You have $2\frac{1}{4}$ miles left to hike.

4 Look Back

Add your answer to the first two distances.

$2\frac{3}{4} + 2\frac{1}{2} + 2\frac{1}{4} = 7\frac{1}{2}$ ✓

Practice the Strategy

Use the strategy *act it out*. Tell how you acted out the problem to get your answer.

1. **Pets** There are 18 students in your class. Eight students have a cat and five students have a dog. Two students in your class have both a cat and a dog. How many students have neither a cat nor a dog?

2. **Money** You have 8 quarters, 10 dimes, and 7 nickels. You give half of your dimes and 2 nickels to a friend. Then you spend one fourth of your quarters and one nickel. How much money do you have left?

3. **Gifts** You buy a roll of ribbon 20 yards long. The amounts of ribbon you use to decorate a gift and to make a bow are shown below.

$2\frac{1}{6}$ yards

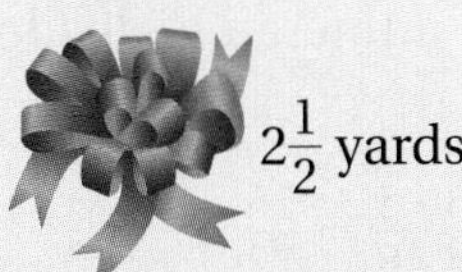

$2\frac{1}{2}$ yards

You decorate 5 gifts. How many bows can you make with the ribbon you have left?

4. **Beads** There are 24 beads in a bowl. Anna takes $\frac{1}{6}$ of the beads. Then John takes two beads. Lena takes $\frac{1}{9}$ of what Anna and John left. Dawn takes $\frac{1}{4}$ of what Lena left, and then Jamal takes five beads. How many beads are left in the bowl?

5. **Lunch Line** You are in a lunch line with 4 students in front of you and 6 students behind you. You let a friend into the line in front of you, who then lets 2 students get in line behind her. Finally, 2 students join the end of the lunch line. How many students are in the lunch line? What is your new position in the lunch line?

Mixed Problem Solving

Use any strategy to solve the problem.

6. **Vacation** On each day of your three day vacation, you can choose one activity. The table below shows your choices. How many different groups of activities can you choose?

Day	Activities
Friday	museum, picnic, bus tour
Saturday	baseball game, bicycling
Sunday	hike, shopping, water park

7. **Fundraising** To raise money for a class trip, you are selling sweatshirts for \$19 and T-shirts for \$11. You have sold 17 items worth a total of \$227. How many of each item have you sold?

8. **Floors** You are choosing a floor covering for the room shown below. It costs \$3 per square foot for carpeting. It costs \$8 per square foot for a wood floor.

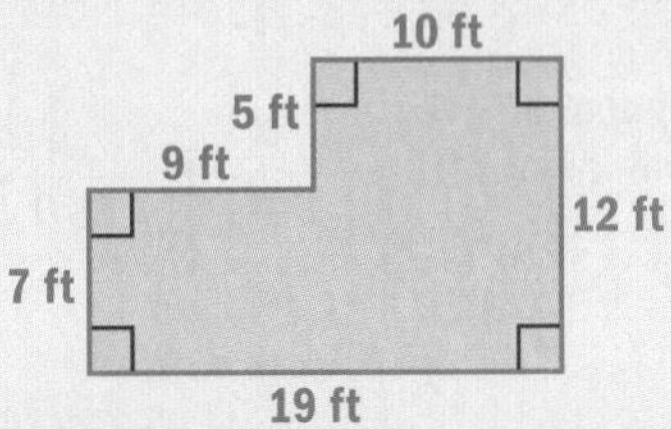

What is the cost to cover the floor with each type of flooring?

Multiplying Fractions

BEFORE	Now	WHY?
You added and subtracted fractions and mixed numbers.	You'll multiply fractions and mixed numbers.	So you can find a moon crater's depth, as in Ex. 19.

In the Real World

Postcards A postcard is $5\frac{1}{2}$ inches long and $3\frac{3}{4}$ inches wide. What is the area of this postcard? In Example 2 on page 231, you will multiply mixed numbers to find the postcard's area.

Multiplication To multiply fractions, you can use the rule below.

Word Watch

Review Words

numerator, p. 707
denominator, p. 707

INDIANA Academic Standards

- Computation (8.2.1)

Multiplying Fractions

Words The product of two or more fractions is equal to the product of the numerators divided by the product of the denominators.

Numbers $\frac{3}{4} \cdot \frac{5}{8} = \frac{3 \cdot 5}{4 \cdot 8} = \frac{15}{32}$

Algebra $\frac{a}{b} \cdot \frac{c}{d} = \frac{a \cdot c}{b \cdot d}$ $(b, d \neq 0)$

EXAMPLE 1 Multiplying Fractions

a. $-\frac{2}{5} \cdot \left(-\frac{2}{3}\right) = \frac{-2 \cdot (-2)}{5 \cdot 3}$ **Use rule for multiplying fractions.**

$= \frac{4}{15}$ **Evaluate numerator and denominator.**

b. $-\frac{3}{10} \cdot \frac{5}{6} = \frac{-3 \cdot 5}{10 \cdot 6}$ **Use rule for multiplying fractions.**

$= \frac{\overset{-1}{\cancel{-3}} \cdot \overset{1}{\cancel{5}}}{\underset{2}{\cancel{10}} \cdot \underset{2}{\cancel{6}}}$ **Divide out common factors.**

$= -\frac{1}{4}$ **Multiply.**

HELP with Review

Remember that the product of two numbers with the same sign is positive. The product of two numbers with different signs is negative.

Mixed Numbers To multiply mixed numbers, first write them as improper fractions.

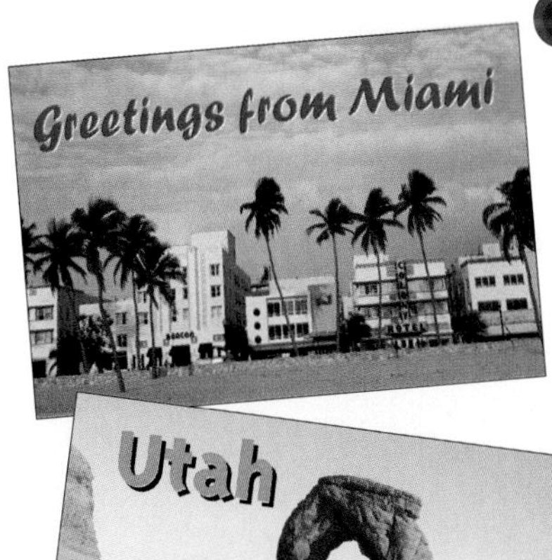

EXAMPLE 2 Multiplying Mixed Numbers

To find the area of the postcard on page 230, use an area formula.

Area = length • width	**Write formula for area of a rectangle.**
$= 5\frac{1}{2} \cdot 3\frac{3}{4}$	**Substitute values.**
$= \frac{11}{2} \cdot \frac{15}{4}$	**Write as improper fractions.**
$= \frac{11 \cdot 15}{2 \cdot 4}$	**Use rule for multiplying fractions.**
$= \frac{165}{8}$, or $20\frac{5}{8}$	**Multiply.**

ANSWER The area of the postcard is $20\frac{5}{8}$ square inches.

Watch Out!

Be careful when you write a negative mixed number as an improper fraction.

$-4\frac{5}{6} = \frac{-4 \cdot 6 + (-5)}{6}$

$-4\frac{5}{6} \neq \frac{-4 \cdot 6 + 5}{6}$

Your turn now **Find the product. Simplify if possible.**

1. $\frac{5}{12} \cdot 15$ **2.** $-\frac{5}{12} \cdot \frac{9}{10}$ **3.** $1\frac{2}{5} \cdot 3\frac{1}{2}$ **4.** $-2\frac{1}{3} \cdot \left(-\frac{3}{4}\right)$

EXAMPLE 3 Evaluating a Variable Expression

Algebra **Evaluate x^2y when $x = -\frac{4}{5}$ and $y = \frac{2}{3}$.**

$x^2y = \left(-\frac{4}{5}\right)^2 \cdot \frac{2}{3}$	**Substitute $-\frac{4}{5}$ for x and $\frac{2}{3}$ for y.**
$= \left(-\frac{4}{5}\right) \cdot \left(-\frac{4}{5}\right) \cdot \frac{2}{3}$	**Write $-\frac{4}{5}$ as a factor 2 times.**
$= \frac{-4 \cdot (-4) \cdot 2}{5 \cdot 5 \cdot 3}$	**Use rule for multiplying fractions.**
$= \frac{32}{75}$	**Multiply.**

Your turn now **Evaluate the expression when $x = -\frac{3}{4}$ and $y = \frac{5}{6}$. Simplify if possible.**

5. $\frac{1}{2}x$ **6.** $2y$ **7.** xy **8.** xy^2

5.3 Exercises

More Practice, p. 731

Getting Ready to Practice

1. **Vocabulary** Copy and complete: The product of two or more fractions is equal to the product of the fractions' _?_ divided by the product of the fractions' _?_.

Find the product. Simplify if possible.

2. $\frac{5}{8} \cdot \frac{7}{16}$
3. $-\frac{9}{4} \cdot \frac{5}{6}$
4. $-4 \cdot \frac{3}{5}$
5. $5\frac{3}{4} \cdot \frac{1}{8}$

6. **Snack Mix** A serving of a snack mix is $\frac{7}{8}$ cup. You need to take 15 servings to your friend's party. How many cups of snack mix should you bring? Explain how you can use estimation to check your answer.

Practice and Problem Solving

HELP with Homework

Example	Exercises
1	7–13, 19
2	14–18
3	20–23

· More Examples
· eTutorial Plus

Find the product.

7. $\frac{7}{11} \cdot \frac{1}{6}$
8. $\frac{4}{5} \cdot \frac{3}{10}$
9. $-\frac{3}{4} \cdot \left(-\frac{2}{9}\right)$
10. $-\frac{5}{6} \cdot \frac{5}{12}$
11. $12 \cdot \frac{3}{8}$
12. $-9 \cdot \frac{1}{9}$
13. $-5 \cdot \left(-\frac{7}{4}\right)$
14. $-4 \cdot 2\frac{9}{16}$
15. $6\frac{2}{3} \cdot 4\frac{1}{12}$
16. $-3\frac{3}{8} \cdot 7\frac{1}{5}$
17. $-8 \cdot \left(-1\frac{4}{5}\right)$
18. $6\frac{3}{16} \cdot \left(-3\frac{1}{5}\right)$

19. **Moon Craters** Simple impact craters on the moon are about $\frac{1}{5}$ as deep as they are wide. Moltke Crater is a simple impact crater on the moon that is 7 kilometers wide. About how deep is Moltke Crater?

Algebra **Evaluate the expression when $a = \frac{5}{8}$ and $b = -\frac{7}{6}$.**

20. $-\frac{1}{4}a$
21. $1\frac{1}{2} \cdot b$
22. $-8a$
23. ab

24. **Critical Thinking** A banana bread recipe uses 3 bananas and $\frac{1}{4}$ cup of butter. You need to make a smaller recipe because you have only 2 bananas. How much butter will you need? Explain.

25. **Act It Out** A section of the town beach is shrinking by $1\frac{3}{4}$ feet per year. Use the *act it out* strategy to find how much the beach will erode in 20 years. Explain how you used the strategy.

Find the area of the figure.

26. 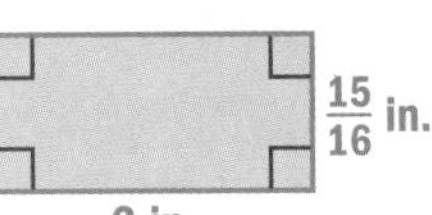

27. 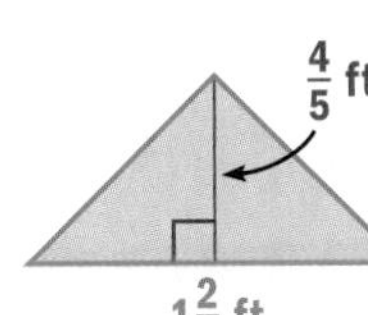

28. 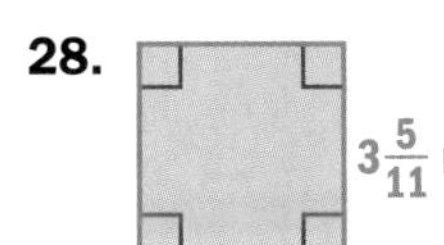

Find the product.

29. $\frac{1}{4} \cdot \left(-\frac{2}{5}\right) \cdot \frac{9}{10}$

30. $\frac{2}{5} \cdot 1\frac{1}{5} \cdot \left(-4\frac{7}{12}\right)$

31. $-9\frac{2}{7} \cdot 1\frac{2}{5} \cdot \frac{3}{4}$

32. Computers One of the first computers, the ENIAC, performed one operation in $\frac{1}{5000}$ second. How long would it take the ENIAC to perform 11,000 operations?

Mosaic tiling

Evaluate the expression.

33. $-\frac{7}{8} + 5\frac{1}{2} \cdot \frac{11}{15}$

34. $\frac{5}{2} \cdot \left(\frac{8}{9} - \frac{5}{12}\right)$

35. $5 - \left(\frac{1}{3} + \frac{1}{6}\right)^2$

36. Challenge Mosaic tiles sometimes measure $\frac{2}{5}$ inch by $\frac{2}{5}$ inch. What area would 500 tiles cover?

Mixed Review 

Multiply or divide. Write your answer as a power. *(Lesson 4.6)*

37. $7^3 \cdot 7^2$

38. $3^5 \cdot 3$

39. $\frac{8^6}{8^4}$

40. $\frac{5^{10}}{5^5}$

Find the sum or difference. *(Lesson 5.2)*

41. $\frac{4}{5} + \frac{7}{10}$

42. $-2\frac{4}{9} + \frac{5}{21}$

43. $\frac{13}{20} - \frac{1}{6}$

44. $-\frac{15}{22} - \frac{9}{16}$

Test-Taking Practice 

INTERNET
State Test Practice
CLASSZONE.COM

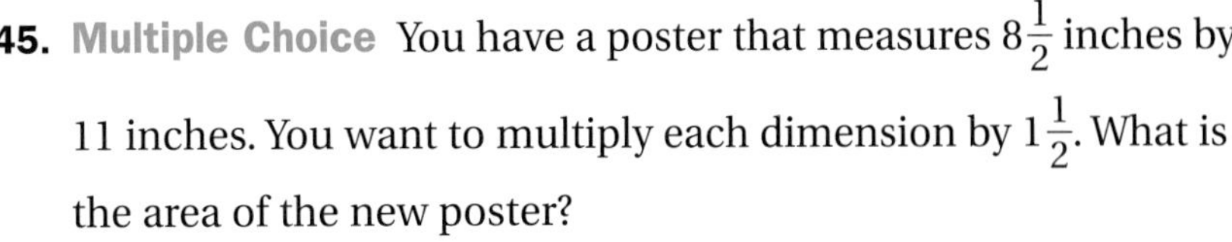

45. Multiple Choice You have a poster that measures $8\frac{1}{2}$ inches by 11 inches. You want to multiply each dimension by $1\frac{1}{2}$. What is the area of the new poster?

A. $93\frac{1}{2}$ in.^{2} **B.** $140\frac{1}{4}$ in.^{2} **C.** $210\frac{3}{8}$ in.^{2} **D.** $280\frac{1}{2}$ in.^{2}

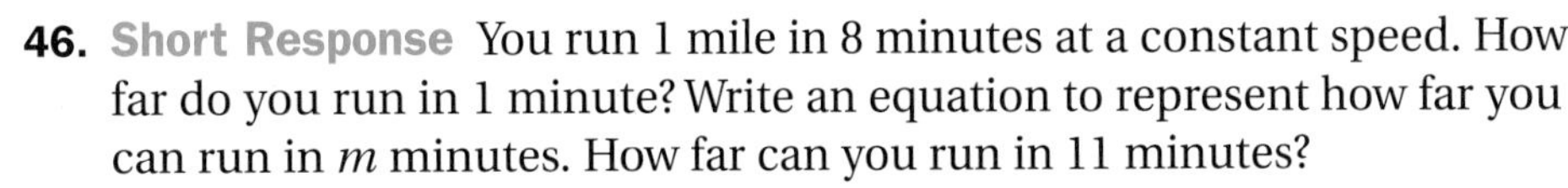

46. Short Response You run 1 mile in 8 minutes at a constant speed. How far do you run in 1 minute? Write an equation to represent how far you can run in *m* minutes. How far can you run in 11 minutes?

Dividing Fractions

BEFORE

You added, subtracted, and multiplied fractions.

Now

You'll divide fractions.

WHY?

So you can find how long your batteries will last, as in Ex. 34.

Word Watch

reciprocal, p. 234
multiplicative inverse, p. 234

INDIANA Academic Standards

- Computation (8.2.1)
- Problem Solving (8.7.1)

Activity You can use models to divide fractions.

1. The model shows that $\frac{3}{4}$ is a part of 6 eight times, so $6 \div \frac{3}{4} = 8$.

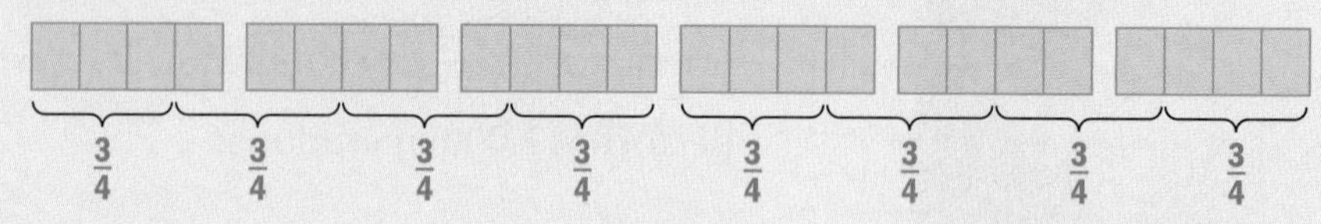

2. Calculate $6 \cdot \frac{4}{3}$. Compare the values of $6 \div \frac{3}{4}$ and $6 \cdot \frac{4}{3}$.

3. Use the model below to evaluate $4 \div \frac{2}{5}$.

4. Calculate $4 \cdot \frac{5}{2}$. Compare the values of $4 \div \frac{2}{5}$ and $4 \cdot \frac{5}{2}$.

5. What fraction can you multiply by 5 to find the value of $5 \div \frac{2}{3}$?

Reciprocals As the activity suggests, dividing a number by a fraction and multiplying the number by the fraction's *reciprocal* give the same result. Two nonzero numbers are **reciprocals** if their product is 1. Reciprocals, like $\frac{3}{7}$ and $\frac{7}{3}$, are also called **multiplicative inverses**.

Dividing Fractions

Words To divide by a fraction, multiply by its reciprocal.

Numbers $\frac{3}{10} \div \frac{4}{7} = \frac{3}{10} \cdot \frac{7}{4} = \frac{21}{40}$

Algebra $\frac{a}{b} \div \frac{c}{d} = \frac{a}{b} \cdot \frac{d}{c} \quad (b, c, d \neq 0)$

with Solving

Notice in part (b) of Example 1 that the reciprocal of a negative number is also a negative number.

EXAMPLE 1 Dividing a Fraction by a Fraction

a. $\frac{5}{6} \div \frac{10}{21} = \frac{5}{6} \cdot \frac{21}{10}$

$= \frac{\overset{1}{\cancel{5}} \cdot \overset{7}{\cancel{21}}}{\underset{2}{\cancel{6}} \cdot \underset{2}{\cancel{10}}}$

$= \frac{7}{4}$, or $1\frac{3}{4}$

b. $\frac{9}{14} \div \frac{-2}{7} = \frac{9}{14} \cdot \frac{7}{-2}$

$= \frac{9 \cdot \overset{1}{\cancel{7}}}{\underset{2}{\cancel{14}} \cdot (-2)}$

$= \frac{9}{-4}$, or $-2\frac{1}{4}$

EXAMPLE 2 Dividing a Fraction by a Whole Number

$\frac{6}{13} \div 3 = \frac{6}{13} \cdot \frac{1}{3}$ **$3 \cdot \frac{1}{3} = 1$, so the reciprocal of 3 is $\frac{1}{3}$.**

$= \frac{\overset{2}{\cancel{6}} \cdot 1}{13 \cdot \underset{1}{\cancel{3}}}$ **Multiply fractions. Divide out common factor.**

$= \frac{2}{13}$ **Multiply.**

Your turn now **Find the quotient. Simplify if possible.**

1. $\frac{5}{8} \div \left(-\frac{7}{10}\right)$ **2.** $\frac{2}{15} \div \frac{8}{9}$ **3.** $-\frac{3}{4} \div \frac{-7}{12}$ **4.** $\frac{6}{7} \div 2$

EXAMPLE 3 Dividing Mixed Numbers

$6\frac{1}{3} \div \left(-2\frac{5}{6}\right) = \frac{19}{3} \div \left(-\frac{17}{6}\right)$ **Write $6\frac{1}{3}$ and $-2\frac{5}{6}$ as improper fractions.**

$= \frac{19}{3} \cdot \left(-\frac{6}{17}\right)$ **Multiply by $-\frac{6}{17}$, the reciprocal of $-\frac{17}{6}$.**

$= \frac{19 \cdot \overset{-2}{\cancel{(-6)}}}{\underset{1}{\cancel{3}} \cdot 17}$ **Multiply. Divide out common factor.**

$= -\frac{38}{17}$, or $-2\frac{4}{17}$ **Multiply.**

✓**Check** Use estimation to check your answer. Because $6 \div (-3)$ is equal to -2, you know that $-2\frac{4}{17}$ is a reasonable answer.

Your turn now **Find the quotient. Simplify if possible.**

5. $6\frac{2}{7} \div 4$ **6.** $-12\frac{1}{4} \div 7$ **7.** $7\frac{1}{3} \div 1\frac{4}{7}$ **8.** $15\frac{3}{4} \div \left(-2\frac{5}{8}\right)$

EXAMPLE 4 Solving an Equation with a Fraction

Photography You use 16 of the 24 pictures of a roll of film on your first day of vacation. At this rate, how long will 4 rolls of film last?

Solution

Write a verbal model to describe the problem. Let d = the number of days.

Number of rolls of film	=	Fraction of roll of film used each day	•	Number of days

$4 = \frac{16}{24}d$ **Write an algebraic model.**

$4 \cdot \frac{24}{16} = \frac{24}{16} \cdot \frac{16}{24}d$ **The multiplicative inverse of $\frac{16}{24}$ is $\frac{24}{16}$.**

$\frac{\cancel{4}^{1}}{1} \cdot \frac{24}{\cancel{16}_{4}} = d$ **Divide out common factor.**

$6 = d$ **Divide.**

ANSWER Four rolls will last six days.

5.4 Exercises

More Practice, p. 731

Getting Ready to Practice

1. **Vocabulary** What is the multiplicative inverse of a number?
2. Write the reciprocal of each of the numbers: $\frac{1}{2}, \frac{4}{7}, -8, 1\frac{1}{2}$.

Find the quotient. Simplify if possible.

3. $\frac{3}{4} \div \frac{1}{8}$
4. $\frac{5}{6} \div \left(-\frac{1}{3}\right)$
5. $\frac{11}{12} \div \frac{11}{16}$
6. $-\frac{5}{6} \div (-2)$
7. $\frac{2}{3} \div 3$
8. $2\frac{1}{2} \div \frac{-9}{14}$
9. $2\frac{2}{3} \div \left(-1\frac{3}{5}\right)$
10. $4\frac{1}{8} \div 1\frac{5}{6}$

11. **Guided Problem Solving** How many hamburgers can you make from 5 pounds of hamburger if you use $\frac{1}{4}$ pound of meat per hamburger?

    (1 Write a verbal model.

    (2 Substitute the given values into the model.

    (3 Solve the equation.

Practice and Problem Solving

Example	Exercises
1	12–15, 32
2	16–19, 28–31
3	20–27
4	33–34

Online Resources
CLASSZONE.COM

- More Examples
- eTutorial Plus

Find the quotient.

12. $\frac{4}{9} \div \frac{4}{7}$ **13.** $-\frac{3}{8} \div \frac{7}{12}$ **14.** $\frac{9}{14} \div \left(-\frac{3}{26}\right)$ **15.** $-\frac{21}{22} \div \frac{-7}{11}$

16. $\frac{8}{11} \div 4$ **17.** $\frac{9}{10} \div (-12)$ **18.** $-\frac{5}{12} \div 10$ **19.** $\frac{63}{8} \div (-9)$

Find the quotient.

20. $5\frac{1}{4} \div 2\frac{1}{3}$ **21.** $7\frac{7}{8} \div \left(-2\frac{1}{4}\right)$ **22.** $12\frac{1}{7} \div 5\frac{5}{6}$ **23.** $-22\frac{2}{3} \div 3\frac{1}{5}$

24. $-9\frac{3}{5} \div (-8)$ **25.** $1\frac{5}{7} \div (-6)$ **26.** $8\frac{4}{13} \div 6\frac{3}{4}$ **27.** $9\frac{9}{14} \div 4\frac{1}{6}$

28. Writing Are the numbers $\frac{1}{9}$ and -9 reciprocals? Explain.

Use mental math to find the quotient.

29. $\frac{1}{2} \div 3$ **30.** $4 \div \frac{1}{2}$ **31.** $1 \div \frac{4}{7}$ **32.** $\frac{2}{3} \div \frac{3}{2}$

33. Dog Food Your dog Bodie eats about $\frac{3}{5}$ of a pound of dog food per day. How long will a five pound bag of dog food last?

34. CD Player Your CD player runs for about $6\frac{1}{2}$ hours on new batteries. If the average length of the CDs in your collection is about $\frac{5}{6}$ hour, how many CDs can you expect to listen to using one new set of batteries?

35. Critical Thinking Juan says, "To divide a fraction by another fraction, rewrite the fractions with common denominators. Then use the formula $\frac{a}{c} \div \frac{b}{c} = \frac{a}{b}$." Does Juan's method work? Explain.

Algebra **Solve the equation.**

36. $\frac{3}{4}a = 15$ **37.** $\frac{7}{10}b = 28$ **38.** $-\frac{9}{17}r = 3$ **39.** $-11 = -9\frac{1}{6}h$

40. Wages Haley earns \$180 working three days a week. On each of those days she works $7\frac{1}{2}$ hours. How much does Haley earn per hour?

41. Survey Two of every five people surveyed, or 350 people, said they prefer spring to fall. How many people were surveyed? Explain how you got your answer.

Algebra **Evaluate the expression when $a = 4$ and $b = 9$.**

42. $\frac{a}{5} \div \frac{8}{150}$ **43.** $\frac{3}{4}a \div \frac{5b}{6}$ **44.** $-\frac{18}{a} \div \frac{b}{16}$ **45.** $\frac{-4}{21} \div \frac{2a}{-b}$

46. Challenge You are creating a board game. You want to cut square game pieces that measure $1\frac{1}{4}$ inches on each side from a piece of paper that measures $8\frac{1}{2}$ inches by 11 inches. How many game pieces can you cut from the paper? Explain.

Mixed Review 

Simplify the variable expression. *(Lesson 4.3)*

47. $\frac{9x^2}{27x}$ **48.** $\frac{24y^4}{15y^2}$ **49.** $\frac{14x^3y}{18xy^3}$ **50.** $\frac{54yz^2}{81xz^2}$

Basic Skills **Write the improper fraction as a mixed number.**

51. $\frac{17}{9}$ **52.** $\frac{16}{5}$ **53.** $\frac{28}{3}$ **54.** $\frac{120}{7}$

Test-Taking Practice 

INTERNET
State Test Practice
CLASSZONE.COM

55. Multiple Choice Solve $\frac{5}{6}a = -15$.

A. -18 **B.** $-\frac{25}{2}$ **C.** $\frac{25}{2}$ **D.** 18

56. Multiple Choice Use the formula $C = (F - 32) \div \frac{9}{5}$ to convert 77°F to °C, where C is degrees Celsius and F is degrees Fahrenheit.

F. 20°C **G.** 25°C **H.** 30°C **I.** 45°C

Who's in First?

The number that makes each equation true represents the place in which the runner finished the race. Find the order in which the runners finished.

Martin $1\frac{2}{?} \div \frac{1}{6} = 10$ **Harriet** $? \div \frac{2}{11} = 22$

Maya $\frac{5}{7} \div \frac{?}{3} = \frac{15}{14}$ **Cornell** $\frac{?}{5} \div \frac{7}{9} = \frac{9}{35}$

5.4 Technology Activity

CALCULATOR

INDIANA: Academic Standards
• Computation (8.2.1, 8.2.3)

Operations with Fractions

GOAL Use a fraction calculator to evaluate expressions with fractions.

You can use a calculator to evaluate expressions with fractions. First, set your calculator to display the answers as fractions or mixed numbers in simplest form.

Press 2nd [FracMode]. Select *A⌴b/c* and press = to set the calculator to mixed number mode.

Press 2nd [FracMode]. Select *Auto* and press = to set the calculator to automatically simplify fractions.

Example **Use a calculator to evaluate the expression.**

	Keystrokes	Display	Answer
a. $\frac{2}{3} - 4\frac{6}{7}$	2 / 3 − 4 UNIT 6 / 7 =	−4⌴4/21	$-4\frac{4}{21}$
b. $-\frac{5}{17} \cdot \left(-\frac{8}{35}\right)$	(−) 5 / 17 × (−) 8 / 35 =	8/119	$\frac{8}{119}$
c. $\frac{3}{10} \div \left(-1\frac{4}{5}\right)$	3 / 10 ÷ (−) 1 UNIT 4 / 5 =	−1/6	$-\frac{1}{6}$

Your turn now **Use a calculator to evaluate the expression.**

1. $\frac{5}{11} + \frac{2}{5}$ **2.** $3\frac{1}{4} + \left(-\frac{6}{7}\right)$ **3.** $7\frac{1}{2} - 6\frac{5}{6}$ **4.** $\frac{2}{5} - \frac{2}{3}$

5. $\frac{7}{9} \cdot 1\frac{1}{3}$ **6.** $\frac{2}{5} \cdot \left(-\frac{3}{4}\right)$ **7.** $9\frac{4}{5} \div \frac{7}{8}$ **8.** $-10\frac{2}{13} \div \left(-3\frac{1}{3}\right)$

9. **Car Care** Rosa's car needs $4\frac{1}{4}$ quarts of oil to run properly. She notices her car has only three fourths of the amount of oil that it needs. How much oil should she add for her car to run properly?

Notebook Review

Review the vocabulary definitions in your notebook.

Copy the review examples in your notebook. Then complete the exercises.

Check Your Definitions

reciprocal, p. 234 multiplicative inverse, p. 234

Use Your Vocabulary

1. What is the product of a number and its reciprocal?

5.1–5.2 Can you add and subtract fractions?

EXAMPLES

a. $\frac{2}{9} + 3\frac{4}{9} = 3 + \left(\frac{2}{9} + \frac{4}{9}\right)$

$= 3\frac{6}{9}$

$= 3\frac{2}{3}$

b. $\frac{9}{14} - \frac{6}{7} = \frac{9}{14} - \frac{12}{14}$

$= \frac{9-12}{14}$

$= -\frac{3}{14}$

Find the sum or difference.

2. $-\frac{5}{12} + \frac{11}{12}$ **3.** $\frac{15}{16} - 2\frac{1}{16}$ **4.** $6\frac{1}{4} - 4\frac{3}{8}$ **5.** $\frac{2x}{3} + \frac{4x}{5}$

5.3 Can you multiply fractions and mixed numbers?

EXAMPLES

a. $-\frac{5}{8} \cdot \frac{3}{10} = -\frac{5 \cdot 3}{8 \cdot 10}$

$= -\frac{\overset{1}{\cancel{5}} \cdot 3}{8 \cdot \underset{2}{\cancel{10}}}$

$= -\frac{3}{16}$

b. $3\frac{2}{3} \cdot \frac{4}{9} = \frac{11}{3} \cdot \frac{4}{9}$

$= \frac{11 \cdot 4}{3 \cdot 9}$

$= \frac{44}{27}$, or $1\frac{17}{27}$

Find the product.

6. $-\frac{6}{7} \cdot \left(-\frac{5}{12}\right)$ **7.** $2\frac{1}{2} \cdot \frac{4}{5}$ **8.** $-3 \cdot 2\frac{5}{6}$ **9.** $-3\frac{1}{3} \cdot \left(-3\frac{1}{4}\right)$

5.4 Can you divide fractions and mixed numbers?

EXAMPLES

a. $\frac{1}{3} \div \frac{5}{6} = \frac{1}{3} \cdot \frac{6}{5}$

$= \frac{1 \cdot \cancel{6}^{2}}{{}_{1}\cancel{3} \cdot 5}$

$= \frac{2}{5}$

b. $2\frac{1}{5} \div 2\frac{3}{4} = \frac{11}{5} \div \frac{11}{4}$

$= \frac{11}{5} \cdot \frac{4}{11}$

$= \frac{{}^{1}\cancel{11} \cdot 4}{5 \cdot \cancel{11}_{1}} = \frac{4}{5}$

☑ **Divide.**

10. $\frac{3}{4} \div \frac{1}{12}$ **11.** $-\frac{5}{9} \div \frac{7}{18}$ **12.** $-2\frac{1}{4} \div \left(-1\frac{2}{7}\right)$

Stop *and* **Think** about Lessons 5.1–5.4

13. **Writing** How can you check your answer to a division problem involving fractions? Use an example to explain.

14. **Critical Thinking** You divide a positive number by a fraction greater than 0 and less than 1. Will the result be *less than, equal to,* or *greater than* the original number? Explain.

Review Quiz 1

Find the sum or difference.

1. $1\frac{5}{8} - \frac{7}{8}$ **2.** $\frac{4}{9} + 3\frac{5}{9}$ **3.** $\frac{x}{12} + \frac{5x}{12}$ **4.** $\frac{4}{9} - \frac{8}{9} + \frac{5}{9}$

5. $\frac{2}{3} + \frac{9}{6}$ **6.** $5\frac{3}{4} - 2\frac{1}{3}$ **7.** $\frac{5}{6} + 2\frac{1}{8}$ **8.** $\frac{3}{10} + 4\frac{2}{5} - 1\frac{1}{2}$

9. **Recipe** A recipe uses $4\frac{2}{3}$ cups of flour. Another recipe uses $4\frac{1}{4}$ cups. If you have 9 cups of flour, can you make both recipes? Explain.

Find the product or quotient.

10. $\frac{7}{12} \cdot \frac{8}{21}$ **11.** $-\frac{11}{12} \cdot \left(-\frac{3}{10}\right)$ **12.** $-\frac{14}{5} \cdot 2\frac{6}{7}$ **13.** $1\frac{1}{8} \cdot (-3)$

14. $\frac{1}{2} \div \frac{5}{6}$ **15.** $\frac{4}{9} \div 8$ **16.** $-\frac{4}{5} \div \frac{3}{2}$ **17.** $-1\frac{3}{4} \div \left(-\frac{7}{12}\right)$

18. **Hair Growth** An average human hair grows about $\frac{1}{2}$ inch per month. How much does a human hair grow in $3\frac{1}{2}$ months?

LESSON
5.5

Fractions and Decimals

BEFORE	Now	WHY?
You divided whole numbers.	You'll write fractions as decimals and decimals as fractions.	So you can analyze breakfast food popularity, as in Exs. 46–48.

Word Watch

rational number, p. 242
terminating decimal, p. 242
repeating decimal, p. 242

INDIANA Academic Standards

- Number Sense (8.1.2)

A **rational number** is a number that can be written as a quotient $\frac{a}{b}$, where a and b are integers and $b \neq 0$. The diagram shows how rational numbers, integers, and whole numbers are related.

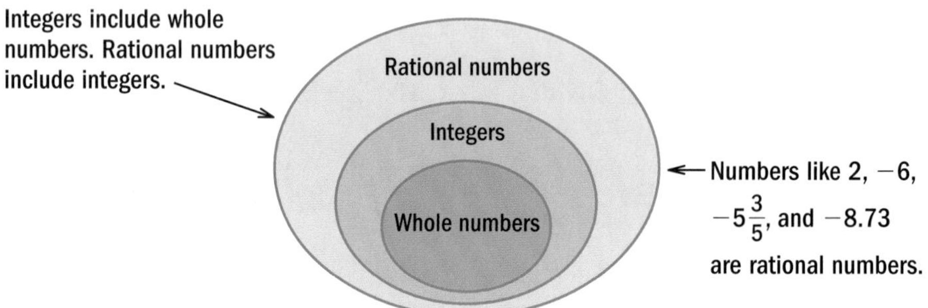
Integers include whole numbers. Rational numbers include integers.
Rational numbers
Integers
Whole numbers
Numbers like 2, −6, $-5\frac{3}{5}$, and −8.73 are rational numbers.

To write any rational number $\frac{a}{b}$ as a decimal, divide a by b. If the quotient has a remainder of zero, the result is a **terminating decimal**. If the quotient has a digit or group of digits that repeats without end, the result is a **repeating decimal**.

EXAMPLE 1 Writing Fractions as Decimals

To write a fraction as a decimal, divide the numerator by the denominator.

a. $\frac{5}{11} = 11\overline{)5.0000\ldots}$, quotient $0.4545\ldots$

$$\begin{array}{r} 44 \\ \hline 60 \\ 55 \\ \hline 50 \\ 44 \\ \hline 60 \\ 55 \\ \hline \end{array}$$

ANSWER The quotient 0.4545. . . is a repeating decimal. To indicate this, place a bar over the repeating digits: $\frac{5}{11} = 0.\overline{45}$.

b. $\frac{7}{20} = 20\overline{)7.00}$, quotient 0.35

$$\begin{array}{r} 60 \\ \hline 100 \\ 100 \\ \hline 0 \end{array}$$

ANSWER The remainder is zero, so $\frac{7}{20} = 0.35$, a terminating decimal.

Indigo bunting

EXAMPLE 2 Ordering Rational Numbers

Biology The table lists the lengths of five finches. Order the finches from shortest to longest.

Finch Species	Length (inches)
House finch	$5\frac{5}{8}$
Painted bunting	5.25
Lazuli bunting	$5\frac{7}{16}$
Purple finch	$5\frac{3}{4}$
Indigo bunting	5.5

Solution

Write mixed numbers as decimals.

$5\frac{5}{8} = 5.625$ $\quad 5\frac{7}{16} = 5.4375$

$5\frac{3}{4} = 5.75$

Then graph all the finches' lengths on a number line.

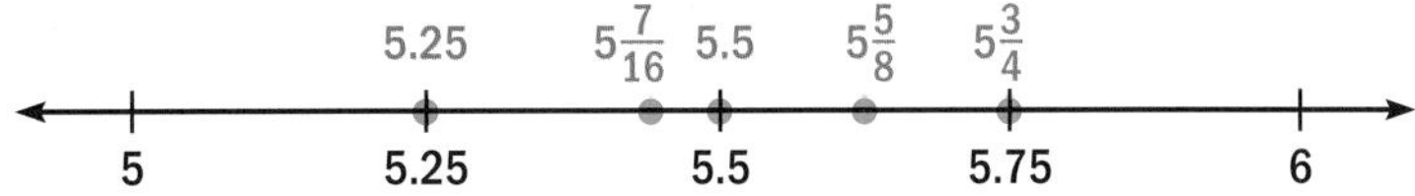

ANSWER From shortest to longest: painted bunting, lazuli bunting, indigo bunting, house finch, purple finch.

Your turn now **Order the numbers from least to greatest.**

1. $0.51, \frac{3}{5}, \frac{11}{20}, \frac{2}{3}, 0.62$
2. $-1\frac{1}{8}, -1\frac{3}{7}, -1.1, -1.43, -1\frac{4}{15}$

Terminating Decimals To write a terminating decimal as a fraction or mixed number, use the place value of the decimal's last digit to determine the denominator. For example, you can write 0.37 as $\frac{37}{100}$, or thirty-seven hundredths, because 7 is in the hundredths' place.

EXAMPLE 3 Writing Terminating Decimals as Fractions

Write the decimal as a fraction or mixed number.

a. 0.4 **b.** −1.905

Solution

a. $0.4 = \frac{4}{10}$ 4 is in the tenths' place.

$= \frac{2}{5}$

b. $-1.905 = -1\frac{905}{1000}$ 5 is in the thousandths' place.

$= -1\frac{\cancel{905}^{181}}{\cancel{1000}_{200}}$

$= -1\frac{181}{200}$

Repeating Decimals To write a repeating decimal as a fraction or mixed number, form two equivalent equations by multiplying by a power of 10. Then subtract the equations.

with Notetaking

You may wish to copy examples into your notebook that show writing repeating decimals as fractions. Include examples with one, two, and three repeating digits.

EXAMPLE 4 Writing Repeating Decimals as Fractions

To write $0.\overline{48}$ as a fraction, let $x = 0.\overline{48}$, or 0.484848 . . . .

(1) The number has 2 repeating digits, so multiply by 100. Let $100x = 48.\overline{48}$, or 48.484848 . . . .

(2) Then subtract x from $100x$.

$$\begin{aligned} 100x &= 48.484848\ldots \\ -\quad x &= 0.484848\ldots \\ \hline 99x &= 48.000000\ldots \end{aligned}$$

(3) Solve for x. Simplify. $x = \frac{48}{99}$, or $\frac{16}{33}$

ANSWER The decimal $0.\overline{48}$ is equivalent to the fraction $\frac{16}{33}$.

Your turn now **Write the decimal as a fraction or mixed number.**

3. 0.3 **4.** 0.62 **5.** −2.45 **6.** −1.24

7. $-0.\overline{7}$ **8.** $-10.\overline{1}$ **9.** $0.\overline{24}$ **10.** $0.8\overline{3}$

Exercises

More Practice, p. 731

Getting Ready to Practice

Vocabulary **Tell whether the number is included in each of the following number groups: *rational number, integer, whole number.***

1. 0 **2.** 0.55 **3.** −14 **4.** $0.\overline{3}$

Write the fraction or mixed number as a decimal.

5. $\frac{4}{5}$ **6.** $2\frac{1}{4}$ **7.** $\frac{1}{3}$ **8.** $1\frac{5}{8}$

Write the decimal as a fraction or mixed number.

9. 0.6 **10.** −1.02 **11.** $0.\overline{8}$ **12.** $0.\overline{53}$

13. **Caterpillars** Write the following lengths of caterpillars in order from least to greatest: $1\frac{7}{8}$ inches, 1.8 inches, $2\frac{1}{9}$ inches, 2.1 inches.

Practice and Problem Solving

HELP with Homework

Example	Exercises
1	14–25, 44–45
2	42, 43, 46
3	26–33
4	34–41

Online Resources
CLASSZONE.COM

- More Examples
- eTutorial Plus

Write the fraction or mixed number as a decimal.

14. $\frac{3}{4}$ **15.** $-\frac{1}{9}$ **16.** $-\frac{12}{25}$ **17.** $\frac{7}{12}$

18. $-\frac{4}{25}$ **19.** $\frac{27}{50}$ **20.** $3\frac{11}{16}$ **21.** $-\frac{33}{80}$

22. $\frac{8}{15}$ **23.** $-14\frac{7}{11}$ **24.** $-\frac{14}{33}$ **25.** $\frac{27}{44}$

Write the decimal as a fraction or mixed number.

26. -0.48 **27.** -0.56 **28.** 1.31 **29.** 2.79

30. 0.365 **31.** 7.253 **32.** -0.0012 **33.** -5.0032

34. $0.\overline{2}$ **35.** 0.8 **36.** $-0.1\overline{5}$ **37.** $0.\overline{15}$

38. $0.\overline{63}$ **39.** $0.\overline{042}$ **40.** $-0.\overline{243}$ **41.** $20.2\overline{07}$

Order the numbers from least to greatest.

42. $-\frac{4}{5}, -\frac{3}{10}, -\frac{3}{8}, -0.2, -0.4$

43. $9\frac{3}{4}, 9.74, 9\frac{5}{7}, 9.72, 9\frac{9}{13}$

44. Stock Listings The New York Stock Exchange once used fractions to list the values of its stocks. It switched to decimals in 2001. Write the following stock prices as decimals rounded to the nearest cent.

$$\$5\frac{1}{4}, \$44\frac{1}{2}, \$53\frac{3}{8}, \$17\frac{7}{16}$$

45. Look for a Pattern Write the fractions $\frac{1}{11}, \frac{2}{11}$, and $\frac{3}{11}$ as decimals.

Use your results to predict the decimal forms of $\frac{4}{11}$ and $\frac{5}{11}$.

Extended Problem Solving In Exercises 46–48, use the table below. It tells the fraction of students in a survey that named each breakfast food as their favorite.

Breakfast food	Bagels	Bacon	Eggs	Cereal	Pancakes
Fraction of students	$\frac{1}{8}$	$\frac{1}{12}$	$\frac{3}{16}$	$\frac{1}{4}$	$\frac{3}{25}$

46. Order Write each fraction as a decimal and order the foods from most popular to least popular.

47. Compare How many more students picked the most popular food than the least popular food if 1200 students responded to the survey?

48. Analyze How many of the 1200 students did not choose any of the foods shown?

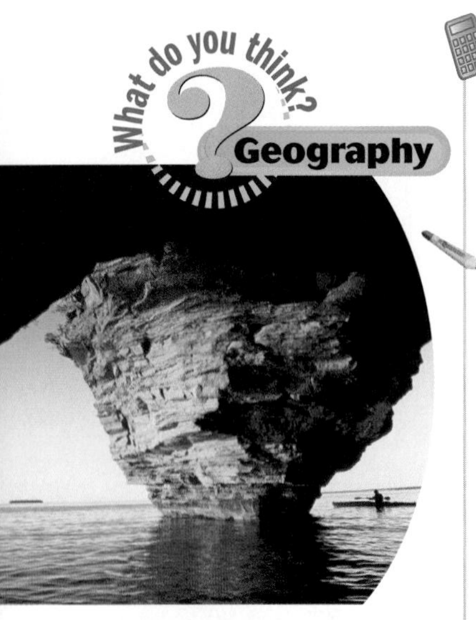

■ **Lake Superior**

Lake Superior has a surface area of about 32,000 square miles. About what fraction of the 182,000 square miles of U.S. water surface area is this? Write this fraction as a decimal.

49. Area The total area of the United States is about 3,718,000 square miles. The portion of this area that is covered by water is $\frac{182,000}{3,718,000}$. Express this fraction as a decimal rounded to three places. About what fraction of the area of the United States is covered by water?

50. Writing Jim says, "Write a mixed number as a decimal by writing it as an improper fraction, and then dividing." Estela says, "Just convert the fraction part of a mixed number to a decimal, and then you can add that to the whole number part." Do both methods work? Explain why or why not.

51. Challenge In the following expressions, $x > 0$. Order the expressions from least to greatest: $x, \frac{x}{5}, \frac{x}{3}, \frac{x}{7}, \frac{x}{8}, \frac{x}{6}, \frac{x}{2}, \frac{x}{4}$.

52. Critical Thinking Find a rational number between $\frac{1}{6}$ and $\frac{2}{9}$. Explain your reasoning.

Mixed Review

Solve the equation using mental math. *(Lesson 1.5)*

53. $s - 7 = 10$ **54.** $4d = 24$ **55.** $5 + t = 18$

Choose a Strategy Use a strategy from the list to solve the following problem. Explain your choice of strategy.

56. You are racing with Al, Sue, and Kim. In how many orders can you and your friends finish the race?

Problem Solving Strategies
- Guess, Check, and Revise
- Make a List
- Draw a Diagram

Basic Skills Estimate the sum or difference.

57. 129 + 42 **58.** 457 + 301 **59.** 91 − 28 **60.** 217 − 188

Test-Taking Practice

INTERNET
State Test Practice
CLASSZONE.COM

61. Multiple Choice Which list is in order from least to greatest?

A. $\frac{1}{7}$, 0.125, 0.45, $\frac{4}{9}$ **B.** $\frac{1}{7}$, 0.125, $\frac{4}{9}$, 0.45

C. 0.125, $\frac{1}{7}$, $\frac{4}{9}$, 0.45 **D.** 0.125, $\frac{1}{7}$, 0.45, $\frac{4}{9}$

62. Multiple Choice In a class, $\frac{22}{25}$ of the students are right-handed. What is another way to express this number?

F. 0.22 **G.** 0.25 **H.** 0.47 **I.** 0.88

Adding and Subtracting Decimals

BEFORE	Now	WHY?
You added and subtracted fractions.	You'll add and subtract decimals.	So you can compare snowfall amounts, as in Ex. 34.

Word Watch

front-end estimation, p. 248

INDIANA
Academic Standards

- Computation (8.2.1, 8.2.4)
- Algebra and Functions (8.3.8)

In the Real World

Dancing The table shows the amounts of money (in billions of dollars) that people in the United States spent on dance studios, schools, and halls. How much was spent in 1995 and 1996? How much more was spent in 1998 than in 1997?

Money Spent on Dancing

Year	Dollars (billions)
1994	0.906
1995	0.947
1996	1.046
1997	1.08
1998	1.138

You can use a vertical format to add or subtract decimals. Begin by lining up the decimal points. Then add or subtract as with whole numbers. Be sure to include the decimal point in your answer.

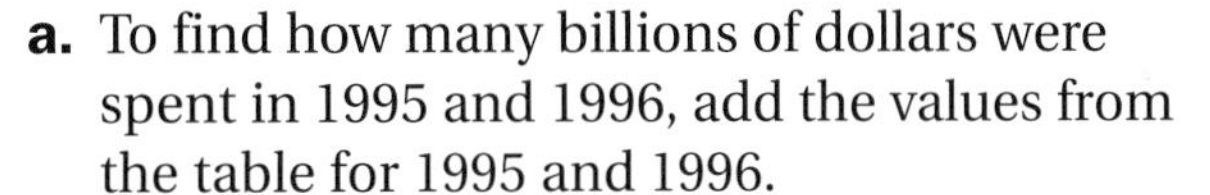

EXAMPLE 1 Adding and Subtracting Decimals

a. To find how many billions of dollars were spent in 1995 and 1996, add the values from the table for 1995 and 1996.

$$\begin{array}{r} 0.947 \\ +\ 1.046 \\ \hline 1.993 \end{array}$$

ANSWER In 1995 and 1996, 1.993 billion dollars was spent.

b. To find how much more was spent in 1998 than in 1997, subtract the value for 1997 from the value for 1998.

$$\begin{array}{r} 1.138 \\ -\ 1.080 \\ \hline 0.058 \end{array}$$

Use a zero as a placeholder.

ANSWER In 1998, 0.058 billion dollars more was spent than in 1997.

Your turn now **Find the sum or difference.**

1. $-12.5 + (-4.55)$
2. $8.93 + 0.367$
3. $7.624 + (-0.05)$
4. $8.91 - 2.745$
5. $-5.3 - 11.49$
6. $5.376 - (-0.8)$

EXAMPLE 2 Solving Equations with Decimals

a.

$y - 1.537 = 6.48$	Original equation
$y - 1.537 + \mathbf{1.537} = 6.48 + \mathbf{1.537}$	**Add 1.537 to each side.**
$y = 8.017$	Simplify.

b.

$x + (-0.34) = 4.27$	Original equation
$x + (-0.34) + \mathbf{0.34} = 4.27 + \mathbf{0.34}$	**Add 0.34 to each side to undo adding −0.34.**
$x = 4.61$	Simplify.

Estimating You can estimate sums using **front-end estimation**. Add the front-end digits to get a low estimate. Then use the remaining digits to adjust the sum to a closer estimate.

EXAMPLE 3 Using Front-End Estimation

Theater You want to estimate the cost of supplies for a play. Is the cost of the items shown (excluding tax) more or less than your $50 budget?

Theater Supplies	
cowboy hat	$18.97
cotton fabric	$9.49
rope	$3.49
safety pins	$2.19
picnic basket	$16.77

Solution

Use front-end estimation.

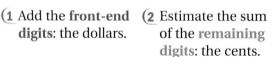

(1) Add the **front-end digits**: the dollars.

$18.97
$9.49
$3.49
$2.19
$16.77
$48

(2) Estimate the sum of the **remaining digits**: the cents.

$18.97 — $1
$9.49, $3.49 → $1
$2.19, $16.77 → $1
$3

(3) Add your results.

$48
+ $3
$51

ANSWER The cost of the items is more than your $50 budget.

Your turn now **Solve the equation.**

7. $x + 1.38 = 2.55$ **8.** $z - 5.3 = 16.29$ **9.** $y - (-0.83) = 0.48$

10. Use front-end estimation to estimate the sum $1.95 + $7.49 + $3.50.

5.6 Exercises

More Practice, p. 731

Getting Ready to Practice

1. **Vocabulary** Copy and complete: You can get a low estimate of 13.56 + 11.42 + 25.94 by adding the front-end digits _?_, _?_, and _?_.

2. **Find the Error** Describe and correct the error in the solution.

$$\begin{array}{r} 10.43 \\ +\ 7.521 \\ \hline 8.564 \end{array}$$

Find the sum or difference.

3. 1.35 + 6.02
4. 14.1 − 3.662

Solve the equation.

5. $x + 2.9 = 5.3$
6. $y - 4.15 = -4.26$
7. $z - (-7.7) = 13.31$

Use front-end estimation to estimate the sum.

8. 2.32 + 6.69 + 8.50 + 4.46
9. 10.23 + 6.98 + 9.05 + 5.80

10. **Sales Tax** Your purchase costs $9.87 plus sales tax of $.49. What is the total amount you pay?

Practice and Problem Solving

HELP with Homework

Example	Exercises
1	11-25, 34, 36
2	26-31
3	32-33, 35

· More Examples
· eTutorial Plus

Find the sum or difference.

11. 30.193 + 7.91
12. 2.507 + 0.586
13. −6.08 + 2.661
14. −0.37 + (−1.8)
15. 6.8 + (−1.812)
16. −12.09 + 1.20
17. 3.28 + (−4.91)
18. 1.46 + (−1.564)
19. 1.57 − 9.28
20. 68.79 − 9.18
21. 15.7 − (−6.4)
22. −0.99 − 0.304
23. 25.885 − 6.9
24. 29.1 − (−3.05)
25. −4.22 − 0.807

Algebra **Solve the equation.**

26. $y + 1.5 = 37$
27. $-2.8 + x = 4.51$
28. $10.4 = 12.46 + z$
29. $7.81 = 7.98 + y$
30. $z + (-3.19) = 5.83$
31. $x - 0.013 = -6.36$

Use front-end estimation to estimate the sum.

32. 5.62 + 4.89 + 3.44 + 9.98
33. 23.70 + 16.12 + 5.96 + 14.18

34. **Snowfall** Chicago's average snowfall in December is 11.2 inches. In 2001, only 1.6 inches fell in December. In inches, how much below average was this?

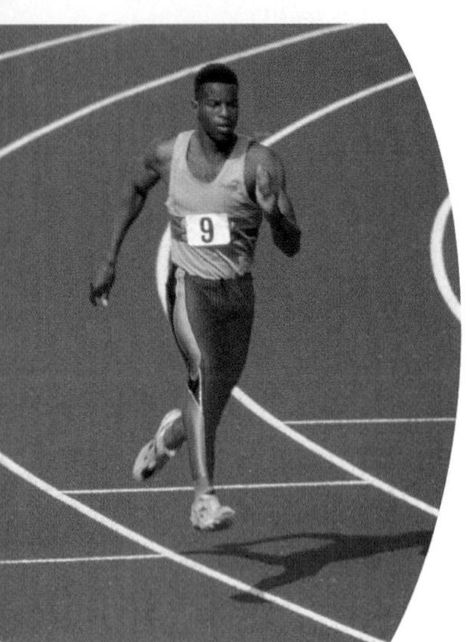

35. **Critical Thinking** The number 29.32 can be written as the sum $20 + 9 + 0.3 + 0.02$. Write 345.692 as a sum in this form.

36. **Track** You run 400 meters in 58.01 seconds. What is the difference of your time and the school record of 55.49 seconds?

Geometry Find the perimeter of the figure.

37. 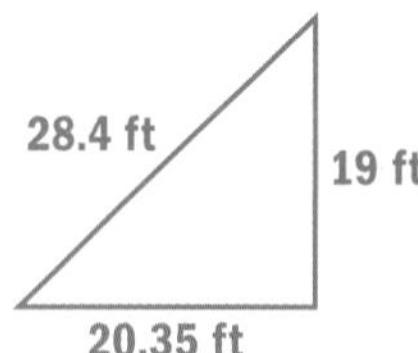

38. 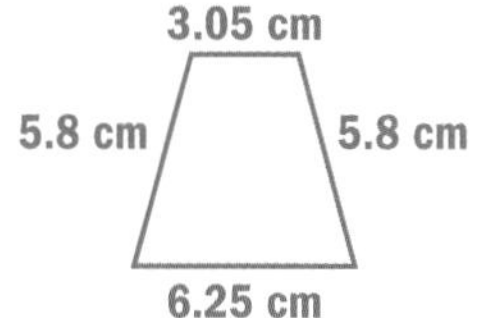

39. 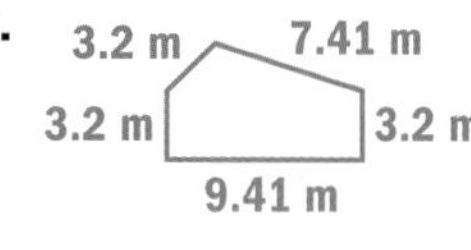

40. **Banking** Use the bank record for the month of January. The beginning balance was \$83.47. Estimate the balance at the end of the month. Then find the exact balance.

Date	Transaction	Deposit	Withdrawal
1/02	deposit	\$50	
1/10	groceries		\$75.35
1/16	bookstore		\$12.95
1/22	deposit	\$112.81	
1/29	video rentals		\$13.08
1/31	computer game		\$21.98

Challenge Find the sum or difference. Write your answer in decimal form.

41. $6.28 + \frac{5}{2}$ 42. $\frac{3}{8} + 4.6$ 43. $12.853 - \frac{3}{4}$ 44. $\frac{9}{20} - 0.35$

Mixed Review 

Simplify the expression using only positive exponents. *(Lesson 4.7)*

45. -12^0 46. $3^{-2} \cdot 3^5$ 47. $\frac{b^{-4}}{b^{10}}$ 48. $\frac{32m^{-8}}{8m^2}$

Find the product or quotient. Simplify if possible. *(Lessons 5.3, 5.4)*

49. $-\frac{8}{9} \cdot \left(\frac{-5}{7}\right)$ 50. $5\frac{3}{7} \cdot \frac{21}{22}$ 51. $-5 \div \left(\frac{-2}{3}\right)$ 52. $6\frac{5}{12} \div 2\frac{3}{4}$

Test-Taking Practice 

INTERNET
State Test Practice
CLASSZONE.COM

53. **Multiple Choice** When adding two positive decimals that are less than 1, the sum is always __?__.

A. less than 1 **B.** negative **C.** more than 1 **D.** positive

54. **Short Response** Plot the following points in a coordinate plane. Then connect the points to form a rectangle and find its perimeter.
$A(1.25, 3.5)$, $B(4.25, 3.5)$, $C(4.25, 6.75)$, $D(1.25, 6.75)$

Multiplying and Dividing Decimals

BEFORE	Now	WHY?
You multiplied and divided integers and fractions.	You'll multiply and divide decimals.	So you can find how many balloons you can buy, as in Ex. 24.

Word Watch

leading digit, p. 251

INDIANA Academic Standards

- Computation (8.2.1)

In the Real World

Rafting You travel downstream in a raft at a rate of about 4.3 miles per hour. How far will you travel in 2.5 hours?

Multiplying Decimals

Words Multiply decimals as you do whole numbers. Then place the decimal point. The number of decimal places in the product is the total number of decimal places in the factors.

Numbers 2.25 (2 places) × 8.9 (1 place) = 20.025 (3 places)

EXAMPLE 1 Multiplying Decimals

To find how far you travel in the problem above about rafting, substitute the given values into the distance formula. Distance = rate • time, so distance = 4.3 • 2.5.

$$\begin{array}{r l} 4.3 & \text{1 decimal place} \\ \times\ 2.5 & \text{+1 decimal place} \\ \hline 215 & \\ 86 & \\ \hline 10.75 & \text{2 decimal places} \end{array}$$

ANSWER You will travel about 10.75 miles.

A number's **leading digit** is its leftmost nonzero digit. To check that a product is reasonable, round each factor to its leading digit and multiply.

4.3 • 2.5 → Round factors to leading digit. → 4 • 3 = 12 ✓

Your turn now **Multiply. Show that your answer is reasonable.**

1. −7.39 • 2.1
2. 19.62 • 5.07
3. 1.13 • 0.04
4. −0.85 • (−8)

Dividing Decimals

Words When you divide by a decimal, multiply both the divisor and the dividend by the power of ten that will make the divisor an integer. Then divide.

Numbers $2.75\overline{)15.125}$ **Multiply by 100.** $\begin{array}{r} 5.5 \\ 275\overline{)1512.5} \end{array}$

EXAMPLE 2 Dividing Decimals

To find the quotient 60.102 ÷ 6.3, multiply the divisor and dividend by 10. Move the decimal points 1 place to the right.

$6.3\overline{)60.102}$ **Move decimal points.** $63\overline{)601.02}$

Then divide. $\begin{array}{r} 9.54 \\ 63\overline{)601.02} \end{array}$

✓**Check** To check that the quotient is reasonable, round the quotient and the divisor to the leading digit. Then multiply. The result should be close in value to the dividend.

$9.54 \cdot 6.3$ **Round.** $10 \cdot 6 = 60$ ✓

EXAMPLE 3 Using Zeros as Placeholders

To find some quotients, you may need to use zeros as placeholders.

Placeholder in Dividend

$6 \div 1.2$

$1.2\overline{)6.0}$ Zero as placeholder

$\begin{array}{r} 5 \\ 12\overline{)60} \\ \underline{60} \\ 0 \end{array}$

Placeholder in Quotient

$0.0126 \div 1.8$

$1.8\overline{)0.0126}$

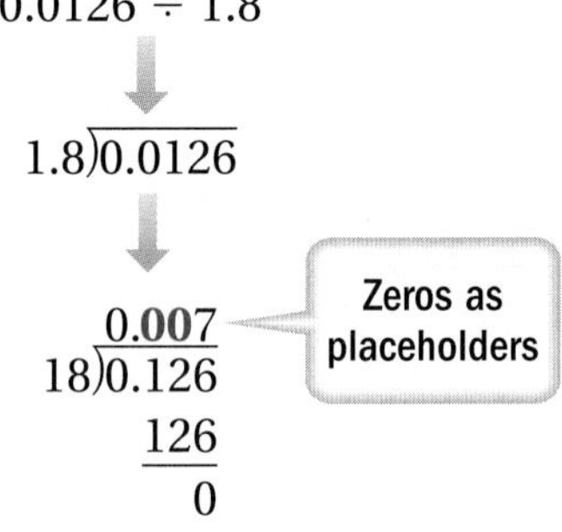

$\begin{array}{r} 0.007 \\ 18\overline{)0.126} \\ \underline{126} \\ 0 \end{array}$ Zeros as placeholders

Your turn now **Find the quotient.**

5. $1.6 \div 0.04$ **6.** $0.632 \div 0.79$ **7.** $-13 \div (-0.65)$

8. $-4.365 \div (-4.5)$ **9.** $0.3744 \div 1.56$ **10.** $-0.0108 \div 2.7$

Getting Ready to Practice

1. **Vocabulary** Copy the division problem. Use the words *quotient*, *dividend*, and *divisor* to label each number.

$$\underline{?} \longrightarrow 9\overline{)7.2} \longleftarrow \underline{?} \qquad 0.8 \longleftarrow \underline{?}$$

Multiply or divide. Show that your answer is reasonable.

2. 7.8 • 2.6
3. 3.75 • 0.4
4. 13.2 ÷ 1.1
5. 0.5 ÷ 1.25

6. **Guided Problem Solving** A mother rhinoceros weighs 3600 pounds. Her baby weighs 0.38 of her weight. How much does the baby weigh? Explain why your answer is reasonable.

(1) Write a verbal model to describe the problem.

(2) Substitute the given values and solve.

(3) Check to see that your answer is reasonable.

Practice and Problem Solving

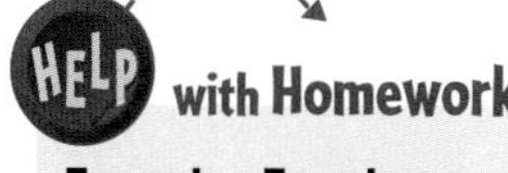

HELP with Homework

Example	Exercises
1	7-22, 23, 25
2	7-22, 24, 26
3	7-22

· More Examples
· eTutorial Plus

Find the product or quotient.

7. 25 • 0.2
8. 2.4 • 0.3
9. −8.2 • 0.7
10. 13.65 • 1.1
11. 4.8 ÷ 1.2
12. 4.9 ÷ 0.07
13. 5 ÷ (−0.1)
14. −8 ÷ (−3.2)
15. 5.41 • 0.35
16. −0.57 ÷ 0.38
17. 4.844 ÷ 0.56
18. −2.687 • (−9)
19. 37.41 ÷ 4.3
20. 0.098 • 0.55
21. 6.025 • 48.2
22. 1.11 ÷ 0.925

23. **Find the Error** Describe and correct the error in the solution.

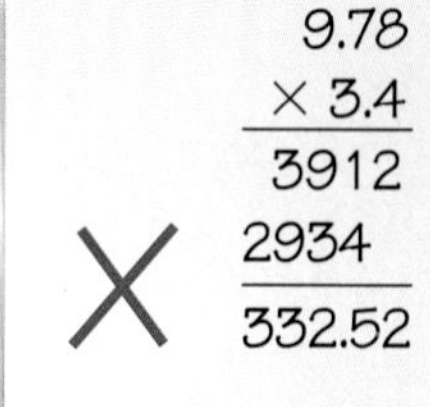

24. **Balloons** You are buying balloons that cost $.89 per package to decorate for a school dance. You have $14.75 to spend. How many packages of balloons can you buy?

25. **Look for a Pattern** Copy and complete the table by multiplying each number in the leftmost column by the number at the top of each other column. Describe the pattern.

×	1	0.1	0.01	0.001	0.0001
87	87	8.7	?	?	?
356	356	?	?	?	?
1200	?	?	?	?	?

Kilauea Volcano, Hawaii

26. **Lava Flows** A lava flow is a stream of molten rock that pours from an erupting vent. A lava flow travels 15.5 miles down a steep slope in 2.5 hours. Find the average rate at which the flow travels. Write your answer in miles per hour. Explain why your answer is reasonable.

Algebra **Solve the equation.**

27. $9 = \frac{a}{-0.9}$ **28.** $\frac{c}{4.5} = 0.16$ **29.** $1.2x = 0.321$ **30.** $-8.25y = -3.3$

Evaluate the expression.

31. $3.4^3 + 5.1 \div 1.7 - 4.89$ **32.** $6.2 \cdot (18.77 - 6.27) + 9.1^2$

33. **Writing** Explain how 4.6 divided by 0.23 is related to 460 divided by 23. Are the quotients the same? Why?

34. **Postal Rates** The table shows rates to mail a first class letter. How much does it cost to mail a first class letter that weighs 3.5 ounces?

First ounce or fraction of ounce	$.37
Each additional ounce or fraction	$.23

35. **Critical Thinking** How many decimal places does 1.3^1 have? 1.3^2? 1.3^3? 1.3^7? Explain your reasoning.

36. **Challenge** One micron is equal to 0.001 millimeter. If a bacteria is 4 microns wide, how many times would you have to magnify it for the bacteria to appear 1 millimeter wide?

Mixed Review

Write the number in standard form. *(Lesson 4.8)*

37. 6.89×10^9 **38.** 1.3×10^{-12} **39.** 7.405×10^{-6}

Order the numbers from least to greatest. *(Lesson 5.5)*

40. $2.32, \frac{9}{4}, 2.5, 2\frac{3}{10}, 2, \frac{11}{5}$ **41.** $-\frac{9}{20}, -0.46, -\frac{3}{8}, -\frac{5}{12}, -0.4$

Basic Skills **Find the quotient.**

42. $55 \div 6$ **43.** $127 \div 5$ **44.** $307 \div 29$ **45.** $8607 \div 42$

Test-Taking Practice

INTERNET
State Test Practice
CLASSZONE.COM

46. **Multiple Choice** The quotient $-0.57 \div 0.38$ is __?__.

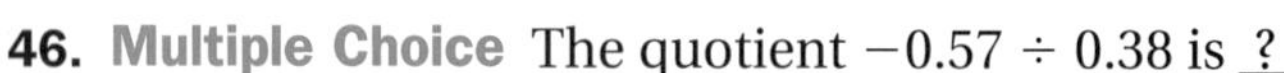

A. an integer **B.** negative **C.** more than 1 **D.** positive

47. **Short Response** You have $75 to spend on party decorations that cost $4.89 per bag, including tax. Find how many bags you can buy. Estimate to check that your answer is reasonable. Show your work.

5.8 Hands-on Activity

GOAL

Collect and analyze data.

MATERIALS

- number cubes

Collecting and Analyzing Data

You can collect data and find a number that represents the data. The *median* is the middle value when the values are written in order. The *mode* is the value that occurs most often.

Explore 1 **Collect data by rolling two number cubes to explore how often each sum occurs.**

1 Roll a pair of number cubes eleven times and record the results.

3 + 2 = 5 **4 + 4 = 8** **6 + 6 = 12** **1 + 2 = 3** **1 + 6 = 7** **2 + 1 = 3**

5 + 3 = 8 **4 + 1 = 5** **1 + 5 = 6** **2 + 6 = 8** **2 + 2 = 4**

2 Add the sums together. Divide by the number of rolls to find the mean.

$$\frac{5 + 8 + 12 + 3 + 7 + 3 + 8 + 5 + 6 + 8 + 4}{11} = \frac{69}{11} \approx 6.3$$

3 Order the sums. Find the median and the mode.

3, 3, 4, 5, 5, 6, 7, 8, 8, 8, 12

middle number (6) most frequent number (8, 8, 8)

4 Which sum do you think occurs most often? Compare your results with other groups.

Your turn now **Find the mean, median, and mode of the data set.**

1. 4.2, 6.1, 3.8, 4.1, 10.2, 9.6, 6.1, 7.3, 2.1, 2.4, 9.8

2. 105, 121, 42, 78, 77, 63, 108, 32, 33, 121, 64

3. $2\frac{1}{2}, 7\frac{3}{4}, 9\frac{1}{4}, 7\frac{1}{2}, 4\frac{3}{8}, 7\frac{3}{4}, 3\frac{7}{8}$

Explore 2

Collect data about the number of letters in the last name of each student in your class.

1. Find the shortest and longest names so you can make a frequency table.

2. Count the number of letters in each name. Make a tally mark for each name.

3. Find the most frequent name length. This is the mode.

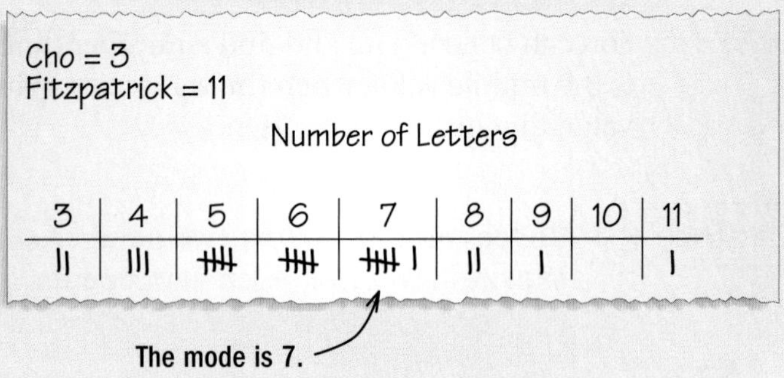

Cho = 3
Fitzpatrick = 11
Number of Letters
3 | 4 | 5 | 6 | 7 | 8 | 9 | 10 | 11
The mode is 7.

4. Find the mean number of letters in the last names.

5. Can you use the mean to describe the average length of a last name in your class? Can you use the mode? Explain.

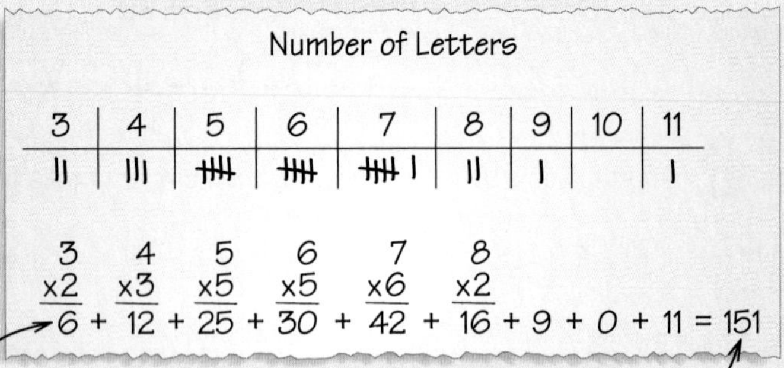

You can multiply to count the number of letters for each column. Then add the column totals.

Divide by the number of students. The mean is $151 \div 25 \approx 6$.

Your turn now

4. A new student whose last name has 16 letters joins your class. If you add "16" to your data, how does this affect the mean and the mode? Explain.

Stop *and* Think

5. **Writing** You are designing a form to collect data. Students will write their last names in a row of small boxes, one letter per box. How many boxes do you think the form should provide? Explain.

Mean, Median, and Mode

BEFORE	Now	WHY?
You used tables and graphs to analyze data sets.	You'll describe data sets using mean, median, mode, and range.	So you can describe World Series attendance, as in Ex. 14.

mean, p. 257
median, p. 257
mode, p. 257
range, p. 258

INDIANA Academic Standards

- Data Analysis and Probability (8.6.3)

In the Real World

Biology A marine biologist records the locations of deep sea jellies in relation to the ocean surface. Jellies are found at −2278 feet, −1875 feet, −3210 feet, −2755 feet, −2407 feet, and −2901 feet. What is the average location of a deep sea jelly?

Three types of averages can be used to describe a data set.

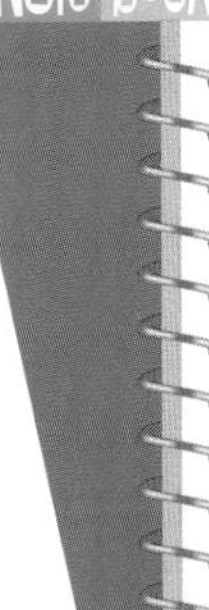

Averages

The **mean** of a data set is the sum of the values divided by the number of values.

The **median** of a data set is the middle value when the values are written in numerical order. If a data set has an even number of values, the median is the mean of the two middle values.

The **mode** of a data set is the value that occurs most often. A data set can have no mode, one mode, or more than one mode.

EXAMPLE 1 Finding a Mean

To find the mean of the 6 locations of the deep sea jellies in the problem above, divide the sum of the locations by 6.

$$\text{Mean} = \frac{-2278 + (-1875) + (-3210) + (-2755) + (-2407) + (-2901)}{6}$$

$$= \frac{-15{,}426}{6}$$

$$= -2571$$

ANSWER The mean location in relation to the ocean surface is −2571 ft.

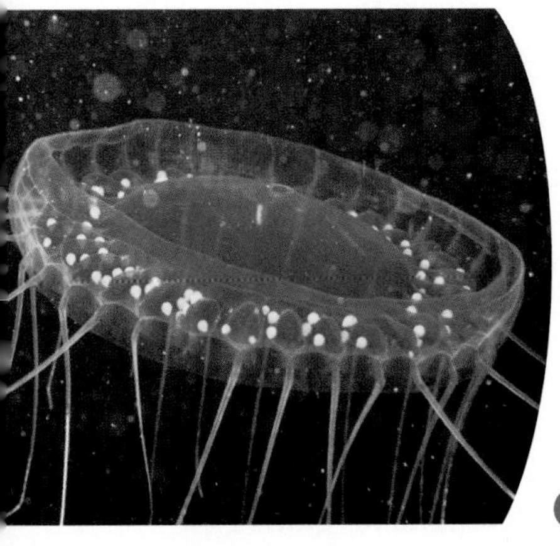
Deep sea jelly

Your turn now **Find the mean of the data.**

1. −3°C, 44°C, −11°C, 9°C, −21°C **2.** $12\frac{1}{2}$ in., $14\frac{3}{4}$ in., $20\frac{1}{2}$ in., $16\frac{3}{4}$ in.

Range The **range** of a data set is the difference of the greatest value and the least value.

EXAMPLE 2 Finding Median, Mode, and Range

Movies **Find the median, mode(s), and range of the movie prices below.**

\$7.20, \$13.25, \$14.94, \$16.56, \$18.74, \$19.99, \$19.99, \$29.49

Median: The data set has an even number of prices, so the median is the mean of the two middle values, \$16.56 and \$18.74.

$$\text{Median} = \frac{\$16.56 + \$18.74}{2} = \frac{\$35.30}{2} = \$17.65$$

Mode: The price that occurs most often is \$19.99. This is the mode.

Range: Find the difference of the greatest and the least values.

$$\text{Range} = \$29.49 - \$7.20 = \$22.29$$

Watch Out!

If the data are not ordered, you need to order the data so you can find the median.

Your turn now **Find the median, mode(s), and range of the data.**

3. 14, 13, 20, 24, 15, 10, 22, 17, 18

4. 9, 7, 4, 9, 4, 10, 5, 14, 9, 4

EXAMPLE 3 Choosing a Representative Average

Ice Cream Groups A and B try a new ice cream flavor and rate it on a scale of 1 to 10 as shown. Which average best represents each group?

Group A Ratings

1, 2, 3, 3, 5, 5, 5, 7, 8, 10

Group B Ratings

1, 1, 1, 2, 3, 4, 4, 9, 10, 10

Solution

Group A

$$\text{Mean} = \frac{49}{10} = 4.9$$

$$\text{Median} = \frac{5 + 5}{2} = \frac{10}{2} = 5$$

Mode: 5

ANSWER The mean, median, and mode are very close. So each average is a fair representation of the ratings as a group.

Group B

$$\text{Mean} = \frac{45}{10} = 4.5$$

$$\text{Median} = \frac{3 + 4}{2} = \frac{7}{2} = 3.5$$

Mode: 1

ANSWER The mean is higher than all but 3 ratings. The mode is equal to the lowest rating. So, mean and mode are not good choices. The median best represents the ratings.

5.8 Exercises

More Practice, p. 731

Getting Ready to Practice

Vocabulary **In Exercises 1–3, use the data set 6, 12, 4, 15, 10, 6, 2, 9. Complete the statement using *mean, median, mode, or range.***

1. The _?_ is 8.
2. The _?_ is 6.
3. The _?_ is 13.

Find the mean, median, mode(s), and range of the data.

4. 8.98, 3.67, 11.13, 8.98, 11.24
5. −71, −56, −62, −44, −56, −47

6. **Find the Error** Describe and correct the error in the solution.

3, 6, 5, 2, 8, 9, 5, 8, 1, 5, 10, 8
The mode of the data set is 5.

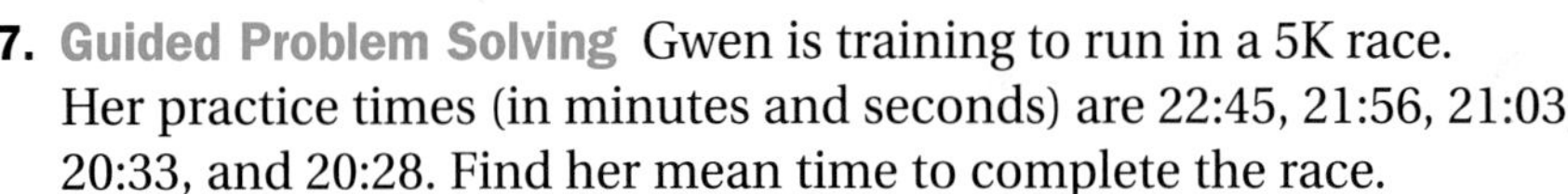

7. **Guided Problem Solving** Gwen is training to run in a 5K race. Her practice times (in minutes and seconds) are 22:45, 21:56, 21:03, 20:33, and 20:28. Find her mean time to complete the race.
   (1) Change Gwen's practice times to seconds.
   (2) Find the sum of the practice times. Divide by the number of times.
   (3) Convert your answer to minutes and seconds.

Practice and Problem Solving

Find the mean, median, mode(s), and range of the data.

8. Distances: 16 km, 23 km, 11 km, 6 km, 15 km, 23 km, 17 km, 16 km
9. Weekly hits at a Web site: 115, 157, 289, 185, 164, 225, 185, 208
10. Golf scores: −2, 0, 3, 1, 0, −1, 2, −2, −3, 0, 4, 1
11. Elevations: 127 ft, −8 ft, 436 ft, 508 ft, −23 ft, 47 ft
12. Daily calories: 2000, 1872, 2112, 2255, 2080, 1795, 1977
13. Shoe lengths: $10\frac{3}{4}$ in., $9\frac{1}{2}$ in., $8\frac{7}{8}$ in., $10\frac{1}{2}$ in., $8\frac{3}{8}$ in., $10\frac{1}{2}$ in.

Example	Exercises
1	8-13, 14-16
2	8-13, 14, 16
3	14, 17

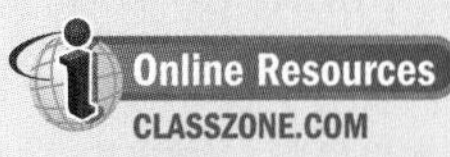

· More Examples
· eTutorial Plus

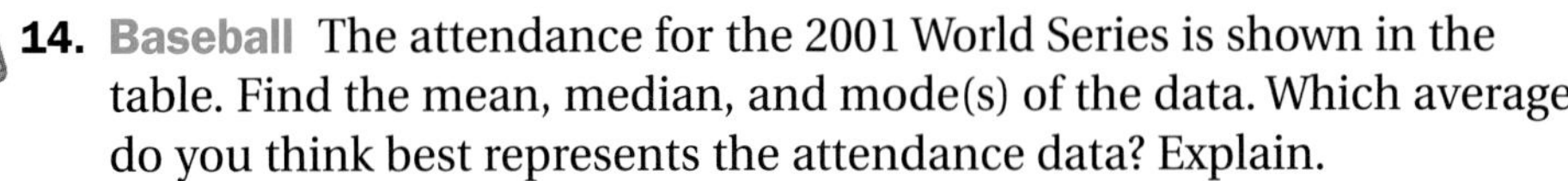

14. **Baseball** The attendance for the 2001 World Series is shown in the table. Find the mean, median, and mode(s) of the data. Which average do you think best represents the attendance data? Explain.

Game	1	2	3	4	5	6	7
Attendance	49,646	49,646	55,820	55,863	56,018	49,707	49,589

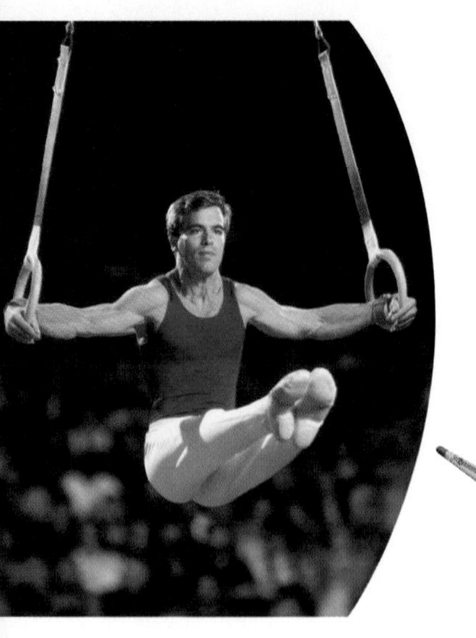

15. Gymnastics A gymnast's performance is rated by six judges. The highest and lowest scores are dropped, and the mean of the remaining four scores is the final score awarded. Find the final score of each gymnast based on the judge's ratings given. Whose final score is the highest?

	Judge 1	Judge 2	Judge 3	Judge 4	Judge 5	Judge 6
Isaac	9.5	9.1	9.3	9.3	9.6	9.4
Carl	9.8	9.7	9.3	9.7	9.6	9.4
Kurt	9.4	9.3	9.3	9.5	9.5	9.6

16. Writing Why does it make sense to find the median of a data set with an even number of values by finding the mean of the middle values?

17. Salary You are researching the average salaries for several different careers. Would you rather know the mean, median, or mode(s) of the salaries for each career? Explain your reasoning.

18. Lakes The average depth of a local lake is reported to be 2 feet. You want to know if you can wade across the lake. What information might be concealed when depth is reported as an average?

19. Algebra Find the mean of $3b$, $5b$, b, $6b$, $-6b$, and $-2b$.

20. Bowling You are bowling three games. In the first two games, you score 125 and 113 points. How many points do you need in the third game to have a mean score of 126 points?

21. Compare and Contrast Jerry and Roberta find the mean of $-2a$, a, $3a$, $6a$, and $9a$ when $a = 2.5$, as shown below. Do both methods work? If so, which method do you prefer? Explain.

Jerry

$-2a = -5 \quad a = 2.5 \quad 3a = 7.5$

$6a = 15 \quad 9a = 22.5$

$$\frac{-5 + 2.5 + 7.5 + 15 + 22.5}{5} = \frac{42.5}{5}$$

$$= 8.5$$

Roberta

$$\frac{-2a + a + 3a + 6a + 9a}{5} = \frac{17a}{5}$$

$$= \frac{17 \cdot 2.5}{5}$$

$$= 8.5$$

22. Number Sense Make two different lists of numbers that have a mean of 8 and a median and mode of 10.

23. Challenge The table shows the numbers of points you scored during your first 14 basketball games of the 15-game season. By halftime of your final game, you have scored 7 points. How many points do you need to score in the second half to have a mean of 10 points per game?

Game	1	2	3	4	5	6	7	8	9	10	11	12	13	14
Points	15	8	7	10	12	4	20	13	7	7	5	3	10	14

Mixed Review

Find the quotient. *(Lesson 2.5)*

24. $\frac{-39}{13}$ **25.** $\frac{200}{-40}$ **26.** $\frac{-44}{-11}$ **27.** $\frac{0}{-197}$

Solve the equation. *(Lessons 3.1–3.3)*

28. $x - 15 = -10$ **29.** $-8 + x = -24$ **30.** $-7x = 84$

31. $-\frac{1}{6}x = -11$ **32.** $3x - 28 = -37$ **33.** $-\frac{x}{4} + 12 = 16$

Test-Taking Practice

INTERNET
State Test Practice
CLASSZONE.COM

34. Extended Response **The table shows attendance at school dances for a year.**

Make a bar graph of the data. Find the mean and median attendance. The student council wants to find the total amount of money collected from students for admission to the dances. Would they find the bar graph, the mean, or the median most useful? Explain.

Dance	Number of Students
Fall	97
Winter Ball	88
Valentine's Day	133
Spring Fling	210
End of Year	198

What other information is also needed to find how much money was collected?

The Prize is Right!

You are a contestant on a television game show. To win a trip you must find the prices of the five items in a shopping cart.

The game show host gives you four hints about the prices.

- The mean of the prices is $1.68.
- The mode of the prices is $1.50.
- The median of the prices is $1.65.
- One item costs $.10 more than the median.

List the prices of the items in the cart in order from least to greatest.

Notebook Review

Review the vocabulary definitions in your notebook.

Copy the review examples in your notebook. Then complete the exercises.

Check Your Definitions

rational number, p. 242
terminating decimal, p. 242
repeating decimal, p. 242
front-end estimation, p. 248
leading digit, p. 251
mean, p. 257
median, p. 257
mode, p. 257
range, p. 258

Use Your Vocabulary

1. Name three averages you can use to represent a data set.

5.5 Can you order rational numbers?

EXAMPLE Order the numbers 3.7, $3\frac{5}{8}$, 3.6, and $3\frac{2}{3}$ from least to greatest.

$3\frac{5}{8} = 3.625$ $\quad$ $3\frac{2}{3} = 3.\overline{6}$ $\quad$ So, the order is 3.6, $3\frac{5}{8}$, $3\frac{2}{3}$, 3.7.

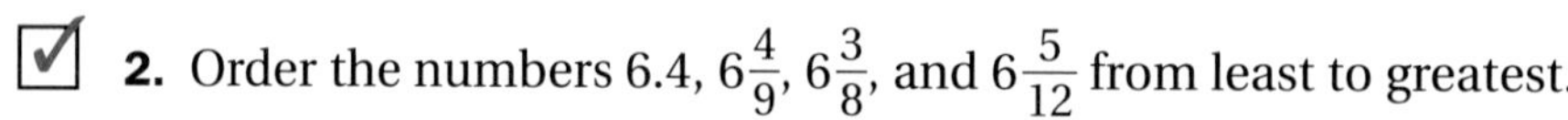

2. Order the numbers 6.4, $6\frac{4}{9}$, $6\frac{3}{8}$, and $6\frac{5}{12}$ from least to greatest.

5.6–5.7 Can you perform operations with decimals?

a.
$$\begin{array}{r} 14.02 \\ +\ 9.80 \\ \hline 23.82 \end{array}$$

b.
$$\begin{array}{r} 20.500 \\ -\ 3.764 \\ \hline 16.736 \end{array}$$

c.
$$\begin{array}{rl} 14.75 & \text{2 decimal places} \\ \times\ 1.3 & \text{+1 decimal place} \\ \hline 4425 & \\ 1475 & \\ \hline 19.175 & \text{3 decimal places} \end{array}$$

d. $4.26\overline{)21.726} \rightarrow 426\overline{)2172.6}$, quotient 5.1

Find the sum, difference, product, or quotient.

3. 1.2 + 0.67
4. 33.2 + 9.398
5. 3.16 − 1.845
6. 90.3 − (−7.81)
7. 6.24 • 0.375
8. 3.348 • 0.9
9. 66.96 ÷ (−2.7)
10. 18.91 ÷ 9.455

5.8 Can you find mean, median, mode, and range?

EXAMPLE Find the mean, median, mode(s), and range of the data set: 4, 5, 6, 6, 7, 9, 11, and 12.

$$\text{Mean} = \frac{4 + 5 + 6 + 6 + 7 + 9 + 11 + 12}{8} = \frac{60}{8} = 7.5$$

$$\text{Median} = \frac{6 + 7}{2} = \frac{13}{2} = 6.5$$

Mode = 6 Range = 12 − 4 = 8

☑ **Find the mean, median, mode(s), and range of the data set.**

11. 25, 20, 30, 22, 24, 23, 24

12. 7.2, 7.3, 7.5, 7.7, 7.9, 7.2, 7.7, 7.1

Stop *and* Think about Lessons 5.5–5.8

13. **Critical Thinking** Write an example of a data set whose mode is greater than its mean.

14. **Writing** Explain why terminating decimals and repeating decimals are rational numbers. Use examples.

Review Quiz 2

Write the fraction as a decimal or the decimal as a fraction.

1. $\frac{1}{25}$ **2.** $\frac{4}{9}$ **3.** 0.58 **4.** $0.\overline{2}$

Find the sum or difference.

5. −2.301 + 8.4 **6.** 15.25 + 9.636 **7.** 14.65 − 3.608 **8.** 3.2 − (−0.225)

Find the product or quotient.

9. −15.3 • 0.48 **10.** 3.88 • 0.9 **11.** 0.162 ÷ 2.7 **12.** 2.07 ÷ 0.225

13. **Racing Camel** A racing camel can travel at a speed of 11.75 miles per hour. How far does it travel in 0.02 hour at this speed?

14. **Tornadoes** The table shows the numbers of tornadoes in the United States from 1995–2001. Find the mean, median, mode(s), and range.

Year	1995	1996	1997	1998	1999	2000	2001
Tornadoes	1234	1173	1148	1424	1342	1071	805

Chapter Review

Vocabulary

reciprocal, p. 234
multiplicative inverse, p. 234
rational number, p. 242
terminating decimal, p. 242
repeating decimal, p. 242
front-end estimation, p. 248
leading digit, p. 251
mean, p. 257
median, p. 257
mode, p. 257
range, p. 258

Vocabulary Review

Copy and complete the statement.

1. The fractions $\frac{3}{5}$ and $\frac{5}{3}$ are _?_ because their product is 1.
2. If the remainder of the quotient $\frac{a}{b}$ is 0, then the decimal form of $\frac{a}{b}$ is a _?_ decimal.
3. You can use _?_ when you do not need to find an exact sum of a set of numbers.
4. A value that occurs most often in a data set is a _?_.
5. For a data set, the sum of the values divided by the number of values is the _?_.
6. The difference of the greatest value and the least value of a data set is the _?_.

Review Questions

Find the sum or difference. *(Lessons 5.1, 5.2)*

7. $\frac{8}{9} + \frac{4}{9}$
8. $-3\frac{5}{8} + \frac{7}{8}$
9. $-\frac{19}{25} - \frac{11}{25}$
10. $\frac{3}{10} - \frac{7}{10} - \frac{9}{10}$
11. $\frac{3}{5} + \frac{1}{4}$
12. $\frac{3}{5} - \frac{2}{3}$
13. $6\frac{2}{7} + \left(-7\frac{1}{8}\right)$
14. $-9\frac{3}{4} - 4\frac{2}{3}$
15. $-\frac{7n}{9} - \frac{5n}{9}$
16. $-\frac{m}{4} + \left(-\frac{m}{4}\right)$
17. $\frac{3}{c} - \frac{7}{2c}$
18. $\frac{5v}{3} + \frac{4v}{5}$

19. **Coins** A quarter's width is about $\frac{15}{16}$ inch. A dime's width is about $\frac{11}{16}$ inch. How much wider is a quarter? *(Lesson 5.1)*

20. **Robots** It took Central High's robot team $107\frac{1}{3}$ hours of labor to build their robot. East High built their robot in $111\frac{5}{6}$ hours. How much longer did East High School take to build their robot? *(Lesson 5.2)*

Review Questions

Find the product or quotient. *(Lessons 5.3, 5.4)*

21. $-\frac{5}{8} \cdot \frac{2}{5}$

22. $-\frac{9}{5} \cdot \left(-\frac{11}{15}\right)$

23. $-6\frac{3}{7} \cdot 2\frac{1}{2}$

24. $4 \cdot \left(-3\frac{5}{12}\right)$

25. $\frac{9}{21} \div 5$

26. $\frac{13}{18} \div \frac{5}{6}$

27. $5\frac{8}{11} \div \left(-\frac{3}{4}\right)$

28. $12\frac{1}{2} \div 4\frac{1}{6}$

Solve the equation. *(Lesson 5.4)*

29. $\frac{5}{6}x = 25$

30. $\frac{2}{3}b = \frac{8}{9}$

31. $-\frac{9}{10}y = 6\frac{3}{7}$

32. $\frac{4}{9}a + 4\frac{1}{3} = 5\frac{2}{3}$

Order the numbers from least to greatest. *(Lesson 5.5)*

33. $2\frac{3}{10}, \frac{11}{5}, 2.32, \frac{5}{2}, 2.25, 2$

34. $-0.45, -\frac{3}{8}, -\frac{5}{12}, -0.4, -0.46$

Find the sum, difference, product, or quotient. *(Lessons 5.6, 5.7)*

35. $5.2 + 20.68$

36. $0.103 + 0.7$

37. $9.6 - 3.555$

38. $-4.23 - 8.093$

39. $16.7 \cdot (-3.2)$

40. $43.4 \cdot 0.13$

41. $3.434 \div 8.08$

42. $-13 \div (-0.52)$

Newborn Animals **In Exercises 43 and 44, use the table. It shows approximate weights, in pounds, of several newborn animals.** *(Lesson 5.6)*

Newborn Animal	Birth Weight (lb)
Hippopotamus	93
Grizzly bear	1
Giant panda	0.29
Giraffe	150
Polar bear	2.09
Gentoo penguin	0.21

43. How much more does the hippopotamus weigh than the gentoo penguin?

44. How much more does the polar bear weigh than the giant panda?

45. Icebergs When an iceberg broke free from Antarctica in May of 2002, it was about 34.5 miles long and 6.9 miles wide. About how much area did the iceberg cover? *(Lesson 5.7)*

46. Cats A tiger at a zoo has a mass of 144.9 kilograms. This is 40.25 times the mass of a house cat. What is the mass of the house cat? *(Lesson 5.7)*

Find the mean, median, mode(s), and range of the data set. *(Lesson 5.8)*

47. Temperatures (°C): $-7, -1, 0, 8, 4, 2, -7, 2$

48. Jumps (meters): 14.6, 19.2, 11, 16.5, 12, 11, 10.9

49. Hand widths (in.): $3\frac{1}{2}, 2\frac{7}{8}, 3\frac{1}{8}, 3\frac{1}{4}, 2\frac{3}{4}$

50. Bike trails (km): 7, 8.3, 17.1, 4.8, 3.9, 7, 4.8, 13.1

Chapter Test

Find the sum or difference.

1. $4\frac{5}{11} - 2\frac{6}{11}$

2. $\frac{9}{16} - \left(-\frac{11}{16}\right)$

3. $-\frac{5}{6} + \frac{1}{8}$

4. $\frac{3}{7} + \left(-\frac{8}{21}\right) + \frac{2}{3}$

5. **Roller Coaster** Yesterday you had to wait in line for $1\frac{3}{4}$ hours to ride a roller coaster. Today you waited $1\frac{1}{4}$ hours. How much longer did you wait yesterday?

Find the product or quotient.

6. $\frac{2}{9} \cdot (-4)$

7. $\frac{5}{2} \cdot \frac{4}{15}$

8. $3\frac{1}{2} \div 2$

9. $7\frac{3}{4} \div 2\frac{7}{12}$

10. **Balloons** You are inflating balloons for a party. If you can inflate one balloon in $\frac{5}{6}$ minute, how many balloons can you inflate in $\frac{1}{2}$ hour?

Write the fraction as a decimal or the decimal as a fraction.

11. $\frac{7}{20}$

12. $\frac{3}{40}$

13. 0.0082

14. $0.\overline{4}$

Find the sum, difference, product, or quotient.

15. $6.2 - 5.984$

16. $2.608 + 12.93$

17. $0.7992 \div 0.333$

18. $-34.69 \cdot 12.7$

Bagels **In Exercises 19 and 20, use the table. It shows the approximate supermarket sales of three types of bagels (in billions of dollars) in the year 2000 in the United States.**

Bagel	Sales (billions)
Frozen	$.145
Refrigerated	$.072
Fresh	$.42

19. How much greater were the sales for frozen bagels than the sales for refrigerated bagels?

20. What is the total amount of supermarket sales of all three types of bagels?

21. **Algebra** Evaluate $0.2x$ and $\frac{x}{0.2}$ when $x = -4.1$, 0.06, and 1.8.

22. **Energy Bill** A gas supplier charges 64.5 cents per therm of gas used. How much does it cost for 116 therms of gas?

23. **Studying** Twelve students spent 2, 5, 3, 7, 10, 9, 8, 7, 6, 7, 6, and 2 hours studying. Find the mean, median, mode(s), and range of the data.

Chapter Standardized Test

Test-Taking Strategy Mark unanswered questions in your test booklet so you can find them quickly when you go back.

Multiple Choice

1. What is the sum of $11\frac{5}{9}$ and $-14\frac{11}{12}$?

A. $-3\frac{13}{36}$ **B.** $-3\frac{1}{3}$ **C.** $-2\frac{13}{36}$ **D.** $-2\frac{33}{108}$

2. You have hiked $2\frac{1}{10}$ miles of a 5 mile trail. How much farther must you hike?

F. $1\frac{9}{20}$ miles **G.** $2\frac{9}{10}$ miles

H. $3\frac{1}{10}$ miles **I.** $7\frac{1}{10}$ miles

3. You need $4\frac{1}{3}$ yards of fabric to make a costume for your dance team. How much fabric do you need to make 7 costumes?

A. $11\frac{1}{3}$ yards **B.** $18\frac{2}{3}$ yards

C. $28\frac{1}{3}$ yards **D.** $30\frac{1}{3}$ yards

4. What is the quotient of $-\frac{3}{4}$ and $\frac{5}{2}$?

F. $-1\frac{3}{20}$ **G.** $-\frac{7}{20}$ **H.** $-\frac{3}{10}$ **I.** $-\frac{3}{20}$

5. You order pants for \$25.60, two shirts for \$15.99 each, and socks for \$6.35. Estimate your cost.

A. about \$46 **B.** about \$48

C. about \$54 **D.** about \$64

6. By what number can you divide $\frac{5}{6}$ to get the quotient $\frac{5}{9}$?

F. $\frac{1}{3}$ **G.** $\frac{2}{3}$ **H.** $\frac{3}{2}$ **I.** 2

7. What is the value of x when $\frac{3}{4}x = \frac{9}{16}$?

A. $\frac{3}{16}$ **B.** $\frac{3}{4}$ **C.** 3 **D.** 4

8. Solve $1.312 + x = 15.6$.

F. 2.48 **G.** 11.56

H. 14.288 **I.** 15.4688

9. You use 0.75 meter of wire to hold together bunches of flowers. How many bunches can you make with 15 meters of wire?

A. 2 **B.** 20 **C.** 200 **D.** 2000

10. Which fraction is greater than 0.34?

F. $\frac{5}{16}$ **G.** $\frac{1}{3}$ **H.** $\frac{55}{162}$ **I.** $\frac{8}{23}$

11. What is the median of the data set -2, 0.4, 1, -2.6, 4.5, -3.7, 1, 3?

A. 0.2 **B.** 0.7 **C.** 1 **D.** 2.275

Short Response

12. Your rectangular garden is 3.4 meters by 2.6 meters. Your friend's square garden has sides of 2.9 meters. Whose garden has a greater area?

Extended Response

13. Your most recent phone calls lasted 1, 2, 5, 46, 2, 8, 5, 3, 7, and 2 minutes. Find the mean, median, and mode(s) of the phone call lengths. Use your understanding of mean, median, and mode to explain which of these averages is most representative of the phone calls.

CHAPTER 6

Multi-Step Equations and Inequalities

BEFORE

In previous chapters you've...

- Solved equations that required using one or two steps
- Solved one-step inequalities

Now

In Chapter 6 you'll study...

- Solving multi-step equations
- Solving equations that have variables on both sides
- Using multi-step inequalities to solve real-world problems

WHY?

So you can solve real-world problems about...

- Venus flytraps, p. 271
- fundraising, p. 274
- drumming, p. 278
- bowling, p. 296

Internet Preview
CLASSZONE.COM

- eEdition Plus Online
- eWorkbook Plus Online
- eTutorial Plus Online
- State Test Practice
- More Examples

Chapter Warm-Up Game

Review skills you need for this chapter in this quick game. Work with a partner.

Key Skill:
Solving one- and two-step equations

TREASURE HUNT

MATERIALS

- 1 number cube
- 1 Treasure Hunt board
- 20 red markers
- 20 yellow markers

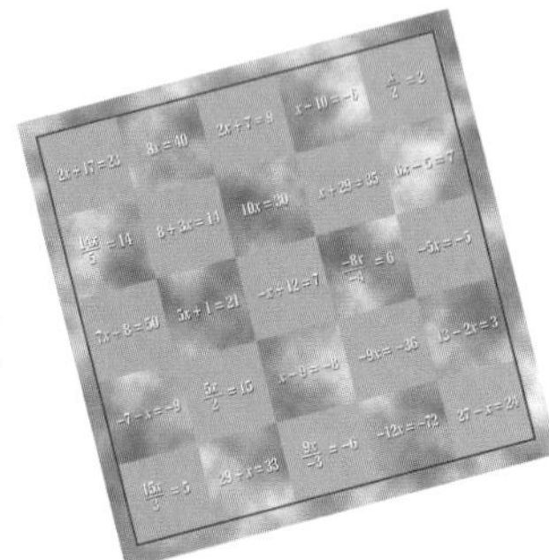

PREPARE Each player gets 20 markers of the same color. On your turn, follow the steps on the next page. You can challenge the other player when you believe they have covered an incorrect space.

1 ROLL a number cube. This is your solution.

2 COVER an equation that has your solution with a marker. If there are no equations that have your solution, you cannot place a marker and it is the next player's turn. Each space you cover is a piece of treasure.

3 CHECK that you cover a correct space for your roll. If you cover an incorrect space, then you must remove your marker and it is the next player's turn.

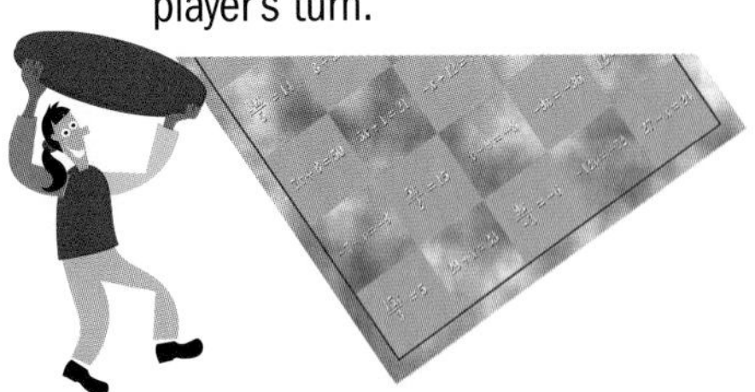

HOW TO WIN Be the player with the most spaces covered (the most treasure collected) when all spaces on the board are covered.

Stop *and* Think

1. **Writing** If the only spaces left on the board are $5x + 1 = 21$, $-7 - x = -9$, and $11 - 2x = 3$, what is the best number to roll? What is the second best number to roll? Explain.
2. **Critical Thinking** How many spaces on the board have a solution of 5? Explain how you found your answer.

Getting Ready to Learn

Word Watch

Review Words

perimeter, p. 33
distributive property, p. 85
like terms, p. 86
inequality, p. 140
reciprocal, p. 234

Review What You Need to Know 

Using Vocabulary **Copy and complete using a review word.**

1. The _?_ of a figure is the sum of its side lengths.

2. The four _?_ symbols are $<$, $>$, $\leq$, and $\geq$.

3. To divide by a fraction, you multiply by its _?_.

Simplify the expression by combining like terms. *(p. 85)*

4. $3 - 2x + 4$ **5.** $4x + 5 + x - 1$ **6.** $-2(3x + 1)$ **7.** $5(x - 4) - x$

Solve the equation. Check your answer. *(p. 119)*

8. $2x - 1 = 3$ **9.** $-3x - 2 = 7$ **10.** $4 - x = 12$ **11.** $13 = 2x + 3$

Solve the inequality. Then graph its solution. *(pp. 140, 146)*

12. $x + 5 < 18$ **13.** $x - 4 \geq -6$ **14.** $-6x \leq 54$ **15.** $\frac{4}{5}x > 20$

You should include material that appears on a notebook like this in your own notes.

Know How to Take Notes

Recording the Process Copy examples your teacher explains during class. Be sure to record each step of the solution to help you remember the process.

Solving Two-Step Equations

$-2x - 3 = 11$	Original equation
$-2x - 3 + 3 = 11 + 3$	Add 3 to each side.
$-2x = 14$	Simplify.
$\frac{-2x}{-2} = \frac{14}{-2}$	Divide each side by -2.
$x = -7$	Simplify.

Call attention to important steps in examples.

In Lesson 6.3, recording each step of the solution may help you remember the process for solving equations involving fractions and decimals.

Solving Multi-Step Equations

BEFORE	Now	WHY?
You solved equations that required using one or two steps.	You'll solve equations that require using two or more steps.	So you know how long to save to buy a mountain bike, as in Ex. 26.

Word Watch

Review Words

distributive property, p. 85
like terms, p. 86

INDIANA Academic Standards

- Algebra and Functions (8.3.1)
- Problem Solving (8.7.10)

In the Real World

Science For a science fair, you perform an experiment to see how the number of Venus flytrap seeds planted in a cup affects plant growth. In each cup, you plant either 5 seeds or 10 seeds. You want to use an equal number of cups for each seed amount. You have 75 seeds. How many cups do you need?

Before using inverse operations to solve an equation, check to see if you can simplify one or both sides of the equation by combining like terms.

EXAMPLE 1 Writing and Solving a Multi-Step Equation

To find the number of cups for each seed amount, first write a verbal model. Let c = the number of cups for each seed amount.

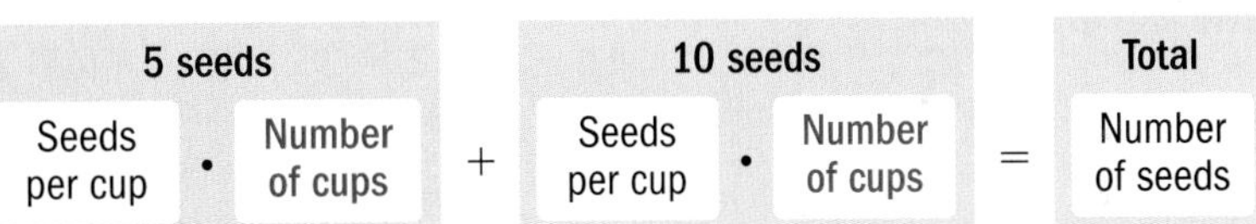

5 seeds
Seeds per cup · Number of cups
+
10 seeds
Seeds per cup · Number of cups
=
Total
Number of seeds

$5c + 10c = 75$ **Write algebraic model.**

$15c = 75$ **Combine like terms.**

$\frac{15c}{15} = \frac{75}{15}$ **Divide each side by 15.**

$c = 5$ **Simplify.**

ANSWER You can plant five cups with 5 seeds and five cups with 10 seeds.

✓ **Check** Substitute 5 for c in original equation.

$5(5) + 10(5) \stackrel{?}{=} 75$

$25 + 50 \stackrel{?}{=} 75$

$75 = 75$ ✓

EXAMPLE 2 Combining Like Terms

$3x + 12 - 4x = 20$	Original equation
$-x + 12 = 20$	Combine like terms: $3x - 4x = -x$.
$-x + 12 - 12 = 20 - 12$	Subtract 12 from each side.
$-x = 8$	Simplify.
$\frac{-x}{-1} = \frac{8}{-1}$	Divide each side by −1.
$x = -8$	Simplify.

Your turn now **Solve the equation. Then check the solution.**

1. $-6 = 11w - 5w$ **2.** $4p + 10 + p = 25$ **3.** $-8r - 2 + 7r = -9$

Before you combine like terms in an equation, you may have to use the distributive property.

HELP with Review

When distributing a negative number, remember to distribute the negative sign to *each* term inside the parentheses. For help with the distributive property, see p. 85.

EXAMPLE 3 Using the Distributive Property

$6n - 2(n + 1) = 26$	Original equation
$6n - 2n - 2 = 26$	Distributive property
$4n - 2 = 26$	Combine like terms.
$4n - 2 + 2 = 26 + 2$	Add 2 to each side.
$4n = 28$	Simplify.
$\frac{4n}{4} = \frac{28}{4}$	Divide each side by 4.
$n = 7$	Simplify.

✓**Check** Substitute 7 for n in the original equation.

$$6(7) - 2(7 + 1) \stackrel{?}{=} 26$$

$$6(7) - 2(8) \stackrel{?}{=} 26$$

$$42 - 16 \stackrel{?}{=} 26$$

$$26 = 26 \checkmark$$

Your turn now **Solve the equation. Then check the solution.**

4. $3(x - 9) = -39$ **5.** $z + 4(6 - z) = 21$ **6.** $8 = -7(y + 1) + 2y$

Clearing Fractions In equations involving a fraction, you may want to multiply each side by a number to change the equation into an equivalent equation that does not have fractions.

EXAMPLE 4 Solving an Equation with a Fraction

$\frac{3x+10}{4} = 7$	Original equation
$\frac{3x+10}{4} \cdot 4 = 7 \cdot 4$	Multiply each side by 4.
$3x + 10 = 28$	Simplify.
$3x + 10 - 10 = 28 - 10$	Subtract 10 from each side.
$3x = 18$	Simplify.
$\frac{3x}{3} = \frac{18}{3}$	Divide each side by 3.
$x = 6$	Simplify.

6.1 Exercises

More Practice, p. 732

Getting Ready to Practice

Vocabulary **Identify the like terms in the expression.**

1. $5x + 6 - 2 - 9x$ **2.** $8y + 3x - 1 + 6y$ **3.** $-t - 15 + 1 - 20$

Solve the equation. Then check the solution.

4. $8b + 2b - 4 = 6$ **5.** $-n - 9 + 8n = 26$ **6.** $5(w - 7) = -15$

7. $m + 3(m - 4) = 16$ **8.** $\frac{k-6}{2} = -10$ **9.** $\frac{z+2}{7} = 12$

10. **Guided Problem Solving** Tickets to the county fair cost \$8 each. Seventy people purchased their tickets in advance and the rest bought them at the gate. The revenue from ticket sales is \$2560. How many people bought their tickets at the gate?

(1) Use the verbal model to write an equation to find the number of tickets sold at the gate.

Price per ticket • (Tickets sold in advance + Tickets sold at gate) = Total revenue

(2) Solve the equation. Then check the solution.

Practice and Problem Solving

Example	Exercises
1	24, 26
2	11-23
3	11-23
4	11-23

CLASSZONE.COM

· More Examples
· eTutorial Plus

Decide whether the given value is a solution of the equation. If not, find the solution.

11. $7x - 3x - 8 = -32; x = 6$

12. $2y - 5(y + 1) = 25; y = -10$

13. $\frac{4m - 3}{3} = 3; m = 2$

14. $2 - 8a + 3a = 17; a = -3$

Solve the equation. Then check the solution.

15. $4x - 7 - 7x = -1$

16. $-2z + 6z - 9 = 15$

17. $-22 + 3k + 6 = -28$

18. $-2(m + 7) = -22$

19. $5(3 - 2n) = 65$

20. $-4 = -1 - 3(2p + 3)$

21. $\frac{5a - 2}{3} = -9$

22. $\frac{2b + 8}{5} = -12$

23. $\frac{c - 5}{8} = 4$

24. Fundraiser You are collecting money during a student council T-shirt sale. Today you collected money from Maria for 13 shirts, money from Kevin for 9 shirts, and money from Emma for 10 shirts. You collected a total of $352. How much did each T-shirt cost?

25. Measurement The perimeter of the rectangle is $3(x - 8)$ millimeters. Use a ruler to measure the rectangle and find the perimeter. Then find the value of x.

26. After-school Job You are saving to buy a mountain bike that costs $225. You already have $25. Each week, you make $15 babysitting and $25 working at a grocery store. Write a verbal model for the money you have using *Money already saved, Weeks, Babysitting money per week, Grocery store money per week,* and *Price of mountain bike.* Use the verbal model to write an equation. In how many weeks will you have enough money?

Solve the equation. Then check the solution.

27. $5y - 2y + 9y = -16$

28. $8k - 4 - 3k - 17 = -21$

29. $7t - 3(1 + t) = -19$

30. $2z - 4(9 - 3z) = 62$

31. $-10 = 6n - (3n + 12)$

32. $\frac{m - 14}{9} = -27$

33. $-11 = \frac{24 - b}{13}$

34. $-34 = \frac{3d + 8}{3}$

Geometry Write an equation for the area of the triangle. Then solve for x.

35. The lengths are in inches. The area is 228 square inches.

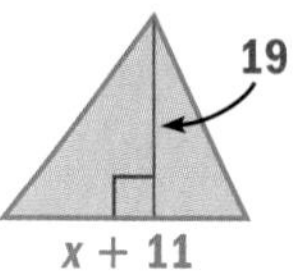

36. The lengths are in meters. The area is 918 square meters.

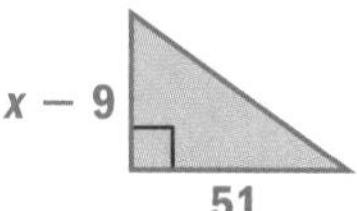

37. Critical Thinking Suppose you want to solve an equation that involves parentheses, such as $3(x + 2) = 9$. You might use the distributive property to rewrite the left side. Would the result be the same if instead you first divide each side by 3? Explain.

38. Number Sense Sara has \$20 to spend at a yard sale. She decides to buy a teapot and as many sets of teacups and saucers as she can afford. The teacups are \$2 each and the saucers are \$1 each. She figures that she can buy 8 teacups and 8 saucers. How can you tell that she's made an error without knowing the cost of the teapot?

39. Geometry Find the values of x and y so that the rectangle and the triangle have the same perimeter. What is the perimeter?

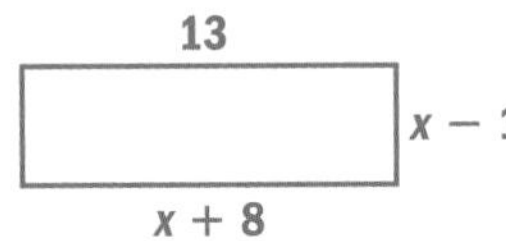

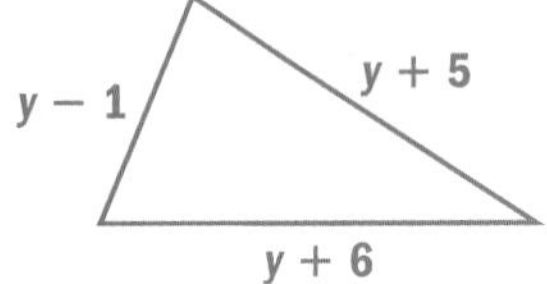

40. Challenge You have \$12 to spend on earrings. You can calculate the sales tax by multiplying the price by 0.05. What is the most that the earrings can cost before the sales tax is added on?

Mixed Review 

Copy and complete the statement with <, >, or =. *(Lesson 4.8)*

41. 1.54×10^{-5} ? 1.54×10^{-6}

42. 0.57×10^{4} ? 5.7×10^{4}

Find the mean, median, mode(s), and range of the data. *(Lesson 5.8)*

43. 35, 32, 31, 32, 35, 32, 37, 38, 34

44. 101, 100, 101, 105, 112, 105

Basic Skills **Find the unknown number.**

45. 8 hours = ? seconds

46. 3 days = ? minutes

Test-Taking Practice 

INTERNET
State Test Practice
CLASSZONE.COM

47. Multiple Choice What is the value of v in the equation $3 + 8v - 9v = 21$?

A. -24 **B.** -18 **C.** 18 **D.** 24

48. Short Response Your summer job is to paint and hang wallpaper in people's homes. You charge x dollars per hour for painting and $(x + 5)$ dollars per hour for hanging wallpaper. In one week, you paint for 12 hours and wallpaper for 15 hours. Your expenses for the week are \$430. Your profit for the week is \$590. How much do you charge per hour for painting and hanging wallpaper? Write a verbal model and an algebraic equation. Then solve the algebraic equation.

6.2 Problem Solving Strategies

INDIANA: Academic Standards
• Problem Solving (8.7.1)

Work Backward

- Guess, Check, and Revise
- Look for a Pattern
- Draw a Diagram
- Write an Equation
- **Work Backward**
- Act It Out
- Solve a Simpler Problem

Problem At the beginning of the year your class divides into seven equal study groups. Then your group joins another group, and two students leave your group when they change classes. Now there are four students in your group. How many students were in your class at the beginning of the year?

1 Read and Understand

Read the problem carefully.

- You know how the class divided and how your group changed.
- You need to find the number of students in the class at the beginning of the year.

2 Make a Plan

Decide on a strategy to use.

One way to solve the problem is to work backward. Start with the final number of students in your group and undo each change that your group went through.

3 Solve the Problem

Reread the problem. Work backward from the final number of students.

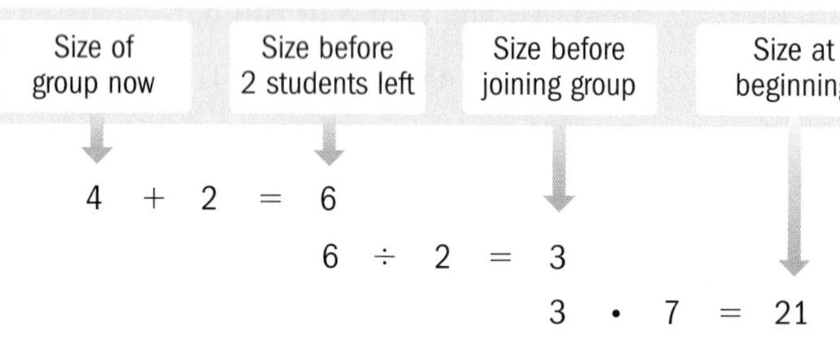

ANSWER **There were 21 students at the beginning of the year.**

4 Look Back

Check your answer. Start with your solution and reread the problem, calculating as you read.

At the beginning of the year your class	21
divides into seven equal study groups.	$21 \div 7 = 3$
Then **your group joins another** group,	$3 \cdot 2 = 6$
and **two students leave** your group.	$6 - 2 = 4$
Now there are **four students** in your group.	4 ✓

Practice the Strategy

Use the strategy *work backward.*

1. **Road Trip** In the last 3 days you've driven 720 miles, 650 miles, and 800 miles. Your car's odometer reads 20,490 miles. What did the odometer read three days ago?

2. **Money** You put half of your money in the bank. The next day you receive your $10 allowance and buy jeans for $25. You have $17 left. Copy and complete the diagram to find out how much money you started with.

Put money in bank		Received allowance		Bought jeans	
?	$\underline{?}$ →	?	$\underline{?}$ →	?	$\underline{?}$ → $17
← $\underline{?}$		← $\underline{?}$		← $\underline{?}$	

3. **Phone Card** Jill uses three fifths of the minutes on her phone card to call her brother, 15 minutes to call a friend, and 5 minutes to order a pizza. If she has 4 minutes left, how many minutes were on the card before she called her brother?

4. **Studying** You spend one hour on math homework and 45 minutes studying for each of your 3 tests. If you finish studying at 6:30 P.M., what time did you start?

5. **Notebook** You use half of your notebook for your research paper and two thirds of the remaining paper for class notes. You have ten pages left for homework. How many pages are in your notebook?

6. **CD Burning** Some friends are recording songs on a CD. The first fifth of the CD has songs from Alex's favorite band. The next 12 minutes are songs Henrique chose. One third of the time remaining is filled with Brian's favorite songs. Sally chose songs for the next 32 minutes. How many minutes of music did they record?

Mixed Problem Solving

Use any strategy to solve the problem.

7. **Consecutive Odd Numbers** The sum of three consecutive odd numbers is 501. What is the value of each number?

8. **Traveling** The following directions describe the path Denzel takes to his friend's house from school.
   - First he travels 5 miles north and then 8 miles west.
   - Next he travels 2 miles north and then 3 miles east.
   - Finally he travels 1 mile south.

   Draw a map showing Denzel's path from school to his friend's house.

9. **Population** The table shows the population of a small town over 15 years. If the population continues to grow in this manner, in what year will the population reach 160,000?

Year	Population
1987	5,000
1992	10,000
1997	20,000
2002	40,000

10. **Getting Ready** Each morning, Angie needs half an hour to shower and dress, 15 minutes to eat, and 5 minutes to brush her teeth. It takes her 15 minutes to walk to school. What is the latest Angie can get up and still arrive at school by 8:10 A.M.?

Solving Equations with Variables on Both Sides

BEFORE	Now	WHY?
You solved equations that had variables on one side.	You'll solve equations that have variables on both sides.	So you can determine the cost of party supplies, as in Ex. 27.

Word Watch

Review Words

perimeter, p. 33
distributive property, p. 85
like terms, p. 86

INDIANA Academic Standards

- Algebra and Functions (8.3.1)
- Measurement (8.5.4)

Activity **Use algebra tiles to model and solve an equation.**

1. Represent the equation $2x + 3 = x + 5$ using algebra tiles.

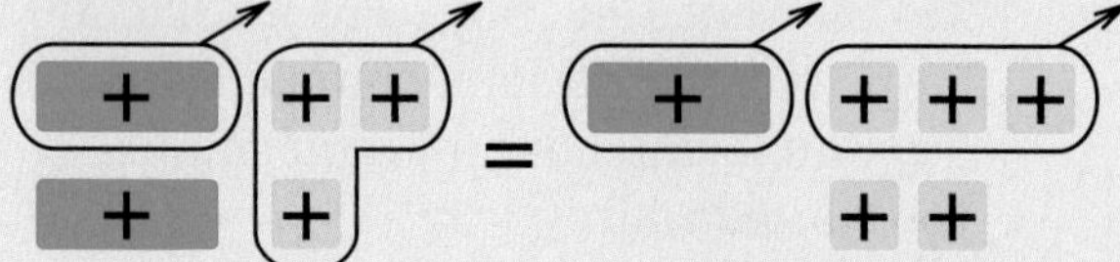

2. Remove one x-tile and three 1-tiles from each side.

3. The solution is 2.

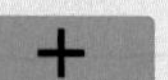

Use algebra tiles to solve the equation.

1. $2x + 7 = 3x + 2$ **2.** $5x - 2 = 3x + 6$ **3.** $4x - 1 = x - 7$

To solve equations with variables on both sides, collect like terms on the same side.

EXAMPLE 1 Collecting Like Terms

Drum lessons at the youth center cost \$8 for members and \$12 for nonmembers. Membership is \$24. For what number of lessons is the cost the same for a member and a nonmember?

Solution

Cost for member						Cost for nonmember		
Member fee	+	Price for members	·	**Number of lessons**	=	Price for nonmembers	·	**Number of lessons**

$24 + 8n = 12n$ Let n = the number of lessons.

$24 = 4n$ Subtract $8n$ from each side.

$6 = n$ Divide each side by 4.

ANSWER Six lessons cost the same for members and nonmembers.

EXAMPLE 2 Finding the Perimeter of a Triangle

Each side of the triangle has the same length. What is the perimeter of the triangle?

5x + 9
7x + 5

Solution

$5x + 9 = 7x + 5$	Write an equation.
$5x + 9 - 5x = 7x + 5 - 5x$	Subtract $5x$ from each side.
$9 = 2x + 5$	Simplify.
$9 - 5 = 2x + 5 - 5$	Subtract 5 from each side.
$4 = 2x$	Simplify.
$\frac{4}{2} = \frac{2x}{2}$	Divide each side by 2.
$2 = x$	Simplify.

Because $5x + 9 = 5(2) + 9 = 19$, each side of the triangle is 19 units long.

The three sides of the triangle are the same length, so the perimeter is $3 \cdot 19$, or 57, units.

ANSWER The perimeter of the triangle is 57 units.

Watch Out!

In Example 2, don't think that because $x = 2$, each side of the triangle has length 2 units. You must substitute 2 into the expressions for side length.

Sometimes you can use the distributive property to simplify one or both sides of an equation before you solve.

EXAMPLE 3 Using the Distributive Property

$21x = 3(2x + 30)$	Original equation
$21x = 6x + 90$	Distributive property
$21x - 6x = 6x + 90 - 6x$	Subtract $6x$ from each side.
$15x = 90$	Simplify.
$\frac{15x}{15} = \frac{90}{15}$	Divide each side by 15.
$x = 6$	Simplify.

Your turn now **Solve the equation.**

1. $4a + 5 = a + 11$
2. $3n + 7 = 2n - 1$
3. $-6c + 1 = -9c + 7$
4. $28 - 3s = 5s - 12$
5. $4(w - 9) = 7w + 18$
6. $2(y + 4) = -3y - 7$

6.2 Exercises

More Practice, p. 732

INTERNET eWorkbook Plus CLASSZONE.COM

Getting Ready to Practice

1. **Vocabulary** What is the perimeter of a rectangle?
2. Is 5 a solution of the equation $4x - 2 = 3x + 12$?

Solve the equation. Then check the solution.

3. $3x = 2x + 5$
4. $5x = 2(x + 5)$
5. $x = 5(2x + 3)$
6. **Geometry** Each side of the triangle has the same length. What is the perimeter of the triangle?

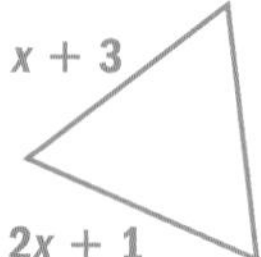

Practice and Problem Solving

HELP with Homework

Example	Exercises
1	7-15, 19-21, 26-27
2	16-18
3	16-18, 22-25

· More Examples
· eTutorial Plus

Solve the equation.

7. $7x = x + 18$
8. $7m = 4m + 21$
9. $30 - 2s = 4s$
10. $81 + 2k = 5k$
11. $13q - 48 = -3q$
12. $-11r = -4r + 56$
13. $5z - 43 = 2z + 80$
14. $16y - 43 = 4y + 65$
15. $8f + 11 = -7f - 19$

Geometry Find the perimeter of the triangle or rectangle. The sides of each triangle are equal in length.

16. 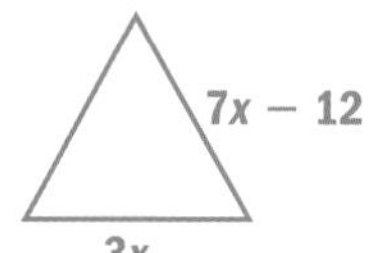

17. 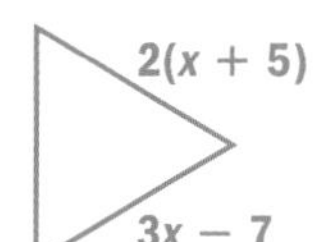

18. 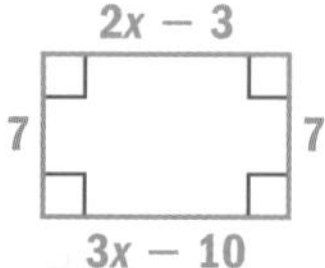

19. **Saving** David has \$32 and is saving \$8 each week. Emily has \$56 and is saving \$6 each week. When will David and Emily have the same amount of money?

Solve the equation.

20. $-1 + 11a = 6 - 3a$
21. $9b - 10 = -b - 18$
22. $3(t - 7) = 6t$
23. $-3h = 9(2 - 3h)$
24. $-n = 2(n - 33)$
25. $3d = 9(d - 1)$
26. **Working Backward** Mark had \$20 before he began earning the same amount each week at his new job. He used half of his first week's pay to pay back a loan. He spent \$15 at the movies and \$12 on a book, and got \$25 for his birthday. After his second paycheck he had \$20 less than two weeks' pay combined. How much is his paycheck?

27. **Party Supplies** You are decorating for a school picnic. Balloons cost \$8 for a dozen but cost more if bought individually. With the money you have, you can buy 7 dozen and 5 single balloons, or 75 single balloons. How much is one balloon? How much money do you have?

Solve the equation.

28. $5p + 4 = 11p - 2 - p$
29. $-5g + 3 = -3g + 6g$
30. $3(j + 4) = -2j + j$
31. $5(t + 7) = 2(2t + 7)$
32. $2(c + 6) = 5(c + 12)$
33. $6(s - 4) = 3(s + 9)$

34. **Critical Thinking** How many different values of x will make the equation $2(x + 3) = 2x + 6$ true? Explain your answer.

35. **Challenge** In 1999, there were 3940 museums and some number of historical sites in the United States. The total number of these attractions was 376 more than five times the number of historical sites. How many historical sites were there in the United States in 1999?

Mixed Review 

Find the least common denominator of the fractions. *(Lesson 4.5)*

36. $\frac{1}{2}, \frac{2}{3}, \frac{5}{6}$
37. $\frac{2}{9}, \frac{3}{4}, \frac{11}{12}$
38. $\frac{4}{5}, \frac{1}{2}, \frac{3}{70}$

Find the sum or difference. *(Lesson 5.6)*

39. $7.31 + 2.248$
40. $10.26 - 3.72$
41. $16.508 + 4.53$

Solve the equation. *(Lesson 6.1)*

42. $5c + 24 - 3c = 2$
43. $3(2z - 3) = 75$
44. $7x - 2(x - 11) = -23$
45. $3b - 5b = -14$
46. $4(x - 7) = 4$
47. $\frac{y + 3}{5} = 10$

Test-Taking Practice 

INTERNET
State Test Practice
CLASSZONE.COM

48. **Multiple Choice** One phone card charges \$.025 a minute with a \$.50 monthly fee. Another card charges \$.038 a minute with no monthly fee. You need a card for 3 months. Which equation could you use to find the number of minutes for which both cards cost the same?

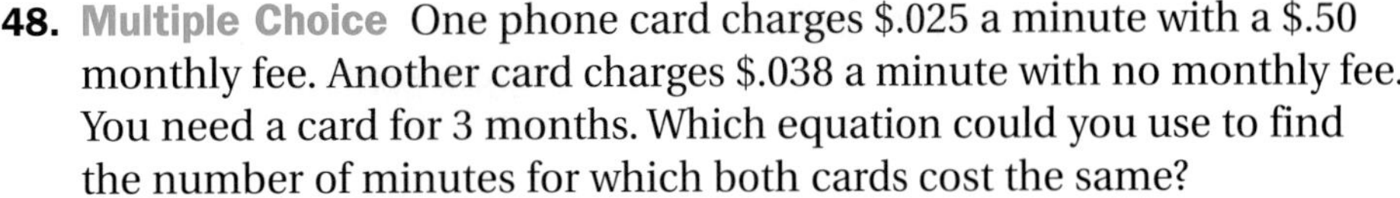

A. $0.025x = 0.038x + 3(0.50)$
B. $0.025x + 3(0.50) = 0.038x$
C. $0.025x = 0.038x$
D. $0.025x + 0.50 = 0.038x$

49. **Multiple Choice** What is the value of x in the equation $5x + 14 = 3x - 12$?

F. -26 **G.** -13 **H.** -1 **I.** 1

Solving Equations Involving Fractions and Decimals

BEFORE	Now	WHY?
You solved equations involving whole numbers.	You'll solve equations with fractions and decimals.	So you can determine the size of a lawn, as in Ex. 18.

Word Watch

Review Words

least common denominator (LCD), p. 192

INDIANA Academic Standards

- Algebra and Functions (8.3.1)
- Problem Solving (8.7.1)

In the Real World

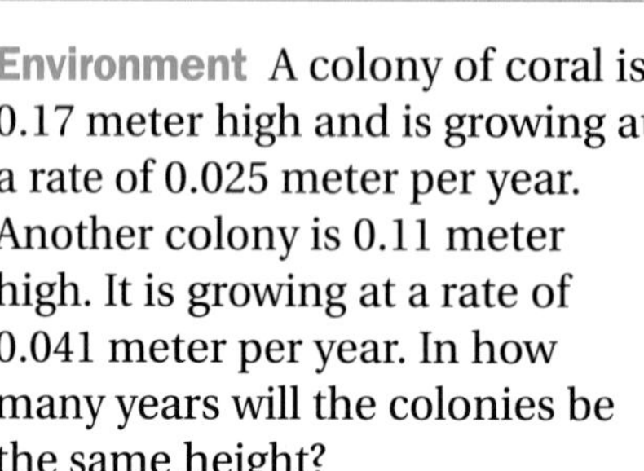

Environment A colony of coral is 0.17 meter high and is growing at a rate of 0.025 meter per year. Another colony is 0.11 meter high. It is growing at a rate of 0.041 meter per year. In how many years will the colonies be the same height?

EXAMPLE 1 Solving an Equation Involving Decimals

To solve the coral problem, you need to solve an equation involving decimals. First write a verbal model. Let n = the number of years.

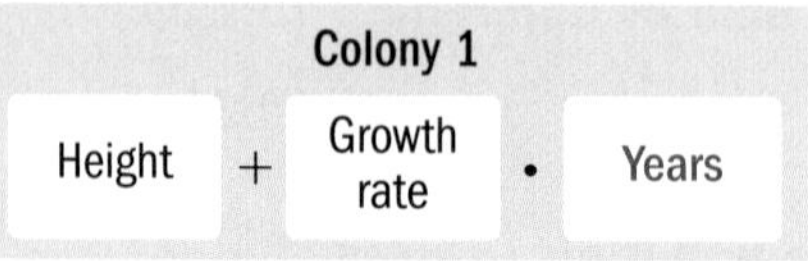

Colony 1						Colony 2				
Height	+	Growth rate	•	Years	=	Height	+	Growth rate	•	Years

$0.17 + 0.025n = 0.11 + 0.041n$	Write algebraic model.
$0.17 = 0.11 + 0.016n$	Subtract $0.025n$ from each side.
$0.06 = 0.016n$	Subtract 0.11 from each side.
$\frac{0.06}{0.016} = \frac{0.016n}{0.016}$	Divide each side by 0.016.
$3.75 = n$	Simplify.

ANSWER The colonies will be the same height in a little less than 4 years.

HELP with Notetaking

In Example 1, some of the steps are not shown. You may want to identify these steps and include them in your notes.

Your turn now **Write a verbal model. Then solve.**

1. You and a friend are buying snowboarding gear. You buy a pair of goggles that costs $39.95 and 4 tubes of wax. Your friend buys a helmet that costs $54.95 and 2 tubes of wax. If you each spend the same amount, how much does each tube of wax cost?

Clearing Decimals The multiplication property of equality allows you to multiply each side of an equation by the same number, so you can clear decimals from an equation if you wish.

To clear decimals, multiply each side of the equation by a power of ten that will make all the coefficients integers. In Example 2, multiply by 100.

EXAMPLE 2 Solving an Equation Involving Decimals

$1.4x - 1.8 + 2.35x = 0.21$	**Original equation**
$(1.4x - 1.8 + 2.35x)100 = (0.21)100$	**Multiply each side by 100 to clear decimals.**
$140x - 180 + 235x = 21$	**Simplify.**
$375x - 180 = 21$	**Combine like terms.**
$375x = 201$	**Add 180 to each side.**
$\frac{375x}{375} = \frac{201}{375}$	**Divide each side by 375.**
$x = 0.536$	**Simplify.**

Clearing Fractions When solving an equation with fractions, you can multiply each side by the LCD to clear the fractions.

EXAMPLE 3 Solving an Equation Involving Fractions

$\frac{3}{10}x = -\frac{1}{6}x + \frac{7}{10}$	**Original equation**
$\left(\frac{3}{10}x\right)30 = \left(-\frac{1}{6}x + \frac{7}{10}\right)30$	**Multiply each side by the LCD, 30.**
$\left(\frac{3}{10}x\right)30 = \left(-\frac{1}{6}x\right)30 + \left(\frac{7}{10}\right)30$	**Distributive property**
$\frac{3 \cdot \cancel{30}^{3}}{{}_{1}\cancel{10}}x = -\frac{1 \cdot \cancel{30}^{5}}{{}_{1}\cancel{6}}x + \frac{7 \cdot \cancel{30}^{3}}{{}_{1}\cancel{10}}$	**Divide out common factors.**
$9x = -5x + 21$	**Simplify.**
$14x = 21$	**Add 5*x* to each side.**
$x = \frac{21}{14} = \frac{3}{2}$, or $1\frac{1}{2}$	**Divide each side by 14. Simplify.**

Your turn now **Solve the equation. Then check the solution.**

2. $-1.7k + 6.7k = 13.1$ **3.** $1.2n - 0.24 = 0.7n$ **4.** $8.3 - 8y = 1.2y + 6$

5. $\frac{4}{5}x + 3 = -\frac{7}{10}$ **6.** $2s - 1\frac{1}{4}s = \frac{1}{3}$ **7.** $\frac{5}{6}v + \frac{5}{8} = \frac{3}{8}v$

6.3 Exercises

More Practice, p. 732

Getting Ready to Practice

1. Vocabulary Copy and complete: 24 is the _?_ of $\frac{1}{4}$, $\frac{5}{6}$, and $\frac{3}{8}$.

Tell what number you would multiply each side of the equation by to eliminate the decimals or fractions. Then solve the equation.

2. $1.5a - 1.2 = 1.8a$ **3.** $5.85b = 8.68 + 3.68b$ **4.** $0.5c + 3.49 - 2c = 4$

5. $\frac{3}{8}m + \frac{7}{8} = 2m$ **6.** $-\frac{4}{15}n + \frac{2}{3} = \frac{2}{5}n$ **7.** $-\frac{1}{5}p + \frac{3}{4}p = 11$

8. Find the Error Describe and correct the error in the solution.

X

$1.5x + 0.25 = 1.6x$

$15x + 25 = 16x$

$25 = x$

Practice and Problem Solving

HELP with Homework

Example	Exercises
1	23-24
2	9-16, 19-22
3	9-16, 18-23

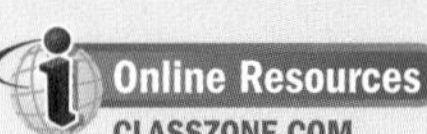

· More Examples
· eTutorial Plus

Solve the equation. Then check the solution.

9. $r + 8.2 + 0.4r = -8.6$

10. $1.5s - 1.2 - s = 0.5$

11. $5.3 + u = 3.2u - 2.7$

12. $4.93 - 9.20v = 0.66v$

13. $p - \frac{4}{9}p = -\frac{7}{9}$

14. $\frac{3}{10} - w = \frac{4}{5} - \frac{3}{5}w$

15. $\frac{1}{6}x + \frac{2}{3}x = 1$

16. $\frac{7}{4}z - \frac{1}{6} = \frac{17}{6} + \frac{3}{4}z$

17. Estimation Round each coefficient and constant in the equation $6.95x - 2.13 = 1.8x + 3.07$ to the nearest integer. Solve the new equation. What does your answer tell you about the answer to the original equation? Solve the original equation. Compare your answers.

18. Mowing the Lawn You mow $\frac{1}{5}$ of the lawn and your sister mows $\frac{2}{5}$ of the lawn. The two of you mow a total of 2400 square feet. What is the area of the lawn? How much area is left to mow?

Solve the equation. Then check the solution.

19. $-2.67g - 8.4 = 6.072 + 0.03g$

20. $0.25(66 + 42.4h) = 3.1652$

21. $\frac{3}{8} + \frac{9}{20}m = \frac{23}{20} + \frac{7}{8}m$

22. $6\frac{4}{5}n - \frac{8}{9} = \frac{7}{15}n$

23. Fabric At a fabric store you buy a clothes pattern for $7. You also buy $\frac{3}{4}$ yard of red fabric, $2\frac{1}{2}$ yards of purple fabric, and $\frac{7}{8}$ yard of blue fabric. The total cost is $23.50. If all three fabrics are the same price per yard, how much do you spend on each fabric?

24. Art Supplies Joyce buys scissors for $6.20 and 7 packages of paper. Paul buys paints for $9.94 and 5 packages of paper. They each spend the same amount, and each package of paper costs the same amount. How much does each package of paper cost?

25. Critical Thinking If you multiply each side of an equation by a common multiple of the denominators that is not the LCD, should you still get the correct answer? Explain.

26. Challenge Your batting average was 0.245 for your first baseball game and 0.251 for your second. After your third game your *overall* batting average is 0.250. What was your batting average for your third game?

Mixed Review

Evaluate the expression. *(Lessons 5.2, 5.3, 5.6, 5.7)*

27. $6.239 + 12.2$ **28.** $5\frac{1}{2} - 2\frac{3}{8}$ **29.** 4.1×8.235 **30.** $\frac{4}{9} \times \frac{11}{13}$

Solve the equation. *(Lesson 6.2)*

31. $6n + 11 = 2n - 1$ **32.** $16 - 3s = 2s - 14$ **33.** $-3(w - 7) = 5w + 3$

Basic Skills **Write an equivalent expression.**

34. $9(8 + x)$ **35.** $-15(y - 4)$ **36.** $-z(4 + 3 - 5)$

Test-Taking Practice

INTERNET
State Test Practice
CLASSZONE.COM

37. Multiple Choice At a basketball game, you buy 10 raffle tickets. Your friend buys a T-shirt for $13.50 and 1 raffle ticket. If you each spend the same amount, which equation can you use to find how much each raffle ticket costs?

A. $11x = 13.5$ **B.** $13.5 = 10x + x$

C. $10x + 13.5 = x$ **D.** $10x = 13.5 + x$

38. Multiple Choice At the deli, Swiss cheese costs $3.95 per pound and turkey costs $4.75 per pound. You buy the same amount of each and spend $13.05. How much did you buy of each?

F. 0.15 pound **G.** 0.18 pound **H.** 1.5 pounds **I.** 1.8 pounds

Notebook Review

Review the vocabulary definitions in your notebook.

Copy the review examples in your notebook. Then complete the exercises.

Check Your Definitions

perimeter, p. 33
distributive property, p. 85
like terms, p. 86
least common denominator (LCD), p. 192

Use Your Vocabulary

1. In your own words, explain how to combine like terms.

6.1–6.2 Can you solve multi-step equations?

EXAMPLE Solve $4(x - 8) = -x + 4 + 7x$.

$4(x - 8) = -x + 4 + 7x$	Original equation
$4x - 32 = 6x + 4$	Use the distributive property and combine like terms.
$-32 = 2x + 4$	Subtract $4x$ from each side.
$-36 = 2x$	Subtract 4 from each side.
$-18 = x$	Divide each side by 2.

☑ **Solve the equation.**

2. $-2x + 8 + x = 12$ **3.** $4z = 8(3 + z)$ **4.** $-6 + 10a = 3 - 2a$

6.3 Can you solve equations involving fractions and decimals?

EXAMPLE Solve $\frac{3}{4}y = \frac{1}{6}y - 4$.

$\frac{3}{4}y = \frac{1}{6}y - 4$	Original equation
$9y = 2y - 48$	Multiply each side by the LCD, 12.
$9y - 2y = 2y - 48 - 2y$	Subtract $2y$ from each side.
$7y = -48$	Simplify.
$y = -\frac{48}{7}$, or $-6\frac{6}{7}$	Divide each side by 7.

Solve the equation.

5. $-3.5a - 19.5 + 9.8a = 10.74$

6. $3\frac{1}{4} - 6b = 1\frac{1}{2} + 2\frac{3}{4}b$

Stop and Think about Lessons 6.1–6.3

7. **Writing** Explain how you can clear the decimals from the equation $16.2 - 4.32x = 10.8 + 0.023x$ before solving for x.

Review Quiz 1

Solve the equation.

1. $2(x + 16) = 46$
2. $79 = 10x - 23 + 7x$
3. $-108 = -16(x + 5) + 9x$
4. $12n = 17 - 22n$
5. $27.2m + 15.7 = -85.94 + 0.8m$
6. $\frac{1}{2}v + \frac{11}{12} - \frac{5}{4}v = -\frac{5}{12}$
7. **Geometry** Find the perimeter of the rectangle. The lengths are measured in feet.

4y − 12

2x − 3

7x − 18

y + 3

8. **Color Printer** You have \$445 to buy a printer. You find one that costs \$235. It uses a black ink cartridge that costs \$30 and a color ink cartridge that costs \$40. Write and solve an equation to determine how many pairs of ink cartridges you can buy for the printer.

Going Bananas

Solve each equation and use the value to move the monkey that number of spaces in the direction indicated. This will lead the monkey to his favorite set of bananas.

1. $x - 5 = 2x - 8$; right
2. $-4x = 2(x - 6)$; up
3. $\frac{1}{2}x = \frac{1}{3}x - \frac{1}{2} + \frac{4}{3}$; left
4. $5(3x + 6) = 9(6x - 1)$; down

6.4 Hands-on Activity

INDIANA: Academic Standards
- Geometry (8.4.1)

GOAL

Find the relationship between diameter and circumference.

MATERIALS

- metric tape measure or ruler
- string
- paper and pencil

Diameter and Circumference

In this activity, you will investigate the relationship between the diameter and circumference of a circle.

The *diameter* is the distance across a circle through the center.

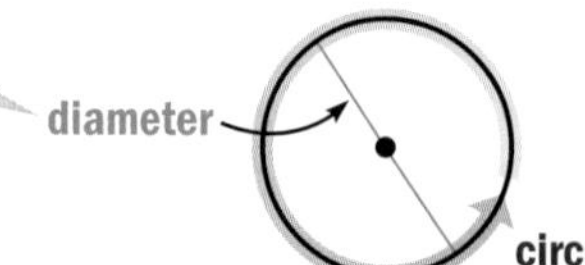

The *circumference* is the distance around a circle.

Explore 1 Find the diameter and circumference of circular objects.

Measure the diameter and circumference of several circular objects. If necessary, wrap a string around the object and measure the length of the string with a ruler. Record the measurements in a table like the one below.

Object	Diameter	Circumference	$\frac{\text{Circumference}}{\text{Diameter}}$
Water bottle	65 mm	206 mm	?
Tuna can	84 mm	264 mm	?
Clock	174 mm	549 mm	?
Quarter	24 mm	74 mm	?
Mug	82 mm	261 mm	?

Your turn now

1. Find the quotient of the circumference and the diameter for each object you measured. Round to the nearest hundredth if necessary. Record the quotients in another column of the table.
2. What do you notice about the numbers in the new column of your table?

Explore 2 Write a circumference formula.

1 Find an average of the quotients $\frac{\text{circumference}}{\text{diameter}}$ in your table. How does your average compare to the averages found by the other students in your class?

2 Find an average of the quotients $\frac{\text{circumference}}{\text{diameter}}$ collected by your whole class.

3 Use the result in Step 2 to write a formula for the circumference of a circle in terms of the diameter.

Your turn now **Use the formula you wrote in Step 3 above to calculate the circumference of the circle given its diameter *d*.**

3. $d = 64$ mm

4. $d = 140$ mm

5. $d = 36$ cm

6. $d = 20$ cm

7. $d = 4$ in.

8. $d = 1.25$ in.

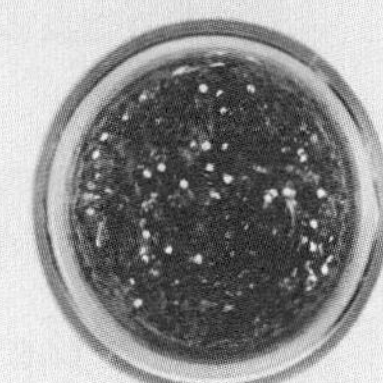

Stop and Think

9. Writing Write a formula for the diameter of a circle in terms of the circumference.

Solving Equations Involving Circumference

BEFORE	Now	WHY?
You solved equations involving fractions and decimals.	You'll solve equations involving the circumference of a circle.	So you can find the diameter of a clock, as in Ex. 28.

Word Watch

circle, p. 290
center, p. 290
radius, p. 290
diameter, p. 290
circumference, p. 290
pi (π), p. 290

INDIANA Academic Standards

- Algebra and Functions (8.3.1)
- Geometry (8.4.1)

A **circle** is the set of all points in a plane that are the same distance from a fixed point called the **center**. The distance from the center to any point on the circle is the **radius**. The **diameter** is the distance across the circle through the center.

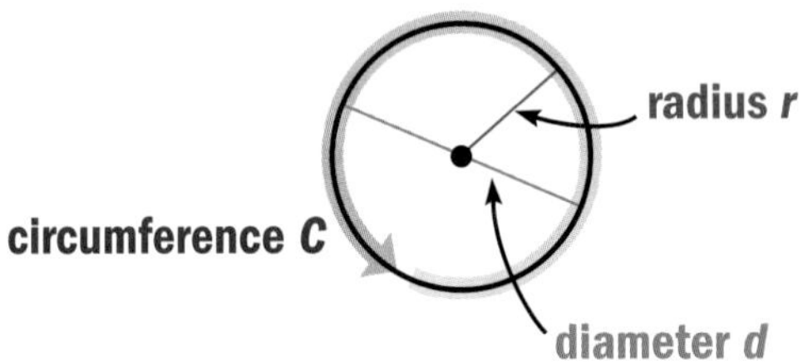

The **circumference** of a circle is the distance around the circle. For every circle, the quotient of its circumference and its diameter is the same: about 3.14159. This constant is represented by the Greek letter **pi**, π. You can approximate π using 3.14, $\frac{22}{7}$, or the π key on a calculator.

Circumference of a Circle

Words The circumference of a circle is the product of π and the diameter.

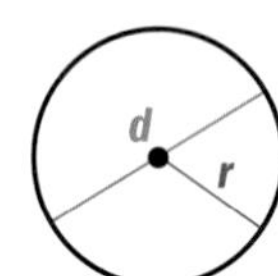

Algebra $C = \pi d$ or $C = 2\pi r$

EXAMPLE 1 Using Radius to Find Circumference

Find the circumference of a circle with a radius of 11 meters.

Solution

$C = 2\pi r$	Circumference formula
$\approx 2(3.14)(11)$	Substitute 3.14 for π and 11 for r.
$= 69.08$	Multiply.

ANSWER The circumference is about 69.08 meters.

with Solving

When deciding whether to use $\frac{22}{7}$ for π, look for numbers that are divisible by 22 or 7.

EXAMPLE 2 Using Diameter to Find Circumference

Find the circumference of the circle.

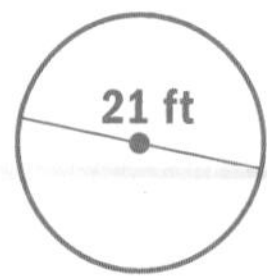

Solution

The measure shown is a diameter, so use the circumference formula that involves the diameter.

$C = \pi d$	**Circumference formula**
$\approx \frac{22}{\cancel{7}_1} \cdot \cancel{21}^3$	**Substitute. Use $\frac{22}{7}$ for π because 21 is divisible by 7.**
$= 66$	**Multiply.**

ANSWER The circumference is about 66 feet.

Your turn now **Find the circumference of the circle. Use 3.14 or $\frac{22}{7}$ for π. Explain your choice of value of π.**

1.

2.

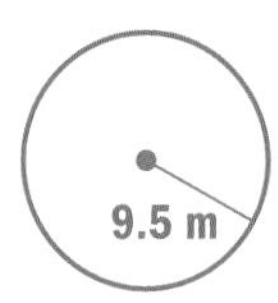

3.

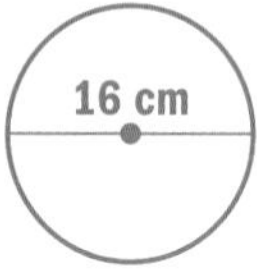

4. diameter = 32 in. **5.** diameter = 140 ft **6.** radius = 1.5 km

What do you think? Recreation

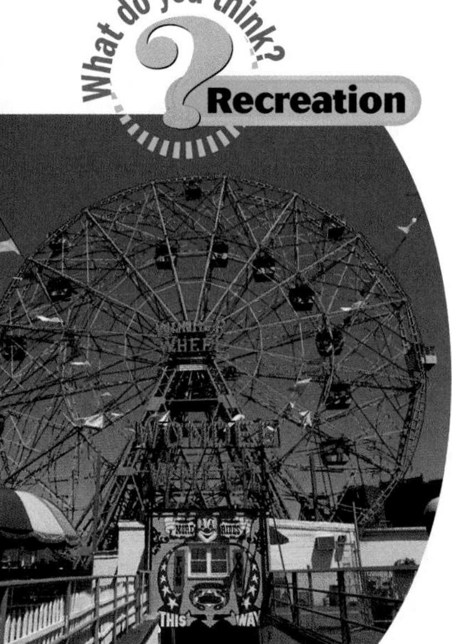

Ferris Wheels

This ride has 16 swinging cars and 8 stationary cars, and it can hold 144 people at a time. How many people can ride in each car?

EXAMPLE 3 Finding Diameter in Real Life

Ferris Wheel **A ferris wheel has a circumference of about 423.9 feet. Find its diameter.**

Solution

You are asked to find the diameter, so use the circumference formula that involves diameter.

$C = \pi d$	**Circumference formula**
$423.9 \approx 3.14d$	**Substitute 423.9 for C and 3.14 for π.**
$\frac{423.9}{3.14} \approx \frac{3.14d}{3.14}$	**Divide each side by 3.14.**
$135 \approx d$	**Simplify.**

ANSWER The diameter is about 135 feet.

with Review

For help with reciprocals, see p. 234.

EXAMPLE 4 Using Circumference to Find the Radius

A circle has a circumference of 88 inches. Find the radius.

Solution

$C = 2\pi r$	Circumference formula
$88 \approx 2\left(\frac{22}{7}\right)r$	Use $\frac{22}{7}$ for π.
$88 \approx \frac{44}{7}r$	Simplify.
$\overset{2}{\cancel{88}} \cdot \frac{7}{\cancel{44}_1} \approx \frac{44}{7}r \cdot \frac{7}{44}$	Multiply each side by $\frac{7}{44}$, the reciprocal of $\frac{44}{7}$.
$14 \approx r$	Simplify.

ANSWER The radius is about 14 inches.

Your turn now **Use 3.14 or $\frac{22}{7}$ for π. Explain your choice of value of π.**

7. A circle has a circumference of 20.41 inches. Find the diameter.
8. A circle has a circumference of 132 inches. Find the radius.

6.4 Exercises

More Practice, p. 732

Getting Ready to Practice

1. **Vocabulary** Draw and label a circle with a radius and a diameter.

Find the indicated measurement, where r = radius, d = diameter, and C = circumference. Use 3.14 or $\frac{22}{7}$ for π. Explain your choice.

2. $d = 56$ m, $C = \underline{?}$
3. $C = 66$ in., $r = \underline{?}$
4. $r = 6\frac{1}{4}$ ft, $C = \underline{?}$
5. $d = 11$ cm, $C = \underline{?}$
6. $C = 3.14$ m, $r = \underline{?}$
7. $C = 330$ yd, $d = \underline{?}$
8. **Find the Error** Describe and correct the error in the solution.

4.5 in.

X

$C = 2 \cdot \pi \cdot \text{radius}$

$\approx 2(3.14)(4.5)$

$= 28.26$ inches

Practice and Problem Solving

Example	Exercises
1	12-20
2	12-20, 23
3	28-29
4	12-20

Online Resources
CLASSZONE.COM

· More Examples
· eTutorial Plus

Measurement **Use a ruler to find the indicated measure. Then use the measure to find the circumference of the circle. Use 3.14 for π.**

9.

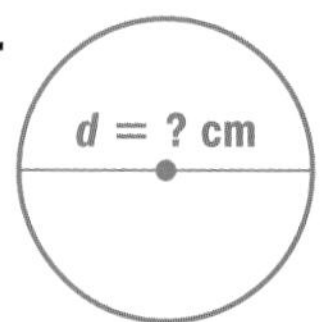

10.

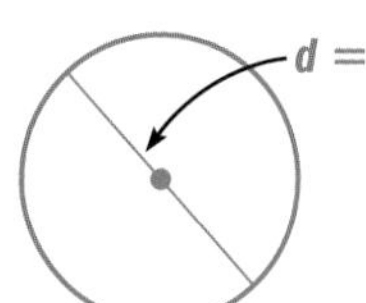

11.

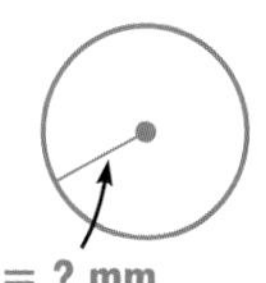

In Exercises 12–20, find the indicated measurement, where r = radius, d = diameter, and C = circumference. Use 3.14 or $\frac{22}{7}$ for π.

12. $C = 44$ m

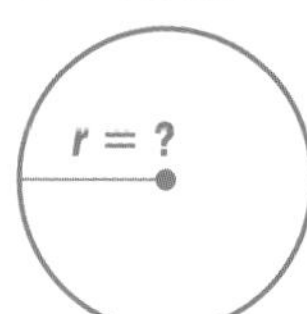

13. $C = 157$ yd

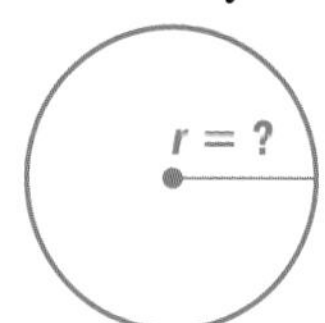

14. $C = 235.5$ cm

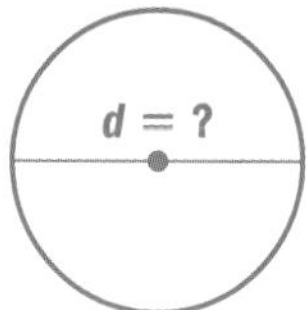

15. $r = 10$ mm, $C = \underline{?}$ **16.** $r = 21$ ft, $C = \underline{?}$ **17.** $d = 14$ in., $C = \underline{?}$

18. $d = 15$ mi, $C = \underline{?}$ **19.** $C = 33$ km, $d = \underline{?}$ **20.** $C = 628$ cm, $r = \underline{?}$

21. **Estimation** Use mental math to solve Exercises 9–11 again, using 3 for π. How can these estimates help you to check your answers?

22. **Critical Thinking** Find the circumferences of circles with the radii 1, 2, 4, 8, and 16 meters. Leave your answers in terms of π. Then compare the circumferences. What happens to the circumference of a circle as its radius doubles?

23. **Dome** The diameter of the U.S. Capitol Building's dome is 96 feet at its widest point. Find its circumference. Use 3.14 for π.

24. **Writing** Look up the word *circumnavigate* in the dictionary. How is the definition like the definition of *circumference*?

Extended Problem Solving **Adventurer Mike Horn traveled around the world as close to the equator as possible without using any motorized transportation.**

25. **Calculate** The radius of Earth is 3963 miles. Approximate its circumference. Use 3.14 for π.

26. **Compare** In order to avoid some dangerous areas, Mike Horn actually traveled 29,000 miles. About how much farther did Mike Horn travel than if he had followed the equator?

27. **Analyze** To the nearest mile, find what the radius of Earth would be if its circumference was 29,000 miles. Use 3.14 for π.

28. **Clock Face** The Great Clock of Westminster rings the bell known as "Big Ben" in London, England. The circumference of the clock face is about 72 feet 3 inches. What is the diameter of the clock face in feet? Use 3.14 for π. Round your answer to the nearest hundredth.

29. **Fashion** To measure the leg opening of a pair of flared jeans, you flatten them out and measure the width. The width is 12 inches, which is half the circumference. What is the diameter of the leg opening? Use 3.14 for π. Round your answer to the nearest hundredth.

Challenge Two circles are *concentric* if they share a center, as in the diagrams below. The circumference of the outer circle is given. Find x. Use 3.14 for π. (All measures are in meters.)

30. $C = 100.48$ m

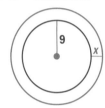

31. $C = 109.9$ m

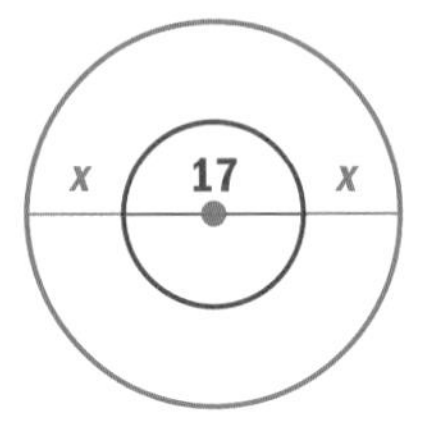

32. $C = 94.2$ m

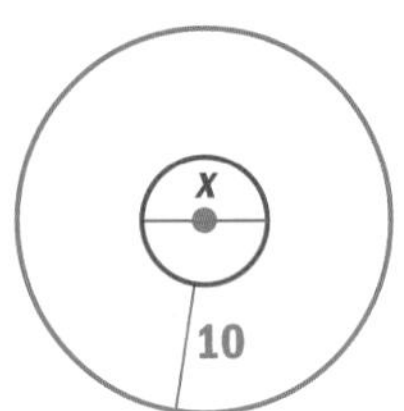

Mixed Review

Plot the point in a coordinate plane. *(Lesson 2.8)*

33. $A(6, -10)$ 34. $B(-4, 4)$ 35. $C(-2, -6)$ 36. $D(-12, 0)$

Solve the inequality. *(Lessons 3.6, 3.7)*

37. $-15 + x \leq 8$ 38. $r + 11 > 6$ 39. $-4a \geq -8$ 40. $3m < -63$

Solve the equation. *(Lesson 6.1)*

41. $-4n - 9 + 5n = -6$ 42. $20 = 8c + 2 + c$ 43. $6 + 2(5 - z) = 7$

Test-Taking Practice

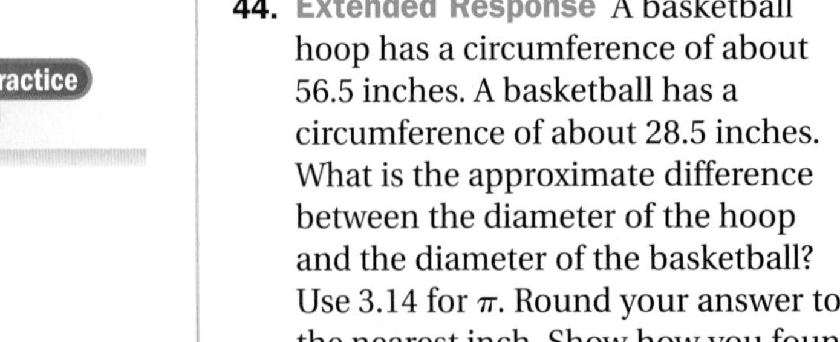

44. **Extended Response** A basketball hoop has a circumference of about 56.5 inches. A basketball has a circumference of about 28.5 inches. What is the approximate difference between the diameter of the hoop and the diameter of the basketball? Use 3.14 for π. Round your answer to the nearest inch. Show how you found your answer.

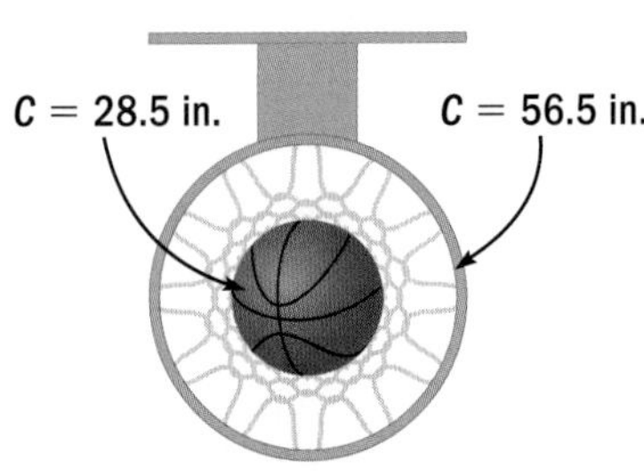

Solving Multi-Step Inequalities

BEFORE	Now	WHY?
You solved multi-step equations and one-step inequalities.	You'll use two or more steps to solve inequalities.	So you can determine how much a salesperson must sell, as in Ex. 21.

Review Words

distributive property, p. 85
like terms, p. 86
inequality, p. 140

INDIANA
Academic Standards

- Algebra and Functions (8.3.1)
- Problem Solving (8.7.1)

Activity Use a table to solve the inequality $x + 4 \geq 3x$.

1. Copy and complete the table.

x	$x + 4$	$3x$	Is $x + 4 \geq 3x$?
−1	3	−3	Yes
0	?	?	?
1	?	?	?
2	?	?	?
3	?	?	?
4	?	?	?

2. For what values of x is the inequality true? What do you think is the solution of the inequality? Explain your reasoning.

3. How is the solution of $4x + 3 > 9x - 7$ different from the solution in Part 2?

4. If you substitute a number less than −1 for x in the inequality above, will the inequality be true? Explain.

In Lessons 6.1 through 6.3, you solved multi-step equations algebraically. You can use many of the same steps to solve multi-step inequalities.

HELP with Review

For help with solving inequalities, see pp. 140 and 146.

EXAMPLE 1 Solving and Graphing a Two-Step Inequality

$10 + 4y < 18$ Original inequality

$10 + 4y - 10 < 18 - 10$ Subtract 10 from each side.

$4y < 8$ Simplify.

$\frac{4y}{4} < \frac{8}{4}$ Divide each side by 4.

$y < 2$ Simplify.

0 1 2 3 4 5

Use an open circle and draw the arrow to the left.

EXAMPLE 2 Combining Like Terms

$3x - 8 < -x + 4$	Original inequality
$3x - 8 - 3x < -x + 4 - 3x$	Subtract $3x$ from each side.
$-8 < -4x + 4$	Combine like terms.
$-8 - 4 < -4x + 4 - 4$	Subtract 4 from each side.
$-12 < -4x$	Simplify.
$\frac{-12}{-4} > \frac{-4x}{-4}$	Divide each side by -4 and reverse the inequality symbol.
$3 > x$	Simplify.

To check your solution, substitute different values for x in the original inequality. Choose a value less than 3, a value greater than 3, and 3.

Your turn now **Solve the inequality. Then graph the solution.**

1. $-7z + 15 \geq 57$ **2.** $11n + 36 < 3n - 4$ **3.** $9(y - 2) > -16$

EXAMPLE 3 Writing and Solving a Multi-Step Inequality

Charity Bowling You are organizing a bowling night for charity. Each ticket costs \$10 and includes shoe rental. Shoes cost you \$5 per pair and door prizes cost you \$50. How many people need to attend for you to raise at least \$200?

Solution

To find the amount you can raise, subtract the total costs from the total ticket sales. Let $x =$ the number of people.

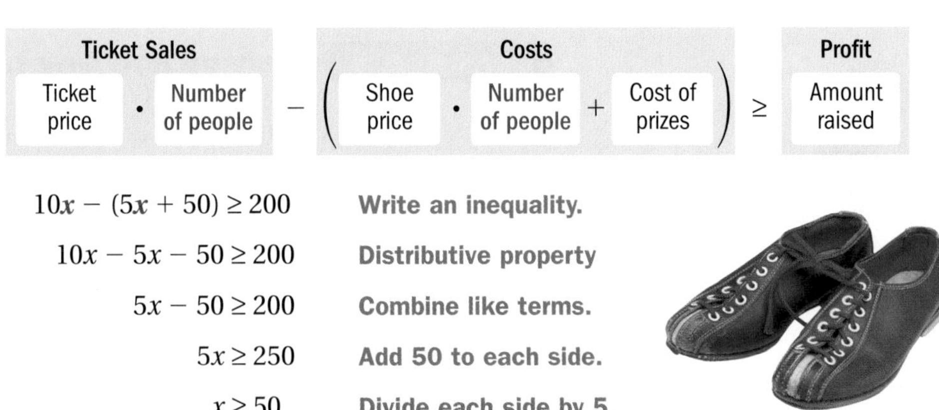

$10x - (5x + 50) \geq 200$	Write an inequality.
$10x - 5x - 50 \geq 200$	Distributive property
$5x - 50 \geq 200$	Combine like terms.
$5x \geq 250$	Add 50 to each side.
$x \geq 50$	Divide each side by 5.

ANSWER At least 50 people need to attend the bowling night.

6.5 Exercises

More Practice, p. 732

INTERNET
eWorkbook Plus
CLASSZONE.COM

Getting Ready to Practice

1. **Vocabulary** Write the meanings of the symbols <, >, ≤, and ≥.

Solve the inequality. Then graph the solution.

2. $5x - 8 < 2$
3. $2x + 1 \geq -7$
4. $-3x + 4 \leq -11$
5. $x - 13 - 2x > 2$
6. $4x - 8 \geq 7x + 1$
7. $1 < 3(x - 1)$
8. **Find the Error** Describe and correct the error in the solution.

$$9 - 2x \leq 3$$
$$-2x \leq -6$$
$$\frac{-2x}{-2} \leq \frac{-6}{-2}$$
$$x \leq 3$$

X

Practice and Problem Solving

HELP with Homework

Example	Exercises
1	9–20
2	15–20
3	21–23

· More Examples
· eTutorial Plus

Solve the inequality. Then graph the solution.

9. $4a + 7 \geq 11$
10. $16 < 3b + 22$
11. $7 - 2p \geq -5$
12. $-3y + 2 < -16$
13. $-2w + 6 < 2$
14. $23s - 30 \leq 39$
15. $12c + 12 > 48c$
16. $5x - 14 \leq 2x + 7$
17. $5 - 4z > 17 - z$
18. $10 \geq 5(3 + t)$
19. $2(5 + n) \leq 6$
20. $-3(d + 2) < -3$
21. **Sales** A salesperson in a clothing store earns \$350 per week plus a 20% commission on the clothes she sells. She wants to know how much she has to sell in one week to earn at least \$500 that week. Solve the inequality $350 + 0.2x \geq 500$. What does the solution mean in this situation?
22. **Video Games** You are approaching the high score of 18,550 on a video game where you have to catch discs for 150 points each. Your current score is 16,000. You want to know how many more discs you need to catch to have a new high score. Use the verbal model to write an inequality. Then solve the inequality. What does the solution mean in this situation?

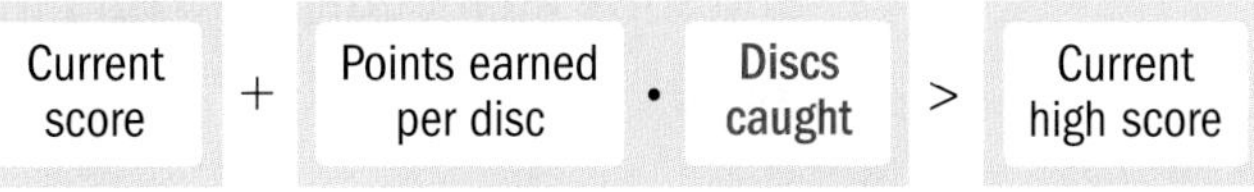

Boston Marathon

Edith Hunkeler of Switzerland won the women's wheelchair division of the Boston Marathon in 2002. She finished the 26.2 mile race in 1 hour, 45 minutes, and 57 seconds. What was her mean speed?

23. **Boston Marathon** You are planning to compete in the Boston Marathon. To officially enter, you have to raise at least \$1500 for charity. You've already raised \$925 by asking people to pledge \$25 each. How many more \$25 pledges do you need to enter?

Money already raised	+	Amount per pledge	•	Additional pledges	≥	Minimum required

Use the verbal model to write and solve an inequality to find the number p of additional pledges that will satisfy the donation requirements.

24. **Writing** Describe how solving an inequality is similar to solving an equation and how it is different from solving an equation.

Solve the inequality.

25. $\frac{1}{2}k - 6 \le -\frac{1}{6}k$

26. $\frac{1}{3}m - \frac{1}{2}m > -4$

27. $-\frac{1}{4}d - \frac{2}{5}d \le 13$

28. $4.56h - 7.912 \ge 1.12h$

29. $4.32 - 0.14x < 0.76x$

30. $0.5w > 12.53 - 0.2w$

31. $3.7z \le 33.32 - 3.1z$

32. $-0.6y - 3.79 + 5.2y < 19.67$

33. **Magazines** It costs a magazine publisher \$1.20 to produce each magazine. Overhead costs, such as salaries and office space, are \$25,000 per month. The publisher sells the magazine for \$3.95. How many magazines does the publisher need to produce and sell each month to make a profit?

Price per magazine
•
Number of magazines
−
Cost per magazine
•
Number of magazines
≥
Overhead costs

Use the verbal model to write and solve an inequality. What does the solution mean in this situation?

Challenge **Solve the inequality. Then graph the solution.**

34. $\frac{2}{3}x + \frac{4}{3} - \frac{3}{4}x < -\frac{3}{4}$

35. $\frac{2}{3}x + 18 \ge 5 - \frac{4}{7}x$

36. $0.05a + 9.367 - 1.65a \le 5.44$

37. $2.3x - 52.46 \le -0.9(x - 117)$

Number Sense **For Exercises 38–40, use the information below. Then tell what the solution represents in this situation and why it cannot be correct.**

You and your sisters have \$25 to spend at a baseball game. You buy 3 ice creams for \$4 each, then use the rest for \$3 drinks. You write and solve an inequality to find the number of drinks you can afford.

38. $d < 120$

39. $d \le 0$

40. $d \ge 4$

Mixed Review 

Choose a Strategy **Use a strategy from the list to solve the following problem. Explain your choice of strategy.**

Problem Solving Strategies
- Guess, Check, and Revise
- Make a List
- Draw a Diagram

41. You are making a sandwich. For bread, you can use either white or wheat. For meat, you can use turkey, ham, or roast beef. Finally, you can have mustard, mayonnaise, or neither. How many different kinds of sandwiches can you make?

Find the mean, median, and mode(s) of the data set. *(Lesson 5.8)*

42. 3.22, 4.45, 6.13, 6.27, 6.34 **43.** 14, 22, 22, 23, 25, 28

Solve the equation. *(Lesson 6.3)*

44. $3.3c - 2.1 = 7.8$ **45.** $4.8 - 2.3x = -3.02$ **46.** $23.06 + 4.3y = 6.72$

Test-Taking Practice 

47. Multiple Choice You are making some items to sell at a fair. The materials cost \$55. You decide to sell each item for \$2. You want to make a profit of at least \$100. Which inequality can you use to find the number of items you need to sell?

A. $2x - 55 \le 100$ **B.** $2x - 55 \ge 100$

C. $2x + 55 \ge 100$ **D.** $2x + 55 \le 100$

48. Multiple Choice Solve the inequality $-3b + 9 - 11b < 65$.

F. $b < -4$ **G.** $b > -4$ **H.** $b < 4$ **I.** $b > 4$

BrAIN GAME

City Solutions

Fill in the blanks with variables so that each inequality on the right is the solution of an inequality on the left. When you are finished, the letters will spell out the name of a city found in 12 states.

1. $2a + 7 - 3a \ge 12$ $\underline{?} < 1$

2. $4p + 1 > 9p - 4$ $\underline{?} \le -5$

3. $s - 2(s + 1) > 3$ $\underline{?} \ge 5$

4. $12 \le -3r - 13 + 8r$ $\underline{?} > 1$

5. $-i + 4 + 7i > 10$ $\underline{?} < -5$

6.5 Technology Activity

SPREADSHEET

INDIANA: Academic Standards
• Algebra and Functions (8.3.1)

Solving Inequalities

GOAL Use a spreadsheet and truth functions to solve inequalities.

Example **Solve the inequality $3x + 2 < 2x - 6$.**

Solution

1. Enter the integers -10 to 10 in column A. Column A contains possible solutions of the inequality.

2. Type the formula "=3*A2 + 2" in cell B2. Use the fill down feature. Column B contains values of the left side of the inequality.

B2	=3*A2+2			
	A	**B**	**C**	**D**
1	x-values	3x + 2		
2	–10	–28		
3	–9	–25		
4	–8	–22		
5	–7	–19		

3. Type the formula "=2*A2 − 6" in cell C2. Use the fill down feature. Column C contains values of the right side of the inequality.

4. Type the truth function "=B2 < C2" in cell D2. Use the fill down feature. Column D tells whether the inequality is true or false for the x-value in that row.

C4	=2*A4–6			
	A	**B**	**C**	**D**
1	x-values	3x + 2	2x – 6	B < C?
2	–10	–28	–26	True
3	–9	–25	–24	True
4	–8	–22	–22	False
5	–7	–19	–20	False

HELP with Technology
A *truth function* compares values and returns *True* or *False*.

ANSWER The solution is all numbers less than -8.

Your turn now **Use spreadsheet software to solve the inequality.**

1. $13 - 3y > -2y$ **2.** $7 - 2s < s - 2$ **3.** $2n - 10 \geq 12n$

4. $p + 16 \leq -3p$ **5.** $-2t + 9 > -5t$ **6.** $x - 3 < 5x + 1$

7. **Shopping** Dani has \$10 to buy school supplies. A notebook costs \$1.50, a pencil costs \$.25, and a pen costs \$.95. She needs two notebooks, three pens, and a few pencils. How many pencils can she buy?

Problem Solving and Inequalities

BEFORE

You solved multi-step inequalities.

Now

You'll use multi-step inequalities to solve real-world problems.

WHY?

So you can determine how many CDs you can buy, as in Ex. 16.

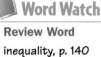

Word Watch

Review Word

inequality, p. 140

INDIANA Academic Standards

- Algebra and Functions (8.3.1)
- Problem Solving (8.7.1)

In the Real World

Season Tickets Individual tickets for a college hockey game cost \$8 each plus a one-time transaction fee of \$5. You can buy a season ticket for \$99. How many games would you have to attend so that buying a season ticket is a better value than buying individual tickets?

EXAMPLE 1 Writing and Solving an Inequality

To decide how many games you would have to attend so that buying a season ticket is a better value than buying individual game tickets, write and solve an inequality.

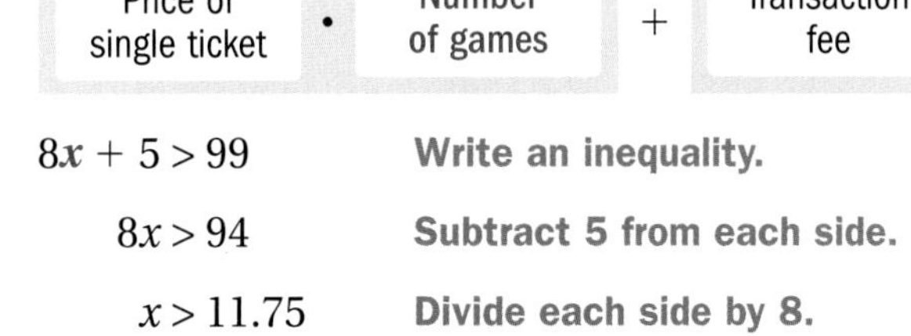

$8x + 5 > 99$ **Write an inequality.**

$8x > 94$ **Subtract 5 from each side.**

$x > 11.75$ **Divide each side by 8.**

ANSWER It doesn't make sense to attend 11.75 games. So you would have to attend 12 or more games to make buying a season ticket a better value than buying individual tickets.

Your turn now **Look back at Example 1.**

1. Check that the solution in Example 1 is reasonable.
2. Individual tickets for a college basketball game cost \$12 each plus a one-time transaction fee of \$8. A season ticket costs \$125. How many games would you have to attend so that buying a season ticket is a better value than buying individual tickets?

Writing Inequalities The following common sentences indicate the four types of inequalities.

$a < b$	$a > b$
a is less than *b*. *a* is fewer than *b*.	*a* is greater than *b*. *a* is more than *b*.
$a \leq b$	$a \geq b$
a is less than or equal to *b*. *a* is at most *b*. *a* is no more than *b*.	*a* is greater than or equal to *b*. *a* is at least *b*. *a* is no less than *b*.

HELP with Reading

The phrase "*a* more than *b*" means $b + a$, while "*a* is more than *b*" means $a > b$.

EXAMPLE 2 Translating Verbal Sentences

Write the sentence as an inequality.

a. Six times the difference of a number and 3 is more than 24.

b. Nine more than 4 times a number is at least 30 plus 11 times the number.

Solution

First decide which inequality symbol to use. Then substitute numbers, variables, and operation symbols.

a. The phrase "is more than" means >.

6 times the difference of a number and 3 **is more than** 24.

$6 \quad \cdot \quad (x - 3) \quad > \quad 24$

ANSWER The inequality is $6(x - 3) > 24$.

b. The phrase "is at least" means ≥.

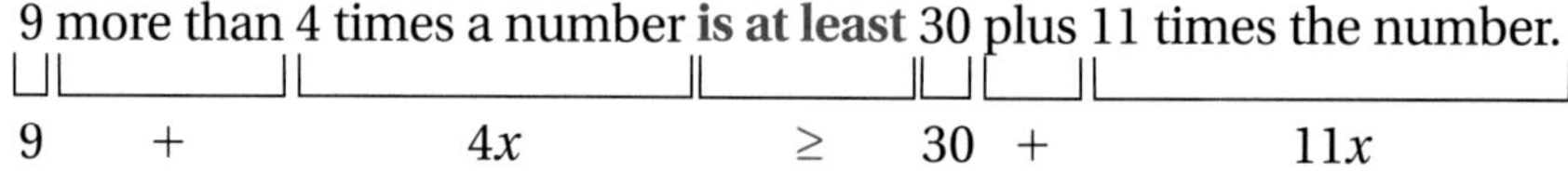
9 more than 4 times a number is at least 30 plus 11 times the number.
9 + 4x ≥ 30 + 11x

ANSWER The inequality is $9 + 4x \geq 30 + 11x$.

Your turn now **Write the sentence as an inequality. Let *x* represent the unknown number.**

3. Six times the sum of a number and 8 is no more than 12 less than twice the number.

4. The difference of a number and 4 is less than 10 more than 3 times the number.

EXAMPLE 3 Writing and Solving an Inequality

Owning a Business You use the Internet to sell mousepads. You pay a wholesaler \$6 for each mousepad. You then sell the mousepads for \$10 each. You pay \$21 per month for Web page hosting. How many mousepads should you sell each month to earn a profit?

Solution

To earn a profit, your revenue must be greater than your expenses.

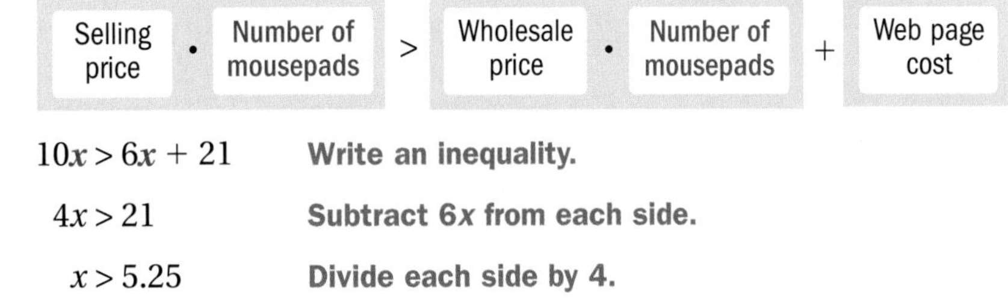

$10x > 6x + 21$	**Write an inequality.**
$4x > 21$	**Subtract $6x$ from each side.**
$x > 5.25$	**Divide each side by 4.**

ANSWER You cannot sell part of a mousepad. So, you should sell at least 6 mousepads per month to earn a profit.

Getting Ready to Practice

Vocabulary **Write the sentence as an inequality. Let x represent the unknown number.**

1. A number is at least 5.
2. A number plus 5 is greater than 9.
3. Eight minus a number is at most 6.
4. Four times a number is less than 28.
5. **Guided Problem Solving** You have \$200 to spend on a health club membership. The initial fee to join is \$50. There is a monthly fee of \$32. For how many months can you be a member without spending more than \$200?

   (1 Write a variable expression for the total cost of a health club membership.

   (2 Use the expression from Step 1 to write an inequality.

   (3 Solve the inequality and check that the answer makes sense. Explain what the solution means in the situation.

Practice and Problem Solving

Example Exercises

Example	Exercises
1	16–18
2	6–13
3	16–18

Online Resources
CLASSZONE.COM

· More Examples
· eTutorial Plus

Write the sentence as an inequality. Let x represent the unknown number. Then solve the inequality.

6. A number plus 2 is at most 6.

7. Nine is less than a number plus 1.

8. Seven less than a number is more than 14.

9. Eight times a number is at least 40.

Matching In Exercises 10–13, match the verbal sentence with the inequality.

A. $4(x + 2) \geq 18$ **B.** $4x + 2 < 18$ **C.** $2x - 4 > 18$ **D.** $2(x - 4) \leq 18$

10. Four times the sum of a number and 2 is at least 18.

11. The difference of 2 times a number and 4 is more than 18.

12. Two times the difference of a number and 4 is no more than 18.

13. The sum of 4 times a number and 2 is fewer than 18.

14. **Writing** Write a real-world problem that can be solved using the inequality $5 + 8x \leq 31$. Solve the inequality and explain what the solution means in the situation.

15. **Critical Thinking** Explain the difference between *3 less than a number* and *3 is less than a number.*

16. **Buying CDs** Each CD you order online costs \$12. Shipping and handling charges are \$4. You have \$50 to spend. Use the verbal model to write and solve an inequality. How many CDs can you buy?

Cost of CD	•	Number of CDs	+	Shipping charges	$\overset{?}{\leq}$	Money you have

17. **Teen Club** A teen club has weekly dances. You can become a member of the club for \$30 a year and pay only \$4 to attend each dance. Otherwise, each dance costs \$6. How many dances do you have to attend so that becoming a member will cost less than paying the nonmember rate?

18. **Signatures** To get a question on a state ballot, you need at least 419,260 signatures on a petition. You've collected 209,260 signatures and have 30 days to collect the rest. Find the mean number of signatures you need to collect per day.

19. **Snowstorm** School will be cancelled if there are at least 6 inches of snow at 6 A.M. There are 2 inches of snow at 7:00 P.M. the night before. The snow is predicted to continue falling at a rate of 0.5 inch per hour. Write an inequality to represent the situation. When will there be at least 6 inches of snow? Will there be school the next day? Explain.

20. **Express Mail** A package sent via Express Mail must be no more than 108 inches in total length and girth. You want to wrap as many boxes together as possible to send as one package. Each box is the same size. Write and solve an inequality to find how many boxes you could wrap as one package if they are arranged as shown.

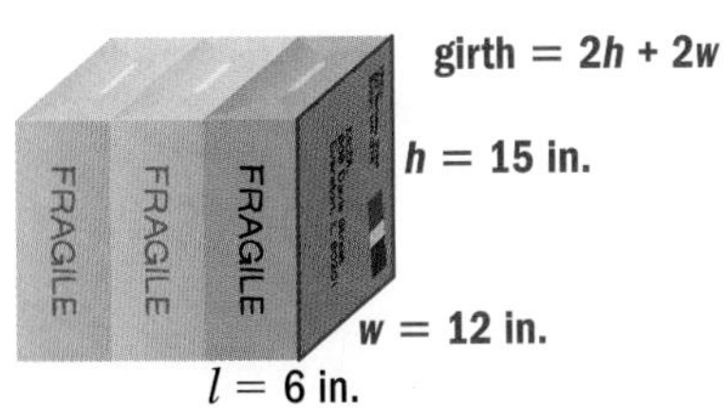

Extended Problem Solving **Town Taxi charges $2.00 plus $.40 for every $\frac{1}{5}$ mile. City Cab charges $2.50 plus $.25 for every $\frac{1}{7}$ mile.**

21. **Interpret** Write expressions for the total cost of a ride with Town Taxi and the total cost of a ride with City Cab.

22. **Compare** For what distances does City Cab cost less than Town Taxi? Express your answer as an inequality.

23. **Analyze** Use the expressions from Exercise 21 to express the distances that Town Taxi costs less than City Cab.

Mixed Review

Find the indicated measurement, where r = radius, d = diameter, and C = circumference. Use 3.14 for π. *(Lesson 6.4)*

24. $d = 27$ m, $r = \underline{?}$ 25. $r = 34$ in., $C = \underline{?}$ 26. $C = 62.8$ ft, $d = \underline{?}$

Basic Skills **Evaluate the expression.**

27. $9 + (10 - 8)^4 \times 5$ 28. $3 + 50 \div 5^2 - 8$ 29. $275 - 2(3 + 2)^3$

Test-Taking Practice

INTERNET
State Test Practice
CLASSZONE.COM

30. **Multiple Choice** While at camp, you call your parents from a pay phone. The first minute costs you $.25 and each additional minute costs you $.10. You have $1.65 in change. Solve the inequality $0.25 + 0.10m \le 1.65$. How many additional minutes m can you talk?

A. less than 14 **B.** no more than 14

C. at most 19 **D.** fewer than 19

31. **Short Response** Your scores on the last 3 bowling games are 90, 92, and 115. What do you need to score in the next game to have a mean of at least 100? Write and solve an inequality.

Notebook Review

Review the vocabulary definitions in your notebook.

Copy the review examples in your notebook. Then complete the exercises.

Check Your Definitions

circle, p. 290	radius, p. 290	circumference, p. 290
center, p. 290	diameter, p. 290	pi (π), p. 290

Use Your Vocabulary

1. Copy and complete: Pi is the quotient of a circle's _?_ and its _?_.

6.4 Can you solve equations involving circumference?

EXAMPLE Find the circumference of a circle with diameter 30.5 cm.

$C = \pi d$ — **Circumference formula**

$\approx (3.14)(30.5)$ — **Substitute 3.14 for π and 30.5 for d.**

$= 95.77$ cm — **Multiply.**

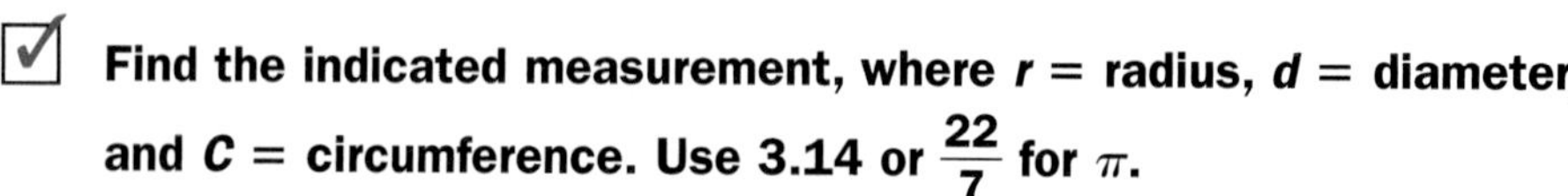

Find the indicated measurement, where r = radius, d = diameter, and C = circumference. Use 3.14 or $\frac{22}{7}$ for π.

2. $r = 7; C = \underline{?}$ **3.** $C = 121; d = \underline{?}$ **4.** $C = 314; r = \underline{?}$

6.5 Can you solve multi-step inequalities?

EXAMPLE Solve $-5(x + 9) \geq 30$.

$-5(x + 9) \geq 30$ — **Original inequality**

$-5x - 45 \geq 30$ — **Distributive property**

$-5x \geq 75$ — **Add 45 to each side.**

$x \leq -15$ — **Divide each side by -5 and reverse the inequality symbol.**

Solve the inequality.

5. $2b - 32 < 52$ **6.** $5j - 18 > 18 - j$ **7.** $6y \leq 3(9 + y)$

6.6 Can you write and solve an inequality?

EXAMPLE You and 3 friends plan to use a $50 gift certificate to pay for dinner. You order an appetizer that costs $6. What is the most each of you can spend so the total cost of the meal is no more than $50?

Number of people	$\cdot$	Cost per person	$+$	Price of appetizer	$\leq$	Amount of gift certificate

$4x + 6 \leq 50$ **Write an inequality.**

$4x \leq 44$ **Subtract 6 from each side.**

$x \leq 11$ **Divide each side by 4.**

ANSWER The most that each of you can spend is $11.

8. You want to work out for at least 45 minutes. You jog for 20 minutes, then divide your time evenly among the stationary bike, stair machine, and rowing machine. How long should you use each machine?

Stop and Think about Lessons 6.4–6.6

9. Writing Describe how you know which inequality symbol to use when translating a sentence.

Review Quiz 2

Find the indicated measurement, where r = radius, d = diameter, and C = circumference. Use 3.14 or $\frac{22}{7}$ for π.

1. $d = 28$ in., $C = \underline{?}$

2. $C = 150$ cm, $r = \underline{?}$

Solve the inequality.

3. $-8a - 10 > 14$

4. $3z \leq 35 - 2z$

5. $5b \geq 2(b + 2.25)$

Write the sentence as an inequality. Then solve.

6. Two less than six times a number is at least forty.

7. Five times the sum of four and a number is greater than ten.

8. Video Games Your current score in a video game is 33,600 points. At each level you earn 2500 points for catching objects and 1700 points for overcoming the obstacles. How many more levels must you go through to beat your high score of 54,000?

CHAPTER 6

Chapter Review

Vocabulary

circle, p. 290
center, p. 290
radius, p. 290
diameter, p. 290
circumference, p. 290
pi (π), p. 290

Vocabulary Review

Copy and complete the statement.

1. A _?_ is the set of all points in a plane that are the same distance from a fixed point called the center.

2. You can approximate _?_ with the decimal 3.14 or the fraction $\frac{22}{7}$.

Matching **Match the word with the correct definition.**

3. diameter

4. circumference

5. radius

A. the distance around a circle

B. the distance across a circle through the center

C. the distance from the center to any point on the circle

Review Questions

Solve the equation. *(Lessons 6.1–6.3)*

6. $6a - 14a = 96$

7. $18 + 4(p - 9) = 6$

8. $4(12 + z) - z = -192$

9. $7c - 10 = c + 44$

10. $6(t - 5) = 2(t + 5)$

11. $-7b + 10 = -11 - 4b$

12. $\frac{11}{16}n - 3 + \frac{1}{4}n = \frac{7}{4}$

13. $5s + 3\frac{1}{8} = \frac{5}{24} - 2s$

14. $5(m - 9) = 13 - 4(10 + m)$

15. Find the Error Describe and correct the error made in finding the perimeter of the rectangle. *(Lesson 6.2)*

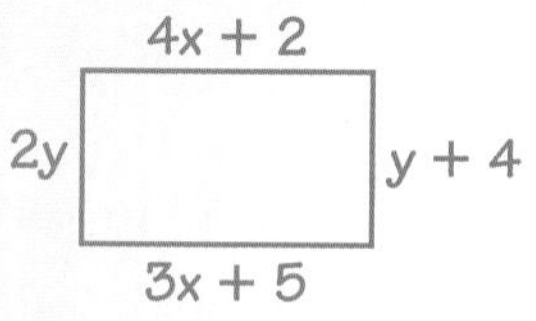

✗ $4x + 2 = 3x + 5$
$x = 3$
$2y = y + 4$
$y = 4$
$P = 2(3) + 2(4) = 14$

16. Critical Thinking What number would you multiply the equation $\frac{5}{9} + \frac{3}{4}x = \frac{2}{3}x - \frac{1}{6}$ by to clear the fractions? *(Lesson 6.3)*

Review Questions

17. **Rowing Teams** Fifty more than twice the number of women's rowing teams is equal to eighty-seven less than three times the number of women's rowing teams. Write and solve an equation to find the number of women's rowing teams. *(Lesson 6.2)*

18. **Recycling Deposit** When you buy a can of soda, you pay for the soda and you pay a \$.05 recycling deposit. You pay \$4.56 for a 12-pack of soda. How much did each soda cost before the deposit? *(Lesson 6.3)*

19. **Race** You and a friend are running in a race for a charity event. You have completed $\frac{3}{8}$ of the race. Your friend has completed $\frac{1}{4}$ of the race and is $\frac{3}{16}$ mile behind you. How long (in miles) is the race? *(Lesson 6.3)*

Find the indicated measurement, where r = radius, d = diameter, and C = circumference. Use 3.14 or $\frac{22}{7}$ for π. *(Lesson 6.4)*

20. $C = \underline{?}$

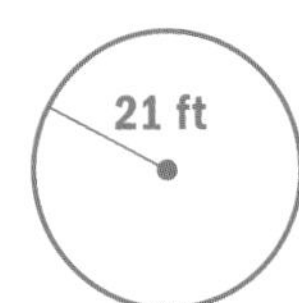

21. $C = \underline{?}$

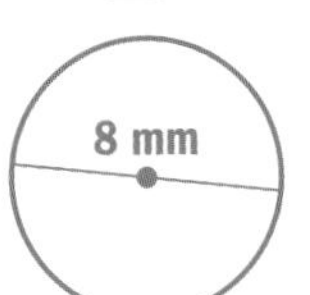

22. $C = 62.8$ mm

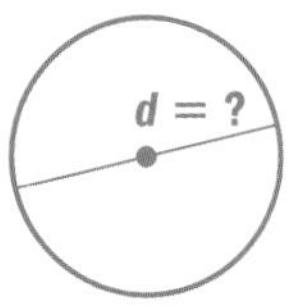

23. $C = 12$ in.

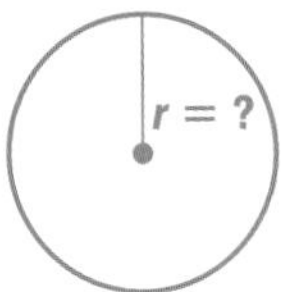

24. **Dome** The Minnesota State Capitol Building has one of the largest unsupported marble domes in the world, with a diameter of 89 feet at its widest point. Find its circumference using 3.14 for π. *(Lesson 6.4)*

Solve the inequality. Graph the solution. *(Lesson 6.5)*

25. $-5 < 3x + 16$

26. $\frac{2}{3}h - 3 \geq 1$

27. $6 - \frac{2}{5}a > 2$

28. $m + 4(5 - m) > -7$

29. $6 - (g - 7) \leq 6 - 8g$

30. $2(3k + 1) \leq 5(k - 6)$

Write the sentence as an inequality. Then solve the inequality. *(Lesson 6.6)*

31. Fourteen minus three times a number is at most eleven.

32. Nine plus four times a number is less than twenty-one.

33. Seven times the difference of fifteen and a number is at least fifty-six.

34. **School Fundraiser** You are selling magazine subscriptions for a school fundraiser. If you sell at least 75 subscriptions in 2 weeks you win a prize. You sold 26 subscriptions in one week. What is the mean number of subscriptions you have to sell per day to sell at least 75 total? *(Lesson 6.6)*

CHAPTER 6

Chapter Test

Solve the equation.

1. $-3z + 17 + 12z = 11$
2. $m - 6(m + 10) = 50$
3. $7(12 - r) = -84$
4. $3b + 4 = b - 4$
5. $-25 - a = 2a + 20$
6. $3(2x - 11) = 3(x + 10)$
7. $\frac{3n - 5}{10} = 7$
8. $\frac{-3r + 54}{5} = 2r + 3$
9. $\frac{3}{5}w = 5w + \frac{22}{25}$
10. **Shopping** You bought a new shirt for \$15.95 and 5 pairs of socks. Your friend bought 10 pairs of socks and spent \$4.20 less than you. How much did each pair of socks cost?
11. **Newspapers** In 1999 there were 1647 daily and 7471 weekly newspapers published in the United States, as well as x other kinds of newspapers. The total number of newspapers was 700 greater than seven times the number x. How many newspapers were published in 1999 that were not daily or weekly?

Find the indicated measurement, where r = radius, d = diameter, and C = circumference. Use 3.14 or $\frac{22}{7}$ for π.

12. $d = 12.3$ mm, $C = \underline{?}$
13. $C = 22$ in., $r = \underline{?}$
14. $C = 9.42$ ft, $d = \underline{?}$
15. **Tetherball** A tetherball pole is 12 feet high. The tetherball is attached to the top of the pole with a string so that the ball hangs 2 feet above the ground. How long is the string attached to the tetherball? What is the circumference of the largest path that the ball could make through the air around the pole? Use 3.14 for π.

Solve the inequality. Then graph the solution.

16. $6n + 19 \le 7$
17. $10 - 3x > 25$
18. $9c - 8 \ge 3c + 16$
19. $3(k + 3) > k - 1$
20. $8y + 3y + 36 \le 124$
21. $w - 4(w + 5) < -8$

Write the sentence as an inequality. Then solve the inequality.

22. Nine added to the product of 11 and a number is at most 4.
23. A number times 2 minus 13 is less than the number plus 8.
24. Seven times the difference of 12 and a number is at least 14.

Chapter Standardized Test

Test-Taking Strategy **Work at a pace that is right for you. Do not worry about how fast others are working.**

Multiple Choice

1. What is the radius of a circle whose circumference is 110 inches? Use $\frac{22}{7}$ for π.

A. $17\frac{1}{2}$ inches **B.** 35 inches

C. $172\frac{6}{7}$ inches **D.** $345\frac{5}{7}$ inches

2. Solve $9 + \frac{1}{4}x = -1\frac{1}{8} - \frac{1}{2}x$.

F. $-13\frac{1}{2}$ **G.** $-10\frac{1}{2}$

H. $-7\frac{19}{32}$ **I.** 3

3. Solve $4x + 9 \geq -7$.

A. $x \leq -4$ **B.** $x \leq \frac{1}{2}$

C. $x \geq -4$ **D.** $x \geq \frac{1}{2}$

4. All three sides of the triangle have equal length. What is the perimeter?

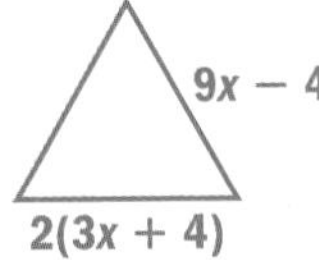

F. 96 units **G.** 32 units

H. 12 units **I.** 4 units

5. A dome has a diameter of 50 feet at its widest point. What is its circumference? Use 3.14 for π.

A. 314 feet **B.** 157 feet

C. 78.5 feet **D.** 39.25 feet

6. Solve $4(x + 5) = x - 19$.

F. -13 **G.** $\frac{1}{4}$ **H.** $\frac{1}{3}$ **I.** 19

7. The circumference of a checker is about 2.355 inches. What is its diameter? Use 3.14 for π.

A. 0.375 inch **B.** 0.75 inch

C. 7.3947 inches **D.** 14.7894 inches

8. Which inequality represents the sentence *ten plus the product of four and a number is at most 9*?

F. $10n + 4 \geq 9$ **G.** $10n + 4 \leq 9$

H. $10 + 4n \geq 9$ **I.** $10 + 4n \leq 9$

9. What is the value of x in the equation $6 - 9(x - 3) = -12$?

A. -5 **B.** $-2\frac{1}{3}$ **C.** $2\frac{1}{3}$ **D.** 5

Short Response

10. You are buying 2.2 pounds of bubble gum that costs $4.50 per pound and lollipops that cost $1.70 per pound. You can't spend more than $15. How many pounds of lollipops can you buy? Explain your reasoning.

Extended Response

11. Each ride on the subway costs $1.25. If you buy a monthly pass for $47, you can ride as often as you want. Write and solve an inequality that models the number of times you need to ride the subway so that buying a pass costs less than paying for each ride. Explain how to use the solution to find the minimum number of times you must ride the subway.

The Physics of Basketball

Dropping Basketballs

The energy with which a basketball hits the ground affects how high the ball will bounce. When a ball is dribbled, several factors affect this energy, including the energy transmitted to the ball by your hand.

When a ball is dropped, the energy with which it hits the ground depends *only* on the mass of the ball, gravity, and the height from which the ball is dropped. Use the equation below to calculate this energy.

Energy E (in Joules) = mass m (in kilograms) × acceleration due to gravity g × height h (in meters)

$$E = mgh$$

For objects on Earth, the acceleration due to gravity g is about 9.8 meters per second squared. You can rewrite the equation above as follows.

$$E = 9.8mh$$

1. Copy and complete the table below. The mass of a typical basketball is 0.6 kilogram. Find the energy with which the ball hits the ground when dropped from each height in the table.

Height (meters)	0.5	1	1.5	2	2.5
Energy (Joules)	?	?	?	?	?

2. You drop a basketball with a mass of 0.6 kilogram. It hits the ground with 12 Joules of energy. From what height did you drop it?

3. You drop a ball from 3 meters and it hits the ground with 15 Joules of energy. What is the mass of the ball?

4. **Writing** Explain how the energy with which a ball hits the ground changes as you increase the height from which you drop it.

5. **Critical Thinking** You drop two identical basketballs from two different heights. One height is twice as great as the other. How will the energies of the two balls as they hit the ground compare? Explain.

Bouncing Basketballs

How high a ball bounces is affected by how bouncy the ball is. For example, a fully inflated basketball bounces higher than a partially inflated one, if both balls hit the ground with the same energy. The fully inflated ball is more bouncy.

You can express the bounciness of a ball by finding the ratio of the bounce height to the drop height. Height is measured from the bottom of the ball to the ground. A standard basketball inflated for game play has a bounciness ratio of about 0.6.

$$\frac{\text{Bounce height (in meters)}}{\text{Drop height (in meters)}} \approx 0.6$$

A ball's bounce height is the height of the *first* bounce.

6. You drop a standard basketball 3 meters. About how high will it bounce on its first bounce?

7. You drop a standard basketball. It bounces to a height of 2 meters on its first bounce. From about what height was it dropped?

8. **Critical Thinking** A ball drops 1.5 meters. It bounces 0.6 meters. Is this ball more or less bouncy than a standard basketball? Explain.

9. **Challenge** You drop a standard basketball 6 meters. Explain how to use the bounciness ratio to find how high the ball bounces on its second bounce. Then find the height of the second bounce.

Project IDEAS

- **Experiment** Design and carry out an experiment to compare the bounciness of several types of ball. Describe your experiment and present your results.
- **Report** A given ball may be designed to perform well during the play of the game in which it is commonly used. Choose a sport and find information on the design of the balls and other equipment used in the sport. Present your findings to the class.
- **Research** The unit of energy called the Joule was named after the scientist James Prescott Joule. Find out more about James Prescott Joule and his work. Present your findings to the class.
- **Career** A variety of professionals do scientific research to study how athletes can improve performance and avoid injury. Investigate some of these careers and present your findings to the class.

CHAPTER

7 Ratio, Proportion, and Percent

BEFORE

In previous chapters you've...

- Found equivalent fractions
- Rewritten fractions and decimals

Now

In Chapter 7 you'll study...

- Finding ratios and unit rates
- Writing and solving proportions
- Solving percent problems
- Rewriting fractions, decimals, and percents
- Finding probabilities of events

WHY?

So you can solve real-world problems about...

- lightning, p. 318
- crocodiles, p. 329
- guitars, p. 342
- beaches, p. 347

Internet Preview
CLASSZONE.COM

- eEdition Plus Online
- eWorkbook Plus Online
- eTutorial Plus Online
- State Test Practice
- More Examples

Chapter Warm-Up Games

Review skills you need for this chapter in these quick games.

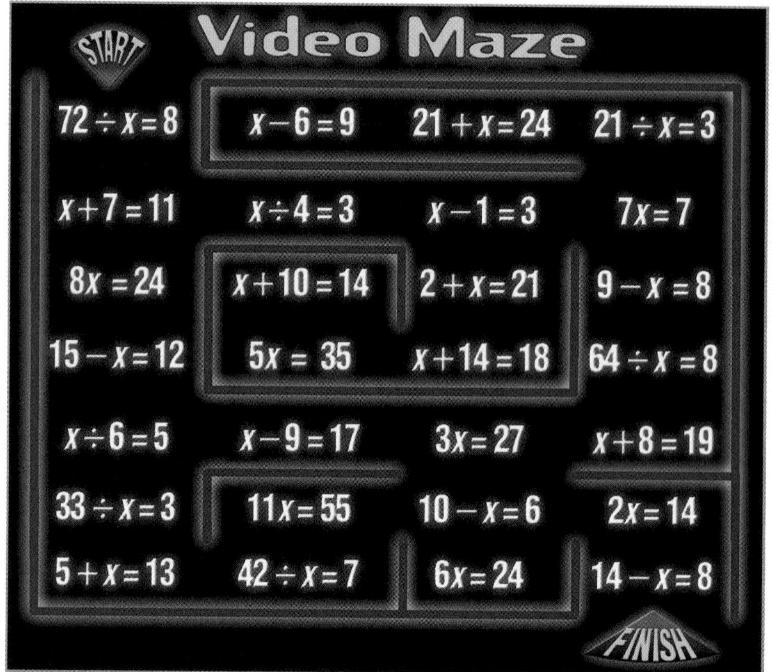

Key Skill:
Solving equations

Find a path through the maze from start to finish.

- Then find the sum of all the solutions of the equations to find your total number of points.
- Which path has the least number of points?

Key Skill:
Performing operations on decimals

Find your way from start to finish in the maze above.

- Evaluate each expression. Then move to the nearest expression that begins with the number that is the value of the previous expression.
- For example, if you start from 5.3 + 4.2 and your choices are 1.4 + 7.2 and 9.5 − 8, you would move to 9.5 − 8 because 5.3 + 4.2 = 9.5.

Stop *and* Think

1. **Writing** A student says that a decimal divided by a decimal is never a whole number. Explain the error in the student's reasoning.
2. **Critical Thinking** How many different paths are there through the *Video Maze* that do not cover the same ground more than once?

Getting Ready to Learn

Word Watch

Review Words

data, p. 5
equation, p. 28
formula, p. 33
simplest form, p. 179
equivalent fractions, p. 179

Review What You Need to Know 

Using Vocabulary **Copy and complete using a review word.**

1. The fraction $\frac{1}{2}$ is in _?_, but $\frac{2}{4}$ is not.

2. The fractions $\frac{2}{3}$ and $\frac{4}{6}$ are _?_.

Solve the equation. *(p. 113)*

3. $\frac{x}{7} = 3$ 4. $\frac{x}{-2} = 4$ 5. $-9x = 108$ 6. $8x = 56$

7. You have 15 pairs of socks in your drawer, including exactly 6 pairs of black socks. What fraction of your socks are black? *(p. 179)*

Order the numbers from least to greatest. *(p. 242)*

8. $0, -0.25, \frac{1}{3}, -1.11, \frac{9}{8}, \frac{12}{9}$ 9. $-\frac{7}{8}, 1.28, \frac{1}{12}, -0.02, 0.34, \frac{10}{3}$

You should include material that appears on a notebook like this in your own notes.

Know How to Take Notes

Taking Notes in Class When your teacher answers your question in class, include the answer in your notes.

Writing Decimals as Fractions

$0.007 = \frac{7}{1000}$ 0.007 has 3 decimal places.
1000 has 3 zeros.

$0.13 = \frac{13}{100}$ 0.13 has 2 decimal places.
100 has 2 zeros.

Number of decimal places equals number of zeros!

As you work on solving proportions in Chapter 7, be sure to ask questions about things you don't understand and write the answers in your notes.

Ratios and Rates

BEFORE	Now	WHY?
You found equivalent fractions.	You'll find ratios and unit rates.	So you can tell whether a TV has a wide screen, as in Ex. 22.

ratio, p. 317
equivalent ratios, p. 317
rate, p. 318
unit rate, p. 318

INDIANA Academic Standards

- Algebra and Functions (8.3.7)
- Measurement (8.5.2, 8.5.3)
- Problem Solving (8.7.1)

Activity **You can compare side lengths and perimeters of squares.**

1. Copy and complete the table using the squares shown. Write the relationship between the side length and the perimeter of each square as a fraction in simplest form.

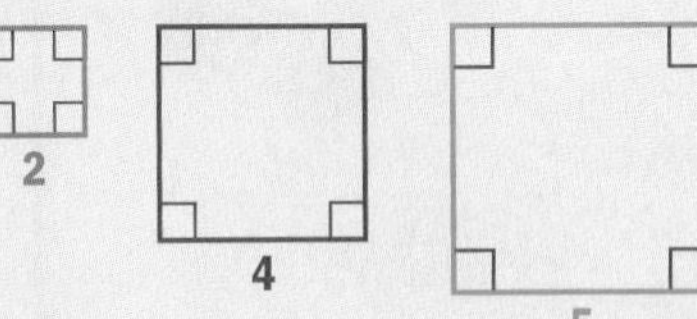

2. What do you notice about the fractions in the table?

3. Describe the relationship between the side length and the perimeter of a square with side length s.

Side length	2	4	5
Perimeter	?	?	?
$\frac{\text{Side length}}{\text{Perimeter}}$	?	?	?

In the activity, you used a *ratio* to reach a conclusion about the relationship between the side length and the perimeter of a square. A **ratio** uses division to compare two numbers. You can write the ratio of a to b ($b \neq 0$) in three ways.

$$\frac{a}{b} \qquad a:b \qquad a \text{ to } b$$

Ratios that have the same value are called **equivalent ratios**.

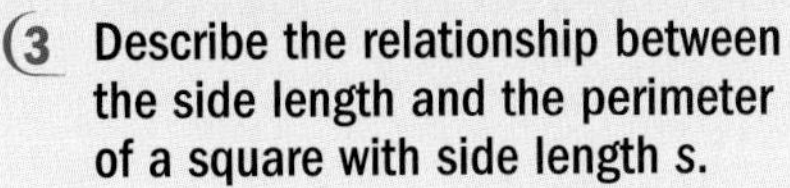

EXAMPLE 1 Writing a Ratio

Skiing A ski resort has 15 easy, 25 intermediate, 7 difficult, and 11 expert-only trails. Write the ratio intermediate trails : easy trails in three ways.

$$\frac{\text{intermediate trails}}{\text{easy trails}} = \frac{25}{15} = \frac{5}{3}$$ Write as a fraction and simplify.

ANSWER The ratio can be written as $\frac{5}{3}$, 5 : 3 , or 5 to 3.

Your turn now **Use the information in Example 1 to write the ratio as a fraction in simplest form and two other ways.**

1. easy trails to difficult trails
2. expert-only trails to easy trails

Rates A **rate** is a ratio of two quantities that have *different* units. Two rates are equivalent if they have the same value.

EXAMPLE 2 Finding an Equivalent Rate

Weather Lightning strikes about 100 times per second around the world. About how many times does lightning strike per minute around the world?

Solution

Use the fact that 60 sec = 1 min. So, $\frac{60 \text{ sec}}{1 \text{ min}}$ is equivalent to 1.

$$\frac{100 \text{ times}}{1 \text{ sec}} = \frac{100 \text{ times}}{1 \cancel{\text{sec}}} \cdot \frac{60 \cancel{\text{sec}}}{1 \text{ min}}$$ Multiply by a fraction that is equivalent to 1.

$$= \frac{6000 \text{ times}}{1 \text{ min}}$$ Simplify.

ANSWER Lightning strikes about 6000 times per minute around the world.

Unit Rates A **unit rate** is a rate that has a denominator of 1 unit. To write a unit rate, find an equivalent rate with a denominator of 1 unit.

with Review

For help with equivalent fractions, see p. 179.

EXAMPLE 3 Finding a Unit Rate

Write −24 feet per 5 seconds as a unit rate.

$$\frac{-24 \text{ ft}}{5 \text{ sec}} = \frac{-24 \div 5}{5 \div 5}$$ Divide numerator and denominator by 5 to get a denominator of 1 unit.

$$= \frac{-4.8}{1}$$ Simplify.

ANSWER The unit rate is −4.8 feet per second.

✓**Check** Round −4.8 ft/sec to −5 ft/sec. The product $-5 \cdot 5 = -25$, which is about −24, so your answer is reasonable.

Your turn now **Write your answer as a rate.**

3. A water pump moves 2 gallons of water per second. How many gallons of water are pumped per minute?

Write the rate as a unit rate.

4. $\frac{114 \text{ points}}{6 \text{ games}}$ **5.** $\frac{365 \text{ people}}{5 \text{ months}}$ **6.** $\frac{329 \text{ miles}}{10 \text{ gallons}}$ **7.** $\frac{-49 \text{ m}}{14 \text{ sec}}$

7.1 Exercises

More Practice, p. 733

Example	Exercises
1	10-17, 27-28
2	18-21
3	23-26

- More Examples
- eTutorial Plus

Getting Ready to Practice

1. **Vocabulary** Copy and complete: Three gallons to \$4.50 and five gallons to \$7.50 are equivalent _?_.

Write the ratio as a fraction in simplest form and two other ways.

2. $\frac{12}{36}$ 3. $\frac{15}{10}$ 4. $\frac{6}{4}$

Tell whether the ratios are equivalent.

5. $\frac{5}{2}$ and $\frac{20}{8}$ 6. 12 to 3 and 6 to 2 7. 6 : 18 and 10 : 30

8. **Wages** You are paid \$47.25 for working 7 hours. How much are you paid per hour?

9. **Find the Error** Describe and correct the error in the solution.

Find an equivalent rate of 14 times a day.

$$\frac{14 \text{ times}}{\text{day}} \cdot \frac{1 \text{ week}}{7 \text{ days}} = \frac{2 \text{ times}}{\text{week}}$$

Practice and Problem Solving

Write the ratio as a fraction in simplest form and two other ways.

10. $\frac{33}{22}$ 11. $\frac{20}{25}$ 12. $-8:6$ 13. 35 to 49

14. 51 to 17 15. 26 : 39 16. $\frac{27}{42}$ 17. $\frac{-12}{4}$

Measurement **Write the equivalent rate.**

18. $\frac{60 \text{ miles}}{\text{hour}} = \frac{? \text{ miles}}{\text{minute}}$ 19. $\frac{32 \text{ ounces}}{\text{serving}} = \frac{? \text{ pounds}}{\text{serving}}$

20. $\frac{105 \text{ min}}{\text{game}} = \frac{? \text{ h}}{\text{game}}$ 21. $\frac{\$1.44}{\text{ft}} = \frac{\$?}{\text{yd}}$

22. **Television** The aspect ratio of a TV screen is the ratio of its length to its width. The aspect ratio of a *standard* TV screen is 4 : 3. The aspect ratio of a *wide screen* TV in the United States is 16 : 9. Describe how you would tell whether a TV has a standard or wide screen given the length and width of the screen.

Write the rate as a unit rate.

23. $\frac{\text{24 adults}}{\text{6 cars}}$ 24. $\frac{-\text{34 meters}}{\text{8 seconds}}$ 25. $\frac{\text{3 pounds}}{\$2}$ 26. $\frac{\text{610 rotations}}{\text{5 minutes}}$

Write the ratio of shaded to unshaded squares.

27. 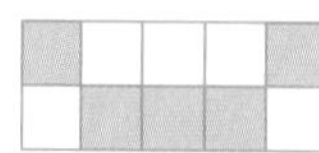

28. 

Find the value of the variable that makes the ratios equivalent.

29. $\frac{x}{8} = \frac{4}{16}$ 30. $\frac{9}{c} = \frac{27}{30}$ 31. $\frac{6}{10} = \frac{15}{n}$ 32. $\frac{2}{12} = \frac{z}{18}$

33. **Writing** About one out of every ten people is left-handed. How many people in your math class would you predict to be left-handed? Explain.

34. **Running Speed** At top speed, a greyhound can run 330 feet in 5 seconds, a roadrunner can run 75 feet in 3 seconds, and a cheetah can run 198 feet in 2 seconds. Write each speed as a unit rate. Which animal is the fastest? Which animal is the slowest?

35. **Population Density** New Jersey's population in 2000 was about 8,414,000. New Jersey's area is 7417 square miles. What was the population per square mile, or *population density*, in New Jersey in 2000? Round to the nearest whole number.

36. **Challenge** You can buy your favorite crackers in a 10 ounce box or a 1 pound box. The 10 ounce box costs \$2.69 and the 1 pound box costs \$3.28. Which is the better buy? Explain.

Mixed Review 

37. Find the radius of a circle with a circumference of 39.25 feet. Use 3.14 for π. *(Lesson 6.4)*

38. Solve the inequality $10y + 4 < 24$ and graph the solution. *(Lesson 6.5)*

Basic Skills **Solve the equation.**

39. $3c = 18$ 40. $9x = -81$ 41. $\frac{v}{4} = -2$ 42. $\frac{n}{10} = 8$

Test-Taking Practice 

43. **Multiple Choice** Which rate is equivalent to 232 miles per 4 hours?

A. $\frac{\text{58 mi}}{\text{4 h}}$ B. $\frac{\text{174 mi}}{\text{3 h}}$ C. $\frac{\text{232 mi}}{\text{3 h}}$ D. $\frac{\text{116 mi}}{\text{1 h}}$

44. **Short Response** Emily runs 1600 meters in 5 minutes 30 seconds, and Megan runs 800 meters in 2 minutes 40 seconds. Who has the faster average speed? Explain your reasoning.

7.2 Hands-on Activity

GOAL

Make scale drawings.

MATERIALS

- ruler
- grid paper
- colored pencils
- magazine

Making a Scale Drawing

A *scale drawing* of an object preserves ratios of lengths but is either smaller or larger than the original object.

Explore

Make an enlarged drawing of the picture.

1. Draw a grid on the original picture.

2. On your grid paper, draw a rectangle that is the same number of units long and wide as the picture you want to enlarge. These unit squares should be bigger than the grid squares on the original picture.

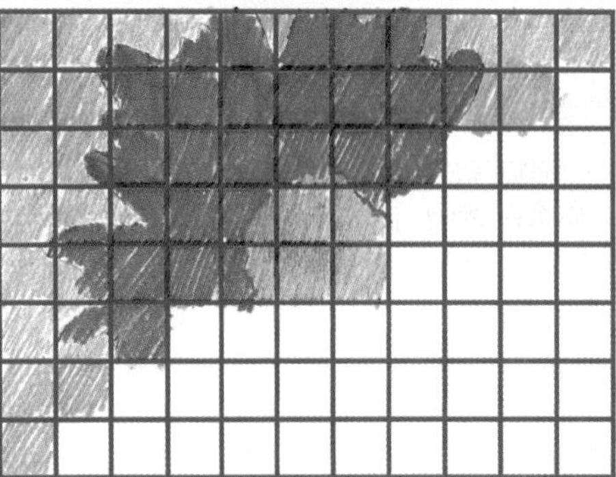

3. Starting in a corner, copy the image that appears in the corresponding corner of the original onto your grid paper. Continue copying the image one block at a time until you have drawn the entire picture.

4. The *scale* of the drawing is the ratio of corresponding measurements of the copy to the original. Measure the width of the copy and of the original. What is the scale of your drawing?

Your turn now

1. Cut out a picture from a magazine and create an enlarged scale drawing of it. Measure the original picture and the enlarged drawing to determine the scale.

2. Is the ratio of the area of a unit square in the copy to the area of a unit square in the original the same as the ratio of their sides? Explain.

Stop *and* Think

3. **Critical Thinking** What would happen if different scales were used in the same drawing?

Writing and Solving Proportions

BEFORE	Now	WHY?
You wrote ratios.	You'll write and solve proportions.	So you can find the dimensions of a model car, as in Ex. 35.

Word Watch

proportion, p. 322
cross products, p. 323
scale model, p. 324
scale, p. 324

INDIANA Academic Standards

- Measurement (8.5.3)
- Problem Solving (8.7.1)

In the Real World

Rhinoceros Beetles An adult rhinoceros beetle weighs only 0.525 ounce but can carry about 446.25 ounces on its back. If a person were as strong as a rhinoceros beetle, how much weight could a 100 pound person carry?

A **proportion** is an equation that states that two ratios are equivalent.

$$\frac{a}{b} = \frac{c}{d},\ b \neq 0,\ d \neq 0$$

The proportion above is read "a is to b as c is to d."

EXAMPLE 1 Writing and Solving a Proportion

To answer the question about strength above, write and solve a proportion.

	Beetle	Person
Carries	446.25	x
Weighs	0.525	100

Use a table to set up a proportion.

$\frac{446.25}{0.525} = \frac{x}{100}$ Write a proportion.

$\frac{446.25}{0.525} \cdot 100 = \frac{x}{100} \cdot 100$ Multiply each side by 100.

$85{,}000 = x$ Simplify.

ANSWER If human strength were proportional to that of a rhinoceros beetle, a 100 pound person could carry 85,000 pounds.

HELP with Solving

In Example 1, the ratios in the proportion use the following units: $\frac{\text{ounces}}{\text{ounces}}$ and $\frac{\text{pounds}}{\text{pounds}}$.

Your turn now Solve the proportion.

1. $\frac{n}{12} = \frac{3}{4}$
2. $\frac{50}{20} = \frac{z}{16}$
3. $\frac{250}{30} = \frac{t}{51}$

Cross Products The proportion $\frac{a}{b} = \frac{c}{d}$ has **cross products** ad and bc.

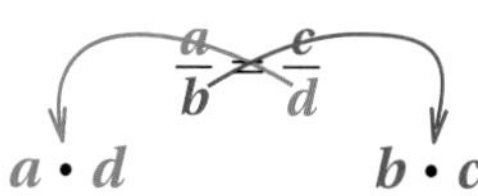

You can use cross products to solve a proportion. You can also use cross products to check whether two ratios form a proportion.

Cross Products Property

Words The cross products of a proportion are equal.

Algebra If $\frac{a}{b} = \frac{c}{d}$, where b and d are nonzero numbers, then $ad = bc$.

Numbers Because $\frac{3}{4} = \frac{9}{12}$, you know that $3 \cdot 12 = 4 \cdot 9$.

EXAMPLE 2 Using the Cross Products Property

$\frac{6.8}{15.4} = \frac{40.8}{m}$ Original proportion

$6.8 \cdot m = 15.4 \cdot 40.8$ Cross products property

$6.8m = 628.32$ Multiply.

$\frac{6.8m}{6.8} = \frac{628.32}{6.8}$ Divide each side by 6.8.

$m = 92.4$ Simplify.

✓**Check** You can check your solution by finding the cross products of the proportion. If the cross products are equal, the solution is correct.

$\frac{6.8}{15.4} \stackrel{?}{=} \frac{40.8}{92.4}$ Substitute 92.4 for m in original proportion.

$6.8 \cdot 92.4 \stackrel{?}{=} 15.4 \cdot 40.8$

$628.32 = 628.32$ ✓

Your turn now Solve the proportion. Then check your solution.

4. $\frac{6}{c} = \frac{54}{99}$ **5.** $\frac{n}{14} = \frac{63}{98}$ **6.** $\frac{2.1}{0.9} = \frac{27.3}{y}$

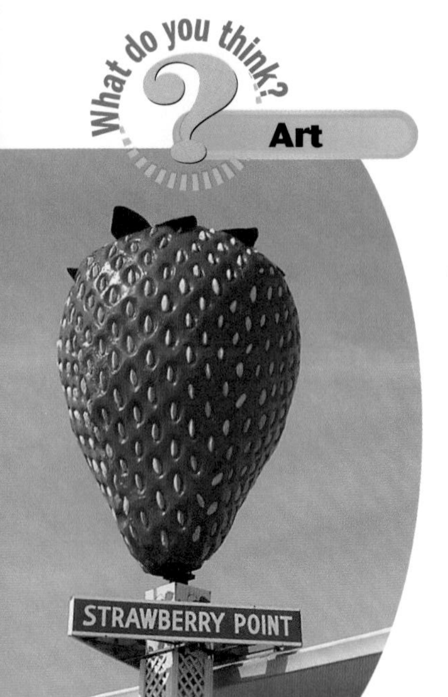

Sculpture

How many inches tall is the giant strawberry? Write the scale of the strawberry sculpture without units.

Scale The dimensions of a **scale model** are proportional to the dimensions of the actual object. The **scale** gives the relationship between the model's dimensions and the actual object's dimensions. A scale can be written as a ratio with or without units. For example, the scale 1 in. : 3 ft can also be written as 1 : 36.

EXAMPLE 3 Using a Scale

Sculpture Strawberry Point, Iowa, has a strawberry sculpture that is 15 feet tall. If the scale of this model is 10 feet to 1 inch, how tall was the original strawberry?

Solution

$$\text{Scale} = \frac{\text{Height of strawberry model}}{\text{Height of original strawberry}}$$ **Write a verbal model.**

$$\frac{10 \text{ ft}}{1 \text{ in.}} = \frac{15 \text{ ft}}{h \text{ in.}}$$ **Write a proportion.**

$$10h = 15$$ **Cross products property**

$$h = 1.5$$ **Divide each side by 10.**

ANSWER The height of the original strawberry was 1.5 inches.

7.2 Exercises

More Practice, p. 733

Getting Ready to Practice

1. **Vocabulary** Describe how to use cross products to solve a proportion.

Solve the proportion. Then check your solution.

2. $\frac{1}{2} = \frac{x}{6}$ 3. $\frac{2}{3} = \frac{4}{z}$ 4. $\frac{6}{a} = \frac{3}{1}$ 5. $\frac{c}{10} = \frac{3}{5}$

6. **Find the Error** Describe and correct the error in solving the proportion.

$\frac{3}{9} = \frac{12}{m}$ ✗

$9m = 3 \cdot 12$

$9m = 36$

$m = 4$

7. **Cars** A car moving at a constant speed travels 88 feet in 2 seconds. Use a proportion to find how many feet it travels in one minute.

Practice and Problem Solving

Example	Exercises
1	12-19
2	8-19, 25-27
3	20-23

CLASSZONE.COM

- More Examples
- eTutorial Plus

Decide Tell whether the ratios form a proportion.

8. $\frac{3}{4} \stackrel{?}{=} \frac{6}{8}$ **9.** $\frac{1}{2} \stackrel{?}{=} \frac{2}{5}$ **10.** $\frac{14}{21} \stackrel{?}{=} \frac{21}{35}$ **11.** $\frac{15}{45} \stackrel{?}{=} \frac{45}{135}$

Solve the proportion.

12. $\frac{3}{8} = \frac{x}{32}$ **13.** $\frac{4}{c} = \frac{20}{45}$ **14.** $\frac{39}{13} = \frac{9}{d}$ **15.** $\frac{68}{12} = \frac{51}{p}$

16. $\frac{67.2}{g} = \frac{16.8}{3.3}$ **17.** $\frac{t}{29.4} = \frac{5.5}{4.2}$ **18.** $\frac{f}{5.4} = \frac{483}{18.9}$ **19.** $\frac{712}{8.8} = \frac{x}{18.7}$

Scale Models You use a scale of 1 inch to 20 feet to make scale models of buildings. A building's actual height is given. Find the model's height.

20. $h = 100$ ft **21.** $h = 240$ ft **22.** $h = 316$ ft **23.** $h = 545$ ft

24. **Mental Math** Explain how you can use equivalent fractions and mental math to solve $\frac{5}{x} = \frac{10}{16}$.

25. **Earnings** You earn $54 mowing 3 lawns. You charge the same amount for each lawn. How much would you earn if you mowed 5 lawns?

Extended Problem Solving To produce one pound of honey, the bees from a hive fly over 55,000 miles and visit about 2 million flowers.

26. About how many flowers are visited to make 10 ounces of honey?

27. About how many miles do the bees fly to make 10 ounces of honey?

28. **Explain** What is the mean number of flowers visited per mile traveled? Explain your reasoning.

EXAMPLE Finding the Value of x

$\frac{30}{2 + x} = \frac{6}{7}$	Original proportion
$7 \cdot 30 = 6(2 + x)$	Cross products property
$210 = 12 + 6x$	Multiply and use distributive property.
$33 = x$	Solve the two-step equation for *x*.

In Exercises 29–31, find the value of *x*.

29. $\frac{2}{x + 2} = \frac{18}{27}$ **30.** $\frac{x - 2}{8} = \frac{30}{40}$ **31.** $\frac{9}{5} = \frac{36}{x - 3}$

Challenge Find the value of each variable.

32. $\frac{4}{12} = \frac{3}{x} = \frac{y}{21}$ **33.** $\frac{7}{12} = \frac{a}{72} = \frac{28}{b}$ **34.** $\frac{8}{5} = \frac{n}{7} = \frac{21}{p}$

35. Model Car A toy manufacturer plans to make a model version of a car using a scale of 1 inch to 43 inches. The actual vehicle is 215 inches long, 75.25 inches wide, and 53.75 inches high. Find the length, width, and height of the model car.

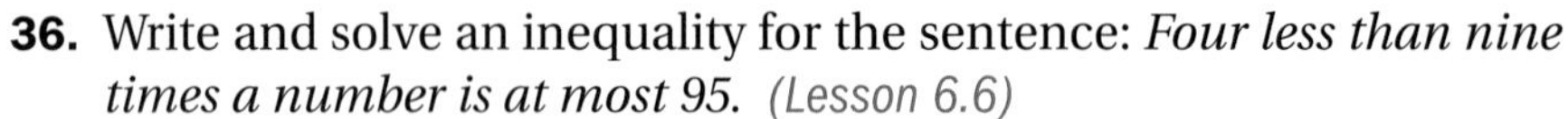

Mixed Review

36. Write and solve an inequality for the sentence: *Four less than nine times a number is at most 95.* *(Lesson 6.6)*

Write the rate as a unit rate. *(Lesson 7.1)*

37. $\frac{\text{42 people}}{\text{14 taxis}}$ **38.** $\frac{\text{258 miles}}{\text{6 hours}}$ **39.** $\frac{\text{36 dogs}}{\text{18 households}}$

Test-Taking Practice

40. Multiple Choice Solve $\frac{12}{15} = \frac{x}{25}$.

A. 31 **B.** 21 **C.** 20 **D.** 4

41. Multiple Choice The scale on a map is $\frac{1}{4}$ inch : 20 miles. The distance from Montgomery, Alabama, to Atlanta, Georgia, is about 2 inches on the map. About how far is it from Montgomery to Atlanta?

F. 20 miles **G.** 80 miles **H.** 160 miles **I.** 200 miles

Balancing Act

The middle person below is holding the same weight on both trays. What shapes do you need to add to the other people's trays to balance the weights they are holding?

Solving Percent Problems

BEFORE You solved proportions.

Now You'll solve percent problems using proportions.

WHY? So you can find the length of a crocodile, as in Ex. 19.

percent, p. 327

INDIANA Academic Standards

- Computation (8.2.1)
- Algebra and Functions (8.3.1)
- Measurement (8.5.3)

In the Real World

Environment A service club is planting seedlings as part of an erosion prevention project. Out of 240 newly planted seedlings, 15 are laurel sumac. What *percent* of the seedlings are laurel sumac?

The word *percent* means "per hundred." A **percent** is a ratio whose denominator is 100. The symbol for percent is %.

Solving Percent Problems

To represent "a is p percent of b," use the proportion

$$\frac{a}{b} = \frac{p}{100}$$

where a is part of the base b and p%, or $\frac{p}{100}$, is the percent.

EXAMPLE 1 Finding a Percent

To find the percent of seedlings that are laurel sumac as described above, use a percent proportion.

$$\frac{a}{b} = \frac{p}{100}$$ Write a percent proportion.

$$\frac{15}{240} = \frac{p}{100}$$ Substitute 15 for *a* and 240 for *b*.

$$\frac{15}{240} \cdot 100 = \frac{p}{100} \cdot 100$$ Multiply each side by 100.

$$6.25 = p$$ Simplify.

ANSWER Of the seedlings, 6.25% are laurel sumac.

Your turn now **Use a percent proportion.**

1. 126 is what percent of 150?
2. 84 is what percent of 70?

EXAMPLE 2 Finding Part of a Base

School Newspaper Your school newspaper's budget this year is 160% of last year's budget, which was \$2125. What is this year's budget?

Solution

$\frac{a}{b} = \frac{p}{100}$ — Write a percent proportion.

$\frac{a}{2125} = \frac{160}{100}$ — Substitute 2125 for b and 160 for p.

$\frac{a}{2125} \cdot 2125 = \frac{160}{100} \cdot 2125$ — Multiply each side by 2125.

$a = 3400$ — Simplify.

ANSWER This year's budget is \$3400.

The Eagle

September 2004 ❖ Beauford's Oldest Paper

Votes Still Being Counted in Student Race

by Henry Deere

The student council race still isn't over. All the votes are in, but they haven't all been counted yet. Half of the votes were counted and tallied, but the election committee lost the tally. Now the votes must be recounted.

Elizabeth Smith said that the committee expected the votes to be counted by the end of the week. "I'm sorry about our mess-up," she said. "No one knows where the tally went."

Candidates shouldn't worry, though. "None of the original votes have been lost," Elizabeth said.

Five students are running for president, two for vice president, three for secretary, and two for treasurer. When told the results would be delayed, one candidate for president, Marc Chan said, "That's cool. Just as long as they get them counted soon. We're ready to know, but we can wait a few more days."

Of the 685 students in the school, 589 voted in this school wide election.

Fall Dance Planned for October

by Catherine Gant

The Dance Committee has announced that the fall dance will be held on October 15, 2004. The dance will be open to all students at the school. Students will not be allowed to bring friends from other schools.

The Dance Committee is looking for people to help out with the dance. They need people to take money at the door, sell refreshments, and help to decorate the gym. If you are interested in helping out, see Mrs. Calligan.

EXAMPLE 3 Finding a Base

Find the number of which 24 is 0.8%.

$\frac{a}{b} = \frac{p}{100}$ — Write a percent proportion.

$\frac{24}{b} = \frac{0.8}{100}$ — Substitute 24 for a and 0.8 for p.

$24 \cdot 100 = b \cdot 0.8$ — Cross products property

$3000 = b$ — Divide each side by 0.8 and simplify.

ANSWER The number of which 24 is 0.8% is 3000.

HELP with Notetaking

In your notes, you may want to include each step of the process of solving a percent proportion.

Summary of Percent Problems

Question	Method	Proportion
a is what percent of b?	Solve for p.	$\frac{a}{b} = \frac{p}{100}$
What number is p% of b?	Solve for a.	$\frac{a}{b} = \frac{p}{100}$
a is p% of what number?	Solve for b.	$\frac{a}{b} = \frac{p}{100}$

Your turn now **Use a percent proportion.**

3. What number is 0.5% of 65?

4. 260 is 325% of what number?

More Practice, p. 733

Getting Ready to Practice

1. **Vocabulary** Copy and complete: Another way to say 25 songs of 100 is to say 25 _?_ of the songs.

Use a percent proportion.

2. 6 is what percent of 75?
3. 27 is what percent of 108?
4. What number is 45% of 246?
5. 209 is 38% of what number?
6. **Guided Problem Solving** You ask 356 people if they enjoy drawing. Of these people, 89 say they do like to draw. What percent of the people surveyed like to draw?
   (1 Write a percent proportion.
   (2 Substitute the known values for the variables.
   (3 Solve the proportion.

Practice and Problem Solving

In Exercises 7–18, use a percent proportion.

7. 5 is what percent of 125?
8. 39 is what percent of 50?
9. 756 is what percent of 840?
10. 111 is what percent of 740?
11. What number is 45% of 245?
12. What number is 30% of 120?
13. What number is 76% of 775?
14. What number is 66% of 95?
15. 179.2 is 32% of what number?
16. 16.1 is 35% of what number?
17. 481 is 52% of what number?
18. 351 is 78% of what number?
19. **Reptiles** The largest crocodiles alive today are 24 feet in length. Recently, researchers discovered bones of an ancient crocodile. It was 167% as long as today's crocodiles. How long was the ancient crocodile?
20. **Water** A child's body is approximately 75% water. About how many pounds of a 60 pound child's weight is water?

Example	Exercises
1	7-18, 21-26
2	7-26
3	7-18, 21-26

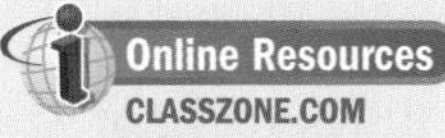

· More Examples
· eTutorial Plus

In Exercises 21–26, use a percent proportion.

21. 567 is what percent of 420?
22. 1.26 is what percent of 42?
23. What number is 520% of 550?
24. What number is 0.36% of 675?
25. 918 is 170% of what number?
26. 79 is 0.01% of what number?

27. **Number Sense** One day, 32 of 80 people wear a red shirt to school. What percent of the 80 people did *not* wear a red shirt to school?

28. **Critical Thinking** Explain how to find 10% of 400 without writing a proportion.

Write and solve the percent problem in terms of *y*.

29. What number is 50% of $8y$?

30. $3y$ is 60% of what number?

31. **Weekends** There are about 52 weeks in a year and two weekend days each week. About what percent of the year falls on a weekend? Round your answer to the nearest tenth of a percent.

32. **Dilophosaurus** You buy your little brother a scale model of a Dilophosaurus. The scale of the model is 1 inch to 3 feet 4 inches. Use the scale to find what percent the model's height is of the actual height.

33. **Challenge** You use a photocopier to reduce an 8 inch by 10 inch photograph. When you press the reduction button, it reduces the length and width by the same percent. What is the new area if you reduce the photograph to 64% of its original size and then reduce the result to 78% of its size? What is the new area if you reduce to 78% first and then to 64%? Compare the two values.

34. **Marathon** Of the 23,513 people who entered the Honolulu Marathon one year, 19,236 finished. What percent of the runners finished? Round your answer to the nearest tenth of a percent.

Mixed Review

Write the decimal as a fraction or mixed number. *(Lesson 5.5)*

35. 1.86

36. 8.714

37. 0.624

Find the product or quotient. *(Lesson 5.7)*

38. 0.023×8.45

39. 47.1×0.96

40. $11.48 \div 8.2$

Test-Taking Practice

41. **Multiple Choice** You decide to save 20% of all the money that you earn. One month you earn $90. How much do you save?

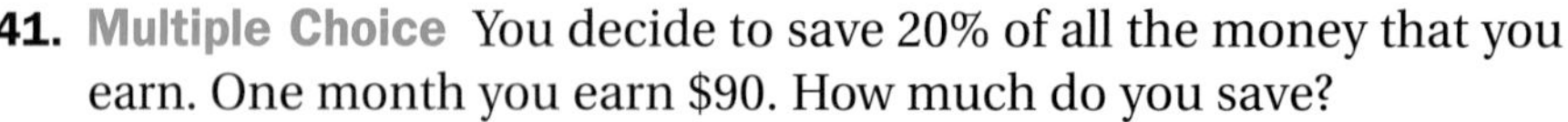

A. $18 **B.** $20 **C.** $22 **D.** $70

42. **Short Response** You read in your school newspaper that 560 of the students at your school belong to a school club, and 875 students attend your school. Write a proportion to determine the percent of students in your school who belong to a club. Solve the proportion.

Fractions, Decimals, and Percents

BEFORE	Now	WHY?
You wrote fractions as decimals and decimals as fractions.	You'll rewrite fractions, decimals, and percents.	So you can express circle graph sectors as percents, as in Ex. 46.

circle graph, p. 331

INDIANA Academic Standards
- Computation (8.2.4)
- Measurement (8.5.2)

In the Real World

Survey The *circle graph* below shows the results of a survey of how 500 students prefer to spend time. What percent of students prefer to spend time with friends?

How Do You Prefer To Spend Your Time?

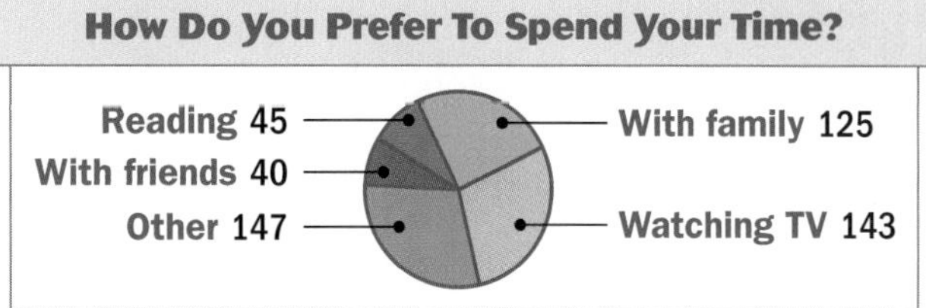

A **circle graph** represents data as parts of a circle. Each part is a percent of the data. The sum of the percents must equal 100% because the circle graph represents all of the data. Each part is also a fraction of the data. The sum of the fractions must equal 1.

EXAMPLE 1 Writing a Fraction as a Percent

The fraction of students who prefer to spend time with friends is $\frac{40}{500}$. To write this fraction as a percent, write a percent proportion and solve for p.

$$\frac{40}{500} = \frac{p}{100}$$ **Write a percent proportion.**

$$\frac{40}{500} \cdot 100 = \frac{p}{100} \cdot 100$$ **Multiply each side by 100.**

$$8 = p$$ **Simplify.**

ANSWER 8% of the students prefer to spend time with friends.

Your turn now **Write the fraction as a percent.**

1. $\frac{4}{5}$ **2.** $\frac{27}{50}$ **3.** $\frac{1}{20}$ **4.** $\frac{3}{8}$

To write a decimal as a percent, write the decimal as a fraction with a denominator of 100. The numerator is the percent. For example:

$$0.89 = \frac{89}{100} = 89\%$$

So, 0.89 = 89%. Notice that 0.89 can be written as a percent by moving the decimal point two places to the right and adding a percent sign.

HELP with Solving

Make sure you move the decimal point two places to the right. Add a zero on the right if necessary, as in part (b) of Example 2.

EXAMPLE 2 Writing Decimals as Percents

Write the decimal as a percent.

a. $0.63 = 0.63$
$= 63\%$

b. $2.7 = 2.70$
$= 270\%$

c. $0.007 = 0.007$
$= 0.7\%$

To write a percent as a decimal, remove the % sign and move the decimal point two places to the left. To write a percent as a fraction, write *n*% as $\frac{n}{100}$ and simplify.

EXAMPLE 3 Writing Percents as Decimals and Fractions

Write the percent as a decimal and as a fraction.

As a decimal	As a fraction
a. $0.32\% = 00.32\%$	$0.32\% = \frac{0.32}{100}$
$= 0.0032$	$= \frac{32}{10{,}000} = \frac{2}{625}$
b. $120\% = 120\%$	$120\% = \frac{120}{100}$
$= 1.2$	$= \frac{6}{5} = 1\frac{1}{5}$
c. $2.5\% = 02.5\%$	$2.5\% = \frac{2.5}{100}$
$= 0.025$	$= \frac{25}{1000} = \frac{1}{40}$

Your turn now **Write the decimal as a percent.**

5. 0.62 **6.** 0.9 **7.** 0.248 **8.** 5.09

Write the percent as a decimal and as a fraction in simplest form.

9. 45% **10.** 214% **11.** 77.5% **12.** 0.5%

EXAMPLE 4 Ordering Fractions, Decimals, and Percents

Order the numbers from least to greatest: 8.7%, $\frac{1}{8}$, and 0.1.

Write 8.7% as a decimal: 8.7% = 08.7% = 0.087

Write $\frac{1}{8}$ as a decimal: $\frac{1}{8}$ = 0.125

Use a number line to order the decimals.

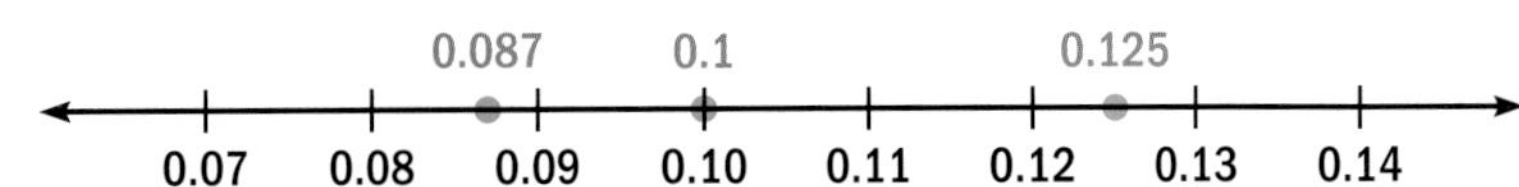

ANSWER The numbers ordered from least to greatest are 8.7%, 0.1, and $\frac{1}{8}$.

Your turn now **Order the numbers from least to greatest.**

13. 41%, $\frac{9}{20}$, 0.389 **14.** $\frac{9}{10}$, 0.099, 95% **15.** 1.5, 145%, $\frac{7}{5}$

7.4 Exercises

More Practice, p. 733

Getting Ready to Practice

1. Vocabulary In a circle graph, what is the sum of the percents? What is the sum of the fractions?

Write the decimal or fraction as a percent.

2. 0.1 **3.** 0.09 **4.** $\frac{5}{8}$ **5.** $\frac{3}{2}$

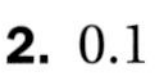

Write the percent as a decimal and as a fraction in simplest form.

6. 80% **7.** 12.5% **8.** 7.5% **9.** 110%

10. Sleeping You survey 48 people and find that 18 of them sleep eight hours a night. What percent sleep eight hours a night?

11. Find the Error Describe and correct the error in writing 0.001 as a percent.

✗ $0.001 = \frac{1}{100} = 1\%$

Practice and Problem Solving

HELP with Homework

Example	Exercises
1	12–27, 45–48
2	12–27
3	28–39
4	40–43

Online Resources
CLASSZONE.COM

- More Examples
- eTutorial Plus

Write the decimal or fraction as a percent.

12. 1.27 **13.** 0.057 **14.** 0.039 **15.** 0.004

16. $\frac{1}{80}$ **17.** $\frac{3}{20}$ **18.** $\frac{31}{10}$ **19.** $\frac{4}{800}$

20. 47.3 **21.** 1.056 **22.** $\frac{1}{125}$ **23.** $\frac{105}{200}$

24. $\frac{5}{9}$ **25.** $\frac{128}{150}$ **26.** 0.0028 **27.** 0.7

Write the percent as a decimal and as a fraction.

28. 40% **29.** 87% **30.** 32.5% **31.** 101%

32. 1% **33.** 4.2% **34.** 200.2% **35.** 124%

36. 187.09% **37.** 0.4% **38.** 0.78% **39.** 44.55%

Order the numbers from least to greatest.

40. 0.022, $\frac{9}{40}$, 22%, 0.228, $\frac{28}{125}$

41. 6.6%, $\frac{3}{50}$, 0.0606, 0.6%, 0.606

42. $\frac{4}{7}$, 0.058, 58, 58%, 0.58%

43. 212%, 21.2, $\frac{21}{100}$, 0.212, $\frac{21}{10}$

44. **Critical Thinking** If a fraction is greater than 1, what do you know about the equivalent percent?

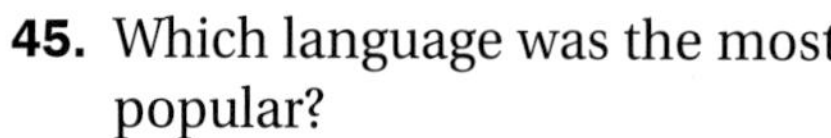

Languages The circle graph shows the world languages that U.S. high school students studied in a recent year. Each fraction in the graph represents part of the total number of U.S. high school students who studied a world language.

45. Which language was the most popular?

46. What percent of the students studied German?

47. What percent of the students studied French or German?

48. What percent of the students did *not* study Spanish?

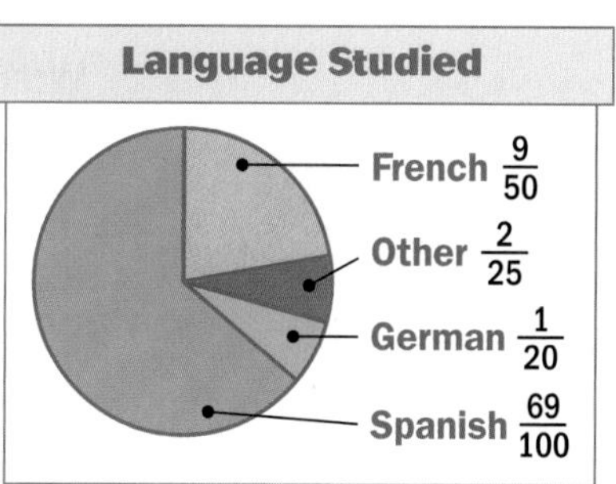

Copy and complete the statement using <, >, or =.

49. $\frac{1}{4}$ _?_ 26% **50.** 450% _?_ $\frac{9}{2}$ **51.** $\frac{13}{25}$ _?_ 0.5

52. 0.0825 _?_ $\frac{17}{200}$ **53.** 4.5% _?_ 0.045 **54.** 101% _?_ 0.101

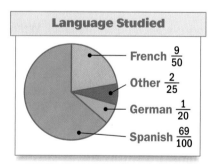

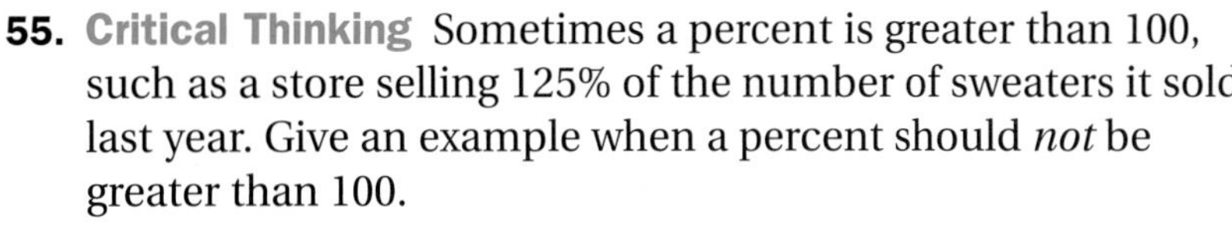

55. **Critical Thinking** Sometimes a percent is greater than 100, such as a store selling 125% of the number of sweaters it sold last year. Give an example when a percent should *not* be greater than 100.

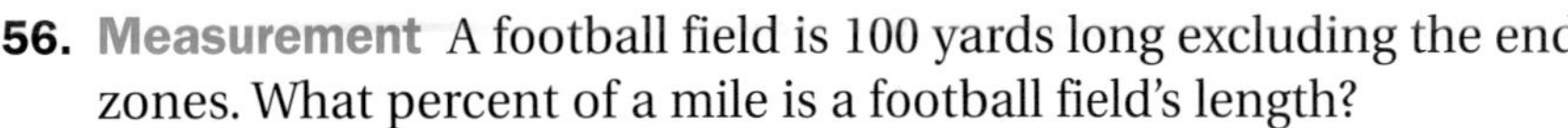

56. **Measurement** A football field is 100 yards long excluding the end zones. What percent of a mile is a football field's length?

57. **Challenge** Use graph paper to illustrate 45% and 4.5%.

58. **Explain** The table shows the percents of people who buy various types of music. Explain why the data should not be represented in a circle graph. Then find an appropriate way to display the data.

Music	Percent
Rock	24.4%
Pop	12.1%
Rap	11.4%
R&B	10.6%
Country	10.5%

Mixed Review 

Write the sentence as an inequality. Then solve. *(Lesson 6.6)*

59. The sum of 13 and 4 times a number is at most 9.

60. Eight less than the quotient of a number and 6 is greater than -7.

Choose a Strategy **Use a strategy from the list to solve the following problem. Explain your choice of strategy.**

61. You work for 4 hours. You spend $5.75 of the money you earn on a movie ticket and $2 on popcorn. Then your sister gives you $3 she owes you. You now have $19.25. How much were you paid per hour?

> Problem Solving Strategies
> - Guess, Check, and Revise
> - Draw a Diagram
> - Work Backward
> - Solve a Simpler Problem

Basic Skills **Find the product or quotient.**

62. 9.2×13.4 **63.** $41.3 \div 11.8$ **64.** $9.9 \div 4.5$ **65.** 1.98×6

Test-Taking Practice 

66. **Multiple Choice** Which numbers are in order from least to greatest?

A. $0.25, 2.5\%, \frac{2}{7}$ **B.** $2.5\%, 0.25, \frac{2}{7}$ **C.** $0.25, \frac{2}{7}, 2.5\%$ **D.** $2.5\%, \frac{2}{7}, 0.25$

67. **Multiple Choice** Which choice shows 53.72% written as a decimal?

F. 5372 **G.** 53.72 **H.** 5.372 **I.** 0.5372

Notebook Review

Review the vocabulary definitions in your notebook.

Copy the review examples in your notebook. Then complete the exercises.

Check Your Definitions

ratio, p. 317	proportion, p. 322	scale, p. 324
equivalent ratios, p. 317	cross products, p. 323	percent, p. 327
rate, unit rate, p. 318	scale model, p. 324	circle graph, p. 331

Use Your Vocabulary

1. Copy and complete: In a(n) _?_, the cross products are equal.

7.1 Can you write a unit rate?

EXAMPLE Write 282 miles per 6 hours as a unit rate.

$\frac{282 \text{ miles}}{6 \text{ hours}} = \frac{282 \div 6}{6 \div 6}$ Divide numerator and denominator by 6.

$= \frac{47}{1}$ Simplify.

ANSWER The unit rate is 47 miles per hour.

Write the rate as a unit rate.

2. 30 feet per 4 seconds

3. \$3.36 per 2 gallons

7.2–7.3 Can you solve percent problems?

EXAMPLE 36 is 15% of what number?

$\frac{a}{b} = \frac{p}{100}$ Write a percent proportion.

$\frac{36}{b} = \frac{15}{100}$ Substitute 36 for *a* and 15 for *p*.

$36 \cdot 100 = 15b$ Cross products property

$240 = b$ Divide each side by 15.

Use a percent proportion.

4. 72 is what percent of 1200?

5. What number is 95% of 26?

7.4 Can you rewrite percents, decimals, and fractions?

EXAMPLE Write 28% as a decimal and as a fraction.

$28\% = 28\% = 0.28$ Remove % sign and move decimal point two places to the left.

$28\% = \frac{28}{100} = \frac{7}{25}$ Write as a fraction and simplify.

ANSWER 28% can be written as 0.28 or $\frac{7}{25}$.

Write the percent as a decimal and as a fraction.

6. 74% **7.** 3.8% **8.** 16.8% **9.** 130%

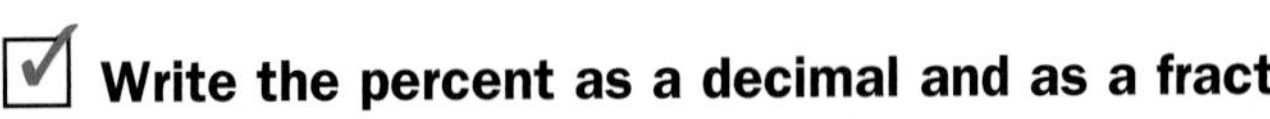

about Lessons 7.1–7.4

10. Writing Explain how to use the cross products property to check if two ratios form a proportion.

Review Quiz 1

A box of animal crackers contains 6 gorillas, 5 bears, 4 camels, 2 monkeys, 2 sheep, and 1 lion. Write the ratio in simplest form.

1. gorillas to sheep **2.** monkeys to camels **3.** bears to lions

Find the value of the variable.

4. $\frac{a}{72} = \frac{5}{6}$ **5.** $\frac{2}{3} = \frac{7}{x}$ **6.** $\frac{18}{27} = \frac{y}{3}$

7. $\frac{6}{8} = \frac{b}{28}$ **8.** $\frac{12}{c} = \frac{23}{92}$ **9.** $\frac{z+1}{8} = \frac{95}{19}$

10. Clothing You save 40% when buying a shirt that originally cost $29. How much do you save?

Gardening **The circle graph shows the numbers of flowers that you planted in a flowerbed.**

11. How many flowers did you plant?

12. What percent of the flowerbed is roses?

13. What two types of flowers combine to equal 70%?

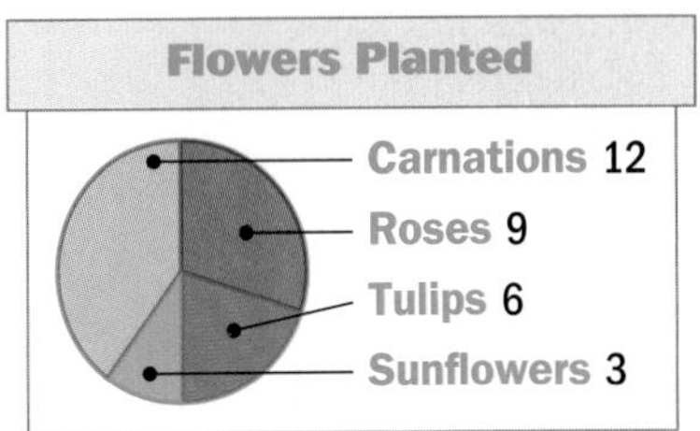

Percent of Change

BEFORE	Now	WHY?
You solved problems with percents.	You'll solve problems with percent of increase or decrease.	So you can find tons of hazelnuts produced, as in Ex. 19.

Word Watch

percent of change, p. 338
percent of increase, p. 338
percent of decrease, p. 338

INDIANA Academic Standards

- Computation (8.2.1)
- Algebra and Functions (8.3.7)

In the Real World

Bears During the summer, a bear's heart rate is about 60 beats per minute, but it can drop to as low as 8 beats per minute during winter. What is the *percent of change* in a bear's heart rate from the summer rate to the winter low rate?

A **percent of change** shows how much a quantity has increased or decreased in relation to the original amount. When the new amount is greater than the original amount, the percent of change is called a **percent of increase**. When the new amount is less than the original amount, it is called a **percent of decrease**.

Percent of Change

Use the following equation to find the percent of change.

$$\text{Percent of change, } p\% = \frac{\text{Amount of increase or decrease}}{\text{Original amount}}$$

For help with repeating decimals, see p. 242.

EXAMPLE 1 Finding a Percent of Decrease

To find the percent of decrease in a bear's heart rate as described above, use the percent of change equation.

$p\% = \frac{60 - 8}{60}$ **Write amount of decrease and divide by original amount.**

$= \frac{52}{60}$ **Subtract.**

$= 0.86\overline{6}$ **Write fraction as a decimal.**

ANSWER The percent of decrease is about 86.7%.

EXAMPLE 2 Finding a Percent of Increase

School A school had 825 students enrolled last year. This year, 870 students are enrolled. Find the percent of increase.

Solution

$p\% = \frac{870 - 825}{825}$ — **Write amount of increase and divide by original amount.**

$= \frac{45}{825}$ — **Subtract.**

$= 0.05\overline{45}$ — **Write fraction as a decimal.**

ANSWER The percent of increase is about 5.5%.

Watch Out!

Make sure you use the original amount, not the new amount, in the denominator when finding a percent of change.

Your turn now **Tell whether the change is an *increase* or *decrease*. Then find the percent of change.**

1. Original amount: 50
New amount: 36

2. Original amount: 10
New amount: 29.5

3. Original amount: 90
New amount: 110

Decimal Method A shortcut to finding a percent of a number is to write the percent as a decimal and then find the product of the decimal and the number. For example, 10% of 60 = 0.10(60) = 6.

Everglades

During the wet season, water flows south through the Everglades at a rate of 100 feet per day. How many days does it take water to flow one mile?

EXAMPLE 3 Using Percent of Increase

Everglades From October to November one year, there was about a 27.4% increase in attendance at Everglades National Park. There were 59,084 visitors in October. About how many people visited in November?

Solution

(1) Find the increase.

Increase = **27.4%** of 59,084

= **0.274**(59,084) — **Write 27.4% as a decimal.**

≈ 16,189 — **Multiply.**

(2) Add the increase to the original amount.

New Amount ≈ 59,084 + 16,189

= 75,273

ANSWER About 75,273 people visited the park in November.

7.5 Exercises

More Practice, p. 733

Getting Ready to Practice

1. **Vocabulary** Copy and complete: When the original amount is less than the new amount, the percent of change is called a(n) _?_.

Tell whether the change is an *increase* or *decrease*. Then find the percent of change.

2. Original amount: 10
   New amount: 14
3. Original amount: 20
   New amount: 16

Find the new amount.

4. 78 is decreased by 22%.
5. 105 is decreased by 78%.
6. **Tennis** In 1975, there were 130,000 tennis courts in the United States. This number increased by 69% from 1975 to 1985. The number then increased by 9% from 1985 to 1995. How many tennis courts were there in the United States in 1985 and in 1995?
   (1) Find the number of tennis courts in 1985.
   (2) Find the amount of the second increase.
   (3) Find the number of tennis courts in 1995.

Practice and Problem Solving

Decide **Tell whether the change is an *increase* or *decrease*. Then find the percent of change.**

7. 10 rabbits to 16 rabbits
8. 360 pounds to 352 pounds
9. $33,300 to $31,080
10. 12,200 voters to 13,908 voters
11. 50 minutes to 45 minutes
12. 350 meters to 420 meters

Example	Exercises
1	7–12
2	7–12
3	13–19

Online Resources
CLASSZONE.COM
· More Examples
· eTutorial Plus

Find the new amount.

13. 1100 is increased by 4%.
14. 24,700 is decreased by 13%.
15. 8 is increased by 60%.
16. 65 is decreased by 30%.
17. 88,450 is decreased by 12.5%.
18. 26,856 is increased by 14.6%.
19. **Hazelnuts** Oregon produces 98% of the hazelnuts grown in the United States. One year, Oregon produced 46,650 tons of hazelnuts. The crop decreased by 67% the following year. How many tons of hazelnuts were produced in Oregon the second year?

Find the percent of increase or decrease.

20. x to $4x$ **21.** $6b$ to $9b$ **22.** y to $\frac{3}{8}y$ **23.** $4.5a$ to $2.25a$

In Exercises 24–27, tell whether the statement is *true* or *false*. Explain your reasoning.

24. An increase from 1 to 3 is a 200% increase.

25. Multiplying a number by 5 is a 500% increase.

26. Multiplying a number by $\frac{1}{4}$ is a 25% decrease.

27. Dividing a number by 5 is an 80% decrease.

28. **Coins** In 1996, a 1943 copper penny was sold for $82,500. What was the percent of increase in the penny's value in 1943 to the value it was sold for in 1996?

29. **Population** The population of the United States in 1992 was about 255,374,000. In 2002, it was about 280,562,000. Find the approximate percent of increase to the nearest tenth.

30. **Challenge** A number increases by 50%, then decreases by 50%. What is the percent of change from the original number to the final number?

31. **Enlargements** You have a photograph that is 6 inches by 4 inches. You want to enlarge it so that these dimensions are increased by 50%. What will the new dimensions be? What will be the percent of increase in the area of the new photograph?

Mixed Review

Find the product or quotient. *(Lesson 5.7)*

32. $4.412 \cdot 0.36$ **33.** $-6.7 \cdot 0.8$ **34.** $-0.91 \div 0.35$

Solve the equation. *(Lesson 6.3)*

35. $14.2 + 1.4x = -5.4$ **36.** $0.2s - 1.3 = 0.3$ **37.** $1.14y - 2 = y + 1.64$

Basic Skills **Solve the equation.**

38. $7x = 63$ **39.** $1.5c = 18$ **40.** $2.5n = 80$

Test-Taking Practice

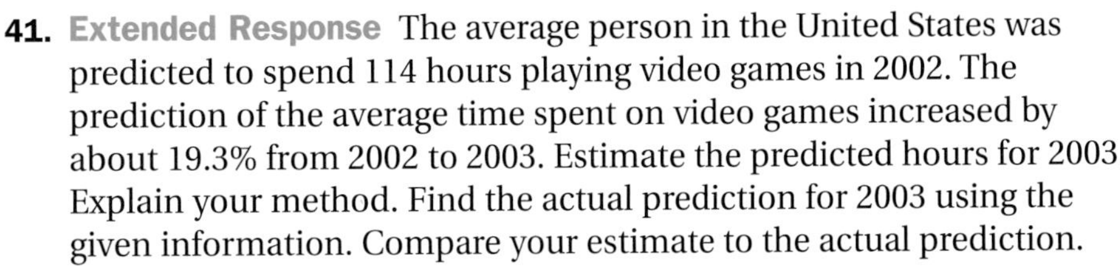

41. **Extended Response** The average person in the United States was predicted to spend 114 hours playing video games in 2002. The prediction of the average time spent on video games increased by about 19.3% from 2002 to 2003. Estimate the predicted hours for 2003. Explain your method. Find the actual prediction for 2003 using the given information. Compare your estimate to the actual prediction.

Percent Applications

BEFORE

You solved problems with percent of increase or decrease.

Now

You'll solve percent application problems.

WHY?

So you can find the sale price of a pair of jeans, as in Ex. 18.

In the Real World

Guitars You are shopping for a guitar and find one with an original price of \$160. The store is offering a 30% *discount* on all guitars. What is the sale price of the guitar?

markup, p. 342
discount, p. 342

INDIANA
Academic Standards
- Computation (8.2.1)
- Problem Solving (8.7.1)

Markup and Discount A retail store buys items from manufacturers at *wholesale prices*. The store then sells the items to customers at *retail prices*. The increase in the wholesale price of an item is a **markup**. A decrease in the price of an item is a **discount**. You can find the retail price or sale price of an item using the equations below.

Retail price = Wholesale price + Markup

Sale price = Original price − Discount

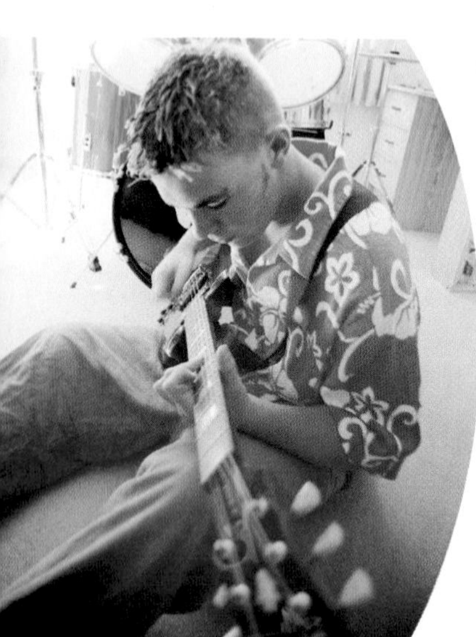

EXAMPLE 1 Finding a Sale Price

To find the sale price of the guitar above, use the sale price equation.

Solution

(1) Find the amount of the discount.

Discount = 30% of \$160

= 0.3(160) **Write 30% as a decimal.**

= 48 **Multiply.**

(2) Subtract the discount from the original price.

160 − 48 = 112

ANSWER The sale price of the guitar is \$112.

Your turn now **Find the sale price.**

1. Original price: \$25
   Percent discount: 10%

2. Original price: \$85.50
   Percent discount: 30%

EXAMPLE 2 Finding a Retail Price

Clothing A shirt has a wholesale price of \$16. The percent markup is 120%. What is the retail price?

HELP with Solving

Remember that the markup must be added to the wholesale price to find the retail price.

Solution

(1) Find the amount of the markup.

$$\text{Markup} = 120\% \text{ of } \$16$$

$= 1.2(16)$ **Write 120% as a decimal.**

$= 19.2$ **Multiply.**

(2) Add the markup to the wholesale price.

$$16 + 19.2 = 35.2$$

ANSWER The retail price of the shirt is \$35.20.

Sales Tax and Tips Sales tax and tips are amounts that are added to the price of some purchases. Sales tax and tips are usually calculated using a percent of the purchase price.

EXAMPLE 3 Finding Sales Tax

Compact Disc Player A portable CD player costs \$48 before tax. The sales tax is 4.5%. What is the total cost?

Solution

(1) Find the amount of the sales tax.

$$4.5\% \text{ of } \$48 = 0.045(48)$$

$$= 2.16$$

(2) Add the sales tax to the price of the portable CD player.

$$48 + 2.16 = 50.16$$

ANSWER The total cost of the CD player is \$50.16.

Your turn now **Find the retail price.**

3. Wholesale price: \$64
Percent markup: 85%

4. Wholesale price: \$35
Percent markup: 110%

Find the total cost.

5. Price: \$8.90
Sales tax: 5%

6. Price: \$54.07
Sales tax: 7%

EXAMPLE 4 Finding Sales Tax and Tip

Restaurants Your food bill at a restaurant is \$24. You leave a 20% tip. The sales tax is 6%. What is the total cost of the meal?

Solution

(1) Find the amount of the tip.

$$20\% \text{ of } \$24 = 0.20(24)$$
$$= 4.8$$

(2) Find the amount of the sales tax.

$$6\% \text{ of } \$24 = 0.06(24)$$
$$= 1.44$$

(3) Add the food bill, tip, and sales tax.

$$24 + 4.8 + 1.44 = 30.24$$

ANSWER The total cost of the meal is \$30.24.

Your turn now **Find the total cost.**

7. Your food bill at a restaurant is \$35. The sales tax is 5%. You leave a 15% tip. What is the total cost of the meal?

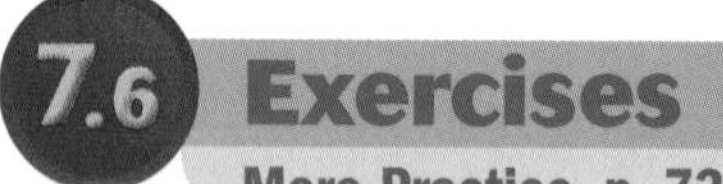

Exercises

More Practice, p. 733

Getting Ready to Practice

1. **Vocabulary** Copy and complete: To find the retail price, add the _?_ to the wholesale price.

Find the sale price or retail price.

2. Original price: \$60
   Percent discount: 15%
3. Original price: \$28.50
   Percent discount: 60%
4. Wholesale price: \$25
   Percent markup: 65%
5. Wholesale price: \$14.50
   Percent markup: 140%

6. **Lamps** A lamp costs \$25.75. The sales tax is 4%. What is the total cost?
7. **Restaurants** Your food bill at a restaurant is \$30. You leave a 20% tip. The sales tax is 6%. What is the total cost of the meal?

Practice and Problem Solving

Example	Exercises
1	8-13, 20-25
2	8-13, 20-25
3	14-17
4	14-17

Online Resources
CLASSZONE.COM
· More Examples
· eTutorial Plus

Find the sale price or retail price. Round to the nearest cent.

8. Original price: \$42
Percent discount: 30%

9. Wholesale price: \$19
Percent markup: 110%

10. Wholesale price: \$16.49
Percent markup: 130%

11. Original price: \$22.40
Percent discount: 25%

12. Original price: \$54.75
Percent discount: 20%

13. Wholesale price: \$65.40
Percent markup: 55%

Find the total cost. Round to the nearest cent.

14. Original price: \$72
Sales tax: 6%

15. Original price: \$58.40
Sales tax: 5.5%

16. Food bill: \$25.80
Tip: 18%
Sales tax: 4.5%

17. Food bill: \$18
Tip: 20%
Sales tax: 5%

18. **Jeans** The wholesale price of a pair of jeans is \$15. A store marks up the price by 75%. When the jeans don't sell, the store offers a 20% discount. What is the sale price of the jeans?

19. **Critical Thinking** A store is having an end of season sale and offers a discount of 40% on all coats. One week later the store discounts the coats an additional 60%. Is the store giving away the coats for free? Explain your reasoning.

Tell whether the new price is a *discount* or *markup*. Then find the percent of discount or markup.

20. Old price: \$32
New price: \$24

21. Old price: \$45
New price: \$40.50

22. Old price: \$19
New price: \$33.25

23. Old price: \$55
New price: \$121

24. Old price: \$12.50
New price: \$22.50

25. Old price: \$199.99
New price: \$119.99

26. **Writing** People often leave tips between 15% and 20% on restaurant bills. Find both the 15% and 20% tips of a food bill that totals \$24.20. Explain why people often leave a tip between 15% and 20% rather than leaving exactly 15% or 20%.

27. **Tipping** You order a pizza to be delivered. The bill comes to \$12.60. You give the delivery person \$15 and tell them to keep the change. What percent tip did you give? Round to the nearest percent.

28. **DVDs** A DVD has a regular price of \$26 and is on sale for \$16.90. What is the percent discount?

29. **Subscription** A magazine subscription has a regular price of \$24.50. You pay \$14.70 for your subscription. What is the percent discount?

30. **Estimation** The original price of an item is \$42 and the percent of discount is 25%. Explain how to estimate the sale price.

31. **Challenge** A total restaurant bill including sales tax and tip is \$33. The tax is 4% and the tip is 16% of the bill before tax. What was the food bill before tax and tip?

32. **Shopping** A basketball has a wholesale price of \$12 and is marked up 115%. Later it is discounted 15%. The sales tax is 4.5%. Find the final cost of the basketball including tax. Round to the nearest cent.

Mixed Review 

Solve the equation. *(Lesson 6.2)*

33. $4a = a + 9$

34. $n - 2 = 2n - 9$

Use a percent proportion. *(Lesson 7.3)*

35. What number is 35% of 80?

36. 308 is what percent of 440?

Basic Skills **Solve the equation.**

37. $2.4b = 108$

38. $8.5y = 51$

39. $3.5x = 140$

40. $1.6d = 38.4$

Test-Taking Practice 

41. **Multiple Choice** A book costs \$7.95 and is on sale for 15% off. The sales tax is 6%. What is the total cost of the book?

A. \$5.64 B. \$7.16 C. \$7.74 D. \$8.27

42. **Multiple Choice** You and two friends eat at a restaurant and split the total bill evenly. The food bill is \$20.88. Sales tax is 5%. You leave a 20% tip. How much should each person pay?

F. \$6.96 G. \$7.31 H. \$8.35 I. \$8.70

BRAIN GAME

Shrink Ray

Ray invents two zappers that shrink and enlarge things. After shrinking almost everything in the house to 40% of its original size, Ray's mother demands that he return things to normal. What percent setting should he use to zap objects back to their original size?

If Ray had instead used the zapper to enlarge things by 60%, what percent setting would he use on the shrink zapper to get them back to their normal size?

Using the Percent Equation

BEFORE	Now	WHY?
You solved percent problems using proportions.	You'll solve percent problems using the percent equation.	So you can find the interest paid on a bank loan, as in Ex. 25.

Word Watch

interest, p. 348
principal, p. 348
annual interest rate, p. 348

INDIANA
Academic Standards

- Computation (8.2.2)
- Algebra and Functions (8.3.1)

In the Real World

Beaches In a survey of 2000 people, 26.7% said that they had visited a beach during the past year. Find the number of people who said they had visited a beach.

In Lesson 7.3, you solved percent problems with proportions. You can also use the decimal method from Lesson 7.5 to solve percent problems.

The Percent Equation

To represent the statement "*a* is *p* percent of *b*" use the equation:

$a = p\% \cdot b$ *p* part of the base = *p* percent • Base

EXAMPLE 1 Finding Part of a Base

To find the number of people who said they had visited a beach in the past year, use the percent equation.

$a = p\% \cdot b$	Write percent equation.
$= 26.7\% \cdot 2000$	Substitute 26.7 for *p* and 2000 for *b*.
$= 0.267 \cdot 2000$	Write percent as a decimal.
$= 534$	Multiply.

ANSWER The number of people who said they had visited a beach during the past year is 534.

Your turn now **Use the percent equation.**

1. Find 45% of 700.
2. Find 24.5% of 800.

EXAMPLE 2 Finding a Base

Student Council Marc received 273, or 35%, of the votes in the student council election. How many students voted in the election?

Solution

$a = p\% \cdot b$	Write percent equation.
$273 = 35\% \cdot b$	Substitute 273 for *a* and 35 for *p*.
$273 = 0.35 \cdot b$	Write 35% as a decimal.
$780 = b$	Divide each side by 0.35.

ANSWER In the election, 780 students voted.

Your turn now **Solve using the percent equation.**

3. 6.4 is 62.5% of what number?

4. 15 is what percent of 120?

When you borrow money from a bank, you pay back interest as well as the amount you borrowed.

Simple Interest **Interest** is an amount paid for the use of money. **Principal** is the amount you borrow or deposit. When interest is paid only on the principal, it is called simple interest. The percent of the principal you pay or earn per year is the **annual interest rate**.

Simple Interest

Words To find simple interest *I*, find the product of the principal *P*, the annual interest rate *r* written as a decimal, and the time *t* in years.

Algebra $I = Prt$

EXAMPLE 3 Finding Simple Interest

You deposit $500 in a savings account that pays a simple interest rate of 2.5% per year. How much interest will you earn after 18 months?

Solution

$I = Prt$	Write formula for simple interest.
$= (500)(0.025)(1.5)$	Substitute values. 18 months = 1.5 years
$= 18.75$	Multiply.

ANSWER You will earn $18.75 in interest.

Getting Ready to Practice

1. **Vocabulary** Copy and complete: To find simple interest, multiply the annual rate written as a decimal, the time in years, and the _?_.

Solve using the percent equation.

2. What number is 46% of 900?
3. 205 is what percent of 250?
4. 132 is 24% of what number?
5. What number is 95% of 420?
6. **Guided Problem Solving** A savings account pays a 3% annual interest rate. How much must you put in the savings account to earn $100 in interest in 6 months?
   (1 Write the simple interest formula.
   (2 Substitute known values in the formula.
   (3 Solve the equation for P. Round to the nearest cent.

Practice and Problem Solving

HELP with Homework

Example	Exercises
1	7-16
2	7-16
3	17-18

· More Examples
· eTutorial Plus

Solve using the percent equation.

7. What number is 65% of 320?
8. What number is 6% of 450?
9. What number is 120% of 55?
10. What number is 0.4% of 150?
11. 115 is 46% of what number?
12. 26 is 130% of what number?
13. 62.4 is 80% of what number?
14. 289.25 is 89% of what number?
15. 3 is what percent of 600?
16. 291.04 is what percent of 856?

Find the amount of simple interest earned.

17. Principal: $250
    Annual rate: 2%
    Time: 3 years
18. Principal : $940
    Annual rate: 3.5%
    Time: 30 months
19. **Weather** In Charlotte, North Carolina, an average of 112 days of the year have precipitation of 0.01 inch or more. What percent of days in Charlotte have precipitation of 0.01 inch or more? Round your answer to the nearest percent.
20. **Writing** Are the solutions of $\frac{12}{b} = \frac{3}{100}$ and $12 = 3\% \cdot b$ the same or different? Explain your reasoning.

Copy and complete the statement with <, >, or =.

21. 60% of 75 _?_ 75% of 60

22. 30% of 120 _?_ 120% of 30

23. **Look for a Pattern** Copy and complete the table by finding the percent of each number. Describe the relationship you see among the three percents in each row.

	5%	10%	15%
22	?	2.2	?
50	?	?	?
76	?	?	?

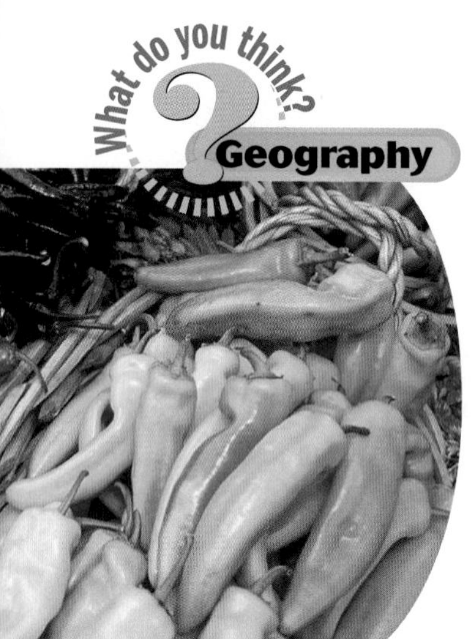

Texas

There are about 10,500 acres of cropland in Texas planted with peppers. What percent of cropland in Texas is planted with peppers? Round to the nearest hundredth of a percent.

24. **Savings** How much money must you deposit in a savings account that pays a 4% simple annual interest rate to earn \$50 in 2 years?

25. **Loan** You borrow \$1200 from the bank. The bank charges an annual simple interest rate of 9.5%. It takes you 15 months to pay back the loan. How much interest do you pay on the loan? What is the total amount that you pay the bank?

26. **Texas** The area of the state of Texas is 171.1 million acres. Of this, 26.9 million acres are cropland. What percent of Texas is cropland? Round your answer to the nearest hundredth of a percent.

27. **Challenge** *Compound interest* on a savings account is earned on both the principal and on any interest that has already been earned. You deposit \$500 into an account that earns 4% compounded annually. How much will you have in your account after the third year? after the sixth year? Round your answers to the nearest cent.

Mixed Review 

Find the quotient. *(Lesson 5.4)*

28. $\frac{8}{3} \div \frac{32}{21}$

29. $\frac{5}{9} \div \frac{2}{3}$

30. $\frac{11}{14} \div \frac{1}{2}$

In Exercises 31–33, solve the equation or inequality. *(Lessons 6.3, 6.5)*

31. $5.4 - 4.6x = 19.2$

32. $\frac{3}{8}u - \frac{1}{2} = \frac{7}{12}$

33. $3n - 27 \le -5n + 64$

34. Solve the proportion $\frac{8}{25} = \frac{7}{d}$. *(Lesson 7.2)*

Test-Taking Practice 

35. **Multiple Choice** What percent of 75 is 30?

A. 30% **B.** 40% **C.** 45% **D.** 75%

36. **Short Response** Vicki hears on the local news that 37.5% of the movie theaters in her city, or 6 theaters, offer discount tickets to students. Write an equation that could be used to determine the number of theaters in Vicki's city. Then solve the equation.

Technology Activity

INDIANA: Academic Standards
• Computation (8.2.2)

Compound Interest

GOAL Use a calculator to compute compound interest.

Compound interest is interest earned on both the principal and on any interest that has already been earned.

Example **Mark deposits $2000 into an account that pays an interest rate of 3.5% compounded annually. He doesn't add or remove money from his account for 4 years. How much money will Mark have in 4 years?**

Solution

The balance of an account after a year can be found by multiplying the principal balance by the quantity one plus the annual interest rate. Use the keystrokes below to find the amount of money in the account in 4 years.

Keystrokes	Display	
2000 [=] [×] 1.035 [=]	2070	In 1 year
[=]	2142.45	In 2 years
[=]	2217.43575	In 3 years
[=]	2295.046001	In 4 years

ANSWER Mark will have $2295.05 in his account in 4 years.

Your turn now **Find the balance of the account earning compound interest.**

1. Principal: $7000
Annual rate: 2%
Time: 4 years

2. Principal: $7000
Annual rate: 4%
Time: 2 years

3. Principal: $1995
Annual rate: 6.5%
Time: 10 years

4. You deposit $1500 into an account that pays an interest rate of 4% compounded annually. Your friend deposits $1500 into an account that pays a simple annual interest rate of 4%. Compare the balances of the two accounts after 5 years.

7.8 Problem Solving Strategies

INDIANA: Academic Standards
• Problem Solving (8.7.1)

Perform an Experiment

- Guess, Check, and Revise
- Look for a Pattern
- Draw a Diagram
- Act It Out
- Perform an Experiment
- Work Backward
- Make a Table

Problem You are playing a board game that involves rolling 2 cubes numbered from 1 to 6. If your cubes sum to an even number, you may advance your game piece forward. If your cubes sum to an odd number, you may not move your piece. Predict the number of times you will be able to move forward in 100 rolls.

1 Read and Understand

Read the problem carefully.

The problem asks you to predict the number of times you will roll two number cubes that sum to an even number in 100 rolls.

2 Make a Plan

Decide on a strategy to use.

Because it might take a while to roll number cubes 100 times, you can make a prediction by performing an experiment. Roll two number cubes 20 times and use the results to make a prediction.

3 Solve the Problem

Reread the problem and perform an experiment.

First, roll two number cubes 20 times and record the results as shown.

Results

5, 12, 7, 9, 4, 8, 7, 6, 6, 3, 8, 4, 7, 5, 6, 9, 2, 4, 10, 11

There are 11 even numbers and 9 odd numbers.

Then, use the results of the experiment to set up and solve a proportion.

$$\frac{\text{Number of even numbers in 20 rolls}}{\text{20 rolls}} = \frac{\text{Number of even numbers in 100 rolls}}{\text{100 rolls}}$$

$$\frac{11}{20} = \frac{x}{100}$$

$$\frac{11}{20} \cdot 100 = \frac{x}{100} \cdot 100$$

$$55 = x$$

You predict that you will get 55 even numbers in 100 rolls.

4 Look Back

To test the accuracy of your prediction, perform another experiment and compare the results.

Practice the Strategy

Use the strategy *perform an experiment.*

1. **Marbles** You conduct an experiment by randomly drawing 10 marbles from a bag of 100 red and blue marbles, and recording how many of each color were drawn. The results of 5 of these experiments are shown below. Estimate how many marbles of each color are in the bag. Explain.

	1	2	3	4	5
Red	6	7	5	7	6
Blue	4	3	5	3	4

2. **Spinner** You are playing a board game that uses a spinner like the one below to determine how many spaces to move. The spinner seems to give the result "5" more often than it should. Describe an experiment you could use to test this assumption. What results would support the assumption?

3. **Names** Write each of the letters of your name on a slip of paper. Place all the slips into a bag and then randomly draw one slip. Record what letter it is, replace it, and repeat the process. Design an experiment to help you predict the number of times you would draw a consonant in 60 draws. Describe your experiment.

4. **Socks** A drawer has exactly 20 white socks and 20 black socks. You randomly draw two socks 100 times and replace them after each draw. Describe an experiment you could use to predict how many times out of 100 you would draw matching socks.

Mixed Problem Solving

Use any strategy to solve the problem.

5. **Shopping** You pick out a sweater and a pair of pants. When you get to the cashier, you find that all sweaters are on sale for 40% off the original price and your bill is $40.40. So, you decide to add two more sweaters to your purchase, bringing the bill to $81.20. How much does one pair of pants cost? What is the original price of one sweater?

6. **Groups** A class is divided into groups of four. Betty, Jamal, Fiona, and Juan are in one group. Each person's name is written on a separate slip of paper. The teacher draws a name each week (and then replaces it for the next week) to find the leader of the group for that week. How often do you predict Fiona's name will be picked in 36 weeks?

7. **Triangles** How many triangles are shown in the figure? Be sure to count triangles of different sizes.

Simple Probability

BEFORE	Now	WHY?
You found ratios.	You'll find probabilities of events.	So you can find the probability of a batter getting a hit, as in Ex. 24.

outcome, event, p. 354
favorable outcome, p. 354
probability of an event, p. 354
theoretical probability, p. 354
experimental probability, p. 355

INDIANA Academic Standards

- Data Analysis and Probability (8.6.6)

Activity You can toss a coin to perform a probability experiment.

1. Copy and complete the table at the right by tossing a coin 20 times.

Number of heads	?
Number of tails	?

2. Use the data to write each ratio below. Then compare the ratios.

a. $\frac{\text{Number of heads}}{\text{Total number of coin tosses}}$ b. $\frac{\text{Number of tails}}{\text{Total number of coin tosses}}$

3. **Comparing Results** Combine your results with those of the other students in your class. Compare the class ratios with your own ratios.

In the activity, you performed an experiment. The possible results of an experiment are **outcomes**. An **event** is a collection of outcomes. Once you specify an event, the outcomes for that event are called **favorable outcomes**. The **probability of an event** is the likelihood that the event will occur.

Probability of an Event

The **theoretical probability** of an event when all outcomes are equally likely is:

$$P(\text{event}) = \frac{\text{Number of favorable outcomes}}{\text{Number of possible outcomes}}$$

EXAMPLE 1 Using Theoretical Probability

Use theoretical probability to predict the number of times a coin will land heads up in 50 coin tosses. There are two equally likely outcomes when you toss the coin, heads or tails.

$$P(\text{heads}) = \frac{\text{Number of favorable outcomes}}{\text{Number of possible outcomes}} = \frac{1}{2}$$

ANSWER You can predict that $\frac{1}{2}$, or 25, of the tosses will land heads up.

An **experimental probability** is based on the results of a sample or experiment. Experimental probability is the ratio of number of favorable outcomes to total number of times the experiment was performed.

A probability can be expressed as a fraction, as a decimal, or as a percent.

EXAMPLE 2 Finding Experimental Probability

You roll a number cube 100 times. Your results are shown. Find the experimental probability of rolling a 6.

Number	Rolls	Number	Rolls
1	17	4	16
2	15	5	14
3	20	6	18

Solution

$$P(\text{rolling a 6}) = \frac{18}{100}$$ ← Number of favorable outcomes / ← Total number of rolls

$$= 0.18 = 18\%$$

ANSWER The experimental probability of rolling a 6 is 18%.

EXAMPLE 3 Using Experimental Probability

You randomly draw a button from a bag of red, blue, green, and yellow buttons 18 times. Each time you record its color and place it back in the bag. There are 80 buttons in the bag. Predict how many are red.

Color	Tally
Red	𝍸 𝍸
Blue	|||
Green	|||
Yellow	||

Solution

1. Find the experimental probability of drawing a red button.

$$P(\text{red}) = \frac{10}{18}$$ ← Number of favorable outcomes / ← Total number of draws

$$= \frac{5}{9}$$ Simplify.

2. Multiply the probability by the total number of buttons and round to the nearest whole number.

$$\frac{5}{9} \times 80 \approx 44$$

ANSWER You can predict that there are 44 red buttons in the bag.

Your turn now **Use the information in Example 3.**

1. There are 18 green buttons in the bag. What is the theoretical probability of drawing a green button at random? What is the experimental probability?

7.8 Exercises

More Practice, p. 733

Getting Ready to Practice

1. **Vocabulary** Copy and complete: The favorable outcomes for rolling an even number on a number cube are _?_, _?_, and _?_.

2. **Socks** You have 4 white socks, 2 black socks, and 2 brown socks. What is the probability that you will choose a black sock at random from these socks?

3. **Find the Error** A student spins a two-color spinner 20 times. The pointer lands on red 7 times and on blue 13 times. Describe and correct the error in the solution.

   Experimental probability of spinning red $= \frac{7}{13}$ ✗

Practice and Problem Solving

Example	Exercises
1	4–9, 20–22
2	10–14
3	15–18

· More Examples
· eTutorial Plus

You randomly draw a tile from a bag that contains 10 A-tiles, 7 E-tiles, 6 I-tiles, 5 O-tiles, and 2 U-tiles. Find the probability of the event.

4. You draw an A.
5. You draw an I.
6. You draw an I or an O.
7. You draw an E or a U.
8. You draw a Z.
9. You draw a vowel.

You roll a number cube 250 times. Your results are shown in the table. Find the experimental probability of the event.

10. You roll a 4.
11. You roll a 2.
12. You roll a number greater than 3.
13. You roll an odd number.
14. You roll a number divisible by 1.

Number	Outcomes	Number	Outcomes
1	40	4	50
2	42	5	35
3	48	6	35

You randomly draw a marble from a bag of 120 marbles. You record its color and replace it. Use the results to estimate the number of marbles in the bag that are the given color.

15. Yellow
16. Green
17. Red
18. Blue

Red	Yellow	Green
7	3	5

19. **Toes** In a survey of 896 people, 409 responded that their second toes are longer than their big toes. What is the probability that a randomly chosen person from the survey has a longer second toe?

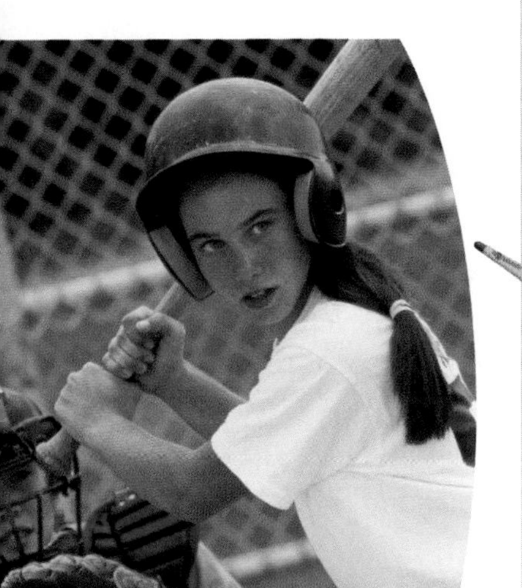

Find the probability of the event.

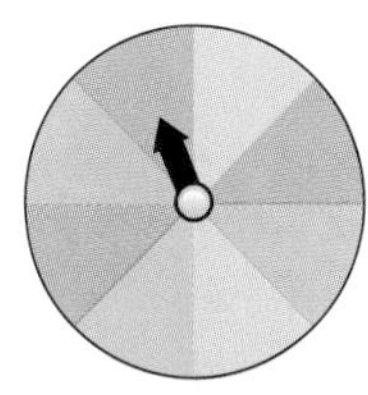

20. *Not* rolling a 2 on a number cube
21. *Not* spinning blue on the spinner
22. *Not* spinning blue, red, or yellow on the spinner
23. **Writing** Describe the difference between experimental and theoretical probability.
24. **Softball** Sharon and Erica are both softball players. Out of 20 times at bat, Sharon got 7 hits. Out of 35 times at bat, Erica got 10 hits. Who do you think is more likely to get a hit her next time at bat? Explain.
25. **Number Cube** Rachel rolled a number cube 24 times and got a 6 once. She thinks that her chances of getting a 6 on her next roll are high. Explain why her chances are no different than on any other roll.
26. **Challenge** You have 15 coins in your pocket: 4 quarters, 3 pennies, 5 dimes, and 3 nickels. Why wouldn't theoretical probability be a good way to predict which coin you pull out of your pocket?

Mixed Review

27. Find the percent of increase from 140 to 154. *(Lesson 7.5)*
28. You deposit $750 in an account with a simple annual interest rate of 2.75%. Find the interest you will earn after 30 months. Round to the nearest cent. *(Lesson 7.7)*

Basic Skills **Find the sum.**

29. $-47 + 19$
30. $20 + (-18)$
31. $-7 + (-25)$
32. $-32 + (-56)$

Test-Taking Practice

INTERNET
State Test Practice
CLASSZONE.COM

33. **Multiple Choice** What is the probability of getting a number divisible by 3 when rolling a number cube?

A. $\frac{3}{10}$ B. $\frac{1}{3}$ C. $\frac{1}{2}$ D. $\frac{2}{3}$

34. **Multiple Choice** In a group of 40 people, 24 prefer dogs to cats. One person is selected at random from the larger group. What is the probability that the person will prefer dogs to cats?

F. 0.16 G. 0.24 H. 0.4 I. 0.6

Notebook Review

Review the vocabulary definitions in your notebook.

Copy the review examples in your notebook. Then complete the exercises.

Check Your Definitions

percent of change, p. 338
percent of increase, p. 338
percent of decrease, p. 338
markup, discount, p. 342
interest, annual interest rate, p. 348
principal, p. 348
outcome, favorable outcome, p. 354
event, probability of an event, p. 354
theoretical probability, p. 354
experimental probability, p. 355

Use Your Vocabulary

1. Describe how to find theoretical probability.

7.5–7.6 Can you find a sale price?

EXAMPLE A pair of shoes has an original price of \$40. What is the sale price after a 15% discount?

$40 \times 0.15 = 6$ **Multiply to find discount.**

$40 - 6 = 34$ **Subtract discount from original price.**

ANSWER The sale price of the shoes is \$34.

✓ **Find the sale price or retail price.**

2. Wholesale price: \$30
Percent markup: 70%

3. Original price: \$72
Percent discount: 18%

7.7 Can you use the percent equation?

EXAMPLE What number is 26% of 300?

$a = p\% \cdot b$ **Write percent equation.**

$a = 26\% \cdot 300$ **Substitute 26 for *p* and 300 for *b*.**

$a = 78$ **Multiply.**

4. 72 is 75% of what number? **5.** What number is 34% of 856?

7.8 Can you find the probability of an event?

EXAMPLE Two scientists spin a Belgian euro coin 250 times and it lands heads up 140 times. Find the experimental probability of the coin landing heads up.

Use the results to find the experimental probability.

$$P(\text{heads}) = \frac{140}{250} \begin{array}{l} \longleftarrow \text{Number of favorable outcomes} \\ \longleftarrow \text{Total number of spins} \end{array}$$

$$= \frac{14}{25} = 0.56 = 56\%$$

6. You randomly draw a marble out of a bag that contains 8 red, 5 yellow, and 4 blue marbles. Find the probability of drawing each color.

Stop *and* Think about Lessons 7.5–7.8

7. **Critical Thinking** You invest $300 at a simple annual interest rate of 3.5% for one year. How much would you need to invest at a 2% simple annual interest rate to earn the same amount of interest that year?

Review Quiz 2

Tell whether the change is an *increase* or *decrease*. Then find the percent of change.

1. Original amount: $120
New amount: $138

2. Original amount: 260 miles
New amount: 169 miles

3. **Retail** A shirt has a $20 wholesale price and is marked up 50%. The sales tax is 5%. What is the total cost of the shirt?

Solve using the percent equation.

4. 75 is 125% of what number?

5. 552.5 is what percent of 85,000?

6. **Koalas** Koalas absorb only about 25% of the fiber they eat. How much fiber is absorbed by a koala that eats 10.5 ounces of fiber per day?

You spin the spinner below 40 times. Predict how many times the spinner lands on the specified color.

7. Red

8. Blue

9. Yellow

CHAPTER 7

Chapter Review

Vocabulary

ratio, equivalent ratios, p. 317
rate, unit rate, p. 318
proportion, p. 322
cross products, p. 323
scale model, scale, p. 324
percent, p. 327
circle graph, p. 331
percent of change, p. 338
percent of increase, p. 338
percent of decrease, p. 338
markup, discount, p. 342
interest, p. 348
principal, p. 348
annual interest rate, p. 348
outcome, p. 354
event, p. 354
favorable outcome, p. 354
probability of an event, p. 354
theoretical probability, p. 354
experimental probability, p. 355

Vocabulary Review

Copy and complete the statement.

1. If you write $\frac{180 \text{ miles}}{3 \text{ hours}}$ as $\frac{60 \text{ miles}}{1 \text{ hour}}$, you have written the rate as a(n) _?_.

2. A(n) _?_ is a ratio whose denominator is 100.

3. The theoretical probability of an event is the ratio of the number of _?_ to the number of _?_.

Match the word with the correct definition.

4. annual interest rate

5. interest

6. principal

A. the amount of money that you borrow or deposit

B. the amount paid for the use of money

C. the percent of the principal that you pay or earn each year

Review Questions

Write the equivalent rate. *(Lesson 7.1)*

7. $\frac{286.8 \text{ m}}{\text{min}} = \frac{? \text{ m}}{\text{sec}}$

8. $\frac{4.2 \text{ in.}}{\text{month}} = \frac{? \text{ in.}}{\text{year}}$

9. $\frac{6 \text{ times}}{\text{min}} = \frac{? \text{ times}}{\text{hour}}$

Solve the proportion. *(Lesson 7.2)*

10. $\frac{5}{13} = \frac{18}{c}$

11. $\frac{48}{36} = \frac{x}{6}$

12. $\frac{n}{12} = \frac{7}{8}$

13. $\frac{25}{b} = \frac{55}{22}$

Review Questions

Use a percent proportion. *(Lesson 7.3)*

14. What number is 500% of 16?

15. 200.2 is 65% of what number?

16. 44 is what percent of 80?

17. 1.7 is what percent of 340?

Write the decimal or fraction as a percent. *(Lesson 7.4)*

18. 0.43

19. 0.003

20. $\frac{3}{10}$

21. $\frac{29}{20}$

Final Project **In Exercises 22–24, use the circle graph. It shows the results of a survey of 300 students who were asked what they would choose for a final project.** *(Lesson 7.4)*

22. What percent of students chose an oral report?

23. What fraction of students chose a visual project? Write the fraction in simplest form.

24. Which final project was chosen by 21% of the students?

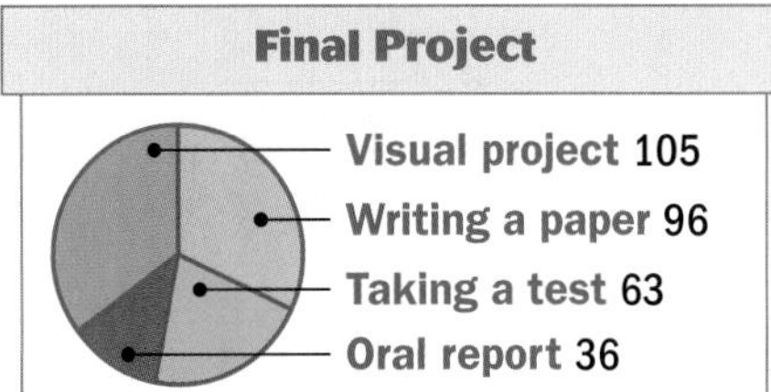

25. Moving A moving van's load changes from 800 to 984 pounds after picking up an appliance. Find the percent of increase. *(Lesson 7.5)*

Find the sale price or retail price. *(Lesson 7.6)*

26. Wholesale price: $22.40
Percent markup: 60%

27. Original price: $21.25
Percent discount: 32%

Find the amount of simple interest earned in 3 years. *(Lesson 7.7)*

28. Principal: $460
Annual rate: 3.5%

29. Principal: $1540
Annual rate: 2.75%

30. Fundraiser At a school fundraiser, the science club made 58% of their money selling juice, 27% selling cookies, and 15% selling apples. The club made $87 selling juice. How much did the club make selling cookies? How much did they make selling apples? *(Lesson 7.7)*

Find the probability of the event. *(Lesson 7.8)*

31. A random 5-digit ZIP code ends with a number less than 5.

32. You roll a number cube and get a 7.

33. A number less than 4 is randomly drawn from the numbers 1, 2, 3, and 4.

Chapter Test

Write the ratio of shaded to unshaded squares.

1. 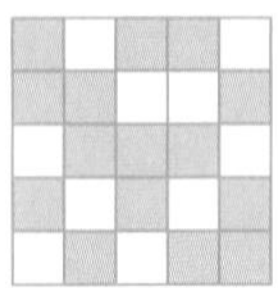
2. 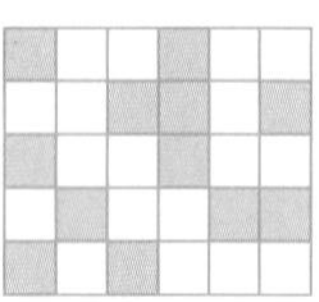
3. 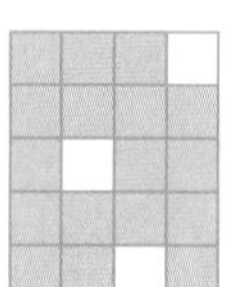
4. 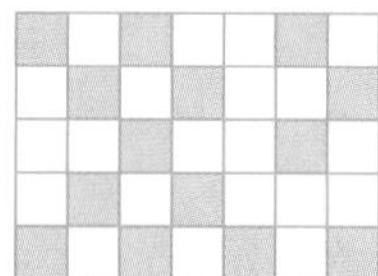

Write the rate as a unit rate.

5. $\frac{156\text{ miles}}{3\text{ hours}}$
6. $\frac{18\text{ servings}}{6\text{ people}}$
7. $\frac{448\text{ cycles}}{5\text{ days}}$
8. $\frac{54\text{ meters}}{21\text{ seconds}}$

Find the value of the variable

9. $\frac{12}{16} = \frac{18}{a}$
10. $\frac{15}{6} = \frac{d}{4}$
11. $\frac{9}{n} = \frac{21}{14}$
12. $\frac{t-3}{12} = \frac{11}{6}$

13. **Maps** The road distance from Miami, Florida, to Columbia, South Carolina, on a map is about 6.7 centimeters. The scale is 1 cm : 150 km. What is the actual distance from Miami to Columbia?

14. **Survey** In a survey, 34%, or 102 people, said they enjoy in-line skating. How many people were surveyed?

Write the percent as a decimal and as a fraction.

15. 0.7%
16. 419%
17. 8%
18. 7.8%

Find the percent of increase or decrease.

19. Original amount: 40
    New amount: 36
20. Original amount: 225
    New amount: 324
21. Original amount: 258
    New amount: 6.45

22. **Food** Your food bill at a restaurant totals $26. There is a 6.5% sales tax and you leave a 16% tip. What is the total cost of the meal?

23. **Recycling** The average person in the United States generates about 4.5 pounds of waste per day. About 30% of this waste is recycled. About how many pounds of waste are recycled per person per day?

A box contains 9 tiles that together spell the word "TENNESSEE." You draw at random one tile from the box. Find the probability of the event.

24. Drawing an E
25. Drawing an S

Chapter Standardized Test

Test-Taking Strategy **Avoid spending too much time on one question. Skip questions you have trouble with, and return to them after you have finished.**

Multiple Choice

1. Which ratio is *not* equivalent to $\frac{3}{7}$?

A. $\frac{9}{21}$ **B.** $\frac{1.5}{3.5}$ **C.** $\frac{300}{700}$ **D.** $\frac{18}{39}$

2. Susan types at a speed of 54 words per minute. What is her typing speed in words per second?

F. 5400 words per second

G. 3240 words per second

H. $1.\overline{1}$ words per second

I. 0.9 word per second

3. Which choice shows $\frac{10 \text{ feet}}{4 \text{ seconds}}$ correctly written as a unit rate?

A. $\frac{5 \text{ ft}}{2 \text{ sec}}$ **B.** $\frac{5 \text{ ft}}{\text{sec}}$ **C.** $\frac{2.5 \text{ ft}}{\text{sec}}$ **D.** $\frac{2 \text{ ft}}{5 \text{ sec}}$

4. A scale model of a school building is 11 inches long and 3 inches high. The actual building is 231 feet long. How tall is the actual building?

F. 21 ft **G.** 33 ft

H. 63 ft **I.** 99 ft

5. Which choice is equal to 0.48?

A. 4.8% **B.** $\frac{2}{5}$

C. $\frac{12}{25}$ **D.** 480%

6. A crowd of 280 people grows to a crowd of 315 people. What is the percent of increase?

F. $11.\overline{1}\%$ **G.** 12.5% **H.** 35% **I.** $88.\overline{8}\%$

7. An item with a wholesale price of $8.40 is marked up 60%. What is the retail price?

A. $3.36 **B.** $5.04 **C.** $13.44 **D.** $14.40

8. You and your friend are leaving a tip after eating dinner. The cost of the dinner is $15.35. You want to leave *about* an 18% tip. How much should you leave as a tip?

F. $1.25 **G.** $2.75 **H.** $8.50 **I.** $18.00

9. You randomly draw a marble from a bag of 3 red, 8 yellow, and 13 blue marbles. What is the probability that the marble is yellow?

A. $\frac{13}{24}$ **B.** $\frac{1}{2}$ **C.** $\frac{1}{3}$ **D.** $\frac{1}{8}$

Short Response

10. You deposit $1350 into a savings account that pays a simple annual interest rate of 2.8%. How much interest will you earn in 15 months? Compare this to the interest you would earn for the same amount of time in an account with a simple annual interest rate of 4%.

Extended Response

11. You draw a marble at random from a bag of red, blue, green, and yellow marbles 24 times. Each time you record its color and place it back in the bag of 75 marbles. The results are shown in the table below. How many of each color marble do you predict are in the bag? Explain.

Red	Blue	Green	Yellow
7	3	5	9

Strategies for Answering
Short Response Questions

Scoring Rubric

Full credit
- answer is correct, *and*
- work and reasoning are included

Partial credit
- answer is correct, but reasoning is incorrect, *or*
- answer is incorrect, but reasoning is correct

No credit
- no answer is given *or*
- answer makes no sense

Problem

You work for your uncle this summer. He pays you $20 on your first day. Each day after that, you will get a raise. You can choose from 2 payment plans. With Plan A, you earn a $5 raise each day. With Plan B, you earn a 20% raise each day. Which plan is a better deal?

Full credit solution

Plan B is a better deal if you work more than 5 days.

Data is used to justify the solution.

Day	1	2	3	4	5	6
Plan A pay	20.00	25.00	30.00	35.00	40.00	45.00
Plan A total	20.00	45.00	75.00	110.00	150.00	195.00
Plan B pay	20.00	24.00	28.80	34.56	41.47	49.76
Plan B total	20.00	44.00	72.80	107.36	148.83	198.59

The question is answered clearly and in complete sentences.

Plan A is better if you work 5 days or less, but Plan B is better if you work more than 5 days. By day 6, the pay with a 20% increase is more than the pay with a $5 raise, so it will continue to be the better plan.

Partial credit solution

I think Plan B is better than Plan A.

The calculations are correct.

Day	1	2	3	4	5	6
Plan A	20.00	25.00	30.00	35.00	40.00	45.00
Plan B	20.00	24.00	28.80	34.56	41.47	49.76

The reasoning is faulty, because the total amount earned was not considered.

The first 4 days, Plan A is better. The next 2 days, Plan B is better. By day 5 Plan B pays you more money, so it is the better plan.

Partial credit solution

The data does not include information past Day 4. So, the answer is incorrect.

Plan A is better. The table shows that over the first four days, Plan A pays out $2.64 more than Plan B.

Day	1	2	3	4
Plan A	20.00	25.00	30.00	35.00
Plan B	20.00	24.00	28.80	34.56
Difference	0	1.00	1.20	0.44

The data is calculated correctly.

No credit solution

The answer is incorrect.

Plan A is better.

Day	1	2	3	4
Plan A	20.00	25.00	30.00	35.00
Plan B	20.00	24.00	26.00	28.00

The data is not calculated correctly.

Your turn now

Score each solution to the short response question below as *full credit*, *partial credit*, or *no credit*. Explain your reasoning.

Watch Out! Be sure to explain your reasoning clearly.

Problem **The Spiff travels 226.8 miles on 14 gallons of gas. The Flyte travels 280 miles on 17.5 gallons of gas. Which car is more fuel efficient?**

1. The Spiff is the more fuel efficient car because it gets 16.2 miles per gallon. The Flyte gets 16 miles per gallon.

2. The Flyte gets 16 miles per gallon, because $280 \div 17.5 = 16$. The Spiff gets 16.2 miles per gallon, because $226.8 \div 14 = 16.2$. The more fuel efficient car gets a greater number of miles per gallon. Because 16.2 is greater than 16, the Spiff is more fuel efficient.

GO ON

PRACTICING Test-Taking Skills

Short Response

1. Joanne is using a map to plan her trip. Measure the distance, in inches, between the two cities on the map. Then use the scale on the map to estimate the actual distance in miles.

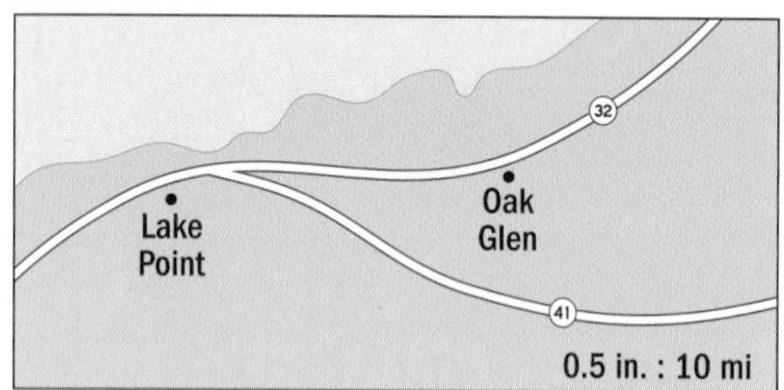

2. John has a pile of quarters. Justin has five more than twice as many quarters as John. Jason has three times as many quarters as John. Justin and Jason have the same number of quarters. How much money does John have? Write your answer in dollars and cents.

3. Amber is shopping for a new watch. The first watch she finds is on sale for 10% off the original price of \$35.95. The second watch she finds is on sale for 20% off the original price of \$38.25. There is an 8% sales tax on both watches. Which watch costs less? Explain your answer.

4. Michelle needs at least \$75 for a school trip. She has \$22 already. Michelle makes \$5 per hour babysitting. How many hours does she need to babysit in order to have enough money for her trip? Write and solve an inequality to answer the question.

5. A bowl contains 5 yellow marbles, 4 green marbles, 3 blue marbles, and 2 red marbles. Kim picks one marble at random. What is the probability that Kim's marble is *not* green? Explain your answer.

6. Vincent's math teacher gives a test every 14 school days, and his English teacher gives a test every 8 school days. Vincent had a math test and an English test today. When will Vincent have an English test and a math test on the same day again? Give the smallest number of school days possible.

7. Ryan, Nelson, and Mia worked together on a project. Ryan completed 35% of the project, and Nelson completed $\frac{2}{5}$ of the project. How much of the project did Mia complete? Give your answer as a fraction and as a percent.

8. A baseball coach counts the number of home runs that each player hits in a season. The table shows the current totals.

Player	Number of Home Runs
Carmine	5
Larry	2
Ray	4
Anthony	6
Michael	0
David	6
Paul	5
Mickey	4
Frank	3

What is the mean number of home runs hit by the team? How many players hit more home runs than this average?

9. Trish parks in front of a parking meter at 2:15 P.M. After 6:00 P.M., she doesn't have to pay to park. The meter only takes quarters, and \$.25 pays for 30 minutes of parking. Trish plans to leave her car in the same place until 8:00 P.M. How much money should she put in the meter? Give your answer in dollars and cents. Explain.

Test-Taking Skills

Multiple Choice

10. A softball team keeps two kinds of bats in the equipment bag. There are 15 metal bats and 9 wooden bats. A player chooses her bat at random. What is the probability that the bat is made of wood?

A. $\frac{3}{8}$ **B.** $\frac{8}{15}$ **C.** $\frac{3}{5}$ **D.** $\frac{5}{8}$

11. The circumference of a circular swimming pool is about 38 feet. What is the best estimate of the pool's diameter?

F. 6 ft **G.** 6.3 ft **H.** 12.1 ft **I.** 12.6 ft

12. A long distance telephone call costs $.25 for the first minute, and each minute after the first costs $.15. How many minutes long is a call that costs $1.75?

A. 9 minutes **B.** 10 minutes

C. 11 minutes **D.** 12 minutes

13. Lucia has 5 quarters for every 7 nickels in her purse. Lucia wants to know how many nickels she has if she has 35 quarters. Which proportion can Lucia use?

F. $\frac{n}{35} = \frac{5}{7}$ **G.** $\frac{35}{n} = \frac{7}{5}$

H. $\frac{5}{n} = \frac{7}{35}$ **I.** $\frac{35}{n} = \frac{5}{7}$

14. What is the prime factorization of 80?

A. $2^4 \cdot 5$ **B.** $2^2 \cdot 4 \cdot 5$

C. $2^3 \cdot 10$ **D.** $2^2 \cdot 20$

15. Three scout troops are each divided into small groups. Every small group has exactly 4 scouts in it, and every scout is in a small group. How many total scouts could be in each of the three troops?

F. 12, 21, 27 **G.** 36, 40, 60

H. 6, 18, 24 **I.** 10, 40, 80

Extended Response

16. Mr. Fay has given his students 20 homework assignments. The table shows the number of homework assignments that each student has completed so far. Find the median number of assignments completed.

Amy	Bill	Dan	Dave	Erin	Jack	Kyle	Matt	Mike	Ron	Tara
17	16	19	20	17	18	17	15	16	19	20

Jillian was left off of Mr. Fay's list by mistake. What is the minimum number of assignments Jillian must complete in order for the median of the group to be 17.5? Explain your answer.

17. Cindy wants to use a 20% discount coupon to buy a coat that originally cost $78. She also wants to use a 10% discount coupon to buy a sweater that originally cost $36. To find the total cost of the items after the discounts, Cindy found the sum of their original prices and subtracted 30% of the total. Explain the mistake that Cindy made. Then show how to find the correct total cost before sales tax.

GO ON

UNIT 2 Chapters 4–7 PRACTICING **Test-Taking Skills**

Cumulative Practice for Chapters 4–7

Chapter 4

Multiple Choice In Exercises 1–7, choose the letter of the correct answer.

1. What is the prime factorization of 54? *(Lesson 4.1)*

   A. $6 \cdot 9$ **B.** $6 \cdot 3^2$ **C.** $2 \cdot 3^3$ **D.** $2^2 \cdot 3^3$

2. What is the greatest common factor of 72 and 90? *(Lesson 4.2)*

   F. 6 **G.** 9 **H.** 12 **I.** 18

3. Which fractions are equivalent? *(Lesson 4.3)*

   A. $\frac{5}{8}, \frac{3}{16}$ **B.** $\frac{15}{30}, \frac{60}{80}$ **C.** $\frac{18}{72}, \frac{7}{28}$ **D.** $\frac{12}{24}, \frac{8}{24}$

4. Which set of fractions is ordered from least to greatest? *(Lesson 4.5)*

   F. $\frac{3}{16}, \frac{1}{4}, \frac{3}{8}, \frac{1}{2}$ **G.** $\frac{3}{8}, \frac{1}{2}, \frac{3}{16}, \frac{1}{4}$

   H. $\frac{3}{8}, \frac{1}{4}, \frac{1}{2}, \frac{3}{16}$ **I.** $\frac{3}{8}, \frac{1}{2}, \frac{1}{4}, \frac{3}{16}$

5. What is the value of the expression $4^2 \cdot 4^3 - 5^3$? *(Lesson 4.6)*

   A. -899 **B.** 81 **C.** 899 **D.** 10,800

6. What is the value of the expression $3 \cdot 3^{-5}$? *(Lesson 4.7)*

   F. $\frac{1}{81}$ **G.** $\frac{1}{5}$ **H.** 45 **I.** 81

7. Which is *not* in scientific notation? *(Lesson 4.8)*

   A. 1×10^6 **B.** 4.4×10^{-2}

   C. 8.03×10^4 **D.** 13.4×10^{-8}

8. **Short Response** Train A leaves the station every 12 minutes. Train B leaves every 15 minutes. A bus leaves every 8 minutes. How often do two trains and a bus depart at the same time? Explain. *(Lesson 4.4)*

9. **Extended Response** A hole at a miniature golf course has 3 doors that swing open on different schedules. You see the 3 doors open at the same time. After 4 seconds, the red door opens again. Two seconds after that, the blue door opens. The red door opens after 2 more seconds. One second later, the yellow door opens. *(Lesson 4.4)*

   a. How often does each door open?

   b. How often do all 3 doors open at the same time? Explain your answer.

Chapter 5

Multiple Choice In Exercises 10–16, choose the letter of the correct answer.

10. You need $4\frac{1}{2}$ yards of fabric for drapes and $3\frac{1}{2}$ yards for a bedspread. How many yards of fabric should you purchase? *(Lesson 5.1)*

    A. $1\frac{1}{2}$ **B.** $7\frac{1}{2}$ **C.** 8 **D.** $8\frac{1}{2}$

11. Find the difference $\frac{18}{21} - \frac{6}{14}$. *(Lesson 5.2)*

F. $\frac{3}{7}$ **G.** $\frac{4}{7}$ **H.** $\frac{6}{7}$ **I.** $\frac{12}{7}$

12. Find the product $-1\frac{1}{2} \cdot \frac{9}{20}$. *(Lesson 5.3)*

A. $-1\frac{9}{20}$ **B.** $-1\frac{1}{20}$ **C.** $-\frac{27}{40}$ **D.** $-\frac{3}{10}$

13. What is the value of a in the equation $\frac{2}{3}a = -12$? *(Lesson 5.4)*

F. -27 **G.** -18 **H.** -12 **I.** -2

14. In your class, $\frac{21}{30}$ of the students ride the bus to school. What is another way to write this number? *(Lesson 5.5)*

A. 0.24 **B.** 0.33 **C.** 0.66 **D.** 0.7

15. What is the value of the expression $-2.643 + (-9.9)$? *(Lesson 5.6)*

F. -12.543 **G.** -11.643

H. 7.257 **I.** 12.543

16. What is the value of the expression $-2.84 \cdot 8.6$? *(Lesson 5.7)*

A. -24.424 **B.** -11.44

C. 5.76 **D.** 24.424

17. **Short Response** Four friends shared a pizza. Each person ate only whole slices. Kerry ate $\frac{1}{6}$ of the pizza, and Amy ate 0.25 of the pizza. Brian ate 0.5 of the pizza. Jeff ate $\frac{1}{12}$ of the pizza. Who ate the most pizza? *(Lesson 5.5)*

18. **Extended Response** Rebecca's long distance plan charges $.10 per minute before 7:00 P.M. and $.05 per minute after 7:00 P.M. Rebecca begins a long distance call at 6:39 P.M. and ends the call at 7:12 P.M. *(Lessons 5.6, 5.7)*

a. Find the cost of the phone call.

b. At 7:15 P.M. Rebecca makes another long distance call. She talks for the same amount of time as she did on the previous call. Find the cost of the second phone call.

c. What is the price difference of Rebecca's first call and her second call?

Chapter 6

Multiple Choice **In Exercises 19–23, choose the letter of the correct answer.**

19. What is the value of n in the equation $3n + 9 + 4n = 2$? *(Lesson 6.1)*

A. -2 **B.** -1 **C.** 1 **D.** 2

20. What is the value of x in the equation $22 + x = 37 + 6x$? *(Lesson 6.2)*

F. -3 **G.** 3 **H.** 6 **I.** 12

21. Find the circumference of the circle. Use 3.14 for π. *(Lesson 6.4)*

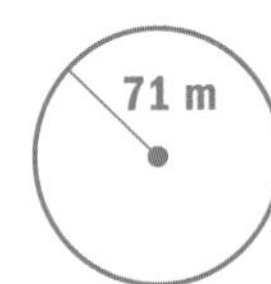

A. 45.22 m **B.** 111.47 m

C. 222.94 m **D.** 445.88 m

22. What is the solution to the inequality $2y - 5 < 7$? *(Lesson 6.5)*

F. $y < -6$ **G.** $y > -6$

H. $y < 6$ **I.** $y > 6$

GO ON

Cumulative Practice continued

23. Mark has $40 to spend on CDs that cost $11.95 each. What is the greatest number of CDs that Mark can buy? *(Lesson 6.6)*

A. 2 **B.** 3 **C.** 4 **D.** 5

24. **Short Response** The diagram shows the approximate measures of a track. Find the perimeter. Explain your steps. Round your answer to the nearest 100. *(Lesson 6.4)*

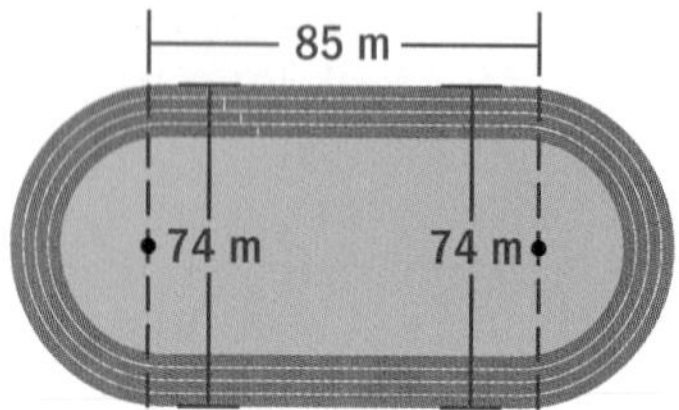

25. **Extended Response** Pat rode his bike at a speed of 9 mi/h. Rick rode at a speed of 8 mi/h. Pat rode 13.5 miles. *(Lesson 6.3)*

a. How many hours and minutes did Pat spend riding?

b. Rick rode his bike for the same amount of time as Pat. How far did Rick ride?

c. Pat and Rick ride at the same speeds for another 45 minutes. Find the total distance traveled by each person.

Chapter 7

Multiple Choice In Exercises 26–31, choose the letter of the correct answer.

26. Lauren types 1040 words in 20 minutes. What is Lauren's typing speed in words per minute? *(Lesson 7.1)*

A. 52 **B.** 104 **C.** 208 **D.** 5700

27. Solve the proportion $\frac{7}{23} = \frac{49}{x}$. *(Lesson 7.2)*

F. 7 **G.** 115 **H.** 161 **I.** 207

28. 18 is what percent of 45? *(Lesson 7.3)*

A. 9% **B.** 40% **C.** 50% **D.** 60%

29. The cost of a concert ticket increased by 4%. The new cost is $31.20. What was the cost before the increase? *(Lesson 7.5)*

F. $18.00 **G.** $29.50 **H.** $30.00 **I.** $31.80

30. What is the total cost of a television priced at $86.90 with 7% sales tax? *(Lesson 7.6)*

A. $66.88 **B.** $80.82 **C.** $89.99 **D.** $92.98

31. Joan invested $100 in an account that pays 5% simple annual interest. What is the account balance after 5 years? *(Lesson 7.7)*

F. $105 **G.** $125 **H.** $150 **I.** $525

32. **Short Response** Houses on your block are numbered 31 through 50. You choose a house at random. What is the probability that the house you choose has a 4 in its number? Explain your answer. *(Lesson 7.8)*

33. **Extended Response** The graph shows the results of a poll in which 504 people would choose to be a zookeeper. *(Lesson 7.4)*

a. How many people chose rodeo star?

b. Find the total number of people who participated in the poll.

c. How many people chose either a veterinarian or a pet store owner?

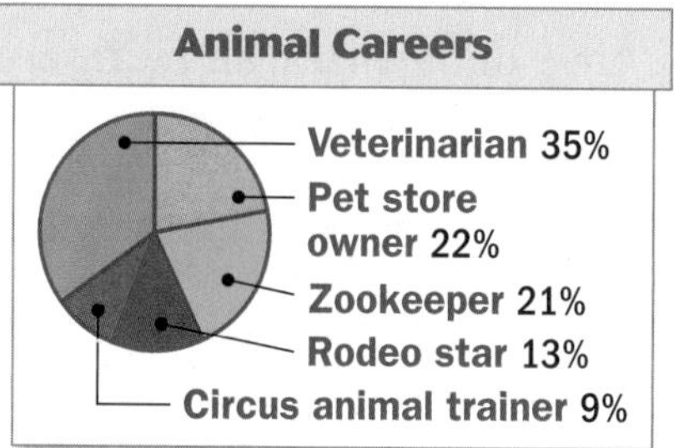

UNIT 3 Geometry and Measurement

Chapter 8 Polygons and Transformations

- Classify angles, triangles, and other polygons.
- Use properties of congruent and similar polygons to solve problems.
- Describe transformations and symmetry of geometric figures.

Chapter 9 Real Numbers and Right Triangles

- Use square roots and the Pythagorean theorem to solve problems.
- Identify rational and irrational numbers.
- Use special relationships in right triangles to solve problems.

Chapter 10 Measurement, Area, and Volume

- Find areas of parallelograms, trapezoids, and circles.
- Find surface areas and volumes of prisms, cylinders, pyramids, and cones.
- Classify and sketch solids.

From Chapter 9, p. 444
How high can you parasail?

Polygons and Transformations

BEFORE

In previous chapters you've...

- Solved equations
- Plotted points in a coordinate plane

Now

In Chapter 8 you'll study...

- Solving equations to find angle measures
- Classifying angles and triangles
- Reflecting, translating, and rotating figures in a coordinate plane

WHY?

So you can solve real-world problems about...

- weaving, p. 378
- referees, p. 384
- geodesic domes, p. 393
- origami, p. 412

Internet Preview
CLASSZONE.COM

- eEdition Plus Online
- eWorkbook Plus Online
- eTutorial Plus Online
- State Test Practice
- More Examples

Chapter Warm-Up Game

Review skills you need for this chapter in this quick game. Work with a partner.

Key Skill:
Plotting points on a coordinate plane

FIND THE FLAGS

MATERIALS

- 2 sheets of grid paper for each player
- Pencils

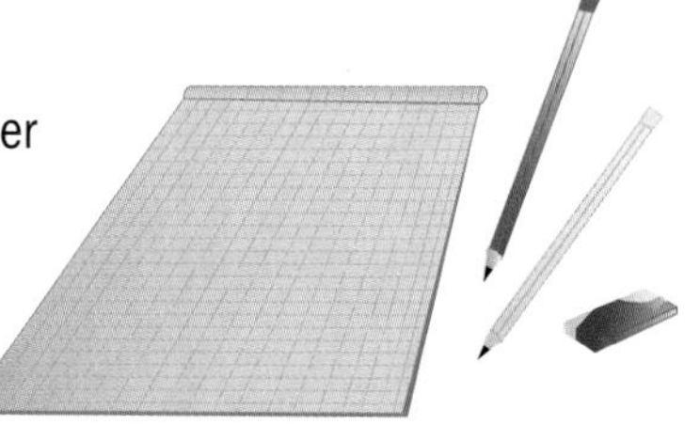

PREPARE Each player draws a coordinate graph on both sheets of grid paper. Each player draws squares along the grid lines passing through the points (7, 0), (0, −7), (−7, 0), and (0, 7). A player secretly marks 4 flags on one graph. A flag is three consecutive points with integer coordinates, either horizontally or vertically. Flags cannot touch the outside borders. On each turn, a player should follow the steps on the next page.

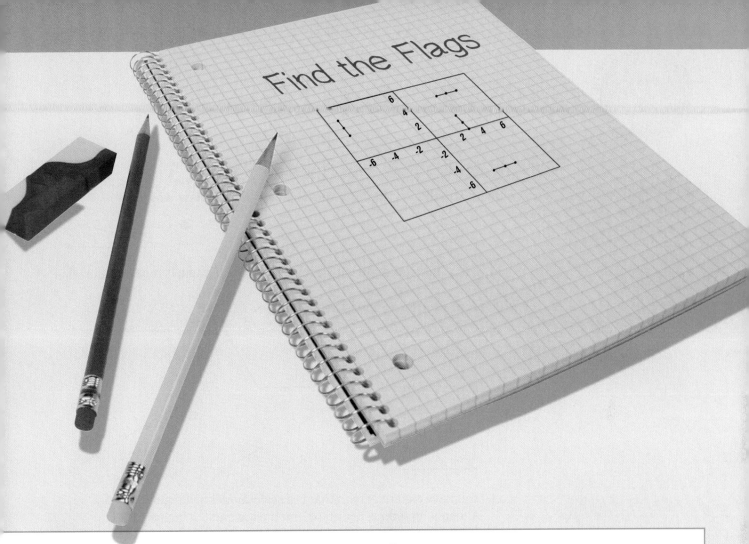

Find the Flags

1 CALL out a point. The other player lets you know if you hit or missed one of their flags.

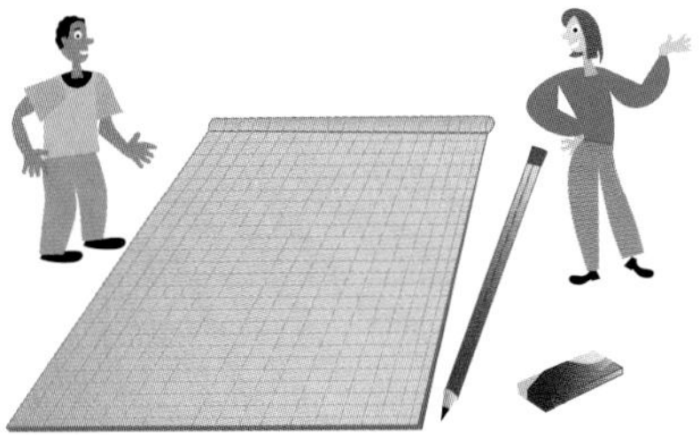

2 MARK a hit with an "X" and a miss with an "O" on your second graph where your flags are not marked. If you hit a flag, you get to go again.

HOW TO WIN Be the first player to hit all the points in the other player's flags.

Stop *and* Think

1. **Writing** How did you decide where to put your flags? Did it work? Explain. What strategy did you use when trying to find the other player's flags? Did it work? Explain.
2. **Critical Thinking** How many points are there (not including any on the border) in each graph? Explain how you got your answer.

Getting Ready to Learn

Word Watch

Review Words

point, p. 718
line, p. 718
ray, p. 718
plane, p. 718
angle, p. 719
vertex, p. 719
degree, p. 721

Review What You Need to Know 

Using Vocabulary **Identify the object with a review word.** *(p. 718)*

1.

2.

3. 

4. Copy and complete with a review word: An angle is measured in _?_.

Use a protractor to measure the angle. *(p. 721)*

5. 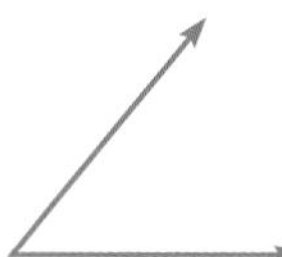

6. 

7. 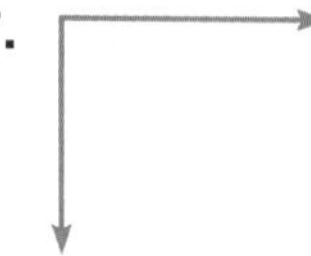

8. 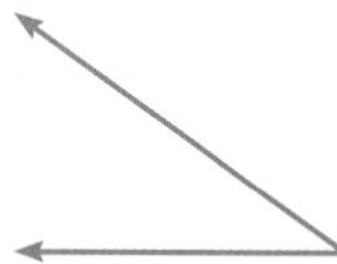

9. 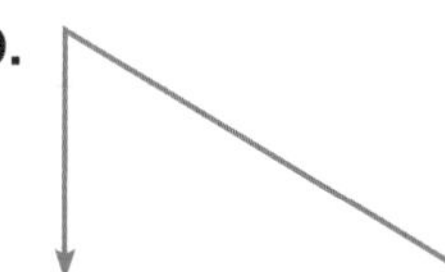

10. 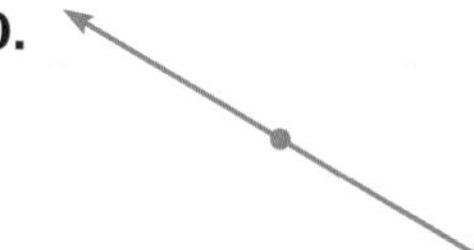

11. You have a giant crayon that is a scale model of a regular crayon. A regular crayon is about 0.25 inch wide and 3.5 inches long. The giant crayon is 6 inches wide. How long is it? *(p. 322)*

Notebook

You should include material that appears on a notebook like this in your own notes.

Know How to Take Notes

Making a Concept Map You will often learn new concepts that are related to each other. It is helpful to organize these concepts in your notes with a map or chart.

A rectangle is a figure with four sides. Its opposite sides are the same length and its angles measure 90°.

A square is a rectangle with sides that are the same length.

In Lesson 8.3, you can use a concept map to organize information about special four-sided shapes.

Parallel Lines Two lines in the same plane that do not intersect are called **parallel lines**. When a line intersects two parallel lines, several pairs of angles that are formed have equal measures.

Angles and Parallel Lines

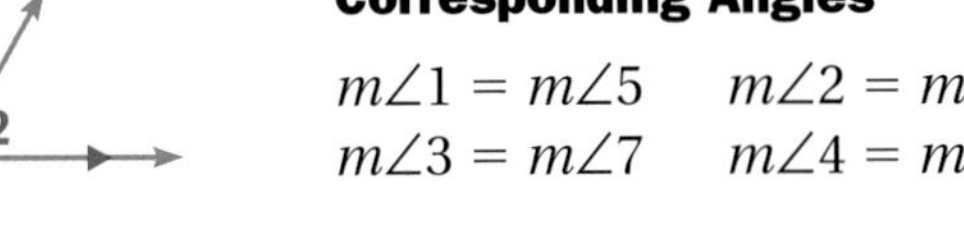

Corresponding Angles

$m\angle 1 = m\angle 5$ $m\angle 2 = m\angle 6$
$m\angle 3 = m\angle 7$ $m\angle 4 = m\angle 8$

Alternate Interior Angles

$m\angle 3 = m\angle 6$ $m\angle 4 = m\angle 5$

Alternate Exterior Angles

$m\angle 1 = m\angle 8$ $m\angle 2 = m\angle 7$

HELP with Solving

Triangles on lines indicate that lines are parallel.

EXAMPLE 3 Using Parallel Lines

Use the diagram to find $m\angle 1$.

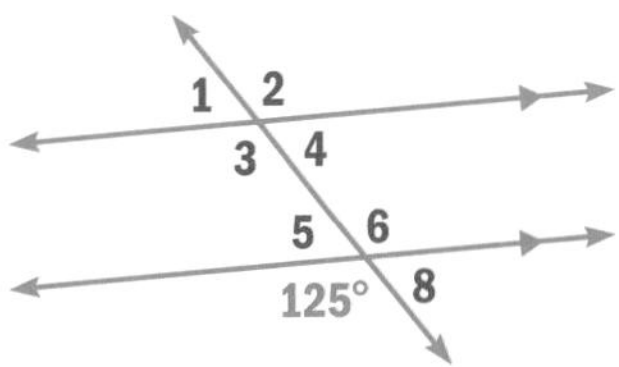

Solution

$\angle 1$ and $\angle 5$ are corresponding angles, so they have equal measures. Find $m\angle 5$.

The angle with measure 125° and $\angle 5$ are supplementary.

$m\angle 5 + 125° = 180°$ Definition of supplementary angles

$m\angle 5 = 55°$ Subtract 125° from each side.

$\angle 1$ and $\angle 5$ have equal measures.

ANSWER $m\angle 1 = 55°$

Your turn now **Find the angle measure.**

9. $m\angle 2$ **10.** $m\angle 3$

11. $m\angle 4$ **12.** $m\angle 6$

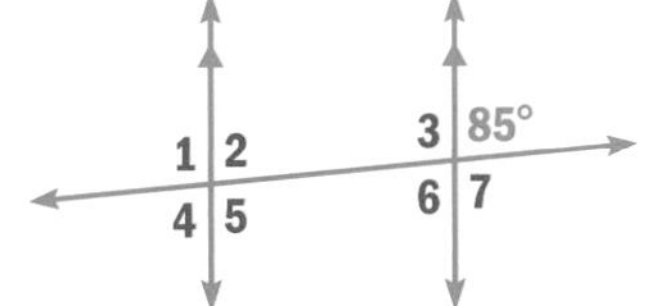

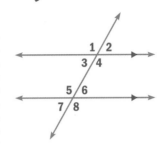

8.1 Exercises

More Practice, p. 734

Getting Ready to Practice

Vocabulary Copy and complete the statement.

1. The sum of the measures of two _?_ angles is 180°.
2. Two lines that intersect to form a right angle are called _?_.

Tell whether the angles are *complementary*, *supplementary*, or *neither*.

3. $m\angle 1 = 62°$, $m\angle 2 = 118°$
4. $m\angle 1 = 51°$, $m\angle 2 = 39°$
5. **Find the Error** Describe and correct the error in the solution.

X $m\angle 2 = 68°$, because vertical angles add up to 180°.

112° 1
3 2

Practice and Problem Solving

HELP with Homework

Example	Exercises
1	6–7, 13
2	8–11
3	14

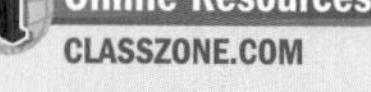

CLASSZONE.COM

- More Examples
- eTutorial Plus

Find the angle measure.

6. $\angle 1$ and $\angle 2$ are complementary, and $m\angle 1 = 56°$. Find $m\angle 2$.
7. $\angle 3$ and $\angle 4$ are supplementary, and $m\angle 4 = 71°$. Find $m\angle 3$.

Find the measures of the numbered angles.

8.

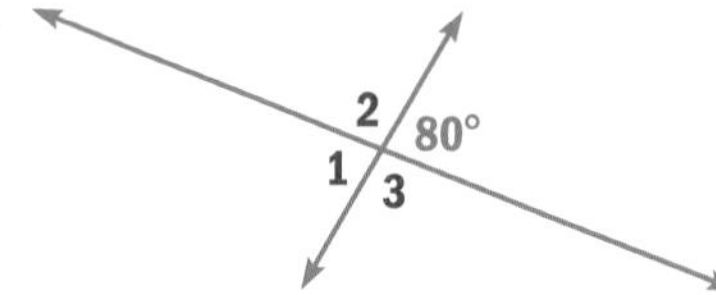

9.

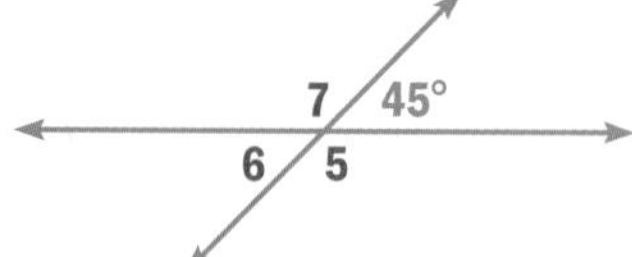

10. **Weaving** Find the angle measures in the weaving if $m\angle 1 = 122°$.

11. **Intersecting Streets** Two streets intersect to form a 75° angle. Sketch the intersection and find the measure of each angle formed.

12. **Writing** Can parallel lines form vertical angles? Explain.

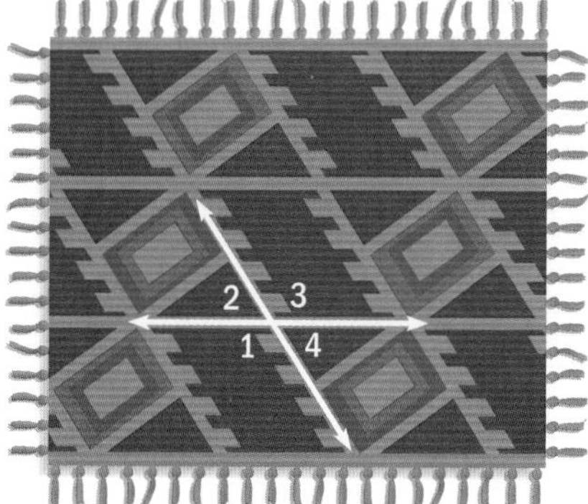

13. Stationery A student designed the stationery border shown here. Explain how to find $m\angle 2$ if $m\angle 1 = 135°$.

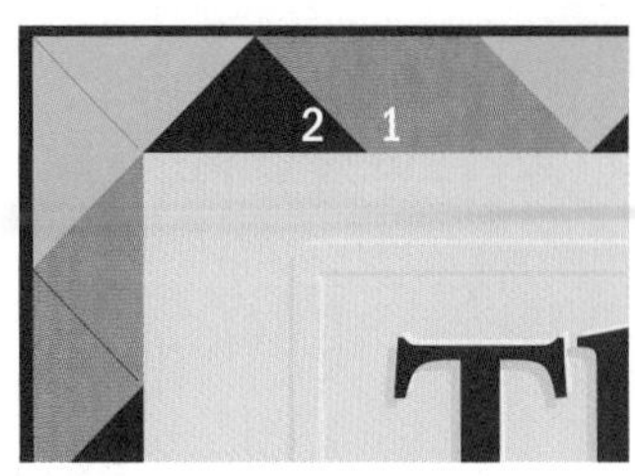

14. In the diagram, $m\angle 4 = 44°$. Find the measure of each angle.

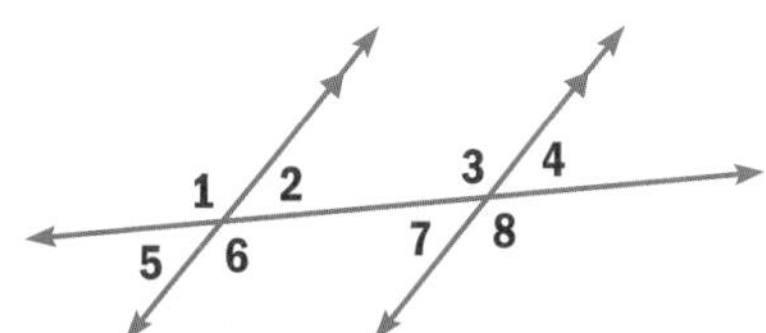

15. Challenge Find the measure of each angle if $m\angle 9 = 106°$.

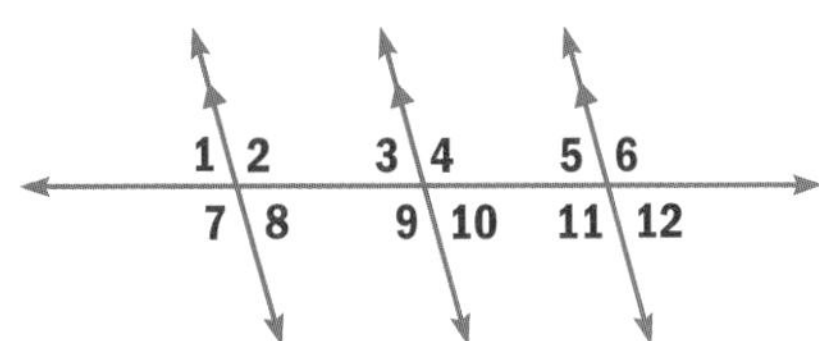

Algebra Find the value of the variable and the angle measures.

16. $m\angle 1 = (5x + 15)°$ and $m\angle 2 = 28x°$

17. $m\angle 6 = (100 - 10y)°$ and $m\angle 3 = 45y°$

18. $m\angle 4 = (7n + 39)°$ and $m\angle 5 = (11n - 13)°$

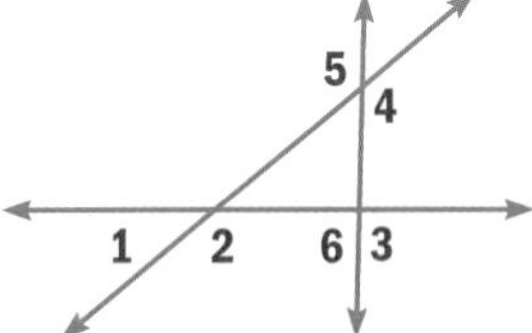

Mixed Review

Write the percent as a fraction in simplest form. *(Lesson 7.4)*

19. 22.6% **20.** 6.5% **21.** 0.45% **22.** 602%

Basic Skills Find the area of a triangle with the given base and height.

23. $b = 3$ in., $h = 2$ in. **24.** $b = 9$ cm, $h = 4$ cm **25.** $b = 13$ ft, $h = 5$ ft

Test-Taking Practice

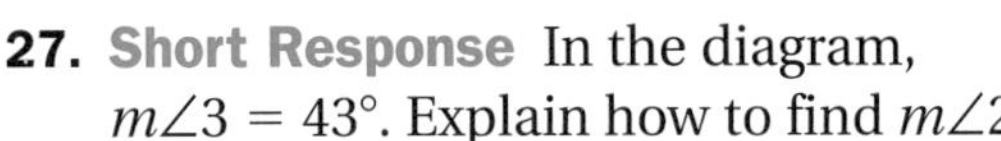

INTERNET
State Test Practice
CLASSZONE.COM

26. Multiple Choice Which angles are complementary?

A. $\angle 1$ and $\angle 2$ **B.** $\angle 2$ and $\angle 3$

C. $\angle 3$ and $\angle 4$ **D.** $\angle 4$ and $\angle 1$

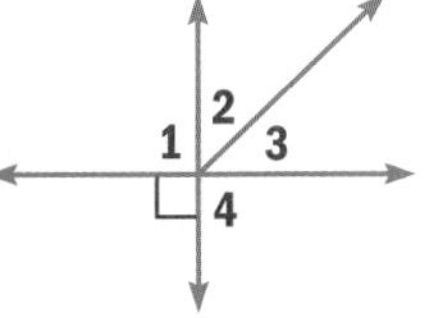

27. Short Response In the diagram, $m\angle 3 = 43°$. Explain how to find $m\angle 2$.

Constructions

GOAL Copy an angle and construct perpendicular lines and parallel lines.

INDIANA Academic Standards
- Geometry (8.4.2)

You can *construct* geometric figures using special tools. A *compass* is used to draw parts of circles called *arcs*. A *straightedge* is used to draw a straight line.

EXAMPLE 1 Copying an Angle

1 Draw an angle. Label its vertex A. Then draw a ray with endpoint X.

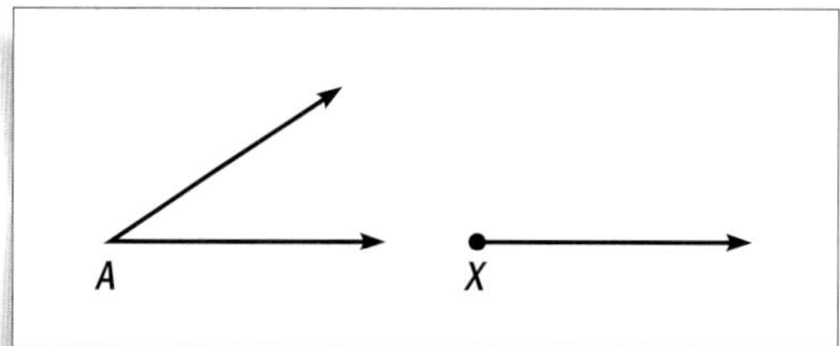

2 Draw an arc with center A. Label B and C on $\angle A$. Use the same compass setting to draw an arc with center X. Label point Y.

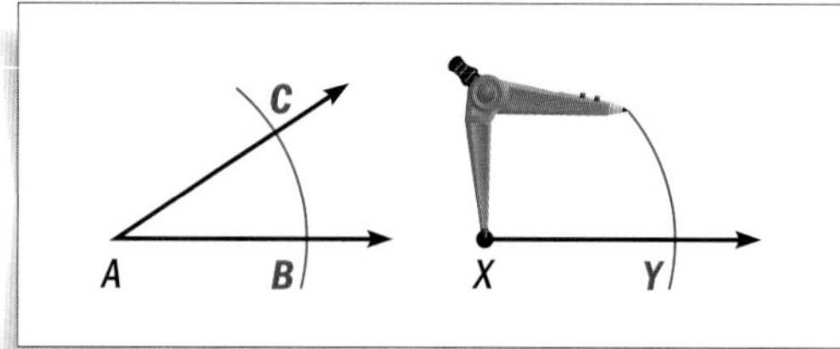

3 Draw an arc with center B that passes through C. Use the same compass setting to draw an arc with center Y. Label point Z.

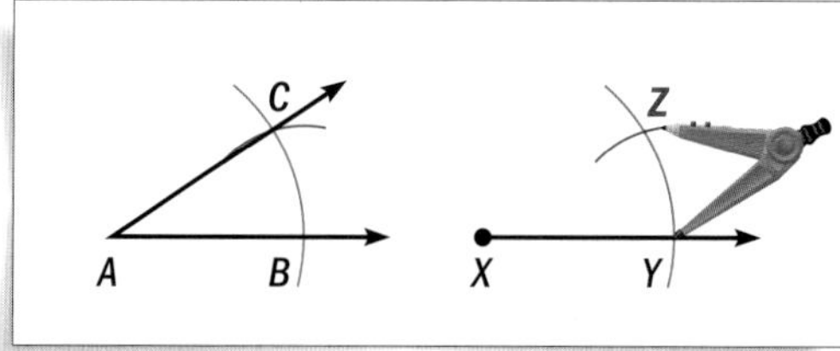

4 Use a straightedge to draw a ray with endpoint X through Z.

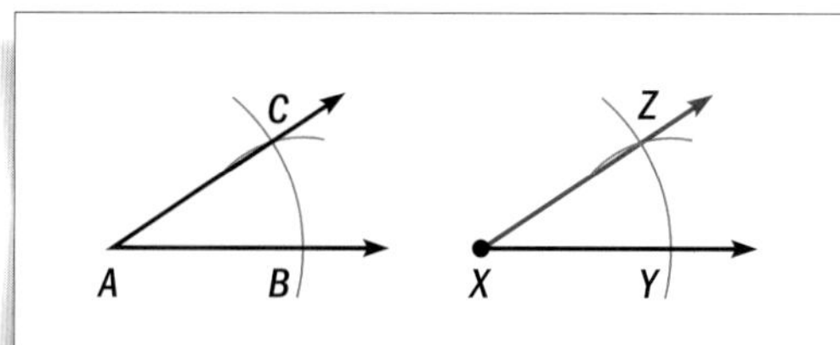

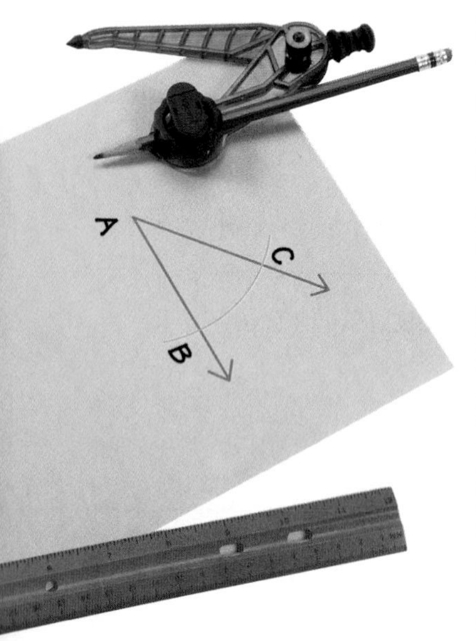

✓ **CHECK** Use a protractor to check that $m\angle A = m\angle X$.

EXAMPLE 2 Constructing a Perpendicular Line

(1) Draw a line and a point *P* not on the line. Draw an arc with center *P* that intersects the line twice. Label *A* and *B*. Using the same compass setting, draw arcs with centers *A* and *B*.

(2) Where the last two arcs intersect label point *Q*. Draw a line through *P* and *Q*. The two lines are perpendicular.

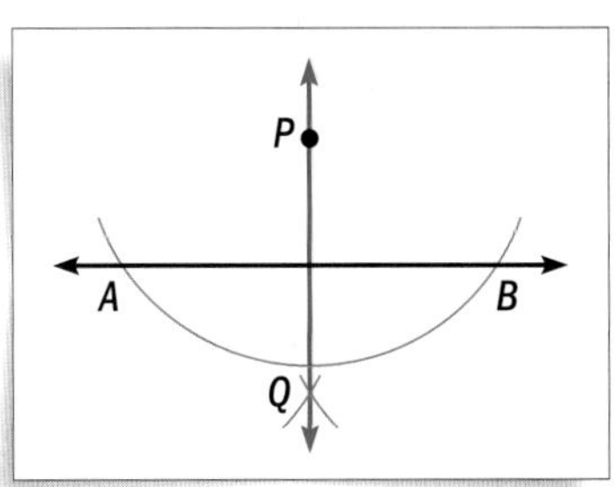

HELP with Solving

The method of construction shown in Example 2 can also work when *P* is on the line through points *A* and *B*. For the last two arcs, use a compass setting greater than half the distance from *A* to *B*.

EXAMPLE 3 Constructing a Parallel Line

(1) Follow the steps in Example 2 to construct perpendicular lines. Label $\angle 1$.

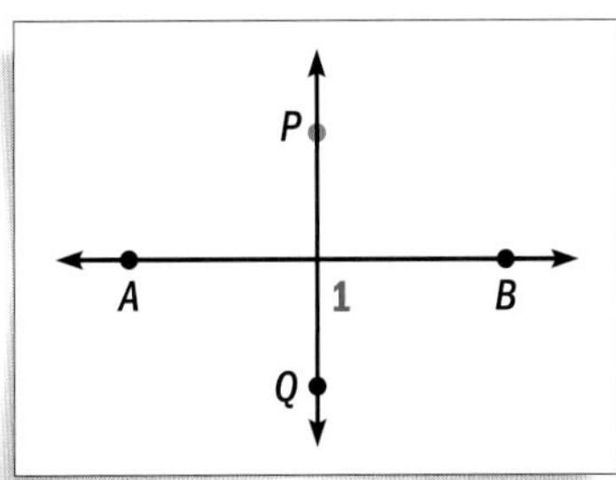

(2) Follow the steps in Example 1 to copy $\angle 1$ at point *P* as shown.

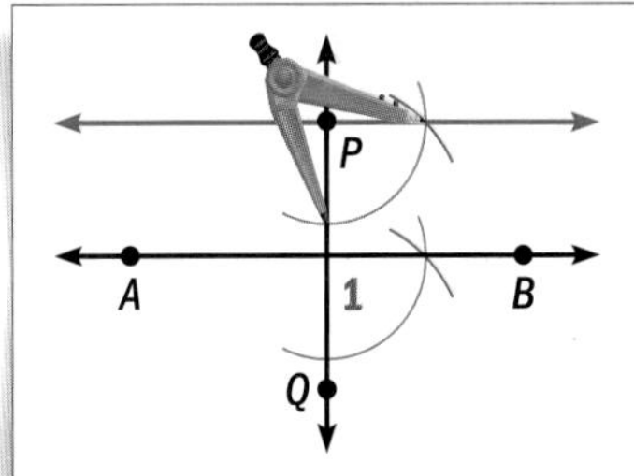

Exercises

Use a protractor to draw an angle with the given measure. Then use a compass and straightedge to copy the angle.

1. 45° **2.** 120° **3.** 135° **4.** 60°

5. Use a compass and a straightedge to construct three parallel lines.

6. Use a compass and straightedge to construct one right triangle.

7. Use a compass and straightedge to construct a rectangle.

Angles and Triangles

BEFORE

You identified pairs of angles.

Now

You'll classify angles and triangles.

WHY?

So you can classify referee signals, as in Exs. 6–8.

Word Watch

acute, right, obtuse angle, p. 382
acute, right, obtuse triangle, p. 382
equilateral, isosceles, scalene triangle, p. 382

INDIANA Academic Standards

- Geometry (8.4.1)

Classifying Angles An angle can be classified by its measure.

Acute angle	**Right angle**	**Obtuse angle**
	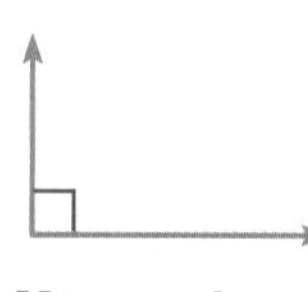	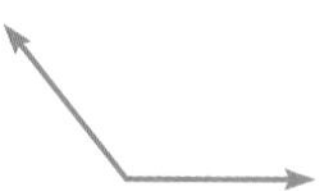
Measure is less than 90°.	Measure is exactly 90°.	Measure is greater than 90° and less than 180°.

Note book

Classifying Triangles

By Angles

An **acute triangle** has three acute angles.

A **right triangle** has one right angle.

An **obtuse triangle** has one obtuse angle.

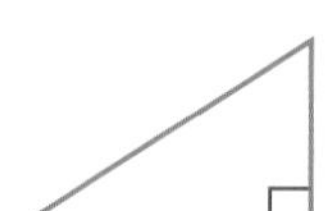

By Sides

An **equilateral triangle** has three sides of equal length.

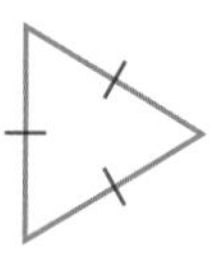

An **isosceles triangle** has at least two sides of equal length.

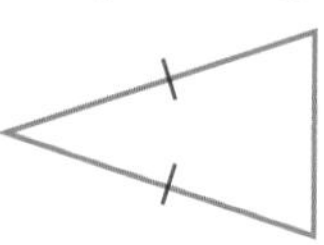

A **scalene triangle** has no sides of equal length.

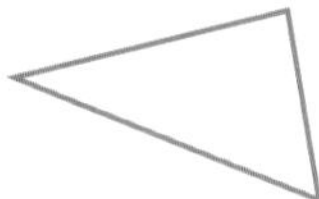

EXAMPLE 1 Classifying a Triangle

Classify the triangle by its side lengths.

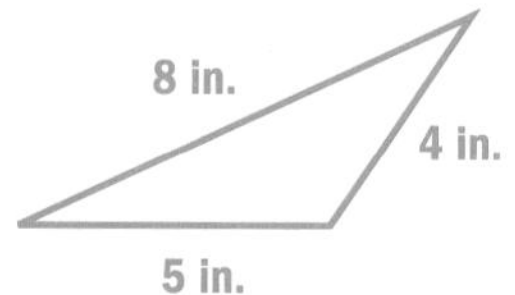

ANSWER The triangle has no sides of equal length. So, it is a scalene triangle.

Find the Flags

1 CALL out a point. The other player lets you know if you hit or missed one of their flags.

2 MARK a hit with an "X" and a miss with an "O" on your second graph where your flags are not marked. If you hit a flag, you get to go again.

HOW TO WIN Be the first player to hit all the points in the other player's flags.

Stop *and* Think

1. **Writing** How did you decide where to put your flags? Did it work? Explain. What strategy did you use when trying to find the other player's flags? Did it work? Explain.
2. **Critical Thinking** How many points are there (not including any on the border) in each graph? Explain how you got your answer.

Getting Ready to Learn

Word Watch

Review Words

point, p. 718
line, p. 718
ray, p. 718
plane, p. 718
angle, p. 719
vertex, p. 719
degree, p. 721

Review What You Need to Know 

Using Vocabulary **Identify the object with a review word.** *(p. 718)*

1.

2.

3.

4. Copy and complete with a review word: An angle is measured in _?_.

Use a protractor to measure the angle. *(p. 721)*

5. 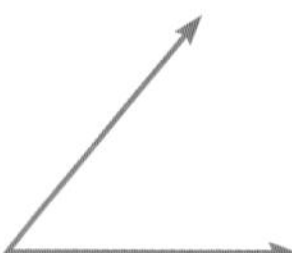

6. 

7. 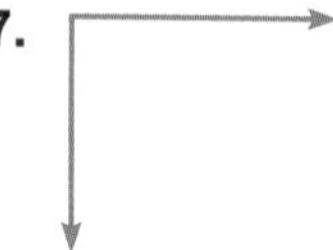

8. 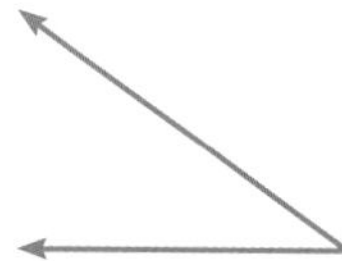

9. 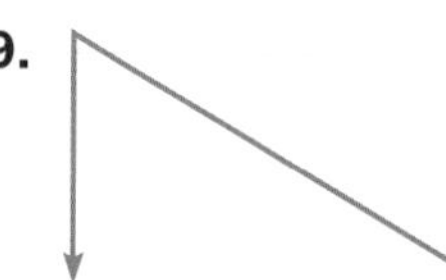

10. 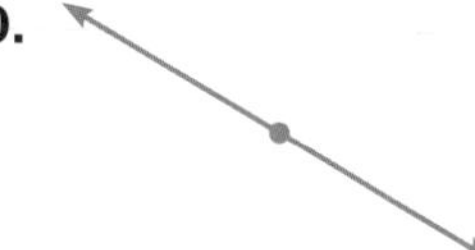

11. You have a giant crayon that is a scale model of a regular crayon. A regular crayon is about 0.25 inch wide and 3.5 inches long. The giant crayon is 6 inches wide. How long is it? *(p. 322)*

Notebook

You should include material that appears on a notebook like this in your own notes.

Know How to Take Notes

Making a Concept Map You will often learn new concepts that are related to each other. It is helpful to organize these concepts in your notes with a map or chart.

A rectangle is a figure with four sides. Its opposite sides are the same length and its angles measure 90°.

A square is a rectangle with sides that are the same length.

In Lesson 8.3, you can use a concept map to organize information about special four-sided shapes.

with Reading

Tick marks in a drawing show that side lengths are equal. Arc marks show that angle measures are equal.

EXAMPLE 2 Classifying a Triangle

Classify the triangle by its angles and by its side lengths.

ANSWER The triangle has one right angle and two sides of equal length. So, it is a right isosceles triangle.

Angles in a Triangle From the figures below, you can see that the sum of the angle measures in the triangle is 180°. This is true for all triangles.

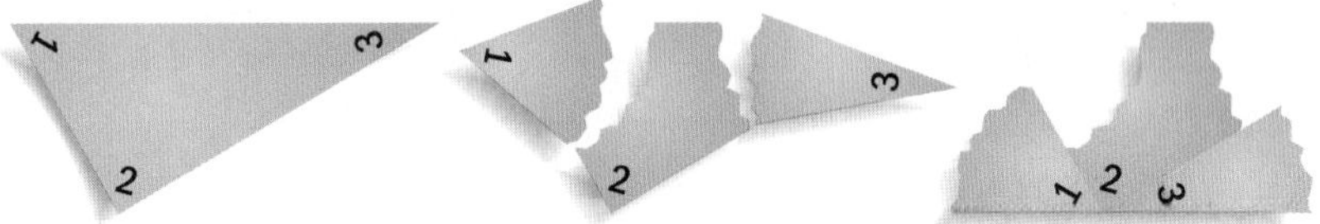

EXAMPLE 3 Finding an Unknown Angle Measure

Find the value of *x*. Then classify the triangle by its angles.

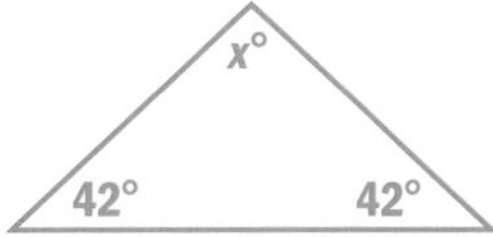

Solution

The sum of the angle measures in a triangle is 180°.

$x° + \mathbf{42°} + \mathbf{42°} = 180°$	**Write an equation.**
$x + \mathbf{84} = 180$	**Add.**
$x + 84 - 84 = 180 - 84$	**Subtract 84 from each side.**
$x = 96$	**Simplify.**

ANSWER The triangle has one obtuse angle, so it is an obtuse triangle.

Your turn now **Find the value of *x*. Then classify the triangle by its angles.**

8.2 Exercises

More Practice, p. 734

Getting Ready to Practice

Vocabulary **Copy and complete the statement.**

1. A(n) ___?___ triangle has no sides of equal length.

Classify the triangle by its side lengths.

2. 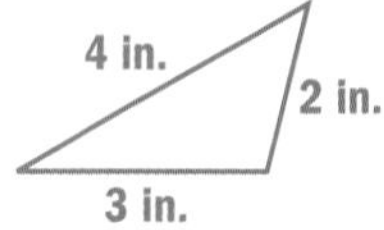

3. 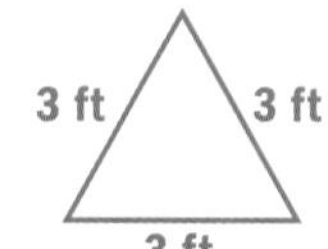

4. 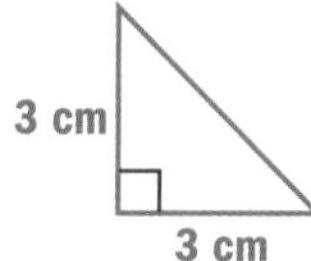

5. **Find the Error** Describe and correct the error in the solution.

The triangle has an acute angle, so it is an acute triangle.
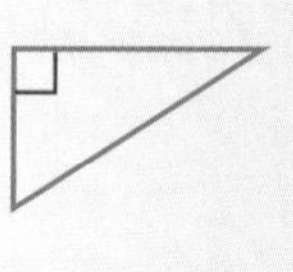

Practice and Problem Solving

Example	Exercises
1	9–11, 15
2	9–11
3	12–14

Online Resources
CLASSZONE.COM
· More Examples
· eTutorial Plus

Estimation **The referee is making calls during a hockey game. Classify the angle made by his arms as *acute*, *obtuse*, or *right*.**

6. Cross Checking

7. Roughing

8. Delayed calling of penalty

Classify the triangle by its side lengths.

9. 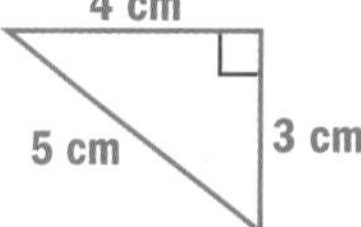

10. 

11. 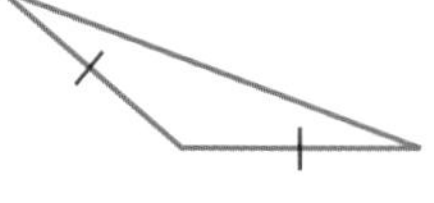

Measurement **Find the value of x. Classify the triangle by its angles.**

12. 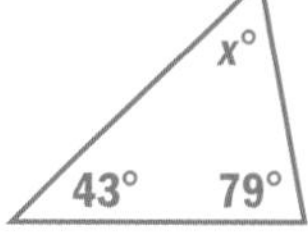

13. 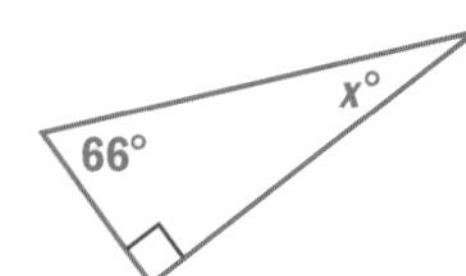

14. 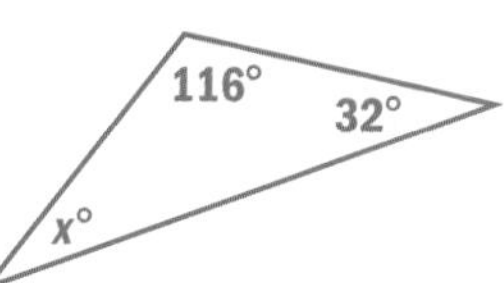

House of Seven Gables
in Salem, Massachusetts

15. **House of Seven Gables** If the two side edges of this gable are the same length, what kind of triangle is formed? Explain.

Writing Can the angles in a triangle have the measures given? Explain.

16. 43°, 48°, 90°

17. 1.5°, 0.5°, 178°

18. 21.3°, 56.7°, 102°

Algebra Find the measure of each angle in the triangle.

19. 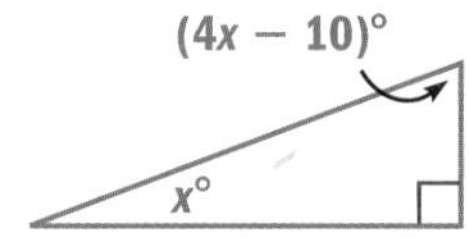

20. 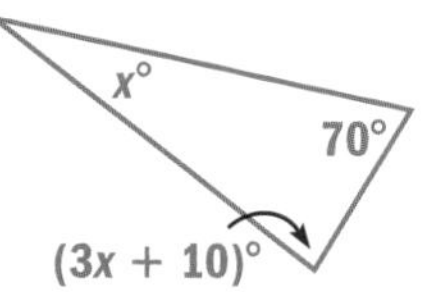

21. 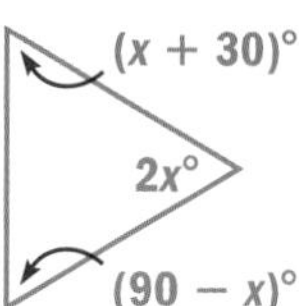

22. **Mental Math** An *equiangular* triangle has three angles with equal measures. Find the measures of those angles.

23. **Measurement** Find the measures of the numbered angles

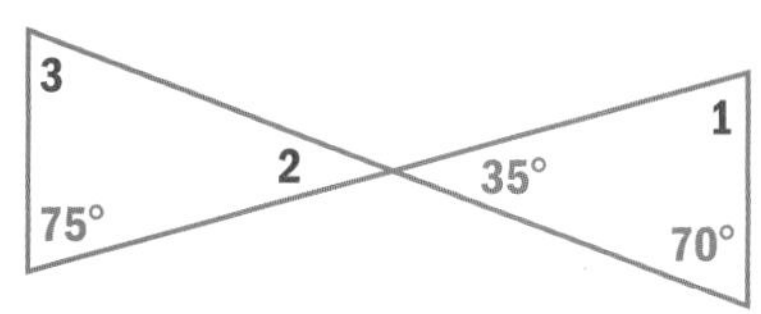

24. **Challenge** Can two angles of a triangle be supplementary? Explain.

Mixed Review

Find the perimeter and area of the rectangle. *(Lesson 1.6)*

25. $l = 2$ yd, $w = 0.6$ yd

26. $l = 13$ m, $w = 12$ m

27. **Geography** Earth's surface is 29.2% land. The total surface area is 510,072,000 square kilometers. Find the total land area. *(Lesson 7.3)*

28. $\angle 3$ and $\angle 4$ are supplementary and $m\angle 4 = 19°$. Find $m\angle 3$. *(Lesson 8.1)*

Test-Taking Practice

INTERNET
State Test Practice
CLASSZONE.COM

29. **Multiple Choice** Find the value of x.

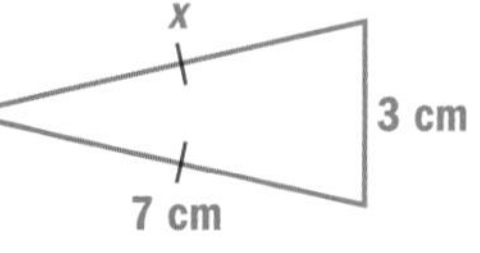

A. 3 cm **B.** 4 cm
C. 7 cm **D.** 10 cm

30. **Multiple Choice** The angles of a triangle measure 110°, 40°, and $x°$. Find the value of x.

F. 30 **G.** 60 **H.** 70 **I.** 80

Quadrilaterals

BEFORE	Now	WHY?
You classified angles and triangles.	You'll classify quadrilaterals.	So you can analyze a design, as in Ex. 17.

quadrilateral, p. 386
trapezoid, p. 386
parallelogram, p. 386
rhombus, p. 386

INDIANA Academic Standards

- Algebra and Functions (8.3.1)
- Geometry (8.4.1)

HELP with Notetaking

You can organize the definitions of quadrilaterals in your notebook using a concept map.

Quadrilaterals A **quadrilateral** is a closed figure with four sides that are line segments. The figures below are special types of quadrilaterals.

Trapezoid

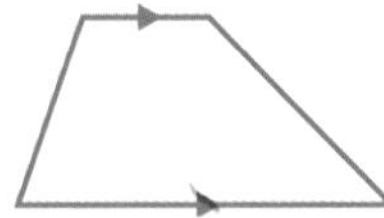

A **trapezoid** is a quadrilateral with exactly 1 pair of parallel sides.

Parallelogram

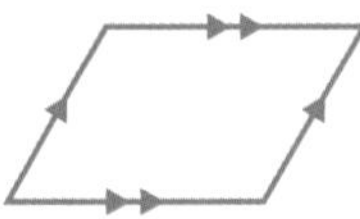

A **parallelogram** is a quadrilateral with both pairs of opposite sides parallel.

Rhombus

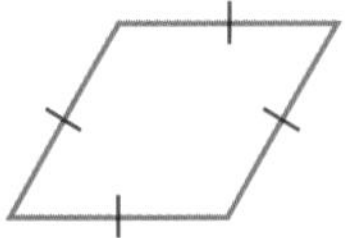

A **rhombus** is a parallelogram with 4 sides of equal length.

Rectangle

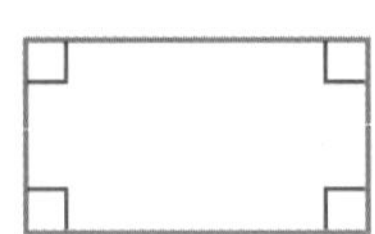

A rectangle is a parallelogram with 4 right angles.

Square

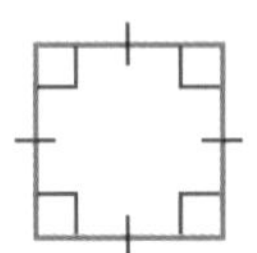

A square is a parallelogram with 4 sides of equal length and 4 right angles.

EXAMPLE 1 Classifying a Quadrilateral

Classify the quadrilateral.

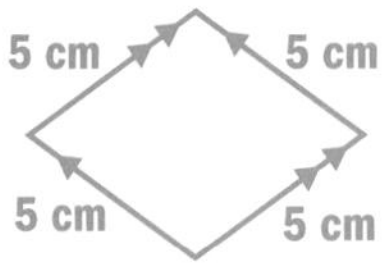

Solution

The quadrilateral is a parallelogram with 4 sides of equal length. So, it is a rhombus.

Your turn now **Classify the quadrilateral.**

1. 

2. 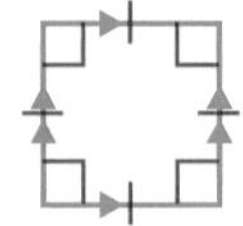

3. 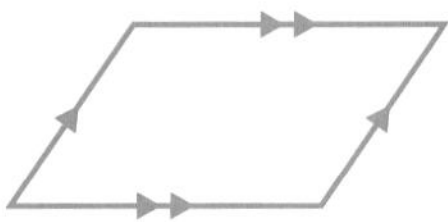

Angle Measures The figures below show that the sum of the angle measures in a quadrilateral is 360°.

Cut a quadrilateral into 2 triangles.

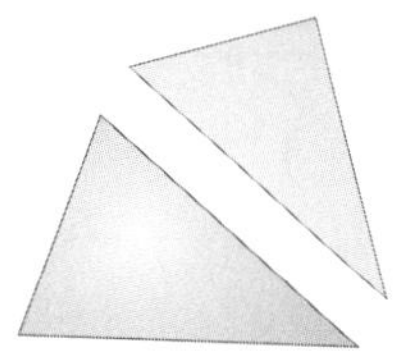

The sum of the angle measures in each triangle is 180°.

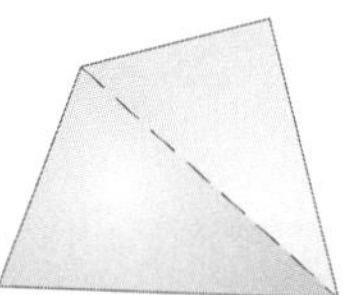

The sum of the angle measures in a quadrilateral is 180° + 180° = 360°.

EXAMPLE 2 Finding an Unknown Angle Measure

Find the value of x.

Solution

The sum of the angle measures in a quadrilateral is 360°.

$x° + 51° + 129° + 129° = 360°$ **Write an equation.**

$x + 309 = 360$ **Add.**

$x = 51$ **Subtract 309 from each side.**

8.3 Exercises

More Practice, p. 734

Getting Ready to Practice

Vocabulary **Copy and complete the statement.**

1. A _?_ is a quadrilateral with both pairs of opposite sides parallel.
2. A _?_ is a quadrilateral with exactly 1 pair of parallel sides.
3. A parallelogram with 4 right angles is a _?_.

Classify the quadrilateral.

4. 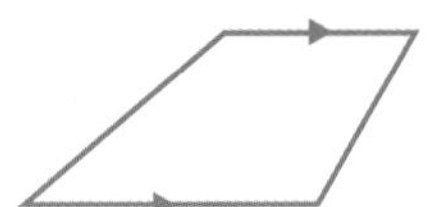

5. 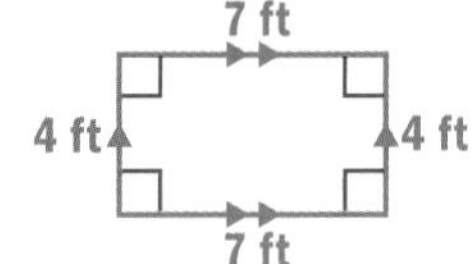

6. 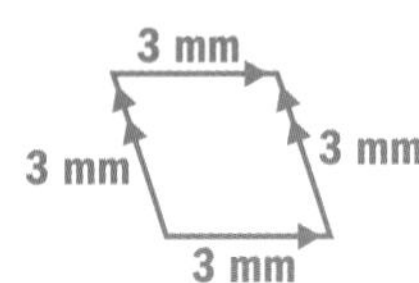

7. The angles of a quadrilateral measure 85°, 74°, 110°, and $x°$. Find the value of x.

Practice and Problem Solving

Example	Exercises
1	8–10
2	11–16

· More Examples
· eTutorial Plus

Measurement Measure the side lengths. Then classify the quadrilateral.

8. 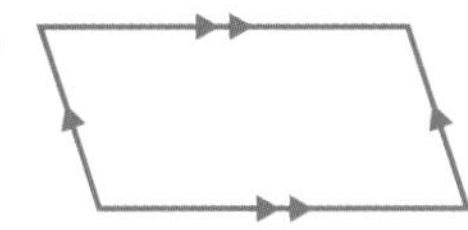

9. 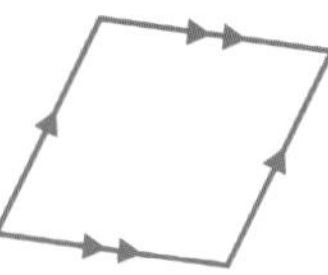

10. 

Find the value of *x*.

11. 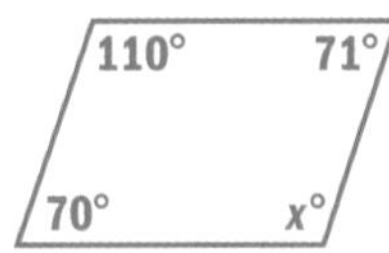

12. 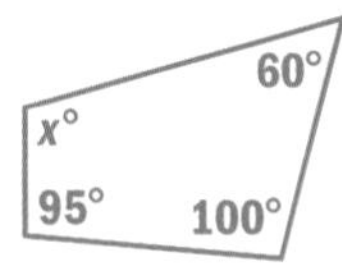

13. 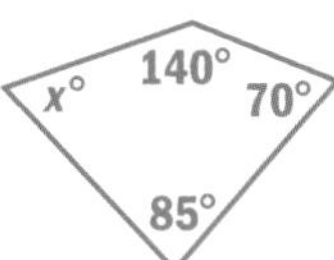

Find the values of *x* and *y*.

14. 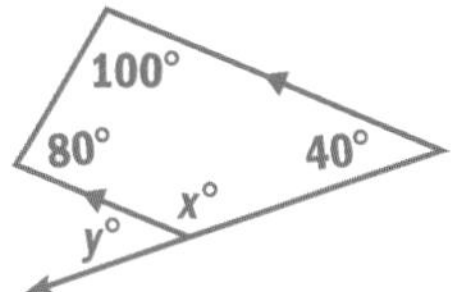

15. 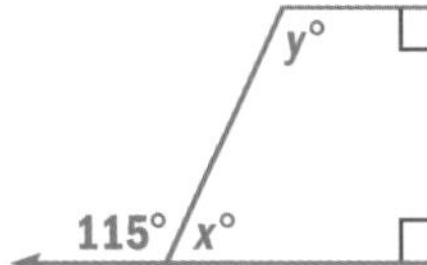

16. 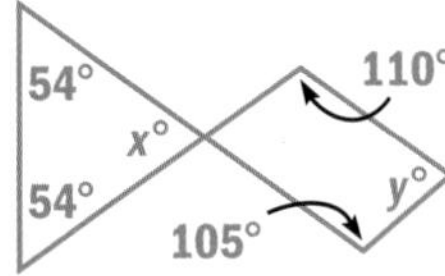

17. Classify each of the quadrilaterals in the design shown below.

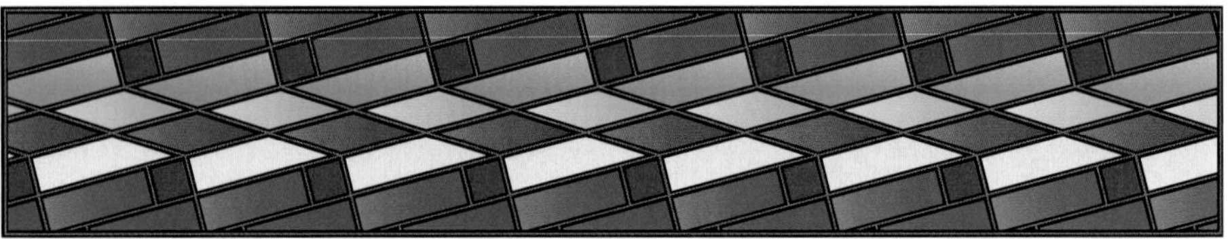

Tell whether the statement is *always*, *sometimes*, or *never* true.

18. A rhombus is also a parallelogram.

19. A rectangle is also a square.

20. A square is also a parallelogram.

21. A triangle is also a quadrilateral.

22. A quadrilateral is also a rectangle.

Find the value of *x* and the unknown angle measures.

23. 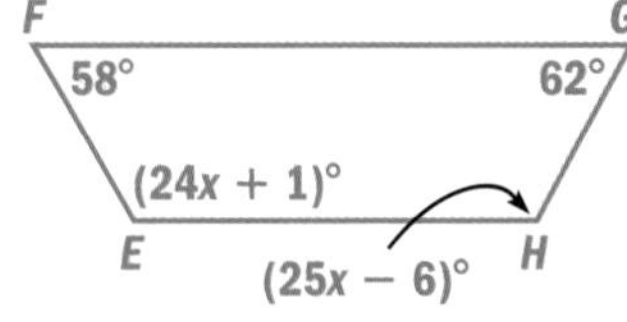

24. 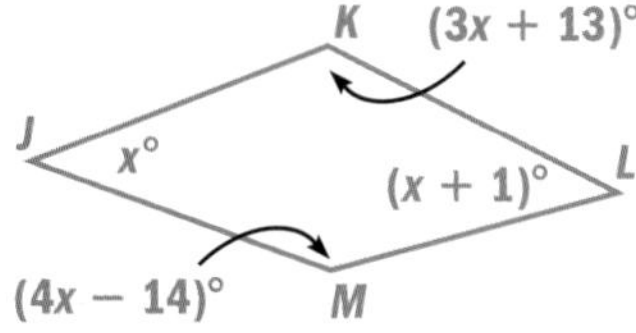

25. **Critical Thinking** What is the greatest number of obtuse angles that a quadrilateral can have? Explain your answer.

26. **Challenge** Find the value of x and y in the diagram. Explain your reasoning.

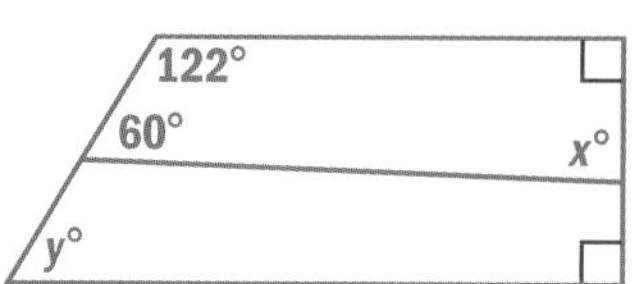

Mixed Review 

In Exercises 27–29, solve the equation. *(Lesson 6.2)*

27. $3x + 12 = 7x - 8$ **28.** $5x + 9 = 3x + 19$ **29.** $-6x + 3 = 4x - 7$

30. Two lines intersect to form a 47° angle. Sketch the lines. Find the measure of each angle in the intersection. *(Lesson 8.1)*

Tell whether the statement is *always*, *sometimes*, or *never* true. *(Lessons 8.1, 8.2)*

31. The measures of complementary angles have a sum of 180°.

32. An obtuse angle measures more than 90°.

33. An isosceles triangle has three sides of equal length.

Test-Taking Practice 

34. **Multiple Choice** Which word can describe two sides of a rectangle?

A. vertical **B.** right **C.** acute **D.** perpendicular

35. **Multiple Choice** Three angles in a quadrilateral are acute. Classify the fourth angle.

F. acute **G.** right **H.** obtuse **I.** straight

Buy Oval Car

Rearrange the letters to make a review word.

1. prizetoad
2. bustoe
3. brushmo
4. tauce
5. allgrapemolar
6. cleanse
7. allearquiet
8. girth
9. catliver
10. includerapper

Polygons and Angles

BEFORE	Now	WHY?
You found angle measures in triangles and quadrilaterals.	You'll find angle measures in polygons.	So you can explore a dome, as in Ex. 24.

polygon, p. 390
regular polygon, p. 390
pentagon, p. 390
hexagon, p. 390
heptagon, p. 390
octagon, p. 390

INDIANA Academic Standards

- Geometry (8.4.1)

Activity **You can use triangles to find the sum of the angle measures in other figures.**

1. Copy the table. Divide each figure into triangles by drawing as many diagonal lines as you can that begin at the point marked.

2. Use your drawings to complete the table.

Shape	Quadrilateral	Pentagon	Hexagon	Octagon
Number of Sides	4	?	?	?
Number of Diagonal Lines	1	?	?	?
Number of Triangles Formed	2	?	?	?
Sum of Angle Measures	360°	?	?	?

3. Use your results to complete a column for a figure with 10 sides.

Polygons A **polygon** is a closed figure whose sides are line segments that intersect only at their endpoints. In a **regular polygon**, all the angles have the same measure and all the sides have the same length.

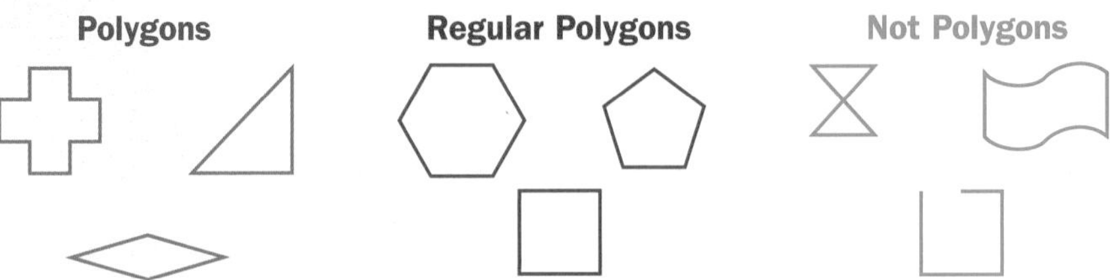

HELP with Reading

You can use n-gon, where n is the number of sides, to identify a polygon if you haven't learned its name. A 13-gon is a 13-sided polygon.

Polygons can be identified by the number of their sides.

Pentagon	Hexagon	Heptagon	Octagon	12-gon
5 sides	6 sides	7 sides	8 sides	12 sides

EXAMPLE 1 Identifying Figures

Is the figure a *polygon*, a *regular polygon*, or *not a polygon*? Explain.

a.

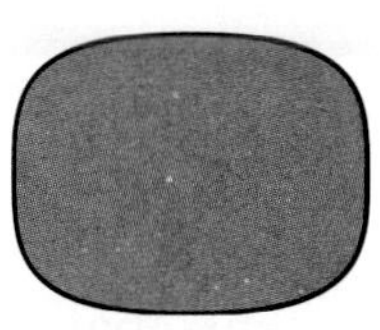

Not a polygon. The figure does not have line segments as sides.

b.

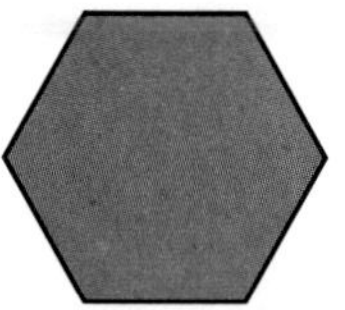

Regular polygon. Its angles have equal measures, and its sides have equal lengths.

Angles In the activity on page 390, you used triangles to find the sum of the angle measures in polygons. In a regular polygon, the measure of one angle is the sum of the angle measures divided by the number of sides.

Angle Measures in a Polygon

Sum of angle measures in an n-gon: $(n - 2) \cdot 180°$

Measure of one angle in a *regular* n-gon: $\dfrac{(n - 2) \cdot 180°}{n}$

EXAMPLE 2 Finding an Angle Measure

Find the measure of one angle in a regular octagon.

A regular octagon has 8 sides, so use $n = 8$.

$\dfrac{(n - 2) \cdot 180°}{n} = \dfrac{(8 - 2) \cdot 180°}{8}$ **Substitute 8 for *n*.**

$= \dfrac{1080°}{8}$ **Simplify numerator.**

$= 135°$ **Divide.**

ANSWER The measure of one angle in a regular octagon is 135°.

Your turn now **Complete the exercise.**

1. Find the sum of the angle measures in a pentagon.

2. Find the measure of one angle in a regular heptagon. Round to the nearest tenth of a degree.

8.4 Exercises

More Practice, p. 734

Getting Ready to Practice

1. **Vocabulary** Copy and complete: A _?_ is a closed figure with sides that are line segments that intersect only at their endpoints.

Tell whether the figure is a *polygon*, a *regular polygon*, or *not a polygon*.

2. 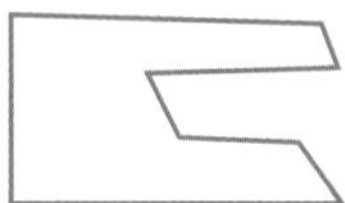
3. 
4. 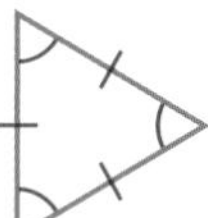

Find the sum of the angle measures in the polygon.

5. 10-gon
6. 9-gon
7. 11-gon
8. 20-gon

9. **Table** A table has 7 sides of equal length and 7 equal angles. Find the measure of one angle to the nearest tenth of a degree.

10. **Find the Error** Describe and correct the error in the solution.

Sum of Angles $= 6 \cdot 180°$

$= 1080°$

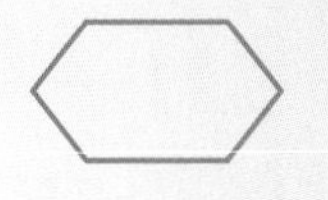

Practice and Problem Solving

Example	Exercises
1	11–13
2	14–17

· More Examples
· eTutorial Plus

Tell whether the swimming pool design is a polygon.

11. 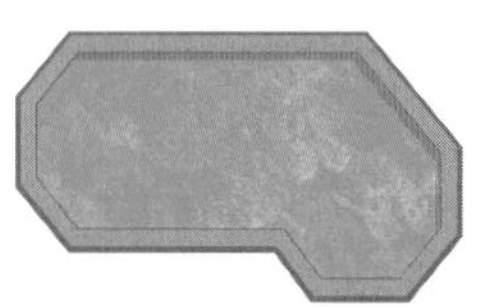
12. 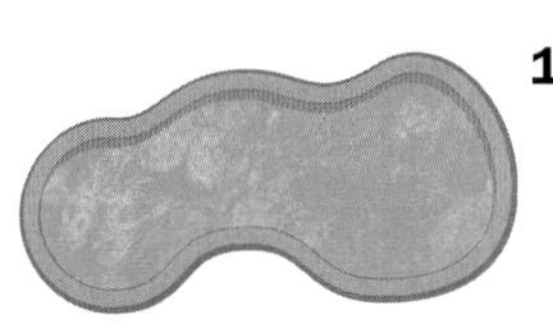
13. 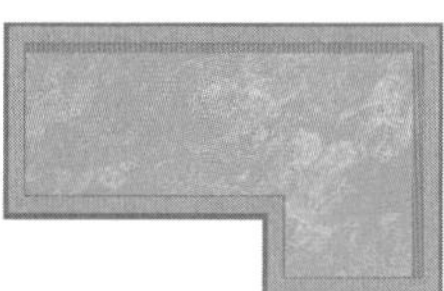

Find the measure of one angle in the polygon.

14. regular 10-gon
15. regular 14-gon
16. regular 15-gon

17. **Calculate** Find the measure of one angle in a regular 115-gon.

Algebra Find the value of *x*.

18. 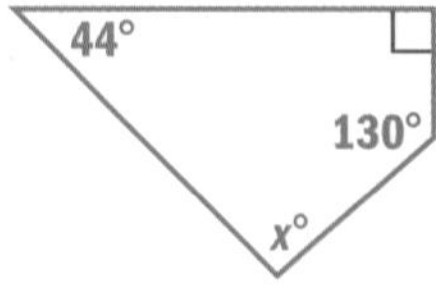

19. 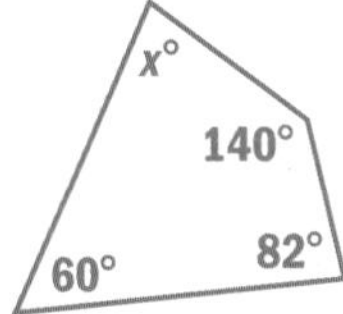

20. 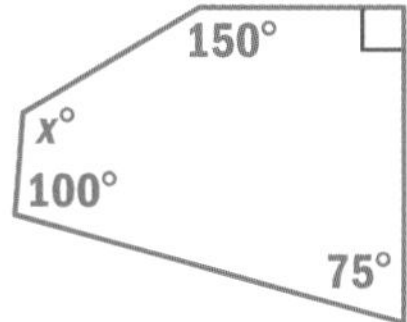

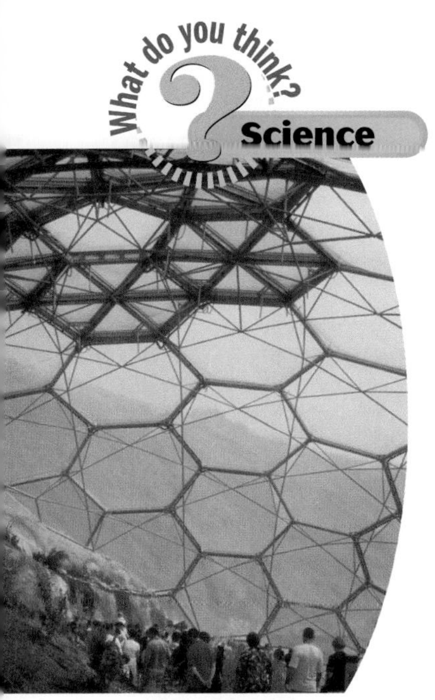

Geodesic Dome

The Eden Project is an environmental center in England made of connected geodesic domes. Its largest dome is 240 meters long. How many feet is this? (1 meter is equal to 3.281 feet.)

Critical Thinking Find the value of *x* and the unknown angle measures.

21. 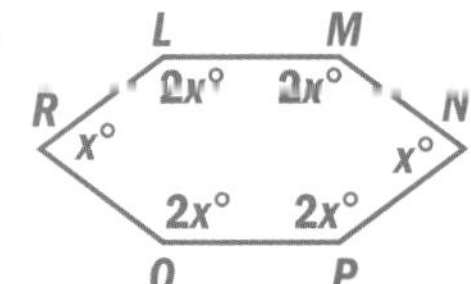

22. 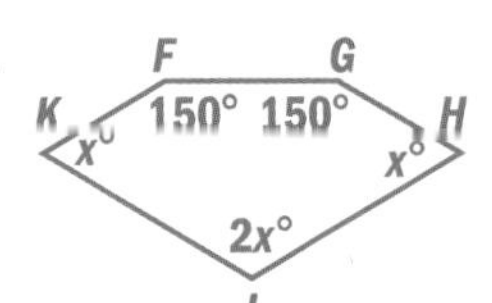

23. 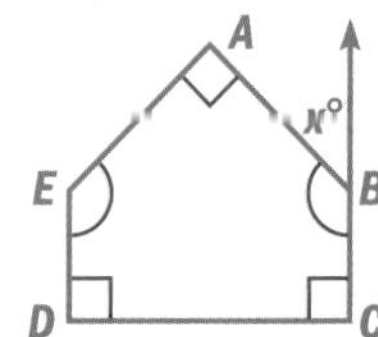

24. **Geodesic Dome** A geodesic dome has some panels that are hexagons. Sketch a regular hexagon, and find the measure of one angle.

25. **Challenge** The sum of the angle measures in a polygon is 1980°. How many sides does it have?

Extended Problem Solving In Exercises 26–28, the angles marked with letters are called *exterior angles*.

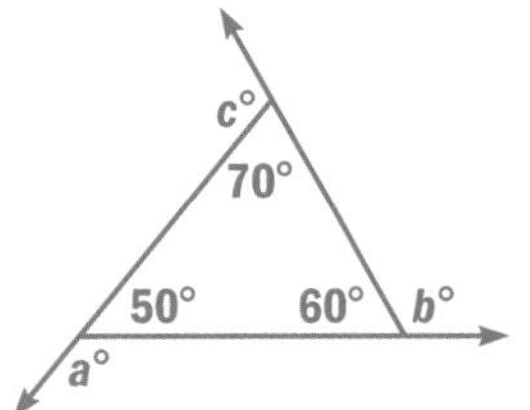

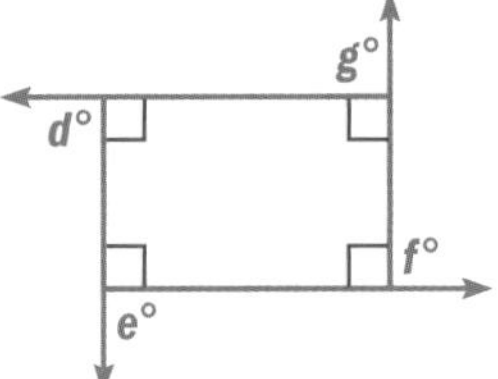

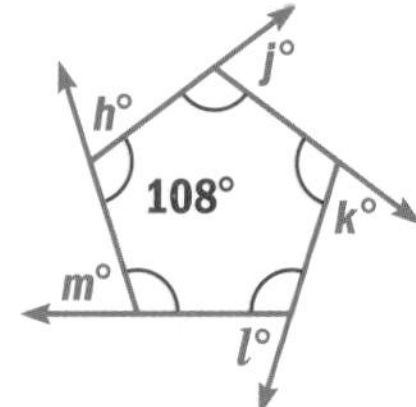

26. **Evaluate** Find the measures of the exterior angles of each polygon.

27. **Calculate** Find the sum of the exterior angle measures for each polygon.

28. **Patterns** Describe a pattern in the sums you found in Exercise 27.

Mixed Review

Write the percent as a fraction in simplest form. *(Lesson 7.4)*

29. 98% **30.** 141.3% **31.** 0.14% **32.** 82.5%

33. The wholesale price of a pair of shoes is $12.75. The retail price of the shoes is $25.95. Find the percent markup. *(Lesson 7.6)*

34. $m\angle 1 = 56°$ and $m\angle 2 = 34°$. Are the angles supplementary? Explain your answer. *(Lesson 8.1)*

Test-Taking Practice

INTERNET
State Test Practice
CLASSZONE.COM

35. **Multiple Choice** Find the measure of one angle in a regular 12-gon.

A. 30° **B.** 60° **C.** 120° **D.** 150°

36. **Multiple Choice** Four angles in a pentagon measure 90°, 85°, 120°, and 130°. What is the measure of the fifth angle?

F. 105° **G.** 115° **H.** 120° **I.** 165°

Notebook Review

Review the vocabulary definitions in your notebook.

Copy the review examples in your notebook. Then complete the exercises.

Check Your Definitions

straight angle, right angle, p. 375
supplementary, complementary angles, p. 375
vertical angles, p. 376
perpendicular lines, p. 376
parallel lines, p. 377
acute, right, obtuse angle, p. 382
acute, right, obtuse triangle, p. 382
equilateral, isosceles, scalene triangle, p. 382
quadrilateral, p. 386
trapezoid, parallelogram, rhombus, p. 386
polygon, regular polygon, p. 390
pentagon, hexagon, heptagon, octagon, p. 390

Use Your Vocabulary

1. **Vocabulary** How many obtuse angles are in an obtuse triangle?

8.1–8.2 Can you find and use angle measures?

EXAMPLE Refer to the diagram to answer parts (a) and (b).

a. Find $m\angle 2$.

The angle with measure 62° and $\angle 2$ are vertical angles, so their measures are equal.

ANSWER $m\angle 2 = 62°$

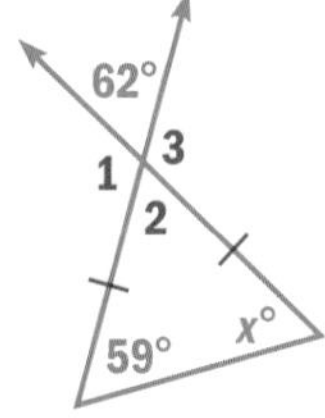

b. Find the value of x. Then classify the triangle.

$x° + 59° + 62° = 180°$ Sum of angle measures is 180°.

$x + 121 = 180$ Add.

$x = 59$ Subtract 121 from each side.

ANSWER The triangle is acute and isosceles.

Find the value of *x*. Classify the triangle by its angles.

2.

3.

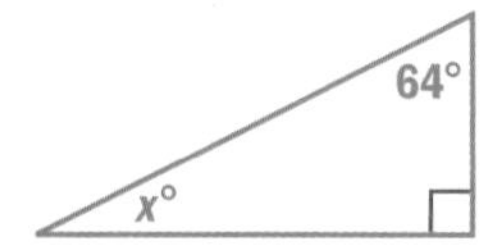

8.3–8.4 Can you find angle measures in polygons?

EXAMPLE Find the measure of one angle in a regular pentagon.

$\frac{(n-2) \cdot 180°}{n}$ **Write the formula for measure of one angle in regular polygon.**

$= \frac{(5-2) \cdot 180°}{5}$ **Substitute 5 for *n*.**

$= 108°$ **Simplify.**

Find the angle measure.

4. Three angles in a quadrilateral measure 203°, 15°, and 90°. Find the measure of the fourth angle.
5. Find the sum of the angle measures in a hexagon.

Stop *and* Think about Lessons 8.1–8.4

6. **Writing** Can a hexagon have two right angles? Draw a diagram and explain your answer.
7. **Illustrate** How many pairs of vertical angles do two intersecting lines form? Draw a diagram and explain your answer.

Review Quiz 1

Tell whether the angles are *complementary*, *supplementary*, or *neither*.

1. $m\angle 1 = 32°, m\angle 2 = 148°$
2. $m\angle 3 = 59°, m\angle 4 = 41°$
3. $m\angle 5 = 12°, m\angle 6 = 78°$
4. $m\angle 7 = 116°, m\angle 8 = 64°$

Can the angles in a triangle have the measures given? Explain.

5. 23°, 57°, 95°
6. 64.6°, 77.3°, 38.1°
7. 155°, 24.9°, 0.1°

Find the value of *x*.

8. 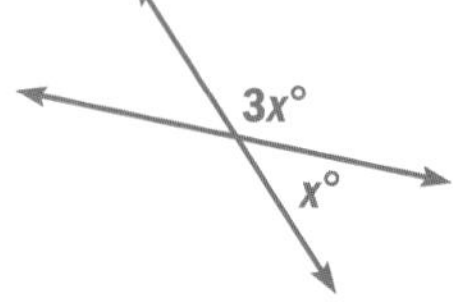

9. 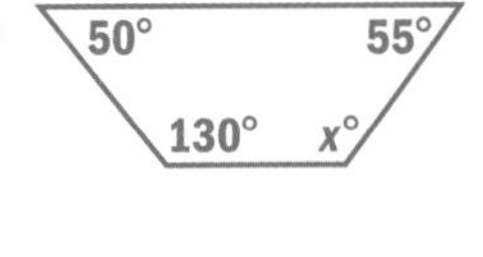

10. 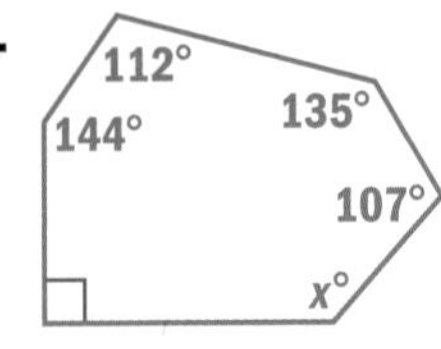

11. Two angles in a triangle measure 75° and 30°. Find the measure of the third angle.

8.5 Hands-on Activity

INDIANA: Academic Standards
- Geometry (8.4.2)

GOAL
Copy a triangle.

MATERIALS
- compass
- straightedge
- protractor

Copying a Triangle

You can use a compass and a straightedge to copy a triangle.

Explore **Use a compass and straightedge to copy a triangle.**

1 Draw a triangle with vertices *A*, *B*, and *C*. Draw a ray with endpoint *P*. Draw an arc with center *A* through point *C*. Use the same compass setting to draw an arc with center *P*. Label point *Q*.

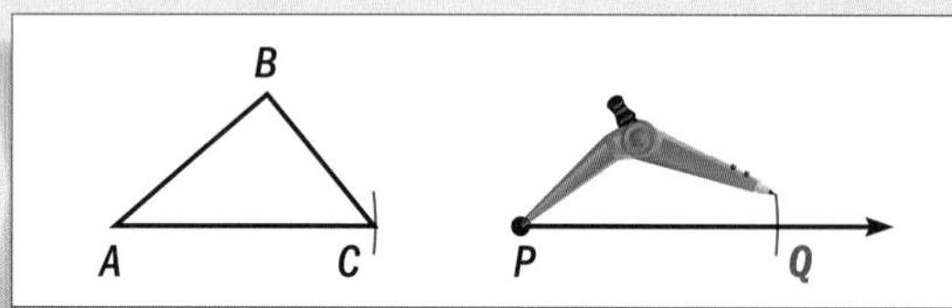

2 Draw an arc with center *C* through point *B*. Use the same compass setting to draw an arc with center *Q*.

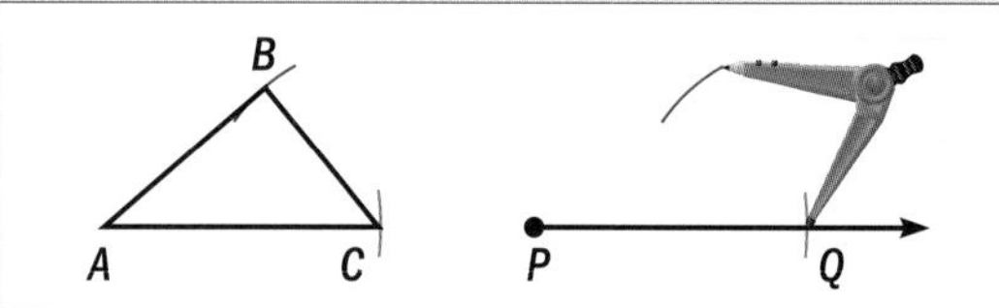

3 Draw an arc with center *A* through point *B*. Use the same compass setting to draw an arc with center *P*. Label point *R*. Connect *P* and *R*. Connect *R* and *Q*.

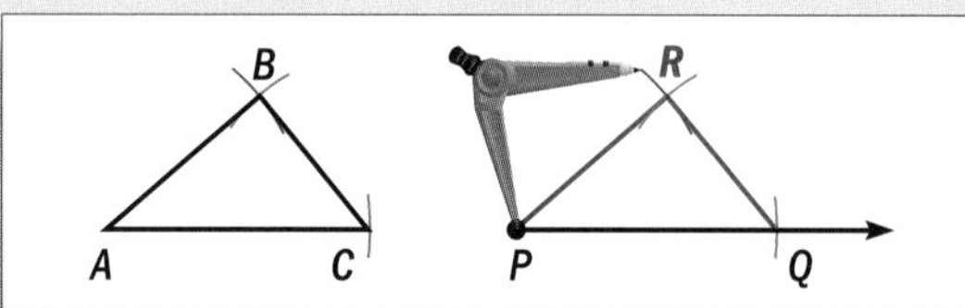

Your turn now **Draw a triangle that fits the description. Then use a compass and straightedge to copy the triangle.**

1. acute **2.** obtuse **3.** right

Stop and Think

4. Critical Thinking Measure the angles of each triangle you copied in Exercises 1–3. What do you notice? Explain.

5. Writing When you use a compass and straightedge to copy a triangle, what measures of the new triangle are identical to the old triangle?

Congruent Polygons

BEFORE	Now	WHY?
You identified polygons.	You'll identify and name congruent polygons.	So you can measure kites, as in Exs. 13 and 14.

congruent sides, p. 397
congruent angles, p. 397
corresponding parts, p. 397

INDIANA Academic Standards

- Geometry (8.4.1)

Congruent sides have equal lengths. **Congruent angles** have equal measures. The symbol ≅ means "is congruent to."

Congruent polygons have the same shape and size. Polygons are congruent if their *corresponding* angles and sides are congruent. **Corresponding parts** are in the same position in different figures. To name congruent polygons, list their corresponding vertices in the same order. In the diagram $\triangle KLM \cong \triangle PQR$.

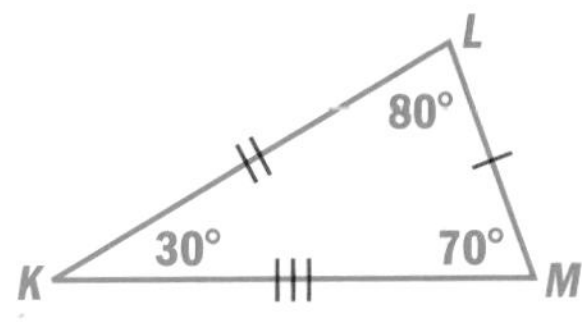

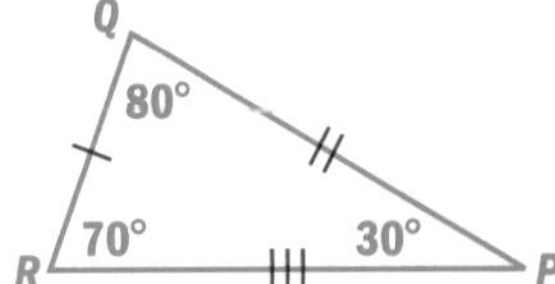

Corresponding angles are congruent.
$\angle K \cong \angle P$ $\angle L \cong \angle Q$ $\angle M \cong \angle R$

Corresponding sides are congruent.
$\overline{LM} \cong \overline{QR}$ $\overline{KL} \cong \overline{PQ}$ $\overline{KM} \cong \overline{PR}$

The side with endpoints *P* and *R*

Naming Corresponding Parts

In the frame below, quadrilateral *ABCD* ≅ quadrilateral *JKLM*. Name all pairs of corresponding angles and sides.

Solution

Corresponding angles are congruent.

$\angle A$, $\angle J$ $\angle B$, $\angle K$

$\angle C$, $\angle L$ $\angle D$, $\angle M$

Corresponding sides are congruent.

$\overline{AB}$, $\overline{JK}$ $\overline{BC}$, $\overline{KL}$

$\overline{CD}$, $\overline{LM}$ $\overline{DA}$, $\overline{MJ}$

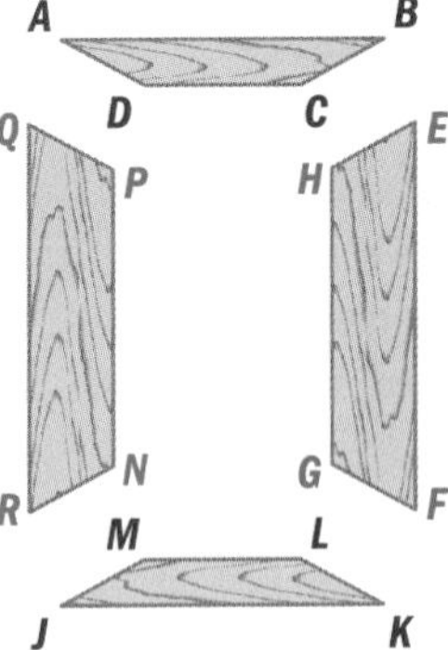

In Example 1, quadrilateral *EFGH* ≅ quadrilateral *QRNP*.

1. Name all pairs of corresponding angles and sides.

$\triangle JKL$ is read "triangle JKL" and refers to the triangle with vertices J, K, and L.

EXAMPLE 2 Using Congruent Polygons

$\triangle JKL \cong \triangle TSR$
Find $m\angle S$.

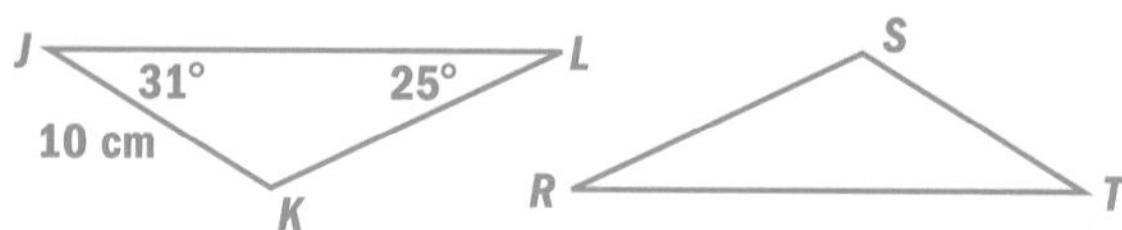

Solution

$\angle K$ and $\angle S$ are corresponding angles, so they have the same measure. Find $m\angle K$.

$m\angle J + m\angle K + m\angle L = 180°$	Sum of angle measures is 180°.
$31° + m\angle K + 25° = 180°$	Substitute given values.
$m\angle K + 56° = 180°$	Combine like terms.
$m\angle K = 124°$	Subtract 56° from each side.

ANSWER Because $m\angle K = m\angle S$, $m\angle S = 124°$.

Your turn now **Find the measure using the triangles in Example 2.**

2. length of $\overline{ST}$ **3.** $m\angle T$ **4.** $m\angle R$

Congruent Triangles You can use the special rules in the chart to tell whether triangles are congruent.

The angle between two sides is sometimes called the *included* angle. The side between two angles is sometimes called the *included* side.

Side-Side-Side (SSS)	If three sides of one triangle are congruent to three sides of another triangle, then the triangles are congruent.	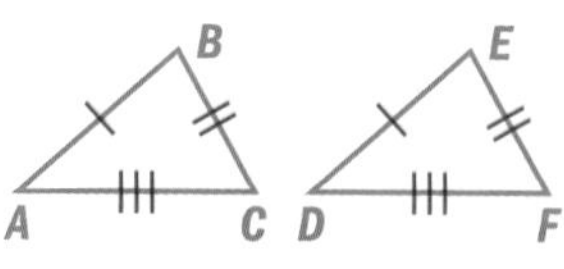 $\triangle ABC \cong \triangle DEF$
Side-Angle-Side (SAS)	If two sides and the angle between them in one triangle are congruent to two sides and the angle between them in another triangle, then the triangles are congruent.	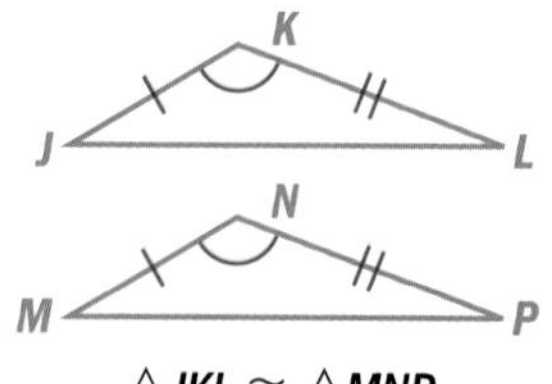 $\triangle JKL \cong \triangle MNP$
Angle-Side-Angle (ASA)	If two angles and the side between them in one triangle are congruent to two angles and the side between them in another triangle, then the triangles are congruent.	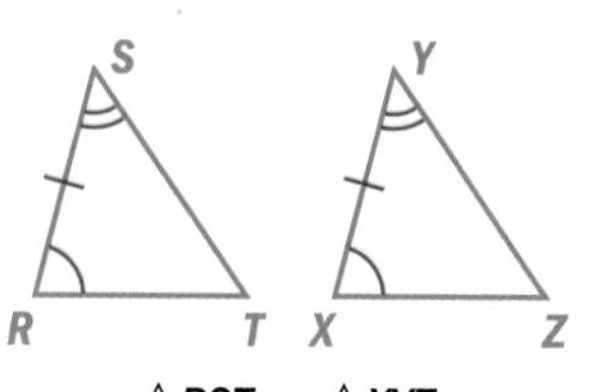 $\triangle RST \cong \triangle XYZ$

EXAMPLE 3 Identifying Congruent Triangles

Name the congruent triangles formed by the bridge cables, and explain how you know that they are congruent.

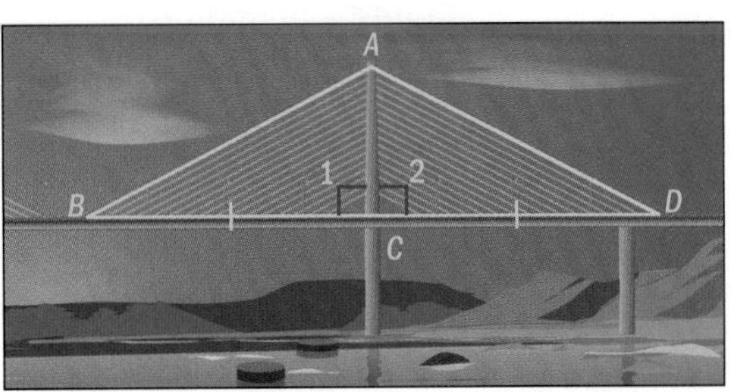

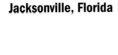

Dames Point Bridge
Jacksonville, Florida

$\overline{CB} \cong \overline{CD}$	Sides are congruent.
$\overline{AC} \cong \overline{AC}$	Side is congruent to itself.
$\angle 1 \cong \angle 2$	Right angles are congruent.

ANSWER $\triangle ACB \cong \triangle ACD$ by Side-Angle-Side.

8.5 Exercises

More Practice, p. 734

Getting Ready to Practice

Vocabulary **Copy and complete the statement.**

1. Two angles with the same measure are _?_.
2. _?_ are in the same position in different figures.

In the diagram, quadrilateral *KLMN* ≅ quadrilateral *SPQR*.

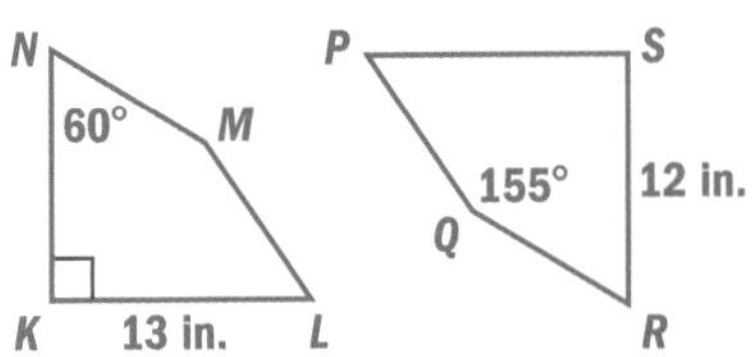

3. Name four pairs of congruent angles.
4. Find $m\angle S$.
5. Find the length of $\overline{NK}$.
6. Find $m\angle R$.
7. **Find the Error** Describe and correct the error in the solution.

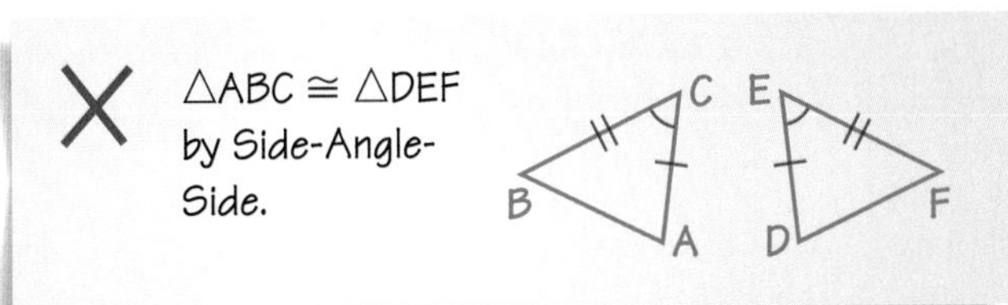

Example	Exercises
1	8-11
2	8-11
3	12-14

Online Resources
CLASSZONE.COM

· More Examples
· eTutorial Plus

Practice and Problem Solving

Measurement Quadrilateral *ABEF* ≅ quadrilateral *DGHC*. Find the unknown measure.

8. length of $\overline{AF}$
9. $m\angle C$
10. length of $\overline{HC}$
11. $m\angle A$

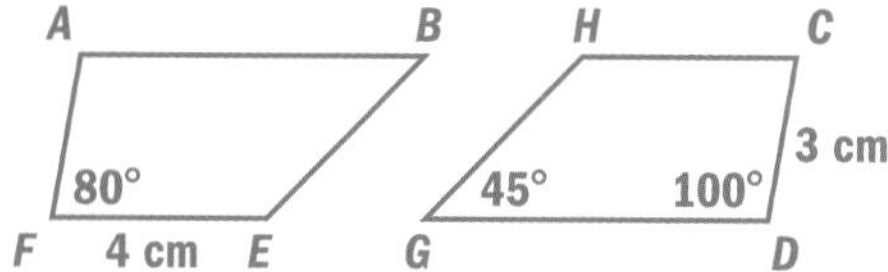

12. Name all the congruent triangles shown. Justify your answer.

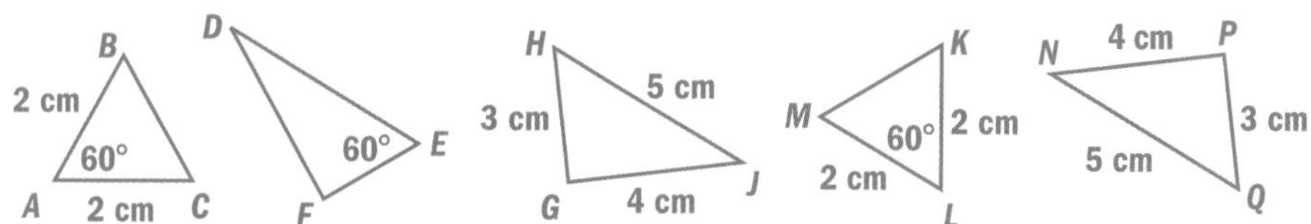

Kites Explain how you know the red triangles in the kite are congruent.

13.

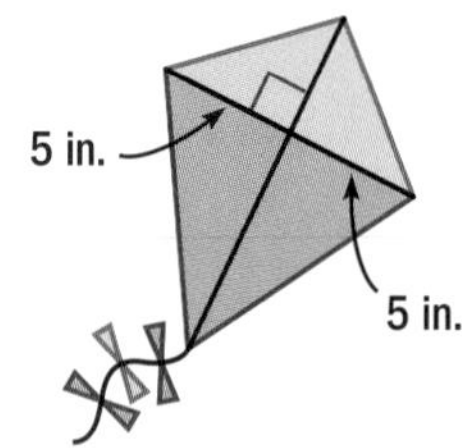

14.

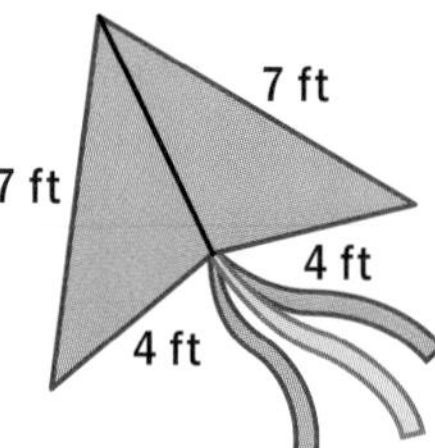

Critical Thinking Explain how you know the triangles are congruent. Then write an equation and solve for *x*.

15.

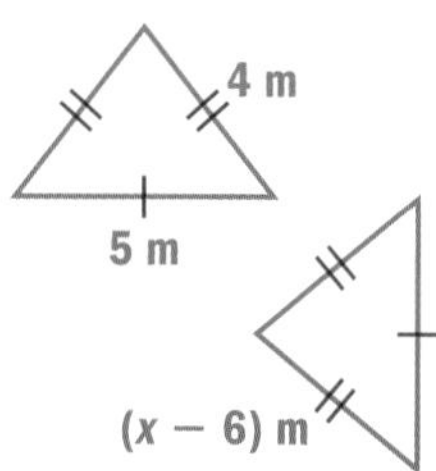

16.

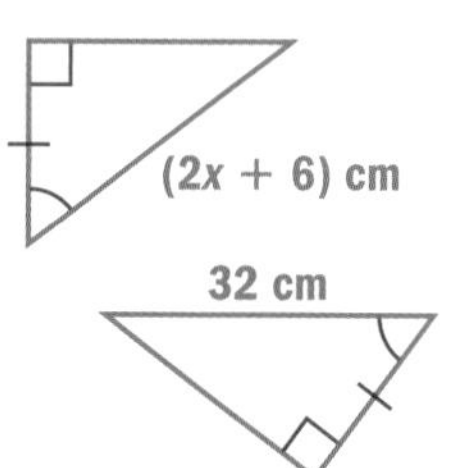

17.

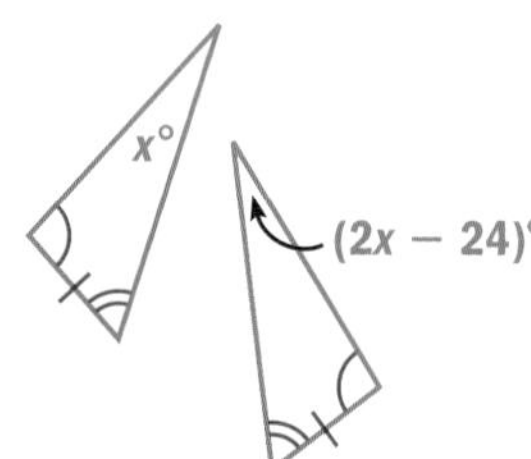

18. **Soccer Field** Some pieces of sod on a field are regular hexagons like the ones shown here. Explain how you know the regular hexagons are congruent.

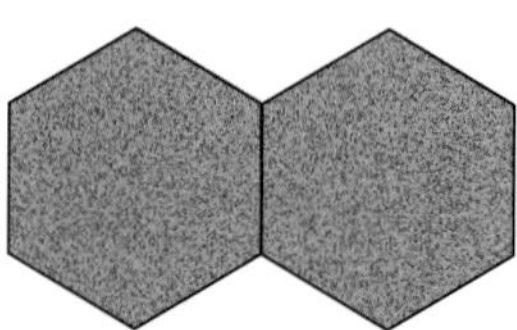

19. **Pockets** Two back pockets on a pair of jeans are congruent. Find $m\angle 1$.

What do you think? Sports

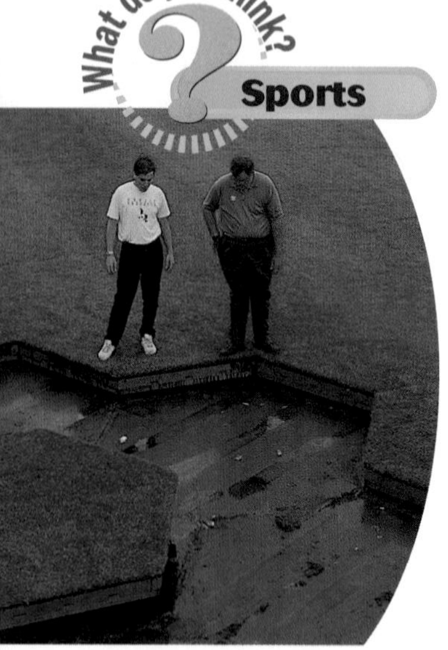

Soccer Field

In 1994, Michigan State University covered the floor of the Silverdome with natural grass for the World Cup tournament. Why do you think hexagons were used in the design?

20. **Pod Shelters** The panels of the pod shelter shown are equilateral triangles. The sides of each triangle are 7 feet long. Explain how you know the panels are congruent triangles.

21. **Challenge** Name the congruent triangles, and explain how you know that they are congruent.

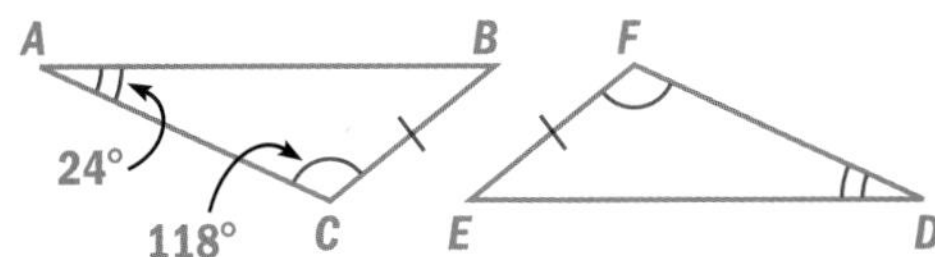

Mixed Review

22. Find 1.25% of 400.

23. Find 65% of 91. *(Lesson 7.7)*

24. If you pick a whole number at random from 1 to 100, what is the probability that the number is a multiple of 5? *(Lesson 7.8)*

Find the value of *x*. *(Lessons 8.3, 8.4)*

25.

26.

Basic Skills **Plot the point in a coordinate plane.**

27. $A(-9, 6)$ **28.** $B(-3, -5)$ **29.** $C(0, -4)$ **30.** $D(4, -1)$

Test-Taking Practice

INTERNET
State Test Practice
CLASSZONE.COM

31. **Multiple Choice** Polygon $ABCD \cong$ polygon $EFGH$. Find $m\angle C$.

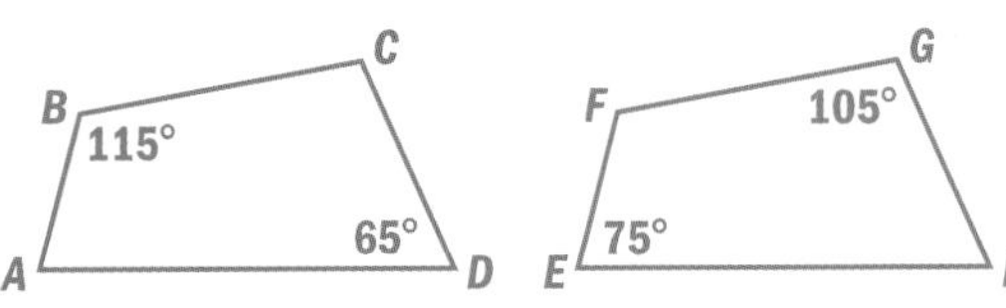

A. 65° **B.** 75° **C.** 105° **D.** 115°

32. **Short Response** Name the congruent triangles and explain how you know that they are congruent.

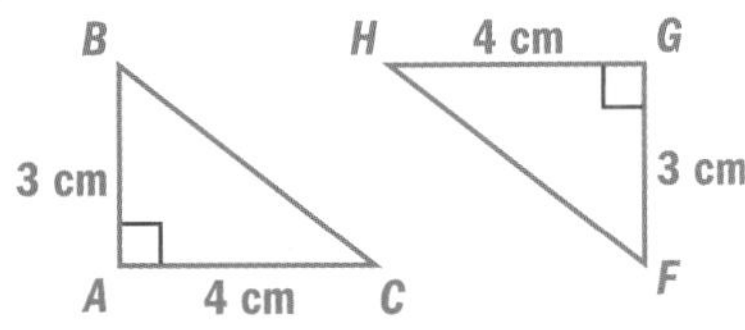

8.6 Problem Solving Strategies

- Guess, Check, and Revise
- Look for a Pattern
- Draw a Diagram
- Write an Equation
- Make a Model
- Act It Out
- Work Backward

Make a Model

Problem You are looking at a picture of a kaleidoscope image. The image includes six red shapes. Tell which red shapes are mirror images of shape 1.

1 Read and Understand

Read the problem carefully.

You need to decide which red shapes are mirror images of shape 1.

2 Make a Plan

Decide on a strategy to use.

You can identify the mirror images by making a model. Trace the kaleidoscope image. Then fold your tracing paper to see if two shapes are mirror images.

3 Solve the Problem

Reread the problem and make a model of the kaleidoscope image using tracing paper.

Trace the outline of the kaleidoscope image and the six red shapes. Also trace the lines that divide the image into six equal parts. Cut out the circle.

Fold the paper once so that shape 1 lies on top of shape 2. You can see that shape 1 and shape 2 line up with each other exactly when you fold the paper. So, shape 2 is a mirror image of shape 1.

Unfold the paper. Now fold it once so that shape 1 lies on top of shape 3. You can see that shape 1 and shape 3 do not line up with each other exactly when you fold the paper. So, shape 3 is not a mirror image of shape 1. Continue to test shapes around the circle

4 Look Back

Which shapes are a mirror images of shape 1? Did you do everything asked in the problem?

Practice the Strategy

Use the strategy *make a model.*

1. **Design** Sketch a kaleidoscope design that includes mirror images of a shape. Divide a circle into six equal parts to make your design. Identify the mirror images.

2. **Bowling Pins** Ten bowling pins are arranged in a triangle, as shown. Explain how you can make the triangle point to the left by moving only three pins.

3. **Seating Arrangements** Alan, David, Mary, Peter, and Scott are sitting on a bench. Alan is between Scott and David. Mary is next to Peter. There is only one person between Mary and Alan, but Mary is not next to Scott. Find two possible seating arrangements.

4. **Boxes** Four boxes of different sizes are stacked on a table, with the largest box on the bottom and the smallest box on the top. You need to move the entire stack of boxes to another table, but you can only move one box at a time. No box can touch the floor, and no box can support a larger box without breaking. You have one extra table to help you. List the moves it takes you to transfer the stack of boxes.

Mixed Problem Solving

Use any strategy to solve the problem.

5. **Hiking** You bring water on a hike. You drink a quarter of the water in the morning and a third of the remaining water at lunch time. In the afternoon, you drink two thirds of the water left in your container. When you get home, there are 16 fluid ounces of water. How much water did you bring on the hike?

6. **Club Planning** The Spanish Club meets every other week. The members decided to have a party during the fifth meeting. The first meeting took place on October 2. Find the date of the party.

7. **Test Scores** John has earned 92, 70, 95, 89, and 90 on his math tests this semester. What score must John receive on his next test to have a mean of 88?

8. **Numbers** You are helping your little sister with her math homework, but you can't read her writing very well. Her sevens and ones look exactly the same. She solved the problem below correctly. Decide which numerals are sevens and which are ones.

```
  211
+ 546
-----
  811
```

Reflections and Symmetry

BEFORE	Now	WHY?
You plotted points in a coordinate plane.	You'll reflect figures and identify lines of symmetry.	So you can find symmetry in starfish, as in Example 4b.

Word Watch

reflection, p. 404
transformation, p. 404
image, p. 404
line symmetry, p. 406

INDIANA Academic Standards

- Geometry (8.4.4)

In the Real World

Reflections The photo illustrates a reflection. A **reflection** creates a mirror image of each point of a figure.

A reflection is a **transformation**, an operation that changes a figure into another figure. The new figure created is called the **image**.

EXAMPLE 1 Identifying a Reflection

Tell whether the red figure is a reflection of the blue figure.

a. 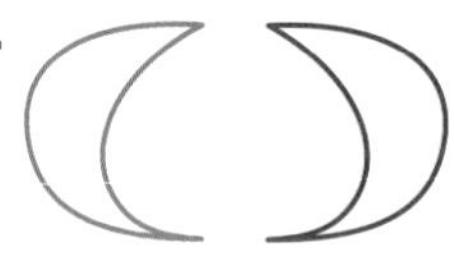

The figure is a reflection.

b. 

The figure is *not* a reflection.

You can describe reflections of figures in a coordinate plane using coordinate notation. The notation $A \rightarrow A'$ is read "*A* goes to *A* prime."

EXAMPLE 2 Reflecting in the y-Axis

Quadrilateral *ABCD* has been reflected in the *y*-axis. Write the coordinates of each vertex of quadrilateral *ABCD* and its image, quadrilateral *A′B′C′D′*.

Solution

Original		Image
$A(-1, 1)$	$\rightarrow$	$A'(1, 1)$
$B(-3, 1)$	$\rightarrow$	$B'(3, 1)$
$C(-4, 3)$	$\rightarrow$	$C'(4, 3)$
$D(-2, 4)$	$\rightarrow$	$D'(2, 4)$

You may have noticed in Example 2 that when a point is reflected in the y-axis, its x-coordinate is multiplied by -1.

Reflections

Reflection in the *x*-axis

Words To reflect a point in the x-axis, multiply its y-coordinate by -1.

	Original		Image
Algebra	(x, y)	$\rightarrow$	$(x, -y)$

Reflection in the *y*-axis

Words To reflect a point in the y-axis, multiply its x-coordinate by -1.

	Original		Image
Algebra	(x, y)	$\rightarrow$	$(-x, y)$

EXAMPLE 3 Reflecting in the x-Axis

Reflect $\triangle PQR$ in the *x*-axis.

Solution

Multiply each y-coordinate by -1.

Original		Image
(x, y)	$\rightarrow$	$(x, -y)$
$P(1, 3)$	$\rightarrow$	$P'(1, -3)$
$Q(4, 4)$	$\rightarrow$	$Q'(4, -4)$
$R(5, 2)$	$\rightarrow$	$R'(5, -2)$

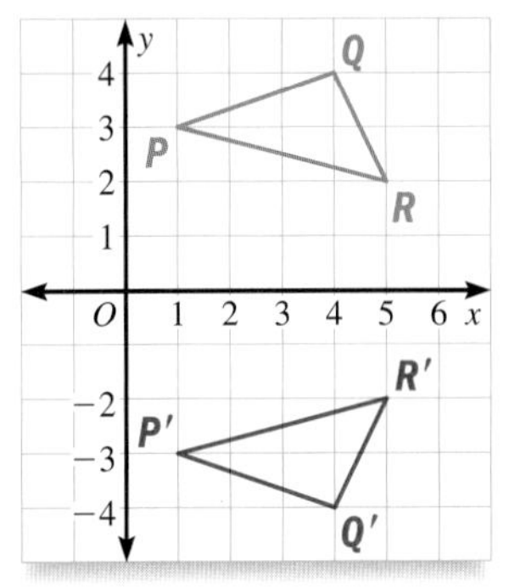

The graph shows $\triangle PQR$ and its reflection $\triangle P'Q'R'$.

Your turn now **Graph the polygon and its image.**

1. Graph the triangle with vertices $J(0, 1)$, $K(0, 4)$, and $L(5, 2)$. Reflect the triangle in the y-axis.
2. Graph the quadrilateral with vertices $S(-3, 2)$, $T(-1, 4)$, $U(-4, 5)$, and $V(-5, 3)$. Reflect the quadrilateral in the x-axis.

Symmetry A figure has **line symmetry** if one half of the figure is a mirror image of the other half. A line of symmetry divides the figure into two congruent parts that are mirror images of each other.

EXAMPLE 4 Identifying Lines of Symmetry

How many lines of symmetry does the picture have?

a. one line of symmetry

b. five lines of symmetry

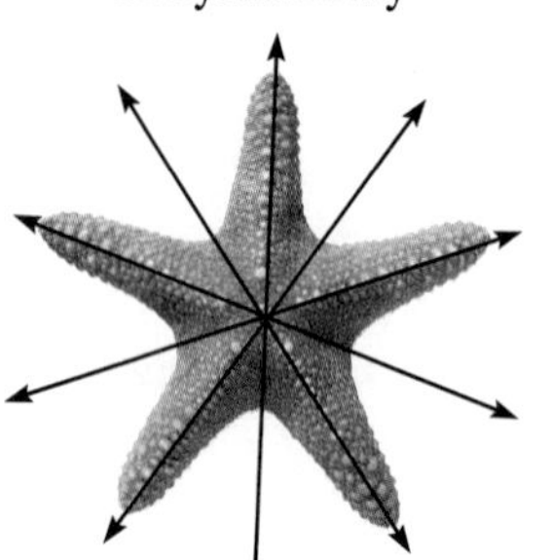

c. no lines of symmetry

8.6 Exercises

More Practice, p. 734

Getting Ready to Practice

Vocabulary Copy and complete the statement.

1. A(n) _?_ creates a mirror image of the original figure.
2. A(n) _?_ is an operation that changes a figure into another figure.

Tell whether the red figure is a reflection of the blue figure.

3. 
4. 
5. 

How many lines of symmetry does the design have?

6. 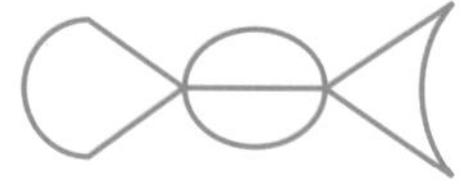
7. 
8. 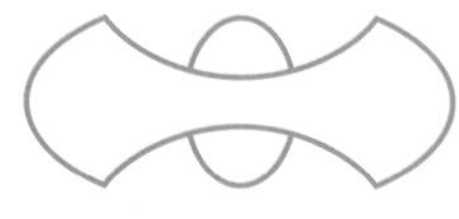

Graph the polygon. Then graph its reflection in the given axis.

9. $K(2, 7), L(3, 3), M(6, 4), N(6, 9)$; x-axis
10. $F(-8, 8), G(-4, 7), H(-3, 3), I(-7, 4)$; y-axis

Practice and Problem Solving

HELP with Homework

Example	Exercises
1	23
2	13–14
3	11–12
4	15–20

Online Resources CLASSZONE.COM

- More Examples
- eTutorial Plus

Graph the polygon. Then graph its reflection in the given axis.

11. $A(3, 6)$, $B(6, 3)$, $C(5, 0)$, $D(1, 1)$; x-axis

12. $Q(-1, 3)$, $R(-3, 6)$, $S(-6, 4)$, $T(-6, 0)$; x-axis

13. $B(2, -1)$, $C(5, 0)$, $D(7, -2)$, $E(0, -6)$; y-axis

14. $P(0, 0)$, $Q(4, 1)$, $R(7, -3)$, $S(2, -7)$; y-axis

Sports **How many lines of symmetry does the diagram have?**

15.

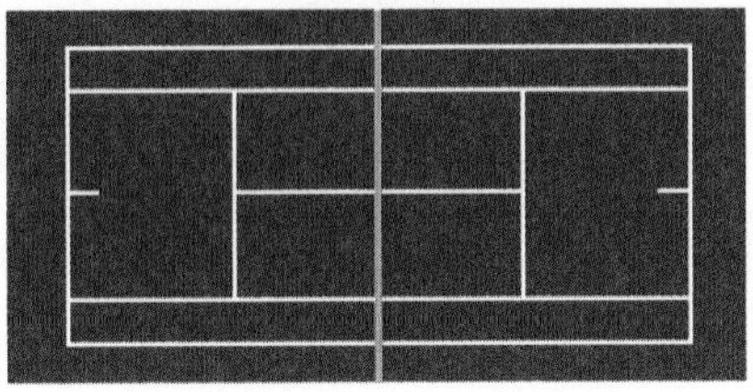

16.

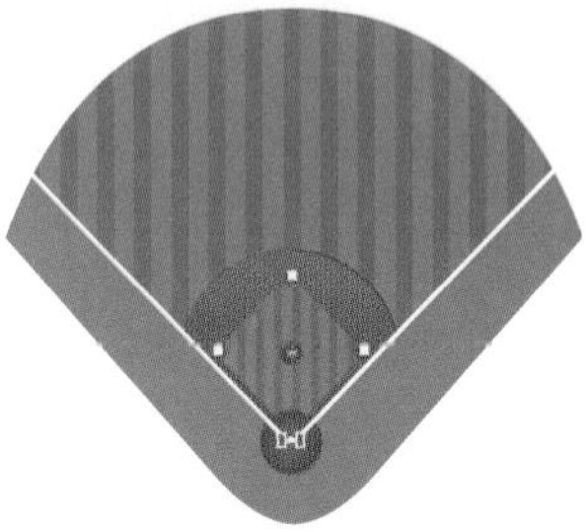

17. Illustrate Draw a quadrilateral with exactly four lines of symmetry. What kind of quadrilateral is this?

Extended Problem Solving **For Exercises 18–20, use the table.**

Sides	3	4	5	6	8
Regular Polygon	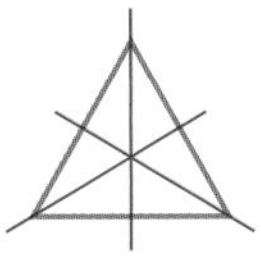	?	?	?	?
Lines of Symmetry	?	?	?	?	?

18. Sketch Copy the table and sketch a regular polygon with the given number of sides in each column. Draw all the lines of symmetry.

19. Evaluate Count the lines of symmetry. Complete the table.

20. Look for a Pattern How is the number of sides related to the number of lines of symmetry?

21. Make a Model Write your name at the top of a piece of tracing paper. Fold the paper and trace your name to create a reflection. Unfold the paper to see your name and its reflection.

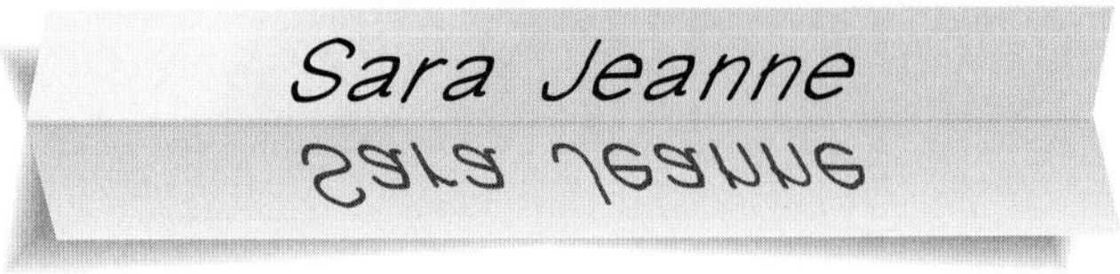

22. **Challenge** Graph the polygon with vertices $S(-6, 0)$, $T(0, 6)$, $V(6, 0)$, $W(2, -4)$, and $X(-2, -4)$. Reflect the polygon in the x-axis and graph its image in the same coordinate plane.

23. **Critical Thinking** A polygon has vertices $A(1, -2)$, $B(5, -1)$, $C(8, -4)$, $D(7, -7)$, and $E(4, -8)$. Reflect the polygon in the x-axis and find the vertices of its image. Then reflect the image in the y-axis. Graph the new image. Is the third polygon a reflection of the original? Explain.

Mixed Review 

In Exercises 24 and 25, find the number. *(Lesson 7.3)*

24. What is 0.8% of 500?

25. 756 is what percent of 270?

26. Find the sum of the angle measures in a 9-gon. *(Lesson 8.4)*

27. Find the measure of one angle in a regular 12-gon. *(Lesson 8.4)*

Test-Taking Practice 

28. **Multiple Choice** Which figure is a reflected image of figure D?

    A. figure A　　**B.** figure B

    C. figure C　　**D.** none

29. **Short Response** Copy figure A and draw all its lines of symmetry. Where do the lines intersect?

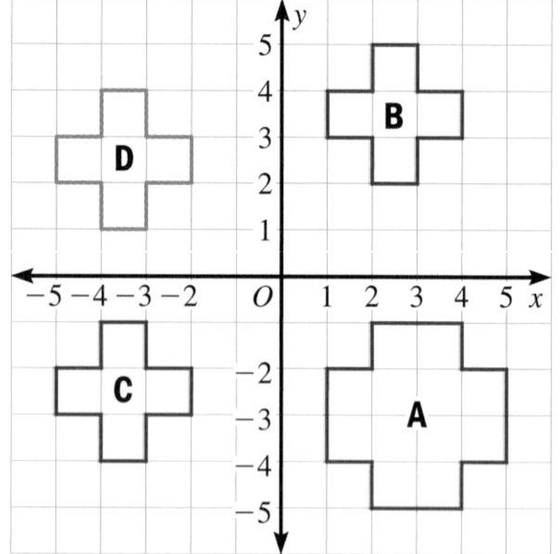

Deep Reflections

Use a mirror to read this quotation from William Shakespeare.

butbyreflection...
...theeyeseesnotitself
...theeyeseesnotitself...
butbyreflection...

Translations and Rotations

BEFORE	Now	WHY?
You reflected figures in a coordinate plane.	You'll translate or rotate figures in a coordinate plane.	So you can describe origami models, as in Exs. 5–6.

translation, p. 409
rotation, p. 410

INDIANA Academic Standards

- Geometry (8.4.4)

Activity You can see how moving a triangle changes its vertices.

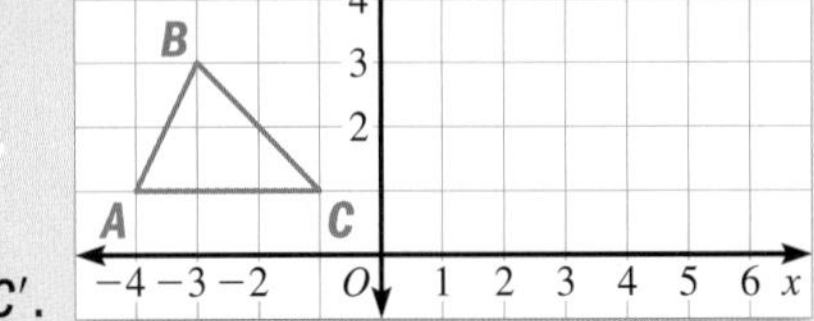

1. Graph an image of *A* by moving it 7 units to the right and 2 units up. Plot the new vertex and label it *A*′.

2. Repeat Step 1 with *B* and *C*. Then connect the vertices to form $\triangle A'B'C'$.

3. How are the coordinates of *A*, *B*, and *C* related to *A*′, *B*′, and *C*′?

In the activity, you transformed $\triangle ABC$ by *sliding* it. A **translation** is a transformation that moves each point of a figure the same distance in the same direction. The image is congruent to the original figure.

To translate a figure in a coordinate plane, you change the coordinates of its points. When *a* and *b* are positive, you can use the guidelines below.

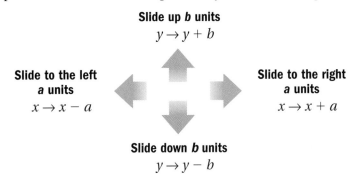

Slide up *b* units
$y \to y + b$

Slide to the left *a* units
$x \to x - a$

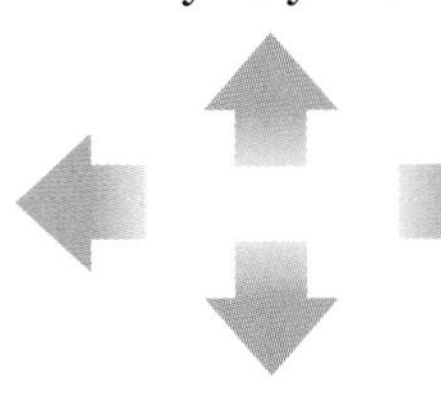

Slide to the right *a* units
$x \to x + a$

Slide down *b* units
$y \to y - b$

EXAMPLE 1 Using Coordinate Notation

Describe the translation from the blue figure to the red figure.

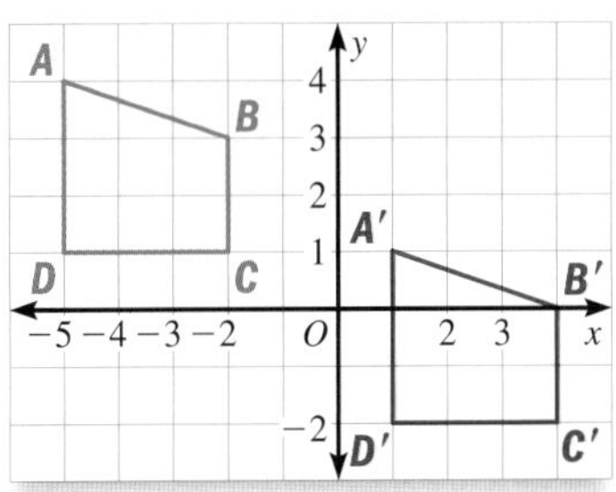

Solution

Each point moves 6 units to the right and 3 units down. The translation is

$(x, y) \to (x + 6, y - 3)$.

Rotations A **rotation** is a transformation that turns each point of a figure the same number of degrees around a common point. In this lesson, figures will always be turned around the origin.

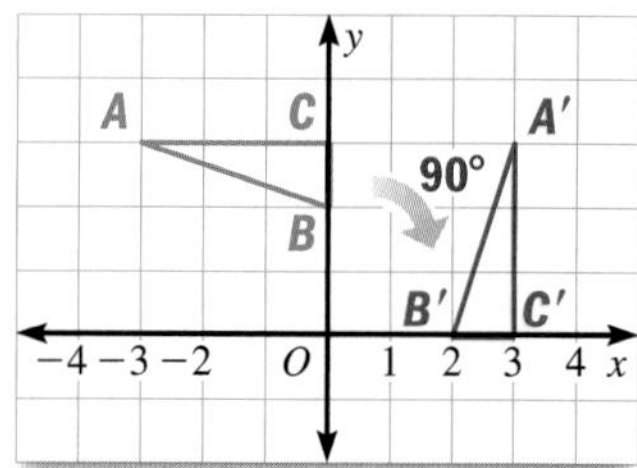

90° Rotations

90° Clockwise Rotation

Words To rotate a point 90° *clockwise,* switch the coordinates, then multiply the new y-coordinate by -1.

Numbers $P(6, 2) \rightarrow P'(2, -6)$ **Algebra** $P(x, y) \rightarrow P'(y, -x)$

90° Counterclockwise Rotation

Words To rotate a point 90° *counterclockwise,* switch the coordinates, then multiply the new x-coordinate by -1.

Numbers $P(5, 3) \rightarrow P'(-3, 5)$ **Algebra** $P(x, y) \rightarrow P'(-y, x)$

with Reading

Clockwise is the direction the hands on a clock turn. Counterclockwise is the opposite direction.

EXAMPLE 2 **Rotating 90° Clockwise**

Rotate quadrilateral *FGHJ* 90° clockwise.

Solution

Original		**Image**
(x, y)	$\rightarrow$	$(y, -x)$
$F(2, 2)$	$\rightarrow$	$F'(2, -2)$
$G(2, 4)$	$\rightarrow$	$G'(4, -2)$
$H(4, 4)$	$\rightarrow$	$H'(4, -4)$
$J(5, 2)$	$\rightarrow$	$J'(2, -5)$

The graph shows $FGHJ$ and $F'G'H'J'$.

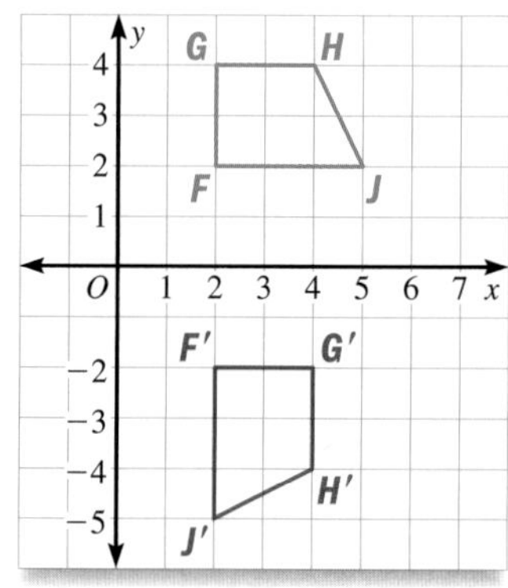

Your turn now **Graph the figure with the given vertices and its image after the rotation.**

1. $A(1, 1)$, $B(3, 1)$, $C(3, 3)$, and $D(1, 4)$; 90° clockwise
2. $K(-1, 3)$, $L(1, 5)$, and $M(2, 3)$; 90° counterclockwise

180° Rotation

Words To rotate a point 180°, multiply its coordinates by -1.

Numbers $P(4, 1) \rightarrow P'(-4, -1)$ **Algebra** $P(x, y) \rightarrow P'(-x, -y)$

EXAMPLE 3 **Rotating 180°**

Rotate $\triangle ABC$ 180°.

Solution

Original		**Image**
(x, y)	$\rightarrow$	$(-x, -y)$
$A(-6, 0)$	$\rightarrow$	$A'(6, 0)$
$B(-5, 2)$	$\rightarrow$	$B'(5, -2)$
$C(-1, 3)$	$\rightarrow$	$C'(1, -3)$

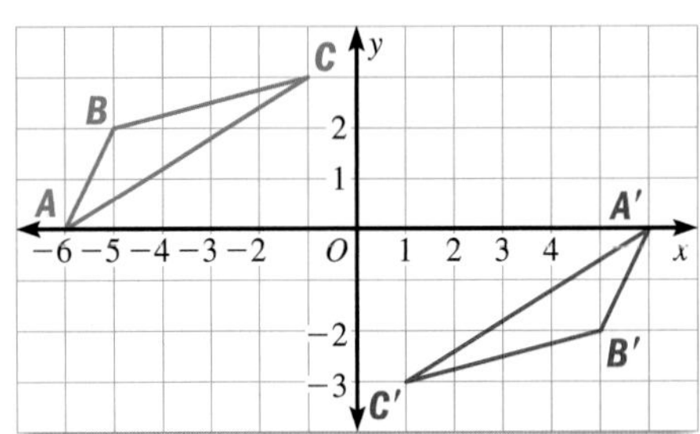

The graph shows $\triangle ABC$ and $\triangle A'B'C'$.

8.7 Exercises

More Practice, p. 734

Getting Ready to Practice

Reflection is a **Fl**ip.
Rotation is a **T**urn.
Translation is a **Sl**ide.

Vocabulary **Name the transformation shown in the graph.**

1.

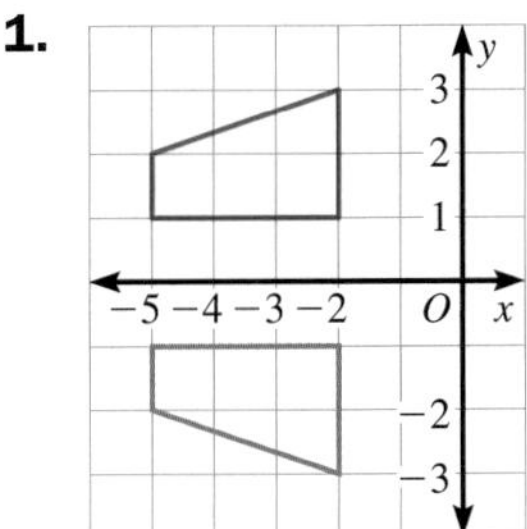

2.

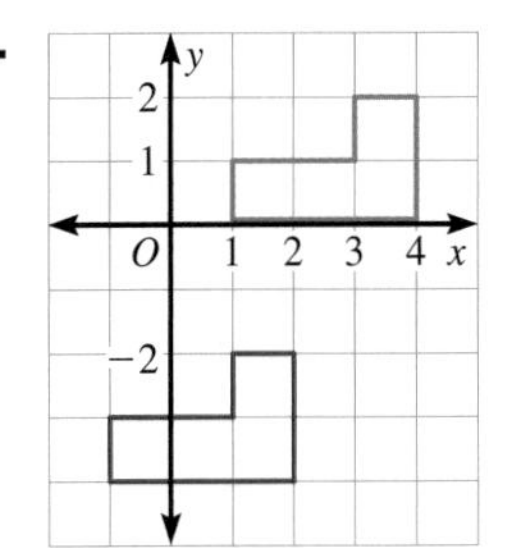

3.

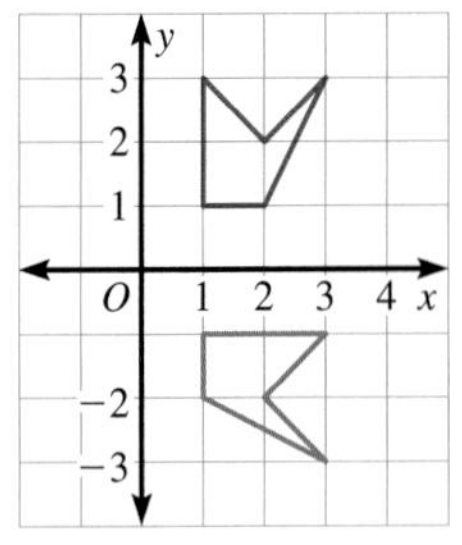

4. **Guided Problem Solving** Rotate $\triangle RST$ 90° counterclockwise.

(1) Graph $\triangle RST$ with vertices $R(-2, -1)$, $S(-5, -2)$, and $T(-4, 2)$.

(2) Find the vertices of the triangle's image.

(3) Graph $\triangle R'S'T'$, the image of $\triangle RST$ after rotation.

Practice and Problem Solving

Example	Exercises
1	15–16
2	20, 23
3	19, 22

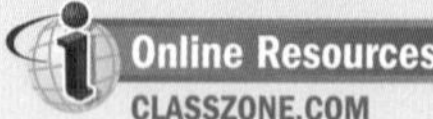

CLASSZONE.COM

· More Examples
· eTutorial Plus

Origami **Describe the transformation shown in the origami model.**

5. 

6. 

Name the type of transformation modeled by the action.

7. riding down an escalator

8. passing food around a table

9. making a handprint in clay

10. playing checkers

11. opening a combination lock

12. going down a water slide

13. riding a carousel

14. looking in a mirror

Use coordinate notation to describe the translation from the blue figure to the red figure.

15. 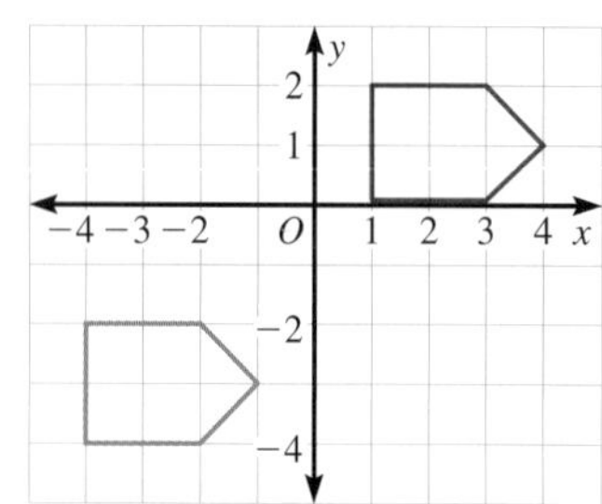

16. 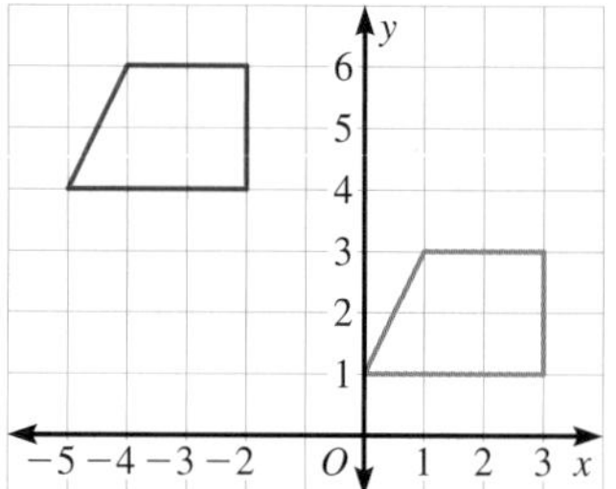

17. $\triangle PQR$ has vertices $P(0, -1)$, $Q(3, -1)$, and $R(5, -3)$. Find the vertices of its image after the translation $(x, y) \to (x - 5, y + 1)$.

18. $\triangle LMN$ has vertices $L(4, 2)$, $M(0, 3)$, and $N(1, 1)$. Find the vertices of its image after the translation $(x, y) \to (x + 1, y - 6)$.

Graph $\triangle LMN$ with vertices $L(2, 0)$, $M(2, 3)$, and $N(6, 0)$. Then graph its image after the given transformation.

19. Rotate 180°.

20. Rotate 90° counterclockwise.

21. Translate using $(x, y) \to (x - 3, y - 4)$.

22. Rotate 180° then translate using $(x, y) \to (x + 1, y + 1)$.

23. Rotate 90° clockwise three times.

24. Translate using $(x, y) \to (x + 3, y)$ then rotate 180°.

For help with quadrants, see p. 91.

25. **Writing** Point A in Quadrant II is rotated 180°. Find the quadrant of point A'. Point B in Quadrant IV is rotated 90° clockwise. Find the quadrant of point B'. Explain your reasoning.

26. **Challenge** The figure is the image of a triangle rotated 90° clockwise and reflected in the y-axis. Graph the original figure.

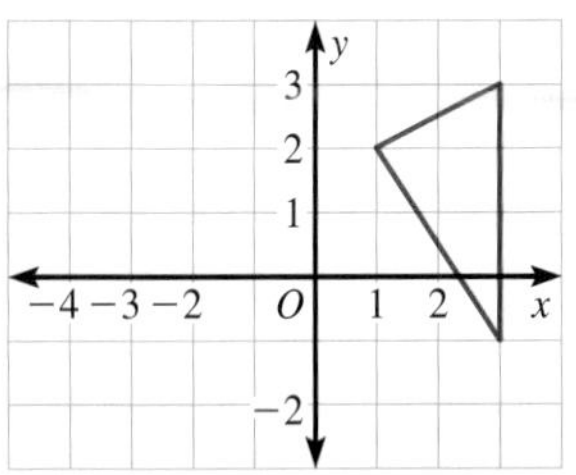

27. **Multiple Methods** Describe four different transformations of the blue square to the red square. You may include combinations of transformations.

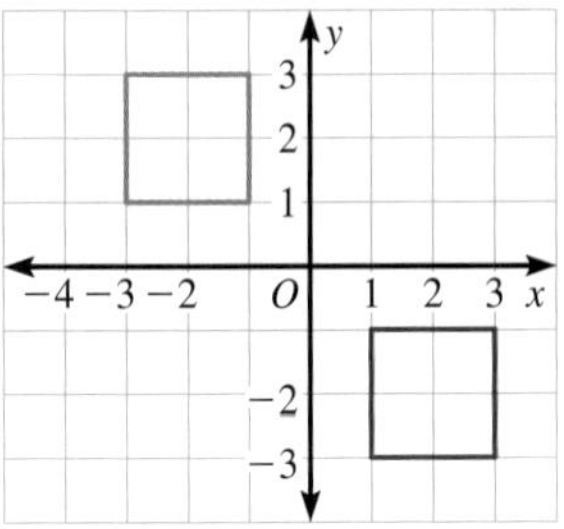

Mixed Review

Solve the proportion. *(Lesson 7.2)*

28. $\frac{a}{25} = \frac{24}{200}$ **29.** $\frac{32}{9} = \frac{c}{108}$ **30.** $\frac{7}{60} = \frac{154}{d}$

Find the value of x. Classify the triangle by its angles. *(Lesson 8.2)*

31.

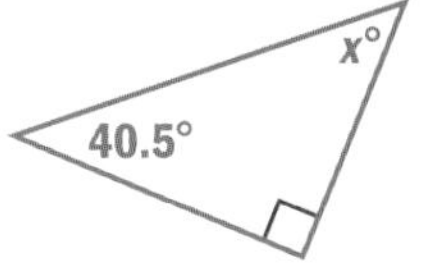

32.

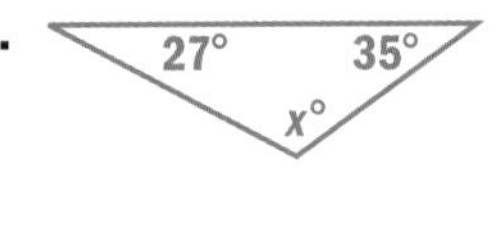

33.

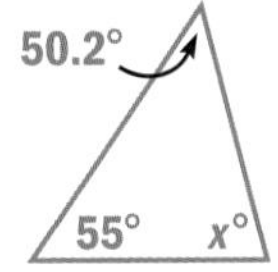

Basic Skills **Find the mean, median, and mode(s).**

34. 39, 45, 43, 28, 45, 48, 39, 45 **35.** 110, 108, 118, 110, 105

Test-Taking Practice

INTERNET State Test Practice CLASSZONE.COM

36. **Extended Response** Rotate the figure 90° clockwise. Reflect the image in the y-axis. Graph the final image. Complete the rule for the double transformation you performed.

$(x, y) \rightarrow (\underline{?}, \underline{?})$

Explain your reasoning.

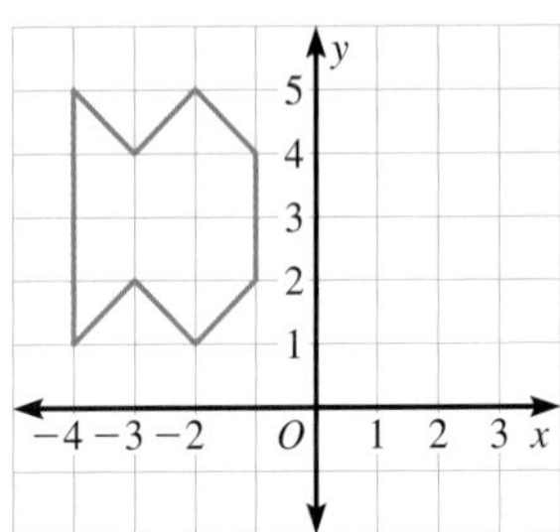

Tessellations

GOAL Decide if a shape tessellates. Create tessellations.

tessellation, p. 414

INDIANA Academic Standards

- Geometry (8.4.4)

Tessellations You can use reflections, rotations, and translations to create a *tessellation*, like the one shown here. A **tessellation** is a repeating pattern of figures that covers a plane with no gaps or overlaps. If a figure can be used to create a tessellation, you say the figure *tessellates*.

EXAMPLE 1 Identifying Tessellating Polygons

Tell whether the polygon tessellates.

a.

Yes, you can create a tessellation by translating a rectangle.

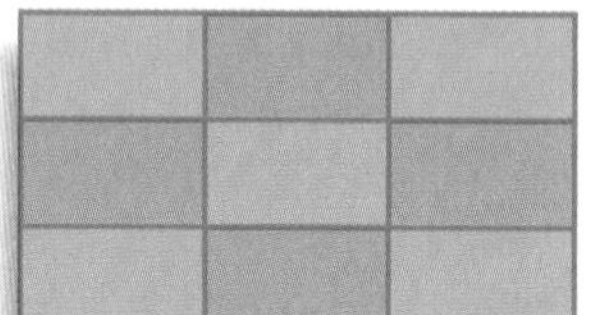

b.

No, regular pentagons will not cover the plane without gaps or overlaps.

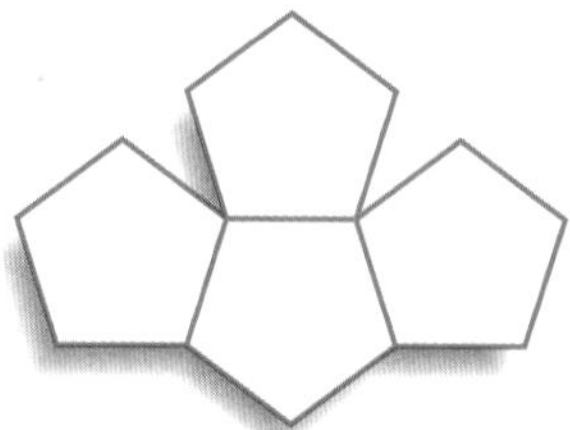

You can create a tessellation by altering a polygon that tessellates.

EXAMPLE 2 Creating a Tessellation

Alter a parallelogram to create a tessellation.

Cut a triangle from the parallelogram.

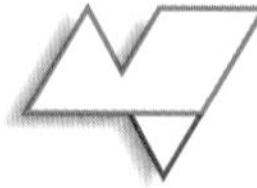

Slide the triangle to the opposite side.

Translate the figure to create a tessellation.

EXAMPLE 3 Creating a Tessellation

Create a tessellation by altering an equilateral triangle.

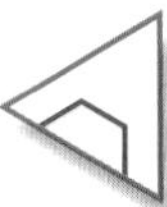

Cut a piece from the triangle.

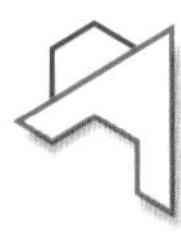

Slide the piece to another side.

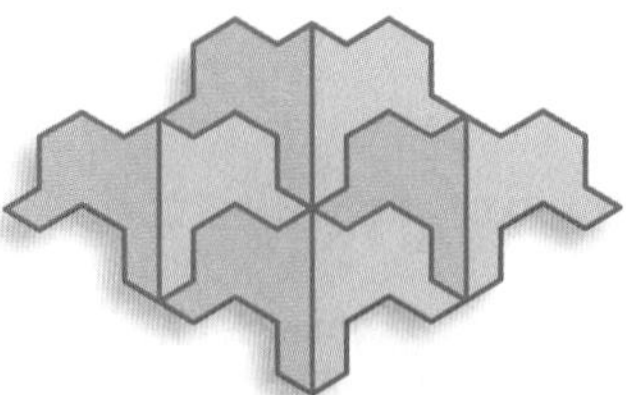

Reflect the figure then translate the pair.

Exercises

Tell whether the figure tessellates.

1. 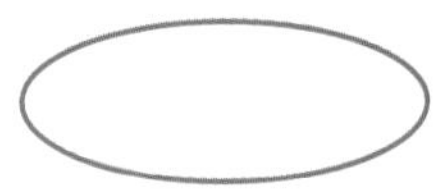

2. 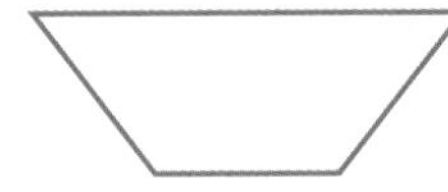

3. 

4. Explain how you can transform the blue shape to create the tessellation.

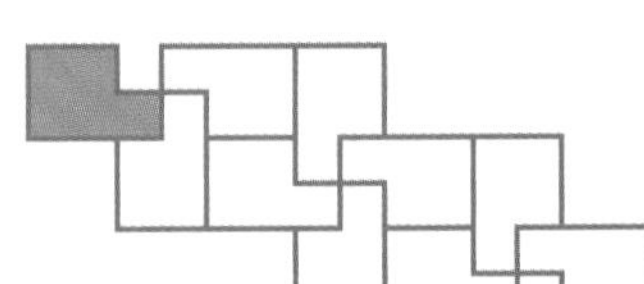

5. Copy and continue the pattern.

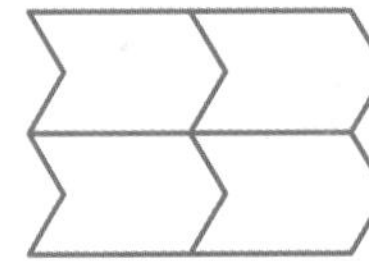

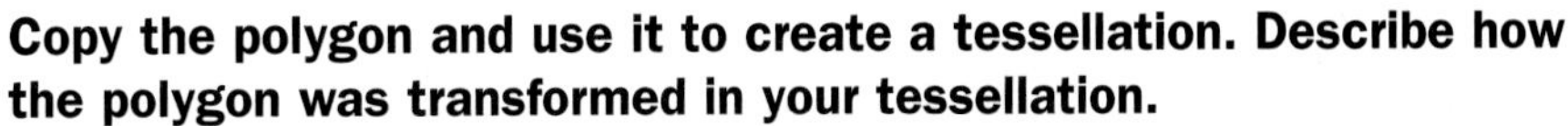

Copy the polygon and use it to create a tessellation. Describe how the polygon was transformed in your tessellation.

6. 

7. 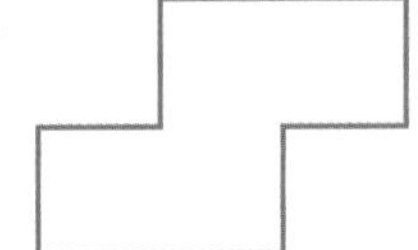

8. 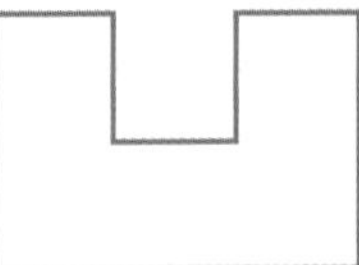

9. **Make a Model** Create a tessellation by altering a rectangle.

10. Create a tessellation by altering a parallelogram that is not a rectangle.

11. Create two different tessellations using the shape at the right.

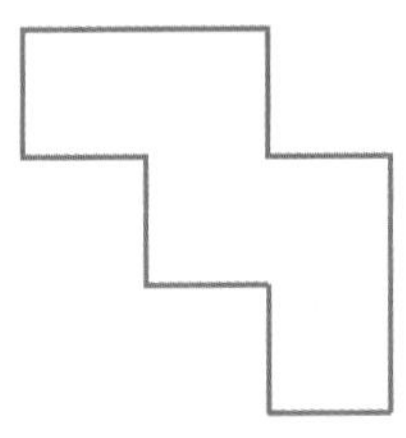

Similarity and Dilations

BEFORE	Now	WHY?
You used congruent polygons to find missing measures.	You'll use similar polygons to find missing measures.	So you can find the height of a sand castle, as in Ex. 14.

similar polygons, p. 416
dilation, p. 418
scale factor, p. 418

INDIANA Academic Standards
- Geometry (8.4.4)
- Measurement (8.5.3)

In the Real World

Television Screens The television screens shown here are different sizes, but they have the same shape. How are they related?

Similar polygons have the same shape, but they can be different sizes. The symbol ~ means "is similar to." When you name similar polygons, list their corresponding vertices in the same order.

Similar Polygons

$\triangle ABC \sim \triangle XYZ$

Corresponding angles are congruent.

$\angle A \cong \angle X \quad \angle B \cong \angle Y \quad \angle C \cong \angle Z$

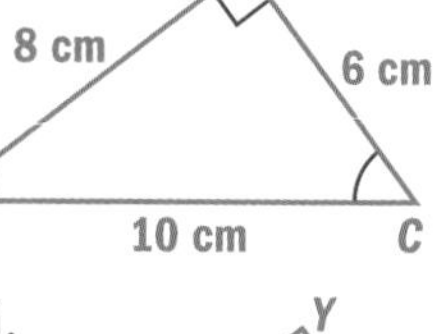

Corresponding side lengths are proportional.

$\frac{AB}{XY} = \frac{BC}{YZ} \quad \frac{BC}{YZ} = \frac{AC}{XZ} \quad \frac{AC}{XZ} = \frac{AB}{XY}$

EXAMPLE 1 Identifying Similar Polygons

Tell whether the television screens are similar.

(1) Corresponding angles are congruent. Each angle measures 90°.
$\angle A \cong \angle E \quad \angle B \cong \angle F \quad \angle C \cong \angle G \quad \angle D \cong \angle H$

(2) Corresponding side lengths are proportional.

$$\frac{30 \text{ inches}}{18 \text{ inches}} = \frac{40 \text{ inches}}{24 \text{ inches}}$$

$$720 = 720$$

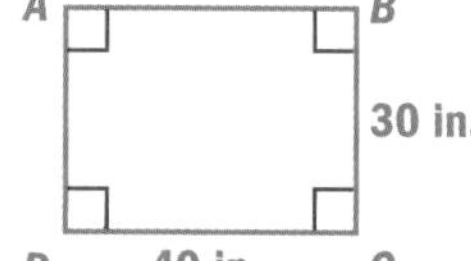

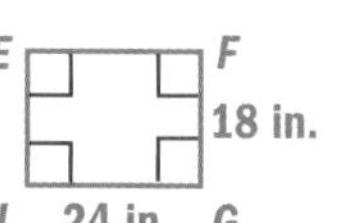

ANSWER Quadrilateral $ABCD \sim$ quadrilateral $EFGH$

For help with writing and solving proportions, see p. 322.

EXAMPLE 2 Using Similar Triangles

In the diagram, $\triangle KLM \sim \triangle NPQ$. Find the value of *y*.

Corresponding side lengths are proportional.

$$\frac{KL}{NP} = \frac{LM}{PQ}$$ **Write a proportion.**

$$\frac{y}{12} = \frac{10}{5}$$ **Substitute given values.**

$$y = 24$$ **Solve the proportion.**

ANSWER The value of *y* is 24 meters.

Your turn now Find the value of *x*.

1. Quadrilateral $ABCD \sim$ quadrilateral $FGHJ$

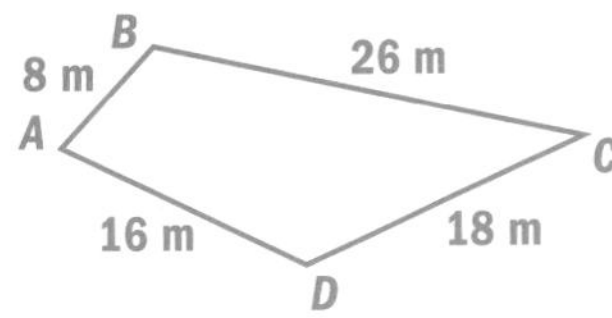

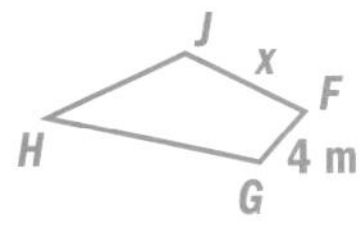

EXAMPLE 3 Using Indirect Measurement

Height Alma is 5 feet tall and casts a 7 foot shadow. At the same time, a tree casts a 14 foot shadow. The triangles formed are similar. Find the height of the tree.

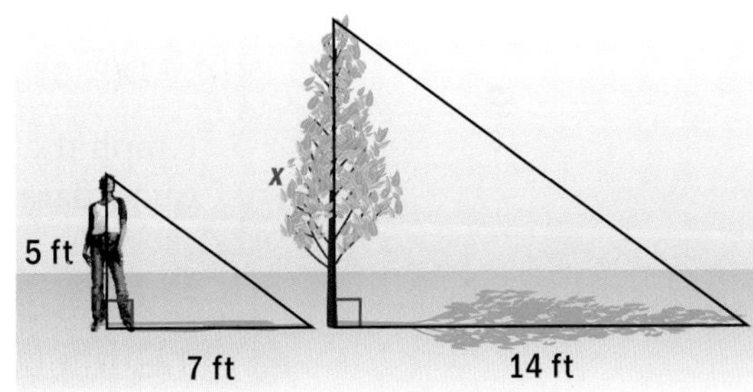

Solution

You can use a proportion to find the height of the tree.

$$\frac{\text{Tree's height}}{\text{Alma's height}} = \frac{\text{Length of tree's shadow}}{\text{Length of Alma's shadow}}$$ **Write a proportion.**

$$\frac{x \text{ feet}}{5 \text{ feet}} = \frac{14 \text{ feet}}{7 \text{ feet}}$$ **Substitute given values.**

$$x = 10$$ **Solve the proportion.**

ANSWER The tree is 10 feet tall.

Dilations A **dilation** stretches or shrinks a figure. The image created by a dilation is similar to the original figure. The **scale factor** of a dilation is the ratio of corresponding side lengths. In this course, the center of dilation will always be the origin.

Dilation

Words To dilate a polygon, multiply the coordinates of each vertex by the scale factor k and connect the vertices.

Numbers $P(4, 1) \rightarrow P'(8, 2)$ **Algebra** $P(x, y) \rightarrow P'(kx, ky)$

Watch Out!

The scale factor is the ratio of corresponding side lengths: $\dfrac{\text{after dilation}}{\text{before dilation}}$

EXAMPLE 4 Dilating a Polygon

Quadrilateral *ABCD* has vertices $A(-1, -1)$, $B(0, 1)$, $C(2, 2)$, and $D(3, 0)$. Dilate using a scale factor of 3.

Solution

Graph the quadrilateral. Find the vertices of the image.

Original		Image
(x, y)	$\rightarrow$	$(3x, 3y)$
$A(-1, -1)$	$\rightarrow$	$A'(-3, -3)$
$B(0, 1)$	$\rightarrow$	$B'(0, 3)$
$C(2, 2)$	$\rightarrow$	$C'(6, 6)$
$D(3, 0)$	$\rightarrow$	$D'(9, 0)$

Graph the image of the quadrilateral.

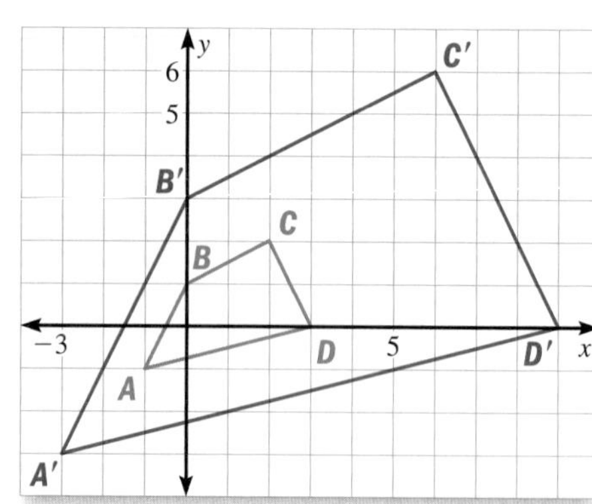

Your turn now **Graph the polygon with the given vertices. Then graph its image after dilation by the scale factor *k*.**

2. Triangle RST has vertices $R(1, 1)$, $S(3, 2)$, and $T(2, 3)$; $k = 2$.
3. Quadrilateral $MNPQ$ has vertices $M(1, 0)$, $N(0, -1)$, $P(-1, 0)$, and $Q(0, 1)$; $k = 4$.
4. Triangle JKL has vertices $J(0, 2)$, $K(6, 4)$, and $L(2, -2)$; $k = \frac{1}{2}$.
5. Quadrilateral $CDGH$ has vertices $C(-6, -6)$, $D(-3, -3)$, $G(0, -3)$, and $H(3, -6)$; $k = \frac{1}{3}$.

Getting Ready to Practice

Vocabulary **Copy and complete the statement.**

1. The ? of a dilation is the ratio of corresponding side lengths.
2. A figure and its image after dilation are always ? .

Watch Out! Remember that corresponding parts are in the same position on different polygons.

Name the similar polygons.

3. 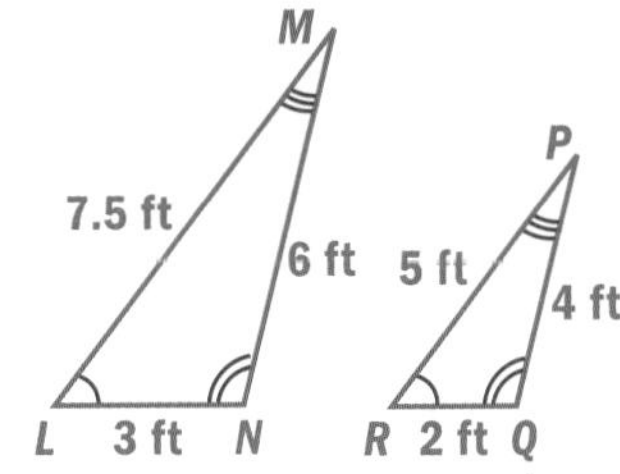

4. 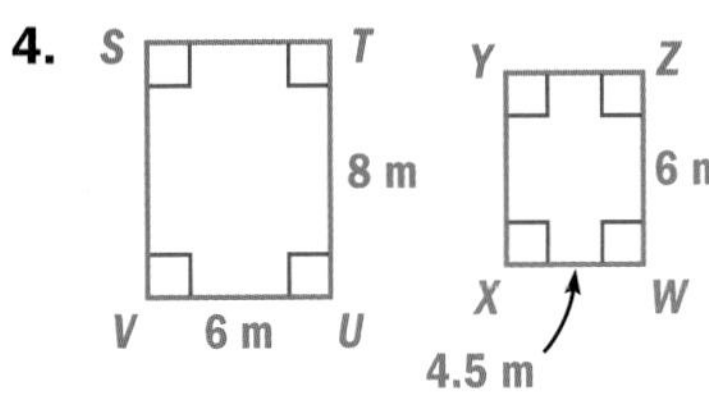

5. **Guided Problem Solving** Dilate $\triangle ABC$ using a scale factor of $\frac{1}{3}$.
   (1) Graph $\triangle ABC$ with vertices $A(3, 6)$, $B(-3, -3)$, and $C(6, 0)$.
   (2) Find the vertices of its image using the scale factor.
   (3) Graph the image.

Practice and Problem Solving

HELP with Homework

Example	Exercises
1	6–7
2	8–13
3	14, 21
4	15–19

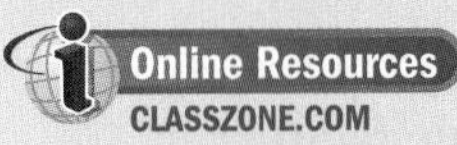

· More Examples
· eTutorial Plus

In Exercises 6 and 7, name the similar polygons.

6. 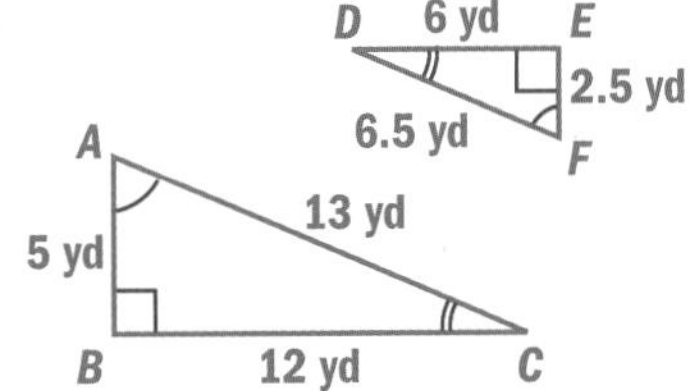

7. 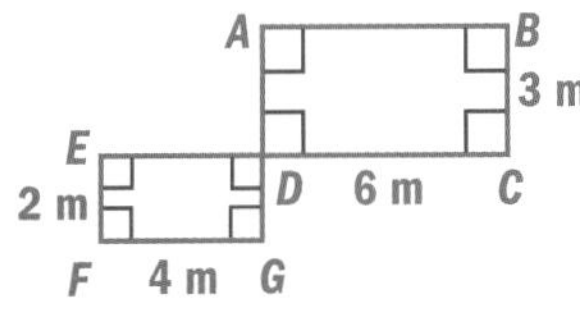

Use the similar triangles to find the value of *x*.

8. $\triangle ABC \sim \triangle DEF$

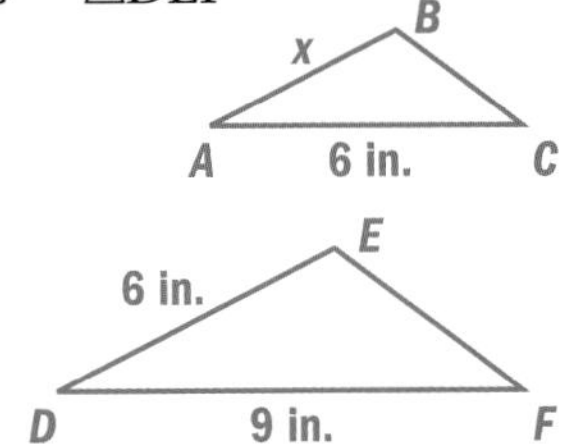

9. $\triangle GHJ \sim \triangle KHM$

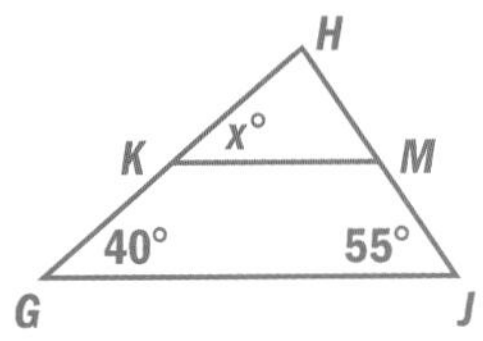

Use the similar polygons to find the value of *x*.

10. Parallelogram *CDFG* is similar to parallelogram *HJLK*.

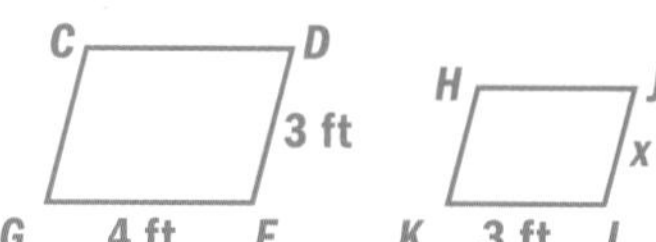

11. Trapezoid *MNPQ* is similar to trapezoid *RSTV*.

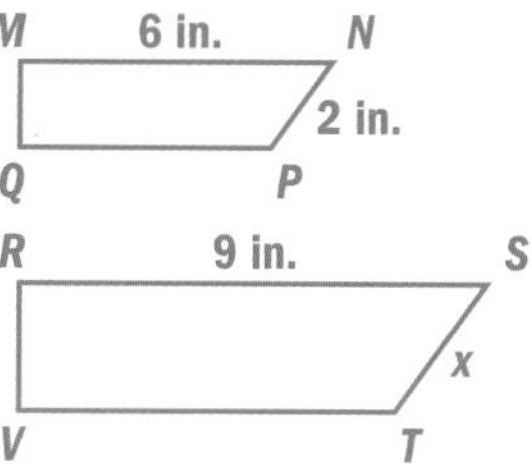

12. $\triangle LMN$ is similar to $\triangle PQR$. Find the value of *x*.

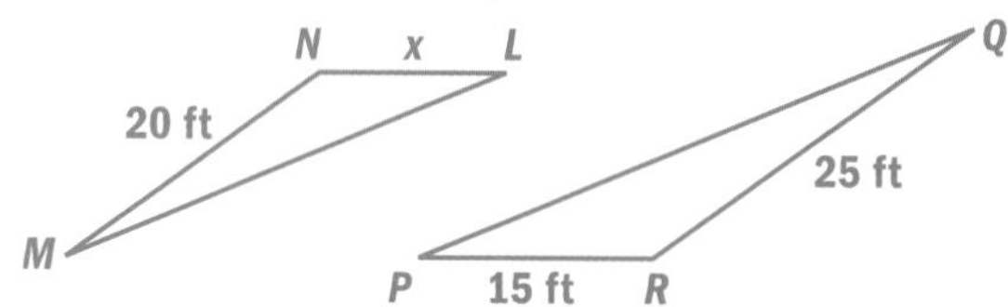

13. Pentagon $ABCDE \sim$ pentagon *FGHJK*. Find the values of *x* and *y*.

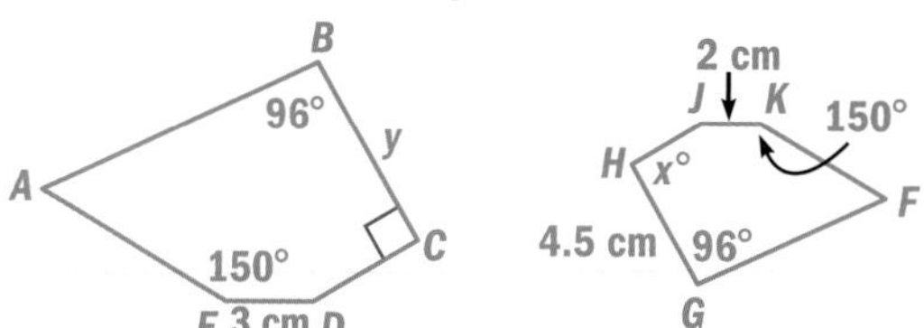

14. Indirect Measurement A sand castle casts an 18 foot shadow. At the same time, your 5 foot friend casts a 20 foot shadow. How tall is the sand castle?

Graph the polygon with the given vertices. Then graph its image after dilation by the scale factor *k*.

15. $W(2, 2)$, $X(0, 4)$, $Y(4, 6)$, $Z(6, 0)$; $k = 3$

16. $B(0, -2)$, $C(4, 2)$, $D(2, 6)$, $E(-2, 6)$, $F(-4, 2)$; $k = \frac{1}{2}$

17. $R(8, 8)$, $S(-4, 4)$, $T(-4, -4)$; $k = \frac{3}{4}$

18. $L(2, -2)$, $M(4, 2)$, $N(-3, 2)$, $P(-1, -2)$; $k = 4$

19. $G(-2, -6)$, $H(-8, -8)$, $J(-6, -2)$, $K(0, 0)$; $k = 1.5$

20. Calculate Pentagon *KLMNP* has vertices $K(24.1, 5.2)$, $L(4.9, 5.3)$, $M(6.8, 0.2)$, $N(3.3, 4.8)$, and $P(25.8, 22.1)$. Use the scale factor 1.8 to find the vertices of its image after dilation.

21. Photo Reduction You reduce a 12 inch by 24 inch photo to $\frac{1}{3}$ of its original dimensions. What are the new dimensions of the photo?

22. Writing Explain why all squares are similar.

23. **Algebra** Hexagon *ABCDEF* is similar to hexagon *PQRSTU*. Find the values of x and y.

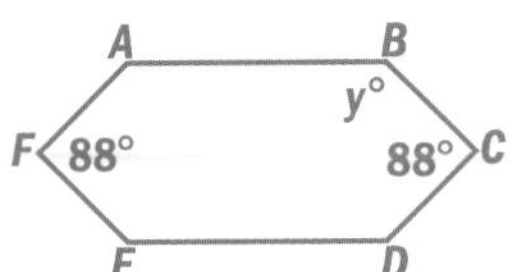

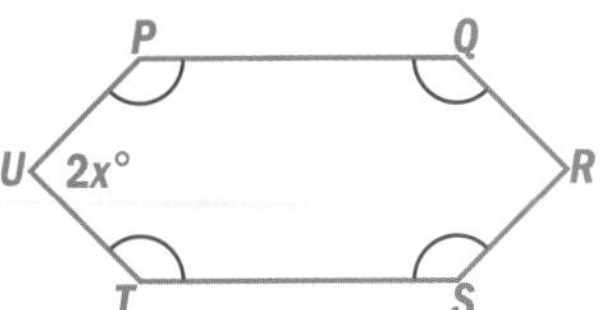

24. **Analyze** If a polygon is dilated by a scale factor of 1, will the image be *larger than, smaller than,* or *identical to* the original polygon? Explain.

25. **Challenge** Name two similar polygons in the diagram. Find their scale factor.

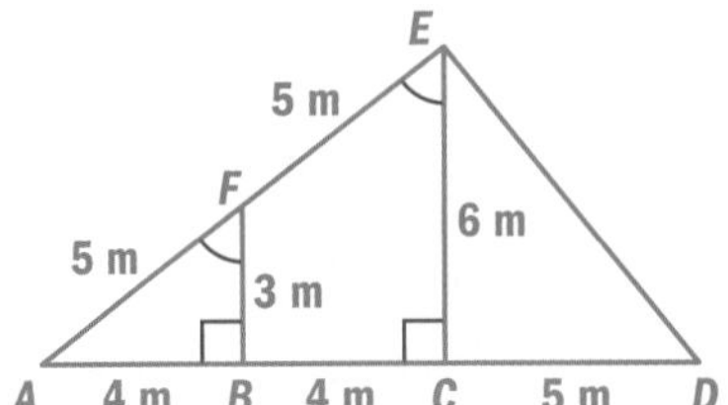

Mixed Review

Choose a Strategy **Use a strategy from the list to solve the following problem. Explain your choice of strategy.**

26. An ice cream stand offers vanilla, chocolate, mint chip, cookie crumble, and strawberry ice cream. Write all the possible 2 scoop cones you can order. How many possibilities are there?

> **Problem Solving Strategies**
> - Look for a Pattern
> - Draw a Diagram
> - Make a List
> - Make a Model

27. You sell your bike for \$50 but owe your parents 45% of the selling price. How much money do you have left after you repay your parents? *(Lesson 7.3)*

28. Graph the polygon with vertices $A(0, 1)$, $B(3, 4)$, $C(9, 3)$, and $D(7, -3)$. Then graph its image after reflection in the x-axis. *(Lesson 8.6)*

Test-Taking Practice

INTERNET
State Test Practice
CLASSZONE.COM

29. **Multiple Choice** Jenny is 5 feet tall and casts a 3 foot shadow. At the same time, a flagpole casts a 15 foot shadow. What mathematical idea can Jenny use to find the height of the flag pole?

A. inequality **B.** congruence **C.** similarity **D.** symmetry

30. **Multiple Choice** Find the length of $\overline{AB}$. $\triangle ABD \sim \triangle BCD$.

F. 6 cm **G.** 7.2 cm

H. 7.5 cm **I.** 11.25 cm

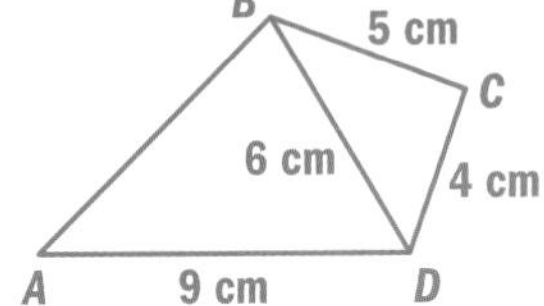

Notebook Review

Review the vocabulary definitions in your notebook.

Copy the review examples in your notebook. Then complete the exercises.

Check Your Definitions

congruent sides, angles, p. 397
corresponding parts, p. 397
reflection, p. 404
transformation, p. 404
image, p. 404
line symmetry, p. 406
translation, p. 409
rotation, p. 410
similar polygons, p. 416
dilation, p. 418
scale factor, p. 418

Use Your Vocabulary

Copy and complete the sentence with a review word.

1. A(n) _?_ creates a mirror image of a figure.

2. A(n) _?_ is a transformation that slides a figure.

8.5 Can you name congruent polygons?

EXAMPLE Name the congruent triangles and explain how you know that they are congruent.

ANSWER $\triangle LMN \cong \triangle SRT$ by Angle-Side-Angle

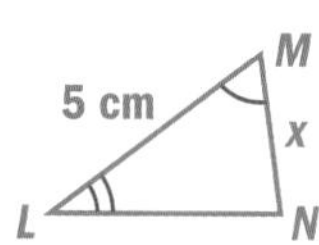

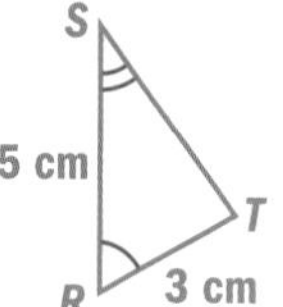

3. Find the value of x using the triangles above.

8.6–8.7 Can you reflect and rotate figures?

EXAMPLE Graph $\triangle ABC$ with vertices $A(1, 3)$, $B(4, 3)$, and $C(3, 1)$. Then graph its reflection in the x-axis.

Original		Image
(x, y)	$\rightarrow$	$(x, -y)$
$A(1, 3)$	$\rightarrow$	$A'(1, -3)$
$B(4, 3)$	$\rightarrow$	$B'(4, -3)$
$C(3, 1)$	$\rightarrow$	$C'(3, -1)$

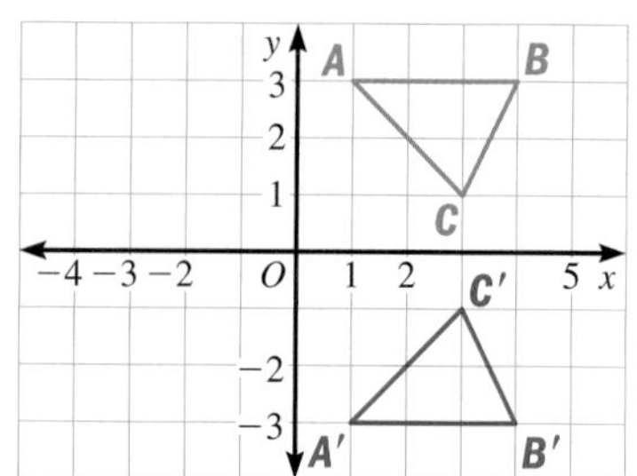

4. Graph the reflection of $\triangle ABC$ in the y-axis.

EXAMPLE Rotate $\triangle KLM$ 90° counterclockwise.

Original		Image
(x, y)	$\rightarrow$	$(-y, x)$
$K(3, 1)$	$\rightarrow$	$K'(-1, 3)$
$L(1, 4)$	$\rightarrow$	$L'(-4, 1)$
$M(3, 3)$	$\rightarrow$	$M'(-3, 3)$

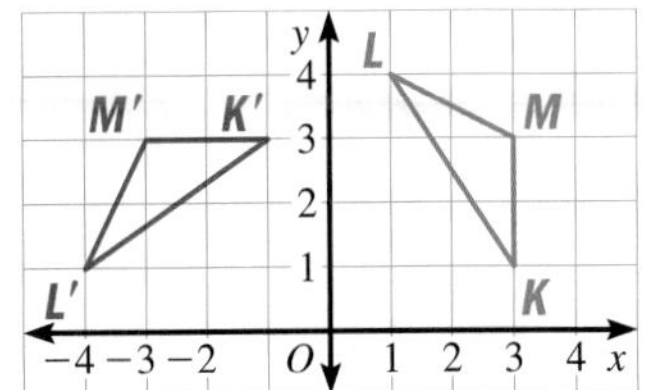

5. Rotate $\triangle KLM$ 180°.

8.8 Can you use similarity to find measures?

EXAMPLE Polygons $ABCD$ and $FGHJ$ are similar. Find the value of x.

$\frac{AB}{FG} = \frac{BC}{GH}$ **Write a proportion.**

$\frac{16}{20} = \frac{x}{15}$ **Substitute.**

$x = 12$ **Solve for *x*.**

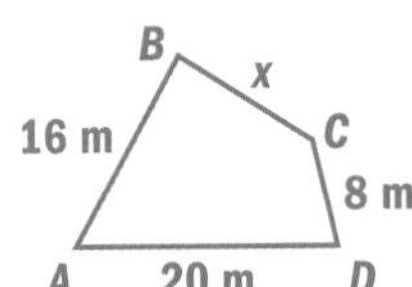

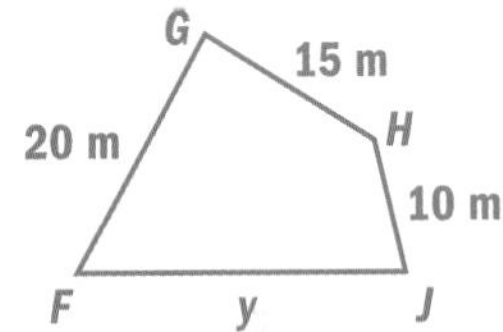

6. Use the similar polygons to find the value of y.

Stop and Think about Lessons 8.5–8.8

7. Writing Explain how dilation affects the perimeter of a figure.

8. Critical Thinking Give a real world example of a 180° rotation.

Review Quiz 2

1. In the diagram, $\triangle ABC \cong \triangle DEF$. Find $m\angle D$.

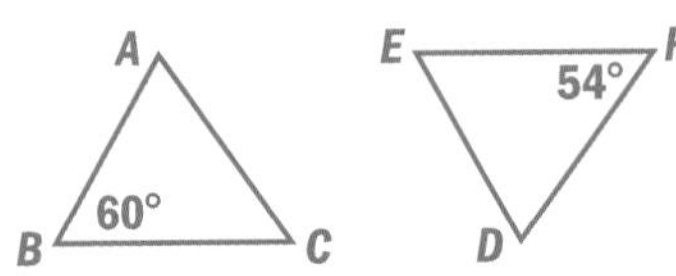

Name the type of transformation modeled by the action.

2. sledding downhill

3. leaving fingerprints

4. spinning in place

5. opening a drawer

6. Graph $\triangle ABC$ with vertices $A(1, 1)$, $B(2, 3)$, and $C(3, 0)$. Dilate the triangle using a scale factor of 4.

Chapter Review

straight angle, right angle, p. 375
supplementary, complementary angles, p. 375
vertical angles, p. 376
perpendicular lines, p. 376
parallel lines, p. 377
acute, right, obtuse angle, p. 382
acute, right, obtuse triangle, p. 382
equilateral, isosceles, scalene triangle, p. 382
quadrilateral, p. 386
trapezoid, parallelogram, rhombus, p. 386
polygon, regular polygon, p. 390
pentagon, hexagon, heptagon, octagon, p. 390
congruent sides, angles, p. 397
corresponding parts, p. 397
reflection, p. 404
transformation, p. 404
image, p. 404
line symmetry, p. 406
translation, p. 409
rotation, p. 410
similar polygons, p. 416
dilation, p. 418
scale factor, p. 418

Vocabulary Review

Matching **Match each word with the correct definition.**

1. transformation	**A.** Two angles whose measures have a sum of 90°
2. reflection	**B.** A transformation that stretches or shrinks a figure
3. parallel lines	**C.** Two angles whose measures have a sum of 180°
4. complementary angles	**D.** A transformation that slides a figure
5. supplementary angles	**E.** A transformation that creates a mirror image of a figure
6. perpendicular lines	**F.** Two lines in the same plane that do not intersect
7. translation	**G.** An operation that changes one figure into another figure
8. dilation	**H.** Two lines that intersect to form a right angle

Review Questions

Find the measure of ∠1. *(Lesson 8.1)*

9.
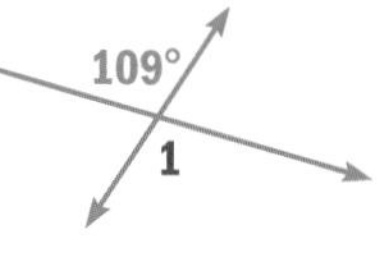

10.
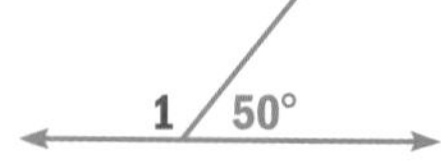

11.
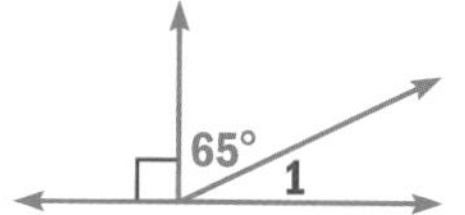

Review Questions

Classify the polygon. *(Lessons 8.2, 8.3)*

12. 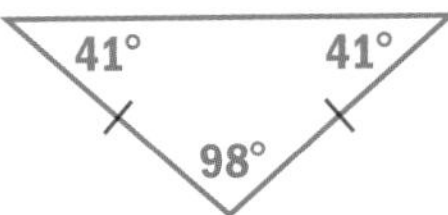

13. 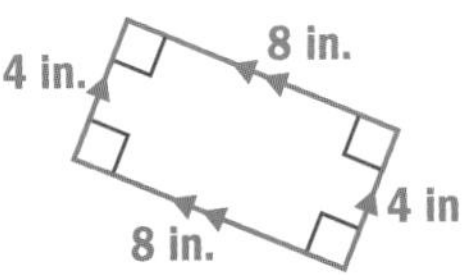

14. 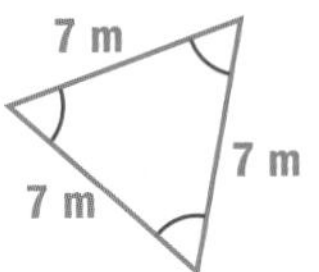

15. Find the sum of the angle measures in a heptagon. *(Lesson 8.4)*

16. Find the measure of one angle in a regular pentagon. *(Lesson 8.4)*

Pentagon *ABCDE* ≅ pentagon *PQRST*. *(Lesson 8.5)*

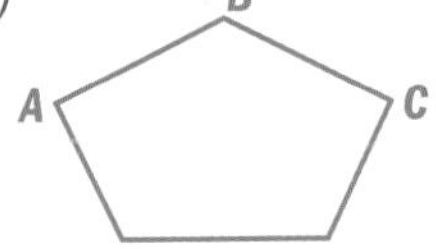

17. Name the congruent corresponding angles.

18. Name the congruent corresponding sides.

Q R P S T

19. Name the congruent triangles and explain how you know they are congruent. *(Lesson 8.5)*

B

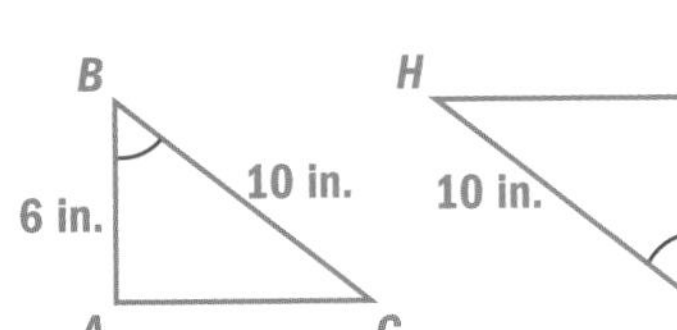

Tell whether the red figure is a reflection of the blue figure. *(Lesson 8.6)*

20. 

21. f ɟ

22. p p

23. g a

24. $\triangle XYZ$ has vertices $X(-1, 1)$, $Y(-3, 1)$, and $Z(-2, 5)$. Reflect $\triangle XYZ$ in the y-axis. Find the vertices of the image. *(Lesson 8.6)*

Rotate the polygon 90° clockwise and graph its image. *(Lesson 8.7)*

25. 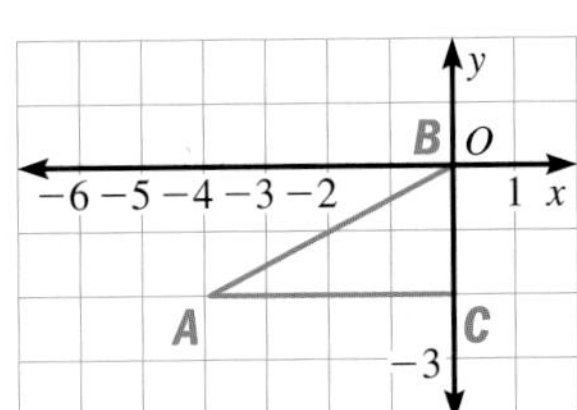

26. 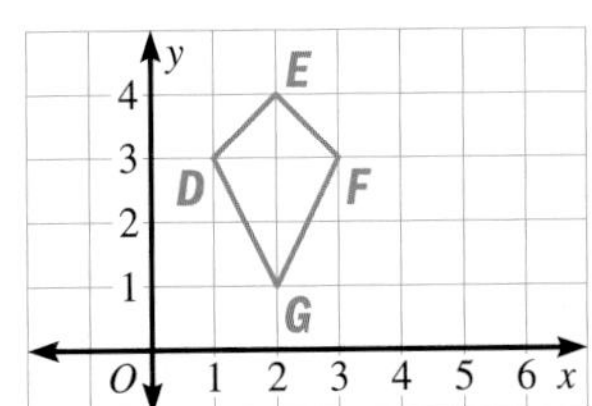

27. 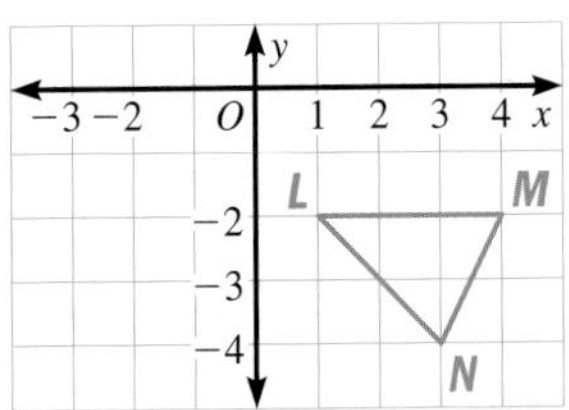

28. **Building Height** A 20 foot flagpole stands beside a building. The flagpole casts a shadow that is 25 feet long. At the same time, the building casts a shadow that is 60 feet long. How tall is the building? *(Lesson 8.8)*

29. A polygon has vertices $A(-2, 0)$, $B(-2, 4)$, $C(-6, 8)$, and $D(-12, 6)$. Dilate it using a scale factor of 2. Find the vertices of the image. *(Lesson 8.8)*

CHAPTER 8

Chapter Test

Find the measures of the numbered angles.

1.

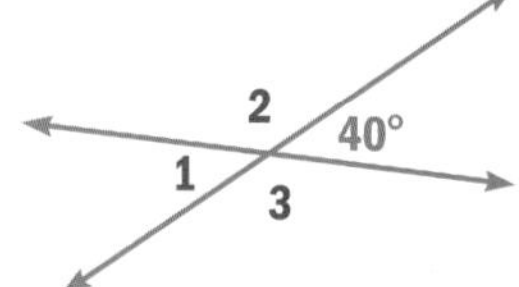

2.

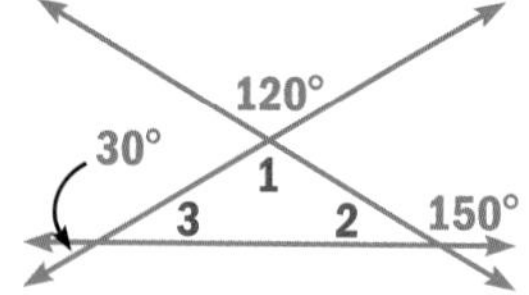

3.

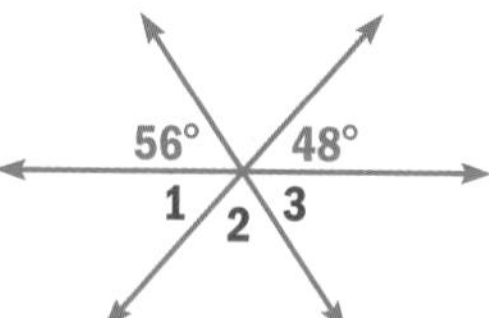

Classify the triangle by its angles.

4.

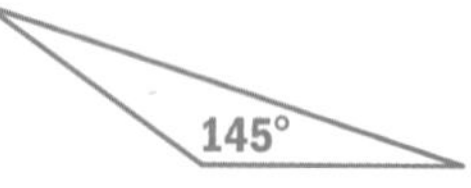

5.

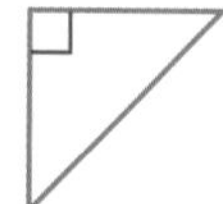

6.

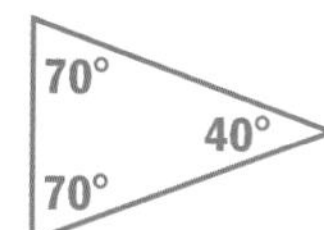

Classify the quadrilateral.

7.

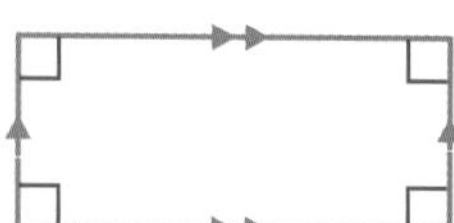

8.

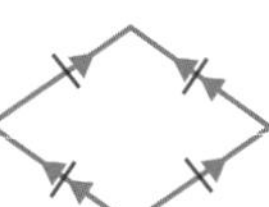

9.

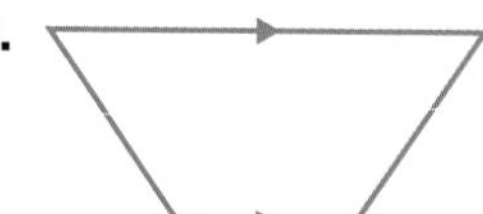

Find the measure of one angle in the polygon.

10. square

11. regular octagon

12. regular 9-gon

13. **Algebra** Write and solve an equation to find the value of x.

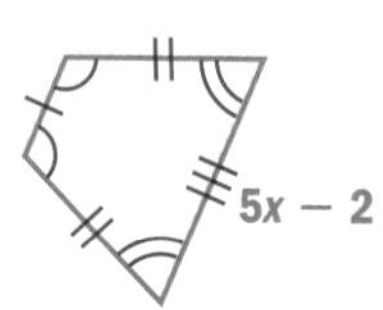

Graph the image of the given transformation.

14. Rotate 180°.

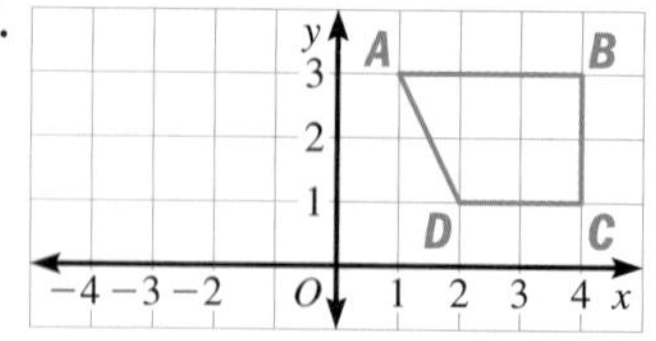

15. Translate using $(x, y) \rightarrow (x - 5, y + 3)$.

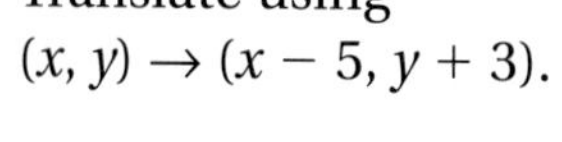

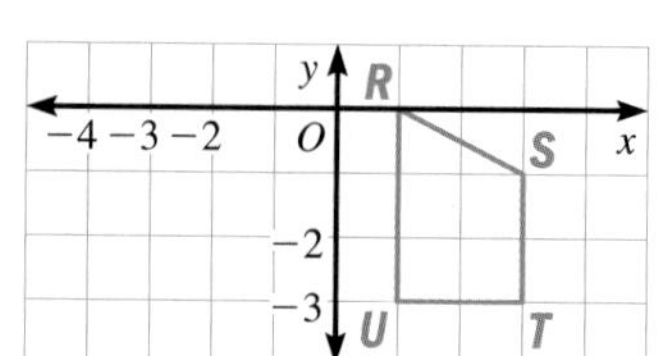

16. **Shadows** Joe is 72 inches tall and has a 108 inch shadow. At the same time, Martha has a 96 inch shadow. How tall is Martha?

Chapter Standardized Test

Test-Taking Strategy **You can make notes, sketches, or graphs in your test booklet to help you solve problems, but you must keep your answer sheet neat.**

Multiple Choice

1. $\angle A$ is supplementary to $\angle B$ and $m\angle A = 62°$. What is $m\angle B$?

A. 28° **B.** 118° **C.** 152° **D.** 298°

2. Which transformation takes the blue figure to the red figure?

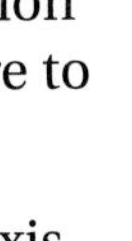

F. reflection in x-axis

G. 90° rotation

H. $(x, y) \to (x + 3, y + 2)$

I. $(x, y) \to (x - 3, y - 2)$

3. Which statement is *not* always true?

A. A rhombus is a figure with four sides.

B. A rhombus has four right angles.

C. A rhombus has parallel opposite sides.

D. A rhombus has four sides of equal length.

4. What is the value of x?

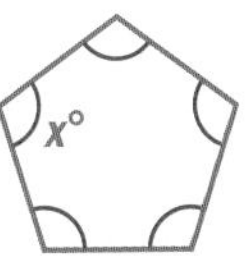

F. 108 **G.** 144

H. 180 **I.** 540

5. What is the sum of the angle measures in a 9-gon?

A. 1260° **B.** 1620° **C.** 2520° **D.** 3240°

6. How many lines of symmetry does the figure have?

F. 0 **G.** 1

H. 2 **I.** 4

7. Which diagram shows a reflection?

A. A A **B.** B B

C. C C **D.** D D

8. $\triangle ABC \sim \triangle DEF$. What is the value of x?

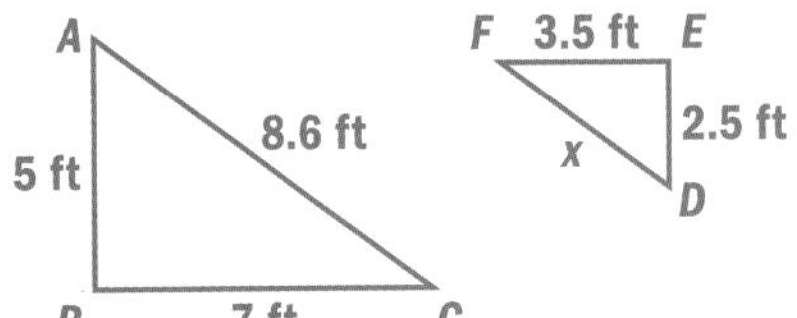

F. 2.5 ft **G.** 3.5 ft **H.** 4.3 ft **I.** 5.1 ft

9. Which statement is *always* true?

A. Supplementary angles are congruent.

B. Complementary angles are congruent.

C. Acute angles are congruent.

D. Vertical angles are congruent.

Short Response

10. Find the value of x and explain your steps.

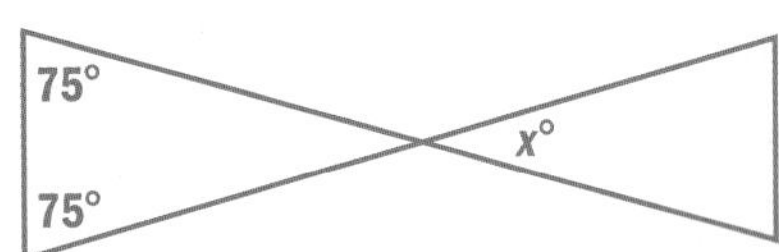

Extended Response

11. Graph $\triangle RST$ with vertices $R(1, 3)$, $S(3, 0)$, and $T(1, 0)$. Graph $\triangle BCA$ with vertices $A(-3, 0)$, $B(-1, 3)$, and $C(-1, 0)$. Explain how you know the two triangles are congruent.

Real Numbers and Right Triangles

BEFORE

In previous chapters you've...

- Found the square of a number
- Investigated rational numbers

Now

In Chapter 9 you'll study...

- Finding square roots
- Classifying real numbers as rational or irrational
- Solving real-world problems using the Pythagorean theorem
- Using trigonometric ratios

WHY?

So you can solve real-world problems about...

- forest rangers, p. 435
- parasailing, p. 444
- softball, p. 456
- totem poles, p. 466

Internet Preview
CLASSZONE.COM

- eEdition Plus Online
- eWorkbook Plus Online
- eTutorial Plus Online
- State Test Practice
- More Examples

Chapter Warm-Up Games

Review skills you need for this chapter in these quick games.

Key Skill:
Evaluating powers

Spin the wheels until all three red lines connect equal values.

- You can turn the wheels one click at a time. Each click moves a wheel one space clockwise.
- How many clicks do you need to turn the left wheel?
- How many clicks do you need to turn the right wheel?

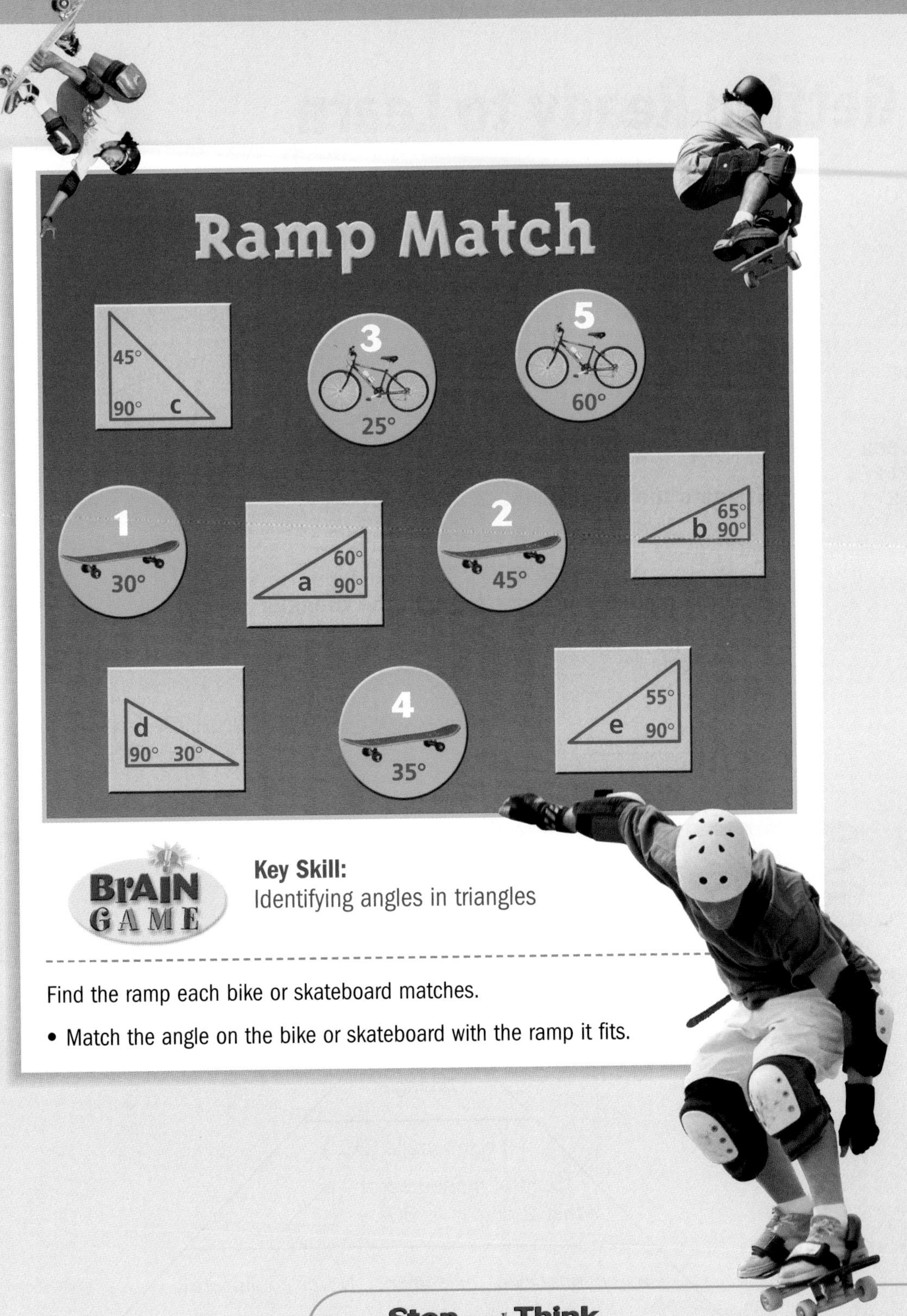

Key Skill:
Identifying angles in triangles

Find the ramp each bike or skateboard matches.

- Match the angle on the bike or skateboard with the ramp it fits.

Stop *and* Think

1. **Critical Thinking** How can you write 4^4 as a power of 2? Explain.
2. **Writing** Explain why a triangular ramp that has angles of 90°, 40°, and 55° cannot exist.

Getting Ready to Learn

Word Watch

Review Words

rational number, p. 242
right angle, p. 375
right triangle, p. 382
equilateral triangle, p. 382
isosceles triangle, p. 382
scalene triangle, p. 382

Review What You Need to Know

Using Vocabulary Use a review word to classify the triangle by its side lengths.

1. 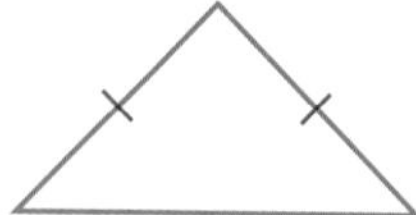

2. 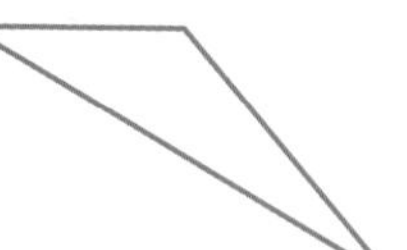

3. 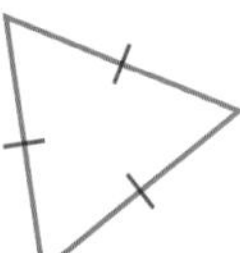

Evaluate the expression. *(p. 20)*

4. $4^2 + 3^2$ **5.** $14^2 - 5^2$ **6.** $27^2 - 3^2$ **7.** $2^2 + 6^2$

Find the measure of each angle in the triangle. *(p. 382)*

8. 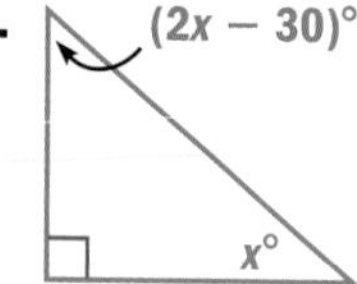

9. 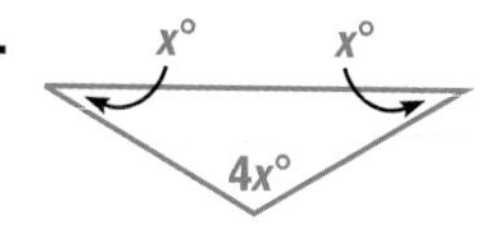

10. 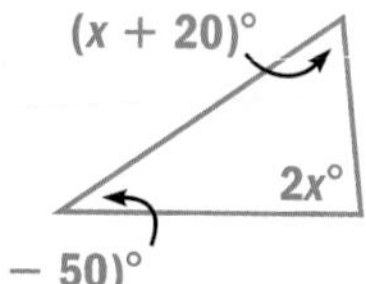

You should include material that appears on a notebook like this in your own notes.

Know How to Take Notes

Illustrating with Examples When you learn a new concept or formula, write it in your notes along with examples and important information.

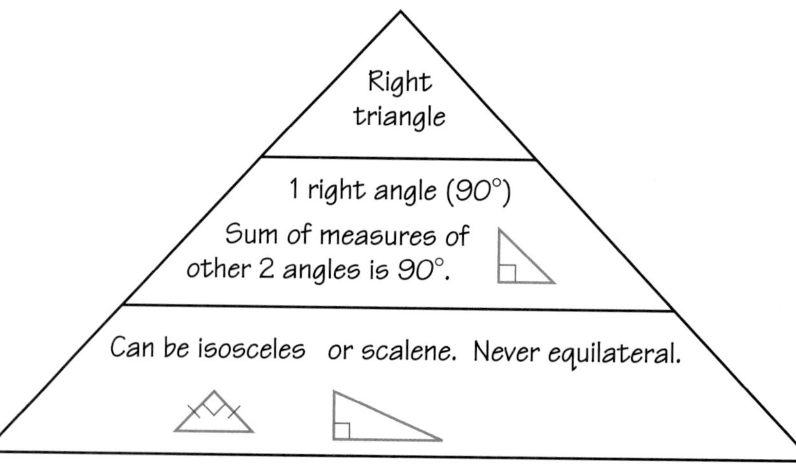

In Lesson 9.3, you will learn a rule about right triangles that you should write in your notebook.

Square Roots

BEFORE	Now	WHY?
You found squares of numbers.	You'll find and approximate square roots of numbers.	So you can find the length of a side of a square pillow, as in Ex. 14.

Word Watch

square root, p. 431
radical expression, p. 431
perfect square, p. 432

INDIANA Academic Standards

- Number Sense (8.1.7)
- Algebra and Functions (8.3.1)

Activity You can find the length of a side of a square if you know its area.

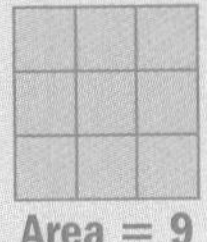

Area = 1 Area = 4 Area = 9

1. Copy and complete the table.

Area of square (square units)	1	4	9	16	25	36
Side length (units)	1	2	3	?	?	?

2. What is the length of each side of a square with an area of 49 square units? 64 square units? 100 square units? 400 square units?

3. What can you say about the length of a side of a square that has an area between 81 and 100 square units?

The numbers 5 and -5 are the *square roots* of 25 because $5^2 = 25$ and $(-5)^2 = 25$. If $m^2 = n$, then m is a **square root** of n.

Every positive number has a positive square root and a negative square root. The symbol $\sqrt{\ }$ is called a *radical sign*. It is used to represent the positive square root. A **radical expression** is an expression that involves a $\sqrt{\ }$.

$\sqrt{25} = 5$ **positive square root**

$-\sqrt{25} = -5$ **negative square root**

Zero has one square root, which is zero.

EXAMPLE 1 Evaluating Square Roots

a. $\sqrt{36} = 6$ because $6^2 = 36$.

b. $-\sqrt{64} = -8$ because $(-8)^2 = 64$.

HELP with Solving

You may want to use the Table of Square Roots on p. 745.

Your turn now Find the square root.

1. $\sqrt{4}$ **2.** $\sqrt{0}$ **3.** $-\sqrt{36}$ **4.** $-\sqrt{81}$

Perfect Squares A **perfect square** is any number that has integer square roots. Some examples of perfect squares are 1, 4, 9, and 16. You can approximate the square roots of a number that is not a perfect square using a number line or a calculator.

EXAMPLE 2 Approximating a Square Root

You can use a number line to approximate $\sqrt{95}$ to the nearest whole number. You know that 95 is between 81 (or 9^2) and 100 (or 10^2), so $\sqrt{95}$ is between 9 and 10.

To decide whether $\sqrt{95}$ is closer to 9 or to 10, find 9.5^2. You can calculate that $9.5^2 = 90.25$ and $(\sqrt{95})^2 = 95$.

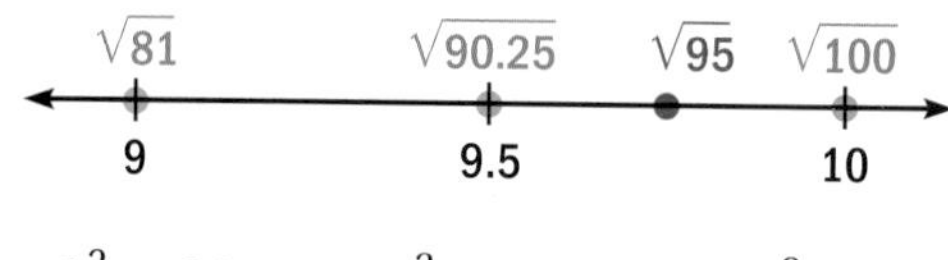

$9^2 = 81$ $\quad 9.5^2 = 90.25$ $\quad 10^2 = 100$

As shown on the number line, $\sqrt{95}$ is between $\sqrt{90.25}$ and $\sqrt{100}$, so it has a value between 9.5 and 10. Therefore, $\sqrt{95}$ is closer to 10 than it is to 9.

ANSWER To the nearest whole number, $\sqrt{95} \approx 10$.

EXAMPLE 3 Using a Calculator

Evaluate the square root. Round to the nearest tenth, if necessary.

a. $\sqrt{441}$ **b.** $-\sqrt{56.25}$ **c.** $\sqrt{8}$ **d.** $-\sqrt{1256}$

Solution

	Keystrokes	Display	Answer
a.	2nd [√] 441 =	21	21
b.	(–) 2nd [√] 56.25 =	–7.5	–7.5
c.	2nd [√] 8 =	2.828427125	2.8
d.	(–) 2nd [√] 1256 =	–35.44009029	–35.4

Your turn now **Approximate to the nearest whole number.**

5. $\sqrt{23}$ **6.** $\sqrt{41}$ **7.** $\sqrt{70}$ **8.** $\sqrt{125}$

Use a calculator to evaluate. Round to the nearest tenth.

9. $\sqrt{236}$ **10.** $\sqrt{11}$ **11.** $-\sqrt{20.96}$ **12.** $-\sqrt{3590}$

EXAMPLE 4 Using a Square Root Equation

Amusement Parks On an amusement park ride, riders stand against a circular wall that spins. At a certain speed, the floor drops out and the force of the rotation keeps the riders pinned to the wall.

The model $s = 4.95\sqrt{r}$ gives the speed needed to keep riders pinned to the wall. In the model, s is the speed in meters per second and r is the radius of the ride in meters. Find the speed necessary to keep riders pinned to the wall of a ride that has a radius of 2.61 meters.

Solution

$s = 4.95\sqrt{r}$	Write equation for speed of the ride.
$= 4.95\sqrt{2.61}$	Substitute 2.61 for r.
$\approx 4.95(1.62)$	Approximate the square root.
$= 8.019$	Multiply.

ANSWER The speed should be about 8.019 meters per second.

EXAMPLE 5 Solving Equations Using Square Roots

a.

$x^2 = 64$	Original equation
$x = \pm\sqrt{64}$	Definition of square root
$x = \pm 8$	Evaluate square roots.

ANSWER The solutions are 8 and -8.

HELP with Reading

The symbol $\pm$ is read *plus or minus.* The statement $x = \pm 8$ means that 8 and -8 are the solutions of $x^2 = 64$.

b.

$z^2 + 14 = 20$	Original equation
$z^2 + 14 - \mathbf{14} = 20 - \mathbf{14}$	Subtract 14 from each side.
$z^2 = 6$	Simplify.
$z = \pm\sqrt{6}$	Definition of square root
$z \approx \pm 2.45$	Approximate square roots.

ANSWER The solutions are about 2.45 and about -2.45.

Your turn now **Approximate the square root. Round to the nearest tenth.**

13. $\sqrt{5}$ **14.** $\sqrt{12}$ **15.** $\sqrt{15}$ **16.** $\sqrt{23}$

Solve the equation. Check your solutions.

17. $t^2 = 36$ **18.** $y^2 - 15 = 10$ **19.** $x^2 + 7 = 16$

9.1 Exercises

More Practice, p. 735

Getting Ready to Practice

1. Vocabulary Copy and complete: A number b is a square root of c if __?__.

Find the two square roots of the number.

2. 9 **3.** 16 **4.** 49 **5.** 121

Use a calculator to approximate the square root. Round to the nearest tenth.

6. $\sqrt{28}$ **7.** $-\sqrt{482}$ **8.** $-\sqrt{34.6}$ **9.** $\sqrt{2440}$

Solve the equation. Check your solutions.

10. $x^2 = 4$ **11.** $b^2 = 49$ **12.** $y^2 + 7 = 56$ **13.** $c^2 - 12 = 69$

14. Guided Problem Solving You want to make a square pillow. You have 729 square inches of material for the front of the pillow. If you use all the material, what is the length of one side of the pillow?

(1) Write an equation.

(2) Use definition of square root to solve the equation.

(3) Evaluate the positive square root.

Practice and Problem Solving

Find the square root.

15. $-\sqrt{1}$ **16.** $\sqrt{100}$ **17.** $\sqrt{144}$ **18.** $-\sqrt{900}$

Approximate the square root to the nearest whole number.

19. $\sqrt{33}$ **20.** $\sqrt{14}$ **21.** $\sqrt{117}$ **22.** $\sqrt{52}$

Use a calculator to evaluate the square root. Round to the nearest tenth, if necessary.

23. $\sqrt{22}$ **24.** $\sqrt{43.56}$ **25.** $-\sqrt{1475}$ **26.** $-\sqrt{6204}$

Solve the equation. Check your solution(s).

27. $x^2 = 0$ **28.** $y^2 = 81$ **29.** $z^2 - 169 = 0$

30. $n^2 - 27 = 94$ **31.** $a^2 + 12 = 48$ **32.** $m^2 + 21 = 421$

33. Critical Thinking Can you find $\sqrt{-25}$? Explain your answer.

HELP with Homework

Example	Exercises
1	15–18
2	19–22
3	23–26
4	34
5	27–32

Online Resources
CLASSZONE.COM
· More Examples
· eTutorial Plus

34. **Fire Tower** A forest ranger is stationed in a 53 foot tall fire tower. The equation for the distance in miles that the ranger can see is $d = \sqrt{1.5h}$, where h is the height in feet above the ground. Find the distance the ranger can see. Round your answer to the nearest tenth.

with Solving

You can use a calculator or the Table of Square Roots on p. 745 to solve Exercises 35–40.

Solve the equation. Round to the nearest hundredth, if necessary. Check your solutions.

35. $x^2 + 8 = 49$ **36.** $y^2 - 31 = 36$ **37.** $62 + z^2 = 198$

38. $t^2 - 44 = 224$ **39.** $c^2 - 35 = 165$ **40.** $57 + m^2 = 253$

Evaluate the expression $\sqrt{x^2 - y^2}$ for the given values.

41. $x = 5, y = 3$ **42.** $x = 10, y = 8$ **43.** $x = 15, y = 12$

Find the two square roots of the number.

44. 0.81 **45.** 1.44 **46.** 1.21 **47.** 1.96

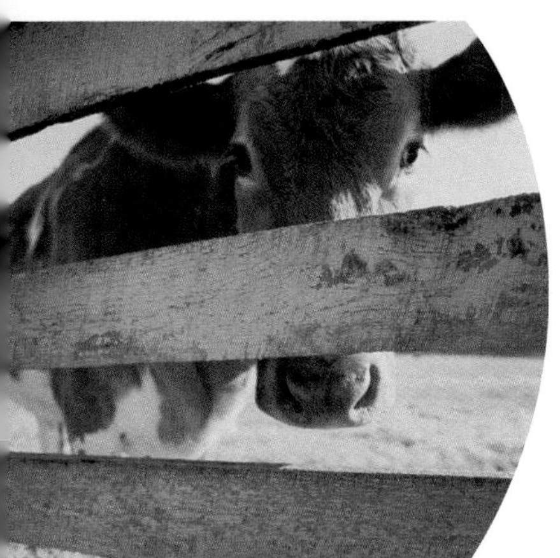

48. **Farming** You want to put a fence around a square plot of land that has an area of 6250 square yards. Find the length of a side, to the nearest tenth of a yard, and then use it to approximate the perimeter of the plot of land.

$A = 6250 \text{ yd}^2$

49. **Home Decorating** You have a square table with an area of 34.5 square feet. You have a tablecloth that measures 60 inches by 60 inches. Is the tablecloth large enough to cover the table? Explain.

50. Evaluate the expression $\sqrt{\sqrt{16}}$.

EXAMPLE Finding a Square Root of a Fraction

$$\sqrt{\frac{9}{16}} = \sqrt{\frac{3}{4} \cdot \frac{3}{4}} = \frac{3}{4}$$ **Definition of square root**

In Exercises 51–55, find the square root.

51. $\sqrt{\frac{1}{4}}$ **52.** $\sqrt{\frac{16}{25}}$ **53.** $\sqrt{\frac{49}{64}}$ **54.** $\sqrt{\frac{81}{100}}$ **55.** $\sqrt{\frac{144}{169}}$

56. **Look for a Pattern** Find the positive square roots of 0.36, 0.0036, 0.000036, and 0.00000036. What pattern do you notice? Using the pattern, predict the positive square root of 0.0000000036.

57. **Challenge** In Example 2, you learned how to approximate the value of a square root to the nearest whole number without using a calculator. Explain how to approximate the value of a square root to the nearest tenth if you have a calculator that cannot evaluate square roots.

Mixed Review

58. **Carnival** Nikki is at a carnival and has \$6. She would like to buy some cotton candy for \$2.25 and use the rest of her money to go on the rides. Each ride costs \$.75. How many rides can she go on? *(Lesson 3.4)*

Tell whether the angles are *complementary*, *supplementary*, or *neither*. *(Lesson 8.1)*

59. $m\angle 1 = 89°$ $m\angle 2 = 31°$

60. $m\angle 1 = 34°$ $m\angle 2 = 56°$

61. $m\angle 1 = 53°$ $m\angle 2 = 127°$

62. $m\angle 1 = 78°$ $m\angle 2 = 102°$

Choose a Strategy **Use a strategy from the list to solve the following problem. Explain your choice of strategy.**

Problem Solving Strategies

- Look for a Pattern
- Draw a Diagram
- Make a Model

63. In how many different ways can three postage stamps be torn from a 3 by 4 sheet of stamps so that the three stamps are still attached to one another?

Basic Skills **Write the decimal as a mixed number.**

64. −1.25

65. 5.35

66. 2.95

67. −9.05

Test-Taking Practice

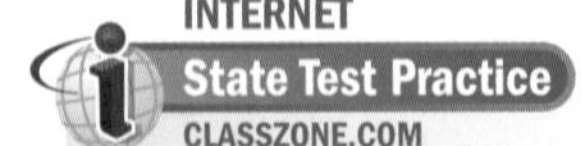

68. **Multiple Choice** Approximate $\sqrt{175}$ to the nearest whole number.

A. 12 **B.** 13 **C.** 14 **D.** 15

69. **Multiple Choice** The area of the square base of a building is 2025 square feet. Find the perimeter of the base of the building.

F. 25 feet **G.** 45 feet **H.** 90 feet **I.** 180 feet

X-cellent Birthday

Augustus De Morgan, a nineteenth century English mathematician, was the first professor of Mathematics at University College, London.

Always interested in strange numerical facts, De Morgan once noted in his writings that he had the distinction of being x years old in the year x^2. If he was born between 1805 and 1815, in what year was he born?

Rational and Irrational Numbers

BEFORE

You investigated rational numbers.

Now

You'll work with irrational numbers.

WHY?

So you can determine how many stencils fill a wall, as in Ex. 24.

irrational number, p. 437
real number, p. 437

INDIANA Academic Standards

- Number Sense (8.1.3)
- Problem Solving (8.7.1)

Recall that a *rational number* is a number that can be written as a quotient $\frac{a}{b}$, where a and b are integers and $b \neq 0$. An **irrational number** is a number that cannot be written as a quotient of two integers. If n is a positive integer and is not a perfect square, then $\sqrt{n}$ and $-\sqrt{n}$ are irrational numbers.

Together, rational numbers and irrational numbers make up the set of **real numbers**. The Venn diagram shows the relationships among numbers in the real number system.

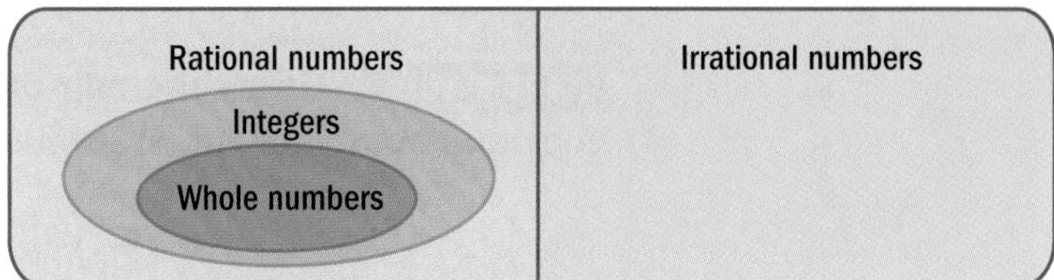

The decimal form of a rational number is either terminating or repeating. The decimal form of an irrational number neither terminates nor repeats.

For help with writing a rational number as a decimal, see p. 242.

EXAMPLE 1 Classifying Real Numbers

	Number	Type	Decimal Form	Type of Decimal
a.	$\frac{3}{4}$	Rational	$\frac{3}{4} = 0.75$	Terminating
b.	$\frac{1}{11}$	Rational	$\frac{1}{11} = 0.0909\ldots = 0.\overline{09}$	Repeating
c.	$\sqrt{3}$	Irrational	$\sqrt{3} = 1.7320508\ldots$	Nonrepeating and nonterminating

Your turn now **Tell whether the number is *rational* or *irrational*. Explain your reasoning.**

1. $\frac{5}{8}$ **2.** $\sqrt{7}$ **3.** $\frac{2}{9}$ **4.** $\sqrt{25}$

EXAMPLE 2 Comparing Real Numbers

Graph the pair of numbers on a number line. Then copy and complete the statement with <, >, or =.

a. $\sqrt{2}$ _?_ 2

b. $\sqrt{\frac{1}{2}}$ _?_ $\frac{1}{2}$

Solution

Use a calculator to approximate the square root and write any fractions as decimals. Then graph the numbers on a number line and compare.

a. $\sqrt{2} \approx 1.4142$ 2

1 1.1 1.2 1.3 1.4 1.5 1.6 1.7 1.8 1.9 2 2.1

So, $\sqrt{2} < 2$.

b. $\frac{1}{2} = 0.5$ $\sqrt{\frac{1}{2}} \approx 0.7071$

0 0.1 0.2 0.3 0.4 0.5 0.6 0.7 0.8 0.9 1

So, $\sqrt{\frac{1}{2}} > \frac{1}{2}$.

Watch Out!

You may need to use parentheses when using a calculator to approximate a square root.

Your turn now **Graph the pair of numbers on a number line. Then copy and complete the statement with <, >, or =.**

5. 4 _?_ $\sqrt{8}$

6. $\sqrt{25}$ _?_ 5

7. $\frac{1}{4}$ _?_ $\sqrt{\frac{1}{4}}$

EXAMPLE 3 Ordering Decimals

Order the decimals $0.4\overline{7}$, $0.\overline{474}$, $0.\overline{47}$, and 0.477 from least to greatest.

Solution

1 Write each decimal out to six decimal places.

Notice that the first two digits after the decimal point are the same for each number.

$0.4\overline{7} = 0.477777...$

$0.\overline{474} = 0.474474...$

$0.\overline{47} = 0.474747...$

$0.477 = 0.477000$

Use the second pair of digits to order the decimals.

2 From least to greatest, the order of the numbers is 0.474474..., 0.474747..., 0.4770, and 0.477777....

ANSWER From least to greatest, the order is $0.\overline{474}$, $0.\overline{47}$, 0.477, and $0.4\overline{7}$.

EXAMPLE 4 Using an Irrational Number

Waves For large ocean waves, the wind speed s in knots and the height of the waves h in feet are related by the equation $s = \sqrt{\frac{h}{0.019}}$. If the waves are about 9.5 feet tall, what must the wind speed be? (1 knot is equivalent to 1.15 miles per hour.)

Solution

$s = \sqrt{\frac{h}{0.019}}$	**Write original equation.**
$= \sqrt{\frac{9.5}{0.019}}$	**Substitute 9.5 for *h*.**
$= \sqrt{500}$	**Divide.**
≈ 22.36	**Approximate square root.**

ANSWER The wind speed must be about 22.36 knots.

Your turn now **Use the equation in Example 4.**

8. Find the wind speed required to produce 15 foot waves.

9.2 Exercises

More Practice, p. 735

Getting Ready to Practice

1. Vocabulary Copy and complete: Numbers that cannot be written as a quotient of two integers are called __?__ numbers.

Tell whether the number is *rational* or *irrational*. Explain your reasoning.

2. $\sqrt{36}$ **3.** $\sqrt{5}$ **4.** $\frac{\sqrt{3}}{8}$ **5.** $\sqrt{\frac{25}{49}}$

Graph the pair of numbers on a number line. Then copy and complete the statement with <, >, or =.

6. $\frac{5}{6}$ __?__ $\sqrt{\frac{5}{6}}$ **7.** $\frac{3}{5}$ __?__ $\sqrt{\frac{36}{100}}$ **8.** 5 __?__ $\sqrt{10}$

9. Dimensions The floor of a square room has an area of 90 square feet. What are the dimensions of the room to the nearest tenth of a foot?

Practice and Problem Solving

with Homework

Example	Exercises
1	10–13
2	14–17
3	18–19
4	36

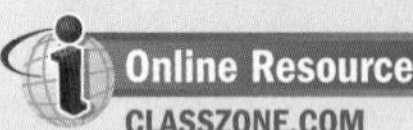

Online Resources
CLASSZONE.COM
- More Examples
- eTutorial Plus

Tell whether the number is *rational* or *irrational*. Explain your reasoning.

10. $\sqrt{144}$ **11.** $\frac{9}{46}$ **12.** 0.30311 **13.** $\sqrt{\frac{3}{5}}$

Graph the pair of numbers on a number line. Then copy and complete the statement with <, >, or =.

14. $\sqrt{\frac{64}{121}}$ $\underline{?}$ $\frac{8}{11}$ **15.** $\sqrt{13}$ $\underline{?}$ 3 **16.** $\sqrt{21}$ $\underline{?}$ 7 **17.** -5 $\underline{?}$ $-\sqrt{25}$

Order the decimals from least to greatest.

18. $0.1\overline{3}, 0.\overline{131}, 0.\overline{13}, 0.133$ **19.** $0.\overline{26}, 0.266, 0.2\overline{6}, 0.\overline{262}$

Evaluate the expression when *a* = 2, *b* = 4, and *c* = 9. Tell whether the result is *rational* or *irrational*.

20. $\sqrt{a+c}$ **21.** $\sqrt{a^2}$ **22.** $\sqrt{bc}$ **23.** $\sqrt{a^2+b^2}$

24. Decorating You are decorating your room. You have a square wall stencil that has an area of 20.25 square inches. Find the length of a side of the stencil. The wall you are decorating is $7\frac{1}{2}$ feet high. How many stencils can you place in a column from the top to the bottom of your wall?

In Exercises 25–27, graph the pair of numbers on a number line. Then copy and complete the statement with <, >, or =.

25. $\sqrt{0.9}$ $\underline{?}$ 0.9 **26.** -7 $\underline{?}$ $-\sqrt{7}$ **27.** $\sqrt{2.25}$ $\underline{?}$ $\frac{3.6}{2.4}$

28. Graph the numbers $-\sqrt{9}$, -8.69, $-\sqrt{45}$, and $-\frac{141}{25}$ on a number line.

Order the numbers from least to greatest.

29. $1.5, \sqrt{8}, -4, -3.75$ **30.** $\sqrt{81}, 10.3, \sqrt{220}, -9$

31. $-\sqrt{12}, -\sqrt{\frac{1}{4}}, -3.5, -\frac{3}{4}$ **32.** $1.02, \sqrt{2.5}, \sqrt{1.25}, \frac{2}{5}$

33. Carpet Your aunt offers you a square piece of carpet that has an area of 110 square feet. You want to use the carpet in a bedroom that measures 10.5 feet by 11.2 feet. Will the carpet fit in the room? Will it be too small? too large? Explain.

34. Critical Thinking Your friend gets a result of 2.645751311 on a calculator and says that it has to be an irrational number. Is your friend right? Explain your reasoning.

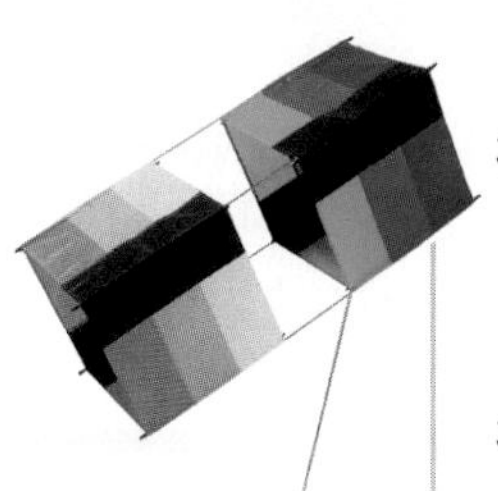

35. **Challenge** Find three rational numbers between $\frac{2}{3}$ and $\frac{3}{4}$. Can you write all of the rational numbers that are between these two numbers? Explain your reasoning.

36. **Box Kites** To calculate the minimum wind speed required to fly a box kite, you can use the formula $m = \sqrt{\frac{w}{A}}$, where m is the minimum wind speed in miles per hour, w is the weight in ounces, and A is the area in square feet of the surface used to lift the kite. Find the minimum wind speed required to lift a box kite with a weight of 5.6 ounces if the area used to lift the kite is 8.71 square feet.

Mixed Review

Simplify. Write the expression using only positive exponents. *(Lessons 4.6, 4.7)*

37. $5a^2 \cdot 6a^9$
38. $d^8 \cdot 4d^{-5}$
39. $-5m^0$
40. $n^{-7} \cdot n^5$
41. $\frac{c^5 \cdot c^3}{c^4}$
42. $\frac{24b^{14}}{8b^9}$
43. $\frac{-8n^8}{12n^{12}}$
44. $\frac{24r^{-5}}{r^3}$

Describe the transformation from the blue figure to the red figure using coordinate notation. *(Lessons 8.6, 8.7)*

45.

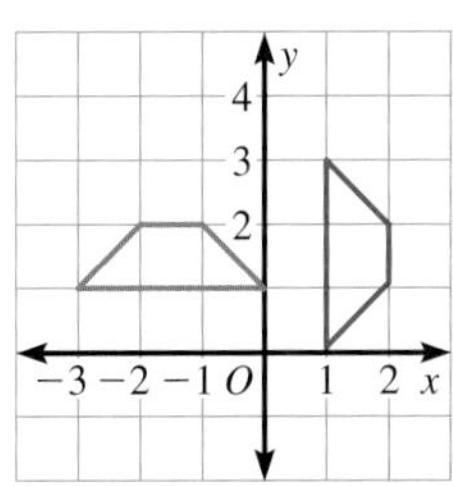

46.

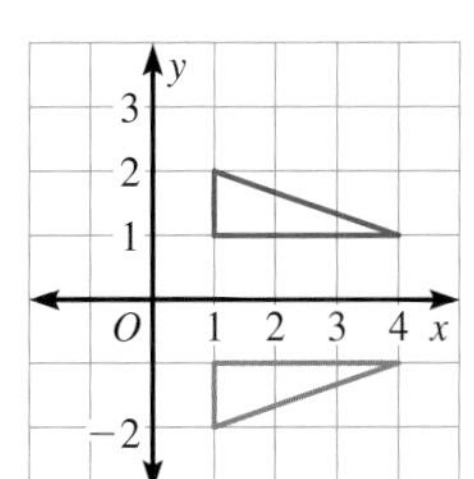

47.

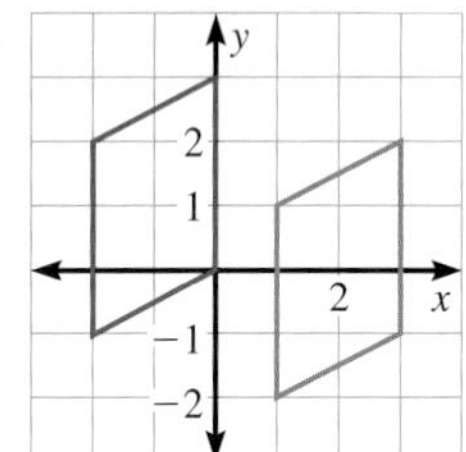

48. You draw a regular hexagon with side lengths of 2 centimeters on an overhead projector transparency. When it is projected, the hexagon is enlarged by a scale factor of 15. Find the perimeter of the image. *(Lesson 8.8)*

Test-Taking Practice

49. **Multiple Choice** Which statement is *not* true?

A. $\sqrt{12} < 4$ **B.** $8 > \sqrt{16}$ **C.** $\sqrt{169} = 13$ **D.** $\sqrt{30} < 5$

50. **Multiple Choice** Which of the following shows the numbers in order from least to greatest?

F. $\sqrt{2}, \sqrt{5}, 1, 2, 3$
G. $1, \sqrt{2}, \sqrt{5}, 2, 3$
H. $1, \sqrt{2}, 2, \sqrt{5}, 3$
I. $1, \sqrt{2}, 2, 3, \sqrt{5}$

9.3 Hands-on Activity

INDIANA: Academic Standards
- Geometry (8.4.5)

GOAL
Use graph paper to relate the side lengths of a right triangle.

MATERIALS
- graph paper
- pen or pencil

Modeling the Pythagorean Theorem

You can use graph paper to find the length of a right triangle's *hypotenuse*, which is the side opposite the right angle.

Explore **Find the length of the hypotenuse of a right triangle with side lengths of three units and four units.**

1. Draw the right triangle on graph paper. The sides of the triangle that form the right angle are called *legs*. For each leg, draw a square that has a leg as one side. What is the sum of the areas of these two squares?

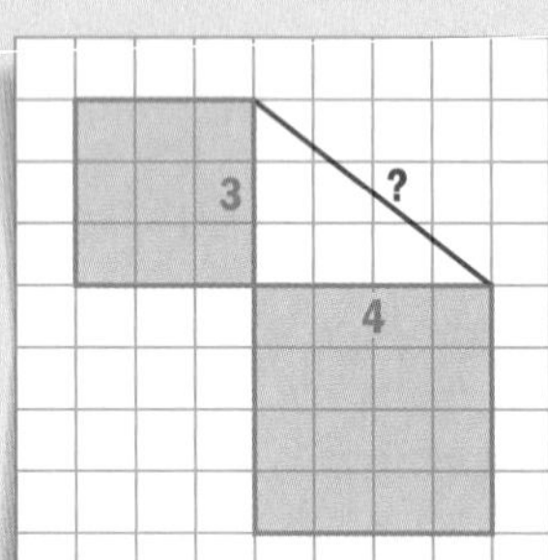

2. Measure the hypotenuse using graph paper. If you draw a square with the hypotenuse as one side, what is its area?

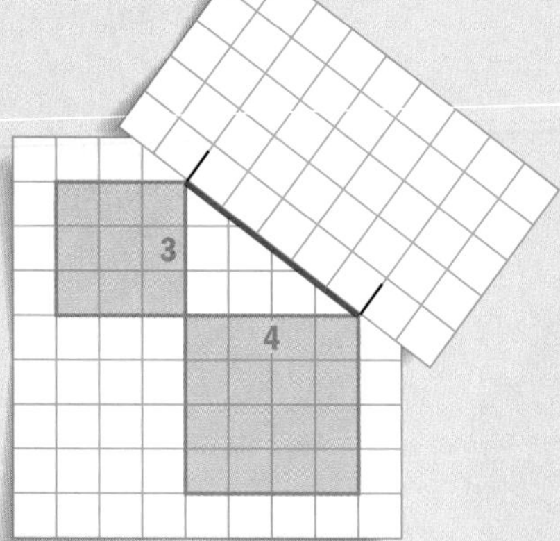

3. Compare the sum of the areas you found in Step 1 to the area you found in Step 2. What do you notice?

Your turn now **Repeat Steps 1–3 for right triangles with legs of the given lengths.**

1. 5, 12 **2.** 6, 8 **3.** 8, 15

Stop and Think

4. Let the lengths of the legs of a right triangle be a and b, and the length of the hypotenuse be c. Write a conjecture about the relationship between the lengths of the legs and the length of the hypotenuse.

The Pythagorean Theorem

BEFORE

You used formulas to solve problems.

Now

You'll use the Pythagorean theorem to solve problems.

WHY?

So you can find the length of a volleyball net support, as in Ex. 21.

Word Watch

INDIANA Academic Standards

- Geometry (8.4.5)
- Problem Solving (8.7.1)

In a right triangle, the sides that form the right angle are called **legs**. The side opposite the right angle is the **hypotenuse**. The lengths of the legs and the hypotenuse are related by the **Pythagorean theorem**.

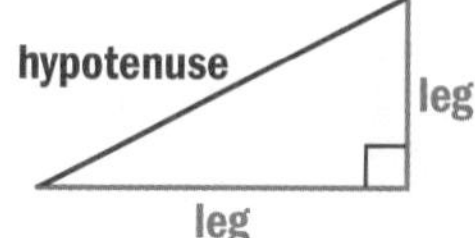

Pythagorean Theorem

Words For any right triangle, the sum of the squares of the lengths of the legs equals the square of the length of the hypotenuse.

$a = 3$, $b = 4$, $c = 5$

Algebra $a^2 + b^2 = c^2$

Numbers $3^2 + 4^2 = 5^2$

EXAMPLE 1 Finding the Length of a Hypotenuse

Find the length of the hypotenuse of a right triangle with leg lengths of 15 inches and 20 inches.

$a^2 + b^2 = c^2$	Pythagorean theorem
$15^2 + 20^2 = c^2$	Substitute 15 for *a* and 20 for *b*.
$225 + 400 = c^2$	Evaluate powers.
$625 = c^2$	Add.
$\sqrt{625} = c$	Take positive square root of each side.
$25 = c$	Evaluate square root.

ANSWER The length of the hypotenuse is 25 inches.

HELP with Notetaking

Be sure to write the Pythagorean theorem in your notebook.

Your turn now Complete the exercise.

1. Find the length of the hypotenuse of a right triangle with leg lengths of 28 inches and 45 inches.

In application problems, you usually need to take only the positive square root. For example, length, speed, and height are positive, so a negative square root would not give a reasonable answer.

EXAMPLE 2 Finding the Length of a Leg

Parasailing You are parasailing. After getting airborne and reaching cruising speed, you are 200 feet directly behind the boat. How high are you above the water to the nearest foot?

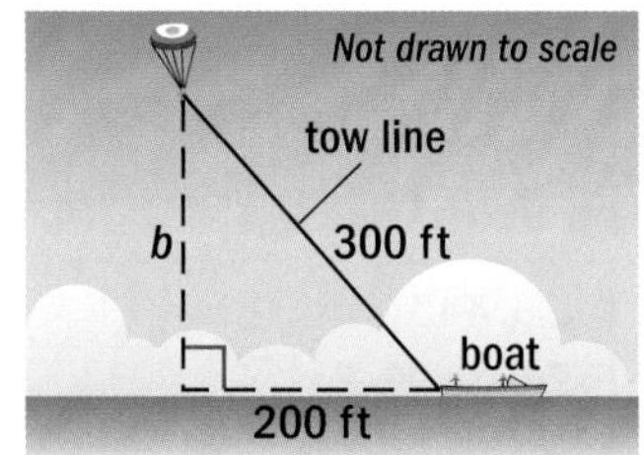

Solution

$a^2 + b^2 = c^2$	**Pythagorean theorem**
$200^2 + b^2 = 300^2$	**Substitute 200 for *a* and 300 for *c*.**
$40{,}000 + b^2 = 90{,}000$	**Evaluate powers.**
$b^2 = 50{,}000$	**Subtract 40,000 from each side.**
$b = \sqrt{50{,}000}$	**Take positive square root of each side.**
$b \approx 223.6068$	**Approximate square root.**

ANSWER You are about 224 feet above the water.

HELP with Solving

If you know the lengths of *any* two sides of a right triangle, you can use the Pythagorean theorem to find the length of the third side.

Your turn now **Find the unknown length. Round to the nearest tenth, if necessary.**

2. c; $a = 7.5$ in.; $b = 18$ in.

3. a; $b = 8$ m; $c = 16$ m

4.

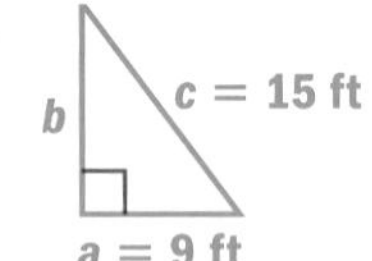

5. **Critical Thinking** Does it matter which leg of a right triangle is labeled a or b? Explain.

Converse of the Pythagorean Theorem The Pythagorean theorem can be written as an if-then statement with two parts.

Theorem If **a triangle is a right triangle**, then $a^2 + b^2 = c^2$.

When you reverse the parts of an if-then statement, the new statement is called the **converse** of the statement.

Converse If $a^2 + b^2 = c^2$, then **the triangle is a right triangle**.

The converse of a statement may or may not be true. The converse of the Pythagorean theorem is true. You can use the converse of the Pythagorean theorem to decide whether a triangle is a right triangle.

EXAMPLE 3 Identifying Right Triangles

Use the converse of the Pythagorean theorem to determine whether the triangle with the given side lengths is a right triangle.

a. $a = 6, b = 8, c = 10$

$$a^2 + b^2 \stackrel{?}{=} c^2$$
$$6^2 + 8^2 \stackrel{?}{=} 10^2$$
$$36 + 64 \stackrel{?}{=} 100$$
$$100 = 100 \checkmark$$

ANSWER A right triangle

b. $a = 10, b = 12, c = 16$

$$a^2 + b^2 \stackrel{?}{=} c^2$$
$$10^2 + 12^2 \stackrel{?}{=} 16^2$$
$$100 + 144 \stackrel{?}{=} 256$$
$$244 \neq 256 \text{ ✗}$$

ANSWER Not a right triangle

9.3 Exercises

More Practice, p. 735

Getting Ready to Practice

1. **Vocabulary** Copy and complete: In a right triangle, the side opposite the right angle is called the _?_.

Let *a* and *b* represent the lengths of the legs of a right triangle, and let *c* represent the length of the hypotenuse. Find the unknown length.

2. $a = 12, b = ?, c = 20$
3. $a = ?, b = 36, c = 39$
4. $a = 9, b = ?, c = 41$
5. $a = 7, b = 24, c = ?$

Use the converse of the Pythagorean theorem to determine whether the triangle with the given side lengths is a right triangle.

6. $a = 3, b = 7, c = 9$
7. $a = 24, b = 45, c = 51$
8. $a = 20, b = 48, c = 52$
9. $a = 16, b = 18, c = 24$
10. **Ladders** A 13 foot ladder is leaning against a building. The bottom of the ladder is 5 feet from the building. How high is the top of the ladder?

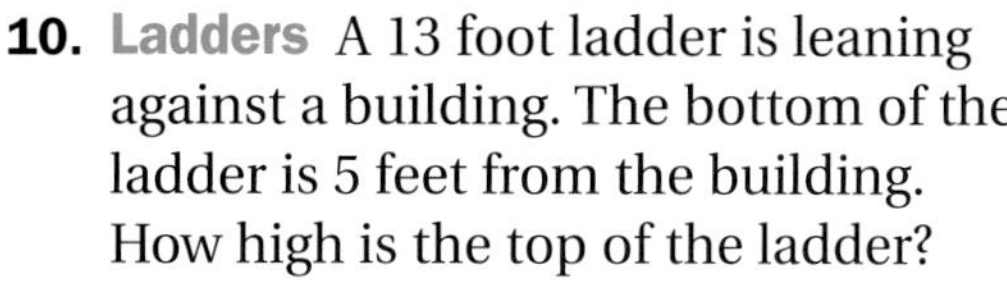

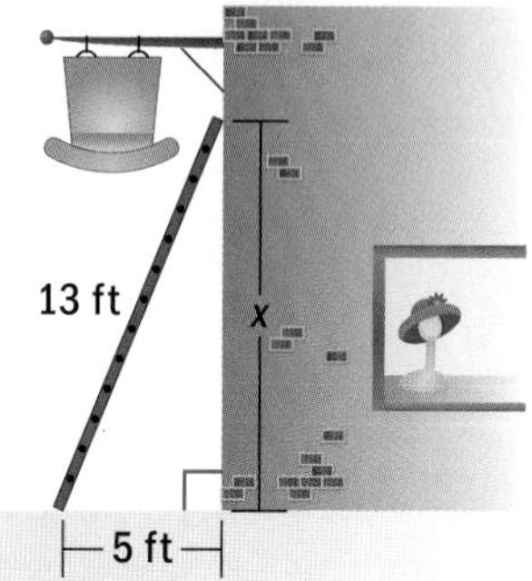

Practice and Problem Solving

HELP with Homework

Example	Exercises
1	11–16
2	11–16, 21
3	17–19

- More Examples
- eTutorial Plus

Find the unknown length. Round to the nearest tenth, if necessary.

11.

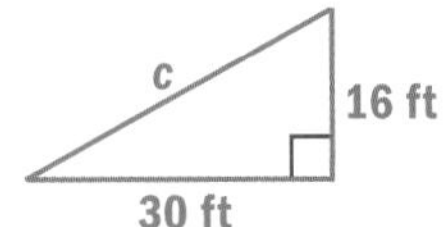

12.

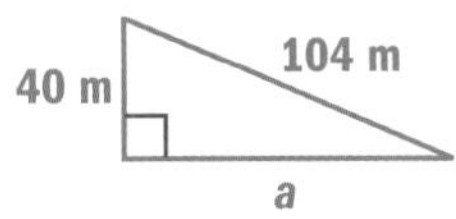

13.

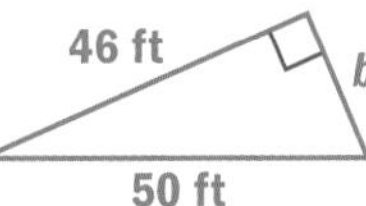

14.

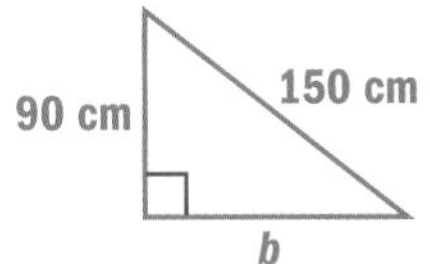

15.

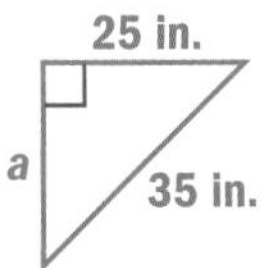

16.

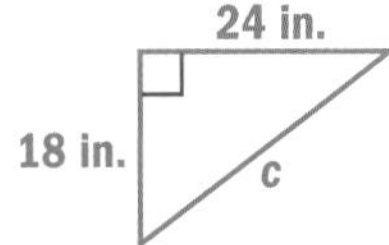

Determine whether the triangle with the given side lengths is a right triangle.

17.

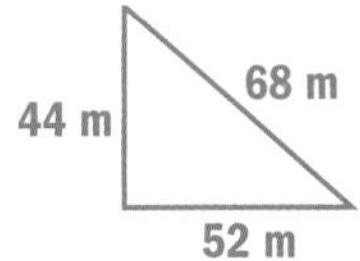

18.

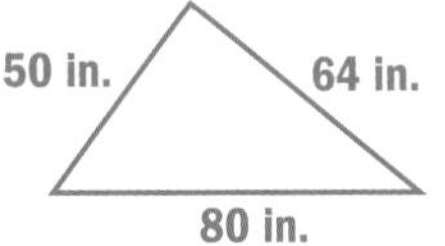

19.

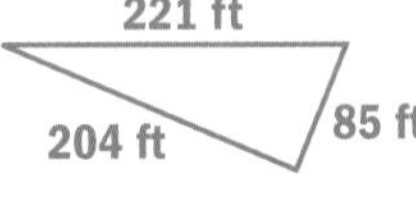

20. Find the Error Describe and correct the error in finding the length of the third side of the right triangle. Round to the nearest tenth of a foot.

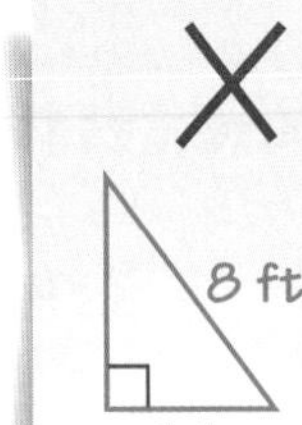

$$a^2 + b^2 = c^2$$
$$6^2 + 8^2 = c^2$$
$$36 + 64 = c^2$$
$$100 = c^2$$
$$10 = c$$

21. Volleyball Net You are setting up a volleyball net. There are two 8 foot poles that hold up the net. You are going to attach each pole to a stake in the ground using a piece of rope. Each stake should be 4 feet from the pole. Assume that the ropes are taut. How long should each rope be? Round to the nearest tenth of a foot.

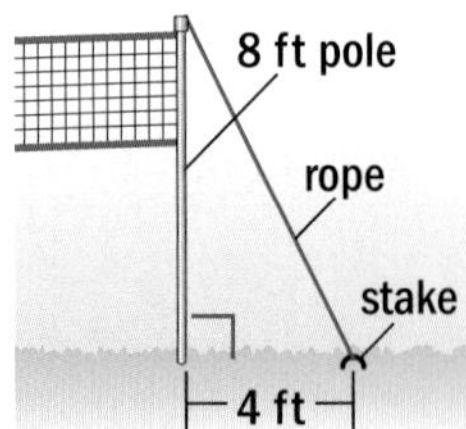

Find the unknown length. Round to the nearest hundredth, if necessary.

22.

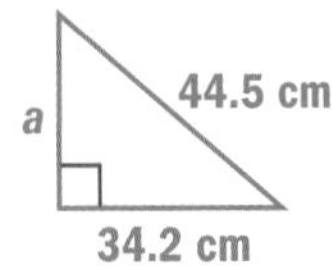

23.

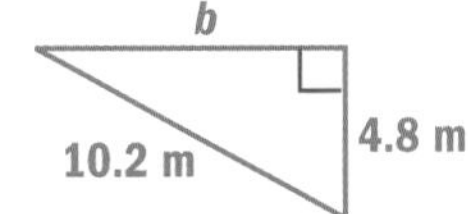

24.

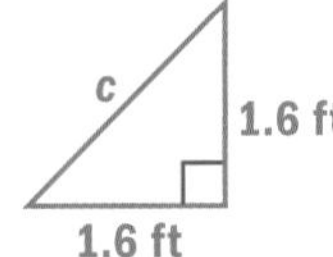

25. Critical Thinking An isosceles right triangle has a hypotenuse with a length of 6 feet. Find the length of each leg. Round to the nearest hundredth of a foot.

Utility Poles

Several states have built nesting platforms on the tops of utility poles to provide safe nesting areas for birds. If a platform is 6 feet wide and the supports meet the pole 6 feet beneath the platform, how long are the supports?

Determine whether the triangle with the given side lengths is a right triangle.

26. $a = 0.65, b = 1.56, c = 1.69$

27. $a = 2.88, b = 0.84, c = 3.2$

28. $a = 0.12, b = 0.16, c = 0.2$

29. $a = 0.75, b = 0.4, c = 0.85$

30. Utility Poles A guy wire with a length of 23.8 meters is attached to a utility pole. The wire is anchored to the ground 9 meters from the base of the pole. How high above the ground is the guy wire attached to the utility pole? Round to the nearest tenth of a meter.

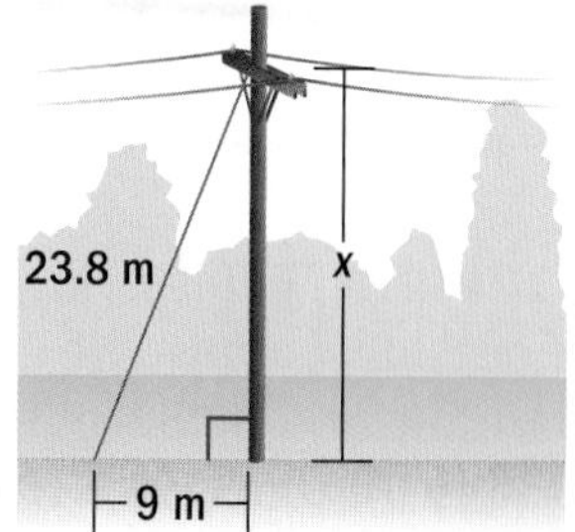

Let *a* and *b* represent the lengths of the legs of a right triangle, and let *c* represent the length of the hypotenuse. Find the unknown length.

31. $a = 1.5, b = ?, c = 2.5$

32. $a = ?, b = 123, c = 139.4$

33. $a = 2.8, b = 4.5, c = ?$

34. $a = 4.5, b = ?, c = 7.5$

35. $a = \sqrt{8}, b = 1, c = ?$

36. $a = ?, b = 2, c = \sqrt{13}$

37. Challenge Draw several different obtuse triangles and measure the lengths of the legs. Let *a* and *b* represent the lengths of the two shorter sides and let *c* represent the length of the longest side. Make a conjecture about the relationship between the lengths of the sides of obtuse triangles.

Mixed Review 

38. In the figure, $ABCD \sim WXYZ$. Find $m\angle D$. *(Lesson 8.8)*

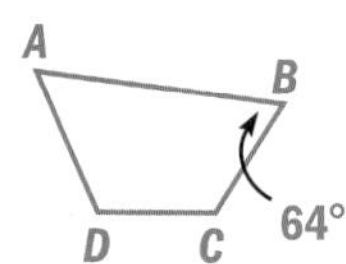

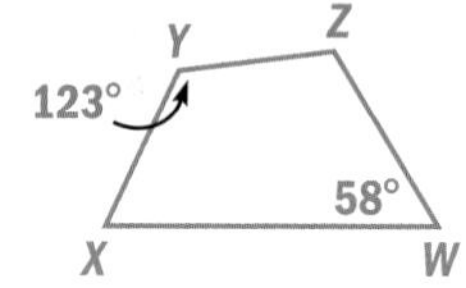

39. Triangle *LMN* has vertices $L(1, 5)$, $M(4, 2)$, and $N(0, 0)$. Dilate the triangle using a scale factor of 3. *(Lesson 8.8)*

Test-Taking Practice 

INTERNET
State Test Practice
CLASSZONE.COM

40. Multiple Choice The hypotenuse of a right triangle has a length of 40 inches, and one of the legs has a length of 32 inches. What is the length of the other leg?

A. 12 inches **B.** 21 inches **C.** 24 inches **D.** 39 inches

41. Short Response Determine whether a triangle with side lengths of 56 feet, 90 feet, and 106 feet is a right triangle. Explain.

9.4 Problem Solving Strategies

INDIANA: Academic Standards
- Geometry (8.4.5)
- Problem Solving (8.7.1)

- Guess, Check, and Revise
- Look for a Pattern
- Make a List
- Act It Out
- Draw a Diagram
- Work Backward
- Solve a Simpler Problem

Draw a Diagram

Problem Jeff is flying a kite. He is holding the end of the kite string about 3 feet above the ground. The length of the string is 35 feet. He is standing about 28 feet from the base of a tree when the wind changes and the kite gets stuck in the tree. About how high off the ground is the kite when it is stuck in the tree?

1 Read and Understand

Read the problem carefully.

You know the height of Jeff's hands above the ground, the length of the kite string, and the distance to the tree. You need to find the height of the kite after it is in the tree.

2 Make a Plan

Decide on a strategy to use.

One way to solve the problem is to draw a diagram of the situation. Then you can use the Pythagorean theorem to find the height of the kite in the tree.

3 Solve the Problem

Reread the problem and draw a diagram.

Show the position of Jeff, the tree, and the kite.

Write known lengths on the diagram. The end of the kite string is about 3 feet above the ground, the string is 35 feet long, and the tree is about 28 feet from Jeff.

Next, use the Pythagorean theorem to find the missing length a.

$$a^2 + b^2 = c^2$$

$$a^2 + 28^2 = 35^2$$

$$a^2 + 784 = 1225$$

$$a^2 = 441$$

$$a = 21$$

$$21 + 3 = 24$$

Length is positive. Find positive square root.

ANSWER The kite is about 24 feet high.

4 Look Back

Be sure that you used all of the necessary information in the problem.

Practice the Strategy

Use the strategy *draw a diagram.*

1. **Utility Pole** A support wire 10 meters long is attached to the top of a utility pole 7 meters tall and is then stretched taut. How far from the base of the pole will the wire be attached to the ground? Round your answer to the nearest tenth of a meter.

2. **Hiking** Eric is hiking from his campsite to a creek. He walks 3.5 miles directly south, 4 miles directly east, then 1.5 miles directly south. Copy and complete the diagram to find how far he is from the campsite.

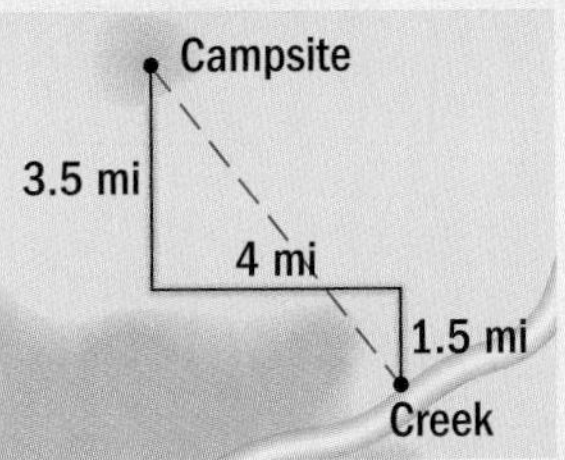

3. **Circus** A cable from the top of a circus tent pole is attached to the ground at a point 15 feet from the base of the pole. If the cable is 40 feet long, how high is the pole? Round your answer to the nearest foot.

4. **Distance** You and your friend live on opposite corners of a square park. You usually ride your bike 1280 feet around the outside of the park to reach your friend's house. Today, you walk diagonally across the park to get to your friend's house. How much shorter is the walking distance than the biking distance? Round your answer to the nearest foot.

5. **Moving** You are moving into a new house. The doorway is 78 inches high and 36 inches wide. Can a round table top with a diameter of 82 inches fit through the doorway?

Mixed Problem Solving

Use any strategy to solve the problem.

6. **Pool** To sanitize a swimming pool, you should use 2 parts per million of chlorine, which can also be written as

$$\frac{\text{2 gallons chlorine}}{\text{1,000,000 gallons water}}.$$

How much chlorine should there be in a pool that holds 20,000 gallons of water?

7. **Advertising** A newspaper charges a base fee of $20 for a color ad plus a charge for each line. The table shows the total cost of several color ads. How much would you expect to pay for a 15 line color ad?

Number of lines	2	4	6	8	10
Total Cost	$36	$52	$68	$84	$100

8. **Money** Your grandmother gave you some money for your birthday. You put half of the money in the bank. Then you go to the mall and spend $12.50 on a DVD and give half of what's left to your younger brother. You now have $2.50 left. How much money did your grandmother give you?

9. **Banking** You have an ATM card for your savings account, but you have forgotten your four-digit personal identification number (PIN). You know the first digit is a 4 and the last three digits contain a 4, 2, and 7. How many possibilities are there for your PIN?

Using the Pythagorean Theorem

BEFORE	Now	WHY?
You found the side lengths of right triangles.	You'll solve real-life problems using the Pythagorean theorem.	So you can find the diagonal length of a swimming pool, as in Ex. 5.

Pythagorean triple, p. 451

INDIANA
Academic Standards
- Geometry (8.4.5)
- Problem Solving (8.7.1)

In the Real World

Boating You and your friend live on opposite sides of a lake. To ride your bicycle to your friend's house, you travel 0.5 mile directly east, then 1.2 miles directly south. How far is it to your friend's house by boat?

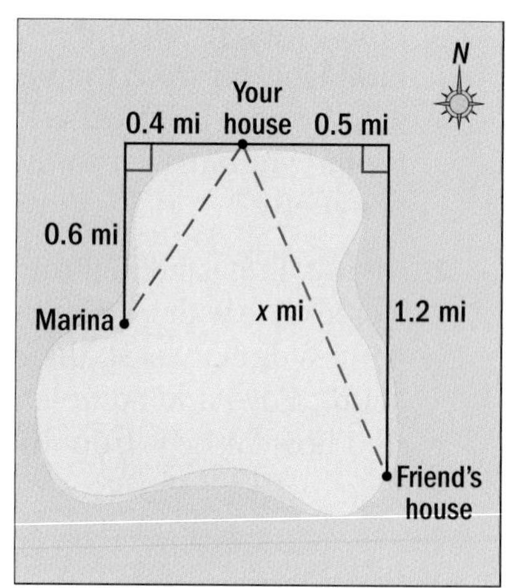

One way to find the distance from your house to your friend's house by boat is to measure the distance *indirectly*. Because the bicycle and boat paths form a right triangle, you can do this using the Pythagorean theorem.

EXAMPLE 1 Using Indirect Measurement

Let a and b represent the lengths of the legs (bicycle paths) of the right triangle. Let x represent the length of the hypotenuse (boat path).

$a^2 + b^2 = x^2$	Pythagorean theorem
$0.5^2 + 1.2^2 = x^2$	Substitute 0.5 for a and 1.2 for b.
$0.25 + 1.44 = x^2$	Evaluate powers.
$1.69 = x^2$	Add.
$1.3 = x$	Take positive square root of each side.

ANSWER It is 1.3 miles to your friend's house by boat.

Your turn now Use the information in the map.

1. To get to the marina from your house, you travel 0.4 mile directly west, then 0.6 mile directly south. How far is it to the marina by boat? Round your answer to the nearest hundredth of a mile.

EXAMPLE 2 Finding Perimeter and Area

Find the perimeter and area of the triangle.

h
17 cm
15 cm

Solution

(1 Find the height of the triangle.

$h^2 + 15^2 = 17^2$	Pythagorean theorem
$h^2 + 225 = 289$	Evaluate powers.
$h^2 = 64$	Subtract 225 from each side.
$h = 8$	Take positive square root of each side.

(2 Use the height to find the perimeter and area.

Perimeter $= 8 + 15 + 17 = 40$

Area $= \frac{1}{2}bh$

$= \frac{1}{2}(15)(8)$

$= 60$

ANSWER The perimeter is 40 cm and the area is 60 cm^2.

HELP with Review

For help with finding the perimeter and area of a triangle, see p. 134.

Your turn now **Complete the exercise.**

2. Find the perimeter and area of the triangle.

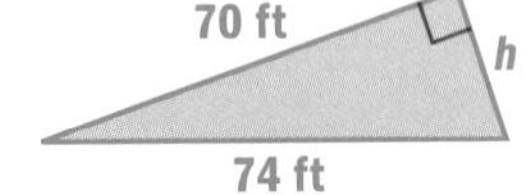

Pythagorean Triples A **Pythagorean triple** is a set of three positive integers *a*, *b*, and *c* such that $a^2 + b^2 = c^2$. For example, the integers 3, 4, and 5 form a Pythagorean triple because $3^2 + 4^2 = 5^2$.

EXAMPLE 3 Identifying a Pythagorean Triple

Determine whether the side lengths of the triangle form a Pythagorean triple.

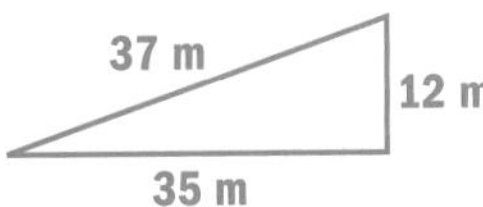

Solution

$a^2 + b^2 = c^2$	Definition of Pythagorean triple
$12^2 + 35^2 \stackrel{?}{=} 37^2$	Substitute 12 for *a*, 35 for *b*, and 37 for *c*.
$144 + 1225 \stackrel{?}{=} 1369$	Evaluate powers.
$1369 = 1369$	Add.

ANSWER Because $12^2 + 35^2 = 37^2$, the side lengths form a Pythagorean triple.

Getting Ready to Practice

1. **Vocabulary** Copy and complete: The integers 5, 12, and 13 form a _?_ because $5^2 + 12^2 = 13^2$.

Find the perimeter of the triangle.

2.

3.

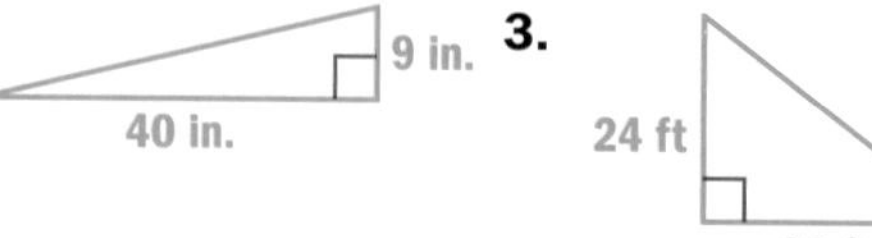

4.

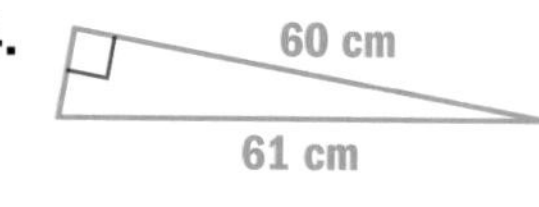

5. **Guided Problem Solving** A rectangular swimming pool has a length of 41 feet and a width of 11 feet. Tina swims the diagonal distance across the pool. About how far does she swim?
   1. Draw a diagram.
   2. Label the known distances.
   3. Use the Pythagorean theorem to find the unknown length. Round your answer to the nearest tenth of a foot.

Practice and Problem Solving

HELP with Homework

Example	Exercises
1	17–19
2	6–11
3	12–15

· More Examples
· eTutorial Plus

Let *a* and *b* represent the lengths of the legs of a right triangle, and let *c* represent the length of the hypotenuse. Find the unknown length. Then find the area and perimeter.

6. $a = 12$ cm, $b = 5$ cm, $c = ?$
7. $a = 8$ ft, $b = ?$, $c = 17$ ft
8. $a = ?$, $b = 4.2$ km, $c = 5.8$ km
9. $a = 4.8$ in., $b = 3.6$ in., $c = ?$
10. $a = 60$ yd, $b = ?$, $c = 601.5$ yd
11. $a = ?$, $b = 117$ m, $c = 125$ m

Determine whether the numbers form a Pythagorean triple.

12. 9, 36, 41
13. 55, 48, 73
14. 39, 80, 89
15. 45, 96, 104

16. **Critical Thinking** Copy and complete the table. Are the Pythagorean triples still Pythagorean triples after they are multiplied by another positive integer? Explain your reasoning.

Pythagorean Triples	3, 4, 5	5, 12, 13	7, 24, 25
Multiply by 2	6, 8, 10	?	?
Multiply by 3	?	?	?
Multiply by 10	?	?	?

Find the measure of *x*.

17. 

18. 

Washington Monument

19. **Bookshelf** You are making a bookshelf. Find x. Round to the nearest inch.

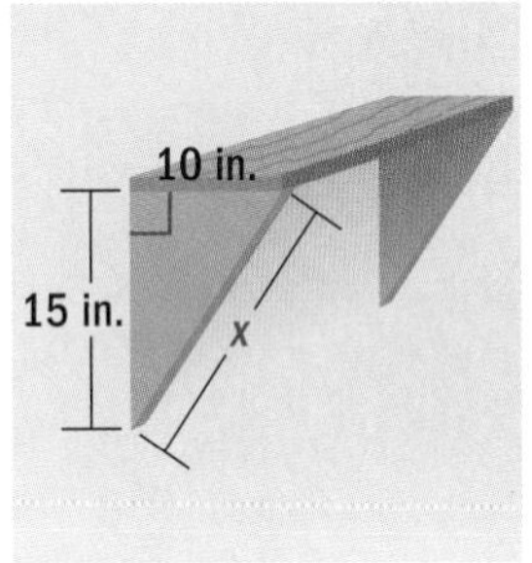

20. **Draw a Diagram** You are standing 500 feet from the Washington Monument. Using a laser range finder on the ground, you measure the distance to the top of the monument to be 747 feet. Find the height of the Washington Monument to the nearest foot.

Find the perimeter of the right triangle given its area and the length of one leg.

21. $a = 6$ m
Area $= 24\text{ m}^2$

22. $a = 8.8$ mi
Area $= 46.2\text{ mi}^2$

23. $a = 84$ cm
Area $= 546\text{ cm}^2$

24. **Challenge** Find the area of the shaded region given $\triangle ABC \sim \triangle ADE$, $AB = 10$ ft, $AC = 6$ ft, and $DE = 16$ ft.

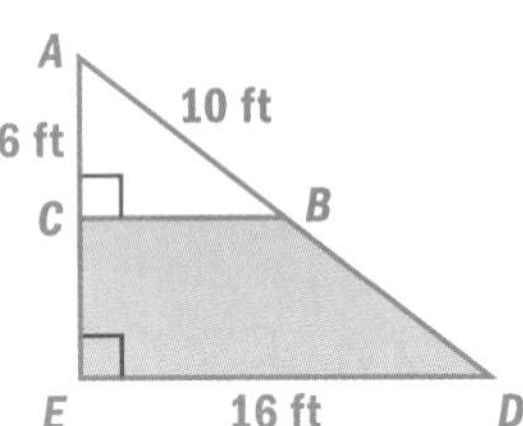

Mixed Review

25. Reflect the polygon with the vertices $A(-3, 3)$, $B(-3, 6)$, $C(-5, 3)$, and $D(-6, 1)$ in the y-axis. Graph the figure and its image. *(Lesson 8.6)*

Find the square root. *(Lesson 9.1)*

26. $\sqrt{9}$

27. $-\sqrt{144}$

28. $-\sqrt{625}$

29. $\sqrt{72.25}$

Test-Taking Practice 

INTERNET
State Test Practice
CLASSZONE.COM

30. **Extended Response** Find the area and perimeter of $\triangle ABC$. Explain how you found your answers. Round your answers to the nearest tenth, if necessary.

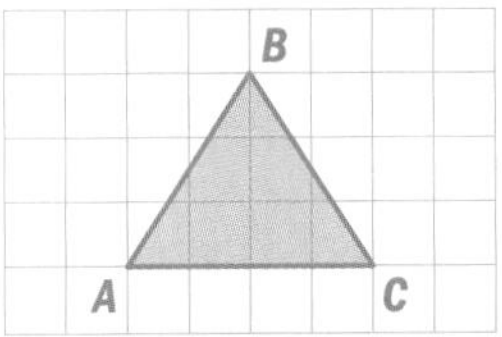

LESSONS 9.1 TO 9.4

Notebook Review

Review the vocabulary definitions in your notebook.

Copy the review examples in your notebook. Then complete the exercises.

Check Your Definitions

square root, p. 431
radical expression, p. 431
perfect square, p. 432
irrational number, p. 437
real number, p. 437
leg, hypotenuse, p. 443
Pythagorean theorem, p. 443
converse, p. 444
Pythagorean triple, p. 451

Use Your Vocabulary

1. Copy and complete: Together, the rational numbers and the irrational numbers make up the set of _?_.

9.1 Can you solve equations using square roots?

EXAMPLE Solve the equation $x^2 - 18 = 4$.

$x^2 - 18 = 4$	Original equation
$x^2 = 22$	Add 18 to each side.
$x = \pm\sqrt{22}$	Definition of square root
$x \approx \pm 4.69$	Approximate square root.

✓ **Solve the equation.**

2. $a^2 = 169$ **3.** $b^2 - 20 = 101$ **4.** $c^2 + 25 = 89$

9.2 Can you compare two real numbers?

EXAMPLE Graph the numbers $\sqrt{7}$ and 3 on a number line. Then complete the statement $\sqrt{7}$ _?_ 3 with <, >, or =.

$\sqrt{7} \approx 2.6458$ 3

2.5 2.6 2.7 2.8 2.9 3 3.1

So, $\sqrt{7} < 3$.

✓ **Graph the pair of numbers on a number line. Then complete the statement with <, >, or =.**

5. $\sqrt{31}$ _?_ 4 **6.** 7 _?_ $\sqrt{59}$ **7.** -9 _?_ $-\sqrt{81}$ **8.** $\sqrt{48}$ _?_ 6.3

9.3–9.4 Can you use the Pythagorean Theorem?

EXAMPLE Find the unknown length.

22 in. a 20 in.

$a^2 + b^2 = c^2$	Pythagorean theorem
$a^2 + 20^2 = 22^2$	Substitute 20 for *b* and 22 for *c*.
$a^2 = 84$	Simplify.
$a \approx 9.2$ in.	Take positive square root of each side.

☑ **Let *a* and *b* represent the lengths of the legs of a right triangle, and let *c* represent the length of the hypotenuse. Find the unknown length.**

9. $a = 8, c = 17$ **10.** $b = 24, c = 40$ **11.** $a = 2.4, b = 0.7$

Stop and Think about Lessons 9.1–9.4

12. Writing Describe how the decimal forms of rational numbers are different from the decimal form of irrational numbers. Give examples to illustrate your answer.

Review Quiz 1

Use a calculator to approximate the square root. Round to the nearest tenth.

1. $\sqrt{50}$ **2.** $\sqrt{18}$ **3.** $-\sqrt{160}$ **4.** $\sqrt{462}$

Solve the equation. Check your solutions.

5. $x^2 = 400$ **6.** $b^2 - 11 = -2$ **7.** $m^2 + 140 = 284$

8. Order the numbers 2.75, $\sqrt{5}$, $\frac{3}{2}$, and -1 from least to greatest.

9. Find the length of the hypotenuse of a right triangle with leg lengths of 12 meters and 16 meters.

10. Antenna How long must a wire be to connect the top of an 8 foot antenna to a hook 5 feet from the base of the antenna? Round your answer to the nearest tenth of a foot.

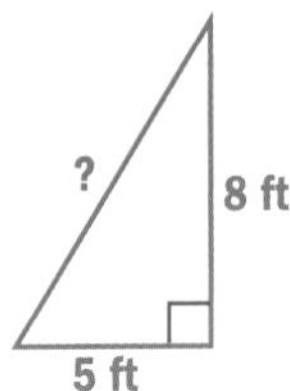

Determine whether the numbers form a Pythagorean triple.

11. 5, 12, 15 **12.** 60, 91, 109

Special Right Triangles

BEFORE	Now	WHY?
You solved real-life problems using the Pythagorean theorem.	You'll use special right triangles to solve real-life problems.	So you can find the depth of a subway station, as in Ex. 13.

In the Real World

Softball The infield of a softball field is a square with a side length of 60 feet. A catcher throws the ball from home plate to second base. How far does the catcher have to throw the ball?

Word Watch

Review Words

equilateral triangle, p. 382
isosceles triangle, p. 382
right triangle, p. 382
scalene triangle, p. 382
leg, p. 443
hypotenuse, p. 443

INDIANA Academic Standards

- Geometry (8.4.5)
- Algebra and Functions (8.3.1)

To find missing side lengths of triangles whose angle measures are 45°-45°-90° or 30°-60°-90°, you can use the special relationships among the side lengths.

45°-45°-90° Triangle

Words In a 45°-45°-90° triangle, the length of the hypotenuse is the product of the length of a leg and $\sqrt{2}$.

Algebra hypotenuse = leg $\cdot \sqrt{2}$

$= x\sqrt{2}$

Diagram

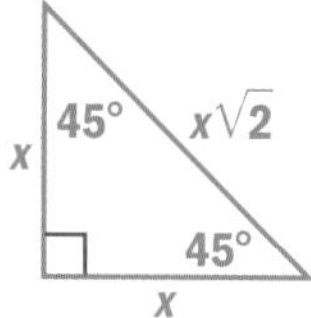

EXAMPLE 1 Using a 45°-45°-90° Triangle

To find the distance from home plate to second base, first draw a diagram. Then use the rule for a 45°-45°-90° triangle.

$$\begin{aligned} \text{hypotenuse} &= \textbf{leg} \cdot \sqrt{2} \\ &= \textbf{60} \cdot \sqrt{2} \\ &\approx 60(1.414) \\ &= 84.84 \end{aligned}$$

Second Base
45°
60 ft
Home Plate
45°

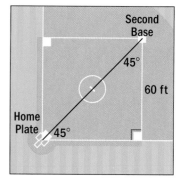

ANSWER A catcher has to throw the ball about 84.84 feet.

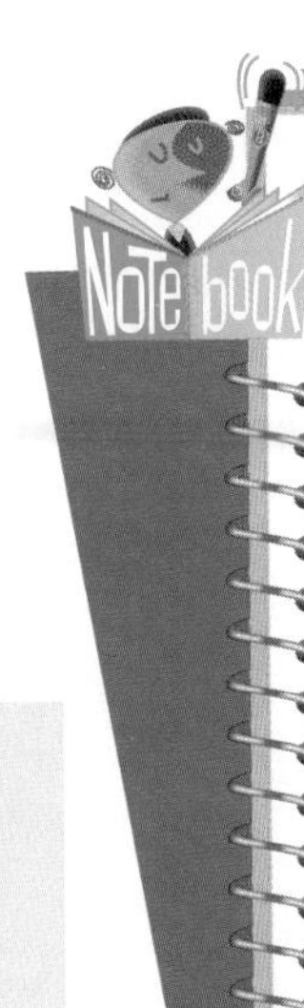

30°-60°-90° Triangle

Words In a 30°-60°-90° triangle, the hypotenuse is twice as long as the shorter leg. The length of the longer leg is the product of the length of the shorter leg and $\sqrt{3}$.

Algebra hypotenuse = 2 • shorter leg

$= 2x$

longer leg = shorter leg • $\sqrt{3}$

$= x\sqrt{3}$

Diagram

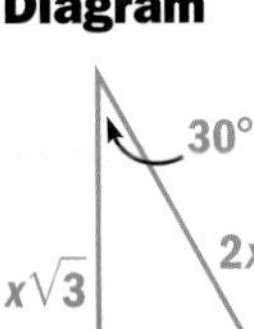

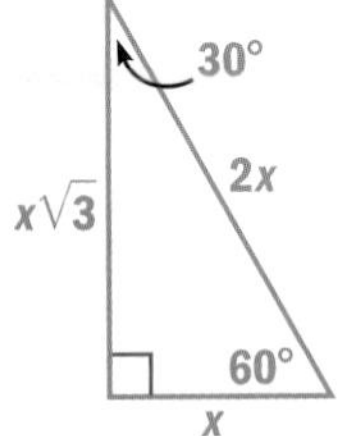

HELP with Solving

In a 30°-60°-90° triangle, the shorter leg is opposite the 30° angle, and the longer leg is opposite the 60° angle.

To give an *exact answer*, leave your answer as a radical expression.

EXAMPLE 2 Using a 30°-60°-90° Triangle

Find the value of each variable in the triangle. Give the exact answer.

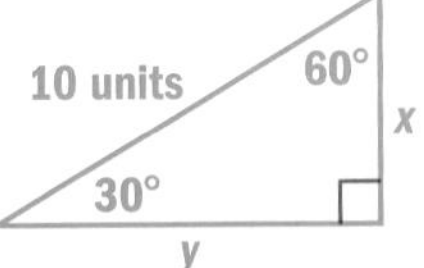

You need to find the length of the shorter leg first in order to find the length of the longer leg.

1. Find the length of the shorter leg.

hypotenuse = 2 • **shorter leg**	**Rule for 30°-60°-90° triangle**
$10 = 2 \cdot x$	**Substitute.**
$5 = x$	**Divide each side by 2.**

2. Find the length of the longer leg.

longer leg = **shorter leg** • $\sqrt{3}$	**Rule for 30°-60°-90° triangle**
$y = 5\sqrt{3}$	**Substitute.**

ANSWER The length of the shorter leg is 5 units. The length of the longer leg is $5\sqrt{3}$ units.

HELP with Solving

You can use the Pythagorean theorem to check the solutions in Examples 1 and 2.

Your turn now **Find the value of each variable. Give exact answers.**

1.

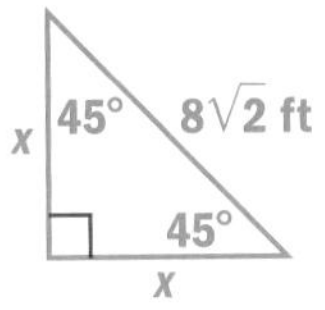

2.

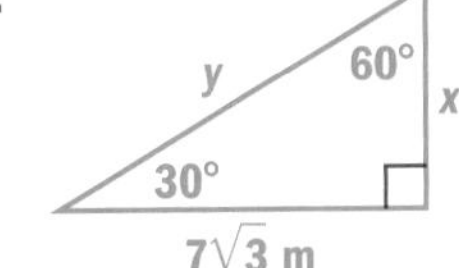

3.

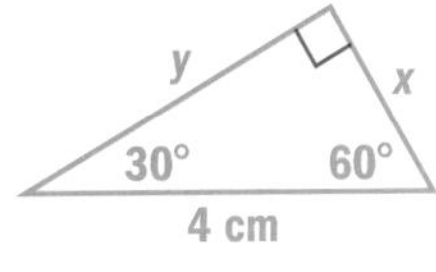

EXAMPLE 3 Using a Special Right Triangle

Water Ski Show The pyramid ski show is a common feature of water parks. Find the horizontal distance from the pyramid to the boat.

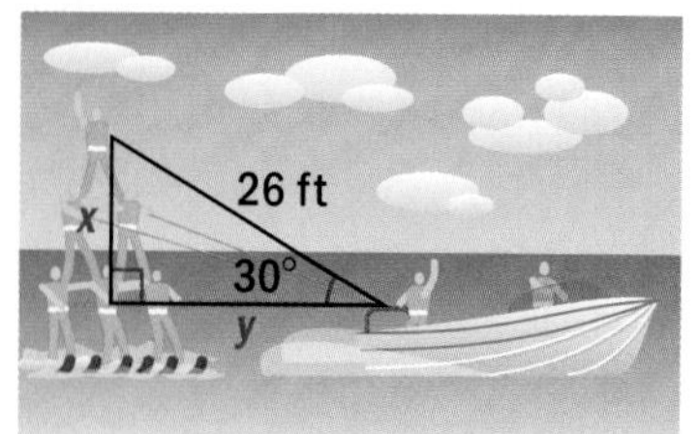

(1) Find the length of the shorter leg.

hypotenuse = 2 • **shorter leg**

$26 = 2 \cdot x$

$13 = x$

(2) Find the length of the longer leg.

longer leg = **shorter leg** • $\sqrt{3}$

$y = 13 \cdot \sqrt{3}$

≈ 22.5166605

ANSWER The horizontal distance is about 23 feet.

9.5 Exercises

More Practice, p. 735

Getting Ready to Practice

1. **Vocabulary** Explain how the length of the hypotenuse in a 45°-45°-90° triangle is related to the length of a leg.

Find the value of the variable. Give the exact answer.

2.

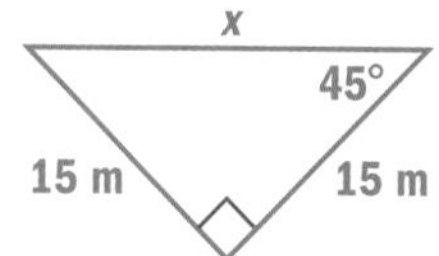

3.

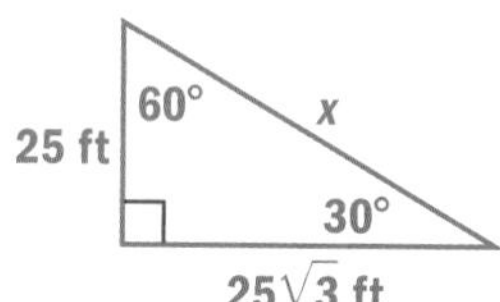

4. **Find the Error** Describe and correct the error in the solution.

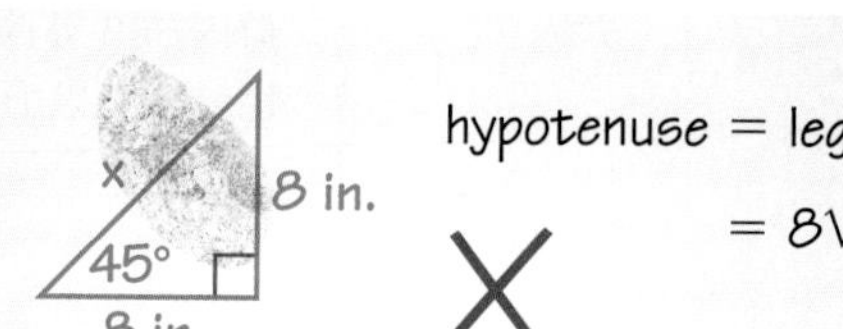

5. **Guided Problem Solving** The hypotenuse of a 30°-60°-90° triangle is $5\sqrt{3}$ inches. Find the length of the longer leg.

(1) Find the length of the shorter leg.

(2) Use the shorter leg to find the length of the longer leg.

Practice and Problem Solving

Example	Exercises
1	6–8
2	9–11
3	13

Online Resources
CLASSZONE.COM

- More Examples
- eTutorial Plus

Find the value of each variable. Give exact answers.

6.

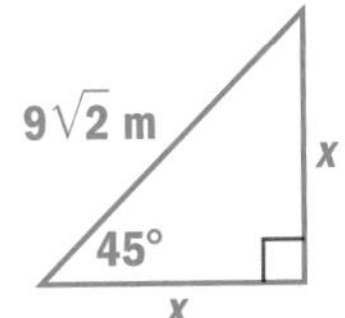

7.

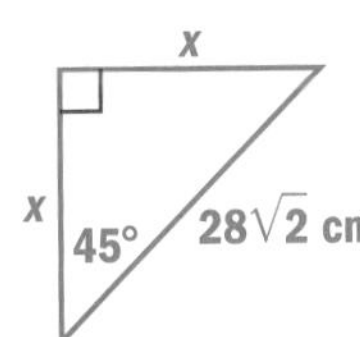

8.

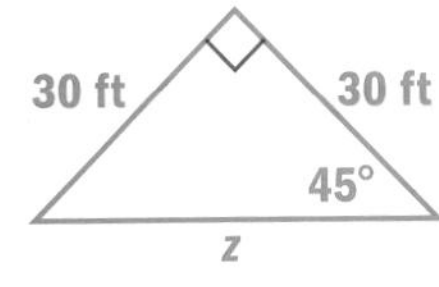

9.

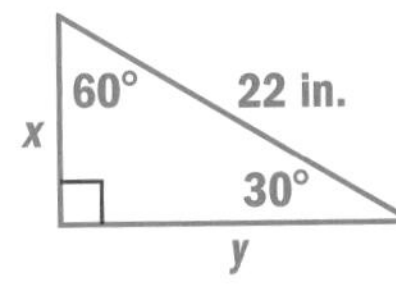

10.

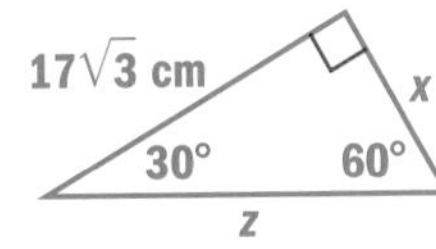

11.

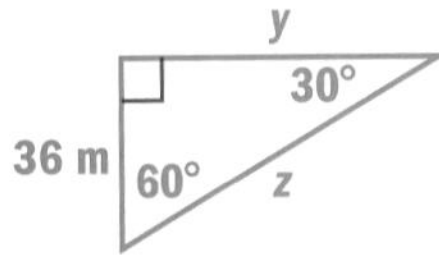

12. Critical Thinking Is it possible to have an equilateral right triangle? Explain your reasoning.

13. Escalator The escalator going down to the main floor of a subway station is 230 feet long and makes a 30° angle with the main floor. How many feet below ground is the subway station?

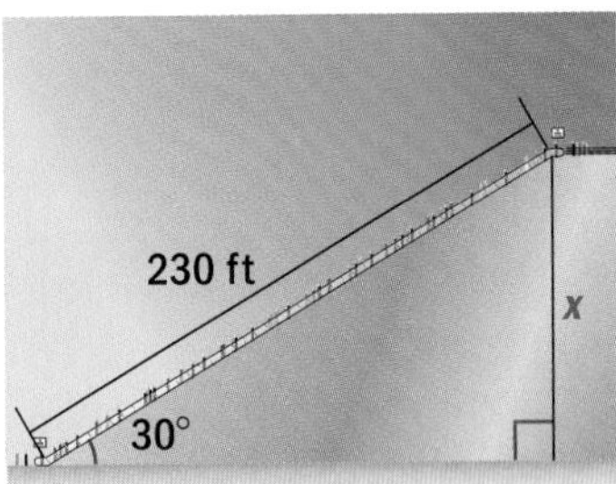

Find the value of each variable. Give exact answers.

14.

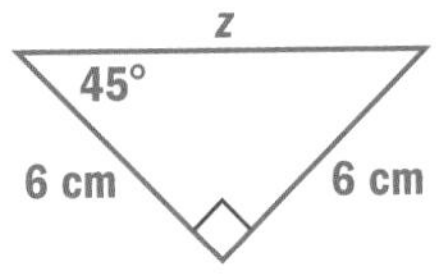

15.

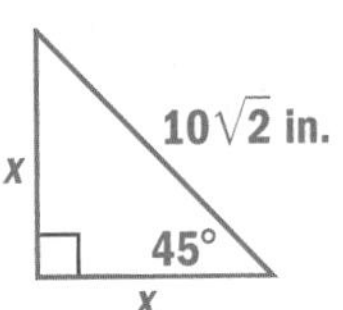

16.

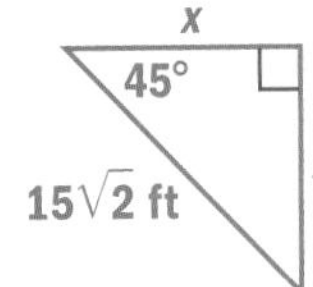

17.

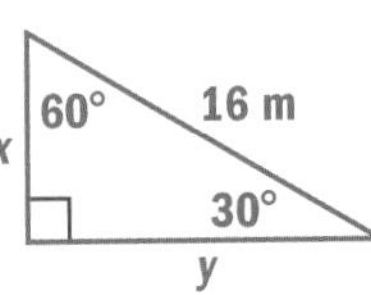

18.

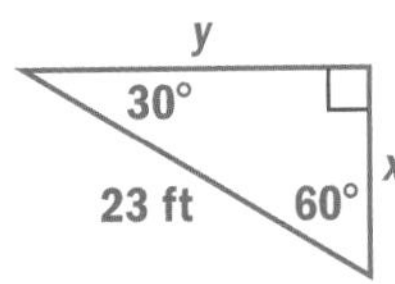

19.

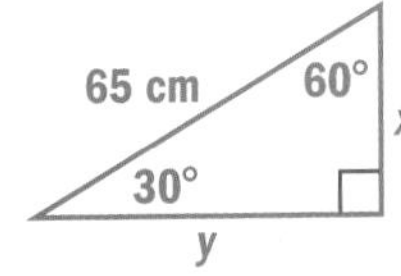

20. Quilting Find the perimeters of the five squares in the diagram of the Snail's Trail quilt pattern at the right. The triangles used in this pattern are 45°-45°-90° triangles. Round your answers to the nearest inch, if necessary.

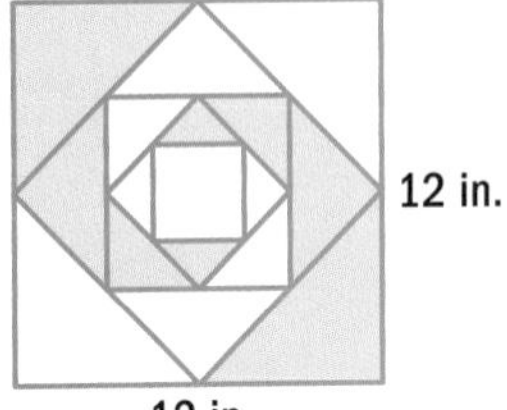

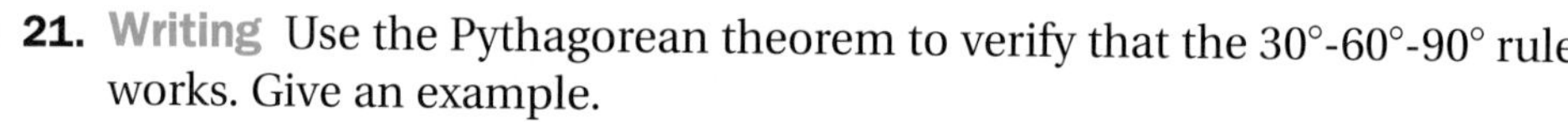

21. **Writing** Use the Pythagorean theorem to verify that the 30°-60°-90° rule works. Give an example.

22. **Critical Thinking** How can you find the area of the triangle shown? (*Hint:* You can fold the triangle in half to create two congruent 30°-60°-90° triangles.)

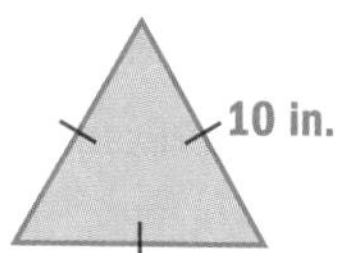

23. **Challenge** In the diagram below, $\triangle ABC \sim \triangle XYZ$. Find all unknown side lengths of the triangles. Give exact answers.

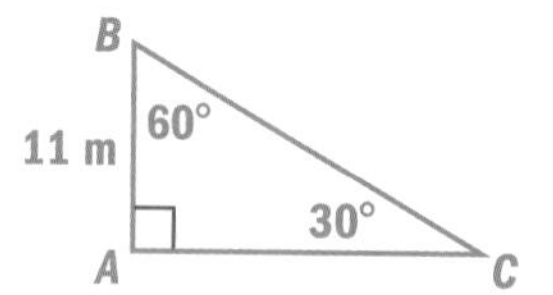

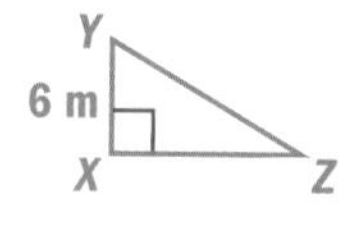

Mixed Review

Find the quotient. *(Lesson 5.4)*

24. $\frac{5}{11} \div \frac{5}{11}$

25. $\frac{3}{10} \div \frac{1}{5}$

26. $\frac{4}{15} \div \left(-\frac{12}{25}\right)$

Write the rate as a unit rate. *(Lesson 7.1)*

27. $\frac{\text{28 people}}{\text{4 teams}}$

28. $\frac{\text{60 meters}}{\text{20 seconds}}$

29. $\frac{\text{488 rotations}}{\text{8 minutes}}$

Basic Skills **Solve the equation.**

30. $165 = -5z$

31. $77 = 7.7p$

32. $19 = \frac{w}{4.2}$

Test-Taking Practice

INTERNET
State Test Practice
CLASSZONE.COM

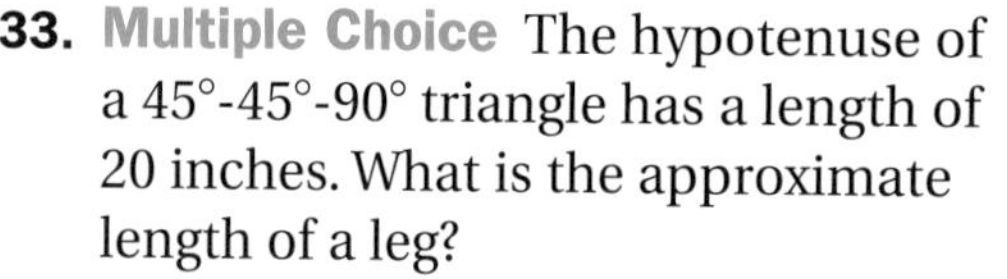

33. **Multiple Choice** The hypotenuse of a 45°-45°-90° triangle has a length of 20 inches. What is the approximate length of a leg?

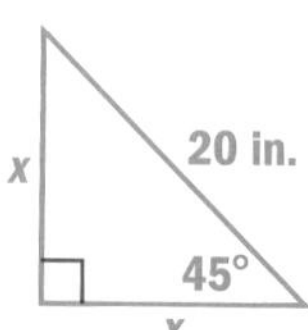

A. 10 inches **B.** 12.5 inches

C. 14.1 inches **D.** 18 inches

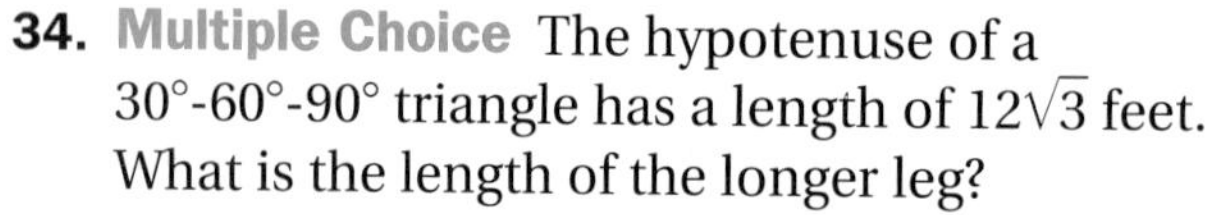

34. **Multiple Choice** The hypotenuse of a 30°-60°-90° triangle has a length of $12\sqrt{3}$ feet. What is the length of the longer leg?

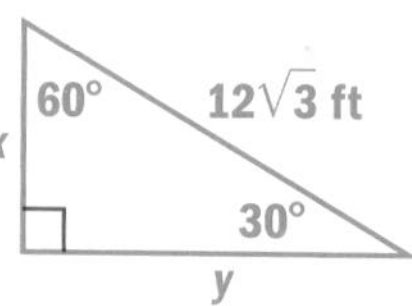

F. 6 feet **G.** $6\sqrt{3}$ feet

H. 18 feet **I.** $18\sqrt{3}$ feet

GOAL

Find the sine and cosine ratios of right triangles.

MATERIALS

- metric ruler
- protractor

Exploring Trigonometric Ratios

You can use a protractor and metric ruler to find the ratios of the length of each leg of a right triangle to the hypotenuse.

Explore **Find ratios of side lengths of similar right triangles.**

1 Draw a 40° angle. Mark tick marks every 5 centimeters along one side.

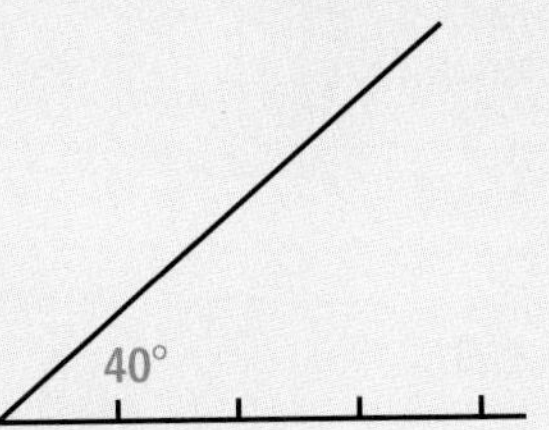

2 Draw perpendicular line segments from four of the tick marks to intersect with the other side of the angle.

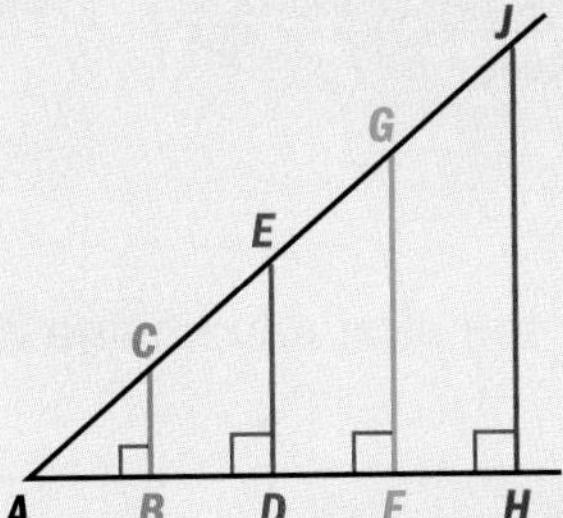

3 There are four similar triangles in your drawing. Measure the legs of each triangle in your drawing to the nearest tenth. Then copy and complete the table. Round your answers to the nearest hundredth.

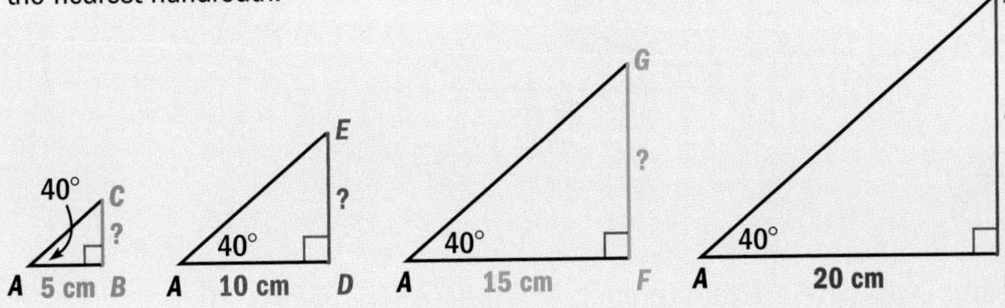

Triangle	Leg 1	Leg 2	Hypotenuse	$\frac{\text{Leg 1}}{\text{Hypotenuse}}$	$\frac{\text{Leg 2}}{\text{Hypotenuse}}$
$\triangle ABC$	5 cm	?	?	?	?
$\triangle ADE$	10 cm	?	?	?	?
$\triangle AFG$	15 cm	?	?	?	?
$\triangle AHJ$	20 cm	?	?	?	?

Explore **Look for a pattern.**

4 Is there a pattern in the ratios $\frac{\text{Leg 1}}{\text{Hypotenuse}}$? If so, what is it?

5 Is there a pattern in the ratios $\frac{\text{Leg 2}}{\text{Hypotenuse}}$? If so, what is it?

6 Repeat Steps 1–5 using a 70° angle. Based on your results, do the ratios depend on the lengths of the right triangles' sides or on the measures of their angles?

The ratios $\frac{\text{Leg 1}}{\text{Hypotenuse}}$ and $\frac{\text{Leg 2}}{\text{Hypotenuse}}$ have special names. They are called the *sine* and *cosine* ratios and can be defined as follows:

$$\sin A = \frac{\text{length of leg opposite } \angle A}{\text{length of hypotenuse}} \qquad \cos A = \frac{\text{length of leg adjacent to } \angle A}{\text{length of hypotenuse}}$$

Your turn now **Find the sine and cosine ratios for $\angle A$ and $\angle B$.**

1. 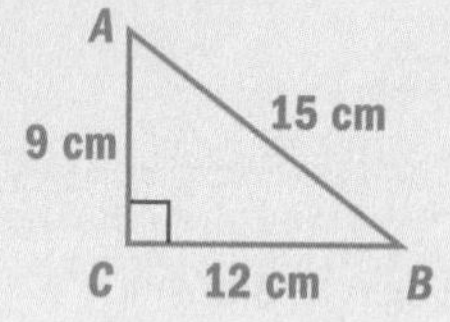

2. 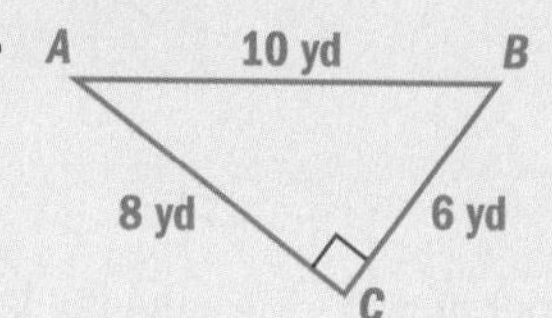

3. 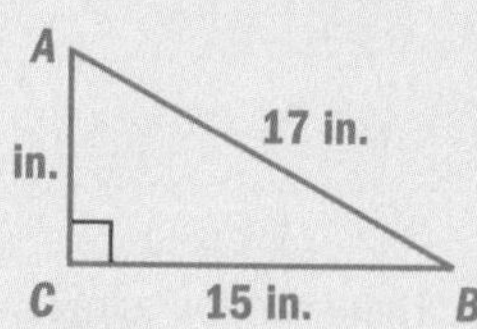

4. 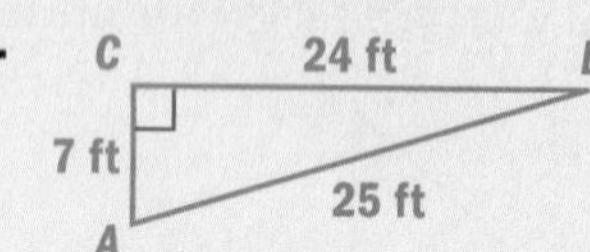

5. 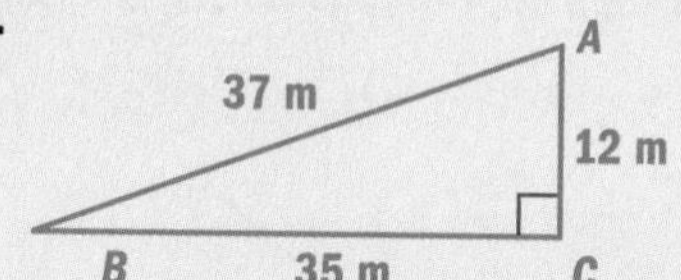

6. 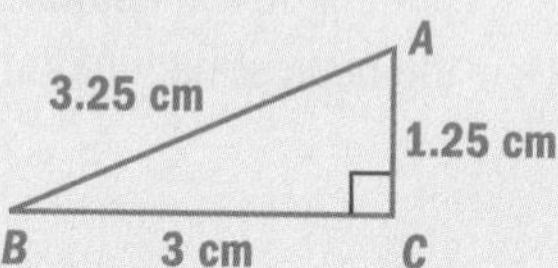

Stop and Think

7. **Critical Thinking** Measure angle A in each triangle in Exercises 1–6. Write the measures in order from least to greatest. Make a table that shows $m\angle A$, $\sin A$, and $\cos A$. Then copy and complete the following two statements using *increases* or *decreases*.

   a. As $m\angle A$ increases from 0° to 90°, the value of $\sin A$ _?_.

   b. As $m\angle A$ increases from 0° to 90°, the value of $\cos A$ _?_.

Using Trigonometric Ratios

BEFORE	Now	WHY?
You found the side lengths of special right triangles.	You'll use trigonometric ratios to find the side lengths.	So you can find the height of a totem pole, as in Ex. 5.

In the Real World

Water Slide A water slide makes an angle of about 18° with the ground. The slide extends horizontally about 64.2 meters. What is the height of the slide? You will see how to solve this problem in Example 5.

trigonometric ratio, p. 463
sine, p. 463
cosine, p. 463
tangent, p. 463

INDIANA
Academic Standards

- Algebra and Functions (8.3.1)
- Measurement (8.5.3)

You can find the height of the water slide using a *trigonometric ratio*. A **trigonometric ratio** is a ratio of the lengths of two sides of a right triangle. The three basic trigonometric ratios are **sine**, **cosine**, and **tangent**. These are abbreviated as *sin*, *cos*, and *tan*.

Trigonometric Ratios

$$\sin A = \frac{\text{side opposite } \angle A}{\text{hypotenuse}} = \frac{a}{c}$$

$$\cos A = \frac{\text{side adjacent to } \angle A}{\text{hypotenuse}} = \frac{b}{c}$$

$$\tan A = \frac{\text{side opposite } \angle A}{\text{side adjacent to } \angle A} = \frac{a}{b}$$

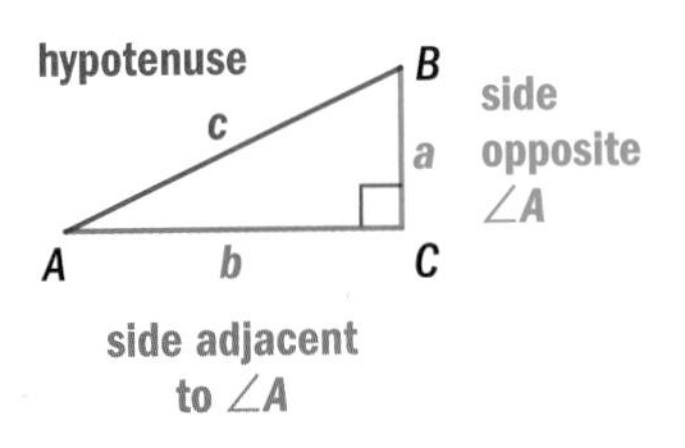

HELP with Solving

Determining the opposite and adjacent sides depends on the angle that is being used. For $\angle Q$, the length of the opposite side is 12 feet, and the length of the adjacent side is 5 feet.

EXAMPLE 1 Finding Trigonometric Ratios

In $\triangle PQR$, write the sine, cosine, and tangent ratios for $\angle P$.

For $\angle P$, the length of the opposite side is 5 feet, and the length of the adjacent side is 12 feet. The length of the hypotenuse is 13 feet.

$$\sin P = \frac{\text{opposite}}{\text{hypotenuse}} = \frac{5}{13}$$

$$\cos P = \frac{\text{adjacent}}{\text{hypotenuse}} = \frac{12}{13}$$

$$\tan P = \frac{\text{opposite}}{\text{adjacent}} = \frac{5}{12}$$

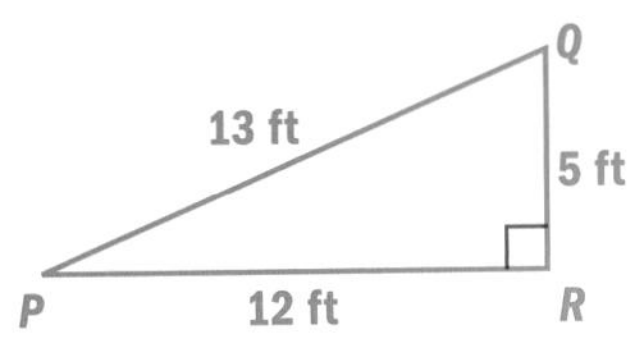

with Technology

When using a calculator to find trigonometric ratios of angles measured in degrees, be sure the calculator is in *degree mode*. You can test this by checking that tan 45° = 1.

EXAMPLE 2 Using a Calculator

Use a calculator to find sine, cosine, and tangent of 30°.

	Keystrokes	Display	Answer
a.	[2nd] [TRIG] [=] 30 [=]	0.5	$\sin 30° = 0.5$
b.	[2nd] [TRIG] [▶] [▶] [=] 30 [=]	0.8660254	$\cos 30° \approx 0.8660$
c.	[2nd] [TRIG] [◀] [◀] [=] 30 [=]	0.5773503	$\tan 30° \approx 0.5774$

Your turn now **Complete the exercise.**

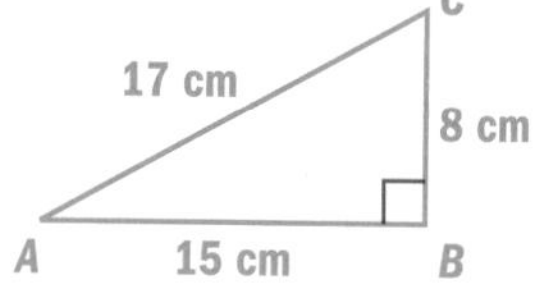

1. For $\triangle ABC$, write the sine, cosine, and tangent ratios for $\angle A$ and $\angle C$.

Use a calculator to approximate the given expression. Round your answer to four decimal places.

2. cos 70° **3.** tan 50° **4.** sin 25° **5.** cos 42° **6.** tan 7°

EXAMPLE 3 Using a Cosine Ratio

Find the value of x in the triangle.

The length of the hypotenuse is 8 inches. The unknown side is adjacent to the given angle. Use cosine of $\angle K$.

$$\cos K = \frac{\text{adjacent}}{\text{hypotenuse}}$$ Definition of cosine

$$\cos 55° = \frac{x}{8}$$ Substitute.

$$0.5736 \approx \frac{x}{8}$$ Use a calculator to approximate cos 55°.

$$0.5736 \cdot 8 \approx \frac{x}{8} \cdot 8$$ Multiply each side by 8.

$$4.5888 \approx x$$ Simplify.

ANSWER The value of x is about 4.59 inches.

Your turn now **Complete the exercise.**

7. Find the value of x in the triangle. Round your answer to the nearest hundredth of a foot.

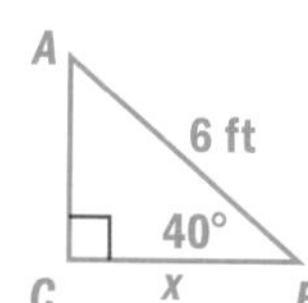

EXAMPLE 4 Using a Sine Ratio

Ski Jump A ski jump is 380 feet long and makes a 27.6° angle with the ground. Find the height of the ski jump.

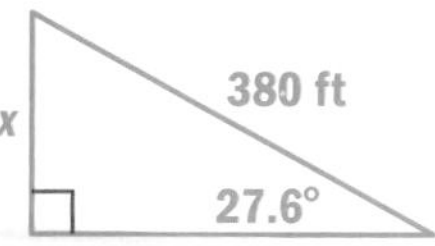

Solution

Use the sine ratio and a calculator to find the value of x.

$\sin 27.6^\circ = \frac{\text{opposite}}{\text{hypotenuse}}$ Definition of sine

$\sin 27.6^\circ = \frac{x}{380}$ Substitute.

$0.4633 \approx \frac{x}{380}$ Use a calculator to approximate sin 27.6°.

$0.4633 \cdot 380 \approx \frac{x}{380} \cdot 380$ Multiply each side by 380.

$176.054 \approx x$ Simplify.

ANSWER The ski jump is about 176 feet high.

EXAMPLE 5 Using a Tangent Ratio

Water Slide To find the height h of the water slide on page 463, use the tangent ratio.

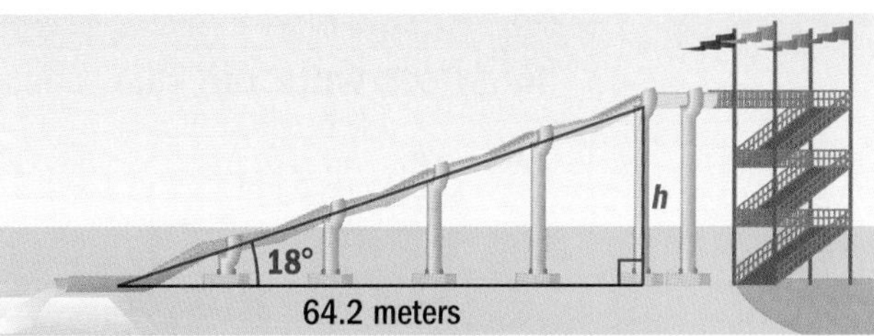

$\tan 18^\circ = \frac{\text{opposite}}{\text{adjacent}}$ Definition of tangent

$\tan 18^\circ = \frac{h}{64.2}$ Substitute.

$0.3249 \approx \frac{h}{64.2}$ Use a calculator to approximate tan 18°.

$0.3249 \cdot 64.2 \approx \frac{h}{64.2} \cdot 64.2$ Multiply each side by 64.2.

$20.85858 \approx h$ Simplify.

ANSWER The height of the water slide is about 21 meters.

9.6 Exercises

More Practice, p. 735

Getting Ready to Practice

Matching Match the term with the correct ratio.

1. sine **2.** cosine **3.** tangent

A. $\frac{\text{adjacent}}{\text{hypotenuse}}$ **B.** $\frac{\text{opposite}}{\text{hypotenuse}}$ **C.** $\frac{\text{opposite}}{\text{adjacent}}$

4. Write the sine, cosine, and tangent ratios in simplest form, for $\angle A$ and $\angle B$ in $\triangle ABC$.

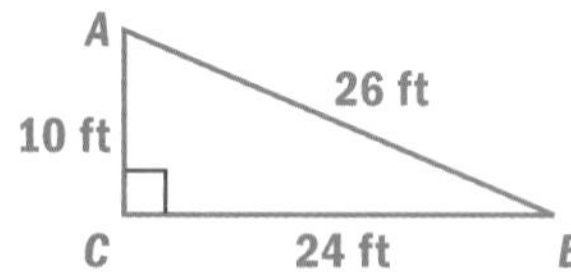

5. **Guided Problem Solving** You stand 50 feet from a totem pole that is perpendicular to the ground. The angle from the point where you stand to the top of the totem pole is 42°. How tall is the totem pole?

(1) Draw a diagram and identify the sides of the triangle.

(2) Write an equation using a trigonometric ratio.

(3) Solve the equation. Round your answer to the nearest foot.

Practice and Problem Solving

In $\triangle PQR$, write the sine, cosine, and tangent ratios for $\angle P$ and $\angle R$.

6.

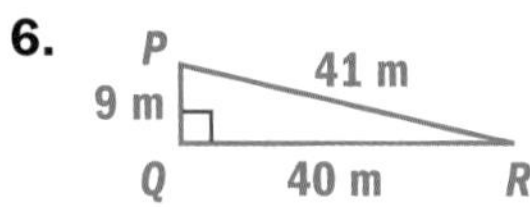

7.

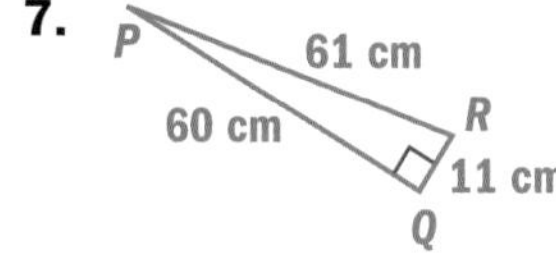

8.

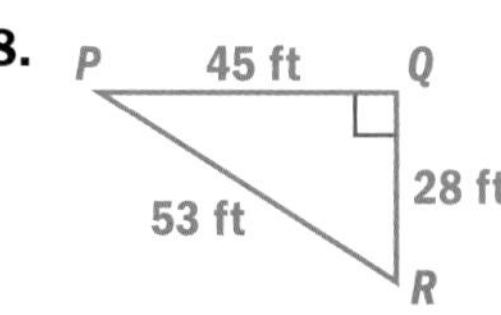

Example	Exercises
1	6-8
2	9-12
3	13-15
4	20, 24-26
5	20, 24-26

· More Examples
· eTutorial Plus

Use a calculator to approximate the given expression. Round your answer to four decimal places.

9. tan 51° **10.** sin 80° **11.** sin 36° **12.** cos 76°

Find the value of *x*. Round your answer to the nearest thousandth.

13.

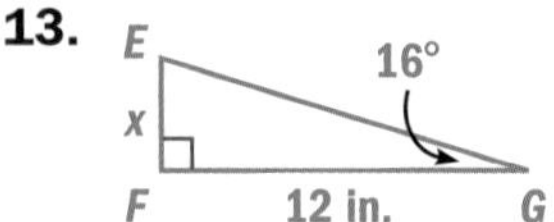

14.

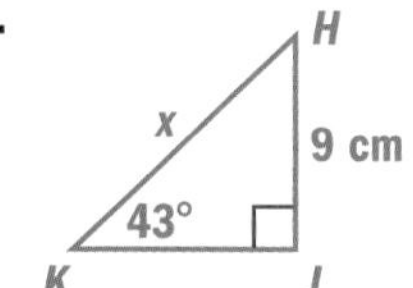

15.

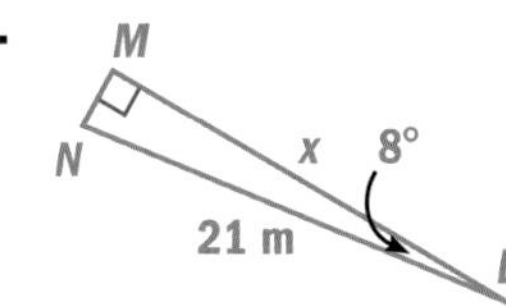

16. **Writing** Explain how to decide which trigonometric ratio (sine, cosine, or tangent) is best for solving a particular problem.

17. **Draw a Diagram** Sketch right triangle ABC that has the given trigonometric ratios: $\tan A = \frac{15}{8}$ and $\cos B = \frac{15}{17}$. Label each side with its length.

18. **Algebra** Write the trigonometric ratios for $\angle A$ and $\angle B$ in $\triangle ABC$.

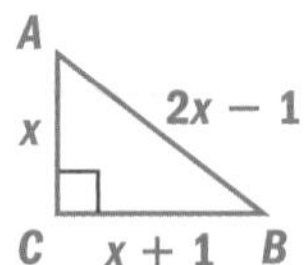

19. **Find the Error** Describe and correct the error in the solution.

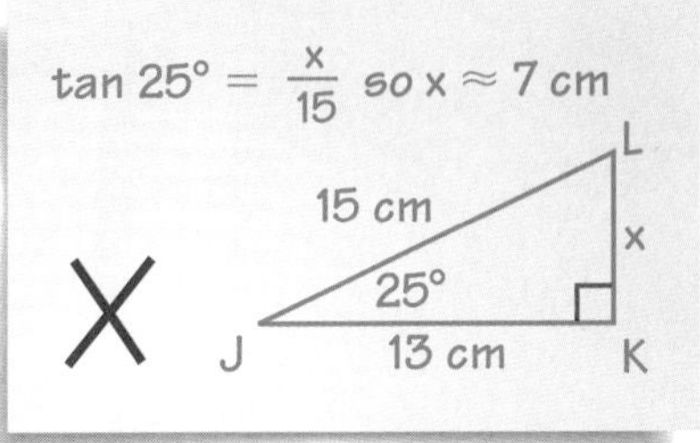

20. **Cats** You are constructing a scratching post and platform for your cat. Find the length x of the scratching post. Round your answer to the nearest tenth of a foot.

Find the value of the unknown angle and side. Then write three trigonometric ratios for $\angle A$.

21.

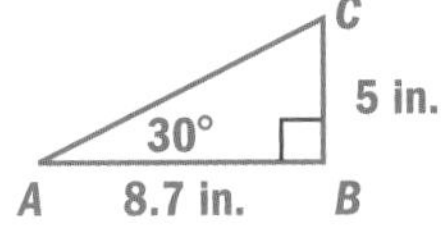

22.

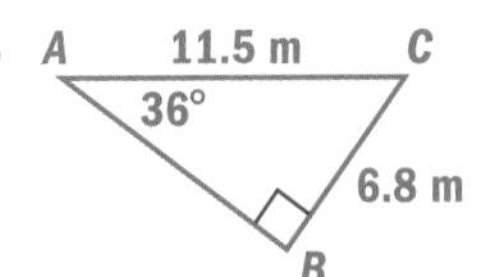

23.

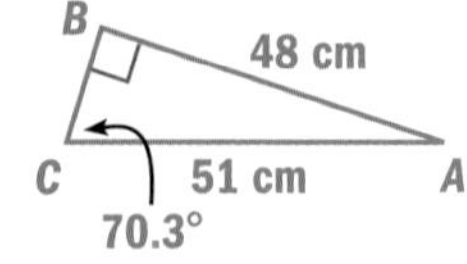

Extended Problem Solving In Exercises 24–26, use the following information. Round your answer to the nearest whole number.

Some whales have been known to dive down to a depth of 3000 meters in search of their favorite food.

24. **Calculate** The whale shown finds food after swimming 2000 m. How deep is the water where the whale found its food?

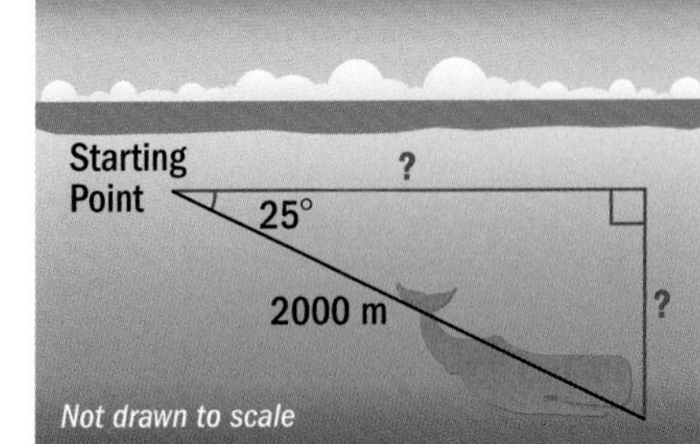

25. **Calculate** How far is the whale along the ocean surface from the point where it started to the point directly above the spot where it found its food?

26. **Compare** Did this whale dive more or less than $\frac{1}{2}$ of the deepest known dive?

Find the perimeter of the triangle. Round your answer to the nearest tenth.

27.

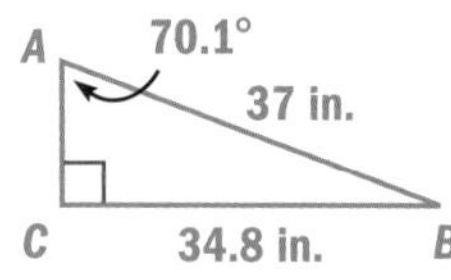

28.

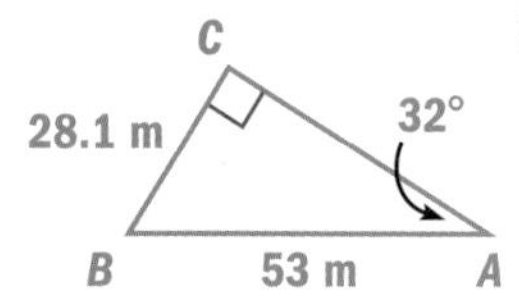

29.

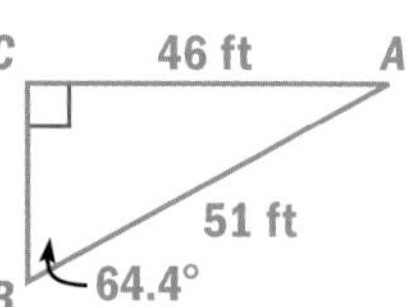

30. Critical Thinking Can the values for the sine or cosine of one of the acute angles in a right triangle be greater than or equal to 1? Explain.

31. Challenge Find the area of the isosceles triangle. Round your answer to the nearest tenth.

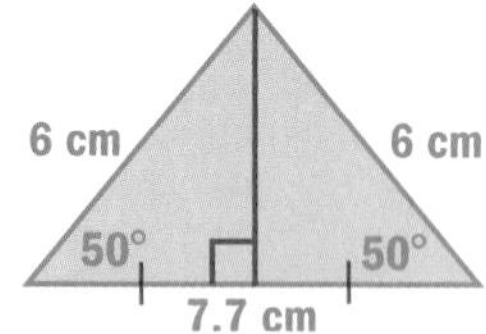

32. Aviation An airplane is at an altitude of 33,000 feet when the pilot starts the descent to the airport. The pilot wants the plane to descend at an angle of 3°. How many miles away from the airport must the descent begin? Round your answer to the nearest mile.

Mixed Review

33. Find the sum of 9.87 and $\frac{43}{50}$. Write your answer in decimal form. *(Lessons 5.5, 5.6)*

34. What type of transformation is modeled by a merry-go-round? *(Lesson 8.7)*

Tell whether the number is *rational* or *irrational*. Explain. *(Lesson 9.2)*

35. $\sqrt{484}$ **36.** $\sqrt{99}$ **37.** $\sqrt{\frac{17}{29}}$ **38.** $\sqrt{\frac{144}{225}}$

Basic Skills **Use the distance formula to find the rate.**

39. $d = 145$ mi, $t = 40$ h **40.** $d = 78$ m, $t = 20$ sec

Test-Taking Practice

INTERNET
State Test Practice
CLASSZONE.COM

41. Multiple Choice What is the cosine of $\angle E$?

A. $\frac{5}{13}$ **B.** $\frac{12}{13}$ **C.** $\frac{13}{5}$ **D.** 13

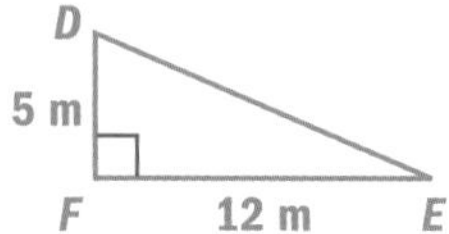

42. Multiple Choice What is the approximate length of side $\overline{AC}$?

F. 7 ft **G.** 10 ft **H.** $7\sqrt{3}$ ft **I.** 14 ft

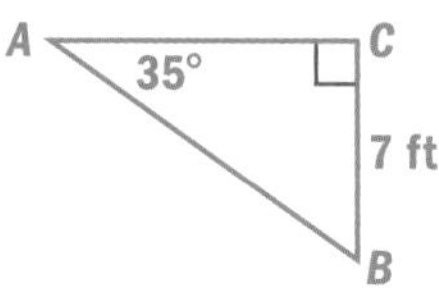

CALCULATOR

9.6 Technology Activity

Finding an Angle Measure

GOAL Use a calculator to find an angle measure using the inverse of a trigonometric ratio.

In some situations, you need to find a particular angle of a given triangle. You can use the inverse of a trigonometric ratio to find the measure of the angle. For example, you can use the inverse tangent feature of your calculator to solve the following problem. The inverse tangent formula is:

$$\text{If } \tan x^\circ = \frac{a}{b}, \text{ then } x^\circ = \tan^{-1}\left(\frac{a}{b}\right).$$

Example **In the 1870s, a cable car system was built in San Francisco. A section of California Street has a vertical height of 76 feet and a horizontal length of 420 feet. Find the angle of the hill, $x°$.**

HELP with Technology

To evaluate an inverse tangent on your calculator, press the 2nd key. Then press the [TRIG] key. Use the right or left arrow to highlight the inverse tangent feature and then press =. Enter the ratio and press = again. The result is the angle measure.

Solution

To find the angle, use inverse tangent.

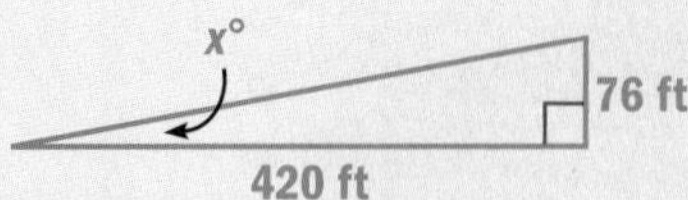

$\tan x^\circ = \frac{\text{opposite}}{\text{adjacent}}$ **Definition of tangent**

$\tan x^\circ = \frac{76}{420}$ **Substitute.**

$x^\circ = \tan^{-1}\left(\frac{76}{420}\right)$ **Definition of inverse tangent**

$x \approx 10.3$ **Use your calculator to approximate.**

ANSWER The angle of the hill is about 10°.

Your turn now **Use a calculator to approximate the expression. Round to the nearest tenth of a degree.**

1. $\tan^{-1}(0.25)$ **2.** $\tan^{-1}(0.14)$ **3.** $\tan^{-1}(0.92)$

4. $\tan^{-1}(1.05)$ **5.** $\tan^{-1}(24.65)$ **6.** $\tan^{-1}(64.25)$

7. **Critical Thinking** Given $\tan^{-1}(0.18)$ and $\tan^{-1}(32.46)$, which one would you expect to represent the largest angle? Why?

LESSONS 9.5 TO 9.6

Notebook Review

Review the vocabulary definitions in your notebook.

Copy the review examples in your notebook. Then complete the exercises.

Check Your Definitions

trigonometric ratio, p. 463
sine, p. 463
cosine, p. 463
tangent, p. 463

Use Your Vocabulary

1. Copy and complete: To write the sine ratio for a given acute angle of a right triangle, you need to know the length of the side _?_ the angle and the length of the _?_.

9.5 Can you find side lengths of special right triangles?

EXAMPLE Find the length of the hypotenuse. Give the exact answer.

hypotenuse = leg • $\sqrt{2}$ **Rule for 45°-45°-90° triangle**

$= 26\sqrt{2}$ **Substitute.**

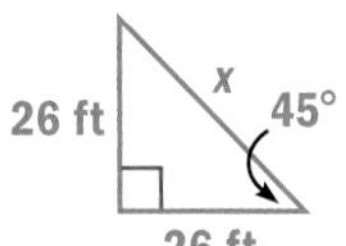

ANSWER The length of the hypotenuse is $26\sqrt{2}$ feet.

Find the value of each variable. Give the exact answer.

2.

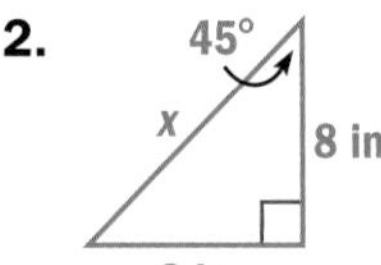

3.

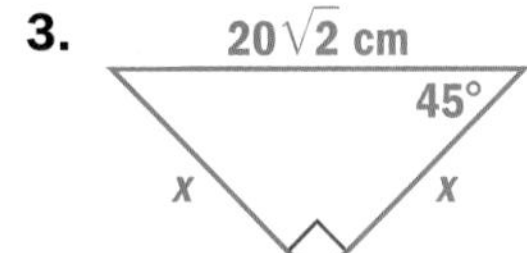

4.

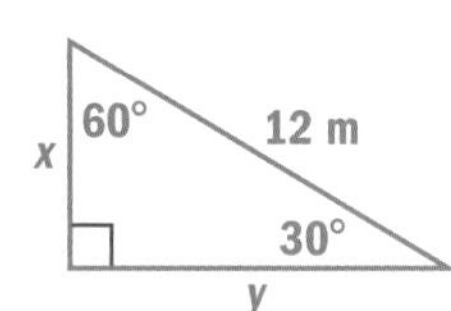

9.6 Can you use trigonometric ratios?

EXAMPLE In $\triangle ABC$, write the sine, cosine, and tangent ratios for $\angle A$.

$$\sin A = \frac{\text{opposite}}{\text{hypotenuse}} = \frac{12}{37}$$

$$\cos A = \frac{\text{adjacent}}{\text{hypotenuse}} = \frac{35}{37}$$

$$\tan A = \frac{\text{opposite}}{\text{adjacent}} = \frac{12}{35}$$

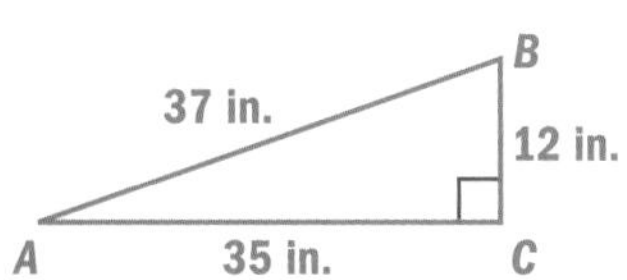

In $\triangle ABC$, write the sine, cosine, and tangent ratios for $\angle A$ and $\angle B$.

5. 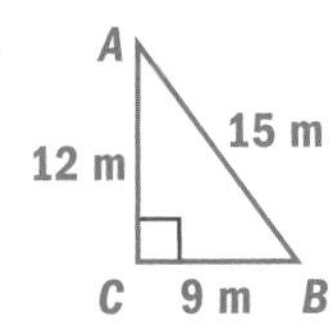

6. 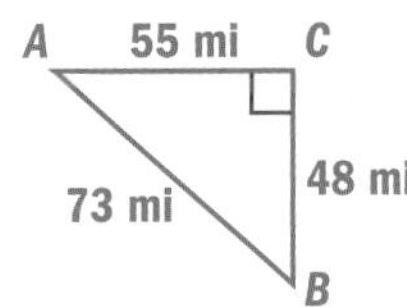

7. 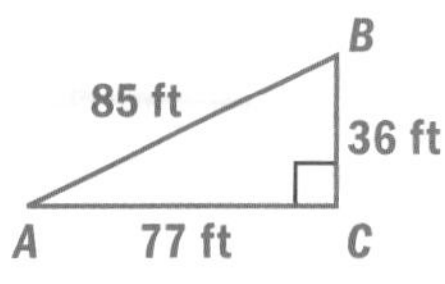

Stop and Think about Lessons 9.5–9.6

8. **Writing** Describe how to find the cosine ratio for one of the acute angles of a right triangle when you know that its sine ratio is $\frac{3}{5}$.

Review Quiz 2

Find the value of each variable. Give exact answers.

1. 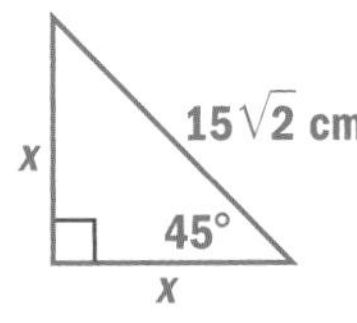

2. 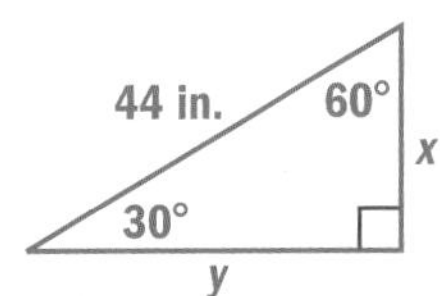

3. 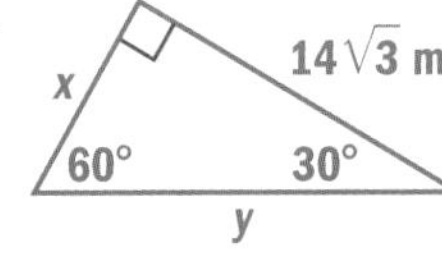

In $\triangle ABC$, write the sine, cosine, and tangent ratios for $\angle A$ and $\angle B$.

4. 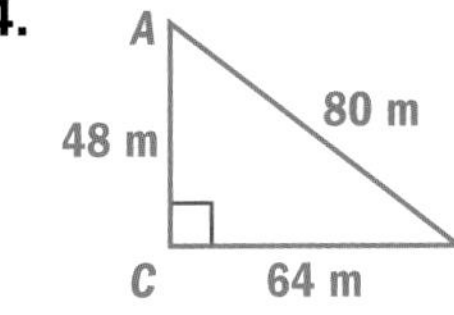

5. 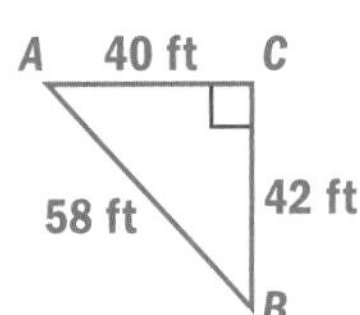

6. 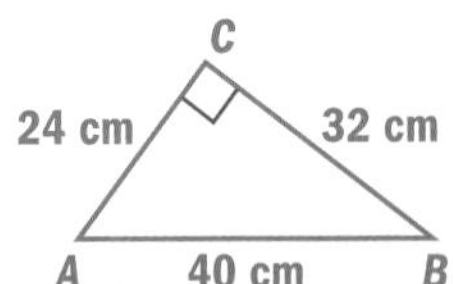

7. **Aviation** If a plane flies 1° off course for 2000 miles, how far away will the plane be from the correct path? Round to the nearest tenth of a mile.

A Real Winner

Replace each expression with the letter of its decimal approximation to find the name of a person who won the Nobel Prize in both physics and chemistry.

cos 15° sin 52° cos 85° sin 60° cos 45°

tan 30° tan 12° sin 5° cos 30° sin 45°

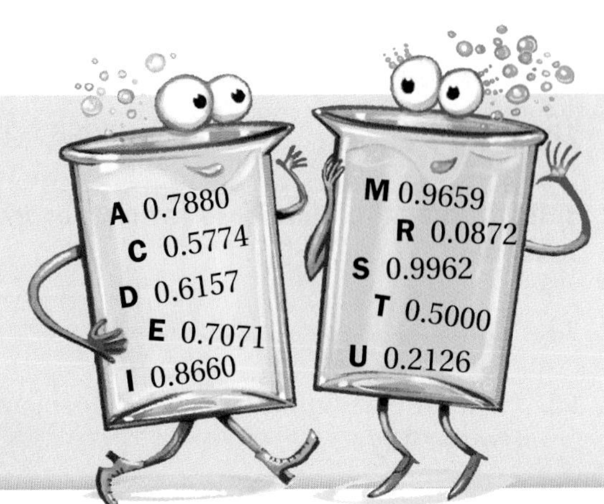

CHAPTER 9

Chapter Review

Vocabulary

square root, p. 431
radical expression, p. 431
perfect square, p. 432
irrational number, p. 437
real number, p. 437
leg, p. 443
hypotenuse, p. 443
Pythagorean theorem, p. 443
converse, p. 444
Pythagorean triple, p. 451
trigonometric ratio, p. 463
sine, p. 463
cosine, p. 463
tangent, p. 463

Vocabulary Review

1. Describe the difference between a *rational number* and an *irrational number*.
2. Give three examples of rational numbers.
3. Give three examples of irrational numbers.
4. Describe how the *lengths of the legs* and *the length of the hypotenuse* of a right triangle are related.

Copy and complete the statement.

5. A(n) _?_ is any number that has integer square roots.
6. In a right triangle, the side opposite the right angle is the _?_.
7. In a 30°-60°-90° triangle, the _?_ leg is opposite the 30° angle.
8. Sine, cosine, and tangent are _?_ ratios.

Review Questions

Use a calculator to approximate the square root. Round to the nearest hundredth, if necessary. *(Lesson 9.1)*

9. $\sqrt{94.09}$
10. $-\sqrt{784}$
11. $-\sqrt{2118}$
12. $\sqrt{941}$

Solve the equation. *(Lesson 9.1)*

13. $m^2 = 196$
14. $a^2 - 1296 = 0$
15. $c^2 - 28 = 36$
16. $x^2 + 15 = 51$

Tell whether the number is *rational* or *irrational*. Explain your reasoning. *(Lesson 9.2)*

17. $\sqrt{100}$
18. $0.\overline{6}$
19. $\frac{16}{25}$
20. $\sqrt{6}$

21. Order the decimals $0.1\overline{8}$, $0.\overline{181}$, $0.\overline{18}$, and 0.188 from least to greatest. *(Lesson 9.2)*

Review Questions

Find the unknown length. *(Lesson 9.3)*

22.

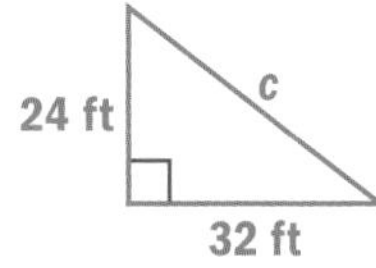

23.

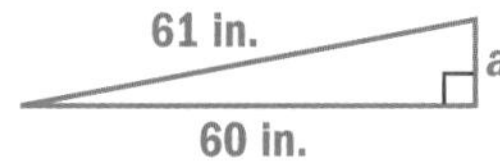

24.

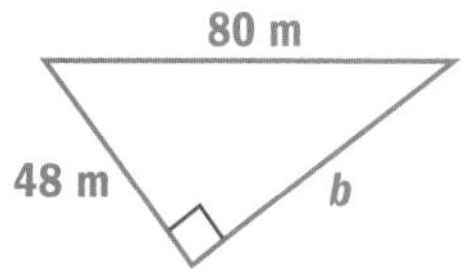

Determine whether the numbers form a Pythagorean triple. *(Lesson 9.4)*

25. 9, 40, 45 **26.** 24, 10, 28 **27.** 72, 54, 90 **28.** 133, 156, 205

29. Ski Lift A ski lift has a horizontal length of 662 meters and a vertical height of 152 meters. Find the length of the ski lift. Round to the nearest hundredth of a meter. *(Lesson 9.4)*

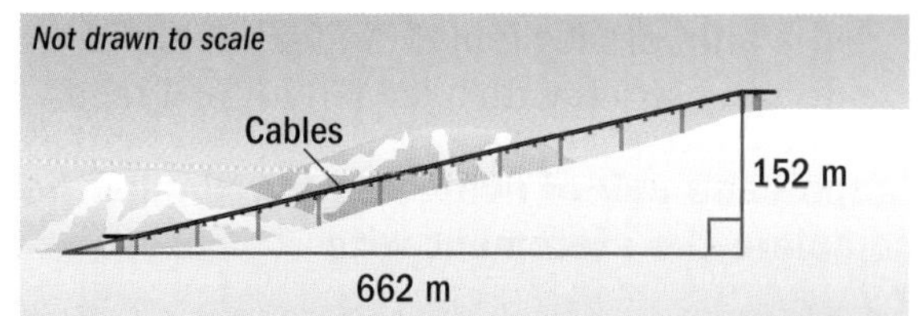

Find the value of each variable. Give exact answers. *(Lesson 9.5)*

30.

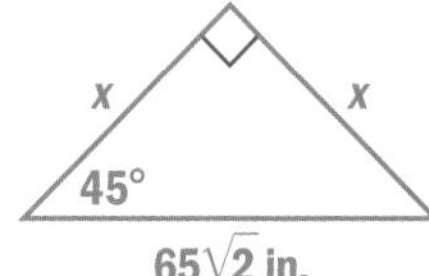

31.

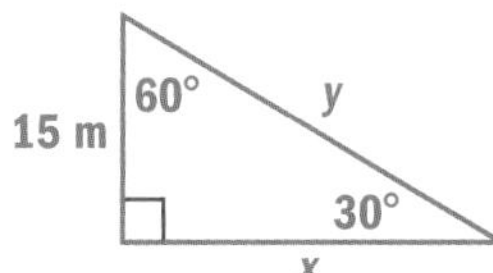

32.

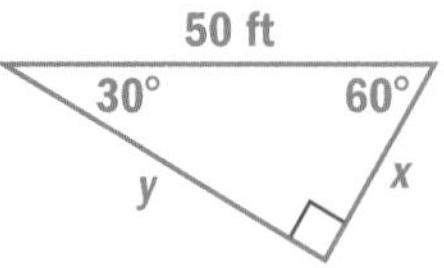

In $\triangle PQR$, write the sine, cosine, and tangent ratios for $\angle P$ and $\angle Q$. *(Lesson 9.6)*

33.

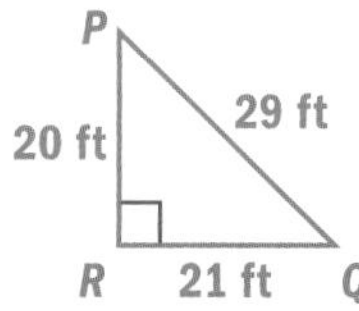

34.

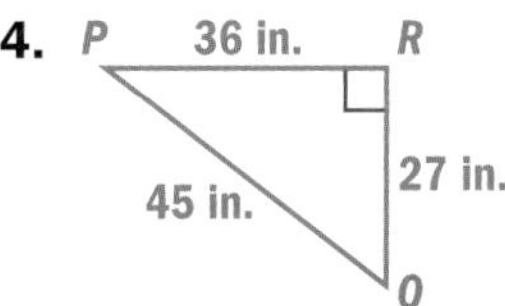

35.

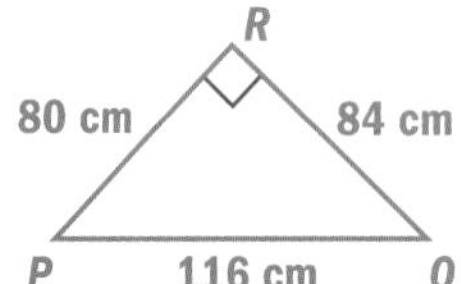

Use a calculator to approximate the given expression. Round your answer to four decimal places. *(Lesson 9.6)*

36. sin 72° **37.** tan 18.5° **38.** cos 49° **39.** tan 40°

40. Skateboard Ramp You are constructing a skateboard ramp like the one shown in the diagram. Find the lengths of the legs of the triangle that supports the ramp. Round your answers to the nearest tenth of a foot. *(Lesson 9.6)*

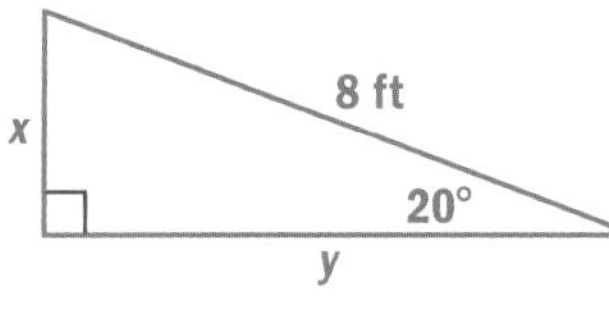

Chapter Test

Solve the equation.

1. $x^2 = 49$ **2.** $m^2 + 41 = 162$ **3.** $n^2 - 63 = 162$ **4.** $a^2 + 88 = 232$

5. Zoology Dr. R. McNeill Alexander studies the motion of animals. From his studies, he determined that the maximum walking speed s, in feet per second, that an animal can walk is $s = 5.66\sqrt{l}$ where l is the animal's leg length, in feet. What is the maximum walking speed for an ostrich with a leg length of 4 feet?

Graph each pair of numbers on a number line. Then copy and complete the statement with <, >, or =.

6. $\sqrt{9}$ __?__ 3 **7.** -11 __?__ $-\sqrt{11}$ **8.** $\sqrt{12}$ __?__ 4

Find the length of the unknown side of the right triangle. Round to the nearest tenth, if necessary. Then find the area and perimeter.

9.

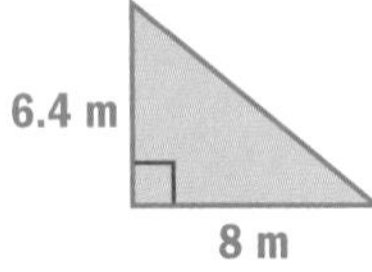

10.

11.

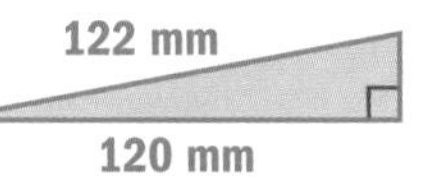

Determine whether the triangle with the given side lengths is a right triangle.

12. $a = 28, b = 96, c = 100$ **13.** $a = 22.5, b = 30, c = 37.5$ **14.** $a = 3.6, b = 5.8, c = 5.9$

Find the value of each variable. Give exact answers.

15.

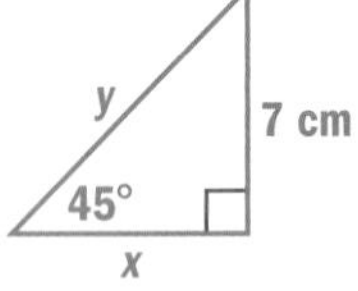

16.

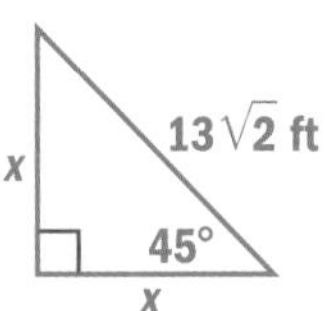

17.

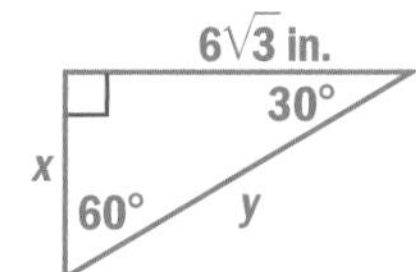

18. Incline In the 1870s, a motorized incline was built in Pittsburgh, PA, to climb the steep hill known as Mt. Washington located at the mouth of the Monongahela River. The track of the incline is 793 feet long and makes a 30° angle with the ground. Find the height of the boarding platform at the top of the incline.

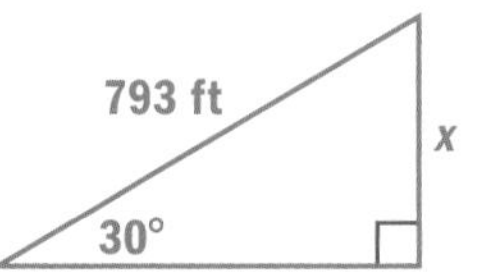

Chapter Standardized Test

Test-Taking Strategy **Some questions involve more than one step. Read each question carefully to be sure you are answering the right question.**

Multiple Choice

1. What is the positive square root of 81?

A. -18 **B.** -9 **C.** 9 **D.** 18

2. Find the value of $\sqrt{x+y}$ when $x = 12$ and $y = 13$.

F. 1 **G.** 5 **H.** 25 **I.** 156

3. The area of the square base of a building is 2704 square feet. Find the perimeter of the base of the building.

A. 52 feet **B.** 104 feet

C. 208 feet **D.** 1352 feet

4. Which number is irrational?

F. $\frac{2}{5}$ **G.** $\sqrt{4}$ **H.** $\sqrt{7}$ **I.** $\sqrt{49}$

5. Which list *is* in order from least to greatest?

A. $-1.5, -\sqrt{15}, -\sqrt{5}, -1$

B. $-\sqrt{15}, -\sqrt{5}, -1.5, -1$

C. $-\sqrt{15}, -1.5, -\sqrt{5}, -1$

D. $-1, -1.5, -\sqrt{5}, -\sqrt{15}$

6. Find the length of the hypotenuse of the right triangle below.

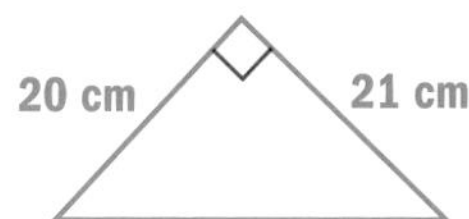

F. 23 cm **G.** 26 cm

H. 29 cm **I.** 32 cm

7. Find the length of the legs of the right triangle. Lengths are given in feet.

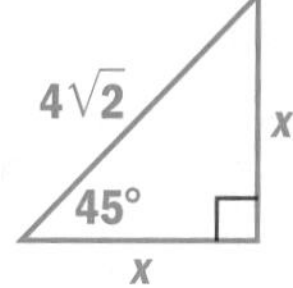

A. 4 feet **B.** 8 feet

C. $8\sqrt{2}$ feet **D.** 16 feet

8. In $\triangle ABC$, find $\sin A$.

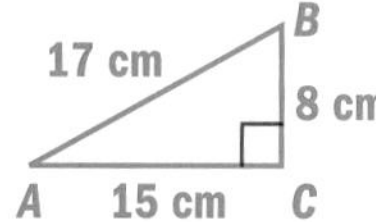

F. $\frac{8}{17}$ **G.** $\frac{8}{15}$ **H.** $\frac{15}{17}$ **I.** $\frac{15}{8}$

Short Response

9. Space Needle You are standing 400 feet from the base of the Space Needle in Seattle, Washington. Using a laser range finder, you measure the distance to the top of the Space Needle to be 725 feet. Find the height of the Space Needle to the nearest foot.

Extended Response

10. Quilting Jenwa is making a quilt using a design based on the pattern shown below. This pattern is a spiral design using right triangles. It is called the Wheel of Theodorus. Working from left to right, use the Pythagorean theorem in each right triangle to find the values of r, s, t, and u. Then identify the 45°-45°-90° triangle in the figure.

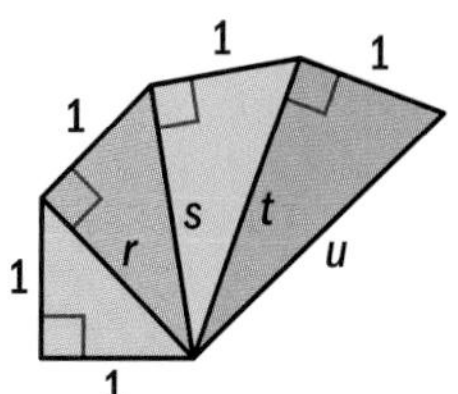

Viewing the STARS

Aiming a Telescope

Earth's atmosphere extends about 1000 kilometers from its surface. As light from stars passes through the atmosphere, some of it is absorbed or scattered by the molecules in the air. Without atmospheric interference, the stars in the night sky would appear much brighter.

An astronomer can minimize this interference by aiming a telescope so that star light passes through as little atmosphere as possible. If you know a star's *angle of elevation*, you can use trigonometry to find how far its light travels through the atmosphere to reach the telescope.

Angle of Elevation In the diagram, light from a star travels a distance of d kilometers through Earth's atmosphere to the telescope. The measure of the star's *angle of elevation* above Earth's surface is $x°$.

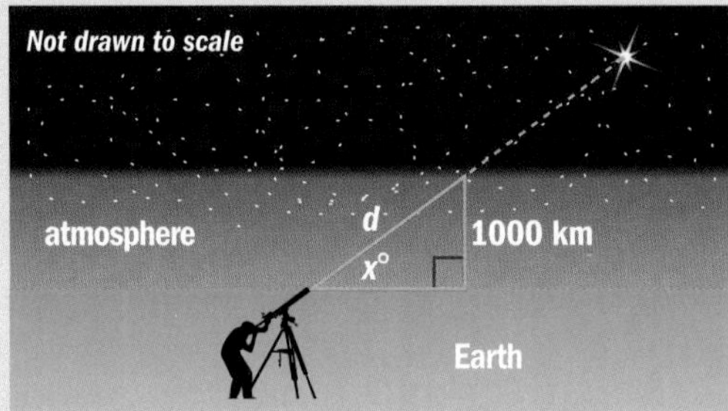

1. Because $\sin x° = \frac{1000}{d}$, you can use the equation $d = \frac{1000}{\sin x°}$ to find d. Copy and complete the table below.

angle of elevation $x°$	10°	20°	30°	40°	50°	60°	70°	80°
distance d (km)								

2. **Critical Thinking** At what angle should you aim a telescope to look through the least amount of atmosphere? Explain your reasoning.

Comparing Observatories

Observatories, buildings devoted to observing the night sky, are often placed at high elevations. Hanle Observatory in India, the world's highest, is about 4.5 kilometers above sea level.

How does raising a telescope's elevation affect the distance a star's light travels through the atmosphere for a given angle of elevation? Use the formula from the previous page to find out.

Telescope at Sea Level

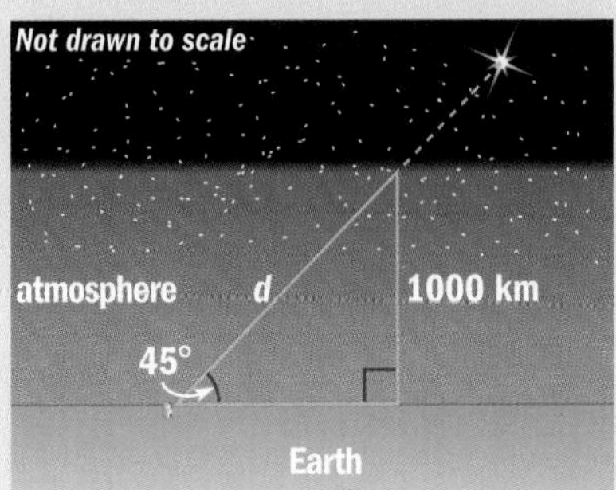

Telescope at Hanle Observatory

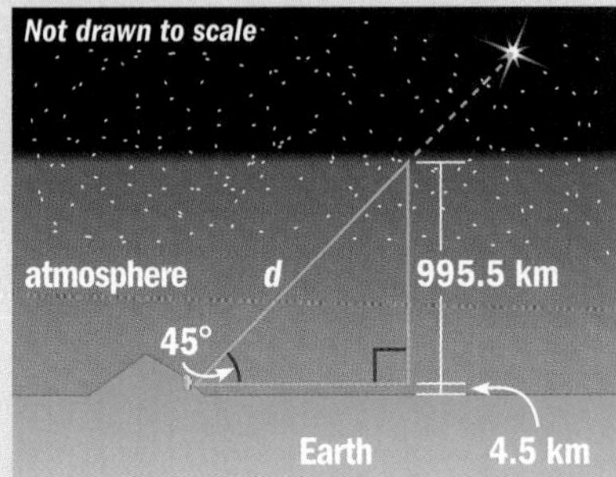

3. Find the distance *d*, in kilometers, that light travels through the atmosphere to reach a telescope at sea level, given an angle of elevation of 45°. Then find the value of *d* for Hanle Observatory.

4. **Critical Thinking** Compare the distances you found in Exercise 3. How does a change in elevation affect *d*? Do you think this difference is significant? Explain.

Project IDEAS

- **Experiment** Measure an object's shadow. Draw a diagram to explain how to use trigonometry to find the object's height if you know the shadow's length and the sun's angle of elevation. Present your findings to the class.
- **Extension** Locate some major astronomical observatories placed at high elevations, and find out why these locations were chosen. Present your findings to the class.
- **Research** The angle of elevation of the moon above Earth's horizon may affect its apparent color. Find out how and why an object's apparent color changes as it moves across the sky. Present your findings to the class.
- **Career** What subjects would you study if you were preparing to be an astronomer? Present your findings to the class.

Measurement, Area, and Volume

BEFORE

In previous chapters you've...

- Found the areas of rectangles
- Identified and sketched polygons

Now

In Chapter 10 you'll study...

- Finding the areas of circles, parallelograms, and trapezoids
- Identifying and sketching three-dimensional figures
- Finding the surface areas and volumes of solids

WHY?

So you can solve real-world problems about...

- architecture, p. 482
- hockey, p. 487
- recycling, p. 515
- swimming pools, p. 517

Internet Preview
CLASSZONE.COM

- eEdition Plus Online
- eWorkbook Plus Online
- eTutorial Plus Online
- State Test Practice
- More Examples

Chapter Warm-Up Game

Review skills you need for this chapter in this quick game. Work with a partner.

Key Skills:
Finding the perimeter, area, or circumference of squares, rectangles, triangles, and circles

MEASURE MATCH

MATERIALS

- 15 Picture Cards

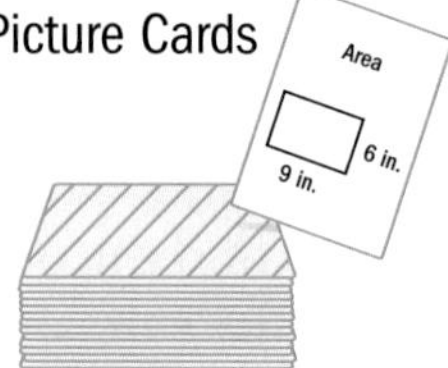

- 15 Measure Cards

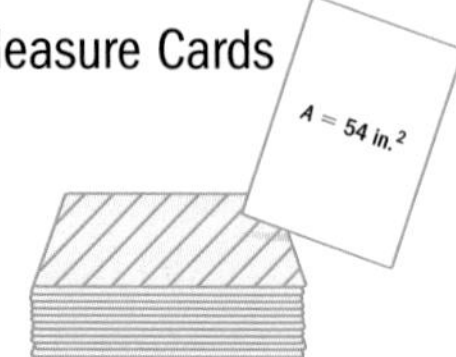

PREPARE Place all cards face down and mix them up. On your turn follow the steps on the next page.

1 TURN over two cards.

2 DECIDE whether the two cards match. Cards match when you turn over a Picture Card and a Measure Card that describes the picture. If the cards match, you may keep them. Otherwise, turn them back over.

3 REMEMBER where the cards are so you can find matching pairs on future turns.

HOW TO WIN

Be the player with the most cards once all the cards have been matched.

Stop *and* Think

1. **Writing** If the Measure Cards did not have *A*, *P*, or *C* on them, would you still be able to tell what was being measured? Explain.
2. **Extension** Design six new cards for *Measure Match*. Three should be Picture Cards and three should be Measure Cards. Make sure each Picture Card matches a Measure Card.

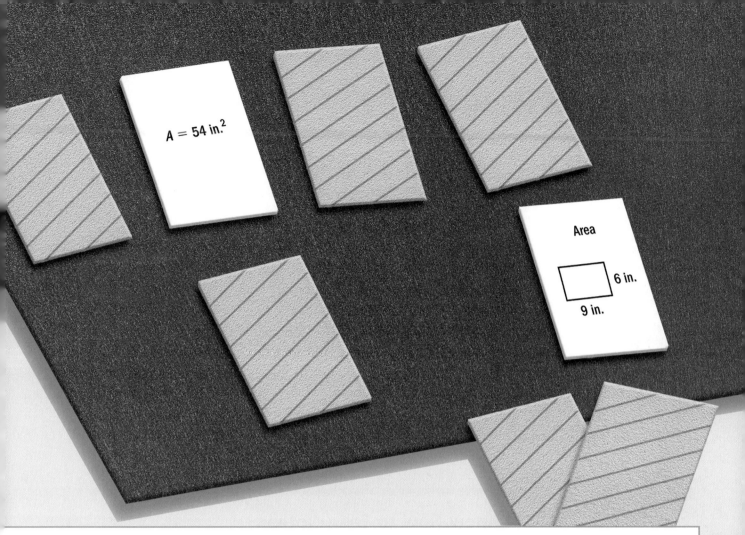

Getting Ready to Learn

Word Watch

Review Words

area, p. 33
base, p. 134
height, p. 134
circle, p. 290
radius, p. 290
pi (π), p. 290
trapezoid, p. 386
parallelogram, p. 386
rhombus, p. 386

Review What You Need to Know 

Using Vocabulary **Classify the figure indicated using a review word.**

1. quadrilateral *ABCD*

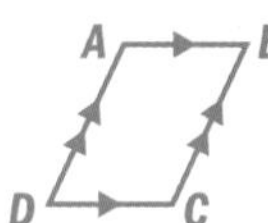

2. $\overline{PQ}$

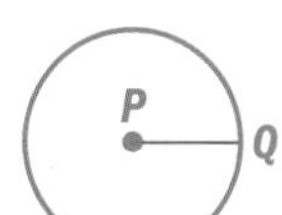

3. quadrilateral *JKLM*

Find the area of the shaded region. *(Lessons 1.6, 3.5)*

4.

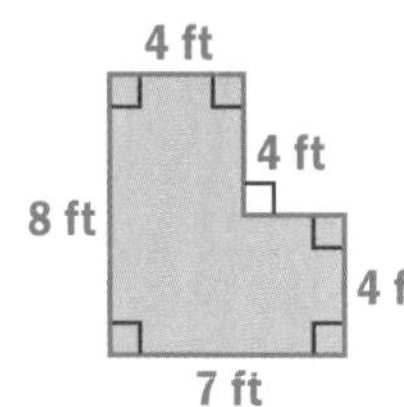

5.

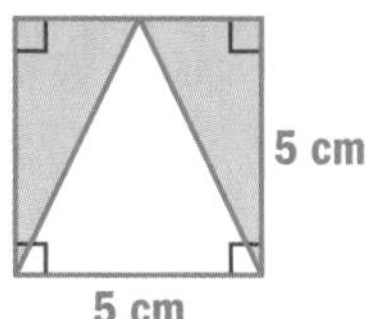

6.

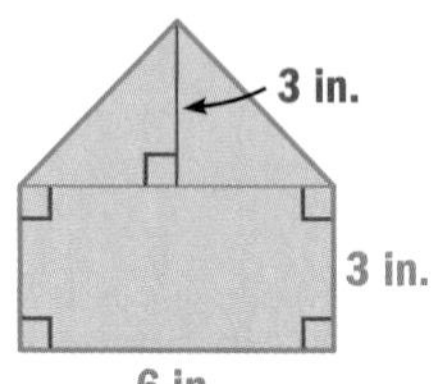

You should include material that appears on a notebook like this in your own notes.

Know How to Take Notes

Using a Concept Grid You can use a concept grid to organize what you know about a topic.

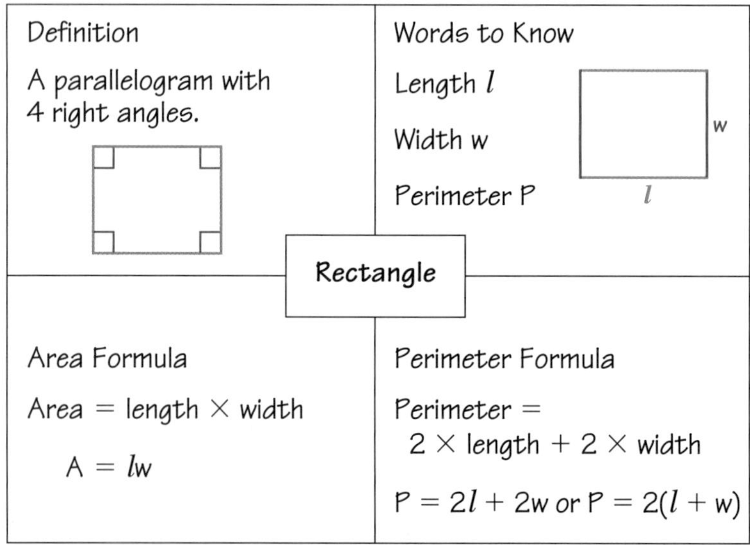

Definition
A parallelogram with 4 right angles.
Words to Know
Length l
Width w
Perimeter P
w
l
Rectangle
Area Formula
Area = length × width
$A = lw$
Perimeter Formula
Perimeter = 2 × length + 2 × width
$P = 2l + 2w$ or $P = 2(l + w)$

In Lesson 10.2, you will learn the formula for the area of a circle. Then you can make a concept grid for circles.

Areas of Parallelograms and Trapezoids

BEFORE	Now	WHY?
You found the areas of triangles and rectangles.	You'll find the areas of parallelograms and trapezoids.	So you can find the area of one side of a podium, as in Ex. 32.

base of a parallelogram, p. 481
height of a parallelogram, p. 481
bases of a trapezoid, p. 482
height of a trapezoid, p. 482

INDIANA
Academic Standards
- Measurement (8.5.4)

The **base of a parallelogram** can be any one of its sides. The **height of a parallelogram** is the perpendicular distance between the base and the opposite side.

The diagram below shows how to change a parallelogram into a rectangle with the same base, height, and area.

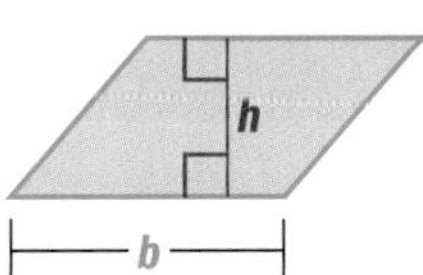

Start with any parallelogram.

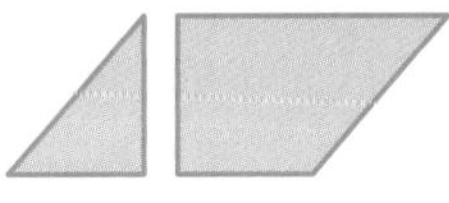

Cut the parallelogram to form a right triangle and a trapezoid.

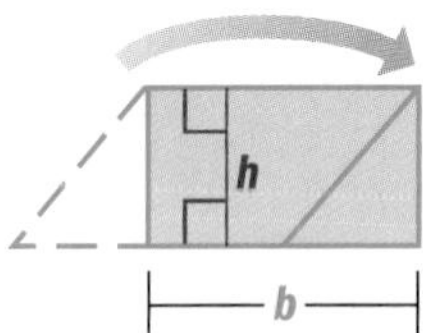

Move the triangle to form a rectangle.

The area of the rectangle is the product of the base and the height, so the formula for the area of the parallelogram is $A = bh$.

Area of a Parallelogram

Words The area of a parallelogram is the product of the base and the height.

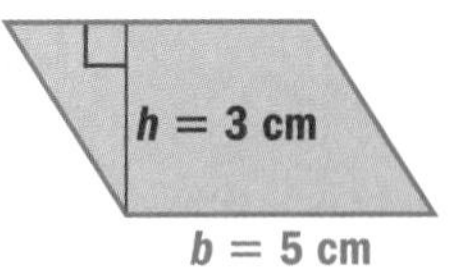

Algebra $A = bh$ **Numbers** $A = 5 \cdot 3 = 15 \text{ cm}^2$

EXAMPLE 1 Finding the Area of a Parallelogram

Find the area of the parallelogram.

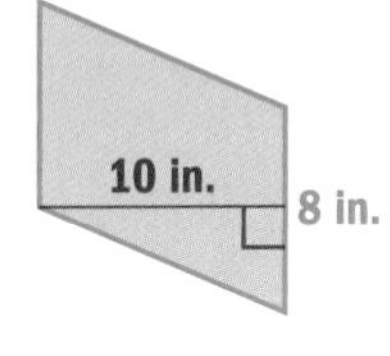

$A = bh$	**Write formula for area.**
$= 8 \cdot 10$	**Substitute 8 for *b* and 10 for *h*.**
$= 80$	**Multiply.**

ANSWER The parallelogram has an area of 80 square inches.

The bases of a trapezoid are labeled b_1 and b_2. You read these labels as "b sub one" and "b sub two." For help with trapezoids, see p. 386.

Trapezoids The **bases of a trapezoid** are its parallel sides. The **height of a trapezoid** is the perpendicular distance between the bases. The diagram below shows how two congruent trapezoids with height h and bases b_1 and b_2 can form a parallelogram with height h and base $b_1 + b_2$.

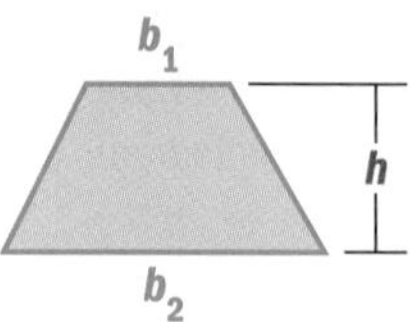

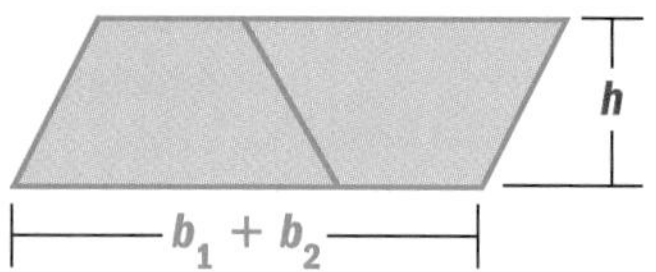

The area of the parallelogram is $(b_1 + b_2)h$, so the area of each trapezoid is $\frac{1}{2}(b_1 + b_2)h$.

Area of a Trapezoid

Words The area of a trapezoid is one half the product of the sum of the bases and the height.

$b_1 = 4$ m
$h = 3$ m
$b_2 = 8$ m

Algebra $A = \frac{1}{2}(b_1 + b_2)h$ **Numbers** $A = \frac{1}{2}(4 + 8)3 = 18 \text{ m}^2$

The Winslow House in River Forest, Illinois

EXAMPLE 2 Finding the Area of a Trapezoid

Architecture The Winslow House was designed by Frank Lloyd Wright. The front part of the roof is a trapezoid. What is its area?

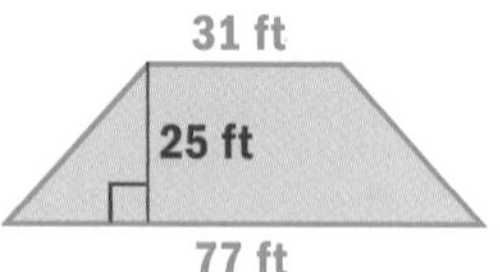

Solution

$A = \frac{1}{2}(b_1 + b_2)h$	Write formula for area of a trapezoid.
$= \frac{1}{2}(31 + 77)25$	Substitute values for b_1, b_2, and h.
$= 1350$	Multiply.

ANSWER The front part of the roof has an area of 1350 square feet.

Your turn now **Sketch the quadrilateral and find its area.**

1. A parallelogram with base 20 meters and height 9 meters
2. A trapezoid with bases of 17 feet and 14 feet and height 6 feet

Getting Ready to Practice

Vocabulary **Write the area formula for the polygon.**

1. parallelogram **2.** triangle **3.** trapezoid

Find the area of the parallelogram or trapezoid.

4.
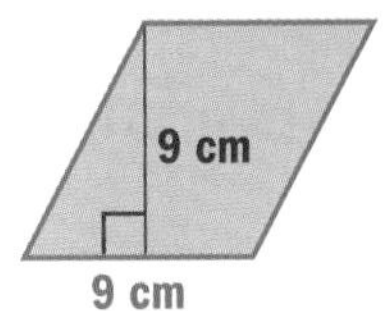

5.
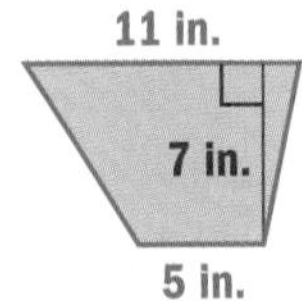

6.
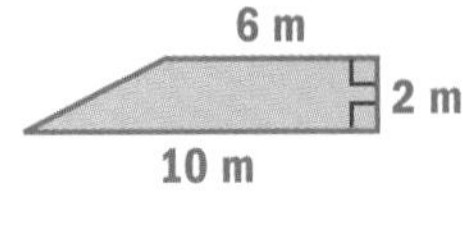

7. Guided Problem Solving You are designing a putting green for a miniature golf course, as shown. Find the area of the green.

(1) Copy the shape and divide it into a trapezoid and a parallelogram.

(2) Find the area of each quadrilateral.

(3) Add the two areas to find the total area.

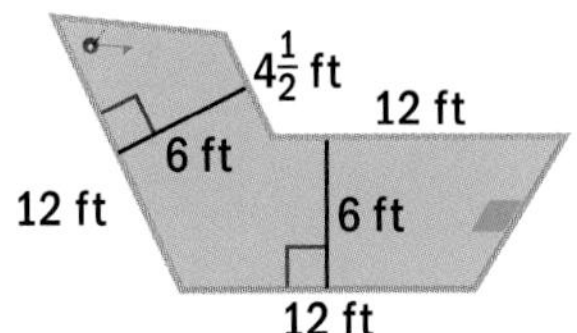

Practice and Problem Solving

HELP with Homework

Example	Exercises
1	8–13, 20
2	15–19

Online Resources
CLASSZONE.COM
· More Examples
· eTutorial Plus

Sketch a parallelogram with base b and height h and find its area.

8. $b = 12$ in., $h = 8$ in. **9.** $b = 9$ ft, $h = 14$ ft **10.** $b = 10$ cm, $h = 22$ cm

Find the area of the parallelogram.

11.
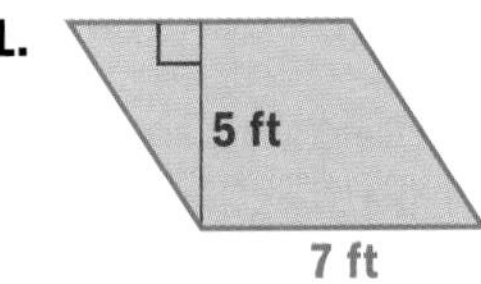

12.
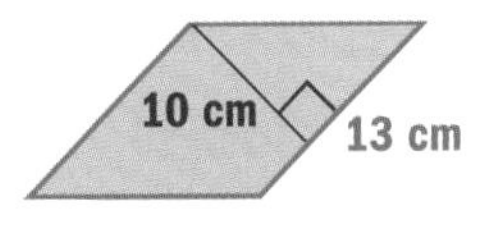

13.
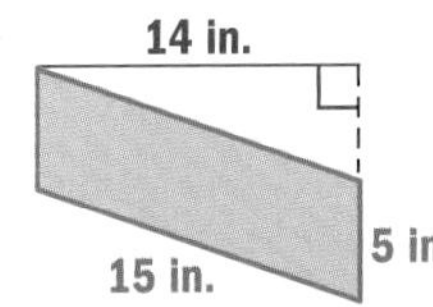

14. Find the Error Describe and correct the error in the solution.

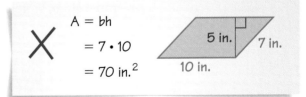

$A = bh$
$= 7 \cdot 10$
$= 70 \text{ in.}^2$

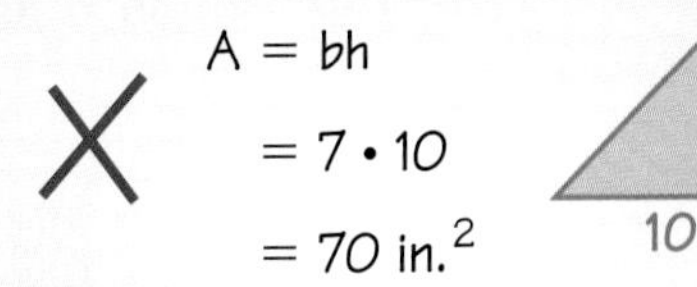

Sketch a trapezoid with bases b_1 and b_2 and height h and find its area.

15. $b_1 = 13$ ft, $b_2 = 7$ ft, $h = 6$ ft **16.** $b_1 = 8$ m, $b_2 = 16$ m, $h = 11$ m

Find the area of the trapezoid.

17. 18 in. 12 in. 9 in.

18. 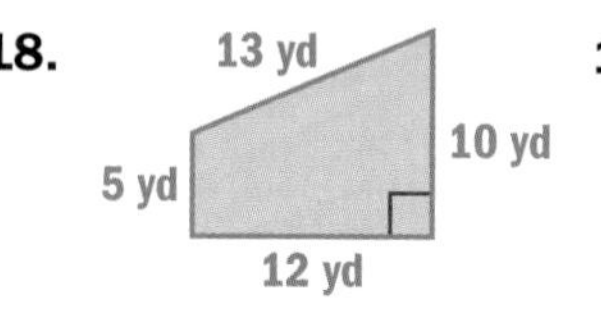

19. 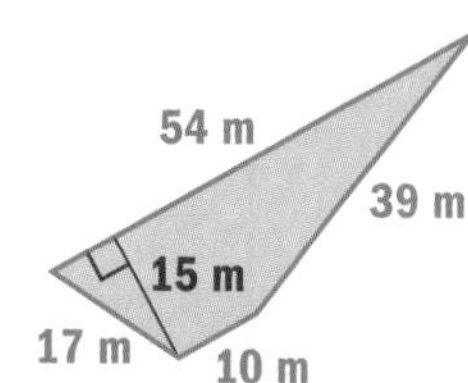

20. Measurement Use a metric ruler to measure the dimensions of the parallelogram in millimeters. Then find the area.

Algebra **Sketch the quadrilateral. Then use an area formula to find the unknown dimension.**

21. A parallelogram has an area of 84 square units. Its height is 12 units. Find the base.

22. A trapezoid has an area of 100 square units. Its bases are 10 units and 15 units. Find the height.

Extended Problem Solving **In Exercises 23–26, use the parallelogram and trapezoid shown.**

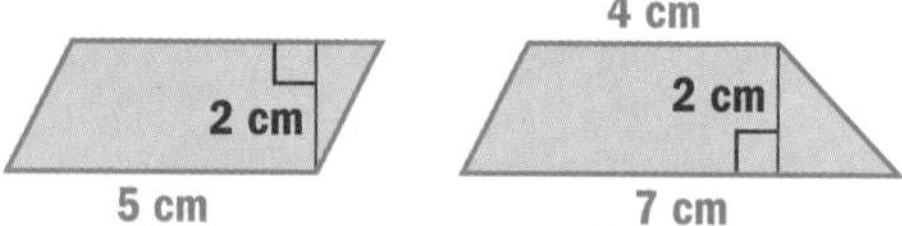

23. Calculate Find the areas of the parallelogram and trapezoid.

24. Compare Double each dimension of the quadrilaterals. Find the new areas. How do the new areas compare to the original areas?

25. Compare Triple each dimension of the original quadrilaterals and find the new areas. How do the new areas compare to the original areas?

26. Critical Thinking Suppose you multiply each dimension by a positive number k. What do you think the new areas would be?

Estimation **Use the given scale and the formula for the area of a trapezoid or a parallelogram to estimate the area of the state.**

27. Nevada

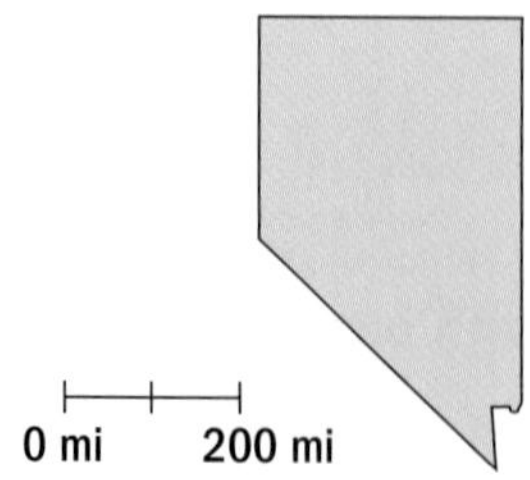

28. Tennessee

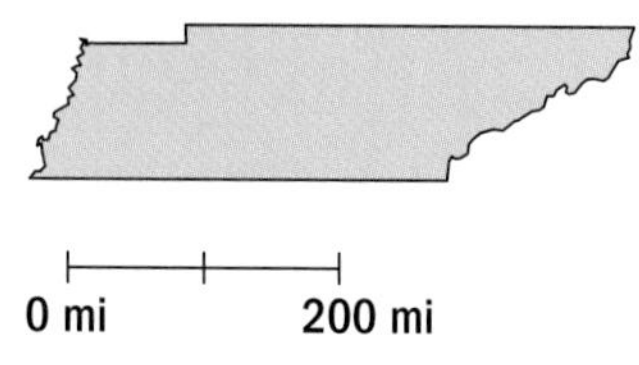

Find the area of the polygon.

29.

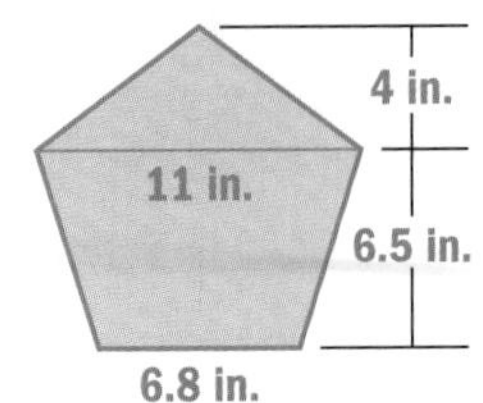

30.

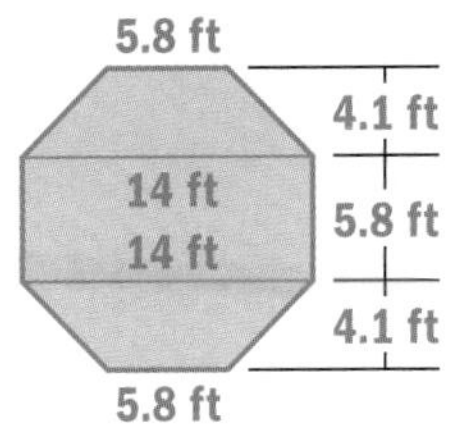

31.

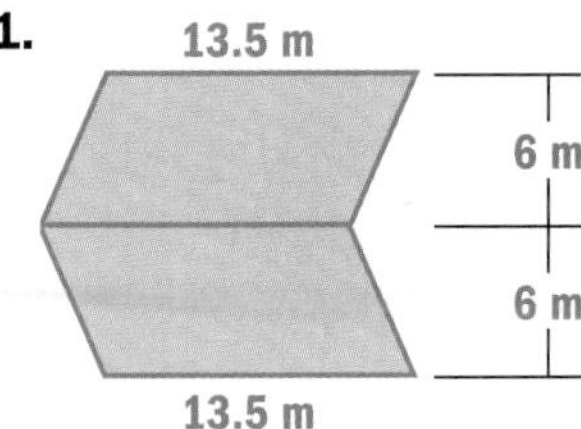

Find the area of the polygon.

32.

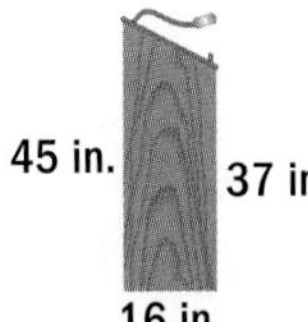

33.

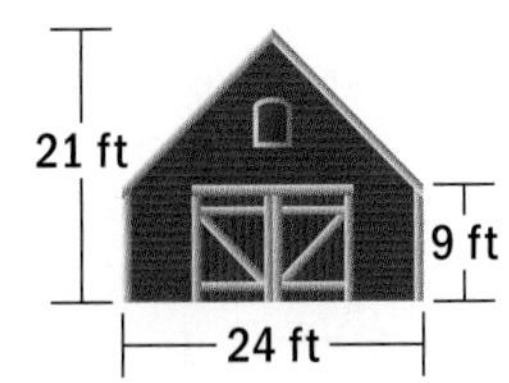

34.

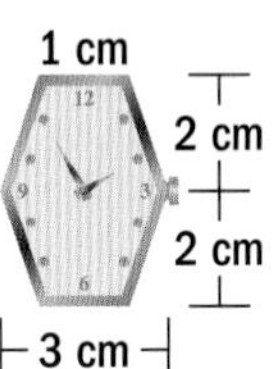

Plot the points in a coordinate plane and connect them to form a parallelogram. Then find the area of the parallelogram.

35. $(-3, -1), (0, 4), (6, 4), (3, -1)$ **36.** $(8, 0), (11, -5), (-2, -5), (-5, 0)$

Challenge **Find the area of the parallelogram or trapezoid.**

37.

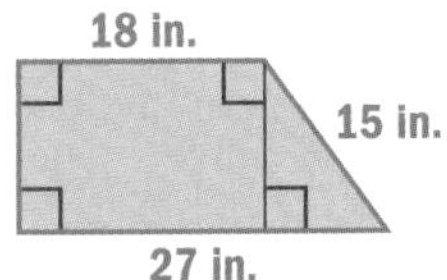

38.

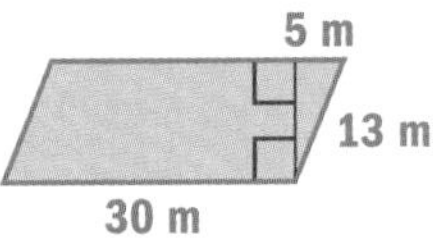

39.

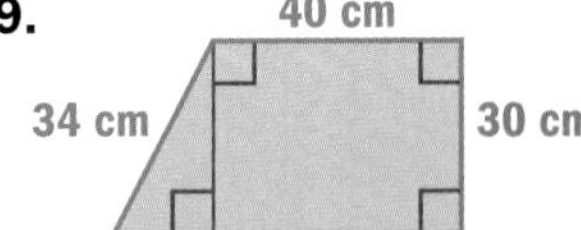

Mixed Review

Find the product. *(Lesson 5.3)*

40. $-\frac{3}{4} \cdot 1\frac{5}{9}$ **41.** $-7 \cdot \left(-\frac{5}{3}\right)$ **42.** $2\frac{3}{8} \cdot \left(-\frac{6}{7}\right)$

43. In $\triangle PQR$, write the sine, cosine, and tangent ratios for $\angle P$ and $\angle R$. *(Lesson 9.6)*

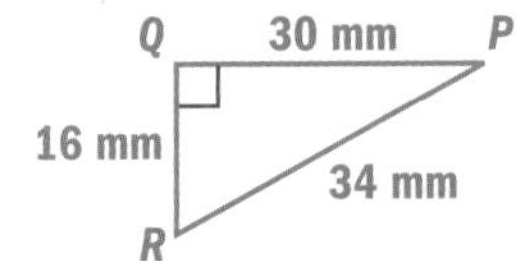

Test-Taking Practice

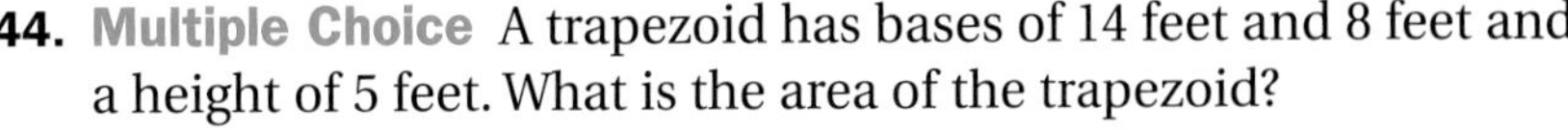

44. Multiple Choice A trapezoid has bases of 14 feet and 8 feet and a height of 5 feet. What is the area of the trapezoid?

A. 55 ft^2 **B.** 76 ft^2 **C.** 91 ft^2 **D.** 110 ft^2

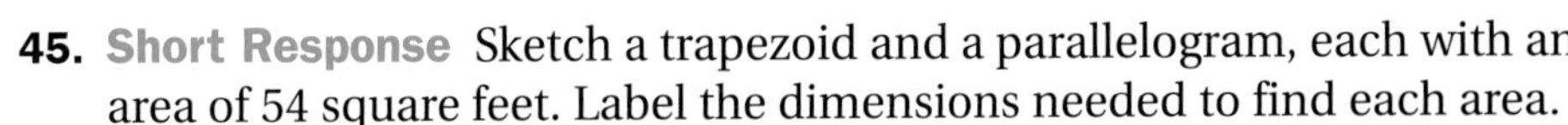

45. Short Response Sketch a trapezoid and a parallelogram, each with an area of 54 square feet. Label the dimensions needed to find each area.

Areas of Circles

BEFORE	Now	WHY?
You found the areas of parallelograms and trapezoids.	You'll find the areas of circles.	So you can find the area of a yard watered by a sprinkler, as in Ex. 22.

Review Words

area, p. 33
circle, p. 290
radius, p. 290
diameter, p. 290
circumference, p. 290
pi (π), p. 290

INDIANA Academic Standards

• Measurement (8.5.4)

Activity You can use a model to find the area of a circle.

1. Draw a circle and cut it into 8 congruent parts. Arrange the pieces of the circle to resemble a parallelogram, as shown below.

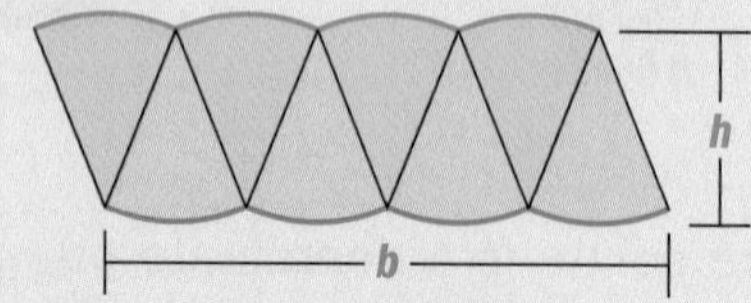

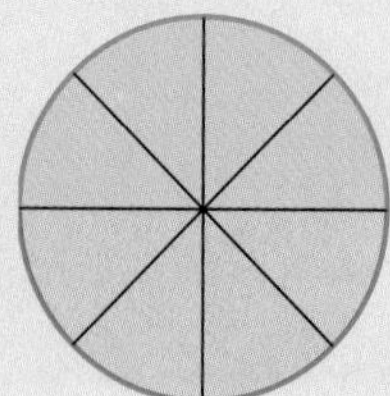

2. Copy and complete: The height of the parallelogram is equal to the __?__ of the circle, and the base of the parallelogram is about equal to one half of the __?__ of the circle.

3. Use the formula for the area of a parallelogram and your answer from Step 2 to find the formula for the area of the circle in terms of r.

The activity suggests the formula given below.

Area of a Circle

Words The area of a circle is the product of π and the square of the radius.

$r = 6$ cm

Algebra $A = \pi r^2$ **Numbers** $A = \pi(6)^2$

EXAMPLE 1 Finding the Area of a Circle

Find the area of a circle with a diameter of 10 inches.

$A = \pi r^2$	Write formula for area of a circle.
$\approx 3.14(5)^2$	Substitute 3.14 for π and 5 for r.
$= 78.5$	Evaluate using a calculator.

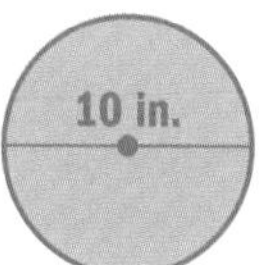

ANSWER The area is about 78.5 square inches.

To help you organize information about circles, you may want to make a concept grid.

EXAMPLE 2 Finding the Radius of a Circle

Find the radius of a circle that has an area of 530.66 square feet.

$A = \pi r^2$	Write formula for area of a circle.
$530.66 \approx (3.14)r^2$	Substitute 530.66 for A and 3.14 for π.
$169 \approx r^2$	Use a calculator to divide each side by 3.14.
$\sqrt{169} \approx r$	Take positive square root of each side.
$13 \approx r$	Evaluate square root.

ANSWER The radius of the circle is about 13 feet.

Your turn now **Find the unknown area or radius of the circle. Use 3.14 for π.**

1. $r = 7$ ft, $A = \underline{?}$ **2.** $d = 3$ km, $A = \underline{?}$ **3.** $A = 628\ \text{cm}^2$, $r = \underline{?}$

EXAMPLE 3 Using the Area of a Circle

Hockey Find the combined area of the two face-off circles of an ice hockey rink.

Solution

The distance between the centers is 44 feet and there is 14 feet between the circles. So,

$$r + 14 + r = 44 \quad \text{and} \quad r = 15.$$

Now use the formula for the area of a circle.

$A = 2\pi r^2$	Area of two circles
$\approx 2(3.14)(15)^2$	Substitute 3.14 for π and 15 for r.
$= 1413$	Evaluate using a calculator.

ANSWER The area of the face-off circles is about 1413 square feet.

Your turn now **Find the area of the shaded region. Use 3.14 for π.**

4.

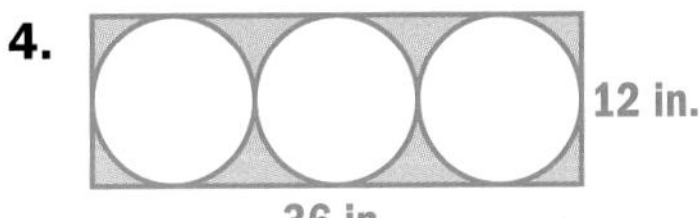

5.

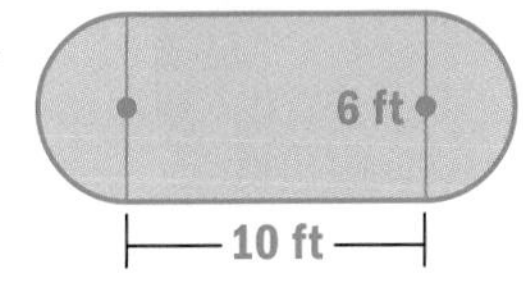

10.2 Exercises

More Practice, p. 736

INTERNET
eWorkbook Plus
CLASSZONE.COM

Getting Ready to Practice

1. **Vocabulary** Copy and complete: The area of a circle is the product of π and the square of the _?_.

Find the area of the circle. Use 3.14 for π.

2. 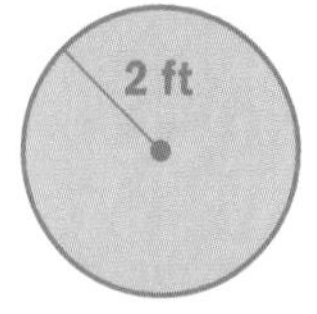

3. 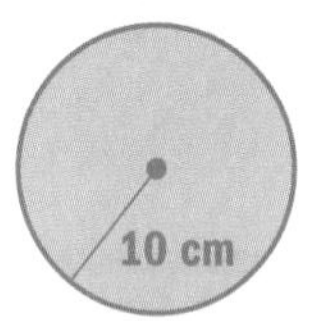

4. 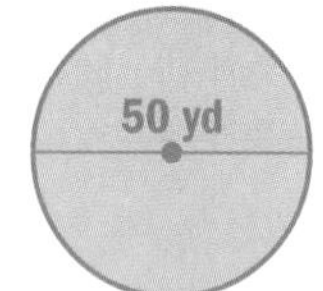

5. Find the radius of a circle that has an area of 154 square meters. Use 3.14 for π.

Practice and Problem Solving

HELP with Homework

Example	Exercises
1	6–15
2	16–21
3	22

Online Resources
CLASSZONE.COM
- More Examples
- eTutorial Plus

Find the area of the circle. Use 3.14 for π.

6. 11 yd

7. 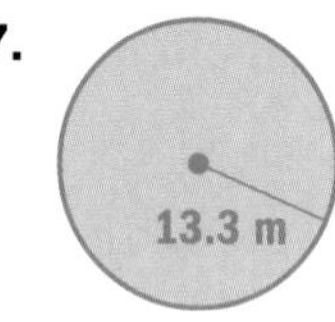

8. 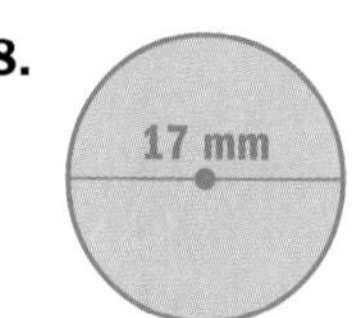

9. 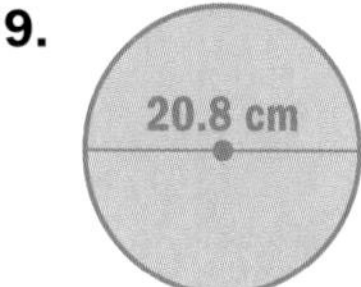

Find the area of the circle with the given radius or diameter. Use 3.14 for π.

10. $r = 9$ cm
11. $r = 10$ ft
12. $r = 30$ m
13. $d = 28$ mm
14. $d = 6$ yd
15. $d = 40$ in.

Find the radius of the circle with the given area. Use 3.14 for π.

16. $A = 28.26\text{ ft}^2$
17. $A = 3.14\text{ m}^2$
18. $A = 200.96\text{ yd}^2$
19. $A = 113.04\text{ in.}^2$
20. $A = 12.56\text{ mm}^2$
21. $A = 254.34\text{ cm}^2$

22. **Sprinklers** You are using a rotating sprinkler to water your yard. The sprinkler rotates in a complete circle. It sprays water a distance of 12 feet. Find the area of the yard that is watered. Use 3.14 for π.

23. **Measurement** Measure the radius of the circle in millimeters. Then find the area of the circle. Use 3.14 for π.

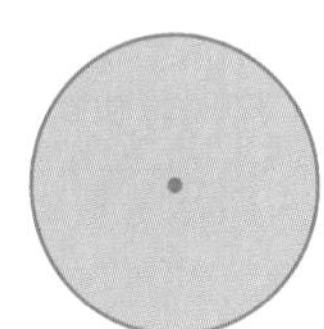

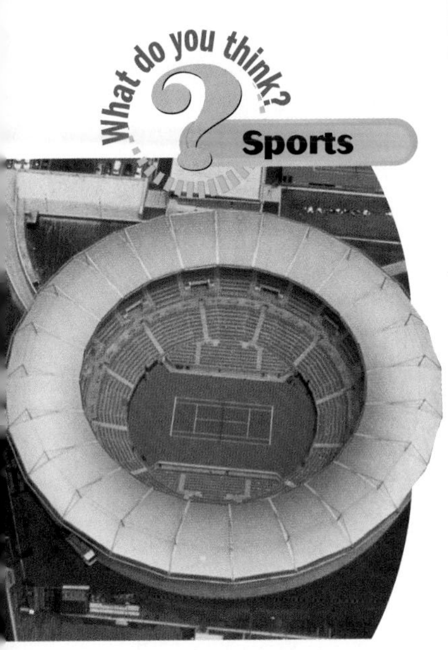

Tennis Center

The roof of the New South Wales Tennis Center has a mass of 70,000 kilograms. The roof was designed using 24 separate panels. What is the mass of each panel?

Find the area of the shaded region. Use 3.14 for π.

24. 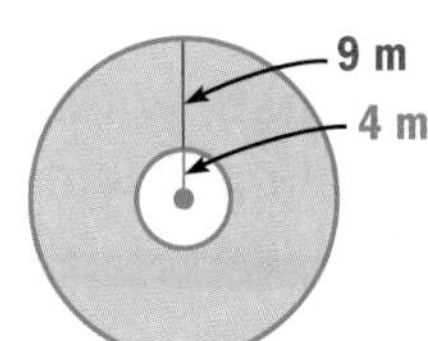

25. 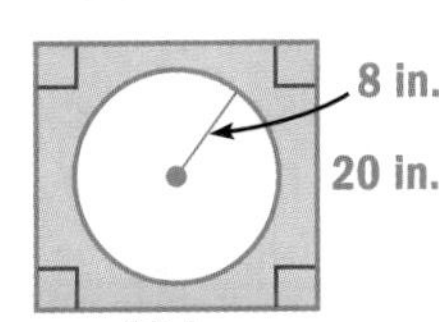

26. 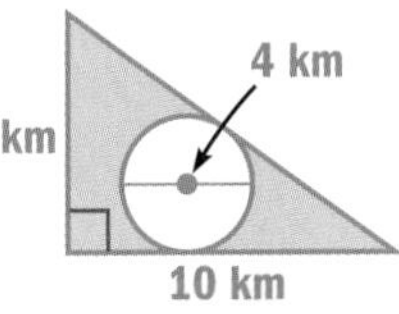

27. Mental Math If the area of a circle is 25π square feet, what is the radius?

28. Tennis Center The roof of the New South Wales Tennis Center in Sydney, Australia, can be approximated by a circle. A level of seats is covered by the ring-shaped roof whose outer diameter is about 100 meters and inner diameter is about 65 meters. What is the area of the roof? Use 3.14 for π.

Algebra Write and solve an equation to find the radius of the circle given its circumference *C*. Then use the radius to find the area of the circle. Use 3.14 for π.

29. $C = 18.84$ ft

30. $C = 81.64$ m

31. $C = 37.68$ cm

32. Critical Thinking Copy and complete the table. Leave your answers in terms of π. What happens to the area of a circle when the radius is multiplied by a number?

Radius r	Area of a circle with radius r	Area of a circle with radius $2r$	Area of a circle with radius $3r$	Area of a circle with radius $4r$
2 in.	4π in.^{2}	?	?	?
3 in.	?	?	?	?
5 in.	?	?	?	?

33. Estimation The diameter of the circle equals the side length of the larger square and the diagonal of the smaller square. The diameter of the circle is 20 millimeters. Find the area of each square and use the areas to estimate the area of the circle. Then calculate the area of the circle and compare it to your estimate. Use 3.14 for π.

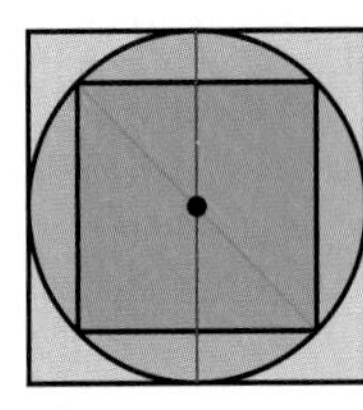

34. Disk Sanders You are using a disk sander to sand a porch that has an area of 11,520 square inches. One disk for the sander has a diameter of 7 inches. Another disk has a diameter of 10 inches. You can sand a surface with the area of five disks in one minute. About how much time would you save by sanding with the larger disk? Round your answer to the nearest minute. Use 3.14 for π.

35. Challenge Find the area of the shaded region. Use 3.14 for π.

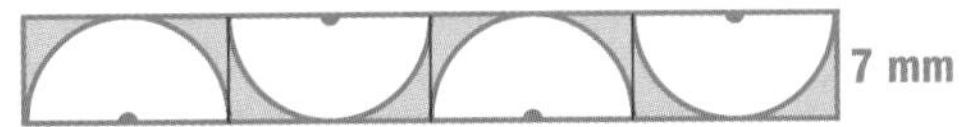

Mixed Review 

Choose a Strategy **Use a strategy from the list to solve the following problem. Explain your choice of strategy.**

> Problem Solving Strategies
> - Make a Table
> - Work Backward
> - Act It Out

36. For each quarter you put in a parking meter you can park your car for 15 minutes. You know you'll be away from your car for up to an hour and 40 minutes. If you have a $10 roll of quarters, how many quarters will you have after you put the necessary amount in the meter?

Tell whether the side lengths form a right triangle. *(Lesson 9.3)*

37. $a = 0.5, b = 0.9, c = 1.06$ **38.** $a = 3.6, b = 4.8, c = 6$

Test-Taking Practice 

39. **Multiple Choice** What is the approximate diameter of a circle with an area of 201 square millimeters? Use 3.14 for π.

A. 8 mm **B.** 16 mm **C.** 32 mm **D.** 64 mm

40. **Short Response** Ty is helping to paint his school's basketball court. Find the total area of the figure and explain how you found it. Use 3.14 for π.

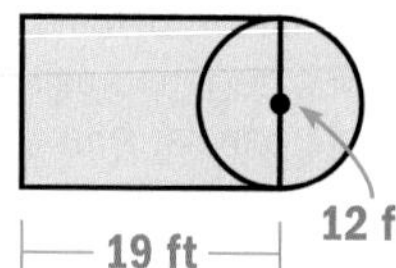

BRAIN GAME

What's the Score?

The center circle of the target has a radius of 3 inches and each ring is 3 inches wide. Find the area of each region in terms of π. Then use the formula below to find the score for each region. Round to the nearest whole number.

$$score = \frac{225\pi}{area}$$

For example, the yellow region has an area of $\pi(3)^2$, or 9π square inches. The score in the yellow region is

$$\frac{225\pi}{area} = \frac{225\pi}{9\pi} = 25.$$

Which player, Greg or Jamie, has a higher score?

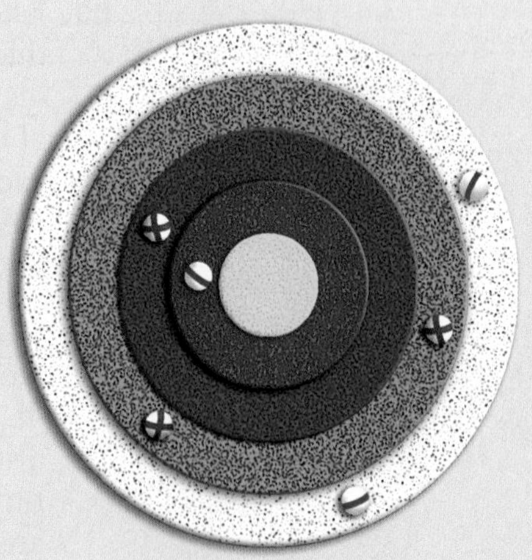

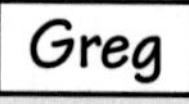

10.2 Technology Activity

SPREADSHEET

INDIANA: Academic Standards
- Measurement (8.5.4)

Comparing Radii of Circles

GOAL Use a spreadsheet to find how the radius of a circle changes when its area changes.

Example

How does the radius of a circle change when its area is multiplied by 4?

1 Create a spreadsheet with an original circle area in cell A1 and the multiplier 4 in cell A2. Enter formulas for the Area column that refer to these cells, as shown.

2 The radius of a circle with area A is given by $\sqrt{\frac{A}{\pi}}$. Enter formulas for the Radius column, as shown.

3 Compare the radii of the two circles by dividing the second radius by the first radius. Enter a formula for this quotient in the Ratio column, as shown.

Comparing Radii

	A	B	C
1	1	Original circle area	
2	4	Multiplier	
3			
4	Area	Radius	Ratio
5	=A1	=SQRT(A5/PI())	
6	=A5*A2	=SQRT(A6/PI())	=B6/B5

4 Change the value of the original circle area in cell A1 several times. What do you notice about the ratio of the radii?

	A	B	C
1	1	Original circle area	
2	4	Multiplier	
3			
4	Area	Radius	Ratio
5	1	0.564190	
6	4	1.128379	2

	A	B	C
1	5	Original circle area	
2	4	Multiplier	
3			
4	Area	Radius	Ratio
5	5	1.261566	
6	20	2.523133	2

	A	B	C
1	15	Original circle area	
2	4	Multiplier	
3			
4	Area	Radius	Ratio
5	15	2.185097	
6	60	4.370194	2

ANSWER When the area of a circle is multiplied by 4, the radius is multiplied by 2.

Your turn now **Find how the radius of a circle changes when its area is multiplied by the given number.**

1. 9 **2.** 16 **3.** 25 **4.** 36

5. **Critical Thinking** How does the radius of a circle change when its area is doubled? tripled? Explain.

6. Explain why $r = \sqrt{\frac{A}{\pi}}$ is the formula for the radius of a circle with area A.

Three-Dimensional Figures

BEFORE	Now	WHY?
You classified and sketched polygons.	You'll classify and sketch solids.	So you can classify solids that form structures, as in Exs. 19–21.

solid, polyhedron, p. 492
face, p. 492
prism, p. 492
pyramid, p. 492
cylinder, p. 492
cone, p. 492
sphere, p. 492
edge, vertex, p. 492

INDIANA
Academic Standards

- Geometry (8.4.3)

A **solid** is a three-dimensional figure that encloses a part of space. A **polyhedron** is a solid that is enclosed by polygons. A polyhedron has only flat surfaces. The polygons that form a polyhedron are called **faces**.

Classifying Solids

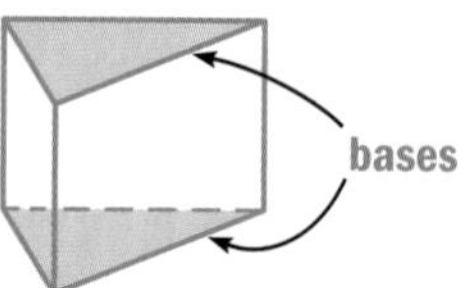

A **prism** is a polyhedron. Prisms have two congruent bases that lie in parallel planes. The other faces are rectangles.

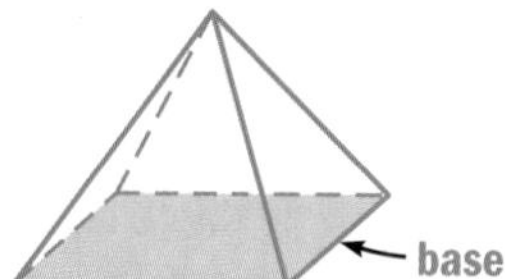

A **pyramid** is a polyhedron. Pyramids have one base. The other faces are triangles.

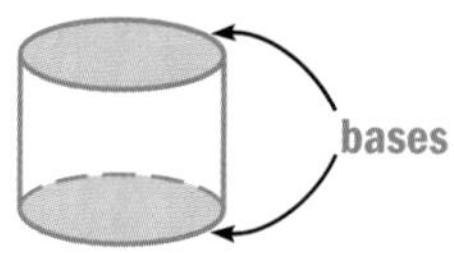

A **cylinder** is a solid with two congruent circular bases that lie in parallel planes.

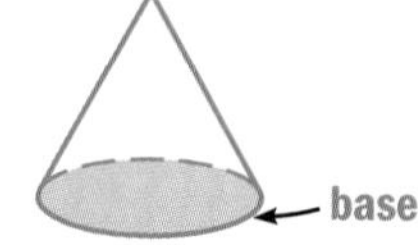

A **cone** is a solid with one circular base.

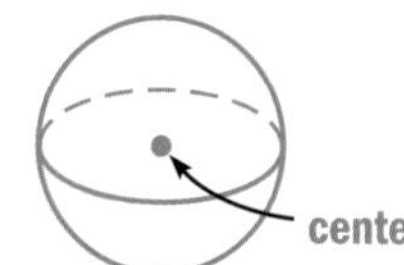

A **sphere** is a solid formed by all points in space that are the same distance from a fixed point called the center.

EXAMPLE 1 Classifying Solids

Classify the solid. Then tell whether it is a polyhedron.

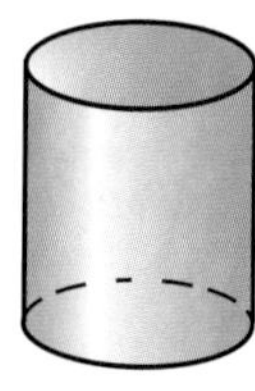

The solid has two congruent circular bases that lie in parallel planes, so it is a cylinder. It is not a polyhedron, because circles are not polygons.

HELP with Vocabulary

The plural of vertex is *vertices*.

The segments where faces meet are called **edges**. A **vertex** of a polyhedron is a point where three or more edges meet.

HELP with Vocabulary

You can name a prism or pyramid using the shape of its base. For example, in Example 2 the base is a pentagon, so the solid is called a pentagonal pyramid.

EXAMPLE 2 Counting Faces, Edges, and Vertices

Classify the solid. Then count the number of faces, edges, and vertices.

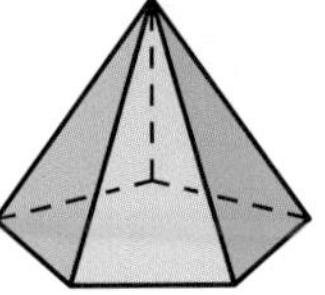

The solid is a pentagonal pyramid.

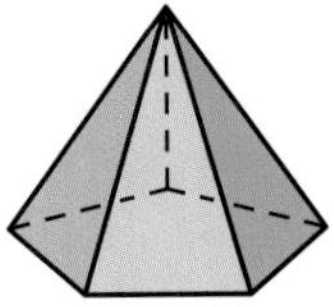

6 faces

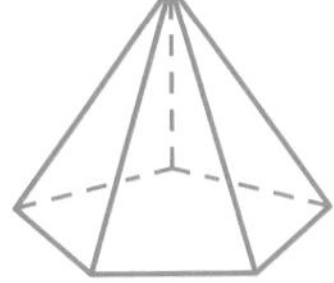

10 edges

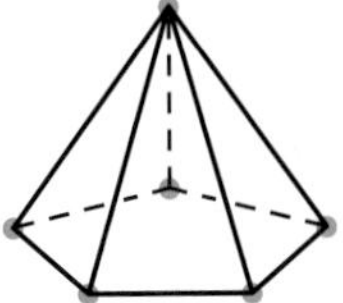

6 vertices

EXAMPLE 3 Sketching a Solid

Show two ways to represent a triangular prism.

Method 1 Sketch the solid.

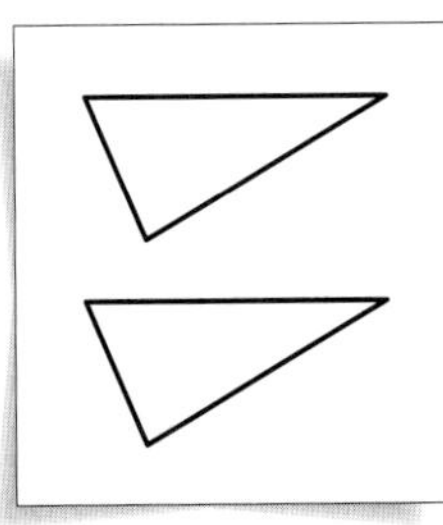

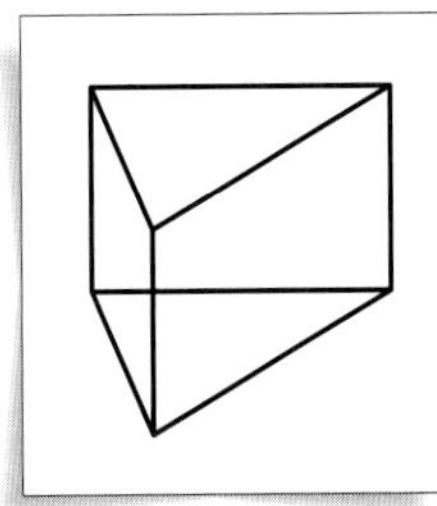

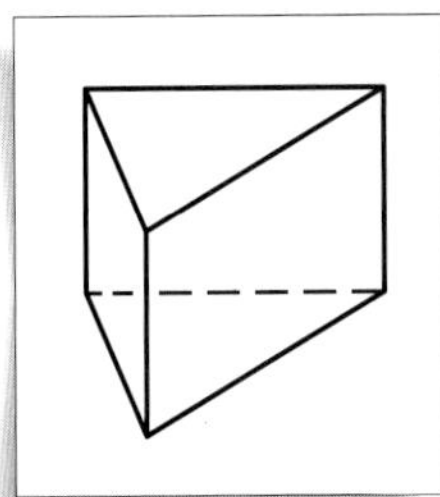

(1) **Sketch two congruent bases.**

(2) **Connect the vertices of the bases.**

(3) **Make any hidden lines dashed.**

Method 2 Sketch the top, front, and side views of the solid.

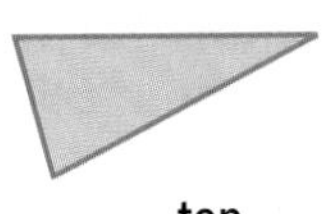

top

front

side

Your turn now **Classify the solid. Then tell whether it is a polyhedron.**

1.

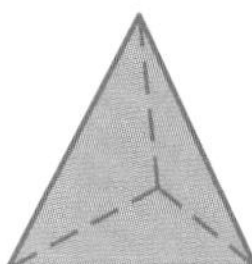

2.

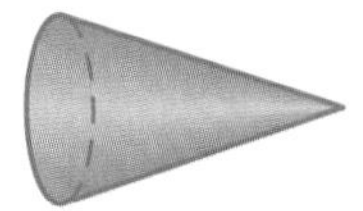

3.

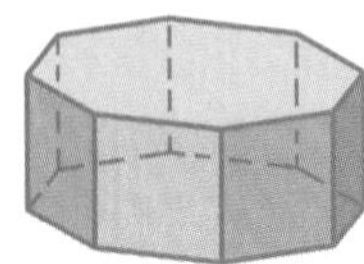

4. Show two ways to represent a rectangular pyramid. Then count the number of faces, edges, and vertices.

10.3 Exercises

More Practice, p. 736

Getting Ready to Practice

Vocabulary **Classify the solid. Then tell whether it is a polyhedron.**

1. 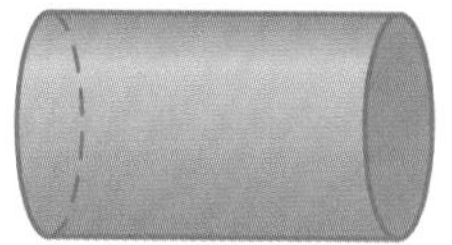

2. 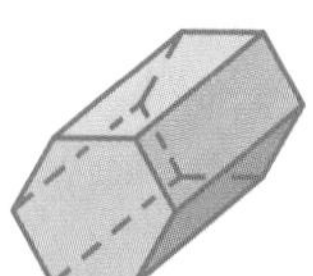

3. 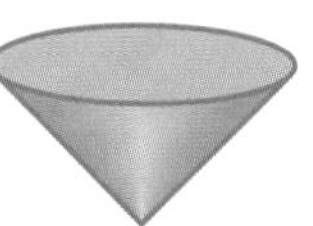

Show two ways to represent the solid. Then count the number of faces, edges, and vertices.

4. triangular pyramid

5. pentagonal prism

6. Guided Problem Solving Sketch a square pyramid.
   1. Sketch a parallelogram for the square base.
   2. Draw a dot centered above the parallelogram.
   3. Connect the vertices of the parallelogram to the dot. Make any hidden lines dashed.

Practice and Problem Solving

Classify the solid. Then tell whether it is a polyhedron.

7. 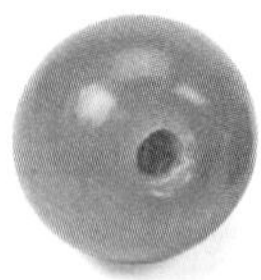

8. 

9. 

In Exercises 10 and 11, show two ways to represent the solid. Then count the number of faces, edges, and vertices.

10. octagonal prism

11. hexagonal prism

12. Writing Give examples of cylinders, cones, and square prisms that you find in your classroom or at home.

Matching **Match the description with the solid.**

13. one circular base
14. two rectangular bases
15. no edges or bases
16. three rectangular faces
17. four triangular faces

A. triangular prism
B. rectangular pyramid
C. rectangular prism
D. cone
E. sphere

HELP with Homework

Example	Exercises
1	7-9, 13-17
2	10-11, 18
3	10-11

Online Resources
CLASSZONE.COM
- More Examples
- eTutorial Plus

18. **Critical Thinking** Copy and complete the table. Use the pattern to write a formula that gives the number of edges in terms of the number of faces and vertices. This is called Euler's Formula.

Figure	Number of faces F	Number of vertices V	Number of edges E	$F + V$
pentagonal pyramid	6	6	10	12
rectangular pyramid	?	?	?	?
triangular prism	?	?	?	?
rectangular prism	?	?	?	?
pentagonal prism	?	?	?	?

Classify the solids that form the structure.

19. 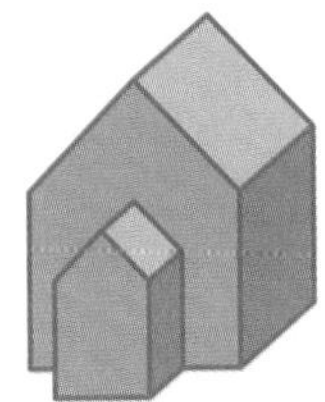

20. 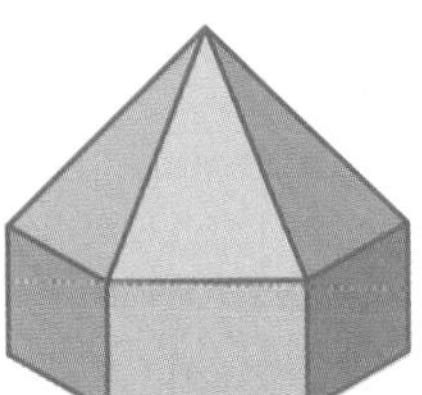

21. 

Sketch the solid with the given views.

22. 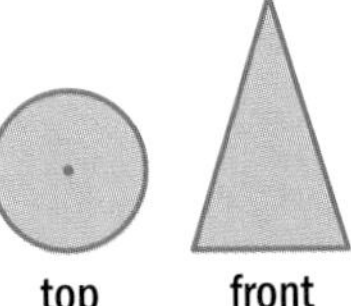

23. 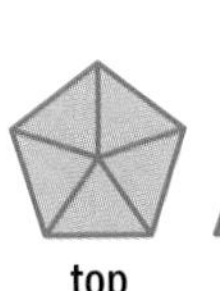 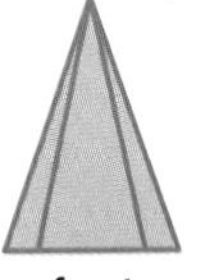 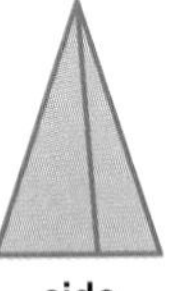

Mixed Review 

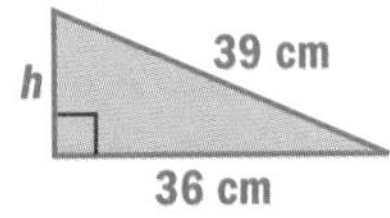

24. Find the value of h. Then find the perimeter and area of the triangle. *(Lesson 9.4)*

25. Find the area of a circle whose diameter is 21 inches. Use 3.14 for π. *(Lesson 10.2)*

Test-Taking Practice 

INTERNET
State Test Practice
CLASSZONE.COM

26. **Multiple Choice** Which of the following solids is a polyhedron?

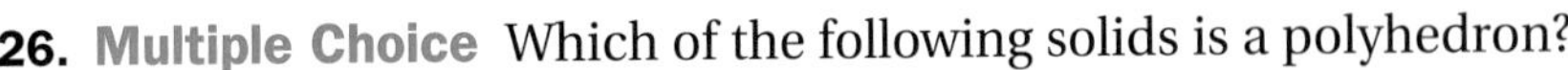

A. sphere **B.** cylinder **C.** cone **D.** pyramid

27. **Multiple Choice** What is the name of the solid shown?

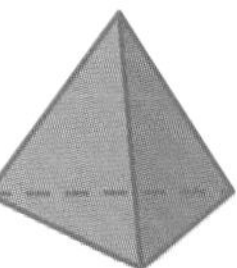

F. cone
G. triangle
H. triangular pyramid
I. triangular prism

Sketching Solids

GOAL Draw views of solids and make isometric drawings.

isometric drawing, p. 496

In Lesson 10.3, you drew the top, front, and side views of several common solids. In the following examples, you will see how to draw the top, front, and side views of more complicated solids.

EXAMPLE 1 Drawing Views of a Solid

Draw the top, front, and side views of the solid.

Solution

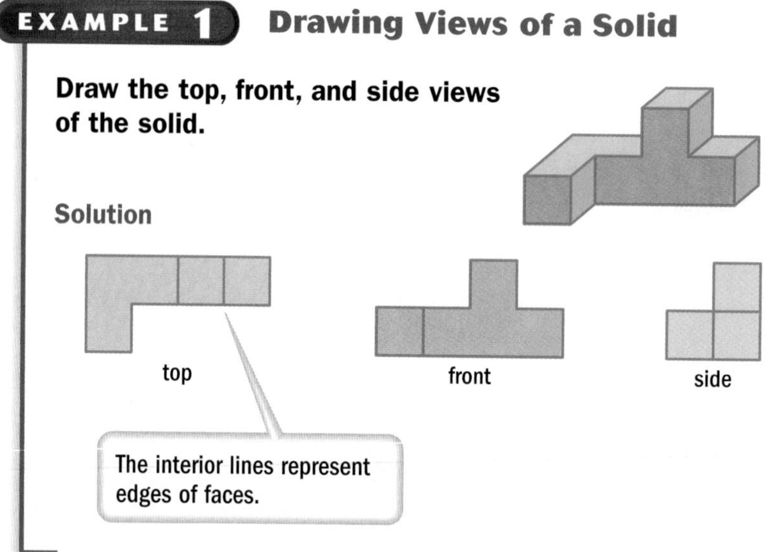

Isometric Drawings An **isometric drawing** is a two-dimensional drawing of a three-dimensional figure. You can create isometric drawings using a grid of dots and a set of three axes that intersect to form 120° angles. Use the dots to guide your drawing.

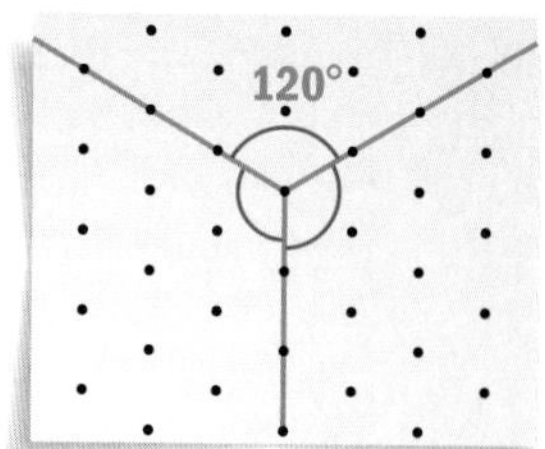

EXAMPLE 2 Creating an Isometric Drawing

Create an isometric drawing of the solid from Example 1.

Solution

The isometric drawing is shown at the right. Each vertical edge of the solid is represented by a vertical line segment.

Add depth to the drawing by shading the top, front, and sides differently.

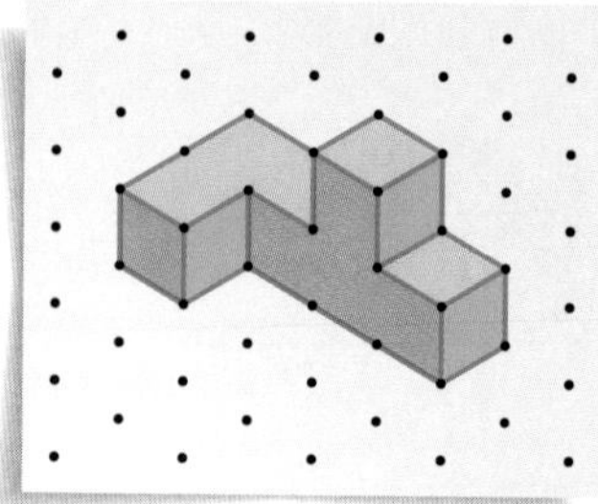

EXAMPLE 3 Interpreting an Isometric Drawing

Draw the top, front, and side views of the solid.

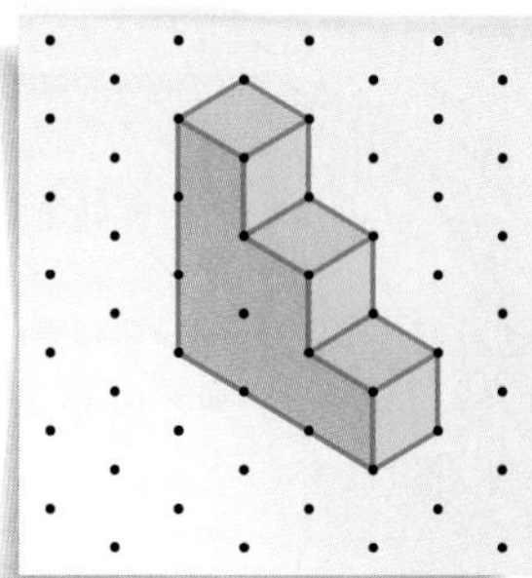

Solution

You can arrange the views this way.

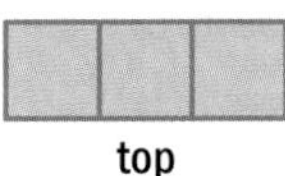

top

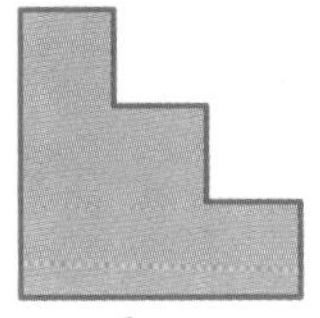

front

side

Exercises

Draw the top, front, and side views of the solid.

1. 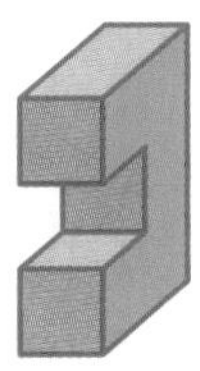

2. 

3. 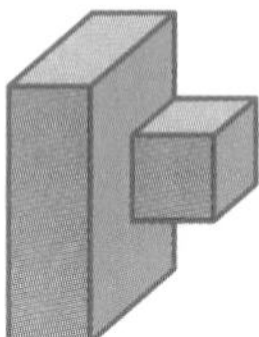

Create an isometric drawing of the solid.

4. 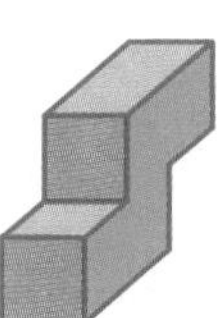

5. 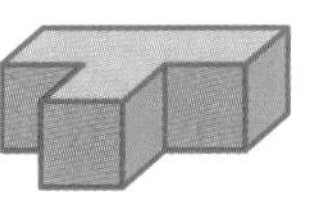

6. 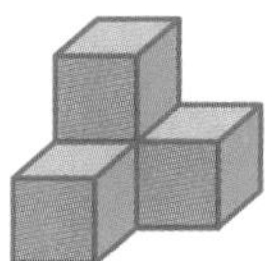

HELP with Solving

For the solids shown here, assume there are no cubes hidden from view except those needed to support the visible ones.

Draw the top, front, and side views of the solid.

7. 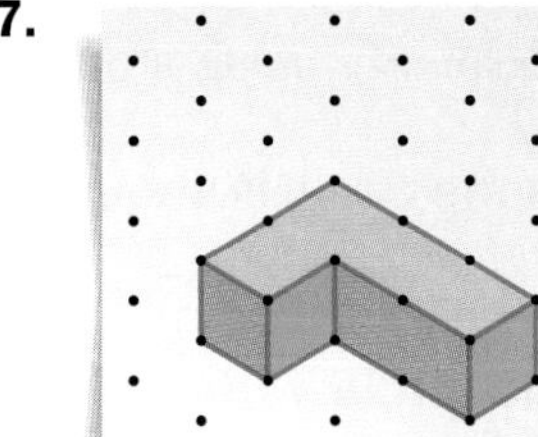

8. 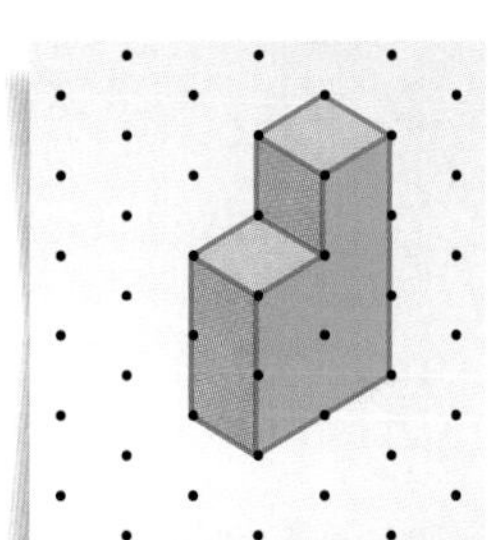

9. 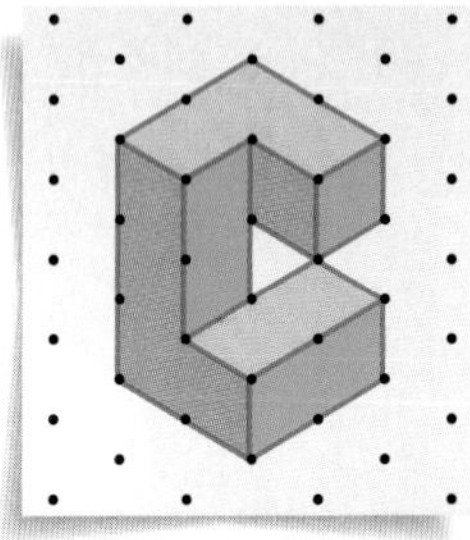

Notebook Review

Review the vocabulary definitions in your notebook.

Copy the review examples in your notebook. Then complete the exercises.

Check Your Definitions

base of a parallelogram, p. 481
height of a parallelogram, p. 481
bases of a trapezoid, p. 482
height of a trapezoid, p. 482
solid, polyhedron, p. 492
face, p. 492
prism, p. 492
pyramid, p. 492
cylinder, p. 492
cone, p. 492
sphere, p. 492
edge, vertex, p. 492

Use Your Vocabulary

1. A(n) _?_ is a solid that is enclosed by polygons.

10.1 Can you find the area of a parallelogram or trapezoid?

EXAMPLE Find the area of the trapezoid.

$A = \frac{1}{2}(b_1 + b_2)h$ — Write formula for area.

$= \frac{1}{2}(12 + 18)(5) = 75$ — Substitute values for b_1, b_2, and h.

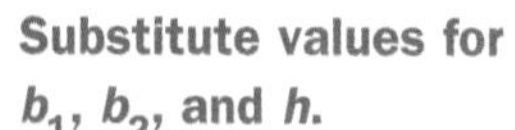

ANSWER The area of the trapezoid is 75 square inches.

2. Find the area of a parallelogram with base 20 feet and height 8 feet.

10.2 Can you find the area of a circle?

EXAMPLE Find the area of the circle. Use 3.14 for π.

$A = \pi r^2$ — Write formula for area of a circle.

$\approx 3.14(3)^2$ — Substitute 3.14 for π and 3 for r.

$= 28.26$ — Evaluate using a calculator.

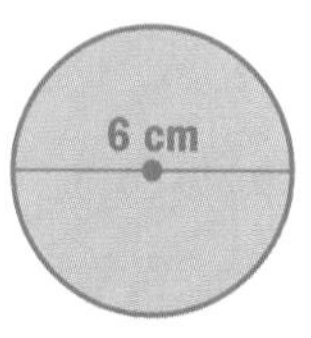

ANSWER The area of the circle is about 28.26 square centimeters.

Find the area of the circle with radius r or diameter d. Use 3.14 for π.

3. $r = 24$ in. **4.** $r = 4$ mm **5.** $d = 18$ yd

10.3 Can you classify three-dimensional figures?

EXAMPLE Count the faces, edges, and vertices of a triangular pyramid.

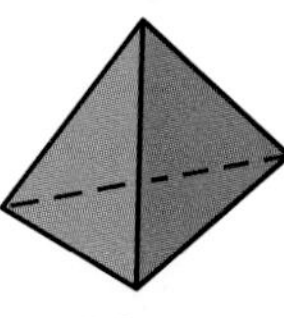

4 faces

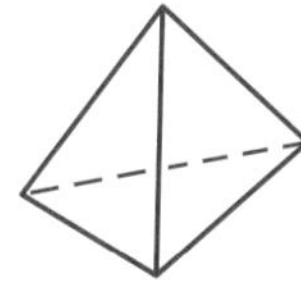

6 edges

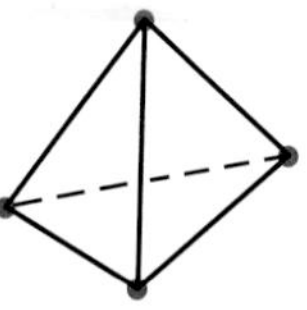

4 vertices

6. Show two ways to represent a square prism.

Stop and Think about Lessons 10.1–10.3

7. **Compare** Explain how a cone and a cylinder are alike and how they are different. Then explain how a cylinder and a prism are alike and how they are different.

8. **Critical Thinking** Can the number of vertices of a prism be odd? Explain.

Review Quiz 1

Find the area of the parallelogram or trapezoid.

1.

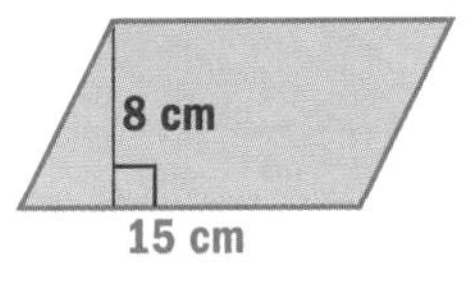

2.

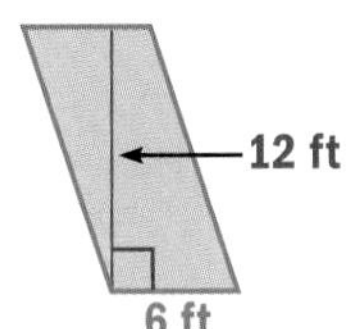

3.

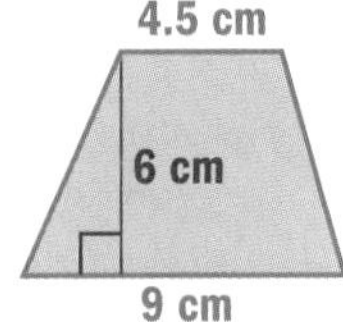

4. A trapezoid has a height of 8 feet. The lengths of the bases are 10 feet and 14 feet. Find the area of the trapezoid.

5. Find the area of a circle with diameter 22 feet. Use 3.14 for π.

Find the radius of the circle with the given area. Use 3.14 for π.

6. $A = 254.34\ \text{ft}^2$ **7.** $A = 452.16\ \text{cm}^2$ **8.** $A = 78.5\ \text{m}^2$

9. Classify the solid. Then tell whether it is a polyhedron.

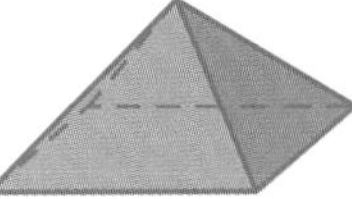

10. Show two ways to represent a pentagonal pyramid. Then count the number of faces, edges, and vertices.

10.4 Problem Solving Strategies

INDIANA: Academic Standards
• Measurement (8.5.4, 8.5.5)

- Guess, Check, and Revise
- Draw a Diagram
- Make a List
- Act It Out
- Break into Parts
- Work Backward
- Make a Table

Break into Parts

Problem Each student in your woodworking class has been assigned to make a mailbox. How much wood will you need to make the mailbox?

1 Read and Understand

Read the problem carefully.

You need to find the amount of wood needed to make the mailbox.

2 Make a Plan

Decide on a strategy to use.

You can solve this problem by breaking it into parts. Find the area of each side of the mailbox. Then add the areas together.

3 Solve the Problem

Reread the problem and break the problem into smaller parts.

Area of bottom: $lw = 18(8)$
$= 144$

Area of left and right sides: $2lh = 2(18)(6)$
$= 216$

Area of two roof pieces: $2(5)(18) = 180$

Area of front door and back door:

Add the area of the two triangles to the area of the two rectangles.

Area of the two triangles: $2\left(\frac{1}{2}\right)(8)(3) = 24$

Area of the two rectangles: $2(8)(6) = 96$

Find the sum of the areas: $A = 144 + 216 + 180 + 24 + 96$
$= 660 \text{ in.}^2$

4 Look Back

Have you found the area of every side of the mailbox? Did you find the total of these areas?

Practice the Strategy

Use the strategy *Break into Parts.*

1. **Mailbox** As an extra credit project, you are making a mailbox with a flat top. The new mailbox is 6 inches wide, 7 inches high, and 12 inches long. How much wood do you need to make this mailbox?

2. **Tiling** You are tiling the L-shaped room shown below. Each tile is 6 inches long by 6 inches wide. How many tiles do you need to tile the room?

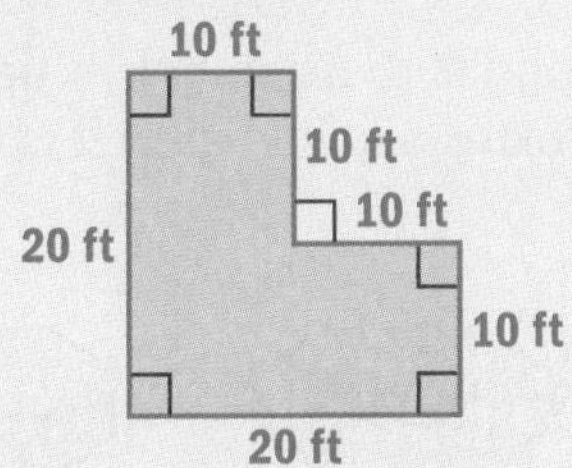

3. **Digits** You are making numbers to hang outside the classrooms in your school. The rooms are numbered 1–100. How many of each digit from 0–9 do you need?

4. **Lawn Mowing** You need about 2 hours to mow 3 acres of land. The total land area in the diagram is one acre, or 43,560 square feet. The house and surrounding plants have an area of 1500 square feet. The driveway is 12 feet wide and 50 feet long. How much time would you need to mow the remaining land area? Round your answer to the nearest minute.

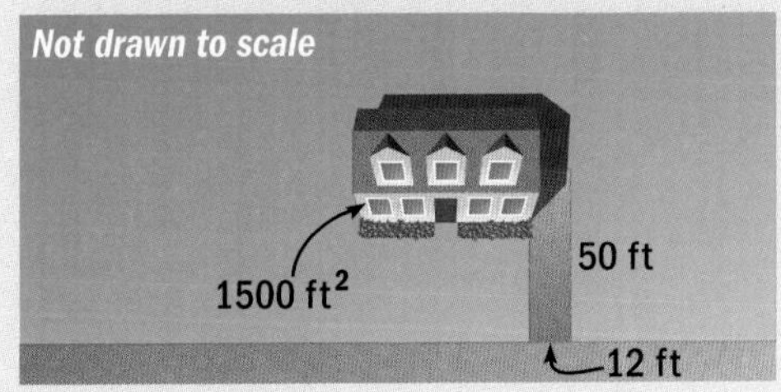

Mixed Problem Solving

Use any strategy to solve the problem.

5. **Food** Paula is making a sandwich with one type of meat, one type of cheese, and one dressing. How many different kinds of sandwiches can she make using the items in the list?

Meat	Cheese	Dressing
Ham	Swiss	Mayonnaise
Turkey	American	Italian dressing
	Cheddar	

6. **Traveling** Ryan left his house at 7:00 A.M. and traveled in his car. He drove 3 miles north, 2.5 miles east, 1 mile south, 1 mile east, 4 miles south, 1.5 miles west, 2 miles north, and 1.5 miles west. At the end of this trip, how far from home was Ryan?

7. **Numbers** The sum of two numbers is 17. The product of the numbers is 52. Find the two numbers.

8. **Clock** One chime of a clock takes 2.5 seconds to complete. At 1:00 the clock chimes once. At 2:00 the clock chimes twice. If the clock chimes in this way every hour, how many seconds will it spend chiming from 1:00 A.M. to 1:05 P.M.?

Surface Areas of Prisms and Cylinders

BEFORE	Now	WHY?
You classified prisms and cylinders.	You'll find the surface areas of prisms and cylinders.	So you can compare two caramels, as in Ex. 18.

Word Watch

net, p. 502
surface area, p. 503

INDIANA Academic Standards

- Measurement (8.5.4, 8.5.5)
- Problem Solving (8.7.1)

In the Real World

Storage Chest You are painting a storage chest. Before you begin painting the chest, you need to find the *surface area.* What is the *surface area* of the chest? You'll find the answer in Example 2.

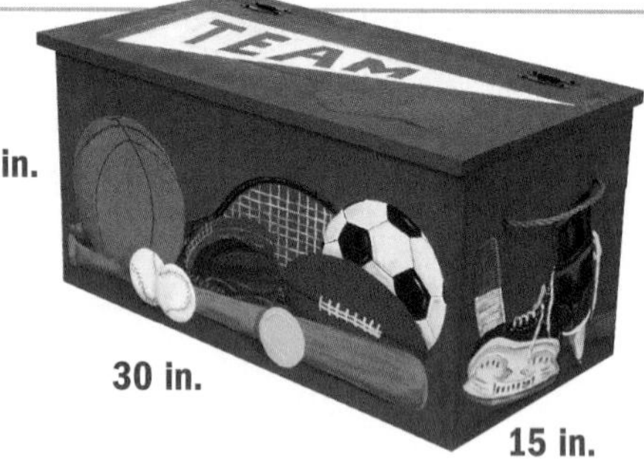

Nets One way to represent a solid is to use a *net.* A **net** is a two-dimensional pattern that forms a solid when it is folded.

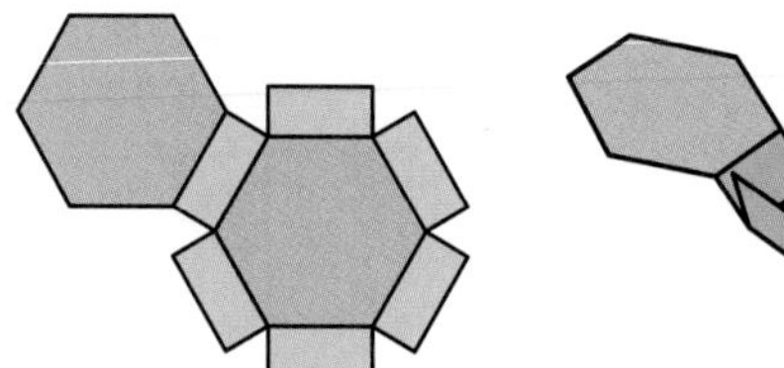
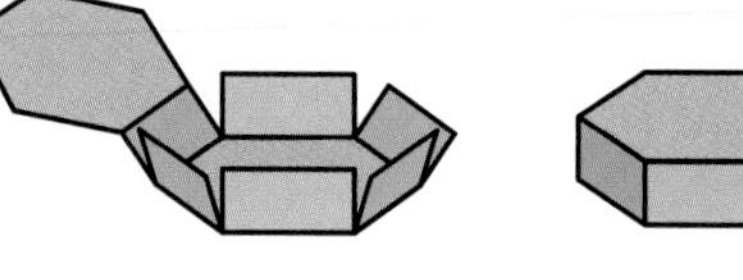
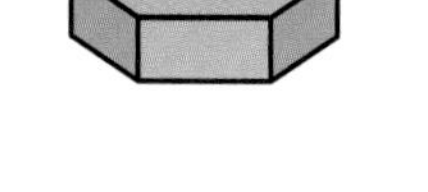

Each polygon of the net represents one face of the solid. There are usually several different possible nets for a given solid.

EXAMPLE 1 Drawing a Net

Draw a net of the triangular prism.

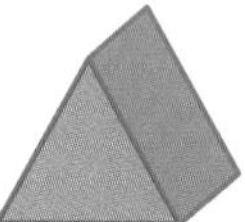

Solution

Method 1 Draw one base with a rectangle adjacent to each side. Draw the other base adjacent to one of the rectangles.

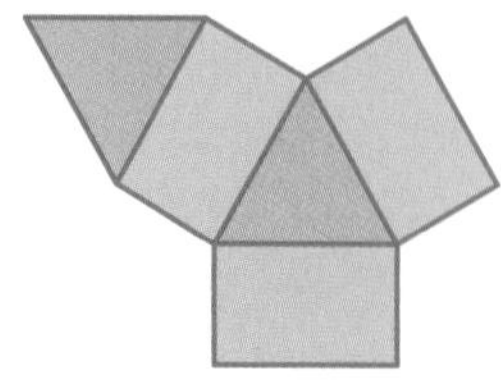

Method 2 For the rectangular faces, draw adjacent rectangles. Draw the bases on opposite sides of one rectangle.

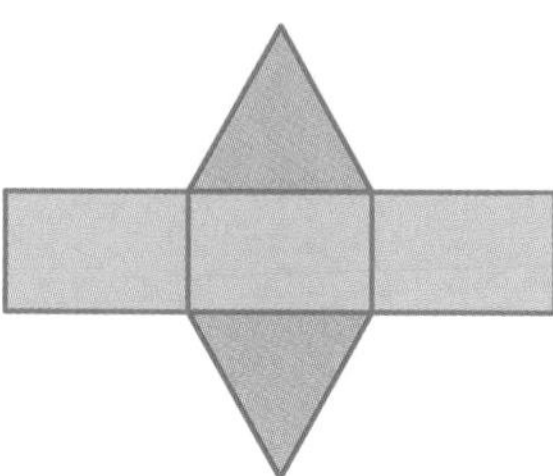

The **surface area** of a polyhedron is the sum of the areas of its faces.

EXAMPLE 2 Using a Net to Find Surface Area

Storage Chest Find the surface area of the storage chest shown on page 502. The chest is 30 inches long, 15 inches wide, and 15 inches high.

Solution

Draw a net of the chest.

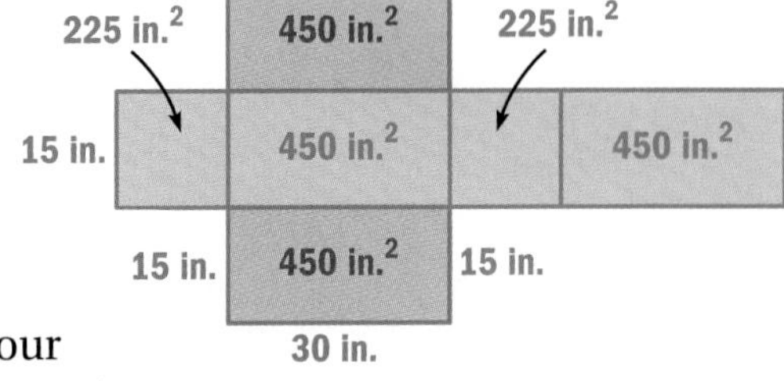

The area of each square face is 15 in. • 15 in. = **225 in.²**

The area of the rectangular face is 30 in. • 15 in. = 450 in.²

There are two square faces and four rectangular faces, so the surface area is 2 • **225 in.²** + 4 • 450 in.² = 2250 in.²

ANSWER The surface area of the storage chest is 2250 square inches.

Notice that in Example 2 the four blue faces form a rectangle that has length equal to the perimeter of the base.

Surface Area of a Prism

Words The surface area of a prism is the sum of twice the area of a base and the product of the base's perimeter and the height.

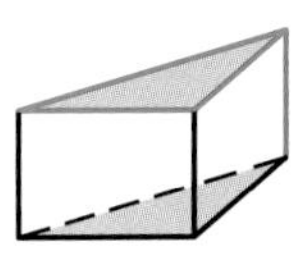

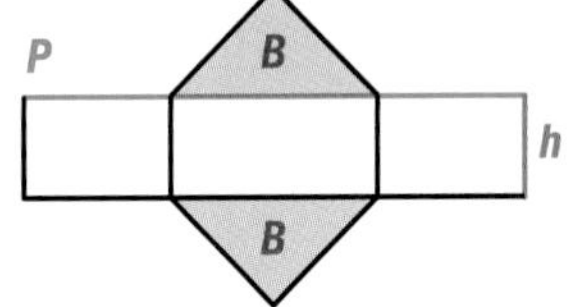

Algebra $S = 2B + Ph$

EXAMPLE 3 Using a Formula to Find Surface Area

Find the surface area of the triangular prism.

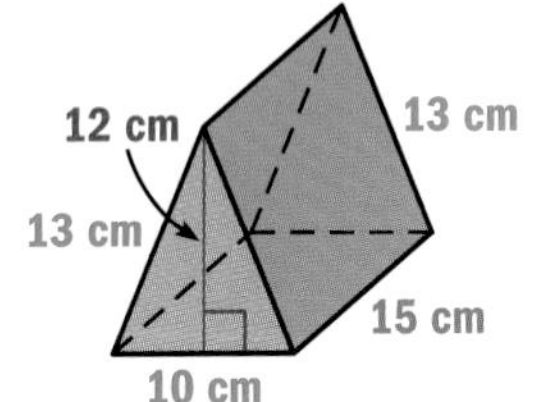

$$S = 2B + Ph$$

$$= 2\left(\frac{1}{2} \cdot 10 \cdot 12\right) + (13 + 13 + 10)15$$

$$= 660$$

ANSWER The surface area of the prism is 660 square centimeters.

Cylinders The net of a cylinder has two circles for the bases. The curved surface of the cylinder becomes a rectangle in the net. The width of the rectangle is the height of the cylinder, and the length of the rectangle is the circumference of the base.

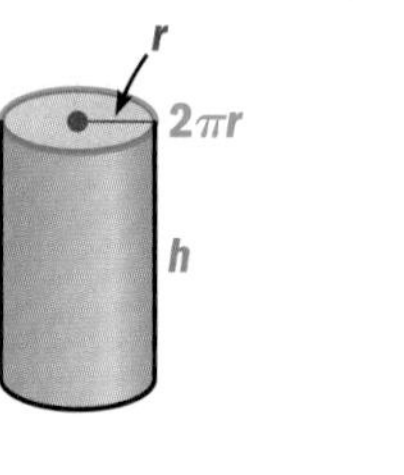

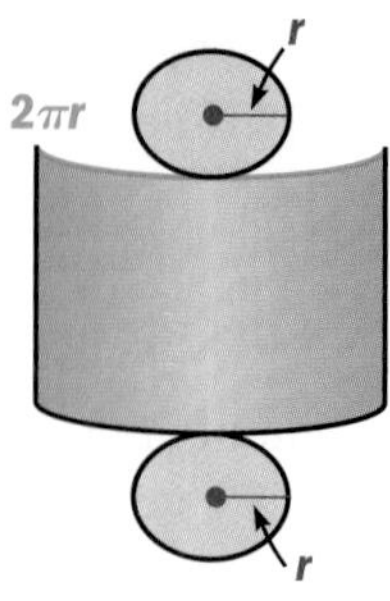

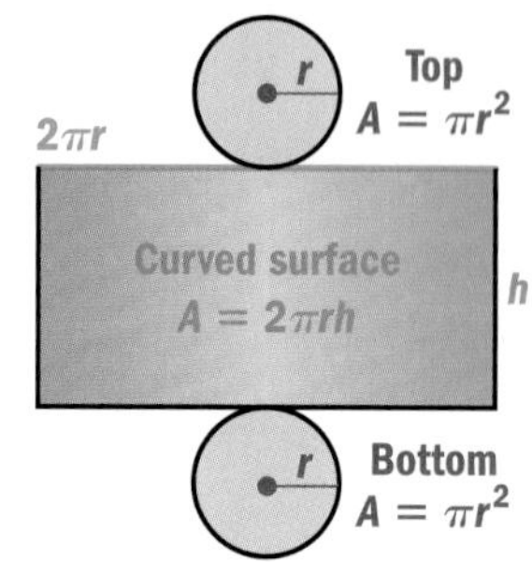

Surface Area of a Cylinder

Words The surface area of a cylinder is the sum of twice the area of a base and the product of the base's circumference and the height.

Algebra $S = 2B + Ch = 2\pi r^2 + 2\pi rh$

EXAMPLE 4 Finding the Surface Area of a Cylinder

Sloppy Joe Find the surface area of the can of sloppy joe sauce.

Solution

The radius is one half the diameter, so $r = 4$ cm.

$S = 2\pi r^2 + 2\pi rh$	Write formula for surface area of a cylinder.
$= 2\pi(4)^2 + 2\pi(4)(10.7)$	Substitute 4 for r and 10.7 for h.
≈ 369.45	Evaluate using a calculator.

ANSWER The surface area of the can is about 369 square centimeters.

HELP with Technology

You can use the π key on your calculator instead of 3.14 when evaluating formulas.

Your turn now Draw a net of the solid. Then find the surface area. Round to the nearest tenth.

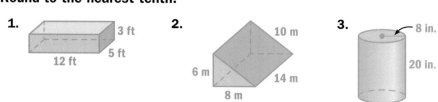

1. 3 ft, 12 ft, 5 ft

2. 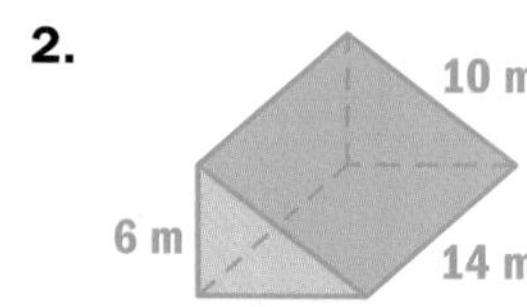

3. 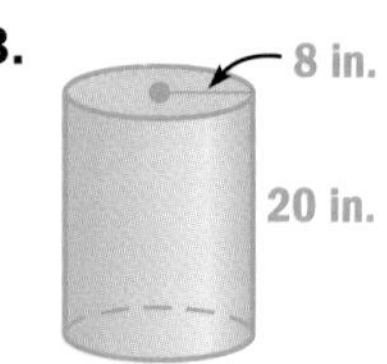

10.4 Exercises

More Practice, p. 736

Getting Ready to Practice

1. **Vocabulary** In your own words, explain what surface area is.

Draw a net. Then find the surface area. Round to the nearest tenth.

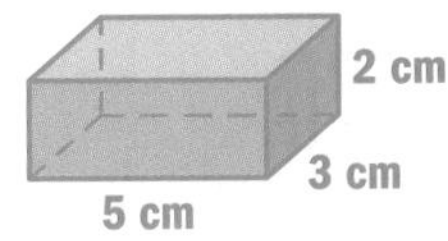

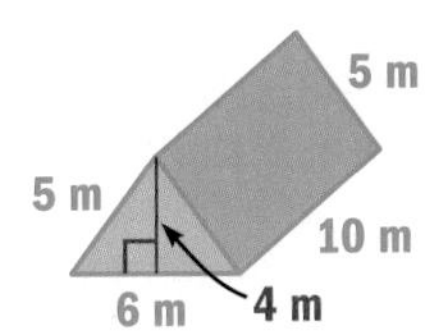

4.

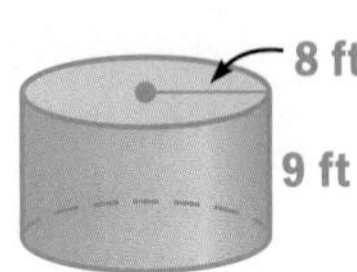

Practice and Problem Solving

Example	Exercises
1	15-17
2	12-17
3	5-8
4	9-17

· More Examples
· eTutorial Plus

Find the surface area of the prism, where *B* is the area of the base, *P* is the perimeter of the base, and *h* is the height.

5. $B = 4 \text{ in.}^2, P = 8 \text{ in.}, h = 5 \text{ in.}$

6. $B = 20 \text{ cm}^2, P = 12 \text{ cm}, h = 3 \text{ cm}$

7. $B = 45 \text{ yd}^2, P = 30 \text{ yd}, h = 2 \text{ yd}$

8. $B = 19.3 \text{ m}^2, P = 16 \text{ m}, h = 0.5 \text{ m}$

Sketch a cylinder with radius *r* and height *h*. Then find its surface area. Round to the nearest tenth.

9. $r = 6 \text{ m}, h = 2 \text{ m}$

10. $r = 1 \text{ ft}, h = 7 \text{ ft}$

11. $r = 10 \text{ cm}, h = 20 \text{ cm}$

Find the surface area of the net. Round to the nearest tenth.

12.

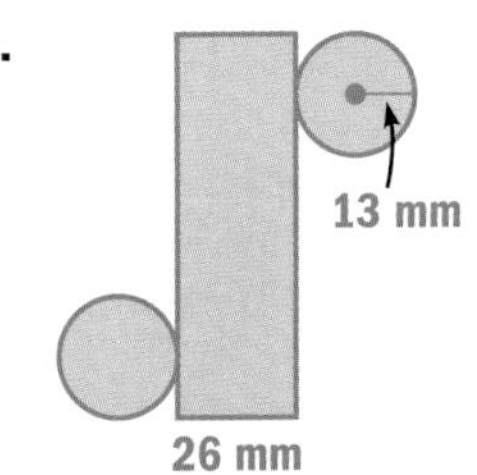

13. 14.

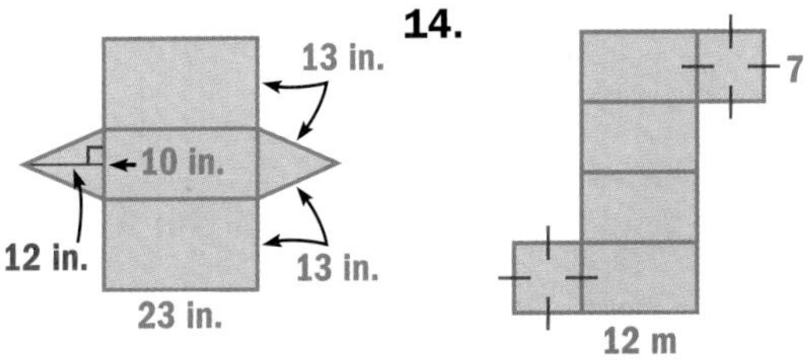

Draw a net. Then find the surface area. Round to the nearest tenth.

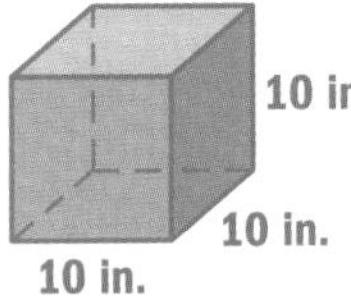

16.

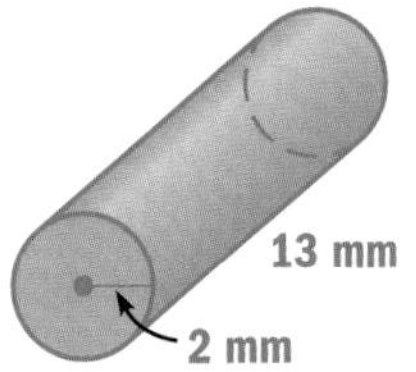

17.

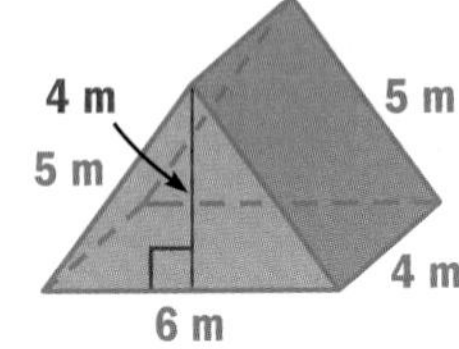

18. **Chocolates** You are dipping caramels into chocolate. Some of the caramels are 1 inch cubes. Others are cylinders that are 1 inch high and 1 inch in diameter. Which shape will require more chocolate?

The Crystal Bridge

Find the surface area of the solid. Round to the nearest tenth.

19. 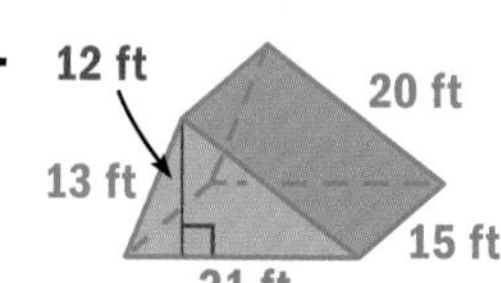

20. 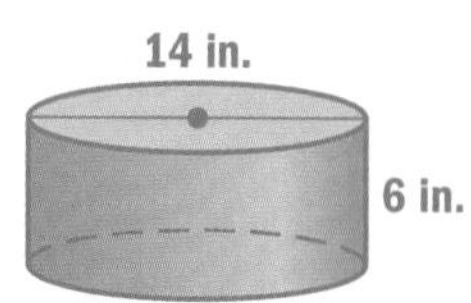

21. 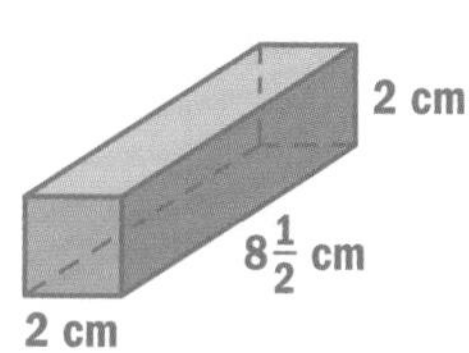

22. **Crystal Bridge** At the Myriad Botanical Gardens in Oklahoma City, there is a tropical conservatory that bridges a small lake. The Crystal Bridge is a cylinder 224 feet long and 70 feet in diameter. Find the surface area of the Crystal Bridge. Round to the nearest tenth.

Breaking into Parts **Draw a net of the solid. Then find the surface area. Round to the nearest tenth.**

23. 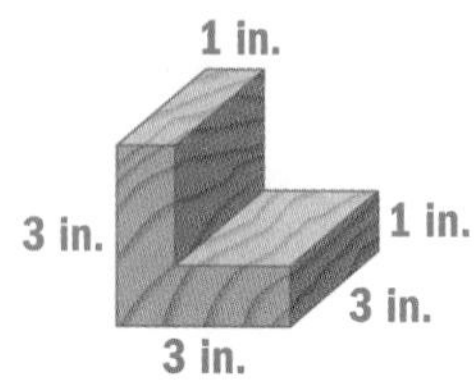

24. 

25. **Challenge** Find the surface area of a triangular prism whose edge lengths are all 1 foot. (*Hint*: Each triangular base can be divided into two 30°-60°-90° triangles.)

Mixed Review 

Tell whether the side lengths form a right triangle. *(Lesson 9.3)*

26. $a = 10, b = 24, c = 26$ **27.** $a = 28, b = 45, c = 53$

Use your calculator to approximate the given value. Round your answer to four decimal places. *(Lesson 9.6)*

28. sin 78° **29.** tan 23° **30.** cos 14° **31.** sin 66°

Find the area of a parallelogram with base *b* and height *h*. *(Lesson 10.1)*

32. $b = 16$ ft, $h = 11$ ft **33.** $b = 12$ in., $h = 18$ in.

Test-Taking Practice 

INTERNET
State Test Practice
CLASSZONE.COM

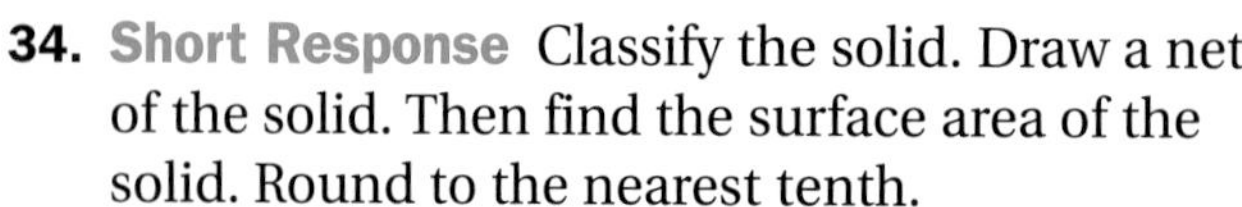

34. **Short Response** Classify the solid. Draw a net of the solid. Then find the surface area of the solid. Round to the nearest tenth.

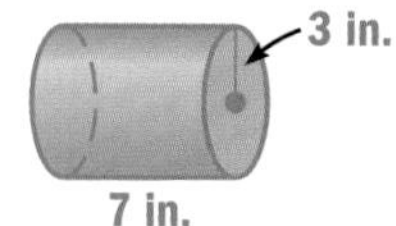

35. **Multiple Choice** What is the surface area of a rectangular prism that is 3 feet long, 2 feet wide, and 9 feet high?

A. 14 ft^2 **B.** 54 ft^2 **C.** 61 ft^2 **D.** 102 ft^2

Surface Areas of Pyramids and Cones

BEFORE

You found the surface areas of prisms and cylinders.

Now

You'll find the surface areas of pyramids and cones.

WHY?

So you can find the surface area of icicles, as in Exs. 25–28.

Word Watch

slant height, p. 507

INDIANA Academic Standards

- Measurement (8.5.4)

The height of a pyramid is the perpendicular distance between the vertex and the base.

The **slant height** l of a regular pyramid is the height of any face that is not the base.

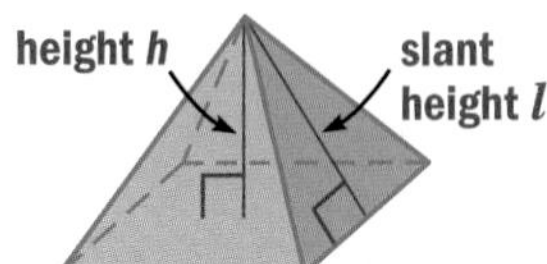

The net for a regular pyramid has a regular polygon as the base and congruent isosceles triangles on each side of the base.

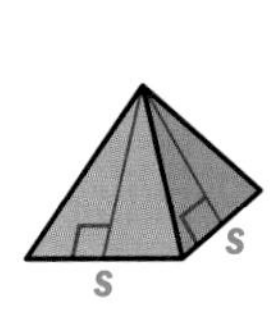

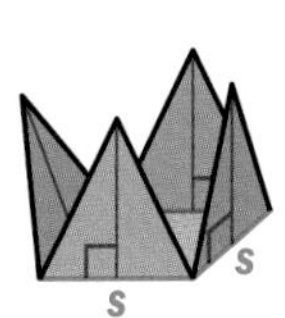

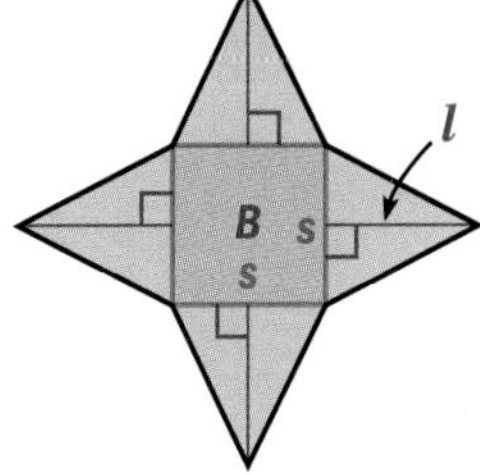

You can use the net of a pyramid to find the surface area of the pyramid.

with Solving

All the pyramids in this lesson have a regular polygon as a base and congruent isosceles triangles as the other faces. The slant height is the same on any face that is not the base.

		Base area		Area of other faces		
Surface area	=	Area of base	+	Number of triangles	×	Area of each triangle
	=	B	+	4	×	$\left(\frac{1}{2}sl\right)$

$$= B + \frac{1}{2}(4s)l$$

$$= B + \frac{1}{2}Pl$$

The product of the number of triangles and the side length of the base is the perimeter of the base.

Surface Area of a Pyramid

Words The surface area of a regular pyramid is the sum of the area of the base and one half the product of the base perimeter and the slant height.

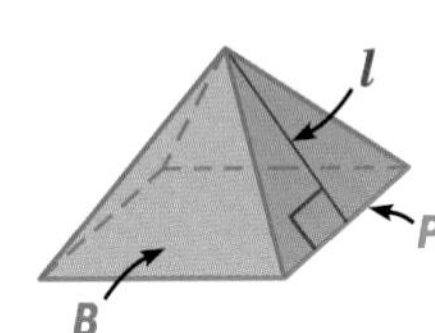

Algebra $S = B + \frac{1}{2}Pl$

EXAMPLE 1 Finding the Surface Area of a Pyramid

Find the surface area of the regular pyramid.

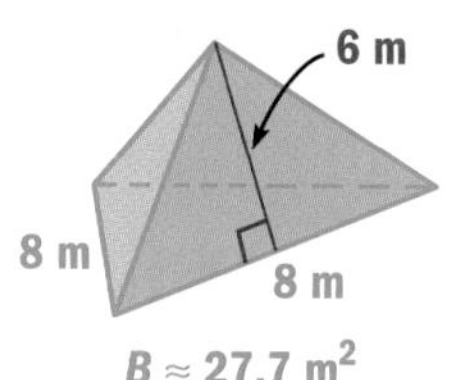

(1) Find the perimeter of the base.

$P = 8 + 8 + 8 = 24$

(2) Substitute into the formula for surface area.

$S = B + \frac{1}{2}Pl$	**Write formula for surface area of a pyramid.**
$\approx 27.7 + \frac{1}{2}(24)(6)$	**Substitute 27.7 for *B*, 24 for *P*, and 6 for *l*.**
$= 99.7$	**Simplify.**

ANSWER The surface area is about 99.7 square meters.

Cones You can use the net of a cone to find its surface area. The curved surface of a cone is part of a circle with radius l, the slant height of the cone. The area of this surface is $A = \pi rl$, where r is the radius of the base of the cone.

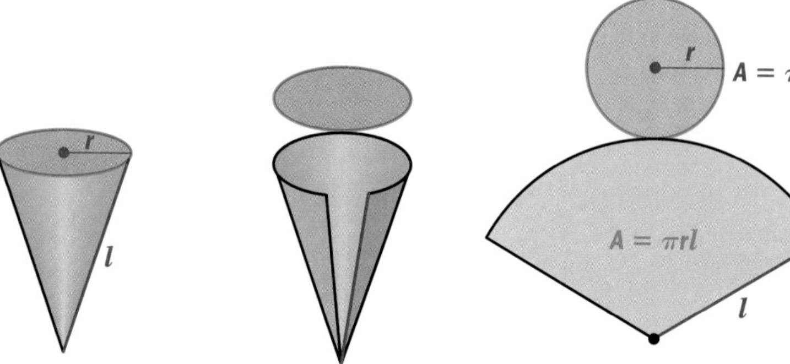

Surface Area of a Cone

Words The surface area of a cone is the sum of the area of the base and the product of pi, the radius of the base, and the slant height.

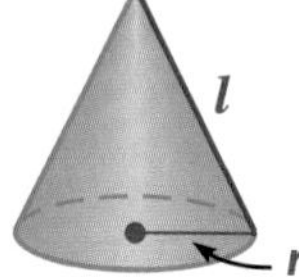

Algebra $S = \pi r^2 + \pi rl$

EXAMPLE 2 Finding the Surface Area of a Cone

Find the surface area of a cone with radius 4 meters and slant height 9 meters.

$S = \pi r^2 + \pi r l$	Write formula for surface area of a cone.
$= \pi(4)^2 + \pi(4)(9)$	Substitute 4 for r and 9 for l.
≈ 163.36	Evaluate using a calculator.

ANSWER The surface area is about 163.36 square meters.

Your turn now **Find the surface area. Round to the nearest tenth.**

1.
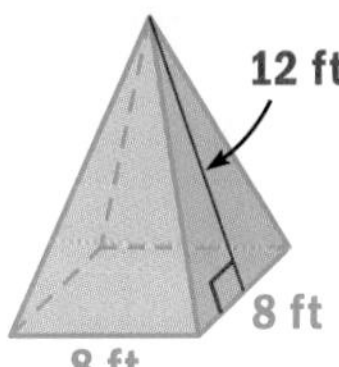

2.
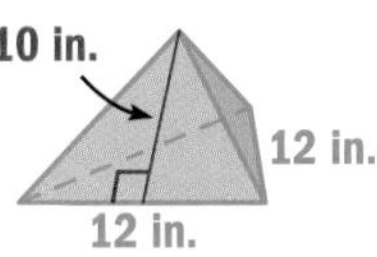

3.
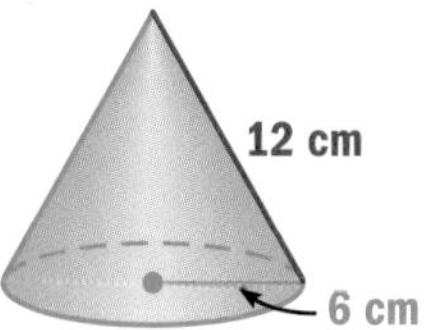

10.5 Exercises

More Practice, p. 736

Getting Ready to Practice

1. **Vocabulary** Draw a square pyramid. Label the height h, slant height l, and base B of the pyramid.

Draw a net of the solid. Then find the surface area. Round to the nearest tenth.

2.
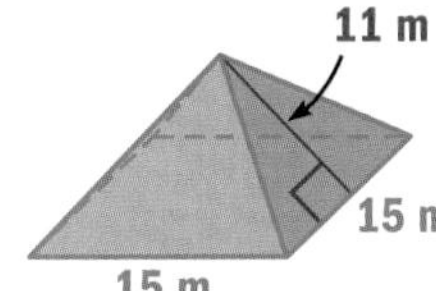

3.
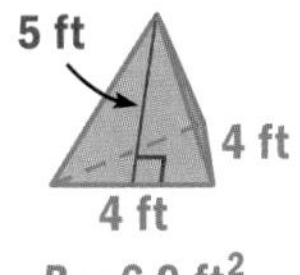

4.
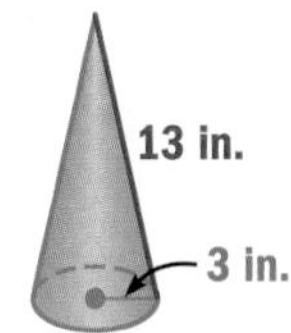

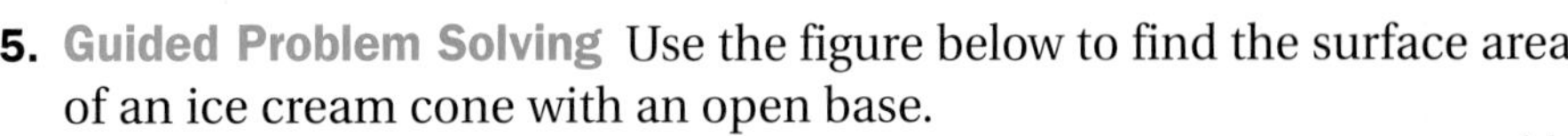

5. **Guided Problem Solving** Use the figure below to find the surface area of an ice cream cone with an open base.

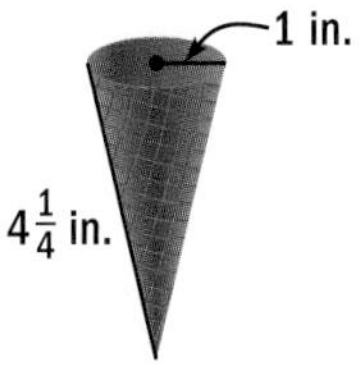

   (1) Write the formula for the surface area of a cone and subtract the area of the base from the formula.

   (2) Substitute the values for slant height and radius.

   (3) Evaluate and round to the nearest tenth.

1 in.

$4\frac{1}{4}$ in.

Practice and Problem Solving

Example	Exercises
1	6-9, 14-19
2	10-19

Online Resources
CLASSZONE.COM

- More Examples
- eTutorial Plus

Find the surface area of the square pyramid with base side length *s* and slant height *l*.

6. $s = 4$ in.
$l = 11$ in.

7. $s = 6$ m
$l = 9$ m

8. $s = 5$ cm
$l = 4.2$ cm

9. $s = 15$ yd
$l = 10$ yd

Find the surface area of the cone with radius *r* and slant height *l*. Round to the nearest tenth.

10. $r = 3$ ft
$l = 8$ ft

11. $r = 2$ in.
$l = 20$ in.

12. $r = 12$ m
$l = 6.5$ m

13. $r = 4$ mm
$l = 5.5$ mm

Draw a net of the solid. Then find the surface area. Round to the nearest tenth.

14.

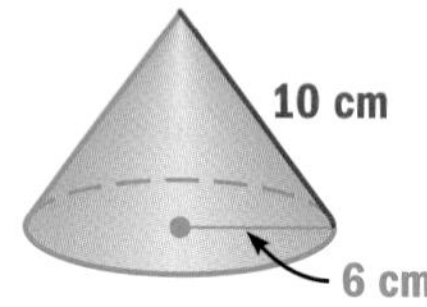

15.

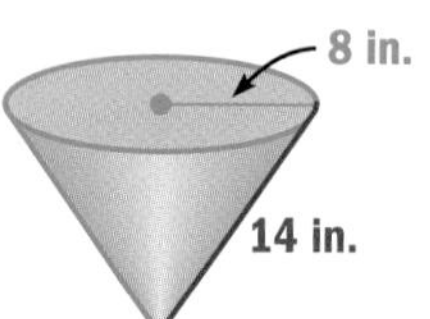

16.

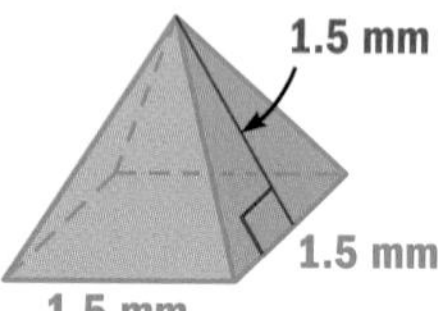

Find the surface area of the solid. Round to the nearest tenth.

17.

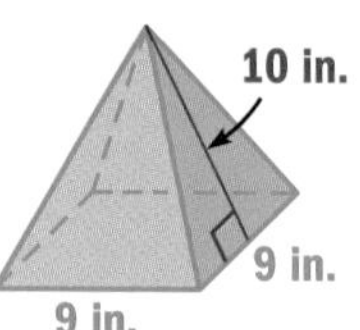

18.

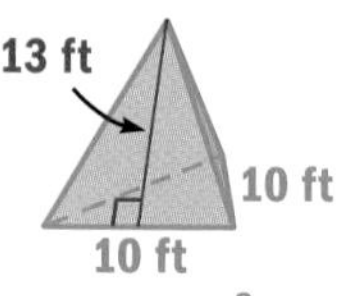

19.

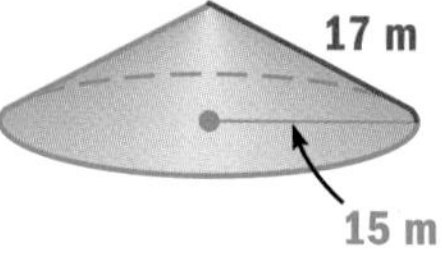

Find the surface area of the net. Round to the nearest tenth.

20.

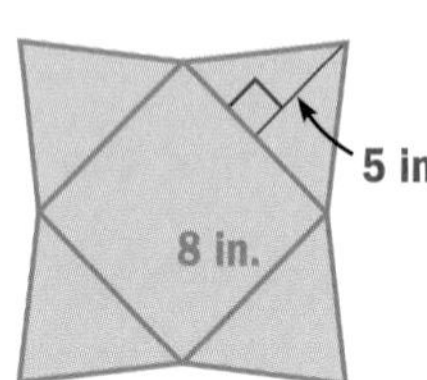

21.

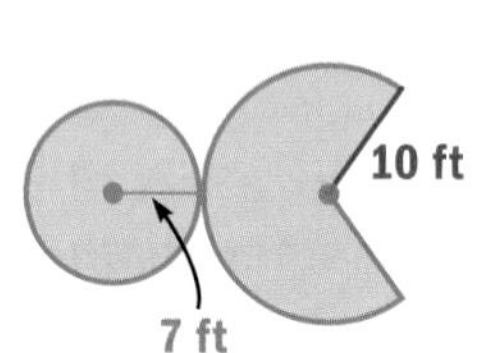

22.

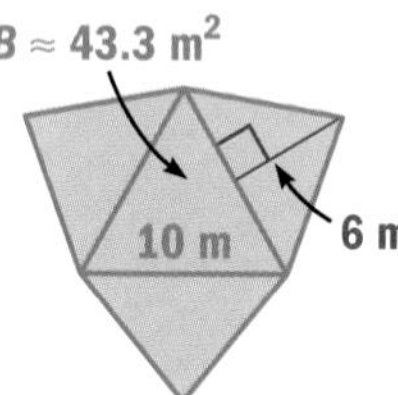

Sports **The formula for the surface area of a sphere is $S = 4\pi r^2$ where *r* is the radius of the sphere. Find the surface area of the sphere. Round to the nearest tenth.**

23.

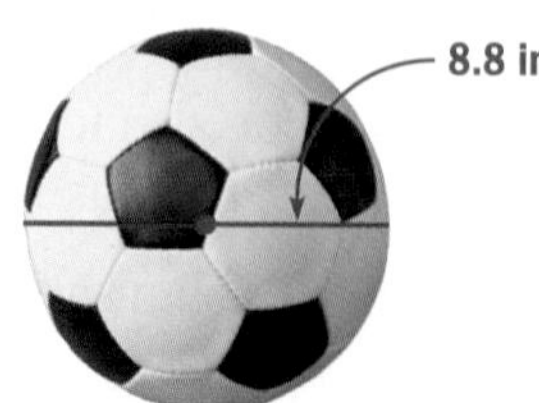

24.

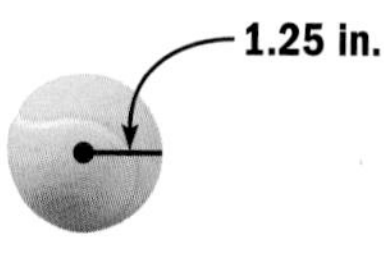

Icicles In Exercises 25–28, use the following information. Find the surface area of the icicle, not including the base, in terms of π. Icicles are shaped like cones. As they melt, icicles change size but stay similar in shape.

25. $r = 1$ in., $l = 6$ in. **26.** $r = 2$ in., $l = 12$ in. **27.** $r = 3$ in., $l = 18$ in.

28. Look for a Pattern Describe the pattern developed in Exercises 25–27. Then predict the surface area of an icicle with a radius of 4 inches and a slant height of 24 inches.

29. Critical Thinking Think of a cone as a special type of pyramid. Substitute the formulas for the area and circumference of a circle into the formula for the surface area of a pyramid. Simplify the expression. What do you notice?

30. Number Sense Which has a greater surface area: a square pyramid with a slant height of 12 units and a base side length of 10 units, or a cone with a slant height of 12 units and a diameter of 10 units?

31. Challenge Find the surface area of the regular hexagonal pyramid shown. In the diagram of its base, all the triangles are congruent.

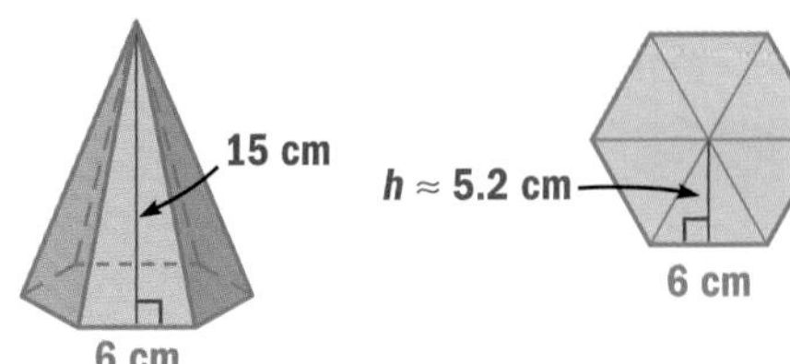

Mixed Review

Tell whether the number is *rational* or *irrational*. *(Lesson 9.2)*

32. $\sqrt{169}$ **33.** $\frac{4}{21}$ **34.** $\frac{\sqrt{7}}{2}$ **35.** $\sqrt{\frac{3}{2}}$

36. Find the surface area of a cylinder with a radius of 3 inches and a height of 8 inches. Round to the nearest tenth. *(Lesson 10.4)*

Test-Taking Practice

INTERNET
State Test Practice
CLASSZONE.COM

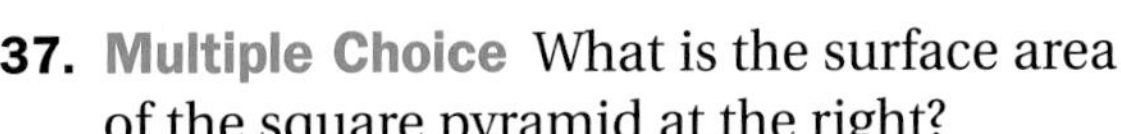

37. Multiple Choice What is the surface area of the square pyramid at the right?

A. 70 m^2 **B.** 95 m^2

C. 119 m^2 **D.** 150.5 m^2

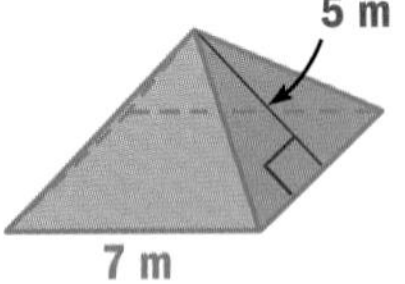

38. Short Response Pablo makes a party hat that is a cone with no base. It has a radius of 4 inches and a slant height of 7 inches. What is the surface area of Pablo's party hat? Monica makes a larger party hat that has a radius and slant height that are twice the lengths of those on Pablo's hat. What is the surface area of Monica's party hat? Round to the nearest tenth.

GOAL
Find the volume of a rectangular prism.

MATERIALS
• sugar cubes

Exploring Volume

The *volume* of a solid is a measure of how much space it occupies. Volume is measured in cubic units. One cubic unit is the amount of space occupied by a cube that measures one unit on each side. This cube is called the *unit cube.*

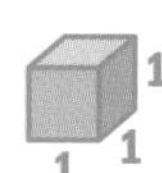

Explore **Find the volume of the rectangular prism.**

To find the volume of the prism shown, first build the prism using sugar cubes to represent unit cubes. Then count the number of cubes you used.

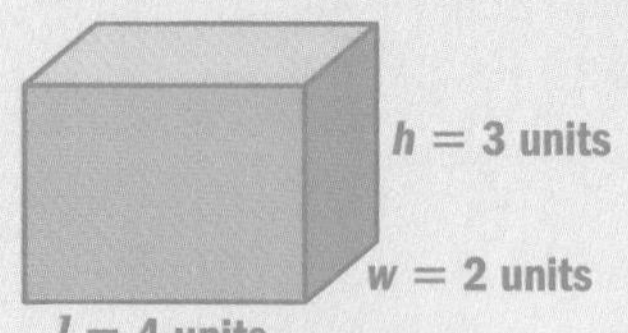

1 It takes 2 rows of 4 cubes, or 8 cubes, to make the bottom of the prism.

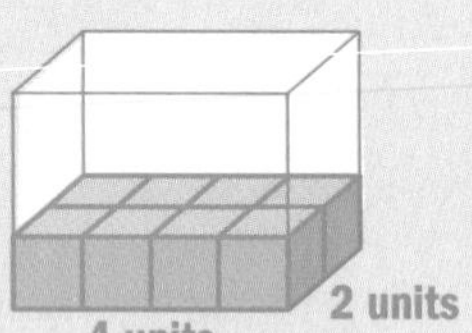

2 It takes 3 layers of 8 cubes, or 24 cubes, to make the prism the right height.

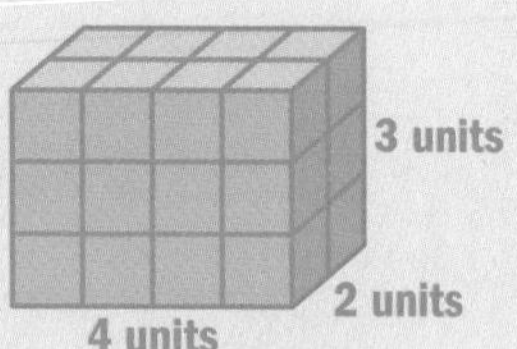

3 Because each cube is 1 cubic unit, the volume of the prism is 24 cubic units.

Your turn now **Use cubes to model the volume of rectangular prisms.**

1. Copy and complete the table to find the volume of the rectangular prism with the given dimensions.

Dimensions of the prism	Cubes to cover the bottom of the prism	Layers of cubes to make the prism	Volume of the prism
4 × 3 × 3	12	3	36
6 × 1 × 2	?	?	?
7 × 5 × 3	?	?	?
4 × 2 × 8	?	?	?

Stop *and* Think

2. **Critical Thinking** Write a formula for the number of cubes that will make a prism of length l, width w, and height h.

Volumes of Prisms and Cylinders

BEFORE	Now	WHY?
You found the surface areas of prisms and cylinders.	You'll find the volumes of prisms and cylinders.	So you can compare the volumes of pools, as in Ex. 28.

In the Real World

volume, p. 513

INDIANA Academic Standards

- Measurement (8.5.4)

Recycling Residents of a community can choose between two recycling bins. Which recycling bin holds more? You will find the answer in Example 3.

The **volume** of a solid is a measure of the amount of space it occupies. Volume is measured in cubic units. One cubic unit is the amount of space occupied by a cube that measures one unit on each side.

Volume of a Prism

Words The volume of a prism is the product of the area of the base and the height.

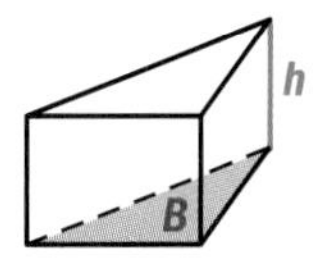

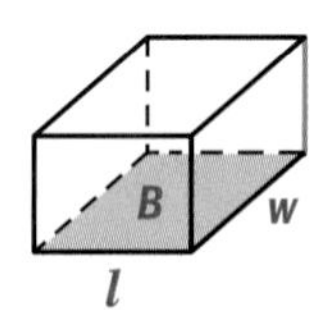

Algebra $V = Bh$

EXAMPLE 1 Finding Volumes of Prisms

Find the volume of the prism.

a.

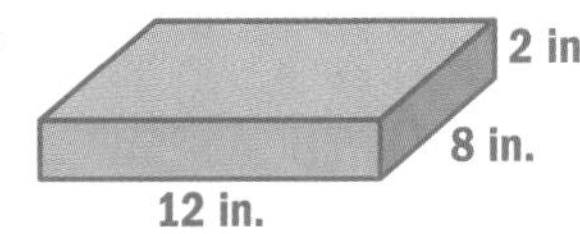

$V = Bh$

$= lwh$

$= 12(8)(2)$

$= 192$

ANSWER The volume is 192 cubic inches.

b.

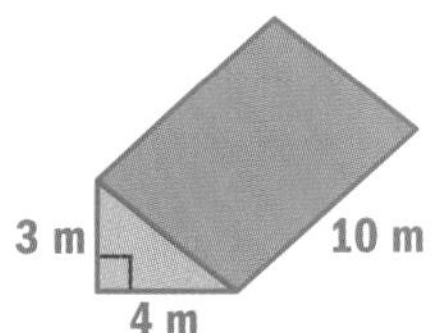

$V = Bh$

$= \frac{1}{2}(4)(3)(10)$

$= 60$

ANSWER The volume is 60 cubic meters.

Watch Out! When you find the volume of a triangular prism, be careful not to confuse the height of the prism with the height of the triangular base.

Because the base of the cylinder is a circle, its area is πr^2.

Volumes of Cylinders The formula for the volume of a cylinder is similar to the formula for the volume of a prism.

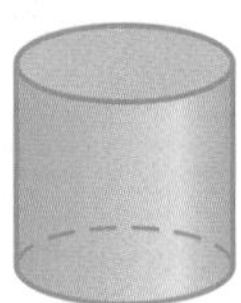

=

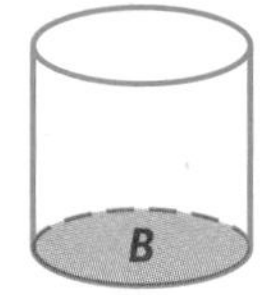

×

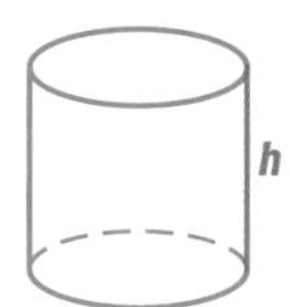

Volume of a cylinder = Area of base × Height

Volume of a Cylinder

Words The volume of a cylinder is the product of the area of a base and the height.

Algebra $V = Bh$

$= \pi r^2 h$

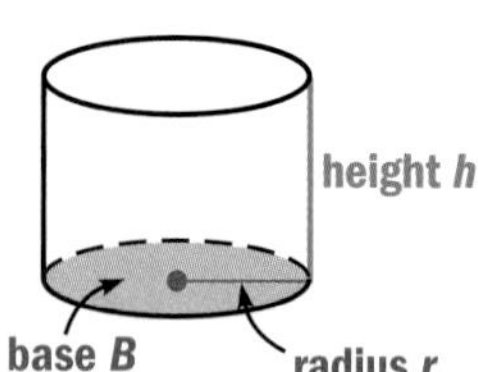

EXAMPLE 2 Finding the Volume of a Cylinder

Find the volume of the cylinder.

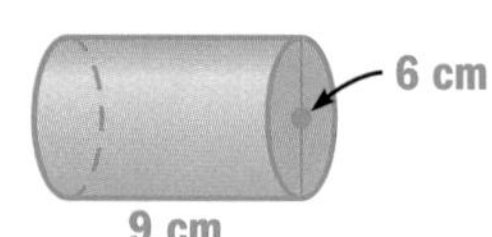

The radius is one half the diameter, so $r = 3$ cm.

$V = Bh$	Write formula for volume.
$= \pi r^2 h$	Write formula for volume of a cylinder.
$= \pi(3)^2(9)$	Substitute 3 for *r* and 9 for *h*.
$= 81\pi$	Simplify.
≈ 254.469	Evaluate using a calculator.

ANSWER The volume is about 254 cubic centimeters.

Your turn now **Find the volume of the solid. Round to the nearest tenth.**

1. 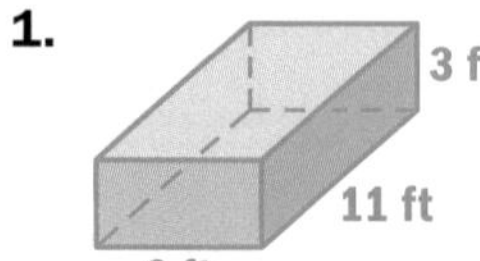

2. 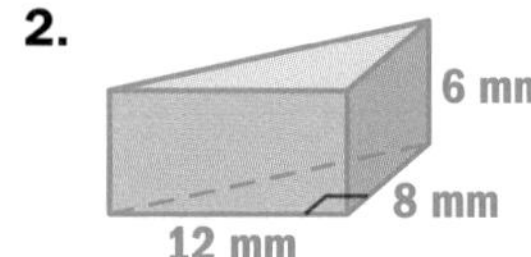

3. 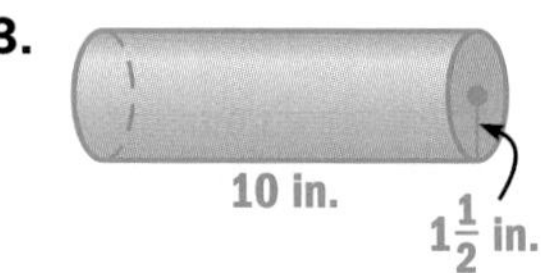

with Reading

When the abbreviation for a unit of measure has an exponent of 3, you read the 3 as "cubic."

ft^3 = cubic feet

cm^3 = cubic centimeters

EXAMPLE 3 Comparing Capacities

Recycling To decide which recycling bin on page 513 can hold more, find the capacity of each bin.

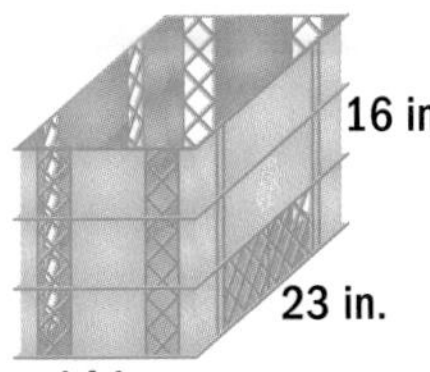

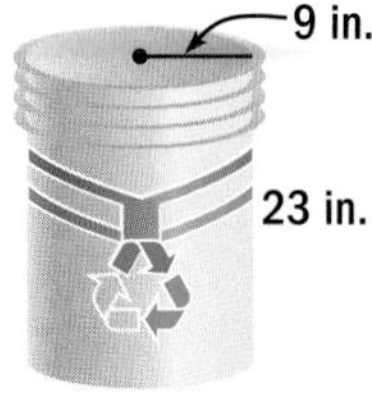

Prism

$V = Bh$

$= lwh$

$= 14(23)(16)$

$= 5152 \text{ in.}^3$

Cylinder

$V = Bh$

$= \pi r^2 h$

$= \pi(9)^2(23)$

$\approx 5852.8 \text{ in.}^3$

ANSWER The cylindrical recycling bin holds more.

10.6 Exercises

More Practice, p. 736

Getting Ready to Practice

1. **Vocabulary** Explain the difference between area and volume.

Find the volume of the solid. Round to the nearest tenth.

2. 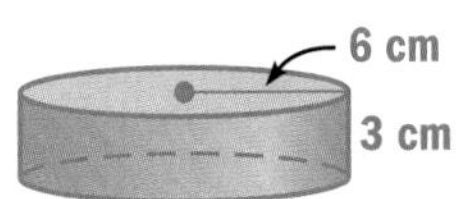

3. 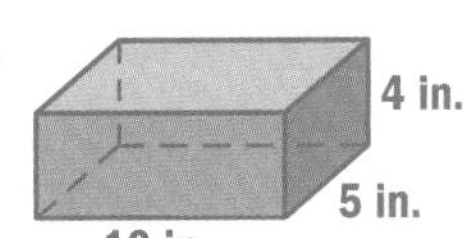

4. 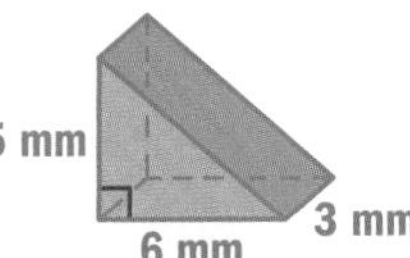

5. **Find the Error** Describe and correct the error in finding the volume of the cylinder.

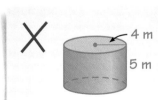

X (4 m, 5 m)

$V = Bh$

$= 2\pi rh$

$= 2\pi(4)(5)$

≈ 125.66

The volume is about 125.66 cubic meters.

Practice and Problem Solving

Example	Exercises
1	6–9, 13–18
2	10–18, 23
3	24

· More Examples
· eTutorial Plus

Find the volume of the rectangular prism.

6. $l = 6$ m, $w = 2$ m, $h = 11$ m

7. $l = 7$ in., $w = 7$ in., $h = 7$ in.

8. $l = 3$ cm, $w = 3.8$ cm, $h = 1.2$ cm

9. $l = 16$ ft, $w = 3$ ft, $h = 2\frac{1}{2}$ ft

Find the volume of the cylinder. Round to the nearest tenth.

10. $r = 4$ ft, $h = 11$ ft

11. $r = 3$ cm, $h = 9$ cm

12. $r = 1.2$ m, $h = 4.5$ m

Find the volume of the solid. If two units of measure are used, give your answer in the smaller units. Round to the nearest tenth.

13.

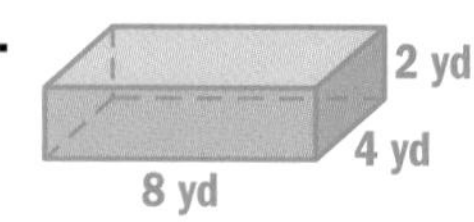

14.

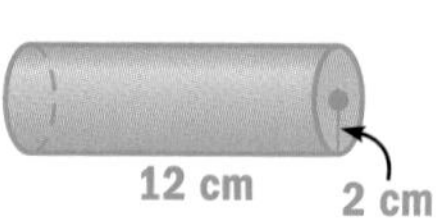

15.

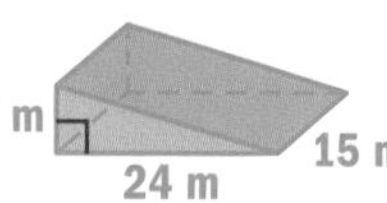

16.

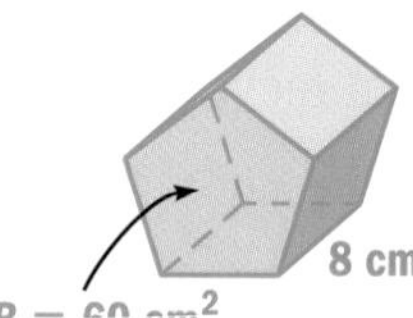

17.

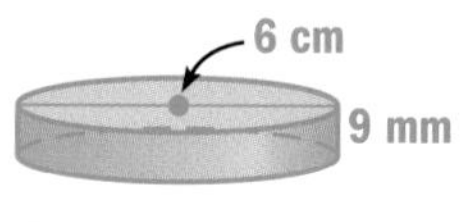

18.

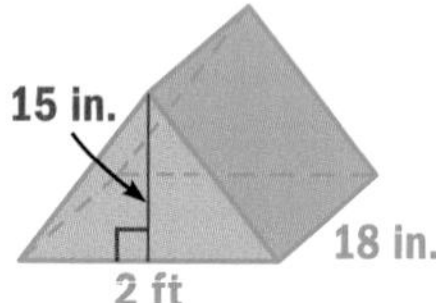

Critical Thinking **In Exercises 19–22, tell whether you would need to calculate *surface area* or *volume* to find the quantity.**

19. The amount of wrapping paper needed to wrap a gift

20. The amount of cereal that will fit in a box

21. The amount of water needed to fill a watering can

22. The amount of frosting needed to decorate a cake

23. **Paint** A paint can is a cylinder 19 centimeters tall and 16 centimeters in diameter. Find the volume of the paint can. Round to the nearest tenth.

24. **Erasers** Find the volume of each eraser in cubic millimeters to the nearest tenth. How many pencil-top erasers would you go through in the time it takes you to go through the larger eraser?

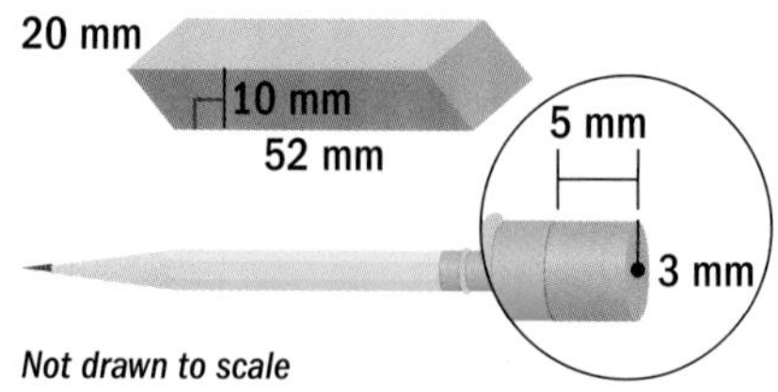

Find the volume of the solid. Round to the nearest tenth.

25.

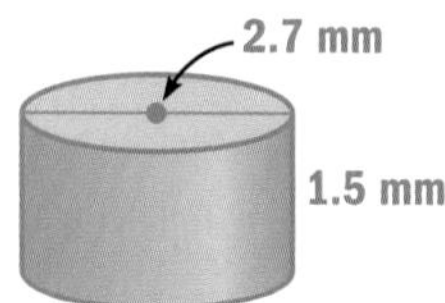

26.

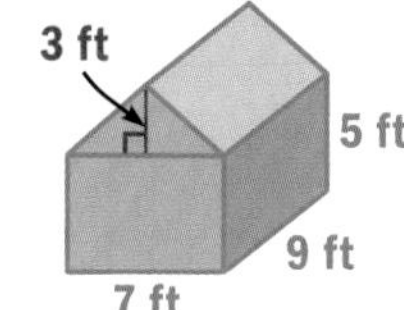

27.

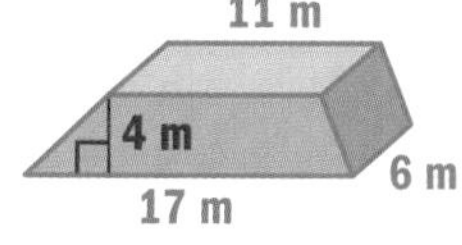

28. **Swimming Pools** A rectangular in-ground pool is 40 feet long, 16 feet wide, and 4 feet deep. A cylindrical above-ground pool has a radius of 12 feet and is 6 feet deep. How many cubic feet of water does each pool hold? Round to the nearest tenth. Which pool holds more?

29. **Salt Shakers** You buy a cylindrical container of salt that has a diameter of 4 inches and a height of 6 inches. Your salt shaker is a rectangular prism that is $1\frac{1}{2}$ inches by $1\frac{1}{2}$ inches by 3 inches. How many times can the salt in the container fill the salt shaker?

30. **Number Sense** Which would have a greater effect on the volume of a cylinder: *doubling the height* or *doubling the radius*? Explain.

31. **Number Sense** Which would have a greater effect on the volume of a long, thin, short box: *doubling the length* or *doubling the width*? Explain.

32. **Challenge** Find the volume of the solid at the right.

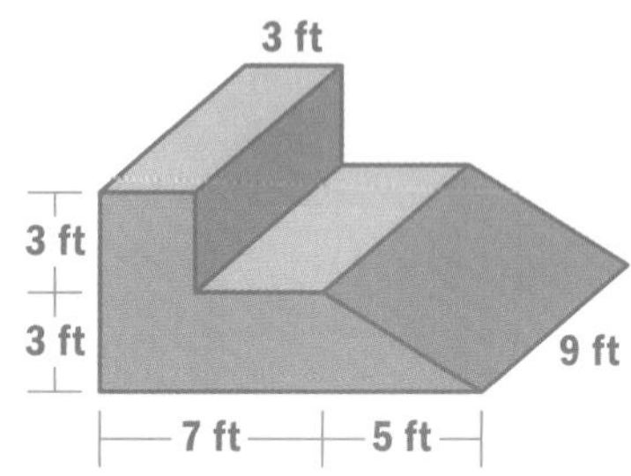

Mixed Review 

Let *a* and *b* represent the lengths of the legs of the right triangle, and let *c* represent the length of the hypotenuse. Find the unknown length. *(Lesson 9.3)*

33. $a = 15, b = ?, c = 39$

34. $a = 16, b = 63, c = ?$

Find the surface area of the solid to the nearest tenth. *(Lesson 10.5)*

35. 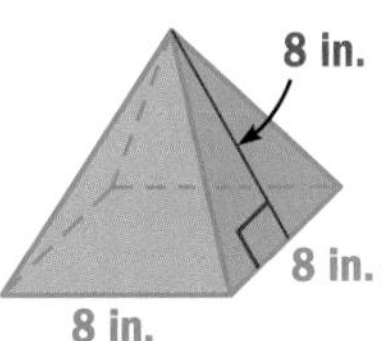

36. 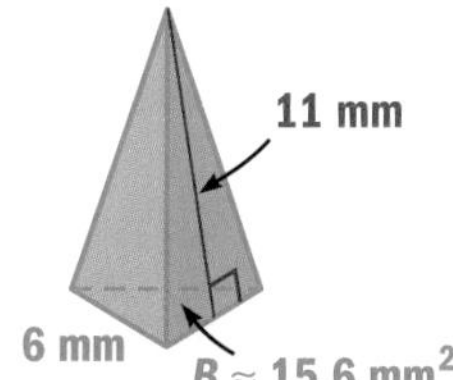

37. 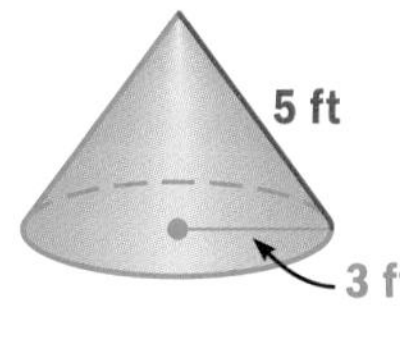

Test-Taking Practice 

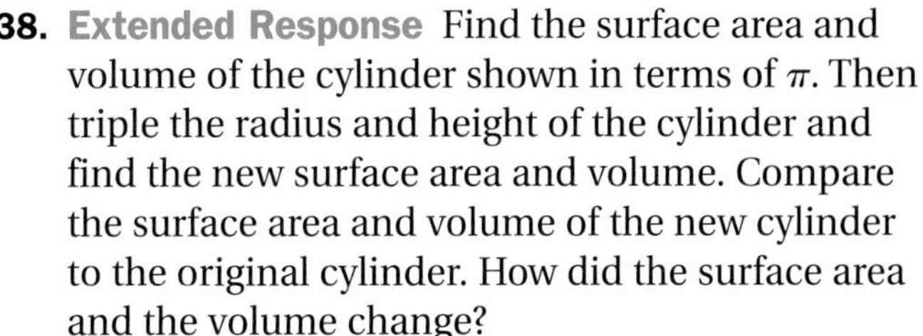

38. **Extended Response** Find the surface area and volume of the cylinder shown in terms of π. Then triple the radius and height of the cylinder and find the new surface area and volume. Compare the surface area and volume of the new cylinder to the original cylinder. How did the surface area and the volume change?

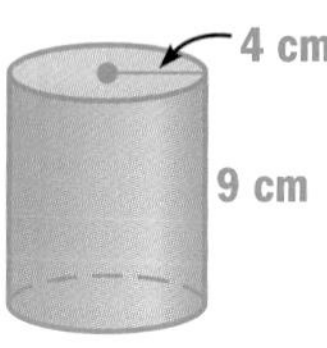

GOAL

Compare the volumes of a prism and a pyramid.

MATERIALS

- tape
- scissors
- metric ruler
- thin cardboard
- popcorn kernels

Comparing Volumes

Compare the volume of a pyramid to the volume of a prism.

Explore

Compare pyramids and prisms.

1. On cardboard, draw the nets shown. Then cut out the nets and use tape to make an open square prism and an open square pyramid.

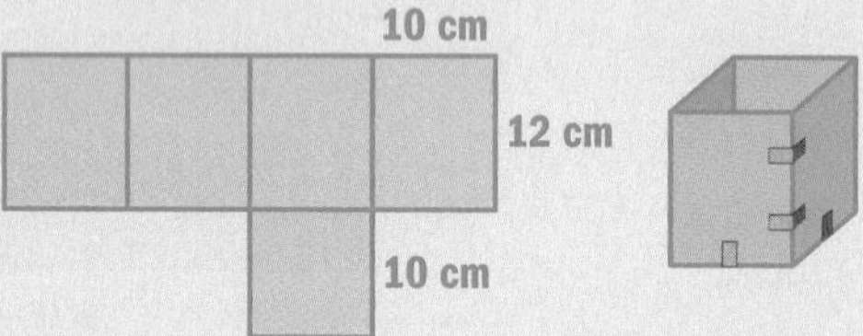

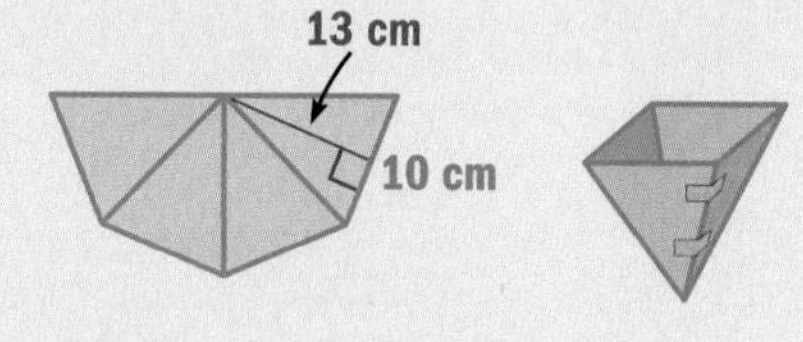

2. Compare the height of the prism to the height of the pyramid. Then compare the base of the prism to the base of the pyramid. What do you notice?

3. Fill the pyramid with popcorn kernels and pour the contents into the prism. Repeat until the prism is full. How many times did you have to empty the pyramid into the prism? Use this number to write the ratio of the volume of the pyramid to the volume of the prism.

Your turn now **Use the formula for the volume of a rectangular prism and the ratio found in the activity to find the volume of the square pyramid.**

1. 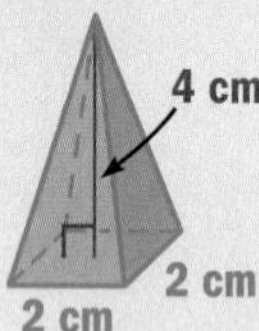

2. 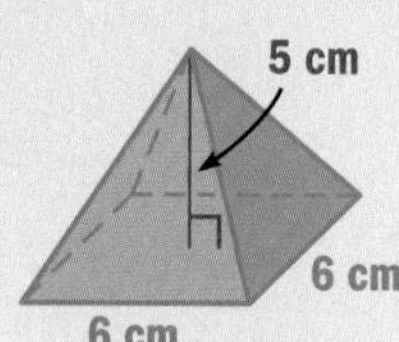

3. 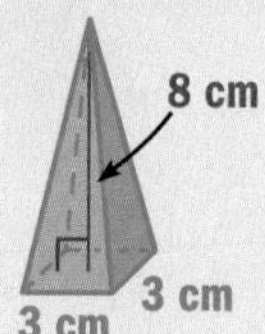

Stop *and* Think

4. **Make a Model** Use the nets shown to make an open cylinder and an open cone. Find the ratio of their volumes.

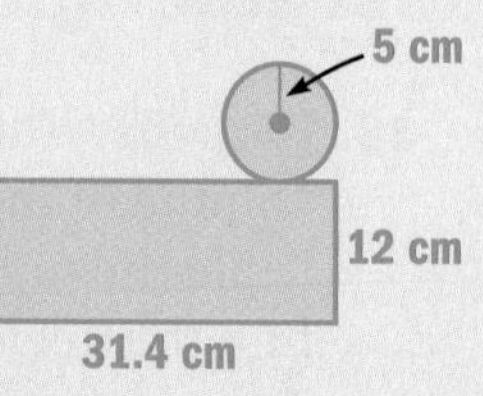

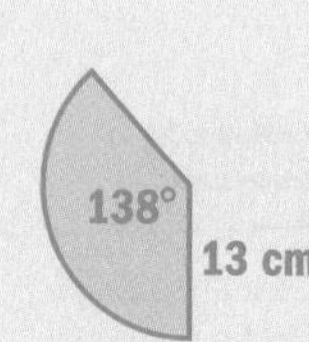

Volumes of Pyramids and Cones

BEFORE	Now	WHY?
You found the volumes of prisms and cylinders.	You'll find the volumes of pyramids and cones.	So you can find the amount of space lit by a spotlight, as in Ex. 26.

In the Real World

Review Words

pyramid, p. 492
cone, p. 492
volume, p. 513

INDIANA Academic Standards

- Measurement (8.5.4)
- Problem Solving (8.7.1)

Famous Buildings The Rainforest Pyramid in Galveston Island, Texas, is the home of many plants, butterflies, fish, and reptiles. This square pyramid has a height of 100 feet, and each side of its base measures 200 feet. What is the volume of the Rainforest Pyramid?

The volumes of a pyramid and a prism with the same base area and the same height are related. The volume of the pyramid is exactly one third the volume of the prism.

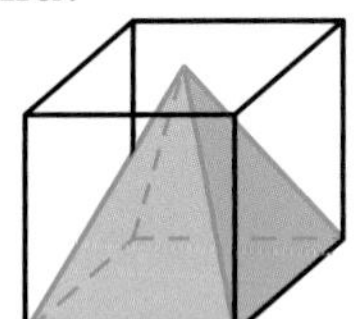

Volume of a Pyramid

Words The volume of a pyramid is one third the product of the area of the base and the height.

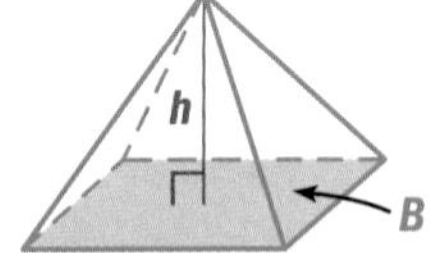

Algebra $V = \frac{1}{3}Bh$

EXAMPLE 1 Finding the Volume of a Pyramid

Find the volume of the Rainforest Pyramid described above using the diagram.

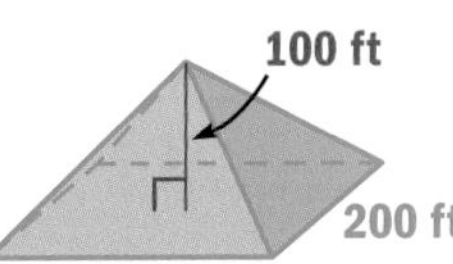

Solution

$V = \frac{1}{3}Bh$ Write formula for volume of a pyramid.

$= \frac{1}{3}(200^2)(100)$ The base is a square, so $B = s^2$.

$= 1{,}333{,}333.\overline{3}$ Evaluate using a calculator.

ANSWER The Rainforest Pyramid has a volume of about 1,300,000 cubic feet.

EXAMPLE 2 Finding the Volume of a Pyramid

Find the volume of the pyramid.

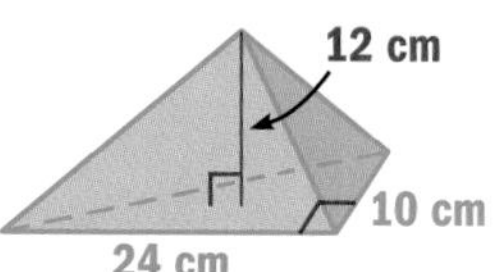

$V = \frac{1}{3}Bh$	**Write formula for volume of a pyramid.**
$= \frac{1}{3}\left(\frac{1}{2} \cdot 24 \cdot 10\right)(12)$	**The base is a triangle, so $B = \frac{1}{2}bh$.**
$= 480$	**Multiply.**

ANSWER The pyramid has a volume of 480 cubic centimeters.

Your turn now **Find the volume of the pyramid.**

1.

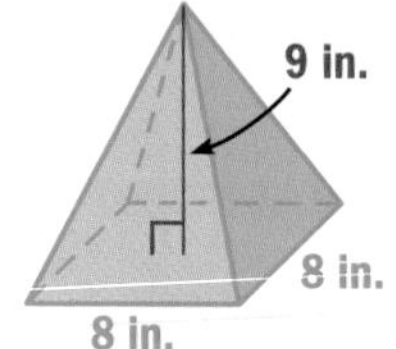

2.

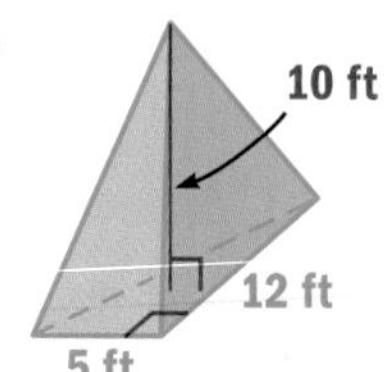

3.

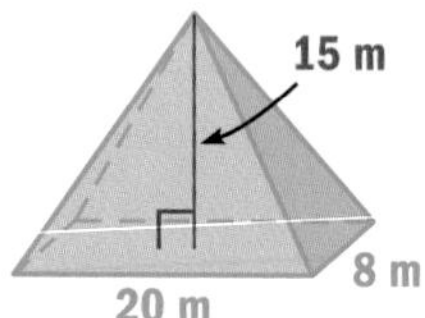

4. **Critical Thinking** Explain how you found the area of the base of each figure in Exercises 1–3.

Volumes of Cones The volume of a cone is related to the volume of a cylinder in the same way the volume of a pyramid is related to the volume of a prism. That is, the volume of a cone is one third the volume of a cylinder with the same base and height.

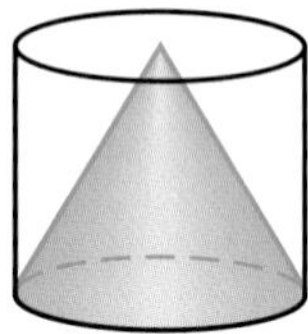

Volume of a Cone

Words The volume of a cone is one third the product of the area of the base and the height.

Algebra $V = \frac{1}{3}Bh = \frac{1}{3}\pi r^2 h$

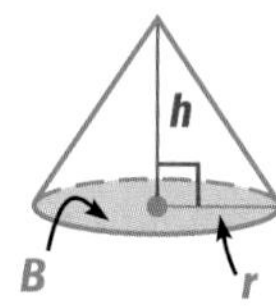

■ **Native Americans**

In the United States, 26 of the 50 states have names that originated from Native American languages. What percent is this?

EXAMPLE 3 **Finding the Volume of a Cone**

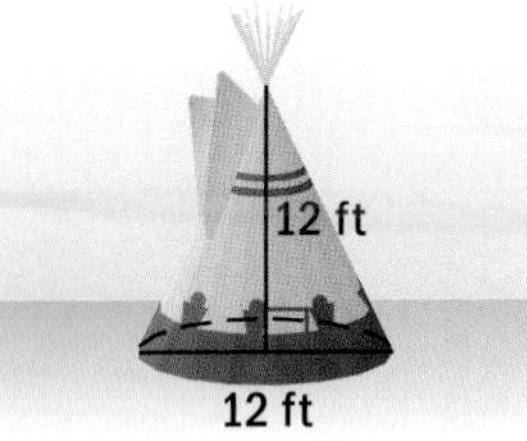

Native Americans Many Native American tribes built tepees that were cone-shaped. A tepee has a height of 12 feet and a base diameter of 12 feet. Approximate the volume of the tepee.

Solution

The radius is one half the diameter, so $r = \frac{1}{2} \cdot 12 = 6$ ft.

$V = \frac{1}{3}\pi r^2 h$	**Write formula for volume of a cone.**
$= \frac{1}{3}\pi(6)^2(12)$	**Substitute 6 for *r* and 12 for *h*.**
$= 144\pi$	**Simplify.**
≈ 452.389	**Evaluate using a calculator.**

ANSWER The tepee has a volume of about 450 cubic feet.

Your turn now **Find the volume of the cone with radius *r* and height *h*. Round to the nearest tenth.**

5. $r = 24$ m, $h = 18$ m **6.** $r = 4$ in., $h = 16$ in. **7.** $r = 15$ ft, $h = 28$ ft

10.7 Exercises

More Practice, p. 736

Getting Ready to Practice

Matching **Match each solid with the *best* formula for its volume.**

1. prism **2.** cylinder **3.** pyramid **4.** cone

A. $V = \frac{1}{3}Bh$ **B.** $V = \pi r^2 h$ **C.** $V = \frac{1}{3}\pi r^2 h$ **D.** $V = Bh$

Find the volume of the solid. Round to the nearest tenth.

5.

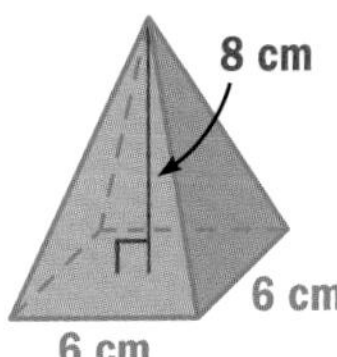

6.

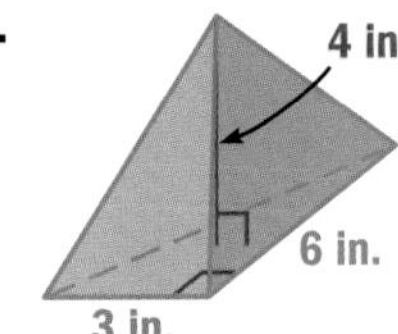

7.

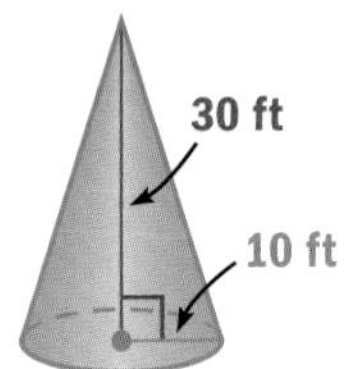

Practice and Problem Solving

Example	Exercises
1	14–16
2	8–16
3	17–25

· More Examples
· eTutorial Plus

Find the volume of the pyramid with base area *B* and height *h*.

8. $B = 9 \text{ in.}^2, h = 4 \text{ in.}$ **9.** $B = 12 \text{ ft}^2, h = 15 \text{ ft}$ **10.** $B = 1.5 \text{ m}^2, h = 0.6 \text{ m}$

Find the volume of the pyramid.

11.

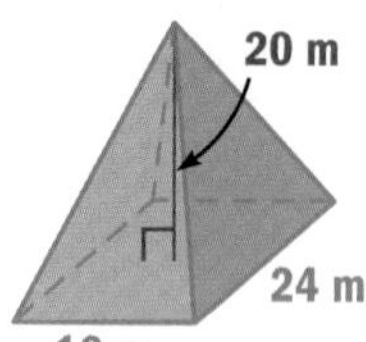

12.

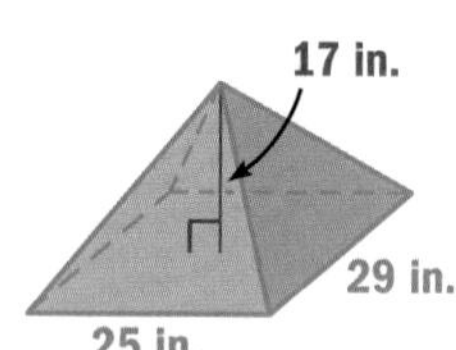

13.

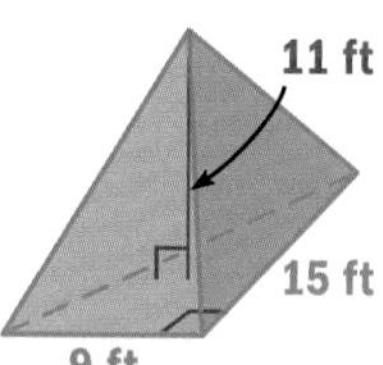

Find the volume of the square pyramid with base side length *s* and height *h*.

14. $s = 5 \text{ m}, h = 4 \text{ m}$ **15.** $s = 12 \text{ yd}, h = 3 \text{ yd}$ **16.** $s = 6 \text{ in.}, h = \frac{1}{2} \text{ in.}$

Find the volume of the cone. If two units of measure are used, give your answer in the smaller units. Round to the nearest tenth.

17.

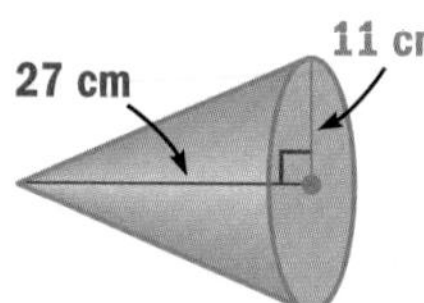

18.

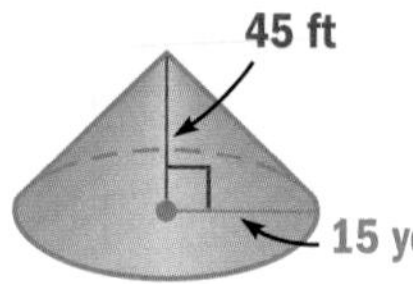

19.

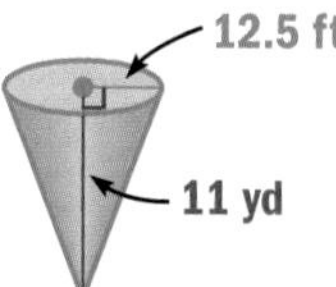

Find the volume of the cone with the given dimensions. If two units of measure are used, give your answer in the smaller units. Round to the nearest tenth.

20. $r = 3 \text{ in.}, h = 7 \text{ in.}$ **21.** $r = 11 \text{ ft}, h = 4 \text{ ft}$ **22.** $r = 1.2 \text{ m}, h = 45 \text{ cm}$

23. $d = 8 \text{ m}, h = 8 \text{ m}$ **24.** $d = 5 \text{ cm}, h = 9 \text{ cm}$ **25.** $d = 3 \text{ ft}, h = 10 \text{ yd}$

26. **Spotlight** The light from a spotlight reaches out in a cone shape from the bulb. The light of the beam extends 24 feet before it hits the floor under the spotlight and creates a circle with a radius of 10 feet. What is the volume of the space directly lit by the spotlight? Round to the nearest tenth.

Find the volume of the pyramid with the given height and the base shown. Round to the nearest tenth.

27. $h = 1.8 \text{ cm}$

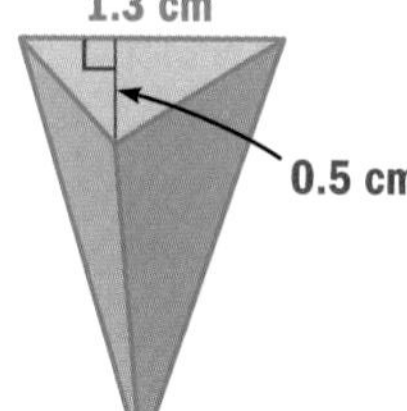

28. $h = 8 \text{ m}$

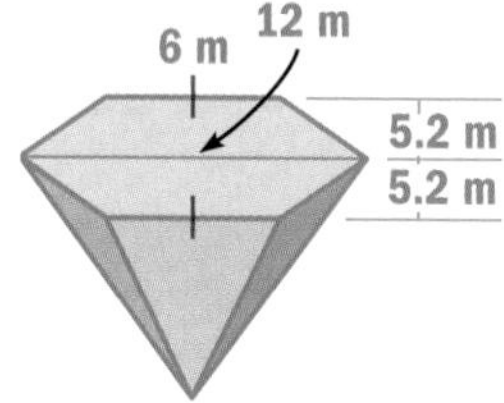

29. Critical Thinking Which would affect the volume of a cone more: *doubling the height* or *doubling the radius*? Explain your reasoning.

Writing Write a sentence describing how to find the volume of the solid. Then write a formula for the volume of the solid.

30.

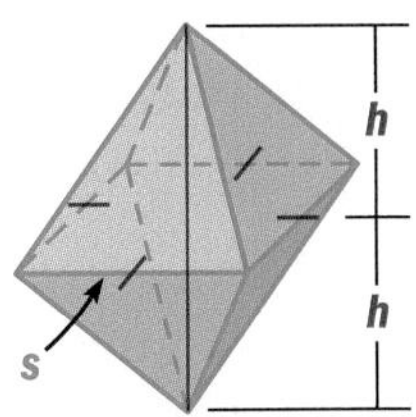

31.

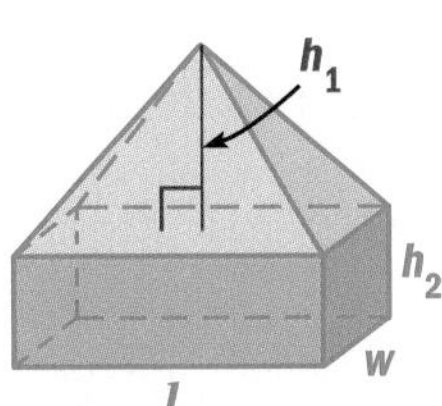

32.

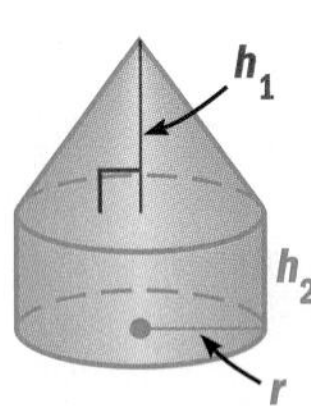

33. Construction A rectangular prism-shaped hole 10 feet by 12 feet by 8 feet is dug into the ground. How tall a pyramid can the excavated dirt form if the base is 10 feet by 10 feet? How tall a cone can it form if the base has a radius of 5 feet? Round your answers to the nearest tenth.

34. Challenge A cone-shaped cup has a height of 11 centimeters and a radius of 4 centimeters. You pour water into the cup until it is 2 centimeters from the top. Sketch the cone. How many fluid ounces of water are in the cup? Round to the nearest tenth. (*Hint*: Use similar triangles and the fact that $1 \text{ cm}^3 \approx 0.0338$ fl oz.)

Mixed Review 

Show two ways to represent the solid. *(Lesson 10.3)*

35. hexagonal prism

36. square pyramid

37. Find the volume of a cylinder with radius 7 inches and height 18 inches. Round to the nearest tenth. *(Lesson 10.6)*

38. Basic Skills The table shows the average high temperatures in Alexandria, Egypt, during the months April through September. Make a bar graph of the data.

Month	April	May	June	July	August	September
Temperature	75° F	79° F	83° F	84° F	86° F	84° F

Test-Taking Practice 

39. Multiple Choice What is the volume of the cone?

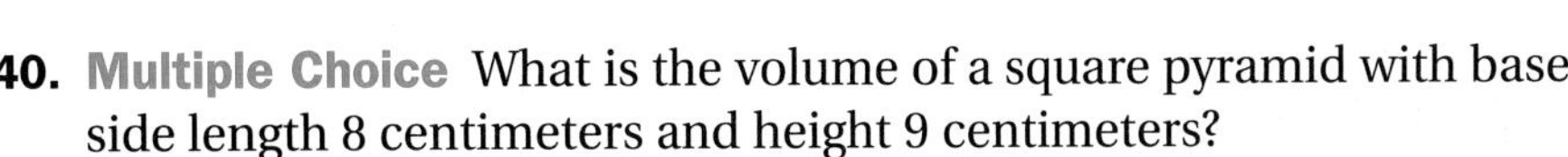

A. $10\pi \text{ ft}^3$ **B.** $21\pi \text{ ft}^3$

C. $49\pi \text{ ft}^3$ **D.** $147\pi \text{ ft}^3$

40. Multiple Choice What is the volume of a square pyramid with base side length 8 centimeters and height 9 centimeters?

F. 72 cm^3 **G.** 192 cm^3 **H.** 576 cm^3 **I.** 648 cm^3

Notebook Review

Review the vocabulary definitions in your notebook.

Copy the review examples in your notebook. Then complete the exercises.

Check Your Definitions

net, p. 502
surface area, p. 503
slant height, p. 507
volume, p. 513

Use Your Vocabulary

1. In your own words, explain what slant height is.

10.4–10.5 Can you find surface areas?

EXAMPLE Find the surface area of the cylinder.

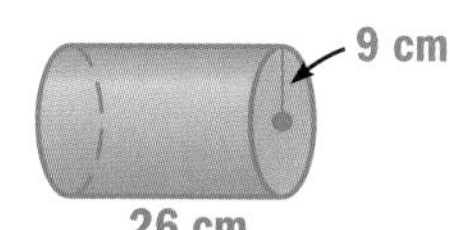

$$S = 2\pi r^2 + 2\pi rh$$

$$= 2\pi(9)^2 + 2\pi(9)(26) \approx 509 + 1470 = 1979$$

ANSWER The surface area of the cylinder is about 1979 square centimeters.

EXAMPLE Find the surface area of the square pyramid.

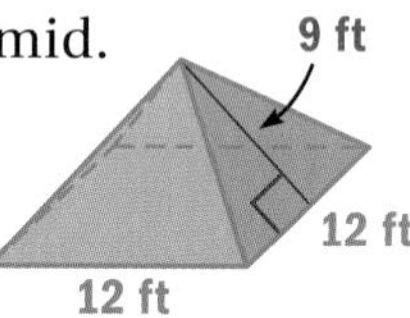

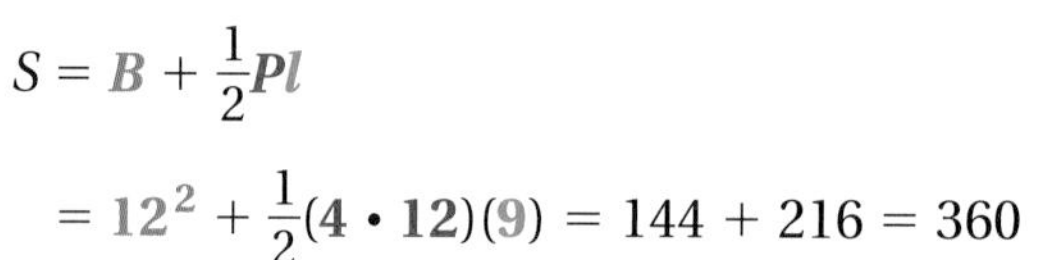

$$S = B + \frac{1}{2}Pl$$

$$= 12^2 + \frac{1}{2}(4 \cdot 12)(9) = 144 + 216 = 360$$

ANSWER The surface area of the pyramid is 360 square feet.

Find the surface area of the solid. Round to the nearest tenth.

2. a cylinder with radius 5 meters and height 10 meters

3. a rectangular prism with length 5 inches, width 2 inches, and height 9 inches

4. a square pyramid with base side length 7 meters and slant height 4 meters

5. a cone with diameter 20 feet and slant height 15 feet

10.6–10.7 Can you find volumes?

EXAMPLE Find the volume of the prism.

$$V = Bh = \frac{1}{2}(7 \cdot 14)(21) = 49 \cdot 21 = 1029$$

ANSWER The volume is 1029 cubic inches.

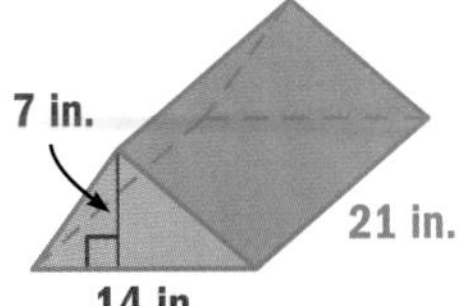

EXAMPLE Find the volume of the cone.

$$V = \frac{1}{3}\pi r^2 h = \frac{1}{3}\pi(7)^2(18) = 294\pi \approx 923.628$$

ANSWER The cone has a volume of about 924 cubic feet.

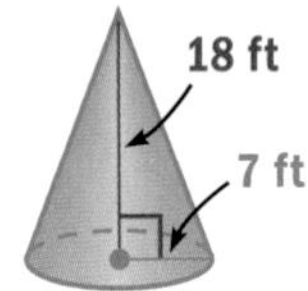

6. Find the volume of a pyramid with base area 27 square meters and height 14 meters.

Stop and Think about Lessons 10.4–10.7

7. Writing What is the difference between area and surface area?

Review Quiz 2

Find the surface area of the solid. Round to the nearest tenth.

1. 6 m 10 m 24 m

2.

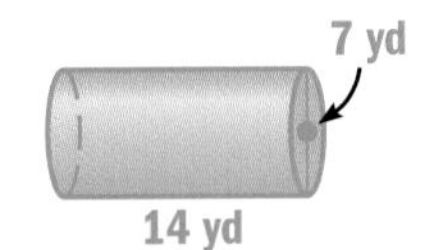

3.

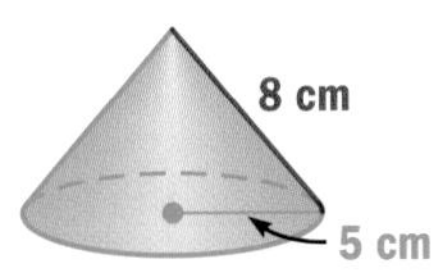

Find the volume of the solid. Round to the nearest tenth.

4.

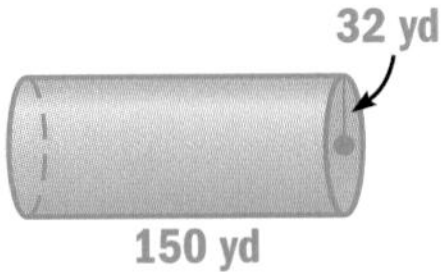

5.

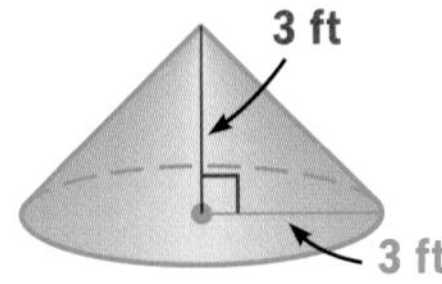

6.

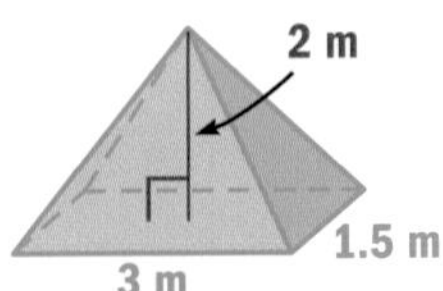

7. Ramp How much cement is needed to make the ramp shown?

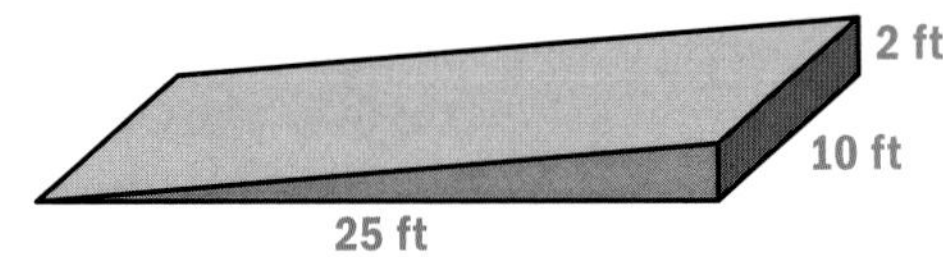

Chapter Review

Vocabulary

base of a parallelogram, p. 481
height of a parallelogram, p. 481
bases of a trapezoid, p. 482
height of a trapezoid, p. 482
solid, polyhedron, p. 492
face, p. 492
prism, p. 492
pyramid, p. 492
cylinder, p. 492
cone, p. 492
sphere, p. 492
edge, vertex, p. 492
net, p. 502
surface area, p. 503
slant height, p. 507
volume, p. 513

Vocabulary Review

Match the figure with its area formula.

1.  **2.** 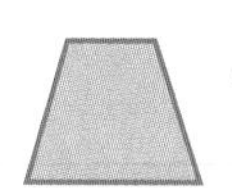 **3.** 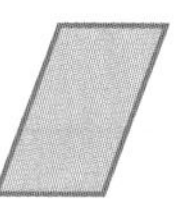 **4.**

A. $A = \pi r^2$ **B.** $A = \frac{1}{2}bh$

C. $A = bh$ **D.** $A = \frac{1}{2}(b_1 + b_2)h$

5. Draw a net of a square prism.

6. How many faces, edges, and vertices does a triangular pyramid have?

Write the formulas for the surface area and the volume of the figure.

7. cylinder **8.** cone

9. pyramid **10.** prism

Review Questions

Find the area of the parallelogram with base *b* and height *h*.
(Lesson 10.1)

11. $b = 16$ ft, $h = 7$ ft **12.** $b = 63$ m, $h = 5.2$ m **13.** $b = 8\frac{1}{4}$ in., $h = 6\frac{5}{11}$ in.

Find the area of the trapezoid with bases b_1 and b_2 and height *h*.
(Lesson 10.1)

14. $b_1 = 20$ cm, $b_2 = 12$ cm, $h = 8$ cm **15.** $b_1 = 6$ yd, $b_2 = 9$ yd, $h = 12$ yd

Find the area of the circle with radius *r* or diameter *d*. Use 3.14 for π.
(Lesson 10.2)

16. $r = 3$ ft **17.** $r = 15$ yd **18.** $d = 80$ cm **19.** $d = 1.5$ m

Review Questions

20. Show two ways to represent a hexagonal prism. Then count the number of faces, edges, and vertices. *(Lesson 10.3)*

21. Draw a net for an octagonal pyramid. How many faces, edges, and vertices does the octagonal pyramid have? *(Lessons 10.3, 10.4)*

Find the surface area of the solid. Round to the nearest tenth.
(Lessons 10.4, 10.5)

22.
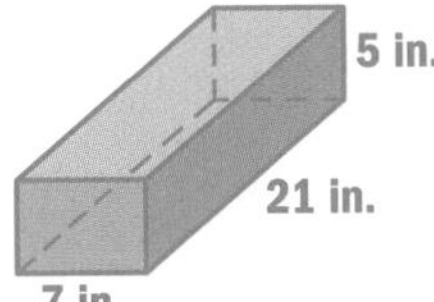

23.
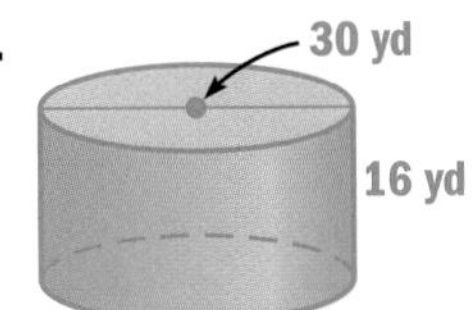

24.
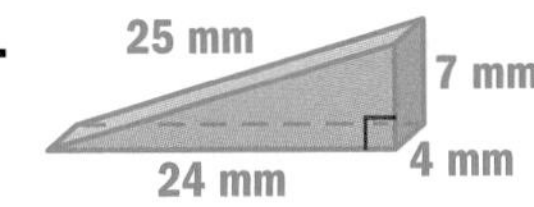

25.
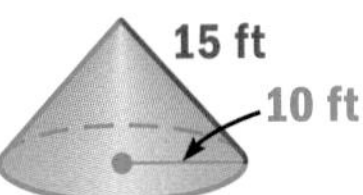

26.
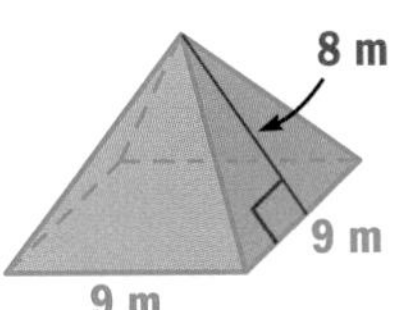

27.
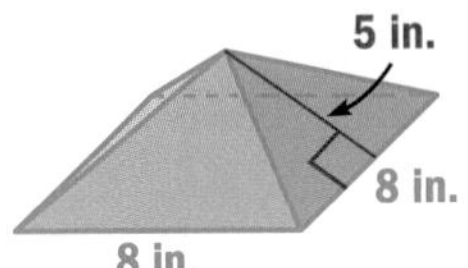

Find the volume of the solid. Round to the nearest tenth.
(Lessons 10.6, 10.7)

28.
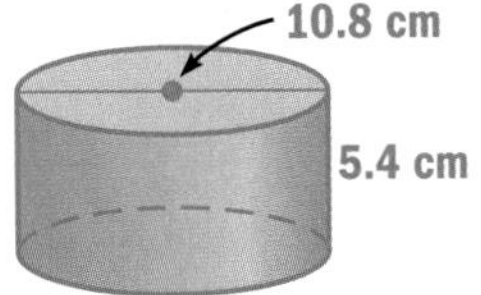

29.
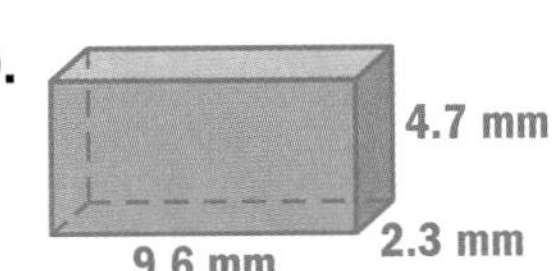

30.
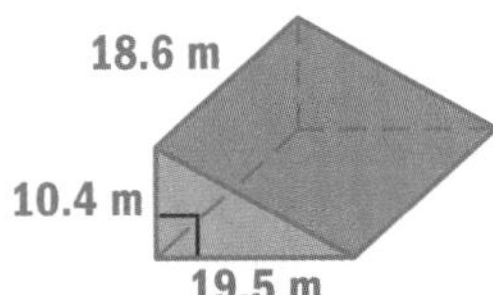

31.
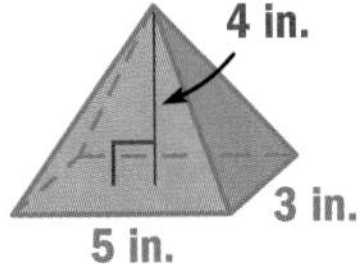

32.
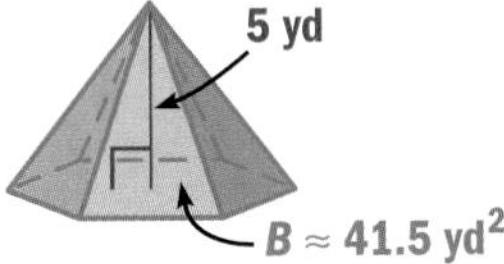

33.
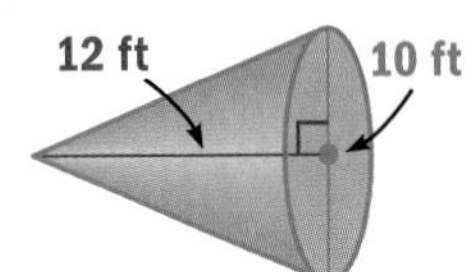

34. Containers A cylinder with a radius of 6 centimeters and a height of 7 centimeters has about the same volume as a rectangular prism with a length of 9 centimeters, a width of 8 centimeters, and a height of 11 centimeters. Which container uses less material to hold the same amount? About how much less material? Round to the nearest tenth. *(Lessons 10.4, 10.6)*

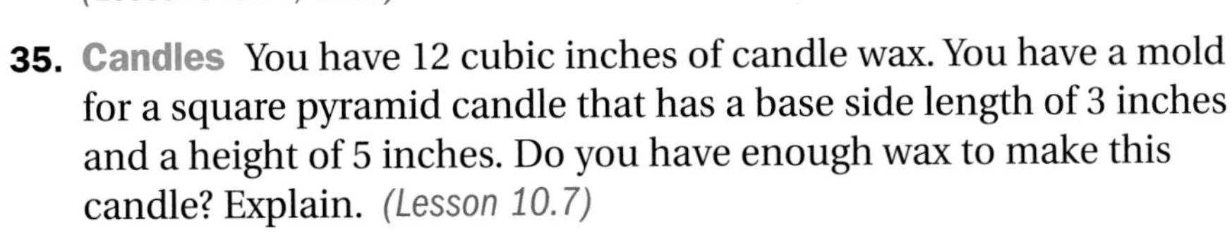

35. Candles You have 12 cubic inches of candle wax. You have a mold for a square pyramid candle that has a base side length of 3 inches and a height of 5 inches. Do you have enough wax to make this candle? Explain. *(Lesson 10.7)*

CHAPTER 10

Chapter Test

Find the area of the parallelogram or trapezoid.

1.

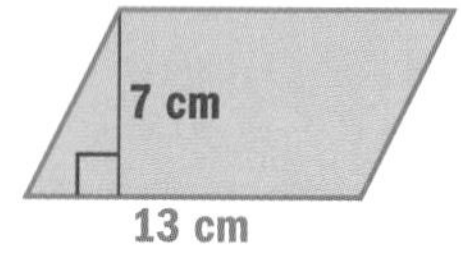

2.

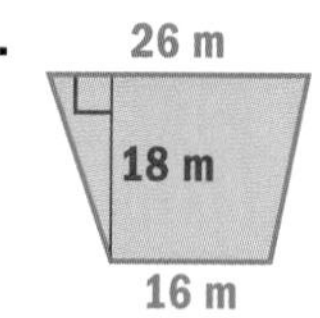

3.

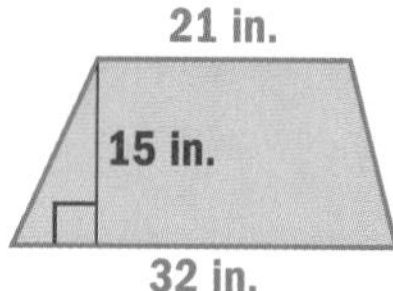

Determine the radius of the circle given its area. Use 3.14 for π.

4. $A = 3.7994 \text{ ft}^2$

5. $A = 0.785 \text{ m}^2$

6. $A = 94.985 \text{ yd}^2$

Classify the solid. Then tell whether it is a polyhedron.

7.

8.

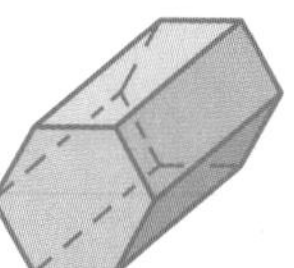

9.

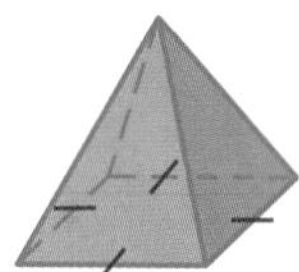

10. Painting You plan to paint the 4 walls and ceiling of a rectangular room with dimensions 15 feet by 12 feet by 8 feet. A can of paint covers 400 square feet. How many cans of paint will you need?

Find the surface area of the solid. Round to the nearest tenth.

11.

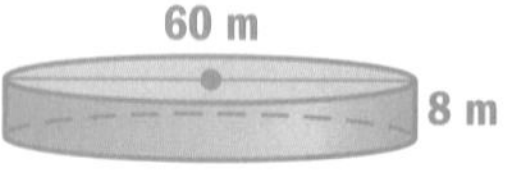

12.

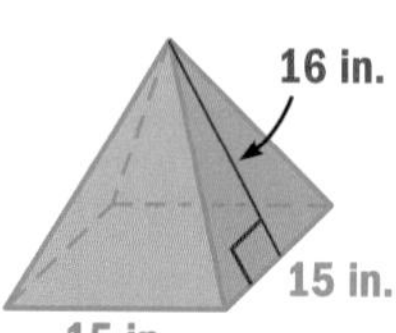

13.

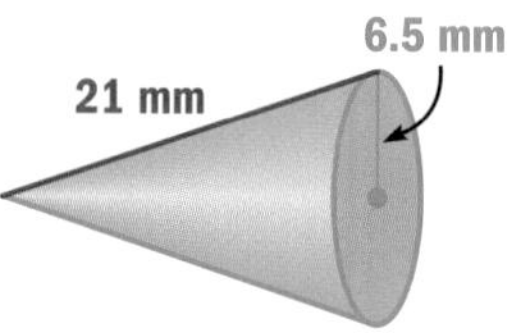

14. Pepperoni A stick of pepperoni is a cylinder, with a radius of 2 centimeters and a length of 12 centimeters. If a slice of pepperoni is 1 cubic centimeter, how many whole slices can be made?

Find the volume of the solid. Round to the nearest tenth.

15.

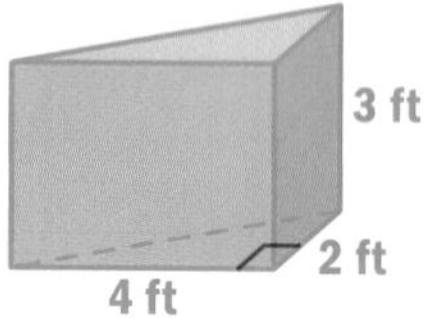

16.

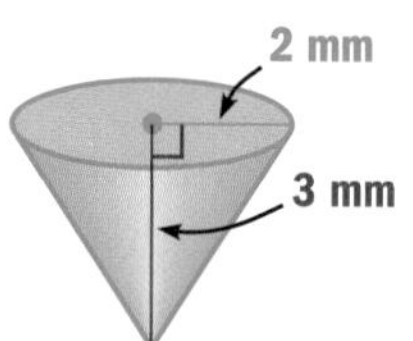

17.

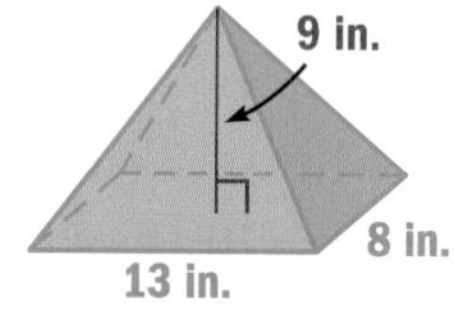

Chapter Standardized Test

Test-Taking Strategy Go back and check as many of your answers as you can.

Multiple Choice

1. A parallelogram has an area of 14 square inches and a base length of 2 inches. What is the height?

   A. 2 in. **B.** 7 in. **C.** 12 in. **D.** 16 in.

2. The diameter of a nickel is 2 centimeters. What is the area of one side of the coin? Use 3.14 for π.

   F. 3.14 cm^2 **G.** 12.56 cm^2
   H. 25.12 cm^2 **I.** 50.24 cm^2

3. How many faces does the figure have?

   A. 3 **B.** 4 **C.** 5 **D.** 6

4. Which of the following statements is true of the prisms?

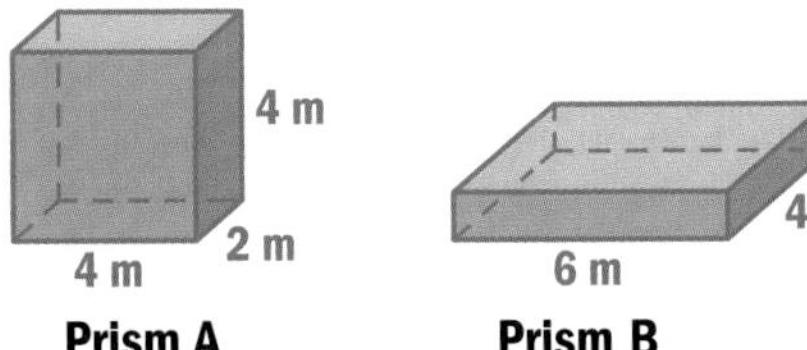

Prism A Prism B

   F. Prism A has a greater surface area than Prism B.

   G. Prism B has a greater surface area than Prism A.

   H. Prism A and Prism B have equal surface areas.

   I. Prism A and Prism B have equal volumes.

5. What is the surface area of a square pyramid with base side length 6 meters and slant height 10 meters?

   A. 36 m^2 **B.** 42 m^2 **C.** 96 m^2 **D.** 156 m^2

6. A pool has a rectangular base measuring 30 feet by 20 feet and is 12 feet deep. What is the volume of the pool?

   F. 240 ft^3 **G.** 600 ft^3
   H. 6000 ft^3 **I.** 7200 ft^3

7. What is the volume of a square pyramid that has a height of 9 feet and a perimeter of 24 feet?

   A. 36 ft^3 **B.** 72 ft^3 **C.** 108 ft^3 **D.** 216 ft^3

8. What is the diameter of a cone with a height of 10 yards and a volume of 92.4 cubic yards? Round to the nearest whole number.

   F. 3 yd **G.** 6 yd **H.** 9 yd **I.** 12 yd

Short Response

9. How does multiplying each dimension by 3 affect the surface area of a cylinder?

Extended Response

10. A company is making two types of aluminum containers. One is a cylinder with a height of 1.25 feet and a diameter of 1 foot. The other is a rectangular prism with a length of 0.75 foot, a width of 0.75 foot, and a height of 1 foot. Aluminum costs $.02 per square foot. How much will it cost to produce each type of container? Round to the nearest cent. Which container holds more?

Strategies for Answering

Context-Based Multiple Choice Questions

Some of the information you need to solve a context-based multiple choice question may appear in a table, a diagram, or a graph.

Problem 1

Ali plants a flower garden in a circle around a tree. The outer edge of the garden has twice the radius of the inner edge. Find the area of the flower garden.

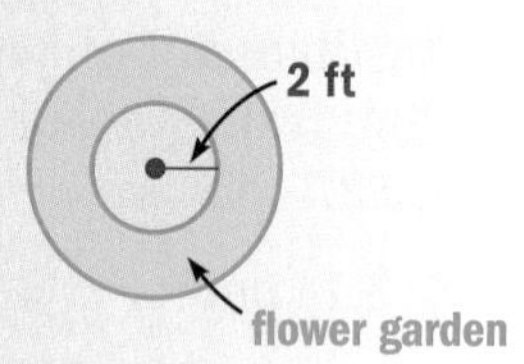

A. 12.56 ft^2 **B.** 25.12 ft^2 **C.** 37.68 ft^2 **D.** 50.24 ft^2

Solution

Read the problem carefully. Decide how you can use the information you are given to solve the problem.

1) You know that the radius of the inner circle is 2 feet and the radius of the outer circle is double the radius of the inner circle, or 4 feet.

Use the areas of both circles to find the area of the garden.

Find the areas of the two circles.

2) Area of inner circle:

radius = 2 ft

$$A = \pi r^2 = \pi \cdot 2^2 = 4\pi$$

Area of outer circle:

radius = 4 ft

$$A = \pi r^2 = \pi \cdot 4^2 = 16\pi$$

Use the areas of the circles to find the area of the garden.

3) Area of garden = Area of outer circle − Area of inner circle

$$A = 16\pi - 4\pi = 12\pi \approx 12 \times 3.14 = 37.68$$

The area of the flower garden is about 37.68 ft^2. The correct answer is C.

Use one of the strategies on pages 156–157.

4) Check to see that the answer is reasonable. Estimate that 16π is about 48 and 4π is about 12. Because $48 - 12 = 36$, C is the most reasonable choice.

Problem 2

Jim walks diagonally across a field. Martha walks along its length and width. The rectangular field is 300 feet wide and 400 feet long. How many feet less does Jim walk than Martha?

F. **1200 feet** **G.** **700 feet** **H.** **500 feet** **I.** **200 feet**

Solution

Read the problem carefully. Remember that the field is a rectangle.

1) Use the information in the problem to make a sketch.

Jim's path
300 ft
400 ft

Use the Pythagorean theorem to find the length of Jim's path. Add to find the length of Martha's path.

2) $a^2 + b^2 = c^2$ Pythagorean theorem
$300^2 + 400^2 = c^2$ Substitute for a and b.
$250{,}000 = c^2$ Solve.
$500 = c$ Evaluate positive square root.

The length of Jim's path is 500 feet.
The length of Martha's path is $300 + 400 = 700$ feet.

Find the difference of the two distances.

3) Martha's distance − Jim's distance
$= 700 - 500$
$= 200$

Jim walks 200 feet less than Martha. The correct answer is I.

Your turn now

Watch Out!

Be sure that you know what question you are asked to answer. Some choices given may be intended to distract you.

1. In Problem 2, Jim and Martha both walk at the rate of 250 ft/min. How many minutes less does Jim walk than Martha?

A. 0.2 min **B.** 0.25 min **C.** 0.8 min **D.** 1.25 min

In Exercises 2–3, use the diagram.

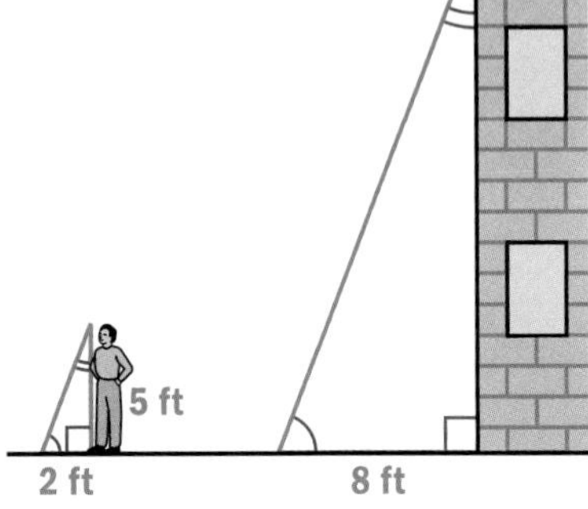

2. What is the height of the building?

F. 10 feet **G.** 16 feet
H. 20 feet **I.** 40 feet

3. How long will the person's shadow be when the building's shadow is 14 feet long?

A. 3 feet **B.** 3.5 feet
C. 4 feet **D.** 7 feet

GO ON

UNIT 3 Chapters 8–10

PRACTICING Test-Taking Skills

Multiple Choice

In Exercises 1 and 2, use the diagram below.

1. Which angles are complementary?

   A. $\angle 1$ and $\angle 2$
   B. $\angle 2$ and $\angle 3$
   C. $\angle 3$ and $\angle 4$
   D. $\angle 1$ and $\angle 4$

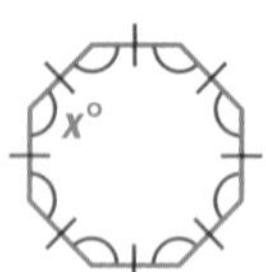

2. Which angles are vertical angles?

   F. $\angle 1$ and $\angle 2$ **G.** $\angle 2$ and $\angle 4$
   H. $\angle 3$ and $\angle 1$ **I.** $\angle 1$ and $\angle 3$

In Exercises 3 and 4, use the diagram below.

$x°$

3. What is the value of x?

   A. 45 **B.** 90 **C.** 135 **D.** 360

4. How many lines of symmetry does the figure have?

   F. 1 **G.** 4 **H.** 8 **I.** 16

5. $\angle B$ and $\angle A$ are supplementary. What is $m\angle B$?

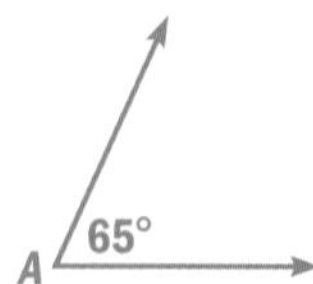

   A. 25° **B.** 35° **C.** 115° **D.** 125°

6. Ben has a rectangular garden that is 12 feet long and 5 feet wide. He plants a row of marigolds along the diagonal of the garden. How long is the row of marigolds?

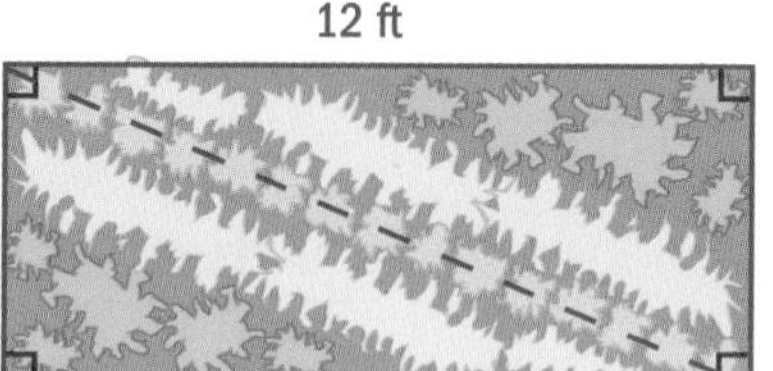

   F. 12 ft **G.** 13 ft **H.** 14 ft **I.** 15 ft

7. What is the area of the parallelogram?

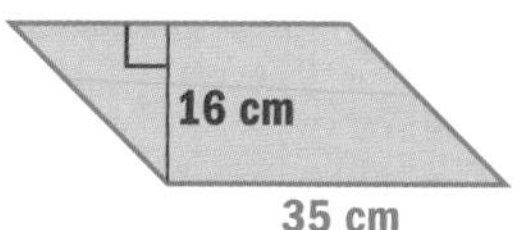

   A. 16 cm^2 **B.** 102 cm^2
   C. 280 cm^2 **D.** 560 cm^2

In Exercises 8 and 9, use the diagram below. The Giant Ocean Tank at the New England Aquarium is a cylinder that is 23 feet deep and 40 feet in diameter.

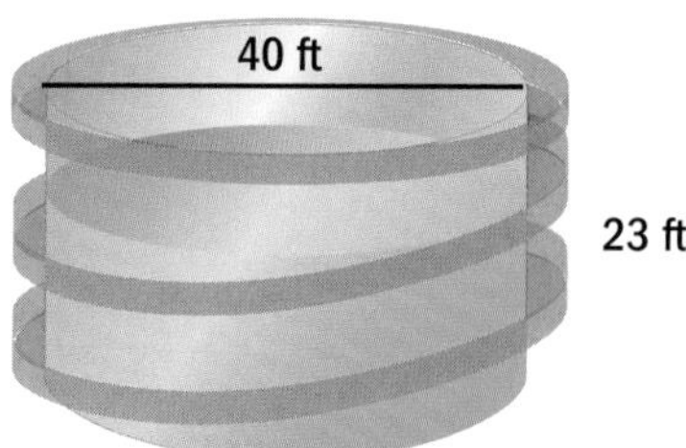

8. Find the area of the curved wall of the tank.

   F. 920 ft^2 **G.** 80π ft^2
   H. 920π ft^2 **I.** 1840π ft^2

9. What is the volume of the tank?

   A. 920π ft^3 **B.** 1720π ft^3
   C. 9200π ft^3 **D.** $18{,}400\pi$ ft^3

Short Response

10. Find the value of x and explain your steps.

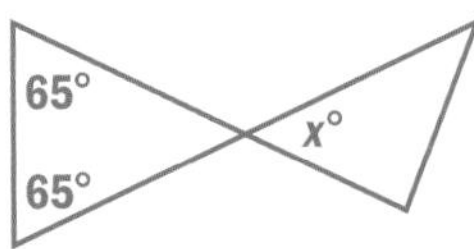

11. An 11 foot ladder leans against a building. The top of the ladder is 7 feet high. How far is the bottom of the ladder from the base of the building?

12. Your town purchases a new fire truck with a 100 foot extension ladder. How close can the fire truck come to a building if the ladder is fully extended at an angle of 45°? Draw a diagram and explain how you found your answer.

13. You stand 15 feet from a flagpole that is perpendicular to the ground. The angle from the point where you stand to the top of the flagpole is 60°. How tall is the flagpole? Explain how you found your answer.

14. The Inuit people of the Arctic use blocks of snow to build igloos in the shape of a half sphere. An igloo is 15 feet in diameter. Find the area of the igloo's floor to the nearest square foot.

15. A radio broadcasts to a circular region with an area of 182 square miles. What is the radius of the region? Round your answer to the nearest tenth of a mile.

Extended Response

16. A boarding ramp extends down from a dock to a ship. The angle of the ramp to the dock changes with the tide. At high tide, the 10 foot ramp meets the dock at an angle of 12°. At low tide, it meets the dock at an angle of 18°. What is the difference in water level to the nearest foot between high tide and low tide?

Draw a diagram and explain how you found your answer.

17. A high school running track surrounds a field that needs to be watered. Write an equation that you can use to find the area enclosed by the track. Explain your reasoning.

Solve the equation to find the area enclosed by the track.

If you water the field at a rate of about $1\frac{1}{4}$ gallons per square foot, about how much water will be used to water the field?

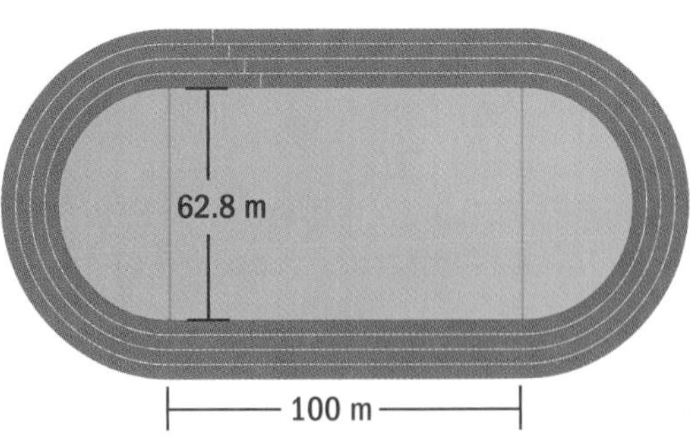

GO ON

Cumulative Practice for Chapters 8–10

Chapter 8

Multiple Choice In Exercises 1–7, choose the letter of the correct answer.

1. $\angle 1$ and $\angle 2$ are complementary, and $m\angle 1 = 62°$. What is $m\angle 2$? *(Lesson 8.1)*

   A. 28° **B.** 38° **C.** 118° **D.** 128°

2. What is the value of x? *(Lesson 8.2)*

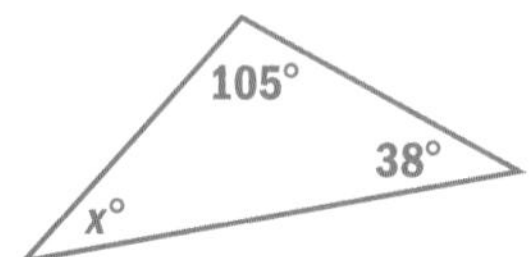

   F. 37 **G.** 67 **H.** 117 **I.** 143

3. Classify the quadrilateral. *(Lesson 8.3)*

   A. rectangle
   B. rhombus
   C. trapezoid
   D. parallelogram

4. What is the sum of the angle measures in a hexagon? *(Lesson 8.4)*

   F. 180° **G.** 540° **H.** 720° **I.** 1080°

5. Triangle ABC is congruent to $\triangle EDF$. Which statement is *not* true? *(Lesson 8.5)*

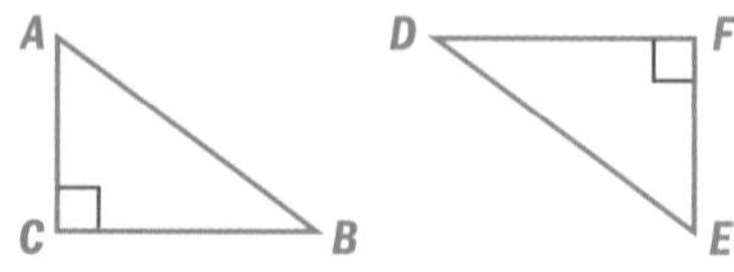

   A. $\overline{AC} \cong \overline{EF}$ **B.** $\overline{CB} \cong \overline{FD}$
   C. $\overline{AB} \cong \overline{DF}$ **D.** $\angle A \cong \angle E$

6. Which transformation is shown? *(Lessons 8.6–8.8)*

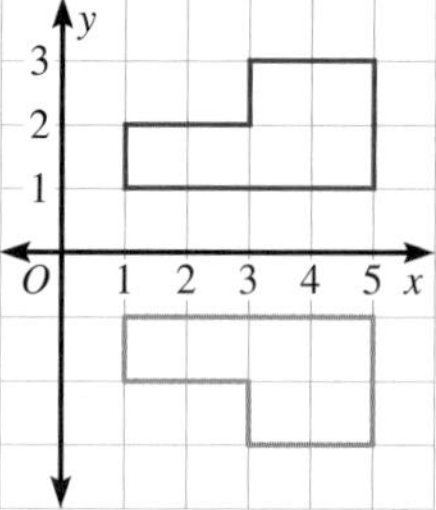

   F. reflection
   G. rotation
   H. translation
   I. dilation

7. You reduce a 20 inch by 36 inch photo to $\frac{1}{4}$ of its original dimensions. What are the new dimensions of the photo? *(Lesson 8.8)*

   A. 4 inch by 6 inch **B.** 4 inch by 9 inch
   C. 5 inch by 6 inch **D.** 5 inch by 9 inch

8. **Short Response** Triangle ABC has vertices $A(-2, -2)$, $B(-4, 0)$, and $C(-2, 3)$. Reflect $\triangle ABC$ in the y-axis. What are the vertices of the image? *(Lesson 8.6)*

9. **Extended Response** In baseball and softball, home plate is a pentagon with three right angles and two congruent obtuse angles. *(Lesson 8.4)*

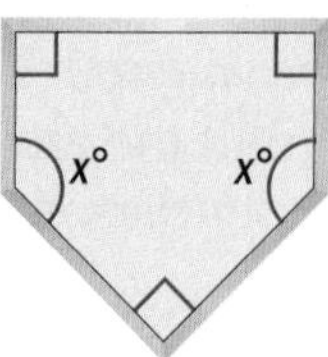

   a. Find the sum of the angle measures of a pentagon.

   b. Write an equation that you can use to find the measure of each obtuse angle.

   c. Solve the equation to find the measure of each obtuse angle.

Chapter 9

Multiple Choice In Exercises 10–17, choose the letter of the correct answer.

10. In 1891, Captain Dansey of the British Royal Artillery designed a square kite for rescuing shipwreck victims. The kite has an area of 81 square feet. What are the dimensions of the kite? *(Lesson 9.1)*

A. 3 ft by 3 ft **B.** 9 ft by 9 ft

C. 18 ft by 18 ft **D.** 81 ft by 81 ft

11. What are the values of a in the equation $a^2 - 81 = 115$? *(Lesson 9.1)*

F. $a = \pm 5.8$ **G.** $a = \pm 9$

H. $a = \pm 10.7$ **I.** $a = \pm 14$

12. Which list shows the numbers in order from least to greatest? *(Lesson 9.2)*

A. $2, \sqrt{3}, \sqrt{7}, \sqrt{11}, 5.5$

B. $\sqrt{3}, 2, \sqrt{7}, \sqrt{11}, 5.5$

C. $2, \sqrt{3}, 5.5, \sqrt{7}, \sqrt{11}$

D. $2, \sqrt{3}, \sqrt{7}, 5.5, \sqrt{11}$

13. What is the value of c? *(Lesson 9.3)*

F. 28 feet

G. 39 feet

H. 45 feet

I. 55 feet

14. The size of a television screen is given by the length of the diagonal of the screen. What size is a television screen that is 28 inches wide and 21 inches high? *(Lesson 9.4)*

A. 24 in. **B.** 32 in. **C.** 35 in. **D.** 40 in.

15. Which set of numbers *is not* a Pythagorean triple? *(Lesson 9.4)*

F. 5, 12, 13 **G.** 9, 40, 41

H. 8, 15, 17 **I.** 6, 24, 25

16. What is the value of x? *(Lesson 9.5)*

A. 7.5 inches

B. 15 inches

C. 21.2 inches

D. 30 inches

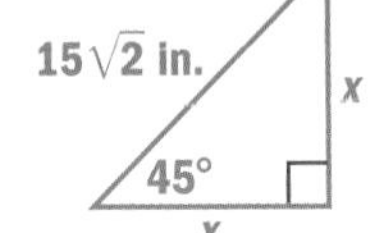

17. In $\triangle ABC$, what is $\tan A$? *(Lesson 9.6)*

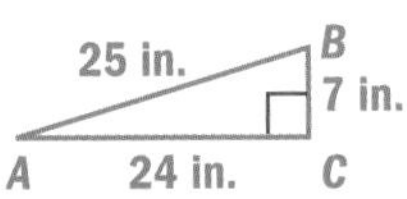

F. $\frac{7}{24}$ **G.** $\frac{7}{25}$ **H.** $\frac{24}{25}$ **I.** $\frac{24}{7}$

18. **Short Response** Julie designs a wheelchair ramp that reaches a door 2 feet above the ground. The ramp makes an angle of 4.76° with the ground. What is the length of the ramp's base to the nearest foot? Draw a diagram and explain your steps. *(Lesson 9.6)*

19. **Extended Response** A jet takes off at an angle of 15° with the ground. The jet's speed is 300 feet per second. *(Lesson 9.6)*

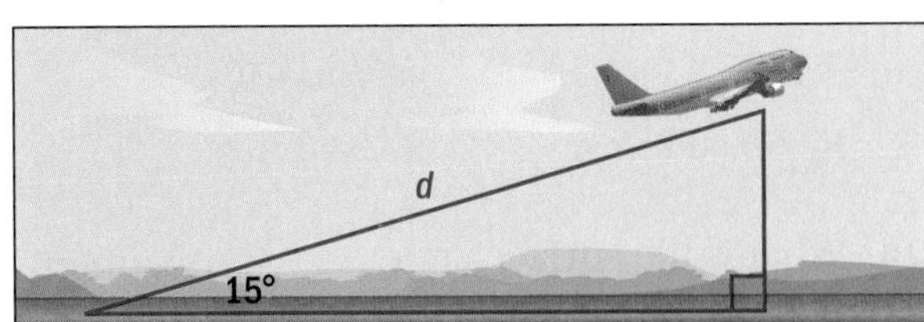

a. How far does the jet travel in 10 seconds?

b. Find the height of the jet 10 seconds after take off.

c. Find the horizontal distance the jet travels after 10 seconds.

Cumulative Practice continued

Chapter 10

Multiple Choice In Exercises 20–26, choose the letter of the correct answer.

20. What is the area of the trapezoid? *(Lesson 10.1)*

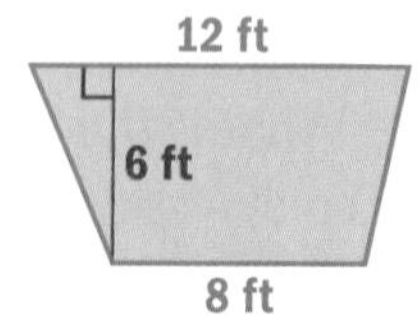

A. 48 ft^2 **B.** 60 ft^2 **C.** 72 ft^2 **D.** 120 ft^2

21. What is the area of the circle? Use 3.14 for π. *(Lesson 10.2)*

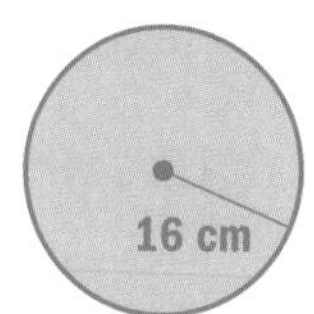

F. 50.24 cm^2 **G.** 256 cm^2

H. 803.84 cm^2 **I.** 4096 cm^2

22. Identify the solid. *(Lesson 10.3)*

A. cone

B. cylinder

C. pyramid

D. triangular prism

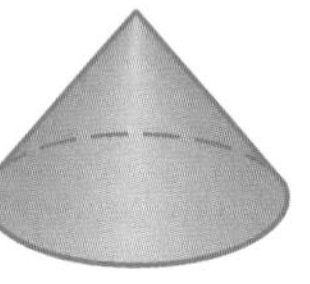

23. What is the approximate surface area of the cylinder? *(Lesson 10.4)*

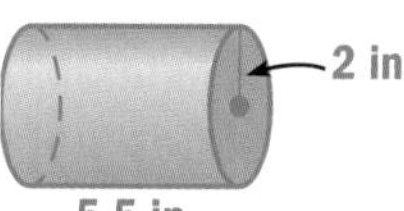

F. 12.56 $in.^2$ **G.** 25.12 $in.^2$

H. 69.08 $in.^2$ **I.** 94.2 $in.^2$

24. What is the surface area of the square pyramid? *(Lesson 10.5)*

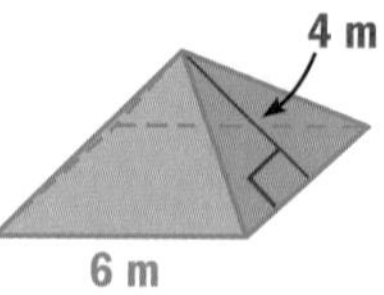

A. 36 m^2 **B.** 48 m^2

C. 84 m^2 **D.** 132 m^2

25. What is the volume of the prism? *(Lesson 10.6)*

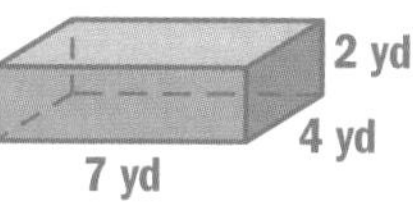

F. 8 yd^2 **G.** 14 yd^2 **H.** 28 yd^3 **I.** 56 yd^3

26. What is the approximate volume of the cone? *(Lesson 10.7)*

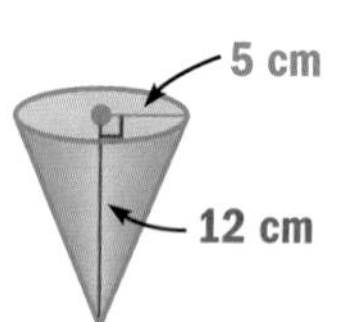

A. 78.5 cm^3 **B.** 314 cm^3

C. 753.6 cm^3 **D.** 942 cm^3

27. Short Response Identify the solid. Then count the number of faces, edges, and vertices. *(Lesson 10.3)*

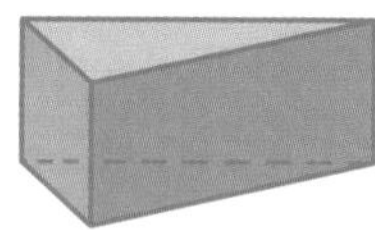

28. Extended Response A movie theater serves a small size of popcorn in a conical container and a large size of popcorn in a cylindrical container. *(Lessons 10.6, 10.7)*

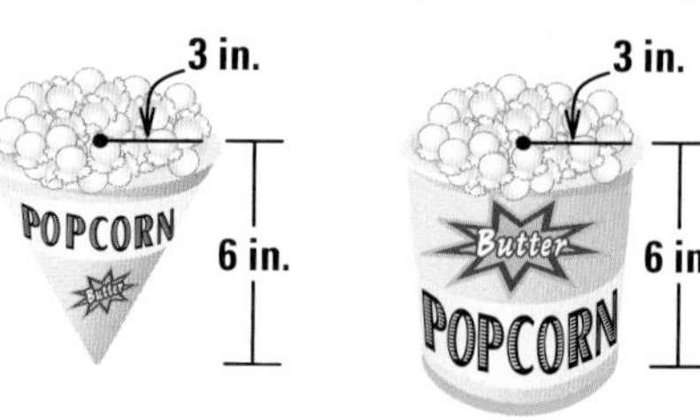

a. What is the volume of the small container?

b. What is the volume of the large container?

c. Which container gives you more popcorn for your money? Explain your reasoning?

Advanced Algebra Topics

Chapter 11 Linear Equations and Graphs

- Write and use functions to predict outcomes.
- Write and solve equations and inequalities.
- Write, evaluate, and graph functions.

Chapter 12 Data Analysis and Probability

- Make and interpret data displays. Choose an appropriate display for a data set.
- Use tree diagrams, the counting principle, and permutations and combinations to solve problems.
- Find probabilities of independent and dependent events.

Chapter 13 Polynomials and Functions

- Simplify and evaluate expressions using exponents.
- Evaluate and graph non-linear equations.

From Chapter 13, p. 679

How many e-mail jokes are sent?

Linear Equations and Graphs

BEFORE

In previous chapters you've...

- Translated verbal sentences into mathematical statements
- Solved equations in one variable

Now

In Chapter 11 you'll study...

- Constructing and interpreting scatter plots
- Finding solutions of equations in two variables
- Writing and graphing equations

WHY?

So you can solve real-world problems about...

- gray whales, p. 543
- inline skates, p. 549
- elevators, p. 552
- hiking, p. 577

Internet Preview
CLASSZONE.COM

- eEdition Plus Online
- eWorkbook Plus Online
- eTutorial Plus Online
- State Test Practice
- More Examples

Chapter Warm-Up Games

Review skills you need for this chapter in these quick games.

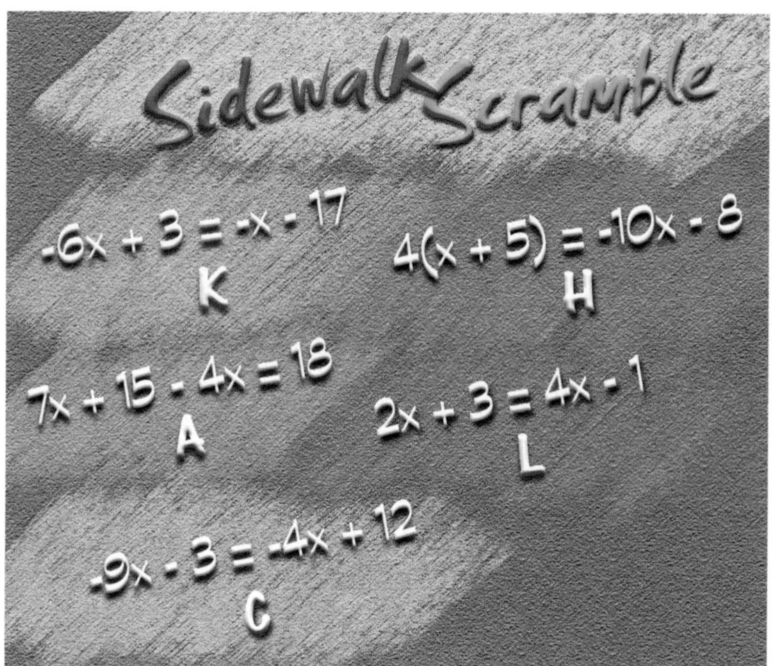

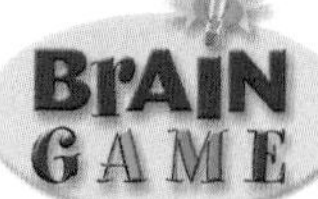

Key Skill:
Solving equations in one variable

Solve the scramble to spell a word associated with sidewalk art.

- Find the solution of each equation.
- Order the equations so that the one with the least solution is first and the one with the greatest solution is last. This will unscramble the letters.

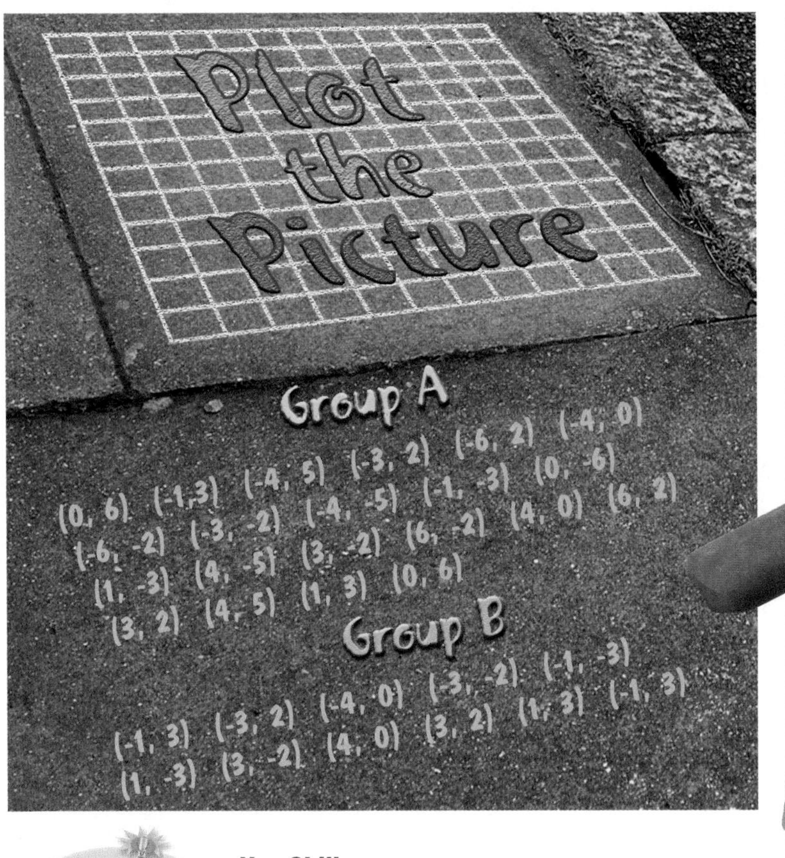

Plot the Picture
Group A
(0, 6) (-1,3) (-4, 5) (-3, 2) (-6, 2) (-4, 0)
(-6, -2) (-3, -2) (-4, -5) (-1, -3) (0, -6)
(1, -3) (4, -5) (3, -2) (6, -2) (4, 0) (6, 2)
(3, 2) (4, 5) (1, 3) (0, 6)
Group B
(-1, 3) (-3, 2) (-4, 0) (-3, -2) (-1, -3)
(1, -3) (3, -2) (4, 0) (3, 2) (1, 3) (-1, 3)

BRAIN GAME

Key Skill:
Plotting points on a coordinate grid

Create a piece of sidewalk art.

- Plot the points listed in Group A on a coordinate grid. Connect each point with a line to the point that follows it.
- Now find and connect the points in Group B in order.

Stop *and* Think

1. **Writing** A student says that in *Sidewalk Scramble* the first step in solving the equation $-6x + 3 = -x - 17$ is to subtract x from both sides. Explain why the student is wrong.
2. **Extension** Design your own piece of sidewalk art. Write directions for making your sidewalk art using points on a coordinate grid.

Getting Ready to Learn

Word Watch

Review Words

coordinate plane, p. 91
x-axis, p. 91
y-axis, p. 91
origin, p. 91
quadrant, p. 91
ordered pair, p. 91
inequality, p. 140
ratio, p. 317

Review What You Need to Know 

1. **Using Vocabulary** Draw a coordinate plane and label the x-axis, y-axis, origin, and third quadrant.

2. Write the ordered pair for each labeled point in the coordinate plane.

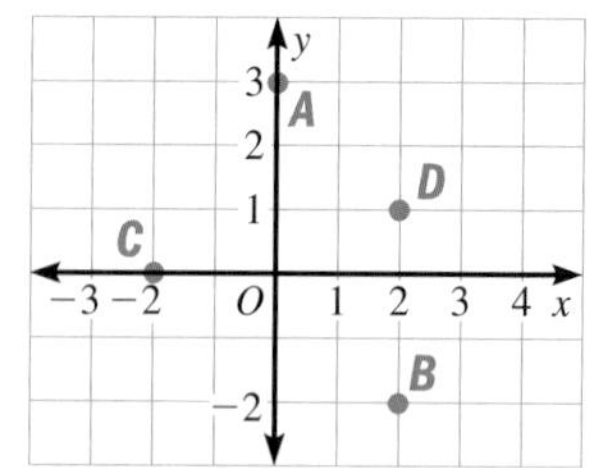

Plot the point in a coordinate plane. *(p. 91)*

3. (0, 4)
4. (−2, 3)
5. (5, −4)
6. (−2, −3)

Solve the equation. *(p. 119)*

7. $3 = 9x - 24$
8. $7 - 8x = 3$
9. $6x + 9 = -45$

Solve the inequality. *(p. 295)*

10. $3x - 4 \leq 5$
11. $-4x - 3 \geq 12$
12. $6 + 2x < 2$

You should include material that appears on a notebook like this in your own notes.

Know How to Take Notes

Write Questions About Homework If you don't know how to solve a homework problem, make a note in you notebook. Leave room to write the answer to your question.

What is the distance from A to C?

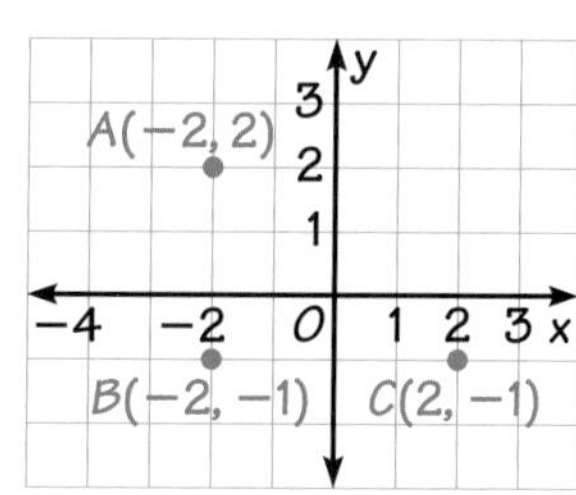

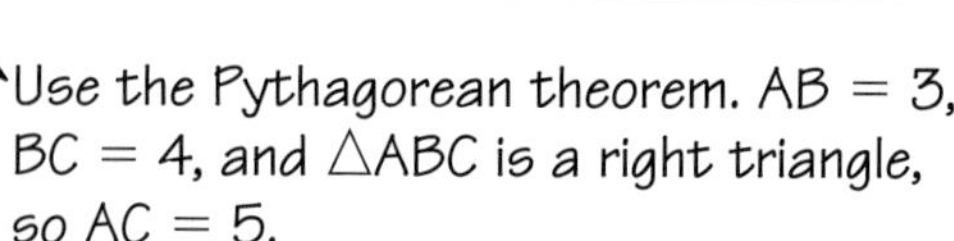

I can't count along the grid from A to C, so how do I solve this?

Use the Pythagorean theorem. AB = 3, BC = 4, and △ABC is a right triangle, so AC = 5.

In Chapter 11, you will learn how the coordinate plane is related to equations. Be sure to find answers to any questions you have.

Relations and Functions

BEFORE	Now	WHY?
You translated verbal sentences into algebraic models.	You'll use tables to represent functions.	So you can find the amount of formula consumed, as in Ex. 8.

In the Real World

Word Watch

relation, p. 541
input, p. 541
output, p. 541
function, p. 541
domain, p. 542
range, p. 542

INDIANA Academic Standards

- Algebra and Functions (8.3.5, 8.3.8)

Fundraisers Your soccer team is selling glow sticks to raise money. The team paid \$50 for a case of 48 glow sticks and sells each glow stick for \$3. How many glow sticks does the team need to sell to start earning a profit? You will answer this question in Example 2.

A **relation** is a set of ordered pairs that relates an **input** to an **output**. A relation can be written as a set of ordered pairs or by using an *input-output table.*

(Input, Output)
(2, 5)
(4, 7)
(−1, 15)
(0, 0)

Input	Output
2	5
4	7
−1	15
0	0

A relation is a **function** if for each input there is exactly one output. In a function, you can say that the output is a *function of* the input.

EXAMPLE 1 Identifying Functions

Watch Out! In a function, two different inputs can have the same output, but each input must have *exactly one* output.

Tell whether the relation is a function. Explain your answer.

a. (0, 2), (1, 4), (2, 6), (3, 8)

ANSWER The relation is a function. Each input has exactly one output.

b.

Input	9	9	25	25
Output	3	−3	5	−5

ANSWER The relation is *not* a function. Both 9 and 25 have two outputs.

Your turn now **Tell whether the relation is a function.**

1. (−2, 4), (2, 4), (4, 2), (−2, −4)

2.

Input	−2	0	2	4
Output	4	0	4	16

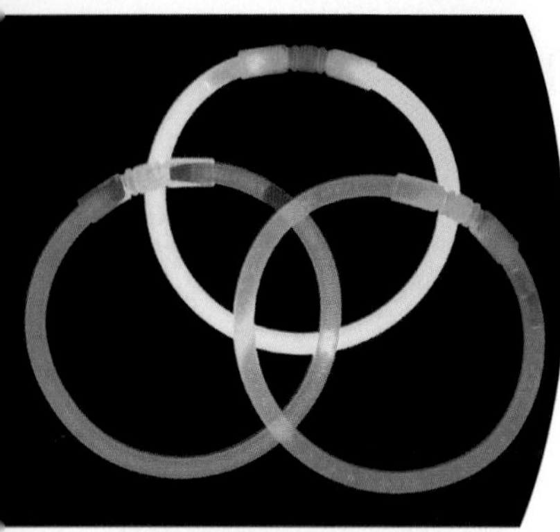

Domain and Range The **domain** of a function is the set of all possible input values. The **range** of a function is the set of all possible output values. A *function rule* assigns each number in the domain to exactly one number in the range.

EXAMPLE 2 Evaluating a Function

Fundraising To solve the problem on page 541, use the function rule $P = 3g - 50$, where P is the profit in dollars and g is the number of glow sticks your team sells.

Solution

First, make a table to determine how many glow sticks your soccer team needs to sell to start earning a profit.

Input g	Function	Output P
0	$P = 3(0) - 50$	-50
10	$P = 3(10) - 50$	-20
16	$P = 3(16) - 50$	-2
17	$P = 3(17) - 50$	1

There are 48 glow sticks, so the domain is 0, 1, 2, 3, . . . , 48. The range is $-50, -47, -44, -41, \ldots, 94$.

HELP with Solving

In Example 2, a negative output value indicates a loss of money for the team.

ANSWER Your soccer team needs to sell at least 17 glow sticks.

EXAMPLE 3 Writing a Function Rule

Write a function rule that relates *x* and *y*.

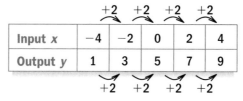

Input x	-4	-2	0	2	4
Output y	1	3	5	7	9

(Inputs increase by +2, +2, +2, +2; outputs increase by +2, +2, +2, +2.)

To write a function rule, try to find an equation of the form $y = ax + b$. You can look at differences in the function to find values of a and b.

1. The value of a is $\frac{\text{change in output}}{\text{change in input}}$.

   $a = \frac{2}{2} = 1$ $\qquad y = 1x + b$

2. To find b, choose an input-output pair to substitute for x and y.

   Let $(x, y) = (0, 5)$ $\qquad 5 = 1(0) + b$, so $b = 5$

ANSWER A function rule that relates x and y is $y = x + 5$.

✓**Check** $3 = -2 + 5$ **Substitute (−2, 3) in function rule.**

11.1 Exercises

More Practice, p. 737

Getting Ready to Practice

1. **Vocabulary** Copy and complete: A relation that has exactly one output value for each input is a(n) _?_.

Tell whether the relation is a function.

2. (3, 0), (0, 6), (1, 5), (3, 7) (−1, 2), (5, 1), (−3, 0)

3.

Input	−2	3	8	13
Output	0	0	0	0

Copy and complete the table of values for the function rule.

4. $y = x - 3$

5. $5x + y = 13$

Input *x*	−1	0	1	2
Output *y*	?	?	?	?

Write a function rule that relates *x* and *y*.

6.

Input *x*	−1	0	1	2
Output *y*	5	6	7	8

7.

Input *x*	0	1	2	3
Output *y*	0	−5	−10	−15

8. **Whale Calf** A gray whale calf was nursed back to health with milk-based formula. The table shows the amounts of formula, in gallons, the whale consumed every 3 to 4 hours. Use the table to write a function rule.

Number of times fed	Total amount consumed (gal)
1	2
2	4
3	6
4	8

Practice and Problem Solving

HELP with Homework

Example	Exercises
1	9-12
2	13-16
3	17-18

· More Examples
· eTutorial Plus

Tell whether the relation is a function. Explain your answer.

9. (4, 5), (2, −3), (4, 9), (−2, −3)

10. (−3, 7), (3, 7), (7, 3), (−7, −3)

11.

Input	−3	−2	0	2
Output	9	4	0	4

12.

Input	4	4	2	5
Output	2	−2	5	−5

Make an input-output table for the function rule. Use a domain of −2, −1, 0, 1, and 2. Identify the range.

13. $y = x - 1$

14. $y = -\frac{1}{4}x$

15. $y = 5x$

16. $y = x^2$

Write a function rule that relates x and y.

17.

Input x	1	2	3	4
Output y	5	10	15	20

18.

Input x	-3	-2	-1	0
Output y	-12	-8	-4	0

19. **Recycling** Stanley receives \$.75 per pound of aluminum cans he recycles. Is the weight of cans he recycles a function of the number of cans? Explain.

20. **Tickets** Ashley is buying movie tickets that are all the same price. Is the total cost a function of the number of tickets? Explain.

Write a function rule that relates r and t.

21.

Input r	1	2	3	4
Output t	1	4	7	10

22.

Input r	0	1	2	3
Output t	2	1.5	1	0.5

23. **Writing** Your friend says that the input-output table below represents a function. Is your friend correct? Explain why or why not.

Input x	-9	-4.5	0	4.5	9
Output y	81	20.25	0	20.25	81

24. **Challenge** Explain why the distance you travel on your bike is not always a function of the time you spend riding your bike. Describe a situation when it would be a function.

Mixed Review

Find the surface area of the solid. *(Lessons 10.4–10.5)*

25. 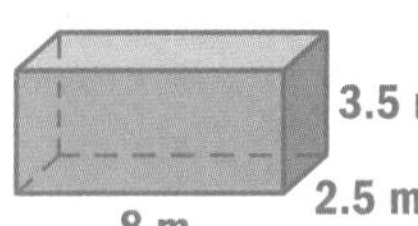

26. 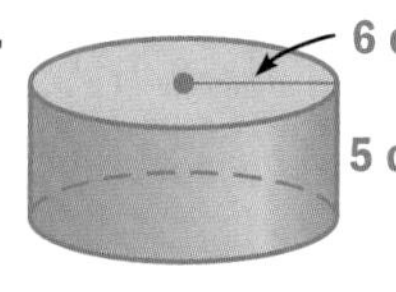

27. 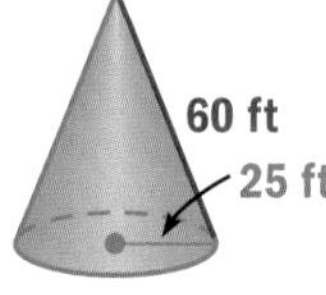

Test-Taking Practice

INTERNET
State Test Practice
CLASSZONE.COM

28. **Multiple Choice** The function rule $y = 3x$ relates x and y in which set of ordered pairs?

A. (0, 0), (3, 1), (6, 2), (9, 3) **B.** (0, 0), (1, 3), (2, 6), (3, 9)

C. (0, 3), (1, 4), (2, 5), (3, 6) **D.** (0, -3), (1, -2), (2, -1), (3, 0)

29. **Multiple Choice** Which of the following relations is *not* a function?

F. (2, 3), (4, 3), (6, 7), (9, 2) **G.** (2, 3), (4, 5), (6, 4), (5, 4)

H. (-1, 8), (0, 11), (1, 8), (5, 4) **I.** (3, 5), (4, 3), (4, 6), (6, 9)

Scatter Plots

BEFORE	Now	WHY?
You found a function rule given a table of values.	You'll make and interpret scatter plots.	So you can compare study time to test score, as in Ex. 6.

scatter plot, p. 545

INDIANA Academic Standards

- Data Analysis and Probability (8.6.5)

In the Real World

NASA NASA's Crawler Transporter is a large vehicle that moves the space shuttle and its launch platform to the launch pad. The crawler uses about 126 gallons of fuel to travel 1 mile.

The table below shows the amount of fuel that is used to travel different numbers of miles. How can you present this information using a graph?

Distance (miles)	1	2	3	4	5	6
Amount of fuel (gallons)	126	252	378	504	630	756

You can represent the information using a *scatter plot*. A **scatter plot** is the graph of a collection of ordered pairs.

EXAMPLE 1 Making and Interpreting a Scatter Plot

You can represent and make conclusions about the information above using a scatter plot.

To make a scatter plot, graph the ordered pairs from the table.

(1, 126), (2, 252), (3, 378),

(4, 504), (5, 630), (6, 756)

Put *Distance* on the horizontal axis and *Fuel used* on the vertical axis.

NASA Crawler Transporter

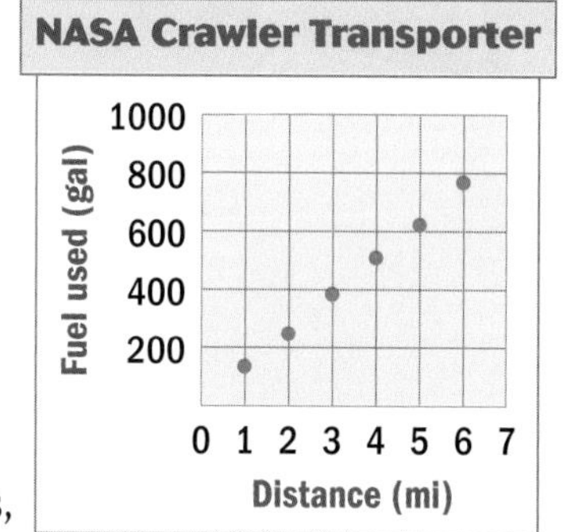

ANSWER As the distance traveled increases, the amount of fuel used increases. There is exactly one output for each input, so this is a function.

NASA's Crawler Transporter

Make a scatter plot of the data.

1.

c	-2	-1	0	1
d	-5	-4	-3	-2

2.

x	0	3	6	9
y	-2	-4	-6	-8

Interpreting Scatter Plots Scatter plots show what kind of relationship exists between two sets of data.

Positive relationship	**Negative relationship**	**No relationship**
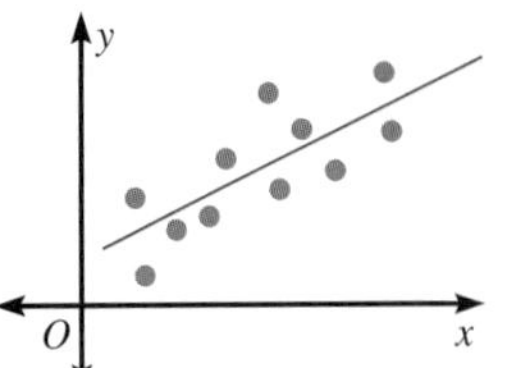	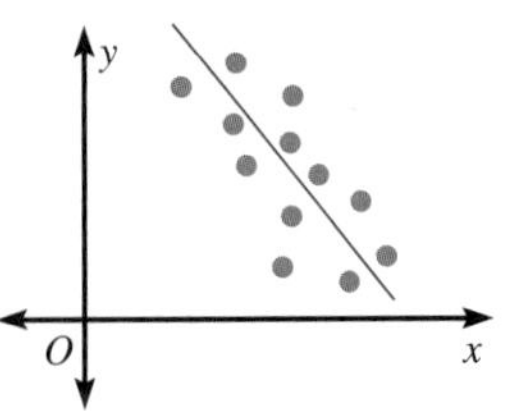	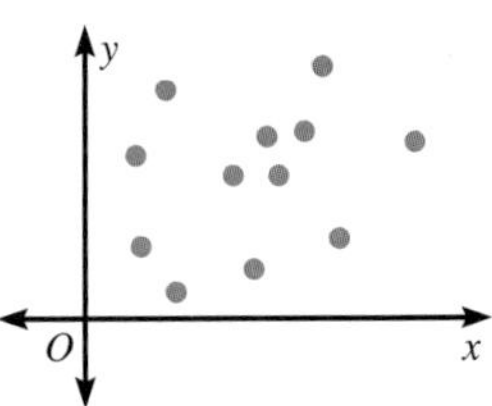
The y-coordinates tend to increase as the x-coordinates increase.	The y-coordinates tend to decrease as the x-coordinates increase.	No pattern exists between the coordinates.

EXAMPLE 2 Interpreting a Scatter Plot

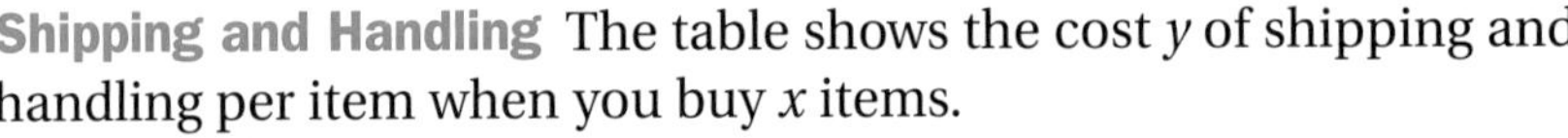

Shipping and Handling The table shows the cost y of shipping and handling per item when you buy x items.

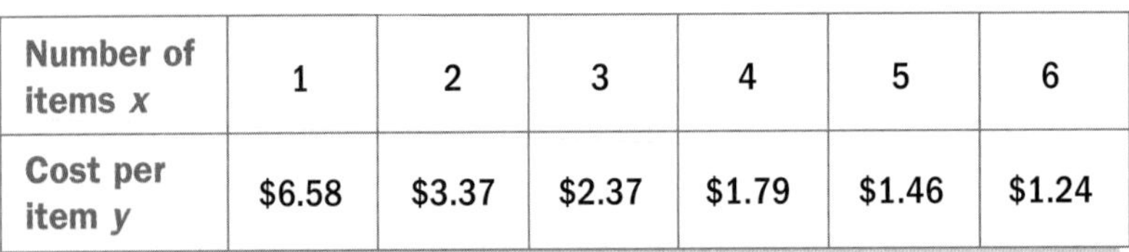

Number of items x	1	2	3	4	5	6
Cost per item y	\$6.58	\$3.37	\$2.37	\$1.79	\$1.46	\$1.24

a. Make a scatter plot of the data. Tell whether x and y have a *positive relationship*, a *negative relationship*, or *no relationship*.

b. Estimate the cost of shipping and handling per item if you buy eight items.

Solution

a. In the scatter plot, the y-coordinates decrease as the x-coordinates increase.

ANSWER The quantities have a negative relationship.

b. To estimate the shipping and handling cost per item to buy eight items, draw a curve that shows the overall pattern of the data, as shown. The curve looks like it will pass through the point (8, 1).

ANSWER The shipping and handling cost per item, if you buy eight items, is about \$1.

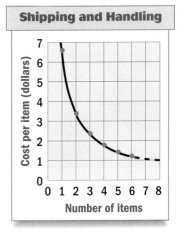

Shipping and Handling

Cost per item (dollars)

Number of items

11.2 Exercises

More Practice, p. 737

Getting Ready to Practice

1. **Vocabulary** Copy and complete: A(n) _?_ is a graph of a collection of ordered pairs.

2. **Guided Problem Solving** The table shows the number of cookbooks sold at a bookstore in each of the six years it has been open. Predict the number of cookbooks that will be sold in the ninth year.

Year x	1	2	3	4	5	6
Books y	450	650	700	800	1100	1250

(1) Make a scatter plot.

(2) Describe the relationship between the variables.

(3) Estimate the number of cookbooks that will be sold in the ninth year by sketching a curve that follows the trend of the data.

Practice and Problem Solving

HELP with Homework

Example	Exercises
1	6-9
2	3-5, 8-9

- More Examples
- eTutorial Plus

Tell whether *x* and *y* have a *positive relationship*, a *negative relationship*, or *no relationship*.

3. 4. 5.

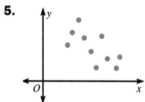

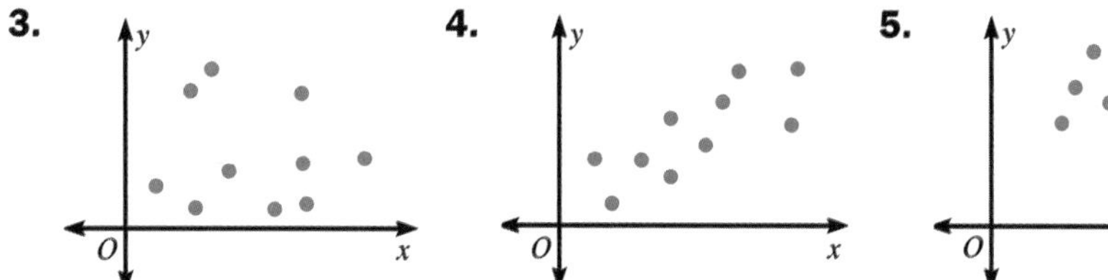

Make a scatter plot of the data. What conclusions can you make?

6.

Hours spent studying	Test score (percent)
1	70
2	80
3	85

7.

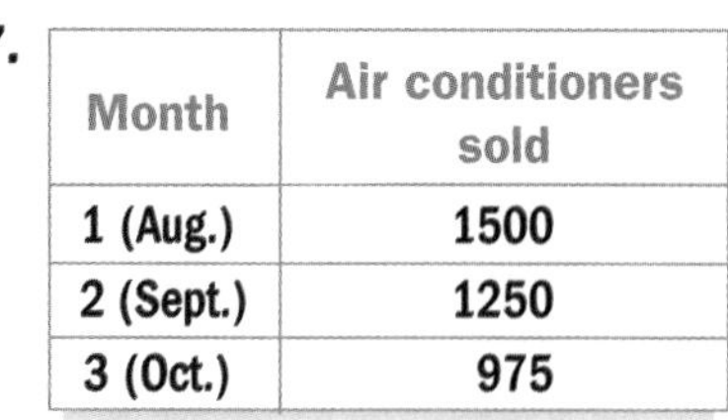

Month	Air conditioners sold
1 (Aug.)	1500
2 (Sept.)	1250
3 (Oct.)	975

Make a scatter plot of the data. Describe the relationship between the variables. Use the relationship to find the next ordered pair.

8.

x	1	2	3	4	5
y	5	10	15	20	?

9.

x	3	4	5	6	7
y	3	6	9	12	?

In Exercises 10–12, what type of relationship might you expect for the given data?

10. The height of a student in 8th grade and a test score of the student

11. The size of a pizza and the price of a pizza

12. The amount of money you give back to your friend and the amount you still owe

13. **Writing** A newspaper claims there is a strong relationship between the weather on the day of an election and voter turnout. What do you think the newspaper means? Could the newspaper use a scatter plot to support its claim? If so, what would the labels on each axis be?

14. **Geometry** Make a table showing several values of length and width of a rectangle whose perimeter is 12 inches. Make a scatter plot of the data. Draw a curve that shows the overall pattern of the data. Predict the width of a rectangle when the length is 3.5 inches.

Mixed Review 

Find the area of a trapezoid with bases b_1 and b_2 and height h. *(Lesson 10.1)*

15. $b_1 = 14$ m, $b_2 = 16$ m, $h = 6$ m **16.** $b_1 = 21$ ft, $b_2 = 32$ ft, $h = 18$ ft

17. Draw the net of a triangular pyramid. *(Lesson 10.3)*

Make a table of values for the function. Use a domain of −2, −1, 0, 1, and 2. Identify the range. *(Lesson 11.1)*

18. $y = 0.7x$ **19.** $y = 3x + 4$ **20.** $y = 0.4x - 1$

Basic Skills **Solve the equation.**

21. $t - 4 = 15$ **22.** $6 + x = 27$ **23.** $z + 17 = 36$ **24.** $w - 13 = 42$

Test-Taking Practice 

Use the information in the table.

Basketball	
Height (in inches)	Avg. points per game
71	3
73	10
75	4
83	19
84	20
90	24

25. **Multiple Choice** Describe the relationship shown in the data.

A. positive **B.** negative

C. none **D.** not enough information

26. **Multiple Choice** Predict how many points a player who is 77 inches tall could make.

F. 15 **G.** 25 **H.** 65 **I.** 85

Equations in Two Variables

BEFORE	Now	WHY?
You found solutions of equations in one variable.	You'll find solutions of equations in two variables.	So you can find how long it takes to pay back a loan, as in Ex. 29.

Word Watch

solution of an equation in two variables, p. 549

INDIANA Academic Standards

- Algebra and Functions (8.3.5)
- Problem Solving (8.7.11)

In the Real World

In-line Skates At a sports store, it costs \$7 per hour to rent in-line skates plus \$10 for the safety equipment. The total cost can be modeled by the equation $C = 10 + 7h$, where C is the total cost in dollars and h is the number of hours skated. What are some possible costs for renting in-line skates?

A **solution of an equation in two variables** is an ordered pair whose values make the equation true. For example, (2, 3) is a solution of $x + y = 5$ because $2 + 3 = 5$.

EXAMPLE 1 Evaluating an Equation in Two Variables

a. Make a table for $C = 10 + 7h$ to find some possible costs for renting in-line skates.

b. How many hours can you skate if you have \$35?

Solution

a. Substitute several values of h into the equation and solve for C.

***h*-value**	**Substitute for *h*.**	**Solve for *C*.**	**Solution**
$h = 1$	$C = 10 + 7(1)$	$C = 17$	(1, 17)
$h = 2$	$C = 10 + 7(2)$	$C = 24$	(2, 24)
$h = 3$	$C = 10 + 7(3)$	$C = 31$	(3, 31)
$h = 4$	$C = 10 + 7(4)$	$C = 38$	(4, 38)

Use the solutions to make a table.

Hours skated *h*	1	2	3	4
Total cost *C*	\$17	\$24	\$31	\$38

b. If you have \$35, you can rent in-line skates for about $3\frac{1}{2}$ hours.

EXAMPLE 2 Checking Solutions

Tell whether (7, −6) is a solution of $x + 3y = 14$.

$x + 3y = 14$	Write original equation.
$7 + 3(-6) \stackrel{?}{=} 14$	Substitute 7 for x and −6 for y.
$7 + (-18) \stackrel{?}{=} 14$	Simplify.
$-11 \neq 14$ ✗	Solution does not check.

ANSWER The ordered pair (7, −6) is *not* a solution of $x + 3y = 14$.

When finding solutions of an equation, it can be helpful to rewrite the equation in *function form*. When an equation is in function form it is solved for y.

Function form	Not function form
$y = -2x + 15$	$2x + y = 15$

HELP with Solving

Generally, an equation involving two variables has an infinite number of solutions.

EXAMPLE 3 Finding Solutions of an Equation

Solve the equation $4x + y = 15$ for y. List four solutions.

(1) Rewrite the equation in function form.

$4x + y = 15$	Write original equation.
$y = 15 - 4x$	Subtract $4x$ from each side.

(2) Evaluate the equation for several x-values.

x-value	Substitute for x.	Solve for y.	Solution
$x = -1$	$y = 15 - 4(-1)$	$y = 19$	(−1, 19)
$x = 0$	$y = 15 - 4(0)$	$y = 15$	(0, 15)
$x = 1$	$y = 15 - 4(1)$	$y = 11$	(1, 11)
$x = 2$	$y = 15 - 4(2)$	$y = 7$	(2, 7)

ANSWER Four solutions are (−1, 19), (0, 15), (1, 11), and (2, 7).

Your turn now **Tell whether the ordered pair is a solution of the equation.**

1. $y = 3x - 7$; (6, 5)

2. $-2x - 4y = 12$; (−4, −1)

List four solutions of the equation.

3. $y = -2x + 6$

4. $15x + 3y = 12$

More Practice, p. 737

Getting Ready to Practice

1. **Vocabulary** Copy and complete: A(n) _?_ of an equation in two variables is an ordered pair.

Rewrite the equation in function form.

2. $3x + y = 19$
3. $-4x + 2y = 8$
4. $-10x - 5y = -15$

5. **Find the Error** Describe and correct the error made when a student was asked to decide whether $(-5, 4)$ is a solution of $2x + 3y = -7$.

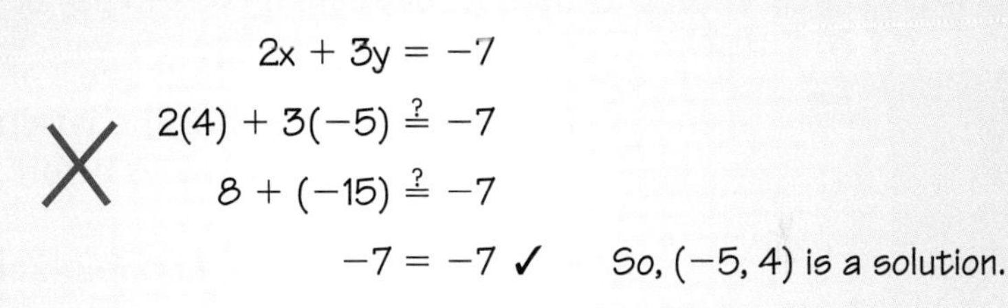

6. **Skateboard Wheels** Your skateboard club decides to replace each club member's wheels for a competition. Sets of four wheels sell for \$24 plus a \$14 shipping and handling cost added to the total. Use the equation $C = 24n + 14$, where C is the total cost in dollars and n is the number of sets of wheels ordered. If the final cost is \$182, how many sets of wheels were bought?

Practice and Problem Solving

HELP with Homework

Example	Exercises
1	7-9, 29
2	10-15, 19-22
3	16-18, 23-28

Online Resources CLASSZONE.COM
- More Examples
- eTutorial Plus

Copy and complete the table for the equation.

x	−5	0	5	10
y	?	?	?	?

7. $y = x + 8$
8. $y = 4 - 3x$
9. $y = -20 + x$

Tell whether the ordered pair is a solution of the equation.

10. $y = 4x + 2$; $(2, 10)$
11. $y = -2x + 5$; $(7, 5)$
12. $y = 6 - x$; $(-3, 3)$
13. $y = 13 - 5x$; $(4, -7)$
14. $y = 6x + 7$; $(2, 21)$
15. $y = 3x - 26$; $(6, -8)$

List four solutions of the equation.

16. $y = -2x + 5$
17. $y = -10 + (-4x)$
18. $y = \frac{1}{2}x - 1$

Calculator Tell whether the ordered pair is a solution of the equation.

19. $3x - y = 71.2$; $(-4.6, 8.2)$

20. $8x + y = 25$; $(2.25, 1.75)$

21. $x + 4y = 28.75$; $(3.23, 6.38)$

22. $x - 2y = -10.42$; $(-5.22, -7.82)$

List four solutions of the equation.

23. $y = 2x - 13$

24. $y = 16x + 24$

25. $-5x + 3 = y$

26. $y = -x + 17$

27. $y = -51 - 6x$

28. $y = \frac{1}{3}x - 5$

29. Loan Your friend agrees to lend you \$15 to buy a toy rocket. You promise to pay your friend \$.75 each week until you have paid back the full \$15. Use the equation $P = 15 - 0.75n$, where P is the amount of money in dollars that you have left to pay and n is the number of weeks, to find the number of weeks it takes to pay back your friend.

30. Critical Thinking In Example 3 of the lesson, you solved the equation for y before substituting the x-values. Will you get the same solutions if you substitute the x-values before solving for y?

Solve the equation for *y*. List four solutions of the equation.

31. $x + y = 8$

32. $42 = 4x + y$

33. $33 = -3x + y$

34. $4y = 8x + 12$

35. $5y + 15x = 10$

36. $-32 = 4x - 12y$

Write an equation in two variables for the values in the table.

37.

x	-1	0	1	2
y	2	4	6	8

38.

x	0	2	4	6
y	2	3	4	5

39. Estimation Estimate the values of $9x$ and $8y$ to explain why $\left(\frac{8}{3}, \frac{-7}{10}\right)$ is not a solution of $9x + 8y = 16$.

40. Glass Elevator An elevator is at a height of 800 feet. It is descending at a rate of 150 feet per minute. Use the equation $h = 800 - 150m$, where h is the height of the elevator in feet and m is the time in minutes. What is the height of the elevator after 5 minutes? How long will it take the elevator to reach a height of 0 feet?

41. Challenge Find the ordered pair that is the solution of both of the equations $y = -2x + 3$ and $y = 0.5x - 2$.

42. Carnival You can go to the carnival for 2 hours. You know that each ride takes about 10 minutes (including the wait in line), and you also want to spend time playing games. Write an equation in two variables to model this situation. If you go on 8 rides, how long can you play games?

Mixed Review

43. Plot (2, 3), (−6, 0), (−5, −1), and (8, −4) in a coordinate plane. *(Lesson 2.8)*

44. Find the area of a circle whose diameter is 25 inches. Use 3.14 for π. *(Lesson 10.2)*

Make a table of values for the function. Use a domain of −2, −1, 0, 1, and 2. Identify the range. *(Lesson 11.1)*

45. $4x + 8y = 16$ **46.** $6x + 3y = 36$ **47.** $14x + 7y = 56$

Basic Skills **Solve the equation.**

48. $6x - 4.25 = 3.55$ **49.** $14.98 + 2.4y = -6.02$

Test-Taking Practice

50. Short Response To join the summer movie club at your local theater, you pay a fee of $25. Then each movie you see is only $3. This situation can be modeled by the equation $C = 25 + 3m$, where C is the total cost in dollars and m is the number of movies you see. Copy and complete the table. If you can spend $60 on the movie club this summer, how many movies can you see?

Movies seen m	Total cost C
1	?
5	?
10	?
25	?

51. Multiple Choice Which ordered pair is a solution of the equation $y = -3x + 11$?

A. (−2, 17) **B.** (0, −11) **C.** (2, 3) **D.** (−1, −14)

Late Night Show

Each ordered pair is a solution of exactly one lettered equation. Write the appropriate letters in the blanks to find what kind of show the boy can expect to see.

?	?	?	?	?	?	?	?	?	?	?
(4, 1)	(9, 12)	(1, 9)	(3, 2)	(2, 5)	(4, 4)	(1, 9)	(17, 9)	(7, 24)	(0, 2)	(8, 15)

L. $y = 2x - 6$ **A.** $x + y = 10$ **T.** $4x + y = 20$ **E.** $y = 2x + 1$

I. $6x - y = 18$ **N.** $2y = 6x - 14$ **R.** $y = x - 8$ **U.** $y = \frac{1}{3}x + 2$

M. $x + 3y = 53$ **P.** $y = \frac{3}{2}x - 5$ **S.** $x + y = 6$ **O.** $y = x + 1$

Problem Solving Strategies

INDIANA: Academic Standards
• Algebra and Functions (8.3.8) • Problem Solving (8.7.1)

Make a Table

- Guess, Check, and Revise
- Look for a Pattern
- Draw a Diagram
- Act It Out
- Make a Table
- Work Backward
- Make a Model

Problem At the beginning of swimming class John can swim 4 laps. Starting after the first week, his swimming teacher wants him to swim 2 laps more than the week before until the end of the 7 week class. At this rate, how many laps will John be able to swim during the last week of class?

1 Read and Understand

Read the problem carefully.

You need to use the pattern to find the number of laps John can swim after a given number of weeks.

2 Make a Plan

Decide on a strategy to use.

One way to solve the problem is to make a table of values. Then extend the pattern until you find the answer.

3 Solve the Problem

Reread the problem and make a table.

First, make a table and enter the information given.

In week 1, John swims 4 laps. In week 2, he swims $4 + 2$, or 6 laps. Each week he swims 2 more laps.

You know that the swimming class is 7 weeks long, so extend your table following the pattern to fill it in.

ANSWER John will be swimming 16 laps during the last week of the 7 week class.

W (weeks)	A (laps)
1	4
2	6
3	8
4	10
5	12
6	14
7	?

4 Look Back

Compare the information in your table to the original problem to be sure you've used the information correctly.

Practice the Strategy

Use the strategy *make a table*.

1. **Diving** Copy and complete the table below representing the depth in feet of a deep-sea diver, currently 160 feet below the surface, ascending at a rate of 20 feet every 4 minutes.

Time (minutes)	4	8	12	16
Depth (feet)	?	?	?	?

2. **Training** Extend the table below using the pattern to find out how many miles you will run in week 10 of training for a race.

Week	1	2	3	4
Distance (miles)	3	3.5	4	4.5

3. **Hot-Air Balloon** A hot-air balloon has just taken off. The balloon is currently 10 feet off the ground and is rising at a rate of 2 feet per second. What is the height of the balloon after 25 seconds?

4. **Reading** You were assigned to read a book over your 2 week spring vacation. The book has 256 pages, so you decide to read 32 pages each day. At this rate when will you finish the book?

5. **DVD Players** Casey and Krystal are each saving money to buy a DVD player that costs $160. Casey already has $55 saved. He will add $7 every week to his fund. Krystal does not have any money saved. She will put $16 in her fund every week until she can afford it. Who will be able to purchase a DVD player first?

Mixed Problem Solving

Use any strategy to solve the problem.

6. **Number Sense** The cube of what number is 3375?

7. **Folding** You are trying to divide a sheet of paper into rectangles by folding it into thirds. You fold the paper 3 times into thirds without opening it. How many of the smallest rectangles do you have as a result? How many of the smallest rectangles will you have if you fold the paper into thirds one more time?

8. **Clothing** The sale price of a rack of sweaters is 80% of the original price. A month later, the sweaters sold for $23.20 each, which is two dollars less than 70% of the sale price. What is the original price of one of the sweaters?

9. **Running** Leslie and Todd each ran in a race. Leslie ran in the girls' 12–16 year old division on a 10 mile track and Todd ran in the boys' 10–12 year old division on an 8 mile track. Leslie came in second place with a time of 1 hour and 20 minutes. Todd came in first place with a time of 1 hour and 8 minutes. Who ran faster?

10. **Surface Area** Find the surface area of the solid shown below.

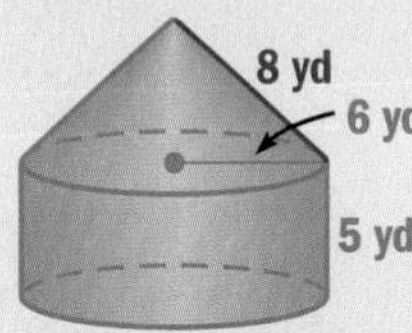

Graphs of Linear Equations

BEFORE	Now	WHY?
You found solutions of equations in two variables.	You'll learn to sketch the graph of a linear equation.	So you can find the amount you pay on a payment plan, as in Ex. 28.

linear equation, p. 556

INDIANA
Academic Standards

- Algebra and Functions (8.3.5, 8.3.7)

Activity **You can graph a function by plotting ordered pairs from a table of values.**

1 Copy and complete the table of values using the equation $y = 3x + 2$.

x	−4	−2	0	2	4
y	−10	?	2	?	?

2 Graph each ordered pair (x, y) in a coordinate plane.
$(-4, -10), (-2, ?), (0, 2), (2, ?), (4, ?)$

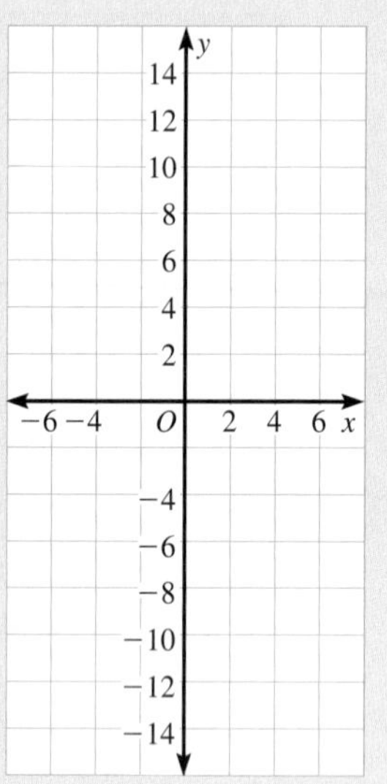

3 Connect the points. What pattern do you notice?

4 Find several more solutions of $y = 3x + 2$. Locate each solution in your coordinate plane. What do you notice?

5 Make a conjecture about the graph of all solutions of $y = 3x + 2$.

Linear Equations In the activity, you graphed solutions of a *linear equation.* A **linear equation** in two variables is an equation in which the variables appear in separate terms and each variable occurs only to the first power. The graph of a linear equation is a line.

Linear equations	**Not linear equations**
$y = x - 1$	$24 = rt$
$3p + 5q = 16$	$a^2 + b^2 = c^2$
$s = 0.2t$	

The equation $24 = rt$ is not linear because it has two variables in the same term. The equation $a^2 + b^2 = c^2$ is not linear because the variables are squared.

with Solving

The arrowheads on the graph in Example 1 indicate that the line extends forever in both directions.

EXAMPLE 1 Graphing a Linear Equation

Graph $y = \frac{1}{2}x + 1$.

Solution

1. Choose several x-values and make a table of values.

x	−4	−2	0	2	4
y	−1	0	1	2	3

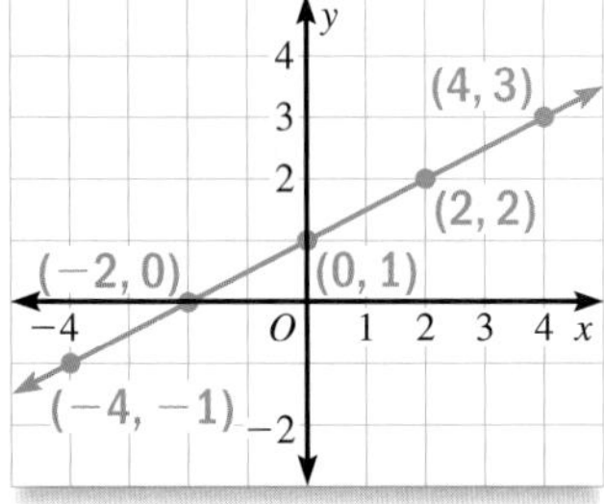

2. List the solutions as ordered pairs.

   (−4, −1), (−2, 0), (0, 1), (2, 2), (4, 3)

3. Graph the ordered pairs. Then draw a line through them.

ANSWER The line is the graph of $y = \frac{1}{2}x + 1$.

Your turn now **Graph the linear equation.**

1. $y = x + 4$ **2.** $y = -2x - 3$ **3.** $y = \frac{1}{2}x - 7$ **4.** $y - x = 6$

What do you think? **Biology**

Hair Growth

If human hair grows at a rate of $\frac{1}{2}$ inch per month, how much does your hair grow in one year? in one and a half years?

EXAMPLE 2 Using the Graph of a Linear Equation

Hair Sue's hair is 3 inches long. If her hair grows $\frac{1}{2}$ inch per month, you can model the length l of her hair in inches using the equation $l = \frac{1}{2}m + 3$ where m is the time in months.

a. Graph $l = \frac{1}{2}m + 3$.

b. Estimate how many months it will take Sue to grow her hair to $5\frac{1}{2}$ inches.

Solution

a. Make a table of values.

m	0	1	2	3
l	3	$3\frac{1}{2}$	4	$4\frac{1}{2}$

Then graph each solution and draw a ray through the points.

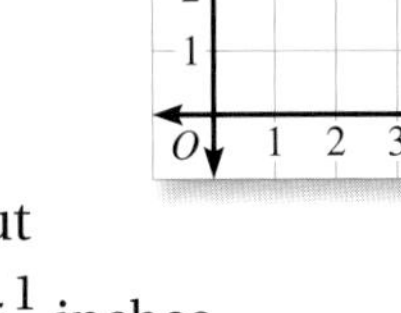

b. The graph shows that it will take about 5 months for Sue to grow her hair to $5\frac{1}{2}$ inches.

Vertical and Horizontal Lines Some linear equations have only one variable. The graphs of these equations are vertical or horizontal lines.

Vertical and Horizontal Lines

The graph of $x = a$ is the vertical line passing through $(a, 0)$.

The graph of $y = b$ is the horizontal line passing through $(0, b)$.

Watch Out! A vertical line *does not* represent a function, because one input has infinitely many outputs. A horizontal line *does* represent a function.

EXAMPLE 3 Graphing Vertical and Horizontal Lines

a. The graph of $x = -2$ is the vertical line through $(-2, 0)$.

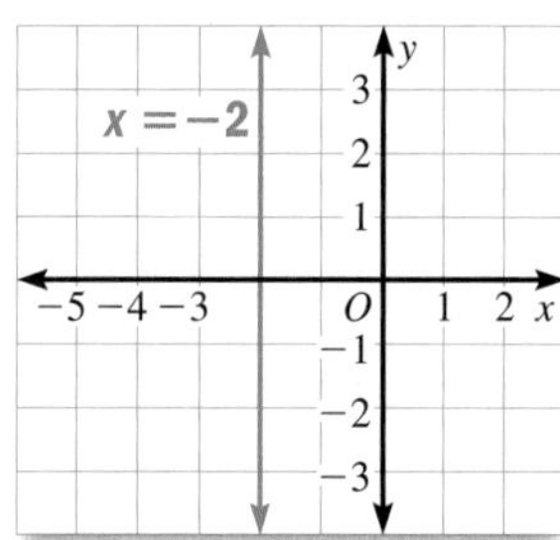

For all values of y, the x-value is -2.

b. The graph of $y = 4$ is the horizontal line through $(0, 4)$.

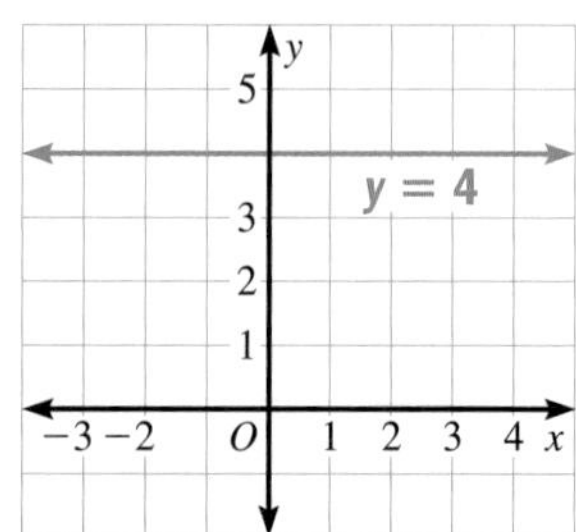

For all values of x, the y-value is 4.

11.4 Exercises

More Practice, p. 737

Getting Ready to Practice

1. Vocabulary Copy and complete: When you graph the solutions of a linear equation, the points form a(n) _?_.

Make a table of values for the equation.

2. $3x - y = -2$ **3.** $y + 4 = 0$ **4.** $-6x + 2y = 16$

Match the equation with the description of its graph.

5. $y = -16$ **6.** $x = 20$ **7.** $y = x + 1$

A. vertical line **B.** horizontal line **C.** slanted line

Practice and Problem Solving

with Homework

Example	Exercises
1	14-25
2	28
3	14-27, 29

CLASSZONE.COM

- More Examples
- eTutorial Plus

Tell whether the equation is a linear equation.

8. $3x + y = 8$ **9.** $2y - 5x = 10$ **10.** $9x^2 = y + 4$

Find three ordered pairs that are solutions of the given equation.

11. $y = x - 2$ **12.** $y = 3x + 4$ **13.** $y = 6$

Graph the linear equation.

14. $y = x + 9$ **15.** $y = x + 10$ **16.** $y = x - 14$

17. $y = 8x$ **18.** $y = -2x + 1$ **19.** $y = -7x + 8$

20. $y = -5x - 6$ **21.** $y = \frac{1}{2}x + 5$ **22.** $y = -\frac{1}{4}x + 12$

23. $y = 9$ **24.** $x = 8$ **25.** $x = -17$

Critical Thinking **Write the equation of the line.**

26.

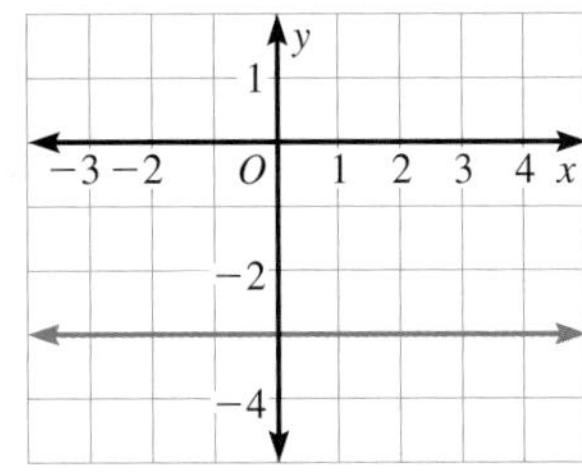

27.

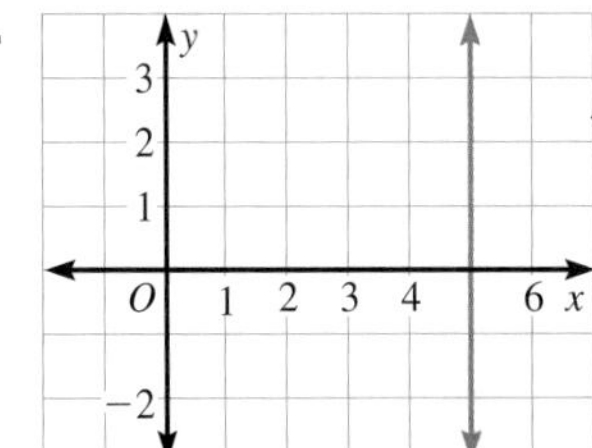

28. Buying a Camera You are taking a photography class and need a digital camera. The payment plan for the camera can be modeled by the equation $C = 10m + 50$, where C is the total amount paid and m is the number of months. Graph the equation and then estimate how much you pay in 12 months.

29. Critical Thinking Graph the equations $x = -3$ and $y = 5$ on the same coordinate grid. Then write the coordinates of the point where the lines intersect. Explain how you can find the coordinates of this point without graphing.

Graph the linear equation.

30. $x - y = 0$ **31.** $10x = -2y$ **32.** $16x - 4y = 8$

33. $9x + 3y = 18$ **34.** $x - 5y = -5$ **35.** $3x - 2y = 6$

36. Savings Account Janet is saving money for a vacation. She has \$80 saved and plans to add \$15.50 to her savings each month. The equation $y = 15.50x + 80$, where y is the amount of money Janet has saved and x is the number of months, models this situation. Make a table of values and graph the equation. Use your graph to estimate when Janet will have \$250.

37. Write the equation of the horizontal line that passes through point A.

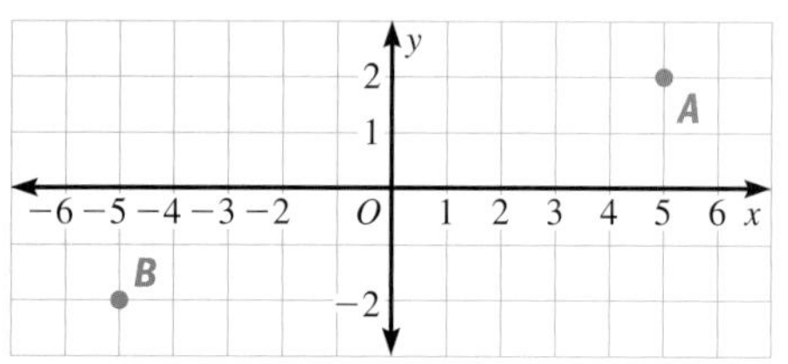

38. Write the equation of the vertical line that passes through point B.

39. **Writing** Explain how to find the equation of a line that is parallel to the x-axis and lies 8.6 units below it.

40. **Challenge** Copy and complete the table for the equation $y = x^2$. Then graph the equation. How can you tell that $y = x^2$ is not a linear equation from looking at the graph? How can you tell from the equation that it is not a linear equation?

x	−2	−1	0	1	2
y	?	?	0	?	?

Mixed Review

Find the area of the parallelogram with height h and base b. *(Lesson 10.1)*

41. $h = 10, b = 14$ **42.** $h = 17, b = 23$ **43.** $h = 32, b = 33$

44. Decide whether the relation is a function: (0, 0), (1, −1), (−1, −1), (2, −2). *(Lesson 11.1)*

45. Copy and complete the table for the equation $6x - 2y = 4$. *(Lesson 11.3)*

x	−4	−2	0	1	2	5
y	?	?	−2	?	?	?

Basic Skills **Solve the equation.**

46. $-8n = -240$ **47.** $\frac{x}{6} = -42$ **48.** $\frac{z}{12} = 4$

Test-Taking Practice

INTERNET
State Test Practice
CLASSZONE.COM

49. **Multiple Choice** Which equation is not linear?

A. $y = \frac{1}{2}x + 6$ **B.** $2x + 3y = 6$ **C.** $y = x^2 - 6$ **D.** $2x = 6 - 3y$

50. **Short Response** The monthly charge for a local cell phone calling plan can be modeled by the linear equation $C = 0.05t + 5.95$, where C is the total monthly cost in dollars and t is the number of minutes used per month. Make a table of values and graph the equation.

11.4 Technology Activity

GRAPHING CALCULATOR

INDIANA: Academic Standards
- Algebra and Functions (8.3.5)

Graphing Linear Functions

GOAL Use a graphing calculator to graph linear functions.

Example **Graph the equation $x - 2y = 6$.**

Solution

1 Rewrite the equation so that it is in function form: $y = \frac{1}{2}x - 3$.

2 Use the following keystrokes on a graphing calculator to enter the function:

Keystrokes

Display

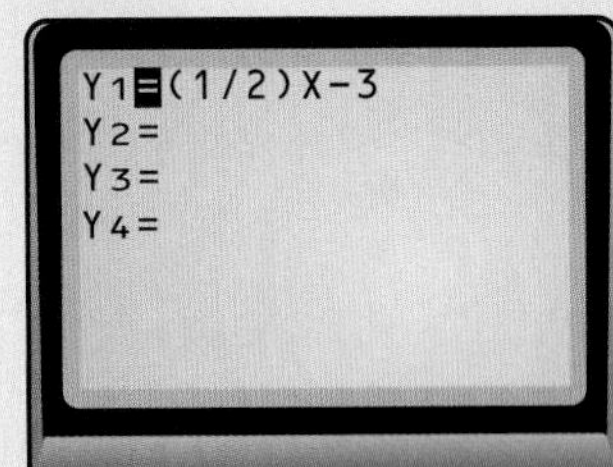

Use the WINDOW feature to set the size of the graph.

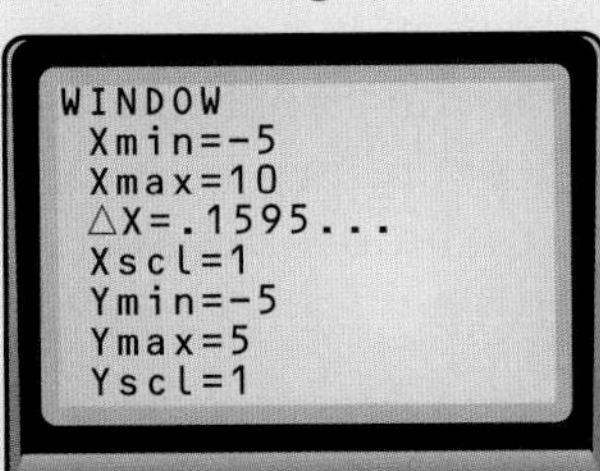

View the graph by pressing the GRAPH button.

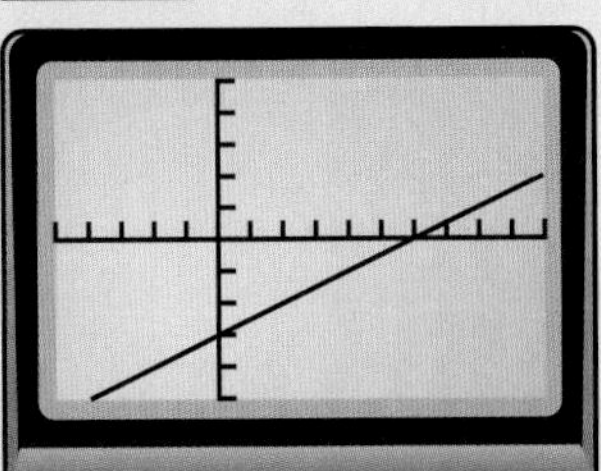

Your turn now **Use a calculator to graph the equation.**

1. $y = 2x - 5$ **2.** $y = 5x + 10$ **3.** $x - y = 11$ **4.** $x + y = 6$

Tell whether the viewing window is appropriate for the graph of the equation. If not, give an appropriate window for it.

5. $y = 4x + 5$

```
Xmin=-5
Xmax=5
△X=.1063...
Ymin=-5
Ymax=5
```

6. $y = 2x + 14$

```
Xmin=-5
Xmax=5
△X=.1063...
Ymin=-5
Ymax=5
```

Notebook Review

Review the vocabulary definitions in your notebook.

Copy the review examples in your notebook. Then complete the exercises.

Check Your Definitions

relation, p. 541
input, p. 541
output, p. 541
function, p. 541
domain, p. 542
range, p. 542
scatter plot, p. 545
solution of an equation in two variables, p. 549
linear equation, p. 556

Use Your Vocabulary

1. Vocabulary Copy and complete: Two ways to represent a relation are writing the ordered pairs and using a(n) _?_.

11.1–11.2 Can you write and plot a function rule?

EXAMPLE Write a function rule that relates x and y. Then make a scatter plot of the data.

Input x	−1	0	1	2
Output y	−6	−5	−4	−3

ANSWER Because each output is 5 less than the corresponding input, a rule for this function is $y = x - 5$. In the scatter plot, the y-coordinates increase as the x-coordinates increase. So the quantities have a positive relationship.

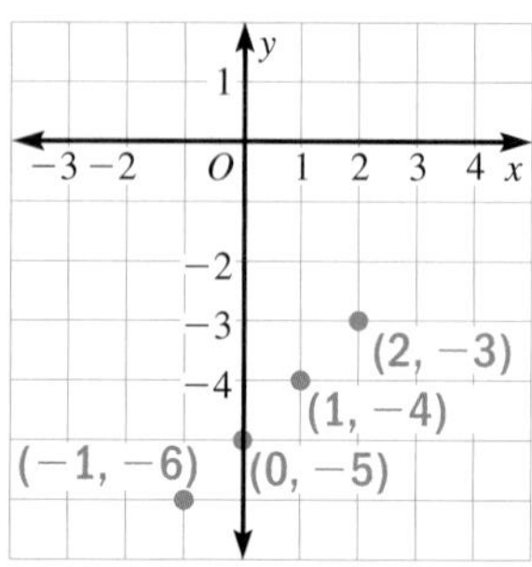

Write a function rule that relates x and y.

2.

x	−2	−1	0	1	2
y	8	4	0	−4	−8

3.

x	−6	−3	0	3	6
y	−3	0	3	6	9

4. Make a scatter plot of the data. Describe the relationship.

x	1	1.5	2	2.5	3
y	10	15	20	25	30

11.3–11.4 Can you graph linear equations?

EXAMPLE Graph the equation $y = 2x + 1$.

Choose 3 values for x. Substitute each value into the equation and solve for y.

x-value	Substitute for x.	Solve for y.	Solution
$x = -1$	$y = 2(-1) + 1$	$y = -1$	$(-1, -1)$
$x = 0$	$y = 2(0) + 1$	$y = 1$	$(0, 1)$
$x = 1$	$y = 2(1) + 1$	$y = 3$	$(1, 3)$

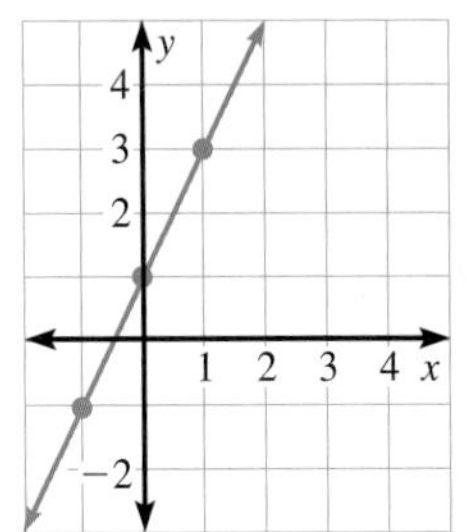

List three solutions of the equation and then graph it.

5. $2x + y = 5$ **6.** $-9x + 3y = -18$ **7.** $4y - x = 16$

Stop and Think about Lessons 11.1–11.4

8. Writing The ordered pair (2, 3) is a solution of $8 = 2y + x$. It is also a solution of $4y = -2x + 16$. Explain why every solution of $8 = 2y + x$ is also a solution of $4y = -2x + 16$.

Review Quiz 1

1. Make a table of values for $y = -\frac{1}{3}x$. Use a domain of 0, 1, 2, and 3. Identify the range.

2. Is $(5, -4)$ a solution of the equation $x - 6y = 29$?

List three solutions of the equation and then graph it.

3. $7y + x = 21$ **4.** $-5x - 2y = -20$ **5.** $-3x + 9y = -18$

Write a function rule that relates x and y.

6. $(-2, 0), (-1, 1), (0, 2), (1, 3), (2, 4)$

7. $(-3, -5), (0, 1), (3, 7), (6, 13), (9, 19)$

8. Fundraising An art club raised \$120 for supplies by selling pottery made by students. Mugs cost \$4 and bowls cost \$2. Make an input-output table and a graph for the equation $4x + 2y = 120$, where x is the number of mugs sold and y is the number of bowls sold. Suppose the art club sold 20 mugs. How many bowls did it sell?

Using Intercepts

BEFORE	Now	WHY?
You graphed linear equations.	You'll find x- and y-intercepts of a line.	So you can find the number of CDs you can buy, as in Ex. 4.

x-intercept, p. 564
y-intercept, p. 564

INDIANA Academic Standards

- Algebra and Functions (8.3.5)

Intercepts The **x-intercept** of a graph is the x-coordinate of the point where the graph crosses the x-axis. The graph of $2x + 3y = 12$ crosses the x-axis at (6, 0), so its x-intercept is 6.

The **y-intercept** is the y-coordinate of the point where the graph intersects the y-axis. The graph of $2x + 3y = 12$ crosses the y-axis at (0, 4), so its y-intercept is 4.

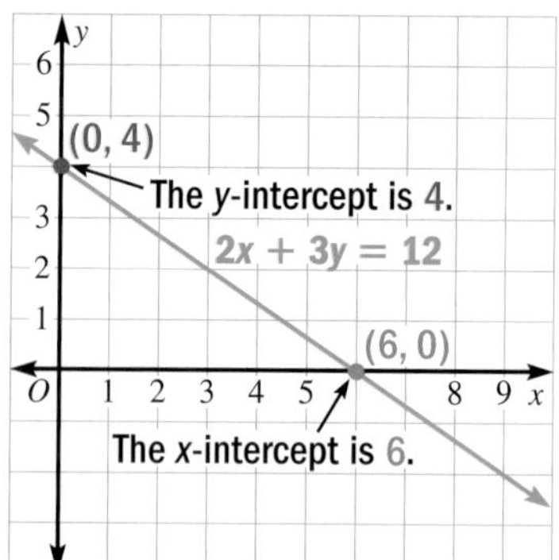

Finding Intercepts

To find the x-intercept of a line, substitute 0 for y into the equation and solve for x.

To find the y-intercept of a line, substitute 0 for x into the equation and solve for y.

EXAMPLE 1 Finding Intercepts

Find the intercepts of the graph of $y = \frac{1}{2}x - 5$.

To find the x-intercept, let $y = 0$ and solve for x.

$$y = \frac{1}{2}x - 5$$
$$0 = \frac{1}{2}x - 5$$
$$5 = \frac{1}{2}x$$
$$10 = x$$

To find the y-intercept, let $x = 0$ and solve for y.

$$y = \frac{1}{2}x - 5$$
$$y = \frac{1}{2}(0) - 5$$
$$y = 0 - 5$$
$$y = -5$$

ANSWER The x-intercept is 10 and the y-intercept is -5. The graph of the equation contains the points (10, 0) and (0, -5).

Graphing The intercepts tell you the points where a line intersects the x-axis and the y-axis. You can use these points to graph a line.

EXAMPLE 2 Using Intercepts to Graph a Line

HELP with Notetaking

Be sure to write down in your notebook that the intercepts of a line are numbers, not points.

Graph the line with an x-intercept of -3 and a y-intercept of 2.

The x-intercept is -3, so plot the point $(-3, 0)$. The y-intercept is 2, so plot the point $(0, 2)$.

Draw a line through the two points.

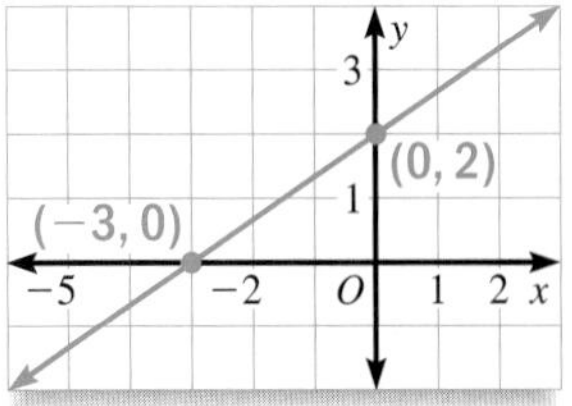

Your turn now **Find the intercepts of the graph of the equation. Then graph the line using the intercepts.**

1. $5x + 3y = 18$
2. $-2x + y = -10$
3. $3x + y = -1$

EXAMPLE 3 Using and Interpreting Intercepts

Fitness Pamela runs and walks with her dog on a trail that is 8 miles long. She can run 4 miles per hour and walk 2 miles per hour. Graph the equation $4x + 2y = 8$, where x is the number of hours running and y is the number of hours walking. What do the intercepts represent?

Solution

(1) Find the x-intercept.

To find the x-intercept, let $y = 0$ and solve for x.

$$4x + 2y = 8$$
$$4x + 2(0) = 8$$
$$4x = 8$$
$$x = 2$$

(2) Find the y-intercept.

To find the y-intercept, let $x = 0$ and solve for y.

$$4x + 2y = 8$$
$$4(0) + 2y = 8$$
$$2y = 8$$
$$y = 4$$

(3) The x-intercept is 2 and the y-intercept is 4. So the points $(2, 0)$ and $(0, 4)$ are on the graph. Plot these points and draw a line through them.

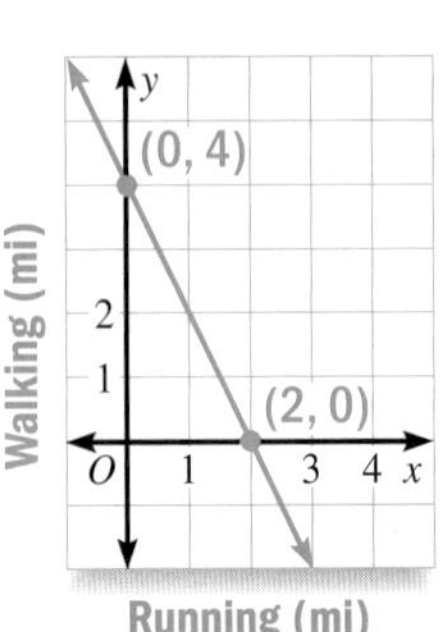

ANSWER The x-intercept represents how many hours it would take if Pamela runs the entire time. The y-intercept represents how many hours it would take if Pamela walks the entire time.

11.5 Exercises

More Practice, p. 737

Getting Ready to Practice

1. **Vocabulary** Copy and complete: A line passes through the points (3, 0) and (0, 5). So, the _?_ is 5 and the _?_ is 3.

Identify the x-intercept and the y-intercept.

2. 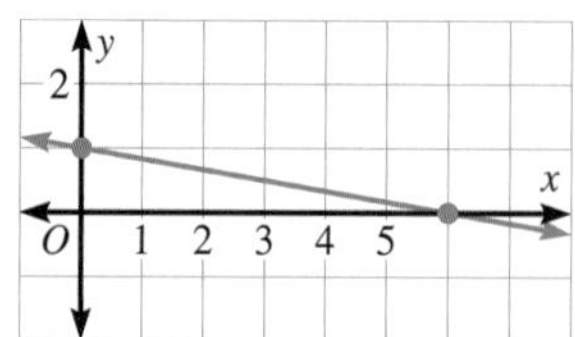

3. 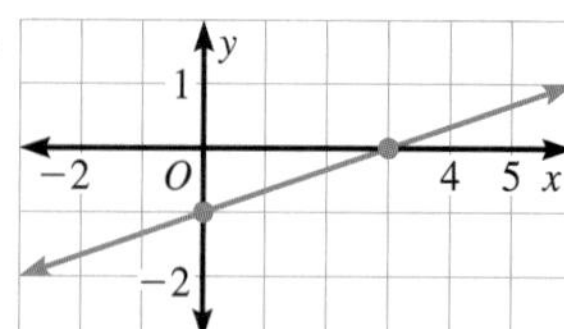

4. **Guided Problem Solving** You have \$60 to spend. CDs are \$12 each and videos are \$10 each. The number of each item you can buy is modeled by the equation $12x + 10y = 60$. Graph the equation and explain what the intercepts represent.

   (1 Find the intercepts.

   (2 Graph the equation.

   (3 Decide what x and y represent in the equation. Explain what the intercepts represent.

Practice and Problem Solving

HELP with Homework

Example	Exercises
1	5-10
2	11-13
3	14

· More Examples
· eTutorial Plus

Find the intercepts of the graph of the equation.

5. $y = 6x - 3$
6. $y = 2x + 4$
7. $y = 5x + 10$
8. $x + 9y = 18$
9. $4x + 5y = 20$
10. $7x - 9y = -63$

Graph the line that has the given intercepts.

11. x-intercept: 9
    y-intercept: 4
12. x-intercept: -3
    y-intercept: 1
13. x-intercept: 6
    y-intercept: -10

14. **Riding the Bus** You are riding the bus home from school. After x minutes, the number of miles from home y is given by $2x + 3y = 18$. Find the intercepts. Then graph the equation. What do the intercepts represent?

15. **Critical Thinking** If the x-intercept of a line is positive and the y-intercept is negative, does the line slant up or down from left to right? Explain your reasoning.

Find the intercepts of the graph of the equation.

16. $y = 9$
17. $y = 14$
18. $x = 21$

Graph the equation using intercepts.

19. $y = 5x - 15$
20. $y = -2.5x + 6.5$
21. $8x + 10y = 30$
22. $y = \frac{1}{2}x + 1$
23. $y = -\frac{2}{3}x + 2$
24. $y = \frac{3}{4}x - \frac{1}{2}$

Find the intercepts of the graph of the equation. Round to the nearest hundredth.

25. $y = -2.14x + 3.65$
26. $y = 1.95x - 12.05$
27. $y = -4.12x - 15.01$
28. **Critical Thinking** What kind of line has no y-intercept?
29. **Investing** A bank offers a savings account at a 2% simple annual interest rate and a certificate of deposit at a 5% simple annual interest rate. You want to earn \$100 in interest the first year. The equation $0.02s + 0.05c = 100$ models the situation. Find the intercepts of the graph of the equation. What do they represent in terms of the situation?

Mixed Review

30. Evaluate the expression $\frac{6a^2b}{2ab^2}$ when $a = 9$ and $b = 4$. *(Lesson 4.3)*

Graph the equation. *(Lesson 11.4)*

31. $y = \frac{3}{4}x + 5$
32. $y = 2x - 6$
33. $y = -7x + 4$

Basic Skills **Use the formula $d = rt$ to find the rate.**

34. $d = 460$ mi, $t = 8$ h
35. $d = 720$ km, $t = 12$ h

Test-Taking Practice

INTERNET
State Test Practice
CLASSZONE.COM

36. **Multiple Choice** What is the y-intercept of the graph of $2x - y = 4$?

    A. -4 B. -1 C. 2 D. 4

37. **Short Response** Melissa needs to have a total of 10 prizes for a school contest. She has two choices: school T-shirts that come in orders of 4, and CD gift certificates that come in packs of 2. Melissa knows that the number of each prize group she can buy is represented by the equation $4x + 2y = 10$. Melissa graphs the line. What do the intercepts tell her about the prizes she can buy?

11.6 Hands-on Activity

INDIANA: Academic Standards
- Algebra and Functions (8.3.6)

GOAL
Understand slope as a measure of steepness.

MATERIALS
- pencil
- graph paper

Finding the Slope of a Line

You can describe the steepness of a line using its *slope*, or ratio of vertical change (rise) to horizontal change (run) in any two points on a line. You can find slope using the formula: $slope = \frac{rise}{run}$.

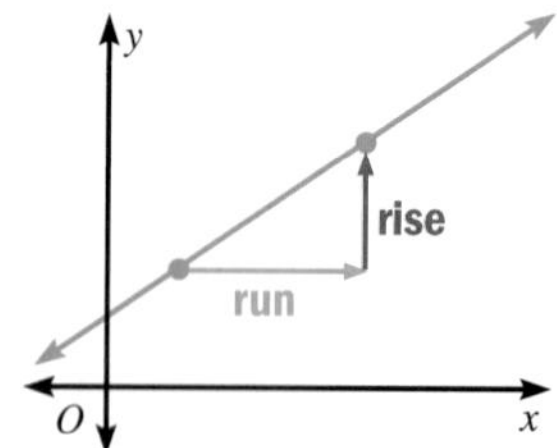

Explore 1 **Find the slope of the line passing through the points (2, 3) and (6, 5).**

1 Plot the points (2, 3) and (6, 5) on a coordinate grid. Using a straightedge draw a line through the points.

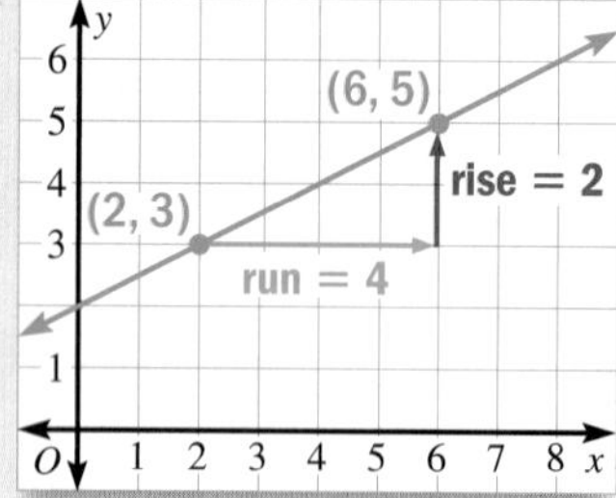

2 Find the rise. Then find the run. Substitute for rise and run in the formula for slope.

$$\text{slope} = \frac{\text{rise}}{\text{run}} = \frac{2}{4} = \frac{1}{2}$$

The slope of the line passing through the points (2, 3) and (6, 5) is $\frac{1}{2}$.

Your turn now **Use the formula for slope.**

1. Find the slope of the line passing through the points (−1, 1) and (−3, 5).
   (1 Plot the points (−1, 1) and (−3, 5) on a coordinate plane using graph paper. Then draw a line through the points.
   (2 Find the rise. Then find the run. Substitute for rise and run in the formula for slope.
2. Using the points (5, 6) and (−2, 3), what operation can you perform on the *y*-coordinates to find the rise? What operation can you perform on the *x*-coordinates to find the run?

Explore 2 Use two points to find the slope of a line.

1 Copy the graph.

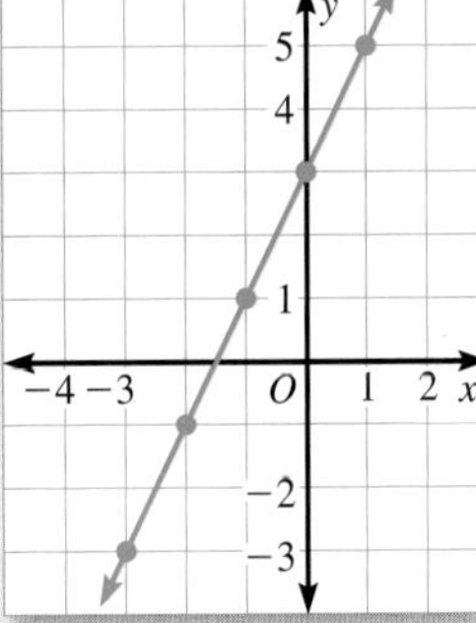

2 Choose two points on the line. Find the rise and run. Calculate the slope.

3 Choose a different pair of points on the line. Find the rise and run. Calculate the slope.

4 What pattern do you notice in your answers to Steps 2 and 3? Make a conjecture about the slope of a line.

Your turn now **Find the slope of the line passing through the points.**

3. $(1, 4), (4, 2)$
4. $(1, -3), (5, -2)$
5. $(-3, 4), (0, 6)$
6. $(7, 8), (-1, -5)$
7. $(-2, 6), (0, -3)$
8. $(-9, 3), (3, -9)$

9. If a line falls from left to right, what can you say about the rise and run?

10. If a line rises from left to right, what can you say about the rise and run?

11. Compare a line with slope greater than 1 to a line with slope between 0 and 1.

Find the slope of the line.

12.

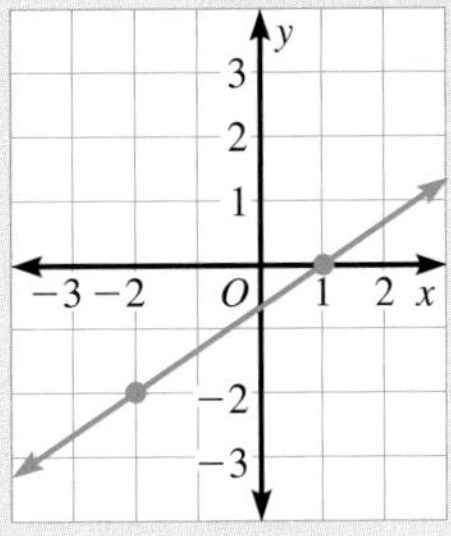

13.

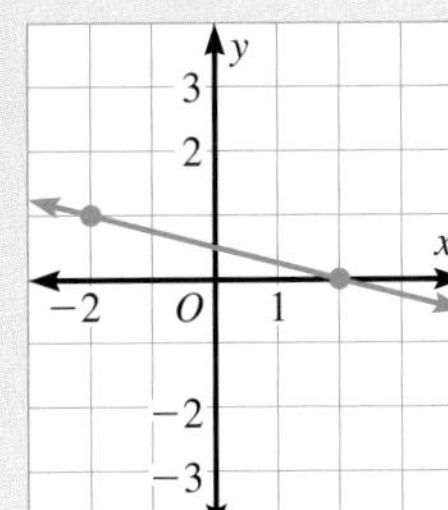

14.

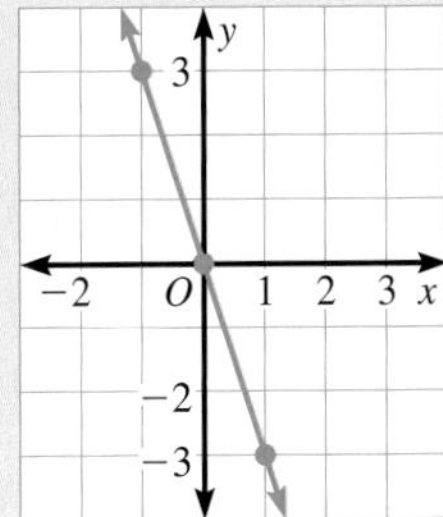

Stop and Think

15. **Challenge** What is the slope of the line passing through the points (a, b) and (c, d)?

Slope

BEFORE	Now	WHY?
You graphed linear equations.	You'll find and interpret slopes of lines.	So you can find the slope of the roof of a birdhouse, as in Ex. 9.

slope, p. 570
rise, p. 570
run, p. 570

INDIANA Academic Standards

- Algebra and Functions (8.3.6)

In the Real World

Cogwheel Railways The Mount Pilatus Railway in the Swiss Alps is the steepest cogwheel railway in the world. The track rises about 20 feet vertically for every 50 feet it runs horizontally. What is the steepness of the track?

You can describe steepness using *slope*. The **slope** of a nonvertical line is the ratio of its vertical change, called the **rise**, to its horizontal change, called the **run**.

EXAMPLE 1 Finding Slope

The diagram shows the rise and the run of the Mount Pilatus Railway.

$$\text{slope} = \frac{\text{rise}}{\text{run}} = \frac{\overset{2}{\cancel{20\text{ ft}}}}{\underset{5}{\cancel{50\text{ ft}}}} = \frac{2}{5}$$

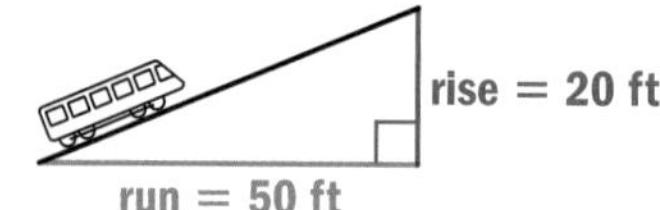

ANSWER The railway has a slope of $\frac{2}{5}$.

Slope of a Line

The slope m of a nonvertical line passing through the points (x_1, y_1) and (x_2, y_2) is

$$m = \frac{\text{rise}}{\text{run}} = \frac{y_2 - y_1}{x_2 - x_1}$$

The slope of a line is the same no matter which two points you choose to use in the formula.

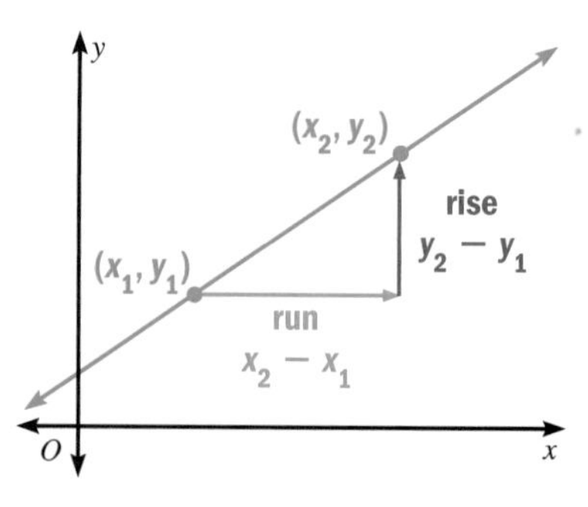

HELP with Vocabulary

The rise is the change in y and the run is the change in x.

EXAMPLE 2 Positive and Negative Slope

Find the slope of the line.

a.

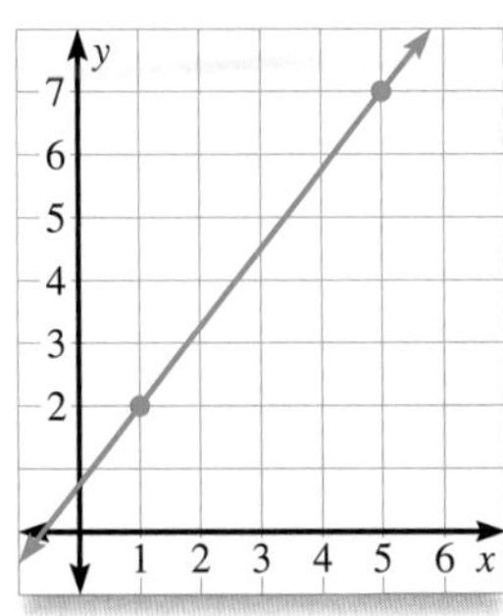

$$m = \frac{\text{rise}}{\text{run}} = \frac{y_2 - y_1}{x_2 - x_1}$$

$$= \frac{7 - 2}{5 - 1}$$

$$= \frac{5}{4}$$

ANSWER The slope is $\frac{5}{4}$.

b.

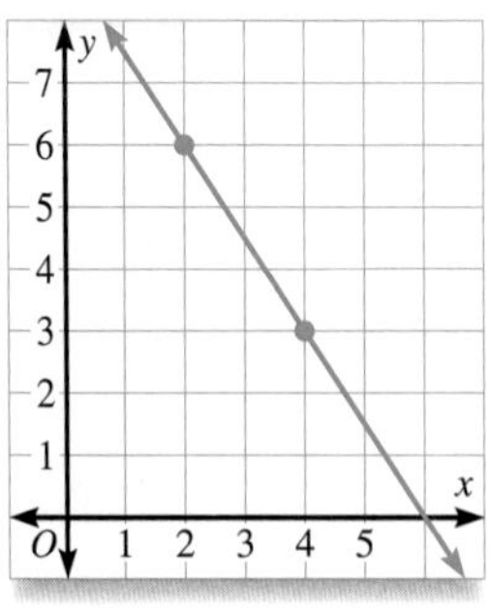

$$m = \frac{\text{rise}}{\text{run}} = \frac{y_2 - y_1}{x_2 - x_1}$$

$$= \frac{3 - 6}{4 - 2}$$

$$= \frac{-3}{2}, \text{ or } -\frac{3}{2}.$$

ANSWER The slope is $-\frac{3}{2}$.

HELP with Review

For help with subtracting integers, see p. 63.

Your turn now **Find the slope of the line passing through the points.**

1. (2, 1), (6, 4) **2.** (0, 6), (10, 0) **3.** (−3, −4), (5, 2)

EXAMPLE 3 Zero and Undefined Slope

Find the slope of the line.

a.

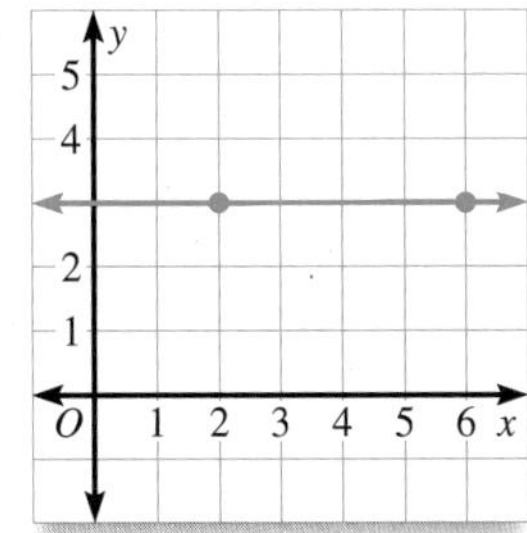

$$m = \frac{\text{rise}}{\text{run}} = \frac{y_2 - y_1}{x_2 - x_1}$$

$$= \frac{3 - 3}{6 - 2} = \frac{0}{4} = 0$$

ANSWER The slope is 0.

b.

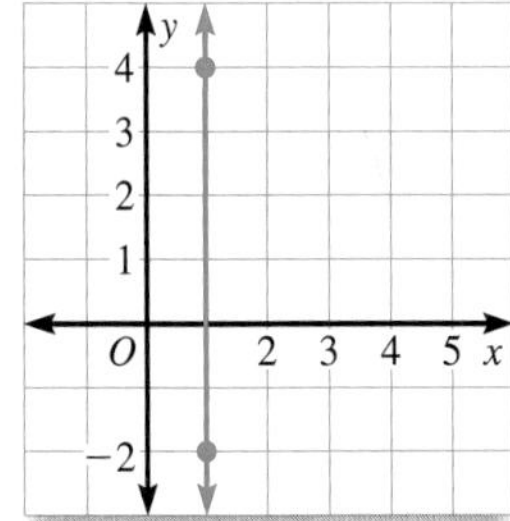

$$m = \frac{\text{rise}}{\text{run}} = \frac{y_2 - y_1}{x_2 - x_1}$$

$$= \frac{4 - (-2)}{1 - 1} = \frac{6}{0}$$

ANSWER The slope is undefined.

Watch Out!

When finding the slope of a line, make sure that you are using the *x*- and *y*-coordinates in the same order.

Summary of Slope

A line with *positive* slope rises from left to right.

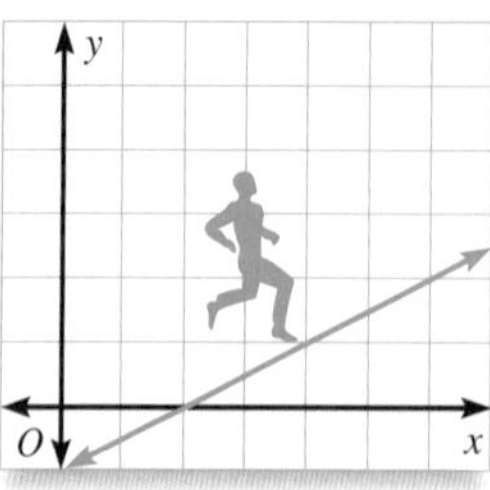

A line with *negative* slope falls from left to right.

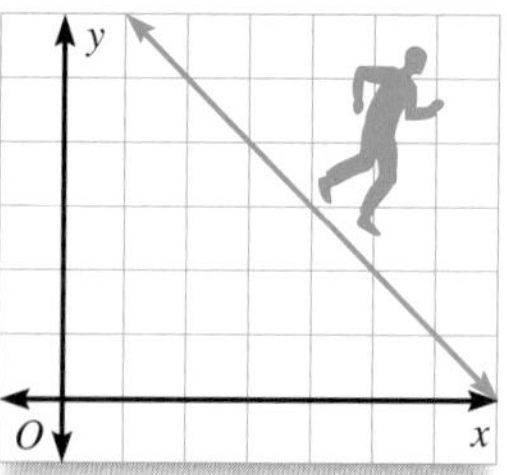

A line with *zero* slope is horizontal.

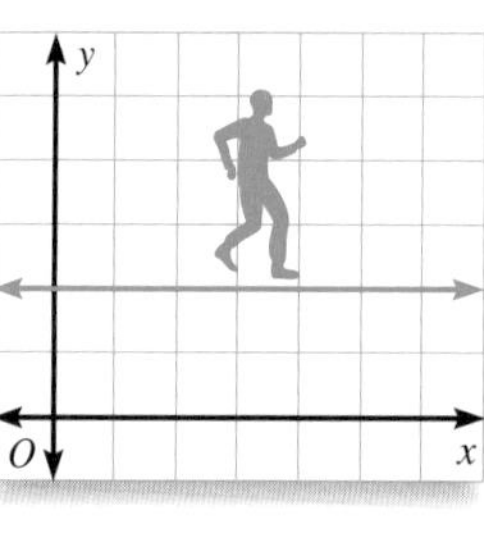

A line with *undefined* slope is vertical.

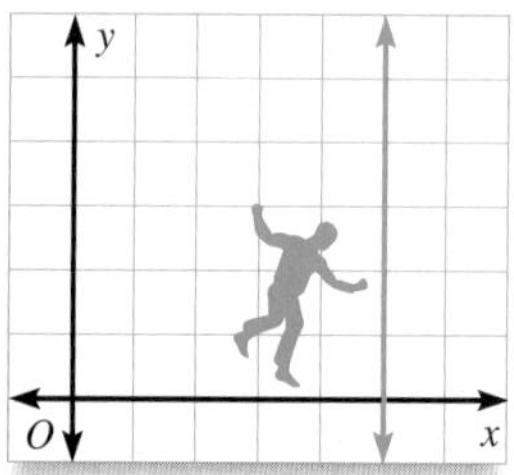

11.6 Exercises

More Practice, p. 737

Getting Ready to Practice

Vocabulary Copy and complete the statement.

1. The change in the y-coordinates is called the _?_.
2. The change in the x-coordinates is called the _?_.

Sketch a line with the given type of slope.

3. negative
4. undefined
5. positive
6. zero

Birdhouse Use the red line on the diagram of a birdhouse.

7. What is the rise of the roof?
8. What is the run of the roof?
9. What is the slope of the roof?

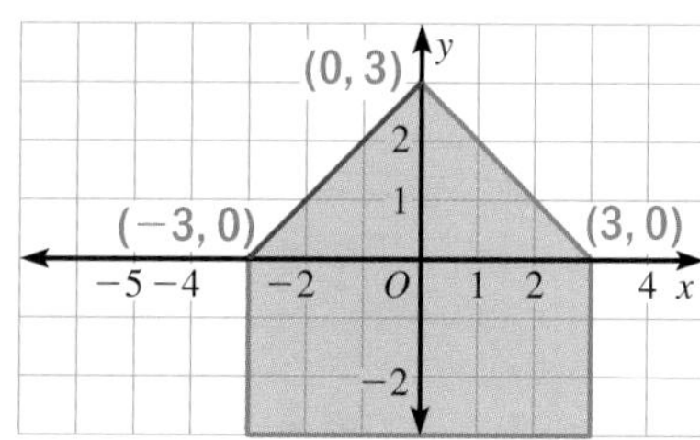

Practice and Problem Solving

with Homework

Example	Exercises
1	26
2	10-26
3	10-25

Online Resources
CLASSZONE.COM

- More Examples
- eTutorial Plus

Write the coordinates of the two points on the line. Then find the slope.

10. 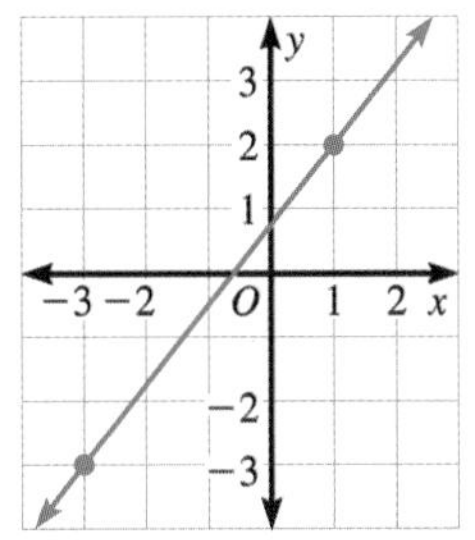

11. 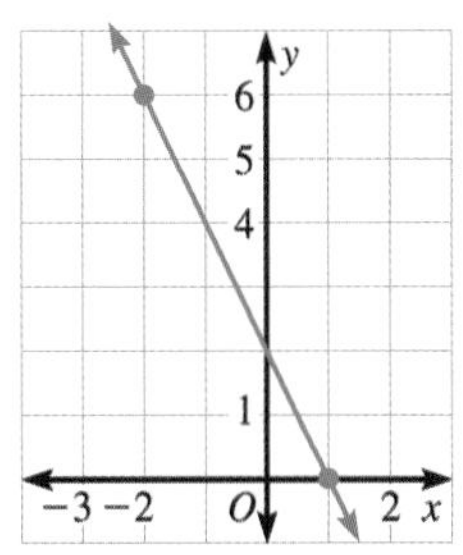

12. 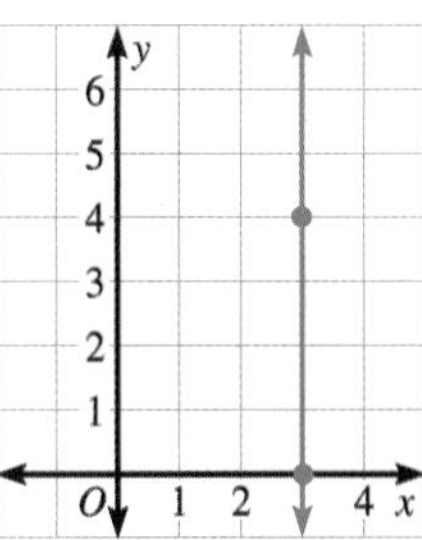

Find the slope of the line passing through the points.

13. $(-4, 8), (6, 6)$ **14.** $(1, 4), (1, -7)$ **15.** $(-2, -4), (4, 2)$

16. $(-5, 4), (3, 4)$ **17.** $(5, 8), (0, 5)$ **18.** $(-3, 1), (-3, -2)$

19. $(-6, -2), (6, -7)$ **20.** $(9, -8), (15, -8)$ **21.** $(12, 22), (-20, 19)$

The three points are vertices of a triangle. Plot and connect the points. Then find the slope of each side of the triangle.

22. $A(0, 0), B(0, 8), C(6, 0)$ **23.** $D(-3, 4), E(4, 1), F(-1, -7)$

24. $G(0, 6), H(4, 0), J(-4, 0)$ **25.** $K(-5, 1), L(-1, -4), M(-2, 4)$

26. **Tides** The pictures show a floating dock at low and high tide. Find the slopes of the ramp in both pictures. Is the ramp steeper at high tide or at low tide?

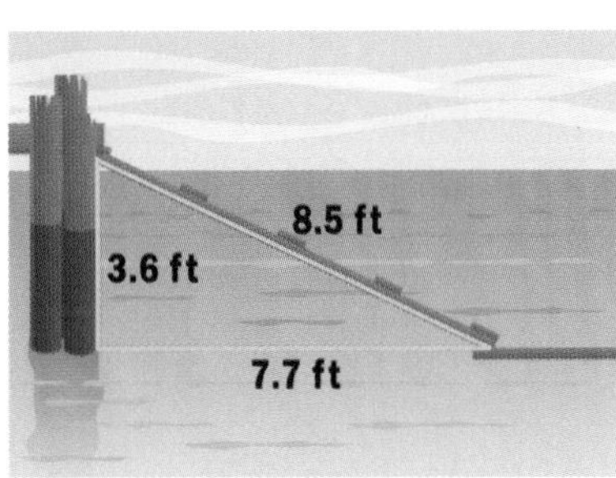

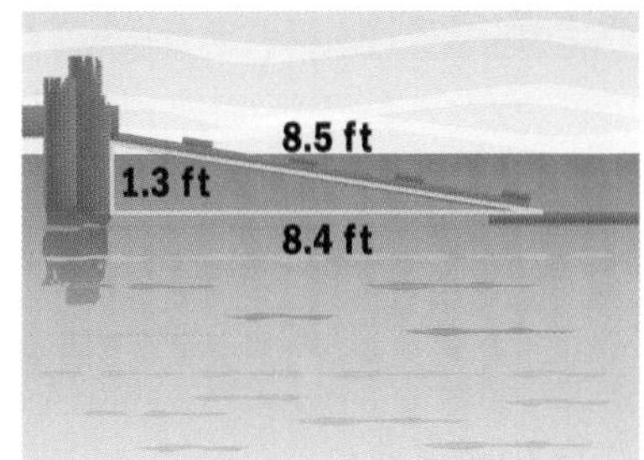

27. **Writing** One line passes through the points $M(1, 1)$ and $N(3, 4)$ and another line passes through the points $P(2, 5)$ and $Q(5, 8)$. Which line has a greater slope? Explain how you can tell by graphing the two lines. Explain how you can tell by calculating the slopes of the lines.

28. **Algebra** A line contains the points (p, q) and $(p + 2, q + 2)$. Find the slope of the line.

29. **Critical Thinking** When you have selected two points on a line to find its slope, does it matter which is (x_1, y_1) and which is (x_2, y_2)? Explain. Give examples to justify your reasoning.

30. **Ski Jump** A ski slope has a starting altitude of 2800 meters and an ending altitude of 1886 meters. The length of the ski slope is about 3299 meters. What is the approximate slope of the ski slope? Round to the nearest hundredth.

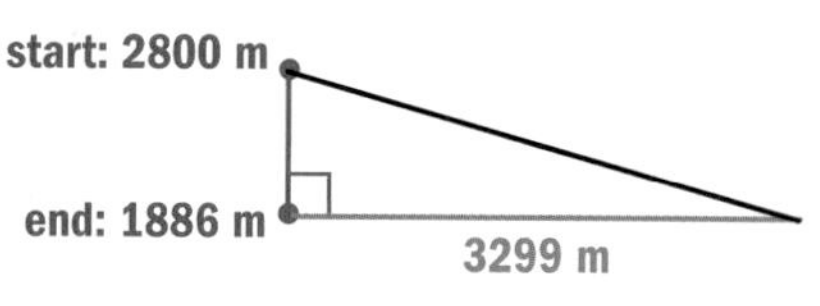

Challenge Find the missing value(s) using the given slope and points.

31. $m = \frac{7}{4}$ and $(x, -7)$, $(16, 0)$

32. $m = 0$ and $(0, 7)$, $(3, y)$

33. $m = \frac{1}{2}$ and $(0, 0)$, $(x, 2)$, $(6, y)$

34. $m = -3$ and $(2, -6)$, $(x, 9)$, $(-1, y)$

Mixed Review

35. The table shows the number of runs scored in each inning of a seven-inning softball game. Make a scatter plot of the data. Tell whether the two quantities have a *positive relationship*, a *negative relationship*, or *no relationship*. (Lesson 11.2)

Inning	1	2	3	4	5	6	7
Runs	0	0	4	2	1	0	1

Tell whether the ordered pair is a solution of the equation $y = -x + 5$. (Lesson 11.3)

36. $(4, 1)$

37. $(-9, 14)$

38. $(10, 15)$

39. $(-31, -26)$

Basic Skills Solve the equation.

40. $-7r + 15 = 29$

41. $42 = \frac{t}{3} + 21$

42. $6s - 5 = 2s$

Test-Taking Practice

43. **Multiple Choice** What is the slope of the line shown in the graph?

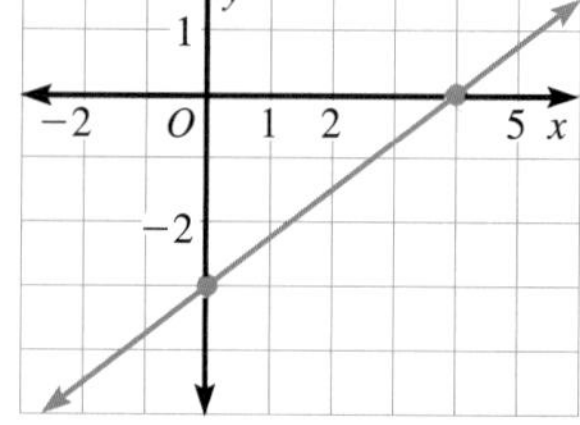

A. $-\frac{4}{3}$

B. $-\frac{3}{4}$

C. $\frac{3}{4}$

D. $\frac{4}{3}$

44. **Multiple Choice** A line passes through the points $(10, 0)$ and $(x, -5)$ and has a slope of $\frac{1}{2}$. What is the value of x?

F. -20

G. -5

H. 0

I. 5

11.7 Hands-on Activity

INDIANA: Academic Standards
- Algebra and Functions (8.3.6)

GOAL
Find how slope, *y*-intercept, and an equation can relate.

MATERIALS
- pencil
- graph paper

Slope-Intercept Form

You can find the slope and *y*-intercept of a line by looking at its equation in *slope-intercept form.*

Explore 1 Find the slope and *y*-intercept of $y = 4x + 3$.

1 Make a table of values for the equation $y = 4x + 3$.

x	0	1	2
y	3	7	11

2 Plot points and draw a line.

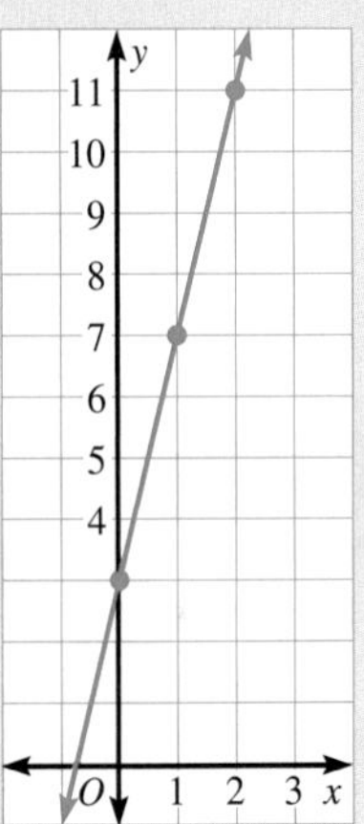

3 Use the graph to find the slope and *y*-intercept of $y = 4x + 3$.

slope $= \frac{4}{1} = 4$ *y*-intercept $= 3$

Your turn now Use a graph to answer Exercises 1–3.

1. Copy and complete the table of values for $y = -2x - 1$.

x	-1	0	1
y	?	?	?

2. Plot the points and draw a line.
3. Use the graph to find the slope and *y*-intercept.
4. Copy and complete the table.

Equation	Slope	*y*-intercept
$y = 4x + 3$	?	?
$y = -2x - 1$	?	?

Explore 2 **Find the slope and *y*-intercept of $y = 3x + 5$.**

1 Make a table of values for the equation $y = 3x + 5$.

x	1	2	3
y	8	11	14

2 Calculate the slope of the line from the points.

$$m = \frac{y_2 - y_1}{x_2 - x_1} = \frac{11 - 8}{2 - 1} = 3$$

3 Calculate the *y*-intercept by substitution.

$$y = 3x + 5 = 3(0) + 5 = 5$$

4 Add $y = 3x + 5$ to your table from Exercise 4.

5 Use your table to make a conjecture about using an equation of a line to find the slope and *y*-intercept of the line.

Your turn now **Graph the line using a table of values. Then use the graph to find the slope and *y*-intercept.**

5. $y = 5x - 7$ **6.** $y = -3x + 2$ **7.** $y = -\frac{2}{3}x - 6$ **8.** $y = \frac{5}{4}x + 1$

Solve the equation for *y*. Make a table of values for the equation. Calculate the slope and *y*-intercept.

9. $y + 2 = \frac{1}{2}x$ **10.** $3y = -2x + 9$ **11.** $y + 4x = -5$ **12.** $6x - 2y = 10$

13. Does your conjecture in Step 5 still seem to be true?

Stop and Think

14. What does m stand for in the equation $y = mx + b$? What does b stand for in the equation $y = mx + b$?

Slope-Intercept Form

BEFORE	Now	WHY?
You graphed equations using intercepts.	You'll write and graph equations in slope-intercept form.	So you can determine how many bracelets you must sell, as in Ex. 21.

slope-intercept form, p. 577

INDIANA Academic Standards

- Algebra and Functions (8.3.6)

In the Real World

Hiking You are hiking a trail on Mount Rainier in Washington. At the base of the trail, the temperature is 50.9°F. The temperature changes at a rate of −0.005°F per foot as you hike up. What equation can you use to find the temperature after you hike up 1000 feet?

One way to write an equation is to use *slope-intercept form.*

Slope-Intercept Form

Words The linear equation $y = mx + b$ is written in **slope-intercept form**. The slope is m. The y-intercept is b.

Algebra $y = mx + b$ **Numbers** $y = 3x + 2$

For help with rewriting equations, see p. 549.

EXAMPLE 1 Identifying Slopes and y-Intercepts

Find the slope and y-intercept of the line.

a. $y = x - 3$ **b.** $-4x + 2y = 16$

Solution

a. The equation $y = x - 3$ can be written as $y = 1x + (-3)$.

ANSWER The line has a slope of 1 and a y-intercept of -3.

b. Write the equation $-4x + 2y = 16$ in slope-intercept form.

$-4x + 2y = 16$ Write original equation.

$2y = 4x + 16$ Add $4x$ to each side.

$y = 2x + 8$ Divide each side by 2.

ANSWER The line has a slope of 2 and a y-intercept of 8.

EXAMPLE 2 Graphing Using Slope-Intercept Form

Graph the equation $y = \frac{1}{2}x + 3$.

Solution

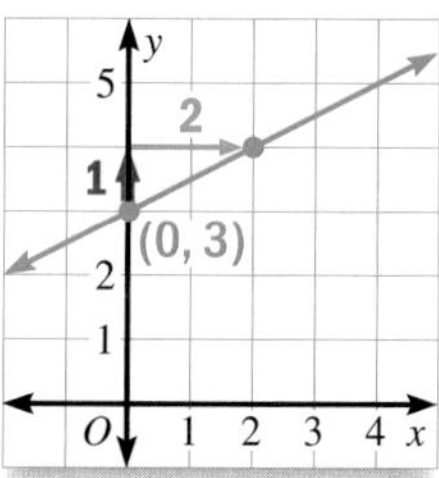

1. The y-intercept is 3, so plot the point (0, 3).
2. The slope is $\frac{1}{2}$, so plot a second point by moving up 1 unit and right 2 units.
3. Draw a line through the points.

Your turn now **Find the slope and y-intercept of the graph of the equation. Then graph the equation.**

1. $y = 2x + 5$ **2.** $-x + y = 6$ **3.** $y = \frac{1}{4}x$

EXAMPLE 3 Using Slope-Intercept Form

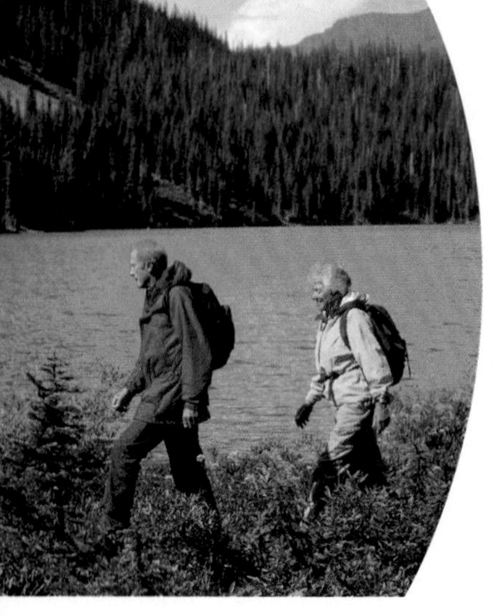

To answer the question on page 577, you can write an equation in slope-intercept form to find the temperature after hiking up 1000 feet.

Solution

1. Write a verbal model.

2. Write an algebraic model in slope-intercept form.

The temperature changes at a rate of -0.005°F per foot, so $m = -0.005$. The initial temperature is 50.9°F, so $b = 50.9$. Let y be the temperature and x be the change in altitude.

$y = mx + b$ **Write slope-intercept form.**

$y = -0.005x + 50.9$ **Substitute -0.005 for m and 50.9 for b.**

3. To find the temperature after hiking up 1000 feet, find the value of y when $x = 1000$.

$y = -0.005x + 50.9$ **Write the equation.**

$= -0.005 \cdot (1000) + 50.9$ **Substitute 1000 for x.**

$= 45.9$ **Simplify.**

ANSWER The temperature after hiking up 1000 feet is 45.9°F.

11.7 Exercises

More Practice, p. 737

INTERNET
eWorkbook Plus
CLASSZONE.COM

Getting Ready to Practice

1. **Vocabulary** Identify the slope and y-intercept of the graph of the equation $y = -5x + 7$.

Rewrite the equation in slope-intercept form.

2. $x - y = -2$
3. $2x = y + 5$
4. $8x - 4y = 32$

Find the slope and y-intercept of the graph of the equation.

5. $y = x + 3$
6. $y = 6 - x$
7. $1 = 2x - y$
8. **Find the Error** Describe and correct the error made by a student while graphing the equation $y = -2x - 1$.

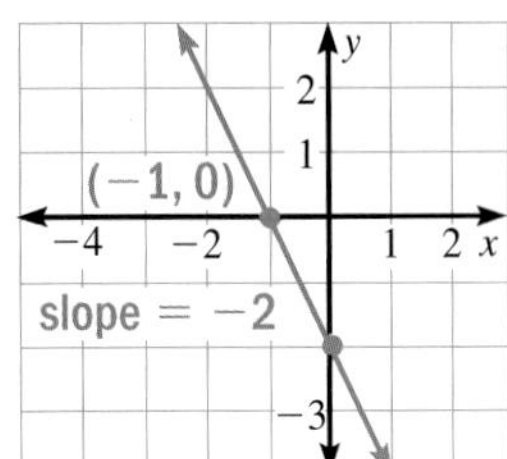

Practice and Problem Solving

HELP with Homework

Example	Exercises
1	9–20
2	9–14
3	21

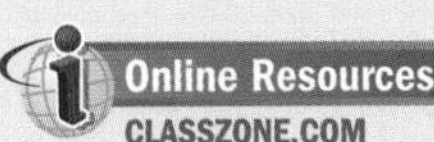

- More Examples
- eTutorial Plus

Find the slope and y-intercept of the graph of the equation. Then graph the equation.

9. $y = x - 8$
10. $y = 3$
11. $y = -x + 7$
12. $y = x - \frac{1}{2}$
13. $y = \frac{2}{3}x - 4$
14. $y = \frac{1}{5}x$

Rewrite in slope-intercept form. Then find the slope and y-intercept of the line.

15. $y = 10 - 6x$
16. $y - 9 = -\frac{3}{4}x$
17. $\frac{2}{3}x - y = 3$
18. $2y + 2x = 12$
19. $y + 12x = 0$
20. $13x - 11y = 143$
21. **Bracelets** You make and sell bracelets. You buy \$28 in supplies and sell the bracelets for \$3.50 each. Your profit can be modeled by $p = 3.50b - 28$ where p is the profit and b is the number of bracelets sold. Graph the equation. How many bracelets do you need to sell to make a profit?

Write the equation of the graph in slope-intercept form.

22. 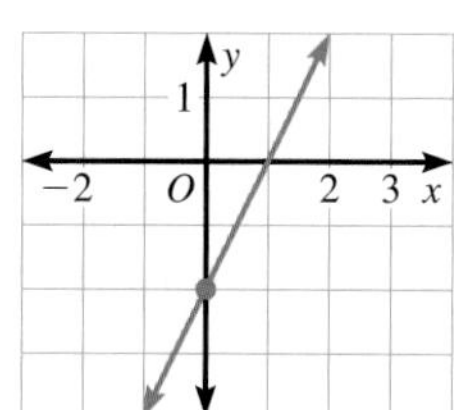

23. 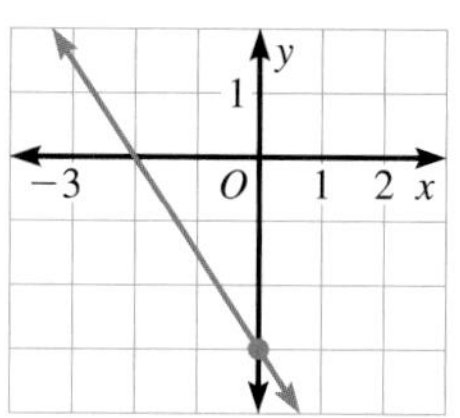

24. **Critical Thinking** Write the equations of two lines that have the same slope but different y-intercepts. Graph the lines. Do the lines appear to be *parallel, perpendicular,* or *neither*? Explain.

25. **Crickets** The number of chirps per minute made by a cricket can be modeled by the equation $c = 4t - 156$, where c is the number of chirps per minute and t is the temperature in degrees Fahrenheit. Graph the equation. What does the x-intercept mean in terms of the temperature and the number of chirps per minute?

26. **Critical Thinking** When two lines are perpendicular and neither has a slope of zero, the product of their slopes is -1. Write the equation of the line that is perpendicular to and has the same y-intercept as the line $y = 2x + 8$. Then graph both lines to check that they are perpendicular.

27. **Challenge** Write the equation $ax + by + c = 0$, where b is not equal to 0, in slope-intercept form.

Mixed Review 

Write the sentence as an inequality, letting x represent the variable. Then solve the inequality. *(Lesson 6.6)*

28. Six is less than a number plus 8.

29. Five times a number is greater than or equal to thirty-five.

Find the volume of the figure. *(Lessons 10.6, 10.7)*

30. A cylinder with radius 3 inches and height 7 inches

31. A pyramid with base area 25 square feet and height 9 feet

Basic Skills **Solve the inequality. Then graph its solution.**

32. $a + 3 \leq -7$

33. $8 < 2 + t$

34. $n - 4 > 7$

Test-Taking Practice 

INTERNET
State Test Practice
CLASSZONE.COM

35. **Extended Response** You and two friends decide to rent one canoe. It costs \$9 an hour to rent the canoe and \$12 for a ride back to the starting point. Graph the equation $c = 9h + 12$ to see the possible costs of renting a canoe. If the maximum amount that each of you wants to spend is \$16, for how many hours can you rent a canoe?

Systems of Equations

GOAL Solve systems of linear equations.

system of linear equations, p. 581
solution of a linear system, p. 581

INDIANA
Academic Standards

- Algebra and Functions (8.3.2)

A **system of linear equations** is a set of two or more linear equations with the same variables. A **solution of a linear system** is an ordered pair that is a solution of each equation in the system.

In the system of equations below, (**3**, **2**) is a solution.

System of equations	**Check**
$2x + 4y = 14$	$2(\mathbf{3}) + 4(\mathbf{2}) = 6 + 8 = 14$ ✓
$3x - 5y = -1$	$3(\mathbf{3}) - 5(\mathbf{2}) = 9 - 10 = -1$ ✓

If a system of linear equations has a solution, then the graphs of the equations intersect.

EXAMPLE 1 Solving a System of Equations by Graphing

Solve the linear system: $x + y = 5$ **Equation 1**

$y = 2x - 1$ **Equation 2**

Solution

1. Write each equation in slope-intercept form.

Equation 1	**Equation 2**
$x + y = 5$	$y = 2x - 1$
$y = -x + 5$	

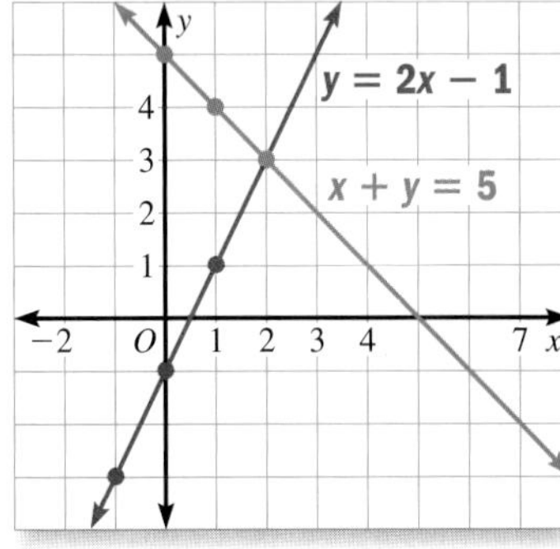

2. Graph both equations.
3. Estimate the point of intersection using the graph. It appears that the point of intersection is (2, 3).
4. Check whether (2, 3) is the solution by substituting 2 for x and 3 for y in each of the equations.

Equation 1	**Equation 2**
$x + y = 5$	$y = 2x - 1$
$2 + 3 \stackrel{?}{=} 5$	$3 \stackrel{?}{=} 2(2) - 1$
$5 = 5$ ✓	$3 = 3$ ✓

ANSWER The solution is (2, 3).

EXAMPLE 2 Solving Linear Systems by Substitution

Solve the linear system: $x + 4y = 4$ **Equation 1**

$x - y = -6$ **Equation 2**

Solution

1 Choose an equation to solve for one of the variables.

$x - y = -6$ Write Equation 2.

$x = y - 6$ Add y to each side.

2 Substitute $y - 6$ for x in Equation 1. Then solve for y.

$x + 4y = 4$ Write Equation 1.

$(y - 6) + 4y = 4$ Substitute $y - 6$ for x.

$5y - 6 = 4$ Combine like terms.

$5y = 10$ Add 6 to each side.

$y = 2$ Divide each side by 5.

3 Substitute 2 for y in the original Equation 2 and solve for x.

$x - y = -6$ Write Equation 2.

$x - 2 = -6$ Substitute 2 for y.

$x = -4$ Add 2 to each side.

ANSWER The solution is $(-4, 2)$.

HELP with Solving

When solving by substitution, solve for the variable that is easier to isolate. You will get the same solution whether you begin by solving for x or for y.

Exercises

Estimate the solution of the linear system using a graph. Then check the solution using algebra.

1. $y = -x + 3$
   $y = x + 1$
2. $x - y = 1$
   $5x - 4y = 0$
3. $y = 2x - 15$
   $x = -2y$

Solve the linear system by substitution.

4. $x = 4$
   $x + y = 2$
5. $a + b = 4$
   $4a + b = 1$
6. $2w - z = -2$
   $4w + z = 20$
7. **Trading Cards** You have 100 trading cards and your friend has 20. Every day you give your friend one card. Use the equations $c = 100 - d$ and $c = 20 + d$ to model this situation. Graph the two equations and find when you both will have the same number of cards.

Graphs of Linear Inequalities

BEFORE	Now	WHY?
You graphed linear equations.	You'll graph linear inequalities.	So you can find how much water you can bring on a trip, as in Ex. 34.

Activity You can use a graph to model linear inequalities.

1. Sketch the graph of $y = x - 1$.

2. Graph and label the following points in your coordinate plane.

   $A(0, 0)$, $B(-3, -2)$, $C(4, -3)$, $D(0, -4)$

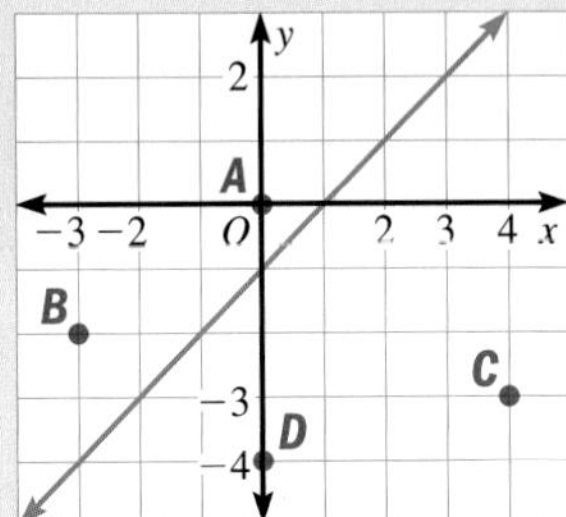

3. Which of the points in Step 2 make the inequality $y < x - 1$ true? Draw a circle around these points.

4. Which of the points in Step 2 make the inequality $y > x - 1$ true? Draw a square around these points.

5. Make a conjecture about the solutions of $y < x - 1$ and the solutions of $y > x - 1$.

Word Watch

linear inequality, p. 583
solution of a linear inequality, p. 583
half-plane, p. 584

INDIANA Academic Standards

- Algebra and Functions (8.3.1, 8.3.5)
- Problem Solving (8.7.1)

In the activity, you investigated solutions of linear inequalities. Some examples of **linear inequalities** in two variables are $y \le 2x + 5$, $2x + 5y < 7$, and $4x + y \ge -6$.

An ordered pair (x, y) is a **solution of a linear inequality** if the inequality is true when the values of x and y are substituted into the inequality.

HELP with Solving

The symbol $\not\le$ means *not less than or equal to.* It is equivalent to the symbol >, which means *greater than.*

EXAMPLE 1 Checking Solutions of a Linear Inequality

Tell whether the point is a solution of $3x - 4y \le -8$.

(x, y)	$3x - 4y$	$3x - 4y \overset{?}{\le} -8$	Conclusion
a. $(0, 0)$	$3(0) - 4(0) = 0$	$0 \not\le -8$	$(0, 0)$ is *not* a solution.
b. $(-1, 4)$	$3(-1) - 4(4) = -19$	$-19 \le -8$	$(-1, 4)$ is a solution.

Your turn now **Is the ordered pair a solution of $2x + 3y < 5$?**

1. $(0, 0)$ **2.** $(-4, 2)$ **3.** $(5, -1)$ **4.** $(1, 1)$

HELP with Vocabulary

A line divides a coordinate plane into two half-planes.

The graph of a linear inequality in two variables is a **half-plane**. The shaded region includes all the solutions of the inequality.

A solid line indicates that points on the line *are* solutions of an inequality. A dashed line indicates that points on the line are *not* solutions.

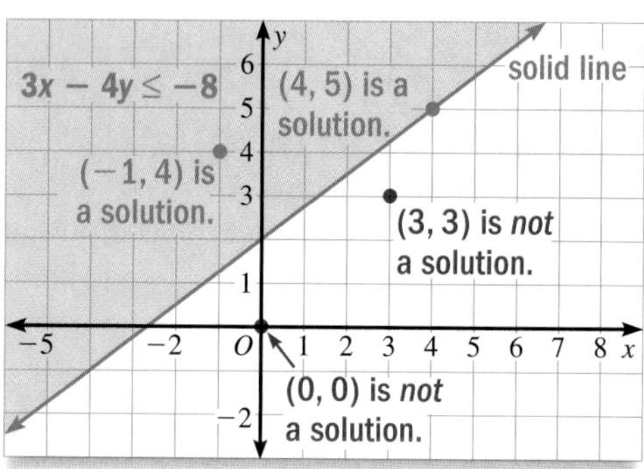

Graphing Linear Inequalities

1. Change the inequality symbol to "=." Graph the equation. Use a dashed line for < or >. Use a solid line for ≤ or ≥.
2. Test a point in one of the half-planes to check whether it is a solution of the inequality.
3. If the test point is a solution, shade its half-plane. If the test point is not a solution, shade the other half-plane.

EXAMPLE 2 Graphing a Linear Inequality

HELP with Solving

You can use any point not on the line as a test point. Using (0, 0) is convenient because 0 is substituted for each variable.

Graph $y - 2x > 3$.

(1) Change > to = and write the equation in slope-intercept form.

$y - 2x = 3$ **Replace > with = sign.**

$y = 2x + 3$ **Add $2x$ to each side.**

Graph the line that has a slope of 2 and a y-intercept of 3. Because the inequality is >, use a dashed line.

(2) Use (0, 0) as a test point.

$y > 2x + 3$

$0 \overset{?}{>} 2(0) + 3$

$0 \not> 3$ **(0, 0) is not a solution.**

(3) Shade the half-plane that does *not* contain (0, 0).

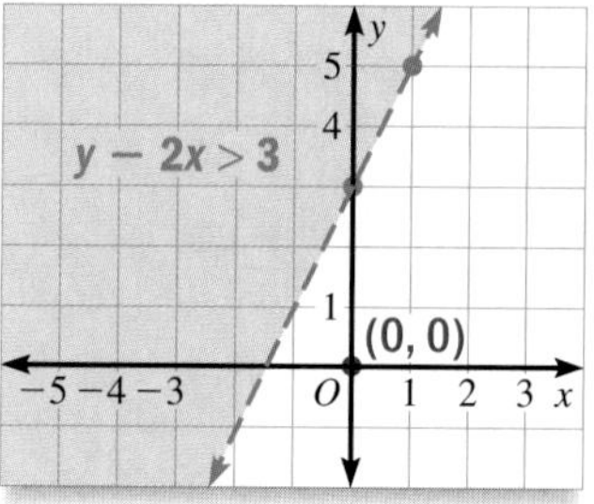

Your turn now **Graph the inequality.**

5. $y < x + 1$ **6.** $3x + y \ge 3$ **7.** $x - 2y \ge -1$ **8.** $y \ge -2$

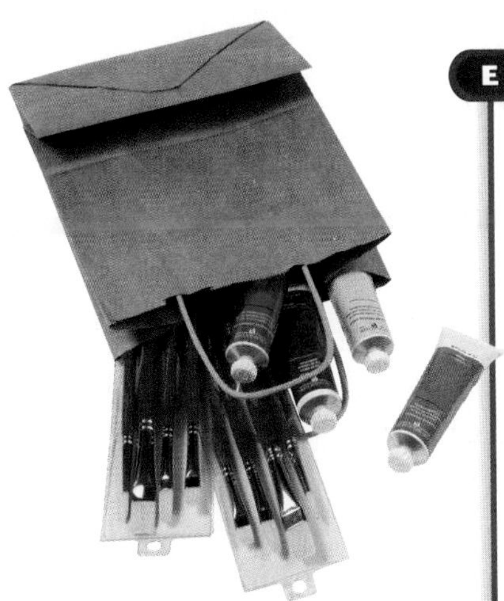

EXAMPLE 3 Using the Graph of a Linear Inequality

Art Supplies You are buying art supplies for your art club. You have \$40 to spend. Tubes of paint cost \$6 each and brushes cost \$4 each. The inequality $6x + 4y \le 40$, where x represents the number of tubes of paint and y represents the number of brushes, models this situation. How many tubes of paint and how many brushes can you buy with \$40?

a. Graph the inequality.

b. Use the graph to find a solution. Then interpret the solution.

Solution

a. Graph the equation $y = -\frac{3}{2}x + 10$.

Use a solid line.

Use (0, 0) as a test point.

$6(0) + 4(0) \stackrel{?}{\le} 40$

$0 \le 40$ ✓

Shade the half-plane that contains (0, 0).

b. One solution is (4, 4). This means that you can buy 4 tubes of paint and 4 brushes.

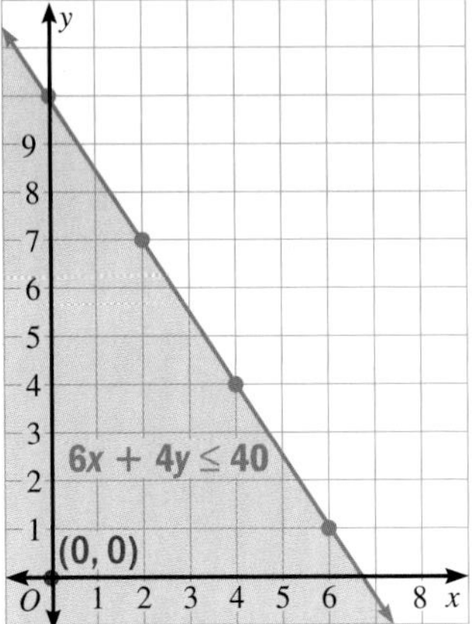

HELP with Solving

In Example 3, all points in the shaded region and on the line are solutions of the inequality. However, negative and fractional solutions do not make sense. You cannot buy a negative number of items, and you cannot buy part of an item.

11.8 Exercises

More Practice, p. 737

INTERNET eWorkbook Plus CLASSZONE.COM

Getting Ready to Practice

1. **Vocabulary** When graphing the inequality $y < 2x + 1$, the graphed dashed line divides the coordinate plane into two _?_.

Tell whether the point is a solution of the inequality $6x + 3y > 24$.

2. (2, 3) 3. (4, 5) 4. (5, 4) 5. (3, 2)

Graph the inequality.

6. $y > 14 - 4x$ 7. $y < x + 5$ 8. $3x - 4 \ge y$ 9. $y + 3 \ge 4x$

10. **Trail Mix** You are making a trail mix of peanuts and raisins. You have \$6.00 to spend on trail mix. Peanuts cost \$2.00 per pound and raisins cost \$1.50 per pound. How much of each item can you buy? Graph the inequality $2x + 1.50y \le 6$ to find different combinations of pounds of peanuts and raisins that you could buy to use in your trail mix.

Practice and Problem Solving

Example	Exercises
1	11–14, 16–19
2	16–31
3	32–34

Online Resources
CLASSZONE.COM

· More Examples
· eTutorial Plus

Tell whether the point is a solution of the inequality.

11. $5x + y \le 17$; (1, 2)

12. $3x + 7y < 20$; (−11, 2)

13. $9x + 12y > 26$; (3, −4)

14. $11x + 18y \ge 31$; (−6, −7)

15. Writing Explain how you can tell when to use a solid line and when to use a dashed line when graphing an inequality.

Matching **Match the inequality with its graph.**

16. $y \le 2x + 1$ **17.** $y < 2x + 1$ **18.** $y > 2x + 1$ **19.** $y \ge 2x + 1$

A.

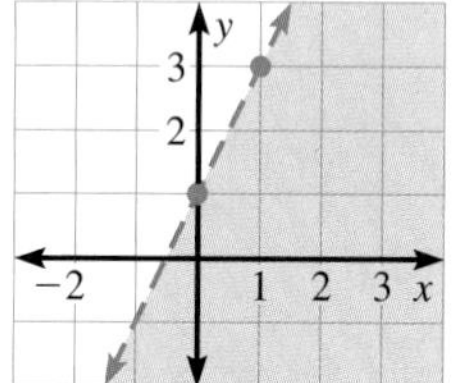

B.

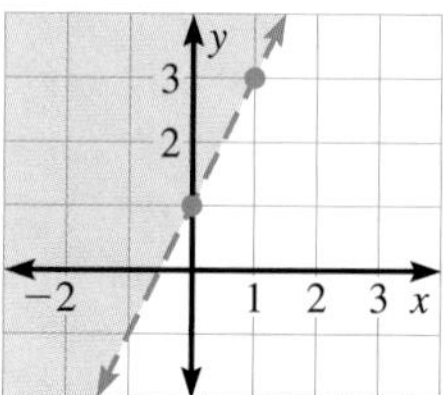

C.

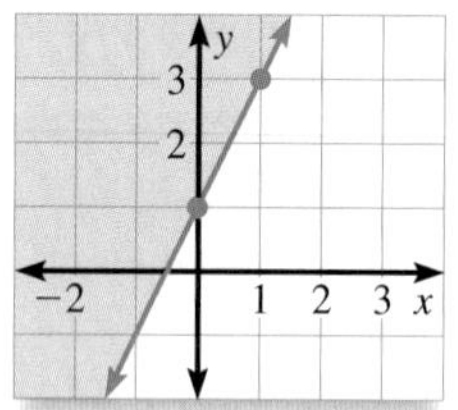

D.

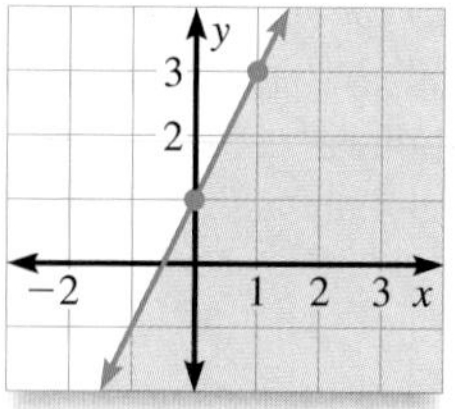

Graph the inequality.

20. $y < x + 6$

21. $y > 9 - 2x$

22. $y \ge 3x - 7$

23. $y \le 4x - 12$

24. $y < 7x + 19$

25. $4x - 13 > y$

26. $5x \le 45$

27. $22 < 2x$

28. $6y > 36$

29. $8y > 64$

30. $-96 \le -3x$

31. $-2y \ge 74$

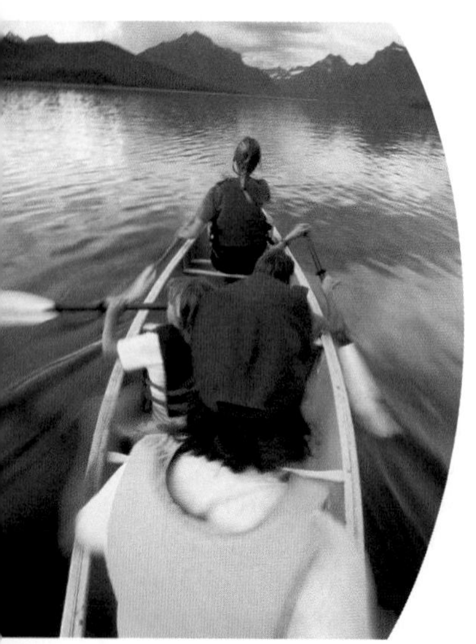

Extended Problem Solving **In Exercises 32–34, use the information about Catherine's canoe trip.**

Catherine is going on a canoe trip. She has to carry a backpack containing the food and water she will need. Catherine can take no more than 10 pounds in her backpack. A bottle of water weighs 16 ounces and a sandwich and fruit weigh 12 ounces.

32. The inequality $16x + 12y \le 160$ models the situation, where x is the number of water bottles and y is the number of meals. How many meals can Catherine take with her if she brings 4 bottles of water?

33. Graph the inequality.

34. Using the graph, find the maximum number of bottles of water Catherine can carry when she packs 2 meals in her backpack.

35. **Writing** Explain how you can write an inequality that represents the half-plane that is *not* the solution of the inequality $5x + y \geq 2$.

36. **Critical Thinking** If you graph the inequalities $y < x + 3$ and $y > x + 3$, do you cover all of the points in the plane? Explain.

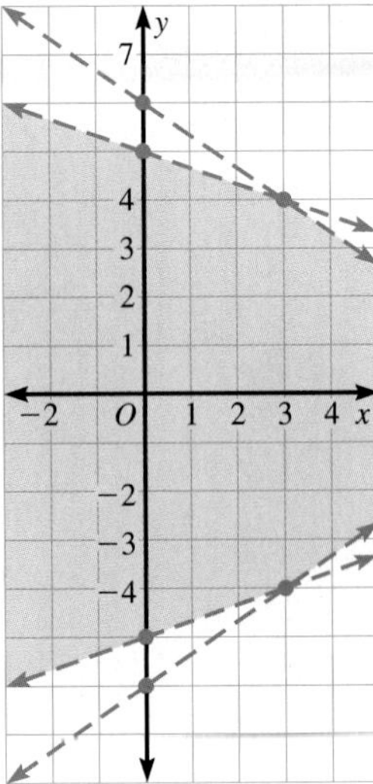

37. **Challenge** The graph at the right represents all the points that are solutions to four inequalities. The equations used to graph the inequalities are

$y = -\frac{1}{3}x + 5$, $y = \frac{1}{3}x - 5$, $y = \frac{2}{3}x - 6$, and

$y = -\frac{2}{3}x + 6$. What are the four inequalities?

Mixed Review

38. Find the intercepts of $4x + 18y = 36$. *(Lesson 11.5)*

39. Find the slope of the line that passes through $(-3, -4)$ and $(7, 8)$. *(Lesson 11.6)*

Basic Skills Write the decimal as a fraction in simplest form.

40. 1.34 **41.** 3.75 **42.** 8.125 **43.** 7.164

Test-Taking Practice 

INTERNET
State Test Practice
CLASSZONE.COM

44. **Multiple Choice** The graph shows how many child tickets y and how many adult tickets x need to be sold at a fundraiser to meet the goal. Which inequality describes the graph?

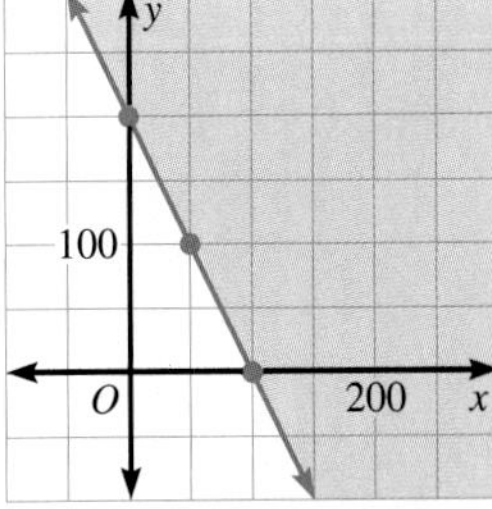

A. $y \leq 2x + 200$ **B.** $y \geq 2x + 200$

C. $y \leq -2x + 200$ **D.** $y \geq -2x + 200$

45. **Multiple Choice** Sonya can spend up to \$125 on decorations for a dance. A bag of balloons costs \$4 and a roll of streamers costs \$2. She uses $4x + 2y \leq 125$ to find how much she can buy, where x is the number of bags of balloons and y is the number of rolls of streamers. Which of the following is a solution?

F. (30, 6) **G.** (30, 4) **H.** (25, 15) **I.** (25, 12)

Notebook Review

Review the vocabulary definitions in your notebook.

Copy the review examples in your notebook. Then complete the exercises.

Check Your Definitions

x-intercept, p. 564
y-intercept, p. 564
slope, p. 570
rise, run, p. 570
slope-intercept form, p. 577
linear inequality, solution, p. 583
half-plane, p. 584

Use Your Vocabulary

1. Vocabulary Copy and complete: In the equation $y = 4x - 9$, 4 is the __?__ and -9 is the __?__.

11.5–11.7 Can you use slope and y-intercepts?

EXAMPLE Find the slope of the line passing through (0, 3) and (4, 6).

The slope can be found by calculating

$$\frac{y_2 - y_1}{x_2 - x_1} = \frac{6 - 3}{4 - 0} = \frac{3}{4}$$

✓ **Find the slope of the line passing through the two points.**

2. (−1, 0) and (5, 8) **3.** (8, 7) and (−2, 3) **4.** (0, 11) and (6, 1)

EXAMPLE Graph $y = \frac{3}{4}x + 3$.

Since $y = \frac{3}{4}x + 3$ is already in slope-intercept form, you know that $\frac{3}{4}$ is the slope and 3 is the y-intercept of the graph of the equation. To graph the equation, first plot the point (0, 3). Then use the slope to find another point on the line.

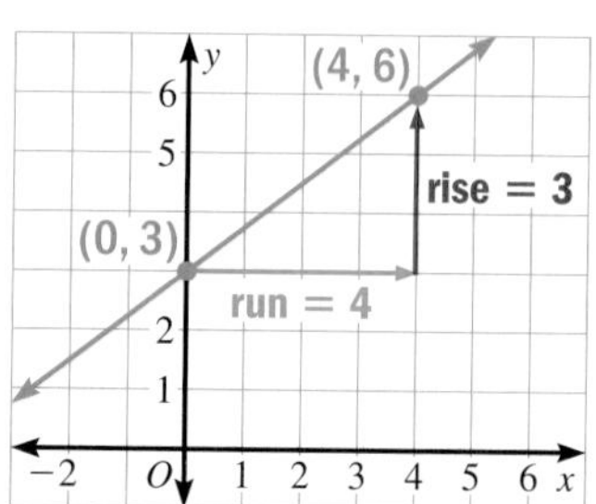

✓ **Find the slope and y-intercept of the graph of the equation. Then graph the equation.**

5. $y = 5x + 20$ **6.** $2x - 3y = -12$ **7.** $x + 4y = 18$

11.8 Can you graph linear inequalities?

EXAMPLE Graph $y > -2x + 4$.

The graph of $y = -2x + 4$ has a slope of -2 and a y-intercept of 4.

Because the inequality is >, use a dashed line.

Use (0, 0) as a test point:

$0 \overset{?}{>} -2(0) + 4$

$0 \not> 4$ **(0, 0) is not a solution.**

Shade the half-plane that does not include (0, 0).

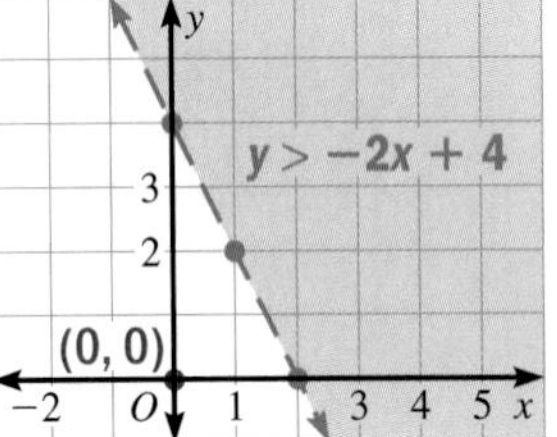

Graph the inequality.

8. $y < x - 4$ **9.** $y \geq 2x - 3$ **10.** $x + y > 6$ **11.** $x - y \leq -5$

Stop and Think about Lessons 11.5–11.8

12. **Critical Thinking** Graph $y = 3x + 5$ and $y = 3x - 2$. What do you notice about the lines?

Review Quiz 2

Find the intercepts of the graph of the equation.

1. $y = 2x + 3$ **2.** $2y + x = 6$ **3.** $x = 3$

Find the slope of the line passing through the points.

4. (3, 4), (5, 7) **5.** (−1, −3), (0, 0) **6.** (−5, 3), (4, 3)

Find the slope and y-intercept of the graph of the equation. Then sketch its graph.

7. $y = \frac{6}{5}x - 2$ **8.** $-5x - 5y = -20$ **9.** $y = -x$

Graph the inequality. Then list three solutions of the inequality.

10. $y > x - 3$ **11.** $x - 3y \leq -9$ **12.** $6x + 7y < -21$

13. **Car Wash** Your club holds a car wash for three hours to raise money for a charity. The equation $10x + 15y = 180$ describes the amount of time it takes to wash small and large vehicles respectively. Find the intercepts of the equation. What do they represent? Graph the equation.

Chapter Review

Vocabulary

relation, p. 541
input, p. 541
output, p. 541
function, p. 541
domain, p. 542
range, p. 542
scatter plot, p. 545
solution of an equation in two variables, p. 549
linear equation, p. 556
x-intercept, p. 564
y-intercept, p. 564
slope, p. 570
rise, run, p. 570
slope-intercept form, p. 577
linear inequality, solution, p. 583
half-plane, p. 584

Vocabulary Review

In Exercises 1–3, copy and complete the statement.

1. The graph of a linear inequality in two variables is a(n) _?_.
2. For a function, the set of all possible input values is called the _?_, and the set of all possible output values is called the _?_.
3. The slope of a nonvertical line is the ratio of its _?_ to its _?_.
4. Explain in your own words how to find the x-intercept and the y-intercept of the graph of an equation.
5. Describe a real-life situation that can be represented by a linear equation. What does the slope of the line tell you about the situation?
6. Write the steps you would take to graph a linear inequality.

Review Questions

Tell whether the relation is a function. Explain your answer. *(Lesson 11.1)*

7. (0, 6), (2, 6), (4, 7), (0, 3), (2, 3), (4, 8)

8.

Input	Output
0	−8
1	−11
2	−14
3	−17

9.

Input	Output
−4	12
−2	12
0	12
2	12

10. Make a scatter plot of the data. Then describe the relationship. *(Lesson 11.2)*

Number of muffins sold	12	24	36	48
Profit	\$6	\$12	\$18	\$24

Review Questions

11. Model Plane You buy a battery operated model plane for \$45. It costs you about \$8 each month to replace the batteries. The equation $C = 45 + 8m$, where C is the total cost in dollars and m is the number of months, describes this situation. About how much has the plane cost you in the first year? *(Lesson 11.3)*

Matching Match the equation with its graph. *(Lesson 11.4)*

12. $y = -2x$

13. $y = -2$

14. $x = -2$

A. 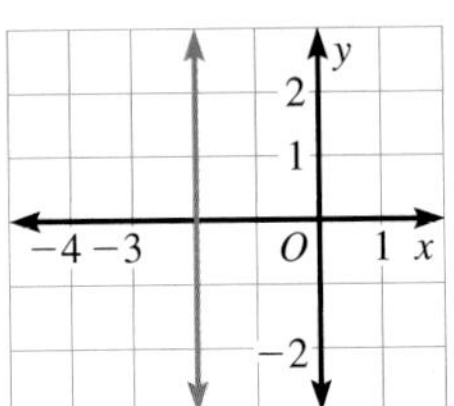

B. 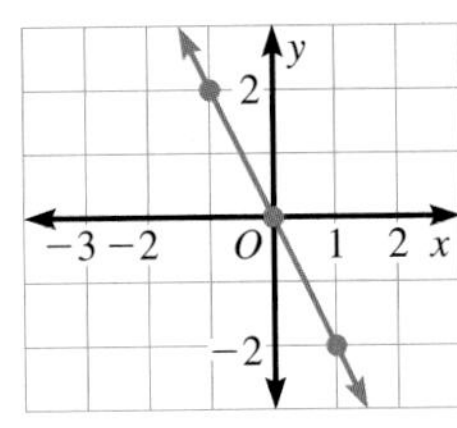

C. 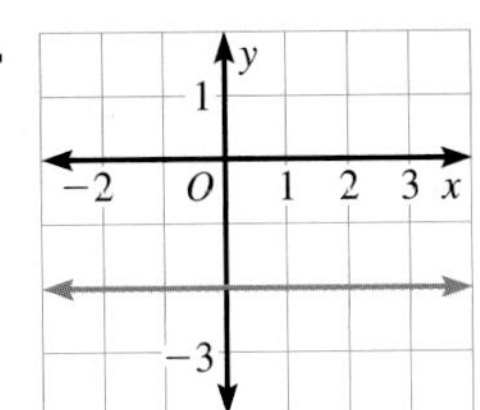

Graph the linear equation. *(Lesson 11.4)*

15. $y = x + 2$

16. $y = -\frac{3}{2}x - 1$

17. $y = 8$

18. Taxes The approximate amount of taxes collected by the Internal Revenue Service from 1980 to 1990 can be modeled by $y = 57.1x + 488$, where y represents taxes, in billions of dollars, and x represents the number of years since 1980. What is the y-intercept of the graph of this equation? What does the y-intercept represent? *(Lesson 11.5)*

Write the coordinates of two points on the line. Then find the slope of the line. *(Lesson 11.6)*

19. 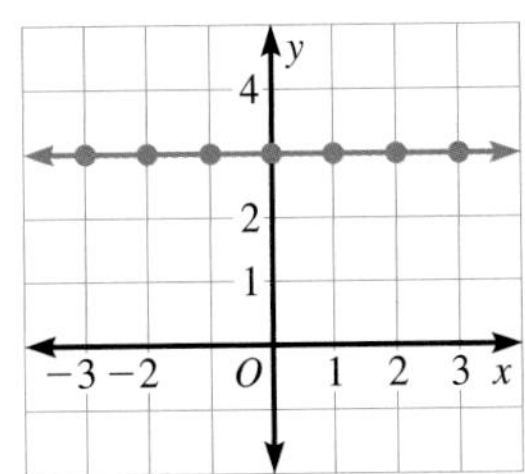

20. 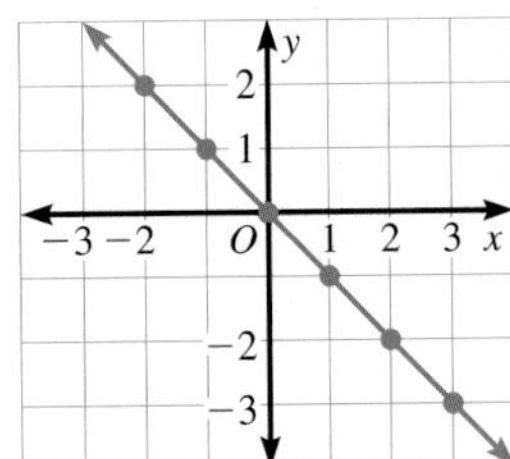

Rewrite the equation in slope-intercept form. Then find the slope and y-intercept of the graph of the equation. *(Lesson 11.7)*

21. $y - 4x = 10$

22. $2y + 6 = x$

23. $-3x - 7y = 21$

Graph the inequality. *(Lesson 11.8)*

24. $6x + 10y < -30$

25. $3x - 7y \geq 21$

26. $4x + 8y \leq 32$

CHAPTER 11

Chapter Test

In Exercises 1 and 2, write a function rule that relates *x* and *y*.

1.

Input x	0	1	2	3
Output y	0	−0.25	−0.5	−0.75

2.

Input x	−2	−1	0	1
Output y	−9	−3	3	9

3. What type of relationship do you expect to find for the number of problems assigned and the time spent doing an assignment?

Tell whether the ordered pair is a solution of the equation $12x + 3y = 21$.

4. $(-1, 11)$ **5.** $(-4, -9)$ **6.** $(2, -15)$ **7.** $(6, -17)$

8. **Temperature** To change a temperature in degrees Celsius C to degrees Fahrenheit F, use the formula $F = \frac{9}{5}C + 32$. Your friend tells you that 45°C is equal to 77°F. Is your friend correct? If not, find the temperature in degrees Fahrenheit.

9. **Gasoline** A scooter uses 1 gallon of gasoline per 60 miles. A linear equation that models the relationship between the number of miles driven n and the amount of gasoline used in gallons g is $n = 60g$. Graph the function and then estimate the number of miles traveled using 12 gallons of gasoline.

Use the diagram of a seesaw.

10. What is the run of the seesaw?

11. What is the rise of the seesaw?

12. What is the slope of the seesaw?

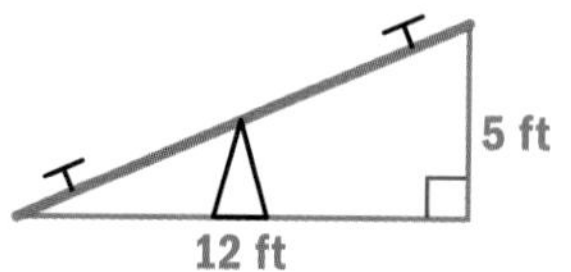

Find the slope and *y*-intercept of the graph of the equation. Then graph the equation.

13. $y = 6x - 3$ **14.** $-5x + y = 1$ **15.** $y = -\frac{1}{4}x$

Graph the inequality.

16. $3x + 6y \geq 12$ **17.** $7x - y \leq 49$ **18.** $8x - 15y > 30$

19. **Gift Card** Ken got a \$25 movie gift card. Matinee shows cost \$4 and evening shows cost \$7. Graph the inequality $4x + 7y \leq 25$. Using the graph, find the greatest number of movies Ken can see.

Chapter Standardized Test

Test-Taking Strategy **When you check your answers, try to use a method other than the one you originally used, to avoid repeating the same mistake.**

Multiple Choice

1. Which of the following relations is *not* a function?

A. (5, 6), (6, 5), (−3, 7), (2, 6)
B. (−5, 6), (5, 6), (−3, 7), (2, 4)
C. (5, 6), (7, 7), (1, −1), (5, 0)
D. (3, 2), (−3, −2), (2, 3), (−2, −3)

2. The scatter plot below shows the average test score of each class on a recent English exam. Describe the relationship shown in the data.

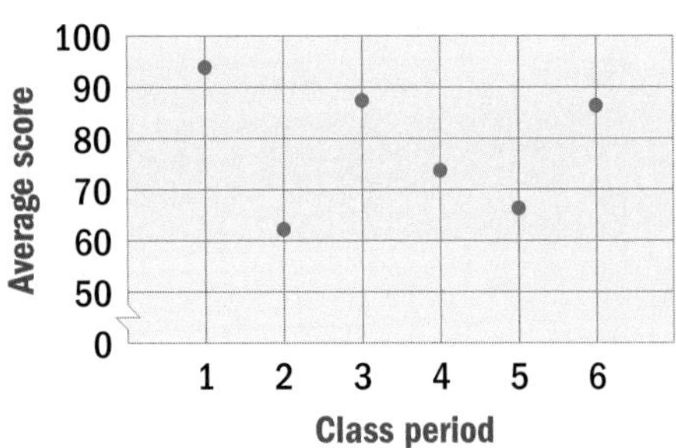

F. positive
G. negative
H. none
I. not enough information

3. Which of the ordered pairs is a solution of the equation $y = 4x - 5$?

A. (−2, −13)
B. (0, 5)
C. (3, 17)
D. (7, 3)

4. What is the slope of the line passing through points (−3, 2) and (4, −5)?

F. −3 **G.** −1 **H.** $\frac{1}{3}$ **I.** 1

5. Which is the slope-intercept form of $9x - 3y = 12$?

A. $-3y = -9x + 12$
B. $x = \frac{1}{3}y + \frac{4}{3}$
C. $y = 3x + 4$
D. $y = 3x - 4$

6. Which equation is represented by the graph?

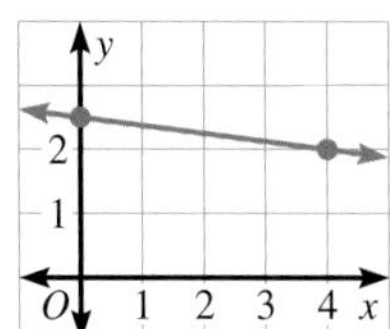

F. $y = -\frac{1}{8}x + 2.5$
G. $y = \frac{1}{8}x + 2.5$
H. $y = -8x + 2.5$
I. $y = 8x + 2.5$

7. What is the value for y in the function table representing $y = x - 7$, when x is 7?

x	3	5	7	9
y	−4	−2	?	2

A. −1 **B.** 0 **C.** 1 **D.** 4

Short Response

8. Graph the inequalities $x + y \leq 5$, $x \geq 0$, and $y \geq 0$. Find the area of the solution region.

Extended Response

9. Your class needs to raise \$120 selling hats and T-shirts. The equation $6x + 5y = 120$, where x is the number of hats sold and y is the number of T-shirts sold, represents the situation. What are the intercepts of the equation? What do they mean in this context?

Data Analysis and Probability

BEFORE

In previous chapters you've...

- Found the median and range of a data set
- Found probabilities of events

Now

In Chapter 12 you'll study...

- Interpreting data displays
- Using permutations and combinations to count possibilities
- Finding the probability of independent and dependent events

WHY?

So you can solve real-world problems about...

- electricity, p. 599
- skateboards, p. 619
- poetry, p. 624
- archery, p. 636

Internet Preview
CLASSZONE.COM

- eEdition Plus Online
- eWorkbook Plus Online
- eTutorial Plus Online
- State Test Practice
- More Examples

Chapter Warm-Up Game

Review skills you need for this chapter in this quick game.

Key Skill:
Interpreting bar and circle graphs

GALAPAGOS GRAPHS

HOW TO PLAY

1 USE the data displays to answer each question. Record the letter for each correct answer.

About how many times larger is Santa Cruz than San Cristobal?
A. 2 **B.** 3 **C.** 4

What is the area of Isabela?
D. 1680 mi^2 **E.** 1771 mi^2 **F.** 1800 mi^2

What percent of the land vertebrate species in the Galapagos Islands are reptiles?
G. 10% **H.** 26% **I.** 30%

2 WRITE the letters of the correct answers to the questions in order. Find the number that corresponds to the letter. Put all three numbers together in the order of the answers. This will tell you the age of the oldest Galapagos tortoise on record.

A. 1 **B.** 2 **C.** 0 **D.** 9 **E.** 5
F. 2 **G.** 7 **H.** 2 **I.** 5

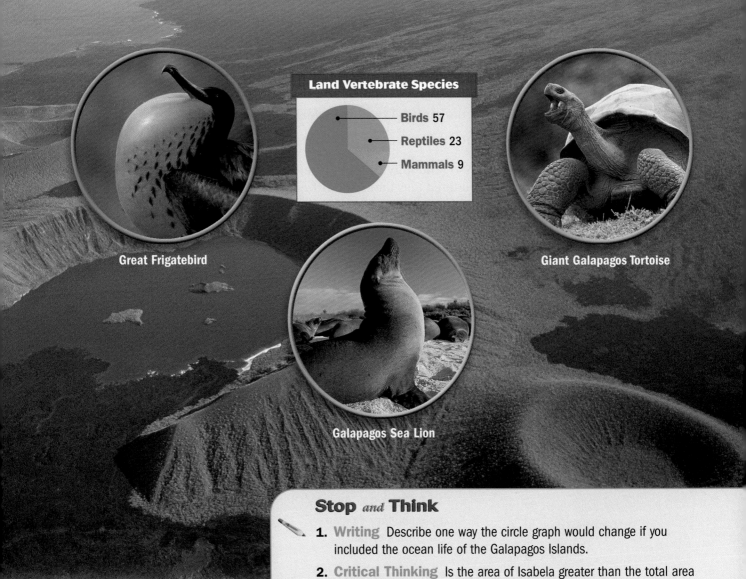

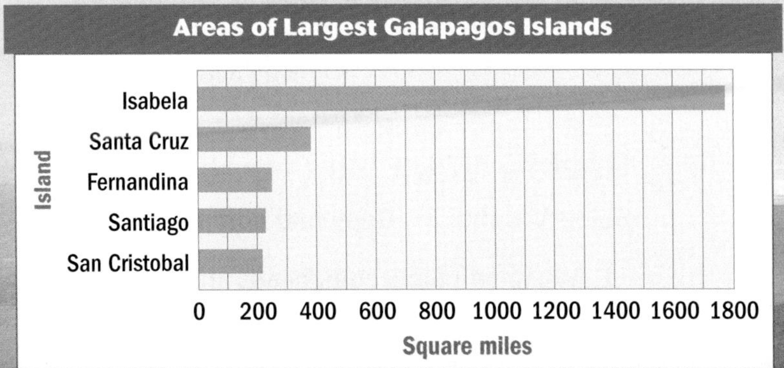

Land Vertebrate Species

Birds 57
Reptiles 23
Mammals 9

Great Frigatebird

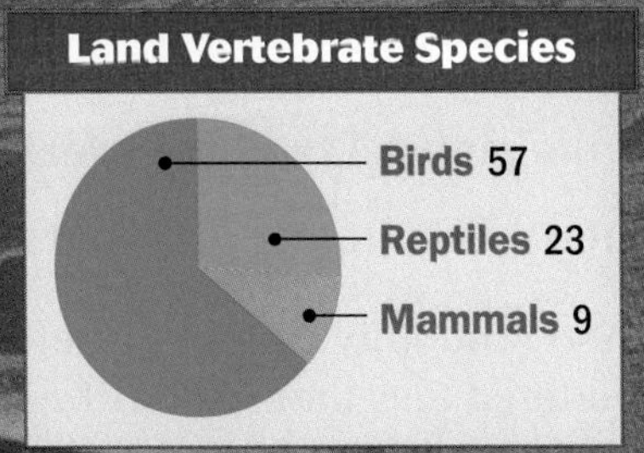

Giant Galapagos Tortoise

Galapagos Sea Lion

Stop *and* Think

1. **Writing** Describe one way the circle graph would change if you included the ocean life of the Galapagos Islands.
2. **Critical Thinking** Is the area of Isabela greater than the total area of the next four largest islands? Explain.

Getting Ready to Learn

Review What You Need to Know 

Using Vocabulary **Copy and complete using a review word.**

1. When you flip a coin, heads and tails are the two possible _?_.

2. Find the sum of the values of a set of data and then divide by the number of data values to find the _?_ of the data.

3. The _?_ is a measure of how likely it is that the event will occur.

Find the mean and the median of the data set. *(p. 257)*

4. 23, 27, 13, 24, 19, 21, 25, 25, 12

5. 0.2, 0.35, 1.33, 1.32, 0.05, 0.5

Find the probability of the event. *(p. 354)*

6. You roll a number cube and get a number greater than 4.

7. You randomly choose the letter A from a bag holding the eight lettered tiles that spell ARKANSAS.

Word Watch

Review Words

data, p. 5
mean, p. 257
median, p. 257
range, p. 258
outcome, p. 354
probability of an event, p. 354

Know How to Take Notes

Contrasting Terms When words have similar meanings, you should emphasize their differences in your notes.

Pairs of Angles

Complementary Angles: The sum of the angle measures is 90°.

Supplementary Angles: The sum of the angle measures is 180°.

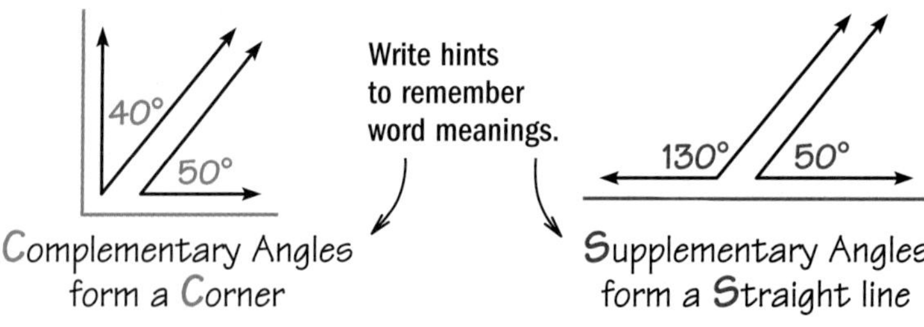
40°
50°
Write hints to remember word meanings.
130°
50°
Complementary Angles form a Corner
Supplementary Angles form a Straight line

In Lesson 12.6, you should note the difference between combinations and permutations.

Notebook

You should include material that appears on a notebook like this in your own notes.

Stem-and-Leaf Plots

BEFORE	Now	WHY?
You organized data using bar graphs and histograms.	You will make and interpret stem-and-leaf plots.	So you can analyze waiting times at a restaurant, as in Ex. 14.

stem-and-leaf plot, p. 597

INDIANA Academic Standards

- Data Analysis and Probability (8.6.4)

In the Real World

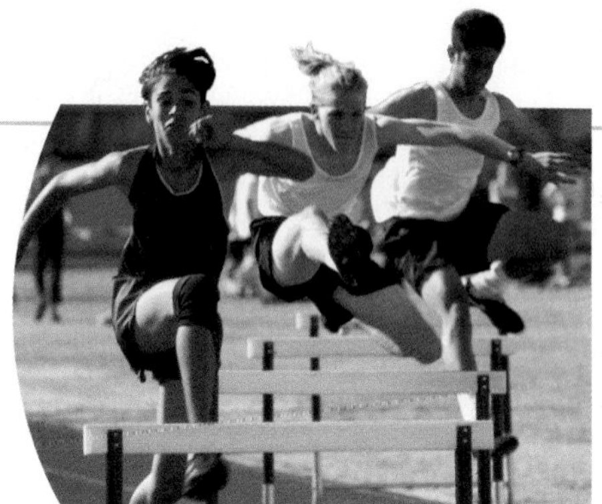

Track Hurdlers entering the 200 meter hurdles at a track meet were ranked according to their qualifying times, in seconds, shown below.

28.6, 29.2, 28.1, 27.5, 29.8, 28.7,
30.2, 29.3, 28.3, 28.9, 29.9, 28.4

How can the data be displayed to show the distribution of the times?

A **stem-and-leaf plot** is a data display that helps you see how data are distributed. You can use a stem-and-leaf plot to order data.

EXAMPLE 1 Making a Stem-and-Leaf Plot

You can display the hurdlers' times given above in a stem-and-leaf plot.

1. The times range from 27.5 to 30.2. Let the **stems** be the digits in the tens' and ones' places. Let the **leaves** be the tenths' digits.
2. Write the stems first. Then record each time by writing its tenths' digit on the same line as its corresponding stem. Include a key that shows what the stems and leaves represent.
3. Make an ordered stem-and-leaf plot.

Unordered Plot

Stem	Leaves
27	5
28	6 1 7 3 9 4
29	2 8 3 9
30	2

Key: 27|5 = 27.5

Ordered Plot

Stem	Leaves
27	5
28	1 3 4 6 7 9
29	2 3 8 9
30	2

Key: 27|5 = 27.5

The leaves for each stem are listed in order from least to greatest.

Your turn now **Make an ordered stem-and-leaf plot of the data.**

1. Video game prices: \$40, \$15, \$10, \$19, \$12, \$24, \$15, \$39, \$51, \$50, \$35, \$20, \$47, \$36, \$30, \$25, \$27, \$29, \$24, \$43, \$29

HELP with Solving

In a stem-and-leaf plot, a stem can be one or more digits. A leaf is usually a single digit.

EXAMPLE 2 Interpreting a Stem-and-Leaf Plot

Biology The stem-and-leaf plot at the right shows the lengths, in millimeters, of young fish in a tank. Use the stem-and-leaf plot to describe the data. What interval includes the most lengths?

Stem	Leaves
4	9
5	
6	1 2 4 7 8 8
7	6 8
8	4

Key: 6 | 8 = 68

Solution

The longest fish is 84 mm and the shortest fish is 49 mm, so the range of lengths is 35 mm. Most of the lengths are in the 60–69 interval.

Double Stem-and-Leaf Plots A double stem-and-leaf plot can be used to compare two sets of data. You read to the left of the stems for one set of data and to the right for the other.

EXAMPLE 3 Making a Double Stem-and-Leaf Plot

Test Scores The data below show the test scores for Beth's class and Marisa's class. Overall, which class had the better test scores?

Beth's class: **95, 86, 79, 79, 58, 68, 90, 63, 71, 81, 82, 94, 64, 76, 77, 79, 83, 91, 83, 68, 74, 71**

Marisa's class: **95, 73, 76, 84, 84, 89, 67, 82, 88, 86, 93, 97, 96, 84, 60, 75, 91, 87, 89, 86, 76, 93**

Solution

You can use a double stem-and-leaf plot to compare the test scores.

Beth's Class		Marisa's Class
8	5	
8 8 4 3	6	0 7
9 9 9 7 6 4 1 1	7	3 5 6 6
6 3 3 2 1	8	2 4 4 4 6 6 7 8 9 9
5 4 1 0	9	1 3 3 5 6 7

Key: 0 | 9 | 1 represents 90 and 91.

ANSWER Marisa's class; it had more scores in the eighties and nineties.

Your turn now **Complete the following exercises.**

2. Make an ordered double stem-and-leaf plot to compare the lengths, in minutes, of the last 10 phone calls made by two friends.

   Kenyon: 12, 8, 17, 5, 23, 29, 21, 34, 16, 28
   Jason: 31, 28, 7, 5, 11, 5, 13, 16, 11, 24

3. In general, who made longer calls, Kenyon or Jason?

Getting Ready to Practice

1. **Vocabulary** Copy and complete: The key for a stem-and-leaf plot says $7|4 = 74$. In the plot, 7 is the _?_ and 4 is the _?_ .

Write the number as it would appear in a stem-and-leaf plot. Identify the stem and the leaf.

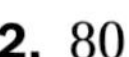

2. 80
3. 117
4. 12.9
5. 4.6

6. **Guided Problem Solving** The data show the times, in minutes, it takes ten students to get ready for school. Make an ordered stem-and-leaf plot of the data. What interval includes the most time values?

   25, 10, 25, 15, 30, 18, 35, 40, 28, 20

   (1 Identify the range of the data.

   (2 Make the stem-and-leaf plot. Include a key.

   (3 Use the plot to find where most of the times fall.

Practice and Problem Solving

Make an ordered stem-and-leaf plot of the data. Identify the interval that includes the most data values.

7. 45, 48, 65, 50, 67, 82, 74, 63
8. 33, 12, 8, 14, 35, 9, 26, 37, 4, 6
9. 108, 95, 89, 112, 109, 94, 103
10. 461, 492, 439, 467, 501, 485
11. 20.2, 22.6, 18.3, 18.7, 22.5, 18.1
12. 5.1, 4.0, 5.3, 3.2, 5.7, 6.9, 5.3

13. **Writing** Explain how you can use an ordered stem-and-leaf plot to find the median value of a set of data.

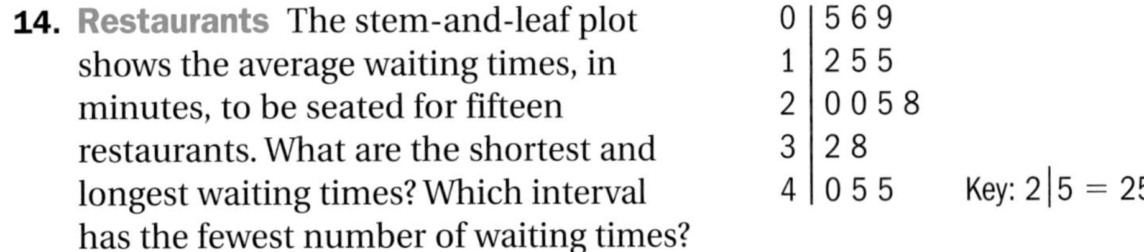

14. **Restaurants** The stem-and-leaf plot shows the average waiting times, in minutes, to be seated for fifteen restaurants. What are the shortest and longest waiting times? Which interval has the fewest number of waiting times?

Stem	Leaves
0	5 6 9
1	2 5 5
2	0 0 5 8
3	2 8
4	0 5 5

Key: $2|5 = 25$

15. **Electricity** The data show the amounts, in dollars, of a family's electric bills for twelve months. Make an ordered stem-and-leaf plot. What is the range? Are the bills more often greater or less than $60?

    95, 58, 47, 78, 43, 65, 84, 72, 55, 84, 96, 59

Example	Exercises
1	7–12
2	13–15, 18
3	16–17, 19

Make an ordered double stem-and-leaf plot of the two sets of data.

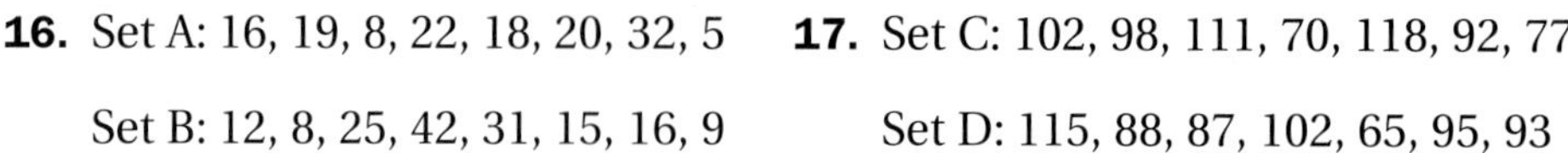

16. Set A: 16, 19, 8, 22, 18, 20, 32, 5

Set B: 12, 8, 25, 42, 31, 15, 16, 9

17. Set C: 102, 98, 111, 70, 118, 92, 77

Set D: 115, 88, 87, 102, 65, 95, 93

18. Critical Thinking Can you make a stem-and-leaf plot from a frequency table? Why or why not?

19. Football The total points that the Cleveland Browns scored in each game of a recent season are given below. Red numbers represent wins and blue numbers represent losses. Make an ordered double stem-and-leaf plot of the data. Describe the relationship between points scored and the outcome of the game.

6, **24**, **23**, **20**, 14, **24**, 21, 12, **27**, **18**, 15, 16, 10, 7, **41**, 7

Extended Problem Solving In Exercises 20–22, use the data below, which show the average monthly temperatures in degrees Fahrenheit (°F) for Los Angeles, California.

56.8, 57.6, 58.0, 60.1, 62.7, 65.7, 69.1, 70.5, 69.9, 66.8, 61.6, 56.9

20. Plot Make an ordered stem-and-leaf plot of the data. What is the range?

21. Convert Convert the data to degrees Celsius (°C) using the formula $C = \frac{5}{9}(F - 32)$. Round to the nearest tenth of a degree.

22. Compare Make an ordered stem-and-leaf plot of the converted data. Compare the two plots. In what ways are they different? Explain.

Mixed Review

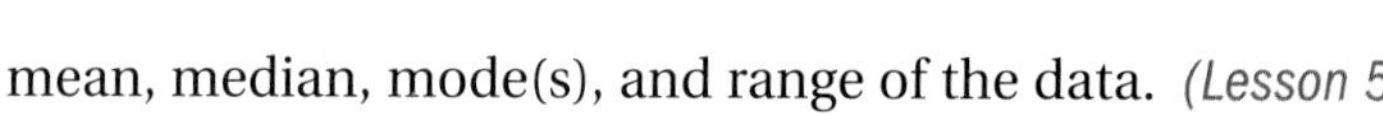

23. Find the mean, median, mode(s), and range of the data. *(Lesson 5.8)*

$-22, 14, 12, 6, -10, 14, 20, 16, -7, -5, 6, -2$

24. Find the slope and y-intercept of the line $7x + 4y = 24$. *(Lesson 11.7)*

Test-Taking Practice

INTERNET
State Test Practice
CLASSZONE.COM

The stem-and-leaf plot shows the ages of people at a birthday party. Use the plot to answer Exercises 25 and 26.

Stem	Leaves
0	6
1	3 7 9
2	0 1 4 5
3	
4	7 9
5	0 1 2 2 2

Key: 4 | 7 = 47

25. Multiple Choice What is the age of the oldest person?

A. 52 **B.** 59 **C.** 60 **D.** 79

26. Multiple Choice What is the median age?

F. 52 **G.** 35 **H.** 30 **I.** 25

Box-and-Whisker Plots

BEFORE

You found the median and range of a data set.

Now

You will make and interpret box-and-whisker plots.

WHY?

So you can analyze camera prices, as in Ex. 12.

Word Watch

box-and-whisker plot, p. 601
lower quartile, p. 601
upper quartile, p. 601
lower extreme, p. 601
upper extreme, p. 601

INDIANA
Academic Standards

- Data Analysis and Probability (8.6.3, 8.6.4)

In the Real World

Bridges The lengths, in meters, of the world's ten longest suspension bridges are listed below. How can you display these data to show how the lengths are distributed?

1280	1118	1990	1074	1298
1067	1624	1158	1090	1410

A **box-and-whisker plot** is a data display that organizes data values into four parts. Ordered data are divided into lower and upper halves by the median. The **lower quartile** is the median of the lower half of the data set. The **upper quartile** is the median of the upper half of the data set.

The **lower extreme** is the least data value and the **upper extreme** is the greatest data value.

HELP with Solving

If a data set has an odd number of values, then the median is not included in either half of the data when determining the quartile values. For help with finding a median, see p. 257.

EXAMPLE 1 Making a Box-and-Whisker Plot

To display the bridge lengths above in a box-and-whisker plot, first order the data to find the median and the quartiles.

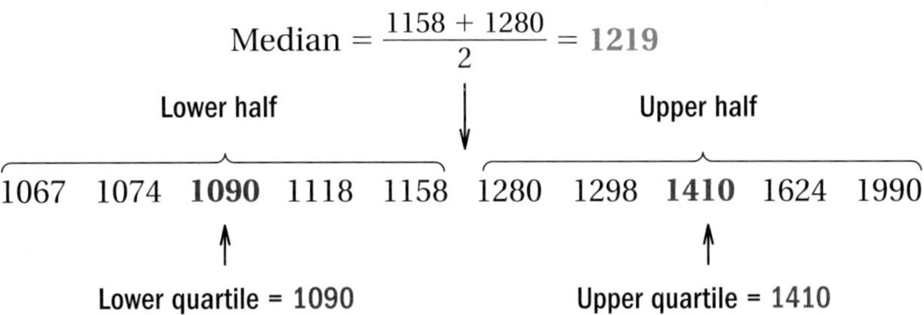

Plot these values below a number line that includes the extremes.

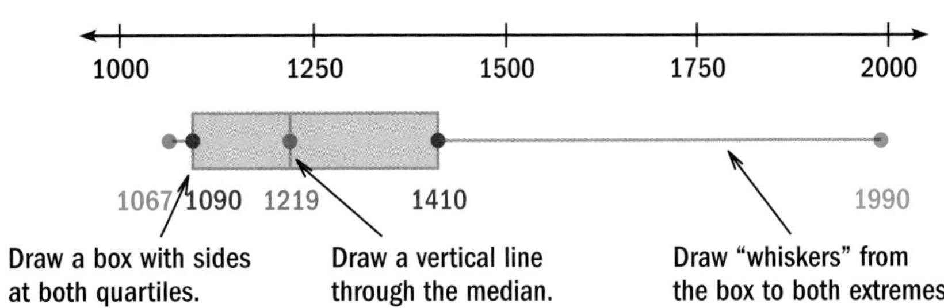

Interpreting a Box-and-Whisker Plot A box-and-whisker plot helps to show how varied, or spread out, the data are. The points divide the data into four parts. Each part represents about one quarter of the data.

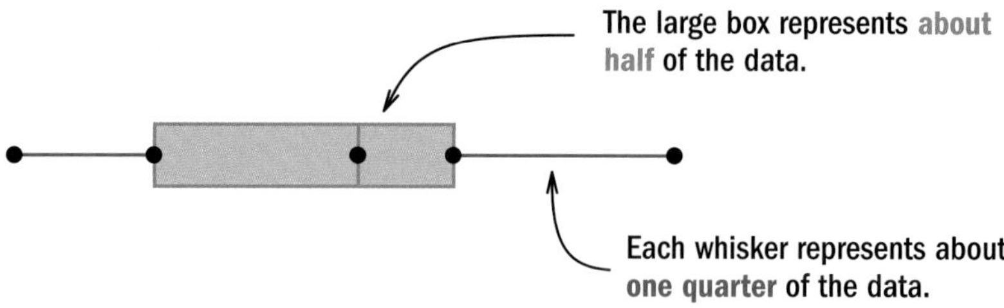

The large box represents about half of the data.
Each whisker represents about one quarter of the data.

You can use box-and-whisker plots to compare two or more data sets.

EXAMPLE 2 Interpreting Box-and-Whisker Plots

Food Science You are testing whether a fertilizer helps tomato plants grow. You give fertilizer to the plants in Group 2, but not to Group 1. The box-and-whisker plots show how much the plants grew, in centimeters, for each group of plants after two weeks.

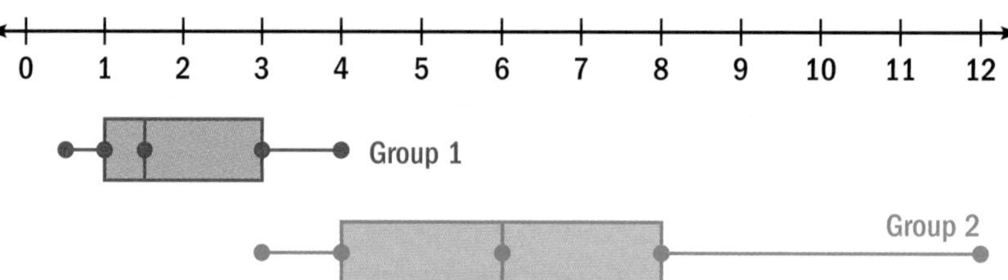

0 1 2 3 4 5 6 7 8 9 10 11 12
Group 1
Group 2

a. About what fraction of the unfertilized plants grew as much as any of the fertilized plants?

b. About what fraction of the fertilized plants grew 4 to 8 centimeters?

Solution

a. Notice that the right whisker for Group 1 overlaps the left whisker for Group 2. So about one quarter of the unfertilized plants grew as much as the any of the fertilized plants.

b. The large box in the plot for Group 2 ranges from 4 to 8, so about one half of the fertilized plants grew 4 to 8 centimeters.

What do you think? Science

Food Science

It takes about 24 pounds of tomatoes to make 7 pints of ketchup. At this rate, how many pounds of tomatoes are used to make a 2 pint bottle of ketchup?

Your turn now **Use a box-and-whisker plot.**

1. Ming worked out for 34, 27, 26, 15, 24, 21, 30, 23, 24, and 35 minutes. Chantelle worked out for 26, 33, 36, 21, 41, 36, 29, 25, 34, and 35 minutes. Make a box-and-whisker plot of the data for each person.
2. Who usually works out longer? Explain.
3. About how often does each person work out for 25–35 minutes?

Getting Ready to Practice

1. **Vocabulary** The median of the lower half of a data set is the _?_ and the median of the upper half of a data set is the _?_.

2. **Guided Problem Solving** You had the following scores while playing a math game: 306, 211, 235, 197, 351, 141, and 227. Make a box-and-whisker plot of your scores. Then predict your next score.

   (1 Find the range and draw a number line.

   (2 Find the median, quartiles, and extremes.

   (3 Draw the box-and-whisker plot.

   (4 Predict a range for your next score. Explain your reasoning.

Practice and Problem Solving

HELP with Homework

Example	Exercises
1	3-13
2	12-15

- More Examples
- eTutorial Plus

In Exercises 3–5, make a box-and-whisker plot of the data.

3. \$67, \$53, \$41, \$33, \$52, \$28, \$70, \$56

4. 327 ft, 419 ft, 9 ft, 299 ft, 111 ft, 0 ft

5. 26 m, 389 m, 878 m, 144 m, 515 m, 404 m

The box-and-whisker plot shows the lengths, in inches, of the jumps of frogs in a frog-jumping contest. Estimate the following values.

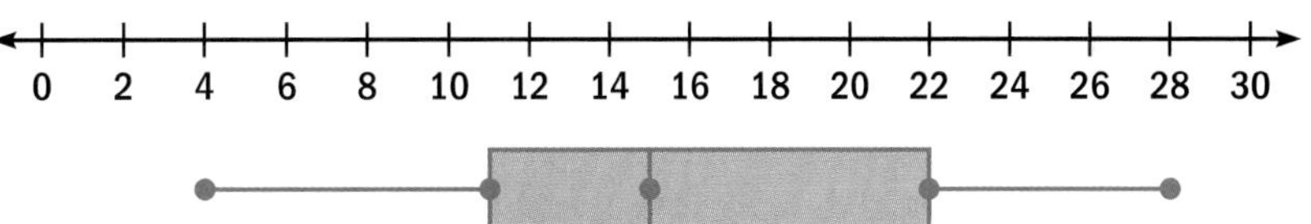

6. range
7. median
8. lower quartile
9. upper quartile
10. lower extreme
11. upper extreme

12. **Camera Prices** The prices of several cameras are \$179.99, \$329.99, \$229.99, \$284.99, \$399.99, \$379.99, \$299.99, \$259.99, and \$259.99. Organize the list of prices from least to greatest. Then make a box-and-whisker plot of the data. What conclusions can you make?

13. **Pumpkins** The weights, in pounds, of 10 giant pumpkins were 853, 811.5, 785, 1020, 826.5, 789, 838, 810, 731, and 822.5. Make a box and-whisker plot of the data. Describe what the plot shows.

14. **Critical Thinking** Explain how making a stem-and-leaf plot can help you to make a box-and-whisker plot.

Lake Area

Three of the world's 10 largest lakes are Great Lakes. The 6 quadrillion gallons in the Great Lakes are 18% of the world's fresh water supply. One quadrillion is equal to one million billions. How much fresh water does the world have?

15. **Basketball** The box-and-whisker plots show the points scored per game for two players. What conclusions can you make about the players' performances? Which player is more consistent? Explain.

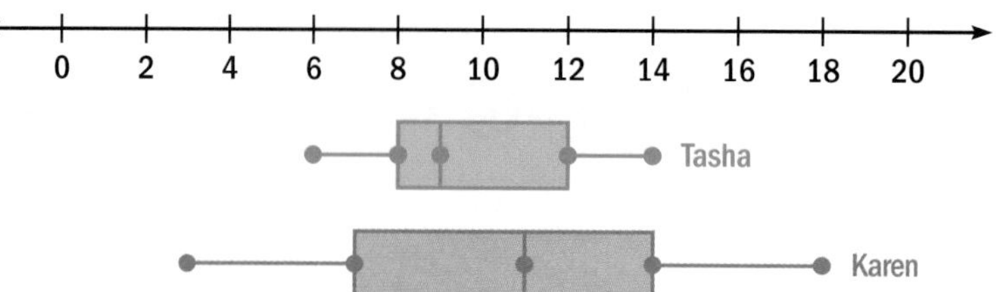

Lake Area In Exercises 16 and 17, use the areas, in square kilometers, of the world's ten largest lakes: 371,000, 84,500, 64,500, 63,500, 62,940, 58,020, 32,000, 31,500, 31,400, and 28,400.

An *outlier* is a data value that is much less or much greater than most of the other values in the data set.

16. Make a box-and-whisker plot of the data. Which value is an outlier?

17. Remove the outlier and then make another box-and-whisker plot. Describe how an outlier affects a box-and-whisker plot.

18. **Challenge** Change one value in the data set 3, 4, 5, 7, 9, 11, 13, 15, 17, 18, 21 so that the median of the set is 13, the lower quartile is 7, and the upper quartile is 17. Explain how you got your answer.

Mixed Review 

19. The table shows the height, in inches, of several players on a soccer team. Make a bar graph of the data. *(Lesson 1.1)*

Name	Ally	Nate	Bob	Inez	Dan	Lisa
Height	68	66	73	66	60	62

Find the x-intercept, y-intercept, and slope of the graph of the equation. Then graph the line. *(Lessons 11.5, 11.6)*

20. $y = 24$ 21. $3x - 5y = 30$ 22. $x = -4$

Test-Taking Practice 

INTERNET
State Test Practice
CLASSZONE.COM

23. **Extended Response** The masses, in grams, of 10 samples from bolt factories A and B are shown. All bolts should be 198.5–202 grams.

Factory A: 199, 201, 200, 198.5, 200.5, 202, 201, 200.8, 200.9, 198.5

Factory B: 201, 200.4, 203, 200.8, 201, 203.4, 200.6, 201, 200.9, 203.1

Make box-and-whisker plots comparing the samples. Describe how well each factory makes bolts within the desired mass range, based on the samples. Then use the plots to compare the factories' performances.

Using Data Displays

BEFORE

You organized data using box-and-whisker plots.

Now

You will organize data using circle graphs and line graphs.

WHY?

So you can represent the areas of boroughs of New York, as in Ex. 13.

Word Watch

circle graph, p. 605
line graph, p. 606

INDIANA Academic Standards

- Data Analysis and Probability (8.6.4)

Circle Graphs A survey asked, "How well can you whistle?" The results are shown in the *circle graph* below. It shows that three out of four people can whistle a tune.

A **circle graph** represents data as sections of a circle. Each section can be labeled using a fraction, decimal, or percent. Because the graph represents all the data, the sum of the sections must equal 1, or 100%.

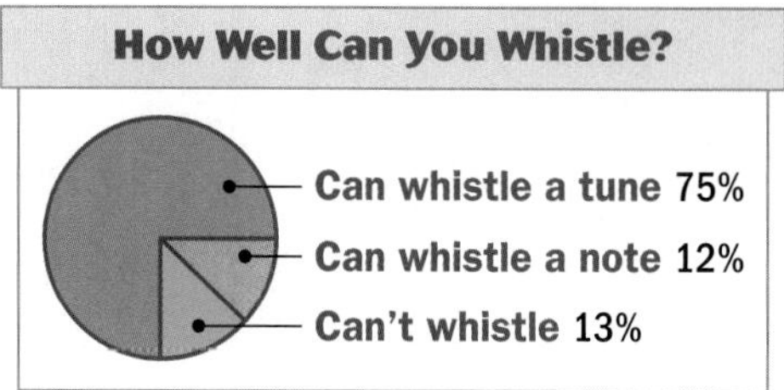

To make a circle graph, find the angle measure to the nearest degree that represents each data value's portion of the whole. The sum of all the angle measures must equal 360°, the number of degrees in a circle.

EXAMPLE 1 Making a Circle Graph

E-mail A survey asked, "How often do you check your e-mail?" Of the 100 people asked, 4 answered *less than weekly,* 23 answered *weekly,* and 73 answered *every day*. You can display the data in a circle graph.

HELP with Solving

In Example 1, you can draw the 14° and 83° angles first. Then the remaining section of the circle will have a measure of 263°.

(1) Use a proportion to find the number of degrees to use to represent each response as a section in a circle graph.

Less than weekly	Weekly	Every day
$\frac{4}{100} = \frac{a}{360°}$	$\frac{23}{100} = \frac{b}{360°}$	$\frac{73}{100} = \frac{c}{360°}$
$a = 14.4° \approx \mathbf{14°}$	$b = 82.8° \approx \mathbf{83°}$	$c = 262.8° \approx \mathbf{263°}$

(2) Draw a circle.

(3) Use a protractor to draw the first angle measure. Then label the section.

(4) Draw and label remaining sections. Include a title.

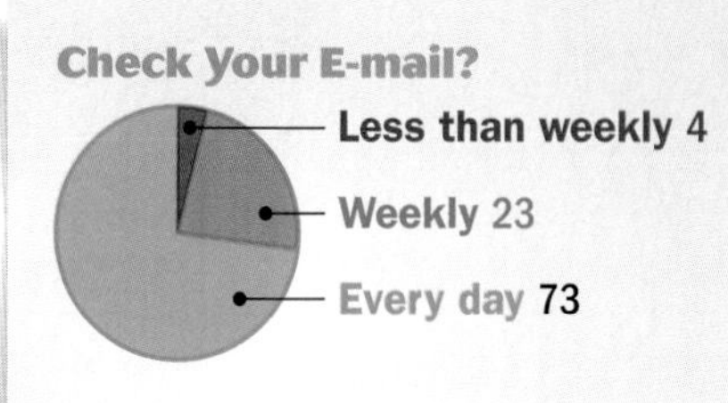

ANSWER The graph shows that the majority of people check their e-mail every day.

Line Graphs A **line graph** represents data that change over time.

EXAMPLE 2 Making a Line Graph

Environment **The table shows the number of insect species on the United States endangered species list. Make a line graph of the data.**

Year	1995	1996	1997	1998	1999	2000	2001
Number	20	20	28	28	28	33	35

Karner Blue Butterfly, endangered since 1992

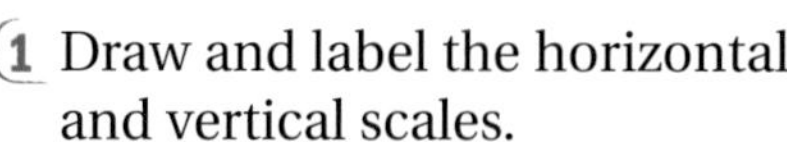

1 Draw and label the horizontal and vertical scales.

2 Plot a point for each data pair.

3 Draw line segments to connect the points.

4 The graph shows an increase over time.

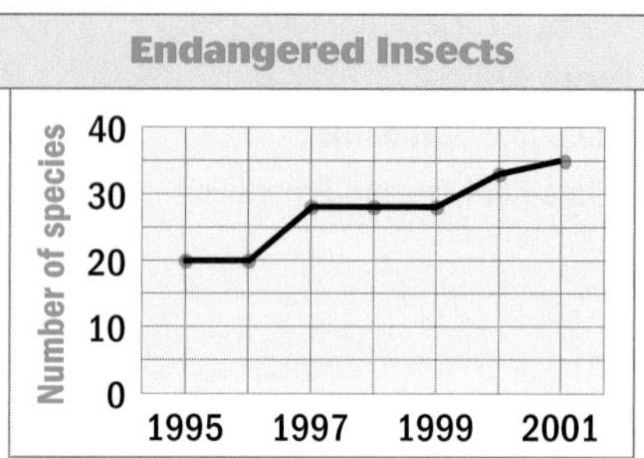

Your turn now **Use the table of polling data.**

1. Make a circle graph of the data for Week 1. What does the graph show?
2. Make a line graph of the data for Ben. What does the graph show?

Who Will You Vote For?			
Week	1	2	3
Ben	55%	50%	40%
Alice	45%	50%	60%

Using appropriate data displays helps you make meaningful conclusions.

Using Appropriate Data Displays

- Use a *circle graph* to represent data as parts of a whole.
- Use a *line graph* to display data over time.
- Use a *stem-and-leaf plot* to order a data set.
- Use a *box-and-whisker plot* to show the data's distribution in quarters, using the median, quartiles, and extremes.
- Use a *bar graph* to display data in distinct categories.
- Use a *histogram* to compare the frequencies of data that are grouped in equal intervals.

EXAMPLE 3 Choosing a Data Display

Choose an appropriate display for the data.

a. The table below shows the results of a survey that asked students if they are going away during summer vacation.

Response	Percent
Yes	48%
No	37%
Don't know	15%

b. The table below shows the results of a survey that asked students about ways they use the Internet.

Purpose	Percent
Research	62%
Shopping	34%
E-mail	45%
News	10%
Browsing	18%

Solution

a. The data add up to 100%, so a circle graph is appropriate.

b. The percents in the categories add up to more than 100%. An appropriate display for the data is a bar graph.

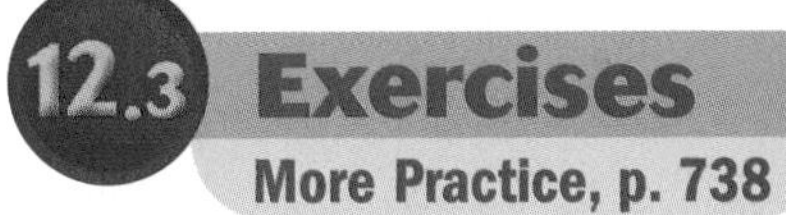

12.3 Exercises

More Practice, p. 738

Getting Ready to Practice

Vocabulary **Copy and complete the statement.**

1. You can use a _?_ to display data as parts of a whole.

2. You can use a _?_ to display changes in a quantity over time.

Convert the value into an angle measure for display in a circle graph.

3. 31% **4.** $\frac{3}{8}$ **5.** 14% **6.** 27 out of 60

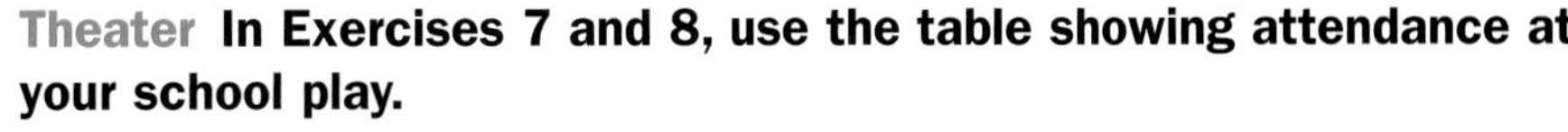

Theater **In Exercises 7 and 8, use the table showing attendance at your school play.**

7. Make a circle graph to display each attendance number as a fraction of total attendance at all four performances.

8. Tickets cost $7 each. Make a line graph that shows how much money was collected from each performance.

Play Attendance	
Friday	130
Saturday (2 P.M.)	231
Saturday (8 P.M.)	291
Sunday	185

Practice and Problem Solving

Example	Exercises
1	9, 12–17
2	10–11, 15–17
3	15–17

Online Resources
CLASSZONE.COM
· More Examples
· eTutorial Plus

9. Snacking The table shows the results of a survey asking students to describe how often they snack. Represent the data in a circle graph.

How Often Do You Snack?	
Never	10%
Rarely	45%
Sometimes	35%
Often	10%

10. New Houses The table below shows the number, in thousands, of new single-family houses sold in the United States each year from 1997 to 2001. Make a line graph of the data. Describe how the data change over time.

Year	1997	1998	1999	2000	2001
Houses sold (thousands)	804	886	880	877	900

11. Music The table below shows the number of people, in millions, who attended symphony orchestra concerts in the United States each year from 1994 to 1998. Make a line graph of the data. What trend does the graph show?

Year	1994	1995	1996	1997	1998
Attendees (millions)	24.4	30.9	31.1	31.9	32.2

The sum of the rounded angle measures in Exercise 13 will not equal 360°. This is the result of *round-off error*. The sum of the unrounded values is 360°.

New York City **The map shows the land area, in square miles, of each of the five boroughs of New York City.**

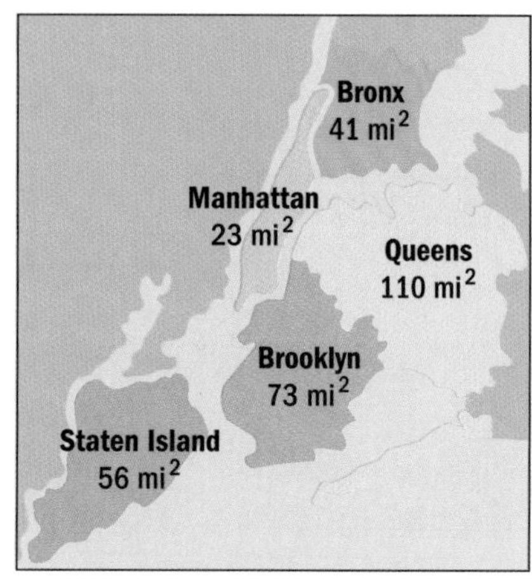

12. Find the percent of the total area of New York City that each borough covers.

13. Represent the data using a circle graph.

14. Use the graph to compare the areas of the boroughs.

Critical Thinking **In Exercises 15–17, tell which type of display you would use for the data described. Explain your reasoning.**

15. You record the temperature at noon every day for a month.

16. You record the temperature at five different locations.

17. You record the high temperature every day for a month, and find how often the daily high temperature falls within each 10 degree temperature interval.

Car Color **In Exercises 18 and 19, use the table. It shows the percent of people who liked the given color for sports and compact cars.**

Color	Silver	Black	Dark blue	White	Dark green	Red	Other
2000	25.4%	14.5%	11.3%	9.8%	6.7%	12.7%	19.6%
2001	22.3%	14.4%	5.0%	11.4%	9.7%	15.8%	21.4%

18. Make a circle graph of the data for 2000 and for 2001.

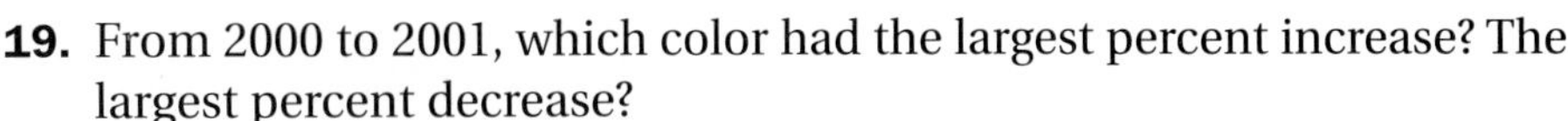

19. From 2000 to 2001, which color had the largest percent increase? The largest percent decrease?

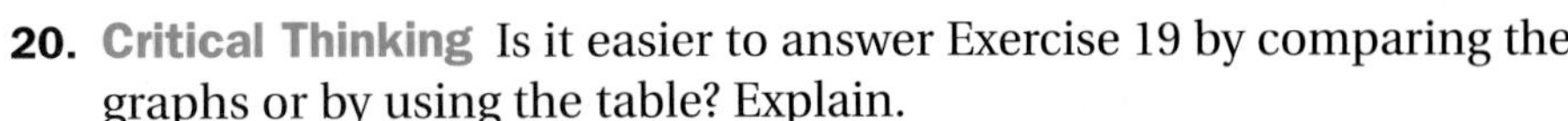

20. **Critical Thinking** Is it easier to answer Exercise 19 by comparing the graphs or by using the table? Explain.

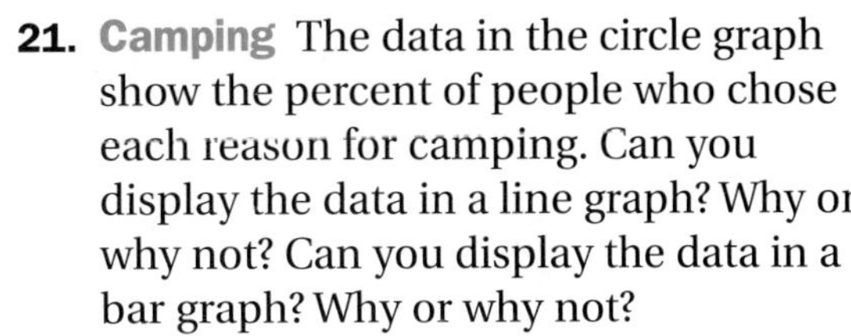

21. **Camping** The data in the circle graph show the percent of people who chose each reason for camping. Can you display the data in a line graph? Why or why not? Can you display the data in a bar graph? Why or why not?

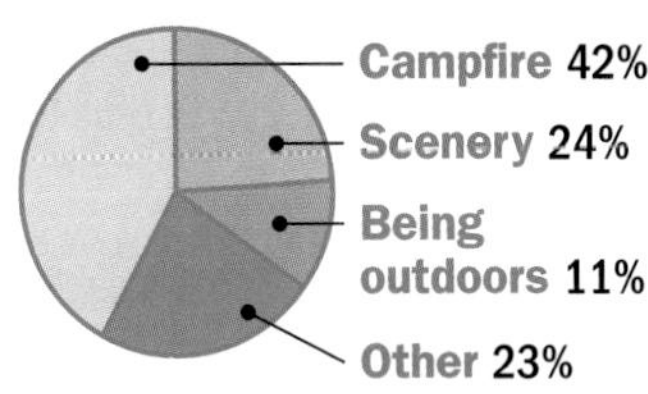

22. **Challenge** Describe a set of data that could be displayed in three different types of data display. Explain how to display it in each.

Mixed Review 

Graph the equation using intercepts. *(Lesson 11.5)*

23. $5x + 2y = 10$ **24.** $8x - 3y = 24$ **25.** $9y - 18x = 27$

26. Make an ordered stem-and-leaf plot of the following data: 17, 10, 11, 15, 21, 34, 26, 16, 36, 24, 37, 20, 18, 31, 39, 29, 28. *(Lesson 12.1)*

Test-Taking Practice 

INTERNET
State Test Practice
CLASSZONE.COM

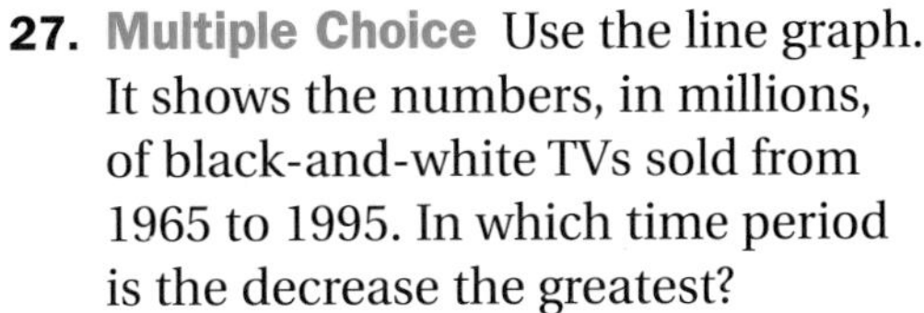

27. **Multiple Choice** Use the line graph. It shows the numbers, in millions, of black-and-white TVs sold from 1965 to 1995. In which time period is the decrease the greatest?

A. 1965–1970 **B.** 1975–1980

C. 1985–1990 **D.** 1990–1995

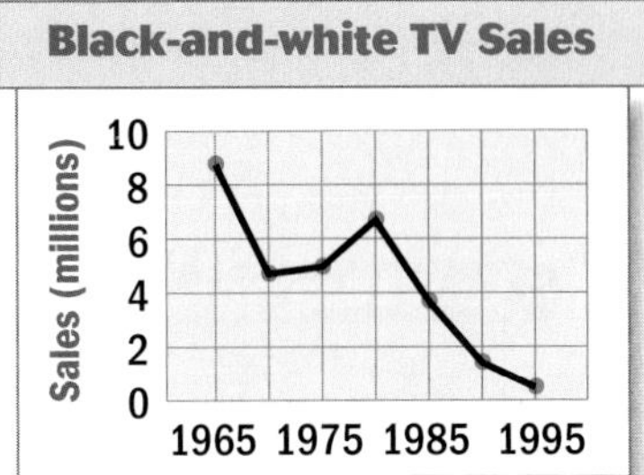

28. **Short Response** You ask 100 people a yes or no question. The possible answers are *yes, no,* and *no answer*. What types of display would be appropriate for this type of data? Explain your reasoning.

12.3 Technology Activity

GRAPHING CALCULATOR

INDIANA: Academic Standards
- Data Analysis and Probability (8.6.4, 8.6.5)

Making Data Displays

GOAL Use a graphing calculator to create data displays.

Example 1 **The table shows the cost, in dollars, of a phone call, based on the length, in minutes, of the call. Make a scatter plot or a line graph on your calculator.**

Minutes	Cost
5	0.5
10	1
15	1.5
20	2
25	2.4
30	2.7

Solution

1 Enter the data into two lists.

L1	L2	L3
5	.5	
10	1	
15	1.5	
20	2	
25	2.4	
30	2.7	

L2(5)=2.4

2 Choose maximums and minimums for the window.

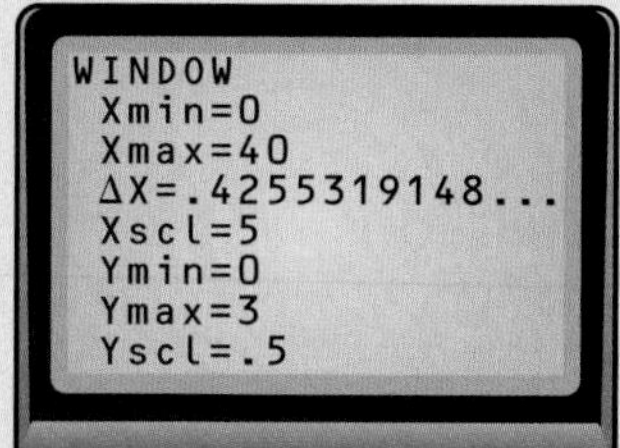

3 Choose a display from the PLOT menu and set the Xlist and Ylist.

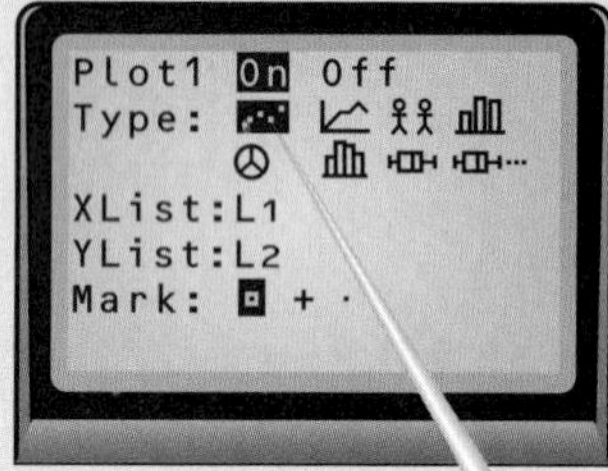

Choose [scatter icon] for a scatter plot or [line icon] for a line graph.

4 Press GRAPH to show the display you have chosen.

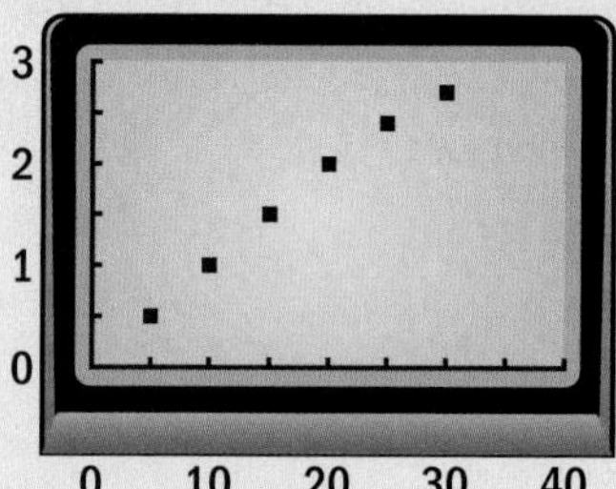

Your turn now **Make a scatter plot and a line graph of the data.**

1.

Year	1997	1998	1999	2000	2001
Rainfall (in.)	21.4	39.8	34.5	26.1	44.9

Example 2 **The table shows the number of people out of 200 surveyed who prefer each type of music. You can use a graphing calculator to make a circle graph of the data.**

Pop	75
Rock	62
Country	43
Classical	20

Solution

1. Press LIST. Then use the TEXT menu to name a list and its categories. Use quotation marks for the first item, so the calculator recognizes that the list is *categorical* (contains words).

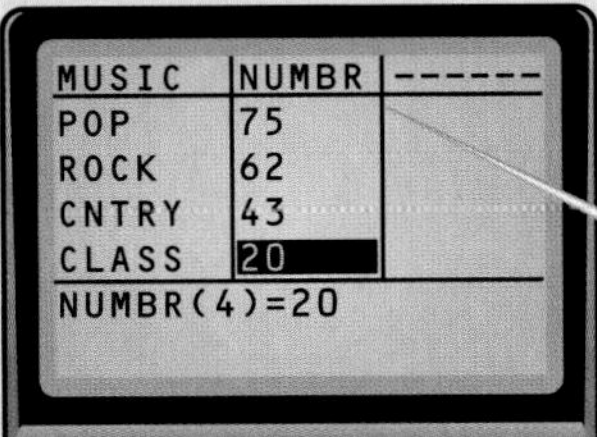

2. Use the PLOT menu to choose the two lists.

3. Press GRAPH to display the circle graph.

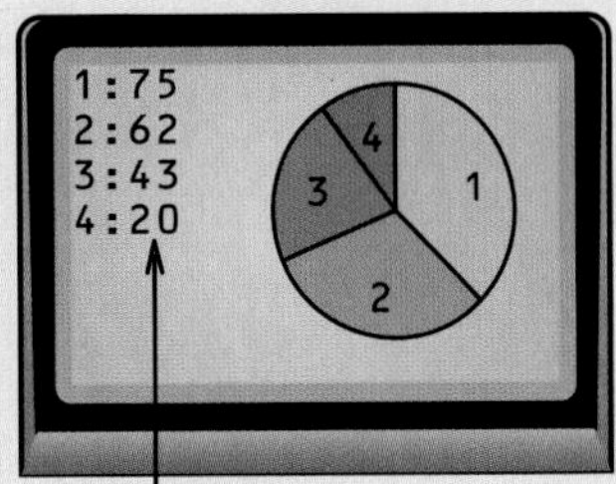

Your turn now **Make a circle graph of the survey data.**

2.

Did You Get Enough Sleep?	
Need more	541
Need less	167
Just right	282
Don't know	21

3.

The last movie I saw I watched...	
in a theater.	410
on a television.	483
on a computer.	21

Misleading Graphs

GOAL Identify and analyze misleading graphs.

Review Words

bar graph, p. 5
line graph, p. 606

When you analyze a graph to make conclusions based on the data displayed, it is important to be aware that the display may be misleading.

EXAMPLE 1 Identifying a Misleading Graph

Attendance Which of the bar graphs that show attendance at an annual rock festival from 1998 to 2002 could be misleading?

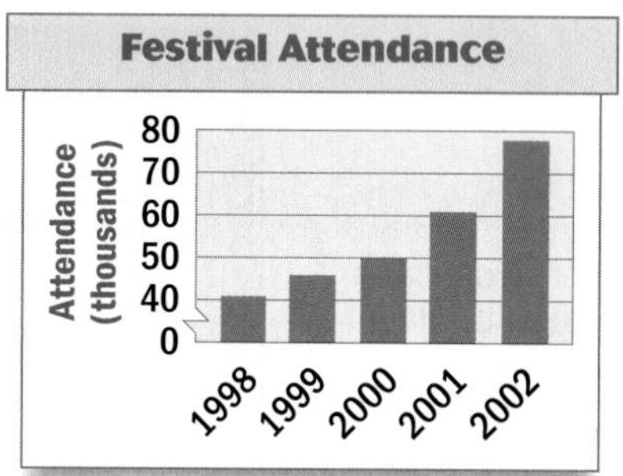

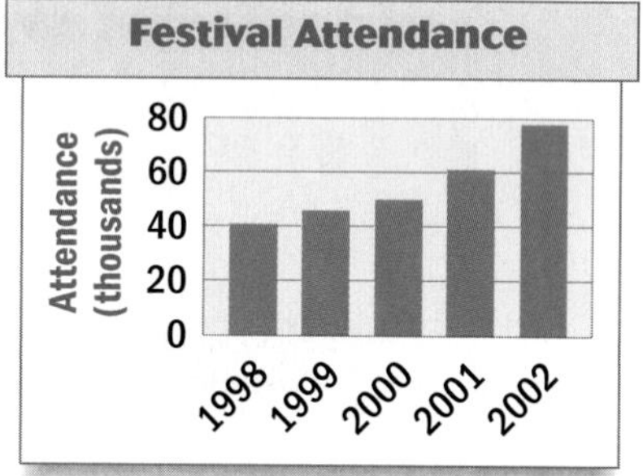

The first graph has a break in the vertical axis, so comparing the bars may lead to incorrect conclusions. It looks as if attendance in 2002 was about three times as great as in 1998, but attendance only doubled during this time. The second graph is less likely to mislead.

HELP with Solving

Remember that the broken axis symbol ⺊ indicates that some of the values in the axis have been left out.

EXAMPLE 2 Analyzing Misleading Graphs

Business The line graphs below display a company's profits and sales for each year from 1998 to 2002. What is misleading about each graph?

a.

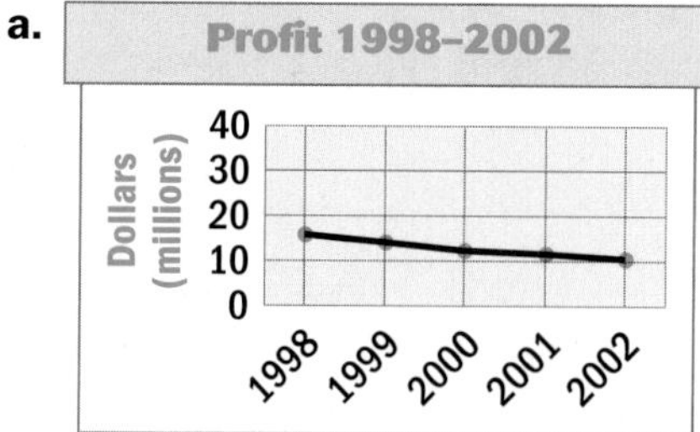

b.

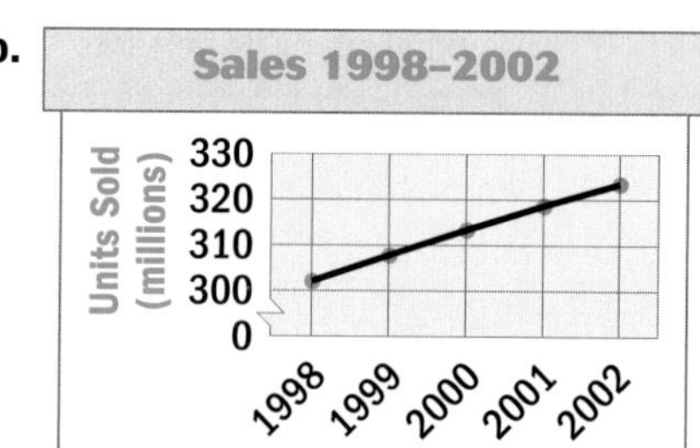

Solution

a. The range of values on the vertical scale is larger than needed. The graph suggests that profits have decreased only slightly, when they have decreased by a third.

b. Because the vertical axis starts at 300, it looks as if sales have risen rapidly. An unbroken axis would show that sales have risen slowly, at less than 2% per year.

EXAMPLE 3 Misleading Comparisons

Compare the average monthly temperatures at two resorts.

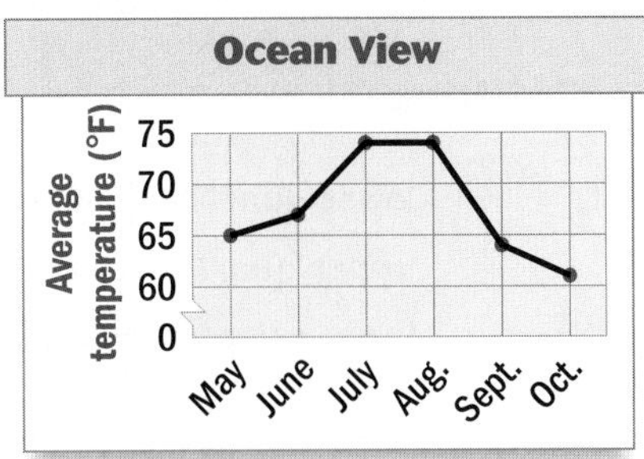

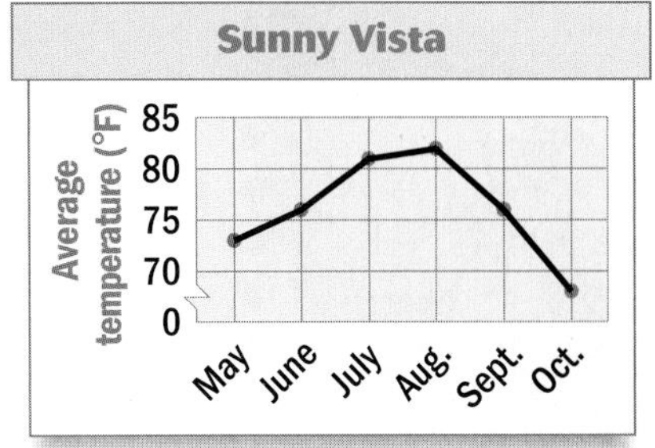

At a glance, the displays suggest that the temperatures are about the same, but the vertical axes are different. When data for both resorts are graphed together, it becomes clear that Sunny Vista has warmer temperatures.

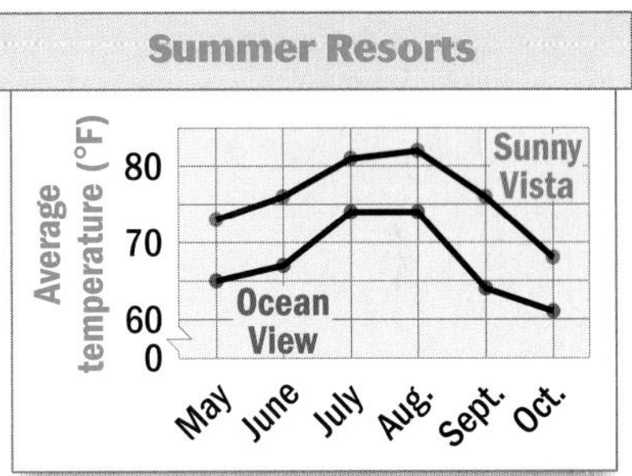

Exercises

Tell whether the data are represented clearly. If the graph is misleading, explain why. Then redraw the graph so that it is not misleading.

1.

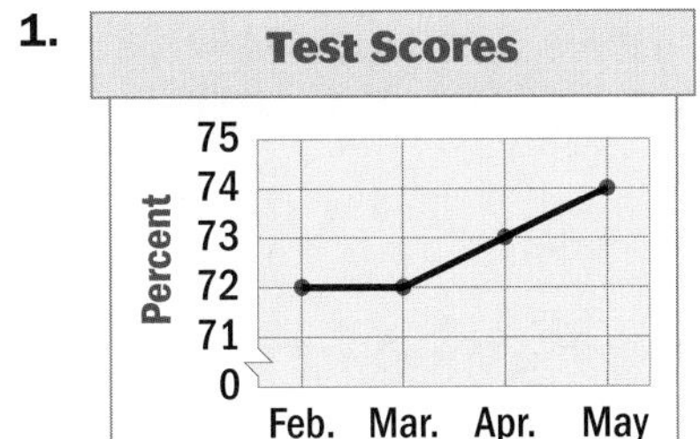

2.

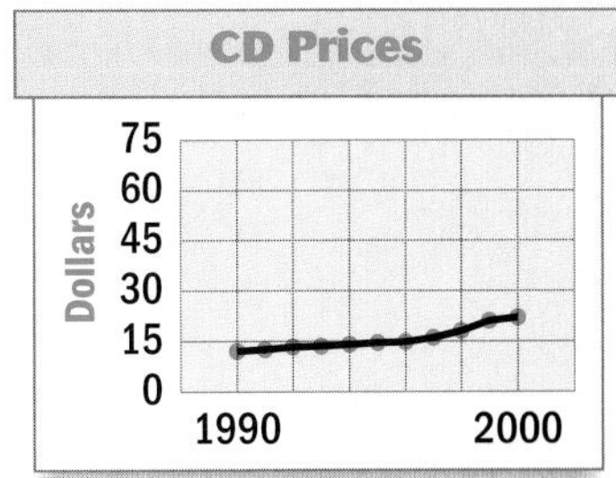

3. **Baseball** The table below shows a baseball pitcher's wins and losses per season. Make a graph that shows a positive performance. Then make another graph that shows a negative performance.

Year	1998	1999	2000	2001	2002
Wins	6	8	10	12	16
Losses	7	9	9	13	14

Notebook Review

Review the vocabulary definitions in your notebook.

Copy the review examples in your notebook. Then complete the exercises.

Check Your Definitions

stem-and-leaf plot, p. 597
box-and-whisker plot, p. 601
lower quartile, p. 601
upper quartile, p. 601
lower extreme, p. 601
upper extreme, p. 601
circle graph, p. 605
line graph, p. 606

Use Your Vocabulary

1. Copy and complete: The _?_ is the least value in a data set and the _?_ is the greatest value in the data set.

12.1–12.2 Can you order and display data?

EXAMPLE Order the data set 24, 29, 35, 32, 22, 20, 43, 27, 41, 31, 26 in a stem-and-leaf plot. Then make a box-and-whisker plot of the data.

2	0 2 4 6 7 9
3	1 2 5
4	1 3

Key: 4 | 1 = 41

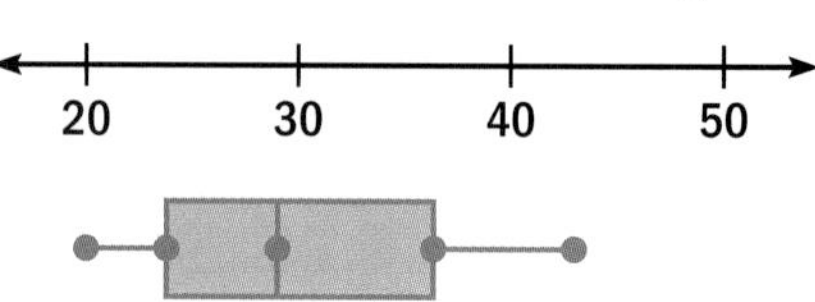

2. Make an ordered stem-and-leaf plot and a box-and-whisker plot of the wind speed data, given in miles per hour: 9, 15, 8, 19, 11, 18, 11, 24, 7, 14.

12.3 Can you use appropriate data displays?

EXAMPLES

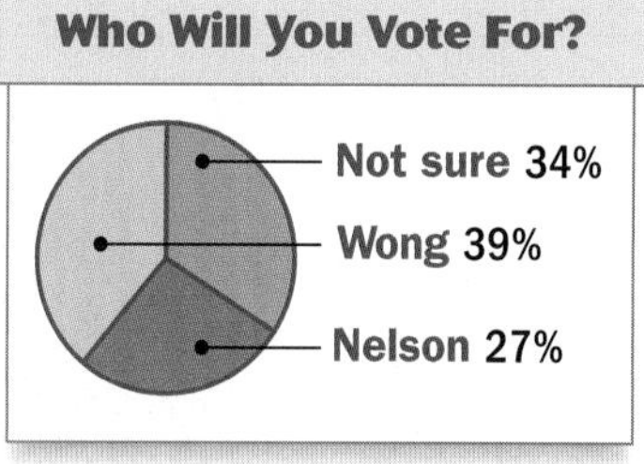

Use a circle graph to represent data as parts of a whole.

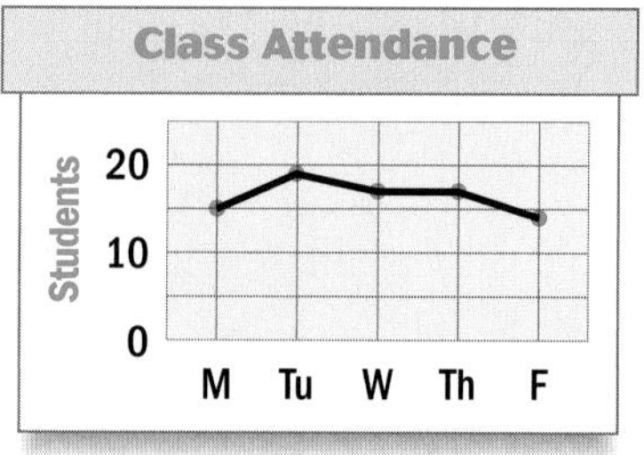

Use a line graph to display changes in a quantity over time.

3. Make a circle graph of survey results where 24% of the people surveyed said *no*, 47% said *yes*, and the rest said *not sure*.

4. The hourly temperatures, in degrees Celsius, starting at 1 P.M. were 33°C, 33°C, 34°C, 37°C, 37°C, and 36°C. Make a line graph of the data.

Stop and Think about Lessons 12.1–12.3

5. **Writing** Describe some real-world data that a double stem-and-leaf plot would help you analyze.

6. **Critical Thinking** Could you display the data from Exercise 3 in a line graph? Explain. What other type of display could be useful?

Review Quiz 1

1. **Attendance** Make an ordered double stem-and-leaf plot comparing the ballpark attendance data below for April and June. Then make a pair of box-and-whisker plots that compare the data. Use the displays to compare April attendance to June attendance.

   April: 1025, 1058, 1030, 997, 990, 1116, 1001, 995, 1122, 1099

   June: 1056, 1125, 1151, 1048, 1123, 1097, 1042, 1164, 1125, 1131

2. **Nuts** Consumption of peanuts per person in the United States was as follows: 1995, 5.7 lb; 1996, 5.7 lb; 1997, 5.9 lb; 1998, 5.9 lb; 1999, 6.4 lb. Make a circle graph or a line graph of the data. Explain your choice.

Safe Cracker

Use the box-and-whisker plot to find the missing leaves in the stem-and-leaf plot of the same group of eight numbers. Take the numbers that the missing leaves represent, and put them in order from least to greatest to find the combination that opens the safe.

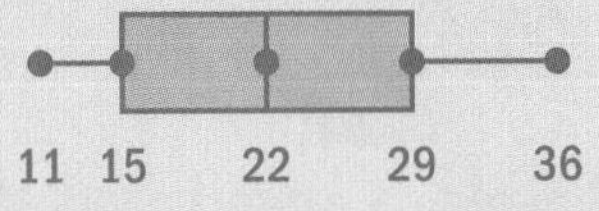

Stem	Leaves
1	1 4 ?
2	0 ? 7
3	1 ?

Key: 1 | 4 = 14

12.4 Problem Solving Strategies

INDIANA: Academic Standards
- Problem Solving (8.7.3)

Solve a Simpler Problem

- Guess, Check, and Revise
- Look for a Pattern
- Draw a Diagram
- Act It Out
- **Solve a Simpler Problem**
- Work Backward
- Make a Table

Problem There are 10 people in a room. They introduce themselves to each other by shaking every other person's hand one time. How many handshakes occur?

1 Read and Understand

Read the problem carefully.

You know that 10 people in a room each shake every other person's hand.

You want to find the total number of handshakes.

2 Make a Plan

Decide on a strategy to use.

By solving a series of simpler problems, you can identify a pattern in the number of handshakes. Then you can extend the pattern to find how many handshakes occur among 10 people.

3 Solve the Problem

Reread the problem and solve a simpler problem.

First, find the number of handshakes between 2 people, 3 people, and so on. You can do this by drawing a diagram. Make a table of your results.

Number of people	2	3	4	5
Number of handshakes	1	3	6	10
Pattern		+2	+3	+4

Extend the pattern to find the number of handshakes among 10 people.

1, 3, 6, 10, 15, 21, 28, 36, 45

+5 +6 +7 +8 +9

ANSWER So, 45 handshakes occur when 10 people shake hands.

4 Look Back

Double-check your calculations to be sure you didn't make any mistakes. You can also use the strategy *act it out* to check your answer.

Practice the Strategy

Use the strategy *solve a simpler problem.*

1. **Restaurants** A restaurant has 28 square tables that seat one person per side. You can join tables together. How many people can fit at two long tables made from all 28 tables? Will it make a difference if the tables are not divided equally?

2. **Triangular Numbers** The dots arranged in a triangle represent triangular numbers.

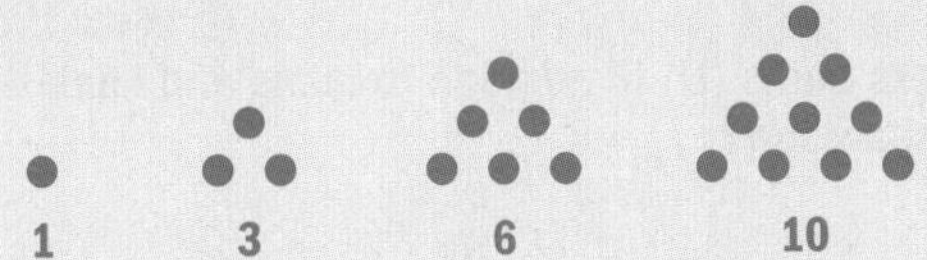

Predict the number of dots in the eighth triangular number.

3. **Tournament** You are planning a small tournament for a chess club. If each of five members plays one game against each of the other members, how many games must you schedule?

4. **House Numbers** The houses on Stanford Street are numbered consecutively from 10 to 132. How many of each digit do you need to form all the house numbers?

5. **Odd Numbers** Find the sum of the first 50 odd whole numbers.

6. **Marching Band** A marching band is in a triangular formation. There is 1 band member in the front row. Each of the other rows contains 2 more band members than the row in front of it. There are 11 rows in all. How many band members are there?

7. **Palindromes** A palindrome is a number that reads the same backward and forward. For example, the number 1 and the number 414 are both palindromes. How many palindromes are there from 1 to 500?

Mixed Problem Solving

Use any strategy to solve the problem.

8. **Walking** Jay and Paul start walking in opposite directions. Jay walks 0.75 mile every 12 minutes, and Paul walks 2.5 miles every 30 minutes. How far apart are they after 1.5 hours?

9. **Games** What is the total number of squares on the checkerboard? Include squares of all sizes.

10. **Prisms** How does doubling the height of each base of a triangular prism affect its volume? How does halving the height of each base affect the volume?

11. **Calendars** What day of the week is the 3117th day after Thursday?

12. **Checking Account** The list below shows deposits and withdrawals this month. If Rodney has $57.68 in his checking account now, how much money did he have before Week 1?

Week 1: He bought a shirt for $18 and a pair of pants for $26.

Week 2: He bought a CD for $14 and lunch for $7.50.

Week 3: He deposited $20.

Counting Methods

BEFORE

You found theoretical and experimental probability.

Now

You will use counting methods to count the number of choices.

WHY?

So you can count the outcomes of an election, as in Ex. 12.

tree diagram, p. 618

INDIANA Academic Standards

- Data Analysis and Probability (8.6.7)

Activity **You can count choices using an organized list.**

You are choosing an outfit. You can choose a T-shirt (T), a button-down shirt (B), or a sweater (S) as a top and jeans (J) or khakis (K) for pants.

 jeans (J)  khakis (K)  T-shirt (T)  button-down (B)  sweater (S)

1. Use the letters to represent possible outfits. One possible outfit is JT, which means jeans and a T-shirt. Make a list of all possible outfits.

2. You decide to consider dress pants (D) in addition to jeans and khakis. How many outfits are possible now?

3. You also decide to include socks as part of the outfit. You can choose between red (R) and green (G). How many outfits are possible now?

In the activity, you made lists to count the number of choices. Another way to count the number of choices is to use a **tree diagram**.

EXAMPLE 1 **Making a Tree Diagram**

You can use a tree diagram to count the number of possible outfits in Step 2 of the activity above.

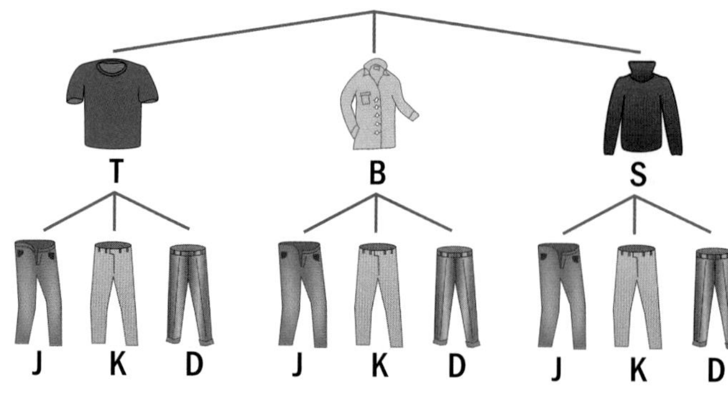

There are 9 different possible outfits.

Another way to count choices is to use the *counting principle.*

The Counting Principle

If one event can occur in m ways, and for each of these a second event can occur in n ways, then the number of ways that the two events can occur together is $m \cdot n$.

This principle can be extended to three or more events.

EXAMPLE 2 Using the Counting Principle

Skateboards To build a skateboard, you can choose one deck and one type of wheel assembly from those shown. To count the number of different skateboards you can build, use the counting principle.

Decks

Wheel Assemblies

$4 \cdot 3 = 12$ **Counting principle**

(4 decks, 3 wheel assemblies)

ANSWER You can build 12 different skateboards.

EXAMPLE 3 Using the Counting Principle

Passwords You are choosing a password that starts with 3 letters and then has 2 digits. How many different passwords are possible?

Solution

$\underbrace{26 \cdot 26 \cdot 26}_{\text{letters}} \cdot \underbrace{10 \cdot 10}_{\text{digits}} = 1{,}757{,}600$ **Counting principle**

ANSWER There are 1,757,600 different possible passwords.

Your turn now **Count the choices.**

1. Your soccer team's uniform choices include yellow and green shirts, white, black, and green shorts, and four colors of socks. Use a tree diagram to find how many different uniforms are possible.

2. In Example 3, suppose that the passwords may not start with an A or use the digit 0. How many different passwords are possible? Explain.

EXAMPLE 4 Finding a Probability

Number Cubes You and three friends each roll a number cube. What is the probability that you each roll the same number?

1 List the *favorable* outcomes. There are 6:

1-1-1-1 2-2-2-2 3-3-3-3 4-4-4-4 5-5-5-5 6-6-6-6

2 Use the counting principle to find the number of *possible* outcomes.

$$\underbrace{6 \cdot 6 \cdot 6 \cdot 6}_{\text{4 number cubes}} = 1296$$

For help with probability, see p. 354.

3 Then use the formula for finding probability.

$$\frac{\text{Number of favorable outcomes}}{\text{Number of possible outcomes}} = \frac{6}{1296} = \frac{1}{216}$$

ANSWER The probability that you each roll the same number is $\frac{1}{216}$.

12.4 Exercises

More Practice, p. 738

Getting Ready to Practice

1. **Vocabulary** Copy and complete: If there are m ways that one event can occur and for each of those there are n ways that a second event can occur, then there are _?_ ways that the two events can occur together.

Make a tree diagram to find the number of choices that are possible. Then check your answer using the counting principle.

2. Choose apple, blueberry, lemon, or cherry pie with juice or tea.
3. Choose a small, medium, or large shirt in red, yellow, or blue.
4. Choose a car or truck with a tape player or a CD player.
5. Choose a hat or scarf in gray, white, or black.
6. **Weekend Plans** You would like to go to the movies, a play, or the zoo. You can invite your cousin or your best friend. You can go on Friday or Saturday. Make a tree diagram to list all of the possibilities. Then use the counting principle to check your answer.
7. **Movies** You and three friends all go to the movies on Friday night. You each pick a movie at random from the four choices. What is the probability that you all pick the same movie to see?

Practice and Problem Solving

HELP with Homework

Example	Exercises
1	8-12, 14, 17
2	8-14, 18
3	8-14, 18
4	15-16

Online Resources
CLASSZONE.COM

- More Examples
- eTutorial Plus

In Exercises 8–11, make a tree diagram to find the number of choices that are possible. Then check your answer using the counting principle.

8. Choose a red, green, blue, or gray ball with a black or silver racquet.

9. Choose one of 6 DVDs and one of 4 CDs.

10. Choose one of 5 essays and one of 3 extra credit questions.

11. Choose a city tour or a park tour with passes to the art or science museum and a trip to the zoo, baseball game, movies, or mall.

12. Class Election The lists show the candidates for offices in a class election. Make a tree diagram to find the number of different ways a president, treasurer, and secretary can be chosen. Then use the counting principle to check your answer.

President	Treasurer	Secretary
☐ Amy	☐ Jessica	☐ Scott
☐ Hector	☐ Michael	☐ Nicole
	☐ Carson	☐ Thomas
		☐ Angela
		☐ Isabel

13. Banking You open a bank account and need to choose a password with 4 characters that can repeat. The password starts with 3 digits and then has 1 letter. How many different passwords are possible?

14. Writing There are 5 CDs and 4 books that you are interested in buying. Describe how to find the number of different pairs of 1 CD and 1 book that you can buy.

15. Coins Six people all flip a coin. What is the probability that they all get heads?

16. States You and Terry randomly choose the name of a state. What is the probability that you both choose a state whose name starts with a T? (Tennessee and Texas are the two states that start with the letter T.)

Extended Problem Solving You are at a grocery store buying flavored water. You can choose lime, lemon, cherry, or orange. You can choose a 0.5-liter, 1-liter, or 2-liter bottle.

17. Draw Make a tree diagram that shows all of the different bottles of flavored water that you can choose.

18. Multiply How many total different bottles can you choose from if 5 new flavors become available?

19. Challenge The sign shows the prices for each bottle size. What are the different total prices that you could be charged for three bottles? What is largest total quantity of water you can buy if you have only $2.60?

Water Sale
0.5 liter — $0.59
1 liter — $0.69
2 liter — $0.99

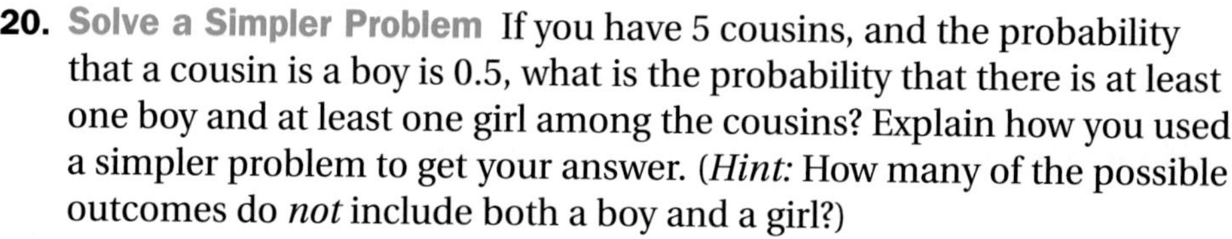

20. **Solve a Simpler Problem** If you have 5 cousins, and the probability that a cousin is a boy is 0.5, what is the probability that there is at least one boy and at least one girl among the cousins? Explain how you used a simpler problem to get your answer. (*Hint:* How many of the possible outcomes do *not* include both a boy and a girl?)

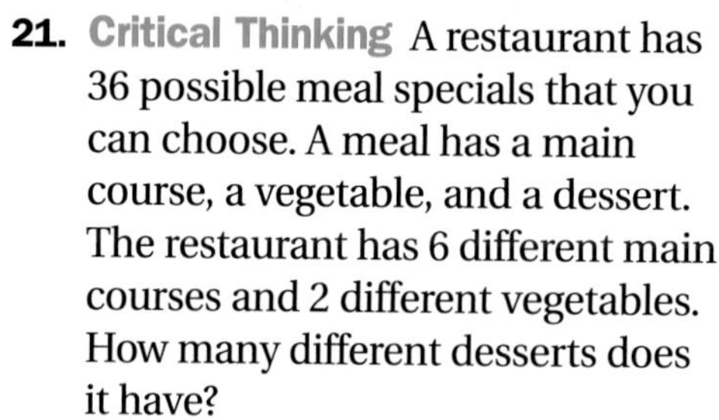

21. **Critical Thinking** A restaurant has 36 possible meal specials that you can choose. A meal has a main course, a vegetable, and a dessert. The restaurant has 6 different main courses and 2 different vegetables. How many different desserts does it have?

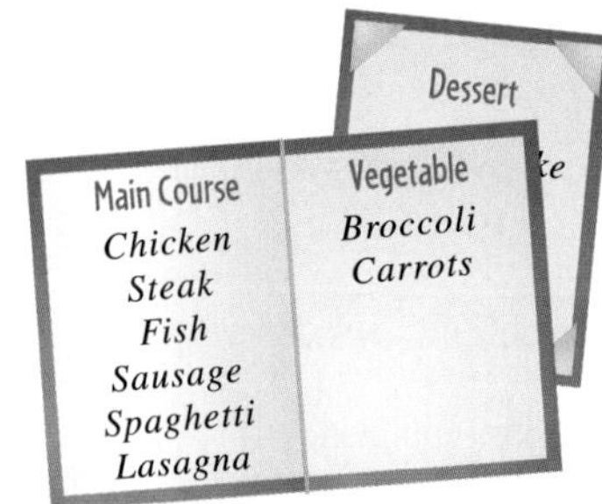

Braille In Exercises 22 and 23, use the following information.

Braille uses arrangements of raised dots to form symbols that represent letters, numbers, and punctuation marks. Braille is read by touching the symbols. Each symbol is a cell of 6 dots arranged in 3 rows of 2. In the cell, certain dots are raised to make a particular symbol.

22. How many different Braille symbols are possible? How many symbols are possible with no raised dots? With 6 raised dots?

23. Are the number of symbols possible with one raised dot the same as the number of symbols possible with 5 raised dots? Explain.

Mixed Review

Find the slope of the line passing through the points. *(Lesson 11.6)*

24. (5, 2), (−4, 2)

25. (−2, 3), (4, 6)

26. (3, 1), (7, −2)

27. The ages, in years, of youth group members are 12, 9, 8, 16, 12, 13, 8, 10, 11, and 17. Make a box-and-whisker plot of the data. *(Lesson 12.2)*

Test-Taking Practice

INTERNET
State Test Practice
CLASSZONE.COM

28. **Multiple Choice** Your computer password has three digits. Which of the expressions would you use to find the total number of possible passwords?

A. $10 + 10 + 10$ **B.** $10 \cdot 10 \cdot 10$ **C.** $10 + 3$ **D.** $10 \cdot 3$

29. **Short Response** You would like a sandwich, a side order, and a drink for lunch. You have a choice of a turkey, tuna, ham, or roast beef sandwich. You may have fruit, salad, or soup as a side order. You may choose juice or iced tea to drink. Make a tree diagram to show all the possible lunches that you can have. Write and evaluate an expression to find the total number of possible lunches.

Permutations

BEFORE	Now	WHY?
You used the counting principle to count possibilities.	You will use permutations to count possibilities.	So you can count the ways you can knit a hat, as in Ex. 20.

Word Watch

permutation, p. 623
factorial, p. 623

INDIANA Academic Standards

- Data Analysis and Probability (8.6.7)

In some arrangements of groups, order is important. For example, the diagram shows the different ways that a group of three dogs could finish first, second, and third at a dog show.

Each arrangement lists the same dogs, but the orders are different. Arrangements such as these are called *permutations.* A **permutation** is an arrangement in which order is important. You can use the counting principle to count permutations.

EXAMPLE 1 Counting Permutations

Music You have five CDs. You can use the counting principle to count the number of permutations of 5 CDs. This is the number of different orders in which you can listen to the CDs.

Choices for 1st CD		Choices for 2nd CD		Choices for 3rd CD		Choices for 4th CD		Choices for 5th CD	
5	•	4	•	3	•	2	•	1	= 120

ANSWER You can listen to the CDs in 120 different orders.

HELP with Solving

You can use $n!$ to find the number of permutations of n objects.

Factorials In Example 1, you evaluated $5 \cdot 4 \cdot 3 \cdot 2 \cdot 1$. You can write $5 \cdot 4 \cdot 3 \cdot 2 \cdot 1$ as 5!, which is read "5 **factorial**."

$5! = 5 \cdot 4 \cdot 3 \cdot 2 \cdot 1$ $\qquad$ $n! = n \cdot (n-1) \cdot (n-2) \cdot \ldots \cdot 1$

The value of 0! is defined to be 1.

Your turn now **Evaluate the factorial.**

1. 3! **2.** 4! **3.** 6! **4.** 1!

EXAMPLE 2 Counting Permutations

Band Competition Twelve marching bands are entered in a competition. You can use the counting principle to count how many ways first, second, and third places can be awarded.

Choices for 1st place		Choices for 2nd place		Choices for 3rd place		
12	•	11	•	10	= 1320	**Counting principle**

ANSWER There are 1320 ways to award the three places.

Permutation Notation Example 2 shows how to find the number of permutations of 12 objects taken 3 at a time. This is written ${}_{12}P_3$.

Permutations

Algebra The number of permutations of n objects taken r at a time can be written as ${}_nP_r$ and evaluated using $\frac{n!}{(n-r)!}$.

Numbers ${}_7P_3 = \frac{7!}{(7-3)!} = \frac{7!}{4!} = \frac{7 \cdot 6 \cdot 5 \cdot \cancel{4} \cdot \cancel{3} \cdot \cancel{2} \cdot \cancel{1}}{\cancel{4} \cdot \cancel{3} \cdot \cancel{2} \cdot \cancel{1}} = 7 \cdot 6 \cdot 5$

EXAMPLE 3 Evaluating a Permutation

Poetry Two students are chosen from a group of 6 to read the first and second poems at the school's poetry reading. To find how many different ways the students can be chosen, find ${}_6P_2$.

$${}_6P_2 = \frac{6!}{(6-2)!} = \frac{6!}{4!}$$ **Use formula.**

$$= \frac{6 \cdot 5 \cdot \cancel{4} \cdot \cancel{3} \cdot \cancel{2} \cdot \cancel{1}}{\cancel{4} \cdot \cancel{3} \cdot \cancel{2} \cdot \cancel{1}}$$ **Divide out common factors.**

$$= 30$$ **Multiply.**

ANSWER There are 30 ways the speakers can be chosen.

with Solving

In Example 3, you can write 6! as $6 \cdot 5 \cdot 4!$ and cancel both 4 factorials.

$$\frac{6 \cdot 5 \cdot 4!}{4!} = 6 \cdot 5$$

Your turn now **Find the number of permutations.**

5. ${}_5P_3$ **6.** ${}_6P_6$ **7.** ${}_8P_7$ **8.** ${}_{100}P_2$

9. In Example 1 on page 623, you found the number of permutations of 5 CDs taken how many at a time? Explain.

Getting Ready to Practice

1. **Vocabulary** Copy and complete: The number of permutations of 15 objects taken 7 at a time can be written as _?_.

Evaluate.

2. 2! **3.** 0! **4.** 7! **5.** 9!

6. ${}_4P_2$ **7.** ${}_9P_6$ **8.** ${}_{10}P_7$ **9.** ${}_5P_5$

10. You have three things to do after you wake up tomorrow. You need to take a shower, eat breakfast, and call your friend. Find the number of permutations and list them.

Practice and Problem Solving

HELP with Homework

Example	Exercises
1	11
2	20–22, 24
3	12–22, 24

Online Resources
CLASSZONE.COM
· More Examples
· eTutorial Plus

11. **Movies** You rent four movies. In how many different orders can you watch the movies?

Find the number of permutations.

12. ${}_3P_1$ **13.** ${}_5P_2$ **14.** ${}_3P_2$ **15.** ${}_9P_3$

16. ${}_{12}P_6$ **17.** ${}_7P_4$ **18.** ${}_{15}P_5$ **19.** ${}_{20}P_3$

20. **Knitting** You are knitting a hat, and you want it to have 3 different colored stripes. You have 6 different colors of yarn. How many different hats could you knit?

21. **Softball** Your softball team has 15 players. Find the number of different ways that the first, second, third, fourth, and fifth batters can be chosen.

22. **After School** You are given a list of 10 activities you can do after school. You are asked to pick your first, second, third, and fourth choices. How many different permutations are possible?

23. **Critical Thinking** Your friend says that $11! = 11 \cdot 10!$. Is your friend correct? Explain.

24. **Gardening** You are planning a garden with 3 rows. Each row will have one type of flower, and none of the rows will be the same. You can choose from the flowers below. Find the number of permutations.

Day Lily

Poppy

Gladiolus

Daffodil

Rose

Sunflower

Tulip

Extended Problem Solving In Exercises 25 and 26, your team is 1 of 15 in a cheerleading competition.

25. If trophies are awarded for first, second, third, and fourth places, in how many different ways can the trophies be awarded?

26. **Compare and Contrast** Suppose the four teams that perform best are all given *excellence* medals instead of first, second, third, and fourth place trophies. In this case, are there more or fewer ways to give the awards than in Exercise 25? Explain.

27. **Challenge** You choose a 6-letter password for your e-mail. Write an expression to represent the number of different passwords you could choose. Explain how this expression changes if you can use each letter only once.

Mixed Review 

28. Find the surface area of a cone that has a slant height of 24 inches and a diameter of 10 inches. Round to the nearest tenth. *(Lesson 10.5)*

29. The table shows the results of a survey that asked students to choose their favorite color. Make a circle graph of the data. *(Lesson 12.3)*

Red	25%
Green	12%
Blue	40%
Other	23%

30. You are making a cake for your younger sister's birthday. You can make vanilla or chocolate cake. You can have white, yellow, or blue frosting. You can make a balloon design or a flower design for the top of the cake. Make a tree diagram to show all of the possible cakes that you could make. *(Lesson 12.4)*

Test-Taking Practice 

31. **Multiple Choice** You go to the cafeteria with five friends. In how many different orders can you and your friends get into the lunch line?

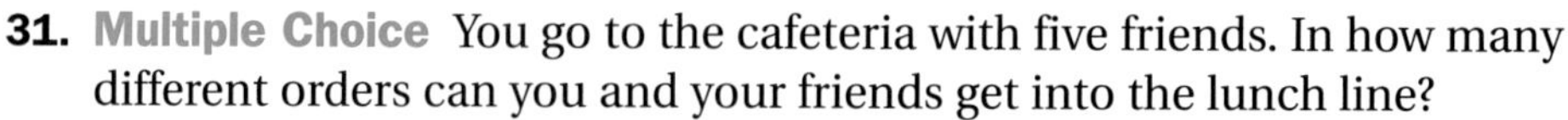

A. 6 **B.** 30 **C.** 120 **D.** 720

32. **Short Response** When you come back from vacation, you want to call Ed, Sue, Ty, and Nestor. You have time to make only two calls. Find the number of different orders in which you can call two friends. Then make a list to show all the different orders.

Combinations

BEFORE	Now	WHY?
You used permutations to count possibilities.	You will use combinations to count possibilities.	So you can count the ways a team can choose captains, as in Ex. 22.

Word Watch

combination, p. 627

In Lesson 12.5, you studied permutations, which are arrangements in which order is important.

A **combination** is a group of items whose order is *not* important. For example, suppose you go to lunch with a friend. You choose milk, soup, and a salad. Your friend chooses soup, a salad, and milk. The order in which the items are chosen does not matter. You both have same meal.

The two meals are the same.

EXAMPLE 1 Listing Combinations

County Fair You have 4 tickets to the county fair and can take 3 of your friends. You can choose from Abby (A), Brian (B), Chloe (C), and David (D). How many different choices of groups of friends do you have?

Solution

List all possible arrangements of three friends. Then cross out any duplicate groupings that represent the same group of friends.

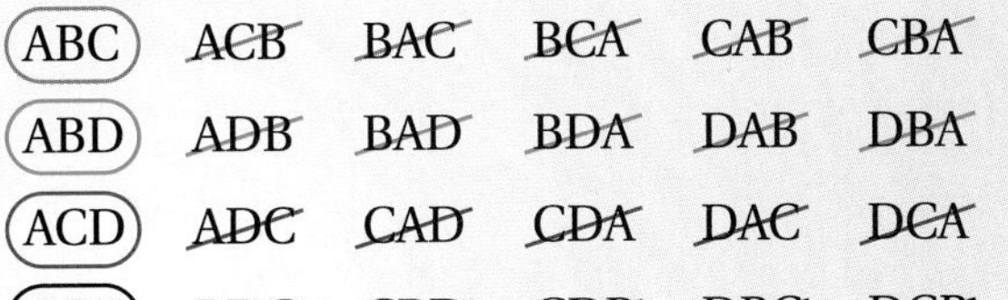

(ABC)	~~ACB~~	~~BAC~~	~~BCA~~	~~CAB~~	~~CBA~~
(ABD)	~~ADB~~	~~BAD~~	~~BDA~~	~~DAB~~	~~DBA~~
(ACD)	~~ADC~~	~~CAD~~	~~CDA~~	~~DAC~~	~~DCA~~
(BCD)	~~BDC~~	~~CBD~~	~~CDB~~	~~DBC~~	~~DCB~~

ABC, ACB, BAC, BCA, CAB, and CBA all represent the same group.

ANSWER You have 4 different choices of groups to take to the fair.

Your turn now

1. In Example 1, the complete list shows the number of *permutations* of 4 items chosen 3 at a time. How many items would be in the complete list if you had to choose from 8 friends?

Combination Notation In Example 1, after you cross out the duplicate groupings, you are left with the number of combinations of 4 items chosen 3 at a time. Using notation, this is written ${}_4C_3$.

Combination Notation

Words To find the number of combinations of n objects taken r at a time, divide the number of permutations of n objects taken r at a time by $r!$.

Numbers ${}_9C_4 = \frac{{}_9P_4}{4!}$

Algebra ${}_nC_r = \frac{{}_nP_r}{r!}$

EXAMPLE 2 Evaluating Combinations

Find the number of combinations.

a. ${}_8C_3$

b. ${}_9C_7$

Solution

a. ${}_8C_3 = \frac{{}_8P_3}{3!}$ — Combination formula

$= \frac{8 \cdot 7 \cdot 6}{3!}$ — ${}_8P_3 = \frac{8!}{(8-3)!} = 8 \cdot 7 \cdot 6$

$= \frac{8 \cdot 7 \cdot \cancel{6}}{\cancel{3} \cdot \cancel{2} \cdot 1}$ — Expand. $3! = 3 \cdot 2 \cdot 1$. Divide out common factors.

$= 56$ — Simplify.

b. ${}_9C_7 = \frac{{}_9P_7}{7!}$ — Combination formula

$= \frac{9 \cdot 8 \cdot 7 \cdot 6 \cdot 5 \cdot 4 \cdot 3}{7!}$ — ${}_9P_7 = \frac{9!}{(9-7)!} = 9 \cdot 8 \cdot 7 \cdot 6 \cdot 5 \cdot 4 \cdot 3$

$= \frac{9 \cdot \overset{4}{\cancel{8}} \cdot \cancel{7} \cdot \cancel{6} \cdot \cancel{5} \cdot \cancel{4} \cdot \cancel{3}}{\cancel{7} \cdot \cancel{6} \cdot \cancel{5} \cdot \cancel{4} \cdot \cancel{3} \cdot \underset{1}{\cancel{2}} \cdot 1}$ — Expand 7!. Divide out common factors.

$= 36$ — Simplify.

Your turn now **Find the number of combinations.**

2. ${}_8C_8$ **3.** ${}_8C_7$ **4.** ${}_7C_2$ **5.** ${}_6C_1$

EXAMPLE 3 Permutations and Combinations

Tell whether the possibilities can be counted using a *permutation* or *combination*. Then write an expression for the number of possibilities.

a. Swimming There are 8 swimmers in the 400 meter freestyle race. In how many ways can the swimmers finish first, second, and third?

b. Track Your track team has 6 runners available for the 4-person relay event. How many different 4-person teams can be chosen?

Solution

a. Because the swimmers can finish first, second, or third, order is important. So the possibilities can be counted by evaluating ${}_8P_3$.

b. Order is not important in choosing the team members, so the possibilities can be counted by evaluating ${}_6C_4$.

HELP with Notetaking

Mutate means to change. For *permutations*, you count changes in the order of items. For *combinations*, objects *combined* in any order represent the same group. You may wish to copy this hint into your notebook.

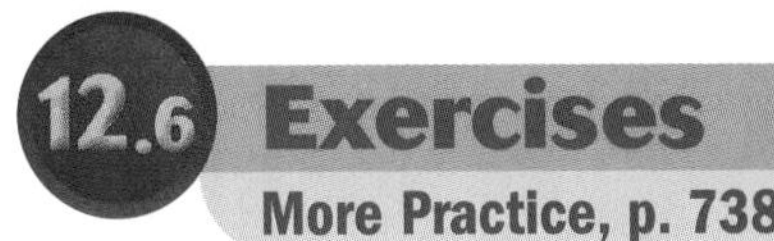

12.6 Exercises

More Practice, p. 738

Getting Ready to Practice

1. Vocabulary Copy and complete: The expression ${}_9C_5$ represents the number of combinations of _?_ objects taken _?_ at a time.

2. Find the Error You choose 3 art projects from the following list: clay, plaster, wood, wire, drawing, painting. Describe and correct the error below in finding the number of possible combinations of 3 projects.

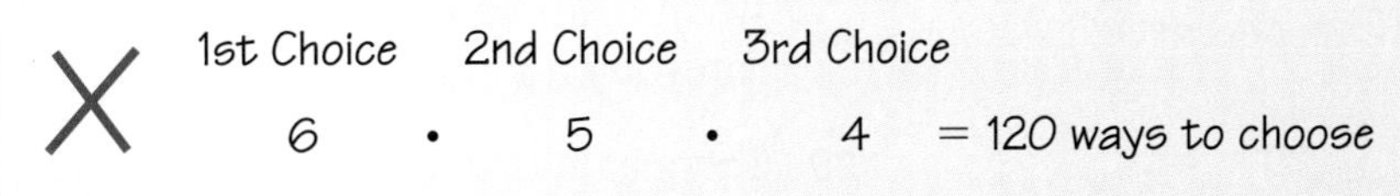

X
1st Choice 2nd Choice 3rd Choice
6 • 5 • 4 = 120 ways to choose

Find the number of combinations.

3. ${}_4C_1$ **4.** ${}_4C_4$ **5.** ${}_7C_6$ **6.** ${}_5C_2$

Tell whether the possibilities should be counted using a *permutation* or *combination*. Then find the answer.

7. Party You are buying balloons for a party. The store has four different colors, and you would like to choose two different colors. How many different pairs of balloon colors can be chosen?

8. Homework You must do homework in math, history, science, and geography. In how many different orders can you do your homework?

Practice and Problem Solving

Example	Exercises
1	9
2	10–21, 22–25
3	26–29

- More Examples
- eTutorial Plus

9. **Essays** For a test, you can choose any 2 essay questions to answer from the 5 questions asked. Make a list and cross out the duplicate choices to show how many different pairs of essay questions you could answer.

Find the number of combinations.

10. $_6C_5$
11. $_6C_6$
12. $_{11}C_9$
13. $_8C_4$
14. $_8C_6$
15. $_8C_1$
16. $_{10}C_8$
17. $_9C_5$
18. $_{11}C_3$
19. $_{13}C_{11}$
20. $_9C_2$
21. $_{100}C_{99}$

22. **Hockey** Your hockey team is choosing 2 team captains from its 18 members. Find the number of combinations that are possible.

23. **Debating** A debate team has 5 members. Your debating club has 12 students. How many different teams can be chosen?

24. **Gardening** You want to grow 4 different vegetables. You can choose from 9 types of seed. Find the number of combinations of 4 vegetables.

25. **Writing** Is it possible to evaluate a combination such as $_3C_4$, $_2C_6$, or $_1C_{10}$? Explain why or why not.

In Exercises 26–29, tell whether the possibilities should be counted using a *permutation* or *combination*. Then find the number of possibilities.

26. **Music** You want to know the number of ways you can play your four favorite songs.

27. **Shopping** You are shopping for a trip and want to buy three sweaters from among a red sweater, a blue sweater, a plaid sweater, a striped sweater, and a turtleneck sweater. How many sets of three sweaters can you choose?

28. **School Colors** Your class is voting for the new school colors. You are asked to choose 2 colors from a list of 8 colors. How many possibilities are there?

29. **Geography** You are coloring the map shown at the right. You want each state to be a different color, and you have 10 possible colors. In how many ways can you color the map? In how many ways can you choose 8 colors?

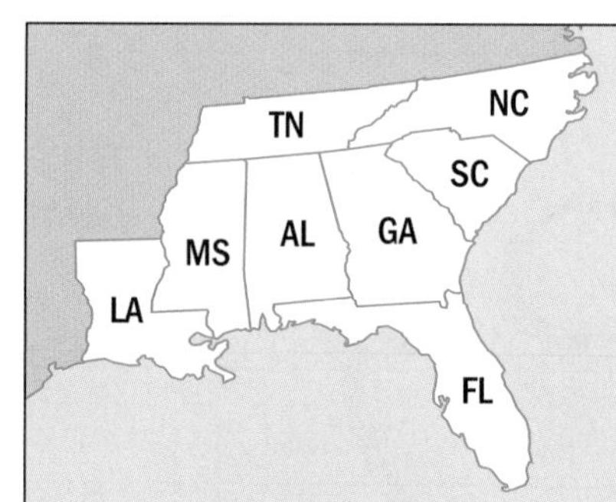

30. **Look for a Pattern** Copy the table. Complete the table by finding the number of combinations. Then describe the pattern.

${}_7C_0$	${}_7C_1$	${}_7C_2$	${}_7C_3$	${}_7C_4$	${}_7C_5$	${}_7C_6$	${}_7C_7$
?	?	?	?	?	?	?	?

Video Games In Exercises 31 and 32, your friend has a collection of 20 video games.

31. You want to borrow four games from your friend. How many different groups of four games can you choose?

32. If you are already sure about two of the game choices, how many different groups of four games can you choose? Explain.

33. **Challenge** What is the value of ${}_nC_r$ when $r = n$? What is the value of ${}_nC_r$ when $n - r = 1$? Explain.

Mixed Review 

Choose a Strategy Use a strategy from the list to solve the following problem. Explain your choice of strategy.

Problem Solving Strategies
- Act It Out
- Solve a Simpler Problem
- Draw a Diagram
- Make a Table

34. A rectangular room is 20 feet by 12 feet, with walls 7.5 feet high. A decorator charges \$.40 per square foot to use paint and \$.70 per square foot for wallpaper. Find the cost to decorate the room with each material.

Find the number of permutations. *(Lesson 12.5)*

35. ${}_{10}P_5$　　36. ${}_{11}P_4$　　37. ${}_{18}P_3$　　38. ${}_{21}P_2$

39. **Basic Skills** You spin the spinner at the right. What is the probability that the spinner lands on blue?

Test-Taking Practice 

INTERNET
State Test Practice
CLASSZONE.COM

40. **Multiple Choice** You are at a fair with four friends. All of you want to ride the roller coaster, but only three people can fit in the first car. How many different groups of three can you and your friends make?

A. 60　　**B.** 24　　**C.** 10　　**D.** 4

41. **Short Response** You have 6 different sweatshirts, and you want to donate some to a charity. Draw a diagram or write an expression so that you can find the number of ways you can donate 2 sweatshirts. Then find the number of ways you can donate 3 sweatshirts.

Probability and Odds

BEFORE
You found the probability of events.

Now
You will find the odds in favor of events.

WHY?
So you can find the odds of a goalie's save, as in Ex. 18.

Word Watch

complementary events, p. 632
unfavorable outcome, p. 633
odds, p. 633

INDIANA Academic Standards

- Data Analysis and Probability (8.6.6)

Activity You can use a spinner to explore probability.

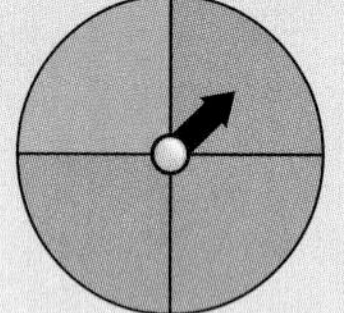

1. What is the probability of the spinner landing on blue? What is the probability of the spinner landing on red?
2. Is it more likely that the spinner will land on blue than red?
3. Find each ratio. Use the ratios to compare the chances of landing on red and on blue.

   a. $\dfrac{\text{number of red sections}}{\text{number of blue sections}}$ b. $\dfrac{\text{number of blue sections}}{\text{number of red sections}}$

4. Explain how to find the probability of the spinner *not* landing on red.

In the activity, the spinner will land on either red or blue. Two events are **complementary** when one event or the other (but not both) must occur. The sum of the probabilities of complementary events is always 1.

When Events A and B are complementary, $P(\text{Event A}) = 1 - P(\text{Event B})$.

HELP with Solving

The probability that Event A occurs and the probability that Event A does *not* occur have a sum of 1 because they are complementary events.

For help with probability, see p. 354.

EXAMPLE 1 Finding Probabilities

Gifts You and seven friends contribute money for a gift. Everyone's name is put in a hat. The person whose name is chosen picks the gift.

a. What is the probability that your name is randomly chosen?

b. What is the probability that your name is randomly *not* chosen?

Solution

a. $P(\text{your name is chosen}) = \dfrac{\text{Number of favorable outcomes}}{\text{Number of possible outcomes}} = \dfrac{1}{8}$

b. $P(\text{your name is not chosen}) = 1 - P(\text{your name is chosen})$

$$= 1 - \frac{1}{8}$$

$$= \frac{7}{8}$$

Your turn now **You are given the probability that an event will occur. Find the probability that the event will not occur.**

1. $P(\text{A}) = \frac{3}{4}$ **2.** $P(\text{A}) = 0.45$ **3.** $P(\text{A}) = 32\%$ **4.** $P(\text{A}) = \frac{7}{10}$

5. The 11 letters in the word MISSISSIPPI are each written on pieces of paper and put in a bag. What is the probability of randomly drawing an S from the bag? What is the probability of randomly *not* drawing an S?

Odds Once you specify the event for which you are finding the probability, outcomes for that event are called *favorable outcomes*. The other outcomes are **unfavorable outcomes**.

When all outcomes are equally likely, the **odds** in favor of an event are equal to the ratio of favorable outcomes to unfavorable outcomes.

$$\textbf{Odds} = \frac{\textbf{Number of favorable outcomes}}{\textbf{Number of unfavorable outcomes}}$$

EXAMPLE 2 Finding Odds

You do a survey asking your class to rank three ice cream flavors. Results for vanilla are shown at the right. What are the odds in favor of a randomly chosen student from your class ranking vanilla first?

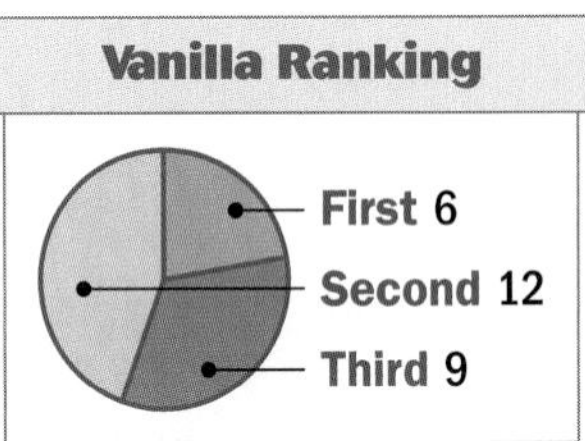

Solution

Vanilla was ranked first by 6 students, so there are 6 favorable outcomes.

It was ranked second by 12 students, and ranked third by 9 students, so there are $12 + 9 = 21$ unfavorable outcomes.

$$\text{Odds} = \frac{\text{Number of favorable outcomes}}{\text{Number of unfavorable outcomes}}$$

$$= \frac{6}{21}$$

$$= \frac{2}{7}$$

ANSWER The odds in favor of a randomly chosen student ranking vanilla first are 2 to 7.

HELP with Reading

Odds are always read as a ratio. For example, $\frac{5}{2}$ is read "five to two," not "five halves."

Your turn now **You choose a card at random from a set of cards numbered 1 to 24. Find the odds in favor of the event.**

6. You choose a 10. **7.** You choose an odd number greater than 7.

Probability and Odds If you know the probability of an event, you can use the following formula to find the odds in favor of that event.

$$\text{Odds} = \frac{\text{Probability event will occur}}{\text{Probability event will not occur}} = \frac{\text{Probability event will occur}}{1 - \text{Probability event will occur}}$$

EXAMPLE 3 Finding Odds Using Probability

Basketball Sean makes 65% of his free throws. What are the odds in favor of Sean making a free throw?

Solution

$\text{Odds} = \frac{0.65}{1 - 0.65}$ **Write percents as decimals.**

$= \frac{0.65}{0.35}$ **Subtract.**

$= \frac{65}{35}$ **Multiply numerator and denominator by 100.**

$= \frac{13}{7}$ **Simplify.**

ANSWER Sean's odds in favor of making a free throw are 13 to 7.

12.7 Exercises

More Practice, p. 738

Getting Ready to Practice

1. **Vocabulary** Copy and complete: Find the ratio of the number of favorable outcomes to the number of unfavorable outcomes to find the _?_ of an event.

You are given the probability that an event will occur. Find the probability that the event will not occur.

2. $P(A) = 84\%$ 3. $P(A) = \frac{2}{5}$ 4. $P(A) = 0.37$ 5. $P(A) = \frac{9}{10}$

You randomly draw a letter tile from a bag. The 8 letters in the word GEOMETRY are in the bag. Find the odds in favor of the event.

6. You choose a G. 7. You choose an E. 8. You choose an S.

9. **Weather** The weather forecast says that there is a 30 percent probability of rain. What are the odds in favor of rain?

Practice and Problem Solving

Example	Exercises
1	10–13, 19–20
2	10–20
3	18, 20

· More Examples
· eTutorial Plus

Find the probability of randomly choosing a red marble from the bag of marbles described. Then find the odds in favor of randomly choosing a blue marble.

10. 3 red and 7 blue marbles

11. 4 red and 9 blue marbles

12. 6 red and 5 blue marbles

13. 6 red, 5 blue, and 3 green marbles

Find the odds in favor of the event described when rolling a number cube.

14. Roll a 3.

15. Roll a number less than 6.

16. Roll a number greater than 2.

17. Roll an odd number less than 5.

18. **Hockey** A hockey goalie has a save percentage of 93%. What are the odds that he makes a save?

19. **Compare** Sam finds the probability of Event A is 0.2. Jan finds the odds in favor of Event A are 1 to 4. Can they both be right? Explain.

20. **Socks** In your sock drawer, you have 20 socks. You have 2 pairs of patterned socks, 4 pairs of gym socks, 3 pairs of striped socks, and 1 pair of black socks. What is the probability that you randomly pull a gym sock from the drawer? What are the odds?

Pizza In Exercises 21–23, use the circle graph. It shows the number of people ordering pizza that order each type of crust.

21. What is the probability that a randomly chosen pizza order is for thin crust?

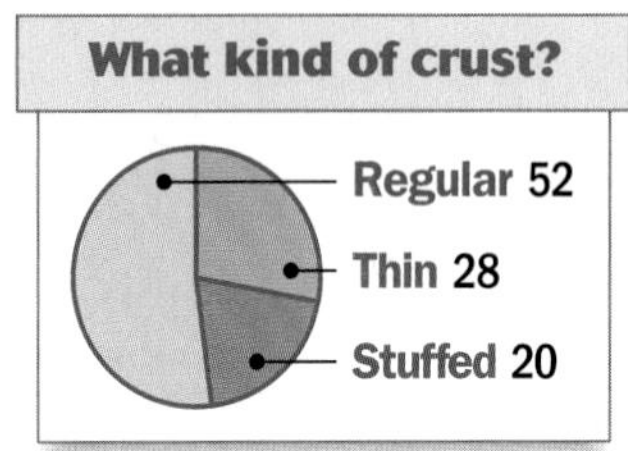

22. What are the odds in favor of a randomly chosen pizza order being for regular crust?

23. What are the odds in favor of a randomly chosen pizza order *not* being for stuffed crust?

Odds Against In Exercises 24 and 25, use the following information. In this lesson, you learned how to find the *odds in favor* of an event. You can also find the *odds against* an event.

$$\text{Odds against} = \frac{\text{Number of unfavorable outcomes}}{\text{Number of favorable outcomes}}$$

24. You choose a chip from a bag of 6 blue, 3 red, and 5 green chips. Find the odds in favor of choosing a green chip. Then find the odds against choosing a green chip.

25. **Challenge** You hear a friend claim that "the odds that you get hit by lightning are a million to one." Is your friend talking about *odds in favor* or *odds against*? Explain your reasoning.

Extended Problem Solving In Exercises 26–28, use the following information.

You make an archery target like the one shown. Assume that when an arrow is shot and hits the target, the arrow is equally likely to hit any point on the target. The probability that an arrow lands within the red bull's-eye circle is given by the following equation.

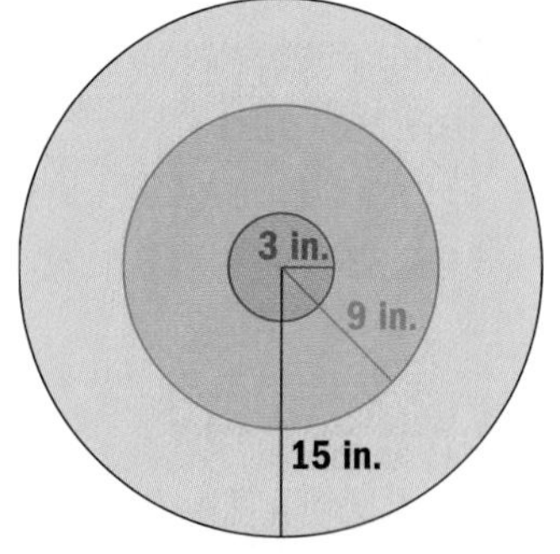

$$P = \frac{\text{Area of bull's-eye}}{\text{Area of target}}$$

26. Geometry What is the area of the bull's-eye? What is the total area of the target? Leave your answers in terms of π.

27. Probability What is the probability that an arrow that hits the target lands within the bull's-eye?

28. Odds What are the odds that an arrow that hits the target lands on the blue region?

Mixed Review 

29. Find the length of the hypotenuse of a right triangle with leg lengths of 24 inches and 45 inches. *(Lesson 9.3)*

Find the slope of the line passing through the points. *(Lesson 11.6)*

30. $(-8, 12), (9, 2)$ **31.** $(7, 5), (-3, 6)$ **32.** $(-1, -5), (-4, -10)$

Basic Skills **Find the product.**

33. $\frac{4}{5} \cdot \frac{7}{12}$ **34.** $\frac{5}{9} \cdot \frac{3}{5}$ **35.** $\frac{1}{8} \cdot \frac{3}{7}$ **36.** $\frac{9}{13} \cdot \frac{5}{6}$

Test-Taking Practice 

INTERNET
State Test Practice
CLASSZONE.COM

37. Multiple Choice You roll a number cube. What is the probability that you will roll a number greater than 4?

A. $\frac{1}{4}$ **B.** $\frac{1}{3}$ **C.** $\frac{1}{2}$ **D.** $\frac{2}{3}$

38. Multiple Choice While playing for your baseball team, you have hit the ball 14 out of 21 times at bat. Based on this record, what are the odds in favor of hitting the ball the next time you are at bat?

F. $\frac{14}{35}$ **G.** $\frac{1}{2}$ **H.** $\frac{2}{3}$ **I.** $\frac{2}{1}$

12.8 Hands-on Activity

INDIANA: Academic Standards
- Data Analysis and Probability (8.6.1, 8.6.6)

GOAL
Use a simulation to explore probability.

MATERIALS
- index cards
- calculator

Probability and Simulations

You can use a simulation to explore probability. A *simulation* is an experiment done to explore the probability of an event.

Explore 1 Simulate a real-world situation.

Do a simulation to find an experimental probability that you and a friend are the 2 students randomly chosen from a group of 8 students.

1 Label eight index cards as shown. Use 1 to represent yourself, 2 to represent your friend, and 3, 4, 5, 6, 7, and 8 to represent the other students.

1	2	3	4
5	6	7	8

2 Shuffle the cards. Randomly draw a card, and then another, without replacing the first. Record whether or not the results represent you and your friend being chosen. Replace the cards.

3 Repeat drawing a pair of cards. Draw a total of 10 pairs. For each pair of cards drawn, record the results.

Use the ratio $\frac{\text{you and friend are chosen}}{\text{total number of pairs drawn}}$ to find the experimental probability that you and your friend are chosen.

Pair	Times Drawn
5, 8	I
7, 2	II
1, 4	I

Your turn now **Use your results from the simulation above.**

1. Combine all the class results. Based on these results, what is the experimental probability that you and your friend are chosen?

Explore 2 Use technology to simulate a real-world situation.

Use your calculator's random integer function to simulate randomly choosing 1 student from a group of 8. Find the experimental probability that any of the students is randomly chosen twice in a row.

1. Use 1, 2, 3, 4, 5, 6, 7, and 8 to represent the students.

2. Clear your calculator screen. Press MATH and choose the PRB menu. Select *randInt(*, the random integer function.

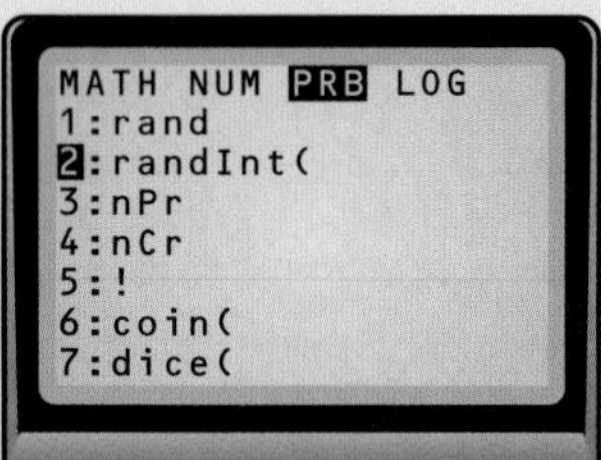

3. Enter **1** , **8** ENTER) to select an integer at random from 1 to 8. Press ENTER again to simulate choosing a student again. Record whether your results represent a match.

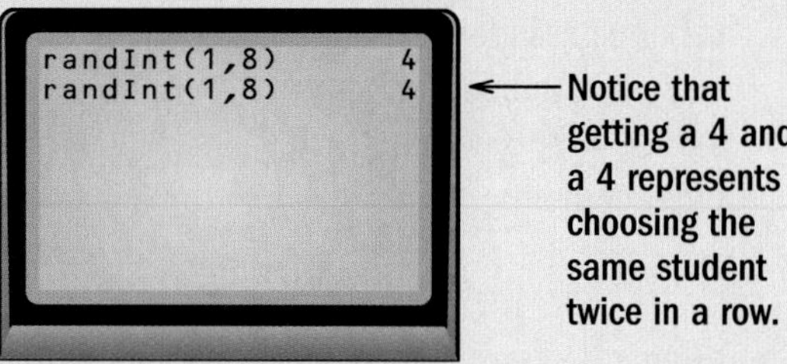

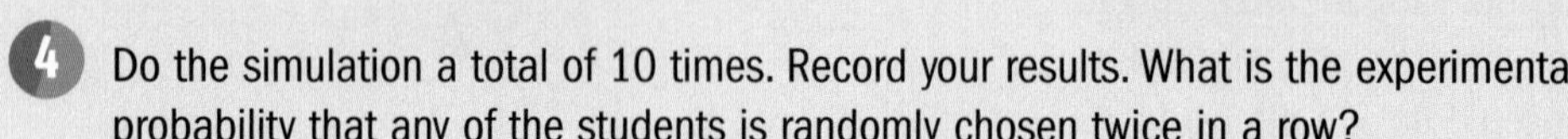

4. Do the simulation a total of 10 times. Record your results. What is the experimental probability that any of the students is randomly chosen twice in a row?

Your turn now **Design a simulation of the situation.**

2. You randomly choose to go to the library, from the choices mall, library, or bowling lanes.

3. You and your friend Chris are randomly chosen from a group of 10 team members to be co-captains.

Stop and Think

4. **Critical Thinking** Refer to Exercise 1 on page 637. Which results do you think are more likely to be close to the theoretical probability that you and your friend are chosen, your results or the class results? Explain.

5. **Writing** Explain how the simulation in Explore 2 above would be different if you wanted to find the probability that you are randomly chosen twice in a row from a group of eight people.

Independent and Dependent Events

BEFORE

You found the probability of an event.

Now

You will study independent and dependent events.

WHY?

So you can find the probability of winning a free snack, as in Ex. 13.

independent events, p. 639
dependent events, p. 639

INDIANA
Academic Standards

- Data Analysis and Probability (8.6.6)

Two events are **independent events** if the occurrence of one event does *not* affect the probability that the other event will occur. Two events are **dependent events** if the occurrence of one event *does* affect the probability that the other event will occur.

Suppose you randomly choose two gumballs one at a time from the jar below. The probability of choosing two red gumballs with replacement is different than the probability without replacement.

Independent Events

First Event

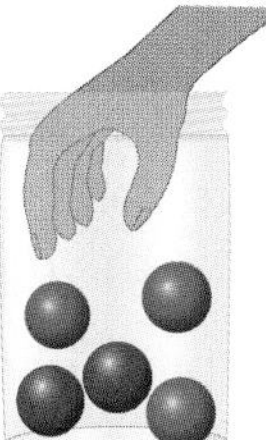

$P(\text{red}) = \frac{2}{5}$

Second Event

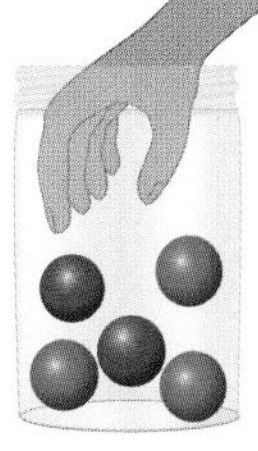

$P(\text{red}) = \frac{2}{5}$

If you replace the gumball, the probability of choosing a red gumball is the same for each choice.

Dependent Events

First Event

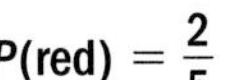

$P(\text{red}) = \frac{2}{5}$

Second Event

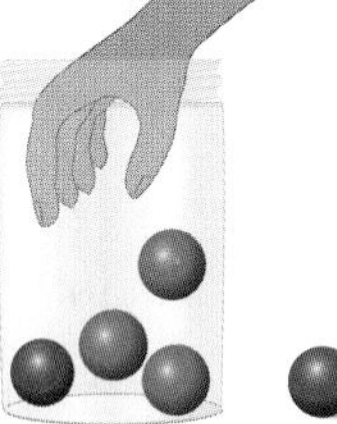

$P(\text{red}) = \frac{1}{4}$

If you don't replace the gumball after choosing, the probability changes.

EXAMPLE 1 Independent and Dependent Events

Tell whether the events are *independent* or *dependent*.

a. You roll a number cube. Then you roll the number cube again.

b. You randomly draw a number from a bag. Then you randomly draw a second number without putting the first number back.

Solution

a. The result of the first roll does not affect the result of the second roll, so the events are independent.

b. There is one fewer number in the bag for the second draw, so the events are dependent.

Multiple Events To find the probability that Event A *and* Event B happen, you multiply probabilities. Because the occurrence of an event may affect the probability of another event, you should determine whether the events are independent or dependent before multiplying.

Probability of Independent Events

For two independent events, the probability that both occur is the product of the probabilities of the events.

$P(\text{A and B}) = P(\text{A}) \cdot P(\text{B})$ **Events A and B are independent.**

EXAMPLE 2 **Probability of Independent Events**

School Fair Your class is raising money by operating a ball toss game. You estimate that about 1 out of every 25 balls tossed results in a win. What is the probability that someone will win on two tosses in a row?

Solution

The tosses are independent events, because the outcome of a toss does not affect the probability of the next toss resulting in a win.

So the probability of each event is $\frac{1}{25}$.

$$P(\text{win and win}) = P(\text{win}) \cdot P(\text{win}) = \frac{1}{25} \cdot \frac{1}{25} = \frac{1}{625}$$

ANSWER The probability of two winning tosses in a row is $\frac{1}{625}$.

Dependent Events If A and B are dependent events, the probability that B occurs given that A also occurs is not the same as the probability of B. So, you should use $P(\text{B given A})$ instead of $P(\text{B})$ to represent the probability that B occurs given that A also occurs.

Probability of Dependent Events

For two dependent events, the probability that both events occur is the product of the probability of the first event and the probability of the second event given that the first event also occurs.

$P(\text{A and B}) = P(\text{A}) \cdot P(\text{B given A})$ **A and B are dependent.**

EXAMPLE 3 Finding Probability of Dependent Events

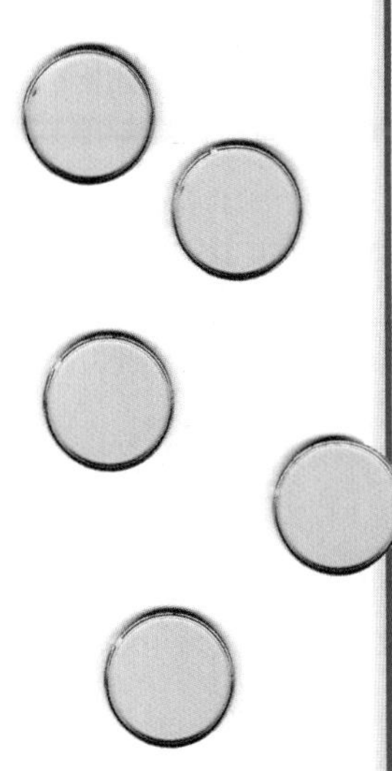

Bingo You are playing the bingo card shown. The caller has 50 numbers left to call. What is the probability that you will get bingo on the next 2 numbers called?

B	I	N	G	O
12	18	41	51	66
7	26	44	54	70
6	27	FREE SPACE	58	63
5	23	39	52	73
3	30	36	57	75

Solution

You need B7 and N44 for bingo. Find the probability of success when each of the next 2 numbers is drawn. Then multiply.

$P(\text{B7 or N44}) = \frac{2}{50} = \frac{1}{25}$ **There are 50 numbers left to call.**

$P(\text{remaining number}) = \frac{1}{49}$ **There are 49 numbers left to call.**

$P(\text{both numbers}) = \frac{1}{25} \cdot \frac{1}{49} = \frac{1}{1225}$ **Multiply the probabilities.**

ANSWER The probability is $\frac{1}{1225}$, or about 0.0008.

Your turn now **Find the probability.**

1. You toss a coin twice. Find the probability of getting two heads.
2. Find the probability for Example 3 if there are 36 numbers left to call.

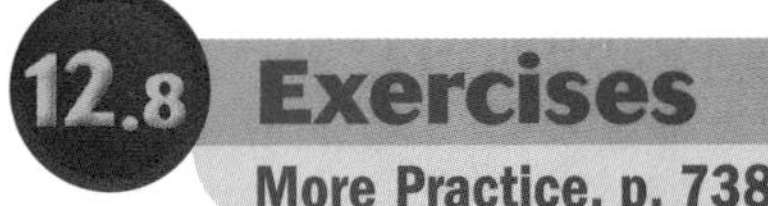

12.8 Exercises

More Practice, p. 738

Getting Ready to Practice

1. **Vocabulary** Copy and complete: When the occurrence of an event does not affect the probability of the next event, the events are __?__.

Tell whether the events are *independent* or *dependent*. Then find the probability.

2. You randomly choose a green marble from a jar of 8 green and 3 blue marbles. You replace the marble and randomly choose another green marble.
3. Your teacher randomly chooses you to give a report. She then randomly chooses Pam from the 22 remaining students.

Practice and Problem Solving

Example	Exercises
1	10–14
2	4–6, 10–14
3	7–14

Online Resources
CLASSZONE.COM
· More Examples
· eTutorial Plus

Events A and B are independent. Find the missing probability.

4. $P(\text{A}) = 0.4$
   $P(\text{B}) = 0.6$
   $P(\text{A and B}) = \underline{?}$

5. $P(\text{A}) = 0.9$
   $P(\text{B}) = \underline{?}$
   $P(\text{A and B}) = 0.09$

6. $P(\text{A}) = \underline{?}$
   $P(\text{B}) = 0.6$
   $P(\text{A and B}) = 0.12$

Events A and B are dependent. Find the missing probability.

7. $P(\text{A}) = 0.75$
   $P(\text{B given A}) = 0.5$
   $P(\text{A and B}) = \underline{?}$

8. $P(\text{A}) = 0.8$
   $P(\text{B given A}) = \underline{?}$
   $P(\text{A and B}) = 0.32$

9. $P(\text{A}) = \underline{?}$
   $P(\text{B given A}) = 0.3$
   $P(\text{A and B}) = 0.039$

In Exercises 10–12, tell whether the events are *independent* or *dependent*. Then find the probability.

10. **Banquet** At a banquet, you can order a main course of a chef's salad, salmon and potatoes, ham and beans, or steak and rice. You can drink water, juice, milk, coffee, or iced tea. If all choices are equally likely, what is the probability that a randomly chosen person orders a chef's salad and juice?

11. **Cookies** You have a jar filled with 5 oatmeal cookies, 6 sugar cookies, 8 frosted cookies, and 9 chocolate cookies. You randomly choose a cookie, keep it, and then choose another. What is the probability that you pick a frosted cookie and then a chocolate cookie?

12. **Buttons** You draw a button at random from the jar at the right. Without replacing the first button, you draw another. What is the probability that you draw a red button and then a yellow button?

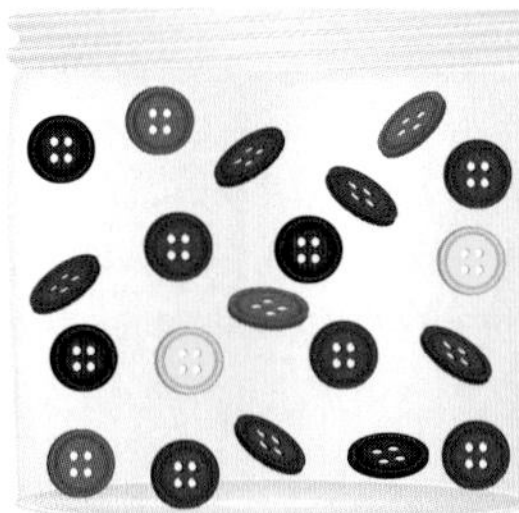

13. **Lucky Plate** Each day, the person who gets the lucky plate wins a free snack from the school cafeteria. The cafeteria sells 127 lunches on Wednesday and 134 lunches on Thursday. What is the probability that you win on both days if you buy lunch both days?

14. **Critical Thinking** What is the probability that when you toss a coin you get heads 7 times in a row? If you have already gotten heads 6 times in a row, what is the probability that you will get heads on the next toss?

15. **Challenge** A brochure says, "If you invested money with us 5 years ago, that money grew by an average of 20%." The brochure also says, "Past performance is no guarantee of future results." Which statement leads you to think that investing money today is independent of past events? Which statement suggests the opposite? Explain.

16. **Elections** A town's election for mayor drew 75% of the town's 800 eligible voters. What is the probability that two different randomly selected people both voted in the election?

Mixed Review 

17. The table shows the amount of time, in minutes, that Cindy ran on the treadmill each day. Make a line graph of the data. Predict how long Cindy will run on Saturday. Explain your reasoning. *(Lesson 12.3)*

Monday	20
Tuesday	25
Wednesday	25
Thursday	35
Friday	41

Basic Skills **Evaluate the expression.**

18. $5 \cdot (11 - 4)$ **19.** $3 + 9 \cdot 6$ **20.** $35 - 21 \div 3$ **21.** $\frac{35}{9 - 2}$

Test-Taking Practice

22. **Multiple Choice** Suppose you spin the spinner at the right twice. What is the probability of landing on a blue region both times?

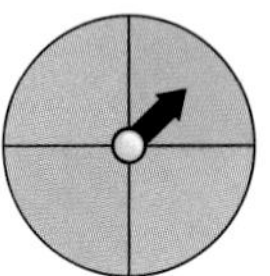

A. $\frac{1}{16}$ **B.** $\frac{1}{8}$ **C.** $\frac{1}{4}$ **D.** $\frac{1}{2}$

23. **Short Response** Your teacher is giving away two prizes by random drawing. She puts 25 students' names into a hat. She draws the first name. Then she chooses a second name without replacing the first name. What is the probability that your name will be chosen first? Does the probability that your name will be chosen second depend on the first outcome? Explain why or why not.

BRAIN GAME

Lucky Numbers

Two balls will be randomly chosen without replacement from the globe shown.

Bo wins if the first ball is blue, and the next ball is a 3 or a 4.

Sherry wins if the first ball is an even number and the next ball is green.

Eva wins if both balls are red.

Who has the best chance of winning?

CHAPTER
12
Special
Topic

Samples

GOAL Identify biased samples and surveys.

Word Watch

population, p. 644
sample, p. 644
random sample, p. 644
biased sample, p. 644

INDIANA
Academic Standards

- Data Analysis and Probability (8.6.2)

One way to collect data about a group is by doing a survey. A **population** is the entire group of people or objects that you want information about. When it is difficult to survey an entire population, a **sample**, or a part of the entire group, is surveyed.

In a **random sample**, each person or object has an equally likely chance of being selected. A non-random sample can result in a **biased sample** that is not representative of the population.

EXAMPLE 1 Identifying Potentially Biased Samples

Costume Dance The student council wants students to help decide on a theme for a costume dance. Students can choose one of the council's three ideas from the options listed at the right.

Which dance theme do you prefer?
Choose one:
☐ movies
☐ famous historical figures
☐ sports and games

Surveying all of the students will take too long, so a sample will be surveyed. Tell whether the survey method could result in a biased sample. Explain.

a. Survey members of the movie club.

b. Survey students as they enter the school.

c. Survey students on the football team.

Solution

a. This method could result in a biased sample because this group is more likely to favor the movie theme.

b. This method is not likely to result in a biased sample because a wide range of students will be surveyed.

c. This method could result in a biased sample because the football players are more likely to favor sports and games.

Survey Questions When you do a survey, you need to phrase the questions so that the responses of the people surveyed accurately reflect their opinions or actions. If not, claims based on the survey results may be biased.

EXAMPLE 2 Identifying Potentially Biased Questions

Tell whether the question could produce biased results. Explain.

a. Do you support the unfair policy of requiring students to do a time-consuming community project? YES ☐ NO ☐

b. Do you like our new apple-nut yogurt flavor, now on sale in stores everywhere? YES ☐ NO ☐

Solution

a. This question suggests that the policy is unfair and that the project is time-consuming. It encourages a response of *no*. So, the question could lead to biased results.

b. The question assumes that the person responding has tried the new yogurt flavor. Those who have not tried the new flavor may not give an accurate opinion. So, the question could lead to biased results.

Exercises

Stadiums **In Exercises 1–3, a city wants to know whether residents favor using public funds to pay for a new baseball stadium. Tell whether the method could result in a biased sample. Explain.**

1. Ask people that call in to a sports radio talk show.
2. Ask every tenth person listed in the phone book.
3. Ask every fifth person who enters the sporting goods store in town.
4. Food A restaurant wants to know what kinds of food to add to its menu to attract new customers. Describe a sampling method that the restaurant can use that is not likely to result in a biased sample.

Tell whether the survey question could produce biased results. Explain your reasoning.

5. Would you rather relax at home while reading a book, or go to a noisy, crowded mall?
6. Allowing messy, dangerous dogs into the park will cause safety and health problems. Will you vote to allow dogs into the park?
7. How often do you buy lunch in the school cafeteria?
8. Do you agree with this store's policy for returning purchases?

Notebook Review

Review the vocabulary definitions in your notebook.

Copy the review examples in your notebook. Then complete the exercises.

Check Your Definitions

tree diagram, p. 618
permutation, p. 623
factorial, p. 623
combination, p. 627
complementary events, p. 632
unfavorable outcome, p. 633
odds, p. 633
independent events, p. 639
dependent events, p. 639

Use Your Vocabulary

1. Vocabulary Copy and complete: A(n) _?_ is an arrangement in which order is important.

12.4 Can you use the counting principle?

EXAMPLE You need to choose one of 3 birdhouse designs and one of 6 possible colors. How many different birdhouses can you build?

ANSWER $3 \cdot 6 = 18$, so you can build 18 different birdhouses.

2. You have 5 designs of birdhouses and 4 colors from which to choose. How many different birdhouses can you build?

12.5–12.6 Can you find permutations and combinations?

EXAMPLE At a swim meet, 10 swimmers are in an event. In how many ways can first, second, third, and fourth place medals be awarded?

The order is important, so find the number of permutations.

$${}_{10}P_4 = \frac{10!}{(10-4)!} = \frac{10!}{6!} = 10 \cdot 9 \cdot 8 \cdot 7 = 5040$$

ANSWER There are 5040 ways to award the medals.

3. You are making a braided rope out of three different colors of yarn. You have seven colors of yarn. In how many ways can you choose the colors so the rope has three different colors?

12.7 Can you find odds?

EXAMPLE You have a bag of 6 red, 5 blue, and 3 white marbles. What are the odds in favor of randomly drawing a red marble from the bag?

ANSWER $\text{Odds} = \dfrac{\text{Number of favorable outcomes}}{\text{Number of unfavorable outcomes}} = \dfrac{6}{8} = \dfrac{3}{4}$

☑ **4.** What are the odds in favor of randomly drawing a white marble ?

12.8 Can you calculate probabilities?

EXAMPLE Tiles with each of the 11 letters in PROBABILITY are in a bag. You randomly draw a tile, replace it, and then randomly draw a second tile. What is the probability that both tiles are I's?

ANSWER $P(\text{I and I}) = P(\text{I}) \cdot P(\text{I}) = \dfrac{2}{11} \cdot \dfrac{2}{11} = \dfrac{4}{121}$

☑ **5.** What is the probability that the first tile is B and the second is L?

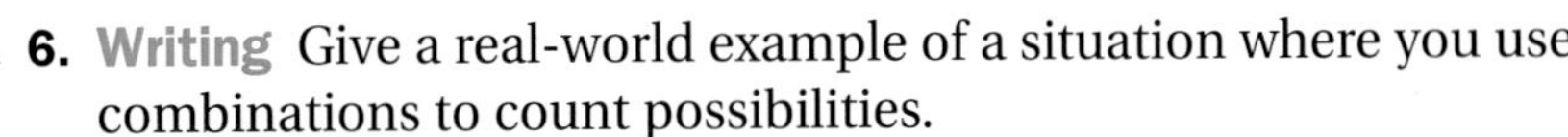

6. Writing Give a real-world example of a situation where you use combinations to count possibilities.

Review Quiz 2

1. **Shoes** You can buy sandals or sneakers in black, brown, tan, or white. Make a tree diagram to show the possible choices for shoes.
2. **Camp** You are scheduling swimming, crafts, canoeing, and softball. How many different schedules of four different activities are possible?
3. **Hockey** Find the number of ways two players can be chosen from 20 team members.
4. **Rain** If the probability that it will rain today is 0.4, what are the odds in favor of rain? What is the probability that it will *not* rain?

Find the probability.

5. You roll a 5 on a 6-sided number cube. Then you roll another 5.
6. A bag has 3 red and 5 blue tiles. You randomly draw a red tile, keep it, and then randomly draw a blue tile.

Chapter Review

Vocabulary

stem-and-leaf plot, p. 597
box-and-whisker plot, p. 601
lower quartile, p. 601
upper quartile, p. 601
lower extreme, p. 601
upper extreme, p. 601
circle graph, p. 605
line graph, p. 606
tree diagram, p. 618
permutation, p. 623
factorial, p. 623
combination, p. 627
complementary events, p. 632
unfavorable outcome, p. 633
odds, p. 633
independent events, p. 639
dependent events, p. 639

Vocabulary Review

Matching **In Exercises 1–6, match the description with the correct word(s).**

1. An arrangement in which order is important
2. An arrangement in which order is not important
3. A graph to display data that fall into distinct categories
4. A graph used to display changes in a quantity over time
5. A plot used to order a data set
6. A plot used to summarize a data set

A. bar graph
B. line graph
C. box-and-whisker plot
D. stem-and-leaf plot
E. combination
F. permutation

7. Copy the box-and-whisker plot at the right. Label the median, upper and lower quartiles, and upper and lower extremes.

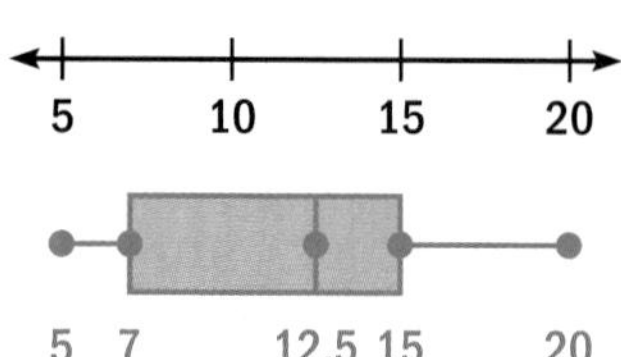

Review Questions

Make an ordered stem-and-leaf plot to organize the data. Identify the interval that includes the most data values. *(Lesson 12.1)*

8. 20, 25, 36, 16, 29, 32, 27, 42

9. 11.2, 7.5, 15.1, 15.7, 15.0, 6.7, 11.3

10. Chess The prices of several chess sets are \$15, \$20, \$38, \$95, \$60, \$45, \$40, \$35, and \$50. Make a box-and-whisker plot of the data. What conclusions can you make? *(Lesson 12.2)*

Review Questions

Ice Cream	50%
Frozen fruit	25%
Ices	10%
Other	15%

11. **Summer Treats** The table shows the favorite summer treats of students surveyed. Represent the data in a circle graph. *(Lesson 12.3)*

12. **Election** Your class is having an election for president, vice president, and secretary. For president there are 4 candidates, for vice president there are 5 candidates, and for secretary there are 3 candidates. No one is running for more than one office. How many groups of winners are possible? *(Lesson 12.4)*

Evaluate the expression. *(Lessons 12.5, 12.6)*

13. ${}_8P_4$ 14. ${}_{10}P_3$ 15. ${}_9C_2$ 16. ${}_6C_1$

17. **Photograph** You and six friends are posing for a photograph. In how many ways can you line up for the photograph if you line up in one row? *(Lesson 12.5)*

In Exercises 18 and 19, tell whether the situation describes a *combination* or a *permutation*. Then find the answer. *(Lessons 12.5, 12.6)*

18. **Pizza** In how many ways can you select 4 different pizza toppings from 12 toppings?

19. **Bobblehead Dolls** You have six different bobblehead dolls, and you want to choose three to give as gifts to Ali, Lin, and Rhea. How many different ways can you do this?

20. **Contest** The probability that you will win a contest is 76%. What is the probability that you will lose the contest? What are the odds that you will lose the contest? *(Lesson 12.7)*

21. **Softball** A softball player has a batting average of 0.350, which means she gets a hit 35% of her times at bat. What are the odds that she will get a hit in her next at bat? *(Lesson 12.7)*

22. **Weather** The weather forecaster says there is a 60% chance that it will snow on Wednesday and a 25% chance that it will snow on Thursday. Find the probability that it will snow on both Wednesday and Thursday. *(Lesson 12.8)*

23. **Cards** Two cards are dealt randomly, one after another, from a deck of cards numbered from 1 through 20. The first card is not returned to the deck before the second is dealt. Find the probability that the first card is a 7 and the second card is a 4. *(Lesson 12.8)*

Chapter Test

In Exercises 1 and 2, make a stem-and-leaf plot. Tell which interval includes the most values. Then make a box-and-whisker plot.

1. 46 kg, 70 kg, 21 kg, 136 kg, 55 kg, 60 kg, 72 kg, 104 kg, 52 kg

2. 12.1 in., 13.5 in., 12.8 in., 10 in., 7 in., 11.2 in., 12.9 in., 11.1 in., 12 in., 13.7 in.

3. **Academy Awards** The lengths, in minutes, of the Best Picture Academy Award winning movies for the years 1990–1999 are 99, 118, 122, 131, 142, 160, 177, 183, 194, and 197. Make a box-and-whisker plot of the data.

4. **Temperature** The record low temperatures in Miami, Florida, are given in the table. Display the data in an appropriate graph.

Month	Jan.	Feb.	Mar.	Apr.	May	Jun.	Jul.	Aug.	Sep.	Oct.	Nov.	Dec.
Temp (°F)	30	32	32	46	53	60	69	68	68	51	39	30

5. **Golf** There are five members on a golf team. Make a tree diagram to count the number of ways you can select a captain and an assistant.

6. **Movies** You and four friends are going to a movie. In how many different orders can you pick your friends up? List all the possible orders.

7. **School Dance** You are making a banner for a school dance and have a choice of 8 colors. You want to use 4 different colors. How many different combinations are possible?

In Exercises 8 and 9, use the circle graph. It shows student replies to *Which animal career would you enjoy?*

Animal Careers

- Veterinarian 35%
- Pet store owner 22%
- Zookeeper 21%
- Rodeo star 13%
- Circus animal trainer 9%

8. What is the probability that a randomly chosen student replied *veterinarian*?

9. What are the odds in favor of a randomly chosen student replying *zookeeper*?

Tell whether the events are *independent* or *dependent*. Then find the probability.

10. You roll a 6 on a number cube. Then you roll again and roll a 2.

11. You have 8 blue marbles and 12 red marbles in a bag. You randomly pick a blue marble on the first draw. Then you randomly pick another blue marble without replacing the first one.

Chapter Standardized Test

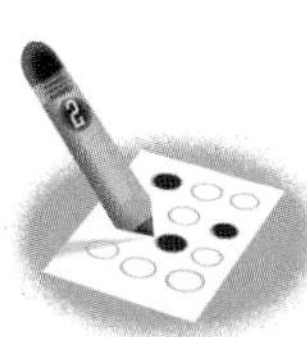

Test-Taking Strategy **Learn as much as you can about a test ahead of time, such as the types of questions and the topics the test will cover.**

Multiple Choice

1. When the number 29 is plotted on a stem-and-leaf plot, the 9 is which of the following?

   A. stem **B.** leaf **C.** key **D.** median

2. What does the number 56 represent on the box-and-whisker plot?

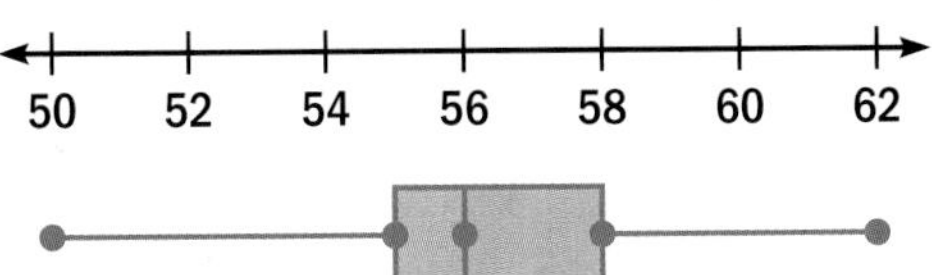

   F. upper quartile **G.** median

   H. lower quartile **I.** lower extreme

3. Which is an appropriate display for the data in the table below?

Favorite sport	Percent of students
Football	17%
Baseball	28%
Basketball	39%
Soccer	8%

   A. bar graph **B.** line graph

   C. circle graph **D.** histogram

4. You are asked to enter a 4-character password for a video game. The password must begin with a letter and end with 3 digits. How many different passwords are possible if you can repeat digits?

   F. 56 **G.** 26,000

   H. 175,760 **I.** 456,976

5. An ice cream parlor has 8 different flavors of ice cream. You would like a dish with 3 scoops of different flavors. How many different dishes can you pick?

   A. 36 **B.** 56

   C. 336 **D.** 40,320

6. There are 200 raffle tickets and 5 are winning tickets. What are the odds in favor of winning with one ticket?

   F. 1 to 40 **G.** 1 to 39

   H. 1 to 199 **I.** 1 to 200

7. You pick randomly from a jar of 12 green, 18 yellow, and 20 red mints. You pick a mint, eat it, and pick another mint. What is the probability that you pick a green mint and then a yellow mint?

   A. $\frac{99}{1225}$ **B.** $\frac{54}{625}$ **C.** $\frac{108}{1225}$ **D.** $\frac{27}{152}$

Short Response

8. There are 30 students auditioning for new openings in a chorus. How many ways can you choose 4 students to be in the chorus?

Extended Response

9. You asked 100 students whether they had shirts of the following colors: blue, yellow, orange. Your results were blue: 94%, yellow: 68%, orange: 43%. Use an appropriate form to display these data. Explain your choice. Then identify another type of display that would not be a good choice for these data. Explain why it would not be a good choice.

INVESTIGATING Robins

Geometric Probability

When a robin hunts for worms, does it search randomly, or can it sense a worm's location? Scientists used geometric probability to investigate this. Geometric probability is based on area. For events dependent on area, you can find the *geometric probability* using the following formula:

$$P(\text{event}) = \frac{\textbf{Area representing favorable outcomes}}{\textbf{Area representing possible outcomes}}$$

There are 4 treasure chests buried in a 5 yard by 10 yard field. Each chest has an area of 1 square yard. Use geometric probability to describe the expected results of searching a randomly chosen spot in the field.

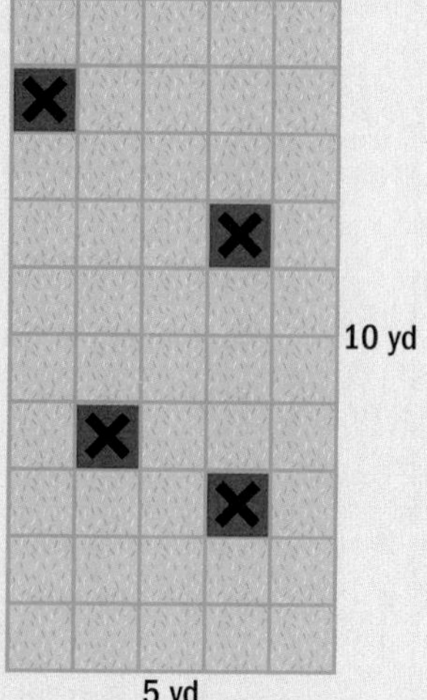

1 Find the area of the treasure chests.

$$4 \text{ chests} \cdot \frac{1 \text{ square yard}}{\text{chest}} = \mathbf{4} \text{ square yards}$$

2 Find the area of the field.

$$5 \text{ yards} \cdot 10 \text{ yards} = \mathbf{50} \text{ square yards}$$

3 Find the geometric probability of finding a treasure chest by random search.

$$P(\text{finding a chest}) = \frac{\textbf{Area of treasure chests}}{\textbf{Area of field}}$$

$$= \frac{\mathbf{4}}{\mathbf{50}} = 0.08$$

So, the geometric probability of finding a chest by random search is 8%.

1. Suppose there are 6 treasure chests in the field. What is the geometric probability of finding a chest by random search?
2. Suppose there are 9 treasure chests in the field, and each has an area of 2 square feet. Find the geometric probability of finding a chest by random search. Remember to measure the field in the same units as the chests.

How Robins Find Worms

To investigate how robins find worms, scientists did a series of experiments. They buried four worms in pans of soil that were marked into a 10 by 10 grid and calculated the geometric probability of a robin finding a worm at random.

Then they let robins search the pan and recorded the percent of the time a worm was found. A robin was counted as finding a worm if the square that it searched contained a worm. The experiment was repeated under different conditions.

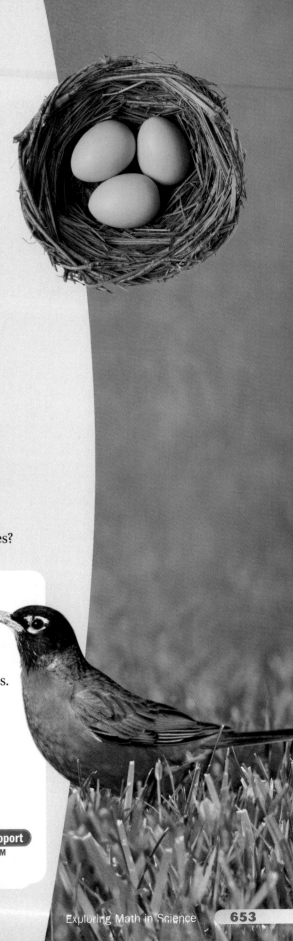

Condition	Correct Finds
Robins could use all senses.	90%
Robins prevented from using visual clues.	50%
White noise decreased robins' ability to hear worms.	59%

3. Find the geometric probability of finding a worm by searching randomly. Write the probability as a percent.
4. The table above shows the percent of attempts in which the robins found worms under each condition. For each condition, compare the percent of correct finds to the geometric probability of randomly finding a worm.
5. **Critical Thinking** What can you conclude from the results of the experiment? How do the results suggest that robins don't search randomly for worms but instead use their senses?

Project IDEAS

- **Experiment** Design and perform an experiment or a search involving geometric probability. Compare the theoretical and experimental geometric probabilities. Explain any discrepancies. Present your findings to the class.
- **Investigate** Learn more about how different birds find food. Present your findings.
- **Research** Look up information about search and rescue techniques. What techniques do people use to increase the probability of finding something? Present your findings.
- **Career** Learn about people who study animal behavior. What sorts of careers do they have? Present your findings.

Polynomials and Functions

BEFORE

In previous chapters you've...

- Simplified expressions by combining like terms
- Graphed linear functions

Now

In Chapter 13 you'll study...

- Simplifying polynomials
- Adding and subtracting polynomials
- Multiplying binomials
- Graphing non-linear functions

WHY?

So you can solve real-world problems about...

- treehouses, p. 663
- baseball, p. 676
- stage design, p. 677
- juggling, p. 680

CLASSZONE.COM

- eEdition Plus Online
- eWorkbook Plus Online
- eTutorial Plus Online
- State Test Practice
- More Examples

Chapter Warm-Up Games

Review skills you need for this chapter in these quick games.

Key Skill:
Using properties of exponents

To break open the piñata on your turn, you need to pick the right stick.

- Evaluate the expression under each stick.
- A stick breaks the piñata if it has the same value as one of the spots.
- Which stick breaks the piñata? Which spot should you hit?

Unmasking Expressions

$x - 4x + 3 + 9x$

$-7x + 8 - 2(3x + 4)$

$5(x - 6) + 10x - 3$

$8x - 3 - 4(2x + 3)$

$4 - (3x - 1) + x$

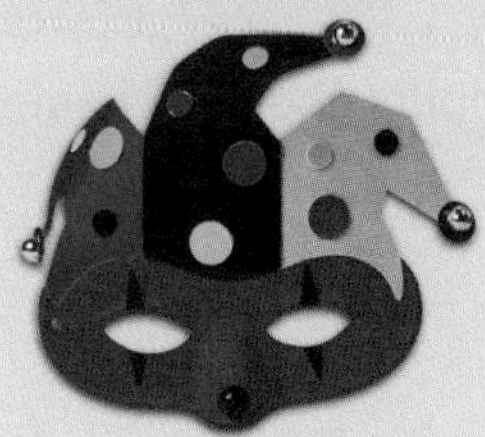

$17 - 4x - 13 + 2x$

John	Maria	Sam	Carol	Vincent	Sophie
$6x + 3$	$-2x + 4$	$-13x$	-15	$-2x + 5$	$15x - 33$

Key Skill:
Combining like terms

Find who is behind each of the masks.

- Match the expression under the mask with the correct simplified expression below a name.

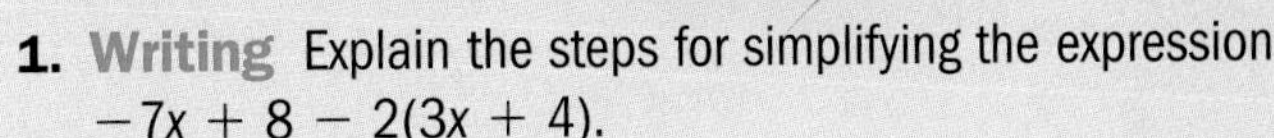

Stop and Think

1. **Writing** Explain the steps for simplifying the expression $-7x + 8 - 2(3x + 4)$.
2. **Critical Thinking** Write $2^5 \cdot 7 \cdot 2^{-1}$ as an expression with only positive exponents.

Getting Ready to Learn

Review What You Need to Know

Word Watch

Review Words

power, p. 20
exponent, p. 20
like terms, p. 86
coefficient, p. 86
monomial, p. 170
function, p. 541

Using Vocabulary **Copy and complete with a review word.**

1. The _?_ of $2x^3$ is 2.
2. A(n) _?_ is a relation that assigns exactly one output value to each input value.
3. A number, a variable, or a product of a number and one or more variables is a(n) _?_.

Simplify the expression. *(p. 85)*

4. $6x - 4 + 4x - 3$
5. $-5(2x + 3) - 4x$
6. $7(3x - 5) - (-x)$
7. $-2x - (-5x)$
8. $-2(-4x - 8)$
9. $-3(3x) + 18x$

Simplify the expression. *(p. 196)*

10. $\frac{y^4}{y^6}$
11. $\frac{5^{37}}{5^{35}}$
12. $x^4 \cdot x^5$

List four solutions of the equation. *(p. 550)*

13. $y = 3x - 5$
14. $y = -2x + 1$
15. $y = \frac{1}{2}x$

You should include material that appears on a notebook like this in your own notes.

Know How to Take Notes

Summarizing Material Summarize the main ideas from different lessons in your notebook. This will help you to see how key ideas are related.

Exponent Rules

Product of Powers

$x^2 \cdot x^3 = x^{2+3}$

$= x^5$

Quotient of Powers

$\frac{x^5}{x^2} = x^{5-2}$

$= x^3$

Zero Exponent

for $x \neq 0$,

$x^0 = 1$

Negative Exponents

for $x \neq 0$,

$x^{-4} = \frac{1}{x^4}$

In Lesson 13.4, you can summarize key ideas about algebra in your notebook.

Polynomials

BEFORE	Now	WHY?
You simplified expressions by combining like terms.	You will simplify polynomials by combining like terms.	So you can find the height of a falling pinecone, as in Example 3.

Word Watch

polynomial, p. 657
binomial, p. 657
trinomial, p. 657
standard form, p. 657

A **polynomial** is a monomial or a sum of monomials. Each monomial in a polynomial is called a *term*. Polynomials are classified by the number of their terms. If a polynomial has more than three terms, it is simply called a polynomial.

Monomial (1 term)	**Binomial** (2 terms)	**Trinomial** (3 terms)
$-2x$	$3x - 2$	$-2a^2 + 3a + 1$
4	$-s^4 + 6s^3$	$3 + 5r - 7r^2$

A polynomial is written in **standard form** if the exponents of the variable decrease from left to right.

Standard Form	**Not Standard Form**
$3x^3 - 2x^2 + 4$	$3 + 5y$
$-2m^6 + 5m^3 - m$	$7t^4 - t^7 - 2t^2 + 3t$

Watch Out!

If you do not see an exponent with a variable, then its exponent is 1.

$2x = 2x^1$

EXAMPLE 1 Writing Polynomials in Standard Form

Write the polynomial in standard form. Classify the polynomial.

a. $x - 9 + 5x^2$

$= x + (-9) + 5x^2$ **Write subtraction as addition.**

$= 5x^2 + x + (-9)$ **Order terms with decreasing exponents.**

ANSWER The polynomial $5x^2 + x - 9$ has 3 terms, so it is a trinomial.

b. $2x - 3x^3$

$= 2x + (-3x^3)$ **Write subtraction as addition.**

$= -3x^3 + 2x$ **Order terms with decreasing exponents.**

ANSWER The polynomial $-3x^3 + 2x$ has 2 terms, so it is a binomial.

Your turn now **Write the polynomial in standard form and classify it.**

1. $4 + b^2 - 8b$ **2.** $-5 + 3x^2$ **3.** $11 + 2n^4 - 7n + 5n^2$

Simplifying Polynomials Remember that *like terms* have the same variables raised to the same powers. To simplify a polynomial, combine like terms by adding their coefficients.

EXAMPLE 2 Simplifying Polynomials

Simplify the polynomial and write it in standard form.

a. $3x^2 + 4x^2 - 2x - 3$

$= (3x^2 + 4x^2) - 2x - 3$ **Group like terms.**

$= 7x^2 - 2x - 3$ **Simplify.**

b. $x^2 + 2 + 4(x^2 - 2x)$

$= x^2 + 2 + 4x^2 - 8x$ **Use the distributive property.**

$= (x^2 + 4x^2) + 2 - 8x$ **Group like terms.**

$= 5x^2 + 2 - 8x$ **Simplify.**

$= 5x^2 - 8x + 2$ **Write in standard form.**

HELP with Review

Remember that $x^2 = 1x^2$. For help with like terms, see p. 85.

Your turn now **Simplify the polynomial and write it in standard form.**

4. $7p + 5p^2 - 2 - 3p^2$

5. $10s^4 - 3s + s^4 - 1$

6. $2(a^2 + 3a - 1) + 2a^2$

7. $8x + 3(2x^2 - x + 1)$

EXAMPLE 3 Evaluating a Polynomial Expression

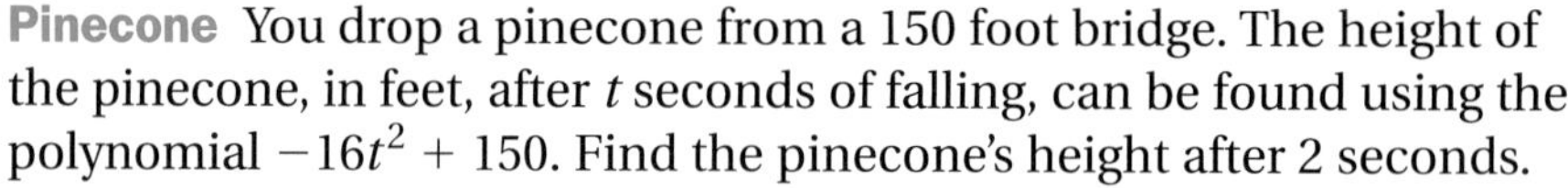

Pinecone You drop a pinecone from a 150 foot bridge. The height of the pinecone, in feet, after t seconds of falling, can be found using the polynomial $-16t^2 + 150$. Find the pinecone's height after 2 seconds.

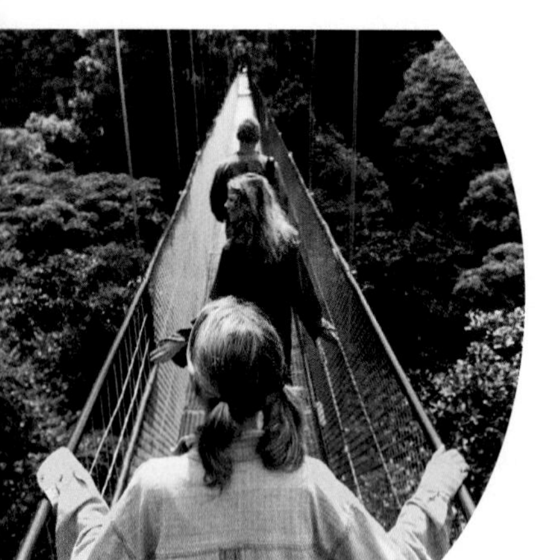

Solution

$-16t^2 + 150 = -16(2)^2 + 150$ **Substitute 2 for *t*.**

$= -16(4) + 150$ **Evaluate the power.**

$= -64 + 150$ **Multiply.**

$= 86$ **Add.**

ANSWER The pinecone's height after 2 seconds is 86 feet.

Your turn now **Find the height of the pinecone in Example 3 after it falls for the given number of seconds.**

8. 0.5 sec

9. 1 sec

10. 1.5 sec

11. 3 sec

Getting Ready to Practice

Vocabulary Classify the polynomial as a *monomial*, a *binomial*, or a *trinomial*.

1. $x^2 + 3x - 7$ **2.** $y - 5$ **3.** $8s^2t$ **4.** $2a^2 + 9a^3 + a$

Write the polynomial in standard form.

5. $7 + 3m$ **6.** $5n - 1 - n^2$ **7.** $4b - 4 + 6b^3$

Simplify the polynomial and write it in standard form.

8. $3x + x^2 - 2x$ **9.** $4 + 5y - 5$ **10.** $-9 + 7m^3 - 2m^3$

11. Find the Error Describe and correct the error in simplifying the polynomial.

X
$-3x^2 - 4(5x + 1)$
$= -3x^2 - 20x - 4$
$= -23x - 4$

Practice and Problem Solving

HELP with Homework

Example	Exercises
1	12-14
2	15-20, 23-26
3	27-30

· More Examples
· eTutorial Plus

Write the polynomial in standard form. Classify the polynomial.

12. $2 - 5y + y^2$ **13.** $-13x^3 + 4x^{10}$ **14.** $3 - r^4 + r + 2r^3$

Simplify the polynomial and write it in standard form.

15. $3x - 4 + x$ **16.** $2c^2 - c^2 + 5c$

17. $4q^3 - 7q^5 + 3q - q^3$ **18.** $7 - 4d^2 - 3d^2 + d$

19. $12 + 3b - 6b + 5$ **20.** $g^3 - 10 + 2g^2 - 5g^3$

Measurement Write a polynomial expression for the perimeter. Simplify the polynomial and write it in standard form.

21.

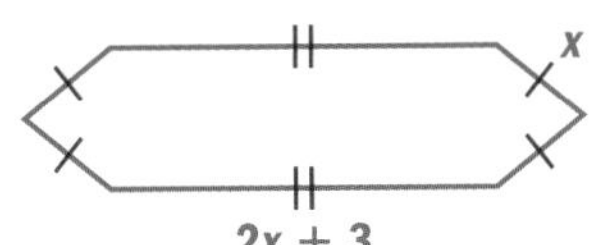

22.

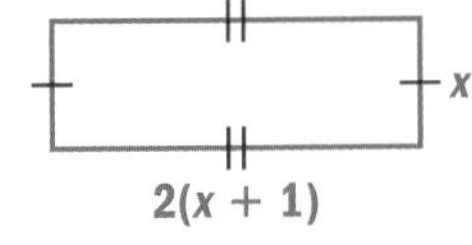

Simplify the polynomial and write it in standard form.

23. $1 + 12m^2 - 5m + 6m - 7$ **24.** $7 - p^3 - 5p^3 + 3p + p - p^3$

25. $3x^2 + 5(x^2 - 3x + 6)$ **26.** $-6(2y^3 - 4y^2 + 1) + 10y^2$

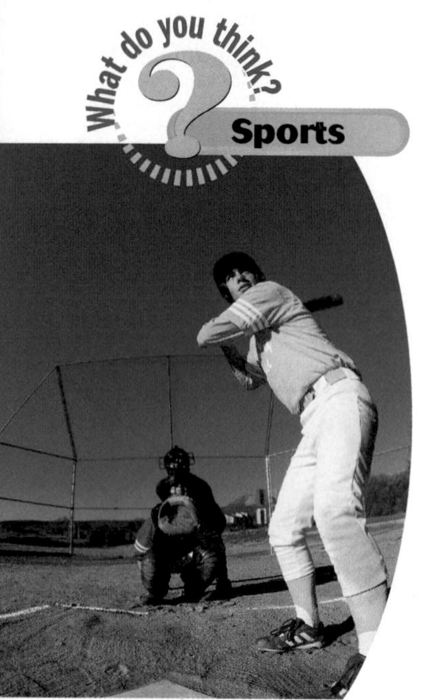

Baseball

A player hits a ball 60 mi/h into right field. The ball has the same height after 2 seconds as it has after 3.5 seconds. How is this possible?

Baseball A player hits a ball 60 mi/h, or 88 ft/sec, toward right field. Evaluate the polynomial $-16t^2 + 88t + 2$ to find the ball's height, in feet, after t seconds.

27. $t = 1.5$ **28.** $t = 2$ **29.** $t = 2.5$ **30.** $t = 3$

Simplify the polynomial and write it in standard form.

31. $-4(t - 3t^2 + 8 - 4t) + 6t^2 - 5$ **32.** $-3(-s^4 + 2s - 6 - s) - 8s + s^4$

Critical Thinking Tell whether the statement is *always, sometimes,* or *never* true.

33. The terms of a trinomial are monomials.

34. A monomial has one factor.

35. A binomial has more than two terms.

Challenge Simplify the polynomial.

36. $3x^2 - 2y + 5x^2 - 4$ **37.** $-16t - 7h + 3t^2 + 4h$

38. $5a - 4(3b + 6) + 4b$ **39.** $-z^2 + 3z - 2(4y - 5z)$

40. **Make a Connection** Find the meaning of the prefix *poly*. Explain what this tells you about the words *polygon* and *polynomial.*

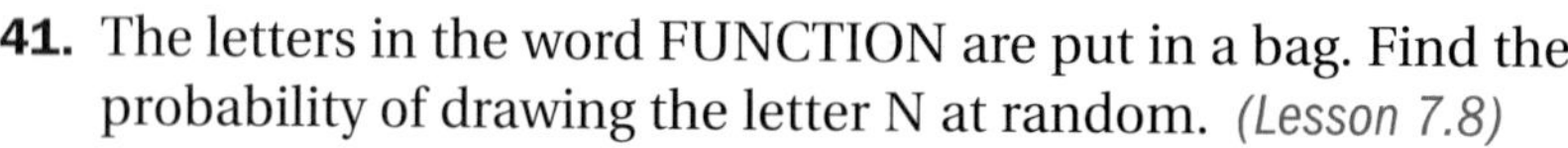

Mixed Review

41. The letters in the word FUNCTION are put in a bag. Find the probability of drawing the letter N at random. *(Lesson 7.8)*

42. Find the volume of the cylinder. Round to the nearest hundredth of a cubic meter. *(Lesson 10.6)*

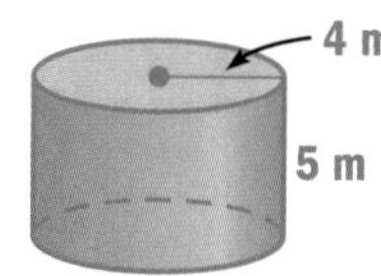

43. Make a stem-and-leaf plot of the data. *(Lesson 12.1)*
38.6, 35.8, 36.3, 34.2, 37.6, 37.5, 36.4, 36.2, 38.6, 36.6

Basic Skills Evaluate the expression.

44. $8(3 + 9)$ **45.** $-3(11 - 4)$ **46.** $-5(7 + 2)$ **47.** $12(6 - 1)$

Test-Taking Practice

INTERNET
State Test Practice
CLASSZONE.COM

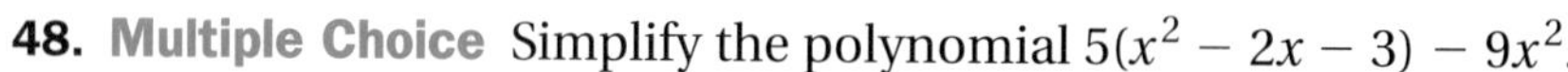

48. **Multiple Choice** Simplify the polynomial $5(x^2 - 2x - 3) - 9x^2$.

A. $4x^2 + 10x - 15$ **B.** $-4x^2 + 10x - 15$

C. $-4x^2 - 15x - 10x$ **D.** $-4x^2 - 10x - 15$

49. **Multiple Choice** Find the value of $-2x^2 - 4x + 7$ when $x = -2$.

F. -9 **G.** 7 **H.** 15 **I.** 23

Adding and Subtracting Polynomials

BEFORE	Now	WHY?
You simplified polynomials.	You'll add and subtract polynomials.	So you can find the area of clay coasters, as in Ex. 29.

Review Words

opposite, p. 54
like terms, p. 86

INDIANA Academic Standards

- Computation (8.2.1)
- Algebra and Functions (8.3.4)
- Measurement (8.5.4)

Activity **You can model polynomial addition with algebra tiles.**

You can model polynomials with algebra tiles.

1. Write the two polynomials represented by the algebra tiles.

2. Group the algebra tiles to model the sum of the polynomials. Draw your model. Write the polynomial that your drawing represents.

3. Use algebra tiles to model the sum of the polynomials below. Write the polynomial that your model represents.

   a. $(3x^2 + 6x + 1) + (x^2 + x)$ **b.** $(2x^2 + 3x + 1) + (4x^2 + x)$

In the activity, you used algebra tiles to add two polynomials. You add polynomials by combining like terms.

EXAMPLE 1 Adding Polynomials Vertically

Find the sum $(-4x^3 + x^2 - 3x - 1) + (4x^2 - 7x + 5)$.

Solution

$-4x^3 + x^2 - 3x - 1$	Write the second polynomial under the first.
$+ \quad 4x^2 - 7x + 5$	Arrange like terms in columns.
$-4x^3 + 5x^2 - 10x + 4$	Add like terms.

In Example 1, you combined like terms vertically. You can also add polynomials by combining like terms horizontally.

with Solving

When you regroup terms, you must move a subtraction or addition sign with the term that follows it.

EXAMPLE 2 Adding Polynomials Horizontally

Find the sum $(2y^2 - 4y + 6) + (y^2 + 3y - 2)$.

Solution

$(2y^2 - 4y + 6) + (y^2 + 3y - 2)$

$= 2y^2 + y^2 - 4y + 3y + 6 - 2$ **Group like terms.**

$= 3y^2 - y + 4$ **Combine like terms.**

Your turn now **Find the sum.**

1. $(6x^2 - 3x + 1) + (3x^2 + 4x - 5)$
2. $(5n^2 + 2n - 9) + (3n^2 - n + 4)$
3. $(y^2 - y + 1) + (-2y^2 + 2y - 1)$
4. $(3p^2 - p - 1) + (p^2 + p - 4)$

Subtracting Polynomials You can subtract a polynomial by adding its *opposite*. To find the opposite of a polynomial, multiply each of its terms by -1. You can subtract polynomials vertically or horizontally.

EXAMPLE 3 Subtracting Polynomials Vertically

Find the difference $(4x^3 + 5x^2 - 2x - 5) - (3x^3 - 4x + 2)$.

Solution

(1) Find the opposite of the second polynomial.

$-(3x^3 - 4x + 2) = -3x^3 + 4x - 2$

(2) Find the sum $(4x^3 + 5x^2 - 2x - 5) + (-3x^3 + 4x - 2)$.

$$\begin{array}{r} 4x^3 + 5x^2 - 2x - 5 \\ + -3x^3 \qquad\quad + 4x - 2 \\ \hline x^3 + 5x^2 + 2x - 7 \end{array}$$

Write the second polynomial under the first.

Arrange like terms in columns.

Add like terms.

Your turn now **Find the difference.**

5. $(4r^2 - r + 8) - (r^2 + 6r - 1)$
6. $(6m^2 + 2m - 3) - (7m^2 + 4)$
7. $(5t^2 + 4t + 1) - (2t^2 + 8t + 11)$
8. $(x^2 + 5x + 7) - (3x^2 - 4x - 2)$

EXAMPLE 4 Finding the Area of a Tree House

Tree House The design for a tree house calls for a rectangular hole in the floor. Write a polynomial expression for the area of the tree house floor.

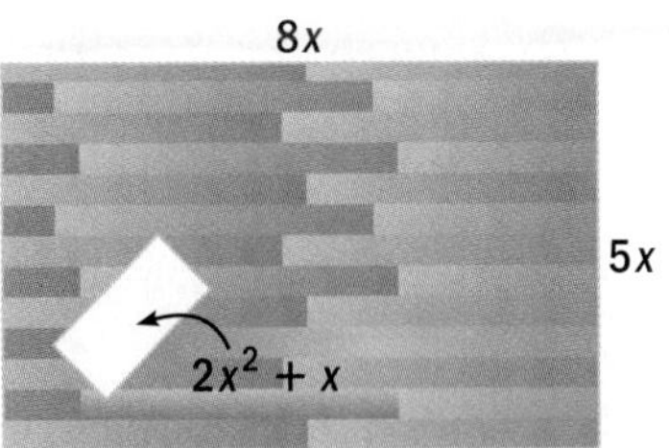

Solution

To find the area of the floor, use the area of the two rectangles.

Area of Large Rectangle

$8x \cdot 5x = 40x^2$

Area of Small Rectangle

$2x^2 + x$

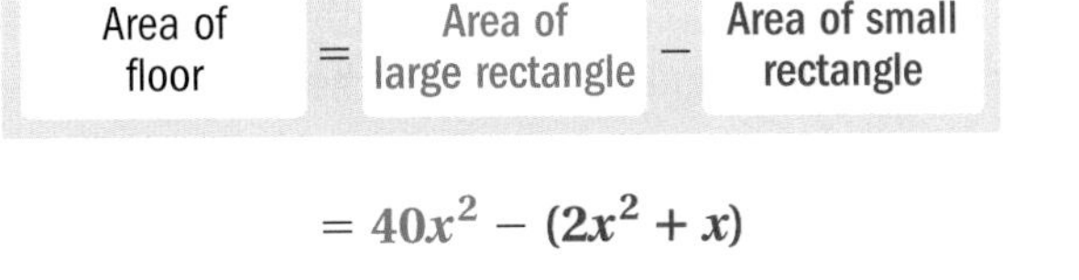

Area of floor = Area of large rectangle − Area of small rectangle

$= 40x^2 - (2x^2 + x)$

$= 40x^2 - 2x^2 - x$ **Distributive property**

$= 38x^2 - x$ **Combine like terms.**

ANSWER A polynomial expression for the area of the floor is $38x^2 - x$.

13.2 Exercises

More Practice, p. 739

Getting Ready to Practice

1. **Vocabulary** Copy and complete: To add polynomials, you should combine _?_.

Find the sum or difference.

2. $(8y + 5) + (4y - 3)$
3. $(7x + 10) - (x - 2)$
4. $(x - 6) + (2x + 9)$
5. $(4p + 1) - (p - 7)$
6. $(5n^2 + 2n + 1) - (4n^2 - 1)$
7. $(-3a + 10) + (2a - 4)$
8. **Find the Error** Describe and correct the error(s) in the solution.

$$\begin{array}{r} -4x^3 + 5x^2 - 7x + 2 \\ +\quad 2x^3 - 6x + 10 \\ \hline -2x^3 - x^2 + 3x + 2 \end{array}$$

Practice and Problem Solving

with Homework

Example	Exercises
1	9-14
2	9-14
3	15-20
4	29

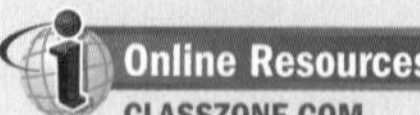

Online Resources CLASSZONE.COM

- More Examples
- eTutorial Plus

Find the sum.

9. $(4x + 7) + (x - 3)$

10. $(-2a - 9) + (a + 4)$

11. $(3n - 7) + (4n + 5)$

12. $(t^2 + 3t) + (3t^2 + 8t)$

13. $(-g^2 + g + 9) + (7g^2 - 6)$

14. $(3z^2 - 2z + 1) + (4z^3 + 3z)$

Find the difference.

15. $(-5d - 1) - (5d + 6)$

16. $(7y + 1) - (3y - 2)$

17. $(2h^2 + 9h) - (13h^2 - h)$

18. $(4x^2 + 9x) - (x^2 + 7x - 1)$

19. $(6r^2 + 2r - 5) - (3r^2 - 9)$

20. $(-4b^3 - 9b + 2) - (b^3 - b + 3)$

Geometry **Write a polynomial expression for the perimeter of the figure. Simplify the polynomial.**

21.

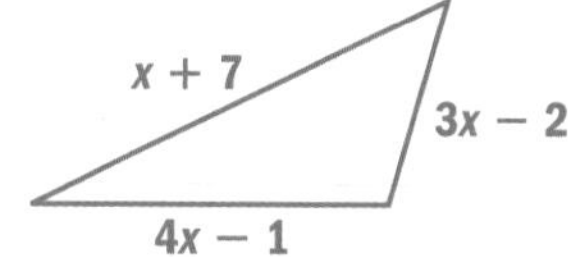

22.

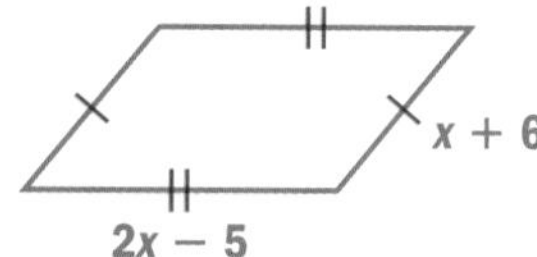

Find the sum or difference.

23. $(2k^2 + 5k) + (4k^2 - 5k)$

24. $(5a^2 + 3a + 8) - (2a^2 - 2a - 9)$

25. $(6x^3 - 12x + 1) + (8x^2 - 4)$

26. $(4p^3 + p^2 - 8) - (7p^3 + 2p + 5)$

27. $(4n - 3) + (9n + 5) - (n - 1)$

28. $(-8m + 1) - (2m - 6) + 5m$

29. **Coasters** To make a set of coasters, you cut identical circles out of a square piece of clay. Write a polynomial expression for the area of clay that remains after you remove the circles. Simplify the polynomial. Is there enough clay left over to make another coaster of the same radius and thickness? Explain your answer.

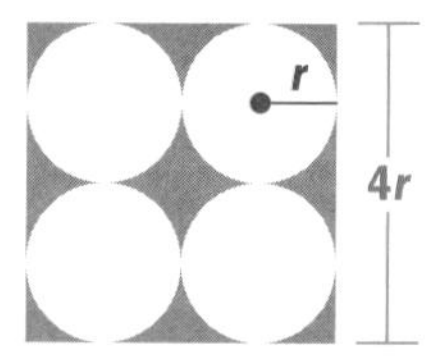

Perform the indicated operations.

30. $-2(5y + 3) - 9(y + 1)$

31. $4(-3s^2 + s - 4) + (5s^2 + s + 7)$

32. $3(q^2 - q) + 2(7q^2 - 2q)$

33. $6(t^3 - t^2 + 3t) - 4(5t^3 + t^2 - t)$

34. $5(4x^3 - 2x^2 + 1) + 3(7x^2 - 5x)$

35. $-7(2v^4 + 3v^2 - 1) - 5(-3v^3 - 6)$

36. **Critical Thinking** Can the sum of two trinomials be a binomial? Give an example to justify your answer.

37. **Challenge** Solve the equation $(2x^2 - 3x + 4) - (2x^2 + x - 8) = 0$.

with Review

For help with surface area of a pyramid, see p. 507.

38. Science Fair You are constructing two wooden pyramids using the designs shown. Write a simplified polynomial expression for the total surface area of the two pyramids.

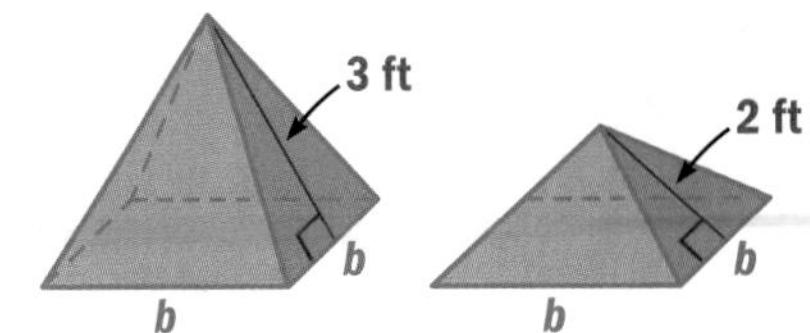

Mixed Review 

Simplify the expression. *(Lesson 4.6)*

39. $b^3 \cdot b^7$ **40.** $\frac{x^{12}}{x^5}$ **41.** $\frac{m^4n^5}{n^2}$ **42.** $\frac{a^2 \cdot a^6}{a^3}$

43. How many different passwords can be made using 4 digits from 0 to 9? *(Lesson 12.4)*

Test-Taking Practice 

INTERNET
State Test Practice
CLASSZONE.COM

44. Multiple Choice Find the sum $(-7x^3 + 4x^2 - 1) + (x^3 - 9x + 3)$.

A. $-6x^3 + 4x^2 - 9x + 2$ **B.** $-8x^3 + 4x^2 - 9x - 4$

C. $-6x^3 + 5x^2 + 2$ **D.** $-8x^3 - 5x^2 + 4$

45. Short Response Explain how to find the difference.
$(x^4 - 3x^3 + 5x + 3) - (x^4 + 2x^3 - 9x^2)$

Polynomial Potions

You need to make six potions using the six ingredients in the laboratory. Each potion is made by adding two ingredients together. Use the list of ingredients and the potion labels to find the secret formulas.

Ingredients

Dog Biscuits
$x^2 - 2x + 2$

Green Slime
$2x^2 - 3x + 1$

Fish Oil
$3x^2 + 5x - 4$

Cotton Balls
$-x^2 - 6x - 2$

Muck
$-3x^2 + 2x - 1$

Nail Polish
$-2x^2 + x - 3$

$-2x - 2$

$5x^2 + 2x - 3$

$x^2 - 9x - 1$

$-8x$

$7x - 5$

$x^2 + 6x - 7$

Monomials and Powers

BEFORE	Now	WHY?
You added and subtracted polynomials.	You will apply properties of exponents to monomials.	So you can find the volume of Saturn, as in Ex. 48.

Review Words

power, p. 20
exponent, p. 20
coefficient, p. 86
monomial, p. 170

INDIANA Academic Standards

- Algebra and Functions (8.3.4)
- Measurement (8.5.5)

Activity You can use the properties of exponents to simplify monomials.

1. Copy and complete the table by expanding each expression, regrouping factors, and simplifying.

Expression	Expand	Regroup	Simplify
$(3x)(4x^2)$	$3 \cdot x \cdot 4 \cdot x \cdot x$	$3 \cdot 4 \cdot x \cdot x \cdot x$	$12x^3$
$(-2x)(5x^4)$	?	?	?
$(xy)^3$	$xy \cdot xy \cdot xy$	$x \cdot x \cdot x \cdot y \cdot y \cdot y$	x^3y^3
$(4x)^2$	?	?	?
$(-3x)^3$	?	?	?

2. What patterns do you notice in the table?

3. Use your results to simplify the expressions $(5x)(2x^3)$ and $(3pq)^2$.

In the activity, you used properties of exponents that you learned in Lesson 4.6 to multiply monomials. To multiply factors that have the same base, add their exponents. Multiply their coefficients.

For help with rules of exponents, see p. 196.

EXAMPLE 1 Multiplying Monomials

Simplify the expression $(2x^3)(-3x)$.

$(2x^3)(-3x) = 2 \cdot x^3 \cdot (-3) \cdot x$ **Expand the expression.**

$= 2 \cdot (-3) \cdot x^3 \cdot x$ **Regroup factors.**

$= -6 \cdot x^3 \cdot x$ **Multiply coefficients.**

$= -6x^4$ **Product of powers property**

Your turn now **Simplify the expression.**

1. $4a(a^2)$ **2.** $(-2m)(7m^2)$ **3.** $(-x)(8x^2)$ **4.** $(y^5)(5y)$

You can use the distributive property and the properties of exponents to find the product of a monomial and a binomial.

EXAMPLE 2 Using the Distributive Property

Simplify the expression $2n(4n^2 - 5)$.

$2n(4n^2 - 5) = (2n)(4n^2) - (2n)(5)$ **Distributive property**

$= 8n^3 - 10n$ **Product of powers property**

Your turn now **Simplify the expression.**

5. $p(2p + 3)$ **6.** $-t^2(-2t + 8)$ **7.** $n^2(5n^2 - 3)$ **8.** $2x(3x - 4)$

In the activity on page 666, you found powers of products. You can use the rule below to simplify a power of a product.

Power of a Product Property

Words To simplify a power of a product, find the power of each factor and multiply.

Algebra $(ab)^m = a^m \cdot b^m$ **Numbers** $(5 \cdot 2)^3 = 5^3 \cdot 2^3$

EXAMPLE 3 Simplifying a Power of a Product

Container The radius of a container is twice its height. Write an expression for the volume of the container. Use the formula $V = \pi r^2 h$.

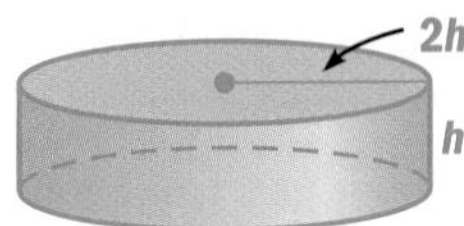

Solution

The radius is twice the height, so $r = 2h$.

$V = \pi(2h)^2 h$ **Substitute 2h for r.**

$= \pi(2^2 \cdot h^2)h$ **Power of a product property**

$= \pi \cdot 4 \cdot h^2 \cdot h$ **Evaluate the power.**

$= 4\pi h^3$ **Product of powers property.**

ANSWER An expression for the volume of the container is $V = 4\pi h^3$.

Power of a Power Property

Words To simplify a power of a power, multiply exponents.

Algebra $(a^m)^n = a^{mn}$ **Numbers** $(5^3)^2 = 5^{3 \cdot 2} = 5^6$

EXAMPLE 4 **Simplifying a Power of a Power**

Simplify the expression $(2y^2)^3$.

$(2y^2)^3 = 2^3 \cdot (y^2)^3$ Power of a product property

$= 8 \cdot y^{2 \cdot 3}$ Power of a power property

$= 8y^6$ Simplify.

Your turn now **Simplify the expression.**

9. $(2^4)^2$ **10.** $(x^6)^2$ **11.** $(5m^3)^2$ **12.** $(a^2b)^2$

13.3 Exercises

More Practice, p. 739

Getting Ready to Practice

Vocabulary **Match the expression with the rule used to simplify it.**

1. $(2y)^5$

2. $(x^2)^7$

3. $3 \cdot x^4 \cdot x^6$

A. power of a power property

B. power of a product property

C. product of powers property

Simplify the expression.

4. $(5x)(7x^6)$ **5.** $2x(x^2 - 1)$ **6.** $(4y)^3$ **7.** $(z^4)^4$

8. **Guided Problem Solving** Simplify the expression $\left(\frac{x}{y}\right)^4$.

(1) Write the expression in expanded form.

(2) Simplify by multiplying numerators and multiplying denominators.

(3) Write a rule you could use to find the power of a quotient.

Practice and Problem Solving

Example	Exercises
1	9-14
2	15-20
3	22-29
4	30-37

- More Examples
- eTutorial Plus

Simplify the expression by multiplying the monomials.

9. $(-4x)(5x^3)$ **10.** $(-16t)(-3t^9)$ **11.** $(-x^2)(-3x)$

12. $(3s)(-2s^3)$ **13.** $(-b^3)(-b^8)$ **14.** $(-y^2)(y^3)$

Simplify the expression by using the distributive property.

15. $m(m + 4)$ **16.** $2w(3w + 1)$ **17.** $-t(t^2 - 4)$

18. $-8x(x^5 + x)$ **19.** $w^2(-2w - 1)$ **20.** $3k^2(12 - k^5)$

21. Seat Cushion You need fabric for a window seat cushion. Use the trapezoid pattern shown to write a polynomial expression for the area of the top of the cushion. Simplify the expression.

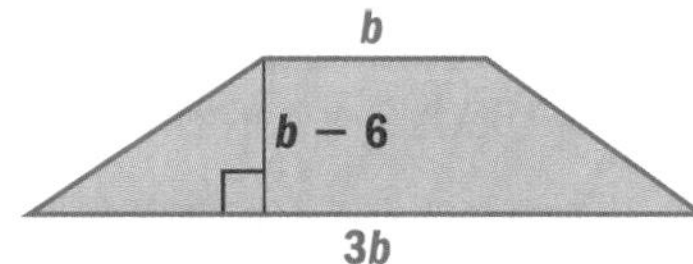

Simplify the expression by using the power of a product property.

22. $(5z)^3$ **23.** $(xyz)^5$ **24.** $(2ab)^4$ **25.** $(-6z)^3$

26. $(-dt)^4$ **27.** $(3rs)^2$ **28.** $(-3xy)^3$ **29.** $(10bh)^5$

Simplify the expression by using the power of a power property.

30. $(t^4)^2$ **31.** $(y^2)^2$ **32.** $(c^2)^9$ **33.** $(x^2)^{10}$

34. $(ab^3)^2$ **35.** $(x^2y^2)^3$ **36.** $(3a^2)^2$ **37.** $(2r^3)^3$

38. Compare and Contrast Explain why $(4y)^2$ is different from $4y^2$.

39. Photo Albums You are making photo albums in different sizes. Each page is twice as long as it is wide and needs a 2 inch margin for binding. Write a polynomial expression for the total area of one page.

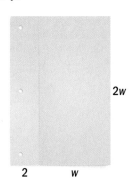

Simplify the expression.

40. $2(5mn^4)^3$ **41.** $-3a^{10}(a^4b^2c)^4$ **42.** $(-2x^4)^3(x^4yz^8)$

43. Critical Thinking Write a ratio comparing the area of the circle to the area of the square. Simplify the ratio. Leave your answer in terms of π.

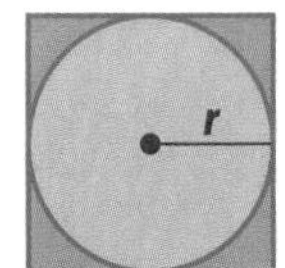

44. **Volume** Write and simplify a polynomial expression for the volume of the square pyramid.

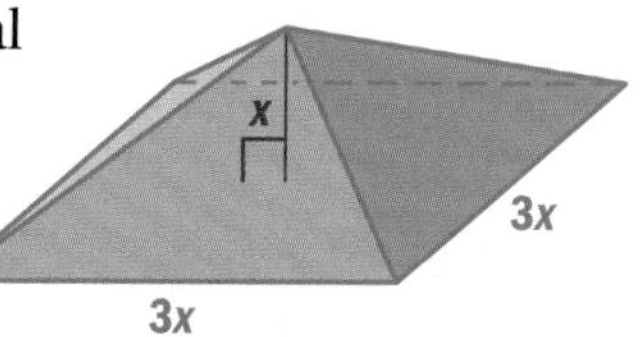

Saturn

The moon Pan orbits within a gap in Saturn's rings. Pan's radius is about 10 kilometers. Compare the volumes of Pan and Saturn.

Scientific Notation Simplify the expression and write it in scientific notation.

45. $(3 \times 10^4)^3$

46. $(9 \times 10^{10})^3$

47. $(5 \times 10^7)^4$

Extended Problem Solving In Exercises 48–50, use the formula $V = \frac{4}{3}\pi r^3$ for the volume of a sphere to find the volumes of spherical objects in our solar system.

48. **Saturn** The radius of Saturn is about 6.0×10^4 kilometers.

49. **Moon of Saturn** The radius of Saturn's moon Dione is about 560 kilometers.

50. **Estimate** Write a ratio comparing the volume of Saturn to the volume of Dione. Use this ratio to estimate how many times larger Saturn is than Dione.

Challenge Simplify the expression.

51. $3[(a^4b^3)^4 \cdot a^8b]^3$

52. $\left(\frac{2x^2}{x}\right)^3$

53. $\frac{(-2xy)^2}{(x^2)^3}$

Mixed Review 

In Exercises 54–57, write the percent as a fraction in simplest form. *(Lesson 7.4)*

54. 55%

55. 71%

56. 29%

57. 18%

58. In one out of every eight holes of mini-golf, you get a hole in one. Find the odds of getting a hole in one on the next hole that you play. *(Lesson 12.7)*

59. Find the probability of rolling first a 2 and then a 4 if you roll a number cube twice. *(Lesson 12.8)*

Test-Taking Practice 

60. **Multiple Choice** Simplify the expression $4a^2(3a + 1)$.

A. $7a^3 + 1$ **B.** $12a^3 + 4a$ **C.** $7a^3 + 4a^2$ **D.** $12a^3 + 4a^2$

61. **Multiple Choice** Simplify the expression $(-2b^4)^3$.

F. $-8b^{12}$ **G.** $8b^7$ **H.** $8b^{12}$ **I.** $-8b^7$

LESSONS 13.1 TO 13.3

Notebook Review

Review the vocabulary definitions in your notebook.

Copy the review examples in your notebook. Then complete the exercises.

Check Your Definitions

polynomial, p. 657
binomial, p. 657
trinomial, p. 657
standard form, p. 657

Use Your Vocabulary

Copy and complete the statement.

1. A polynomial with one term is called a _?_.

2. A _?_ is a monomial or a sum of monomials.

13.1 Can you simplify polynomials?

EXAMPLE Simplify the polynomial $4x^2 - 5(x^2 - x + 3 - 2x)$.

$4x^2 - 5(x^2 - x + 3 - 2x)$

$= 4x^2 - 5x^2 + 5x - 15 + 10x$ **Distributive property**

$= -x^2 + 15x - 15$ **Combine like terms.**

✓ **Simplify the polynomial and write it in standard form.**

3. $10 - 3a^2 + 4a^2 + 8$

4. $6 + z^2 - 3z + z^2 - 5$

13.2 Can you add and subtract polynomials?

EXAMPLE Find the sum $(3x^2 - 2x + 7) + (5x - 9)$.

$3x^2 - 2x + 7$ **Write the second polynomial under the first.**

$+ \quad 5x - 9$ **Arrange like terms in columns.**

$3x^2 + 3x - 2$ **Combine like terms.**

✓ **Find the sum or difference.**

5. $(n^3 + 4n^2 - 9) + (n^3 + n^2 - 2n + 6)$

6. $(2x^2 + 3x - 1) - (7x^2 - x - 5)$

13.3 Can you multiply monomials?

EXAMPLE Simplify the expression $(x^3)(3x)^2$.

$(x^3)(3x)^2 = x^3(3^2 \cdot x^2)$ **Power of a product property**

$= x^3 \cdot 9 \cdot x^2$ **Evaluate the power.**

$= 9x^5$ **Product of powers property**

☑ **Simplify the expression.**

7. $(8x^8)(6x^2)$ **8.** $(6n^3m)^2$ **9.** $(2ab)^4$ **10.** $(4r^2)(r - 5)$

about Lessons 13.1–13.3

11. **Writing** Simplify the expression $(2x)(x^2y)$ and explain your steps.

12. **Critical Thinking** The radius of a cylinder is three times its height. Write a polynomial expression for the surface area of the cylinder using only one variable. Use the formula $S = 2\pi r^2 + 2\pi rh$.

Review Quiz 1

Simplify the polynomial and write it in standard form.

1. $5x^2 + 4x - 3x^2 - 11$

2. $-9y^2 + 7y - 2y + 10 - y$

3. $-5k^3 + 2(3k^3 + k - 4)$

4. $8r^3 - 4r - 5r^3 - 3r + 1$

Find the sum or difference.

5. $(6n^3 - 2n^2) + (n^3 + 7n^2 - 4n)$

6. $(4b^2 - 3b + 8) - (2b^2 - 6)$

7. $(x^2 + 6x + 1) - (2x^2 - 8x + 4)$

8. $(3m^2 + m - 9) + (7m^2 + 2)$

9. **Area** Write a polynomial expression for the area of the floor surrounding the rug in the diagram. Simplify the polynomial.

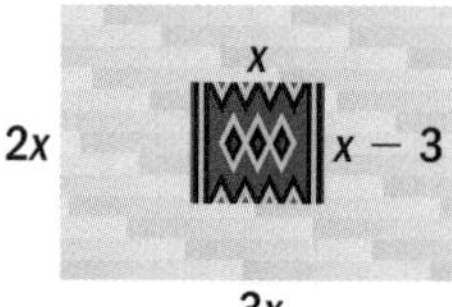

Simplify the expression.

10. $(x^3)(-5x)$

11. $(3t^4)(4t^2)$

12. $(2c^3)^4$

13. $(-2y)^4$

14. $r^3(3r - 4)$

15. $-5d(3d^2 + 2)$

13.4 Hands-on Activity

GOAL

Multiply binomials using algebra tiles.

MATERIALS

- algebra tiles

Multiplying Binomials

You can model binomial multiplication with algebra tiles.

Explore **Model the product $(x + 3)(3x + 2)$ with algebra tiles.**

1 Model each binomial with algebra tiles. Arrange the first binomial vertically and the second binomial horizontally, as shown.

2 The binomials define a rectangular area with length $(3x + 2)$ units and width $(x + 3)$ units. Fill in the region with the appropriate tiles.

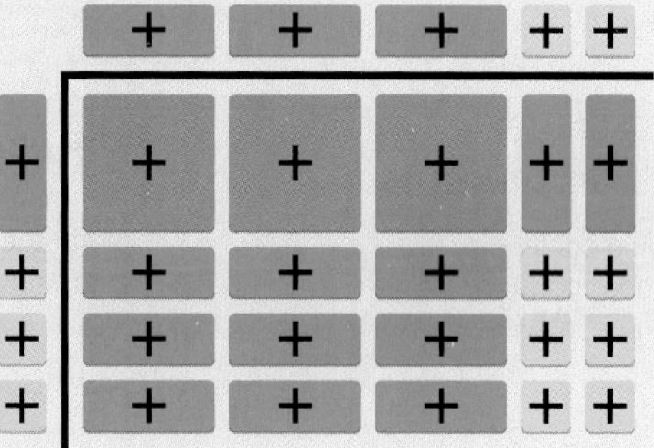

3 The rectangle on the inside of the model represents $3x^2 + 11x + 6$. This is the product of the binomials.

Your turn now **Find the product with algebra tiles. Draw your model.**

1. $(x + 1)(x + 2)$ **2.** $(x + 4)(x + 4)$ **3.** $(x + 2)(2x + 2)$

Stop and Think

Model the expression with algebra tiles. Arrange the tiles in a rectangle. Find the two binomials that have this product.

4. $x^2 + 5x + 6$ **5.** $x^2 + 2x + 1$ **6.** $3x^2 + 8x + 4$

Multiplying Binomials

BEFORE	Now	WHY?
You multiplied monomials and polynomials.	You'll multiply binomials.	So you can find an account balance after 2 years, as in Ex. 22.

Review words

polynomial, p. 657
binomial, p. 657

INDIANA
Academic Standards

- Computation (8.2.1)
- Algebra and Functions (8.3.4)

You can use a visual model to multiply binomials. The model below shows that the product $(x + 2)(3x + 1)$ equals $3x^2 + 7x + 2$.

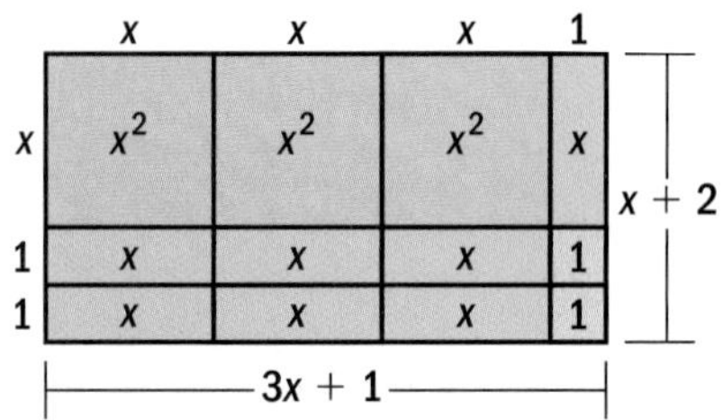

You can multiply two binomials using a table or a vertical method.

HELP with Notetaking

You should summarize key ideas about polynomials in your notebook.

EXAMPLE 1 Multiplying Binomials with a Table

Find the product $(-3x + 2)(8x + 7)$ and simplify.

Write the first polynomial on the left of the table.

	$8x$	7
$-3x$	$-24x^2$	$-21x$
2	$16x$	14

Write the second polynomial above the table.

Multiply to fill in the table.

The product is $-24x^2 - 21x + 16x + 14$. Combine like terms.

ANSWER The product is $-24x^2 - 5x + 14$.

EXAMPLE 2 Multiplying Binomials Vertically

Find the product $(2x - 5)(3x + 4)$ and simplify.

$2x - 5$	**Write the first binomial.**
$\times \quad 3x + 4$	**Write the second binomial.**
$8x - 20$	**Multiply $4(2x - 5)$.**
$6x^2 - 15x$	**Multiply $3x(2x - 5)$. Line up like terms.**
$6x^2 - 7x - 20$	**Add $8x - 20$ and $6x^2 - 15x$.**

with Vocabulary

Compound interest is earned on the original amount of money in an account and on the interest already earned.

EXAMPLE 3 Multiplying Binomials Horizontally

Banking You deposit $1 into a savings account with interest compounded annually. The balance of the account after two years can be found using the expression $(1 + r)^2$, where r represents the interest rate. Expand this expression and simplify.

Solution

To expand the expression, multiply 2 binomials.

$(1 + r)^2 = (1 + r)(1 + r)$	$(1 + r)^2$ means $(1 + r)(1 + r)$.
$= 1(1 + r) + r(1 + r)$	Distributive property
$= 1 + r + r + r^2$	Distributive property
$= 1 + 2r + r^2$	Combine like terms.
$= r^2 + 2r + 1$	Write in standard form.

Your turn now **Find the product and simplify.**

1. $(x + 1)(x + 3)$ **2.** $(b - 4)(b - 3)$ **3.** $(3t - 4)(t + 2)$

The FOIL Method The letters in the word FOIL can help you remember how to multiply binomials. The letters should remind you of the words **F**irst, **O**uter, **I**nner, and **L**ast.

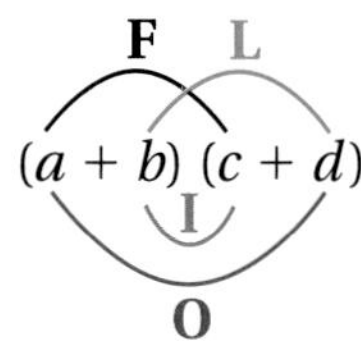

EXAMPLE 4 Multiplying with the FOIL Method

Find the product $(2x + 3)(3x - 1)$ and simplify.

F		O		I		L	
First	+	Outer	+	Inner	+	Last	
$2x \cdot 3x$	+	$2x \cdot (-1)$	+	$3 \cdot 3x$	+	$3 \cdot (-1)$	Group terms.
$6x^2$	+	$(-2x)$	+	$9x$	+	(-3)	Multiply.
		$6x^2 + 7x - 3$					Combine like terms.

Your turn now **Find the product and simplify.**

4. $(d + 6)(d + 5)$ **5.** $(x - 3)(x - 1)$ **6.** $(5s + 3)(2s - 4)$

More Practice, p. 739

INTERNET
eWorkbook Plus
CLASSZONE.COM

Getting Ready to Practice

1. **Vocabulary** Copy and complete: A polynomial with two terms is called a _?_.

HELP with Homework

Example	Exercises
1	9-17
2	9-17
3	22
4	9-17

Online Resources
CLASSZONE.COM
· More Examples
· eTutorial Plus

Find the product and simplify.

2. $3x(x - 4)$
3. $2m(3m + 1)$
4. $-2y(y + 5)$
5. $(y - 4)(y + 1)$
6. $(g + 3)(g + 7)$
7. $(z + 4)(z - 2)$
8. **Find the Error** Describe and correct the error in the solution.

$$(x + 2)(x - 4)$$
$$= x \cdot x + x \cdot 4 + 2 \cdot x + 2 \cdot (-4)$$
$$= x^2 + 4x + 2x - 8$$
$$= x^2 + 6x - 8 \quad \times$$

Practice and Problem Solving

Find the product and simplify.

9. $(x + 9)(x - 2)$
10. $(p + 6)(p + 4)$
11. $(a + 10)(a - 4)$
12. $(2m + 3)(m - 7)$
13. $(3q - 1)(q - 1)$
14. $(b - 3)(9b + 4)$
15. $(6r + 7)(r - 1)$
16. $(t - 1)(-3t - 4)$
17. $(-x - 5)(11x - 12)$

Critical Thinking **Find the product and simplify.**

18. $(x + 3)(x - 3)$
19. $(x - 4)(x + 4)$
20. $(x + 1)(x - 1)$
21. **Look for a Pattern** Describe the pattern in the binomials and their products in Exercises 18–20.
22. **Savings Account** You deposit \$50 into a savings account with interest compounded annually. The expression $50(1 + r)^2$, where r is the interest rate, gives the account balance after 2 years. Expand this expression and simplify. Find the account balance for $r = 0.03$.
23. **Baseball** The middle of a baseball is a cork sphere with a radius of 0.6875 inch. Use the formula $S = 4\pi r^2$ to write a polynomial expression for the surface area of the baseball. Expand the expression and simplify.

0.6875 in.

Find the product and simplify.

24. $\left(\frac{1}{2}x + 2\right)(4x - 6)$ **25.** $(9b - 12)\left(\frac{1}{3}b - 6\right)$ **26.** $(n^2 - 2)(n^2 + 1)$

27. Stage Design You are building a platform on stage for a school talent show. Write and simplify a polynomial expression for the area of the platform using the design shown. Then find the area when x is 5 feet.

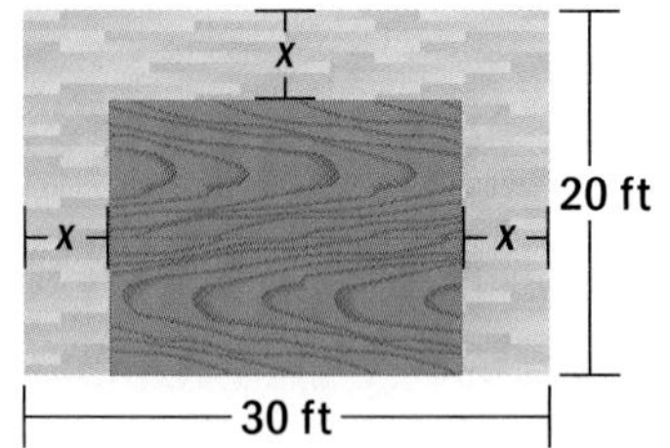

28. Writing Explain why $(x + 3)^2$ does not equal $x^2 + 9$.

29. Challenge Find the product and simplify: $(x + 4)(3x^2 - 2x + 1)$.

30. Savings You put \$20 into a savings account with interest compounded annually. The expression $20(1 + r)^3$, where r is the interest rate, gives the account balance after 3 years. Expand this expression and simplify. Find the account balance for $r = 0.05$.

31. Work Backward Find the unknown binomial in the equation $x^2 + 8x + 7 = (\underline{\ ?\ })(x + 7)$.

Mixed Review

Graph the linear equation. *(Lesson 11.4)*

32. $y = 6x - 4$ **33.** $y = x - 3$ **34.** $y = -2x + 7$

Find the product. *(Lesson 13.3)*

35. $-4r(r + 6)$ **36.** $3c(4c^2 + 2c)$ **37.** $-5x(-3x + 2)$

Basic Skills Plot the point in a coordinate plane.

38. $(2, -9)$ **39.** $(-7, 6)$ **40.** $(-3, -8)$ **41.** $(0, 4)$

Test-Taking Practice

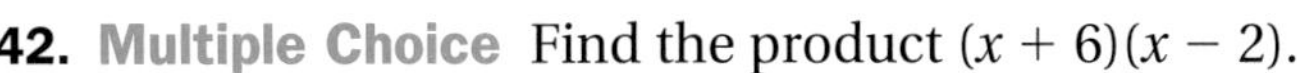

INTERNET
State Test Practice
CLASSZONE.COM

42. Multiple Choice Find the product $(x + 6)(x - 2)$.

A. $x^2 - 4x - 12$ **B.** $x^2 - 4x + 4$

C. $x^2 + 4x + 12$ **D.** $x^2 + 4x - 12$

43. Multiple Choice Find the product $(2x + 1)(x - 5)$.

F. $2x^2 - 9x - 5$ **G.** $x^2 - 9x - 5$

H. $2x^2 + 11x - 5$ **I.** $x^2 + 11x - 5$

13.5 Problem Solving Strategies

INDIANA: Academic Standards
• Problem Solving (8.7.1)

- Look for a Pattern
- Draw a Diagram
- Act It Out
- Work Backward
- Draw a Graph
- Break into Parts

Draw a Graph

Daylight The table below shows the total hours of daylight, to the nearest quarter hour, in Anchorage, Alaska, on the 20th day of each month. The table is missing data for the month of July. Estimate the total hours of daylight on July 20.

Month	Jan.	Feb.	March	April	May	June	July	Aug.	Sept.	Oct.	Nov.	Dec.
Hours of Daylight	$6\frac{3}{4}$	$9\frac{1}{2}$	$12\frac{1}{4}$	$15\frac{1}{4}$	$17\frac{3}{4}$	$19\frac{1}{4}$	?	$15\frac{1}{2}$	$12\frac{1}{2}$	$9\frac{3}{4}$	7	$5\frac{1}{2}$

1 Read and Understand

Read the problem carefully.

You need to estimate the total hours of daylight on July 20.

2 Make a Plan

Decide on a strategy to use.

You can estimate the hours by drawing a graph. Use the table of values to sketch a curve.

3 Solve the Problem

Reread the problem and draw a graph.

The data in the table are ordered pairs. Let the *x*-axis show the date (Jan. 20 = 1, Feb. 20 = 2, etc.). Let the *y*-axis show the hours of daylight. Plot the points in the coordinate plane.

Connect the points with a curve, and use it to estimate the total hours of daylight on July 20.

ANSWER There are about 18 hours of daylight on July 20.

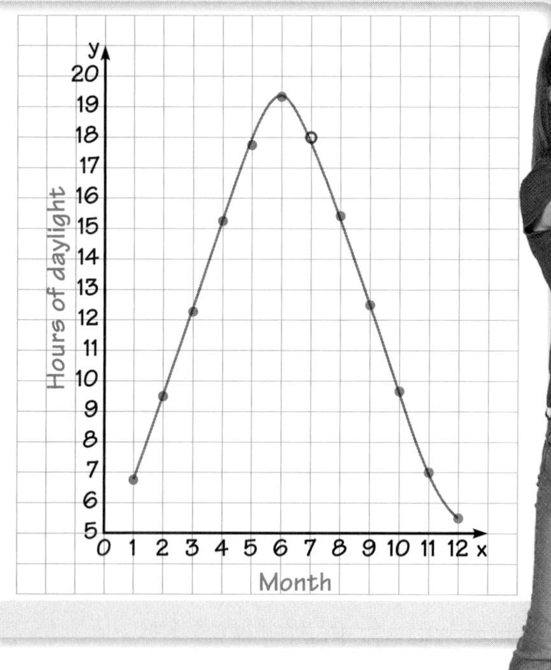

4 Look Back

Because the graph decreases from June to December it is reasonable to say that there are between $19\frac{1}{4}$ and $15\frac{1}{2}$ hours of daylight on July 20. A reasonable estimate is 18 hours.

Practice the Strategy

Use the strategy *draw a graph*.

1. **E-mail** You e-mail two copies of a joke on January 1. Each recipient e-mails two copies of the joke on the day after receiving it. How many e-mails are sent on January 7?

2. **Square Root** Copy and complete the table.

x	1	4	9	16	25	36
$\sqrt{x}$	?	?	?	?	?	?

Estimate the square roots below.

a. $\sqrt{7}$ **b.** $\sqrt{30}$ **c.** $\sqrt{20}$

3. **Cutting** The area of a poster board is 1000 square inches. You repeatedly cut the poster in half, setting aside one half each time. Estimate how many cuts you will make before the area of the remaining piece is less than 1 square inch.

4. **Kiwi Bird** A female kiwi bird weighs from 3 to 9 pounds. A kiwi bird's egg weighs about $\frac{1}{5}$ of the mother's body weight. Estimate the weight of a female bird whose egg weighs less than 0.7 pound.

5. **Tutoring** For each hour you spend tutoring after school, you earn 5 extra-credit points. Make a table that shows how many extra-credit points you can earn for hours you spend tutoring. Estimate how many extra-credit points you would earn after tutoring for 1 hour and 45 minutes.

Mixed Problem Solving

Use any strategy to solve the problem.

6. **Peanut Butter** In a poll, 44% of the people said the best thing to eat with peanut butter is jelly. About 23% chose chocolate. Only 15% preferred marshmallow spread with peanut butter. The rest of the people chose bananas. If 2916 people participated in the poll, about how many people choose bananas with peanut butter?

7. **Draw** Copy the grid. How many squares can you draw by connecting dots?

8. **Encyclopedia** You have a two-volume music encyclopedia. Each volume has 600 pages, and its front and back covers are each 0.4 centimeter thick. If the books sit in the usual order on a shelf, what is the distance, in centimeters, from the first page of Volume 1 to the last page of Volume 2?

9. **Solid** Find the volume of the solid shown. The formula for the volume of a sphere is $V = \frac{4}{3}\pi r^3$. Round to the nearest hundredth of a cubic centimeter.

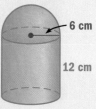

6 cm

12 cm

LESSON 13.5

Non-Linear Functions

BEFORE

You wrote function rules and graphed linear functions.

Now

You'll use function notation and graph non-linear functions.

WHY?

So you can find the height of a falling penny, as in Ex. 11.

Word Watch

function notation, p. 680
vertical line test, p. 681

INDIANA
Academic Standards

- Algebra and Functions (8.3.9, 8.3.10)

In the Real World

Juggling You are juggling three balls. The height of one ball, in feet, is found with the equation $h = -16t^2 + 20t + 3$, where t is seconds that pass after you let go of the ball. Write the equation in function notation. Use this function to find the height of one ball 0.5 second after you let go of it.

In Lesson 11.1, you wrote functions as equations in x and y. You used x to name the input and y to name the output. Sometimes it is useful to use **function notation** instead.

equation in x and y	function notation
$y = 3x - 4$	$f(x) = 3x - 4$

The symbol $f(x)$ is read as "the function of f at x" or "f of x."

EXAMPLE 1 Using Function Notation

Write a function that models the height of a ball x seconds after you let go of it. Use function notation. Evaluate for $x = 0.5$.

Solution

Let $f(x)$ = height in feet and x = time in seconds.

$f(x) = -16x^2 + 20x + 3$ — Write the height equation above in function notation.

$f(\mathbf{0.5}) = -16(\mathbf{0.5})^2 + 20(\mathbf{0.5}) + 3$ — Substitute 0.5 for x.

$f(0.5) = -16(0.25) + 10 + 3$ — Evaluate.

$f(0.5) = 9$

ANSWER The function is $f(x) = -16x^2 + 20x + 3$. The height of the ball is 9 feet after 0.5 second.

Your turn now Rewrite using function notation.

1. $y = x^2$
2. $y = 3x^2 + 4$
3. $y = -\frac{1}{2}x^2$

Graphing Functions The function in Example 1 is non-linear. A non-linear function has a graph that is not a straight line. You can graph non-linear functions by first making a table of values.

HELP with Reading

$f(x)$ does not mean "f times x." It means "the value of the function at x."

EXAMPLE 2 Graphing a Non-Linear Function

Graph the function $f(x) = x^2 - 1$.

(1) Choose several x-values and make a table of values.

x	−2	−1	0	1	2
$f(x)$	3	0	−1	0	3

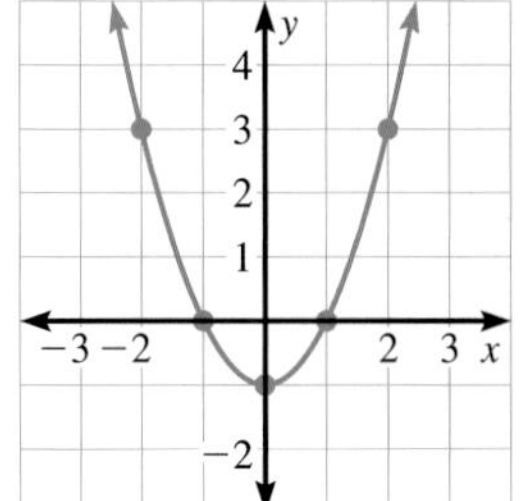

(2) List the solutions as ordered pairs.
(−2, 3), (−1, 0), (0, −1), (1, 0), (2, 3)

(3) Plot the ordered pairs. Then draw a smooth curve through the points, as shown.

Your turn now **Graph the function using a table of values.**

4. $f(x) = -x^2 + 4$ **5.** $f(x) = x^2 + 1$ **6.** $f(x) = 2x^2$

Vertical Line Test You can use the **vertical line test** to tell whether a graph represents a function. If a vertical line intersects the graph at more than one point, then the graph does *not* represent a function. Remember, a function has exactly one output value for each input value.

EXAMPLE 3 Using the Vertical Line Test

Tell whether the graph represents a function.

a.

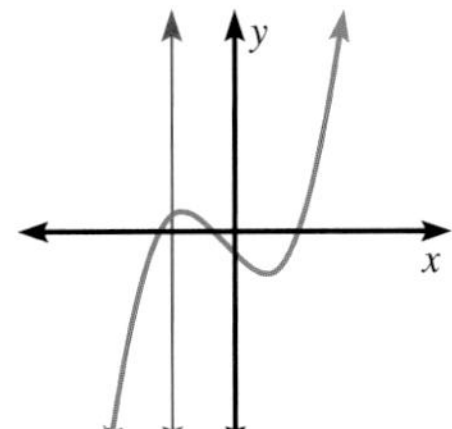

No vertical line intersects the graph at more than one point. So, the graph represents a function.

b.

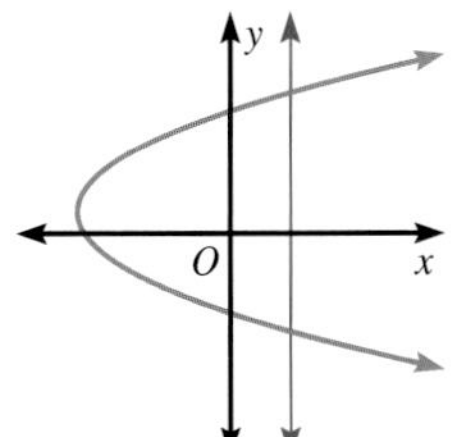

A vertical line intersects the graph at more than one point. So, the graph does *not* represent a function.

Example	Exercises
1	8-11
2	12-17
3	18-20

· More Examples
· eTutorial Plus

Getting Ready to Practice

1. **Vocabulary** Which is written in function notation?

A. $f = 2x + 4$ **B.** $f(x) = 2x + 4$ **C.** $2(f) + 4$

Evaluate the function for $x = -2$, 0, and 2.

2. $f(x) = x^2$
3. $f(x) = x^2 - 5$
4. $f(x) = -3x^2$

Tell whether the graph represents a function.

5. 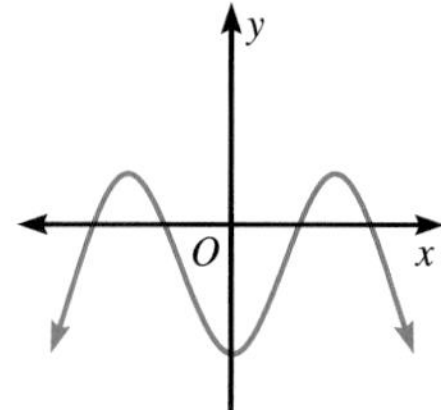

6. 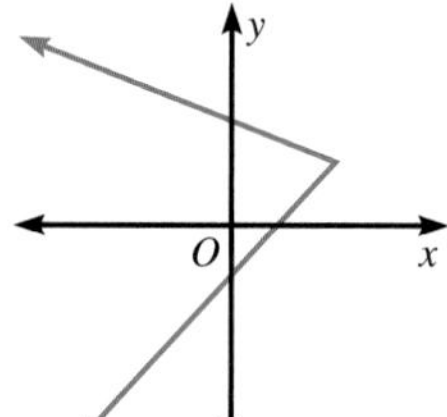

7. 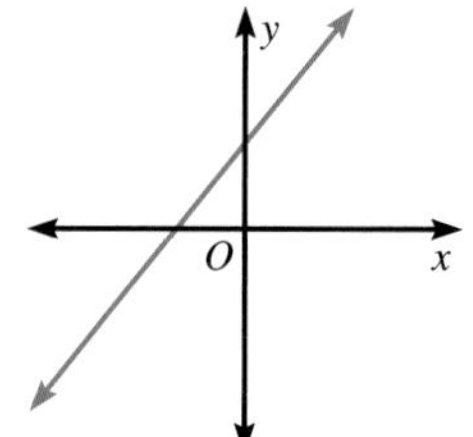

Practice and Problem Solving

Rewrite using function notation.

8. $y = 4x^2$
9. $y = 2x^2 - x$
10. $y = -x^2 + 10$

11. **Penny Drop** You drop a penny into a well and hear it hit the water after 3 seconds. The function $d = -16t^2 + 4$ gives the elevation of the penny, in feet, after it falls for t seconds. Write this in function notation, and find how far the penny falls before hitting the water.

Graph the function using a table of values with $x = -3, -2, -1, 0, 1, 2,$ and 3.

12. $f(x) = 4x^2$
13. $f(x) = x^2 + 8$
14. $f(x) = -x^2 + 5$
15. $f(x) = -x^2$
16. $f(x) = 3x^2 - 4$
17. $f(x) = -2x^2 - 1$

Tell whether the graph represents a function.

18. 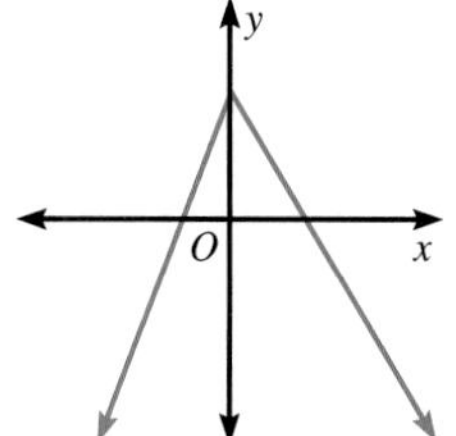

19. 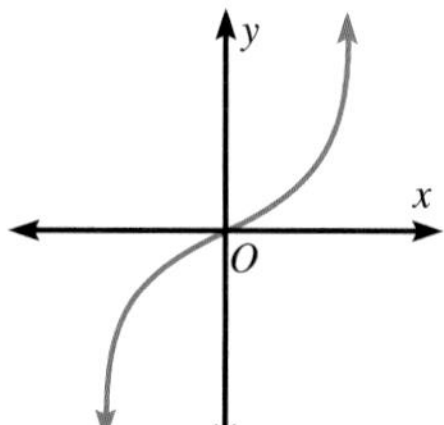

20. 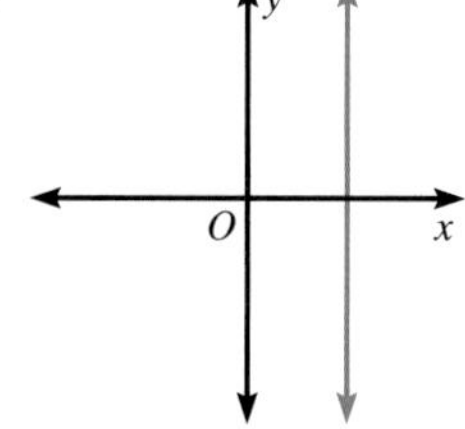

21. **Reflecting Pool** A rectangular reflecting pool is 50 feet long and 30 feet wide, but you do not know how deep the water is. Write a function that you can use to find the volume of water in the pool for different depths.

22. **Baseball** A ball is hit 75 mi/h, or 110 ft/sec, into center field. The height of the ball, in feet, is found with the function $f(x) = -16x^2 + 110x + 3$, where x is the number of seconds after the ball is hit. Graph this function. Use the graph to estimate how many seconds will pass before the ball lands on the ground.

Graph the function using a table of values.

23. $f(x) = -\frac{1}{2}x^2$
24. $f(x) = 5 - 5x^2$
25. $f(x) = 4x^2 + x$
26. $f(x) = x^2 - 3x$
27. $f(x) = (x - 1)^2$
28. $f(x) = (x + 2)^2$

29. **Make a Table** Graph the function $f(x) = x^3$ using a table of values. Describe how the graph of this function is different from the graph of the function $f(x) = x^2$. Be sure to include negative and positive x-values in your table.

30. **Draw a Graph** Write a function for the area of the triangle. Graph the function using a table of values. Estimate the value of x if the area of the triangle is 30 square inches.

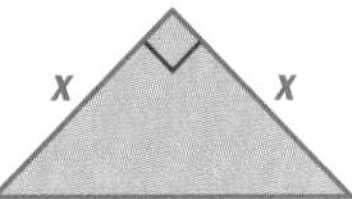

31. **Interpret** Write a function for the area of the rectangle shown. Graph the function using a table of values, and use it to find the greatest possible area of the rectangle. If the rectangle has the maximum area, what are its length and width?

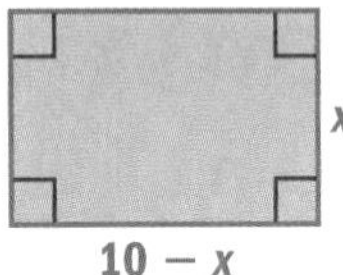

Work Backward **Write a function in function notation for the values in the table.**

32.

x	−2	−1	0	1	2
f(x)	5	2	1	2	5

33.

x	−4	−2	0	2	4
f(x)	−64	−8	0	8	64

34. **Challenge** You deposit \$20 into a savings account that earns 2% interest compounded monthly. The expression $20(1.02)^t$ gives the account balance after t months. Write a function for the account balance, and find the balance after 1, 2, and 3 months.

35. **Population** In 2001, the United States population was about 2.8×10^8 people and growing 0.8% each year. You can predict the future population with the expression $(2.8 \times 10^8)(1.008)^t$, where t is the number of years after 2001. Write the expression as a function and use it to predict the population of the United States in 2005.

Mixed Review

In Exercises 36–43, solve the equation. *(Lesson 3.3)*

36. $3x + 1 = 7$ **37.** $2x - 3 = 5$ **38.** $-x + 1 = 2$ **39.** $6x - 1 = -11$

40. $2x + 5 = -17$ **41.** $2x + 4 = 10$ **42.** $-3x - 4 = 11$ **43.** $5x + 3 = -12$

44. List four solutions of the equation $2x + 4y = -12$. *(Lesson 11.3)*

Find the product and simplify. *(Lesson 13.4)*

45. $(x + 2)(x + 2)$ **46.** $(3z - 2)(2z - 1)$ **47.** $(5a - 1)(a + 3)$

Choose a Strategy **Use a strategy from the list to solve the following problem. Explain your choice of strategy.**

Problem Solving Strategies
- Draw a Diagram
- Break into Parts
- Solve a Simpler Problem

48. You are saving pennies in a coffee can. On the first day, you put one penny in the can. On the second day, you put two pennies in the can. On the third day, you put three pennies in the can. If you continue this method of saving, how many pennies will be in the can on day 100?

Test-Taking Practice

49. Extended Response Graph the four functions below using tables of values. Describe the differences in the graphs. Explain the effect of a negative coefficient on a graph.

$f(x) = x^2$ $f(x) = -x^2$ $f(x) = \frac{1}{2}x$ $f(x) = -\frac{1}{2}x$

Number Crunch

Why was ten afraid of seven?

Use the function $f(x) = 2x^2 - 3x + 7$ to break the code.

?	?	?	?	?	?	?	?	?	?	?	?
−3	5	0	3	−4	1	5	1	5	2	5	6

?	?	?	?	?	?	?	?	?
5	4	−2	−1	−5	6	4	6	5

A	B	C	E	G	H	I	N	S	T	U	V
16	34	7	42	21	12	27	61	6	72	51	9

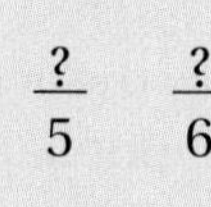

GRAPHING CALCULATOR

INDIANA: Academic Standards
- Algebra and Functions (8.3.10)

Graphing Non-Linear Functions

GOAL Use a graphing calculator to graph non-linear functions.

Example **Use a graphing calculator to compare the functions.**

$y_1 = x^2$ $\quad y_2 = 2x^2$ $\quad y_3 = 3x^2$ $\quad y_4 = 4x^2$

Solution

Use the following keystrokes to enter the functions into a graphing calculator:

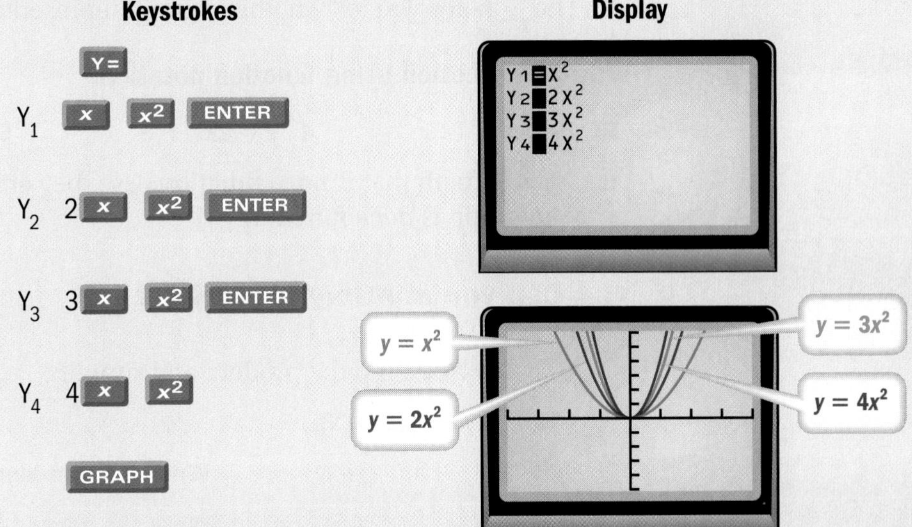

HELP with Technology
You may need to adjust your viewing window in order to see the graphs.

ANSWER The graphs are curves that pass through (0, 0). As the coefficient of x^2 increases, the curve gets narrower.

Your turn now **Graph the functions using a graphing calculator. Describe the pattern in the graphs.**

1. $y = x^2 + 5$ **2.** $y = x^2 - 5$ **3.** $y = x^2 + 7$ **4.** $y = x^2 - 7$

Graph the functions. Describe the pattern in the graphs.

5. $y = -x^2$ **6.** $y = -2x^2$ **7.** $y = -3x^2$ **8.** $y = -4x^2$

Notebook Review

Review the vocabulary definitions in your notebook.

Copy the review examples in your notebook. Then complete the exercises.

Check Your Definitions

function notation, p. 680 vertical line test, p. 681

Use Your Vocabulary

Copy and complete the statement.

1. The equation $f(x) = 7x - 4$ is written using _?_.

2. The _?_ helps you tell whether a graph represents a function.

Write the function using function notation.

3. $y = 5x - 12$ **4.** $y = 2x^3 + 8$ **5.** $y = x^3 + 3x^2 - 10$

6. Draw a graph that is *not* a function. Use the vertical line test to show why your graph is *not* a function.

13.4 Can you multiply binomials?

EXAMPLE Find the product and simplify.

a. $(4x - 7)(2x + 3)$

$4x - 7$	Write the first binomial.
$\times \quad 2x + 3$	Write the second binomial.
$12x - 21$	Multiply $3(4x - 7)$.
$8x^2 - 14x$	Multiply $2x(4x - 7)$. Line up like terms.
$8x^2 - 2x - 21$	Add $12x - 21$ and $8x^2 - 14x$.

b. $(x + 3)(x + 2)$

$= x(x + 2) + 3(x + 2)$ Distributive property

$= x^2 + 2x + 3x + 6$ Distributive property

$= x^2 + 5x + 6$ Combine like terms.

Find the product and simplify.

7. $(x + 5)(x + 7)$ **8.** $(g + 10)(g - 2)$ **9.** $(y - 4)(3y - 1)$

13.5 Can you graph non-linear functions?

EXAMPLE Graph $f(x) = -2x^2 + 5$.

Choose several x-values and make a table of values.

x	−2	−1	0	1	2
$f(x)$	−3	3	5	3	−3

List the solutions as ordered pairs.
(−2, −3), (−1, 3), (0, 5), (1, 3), (2, −3)

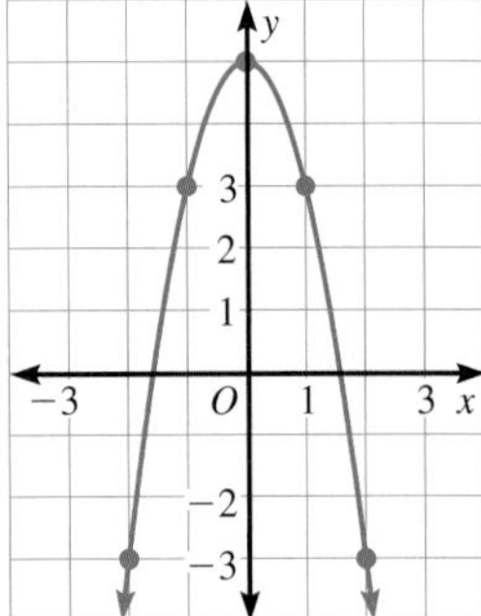

Graph the ordered pairs. Draw a smooth curve through them, as shown.

Graph the function using a table of values.

10. $f(x) = 3x^2$ **11.** $f(x) = -x^2 + 3$ **12.** $f(x) = 2x^2 - 6$

Stop and Think about Lessons 13.4–13.5

13. Writing Explain how you can use the vertical line test to tell whether a graph represents a function.

Review Quiz 2

Find the product and simplify.

1. $(x - 1)(x + 9)$ **2.** $(a + 4)(a + 9)$ **3.** $(m - 2)(m - 8)$

4. $(4y + 5)(y - 2)$ **5.** $(b + 3)(4b - 3)$ **6.** $(3z - 2)(2z - 7)$

Rewrite using function notation.

7. $y = 3x + 9$ **8.** $y = -2x^2 - 4$ **9.** $y = 19 - x + x^2$

Evaluate the function for $x = -2, -1, 0, 1,$ and 2.

10. $f(x) = 2 - x^2$ **11.** $f(x) = \frac{1}{2}x^2 - 6$ **12.** $f(x) = x^2 + x$

Graph the function using a table of values.

13. $f(x) = -x^2 + 1$ **14.** $f(x) = \frac{1}{4}x^2$ **15.** $f(x) = -3x^2 - 4$

Chapter Review

Vocabulary

polynomial, p. 657
binomial, p. 657
trinomial, p. 657
standard form, p. 657
function notation, p. 680
vertical line test, p. 681

Vocabulary Review

Copy and complete the statement.

1. The polynomial $x^3 - 2x + 1$ is a _?_.

2. A polynomial is written in _?_ if the exponents of the variable decrease from left to right.

3. You can use the _?_ to tell whether a graph represents a function.

Classify the polynomial as a *monomial*, a *binomial*, or a *trinomial*.

4. $5x^3 + 2x + 3$ **5.** $5a^3$ **6.** $5y + 3$ **7.** $-r + 3$

Review Questions

Write the polynomial in standard form. *(Lesson 13.1)*

8. $7 - 2a^2 + 10a$ **9.** $5x - 3x^3 - 4 + x^2$ **10.** $4 + 7y^2 - 8y^3 + y$

11. $9t + 8 - t^2 + 6t^3$ **12.** $9 + 2m^5 + m^2 - m^4$ **13.** $25 + n^2 - 3n^4 + 5n$

Simplify the polynomial and write it in standard form. *(Lesson 13.1)*

14. $8k + 1 + 3k + k^2 - 4$ **15.** $5w - 2w + 2w^2 - 8$ **16.** $6p^2 + 9(2p^3 + 3 + p^2)$

17. $3x^2 + 4(7 - x^2 + 4x)$ **18.** $-8(2s - 3s^2 + 7) + 4s^3$ **19.** $4(5y - 2y^2 + 11) - 2y^2$

Find the sum or difference. *(Lesson 13.2)*

20. $(10q^2 - 6) + (q^2 + 1)$ **21.** $(2p^2 + 9p) - (5p^2 + 9p)$

22. $(3x^2 - x + 7) - (6x^2 + 4x - 11)$ **23.** $(7y^2 + y - 4) + (y^2 - y - 1)$

24. $4(m^2 - 3m) + 5(2m^2 - m)$ **25.** $-2(v^3 - v^2 + v) - 3(v^3 + 4v^2)$

Review Questions

Simplify the expression. *(Lesson 13.3)*

26. $(3r^2)^3$

27. $(2xy)^3$

28. $(7z)(-4z)^2$

29. $(-6a^2b^4)^3$

30. $(-c^3)(2c^4)$

31. $(-9n)(-7p^2)^4$

Simplify the expression. *(Lesson 13.3)*

32. $x^2(5x - 7)$

33. $-3a(a^2 - 2a)$

34. $4y(6y^2 - 8y)$

35. $-y^3(-y^2 + 11y)$

36. $7b(14 - 6b^2)$

37. $-6g(3g^2 + 10g)$

Write a polynomial expression for the area of the figure and simplify. *(Lesson 13.3)*

38.

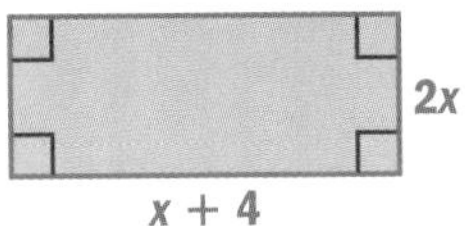

39.

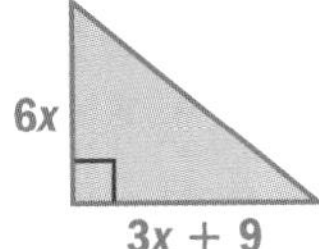

40.

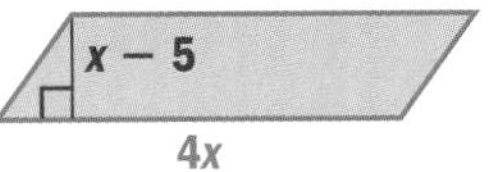

Find the product and simplify. *(Lesson 13.4)*

41. $(t + 3)(t - 4)$

42. $(2x + 3)(x + 5)$

43. $(q - 7)(q - 9)$

44. $(m - 4)(m - 5)$

45. $(3d + 8)(d - 6)$

46. $(h + 3)(2h - 5)$

47. $(2k - 9)(-4k - 1)$

48. $(2n + 6)(3n - 12)$

49. $(-2b + 1)(-b - 4)$

50. Write a polynomial expression for the area of the swimming pool's walkway and simplify. The walkway is x ft wide. *(Lesson 13.4)*

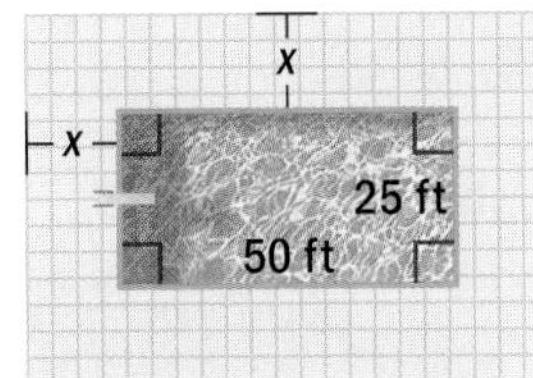

Graph the function using a table of values. *(Lesson 13.5)*

51. $f(x) = x^2 + 3$

52. $f(x) = 7 - x^2$

53. $f(x) = x^2 - 4$

54. $f(x) = 3x^2 + 1$

Tell whether the graph represents a function. *(Lesson 13.5)*

55.

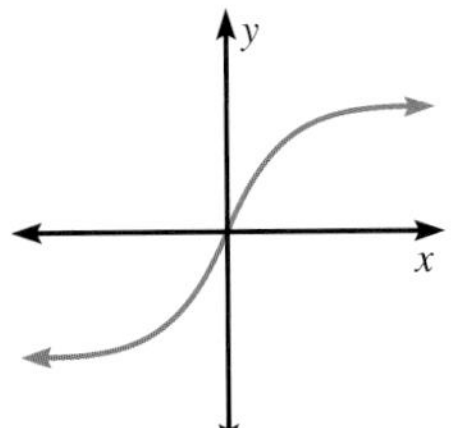

56.

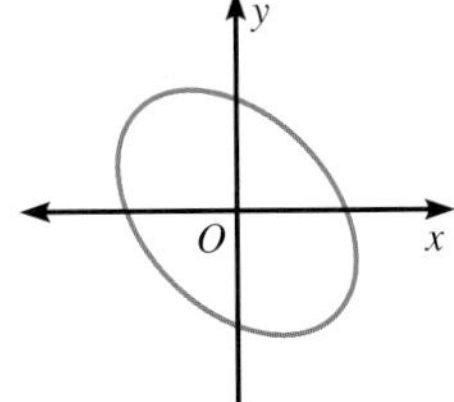

57.

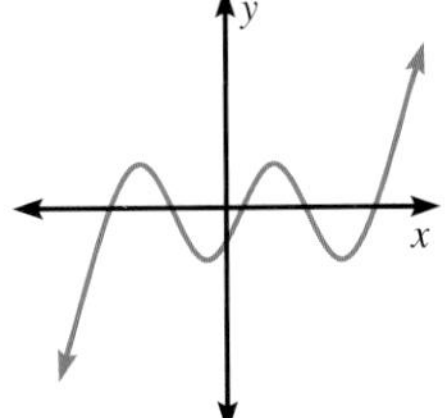

Chapter Test

Simplify the polynomial and write it in standard form.

1. $10x - 7x + 4 + x^2 - 3x + 4$

2. $-y + 6(y^2 - y^3 + 1)$

3. **Apple Picking** An apple falls from a 28 foot tall tree. The height of the apple, in feet, after t seconds of falling, can be found using the polynomial $-16t^2 + 28$. Find the apple's height after 0.5 second.

Find the sum or difference.

4. $(3r^2 + 4r - 7) + (-r^2 - r + 11)$

5. $(4s^2 - 11s) - (s^2 - 6s + 21)$

6. $(4a^5 - a) + (-3a^5 + 1)$

7. $(-y^2 + 12) + (8y^2 - 10)$

8. $(5x^6 - 3x^2 + x) - (4x^2 + 2x)$

9. $(-7z^3 + z^2 - 5) - (z^3 - 3z^2 + 1)$

10. **Perimeter** Write a polynomial expression for the perimeter of the triangle. Simplify the polynomial.

$9x - 5$

$10x - 7$

$x + 2$

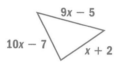

Simplify the expression.

11. $(3a^2)(5a^2b)$

12. $(9z)^2$

13. $(3d^2)^4$

14. $(-2w^4)^3$

15. $(-2p^2)^4$

16. $(x^4y)^8$

17. $(4n^2)(-3n)$

18. $(3r)^3(3r)$

Find the product and simplify.

19. $m^2(3m^2 + 8m)$

20. $7n(n^2 - 2n)$

21. $3p(2p^2 + 3p)$

22. $(2x + 7)(3x + 2)$

23. $(4y + 12)(y - 3)$

24. $(z - 9)(5z + 8)$

Graph the function using a table of values.

25. $f(x) = -5x^2$

26. $f(x) = x^2 + 3$

27. $f(x) = x^2 - 1$

Tell whether the graph represents a function.

28.

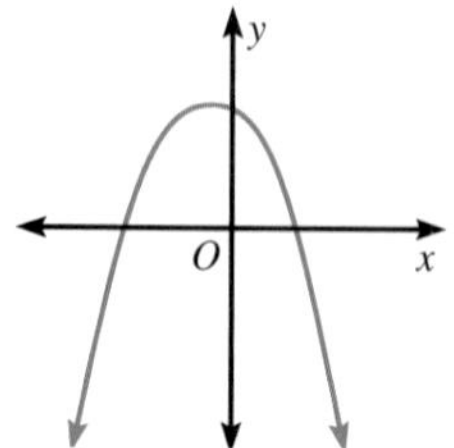

29.

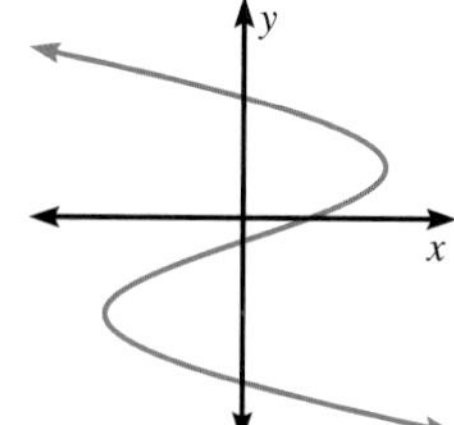

30.

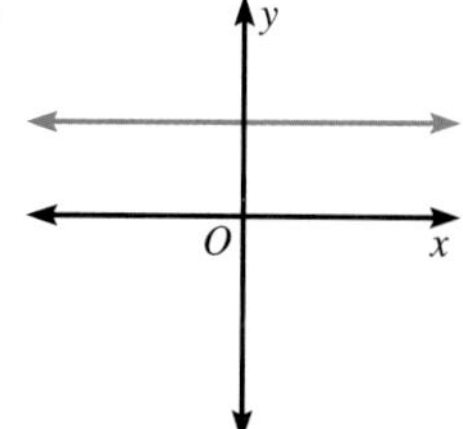

Chapter Standardized Test

Test-Taking Strategy **Think positively during a test. This will help you keep up your confidence and enable you to focus on each question.**

Multiple Choice

1. Simplify the polynomial and write it in standard form.

$10 - 5x^2 + 4x^3 + x^2 - 8$

A. $2 - 4x^2 + 4x^3$ **B.** $4x^3 + 6x^2 + 2$

C. $4x^3 - 4x^2 + 2$ **D.** $2 + 6x^2 + 4x^3$

2. Find the sum.

$(4x^2 + 4x - 5) + (5x^2 - x - 8)$

F. $9x^2 + 3x - 13$ **G.** $9x^2 + 3x - 3$

H. $9x^2 - 3x - 13$ **I.** $9x^2 + 3x + 3$

3. Find the difference.

$(2x^2 - 3x + 2) - (x^2 + 3x + 2)$

A. $x^2 - x$ **B.** $x^2 - 6x$

C. $x^2 + x + 4$ **D.** $x^2 - 6x + 4$

4. Simplify the expression $(2x^2)(x^3y)$.

F. $2x^6y$ **G.** $2xy^5$ **H.** $2x^5y$ **I.** $2x^5y^5$

5. Simplify $11x(x^2 - 2x - 8)$.

A. $11x^3 - 22x^2 + 88$

B. $11x^3 - 22x^2 - 88x$

C. $11x^2 + 22x - 88$

D. $11x^2 + 22x + 88x$

6. Simplify the expression $(5pq)^2$.

F. $10pq$ **G.** $25pq^2$ **H.** $10pq^2$ **I.** $25p^2q^2$

7. Simplify the expression $(-3n^2)^3$.

A. $-27n^6$ **B.** $27n^6$ **C.** $-9n^6$ **D.** $9n^6$

8. Find the product $(x + 3)(x - 4)$ and simplify.

F. $x^2 + 7x - 12$ **G.** $x^2 - x - 12$

H. $x^2 + x - 12$ **I.** $x^2 - x - 7$

9. You deposit \$25 into a savings account with interest compounded annually. The account balance after 2 years is given by the expression $25(r + 1)^2$. Expand this expression and simplify.

A. $25r^2 + 2r + 25$ **B.** $25r^2 + 25r + 1$

C. $25r^2 + 50r + 1$ **D.** $25r^2 + 50r + 25$

10. Find the value of the function for $x = -2$.

$f(x) = -3x^2 + 5$

F. -7 **G.** 7 **H.** 11 **I.** 17

Short Response

11. Write an expression for the area of the rectangle. Simplify the expression, and write it in standard form.

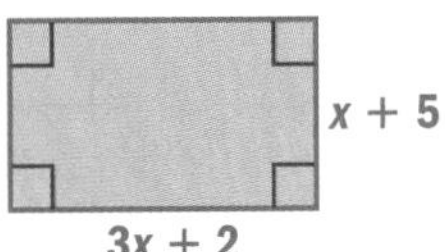

Extended Response

12. Graph each function using a table of values. Explain how the graphs are different.

$f(x) = x^2$

$f(x) = x^2 + 1$

$f(x) = x^2 + 2$

Describe the graph of the function $f(x) = x^2 + 125$.

Scoring Rubric

Full credit
- answer is correct, *and*
- work or reasoning is included

Partial credit
- answer is correct, but reasoning is incorrect, *or*
- answer is incorrect, but reasoning is correct

No credit
- no answer is given, *or*
- answer makes no sense

Strategies for Answering

Extended Response Questions

Problem

A tank contains 30 gallons of water. You pull out the drain plug, and water begins to flow from the tank at a rate of 4 gallons per minute. Make a table and draw a graph that shows the amount of water in the tank as the water drains. After how much time will the tank contain exactly 16 gallons of water? Give your answer in minutes and seconds. Explain how you found your answer.

Full credit solution

In the graph, the horizontal axis shows minutes after pulling the plug, and the vertical axis shows the gallons of water in the tank.

The table and graph are correct and reflect an understanding of the problem.

minutes	gallons
0	30
1	26
2	22
3	18
4	14
5	10
6	6
7	2

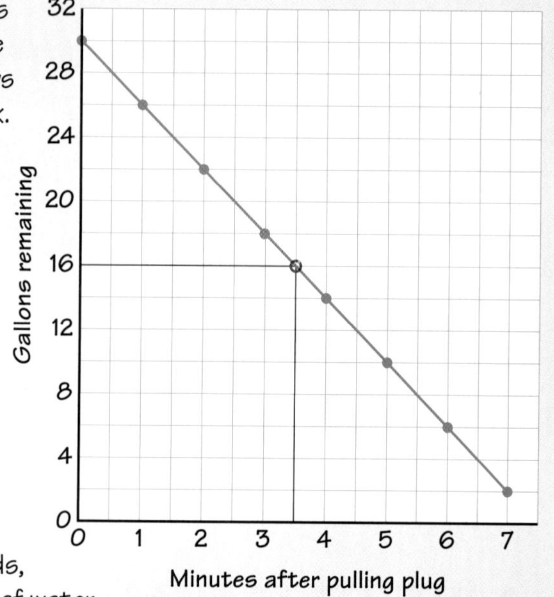

The answer is correct.

After 3 minutes and 30 seconds, the tank will contain 16 gallons of water.

The reasoning behind the answer is explained clearly.

To find my answer, I looked at the graph and saw that the tank will hold 16 gallons at $3\frac{1}{2}$ minutes. Because $\frac{1}{2}$ of a minute equals 30 seconds, I know that the tank will hold 16 gallons of water after 3 minutes and 30 seconds.

Partial credit solution

The table and graph are correct.

minutes	0	1	2	3	4
gallons	30	26	22	18	14

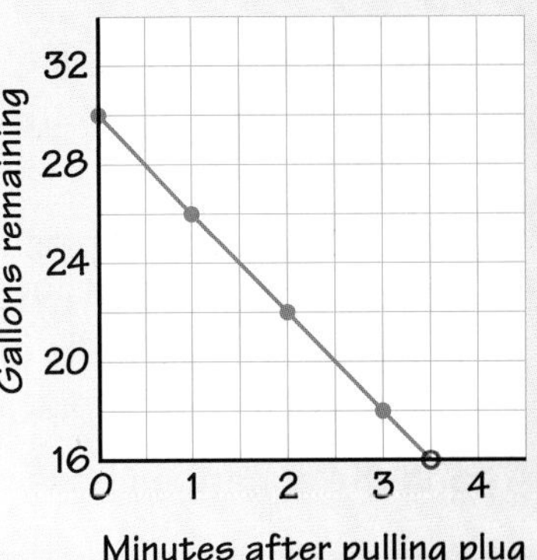

The answer is incorrect.

The tank will hold 16 gallons after 3 minutes and 5 seconds. The graph shows that there are 16 gallons after 3.5 minutes.

No credit solution

The table is correct, but there is no graph.

minutes	0	1	2	3	4
gallons	30	26	22	18	14

The answer is incorrect, and there is no explanation.

The tank will never have exactly 16 gallons in it.

Watch Out!

Scoring is often based on how clearly you explain your reasoning.

Your turn now

1. Score one student's answer to the problem on page 692 as *full credit, partial credit,* or *no credit.* Explain your choice. If you choose *partial credit* or *no credit,* explain how to change the answer so that it earns *full credit.*

minutes	0	1	2	3	4
gallons	30	26	22	18	14

The tank will have 16 gallons after 3 minutes and 30 seconds. The table shows that the tank will have 16 gallons between 3 and 4 minutes. 16 is halfway between 14 and 18. So, the tank must have 16 gallons halfway between 3 and 4 minutes. The tank has 16 gallons at 3 minutes and 30 seconds.

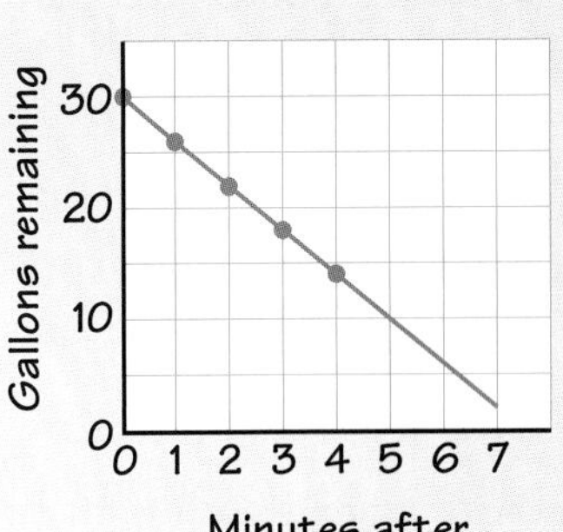

PRACTICING Test-Taking Skills

Extended Response

1. The menu shows the prices of circular cheese pizzas with different diameters and the cost of each topping.

Diameter	Price	Cost of each topping
10 in.	$4.25	$.50
12 in.	$6.25	$.75
14 in.	$7.75	$.75
16 in.	$8.75	$1.00
18 in.	$9.75	$1.25
24 in.	$13.00	$1.75

The price of a 12 inch pizza can be modeled by the equation $p = 0.75t + 6.25$, where t is the number of toppings. Make a table of values that shows the prices of a 12 inch pizza with 1 to 6 toppings.

Graph the equation above using your table of values.

Write and graph an equation for the price of a 10 inch pizza. Which graph has a greater slope? Explain why.

2. The double stem-and-leaf plot shows the heights of 15 football players and 15 basketball players.

What is the height of the tallest football player?

How many basketball players are over 82 inches tall?

In general, are the football players or the basketball players taller? Explain how you used the data to draw a conclusion.

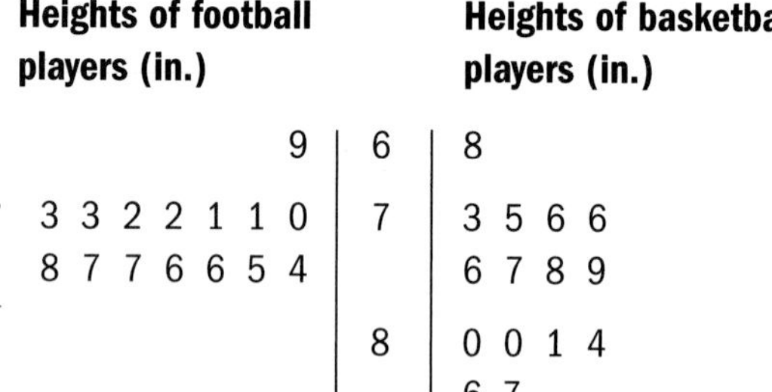

Heights of football players (in.)
Heights of basketball players (in.)
9 | 6 | 8
3 3 2 2 1 1 0 | 7 | 3 5 6 6
8 7 7 6 6 5 4 | | 6 7 8 9
| 8 | 0 0 1 4
| | 6 7

Key: 0 | 7 | 3 = 70 and 73

3. Players spin the two spinners shown and flip a coin. They earn a point for a 1, a point for blue, a point for tails, and a bonus point for getting all three in one turn.

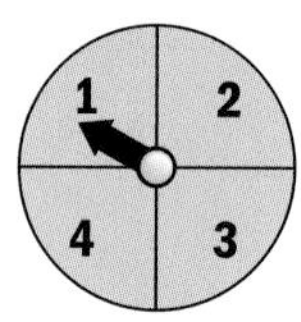

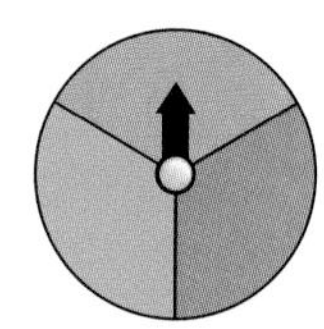

In one turn, what is the probability of spinning a 1? spinning a blue? getting tails?

What is the probability of getting the bonus point? Explain your answer.

4. Write a polynomial expression for the area of each colored region of the figure shown.

Write a polynomial expression for the sum of these areas.

Write an expression for the area of the entire figure as a product of two binomials. Explain how you found your answer.

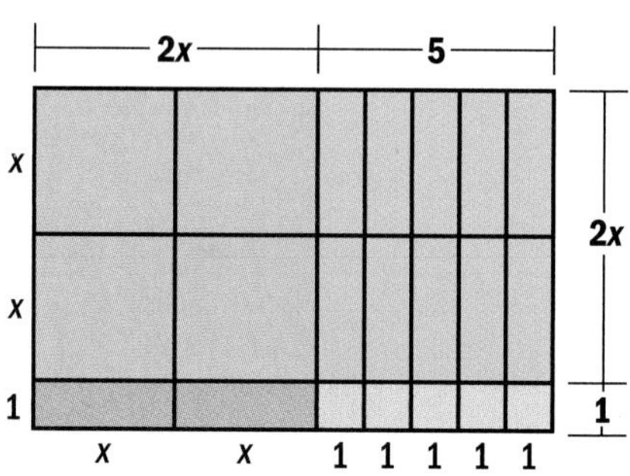

Multiple Choice

5. What is the slope of the line passing through the points (4, −3) and (−2, 5)?

   A. $-\frac{4}{3}$ B. −1 C. $\frac{3}{4}$ D. 1

6. Which equation is represented by the graph?

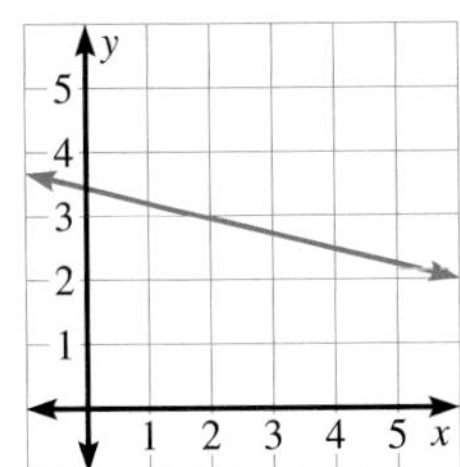

   F. $y = \frac{1}{4}x + 3.5$ G. $y = -\frac{1}{4}x + 3.5$

   H. $y = 4x + 3.5$ I. $y = -4x + 3.5$

7. Your locker combination has 3 numbers from 0 to 15. Each number must be different. How many locker combinations are possible?

   A. 45 B. 48 C. 560 D. 3360

8. Find the difference.
   $(5x^2 - 2x + 3) - (2x^2 - 2x - 3)$

   F. $3x^2 + 6$ G. $3x^2 - 4x$

   H. $3x^2 - 4x + 6$ I. $3x^2 + 4x - 6$

9. Find the product $(x - 6)(x + 3)$ and simplify.

   A. $x^2 - 3x + 9$ B. $x^2 + 9x - 18$

   C. $x^2 - 3x - 18$ D. $x^2 - 9x + 9$

Short Response

10. The table below shows the latitude and a typical minimum temperature in January for each of 6 U.S. cities.

City	Latitude (°N)	Minimum temperature in January (°F)
Anchorage	61	9
Miami	26	60
Helena	47	10
Reno	39	22
Buffalo	43	18
Memphis	35	31

Make a scatter plot of the data. What type of relationship does the scatter plot show between latitude and temperature? Explain.

11. The players of a baseball team hit the following numbers of home runs during one season: 6, 17, 12, 11, 6, 21, 5, 12, 9, 14, 24, 4, 25, 14, 18. Make a box-and-whisker plot of the data. Describe what the plot shows.

12. You roll two number cubes at the same time. What is the probability that the sum of the numbers showing on the two cubes is less than or equal to 5? What is the probability that the sum is greater than 5? Explain how you found your answers.

13. The function $S = 4\pi r^2$ gives the surface area of a sphere with radius r. Write this function in function notation. Graph the function. Estimate the radius of a sphere that has a surface area of 80 square centimeters. Use 3.14 for π. Explain your steps.

GO ON

Cumulative Practice for Chapters 11–13

Chapter 11

Multiple Choice In Exercises 1–8, choose the letter of the correct answer.

1. Which of the following relations is *not* a function? *(Lesson 11.1)*

   A. (0, −3), (1, −1), (2, 1), (3, 3)

   B. (−4, 0), (2, 1), (0, 2), (2, 3)

   C. (0, 5), (2, 0), (4, −5), (−1, 3)

   D. (6, 5), (0, −1), (3, 6), (−2, −1)

2. The scatter plot shows the amount of money spent on supplies each month. What is the best prediction of the amount of money spent in the eighth month? *(Lesson 11.2)*

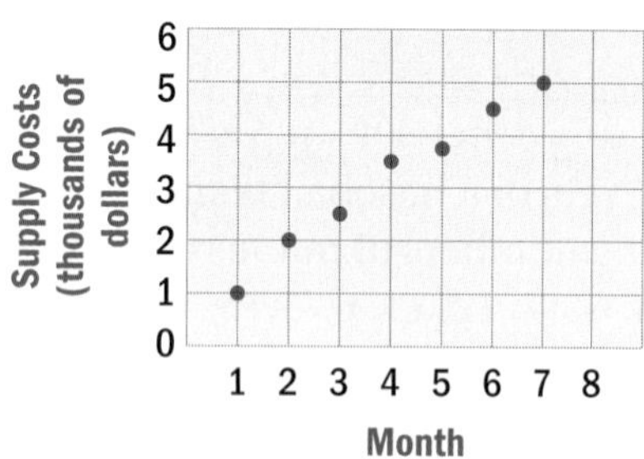

   F. \$45 **G.** \$55 **H.** \$4500 **I.** \$5500

3. Which ordered pair is a solution of the equation $y = -2x + 6$? *(Lesson 11.3)*

   A. (6, −6) **B.** (−4, 3)

   C. (−8, −5) **D.** (7, 7)

4. Which equation is *not* linear? *(Lesson 11.4)*

   F. $y = -2x + 4$ **G.** $3x + 4y = 8$

   H. $y = x^3 - 8$ **I.** $4x = 8 - 2y$

5. What is the x-intercept of the graph of the equation $2x + 3y = 6$? *(Lesson 11.5)*

   A. −3 **B.** −2 **C.** 2 **D.** 3

6. What is the slope of the line? *(Lesson 11.6)*

   F. $-\frac{3}{2}$

   G. 0

   H. 1

   I. $\frac{3}{2}$

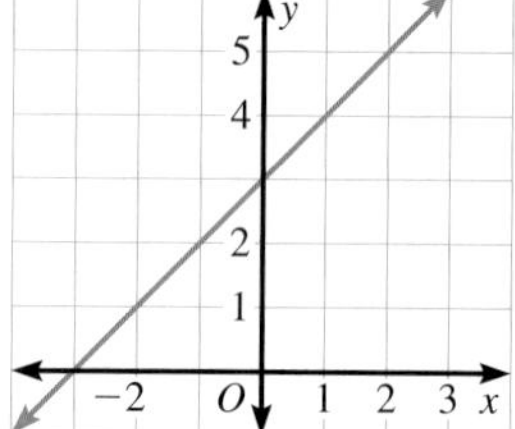

7. A line passes through the points (1, 2) and (2, y) and has a slope of 0. What is the value of y? *(Lesson 11.6)*

   A. −1 **B.** 2 **C.** 3 **D.** 5

8. Which ordered pair is a solution of $5x + 9y < 45$? *(Lesson 11.8)*

   F. (−3, 8) **G.** (4, 6) **H.** (6, −4) **I.** (−2, 12)

9. **Short Response** Write a function rule that relates x and y. *(Lesson 11.1)*

Input x	2	4	6	8
Output y	5	9	13	17

10. **Extended Response** For a party, you rent a karaoke machine for \$50. Food will cost \$6 per person. *(Lesson 11.7)*

    a. Graph the equation $y = 6x + 50$ to see the possible total costs of the party.

    b. How much will it cost to invite 11 people?

    c. You want to spend no more than \$100. How many people can you invite?

Chapter 12

The stem-and-leaf plot shows the number of home runs for each player on a softball team. Use the plot for Exercises 11–12. *(Lesson 12.1)*

Stem	Leaves
0	4 5 7 8
1	2 4 5 6 6 8
2	1 4 5

Key: 2 | 1 = 21

11. What is the greatest number of home runs hit by one player?

A. 4 **B.** 25 **C.** 28 **D.** 52

12. What is the median number of home runs?

F. 12 **G.** 15 **H.** 16 **I.** 21

The box-and-whisker plot shows stereo prices. Use the plot for Exercises 13–14. *(Lesson 12.2)*

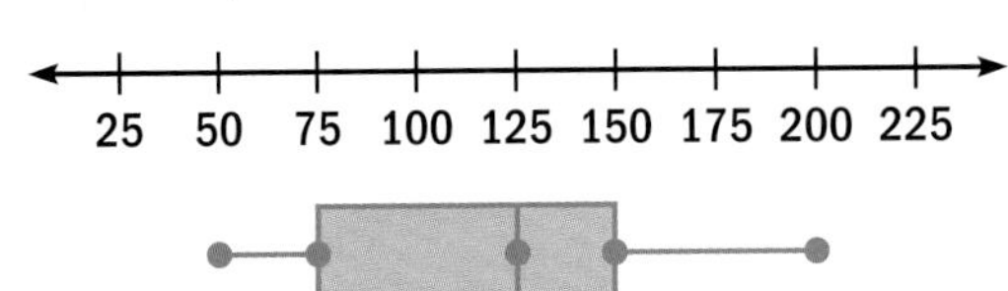

13. What is the lowest stereo price?

A. \$25 **B.** \$50 **C.** \$75 **D.** \$125

14. What is the median price of the stereos?

F. \$75 **G.** \$100 **H.** \$125 **I.** \$150

15. The line graph shows the average number of geese in one area over seven months. Which month had the greatest average number of geese? *(Lesson 12.3)*

A. April

B. May

C. June

D. July

Geese
125
100
75
50
25
0
March April May June July Aug. Sept.

16. You have 3 pairs of shoes, 6 pairs of pants, 4 shirts, and 3 belts. How many different combinations of shoes, pants, shirts, and belts can you make? *(Lesson 12.4)*

F. 16 **G.** 204 **H.** 216 **I.** 313

17. Four cyclists are racing. Trophies are awarded to the people who come in first place and second place. In how many different ways can the trophies be awarded? *(Lesson 12.5)*

A. 2 **B.** 4 **C.** 12 **D.** 24

18. There are 14 pints of rocky road ice cream and 12 pints of fudge almond in a freezer. If Joey chooses a pint at random, what is the probability that he will choose rocky road? *(Lesson 12.7)*

F. $\frac{6}{13}$ **G.** $\frac{7}{13}$ **H.** $\frac{6}{7}$ **I.** $\frac{7}{6}$

19. You roll a number cube once. What are the odds in favor of rolling a four? *(Lesson 12.7)*

A. $\frac{1}{6}$ **B.** $\frac{1}{5}$ **C.** $\frac{1}{4}$ **D.** $\frac{1}{3}$

20. A bag contains 16 red balls and 24 white balls. You draw a ball at random, replace it, and draw a second ball. What is the probability of drawing a red ball and then a white ball? *(Lesson 12.8)*

F. $\frac{1}{384}$ **G.** $\frac{1}{24}$ **H.** $\frac{1}{16}$ **I.** $\frac{6}{25}$

21. A bag contains the letters of the word *Mississippi*. You draw one letter at random, do not replace it, and then draw a second letter. What is the probability of drawing the letter *i* twice? *(Lesson 12.8)*

A. $\frac{12}{121}$ **B.** $\frac{6}{55}$ **C.** $\frac{16}{121}$ **D.** $\frac{8}{55}$

GO ON

Cumulative Practice continued

22. Short Response A group of 10 people travel in 2 cars with 5 people in each car. How many different groups can go in one car? How many ways can the group split into 2 cars? Explain your answers. *(Lesson 12.6)*

23. Extended Response The points that you scored in each basketball game during the season are given below. Red numbers represent games won, and blue numbers represent games lost. *(Lesson 12.3)*

12, 10, 26, 22, 18, 17, 5, 20, 22, 18,
15, 8, 14, 19, 22, 23, 25, 8, 16, 20

a. Use an appropriate display to represent the data.

b. Explain your choice of display.

c. Identify a type of display that is not a good choice for the data. Explain why it is not a good choice.

Chapter 13

Multiple Choice In Exercises 24–30, choose the letter of the correct answer.

24. Simplify the polynomial. *(Lesson 13.1)*
$4(x^2 - 2x - 4) - 2x^2$

A. $-2x^2 + 8x + 16$ **B.** $2x^2 - 8x - 16$
C. $-2x^2 - 8x + 16$ **D.** $2x^2 + 8x + 16$

25. What is the value of $-3x^2 - 5x + 8$ for $x = 3$? *(Lesson 13.1)*

F. -34 **G.** -12 **H.** -6 **I.** 34

26. Find the sum $(2x - 6) + (3x - 9)$. *(Lesson 13.2)*

A. $5x - 15$ **B.** $-x - 3$
C. $x + 3$ **D.** $5x + 15$

27. Find the difference. *(Lesson 13.2)*
$(3x^4 - 2x^2 + 3) - (x^4 + 2x^3 + x^2)$

F. $2x^4 - 2x^3 - 3x^2 + 3$
G. $2x^4 - 2x^3 - x^2 + 3$
H. $2x^4 + 2x^3 - x^2 + 3$
I. $2x^4 - 4x^3 - x^2 + 3$

28. Simplify the expression $(3a^2)(4a + 1)$. *(Lesson 13.3)*

A. $7a^2 + 3a$ **B.** $7a^2 + 1$
C. $12a^3 + 3a^2$ **D.** $12a^3 + 3$

29. Simplify the expression $(3y^2)^3$. *(Lesson 13.3)*

F. $27y^5$ **G.** $3y^5$ **H.** $27y^6$ **I.** $3y^6$

30. Find the product and simplify. *(Lesson 13.4)*
$(3x + 3)(2x - 2)$

A. $6x^2 + 6$ **B.** $6x^2 - 6$
C. $6x^2 + 6x - 6$ **D.** $6x^2 - 6x + 6$

31. Short Response A walnut falls from a tree 75 feet off the ground. The polynomial $-16t^2 + 75$ gives the walnut's height, in feet, after t seconds of falling. Find its height after 1 second and 2 seconds. Estimate how many seconds the walnut falls before hitting the ground. *(Lesson 13.1)*

32. Extended Response Use your graphs to look for a pattern. *(Lesson 13.5)*

a. Graph each function in a coordinate plane.

$f(x) = 3x^2 - 5$
$f(x) = 3x^2 - 3$
$f(x) = 3x^2 - 1$

b. Describe the graph of the function $f(x) = 3x^2 - 100$.

End-of-Course Test

Algebra, Integers, and Equation Solving

1. The table shows the number of visits to your Web site for five days. Make a bar graph of the data.

Days	Mon	Tues	Wed	Thurs	Fri
Visits	12	18	21	25	28

Evaluate the expression.

2. $8 \cdot 4 + 3 \cdot 5$
3. $46 - 25 + 8 \div 2$
4. $(3 + 1)^3 \div 8 - 2$
5. $7a - 4$ when $a = 2$
6. $\frac{9}{2y - 5}$ when $y = 4$
7. x^4 when $x = 5$

Use a number line to order the integers from least to greatest.

8. 65, −13, 19, 61, −19, 34
9. 878, 433, −602, 1074, −1222

Find the sum, difference, product, or quotient.

10. $-61 + (-44)$
11. $-13 + 8 + (-6)$
12. $-49 - (-16)$
13. $85 - (-18) - 12$
14. $5(-8)$
15. $-9(-6)(-4)$
16. $\frac{-64}{8}$
17. $\frac{-55}{-11}$
18. In a local school committee election, 250 votes were cast for two candidates. Candidate A won the election by 10 votes. How many votes did Candidate A receive?
19. Plot and connect points $A(-10, 12)$, $B(10, 12)$, $C(10, -12)$, and $D(-10, -12)$. Identify the figure. Then find the perimeter and area of the figure.

Simplify the expression by combining like terms.

20. $6y + 5y$
21. $8a - 6b + a$
22. $6(x - 7) + 4x + 3$
23. $3(2x + y) - (8 + 5x)$

Solve the equation.

24. $49 = d + 12$
25. $b - 18 = 12$
26. $8 = \frac{56}{x}$
27. $15 = \frac{x}{5}$
28. $4b = -64$
29. $-6x = 72$
30. $5b + 9 = 18$
31. $-21 = 19 - 4x$

Solve the inequality. Then graph the solution.

32. $b + 6 \leq 12$
33. $6 > 8 + t$
34. $-\frac{1}{6}a < 24$
35. $8 \geq -\frac{1}{4}x$

Algebra and Rational Numbers

36. Write the following fractions in simplest form: $\frac{12}{26}, \frac{18}{54}, \frac{16}{82}, \frac{24}{84}$.

Find the GCF and LCM of the numbers.

37. 12, 16, 48 **38.** 16, 32, 64 **39.** 45, 90, 180 **40.** 10, 15, 50

Simplify. Write the expression using only positive exponents.

41. $y^6 \cdot y^4$ **42.** $x^{-7} \cdot x^5$ **43.** $\frac{x^{18}}{x^{11}}$ **44.** $y^8 \cdot y^{-5}$

Find the sum, difference, product, or quotient.

45. $\frac{13}{24} + \left(-\frac{7}{24}\right)$ **46.** $-2\frac{2}{5} - 2\frac{2}{5}$ **47.** $8\frac{1}{2} + 5\frac{1}{4}$ **48.** $11\frac{2}{9} - 14\frac{1}{2}$

49. $5\frac{1}{4} \cdot \left(-4\frac{1}{5}\right)$ **50.** $-3\frac{1}{3} \cdot \left(-8\frac{4}{5}\right)$ **51.** $1\frac{1}{2} \div \left(-3\frac{3}{8}\right)$ **52.** $5\frac{1}{9} \div 2\frac{4}{7}$

53. $7.9 + (-2.344)$ **54.** $-8.1 - (-4.06)$ **55.** $14.66 \cdot 2.1$ **56.** $4.844 \div (-0.56)$

57. Order the numbers from least to greatest: $8\frac{2}{3}$, 8.5, 13.35, $7\frac{2}{3}$, $8\frac{9}{20}$, $8.\bar{6}$, 7.7. Then find the mean, median, and mode(s) of the numbers.

Solve the equation or inequality.

58. $3(b - 9) = -39$ **59.** $-6 = 11a - 5a$ **60.** $3x = 9(x - 1)$ **61.** $6(y - 4) = 3(y + 9)$

62. $\frac{1}{6}n + \frac{2}{3}n = 1$ **63.** $5.9 + c = 3c - 2.1$ **64.** $5a + 8 \geq 12$ **65.** $-2(d + 4) < -4$

66. $\frac{2}{9} = \frac{10}{a}$ **67.** $\frac{x}{4} = \frac{21}{12}$ **68.** $\frac{45}{15} = \frac{y}{1}$ **69.** $\frac{12}{15} = \frac{p}{100}$

Write the number as a percent, as a decimal, and as a fraction.

70. 22.5% **71.** 0.37 **72.** $\frac{13}{20}$ **73.** 0.1%

74. You buy a stereo for $74 plus 8% sales tax. What is your total cost?

75. What is 0.5% of 65? Five is what percent of 125?

76. You draw a tile randomly from a bag that contains 12 B tiles, 6 C tiles, 8 D tiles, and 5 A tiles. What is the probability that you draw a D?

Geometry and Measurement

77. $\angle 1$ and $\angle 2$ are complementary, and $m\angle 1 = 74°$. Find $m\angle 2$.

Find the value of *x*. Then classify the figure.

78.
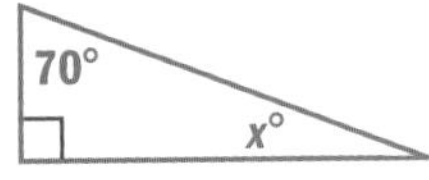

79.
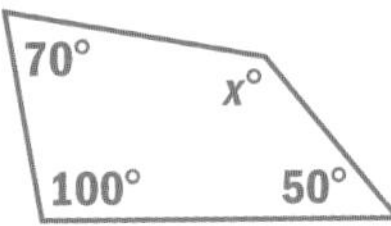

80.
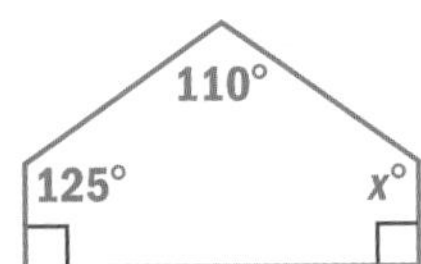

81. Draw $\triangle ABC$ in the coordinate plane with vertices $A(2, 5)$, $B(2, 2)$, and $C(6, 2)$. Draw $\triangle DEF$ congruent to $\triangle ABC$. Then translate $\triangle DEF$ using $(x, y) \longrightarrow (x - 4, y - 7)$. Identify the coordinates of $\triangle DEF$ and $\triangle D'E'F'$.

82. Find the following square roots: $-\sqrt{2}$, $\sqrt{121}$, $\sqrt{81}$, $-\sqrt{400}$

83. Is $\sqrt{\frac{4}{81}}$ a rational or irrational number? $\sqrt{18}$? Explain.

A right triangle has leg lengths *a* and *b* and a hypotenuse of length *c*. Find the unknown length. Then find the triangle's area and perimeter.

84. $a = 12$ cm, $b = 5$ cm, $c = ?$

85. $a = 12$ ft, $b = 16$ ft, $c = ?$

Find the value of each variable. Give exact answers.

86.
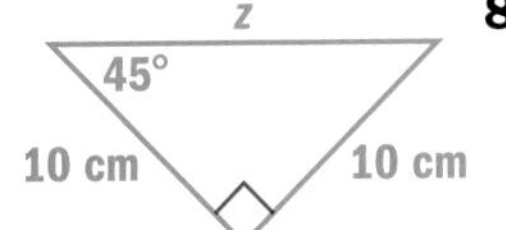

87.
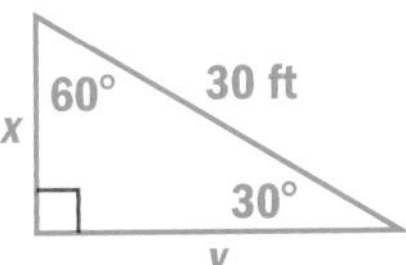

88.
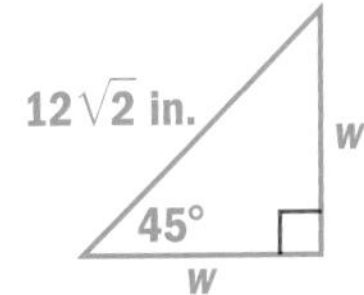

89. Find the area of a trapezoid with bases of 18 feet and 12 feet and a height of 5 feet.

90. What is the area of a circle with a radius of 5 feet? with a diameter of 12 centimeters? Use 3.14 for π.

Find the surface area and volume of the solid. Use 3.14 for π.

91.
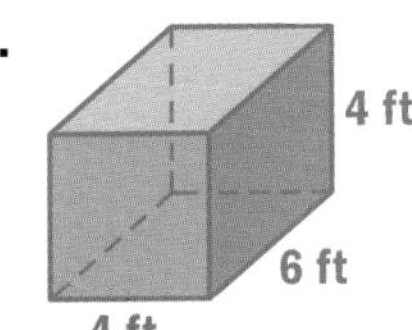

92.
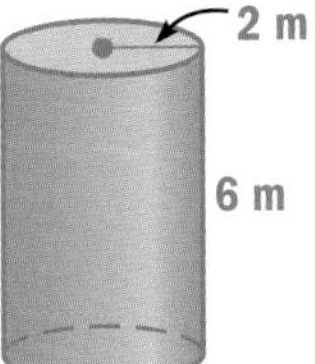

93.
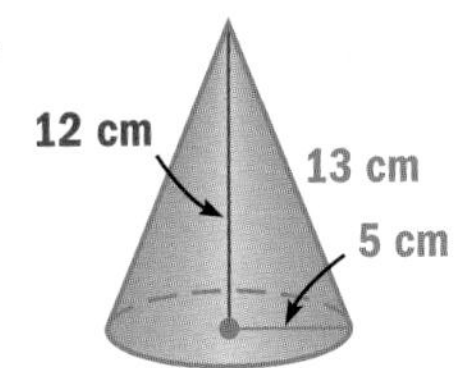

Advanced Algebra Topics

94. Make tables of values for the functions $y = 2x$ and $y = x - 2$. Use a domain of $-2, -1, 0, 1$, and 2. Identify the range of each function.

95. Make a scatter plot of (1, 4), (2, 8), (3, 12), and (4, 16). Describe the relationship between the variables. Then find the next ordered pair.

Graph the equation. Identify the intercepts of the graph.

96. $y = 2x - 12$ **97.** $y = 4 - 3x$ **98.** $y = -x + 17$ **99.** $y = -5x - 6$

100. $y = -\frac{1}{2}x + 5$ **101.** $y = -6x + 8$ **102.** $x + 9y = 18$ **103.** $y = 2x + 4$

104. Find the slope of the line passing through the points (5,8) and (0,5).

105. Rewrite $y + 12x = 6$ and $13x - 11y = 12$ in slope-intercept form. Then find the slope and the y-intercept of the graph of each equation.

106. Tell whether $(-8, -9)$ is a solution of the inequality $12x - 16y \geq 34$.

Make a stem-and-leaf plot and a box-and-whisker plot of the data.

107. 46, 49, 66, 51, 68, 83, 78, 64 **108.** \$68, \$63, \$51, \$43, \$53, \$38, \$60, \$66

109. In an election poll, 32% preferred Atkins, 47% preferred Liu, and 21% were undecided. Make a circle graph of the data.

110. You can choose from 3 sandwiches, 4 drinks, and 2 snacks. How many different sandwich-drink-snack groupings are possible?

Evaluate.

111. ${}_{18}P_2$ **112.** ${}_{14}P_3$ **113.** ${}_9C_6$ **114.** ${}_8C_5$

115. You roll a number cube. What are the odds of getting an odd number?

Simplify the polynomial and write it in standard form.

116. $4x^2 - 5x - 2x^2 + 7x$ **117.** $-3x^2 + 3x - x + 7$

Simplify the expression.

118. $(x^2 - 2x + 5) + (x^2 - 4)$ **119.** $(5y^2 - y - 1) - (y^2 + 4y)$ **120.** $(3x^2 - 4x + 2) + (x^2 + 6x - 5)$

121. $(6x)(8x^6)$ **122.** $(8y)^3$ **123.** $(x^6)^3$

124. $(n - 3)(n - 3)$ **125.** $(4x - 2)(8x - 3)$ **126.** $(12b - 4)(8b + 3)$

127. Graph $f(x) = x^2 + 6$. Use a table of values with $x = 2, 1, 0, -1$, and -2.

Contents of Student Resources

Place Value

The **whole numbers** are the numbers 0, 1, 2, 3, ... A **digit** is any of the numbers 0, 1, 2, 3, 4, 5, 6, 7, 8, or 9. The decimals are numbers such as 121.32, 25.6, and 3.456. For example, the decimal 4.5 has the digits 4 and 5. The place value of each digit in a whole number or a decimal depends on its position within the number. For example, in the number 491,037.892, the 8 has a value of 0.8 or 8×0.1 because it is in the tenths' place.

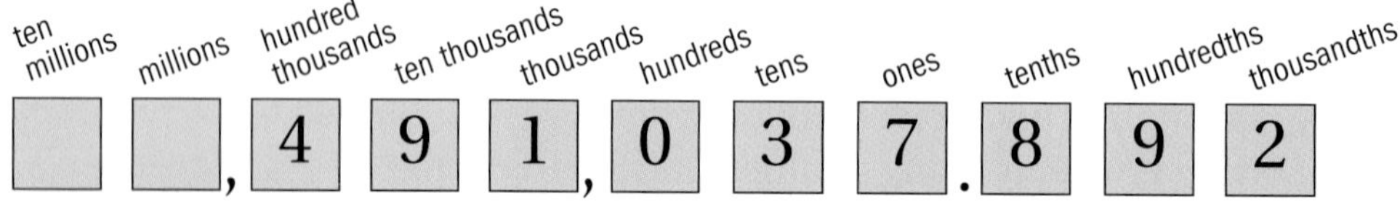

EXAMPLE **Write the number 27,037.6 in expanded form.**

$27{,}037.6 = 20{,}000 + 7000 + 30 + 7 + 0.6$

The zero in the hundreds' position is a placeholder.

$= 2 \times 10{,}000 + 7 \times 1000 + 3 \times 10 + 7 \times 1 + 6 \times 0.1$

EXAMPLE **Write the number in standard form.**

a. $4 \times 1000 + 5 \times 10 + 6 \times 0.1 + 8 \times 0.01$

b. Four million, sixty thousand, five and two thousandths

Solution

a. $4 \times 1000 + 5 \times 10 + 6 \times 0.1 + 8 \times 0.01 = 4000 + 50 + 0.6 + 0.08$

$= 4050.68$

b. Write 4 in the millions' place, 6 in the ten thousands' place, 5 in the ones' place, and the 2 in the thousandths' place. Use zeros as placeholders for the other places. The answer is 4,060,005.002.

Practice

Write the number in expanded form.

1. 56,809 **2.** 3.075 **3.** 1002.003 **4.** 306.405

Write the number in standard form.

5. $5 \times 100{,}000 + 6 \times 10 + 9 \times 1 + 7 \times 0.001$ **6.** Five million, ten and thirty-six thousandths

Rounding

To **round** a number means to approximate the number to a given place value. When rounding, look at the digit to the right of that place value. If the digit to the right is less than 5 (0, 1, 2, 3, or 4), round down. If the digit to the right is 5 or greater (5, 6, 7, 8, or 9), round up.

EXAMPLE **Round the number to the place value of the red digit.**

a. 6932 **b.** 45.674

Solution

a. Because the 9 is in the hundreds' place, round 6932 to the nearest hundred. Notice that 6932 is between 6900 and 7000, so it will round to one of these two numbers.

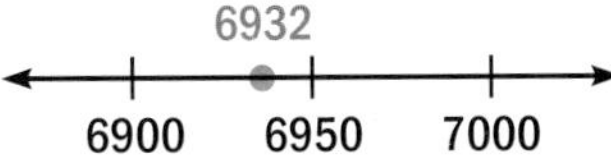

Notice that 6932 is closer to 6900 than to 7000.

The digit to the right of the 9 in the hundreds' place is the 3 in the tens' place. Because 3 is less than 5, round down.

ANSWER 6932 rounded to the nearest hundred is 6900.

b. Because 6 is in the tenths' place, round 45.674 to the nearest tenth. Notice that 45.674 is between 45.6 and 45.7, so it will round to one of these two numbers.

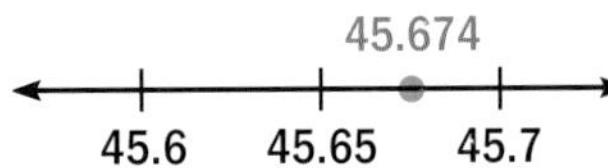

Notice that 45.674 is closer to 45.7 than to 45.6.

The digit to the right of the 6 in the tenths' place is the 7 in the hundredths' place. Because 7 is 5 or greater, round up.

ANSWER 45.674 rounded to the nearest tenth is 45.7.

Practice

Round the number to the place value of the red digit.

1. 1253 **2.** 57,309 **3.** 8.183 **4.** 32.76 **5.** 44,380

6. 12.535 **7.** 452.84 **8.** 998,543 **9.** 62.847 **10.** 640,796

11. 164.479 **12.** 1209.4 **13.** 52.961 **14.** 12,742.5 **15.** 3,501,652

Divisibility Tests

When two nonzero whole numbers are multiplied together, each number is a **factor** of the product. A number is **divisible** by another number if the second number is a factor of the first. For example, $2 \times 5 = 10$, so 2 and 5 are factors of 10, and 10 is divisible by both 2 and 5.

You can use the following tests to test a whole number for divisibility by 2, 3, 4, 5, 6, 8, 9, and 10.

Divisible by 2: The last digit of the number is 0, 2, 4, 6, or 8.
Divisible by 3: The sum of the digits of the number is divisible by 3.
Divisible by 4: The last two digits of the number are divisible by 4.
Divisible by 5: The last digit of the number is 0 or 5.
Divisible by 6: The number is divisible by both 2 and 3.
Divisible by 8: The last three digits of the number are divisible by 8.
Divisible by 9: The sum of the digits of the number is divisible by 9.
Divisible by 10: The last digit of the number is 0.

EXAMPLE **Test the number for divisibility by 2, 3, 4, 5, 6, 8, 9, and 10.**

a. 2736 **b.** 74,420

Solution

a. The last digit of 2736 is 6, so it is divisible by 2 but not by 5 or 10. The sum of the digits is $2 + 7 + 3 + 6 = 18$, so it is divisible by 3 and 9. The last two digits, 36, are divisible by 4, so 2736 is divisible by 4. Because 2736 is divisible by both 2 and 3, it is divisible by 6. The last three digits, 736, are divisible by 8, so 2736 is divisible by 8.

ANSWER 2736 is divisible by 2, 3, 4, 6, 8, and 9.

b. The last digit of 74,420 is 0, so it is divisible by 2, 5, and 10. The sum of the digits is $7 + 4 + 4 + 2 + 0 = 17$, so it is not divisible by 3 or 9. The last two digits, 20, are divisible by 4, so 74,420 is divisible by 4. Because 74,420 is divisible by 2, but not by 3, it is not divisible by 6. The last three digits, 420, are not divisible by 8, so 74,420 is not divisible by 8.

ANSWER 74,420 is divisible by 2, 4, 5, and 10.

Practice

Test the number for divisibility by 2, 3, 4, 5, 6, 8, 9, and 10.

1. 34 **2.** 84 **3.** 285 **4.** 560 **5.** 972
6. 4210 **7.** 2815 **8.** 6390 **9.** 88,004 **10.** 75,432

Mixed Numbers and Improper Fractions

A **fraction** is a number of the form $\frac{a}{b}$ ($b \neq 0$) where a is called the **numerator** and b is called the **denominator**. A number $1\frac{3}{5}$, read as "one and three fifths," is a *mixed number*. A **mixed number** is the sum of a whole number part and a fraction part. An **improper fraction**, such as $\frac{21}{8}$, is any fraction in which the numerator is greater than or equal to the denominator.

EXAMPLE **Write $3\frac{2}{5}$ as an improper fraction.**

$3\frac{2}{5} = \frac{15 + 2}{5}$ 1 whole $= \frac{5}{5}$, so 3 wholes $= \frac{3 \times 5}{5}$, or $\frac{15}{5}$.

$= \frac{17}{5}$ Add.

EXAMPLE **Write $\frac{13}{4}$ as a mixed number.**

1. Divide 13 by 4.

$$\begin{array}{r} 3\text{R}1 \\ 4\overline{)13} \\ \underline{12} \\ 1 \end{array}$$

2. Write the mixed number. $3 + \frac{1}{4} = 3\frac{1}{4}$

Practice

Copy and complete the statement.

1. $7\frac{3}{5} = \frac{?}{5}$ **2.** $3\frac{1}{6} = \frac{?}{6}$ **3.** $\frac{23}{4} = 5\frac{?}{4}$ **4.** $\frac{17}{7} = 2\frac{?}{7}$

Write the mixed number as an improper fraction.

5. $3\frac{1}{2}$ **6.** $1\frac{5}{6}$ **7.** $4\frac{3}{8}$ **8.** $8\frac{5}{7}$ **9.** $10\frac{3}{4}$

Write the improper fraction as a mixed number.

10. $\frac{11}{4}$ **11.** $\frac{15}{2}$ **12.** $\frac{25}{6}$ **13.** $\frac{17}{3}$ **14.** $\frac{33}{8}$

Ratio and Rate

One way to compare numbers is to use a ratio. The **ratio** uses division to compare two numbers. You can write the ratio of a to b as $\frac{a}{b}$, as $a : b$, or as "a to b."

EXAMPLE **There are 15 boys and 17 girls in the band. Write the ratio of the number of boys to girls in the band in three ways.**

$$\frac{\text{Number of boys}}{\text{Number of girls}} = \frac{15}{17} = 15 \text{ to } 17 = 15 : 17$$

A **rate** is a ratio of two quantities that have different units, such as $\frac{150 \text{ miles}}{3 \text{ hours}}$. A **unit rate** is a rate with a denominator of 1 unit.

EXAMPLE **Write the rate $\frac{150 \text{ miles}}{3 \text{ hours}}$ as a unit rate.**

$$\frac{150 \text{ mi}}{3 \text{ h}} = \frac{50 \text{ mi}}{1 \text{ h}} \quad (\div 3 \text{ numerator and denominator})$$

Divide 3 by 3 to get 1, so divide 150 by 3 also.

ANSWER The unit rate is 50 miles per hour.

Practice

The table shows the numbers of boys and girls in Mr. Smith's class and in Ms. Jung's class. Use the table to write the specified ratio.

1. Boys in Mr. Smith's class to girls in Mr. Smith's class
2. Boys in Mr. Smith's class to boys in Ms. Jung's class
3. Girls in Ms. Jung's class to all girls

	Boys	Girls
Mr. Smith's class	13	12
Ms. Jung's class	17	11

Write the rate and unit rate.

4. 8 feet in 2 seconds
5. \$24 for 8 pens
6. 333 miles in 6 hours
7. 280 words in 5 minutes
8. 3 quarts for \$2.50
9. 8 inches in 6 days

Adding and Subtracting Decimals

To add and subtract decimals, start with the digits in the place on the right. Moving to the left, add or subtract the digits one place value at a time, regrouping as needed.

EXAMPLE **Find the sum 0.157 + 0.663.**

1 Add the thousandths. Regroup 10 thousandths as 1 hundredth and 0 thousandths.

$$\begin{array}{r} \scriptstyle 1 \\ 0.157 \\ +\ 0.663 \\ \hline 0 \end{array}$$

2 Add the hundredths. Regroup 12 hundredths as 1 tenth and 2 hundredths.

$$\begin{array}{r} \scriptstyle 11 \\ 0.157 \\ +\ 0.663 \\ \hline 20 \end{array}$$

3 Add the tenths. Place the decimal point in the answer.

$$\begin{array}{r} \scriptstyle 11 \\ 0.157 \\ +\ 0.663 \\ \hline 0.820 \end{array}$$

EXAMPLE **Find the difference 30.7 – 3.8.**

1 Start with the tenths. There are not enough tenths in 30.7 to subtract 8 tenths.

$$\begin{array}{r} 30.7 \\ -\ 3.8 \\ \hline \end{array}$$

2 Move to the ones. There are no ones in 30.7, so regroup 1 ten as 9 ones and 10 tenths.

$$\begin{array}{r} \scriptstyle 9 \\ \scriptstyle 2\ \cancel{10}\ 17 \\ \cancel{3}\cancel{0}.\cancel{7} \\ -\ 3.8 \\ \hline \end{array}$$

3 Subtract. Place the decimal point in the answer.

$$\begin{array}{r} \scriptstyle 9 \\ \scriptstyle 2\ \cancel{10}\ 17 \\ \cancel{3}\cancel{0}.\cancel{7} \\ -\ 3.8 \\ \hline 26.9 \end{array}$$

✓ **Check** Because addition and subtraction are inverse operations, you can check your answer by adding: 26.9 + 3.8 = 30.7.

Practice

Find the sum or difference.

1. 3.56 + 2.74 **2.** 12.7 + 93.8 **3.** 27.5 + 3.6 **4.** 0.923 + 0.179

5. 4.217 + 6.739 **6.** 9.3 − 2.8 **7.** 4.56 − 1.65 **8.** 13.64 − 5.85

9. 38.45 − 19.57 **10.** 741.52 − 48.66 **11.** 56.98 + 0.82 **12.** 100.476 − 4.989

13. 365.57 − 79.38 **14.** 49.86 + 2.65 **15.** 97.156 − 9.092 **16.** 232.543 − 209.692

Skills Review

Adding and Subtracting Fractions

To add two fractions with a common denominator, write the sum of the numerators over the denominator.

Numbers $\frac{2}{5} + \frac{1}{5} = \frac{3}{5}$ **Algebra** $\frac{a}{c} + \frac{b}{c} = \frac{a+b}{c}\ (c \neq 0)$

EXAMPLE **Find the sum $\frac{4}{7} + \frac{6}{7}$.**

$\frac{4}{7} + \frac{6}{7} = \frac{4+6}{7}$ Write sum of numerators over denominator.

$= \frac{10}{7}$ Add.

$= 1\frac{3}{7}$ Write the improper fraction as a mixed number.

To subtract two fractions with a common denominator, write the difference of the numerators over the denominator.

Numbers $\frac{7}{9} - \frac{2}{9} = \frac{5}{9}$ **Algebra** $\frac{a}{c} - \frac{b}{c} = \frac{a-b}{c}\ (c \neq 0)$

EXAMPLE **Find the difference $\frac{10}{11} - \frac{4}{11}$.**

$\frac{10}{11} - \frac{4}{11} = \frac{10-4}{11}$ Write difference of numerators over denominator.

$= \frac{6}{11}$ Subtract.

Practice

Find the sum or difference.

1. $\frac{1}{3} + \frac{1}{3}$ **2.** $\frac{8}{9} + \frac{5}{9}$ **3.** $\frac{6}{7} - \frac{3}{7}$ **4.** $\frac{11}{12} - \frac{4}{12}$ **5.** $\frac{1}{8} + \frac{7}{8}$

6. $\frac{8}{11} + \frac{7}{11}$ **7.** $\frac{13}{15} - \frac{2}{15}$ **8.** $\frac{5}{6} - \frac{4}{6}$ **9.** $\frac{1}{9} + \frac{1}{9}$ **10.** $\frac{10}{11} - \frac{2}{11}$

11. $\frac{11}{12} + \frac{8}{12}$ **12.** $\frac{9}{10} - \frac{6}{10}$ **13.** $\frac{5}{9} - \frac{4}{9}$ **14.** $\frac{9}{16} + \frac{12}{16}$ **15.** $\frac{11}{14} - \frac{2}{14}$

16. $\frac{8}{15} - \frac{8}{15}$ **17.** $\frac{5}{12} + \frac{2}{12}$ **18.** $\frac{8}{10} + \frac{1}{10}$ **19.** $\frac{6}{7} + \frac{5}{7}$ **20.** $\frac{5}{8} - \frac{2}{8}$

Estimation in Addition and Subtraction

To **estimate** a solution means to find an approximate answer. When numbers being added have about the same value, you can use *clustering* to estimate their sum. Another way to estimate is to add the digits in the greatest place, then round the remaining parts of the numbers and add. Finally, add the sums together.

EXAMPLE **Estimate the sum 3836 + 4235 + 3982.**

$$\begin{array}{r} 3836 \\ 4235 \\ +\ 3982 \\ \hline \end{array} \qquad \begin{array}{r} 4000 \\ 4000 \\ +\ 4000 \\ \hline 12{,}000 \end{array}$$

The numbers all cluster around the value 4000.

ANSWER The sum 3836 + 4235 + 3982 is *about* 12,000.

To estimate a difference, first subtract the digits in the greatest place. Then round the remaining parts of the numbers and subtract the lesser number from the greater number. Finally, combine the two differences using addition or subtraction as shown below.

EXAMPLE **Estimate the difference 68,453 − 32,792.**

1. First subtract the digits in the ten thousands' place.

$$\begin{array}{r} 68{,}453 \\ -\ 32{,}792 \\ \hline \end{array} \qquad \begin{array}{r} 60{,}000 \\ -\ 30{,}000 \\ \hline 30{,}000 \end{array}$$

2. Then round the remaining digits to the nearest thousand. Subtract the lesser number from the greater number.

$$\begin{array}{r} 8{,}000 \\ -\ 3{,}000 \\ \hline 5{,}000 \end{array}$$

3. Because the greater remaining number was originally on the *top*, you *add* the differences.

30,000 + 5,000 = 35,000

Note that if the greater remaining number had originally been on the *bottom*, you would *subtract* the differences.

Practice

Estimate the sum or difference.

1. 935 + 887 + 912 **2.** 4967 + 4802 + 5218 **3.** 5971 + 6032 + 7865

4. 8891 − 4932 **5.** 4373 − 2158 **6.** 449,739 − 285,921

Solving Problems Using Addition and Subtraction

You can use the following guidelines to tell whether to use addition or subtraction to solve a word problem.

- Use addition when you need to combine, join, or find a total.
- Use subtraction when you need to separate, compare, take away, find how many are left, or find how many more are needed.

EXAMPLE **You have 36 stamps in your stamp collection. You want to collect 18 more stamps. How many stamps will you have in all?**

You need to combine, so you need to add.

$36 + 18 = 54$

ANSWER You will have 54 stamps in your stamp collection.

EXAMPLE **Your total bill for lunch is \$4.78. You pay with a \$5 bill. How much change do you receive?**

You need to take away, so you need to subtract.

$\$5.00 - \$4.78 = \$.22$

ANSWER You receive \$.22 in change.

Practice

1. You spend \$48 for a coat and \$45 for a pair of shoes. How much do you spend in all?
2. You bought a box of 96 pencils. You gave 28 of the pencils to your friend. How many pencils do you have left?
3. You have \$18. You buy a video for \$15.99. How much money do you have left?
4. You have 24 country CDs and 18 pop CDs. How many country and pop CDs do you have in all?
5. You have 900 minutes a month on your cell phone plan. You have used 652 minutes so far this month. How many minutes do you have left?
6. You have \$149. You make \$24 babysitting. How much money do you have?

Multiplying Fractions

To multiply a fraction by a whole number, multiply the numerator of the fraction by the whole number and write the product over the denominator of the fraction. Simplify if possible.

EXAMPLE **Find the product.**

a. $3 \times \frac{2}{7} = \frac{3 \times 2}{7}$ — **Write the product of the whole number and the numerator over the denominator.**

$= \frac{6}{7}$ — **Multiply.**

b. $\frac{3}{8} \times 5 = \frac{3 \times 5}{8}$ — **Write the product of the whole number and the numerator over the denominator.**

$= \frac{15}{8}$, or $1\frac{7}{8}$ — **Multiply. Then write as a mixed number.**

To multiply two fractions, write the product of the numerators over the product of the denominators. Simplify if possible.

$$\text{product of fractions} = \frac{\text{product of numerators}}{\text{product of denominators}}$$

EXAMPLE **Find the product.**

$\frac{4}{5} \times \frac{2}{3} = \frac{4 \times 2}{5 \times 3}$ — **Use rule for multiplying fractions.**

$= \frac{8}{15}$ — **Multiply.**

Practice

Find the product. Simplify if possible.

1. $6 \times \frac{2}{15}$ **2.** $2 \times \frac{6}{11}$ **3.** $4 \times \frac{5}{9}$ **4.** $8 \times \frac{5}{9}$ **5.** $\frac{3}{4} \times 7$

6. $\frac{4}{7} \times 5$ **7.** $\frac{6}{7} \times 3$ **8.** $\frac{3}{7} \times \frac{6}{11}$ **9.** $\frac{2}{3} \times \frac{4}{5}$ **10.** $\frac{3}{4} \times \frac{1}{7}$

11. $\frac{1}{8} \times \frac{3}{5}$ **12.** $\frac{7}{9} \times \frac{5}{8}$ **13.** $\frac{5}{9} \times \frac{2}{3}$ **14.** $\frac{3}{8} \times \frac{4}{5}$ **15.** $\frac{5}{12} \times \frac{5}{6}$

Multiplication of a Decimal by a Whole Number

To multiply a decimal by a whole number, multiply the entire first number (ignoring the decimal point) by the digit in each place value of the second number to get partial products. Add the partial products. Then place the decimal point in the answer, showing the same number of decimal places as in the decimal.

EXAMPLE **Find the product 31.5 × 206.**

1. Multiply 31.5 by the ones' digit in 206. Ignore the decimal point.

```
   3
  31.5
× 206
  1890
```

2. Skip the 0 in the tens' place, and multiply by the hundreds' digit. Start the partial product in the hundreds' place.

```
   1
  31.5
× 206
  1890
 630
```

3. Add the partial products. The decimal has one decimal place, so show one decimal place in the answer.

```
   31.5
 × 206
   1890
  630
 6489.0
```

Practice

Find the product.

1. 2.3 × 98
2. 0.62 × 46
3. 85 × 7.9
4. 0.56 × 63
5. 2.08 × 14
6. 6.52 × 36
7. 7.24 × 89
8. 8.35 × 16
9. 77.6 × 22
10. 3.45 × 105
11. 453 × 41.2
12. 614 × 6.71
13. 32.6 × 463
14. 71.8 × 934
15. 90.5 × 407
16. 15.36 × 123
17. 3.442 × 276
18. 93.08 × 306
19. 5.436 × 682
20. 60.97 × 708
21. 142.82 × 35
22. 25.987 × 76
23. 32.903 × 55
24. 243.72 × 38
25. 75.032 × 73
26. 380.07 × 114
27. 508.25 × 237
28. 15.456 × 591
29. 36.902 × 205
30. 8257.6 × 459

Dividing Decimals

In a division problem, the number being divided is called the **dividend** and the number it is being divided by is called the **divisor**. The result of the division is called the **quotient**. To **divide** two numbers, you start with the leftmost digit of the dividend and move to the right. Before you start dividing decimals, place the decimal point in the quotient.

EXAMPLE **Find the quotient 5.2 ÷ 8.**

1 Place the decimal point in the quotient directly above the decimal point in the dividend. Then divide as with whole numbers. Because 8 is greater than 5, place a zero above the 5.

$$\begin{array}{r} 0. \\ 8\overline{)5.2} \end{array}$$

divisor → 8 ; dividend ← 5.2

2 Because 8 × 6 = 48, estimate that 8 divides 52 about 6 times. Multiply 6 and 8. Then subtract 48 from 52. Be sure the difference is less than the divisor: 4 < 8.

$$\begin{array}{r} 0.6 \\ 8\overline{)5.2} \\ -\,48 \\ \hline 4 \end{array}$$

3 Add zero as a placeholder. Bring down the zero. Divide 40 by 8 to get 5. Multiply 5 and 8. Subtract 40 from 40. The remainder is zero.

$$\begin{array}{r} 0.65 \\ 8\overline{)5.20} \\ -\,48 \\ \hline 40 \\ -\,40 \\ \hline 0 \end{array}$$

EXAMPLE **Find the quotient 12 ÷ 2.8.**

1 To multiply the divisor and the dividend by 10, move both decimal points 1 place to the right. Then divide as with whole numbers.

$$28\overline{)120}$$

divisor → 28 ; dividend ← 120

2 Because 28 × 4 = 112, estimate that 28 divides 120 about 4 times. Multiply 4 and 28. Then subtract 112 from 120.

$$\begin{array}{r} 4 \\ 28\overline{)120} \\ -\,112 \\ \hline 8 \end{array}$$

3 Be sure the difference is less than the divisor: 8 < 28. So 12 ÷ 2.8 is equal to $4\frac{8}{28}$, or $4\frac{2}{7}$.

$$\begin{array}{r} 4R8 \\ 28\overline{)120} \\ -\,112 \\ \hline 8 \end{array}$$

Practice

Find the quotient.

1. 2.7 ÷ 6 **2.** 3.8 ÷ 4 **3.** 6.8 ÷ 8 **4.** 46.9 ÷ 7 **5.** 13.71 ÷ 3

6. 15 ÷ 2.5 **7.** 8 ÷ 1.3 **8.** 32 ÷ 5.46 **9.** 63 ÷ 7.12 **10.** 75 ÷ 6.357

Skills Review

Estimation in Multiplication and Division

One way to estimate a product or a quotient is to find a range for the product or quotient by finding a low estimate and a high estimate. A low estimate and a high estimate can be found by using *compatible numbers,* which are numbers that make a calculation easier.

EXAMPLE **Find a low and high estimate for the product 56 × 35 using compatible numbers.**

For a low estimate, round both factors *down*. $50 \times 30 = 1500$

For a high estimate, round both factors *up*. $60 \times 40 = 2400$

ANSWER The product 56 × 35 is between 1500 and 2400.

EXAMPLE **Find a low and high estimate for the quotient 23,400 ÷ 45 using compatible numbers.**

When the divisor has more than one digit, round it .

For a *low* estimate, round the divisor *up* and choose a compatible dividend that is *lower* than the original dividend. $50\overline{)20{,}000}$ = 400

For a *high* estimate, round the divisor *down* and choose a compatible dividend that is *higher* than the original dividend. $40\overline{)24{,}000}$ = 600

ANSWER The quotient 23,400 ÷ 45 is between 400 and 600.

Practice

Find a low and high estimate for the product or quotient using compatible numbers.

1. 43 × 16	**2.** 359 × 28	**3.** 852 × 53	**4.** 734 × 76
5. 225 ÷ 6	**6.** 2795 ÷ 7	**7.** 17,934 ÷ 77	**8.** 41,042 ÷ 92
9. 326 × 48	**10.** 612 × 273	**11.** 745 × 158	**12.** 905 × 657
13. 625 × 28	**14.** 809 × 97	**15.** 742 ÷ 8	**16.** 231 ÷ 38
17. 5421 ÷ 7	**18.** 4972 ÷ 18	**19.** 1583 ÷ 82	**20.** 43,789 ÷ 64

Solving Problems Using Multiplication and Division

You can use the following guidelines to tell whether to use multiplication or division to solve a word problem.

- Use multiplication when you need to find the total number of objects that are in groups of equal size or to find a fractional part of another number.
- Use division when you need to find the number of equal groups or the number in each equal group.

EXAMPLE **You baked 48 muffins. You give $\frac{1}{3}$ of them to your friend. How many muffins did you give to your friend?**

You need to find the fractional part of another number, so you need to multiply.

$$48 \cdot \frac{1}{3} = 16$$

ANSWER You gave 16 muffins to your friend.

EXAMPLE **You bought 4 cans of soup for a total of \$3.56. How much did you pay for each can of soup?**

You need to find the amount in each equal group, so you need to divide.

$$3.56 \div 4 = 0.89$$

ANSWER You paid \$.89 for each can of soup.

Practice

1. You bought 6 notebooks. Each notebook cost \$1.58. How much did you pay for all of the notebooks?
2. You have 92 baseball cards. You give $\frac{1}{4}$ of your cards to your friend. How many cards did you give your friend?
3. You have 12 flats of flowers. If each flat contains 48 flowers, how many flowers do you have?
4. You paid \$22.95 for the plates for your party. If you bought 9 packages of plates, how much did you pay for each package?

Points, Lines, and Planes

In geometry, a **point** is usually labeled with an uppercase letter, such as *A* or *B*. Points are used to name *lines, rays,* and *segments.* A **plane** is a flat surface that extends without end in all directions. You can represent a plane by a figure that looks like a floor or a wall.

Words	Diagram	Symbols
A **line** extends without end in two *opposite* directions.	X Y	$\overleftrightarrow{XY}$ or $\overleftrightarrow{YX}$
A **ray** has one **endpoint** and extends without end in *one* direction.	X Y	$\overrightarrow{XY}$
A **segment** has two endpoints.	X Y	$\overline{XY}$ or $\overline{YX}$

EXAMPLE **Identify and name the *line, ray,* or *segment.***

a.

b.

c.

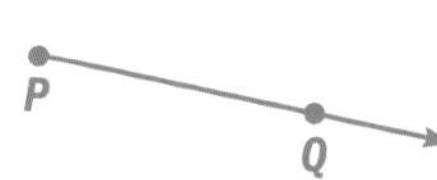

Solution

a. The figure is a segment that can be named $\overline{AB}$.

b. The figure is a line that can be named $\overleftrightarrow{MN}$.

c. The figure is a ray that can be named $\overrightarrow{PQ}$.

Practice

Match the name with the correct figure.

1. $\overline{CD}$

2. $\overleftrightarrow{CD}$

3. $\overrightarrow{CD}$

A.

B.

C.

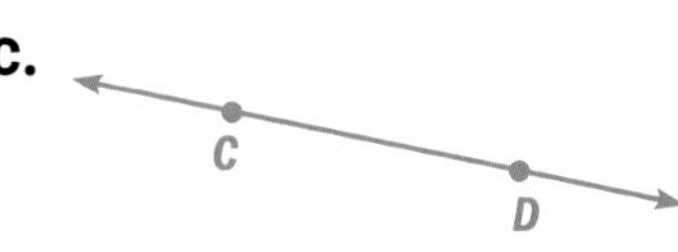

In Exercises 4–7, use the diagram.

4. Name three points.

5. Name two rays.

6. Name two lines.

7. Name a segment that has *S* as an endpoint.

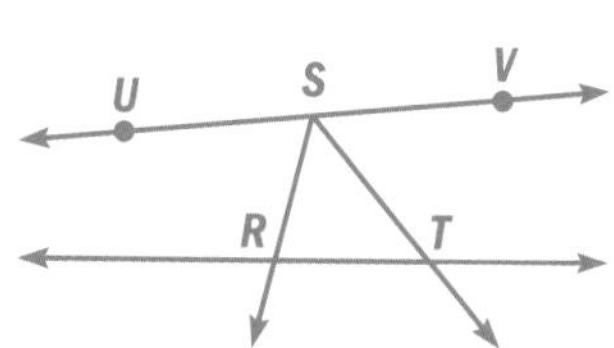

Angles

An **angle** is formed by two rays with the same endpoint. The endpoint is called the **vertex**. The symbol ∠ is used to represent an angle.

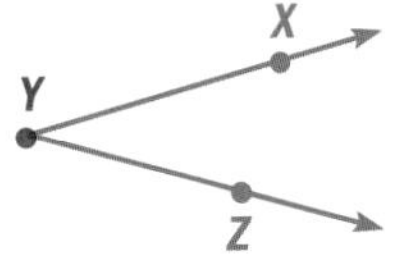

EXAMPLE **Name the angle above in three ways.**

Name the angle by its vertex alone: $\angle Y$

Name the angle by its vertex and two points, with the vertex as the middle point: $\angle XYZ$

Name the angle by its vertex and two points, but reverse the order of the points: $\angle ZYX$

Practice

Match the name with the correct angle.

1. $\angle ABC$

2. $\angle RST$

3. $\angle MNP$

A.

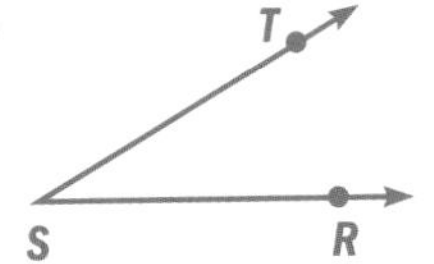

B.

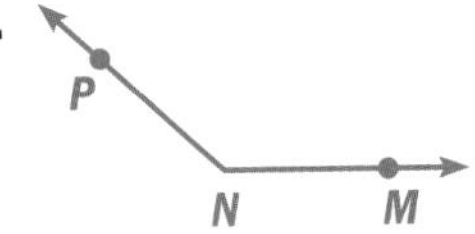

C.

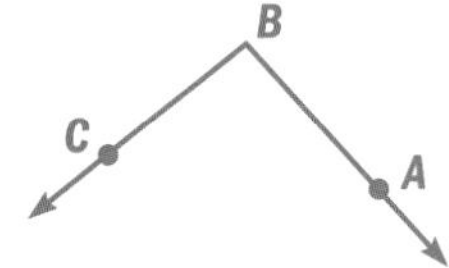

Name the angle in three ways.

4.

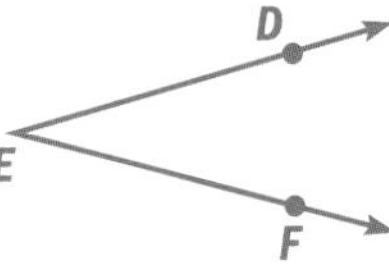

5.

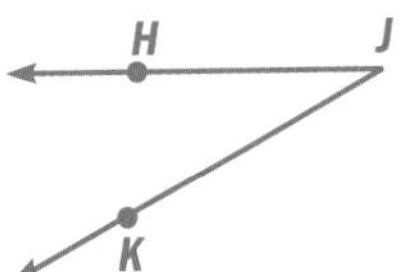

6.

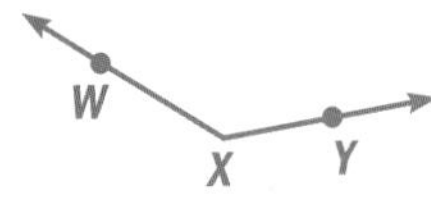

7.

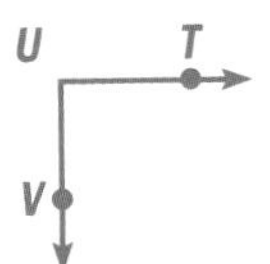

8.

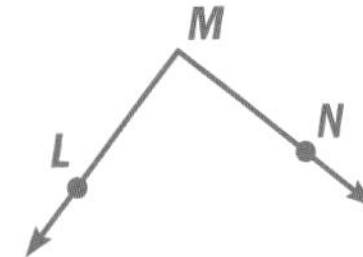

9.

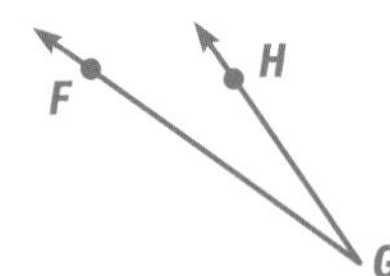

10. Draw a triangle with vertices P, Q, and R. Name each angle of the triangle in three ways.

Using a Ruler

An **inch ruler** has markings for inches, halves of an inch, fourths of an inch, eighths of an inch, and sixteenths of an inch. As the lengths get shorter, so do the markings.

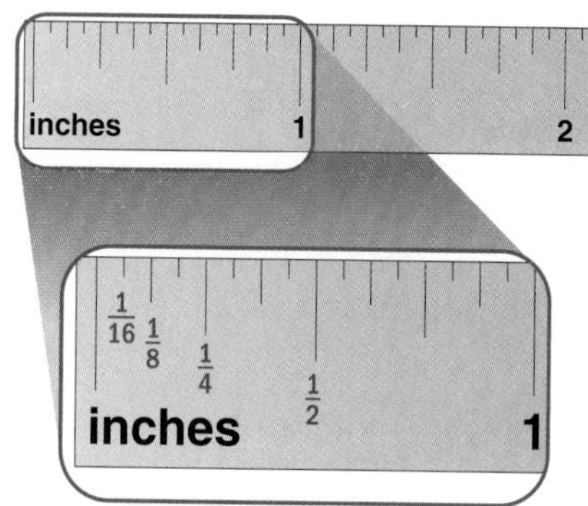

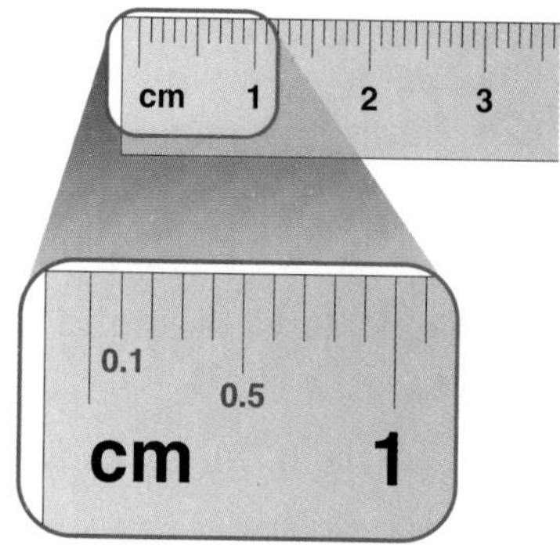

A **centimeter ruler** has markings for centimeters, halves of a centimeter, and tenths of a centimeter (also called *millimeters*). Like an inch ruler, as the lengths get shorter, so do the markings.

EXAMPLE **Use a ruler to draw a segment with the given length.**

a. $2\frac{1}{8}$ inches

b. 3.8 centimeters

Solution

a. Start at the leftmost mark on the ruler.

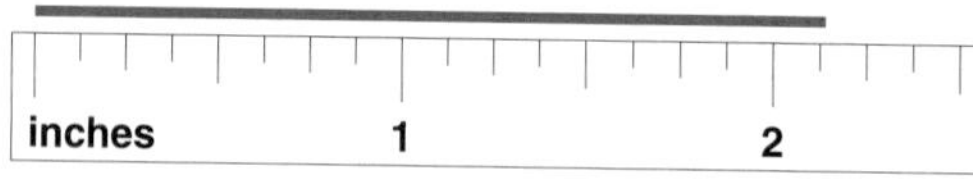

Draw a segment so that the other end is at the first $\frac{1}{8}$ in. mark after 2.

b. Start at the leftmost mark on the ruler.

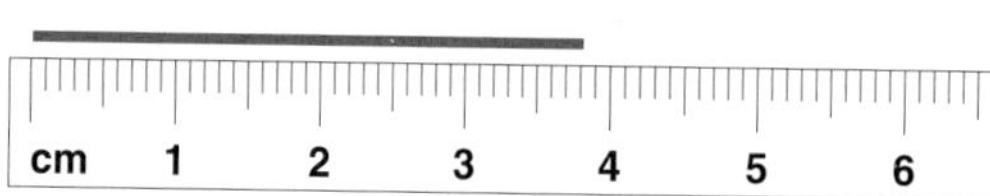

Draw a segment so that the other end is at the 3.8 cm mark.

Practice

Use a ruler to draw a segment with the given length.

1. $\frac{7}{16}$ inch **2.** $4\frac{5}{8}$ inches **3.** 4.3 centimeters **4.** 2.7 centimeters

5. $2\frac{5}{16}$ inches **6.** 6.5 centimeters **7.** 2.9 centimeters **8.** $1\frac{1}{4}$ inches

Skills Review

Using a Protractor

A **protractor** is a tool you can use to draw and measure angles. A unit of measure for angles the **degree** (°). To measure an angle, place the center of the protractor on the vertex of the angle and line up one ray with the 0° line. Then read the measure where the other ray crosses the protractor.

The measure of $\angle XYZ$ is 135°. You can write this as $m\angle XYZ = 135°$.

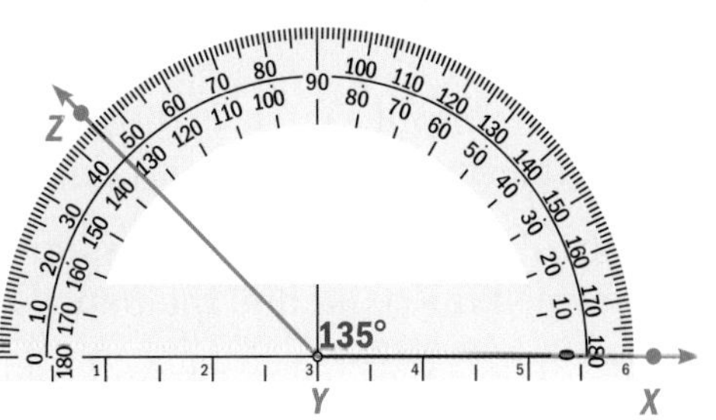

EXAMPLE **Use a protractor to draw an angle that has a measure of 48°.**

1. Draw and label a ray.

2. Place the center of the protractor at the endpoint of the ray. Line up the ray with the 0° line. Then draw and label a point at the 48° mark on the inner scale.

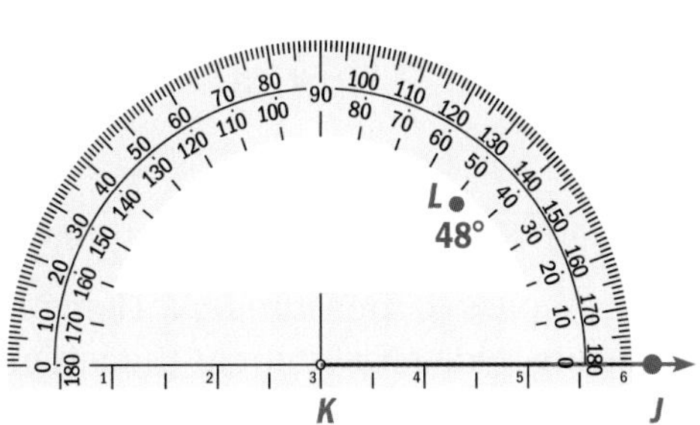

3. Remove the protractor and draw $\overrightarrow{KL}$ to complete the angle.

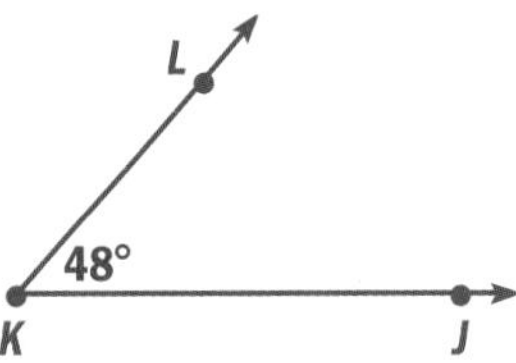

Practice

Use a protractor to measure the angle.

1.

2.

3.

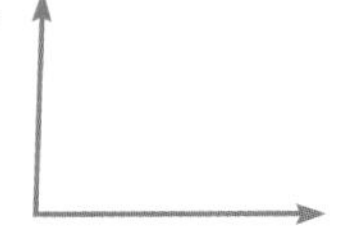

4. Use a protractor to draw angles measuring 46°, 125°, and 73°.

Using a Compass

A **compass** is an instrument used to draw circles. A **straightedge** is any object that can be used to draw a segment.

EXAMPLE **Use a compass to draw a circle with radius 3 cm.**

Recall that the *radius* of a circle is the distance between the center of the circle and any point on the circle.

Use a metric ruler to open the compass so that the distance between the point and the pencil is 3 cm.

Place the point on a piece of paper and rotate the pencil around the point to draw the circle.

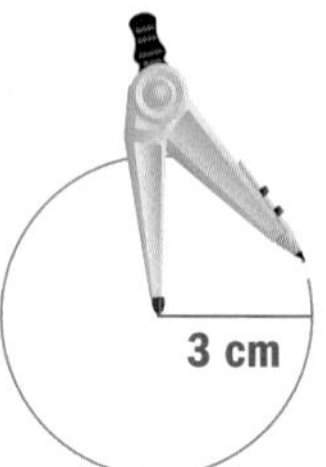

EXAMPLE **Use a straightedge and a compass to draw a segment whose length is the sum of $\overline{MN}$ and $\overline{PQ}$.**

M N P Q

Solution

Use a straightedge to draw a segment longer than both given segments.

Open your compass to measure $\overline{MN}$. Using this compass setting, place the point at the left end of your segment and make a mark that crosses your segment.

Then open your compass to measure $\overline{PQ}$. Using this compass setting, place the point at the first mark you made on your segment and make another mark that crosses your segment.

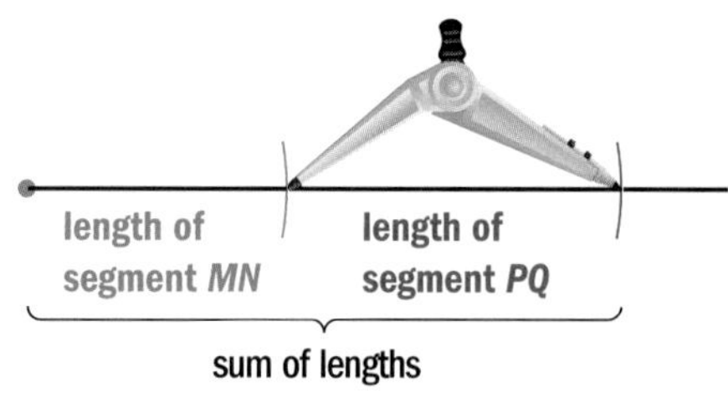

Practice

1. Use a compass to draw a circle with radius 4 cm.
2. Use a straightedge and a compass to draw a segment whose length is the *sum* of the lengths of the two given segments.

   A B

   C D
3. Use a straightedge and a compass to draw a segment whose length is the *difference* of the lengths of the two given segments in Exercise 2.

Reading and Making Line Plots

A **line plot** uses a number line to show how often data values occur.

EXAMPLE **You surveyed 20 of your friends and asked them how many pets they have. Their responses were: 6, 2, 3, 1, 5, 0, 2, 4, 1, 1, 6, 2, 0, 3, 1, 4, 3, 2, 1, 1.**

a. Make a line plot of the data. **b.** What was the most frequent response?

Solution

a.

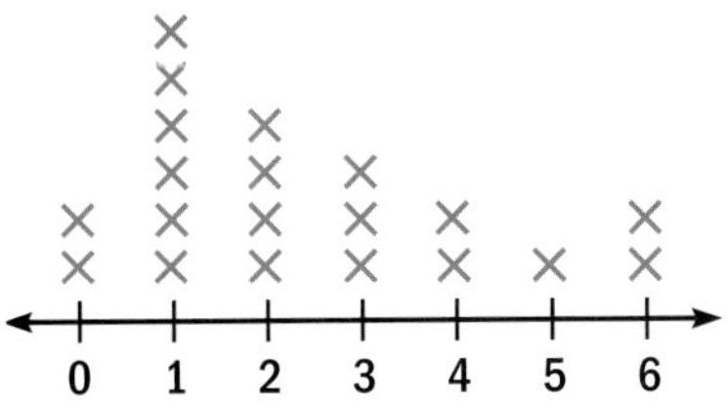

b. The greatest number of ×s is above 1, so 1 was the most frequent response.

Practice

Make a line plot of the data.

1. In a survey, 15 people were asked how many TVs they own. Their responses were: 1, 2, 1, 4, 3, 2, 1, 5, 1, 2, 3, 1, 2, 1, 2.
2. In a survey, 18 people were asked how many times they eat out each week. Their responses were: 2, 4, 1, 3, 5, 6, 3, 7, 2, 1, 4, 8, 5, 4, 3, 4, 1, 2.

Use the line plot below. It shows the results of a questionnaire asking people how many hours they exercise each week.

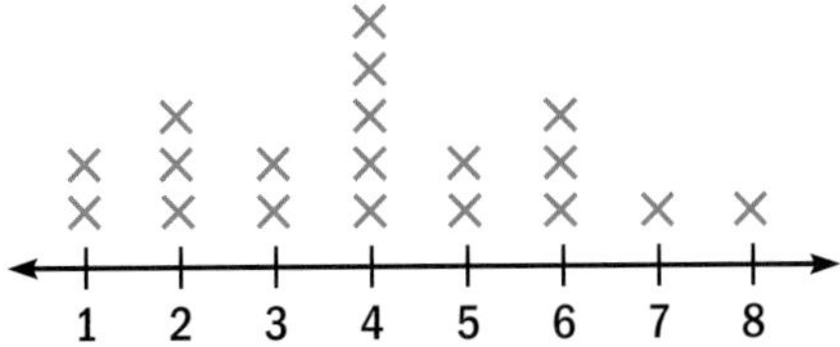

3. How many people completed the questionnaire?
4. How many more people exercise 4 hours each week than exercise 6 hours each week?
5. How many people exercise less than 3 hours each week?

Reading and Making Bar Graphs

Data are numbers or facts. A **bar graph** is one way to display data. A bar graph uses bars to show how quantities in categories compare.

EXAMPLE **The bar graph shows the results of a survey on favorite flavors of ice cream. Which flavor was chosen the most? Which flavor was chosen the least?**

The longest bar on the graph represents the 11 people who chose chocolate. So, chocolate was chosen the most.

The shortest bar represents the 2 students who chose strawberry. So, strawberry was chosen the least.

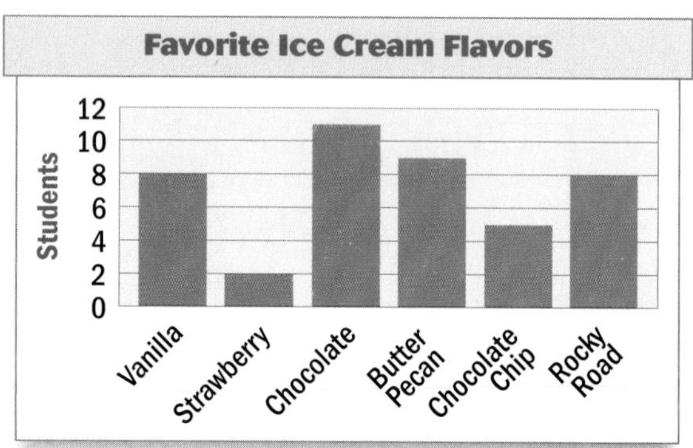

To make a bar graph, choose a title and a scale. Draw and label the axes. Then draw bars to represent the data given.

EXAMPLE **Draw a bar graph for the data given.**

Subject	Number of Students
Math	8
English	15
History	20
Science	16

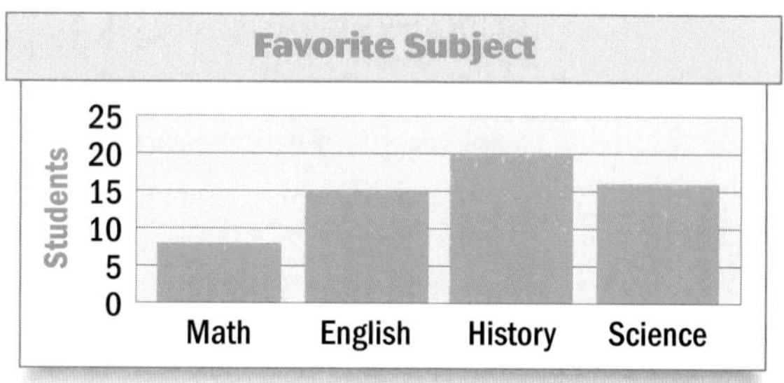

Practice

In Exercises 1–3, use the bar graph of ice cream flavors above.

1. How many students chose butter pecan as a favorite ice cream flavor?
2. How many students chose vanilla as a favorite ice cream flavor?
3. Which two flavors were chosen by the same number of students?
4. Suppose 8 more students took the survey shown in the second example. Draw a new bar graph if 3 of the students chose math, 4 chose history, and 1 chose science.

Reading and Making Line Graphs

Another way to display data is to use a *line graph*. A **line graph** uses line segments to show how a quantity changes over time.

EXAMPLE **The line graph shows plant growth data collected by students every day for 7 days. The greatest increase in growth occurred between what two days? What was the amount of the increase?**

The steepest segment in the line graph is from Monday to Tuesday. The students recorded a height of 1 inch on Monday and a height of 3.5 inches on Tuesday, for an increase of 2.5 inches.

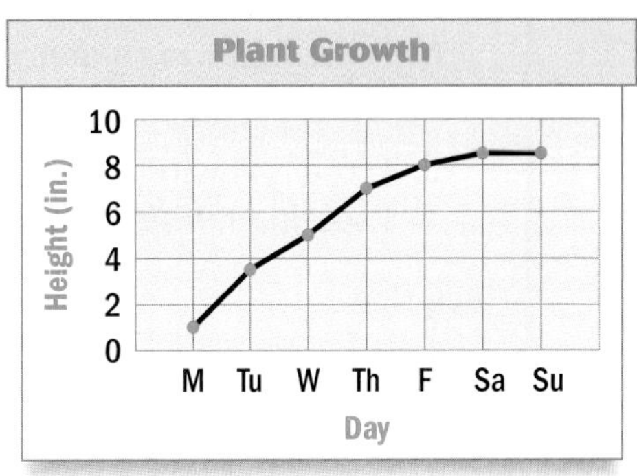

To make a line graph, choose a title and scales. Draw and label the axes. Then plot and connect points to represent the data given.

EXAMPLE **Draw a line graph for the data given.**

Month	Weight of Puppy (pounds)
1	3
2	5.5
3	7
4	11

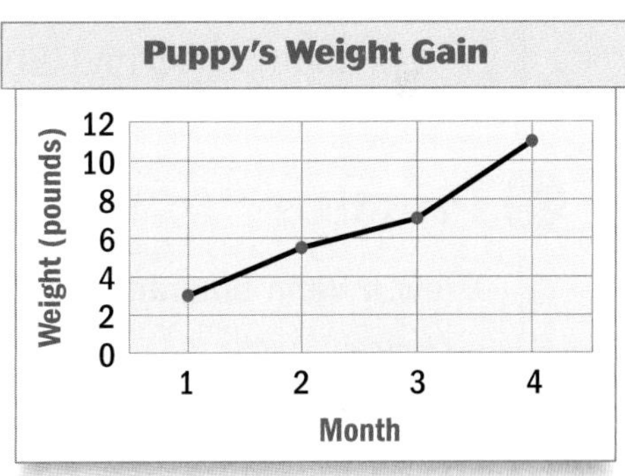

Practice

In Exercises 1 and 2, use the plant growth line graph above.

1. Between which two days was the growth 1 inch?
2. Between which two days did the height remain the same?
3. Suppose in month 5 the puppy in the second example weighed 15 pounds. Copy the graph and add this data to it.

Skills Review

Venn Diagrams and Logical Reasoning

A **Venn diagram** uses shapes to show how sets are related.

EXAMPLE **Draw and use a Venn diagram.**

a. Draw a Venn diagram of the whole numbers from 6 through 19 where set A consists of even numbers and set B consists of multiples of 5.

b. Is the following statement *true* or *false*? Explain. *No even whole number from 6 through 19 is a multiple of 5.*

c. Is the following statement *always, sometimes,* or *never* true? Explain. *A multiple of 5 from 6 through 19 is even.*

Solution

a.

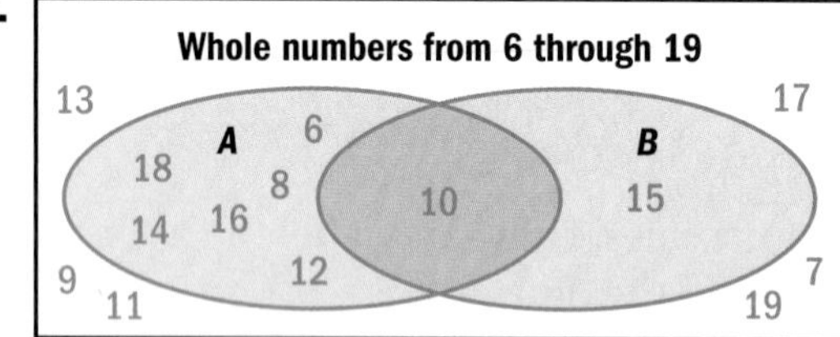

b. False. 10 is an even whole number that is a multiple of 5.

c. Sometimes. It is true that 10 is a multiple of 5 that is even, but 15 is a multiple of 5 that is odd.

Practice

Draw a Venn diagram of the sets described.

1. Of the whole numbers less than 12, set A consists of numbers that are greater than 8 and set B consists of odd numbers.

2. Of the whole numbers less than 10, set C consists of multiples of 3 and set D consists of even numbers.

Use the Venn diagrams you drew in Exercises 1 and 2 to answer the question. Explain your reasoning.

3. Is the following statement *true* or *false*? *There is only one odd number greater than 8 and less than 12.*

4. Is the following statement *always, sometimes,* or *never* true? *A whole number less than 10 is both a multiple of 3 and even.*

Extra Practice

Chapter 1

1.1 The frequency table shows the heights of 30 students.

Height (inches)	54–55.9	56–57.9	58–59.9	60–61.9	62–63.9	64–65.9	66–67.9	68–69.9
Frequency	1	2	4	5	7	6	3	2

1. Make a histogram of the data shown in the frequency table.
2. Which height interval has the greatest number of students?
3. Can you use the histogram to determine the number of students who are between 60 and 69.9 inches tall? Explain.

1.2 Evaluate the expression.

4. $15 - 3 \cdot 2 + 4$
5. $42 \div [(5 - 2) \cdot (1 + 1)]$
6. $2 + \frac{100 - 36}{7 + 9}$
7. $4 \cdot 7 - 8 \cdot 3$
8. $3 + 10 \cdot 5 \div 2$
9. $(11 - 56 \div 8) \cdot 9$

1.3 Evaluate the expression when $r = 1.5$ and $s = 2.4$.

10. $10r + s$
11. $\frac{7s}{r + 0.5}$
12. $8rs$
13. $3(r + s)$

1.4 Evaluate the expression.

14. $24 - (2^3 + 1) \cdot 2$
15. $6^3 \div (2 + 1)^2 + 3$
16. $(8 - 5)^4 + 7 \cdot 5^2$

1.5 In Exercises 17–24, solve the equation using mental math.

17. $5n = 35$
18. $\frac{60}{t} = 4$
19. $12 + w = 75$
20. $41 - a = 23$
21. $9 + b = 17$
22. $63 - c = 10$
23. $6x = 54$
24. $\frac{m}{12} = 9$

1.6 25. Find the perimeter and area of a rectangular garden with a length of 13 feet and a width of 8 feet.

1.6 26. Ramon jogs at a rate of 5 miles per hour. How far does he jog in 1.5 hours?

1.6 27. Find the side length of a square that has a perimeter of 32 centimeters.

1.7 28. You do 5 hours of yard work each day for 4 days and earn $6 per hour. Then you buy 2 concert tickets for $12 each. Use the problem solving plan to find how much money you have left.

Extra Practice

Chapter 2

2.1 Use a number line to order the integers from least to greatest.

1. 33, −24, −43, 7, 19, −2

2. −230, 157, −68, −146, 5, 94

2.1 Write the opposite and the absolute value of the integer.

3. −25 **4.** 467 **5.** 0 **6.** $|-2|$

2.2 Find the sum.

7. 342 + (−751) **8.** −147 + 71 **9.** −89 + 268

10. −29 + (−51) + 36 **11.** −78 + 65 + 13 **12.** 93 + (−57) + (−102)

2.3 Find the difference.

13. −12 − 4 **14.** 10 − 13 **15.** 34 − (−17) **16.** −18 − (−17)

17. 23 − 38 **18.** 81 − (−16) **19.** −9 − (−77) **20.** −63 − 19

2.4 Find the product.

21. (−7)(−50) **22.** 25(−7) **23.** −4(16) **24.** (−12)(−21)

25. −95(0)(−58) **26.** 54(−1)(5) **27.** 8(−2)(−3)(5) **28.** (−14)(4)(6)(9)

2.5 In Exercises 29–32, find the quotient.

29. $\frac{96}{-8}$ **30.** $\frac{-48}{-12}$ **31.** $\frac{0}{4}$ **32.** $\frac{-80}{5}$

2.5 **33.** Find the mean of the data: −8, 6, 3, −20, −9, 4.

2.6 Evaluate the expression. Justify each step.

34. −28 + (74 − 32) **35.** $7\left(2 \cdot \frac{3}{7}\right)$ **36.** (−7.2 + 3.5) + (−3.5)

2.7 Use the distributive property to evaluate or simplify the expression.

37. −5(−3 + 8) **38.** $3(m - 4)$ **39.** $-1(4 + 9r)$ **40.** $8(-4j - 3)$

2.7 Simplify the expression by combining like terms.

41. $-x + 3y - 5y + 6x$ **42.** $2(3k - 6) + 4 + 5k$ **43.** $5a - 3(2a + b) - 7b$

2.8 Plot the point in a coordinate plane and describe its location.

44. $A(3, -2)$ **45.** $B(5, 1)$ **46.** $C(0, -4)$ **47.** $D(-1, -3)$

Chapter 3

Extra Practice

3.1 Solve the equation. Check your solution.

1. $n - 3 = 5$ **2.** $36 = p + 20$ **3.** $-4 = h - 9$ **4.** $27 + z = 51$

3.2 Solve the equation. Check your solution.

5. $32 = \frac{x}{2}$ **6.** $11k = -55$ **7.** $76 = 19r$ **8.** $\frac{y}{-1.4} = -5$

3.3 Solve the equation. Check your solution.

9. $5a - 2 = 33$ **10.** $\frac{d}{3} + 8 = -6$ **11.** $-1 = 14 - 2h$ **12.** $84 - z = 96$

13. $\frac{c}{4} + 7 = 12$ **14.** $47 = -6y + 5$ **15.** $73 = 15 - b$ **16.** $55 = 7t - 8$

3.4 In Exercises 17 and 18, translate the statement into an equation. Then solve the equation.

17. Five less than the product of 6 and a number is 13.

18. The sum of 5 and the quotient of a number and 3 is -1.

3.4 **19.** An auto repair shop charges \$48 per hour for labor plus the cost of parts. Your car needs new parts that cost \$129, and the total cost is \$201. How much time is required to repair the car?

3.5 Find the area and perimeter of the triangle.

20.

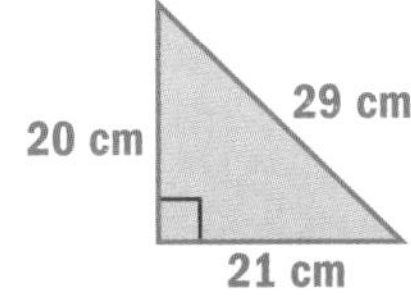

21.

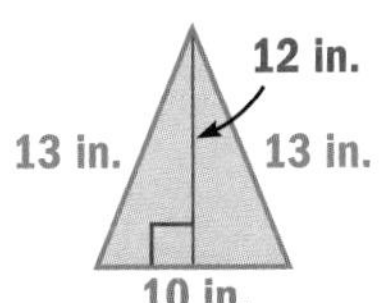

22.

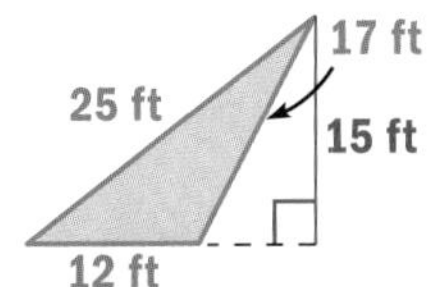

3.5 **23.** A rectangle has an area of 60 square meters and a length of 12 meters. What is the width of the rectangle? What is the perimeter?

3.5 **24.** A square has an area of 81 square feet. What is the length of each side?

3.6 Solve the inequality. Then graph its solution.

25. $4 + j \geq -1$ **26.** $0 < m - 6$ **27.** $z + 4.5 \leq 2$ **28.** $-38 > t - 46$

3.7 Solve the inequality. Then graph its solution.

29. $5x < -25$ **30.** $3 \leq -\frac{1}{3}y$ **31.** $2 \geq \frac{s}{4}$ **32.** $-13k > -65$

Chapter 4

4.1 Write the prime factorization of the number.

1. 72 **2.** 65 **3.** 153 **4.** 196

4.1 Factor the monomial.

5. $25pq$ **6.** $7a^3$ **7.** $22xy^2$ **8.** $54s^2t$

4.2 Find the greatest common factor of the numbers or monomials.

9. 45, 75 **10.** 108, 162 **11.** $6bc, 35abc^2$ **12.** $4p^2, 18qr$

13. $21mn, 9km^2$ **14.** $14x^2y^3, 28xy^2$ **15.** $34w^2z^2, 51w^5z^4$ **16.** $abcdf, a^2d^3gh$

4.3 Write the fraction in simplest form.

17. $\frac{32}{64}$ **18.** $\frac{-15}{39}$ **19.** $\frac{-22}{77}$ **20.** $\frac{17}{51}$

21. $\frac{10x}{45xy}$ **22.** $\frac{-16mn}{40mn}$ **23.** $\frac{-6ab}{4bc}$ **24.** $\frac{28rs}{7rst}$

4.4 Find the least common multiple of the numbers or monomials.

25. 30, 60 **26.** $4x, 18xy^2$ **27.** $5ab^2, 3bc^2$ **28.** $12x^3y, 8x^2y^4$

4.5 Copy and complete the statement with <, >, or =.

29. $\frac{7}{8} \underline{?} \frac{9}{11}$ **30.** $3\frac{3}{5} \underline{?} \frac{11}{3}$ **31.** $\frac{17}{6} \underline{?} 2\frac{13}{18}$ **32.** $1\frac{10}{15} \underline{?} \frac{35}{21}$

33. $\frac{11}{10} \underline{?} 1\frac{1}{8}$ **34.** $\frac{4}{5} \underline{?} \frac{6}{11}$ **35.** $\frac{50}{9} \underline{?} 5\frac{2}{7}$ **36.** $\frac{63}{15} \underline{?} 4\frac{5}{12}$

4.6 Simplify the expression. Write your answer as a power.

37. $z^5 \cdot z$ **38.** $5^8 \cdot 5^4$ **39.** $(-7)^6 \cdot (-7)^3$ **40.** $a^2 \cdot a^4$

41. $\frac{6^9}{6^5}$ **42.** $\frac{(-8)^{12}}{(-8)^2}$ **43.** $\frac{(-v)^7}{(-v)^4}$ **44.** $\frac{c^9}{c}$

4.7 Simplify. Write the expression using only positive exponents.

45. $6k^{-1}$ **46.** $a^3 \cdot a^{-3}$ **47.** $\frac{s^{-3}}{s^4}$ **48.** $n^{-4} \cdot n^{-2}$

4.8 Write the number in scientific notation.

49. 124,000,000 **50.** 0.0000005 **51.** 0.0000791 **52.** 32,100

4.8 Write the number in standard form.

53. 2.7×10^{-3} **54.** 9.09×10^2 **55.** 5.88×10^{11} **56.** 6.2×10^{-8}

Chapter 5

Find the sum or difference.

5.1 **1.** $\frac{7}{8} + \frac{5}{8}$ **2.** $5\frac{1}{5} - 3\frac{4}{5}$ **3.** $-\frac{11m}{15} + \frac{m}{15}$ **4.** $-\frac{5a}{9b} - \frac{4a}{9b}$

5.2 **5.** $\frac{9}{10} - \frac{5}{6}$ **6.** $\frac{2}{5} - \frac{3}{7}$ **7.** $4\frac{1}{4} + 3\frac{7}{8}$ **8.** $-\frac{5}{12} + \frac{11}{16}$

5.3 **Find the product.**

9. $\frac{7}{8} \cdot \frac{3}{14}$ **10.** $5 \cdot \left(-3\frac{1}{4}\right)$ **11.** $-\frac{5}{18} \cdot 1\frac{1}{3}$ **12.** $-1\frac{3}{5} \cdot \left(-2\frac{1}{4}\right)$

5.4 **Find the quotient.**

13. $\frac{5}{9} \div 2$ **14.** $-\frac{7}{12} \div \frac{2}{3}$ **15.** $4\frac{1}{8} \div \left(-1\frac{1}{3}\right)$ **16.** $-2\frac{1}{2} \div (-10)$

5.5 **Write the fraction or mixed number as a decimal. Write the decimal as a fraction or mixed number.**

17. $-\frac{48}{125}$ **18.** $4\frac{11}{12}$ **19.** -0.28 **20.** $0.\overline{72}$

21. 0.006 **22.** -8.34 **23.** $3\frac{7}{8}$ **24.** $-\frac{16}{250}$

5.5 **Order the numbers from least to greatest.**

25. $-\frac{7}{3}, -2\frac{5}{12}, -2.43, -2.5, -2\frac{2}{5}$ **26.** $\frac{18}{5}, 3\frac{1}{3}, 3.8, 3.55, 3\frac{7}{12}$

27. $\frac{26}{5}, 5.3, 5\frac{2}{9}, 5.21, 5\frac{3}{8}$ **28.** $-4.2, -4\frac{1}{6}, -\frac{59}{14}, -4\frac{3}{7}, -4.04$

5.6 **Find the sum or difference.**

29. $7.21 + (-3.4)$ **30.** $-9.8 + (-3.7)$ **31.** $0.8 - (-12.3)$ **32.** $8.217 - 9.68$

33. $-10.2 + (-6.35)$ **34.** $-8.78 + 3.9$ **35.** $3.28 - 11.395$ **36.** $-0.04 - 5.789$

5.7 **Find the product or quotient.**

37. $-8.32 \cdot (-0.47)$ **38.** $-20.51 \cdot 3.14$ **39.** $0.435 \div 0.29$ **40.** $2.072 \div (-0.74)$

41. $4.7 \cdot (-6.78)$ **42.** $-0.14 \cdot (-9.43)$ **43.** $-19.27 \div 2.35$ **44.** $0.224 \div 5.6$

5.8 **Find the mean, median, mode(s), and range of the data.**

45. Finishing times for a race in minutes: 24, 37, 57, 81, 31, 25, 43, 39, 33, 40, 34, 65, 50

46. Daily low temperatures: −6°F, −7°F, −6°F, 5°F, 3°F, 0°F, −3°F

47. Grades on quizzes: 93, 84, 100, 95, 89, 78, 78, 85, 83, 95

Chapter 6

Solve the equation. Then check the solution.

6.1 **1.** $6k - 8 - 4k = 6$ **2.** $16 = 2(s + 9) - 4$ **3.** $5(n + 7) + 1 = -9$

4. $-8 = -3m + 2 + 5m$ **5.** $\frac{7a - 2}{3} = 4$ **6.** $2 = \frac{3 - 4t}{5}$

6.2 **7.** $3a + 2 = 7a + 10$ **8.** $9y - 8 = 6y + 7$ **9.** $5x + 7 = 8(x - 1)$

10. $13v = 7(9 - v)$ **11.** $5(w + 3) = -10w$ **12.** $2(z + 5) = 3z + 14$

6.3 **13.** $2.8y + 8.6 = 9.12 - 1.2y$ **14.** $7.25p - 3 + p = 14.325$ **15.** $7 - 2.65z = -4.4z$

16. $x - \frac{2}{3}x = \frac{3}{4}$ **17.** $\frac{9}{10}n + \frac{1}{5} = \frac{7}{10}n - \frac{3}{5}$ **18.** $\frac{6}{4}r - \frac{21}{8} = \frac{3}{4}r$

6.4 **Find the indicated measurement, where r = radius, d = diameter, and C = circumference. Use 3.14 or $\frac{22}{7}$ for π. Explain your choice of value for π.**

19. $r = \underline{?}$

20. $C = \underline{?}$

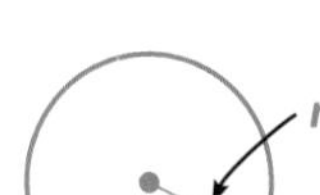

21. $r = \underline{?}$

22. $d = \underline{?}$

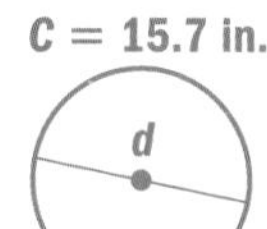

6.5 **Solve the inequality. Then graph the solution.**

23. $19 - 8c > 3$ **24.** $2(7 + n) \leq -10$ **25.** $5s + 3 \geq -7 - 5s$

26. $20 - 11x \geq -2$ **27.** $4(b - 3) > 20$ **28.** $-6y - 13 < 11 + 2y$

6.6 **In Exercises 29–32, write the sentence as an inequality. Let n represent the unknown number. Then solve the inequality.**

29. Twelve more than half a number is at most 8.

30. The difference of 3 times a number and 2 is greater than 7.

31. Four times a number is no less than 16.

32. The quotient of 18 and 6 times a number is less than 3.

6.6 **33.** You want to ride your bike for at least 28 miles. You have already biked for 10 miles. If you bike at a speed of 12 miles per hour, how much longer do you need to bike?

6.6 **34.** Nathan has $20 to spend at a carnival. The carnival has a $10 entrance fee. Ride tickets cost $.75 each. What number of tickets can Nathan buy?

Chapter 7

7.1 **A baseball team had 12 wins, 4 losses, and 2 ties in one season. Write the ratio as a fraction in simplest form and two other ways.**

1. wins to losses

2. losses to games played

3. wins to games played

7.1 **Write the equivalent rate.**

4. $\frac{9000 \text{ tickets}}{6 \text{ hours}} = \frac{? \text{ tickets}}{\text{hour}}$

5. $\frac{240 \text{ tickets}}{\text{hour}} = \frac{? \text{ tickets}}{\text{minute}}$

6. $\frac{7 \text{ meters}}{\text{second}} = \frac{? \text{ meters}}{\text{minute}}$

7.2 **Solve the proportion. Then check your solution.**

7. $\frac{x}{18} = \frac{25}{2}$

8. $\frac{4}{9} = \frac{5}{y}$

9. $\frac{3.6}{n} = \frac{4.8}{12.4}$

10. $\frac{m}{6} = \frac{35}{42}$

7.3 **Use a percent proportion.**

11. 9 is what percent of 75?

12. 42 is 25% of what number?

13. What number is 7% of 128?

14. 7 is what percent of 56?

7.4 **Write the decimal or fraction as a percent.**

15. 0.125

16. 1.42

17. $\frac{18}{25}$

18. $\frac{197}{200}$

7.4 **Write the percent as a decimal and as a fraction.**

19. 31%

20. 55%

21. 175%

22. 1.28%

7.5 **In Exercises 23–25, tell whether the change is an *increase* or *decrease*. Then find the percent of change.**

23. Original amount: 25
New amount: 28

24. Original amount: 144
New amount: 126

25. Original amount: 5000
New amount: 4950

7.6 **26.** A pair of shoes has a wholesale price of $28. The percent markup is 110%. What is the retail price?

7.6 **27.** Your food bill at a restaurant is $18.40. You leave a 15% tip. The sales tax is 5%. Find the total cost of the meal.

7.7 **Solve using the percent equation.**

28. What number is 121% of 412?

29. 13 is 15.6% of what number?

30. 57 is what percent of 76?

31. What number is 0.3% of 28?

7.8 **A bag contains 12 slips of paper numbered from 1 through 12. A slip of paper is chosen at random. Find the probability of the event.**

32. Drawing a number greater than 4

33. Drawing a number that is divisible by 5

Chapter 8

8.1 Find the measure(s) of the numbered angle(s).

1.

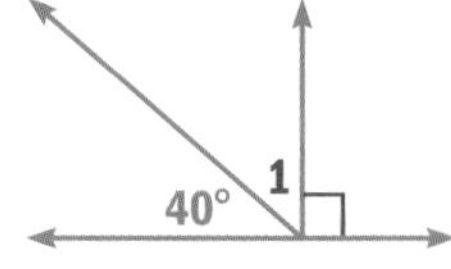

2.

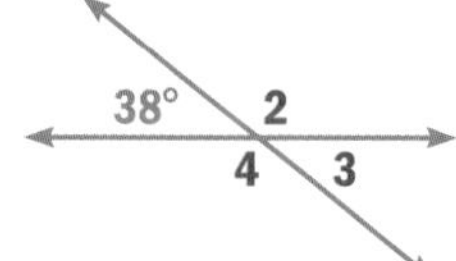

3.

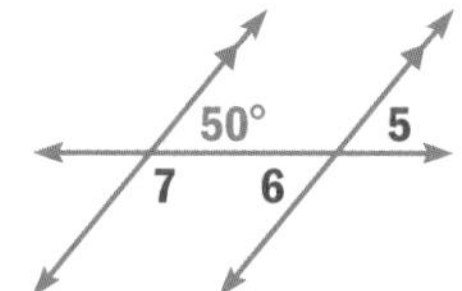

8.2 Find the value of *x*. Classify the triangle by its angles.

4.

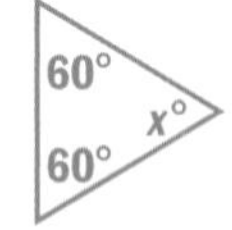

5.

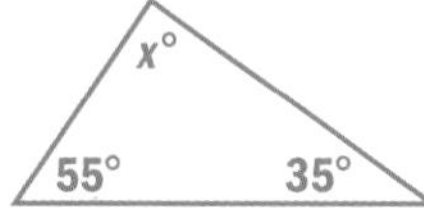

6.

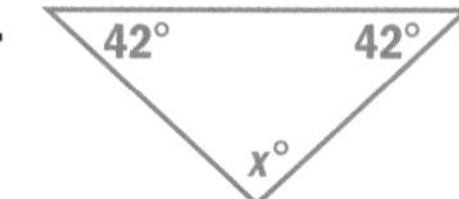

8.3 In Exercises 7–9, classify the quadrilateral.

7.

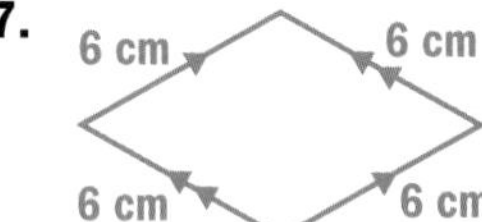

8.

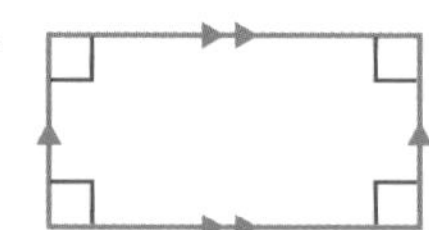

9.

8.4 **10.** Find the sum of the angle measures in an 11-gon.

8.4 **11.** Find the measure of one angle in a regular 18-gon.

8.5 In Exercises 12–14, use the diagrams.

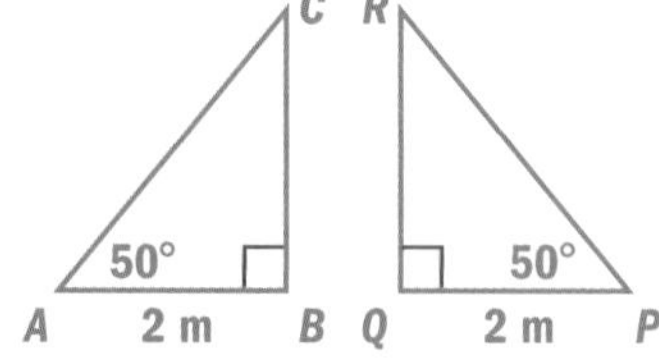

12. Name all pairs of congruent sides.

13. Name all pairs of congruent angles.

14. Explain how you know that $\triangle ABC \cong \triangle PQR$.

Graph $\triangle ABC$ with vertices $A(-2, 4)$, $B(0, 2)$, and $C(-2, -6)$. Then graph its image after the given transformation.

8.6 **15.** Reflect $\triangle ABC$ in the x-axis.

8.6 **16.** Reflect $\triangle ABC$ in the y-axis.

8.7 **17.** Translate $\triangle ABC$ using $(x, y) \rightarrow (x - 1, y + 4)$.

8.7 **18.** Translate $\triangle ABC$ using $(x, y) \rightarrow (x + 2, y - 3)$.

8.7 **19.** Rotate $\triangle ABC$ 90° clockwise.

8.8 **20.** Dilate $\triangle ABC$ by a scale factor of 2.

8.8 **21.** Dilate $\triangle ABC$ by a scale factor of $\frac{1}{2}$.

Chapter 9

9.1 Use a calculator to approximate the square root. Round to the nearest tenth.

1. $\sqrt{52}$ **2.** $\sqrt{9.6}$ **3.** $-\sqrt{738}$ **4.** $-\sqrt{2037}$

9.1 Solve the equation. Check your solutions.

5. $k^2 = 900$ **6.** $h^2 - 5 = 44$ **7.** $153 + z^2 = 378$ **8.** $168 = v^2 - 1$

9. $a^2 + 7 = 88$ **10.** $m^2 = 3600$ **11.** $x^2 - 11 = 53$ **12.** $w^2 + 78 = 478$

9.2 In Exercises 13–16, graph the pair of numbers on a number line. Then copy and complete the statement with <, >, or =.

13. $\sqrt{18}\ \underline{?}\ 4$ **14.** $\sqrt{\frac{9}{16}}\ \underline{?}\ \frac{3}{4}$ **15.** $-8\ \underline{?}\ -\sqrt{70}$ **16.** $\frac{2}{3}\ \underline{?}\ \sqrt{\frac{1}{9}}$

9.2 **17.** Order the decimals 0.12, $0.\overline{1}$, $0.\overline{12}$, 0.123, and $0.\overline{123}$.

9.2 **18.** Order the decimals 0.34, $0.\overline{3}$, $.\overline{34}$, and 0.334 from least to greatest.

9.3 Let *a* and *b* represent the lengths of the legs of a right triangle, and let *c* represent the length of the hypotenuse. Find the unknown length.

19. $a = 21, b = 28, c = \underline{?}$ **20.** $a = \underline{?}, b = 63, c = 65$ **21.** $a = 56, b = \underline{?}, c = 65$

22. $a = 1.5, b = 3.6, c = \underline{?}$ **23.** $a = \underline{?}, b = 100, c = 125$ **24.** $a = 32, b = \underline{?}, c = 68$

9.4 Determine whether the numbers form a Pythagorean triple.

25. 40, 42, 58 **26.** 37, 39, 54 **27.** 15, 112, 113 **28.** 12, 35, 38

9.5 Find the values of the variables. Give exact answers.

29.

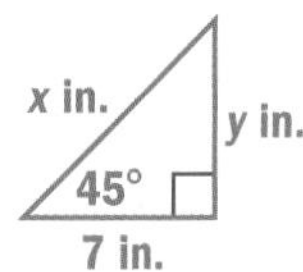

30.

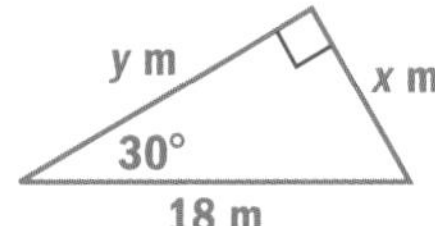

31.

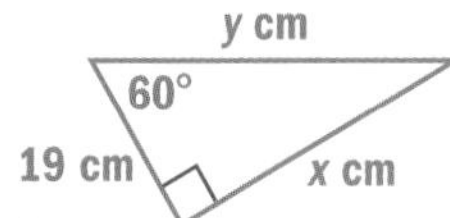

9.6 In $\triangle ABC$, write the sine, cosine, and tangent ratios for $\angle A$ and $\angle B$.

32.

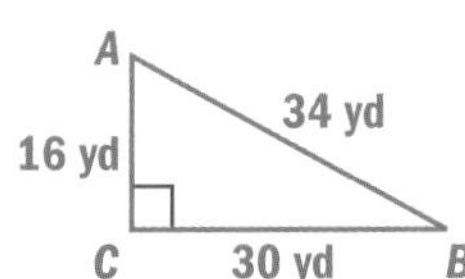

33.

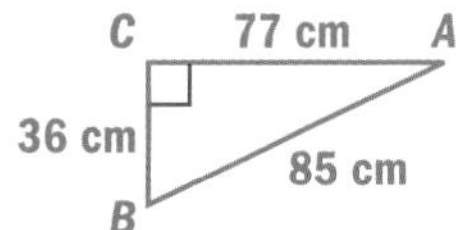

34.

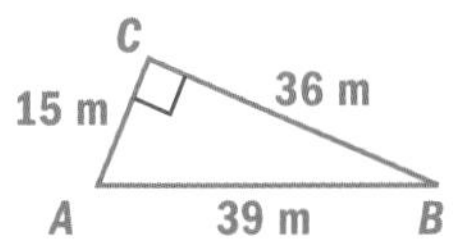

9.6 **35.** Use a calculator to approximate the sine, cosine, and tangent of 62°. Round your answers to four decimal places.

Extra Practice

Chapter 10

10.1 Sketch a parallelogram with base *b* and height *h* and find its area.

1. $b = 15$ in., $h = 13$ in. **2.** $b = 9.4$ ft, $h = 4.8$ ft **3.** $b = 8\frac{1}{3}$ cm, $h = 1\frac{1}{5}$ cm

10.1 Sketch a trapezoid with bases b_1 and b_2 and height *h* and find its area.

4. $b_1 = 9$ m, $b_2 = 16$ m, $h = 18$ m **5.** $b_1 = 40$ yd, $b_2 = 28$ yd, $h = 10.5$ yd

10.2 In Exercises 6–13, find the area of the circle given its radius *r* or diameter *d*. Use 3.14 for π.

6. $r = 18$ mi **7.** $d = 80$ in. **8.** $d = 11$ mm **9.** $r = 2.9$ ft

10. $d = 7.8$ in. **11.** $r = 0.3$ cm **12.** $r = 11$ ft **13.** $d = 16$ mi

10.3 **14.** How many faces, edges, and vertices does a hexagonal pyramid have?

10.3 **15.** Show two ways to represent a cylinder. Tell whether it is a polyhedron.

10.4 Draw a net for the solid. Then find the surface area. Round to the nearest tenth.

16.

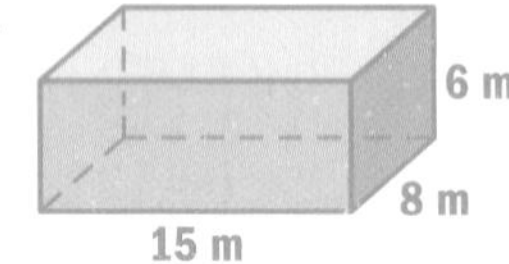

17.

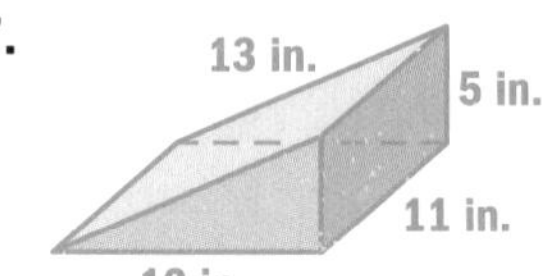

18.

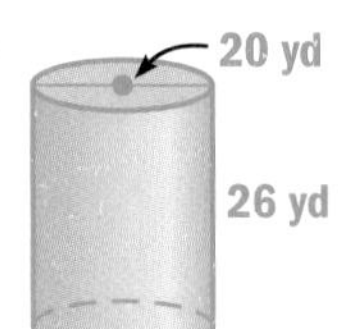

10.5 Find the surface area of the solid. Round to the nearest tenth.

19. A square pyramid with base side length 12 m and slant height 9 m

20. A cone with radius 8 cm and slant height 9 cm

21. A cone with diameter 15 m and slant height 8.2 m

10.6 Find the volume of the solid. Round to the nearest tenth.

22. The prism in Exercise 16

23. The prism in Exercise 17

24. The cylinder in Exercise 18

10.7 Find the volume of the solid. Round to the nearest tenth.

25. A square pyramid with base side length 10 ft and height 8 ft

26. A cone with radius 18 m and height 6 m

27. The triangular pyramid shown at the right

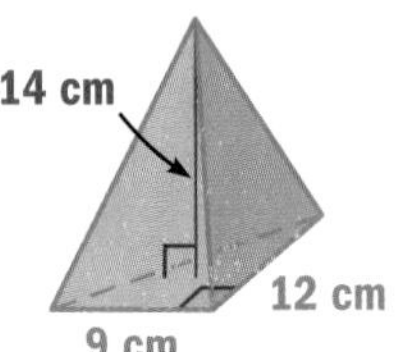

Chapter 11

11.1 **1.** Decide whether the relation $(-3, 3)$, $(-2, 2)$, $(-1, 1)$, $(0, 0)$, $(1, 1)$ is a function. Explain your answer.

11.1 **2.** Make an input-output table for the function $y = 0.5x$. Use a domain of -4, -2, 0, 2, and 4. Identify the range.

11.1 **3.** Write a function rule that relates x and y.

Input x	-5	-3	-1	1
Output y	-6	-4	-2	0

11.2 **4.** Make a scatter plot of the data in Exercise 3. Describe the relationship between x and y.

11.3 Tell whether the ordered pair is a solution of the equation.

5. $y = 3x - 7$; $(1, 4)$ **6.** $4x + y = 5$; $(2, -1)$ **7.** $y = \frac{1}{2}x + \frac{1}{2}$; $(-3, -1)$

11.3 List four solutions of the equation.

8. $y = -x - 3$ **9.** $y = 7 + 2x$ **10.** $y = -\frac{2}{3}x$ **11.** $y = -x$

12. $-x + y = 1$ **13.** $3x + y = -2$ **14.** $x + 2y = 8$ **15.** $-3y + 4x = 7$

11.4 Graph the linear equation.

16. $y = -3$ **17.** $y = \frac{1}{4}x - 2$ **18.** $x = 4$ **19.** $3x + y = 4$

11.5 In Exercises 20–23, find the intercepts of the graph of the equation.

20. $y = -2x + 4$ **21.** $y = 5x - 1$ **22.** $x + 5y = -5$ **23.** $2x - 3y = 12$

11.5 **24.** Graph the line with an x-intercept of 4 and a y-intercept of -1.

11.5 **25.** Graph the line with an x-intercept of -2 and a y-intercept of 10.

11.6 Find the slope of the line passing through the points.

26. $(-2, 3)$, $(6, 1)$ **27.** $(5, 0)$, $(5, -9)$ **28.** $(6, -4)$, $(2, -4)$ **29.** $(7, -5)$, $(-2, -14)$

30. $(-7, 8)$, $(-9, 5)$ **31.** $(-3, -2)$, $(-7, 2)$ **32.** $(4, 9)$, $(3, 13)$ **33.** $(0, 7)$, $(-3, -10)$

11.7 Find the slope and *y*-intercept of the graph of the equation.

34. $y = 3x - 5$ **35.** $y = 2$ **36.** $y = -\frac{1}{3}x + 1$ **37.** $2x - y = 8$

11.8 Graph the inequality.

38. $y > -x - 3$ **39.** $6 \le 3y$ **40.** $5 + 2x > y$ **41.** $4x + 3y \le -12$

Chapter 12

In Exercises 1–3, use the following lengths, in inches, of alligators at an alligator farm: 140, 127, 103, 140, 118, 100, 117, 101, 116, 129, 130, 105, 99, 143.

12.1 **1.** Make an ordered stem-and-leaf plot of the data. Identify the interval that includes the most data values.

12.1 **2.** Find the median and range of the data.

12.2 **3.** Make a box-and-whisker plot of the data. What conclusions can you make?

12.3 **4.** In a survey about favorite kinds of movies, 20 people chose dramas, 4 chose horror movies, 8 chose science fiction, and 18 chose comedies. Represent the data in a circle graph.

12.3 **5.** You want to display the average monthly price of a stock for each month in 2001. What type of display would you use? Explain.

12.4 **6.** You can take one of three different classes in the morning or the afternoon. Make a tree diagram to find the number of choices that are possible.

12.4 **7.** A license plate has 3 digits followed by 3 letters. How many different license plates are possible?

12.5 **In Exercises 8–11, find the number of permutations.**

8. $_7P_2$ **9.** $_{11}P_1$ **10.** $_8P_5$ **11.** $_{10}P_3$

12.5 **12.** There are 8 students in the school play. How many different ways can the cast be arranged in a row?

12.6 **In Exercises 13–16, find the number of combinations.**

13. $_5C_4$ **14.** $_{20}C_2$ **15.** $_6C_3$ **16.** $_{12}C_9$

12.6 **17.** A CD case holds 30 CDs. How many ways can you select 3 CDs from the case?

12.7 **18.** A telephone number is chosen at random. Find the odds that the last digit is greater than 3.

12.8 **19.** You flip two coins. Find the probability that you do *not* get two heads.

12.8 **20.** You and two friends each roll a number cube. What is the probability that all of you roll a 3?

12.8 **21.** Ten slips of paper numbered 1 through 10 are placed in a bag. You draw a slip at random and draw another without replacing the first. Find the probability that both numbers are odd.

Chapter 13

13.1 In Exercises 1–3, simplify the polynomial and write it in standard form.

1. $3 + 5x - x^2 - 7x + 4$ **2.** $2t^4 + t^3 - 6 - 3t^3 + t^2$ **3.** $4(5 - k) + 4k - k^2 + 1$

13.1 **4.** The height, in feet, of a falling pebble after t seconds of falling from a height of 45 feet can be found using the polynomial $-16t^2 + 45$. Find the pebble's height after 1.5 seconds.

13.2 Find the sum or difference.

5. $(3x^2 + 5x - 4) + (-2x^3 + x^2 + 9x)$ **6.** $(-8x^2 - x + 1) - (7x^2 - 5x + 1)$

7. $(4x^3 - 8x^2 + 2) - (x^3 + x^2 - 6x + 5)$ **8.** $(-x^2 - 3x + 7) + (x^2 + 4x - 9)$

9. $(2x^3 - 2x^2 + 1) + (-x^3 + 9x + 5)$ **10.** $(3x^2 - 5x - 10) - (5x^3 + x - 2)$

13.3 Simplify the expression.

11. $(4z)(-7z^5)$ **12.** $(-r^2)(-3r^2)$ **13.** $-3n(2n - 5)$ **14.** $q^3(-q + 2)$

15. $(5ab)^3$ **16.** $(-rst)^4$ **17.** $(p^6)^4$ **18.** $(3y^5)^2$

13.4 Find the product and simplify.

19. $(2x + 1)(x - 5)$ **20.** $(m - 3)(-m + 4)$ **21.** $(d + 6)(d + 4)$

22. $(4y - 3)(4y + 3)$ **23.** $(a - 8)(a - 7)$ **24.** $(5x + 2)(2x - 1)$

13.5 Rewrite using function notation.

25. $y = 2x - 5$ **26.** $y = 3x^2$ **27.** $y = 5x^2 + 1$

13.5 Evaluate the function for $x = -2, -1, 0, 1,$ and 2.

28. $f(x) = 2x^2 + x$ **29.** $f(x) = \frac{1}{4}x^2$ **30.** $f(x) = \frac{1}{2}x^2 - x$

31. $f(x) = -3x^2 + 2x$ **32.** $f(x) = x^2 + 4x$ **33.** $f(x) = -x^2 - 3$

13.5 Graph the function using a table of values.

34. $f(x) = 3x^2$ **35.** $f(x) = -x^2 + 2$ **36.** $f(x) = 2x^2 - 4$

13.5 Tell whether the graph represents a function.

37.

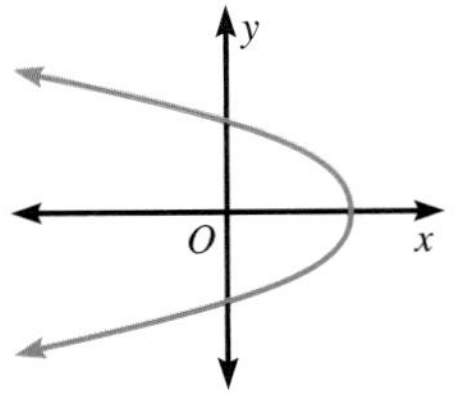

38.

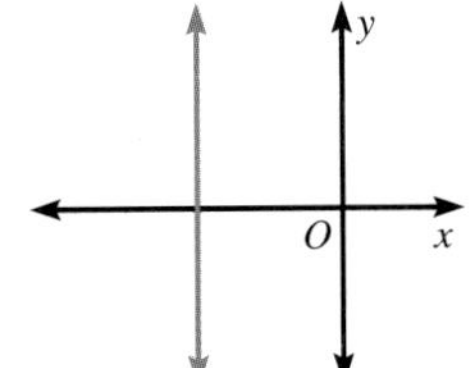

39.

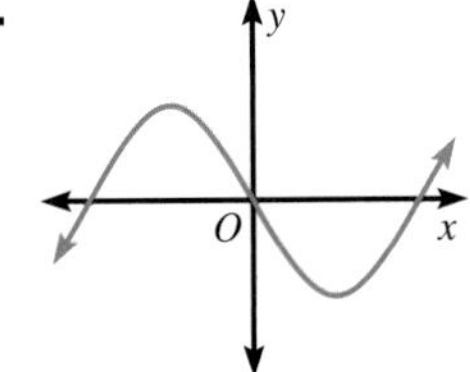

Extra Practice

Table of Symbols

Symbol	Meaning	Page
28.6	decimal point	**4**
$=$	equals, is equal to	**10, 28**
$3 \cdot x$ $3(x)$ $3x$	3 times x	**10, 15**
$\frac{14}{2}$	14 divided by 2	**11**
( )	parentheses—a grouping symbol	**11**
[ ]	brackets—a grouping symbol	**11**
4^3	$4 \cdot 4 \cdot 4$	**20**
$\stackrel{?}{=}$	is equal to?	**26, 29**
$\neq$	is not equal to	**29**
∟	right angle	**33, 375**
$\approx$	is approximately equal to	**39**
$\ldots$	continues on	**53**
-3	negative 3	**53**
-3	the opposite of 3	**54**
$\lvert a \rvert$	the absolute value of a number a	**54**
(x, y)	ordered pair	**91**
$<$	is less than	**141, 302**
$>$	is greater than	**141, 302**
$\leq$	is less than or equal to	**141, 302**
$\geq$	is greater than or equal to	**141, 302**

Symbol	Meaning	Page
$1.1\overline{6}$	repeating decimal 1.16666. . .	**242**
π	pi—a number approximately equal to 3.14	**290**
$a:b, \frac{a}{b}$	ratio of a to b	**317**
%	percent	**327**
$^\circ$	degree(s)	**375, 721**
$\angle A$	angle with vertex point A	**375, 719**
$m\angle B$	the measure of angle B	**375**
$\perp$	is perpendicular to	**376**
$\parallel$	is parallel to	**377**
⟷ ⟷	parallel lines	**377**
$\cong$	is congruent to	**397**
$\overline{AB}$	line segment AB	**397**
$\triangle ABC$	triangle with vertices A, B, and C	**398**
A'	the image of point A	**404**
$\sim$	is similar to	**416**
$\sqrt{a}$	the positive square root of a number a where $a \geq 0$	**431**
$\pm$	plus or minus	**433**
$\nleq$	is not less than or equal to	**583**
3!	3 factorial, or $3 \cdot 2 \cdot 1$	**623**
$f(x)$	the function of f at x	**680**
$\overleftrightarrow{AB}$	line AB	**718**
$\overrightarrow{AB}$	ray AB	**718**

Table of Measures

Time

60 seconds (sec) = 1 minute (min)
60 minutes = 1 hour (h)
24 hours = 1 day (d)
7 days = 1 week (wk)
4 weeks (approx.) = 1 month

365 days, 52 weeks (approx.), 12 months = 1 year
10 years = 1 decade
100 years = 1 century

METRIC	UNITED STATES CUSTOMARY
Length	**Length**
10 millimeters (mm) = 1 centimeter (cm)	12 inches (in.) = 1 foot (ft)
100 cm, 1000 mm = 1 meter (m)	36 in., 3 ft = 1 yard (yd)
1000 m = 1 kilometer (km)	5280 ft, 1760 yd = 1 mile (mi)
Area	**Area**
100 square millimeters (mm^2) = 1 square centimeter (cm^2)	144 square inches $(in.^2)$ = 1 square foot (ft^2)
10,000 cm^2 = 1 square meter (m^2)	9 ft^2 = 1 square yard (yd^2)
10,000 m^2 = 1 hectare (ha)	43,560 ft^2, 4840 yd^2 = 1 acre (A)
Volume	**Volume**
1000 cubic millimeters (mm^3) = 1 cubic centimeter (cm^3)	1728 cubic inches $(in.^3)$ = 1 cubic foot (ft^3)
1,000,000 cm^3 = 1 cubic meter (m^3)	27 ft^3 = 1 cubic yard (yd^3)
Liquid Capacity	**Liquid Capacity**
1000 milliliters (mL), 1000 cubic centimeters (cm^3) = 1 liter (L)	8 fluid ounces (fl oz) = 1 cup (c)
1000 L = 1 kiloliter (kL)	2 c = 1 pint (pt)
	2 pt = 1 quart (qt)
	4 qt = 1 gallon (gal)
Mass	**Weight**
1000 milligrams (mg) = 1 gram (g)	16 ounces (oz) = 1 pound (lb)
1000 g = 1 kilogram (kg)	2000 lb = 1 ton
1000 kg = 1 metric ton (t)	
Temperature Degrees Celsius (°C)	**Temperature** Degrees Fahrenheit (°F)
0°C = freezing point of water	32°F = freezing point of water
37°C = normal body temperature	98.6°F = normal body temperature
100°C = boiling point of water	212°F = boiling point of water

Table of Formulas

Geometric Formulas

Rectangle (p. 33)

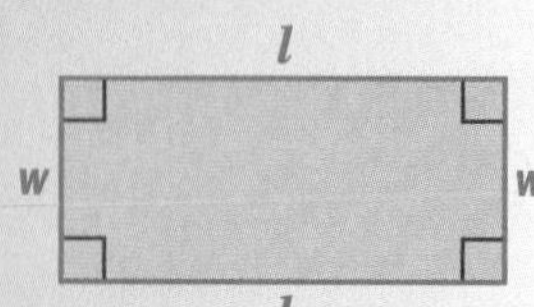

Area
$A = lw$

Perimeter
$P = 2l + 2w$

Square (p. 33)

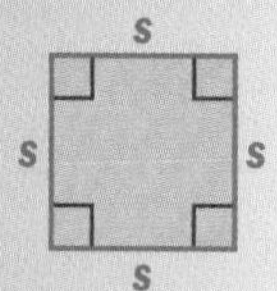

Area
$A = s^2$

Perimeter
$P = 4s$

Triangle (p. 134)

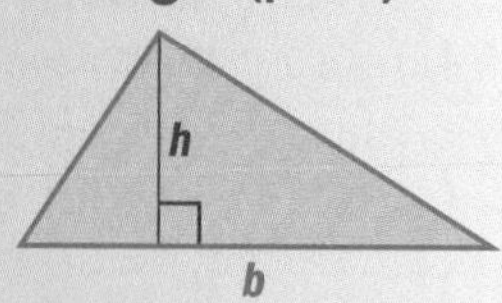

Area
$A = \frac{1}{2}bh$

Parallelogram (p. 481)

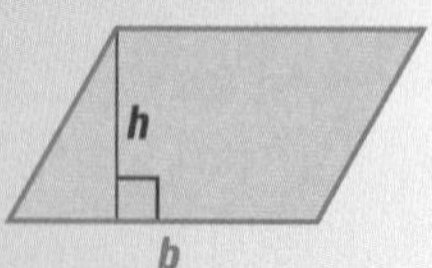

Area

$A = bh$

Trapezoid (p. 482)

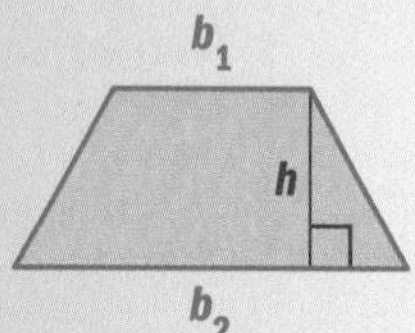

Area

$A = \frac{1}{2}(b_1 + b_2)h$

Circle (pp. 290, 486)

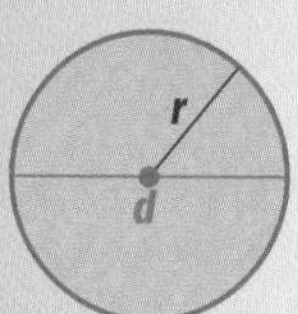

Area
$A = \pi r^2$

Circumference
$C = \pi d$ or
$C = 2\pi r$

Prism (pp. 503, 513)

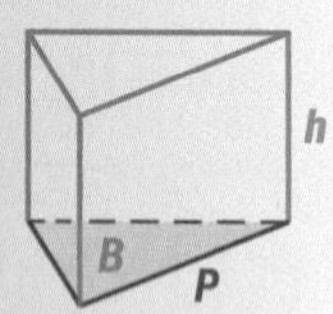

Surface Area
$S = 2B + Ph$

Volume
$V = Bh$

Cylinder (pp. 504, 514)

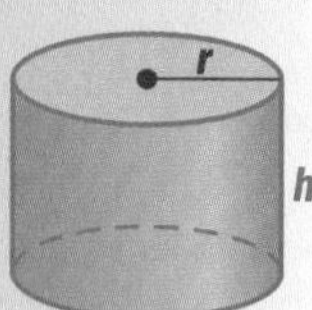

Surface Area
$S = 2\pi r^2 + 2\pi rh$

Volume
$V = \pi r^2 h$

Pyramid (pp. 507, 519)

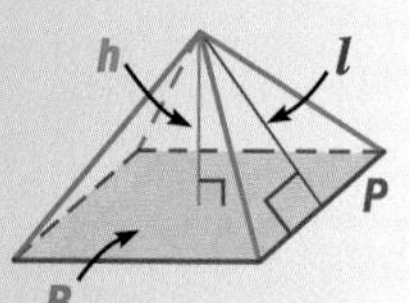

Surface Area
$S = B + \frac{1}{2}Pl$

Volume
$V = \frac{1}{3}Bh$

Cone (pp. 508, 520)

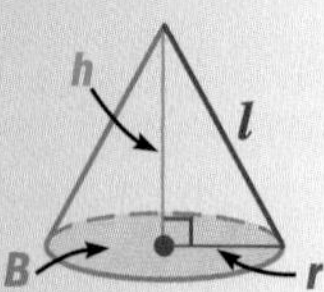

Surface Area
$S = \pi r^2 + \pi rl$

Volume
$V = \frac{1}{3}Bh = \frac{1}{3}\pi r^2 h$

Other Formulas

Distance traveled (p. 34)	$d = rt$ where d = distance, r = rate, and t = time
Simple interest (p. 348)	$I = Prt$ where I = simple interest, P = principal, r = annual interest rate, and t = time in years
Pythagorean theorem (p. 443)	In a right triangle, $a^2 + b^2 = c^2$ where a and b are the lengths of the legs, and c is the length of the hypotenuse.

Table of Properties

Identity Properties (pp. 59, 71)

Addition The sum of a number and the additive identity, 0, is the number.

Numbers $7 + 0 = 7$

Algebra $a + 0 = a$

Multiplication The product of a number and the multiplicative identity, 1, is the number.

Numbers $3 \cdot 1 = 3$

Algebra $a \cdot 1 = a$

Inverse Properties (pp. 61, 73, 234)

Addition The sum of a number and its additive inverse, or opposite, is 0.

Numbers $4 + (-4) = 0$

Algebra $a + (-a) = 0$

Multiplication The product of a nonzero number and its multiplicative inverse, or reciprocal, is 1.

Numbers $\frac{2}{3} \cdot \frac{3}{2} = 1$

Algebra $\frac{a}{b} \cdot \frac{b}{a} = 1\ (a, b \neq 0)$

Commutative Property (p. 80)

Addition In a sum, you can add terms in any order.

Numbers $-2 + 5 = 5 + (-2)$

Algebra $a + b = b + a$

Multiplication In a product, you can multiply factors in any order.

Numbers $3(-6) = -6(3)$

Algebra $ab = ba$

Associative Property (p. 81)

Addition Changing the grouping of terms in a sum will not change the sum.

Numbers $(2 + 4) + 6 = 2 + (4 + 6)$

Algebra $(a + b) + c = a + (b + c)$

Multiplication Changing the grouping of factors in a product will not change the product.

Numbers $(6 \times 2.5) \times 4 = 6 \times (2.5 \times 4)$

Algebra $(ab)c = a(bc)$

Distributive Property (p. 85)

You can multiply a number and a sum by multiplying each term of the sum by the number and then adding these products. The same property applies to subtraction.

Numbers $3(4 + 6) = 3(4) + 3(6)$ $\quad 2(8 - 5) = 2(8) - 2(5)$

Algebra $a(b + c) = a(b) + a(c)$ $\quad a(b - c) = a(b) - a(c)$

Properties of Exponents (pp. 196, 197)

To find the *product of powers* with the same base, add their exponents.

Numbers $5^2 \cdot 5^3 = 5^{2+3} = 5^5$

Algebra $a^b \cdot a^c = a^{b+c}$

To find the *quotient of powers* with the same nonzero base, subtract the denominator's exponent from the numerator's exponent.

Numbers $\frac{7^4}{7^2} = 7^{4-2} = 7^2$ **Algebra** $\frac{a^b}{a^c} = a^{b-c}$

Cross Products Property (p. 323)

The cross products of a proportion are equal.

Numbers Because $\frac{3}{4} = \frac{6}{8}$, $3 \cdot 8 = 4 \cdot 6$.

Algebra If $\frac{a}{b} = \frac{c}{d}$, then $ad = bc$, $b, d \neq 0$.

Finding Squares and Square Roots

EXAMPLE 1 Finding a Square

Find 54^2.

Find 54 in the column labeled *No.* (an abbreviation for *Number*). Read across to the column labeled *Square*.

No.	Square	Sq. Root
51	2601	7.141
52	2704	7.211
53	2809	7.280
54	2916	7.348
55	3025	7.416

ANSWER So, $54^2 = 2916$.

EXAMPLE 2 Finding a Square Root

Find a decimal approximation of $\sqrt{54}$.

Find 54 in the column labeled *No.* Read across to the column labeled *Sq. Root*.

No.	Square	Sq. Root
51	2601	7.141
52	2704	7.211
53	2809	7.280
54	2916	7.348
55	3025	7.416

ANSWER So, to the nearest thousandth, $\sqrt{54} \approx 7.348$.

EXAMPLE 3 Finding a Square Root

Find a decimal approximation of $\sqrt{3000}$.

Find the two numbers in the *Square* column that 3000 is between. Read across to the column labeled *No.*; $\sqrt{3000}$ is between 54 and 55, but closer to 55.

No.	Square	Sq. Root
51	2601	7.141
52	2704	7.211
53	2809	7.280
54	2916	7.348
55	3025	7.416

ANSWER So, $\sqrt{3000} \approx 55$. A more accurate approximation can be found using a calculator: 54.772256.

Table of Squares and Square Roots

No.	Square	Sq. Root
1	1	1.000
2	4	1.414
3	9	1.732
4	16	2.000
5	25	2.236
6	36	2.449
7	49	2.646
8	64	2.828
9	81	3.000
10	100	3.162
11	121	3.317
12	144	3.464
13	169	3.606
14	196	3.742
15	225	3.873
16	256	4.000
17	289	4.123
18	324	4.243
19	361	4.359
20	400	4.472
21	441	4.583
22	484	4.690
23	529	4.796
24	576	4.899
25	625	5.000
26	676	5.099
27	729	5.196
28	784	5.292
29	841	5.385
30	900	5.477
31	961	5.568
32	1024	5.657
33	1089	5.745
34	1156	5.831
35	1225	5.916
36	1296	6.000
37	1369	6.083
38	1444	6.164
39	1521	6.245
40	1600	6.325
41	1681	6.403
42	1764	6.481
43	1849	6.557
44	1936	6.633
45	2025	6.708
46	2116	6.782
47	2209	6.856
48	2304	6.928
49	2401	7.000
50	2500	7.071

No.	Square	Sq. Root
51	2601	7.141
52	2704	7.211
53	2809	7.280
54	2916	7.348
55	3025	7.416
56	3136	7.483
57	3249	7.550
58	3364	7.616
59	3481	7.681
60	3600	7.746
61	3721	7.810
62	3844	7.874
63	3969	7.937
64	4096	8.000
65	4225	8.062
66	4356	8.124
67	4489	8.185
68	4624	8.246
69	4761	8.307
70	4900	8.367
71	5041	8.426
72	5184	8.485
73	5329	8.544
74	5476	8.602
75	5625	8.660
76	5776	8.718
77	5929	8.775
78	6084	8.832
79	6241	8.888
80	6400	8.944
81	6561	9.000
82	6724	9.055
83	6889	9.110
84	7056	9.165
85	7225	9.220
86	7396	9.274
87	7569	9.327
88	7744	9.381
89	7921	9.434
90	8100	9.487
91	8281	9.539
92	8464	9.592
93	8649	9.644
94	8836	9.695
95	9025	9.747
96	9216	9.798
97	9409	9.849
98	9604	9.899
99	9801	9.950
100	10,000	10.000

No.	Square	Sq. Root
101	10,201	10.050
102	10,404	10.100
103	10,609	10.149
104	10,816	10.198
105	11,025	10.247
106	11,236	10.296
107	11,449	10.344
108	11,664	10.392
109	11,881	10.440
110	12,100	10.488
111	12,321	10.536
112	12,544	10.583
113	12,769	10.630
114	12,996	10.677
115	13,225	10.724
116	13,456	10.770
117	13,689	10.817
118	13,924	10.863
119	14,161	10.909
120	14,400	10.954
121	14,641	11.000
122	14,884	11.045
123	15,129	11.091
124	15,376	11.136
125	15,625	11.180
126	15,876	11.225
127	16,129	11.269
128	16,384	11.314
129	16,641	11.358
130	16,900	11.402
131	17,161	11.446
132	17,424	11.489
133	17,689	11.533
134	17,956	11.576
135	18,225	11.619
136	18,496	11.662
137	18,769	11.705
138	19,044	11.747
139	19,321	11.790
140	19,600	11.832
141	19,881	11.874
142	20,164	11.916
143	20,449	11.958
144	20,736	12.000
145	21,025	12.042
146	21,316	12.083
147	21,609	12.124
148	21,904	12.166
149	22,201	12.207
150	22,500	12.247

Equivalent Fractions, Decimals, and Percents

Fraction	Decimal	Percent
$\frac{1}{10}$	0.1	10%
$\frac{1}{8}$	0.125	$12\frac{1}{2}\%$
$\frac{1}{5}$	0.2	20%
$\frac{1}{4}$	0.25	25%
$\frac{3}{10}$	0.3	30%
$\frac{1}{3}$	$0.\overline{3}$	$33\frac{1}{3}\%$
$\frac{3}{8}$	0.375	$37\frac{1}{2}\%$
$\frac{2}{5}$	0.4	40%
$\frac{1}{2}$	0.5	50%
$\frac{3}{5}$	0.6	60%
$\frac{5}{8}$	0.625	$62\frac{1}{2}\%$
$\frac{2}{3}$	$0.\overline{6}$	$66\frac{2}{3}\%$
$\frac{7}{10}$	0.7	70%
$\frac{3}{4}$	0.75	75%
$\frac{4}{5}$	0.8	80%
$\frac{7}{8}$	0.875	$87\frac{1}{2}\%$
$\frac{9}{10}$	0.9	90%
1	1	100%

Glossary

a

	Example
absolute value **(p. 54)** The absolute value of a number a is the distance between a and 0 on a number line. The absolute value of a is written $\|a\|$.	$\|4\| = 4$ $\|-7\| = 7$ $\|0\| = 0$
acute angle **(p. 382)** An angle whose measure is less than 90°.	
acute triangle **(p. 382)** A triangle with three acute angles.	60° 50° 70°
addition property of equality **(p. 110)** Adding the same number to each side of an equation produces an equivalent equation.	If $x - 5 = 2$, then $x - 5 + 5 = 2 + 5$, so $x = 7$. If $x - a = b$, then $x - a + a = b + a$.
additive identity **(p. 59)** The number 0 is the additive identity because the sum of any number and 0 is the original number.	$-7 + 0 = -7$ $a + 0 = a$
additive inverse **(p. 61)** The additive inverse of a number a is the opposite of the number, or $-a$. The sum of a number and its additive inverse is 0.	The additive inverse of 6 is -6, so $6 + (-6) = 0$.
angle **(p. 719)** A figure formed by two rays that begin at a common point, called the vertex.	ray vertex ray
angle of rotation **(p. 410)** In a rotation, the angle formed by two rays drawn from the center of rotation through corresponding points on the original figure and its image.	*See* rotation.
annual interest rate **(p. 348)** In simple interest, the percent of the principal earned or paid per year.	*See* simple interest.
area **(p. 33)** The number of square units covered by a figure.	2 units 7 units *Area* = 14 square units
associative property of addition **(p. 81)** Changing the grouping of terms in a sum does not change the sum.	$(9 + 4) + 6 = 9 + (4 + 6)$ $(a + b) + c = a + (b + c)$
associative property of multiplication **(p. 81)** Changing the grouping of factors in a product does not change the product.	$(2 \cdot 5) \cdot 3 = 2 \cdot (5 \cdot 3)$ $(ab)c = a(bc)$

b

	Example
bar graph (p. 5) A type of graph in which the lengths of bars are used to represent and compare data in categories.	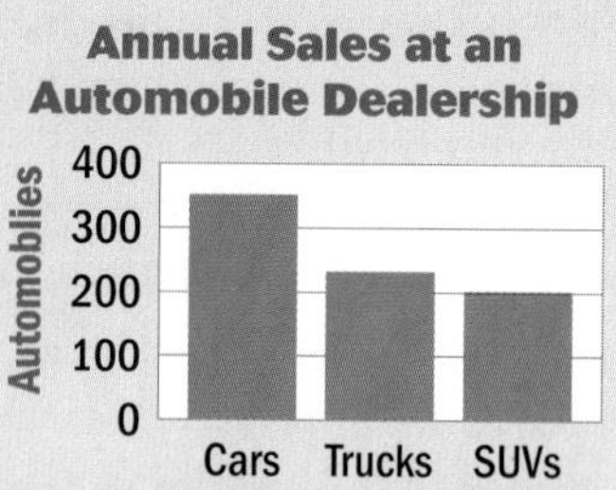 **Annual Sales at an Automobile Dealership** Automobiles: 400, 300, 200, 100, 0 Cars, Trucks, SUVs
base of a parallelogram (p. 481) The length of any side of the parallelogram can be used as the base.	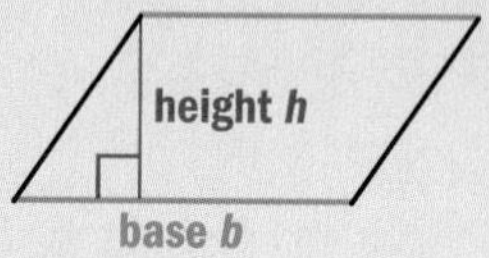 height h base b
base of a power (p. 20) The number or expression that is used as a factor in a repeated multiplication.	In the power 5^3, the base is 5.
base of a triangle (p. 134) The length of any side of the triangle can be used as the base.	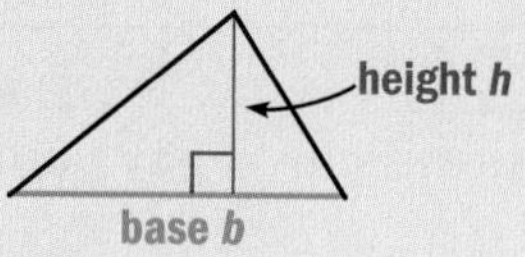 height h base b
bases of a trapezoid (p. 482) The lengths of the parallel sides of the trapezoid.	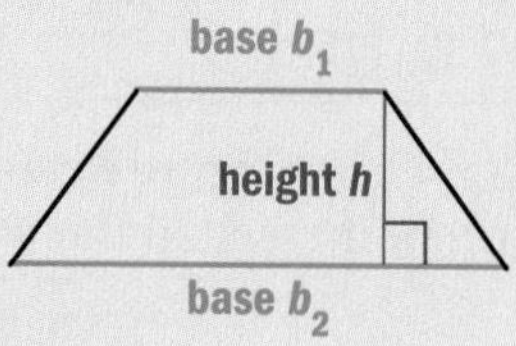 base b_1 height h base b_2
biased sample (p. 644) A sample that is not representative of the population from which it is selected	The members of a soccer team are a biased sample if you want to find the average time students spend playing sports each week.
binomial (p. 657) A polynomial with two terms.	$7y^4 + 9$
box-and-whisker plot (p. 601) A data display that divides a data set into four parts using the lower extreme, lower quartile, median, upper quartile, and upper extreme.	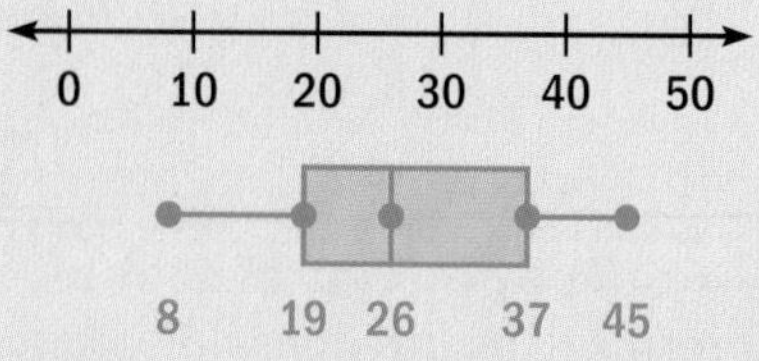 0 10 20 30 40 50 8 19 26 37 45

c

center of a circle (p. 290) The point inside the circle that is the same distance from all points on the circle.	*See* circle.

	Example
center of rotation **(p. 410)** The point about which a figure is turned when the figure undergoes a rotation.	*See* rotation.
circle **(p. 290)** The set of all points in a plane that are the same distance, called the radius, from a fixed point, called the center.	radius center diameter circumference
circle graph **(p. 331, 605)** A circle graph displays data as sections of a circle. The entire circle represents all the data. Each section is labeled using the actual data or using data expressed as fractions, decimals, or percents of the sum of the data.	Siblings Three or more 25% None 10% Two 25% One 40%
circumference **(p. 290)** The distance around a circle.	*See* circle.
coefficient **(p. 86)** The number part of a term that includes a variable.	The coefficient of $7x$ is 7.
combination **(p. 627)** A grouping of objects in which the order is not important.	There are 6 combinations of 2 letters chosen from VASE: VA VS VE AS AE SE
common factor **(p. 173)** A whole number that is a factor of two or more nonzero whole numbers.	The common factors of 8 and 12 are 1, 2, and 4.
common multiple **(p. 186)** A multiple that is shared by two or more numbers.	The common multiples of 4 and 6 are 12, 24, 36, ...
commutative property of addition **(p. 80)** In a sum, you can add terms in any order.	$4 + 7 = 7 + 4$ $a + b = b + a$
commutative property of multiplication **(p. 80)** In a product, you can multiply factors in any order.	$5(-8) = -8(5)$ $ab = ba$
complementary angles **(p. 375)** Two angles whose measures have a sum of 90°.	32° 58°
complementary events **(p. 632)** Two events are complementary when one event or the other (but not both) must occur.	When rolling a number cube, the events "getting an odd number" and "getting an even number" are complementary events.

Glossary

	Example
composite number (p. 169) A whole number greater than 1 that has positive factors other than 1 and itself.	6 is a composite number because its factors are 1, 2, 3, and 6.
cone (p. 492) A solid with one circular base.	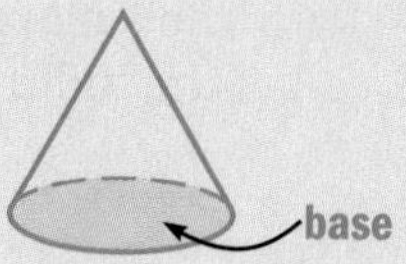 base
congruent angles (p. 397) Angles that have the same measure.	*See* congruent polygons.
congruent polygons (p. 397) Similar polygons that have the same size. For congruent polygons, corresponding angles are congruent and corresponding sides are congruent. The symbol ≅ indicates congruence and is read "is congruent to."	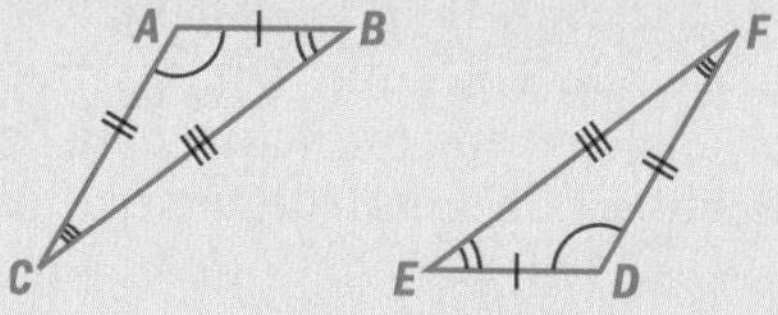 A B C E D F $\triangle ABC \cong \triangle DEF$
congruent sides (p. 397) Sides that have the same length.	*See* congruent polygons.
constant term (p. 86) A term that has a number but no variable.	In the expression $5y + 9$, the term 9 is a constant term.
converse (p. 444) An if-then statement where the hypothesis and conclusion of the original statement have been reversed.	Original: If you clean your room, then it will be neat. Converse: If your room is neat, then you cleaned it.
coordinate plane (p. 91) A coordinate system formed by the intersection of a horizontal number line, called the x-axis, and a vertical number line, called the y-axis.	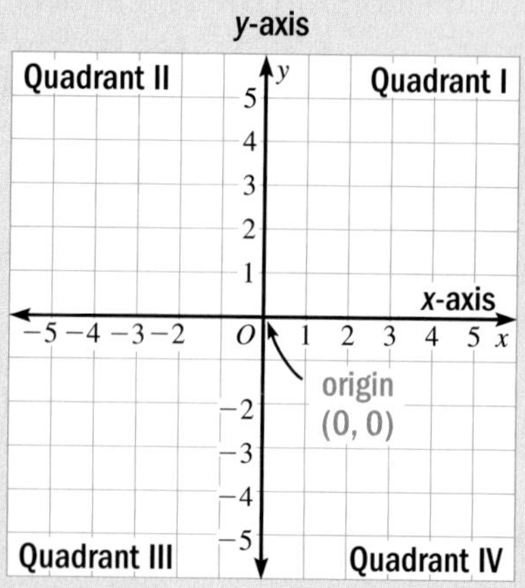 y-axis Quadrant II Quadrant I x-axis origin (0, 0) Quadrant III Quadrant IV

	Example
corresponding angles **(p. 377)** Angles that occupy corresponding positions when a line intersects two other lines.	 $\angle 1$ and $\angle 2$ are corresponding angles.
corresponding parts **(p. 397)** Pairs of sides and angles of polygons that are in the same relative position.	 $\angle A$ and $\angle E$ are corresponding angles. $\overline{AB}$ and $\overline{ED}$ are corresponding sides.
cosine **(p. 463)** The cosine of any acute angle A of a right triangle is the ratio of the adjacent leg to the hypotenuse.	 $\cos A = \frac{b}{c}$
counting principle **(p. 619)** If one event can occur in m ways, and for each of these a second event can occur in n ways, then the number of ways that the two events can occur together is $m \cdot n$. The counting principle can be extended to three or more events.	If a T-shirt is made in 5 sizes and in 7 colors, then the number of different T-shirts that are possible is $5 \cdot 7 = 35$.
cross products **(p. 323)** In a proportion $\frac{a}{b} = \frac{c}{d}$ where $b \neq 0$ and $d \neq 0$, the cross products are ad and bc.	The cross products of the proportion $\frac{2}{3} = \frac{4}{6}$ are $2 \cdot 6$ and $3 \cdot 4$.
cylinder **(p. 492)** A solid with two congruent circular bases that lie in parallel planes.	
d	
data **(p. 5)** Information, facts, or numbers that describe something.	Numbers of cars sold annually at a dealership: 340, 350, 345, 347, 352, 360, 365
degrees **(p. 721)** Unit of measure for angles. The symbol for degrees is °. There are 360° in a circle.	

Glossary

	Example
dependent events (p. 639) Two events such that the occurrence of one affects the likelihood that the other will occur.	A bag contains 5 red and 8 blue marbles. You randomly choose a marble, do not replace it, then randomly choose another marble. The events "first marble is red" and "second marble is red" are dependent events.
diameter of a circle (p. 290) The distance across the circle through the center.	*See* circle.
dilation (p. 418) A transformation that stretches or shrinks a figure.	The scale factor is $\frac{1}{2}$.
discount (p. 342) A decrease in the price of an item.	The original price of a pair of jeans is \$42 but the store sells it for \$29.99. The discount is \$12.01.
distributive property (p. 85) For all numbers a, b, and c, $a(b + c) = ab + ac$ and $a(b - c) = ab - ac$.	$8(10 + 4) = 8(10) + 8(4)$ $3(4 - 2) = 3(4) - 3(2)$
division property of equality (p. 114) Dividing each side of an equation by the same nonzero number produces an equivalent equation.	If $6x = 54$, then $\frac{6x}{6} = \frac{54}{6}$, so $x = 9$. If $ax = b$ and $a \neq 0$, then $\frac{ax}{a} = \frac{b}{a}$.
domain of a function (p. 542) The set of all possible input values for the function.	*See* function.
e	
edge of a polyhedron (p. 492) A line segment where two faces of the polyhedron meet.	face edge vertex

	Example
equation (p. 28) A mathematical sentence formed by setting two expressions equal.	$3 \cdot 6 = 18$ and $x + 7 = 12$ are equations.
equilateral triangle (p. 382) A triangle with three congruent sides.	
equivalent equations (p. 109) Equations that have the same solution(s).	$2x - 6 = 0$ and $2x = 6$ are equivalent equations because the solution of both equations is 3.
equivalent fractions (p. 179) Fractions that represent the same part-to-whole relationship. Equivalent fractions have the same simplest form.	$\frac{6}{8}$ and $\frac{9}{12}$ are equivalent fractions that both represent $\frac{3}{4}$.
equivalent inequalities (p. 141) Inequalities that have the same solution.	$3x \leq 12$ and $x \leq 4$ are equivalent inequalities because the solution of both inequalities is all numbers less than or equal to 4.
equivalent ratios (p. 317) Ratios that have the same value.	$\frac{15}{12}$ and $\frac{25}{20}$ are equivalent ratios because $\frac{15}{12} = 1.25$ and $\frac{25}{20} = 1.25$.
evaluate (p. 10) To find the value of an expression with one or more operations.	$4(3) + 6 \div 2 = 15$
event (p. 354) A collection of outcomes of an experiment.	An event for rolling a number cube is "getting a number divisible by 3."
experimental probability (p. 355) A probability based on a sample or repeated trials of an experiment. The experimental probability of an event is given by: $P(\text{event}) = \frac{\text{Number of favorable outcomes}}{\text{Number of trials or items in sample}}$	During one month, your school bus is on time 17 out of 22 school days. The experimental probability that the bus is on time is: $P(\text{bus is on time}) = \frac{17}{22} \approx 0.773$
exponent (p. 20) A number or expression that represents how many times a base is used as a factor in a repeated multiplication.	In the power 5^3, the exponent is 3.

f

	Example
face of a polyhedron (p. 492) A polygon that is a side of the polyhedron.	*See* edge of a polyhedron.
factor tree (p. 169) A diagram that can be used to write the prime factorization of a number.	54 6 × 9 2 × 3 × 3 × 3
factorial (p. 623) The expression $n!$ is read "n factorial" and represents the product of all integers from 1 to n.	$4! = 4 \cdot 3 \cdot 2 \cdot 1 = 24$
favorable outcomes (p. 354) Outcomes corresponding to a specified event.	When rolling a number cube, the favorable outcomes for the event "getting a number greater than 4" are 5 and 6.
formula (p. 33) An equation that relates two or more quantities such as perimeter, length, and width.	$P = 2l + 2w$
fraction (p. 179) A number of the form $\frac{a}{b}$ ($b \neq 0$) where a is called the numerator and b is called the denominator.	$\frac{5}{7}$ and $\frac{18}{10}$ are fractions.
frequency (p. 6) The number of data values that lie in an interval of a frequency table or histogram.	*See* frequency table *and* histogram.
frequency table (p. 6) A table used to group data values into intervals.	(see table below)
front-end estimation (p. 248) A method for estimating the sum of two or more numbers. In this method, you add the front-end digits, estimate the sum of the remaining digits, and then add the results.	To estimate $3.81 + 1.32 + 5.74$, first add the front-end digits: $3 + 1 + 5 = 9$. Then estimate the sum of the remaining digits: $0.81 + (0.32 + 0.74) \approx 1 + 1 = 2$. The sum is about $9 + 2 = 11$.
function (p. 541) A pairing of each number in a given set with exactly one number in another set. Starting with a number called an input, the function associates with it exactly one number called an output.	(see table below) The input-output table above represents a function.

Frequency table example:

Interval	Tally	Frequency
0–9	||	2
10–19	||||	4
20–29	~~||||~~	5

Function example:

Input x	1	2	3	4
Output y	2	4	6	8

Glossary

	Example
function notation **(p. 680)** An equation that uses $f(x)$ to represent the output of the function f for an input of x.	$f(x) = 5x + 13$ is written using function notation.
g	
graph of an inequality **(p. 140)** On a number line, the set of points that represents the solution of the inequality. (*See* half-plane.)	The graph of the inequality $x < 2$ is shown below. −3 −2 −1 0 1 2 3
greatest common factor (GCF) **(p. 173)** The greatest whole number that is a factor of two or more nonzero whole numbers.	The GCF of 18 and 27 is 9. The GCF of 48, 24, and 36 is 12.
h	
half-plane **(p. 584)** The graph of a linear inequality in two variables.	$y \geq x + 3$
height of a parallelogram **(p. 481)** The perpendicular distance between a side whose length is the base and the opposite side.	*See* base of a parallelogram.
height of a trapezoid **(p. 482)** The perpendicular distance between the bases of the trapezoid.	*See* bases of a trapezoid.
height of a triangle **(p. 134)** The perpendicular distance between a side whose length is the base and the vertex opposite that side.	*See* base of a triangle.
heptagon **(p. 390)** A polygon with seven sides.	
hexagon **(p. 390)** A polygon with six sides.	

Glossary

	Example
histogram **(p. 6)** A graph that displays data from a frequency table. A histogram has one bar for each interval of the frequency table. The height of the bar indicates the frequency for the interval.	**Library Visitors on a Saturday** Frequency: 0, 1, 2, 3, 4, 5, 6 Age (years): 0–9, 10–19, 20–29, 30–39, 40–49
hypotenuse **(p. 443)** The side of a right triangle that is opposite the right angle.	hypotenuse, leg, leg
I	
identity property of addition **(p. 59)** The sum of a number and the additive identity, 0, is the number.	$8 + 0 = 8$ $a + 0 = a$
identity property of multiplication **(p. 71)** The product of a number and the multiplicative identity, 1, is the number.	$4 \cdot 1 = 4$ $a \cdot 1 = a$
image **(p. 404)** The new figure formed by a transformation.	*See* reflection, rotation, *and* translation.
improper fraction **(p. 707)** A fraction whose numerator is greater than or equal to its denominator.	$\frac{8}{7}$ is an improper fraction.
independent events **(p. 639)** Two events such that the occurrence of one does not affect the likelihood that the other will occur.	You toss a coin and roll a number cube. The events "getting heads" and "getting a 6" are independent events.
inequality **(p. 140)** A mathematical sentence formed by placing an inequality symbol between two expressions.	$3 < 5$ and $x + 2 \geq -4$ are inequalities.
input **(p. 541)** A number on which a function operates. An input value is in the domain of the function.	*See* function.
integers **(p. 53)** The numbers . . . , −4, −3, −2, −1, 0, 1, 2, 3, 4, . . . consisting of the negative integers, zero, and the positive integers.	−8 and 14 are integers. $-8\frac{1}{3}$ and 14.5 are *not* integers.

	Example
interest **(p. 348)** The amount earned or paid for the use of money.	*See* simple interest.
inverse operations **(p. 109)** Operations that "undo" each other.	Addition and subtraction are inverse operations. Multiplication and division are also inverse operations.
inverse property of addition **(p. 61)** The sum of a number and its additive inverse, or opposite, is 0.	$5 + (-5) = 0$ $a + (-a) = 0$
inverse property of multiplication **(pp. 73, 234)** The product of a nonzero number and its multiplicative inverse, or reciprocal, is 1.	$\frac{3}{4} \cdot \frac{4}{3} = 1$ $\frac{a}{b} \cdot \frac{b}{a} = 1 \quad (a, b \neq 0)$
irrational number **(p. 437)** A real number that cannot be written as a quotient of two integers. The decimal form of an irrational number neither terminates nor repeats.	$\sqrt{2}$ and 0.313113111. . . are irrational numbers.
isosceles triangle **(p. 382)** A triangle with at least two congruent sides.	

L

leading digit **(p. 251)** The first nonzero digit in a number.	The leading digit of 725 is 7. The leading digit of 0.002638 is 2.
least common denominator (LCD) **(p. 192)** The least common multiple of the denominators of two or more fractions.	The LCD of $\frac{7}{10}$ and $\frac{3}{4}$ is 20, the least common multiple of 10 and 4.
least common multiple (LCM) **(p. 186)** The least number that is a common multiple of two or more whole numbers.	The LCM of 4 and 6 is 12. The LCM of 3, 5, and 10 is 30.
legs of a right triangle **(p. 443)** The two sides of a right triangle that form the right angle.	*See* hypotenuse.
like terms **(p. 86)** Terms that have identical variable parts raised to the same power. (Two or more constant terms are considered like terms.)	In the expression $x + 4 - 2x + 1$, x and $-2x$ are like terms, and 4 and 1 are like terms.
linear equation **(p. 556)** An equation in which the variables appear in separate terms and each variable occurs only to the first power.	$7y = 14x + 21$ is a linear equation.

	Example
linear function **(pp. 556, 681)** A function whose graph is a line or part of a line.	$y = -x + 1$
linear inequality **(p. 583)** An inequality in which the variables appear in separate terms and each variable occurs only to the first power.	$y \leq 2x + 5$ is a linear inequality
line graph **(pp. 606, 725)** A type of graph in which points representing data pairs are connected by line segments. A line graph is used to show how a quantity changes over time.	Average Price of Gold
line of reflection **(p. 404)** The line over which a figure is flipped when the figure undergoes a reflection.	*See* reflection.
line of symmetry **(p. 406)** A line that divides a figure into two parts that are mirror images of each other.	*See* line symmetry.
line symmetry **(p. 406)** A figure has line symmetry if it can be divided by a line, called a line of symmetry, into two parts that are mirror images of each other.	A square has 4 lines of symmetry.
lower extreme **(p. 601)** The least value in a data set.	*See* box-and-whisker plot.
lower quartile **(p. 601)** The median of the lower half of a data set.	*See* box-and-whisker plot.
m	
markup **(p. 342)** The increase in the wholesale price of an item.	The wholesale price of a loaf of bread is \$1 but the store sells it for \$1.59. The markup is \$.59.

	Example
mean **(pp. 75, 257)** The sum of the values in a data set divided by the number of values.	The mean of the data set 85, 59, 97, 71 is $\frac{85 + 59 + 97 + 71}{4} = \frac{312}{4} = 78$.
median **(p. 257)** The middle value in a data set when the values are written in numerical order. If the data set has an even number of values, the median is the mean of the two middle values.	The median of the data set 8, 17, 21, 23, 26, 29, 34, 40, 45 is the middle value, 26.
mixed number **(p. 707)** A number that has a whole number part and a fraction part.	$3\frac{2}{5}$ is a mixed number.
mode **(p. 257)** The value in a data set that occurs most often. A data set can have no mode, one mode, or more than one mode.	The mode of the data set 73, 42, 55, 77, 61, 55, 68 is 55 because it occurs most often.
monomial **(p. 170, 657)** A number, a variable, or a product of a number and one or more variables.	$3xy$, $8x^2$, x, and 14 are monomials.
multiple **(p. 186)** A multiple of a number is the product of the number and any nonzero whole number.	The multiples of 3 are 3, 6, 9, ...
multiplication property of equality **(p. 113)** Multiplying each side of an equation by the same nonzero number produces an equivalent equation.	If $\frac{x}{3} = 7$, then $3 \cdot \frac{x}{3} = 3 \cdot 7$, so $x = 21$. If $\frac{x}{a} = b$ and $a \neq 0$, then $a \cdot \frac{x}{a} = a \cdot b$.
multiplication property of zero **(p. 71)** The product of a number and 0 is 0.	$-4 \cdot 0 = 0$ $a \cdot 0 = 0$
multiplicative identity **(p. 71)** The number 1 is the multiplicative identity because the product of any number and 1 is the original number.	$9 \cdot 1 = 9$ $a \cdot 1 = a$
multiplicative inverse **(p. 73, 234)** The multiplicative inverse of a number $\frac{a}{b}$ $(a, b \neq 0)$ is the reciprocal of the number, or $\frac{b}{a}$. The product of a number and its multiplicative inverse is 1.	The multiplicative inverse of $\frac{3}{2}$ is $\frac{2}{3}$, so $\frac{3}{2} \cdot \frac{2}{3} = 1$.

n	Example
negative integers (p. 53) The integers that are less than zero.	The negative integers are $-1, -2, -3, -4, \ldots$.
net (p. 502) A two-dimensional representation of a solid. This pattern forms a solid when it is folded.	
numerical expression (p. 10) An expression consisting of numbers and operations.	$4(3) + 24 \div 2$

o	
obtuse angle (p. 382) An angle whose measure is greater than 90° and less than 180°.	
obtuse triangle (p. 382) A triangle with one obtuse angle.	120°, 35°, 25°
octagon (p. 390) A polygon with eight sides.	
odds in favor of an event (p. 633) The ratio of favorable outcomes to unfavorable outcomes.	The odds of rolling an even number on a six sided number cube is $\frac{3}{3}$, or 1.
opposites (p. 54) Two numbers that are the same distance from 0 on a number line but are on opposite sides of 0.	-3 and 3 are opposites.
order of operations (p. 10) A set of rules for evaluating an expression involving more than one operation.	To evaluate $3 + 2 \cdot 4$, you perform the multiplication before the addition: $3 + 2 \cdot 4 = 3 + 8 = 11$
ordered pair (p. 91) A pair of numbers (x, y) that can be used to represent a point in a coordinate plane. The first number is the x-coordinate, and the second number is the y-coordinate.	(−2, 1); 1; −2; x; y; −5 −4 −3; 1 2; 1 2

Glossary

	Example
origin **(p. 91)** The point (0, 0) where the x-axis and the y-axis meet in a coordinate plane.	*See* coordinate plane.
outcomes **(p. 354)** The possible results when an experiment is performed.	When tossing a coin, the outcomes are heads and tails.
output **(p. 541)** A number produced by evaluating a function using a given input. An output value is in the range of the function.	*See* function.
P	
parallel lines **(p. 377)** Two lines in the same plane that do not intersect. The symbol $\|$ is used to indicate parallel lines.	a, b; $a \parallel b$
parallelogram **(p. 386)** A quadrilateral with both pairs of opposite sides parallel.	
pentagon **(p. 390)** A polygon with five sides.	
percent **(p. 327)** A ratio whose denominator is 100. The symbol for percent is %.	$\frac{17}{20} = \frac{17 \cdot 5}{20 \cdot 5} = \frac{85}{100} = 85\%$
percent of change **(p. 338)** A percent that shows how much a quantity has increased or decreased in comparison with the original amount: $\text{Percent of change } p = \frac{\text{Amount of increase or decrease}}{\text{Original amount}}$	The percent of change p from 15 to 19 is: $p = \frac{19 - 15}{15} = \frac{4}{15} \approx 0.267 = 26.7\%$
percent of decrease **(p. 338)** The percent of change in a quantity when the new amount of the quantity is less than the original amount.	*See* percent of change.
percent of increase **(p. 338)** The percent of change in a quantity when the new amount of the quantity is greater than the original amount.	*See* percent of change.
perfect square **(p. 432)** A number that is the square of an integer.	49 is a perfect square because $49 = (\pm 7)^2$.

Glossary

	Example
perimeter **(p. 33)** The distance around a figure. For a figure with straight sides, the perimeter is the sum of the lengths of the sides.	7 ft; 4 ft; 4 ft; 7 ft *Perimeter* = 22 ft
permutation **(p. 623)** An arrangement of a group of objects in a particular order.	There are 6 permutations of the 3 letters in the word CAT: CAT ACT TCA CTA ATC TAC
perpendicular lines **(p. 376)** Two lines that intersect to form a right angle. The symbol ⊥ is used to indicate perpendicular lines.	a; b; $a \perp b$
pi (π) **(p. 290)** The ratio of the circumference of a circle to its diameter.	You can use 3.14 or $\frac{22}{7}$ to approximate π.
plane **(p. 718)** A plane can be thought of as a flat surface that extends without end.	
polygon **(p. 390)** A closed geometric figure made up of three or more line segments that intersect only at their endpoints.	**Polygon** **Not a polygon**
polyhedron **(p. 492)** A solid that is enclosed by polygons.	
polynomial **(p. 657)** A monomial or a sum of monomials.	*See* binomial, trinomial, monomial.
population **(p. 644)** In statistics, the entire group of people or objects about which you want information.	If a biologist wants to determine the average age of the elephants in a wildlife refuge, the population consists of every elephant in the refuge.
positive integers **(p. 53)** The integers that are greater than zero.	The positive integers are 1, 2, 3, 4, ...

	Example
power (p. 20) A product formed from repeated multiplication by the same number or expression. A power consists of a base and an exponent.	2^4 is a power with base 2 and exponent 4. $2^4 = 2 \cdot 2 \cdot 2 \cdot 2 = 16$
prime factorization (p. 169) Expressing a whole number as a product of prime numbers.	The prime factorization of 54 is $2 \times 3 \times 3 \times 3 = 2 \times 3^3$.
prime number (p. 169) A whole number greater than 1 whose only positive factors are 1 and itself.	5 is a prime number because its only positive factors are 1 and 5.
principal (p. 348) An amount of money that is deposited or borrowed.	*See* simple interest.
prism (p. 492) A solid, formed by polygons, that has two congruent bases lying in parallel planes.	
probability of an event (p. 354) A number from 0 to 1 that measures the likelihood that the event will occur.	*See* experimental probability *and* theoretical probability.
proportion (p. 322) An equation stating that two ratios are equivalent.	$\frac{3}{5} = \frac{6}{10}$ and $\frac{x}{12} = \frac{25}{30}$ are proportions.
pyramid (p. 492) A solid, formed by polygons, that has one base. The base can be any polygon, and the other faces are triangles.	
Pythagorean theorem (p. 443) For any right triangle, the sum of the squares of the lengths a and b of the legs equals the square of the length c of the hypotenuse: $a^2 + b^2 = c^2$.	$15^2 + 20^2 = 25^2$
Pythagorean triple (p. 451) A set of three positive integers a, b, and c such that $a^2 + b^2 = c^2$.	5, 12, and 13 is a Pythagorean triple.

q	Example
quadrant **(p. 91)** One of the four regions that a coordinate plane is divided into by the x-axis and the y-axis.	*See* coordinate plane.
quadrilateral **(p. 386)** A closed geometric figure made up of four line segments, called sides, that intersect only at their endpoints; a polygon with four sides.	
r	
radical expression **(p. 431)** An expression involving a radical sign, $\sqrt{\ }$.	$\sqrt{3(22+5)}$ is a radical expression.
radius of a circle **(p. 290)** The distance between the center and any point on the circle.	*See* circle.
random sample **(p. 644)** A sample selected in such a way that each member of the population has an equally likely chance to be part of the sample.	A random sample of 5 eighth graders can be selected by putting the names of all eighth graders in a hat and drawing 5 names without looking.
range of a data set **(p. 258)** The difference of the greatest and least values in the data set.	The range of the data set 60, 35, 22, 46, 81, 39 is $81 - 22 = 59$.
range of a function **(p. 542)** The set of all possible output values for the function.	*See* function.
rate **(p. 318)** A ratio of two quantities measured in different units.	An airplane climbs 18,000 feet in 12 minutes. The airplane's rate of climb is $\frac{18{,}000 \text{ ft}}{12 \text{ min}} = 1500 \text{ ft/min}$.
ratio **(p. 317)** A comparison of two numbers using division. The ratio of a to b (where $b \neq 0$) can be written as a to b, as $\frac{a}{b}$, or as $a : b$.	The ratio of 17 to 12 can be written as 17 to 12, as $\frac{17}{12}$, or as 17 : 12.
rational number **(p. 242)** A number that can be written as $\frac{a}{b}$ where a and b are integers and $b \neq 0$.	$6 = \frac{6}{1}$, $-\frac{3}{5} = \frac{-3}{5}$, $0.75 = \frac{3}{4}$, and $2\frac{1}{3} = \frac{7}{3}$ are all rational numbers.
real numbers **(p. 437)** The set of all rational numbers and irrational numbers.	$0, -\frac{5}{9}, 2.75$, and $\sqrt{3}$ are all real numbers.

Glossary

	Example
reciprocals **(p. 234)** Two nonzero numbers whose product is 1.	$\frac{2}{3}$ and $\frac{3}{2}$ are reciprocals.
reflection **(p. 404)** A transformation that creates a mirror image of each point of a figure; also known as a *flip*.	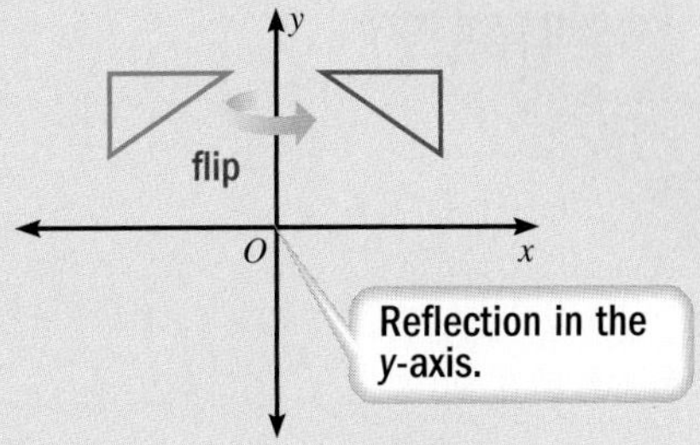 flip Reflection in the *y*-axis.
regular polygon **(p. 390)** A polygon with all sides equal in length and all angles equal in measure.	 **Regular pentagon**
relation **(p. 541)** A set of ordered pairs.	(5, 7), (6, 5), (0, 5), (6, 0) is a relation
relatively prime numbers **(p. 174)** Two or more nonzero whole numbers whose greatest common factor is 1.	9 and 16 are relatively prime because their GCF is 1.
repeating decimal **(p. 242)** A decimal that has one or more digits that repeat without end.	0.7777. . . and $1.\overline{29}$ are repeating decimals.
rhombus **(p. 386)** A parallelogram with four congruent sides.	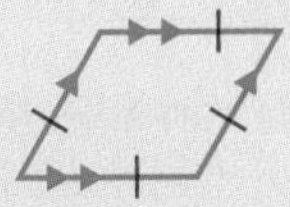
right angle **(p. 375)** An angle whose measure is exactly 90°.	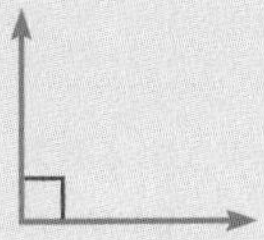
right triangle **(p. 382)** A triangle with one right angle.	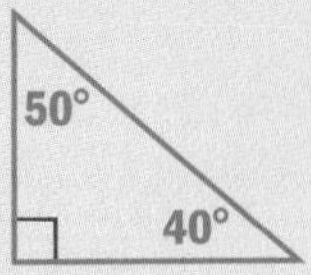 50° 40°
rise **(p. 570)** The vertical change between two points on a line.	*See* slope.

	Example
rotation **(p. 410)** A transformation that rotates a figure through a given angle, called the angle of rotation, and in a given direction about a fixed point, called the center of rotation; also known as a *turn*.	center of rotation y O x turn
rotational symmetry **(p. 410)** A figure has rotational symmetry if a turn of 180° or less produces an image that fits exactly on the original figure.	90° 180° A square has rotational symmetry.
run **(p. 570)** The horizontal change between two points on a line.	*See* slope.
S	
sample **(p. 644)** A part of a population.	To predict the results of an election, a survey is given to a sample of voters.
scale **(p. 324)** In a scale drawing, the scale gives the relationship between the drawing's dimensions and the actual dimensions.	The scale "1 in. : 10 ft" means that 1 inch in the scale drawing represents an actual distance of 10 feet.
scale drawing **(p. 321)** A diagram of an object in which the dimensions are in proportion to the actual dimensions of the object.	1 cm : 12 m
scale factor **(p. 418)** The ratio of corresponding side lengths of a figure and its image after dilation.	*See* dilation.

Glossary

	Example
scale model **(p. 324)** A model of an object in which the dimensions are in proportion to the actual dimensions of the object.	A scale model of the White House appears in Tobu World Square in Japan. The scale used is 1 : 25.
scalene triangle **(p. 382)** A triangle with no congruent sides.	
scatter plot **(p. 545)** The graph of a set of data pairs (x, y), which is a collection of points in a coordinate plane.	
scientific notation **(p. 205)** A number is written in scientific notation if it has the form $c \times 10^n$ where c is greater than or equal to 1 and less than 10, and n is an integer.	In scientific notation, 328,000 is written as 3.28×10^5, and 0.00061 is written as 6.1×10^{-4}.
similar polygons **(p. 416)** Polygons that have the same shape but not necessarily the same size. Corresponding angles of similar polygons are congruent, and the ratios of the lengths of corresponding sides are equal. The symbol ~ is used to indicate that two polygons are similar.	$\triangle LMN \sim \triangle PQR$
simple interest **(p. 348)** Interest that is earned or paid only on the principal. The simple interest I is the product of the principal P, the annual interest rate r written as a decimal, and the time t in years: $I = Prt$.	You deposit \$700 in a savings account that pays a 3% simple annual interest rate. After 5 years, the interest is $I = Prt = (700)(0.03)(5) = \$105$, and your account balance is $\$700 + \$105 = \$805$.
simplest form of a fraction **(p. 179)** A fraction is in simplest form if its numerator and denominator have a greatest common factor of 1.	The simplest form of the fraction $\frac{6}{8}$ is $\frac{3}{4}$.

Glossary

	Example
sine **(p. 463)** The sine of any acute angle A of a right triangle is the ratio of the opposite leg to the hypotenuse.	 $\sin A = \frac{a}{c}$
slant height **(p. 507)** The height of any face that is not the base of a regular pyramid.	
slope **(p. 570)** The slope of a nonvertical line is the ratio of the rise (vertical change) to the run (horizontal change) between any two points on the line.	 The slope of the line above is: $\text{slope} = \frac{\text{rise}}{\text{run}} = \frac{-2}{5} = -\frac{2}{5}.$
slope-intercept form **(p. 577)** The form of a linear equation $y = mx + b$ where m is the slope and b is the y-intercept.	$y = 6x + 8$ is in slope-intercept form.
solid **(p. 492)** A three-dimensional figure that encloses a part of space.	*See* cone, cylinder, prism, pyramid, *and* sphere.
solution of an equation **(p. 28)** A number that makes the equation true when substituted for the variable in the equation.	The solution of the equation $n - 3 = 4$ is 7.
solution of an equation in two variables **(p. 549)** An ordered pair (x, y) that makes the equation true when the values of x and y are substituted into the equation.	(3, 8) is a solution of $y = 3x - 1$.
solution of an inequality **(p. 140)** The set of all numbers that make the inequality true when substituted for the variable in the inequality.	The solution of the inequality $y + 2 > 5$ is $y > 3$.
solution of a linear inequality **(p. 583)** An ordered pair (x, y) that makes the inequality true when the values of x and y are substituted into the inequality.	A solution of $y \geq 2x - 9$ is (5, 1).

	Example
solving an equation (p. 28) Finding all solutions of the equation by using mental math or the properties of equality.	To solve the equation $4x = 20$, find the number that can be multiplied by 4 to equal 20; $4(5) = 20$, so the solution is 5.
sphere (p. 492) A solid formed by all points in space that are the same distance from a fixed point called the center.	
square root (p. 431) A square root of a number n is a number m which, when multiplied by itself, equals n.	The square roots of 81 are 9 and −9 because $9^2 = 81$ and $(-9)^2 = 81$.
standard form (p. 657) A polynomial written with the exponents of the variable decreasing from left to right.	$3x^5 - 8x^3 + 5x^2 + x - 2$ is in standard form.
stem-and-leaf plot (p. 597) A data display that helps you see how data values are distributed. Each data value is separated into a leaf (the last digit) and a stem (the remaining digits). In an ordered stem-and-leaf plot, the leaves for each stem are listed in order from least to greatest.	stems leaves 10 | 8 11 | 2 2 5 12 | 1 3 Key: 10 | 8 = 108
straight angle (p. 375) An angle whose measure is exactly 180°.	
subtraction property of equality (p. 109) Subtracting the same number from each side of an equation produces an equivalent equation.	If $x + 7 = 9$, then $x + 7 - 7 = 9 - 7$, so $x = 2$. If $x + a = b$, then $x + a - a = b - a$.
supplementary angles (p. 375) Two angles whose measures have a sum of 180°.	
surface area of a polyhedron (p. 503) The sum of the areas of the faces of the polyhedron.	 *Surface area* $= 2(6)(4) + 2(6)(3) + 2(4)(3)$ $= 108 \text{ in.}^2$

Glossary

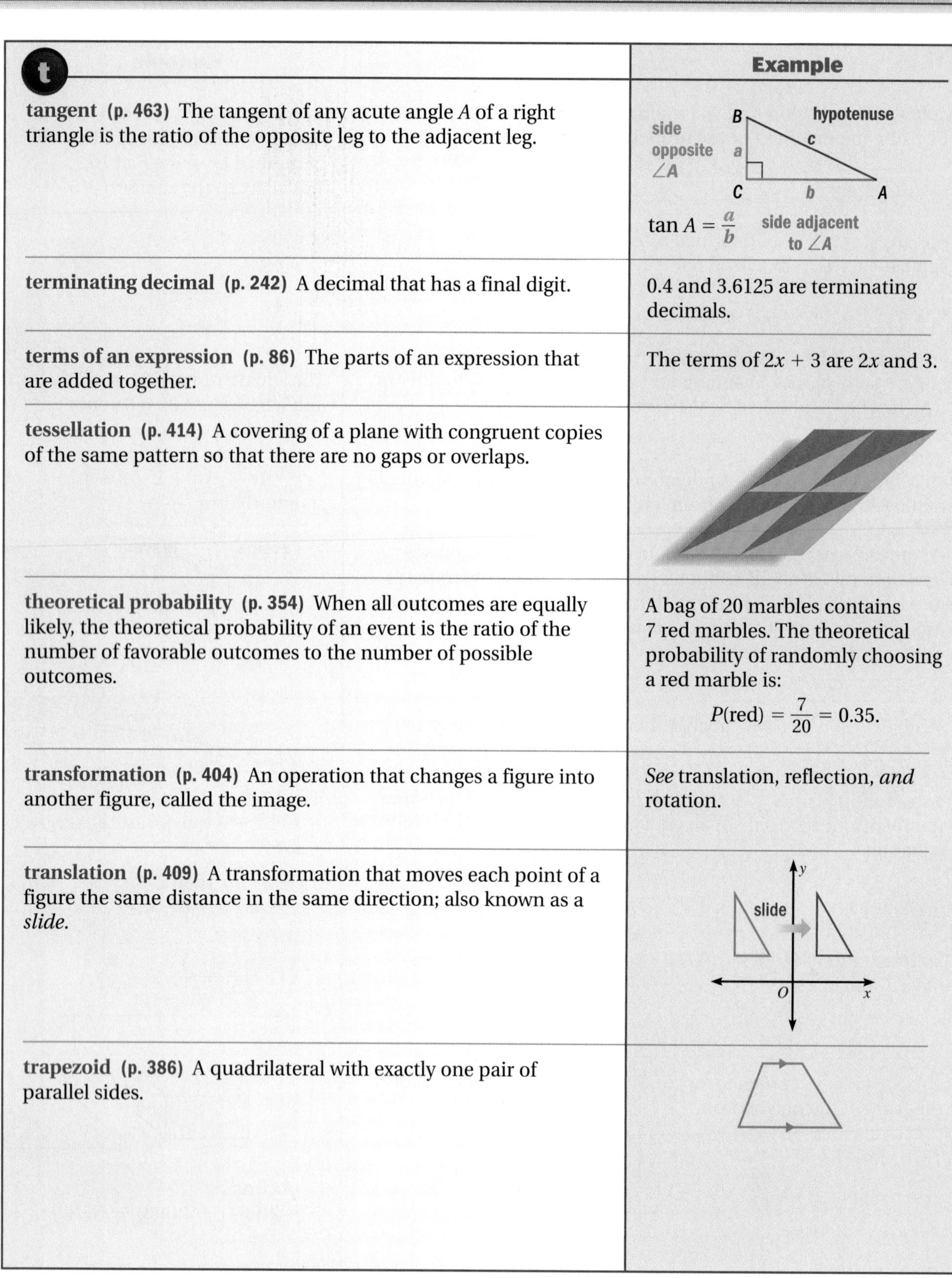

t	Example
tangent **(p. 463)** The tangent of any acute angle A of a right triangle is the ratio of the opposite leg to the adjacent leg.	B, hypotenuse, c, side opposite $\angle A$, a, C, b, A $\tan A = \frac{a}{b}$ side adjacent to $\angle A$
terminating decimal **(p. 242)** A decimal that has a final digit.	0.4 and 3.6125 are terminating decimals.
terms of an expression **(p. 86)** The parts of an expression that are added together.	The terms of $2x + 3$ are $2x$ and 3.
tessellation **(p. 414)** A covering of a plane with congruent copies of the same pattern so that there are no gaps or overlaps.	
theoretical probability **(p. 354)** When all outcomes are equally likely, the theoretical probability of an event is the ratio of the number of favorable outcomes to the number of possible outcomes.	A bag of 20 marbles contains 7 red marbles. The theoretical probability of randomly choosing a red marble is: $P(\text{red}) = \frac{7}{20} = 0.35.$
transformation **(p. 404)** An operation that changes a figure into another figure, called the image.	*See* translation, reflection, *and* rotation.
translation **(p. 409)** A transformation that moves each point of a figure the same distance in the same direction; also known as a *slide*.	y, slide, O, x
trapezoid **(p. 386)** A quadrilateral with exactly one pair of parallel sides.	

Glossary

	Example
tree diagram **(p. 618)** A branching diagram that shows all the possible choices or outcomes of a process carried out in several stages.	H → H, T; T → H, T Outcomes: HH, HT, TH, TT
trigonometric ratio **(p. 463)** A ratio of the lengths of two sides of a right triangle.	*See* sine, cosine, and tangent.
trinomial **(p. 657)** A polynomial with three terms.	$3x^2 + 2x - 4$

u

unfavorable outcome **(p. 633)** An outcome that is not a favorable outcome.	*See* favorable outcome.
unit rate **(p. 318)** A rate that has a denominator of 1 unit.	\$9 per hour is a unit rate.
upper extreme **(p. 601)** The greatest value in a data set.	*See* box-and-whisker plot.
upper quartile **(p. 601)** The median of the upper half of a data set.	*See* box-and-whisker plot.

v

variable **(p. 15)** A symbol, usually a letter, that is used to represent one or more numbers.	In the expression $m + 5$, the letter m is the variable.
variable expression **(p. 15)** An expression that consists of numbers, variables, and operations.	$n - 3$, $\frac{2s}{t}$, and $x + 4yz + 1$ are variable expressions.
verbal model **(p. 11)** A word equation that represents a real-world situation.	Distance traveled = Speed of car • Time traveled
vertex of a polyhedron **(p. 492)** A point where three or more edges of the polyhedron meet.	*See* edge of a polyhedron.
vertical angles **(p. 376)** A pair of opposite angles formed when two lines meet at a point.	1 2 3 4 $\angle 1$ and $\angle 3$ are vertical angles. $\angle 2$ and $\angle 4$ are also vertical angles.

	Example
vertical line test **(p. 681)** If a vertical line intersects a graph at more than one point, then the graph does not represent a function.	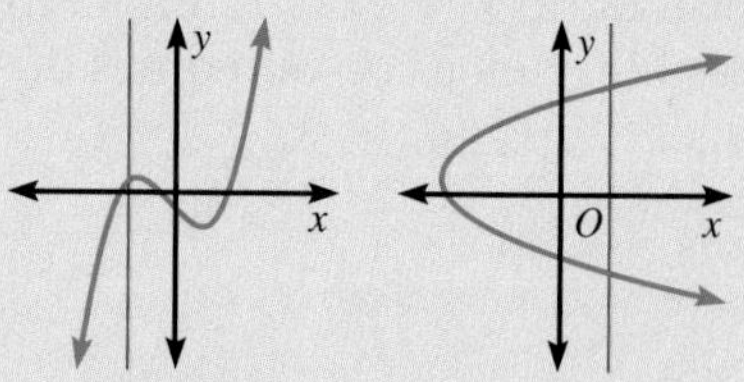
volume of a solid **(p. 513)** The amount of space the solid occupies.	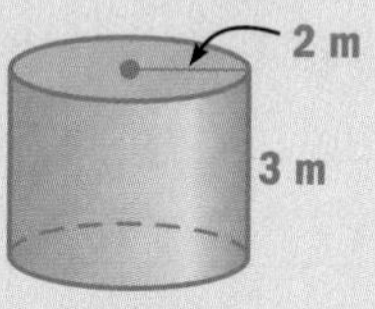 *Volume* $= \pi r^2 h$ $\approx (3.14)(2)^2(3)$ $\approx 37.7\ \text{m}^3$

X

***x*-axis** **(p. 91)** The horizontal number line in a coordinate plane.	*See* coordinate plane.
***x*-coordinate** **(p. 91)** The first number in an ordered pair representing a point in a coordinate plane.	The *x*-coordinate of the ordered pair (−2, 1) is −2.
***x*-intercept** **(p. 564)** The *x*-coordinate of the point where the graph intersects the *x*-axis.	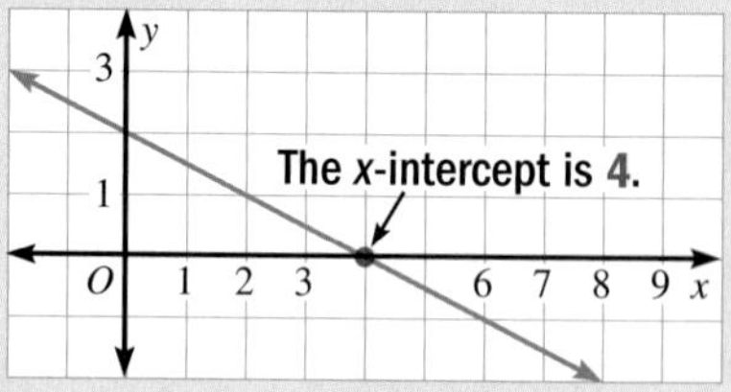

Y

***y*-axis** **(p. 91)** The vertical number line in a coordinate plane.	*See* coordinate plane.
***y*-coordinate** **(p. 91)** The second number in an ordered pair representing a point in a coordinate plane.	The *y*-coordinate of the ordered pair (−2, 1) is 1.
***y*-intercept** **(p. 564)** The *y*-coordinate of the point where the graph intersects the *y*-axis.	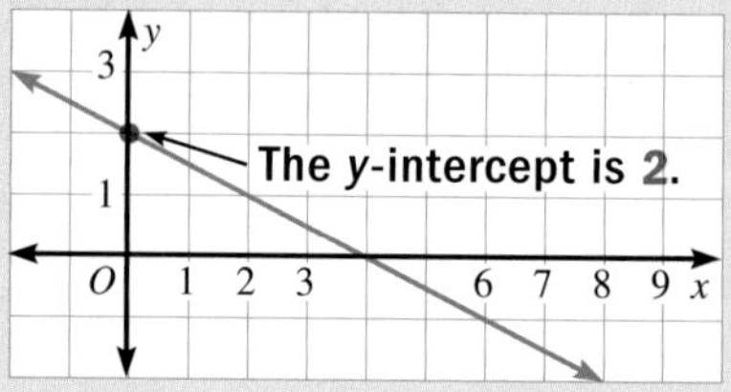

Index

Index

b

c

Index

d

Index

f

Index

g

Index

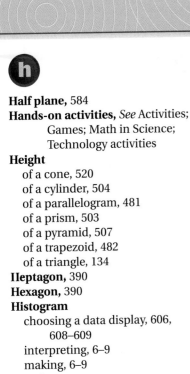

Index

n

O

P

Index

q

Index

S

Index

t

U

V

W

Index

Credits

Photography

iii *top to bottom* Meridian Creative Group, RMIP/Richard Haynes, Michael Girard, Jerry Head Jr.; **vi** Copyright © AFP/Corbis; **vii** Jim Schwabel/Index Stock; **viii** Bobby Model/National Geographic/Getty Images; **ix** Copyright © Tom Stewart/Corbis; **x** Copyright © Reuters NewMedia/Corbis; **xi** Charles Krupa/AP Wide World Photos; **xii** *left* PhotoDisc; *right* Lee Celano/AP Wide World Photos; **xiii** Frank Siteman; **xiv** Paul Sancya/AP Wide World Photos; **xv** Kevin Bartram/The Galveston County Daily News/AP Wide World Photos; **xvi** Scott Spiker/ImageState; **xvii** West Rock/Stone/Getty Images; **xviii** Matthias Clamer/Stone/Getty Images; **1** John Warden/Getty Images; **2** Copyright © Corbis; **3** *left* Copyright © Joseph Sohm; Chromosohm, Inc./Corbis; *right* Copyright © Royalty-Free/Corbis; **5** Diaphor Agency/ Index Stock; **6** Copyright © Alan Schein/ CorbisStockMarket; **7** Copyright © Corbis; **8** Silvia Flores,The Press-Enterprise/AP Wide World Photos; **9** PhotoDisc; **10** Copyright © Mark Richards/PhotoEdit/PictureQuest; **11** Copyright © Galen Rowell/ Corbis; **12** Jerry Trafford; **13** *left* Julie Blum/Columbus Telegram/AP Wide World Photos; *right* Copyright © Becky Luigart-Stayner/Corbis; **15** *top* Copyright © PunchStock; *bottom* Zefa Visual Media-Germany/Index Stock; **17** *top* Greer & Associates, Inc/SuperStock; *bottom left* Stockbyte; *bottom right* PhotoDisc; **18** *left* James Meyer/The Image Bank/Getty Images; *right* Copyright © Comstock; **20** Copyright © Ron Watts/Corbis; **22** PhotoDisc; **23** Eric Wessman/ Photonica; **26** Frank Siteman; **27** Syracuse Newspapers/The Image Works; **29** *both* Copyright © Reuters NewMedia, Inc./Corbis; **31** Copyright © AFP/Corbis; **34** Barbara Strnadova/Photo Researchers, Inc.; **35** Larry West/Photo Researchers, Inc.; **36** Ken Osburn/ Index Stock; **37** Johner/ Photonica; **38** Ted S. Warren/AP Wide World Photos; **42** Kevork Djansezian/AP Wide World Photos; **47** Copyright © Stephen Frink/Corbis; **48** PhotoDisc; **53** Artville; **54** *top left* Copyright © Comstock; *bottom left* Photo by Jerry Trafford, Courtesy of Vintage IWear; *right* Artville; **56** *left* NASA; *right* Ken O'Donoghue; **61** *both* The Picture Desk; **62** Copyright © Bob Daemmrich/PictureQuest; **64** Jeff Hunter/The Image Bank/Getty Images; **66** Tim Haske/Index Stock; **68** Frank Siteman; **69** Copyright © Kwame Zikomo/SuperStock; **70** *top* Shinoda/Photonica; *bottom* Copyright © Stephen Frink/Corbis; **73** *left* Copyright © Corbis; *right, both* PhotoDisc; **75** Copyright © Dean Conger/Corbis; **76** PhotoDisc; **77** Copyright © Paul A. Souders/Corbis; **80** *top* School Division, Houghton Mifflin Company; *bottom* Steve Casimiro/Getty Images; **83** Steven Senne/AP Wide World Photos; **84** *left* Ken O'Donoghue, *right* PhotoDisc; **85** SuperStock; **87, 88** *all* Ken O'Donoghue; **89** Jim Schwabel/Index Stock; **93** Copyright © Bill Ross/Corbis; **94** *top left* Copyright © PhotoDisc/Getty Images; *top right* EyeWire Collection/Getty Images; **99** School Division, Houghton Mifflin Company; **102** *top* Copyright © Galen Rowell/Corbis; *bottom* Copyright © Darrell Gulin/Corbis; **103** *top* Copyright ©Bjorn Backe; Papilio/Corbis; *bottom* Copyright © Richard Hamilton Smith/ Corbis; **104** *all* NASA; **105** *left* NASA; *right* Copyright © NASA/Corbis; **110** Bobby Model/National Geographic/Getty Images; **111** Ken O'Donoghue; **112** Darryl Torckler/Getty Images; **114** Steve Hix/Getty Images; **115** G.D.T./Getty Images; **119** *top* Stockbyte; *bottom* Frank Siteman; **121** Ken O'Donoghue; **123** Dennis O'Clair/Getty Images; **124** Mitchell Funk/Getty Images; **127** *left* Copyright © Image 100/Royalty-Free/Corbis; *right* Ken O'Donoghue; **132** Frank Siteman; **133** Antonio Mo/Getty Images; **135** Copyright © Cosmo Condina; **136** John Warden/ Getty Images; **138** Brand X Pictures; **139** RubberBall Productions/CorbisStockMarket; **140** *left* Ken O'Donoghue; *right* Copyright © Kurt Wittman/Corbis; **143** Adrian Weinbrecht/Getty Images; **144** Copyright © Reuters NewMedia Inc./ Corbis; **147** Art Wolfe/Getty Images; **148** Brand X Pictures; **149** Dale Durfee/Stone/Getty Images; **154** Ryan McVay/PhotoDisc/Getty Images; **163** David Young-Wolff/Stone/Getty Images; **164** Alistair Cowin/Index Stock; **165** *background* Benelux Press/Index Stock; *top left* Stephen Simpson/Taxi/Getty Images; *top right* Copyright © Tom Stewart/Corbis; *bottom left* Benelux Press/Index Stock; **168** *both* Ken O'Donoghue; **170** School Division, Houghton Mifflin Company; **171** National Park Service Historic Photograph Collection; **172** Ken O'Donoghue; **175** *top* School Division, Houghton Mifflin Company; *bottom* Bob Torrez/Stone/Getty Images; **176** *both* PhotoDisc; **177** Courtesy of Jonathan Wheeler; **179** *top* Copyright © Erich Lessing/Art Resource, NY; *center three images* Christie's Images; *bottom image* Eric Kamp/Index Stock; **180** *both* Christie's Images; **181** PhotoDisc; **181** Copyright © PhotoDisc; **182** Claus Meyer/Minden Pictures; **184** Frank Siteman; **185** David Davis/Index Stock; **186** *left* Copyright © Guy Cali/Picturequest; *right* Copyright © Comstock; **188** Copyright © Corbis; **193** Konrad Wothe/Minden Pictures; **194** Copyright © Tom Stewart/Corbis; **195** Steve Miller/AP Wide World Photos; **199** Copyright © NASA/Corbis; **201** *top* Copyright © Roger Holden/Index Stock/PictureQuest; *bottom* Copyright © M. Hans/Vandystadt/Photo Researchers, Inc.; **203** Copyright © MICROFIELD SCIENTIFIC LTD/Photo Researchers, Inc.; **204** *left* Artville; *right* Pho/AP Wide World Photos; **205** *top* Courtesy of Fan Yang; The Science of Bubbles; *center* International Stock/ImageState; **207** NASA; **208** Artville; **213** Robb Helfrick/Index Stock; **214** G.K. & Vikki Hart/The Image Bank/Getty Images; **216** © David Brooks/Corbis; **217** *left* Don Mason/Corbis; *right* School Division, Houghton Mifflin Company; **220** Photo by Shawn Lockhart, courtesy of Southwest Wisconsin Reptiles; **222** David Madison/Stone/Getty Images; **223** David Young-Wolff/Stone/Getty Images; **224** Ryan McVay/PhotoDisc/ PictureQuest; **225** Ken O'Donoghue; **226** Copyright © Reuters NewMedia Inc./Corbis; **228** Frank Siteman; **229** Donna Day/Stone/Getty Images; **230** EyeWire Collection/Getty Images; **231** *top* F. Schussler/Photolink/ Getty Images; *bottom* PunchStock; **232** Ken O'Donoghue; **233** Gianni Cigolini/Image Bank/Getty Images; **236** Copyright © Image 100/Royalty-Free/Corbis; **243** Steve Maslowski/Photo Researchers, Inc.; **244** G.K. & Vikki Hart/The Image Bank/Getty Images; **245** Frank Siteman; **246** Tom Bean/Stone/Getty Images; **247** Frank Siteman; **248** Ken O'Donoghue; **250** Copyright © Peter Adams/Index Stock/PictureQuest; **251** Bruce Leighty/Index Stock; **253** Michael K. Nichols/National Geographic/Getty Images; **254** Brad Lewis/Adventure Photography/ImageState; **257** Copyright © Ralph White/Corbis; **258** Copyright © Tom Stewart/Corbis; **259** PhotoDisc; **260** Copyright © Jon Feingersh/Corbis; **265** Kevin Schafer/The Image Bank/Getty Images; **266** Copyright © Comstock; **269** Ken O'Donoghue; **271** *both* Ken O'Donoghue; **273** Neo Vision/Photonica; **274** Copyright © Chuck Savage/CorbisStockMarket; **275** Ken O'Donoghue; **276** Copyright © Rob Lewine/CorbisStockMarket; **277** Volo Pictures/ Photonica; **278** Stockbyte; **281** Tony Anderson/Taxi/Getty Images; **282** *top* Gary Bell/Taxi/Getty Images; *bottom* Georgette Douwma/Taxi/Getty Images; **285, 288** Ken O'Donoghue; **289** *top row: left, center* Ken O'Donoghue; *right* PhotoDisc; *bottom row: left, right* Ken O'Donoghue; *center* Comstock; **291** Copyright © Alan Schein Photography/Corbis; **294** Frank Siteman; Copyright © Anthony Nex/Corbis; **296** *left* Antonio Mo/Getty Images; *right* Copyright © Comstock; **298** Charles Krupa/AP Wide World Photos; **301** *top* Copyright © Duomo/Corbis; *bottom* Frank Siteman; **303** Ken O'Donoghue; **304** Josef Peter Fankhauser/Getty Images; **312** *left* Copyright © Tony Freeman/Photo Edit; *type background* Copyright © Corbis; **313** Zefa Visual Media Germany/Index Stock; **315** Ken O'Donoghue; **317** Copyright © Marc Muench/Corbis; **318** Copyright © J Silver/SuperStock Images; **319** Frank Siteman; **321** PhotoDisc; **322** Copyright © Wolfgang Kaehler/Corbis; **324** Courtesy of the city of Strawberry Point, Iowa; **325** Copyright © Paul A. Souders/ Corbis; **326** School Division, Houghton Mifflin Company; **327** *top* PhotoDisc; *bottom* Lee Celano/AP Wide World Photos; **328** *left* Ian Shaw/ Stone/Getty Images; *right: inset top* Stockbyte; *inset bottom* Photospin; **329** Stuart Cohen/The Image Works; **330** Ken O'Donoghue; **331** Philip Lee Harvey/Getty Images; **334** C Squared Studios/PhotoDisc/Getty Images; **335** Ken O'Donoghue; **338** PhotoDisc; **339** Copyright © Nik Wheeler/ Corbis; **340** *left* Copyright © Patrik Giardino/Corbis; *right* Corbis; **341** Getty Images; **342** *top* Darrell Gulin/Stone/Getty Images; *bottom* Nick Daly/Stone/Getty Images; **344** Ken O'Donoghue; **345** Copyright © Stockbyte/PunchStock; **346** PhotoDisc; **347** *top* PhotoDisc; *bottom* Copyright © Ariel Skelley/Corbis; **348** PhotoDisc; **349** James L. Stanfield/ National Geographic Image Collection; **350** Inga Spence/Index Stock; **352** Frank Siteman; **353** Daniel Allan/Taxi/Getty Images; **355** Ken O'Donoghue; **357** Don Smetzer/Stone/Getty Images; **361, 362** PhotoDisc; **371** Copyright © Royalty-Free/Corbis; **373** Ken O'Donoghue; **376** Copyright © Mike Chew/Corbis; **379, 380** Ken O'Donoghue; **385** Copyright © Lee Snider/Corbis; **391** *top* Ken O'Donoghue; *bottom*

PhotoDisc; **393** Lionel Glyn Coates/www.bciusa.com; **397** *top* David Young-Wolff/Stone/Getty Images; *bottom* Stockbyte/PunchStock; *frames*: Ken O'Donoghue; **399** Copyright © Richard Cummins/Corbis; **400** Courtesy of Michigan State University, Department of Crop and Soil Sciences; **401** *both* Sanford Ponder www.thepod.net; **402** Frank Siteman; **403** Copyright © Tim Pannell/Corbis; **404** Frank Siteman; **406** *all* PhotoDisc; **412** *top left, right* Ken O'Donoghue; *center left* Copyright © SuperStock Images; **414**, **415** Ken O'Donoghue; **416** Frank Siteman; *televisions*: PhotoDisc; **428** *background* PhotoDisc; *top left* ImageState; *center, both* Ken O'Donoghue; **429** *top left* Joe McBride/Stone/Getty Images; *top right* PhotoDisc/Getty Images; *bottom right* Copyright © Royalty-Free/Corbis; *background insets* PhotoDisc; **432** Ian Shaw/Getty Images; **433** Eunice Harris/Photo Researchers, Inc.; **434** Frank Siteman; **435** Ed Elberfeld/Index Stock; **436** Benelux Press/Index Stock; **439** *left* Rex Ziak/Stone/Getty Images; *right* AP Photo/Goran Stenberg; **440** Ken O'Donoghue; **441** Frank Siteman; **444** Copyright © Royalty-Free/Corbis; **446** Arthur Tilley/Stone/Getty Images; **447** *top* Alan Carey/Photo Researchers, Inc.; *left* Copyright © George Lepp/Corbis; **448** *background* Ken O'Donoghue; *center* Frank Siteman, **449** Sentinel-Tribunc, J.D. Pooley/AP Wide World Photos; **450** *left* Copyright © Tony Freeman/ PhotoEdit, Inc.; *right* School Division, Houghton Mifflin Company; **453** *left* Copyright © Royalty-Free/Corbis; *center* Jeffrey Sylvester/Taxi/ Getty Images; *center right* Ken O'Donoghue; *right* PhotoDisc; **456** *top* Ken O'Donoghue; *bottom* Copyright © Cleve Bryant/PhotoEdit, Inc.; **458** Telegraph Herald, David Raoyal/AP Wide World Photos; **459** Copyright © SuperStock Images; **463** Copyright © Jeff Greenberg/eStock Photography/ PictureQuest; **465** Paul Sancya/AP Wide World Photos; **466** Harvey Lloyd/ Taxi/Getty Images; **468** Greg Kiger/Index Stock; **473** Copyright © Tony Freeman/PhotoEdit, Inc.; **474** Christophe Ratier/Photo Researchers, Inc.; **476** *top left* courtesy of The Planetarium, Armagh, Northern Ireland; *bottom left* Ken Wardius/Index Stock; *type background* Digital Vision Getty Images; **477** *top right* courtesy of The Planetarium, Armagh, Northern Ireland; *top inset* Copyright © Corbis; *bottom* Copyright © Roger Ressmeyer/Corbis; **482** Copyright © Thomas A. Heinz/Corbis; **485** Stockbyte; **487** Mike Powell/Allsport Concepts/Getty Images; **488** David Lees/Taxi/Getty Images; **489** Copyright © Australian Picture Library/ Corbis; **494** *all* Ken O'Donoghue; **495** Copyright © Philip Gould/Corbis; **500** Frank Siteman; **501** Moggy/Stone/Getty Images; **502** courtesy of Kerry Cashman, photo by Ken O'Donoghue; **505** Ken O'Donoghue; **506** Copyright © Dave G. Houser/Corbis; **509** Copyright © Greer & Associates, Inc./SuperStock Images; **510** *left* PhotoDisc; *right, both* Copyright © Corbis; **511** Copyright © Royalty-Free/Corbis; **513** Copyright © Mark Gibson/Corbis; **516** PhotoDisc; **517** David Hanover/ Stone/Getty Images; **519** Kevin Bartram/The Galveston County Daily News/AP Wide World Photos; **521** EyeWire Collection/Getty Images; **537** Copyright © Royalty-Free/Corbis; **539** *left* Jason Hindley/Stone/Getty Images; *right* Ken O'Donoghue; **541**, **542** Frank Siteman; **543** Sea World/ AP Wide World Photos; **544** Copyright © Peter Beck/Corbis; **545** NASA/AP Wide World Photos; **548** Copyright © Royalty-Free/Corbis; **549** *top* Copyright © Brooklyn Productions/Royalty-Free/Corbis; *bottom* Copyright © Merritt Vincent/PhotoEdit, Inc.; **551** Ken O'Donoghue; **552** Copyright © Mark Garten/Corbis; **554** Frank Siteman; **555** Copyright © Corbis; **557** Donna Day/Stone/Getty Images; **559** Antonio Mo/Taxi/Getty Images; **565** Copyright © Kevin Radford/SuperStock; **566** Copyright © Tom Stewart/ Corbis; **570** Jim Schwabel/Index Stock; **572** Nancy R. Cohen/PhotoDisc/ Getty Images; **574** Glyn Kirk/Stone/Getty Images; **577** RO-MA Stock/Index Stock; **578** Copyright © Larry Prosor/SuperStock; **579** Ken O'Donoghue; **580** Copyright © J. H. Robinson/Photo Researchers, Inc.; **585** Ken O'Donoghue; **586** Scott Spiker/ImageState; **591** WEST ROCK/Taxi/Getty Images; **592** Stewart Cohen/Index Stock; **594–595** *background* Tui De Roy/Minden Pictures; **595** *left* Tui De Roy/Minden Pictures; *center* Michio Hoshino/Minden Pictures; *right* Franz Lanting/Minden Pictures; **597** *top* David Young-Wolff/PhotoEdit, Inc.; *bottom* Rubberball/PunchStock; **600** Ron Schwane/AP Wide World Photos; **601** Paul Nicklen/National Geographic/Getty Images; **602** Jason Homa/The Image Bank/Getty Images; **604** The Time Herald, Tony Pitts/ AP Wide World Photos; **606** A. H. Rider/Photo Researchers, Inc.; **607** *top* Stuart Hughs/Stone/Getty Images; *bottom* School Division, Houghton Mifflin Company; **609** Antonio Mo/ Taxi/Getty Images; **616** Frank Siteman; **617** Copyright © Lisette Le Bon/SuperStock; **618** Frank Siteman; **619** Copyright © Roger Allyn Lee/SuperStock Images; **622** Billy Hustace/Stone/Getty Images; **624** Myrleen Cate/Index Stock; **625** *all* PhotoDisc *except 4th from right*: Photospin; **626** Rubberball/PunchStock; **627** *top, both* Ken O'Donoghue; *center left* West Rock/Stone/Getty Images; **629** Ken O'Donoghue; **631** Marc Romanelli/The Image Bank/ Getty Images; **634** Photo by David Gray, Copyright © Reuters 1998; **635** Ken O'Donoghue; **636** Stephen Simpson/ Taxi/Getty Images; **639** School Division, Houghton Mifflin Company; **644** Ken O'Donoghue; **645** Marvin E. Newman/The Image Bank/Getty Images; **648** Dorling Kindersley; **649** Zbigniew Bzdak/The Times of Northwest Indiana/AP Wide World Photos; **652** *left* Copyright © Eric and David Hosking/Corbis; *right* Copyright © Gary W. Carter/Corbis; **653** *top right* PhotoDisc; *bottom right* Copyright © Arthur Morris/Corbis; **654**, **655** *all* Ken O'Donoghue, *except* **655** *bottom row, far right*: Comstock; **658** Matthias Clamer/Stone/ Getty Images; **660** Copyright © Royalty-Free/ Corbis; **663** PhotoDisc/ Getty Images; **664** Ken O'Donoghue; **667** Ken O'Donoghue; **669** Ken O'Donoghue; *inset* Stockbyte; **670** Copyright © NASA/Corbis; **676** PhotoDisc; **677** PhotoDisc/ Getty Images; **678** Frank Siteman; **679** Copyright © Royalty-Free/Corbis; **680** Frank Siteman; **683** Copyright © M.Dillon/Corbis

Illustration

Brian White
19, 30, 43, 60, 67, 72, 95, 116, 128, 145, 177, 189, 200, 221, 237, 238, 261, 280, 287, 299, 320, 326, 333, 346, 389, 408, 420, 436, 445, 467, 471, 522, 546, 553, 582, 599, 615, 620, 642, 643, 665, 682, 684

Rob Dunlavey
268, 269 372, 373, 478, 479

Sam Ward
122

Credits

Selected Answers

Chapter 1

1.1 Getting Ready to Practice (p. 7) **1.** intervals **3.** 3 times **5.** Step 1: histogram; Steps 2–3:

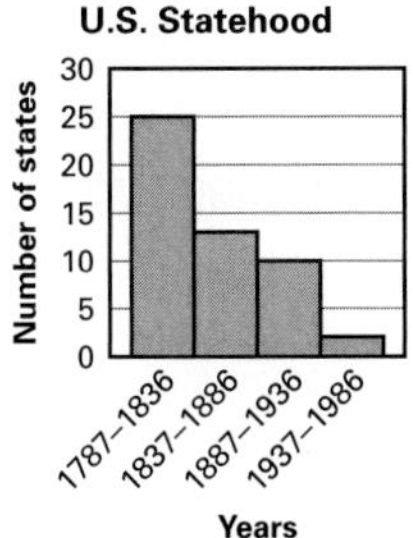

1.1 Practice and Problem Solving (pp. 7–9)
7. department stores **9.** No. *Sample answer:* The category with the most stores might not have the most floor space if each store is small, while a category with fewer stores might have the most floor space if each store is large. **11.** Table; exact amounts are given in a table but may be difficult to read from a bar graph.

13.

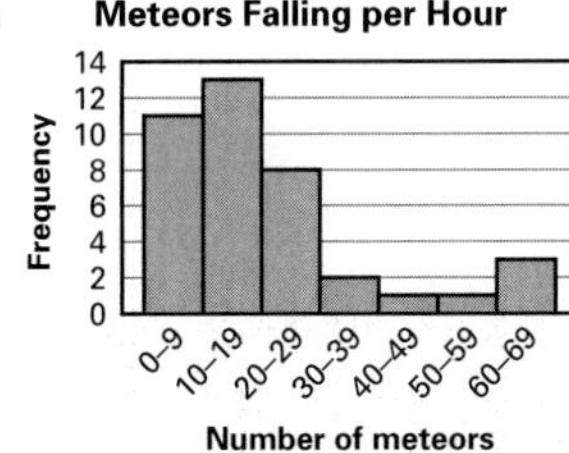

15. 52 hurricanes **17.** No; there does not appear to be a pattern in the data.

19.

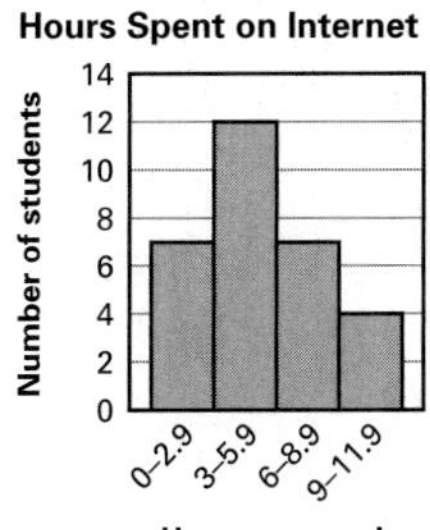

21. about 4000 schools **25.** 136 **27.** 7 **29.** 45.44 **31.** 58.78

1.2 Getting Ready to Practice (p. 12) **1.** Multiply 2 by 5. Add the result (10) to 8. Subtract 4 from this sum (18) to obtain the final result (14). **3.** Multiply 5 by 15; 25. **5.** Subtract 7 from 15; 18. **7.** Subtract 2 from 5; 30. **9.** In the second step, 63 must be divided by 9 before being added to 9: $3 \times 3 + 63 \div 9 = 9 + 63 \div 9 = 9 + 7 = 16$.

1.2 Practice and Problem Solving (pp. 12–13)
11. 29 **13.** 24 **15.** 15 **17.** 5 **19.** \$250 **21.** $\frac{3}{4}$ **23.** 12 **25.** 10.1 **27.** 54.6 **29.** 7 **31.** $12 \div (6 + 4 - 7) = 4$ **33.** 372 cookies **35.** $\times$; $12 \times (4 + 2) = 72$ **37.** 32 students **39.** 4 **41.** 6

1.2 Technology Activity (p. 14) **1.** 106.8 **3.** 7 **5.** 5 **7.** 2 **9.** \$10.44

1.3 Getting Ready to Practice (p. 17) **1.** variable; numerical **7.** 44 **9.** 5

1.3 Practice and Problem Solving (pp. 18–19)
11. 23 **13.** 39.5 **15.** 5 **17.** 6 **19.** $\frac{2}{5}x$ **21.** $12 + x$ **23.** 18 mi **25.** *Sample answer:* Serena is saving to buy a gift for her sister. She starts with \$2 and saves an additional \$8 per week. **27.** $4 + 17n$; \$106 **29.** 32.8 **31.** 96 **33.** 1.6 **35.** 10 **37.** A good answer will include an expression that can only be evaluated correctly by using the order of operations. The explanation of the correct order to use will follow the rules for the order of operations. **39.** $2.75p + 1.25d$; \$13.25 **41.** 50 **43.** 18 **45.** 4095 **47.** 42

1.4 Getting Ready to Practice (p. 22) **1.** *Sample answer:* base $\rightarrow 3^2 \leftarrow$ exponent **3.** 1331 **5.** 64 **7.** 0 **9.** 6 **11.** 7^2 means 7×7; $7^2 = 7 \times 7 = 49$.

1.4 Practice and Problem Solving (pp. 22–23)
13. 3^3; 3 to the third power, or 3 cubed **15.** 6 **17.** 128 **19.** 1 **21.** 109 **23.** 12 **25.** 3 **27.** 16 **29.** 119 **31.** $1000 \cdot 2^3$ **33.** $<$ **35.** 17.17 **37.** 1030.301 **39.** No; $16 \cdot 2^2 = 64$, so the divers have fallen 64 feet after 2 seconds. **41.** 302 **45.** 9 **47.** 6 outfits. *Sample answer:* I used Draw a Diagram because a tree diagram allowed me to find the total number of outfits in an organized way.

1.1–1.4 Notebook Review (pp. 24–25) **1.** Evaluate expressions inside grouping symbols. **2.** The question cannot be answered using the bar graph because the depth does not determine the area of the lake. **3.** Erie **4.** 18 **5.** 3 **6.** 7 **7.** 57 **8.** 1000 **9.** 370 **10.** The number of zeros is the same as the exponent.

1.5 Problem Solving Strategies (p. 27) **1.** 106, 107 **3.** 17 blue chips; 3 green chips **5.** *Sample:*

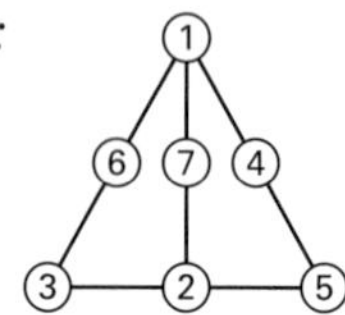

7. twice **9.** Bob, Kelly, Justin, Tim, Michelle

1.5 Getting Ready to Practice (p. 30) **1.** *Sample answer:* $4 + x = 7$; use mental math and ask "4 plus what number is 7?" The answer is 3. **3.** 44 **5.** 7 **7.** yes **9.** no

1.5 Practice and Problem Solving (pp. 30–31) **15.** yes **17.** no **19.** 11 **21.** 29 **23.** 2 **25.** 15 **27.** $14 + r = 43$; 29 in. **29.** $5033 + b = 5396$; 363 lb **31.** $4p = 60$; 15 invitations **37.** $x + 220 = 245$; 25 min **39.** 96 **41.** 6000 **43.** 1000

1.6 Getting Ready to Practice (p. 35) **1.** Area is the surface a figure covers, while perimeter is the distance around the figure. **3.** $P = 30$ in., $A = 56$ in.^{2} **5.** 159 cm

1.6 Practice and Problem Solving (pp. 36–37) **7.** $P = 22$ cm, $A = 24$ cm^2 **9.** $P = 40$ ft, $A = 100$ ft^2 **11.** $P = 72$ in., $A = 324$ in.^{2} **13.** $P = 54$ cm, $A = 182$ cm^2 **15.** 6 m **17.** 9 km/h **19.** 10.5 mi **21.** 225 mi **23.** 90 mi/h **25.** about 4 h **27.** 1560 ft **29.** 2 bags **33.** 9 **35.** 30 **37.** 15.54

1.7 Getting Ready to Practice (p. 41) **1.** Step 1. Read and Understand, Step 2. Make a Plan, Step 3. Solve the Problem, Step 4. Look Back **3.** Step 1: Trains in one hour = people in one hour ÷ people per train, so trains in one hour = people in one hour ÷ (cars per train • passengers per car); Step 2: 45 trains; Step 3: 45 • 20 = 900

1.7 Practice and Problem Solving (pp. 41–43) **5.** 15 h **7.** 16 h **9.** 12 oz **11.** 3, 1 **13.** 9, 5 **15.** \$5060 **17.** $8x$, $10x$ **19.** $31x^2$, $39x^2$ **21.** 7 ft; 49 ft^2 **23.** 5 **25.** 4 **29.** 0 **31.** $P = 38$ in., $A = 48$ in.^{2} **33.** > **35.** >

1.5–1.7 Notebook Review (pp. 44–45) **1.** $P = 2l + 2w$ **2.** 13 **3.** 12 **4.** 3 **5.** 18 **6.** $P = 22$ m, $A = 28$ m^2 **7.** 9 teaspoons **8.** Yes; perimeter is measured in linear units and area is measured in square units.

Chapter Review (pp. 46–47) **1.** histogram **3.** order of operations **5.** base **7.** false **9.** true **11.** No; the age group that includes teenagers also includes other ages. **13.** 1 **15.** 2 • 28.5 − 20; \$37 **17.** 4 **19.** 72 **21.** 225 **23.** 10,000 **25.** 27 **27.** 261 **29.** 7 **31.** $P = 32$ m, $A = 60$ m^2 **33.** $P = 32$ in., $A = 64$ in.^{2} **35.** B, C, and D

Chapter 2

2.1 Getting Ready to Practice (p. 55) **1.** opposites **3.** −130, −56, 0, 62, 74, 120 **5.** 8, 8 **7.** −1327, 1327

2.1 Practice and Problem Solving (pp. 55–56) **9.** > **11.** < **13.** > **15.** > **17.** −20, −12, 18, 44, 59, 64 **23.** Gieselmann Lake **25.** 32 **27.** −29 **29.** 81 **31.** −3 **33.** = **35.** < **37.** Flight crew departs for launch pad. Pilot starts auxiliary power units. Main engine starts. Liftoff. Shuttle clears launch tower, and control switches to the Mission Control Center. **41.** 19 **43.** 34 pages

2.2 Getting Ready to Practice (p. 60) **1.** absolute values **3.** −12 **5.** 0 **7.** −32 **9.** −34 **11.** −17

2.2 Practice and Problem Solving (pp. 61–62) **13.** −3 **15.** 4 **17.** Since the signs are different, the lesser absolute value should be subtracted from the greater absolute value and the sign of the number with the greater absolute value should be used; $-8 + 5 = -3$. **19.** −109 **21.** −82 **23.** 12 **25.** −3 **27.** always **29.** sometimes **31.** *Sample answer:* when you are balancing your checkbook **33.** $-1200 + 800 = -400$; 400 B.C. **35.** 90 **37.** 146 **39.** −1207 **41.** −999 **43.** 0; at **45.** 0; no **47.** 5 **49.** −19 **51.** 122 **53.** 512 **55.** −921, −346, −125, 128, 724

2.3 Getting Ready to Practice (p. 65) **1.** −2 − 6 **3.** −7 **5.** −4 **7.** −10 **9.** −23 **11.** Step 1: 55 ft, 0 ft, 55 ft; Step 2: 55 − 0 = 55 ft, 0 − (−35) = 35 ft, 55 − (−35) = 90 ft; Step 3: 55, 35, 90

2.3 Practice and Problem Solving (pp. 65–67) **13.** 0 **15.** −8 **17.** −27 **19.** 44 **21.** −1000 points **23.** 5 **25.** Subtract −137 from 123. **27.** 42°F

29. −259 **31.** 1802 **33.** −10 **35.** −18 **37.** 12 **39.** −71 **41.** Triassic Period: 37 million yr; Jurassic Period: 64 million yr; Cretaceous Period: 79 million yr **43.** 5 **45.** −31 **49.** 8 **51.** 3 **53.** 2 **55.** 168 **57.** 5649

2.4 Problem Solving Strategies (p. 69) **1.** 55 dots **3.** 144 blue tiles **5.** Scott: 12 yr old, Ben: 15 yr old, Kelly: 9 yr old **7.** $40 **9.** 19 ways

2.4 Getting Ready to Practice (p. 72) **1.** negative **3.** 0 **5.** −6 **7.** 270 **9.** The product of two negative integers is positive; $-8(-12) = 96$.

2.4 Practice and Problem Solving (pp. 72–73) **11.** 17 **13.** 44 **15.** −15 **17.** 32 **19.** −288 **21.** 0 **23.** 70 **25.** −133 **27.** −132 **29.** −4 **31.** −4 **33.** The power is positive when the exponent is even and negative when the exponent is odd. **35.** 64 **37.** 9216 **39.** −$81.70 **41.** −104,832 **43.** −682 **45.** 17 ft **47.** −23 **49.** 15 **51.** 2

2.5 Getting Ready to Practice (p. 76) **1.** mean **3.** 0 **5.** −5 **7.** −3 **9.** −3

2.5 Practice and Problem Solving (pp. 76–77) **11.** 7 **13.** −9 **15.** 7 **17.** 0 **19.** 1 **21.** Always. *Sample answer:* The mean of −3, −5, and −1 is $\frac{-9}{3} = -3$. **23.** 4 **25.** −4 **27.** −1.5 **29.** 0.8 **31.** −29.2°F **35.** 5^5 **37.** b^4 **39.** −72

2.1–2.5 Notebook Review (pp. 78–79)

1. 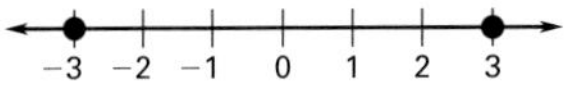

2. −15, −5, 1, 4, 8, 16 **3.** −85, −60, −6, 40, 42, 98 **4.** 38 **5.** −55 **6.** −119 **7.** −66 **8.** −65 **9.** −15 **10.** 312 **11.** −62 **12.** −6 **13.** 4 **14.** Yes. *Sample answer:* The opposite of the sum can be written as $-1(a + b)$. Using the distributive property you get $-a + (-b)$ which is the sum of the opposites.

2.6 Getting Ready to Practice (p. 82) **7.** 45; commutative and associative properties of addition **9.** −290; commutative and associative properties of multiplication **11.** −36; associative property of addition **13.** 15 in.^3

2.6 Practice and Problem Solving (pp. 83–84) **15.** 54; commutative property of multiplication **17.** 9; associative property of addition **19.** 69 **21.** 21 **23.** −700 **25.** −900 **27.** $70x$ **29.** $70 + x$ **31.** No. *Sample answer:* $20 \div 4 = 5$, but $4 \div 20 = 0.2$. **33.** 5.7 **35.** 35 **37.** 420 **39.** $60 **41.** The student grouped the first and last numbers, the second and next to last numbers, and so on, to make 10, and then all of the 10s and the 5 were added to find the sum; 190. **45.** 26 in. and 34 in. *Sample answer:* I used Guess, Check, and Revise because I decided to choose two numbers whose sum was 60 and then check to see if the difference was 8. I revised my guess until it was correct. **47.** $1.35 < 1.53$

2.7 Getting Ready to Practice (p. 87) **1.** like terms: $7x$ and x, $-3y$ and $-6y$; coefficients: 7, −3, −6, 1 **3.** $-7(3) + (-7)(2)$ **5.** $9y$ **7.** $6m + n - 4b$

2.7 Practice and Problem Solving (pp. 88–89) **13.** $9x - 27$ **15.** 56 **17.** $-34z + 884$ **19.** $4r + 2s$ **21.** $5a + 6b$ **23.** $-3x - 9y$ **25.** Add $2.35 and $.65 to get $3.00. Multiply $3.00 by 6 to find the total, $18. **27.** $7y - 14$ **29.** $2x + 2$ **31.** $12d$ **33.** $786.24 **35.** $3x - 5$ **37.** $1.7y - 6.7$ **39.** *Sample answer:* $4(30 + 4) = 120 + 16 = 136$; mental math can be used to multiply and then add. **41.** *Sample answer:* $24(10 + 2) = 240 + 48 = 288$; mental math can be used to multiply and then add. **43.** Yes; by the commutative property of multiplication, $xy = yx$. **47.** −100, −90, −20, 0, 70 **49.** −21 **51.** −700

2.7 Technology Activity (p. 90) **1.** −28,546 **3.** 11,009 **5.** −2,105,804 **7.** −262,890,144 **9.** −101 **11.** about 13,904 km; about 10,428 km

2.8 Getting Ready to Practice (p. 93)

1. 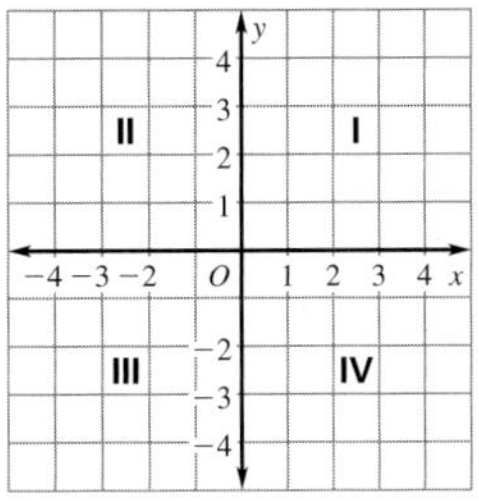

3. (0, 1) **5.** (1, −2)

6-9.

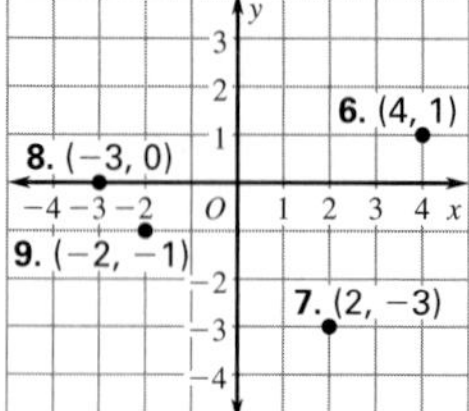

2.8 Practice and Problem Solving (pp. 93-95) **11.** $(-3, 3)$ **13.** $(-5, 0)$ **15.** $(0, -2)$

17-20.

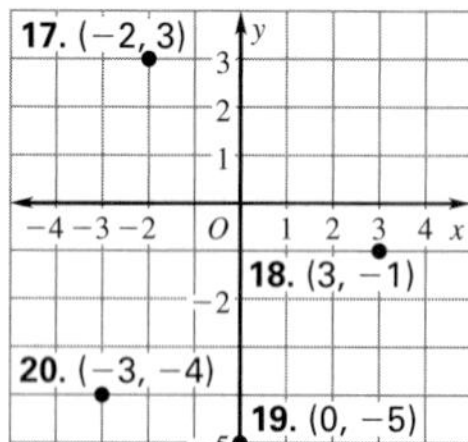

17. Quadrant II
19. y-axis

21.

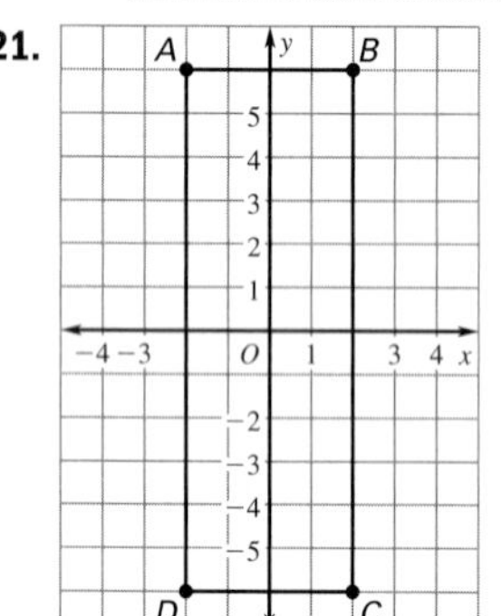

rectangle; 32 units

23. The points lie along a line; \$8.75.

25.

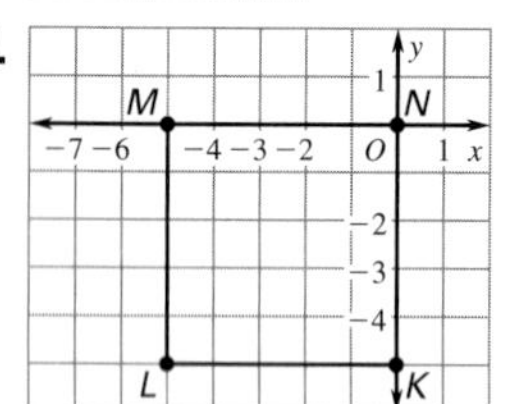

20 units; 25 square units

27. \$.70, \$1.40, \$2.10 **29.** \$4.20

31.

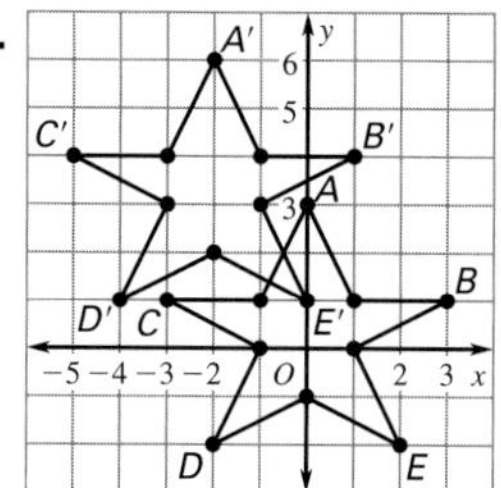

$A(-2, 6)$, $B(1, 4)$, $C(-5, 4)$, $D(-4, 1)$, $E(0, 1)$

33. -1 **35.** $4x + 36$ **37.** $-9z + 18$

2.6-2.8 Notebook Review (pp. 96-97) **1.** -5 **2.** -190 **3.** -1300 **4.** -83 **5.** $27a + 95$ **6.** $76b + 36$ **7.** $-70c + 40$

8-11.

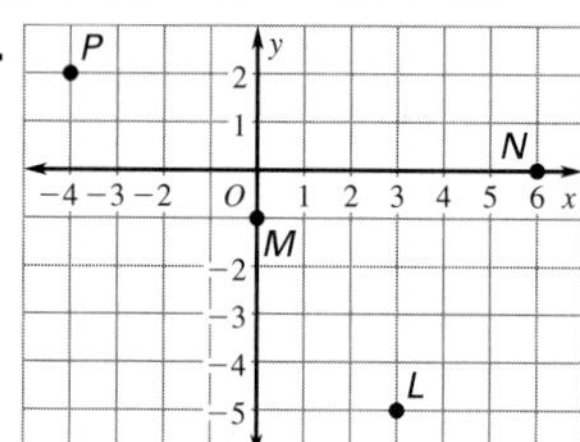

8. Quadrant IV
9. y-axis
10. x-axis
11. Quadrant II

12. Use $4(6 + 0.11) = 4(6) + 4(0.11) = 24 + 0.44 = 24.44$.

Chapter Review (pp. 98-99) **1.** 2; 15, -15

3. 4;

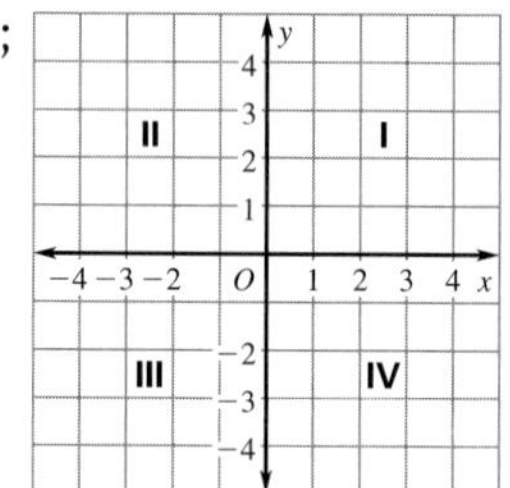

5. coordinate plane **7.** $-42, -31, -5, 8, 11, 53$ **9.** $-22, 22$ **11.** 512, 512 **13.** -172 **15.** 176 **17.** -86 **19.** 79 **21.** -54 **23.** 0 **25.** -192 **27.** -140 **29.** 152 ft **31.** 14 **33.** -9 **35.** 1 **37.** 97; commutative and associative properties of addition **39.** 1900; commutative and associative properties of multiplication **41.** 0; multiplication property of zero **43.** $63 + 77y$ **45.** $7x - 2y$ **47.** \$38.70 **49.** $(-4, 3)$ **51.** $(-2, -3)$

Chapter 3

3.1 Getting Ready to Practice (p. 111) **1.** inverse **3.** 20 **5.** Step 1: Sales tax; Step 2: $54.99 + x = 58.29$; Step 3: \$3.30

3.1 Practice and Problem Solving (pp. 111–112)
7. subtracting 4.5 **9.** 5 **11.** 13 **13.** 2 **15.** 24
17. −28 **19.** 64 **21.** yes **23.** no; $t = 29 - 3$
25. *Sample answer:* There are 55 cats at the shelter. There are 13 more cats than dogs. How many dogs are at the shelter? **27.** 0 **29.** 1 **31.** 4.7 **33.** 8
35. −31 **39.** $3.52
40–43.

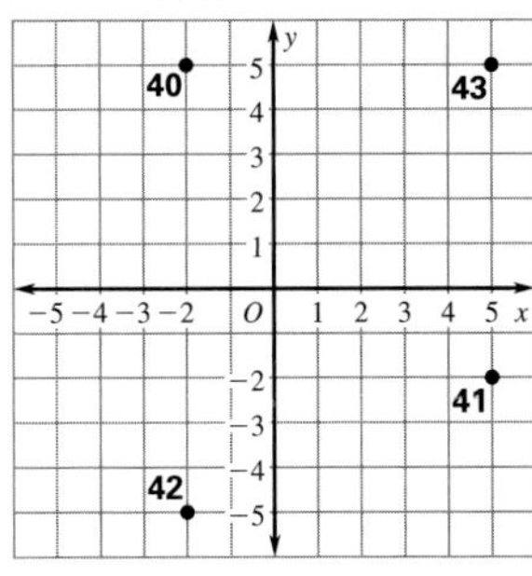

41. Quadrant IV
43. Quadrant I

45. *Sample answer:* 130, 220 **47.** *Sample answer:* 2800, 4000

3.2 Getting Ready to Practice (p. 115) **1.** divide
3. $\frac{y}{9} = -3$ [original equation]; $\frac{y}{9} \cdot 9 = (-3) \cdot 9$ [Multiply each side by 9.]; $y = -27$ [Simplify.]

3.2 Practice and Problem Solving (pp. 115–116)
5. 18 **7.** 70 **9.** 3 **11.** 105 **13.** 216 **15.** 2.5
19. dividing by 5 **21.** subtracting −6, or adding 6
23. −216 **25.** 10 **27.** 29.9 **29.** 30 **31.** 3 **33.** −2.1
35. *Sample answer:* $3x = 18$, $\frac{x}{2} = 3$ **37.** about 17 eggs; about 4 eggs **39.** < **41.** > **43.** sixteen and two hundredths **45.** seven million, five hundred forty thousand, six hundred eighty-eight

3.3 Getting Ready to Practice (p. 121)
1. addition, division; 3 **3.** 3 **5.** 1 **7.** −4

3.3 Practice and Problem Solving (pp. 121–123)
11. 4 **13.** 7 **15.** $\frac{1}{4}$, or 0.25 **17.** 3 **19.** 9 **21.** $-\frac{1}{2}$, or −0.5 **23.** $2\frac{2}{3}$; because 3 miles is an estimate, $3h$ is an estimate for the number of miles of trail cleaned per hour, so the number of hours will also be an estimate. **25.** 7 **27.** $-1\frac{2}{3}$ **29.** 40 **31.** 55
33. −7 **35.** 24 **37.** 19 min **39.** Divide each side by 2; simplify; subtract 3 from each side; simplify.
41. −15 **45.** 132; the summer pass would be cheaper than paying for 40 day passes.
47. *Sample answer:* Choose the summer pass if you go to the pool more than 29 days because it is cheaper. Choose the day pass if you go to the pool 29 days or less because it is cheaper. **49.** 19
51. 48 **53.** 50% **55.** 20%

3.4 Practice and Problem Solving (pp. 126–128)
7. $4 + 5n = 9$; 1 **9.** 16 sandwiches on rye bread
11. *Sample answer:* You buy 5 boxes of your favorite cereal at the store. With the store's double-coupon policy, you save $6 with your coupons. You pay $9 for the cereal. What was the original price of each box? **13.** $7 **15.** $2x + 5 = 12$; 3.5 **17.** $-2n + 3.5 = 7.5$; −2 **19.** 85 people **21.** the number of hours worked **27.** $P = 30$ ft; $A = 36\text{ ft}^2$ **29.** $P = 84$ m; $A = 432\text{ m}^2$ **31.** 35

3.4 Technology Activity (p. 129) **1.** *Sample answer:* $35(4) + 10x = 190$; 5 adults

3.1–3.4 Notebook Review (pp. 130–131)
1. addition and subtraction; multiplication and division **2.** −11 **3.** 42 **4.** 12 **5.** 47 **6.** −11
7. −9 **8.** 27 **9.** −40 **10.** 55 **11.** −4 **12.** 0 **13.** 2
14. 105 envelopes per hour **15.** It uses inverse operations in reverse order to their corresponding operations.

3.5 Problem Solving Strategies (p. 133) **1.** 672 ft^2
3. $118,125 **5.** the room where students share tables **7.** The total number of students is greater than 1238.

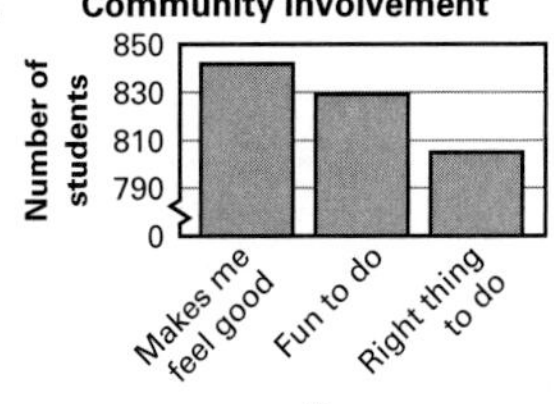

9. 96 ft;

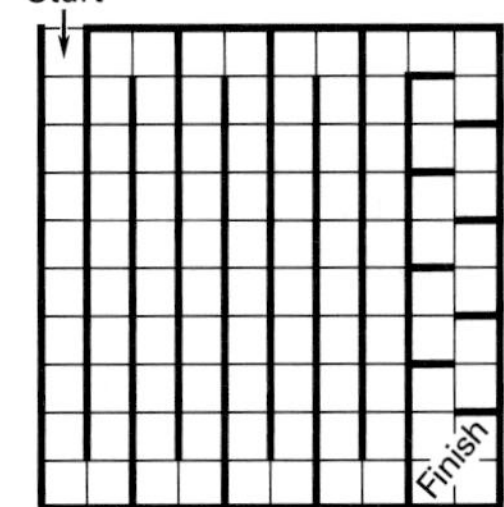

Sample answer: I tried drawing other mazes.

3.5 Getting Ready to Practice (p. 137) **1.** base, height **3.** $A = 4$ cm^2; $P = 8$ cm **5.** Step 1: 42 yd^2; Step 2: 9 yd^2; Step 3: 51 yd^2

3.5 Practice and Problem Solving (pp. 137–139) **7.** $A = 24$ in.^{2}; $P = 32$ in. **9.** 3 ft **11.** 4 cm **13.** 20 m **15.** Area is given in square units; $A = 10$ in.^{2} **17.** 24 in. **19.** $\frac{5}{x}$ m **21.** 16 m^2 **23.** 180 ft^2 **25.** *Sample answer:* about 3 ft by 6 ft; 18 ft^2 **27.** Doubles the area. **29.** Quadruples the area. **31.** No; Kate has 121 square feet and the room has an area of 252 square feet, so Kate has less than half the area of the room. **33.** 37.5 m^2 **35.** -60 **37.** 21 **39.** -32 **41.** 7 **43.** 35 **45.** $>$ **47.** $<$

3.6 Getting Ready to Practice (p. 142)
1. equivalent inequalities
7. $t < -2$; −3 −2 −1 0 1 2 3
9. Step 1: 360; Step 2: $360 + x \geq 425$, $x \geq 65$; Step 3: 60 70 80 90

3.6 Practice and Problem Solving (pp. 143–145) **11.** $x \geq -5$ **13.** $x < 6$ **15.** no **17.** yes **19.** j is greater than -4. **21.** n is less than 0.
23. $t > -3$; −4 −3 −2 −1 0 1 2
25. $r \geq 8$; −2 0 2 4 6 8 10
27. $p > 7$; 2 3 4 5 6 7 8
29. $m \leq 11$; 6 7 8 9 10 11 12
31. $33.96 + x \geq 50$; $x \geq \$16.04$ **33.** 20 min
35. $r < 7.5$; 5 6 7 8
37. $p \geq 3$; −1 0 1 2 3 4 5
39. $t > 4\frac{3}{4}$; 4 5
41. $x \geq 13$ is the solution to $x - 3 \geq 10$. **43.** no **45.** $x > 81$ hertz and $x < 1100$ hertz **47.** y is greater than -2 and y is less than 1. **49.** m is greater than or equal to 4 and m is less than or equal to 11. **53.** -53 **55.** -7 **57.** 9.053

3.7 Getting Ready to Practice (p. 148) **1.** reverse **3.** yes **5.** $m \leq -42$; −50 −46 −42 −38
7. $p > -5$; −6 −5 −4 −3 −2 −1 0

3.7 Practice and Problem Solving (pp. 148–149)
13. $x > 4$; −1 0 1 2 3 4 5
15. $b \leq -360$; −360 −120 0 120 240
17. $g < 6$; −2 0 2 4 6 8 10
19. $c \geq -6$; −8 −6 −4 −2 0 2 4
25. No; there are infinitely many solutions. **33.** You undo the operations in the same way. If you multiply or divide by a negative number in an inequality, you must reverse the direction of the inequality. **35.** $x \geq 80$ **37.** $x \geq \frac{1}{2}$ **41.** 12 cm by 16 cm **43.** 1 **45.** $c \leq 4$; 0 1 2 3 4 5 6
47. $x > 29$; 25 26 27 28 29 30 31 **49.** 72

3.5–3.7 Notebook Review (pp. 150–151)
1. *Sample:*

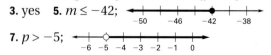

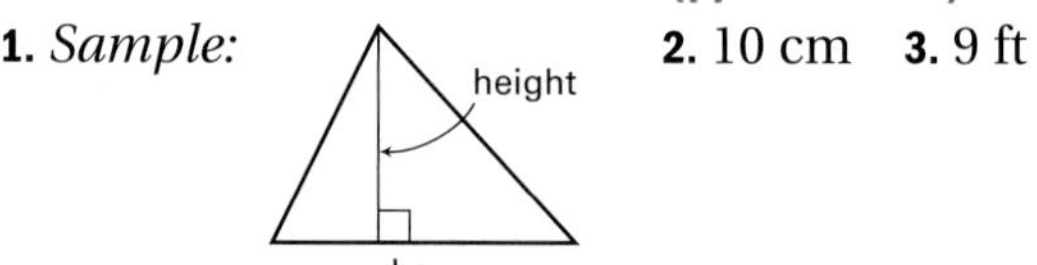

2. 10 cm **3.** 9 ft
4. $h > 24$; 21 22 23 24 25 26 27
5. $k \leq 10$; 0 2 4 6 8 10 12
6. $p > -8$; −10 −8 −6 −4 −2 0 2
7. $d \geq -6$; −10 −8 −6 −4 −2 0 2
8. $d \leq 204$ **9.** $x \leq -100$ **10.** $c > 5$ **11.** $b > -4$ **12.** $c \geq 54$ **13.** 7; the solution to the inequality is $x < 8$ and the greatest integer that is less than 8 is 7.

Chapter Review (pp. 152–153) **1.** Addition and subtraction, multiplication and division; one operation undoes the other. **3.** equivalent equations **5.** 32 **7.** 15 **9.** 40 **11.** 1288 **13.** -3 **15.** 2.4 **17.** Fuel in tank $-$ Fuel used $=$ Fuel left; $\frac{5}{8} - x = \frac{3}{8}$; $x = \frac{2}{8} = \frac{1}{4}$ **19.** 9 **21.** -5 **23.** 27 **25.** -115 **27.** -45 **29.** 18 baskets **31.** 8 m **33.** 20 in.^{2} **35.** 60 yd^2
37. $c \leq 108$; −72 −36 0 36 72 108 144
39. $h > -4$; −5 −4 −3 −2 −1 0 1
41. The inequality sign should not be reversed when subtracting; $x < 10$.

Chapter 4

4.1 Getting Ready to Practice (p. 170) **1.** prime **3.** 1, 3, 9, 27 **5.** 1, 2, 3, 6, 11, 22, 33, 66 **7.** $5 \cdot 11$ **9.** $2^5 \cdot 3$

4.1 Practice and Problem Solving (pp. 171–172) **11.** 1, 2, 17, 34 **13.** 1, 2, 3, 4, 6, 9, 12, 18, 27, 35, 54, 108 **15.** composite **17.** prime **19.** $2^3 \cdot 7$ **21.** $2 \cdot 3 \cdot 17$ **23.** second row: 8; fourth row: 2, 2, 2, 11; $2^3 \cdot 11$ **25.** second row: 2; third row: 2, 21; fourth row: 5, 3, 7; $2 \cdot 3 \cdot 5 \cdot 7$ **27.** $3 \cdot 5 \cdot c \cdot d$ **29.** $3 \cdot 3 \cdot a \cdot a \cdot b \cdot b \cdot b \cdot b$ **31.** 3 stars by 5 stars **33.** 5 stars by 6 stars (or 3 stars by 10 stars, or 2 stars by 15 stars) **35.** 1, 13, 23, 299 **37.** 1, 2, 4, 5, 8, 10, 16, 20, 25, 40, 50, 80, 100, 200, 400 **39.** $2^3 \cdot 5 \cdot 7$ **41.** $3^2 \cdot 5^3$ **43.** *Sample answer:* $3 + 7$ **45.** *Sample answer:* $11 + 17$ **47.** No; 40 is not a factor of 140. **49.** 2 and 3 **53.** $-4a + 4b + 2$ **55.** $y \geq 40$ **57.** 850 ft^2. *Sample answer:* I used Draw a Diagram to draw the spaces and find the area. **59.** *Sample answer:* 7000; 9000 **61.** *Sample answer:* 13; 20

4.2 Getting Ready to Practice (p. 175) **1.** greatest common factor, or GCF **7.** Step 1: $56 = 2 \cdot 2 \cdot 2 \cdot 7$, $68 = 2 \cdot 2 \cdot 17$; Step 2: 2 and 2; Step 3: 4; the greatest number of teams that can be formed is 4, where each has 14 girls and 17 boys.

4.2 Practice and Problem Solving (pp. 176–177) **9.** 7 **11.** 12 **13.** no; 5 **15.** yes **17.** no; 18 **19.** yes **21.** 30 baskets; 2 cans of cranberry sauce, 4 cans of fruit, 3 cans of corn, 2 boxes of muffin mix **23.** $2z^2$ **25.** $4xy^2$ **27.** $15bc$ **29.** always **31.** *Sample answer:* 6 and 25 **33.** 90 bouquets **35.** 12 ft **37.** -8 **39.** $2^2 \cdot 3 \cdot 7$

4.3 Getting Ready to Practice (p. 181) **1.** yes **3.** yes **5.** $\frac{2}{3}$ **7.** $\frac{5}{8}$ **9.** *Sample answer:* $\frac{2}{10}, \frac{3}{15}$ **11.** 64

4.3 Practice and Problem Solving (pp. 182–183) **13.** $\frac{3}{4}$ **15.** $\frac{-1}{8}$, or $-\frac{1}{8}$ **17.** $\frac{b}{2}$ **19.** $\frac{-3t}{10}$, or $-\frac{3t}{10}$ **21.** yes **23.** yes **25.** *Sample answer:* $\frac{1}{2}, \frac{2}{4}$ **27.** *Sample answer:* $\frac{2}{5}, \frac{4}{10}$ **29.** $\frac{1}{3}$ **31.** 1 **33.** $\frac{9}{50}$ **35.** $\frac{8}{25}$ **37.** $\frac{1}{10}$ **39.** For birds, about $\frac{60}{1500} = \frac{1}{25}$ are threatened; a greater fraction of mammals is threatened than birds; $\frac{1}{40}$ (reptiles), $\frac{64}{1541}$ (birds), $\frac{1}{10}$ (mammals). **41.** $\frac{3}{5}, \frac{3}{5}$; yes **43.** $\frac{3}{4}, \frac{5}{8}$; no **45.** $\frac{5}{6}, \frac{5}{6}$; yes **47.** $\frac{3}{4}, \frac{7}{8}$; no **49.** y^2 **51.** $\frac{-4z}{x^2y}$, or $-\frac{4z}{x^2y}$ **53.** no **55.** yes **61.** **63.**

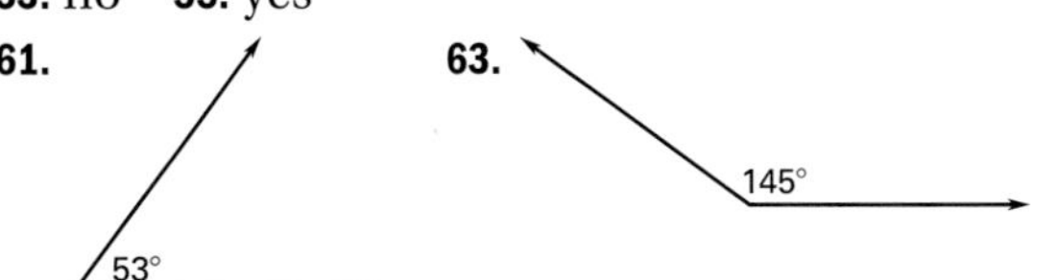

4.4 Problem Solving Strategies (p. 185) **1.** 10 ways **5.** 16 choices **7.** 44 posts **9.** 168 in., or 14 ft

4.4 Getting Ready to Practice (p. 188) **1.** common multiple **7.** 4 is the GCF of 12 and 24. The LCM is $2 \cdot 2 \cdot 2 \cdot 3$, or 24.

4.4 Practice and Problem Solving (pp. 188–189) **9.** multiples of 6: 6, 12, 18, 24, 30, 36, 42; multiples of 21: 21, 42; LCM: 42 **11.** multiples of 10: 10, 20, 30; multiples of 15: 15, 30; LCM: 30 **13.** $17 = 17$, $57 = 3 \cdot 19$; 969 **15.** $125 = 5^3$, $500 = 2^2 \cdot 5^3$; 500 **17.** $8 = 2^3$, $16 = 2^4$, $32 = 2^5$; 32 **19.** $20 = 2^2 \cdot 5$, $24 = 2^3 \cdot 3$, $60 = 2^2 \cdot 3 \cdot 5$; 120 **21.** $49s^3t^2$ **23.** $120c^2d^6$ **25.** 180 sec **27.** 4320 **29.** 4788 **31.** 300 **33.** 60 **35.** $120x^4y^7$ **37.** $495g^4h^5k^3$ **39.** 24 min; 1440 sec **43.** $19x + 20 + 2y$ **45.** 73.7 **47.** 134.77

4.1–4.4 Notebook Review (pp. 190–191) **1.** prime factorization **2.** $2^3 \cdot 5$ **3.** 7 **4.** $5 \cdot 17$ **5.** $2^3 \cdot 3 \cdot 5$ **6.** 16 **7.** 20 **8.** $7a$ **9.** $20y^4$ **10.** $\frac{1}{3}$ **11.** $\frac{3}{20}$ **12.** $\frac{b}{3}$ **13.** $\frac{n^2}{3}$ **14.** 84 **15.** 270 **16.** $50c^2d$ **17.** $36n^3$ **18.** *Sample answer:* When you list the factors of a number, you list all numbers by which the number is divisible, including 1, composite numbers, and the number itself. When you find the prime factorization of a number, you write the number as a product only of its prime factors.

4.5 Getting Ready to Practice (p. 194) **1.** least common multiple or LCM **3.** 20 **5.** 36 **7.** $<$ **9.** $>$

4.5 Practice and Problem Solving (pp. 194–195)
11. > **13.** < **15.** > **17.** $\frac{1}{8}, \frac{5}{16}, \frac{1}{2}, \frac{3}{4}$ **19.** $\frac{15}{16}, \frac{5}{3}, \frac{35}{15}, 2\frac{2}{5}$
23. $\frac{-47}{4}, -11\frac{7}{12}, \frac{-23}{2}, -11\frac{17}{48}, \frac{-34}{3}$ **25.** >
31. $2^4 \cdot 3 \cdot 7$

4.6 Getting Ready to Practice (p. 198) **1.** base
3. yes **5.** no **7.** 4^6 **9.** a^{12} **11.** c **13.** 8^5 **15.** The bases should not be multiplied;. $2^2 \cdot 2^4 = 2^{2+4} = 2^6$.

4.6 Practice and Problem Solving (pp. 199–200)
17. v^{12} **19.** m^{19} **21.** x^4 **23.** y^2 **25.** $(-4)^5$ **27.** 7^4
29. 2^{10} **31.** 9^4 **33.** 5 **35.** 9 **37.** $4y^5$ **39.** $64a^7b^{10}$
41. z^5 **43.** $25n^3$ **45.** 10^{12} **47.** 10^{12} **49.** 2^2 **55.** 157
57. 18 **59.** >

4.7 Getting Ready to Practice (p. 203) **1.** true
3. $\frac{1}{81}$ **5.** $\frac{1}{16}$ **7.** 5^{-3} means $\frac{1}{5^3}$; $5^{-3} = \frac{1}{5^3} = \frac{1}{5 \cdot 5 \cdot 5} = \frac{1}{125}$.

4.7 Practice and Problem Solving (pp. 203–204)
9. $\frac{1}{36}$ **11.** $\frac{1}{625}$ **13.** $\frac{1}{m^4}$ **15.** $\frac{9}{n^3}$ **17.** $\frac{1}{b^6}$ **19.** $\frac{1}{d^{13}}$
21. $\frac{kg}{m \cdot s^2}$ **23.** −8 **25.** 10 **27.** 10^{11} **29.** 10^8 **31.** 10^7
33. never **35.** −25 **37.** 52 **39.** 90 **41.** −17

4.8 Getting Ready to Practice (p. 207) **1.** yes
3. yes **5.** 4.68×10^{-1} **7.** 4,350,000 **9.** 96,200,000

4.8 Practice and Problem Solving (pp. 207–208)
11. 7.9×10^3 **13.** 2.13×10^6 **15.** 4.15×10^{-7}
17. 0.0871 **19.** 0.00000000176
21. 2,830,000,000,000 **23.** 6×10^8 **25.** 6.552×10^{14}
27. 1.5×10^7 **31.** > **33.** 1.066×10^5 **35.** 1.944×10^{-13} **37.** 3.5×10^{11} **39.** 1.19×10^8; 6.205×10^9
41. 1.2×10^{-13} cm **43.** 6 **45.** $\frac{2}{3m}$

4.8 Technology Activity (p. 209) **1.** 2.7115×10^{14}
3. 1.584×10^{-11} **5.** 2.682119205×10^7
7. $1.365853659 \times 10^{-7}$ **9.** about 2.3×10^2

4.5–4.8 Notebook Review (pp. 210–211)
1. scientific notation **2.** > **3.** < **4.** < **5.** = **6.** n^{13}
7. y^{16} **8.** x^2 **9.** c^4 **10.** $\frac{12}{a^5}$ **11.** $\frac{1}{n^3}$ **12.** $\frac{1}{m^{11}}$ **13.** $\frac{1}{c^{13}}$
14. 3.46×10^{10} **15.** 9×10^{-7} **16.** 5.02×10^{-10}

17. *Sample answer:* Use the commutative and associative properties to rewrite the product as $(5 \times 4) \times (10^9 \times 10^{15})$. Use multiplication and the product of powers property to simplify this to 20×10^{24}. Move the decimal point to write the product in scientific notation as 2.0×10^{25}.

Chapter Review (pp. 212–213) **1.** The greatest common factor is the greatest number that is a factor of both numbers. The least common multiple is the smallest number that is a multiple of both numbers. **3.** *Sample answer:* $3x$, $4s^2$, $7ab^3$
5. simplest form **7.** prime factorization **9.** $2 \cdot 3^3$
11. $2 \cdot 3 \cdot 5^2$ **13.** $19 \cdot a \cdot a \cdot b$ **15.** $2 \cdot 2 \cdot 2 \cdot 7 \cdot u \cdot u \cdot v \cdot v$ **17.** 10 **19.** 3 **21.** $9xy$ **23.** $\frac{1}{3}$ **25.** $-\frac{16}{51}$
27. $\frac{c}{3}$ **29.** $\frac{4}{n}$ **31.** 105 **33.** $25m^2n^4$ **35.** 24 sec
37. < **39.** > **41.** 8^4 **43.** 7^2 **45.** $\frac{7}{x^4}$ **47.** $\frac{1}{3w^8}$
49. 0.000658 **51.** 6×10^6 ft³/min; 3.6×10^8 ft³/h

Chapter 5

5.1 Getting Ready to Practice (p. 221)
1. denominator, numerator **3.** $\frac{2}{3}$ **5.** $\frac{1}{5}$ **7.** $1\frac{3}{7}$
9. c **11.** $18\frac{3}{4}$ in.

5.1 Practice and Problem Solving (pp. 222–223)
13. $\frac{1}{9}$ **15.** $-\frac{11}{12}$ **17.** $\frac{1}{5}$ **19.** $-\frac{1}{2}$ **21.** $\frac{8}{15}$ **23.** $-8\frac{2}{5}$
25. $-\frac{n}{7}$ **27.** $-\frac{q}{p}$ **29.** 15 h; $2\frac{2}{3}$ h **31.** $1\frac{11}{18}$ **33.** $\frac{8}{25}$
35. $\frac{15}{16}$ **37.** $-8\frac{1}{5}$ **39.** $3\frac{1}{12}$ **41.** $\frac{1}{4}$ **43.** $1\frac{1}{3}$ **47.** 5
49. −42 **51.** 105 **53.** 1850 **55.** 9 **57.** 24 **59.** 16
61. 1.25

5.2 Getting Ready to Practice (p. 226) **1.** least common denominator or LCD **3.** $1\frac{23}{24}$ **5.** $\frac{36 + x}{9x}$

5.2 Practice and Problem Solving (pp. 226–227)
7. $\frac{5}{8}$ **9.** $\frac{13}{18}$ **11.** $-\frac{1}{32}$ **13.** $-\frac{33}{40}$ **15.** $11\frac{19}{36}$ **17.** $13\frac{8}{35}$
19. $8\frac{1}{3}$ ft **21.** true **23.** false **25.** $\frac{17s}{20}$ **27.** $\frac{77}{50n}$

29. West; traveling east is $\frac{27}{50}$ of the way around the equator, while traveling west is $1 - \frac{27}{50} = \frac{23}{50}$ of the way. Since $\frac{23}{50} < \frac{27}{50}$, traveling west is shorter.

31. $1\frac{11}{72}$ **35.** 0 **37.** -126 **39.** < **41.** <

5.3 Problem Solving Strategies (p. 229)
1. 7 students. *Sample answer:* Choose 18 classmates. Let 2 classmates represent the students that have both a dog and a cat. Six more classmates are needed to represent the students that have a dog and 3 more to represent those that have a cat. There are 7 classmates left over. **3.** 3 bows. *Sample answer:* Let one floor tile represent $\frac{1}{6}$ of a yard. Mark off $13 \cdot 5 = 65$ tiles to represent the amount of ribbon needed to decorate 5 gifts. Mark off 120 tiles to represent the amount of ribbon you have. The difference, 55 tiles, represents the length of ribbon left from which to make bows. Since 15 tiles represent the amount of ribbon needed to make a bow and $55 \div 15 = 3\frac{2}{3}$, 3 bows can be made with the remaining ribbon.
5. 16 students; eighth. *Sample answer:* I had 4 classmates stand in front of me and 6 stand behind me. Then I had another classmate stand in front of me, and then two more classmates stood behind her but in front of me. Then I had 2 more classmates join the end of the line. Counting showed 16 classmates in line, of which I was eighth.
7. 5 sweatshirts and 12 T-shirts

5.3 Getting Ready to Practice (p. 232)
1. numerators, denominators **3.** $-1\frac{7}{8}$ **5.** $\frac{23}{32}$

5.3 Practice and Problem Solving (pp. 232–233)
7. $\frac{7}{66}$ **9.** $\frac{1}{6}$ **11.** $4\frac{1}{2}$ **13.** $8\frac{3}{4}$ **15.** $27\frac{2}{9}$ **17.** $14\frac{2}{5}$ **19.** $1\frac{2}{5}$ km **21.** $-1\frac{3}{4}$ **23.** $-\frac{35}{48}$ **25.** 35 ft. *Sample answer:* Let one floor tile represent $\frac{1}{4}$ foot. Mark off 7 tiles to represent $1\frac{3}{4}$ feet. Mark off 7 tiles 19 more times to get 140 total tiles. Since 140 tiles times $\frac{1}{4}$ foot per tile equals 35, the answer is 35 feet.

27. $\frac{2}{3}$ ft^2 **29.** $-\frac{9}{100}$ **31.** $-9\frac{3}{4}$ **33.** $3\frac{19}{120}$ **35.** $4\frac{3}{4}$ **37.** 7^5 **39.** 8^2 **41.** $1\frac{1}{2}$ **43.** $\frac{29}{60}$

5.4 Getting Ready to Practice (p. 236) **1.** The multiplicative inverse, or reciprocal, of a number is the number that when multiplied by the original number equals 1. **3.** 6 **5.** $1\frac{1}{3}$ **7.** $\frac{2}{9}$ **9.** $-1\frac{2}{3}$ **11.** Step 1: Number of pounds of hamburger = Pounds per hamburger • Number of hamburgers; Step 2: $5 = \frac{1}{4}h$; Step 3: 20 hamburgers

5.4 Practice and Problem Solving (pp. 237–238)
13. $-\frac{9}{14}$ **15.** $1\frac{1}{2}$ **17.** $-\frac{3}{40}$ **19.** $-\frac{7}{8}$ **21.** $-3\frac{1}{2}$ **23.** $-7\frac{1}{12}$ **25.** $-\frac{2}{7}$ **27.** $2\frac{11}{35}$ **29.** $\frac{1}{6}$ **31.** $1\frac{3}{4}$ **33.** about $8\frac{1}{3}$ days **35.** Yes. *Sample answer:* When the two fractions are written with the same denominator c, then they can be represented as $\frac{a}{c}$ and $\frac{b}{c}$. Then $\frac{a}{c} \div \frac{b}{c} = \frac{a}{c} \cdot \frac{c}{b} = \frac{a}{b}$, so Juan's method works. **37.** 40 **39.** $1\frac{1}{5}$ **41.** 875 people. *Sample answer:* I solved the equation $\frac{2}{5}p = 350$. **43.** $\frac{2}{5}$ **45.** $\frac{3}{14}$ **47.** $\frac{x}{3}$ **49.** $\frac{7x^2}{9y^2}$ **51.** $1\frac{8}{9}$ **53.** $9\frac{1}{3}$

5.4 Technology Activity (p. 239) **1.** $\frac{47}{55}$ **3.** $\frac{2}{3}$ **5.** $1\frac{1}{27}$ **7.** $11\frac{1}{5}$ **9.** $1\frac{1}{16}$ qt

5.1–5.4 Notebook Review (pp. 240–241) **1.** 1 **2.** $\frac{1}{2}$ **3.** $-1\frac{1}{8}$ **4.** $1\frac{7}{8}$ **5.** $\frac{22x}{15}$ **6.** $\frac{5}{14}$ **7.** 2 **8.** $-8\frac{1}{2}$ **9.** $10\frac{5}{6}$ **10.** 9 **11.** $-1\frac{3}{7}$ **12.** $1\frac{3}{4}$ **13.** Multiply the answer by the divisor. The answer should be the dividend. *Sample answer:* $\frac{2}{5} \div \frac{5}{6} = \frac{12}{25}$ and $\frac{12}{25} \cdot \frac{5}{6} = \frac{2}{5}$
14. Greater than. *Sample answer:* Since dividing by a number is the same as multiplying by its reciprocal, and the reciprocal of a fraction between 0 and 1 will be greater than 1, the quotient will be greater than the original number.

5.5 Getting Ready to Practice (p. 244)
1. rational number, integer, whole number **3.** rational number, integer **5.** 0.8 **7.** $0.\overline{3}$ **9.** $\frac{3}{5}$ **11.** $\frac{8}{9}$ **13.** 1.8 in., $1\frac{7}{8}$ in., 2.1 in., $2\frac{1}{9}$ in.

5.5 Practice and Problem Solving (pp. 245–246)
15. $-0.\overline{1}$ **17.** $0.58\overline{3}$ **19.** 0.54 **21.** -0.4125 **23.** $-14.\overline{63}$ **25.** $0.6\overline{136}$ **27.** $-\frac{14}{25}$ **29.** $2\frac{79}{100}$ **31.** $7\frac{253}{1000}$ **33.** $-5\frac{2}{625}$ **35.** $\frac{8}{9}$ **37.** $\frac{5}{33}$ **39.** $\frac{14}{333}$ **41.** $20\frac{41}{198}$ **43.** $9\frac{9}{13}$, $9\frac{5}{7}$, 9.72, 9.74, $9\frac{3}{4}$ **45.** $0.\overline{09}$, $0.\overline{18}$, $0.\overline{27}$; $0.\overline{36}$, $0.\overline{45}$ **47.** 200 students **49.** 0.049; $\frac{1}{20}$ **53.** 17 **55.** 13 **57.** *Sample answer:* 170 **59.** *Sample answer:* 60

5.6 Getting Ready to Practice (p. 249) **1.** 13, 11, 25 **3.** 7.37 **5.** 2.4 **7.** 5.61 **9.** 32

5.6 Practice and Problem Solving (pp. 249–250)
11. 38.103 **13.** -3.419 **15.** 4.988 **17.** -1.63 **19.** -7.71 **21.** 22.1 **23.** 18.985 **25.** -5.027 **27.** 7.31 **29.** -0.17 **31.** -6.347 **33.** 60 **35.** $300 + 40 + 5 + 0.6 + 0.09 + 0.002$ **37.** 67.75 ft **39.** 26.42 m **45.** -1 **47.** $\frac{1}{b^{14}}$ **49.** $\frac{40}{63}$ **51.** $7\frac{1}{2}$

5.7 Getting Ready to Practice (p. 253)
1. divisor → $9\overline{)7.2}$ ← dividend, with quotient 0.8 ← quotient **3.** 1.5; $4 \cdot 0.4 = 1.6$ **5.** 0.4; $0.5 \div 1 = 0.5$

5.7 Practice and Problem Solving (pp. 253–254)
7. 5 **9.** -5.74 **11.** 4 **13.** -50 **15.** 1.8935 **17.** 8.65 **19.** 8.7 **21.** 290.405 **23.** The answer should have $2 + 1 = 3$ decimal places; 33.252. **27.** -8.1 **29.** 0.2675 **31.** 37.414 **33.** If you multiply both 4.6 and 0.23 by 100, you get 460 and 23; yes; because you have multiplied $\frac{4.6}{0.23}$ by $\frac{100}{100} = 1$ to get $\frac{460}{23}$. **37.** 6,890,000,000 **39.** 0.000007405 **41.** -0.46, $-\frac{9}{20}$, $-\frac{5}{12}$, -0.4, $-\frac{3}{8}$ **43.** 25 R2 **45.** 204 R39

5.8 Getting Ready to Practice (p. 259) **1.** mean **3.** range **5.** -56; -56; -56; 27 **7.** Step 1: 1365 sec, 1316 sec, 1263 sec, 1233 sec, 1228 sec; Step 2: 6405 sec; 1281 sec; Step 3: 21:21

5.8 Practice and Problem Solving (pp. 259–261)
9. 191; 185; 185; 174 **11.** $181.1\overline{6}$ ft; 87 ft; none; 531 ft **13.** $9\frac{3}{4}$ in.; 10 in.; $10\frac{1}{2}$ in.; $2\frac{3}{8}$ in. **15.** Isaac: 9.375, Carl: 9.6, Kurt, 9.425; Carl's **17.** *Sample answer:* The median; there are equally many salaries above and below it, so it should reflect the most likely salary for me in each career. **19.** $\frac{7b}{6}$ **21.** Yes. *Sample answer:* I prefer Roberta's method because it is shorter and can be used for any value of *a*. **25.** -5 **27.** 0 **29.** -16 **31.** 66 **33.** -16

5.5–5.8 Notebook Review (pp. 262–263)
1. mean, median, mode **2.** $6\frac{3}{8}$, 6.4, $6\frac{5}{12}$, $6\frac{4}{9}$ **3.** 1.87 **4.** 42.598 **5.** 1.315 **6.** 98.11 **7.** 2.34 **8.** 3.0132 **9.** -24.8 **10.** 2 **11.** 24; 24; 24; 10 **12.** 7.45; 7.4; 7.2 and 7.7; 0.8 **13.** *Sample answer:* 3, 4, 12, 12 **14.** They both can be written as ratios. *Sample answer:* $0.2 = \frac{1}{5}$ and $0.\overline{2} = \frac{2}{9}$.

Chapter Review (pp. 264–265) **1.** reciprocals **3.** front-end estimation **5.** mean **7.** $1\frac{1}{3}$ **9.** $-1\frac{1}{5}$ **11.** $\frac{17}{20}$ **13.** $-\frac{47}{56}$ **15.** $-\frac{4n}{3}$ **17.** $-\frac{1}{2c}$ **19.** $\frac{1}{4}$ in. **21.** $-\frac{1}{4}$ **23.** $-16\frac{1}{14}$ **25.** $\frac{3}{35}$ **27.** $-7\frac{7}{11}$ **29.** 30 **31.** $-7\frac{1}{7}$ **33.** 2, $\frac{11}{5}$, 2.25, $2\frac{3}{10}$, 2.32, $\frac{5}{2}$ **35.** 25.88 **37.** 6.045 **39.** -53.44 **41.** 0.425 **43.** 92.79 lb **45.** 238.05 mi^2 **47.** 0.125°C; 1°C; −7°C and 2°C; 15°C **49.** $3\frac{1}{10}$ in.; $3\frac{1}{8}$ in.; no mode; $\frac{3}{4}$ in.

Chapter 6

6.1 Getting Ready to Practice (p. 273) **1.** $5x$ and $-9x$, 6 and -2 **3.** -15, 1, and -20 **5.** 5 **7.** 7 **9.** 82

6.1 Practice and Problem Solving (pp. 274–275)
11. no; -6 **13.** no; 3 **15.** -2 **17.** -4 **19.** -5 **21.** -5 **23.** 37 **25.** length: 40 mm, width: 17 mm, perimeter: 114 mm; 46 **27.** $-1\frac{1}{3}$ **29.** -4 **31.** $\frac{2}{3}$ **33.** 167 **35.** $\frac{19(x + 11)}{2} = 228$; 13

37. Yes. *Sample answer:* If you divide each side by 3, you get $x + 2 = 3$, so $x = 1$. This is the same answer you get using the distributive property. **39.** $x = 5$, $y = 8$; 34 **41.** > **43.** 34, 34, 32, 7 **45.** 28,800

6.2 Problem Solving Strategies (p. 277)
1. 18,320 mi **3.** 60 min **5.** 60 pages **7.** 165, 167, 169 **9.** 2012

6.2 Getting Ready to Practice (p. 280) **1.** the sum of the lengths of the sides, or twice the length plus twice the width **3.** 5 **5.** $-1\frac{2}{3}$

6.2 Practice and Problem Solving (pp. 280–281)
7. 3 **9.** 5 **11.** 3 **13.** 41 **15.** −2 **17.** 132 **19.** 12 wk **21.** $-\frac{4}{5}$ **23.** $\frac{3}{4}$ **25.** $1\frac{1}{2}$ **27.** \$.80; \$60 **29.** $\frac{3}{8}$ **31.** −21 **33.** 17 **37.** 36 **39.** 9.558 **41.** 21.038 **43.** 14 **45.** 7 **47.** 47

6.3 Getting Ready to Practice (p. 284) **1.** least common denominator or LCD **3.** 100; 4 **5.** 8; $\frac{7}{13}$ **7.** 20; 20

6.3 Practice and Problem Solving (pp. 284–285)
9. −12 **11.** $3.\overline{63}$ **13.** $-1\frac{2}{5}$ **15.** $1\frac{1}{5}$ **17.** $7x - 2 = 2x + 3$; 1; it is about 1; about 1.0097; the answers are very close. **19.** −5.36 **21.** $-1\frac{14}{17}$ **23.** \$3 on red, \$10 on purple, and \$3.50 on blue **25.** Yes. *Sample answer:* The extra factor(s) will divide out, so the simplified result will be the same. **27.** 18.439 **29.** 33.7635 **31.** −3 **33.** 2.25 **35.** $-15y + 60$

6.1–6.3 Notebook Review (pp. 286–287)
1. *Sample answer:* To combine like terms, find the terms with the same variable part, including exponents, and add or subtract the coefficients. The result is the coefficient of the term with that same variable part. Constants are like terms. **2.** −4 **3.** −6 **4.** $\frac{3}{4}$ **5.** 4.8 **6.** $\frac{1}{5}$ **7.** Multiply each side by 1000.

6.4 Getting Ready to Practice (p. 292)
1.

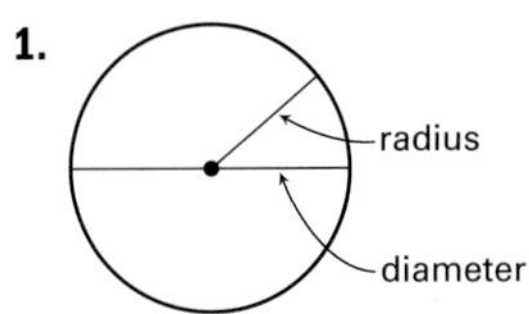

3. 10.5 in.; I used $\frac{22}{7}$ because 66 is divisible by 22. **5.** 34.5 cm; I used 3.14 because 11 is not divisible by 7. **7.** 105 yd; I used $\frac{22}{7}$ because 330 is divisible by 22.

6.4 Practice and Problem Solving (pp. 293–294)
9. 2; 6.28 cm **11.** 7; 44.0 mm **13.** 25 yd **15.** 62.8 mm **17.** 44 in. **19.** 10.5 km **21.** Ex. 9: 6 cm; Ex. 10: 2.25 in.; Ex. 11: 42 mm; the actual answers should be close to these estimates. **23.** about 301 ft **25.** about 24,900 mi **27.** about 4620 mi **29.** 7.64 in. **37.** $x \le 23$ **39.** $a \le 2$ **41.** 3 **43.** $4\frac{1}{2}$

6.5 Getting Ready to Practice (p. 297) **1.** less than; greater than; less than or equal to; greater than or equal to
3. $x \ge -4$;
5. $x < -15$;
7. $x > 1\frac{1}{3}$;

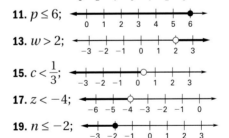

6.5 Practice and Problem Solving (pp. 297–299)
9. $a \ge 1$;
11. $p \le 6$;
13. $w > 2$;
15. $c < \frac{1}{3}$;
17. $z < -4$;
19. $n \le -2$;
21. $x \ge 750$; the salesperson must sell at least \$750 in clothes in that week to make at least \$500 for the week. **23.** at least 23 pledges; $925 + 25p \ge 1500$; $p \ge 23$ **25.** $k \le 9$ **27.** $d \ge -20$ **29.** $x > 4.8$ **31.** $z \le 4.9$ **33.** $3.95m - 1.2m \ge 25{,}000$; $m \ge 9090.\overline{90}$; the publisher must sell at least 9091 magazines each month to make a profit. **39.** *Sample answer:* You cannot buy a negative number of soft drinks.

41. 18 sandwiches. *Sample answer:* I used Make a List to list all of the possibilities. **43.** $22\frac{1}{3}$, 22.5, 22 **45.** 3.4

6.5 Technology Activity (p. 300) **1.** $y < 13$ **3.** $n \le -1$ **5.** $t > -3$ **7.** 16 pencils

6.6 Getting Ready to Practice (p. 303) **1.** $x \ge 5$ **3.** $8 - x \le 6$ **5.** Step 1: $32m + 50$; Step 2: $32m + 50 \le 200$; Step 3: $m \le 4.6875$; you can be a member up to 4 months without spending more than $200.

6.6 Practice and Problem Solving (pp. 304–305) **7.** $9 < x + 1$; $x > 8$ **9.** $8x \ge 40$; $x \ge 5$ **15.** "3 less than a number" is equivalent to the expression $n - 3$, while "3 is less than a number" is equivalent to the inequality $3 < n$. **17.** more than 15 dances **19.** $2 + 0.5n \ge 6$; 3 A.M.; no. *Sample answer:* If there are 6 inches of snow at 3 A.M., and it keeps snowing at the same rate, then there will be 7.5 inches of snow at 6 A.M. **21.** $2 + 0.4 \cdot 5 \cdot m$; $2.50 + 0.25 \cdot 7 \cdot m$ **23.** $m < 2$ mi **25.** 213.52 in. **27.** 89 **29.** 25

6.4–6.6 Notebook Review (pp. 306–307) **1.** circumference; diameter **2.** 44 **3.** 38.5 **4.** 50 **5.** $b < 42$ **6.** $j > 6$ **7.** $y \le 9$ **8.** $8\frac{1}{3}$ min **9.** *Sample answer:* Use < if the expressions "is less than" or "is fewer than" are used. Use > if "is greater than" or "is more than" are used. Use ≤ if "is less than or equal to," "is at most," or "is not more than" are used. Use ≥ if "is greater than or equal to," "is at least," or "is not less than" are used.

Chapter Review (pp. 308–309) **1.** circle **7.** 6 **9.** 9 **11.** 7 **13.** $-\frac{5}{12}$ **15.** In the last step, the values of x and y were substituted for the length and the width to find the perimeter. Instead, the values of x and y must first be substituted into the expressions for the length and width of the rectangle. The length is $4x + 2 = 4(3) + 2 = 14$. The width is $2y = 2(4) = 8$. So, $P = 2(14) + 2(8) = 44$. **17.** $2w + 50 = 3w - 87$; 137 teams **19.** $1\frac{1}{2}$ mi **21.** 25.1 mm **23.** 1.91 in. **25.** $x > -7$;

−8 −7 −6 −5 −4 −3 −2

27. $a < 10$;

0 2 4 6 8 10 12

29. $g \le -1$;

−3 −2 −1 0 1 2 3

31. $14 - 3x \le 11$; $x \ge 1$ **33.** $7(15 - x) \ge 56$; $x \le 7$

Chapter 7

7.1 Getting Ready to Practice (p. 319) **1.** rates **3.** $\frac{3}{2}$, 3 to 2, 3 : 2 **5.** yes **7.** yes **9.** Multiply by $\frac{7 \text{ days}}{1 \text{ week}}$; $\frac{14 \text{ times}}{1 \text{ day}} \cdot \frac{7 \text{ days}}{1 \text{ week}} = \frac{98 \text{ times}}{1 \text{ week}}$.

7.1 Practice and Problem Solving (pp. 319–320) **11.** $\frac{4}{5}$, 4 to 5, 4 : 5 **13.** $\frac{5}{7}$, 5 to 7, 5 : 7 **15.** $\frac{2}{3}$, 2 to 3, 2 : 3 **17.** $\frac{-3}{1}$, −3 to 1, −3 : 1 **19.** 2 **21.** 4.32 **23.** $\frac{4 \text{ adults}}{1 \text{ car}}$ **25.** $\frac{1.5 \text{ lb}}{1 \text{ dollar}}$ **27.** $\frac{5}{5} = \frac{1}{1}$ **29.** 2 **31.** 25 **33.** Check work; $\frac{1}{10}$ of the people in the class are left-handed, so divide the number of people by 10. **35.** 1134 people/mi^2 **37.** 6.25 ft **39.** 6 **41.** −8

7.2 Getting Ready to Practice (p. 324) **1.** Find the cross products and solve the resulting equation to solve the proportion. **3.** 6 **5.** 6 **7.** 2640 ft

7.2 Practice and Problem Solving (pp. 325–326) **9.** no **11.** yes **13.** 9 **15.** 9 **17.** 38.5 **19.** 1513 **21.** 12 in. **23.** 27.25 in. **25.** $90 **27.** 34,375 mi **29.** 1 **31.** 23 **35.** length: 5 in.; width: 1.75 in.; height: 1.25 in. **37.** $\frac{3 \text{ people}}{1 \text{ taxi}}$ **39.** $\frac{2 \text{ dogs}}{1 \text{ household}}$

7.3 Getting Ready to Practice (p. 329) **1.** percent **3.** 25% **5.** 550

7.3 Practice and Problem Solving (pp. 329–330) **7.** 4% **9.** 90% **11.** 110.25 **13.** 589 **15.** 560 **17.** 925 **19.** 40.08 ft **21.** 135% **23.** 2860 **25.** 540 **27.** 60% **29.** $4y$ **31.** 28.5% **35.** $1\frac{43}{50}$ **37.** $\frac{78}{125}$ **39.** 45.216

7.4 Getting Ready to Practice (p. 333) **1.** 100%; 1 **3.** 9% **5.** 150% **7.** 0.125, $\frac{1}{8}$ **9.** 1.1, $1\frac{1}{10}$ **11.** The numerator of the fraction should be 0.1; $0.001 = \frac{0.1}{100} = 0.1\%$.

7.4 Practice and Problem Solving (pp. 334–335)
13. 5.7% **15.** 0.4% **17.** 15% **19.** 0.5% **21.** 105.6% **23.** 52.5% **25.** $85\frac{1}{3}$% **27.** 70% **29.** 0.87, $\frac{87}{100}$ **31.** 1.01, $1\frac{1}{100}$ **33.** 0.042, $\frac{21}{500}$ **35.** 1.24, $1\frac{6}{25}$ **37.** 0.004, $\frac{1}{250}$ **39.** 0.4455, $\frac{891}{2000}$ **41.** 0.6%, $\frac{3}{50}$, 0.0606, 6.6%, 0.606 **43.** $\frac{21}{100}$, 0.212, $\frac{21}{20}$, 212%, 21.2 **45.** Spanish **47.** 23% **49.** $<$ **51.** $>$ **53.** $=$ **55.** *Sample answer:* when referring to part or all of a group of people **59.** $13 + 4x \le 9$; $x \le -1$ **61.** $6. *Sample answer:* I used Work Backward because it allowed me to start with the known final amount and then "undo" each of the steps one at a time. **63.** 3.5 **65.** 11.88

7.1–7.4 Notebook Review (pp. 336–337)
1. proportion **2.** $\frac{7.5 \text{ ft}}{1 \text{ sec}}$ **3.** $\frac{\$1.68}{1 \text{ gal}}$ **4.** 6% **5.** 24.7 **6.** 0.74, $\frac{37}{50}$ **7.** 0.038, $\frac{19}{500}$ **8.** 0.168, $\frac{21}{125}$ **9.** 1.3, $1\frac{3}{10}$ **10.** If the cross products are equal, then the ratios form a proportion.

7.5 Getting Ready to Practice (p. 340)
1. increase **3.** decrease; 20% **5.** 23.1

7.5 Practice and Problem Solving (pp. 340–341)
7. increase; 60% **9.** decrease; $6.\overline{6}$% **11.** decrease; 10% **13.** 1144 **15.** 12.8 **17.** 77,393.75 **19.** about 15,390 tons **21.** 50% increase **23.** 50% decrease **25.** False; multiplying by 5 gives a 400% increase. **27.** True; to find an 80% decrease, multiply by 80% and subtract. The final result is 20% of the original number, and finding 20% of a number is the same as dividing by 5. **29.** 9.9% **31.** 9 in. by 6 in.; 125% **33.** −5.36 **35.** −14 **37.** 26 **39.** 12

7.6 Getting Ready to Practice (p. 344) **1.** markup **3.** $11.40 **5.** $34.80 **7.** $37.80

7.6 Practice and Problem Solving (pp. 345–346)
9. $39.90 **11.** $16.80 **13.** $101.37 **15.** $61.61 **17.** $22.50 **21.** discount; 10% **23.** markup; 120% **25.** discount; about 40% **27.** 19% **29.** 40% **33.** 3 **35.** 28 **37.** 45 **39.** 40

7.7 Getting Ready to Practice (p. 349)
1. principal **3.** 82% **5.** 399

7.7 Practice and Problem Solving (pp. 349–350)
7. 208 **9.** 66 **11.** 250 **13.** 78 **15.** 0.5% **17.** $15 **19.** 31% **21.** $=$ **23.** Row 1: 1.1, 3.3; Row 2: 2.5, 5, 7.5; Row 3: 3.8, 7.6, 11.4; for 22, the number increased by 1.1 each time; for 50, the number increased by 2.5 each time; for 76, the number increased by 3.8 each time. **25.** $142.50; $1342.50 **29.** $\frac{5}{6}$ **31.** −3 **33.** $n \le 11\frac{3}{8}$

7.7 Technology Activity (p. 351) **1.** $7577.03 **3.** $3744.89

7.8 Problem Solving Strategies (p. 353) **1.** 62 red, 38 blue. *Sample answer:* In the 5 trials, 31 red marbles were chosen and 19 blue marbles were chosen. So $\frac{31}{50} = \frac{x}{100}$, or $x = 62$, and $\frac{19}{50} = \frac{y}{100}$, or $y = 38$. **3.** *Sample answer:* Draw and then replace a letter 20 times and record the results. Write a proportion comparing the ratio of the number of consonants drawn in the experiment to the ratio that would be drawn in 60 trials. Solve the proportion to find the predicted number of consonants drawn. **5.** $20; $34 **7.** 27 triangles

7.8 Getting Ready to Practice (p. 356) **1.** 2, 4, 6 **3.** The experimental probability is the ratio of favorable outcomes to total outcomes, not to unfavorable outcomes as shown. The number of total outcomes is 20, so the experimental probability of spinning red is $\frac{7}{20}$.

7.8 Practice and Problem Solving (pp. 356–357)
5. $\frac{1}{5}$ **7.** $\frac{3}{10}$ **9.** 1 **11.** 16.8% **13.** 49.2% **15.** 24 **17.** 56 **19.** about 46% **21.** $\frac{3}{4}$ **25.** *Sample answer:* Each time she rolls the number cube has no effect on any other time she rolls the number cube. **27.** 10% **29.** −28 **31.** −32

7.5–7.8 Notebook Review (pp. 358–359) **1.** Find the ratio of the number of favorable outcomes to the number of possible outcomes. **2.** $51 **3.** $59.04 **4.** 96 **5.** 291.04 **6.** red: $\frac{8}{17}$; yellow: $\frac{5}{17}$; blue: $\frac{4}{17}$ **7.** $525

Chapter Review (pp. 360–361) **1.** unit rate **3.** favorable outcomes; possible outcomes **7.** 4.78 **9.** 360 **11.** 8 **13.** 10 **15.** 308 **17.** 0.5% **19.** 0.3% **21.** 145% **23.** $\frac{7}{20}$ **25.** 23% **27.** \$14.45 **29.** \$127.05 **31.** $\frac{1}{2}$ **33.** $\frac{3}{4}$

Chapter 8

8.1 Getting Ready to Practice (p. 378) **1.** supplementary **3.** supplementary **5.** Vertical angles have the same measure, so $m\angle 2 = 112°$.

8.1 Practice and Problem Solving (pp. 378–379) **7.** 109° **9.** $m\angle 6 = 45°$, $m\angle 5 = m\angle 7 = 135°$

11.

105° 75°
75° 105°

13. *Sample answer:* Together, the angles form a straight angle, so the sum of their measures is 180°. So, $135° + m\angle 2 = 180°$, and $m\angle 2 = 180° - 135° = 45°$. **17.** $y = 2$; $m\angle 6 = 90°$, $m\angle 3 = 90°$ **19.** $\frac{113}{500}$ **21.** $\frac{9}{2000}$ **23.** 3 in.^{2} **25.** 32.5 ft^2

Special Topic Exercises (p. 381) **1-7.** Sample answers are given.

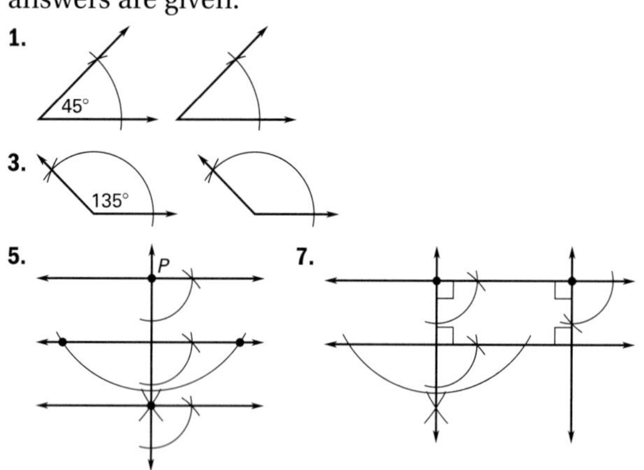

8.2 Getting Ready to Practice (p. 384) **1.** scalene **3.** equilateral **5.** The triangle has one right angle, so it is a right triangle.

8.2 Practice and Problem Solving (pp. 384–385) **7.** right **9.** scalene **11.** isosceles **13.** 24; right **15.** Isosceles; an isosceles triangle has two sides of equal length. **17.** Yes; the sum of the measures of the angles is 180°. **19.** 20°, 70°, 90° **21.** 60°, 60°, 60° **23.** $m\angle 1 = 75°$, $m\angle 2 = 35°$, $m\angle 3 = 70°$ **25.** 5.2 yd, 1.2 yd^2 **27.** 148,941,024 km^2

8.3 Getting Ready to Practice (p. 387) **1.** parallelogram **3.** rectangle **5.** parallelogram, rectangle **7.** 91

8.3 Practice and Problem Solving (pp. 388–389) **9.** 1.6 cm; parallelogram, rhombus **11.** 109 **13.** 65 **15.** $x = 65$, $y = 115$ **17.** dark blue rectangle, red square, green trapezoid, light blue parallelogram, purple parallelogram, yellow trapezoid **19.** sometimes **21.** never **23.** 5; $m\angle E = 121°$, $m\angle H = 119°$ **27.** 5 **29.** 1 **31.** never **33.** sometimes

8.4 Getting Ready to Practice (p. 392) **1.** polygon **3.** not a polygon **5.** 1440° **7.** 1620° **9.** 128.6°

8.4 Practice and Problem Solving (pp. 392–393) **11.** yes **13.** yes **15.** about 154° **17.** about 176.9° **19.** 78 **21.** $x = 72$; $m\angle R = m\angle N = 72°$; $m\angle L = m\angle M = m\angle P = m\angle Q = 144°$ **23.** $x = 45$; $m\angle B = m\angle E = 135°$ **27.** 360°; 360°; 360° **29.** $\frac{49}{50}$ **31.** $\frac{7}{5000}$ **33.** about 103.5%

8.1–8.4 Notebook Review (pp. 394-395) **1.** one **2.** 122; obtuse **3.** 26; right **4.** 52° **5.** 720° **6.** Yes; *Sample answer:* The sum of the other four angles just needs to be 540°.

7. Two;

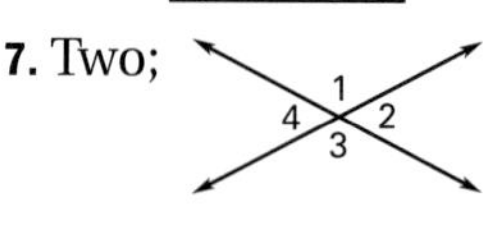

Sample answer: There are two pairs of angles that do not share a side: $\angle 1$ and $\angle 3$, and $\angle 2$ and $\angle 4$.

8.5 Getting Ready to Practice (p. 399) **1.** congruent **3.** $\angle K$ and $\angle S$, $\angle L$ and $\angle P$, $\angle M$ and $\angle Q$, $\angle N$ and $\angle R$ **5.** 12 in. **7.** The corresponding vertices are not listed in the correct order; $\triangle ABC \cong \triangle DFE$ by Side-Angle-Side.

8.5 Practice and Problem Solving (pp. 400–401)
9. 80° **11.** 100° **13.** Side-Angle-Side **15.** Side-Side-Side; $x - 6 = 4$; 10 **17.** Angle-Side-Angle; $2x - 24 = x$; 24 **19.** 127.5° **23.** 59.15 **25.** 103
27–30.

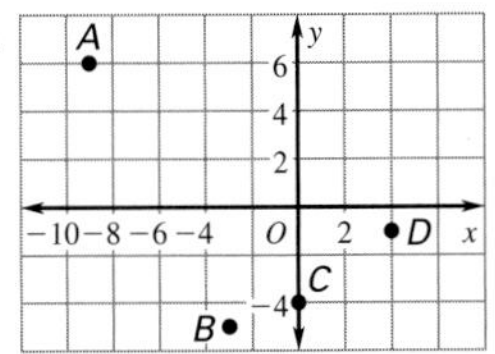

8.6 Problem Solving Strategies (p. 403)
1. *Sample:*

mirror images: 1 and 2, 3 and 4, 5 and 6, 1 and 6, 2 and 3, 4 and 5, 1 and 4, 2 and 5, 3 and 6

3. Scott, Alan, David, Mary, Peter; Scott, Alan, Peter, Mary, David **5.** 96 oz **7.** 92

8.6 Getting Ready to Practice (p. 406)
1. reflection **3.** no **5.** no **7.** none

8.6 Practice and Problem Solving (pp. 407–408)
11.

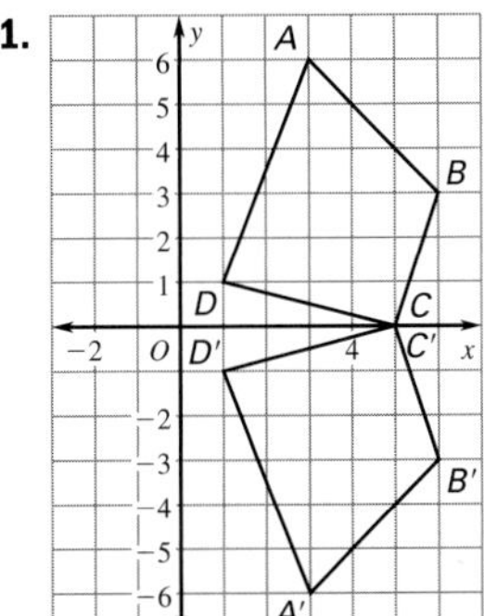

13.

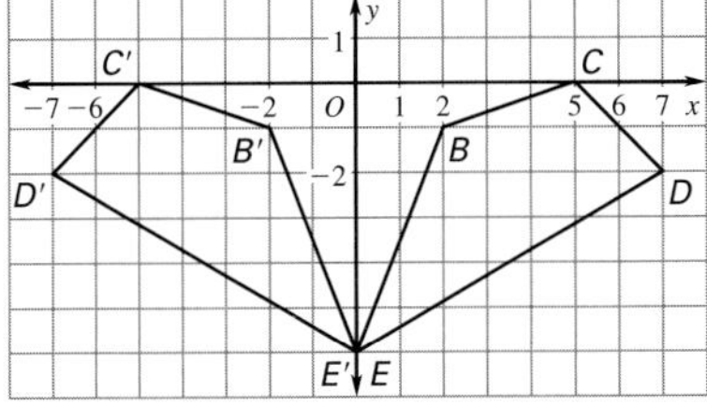

15. two

17.

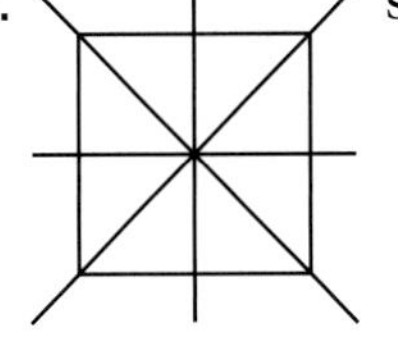

square

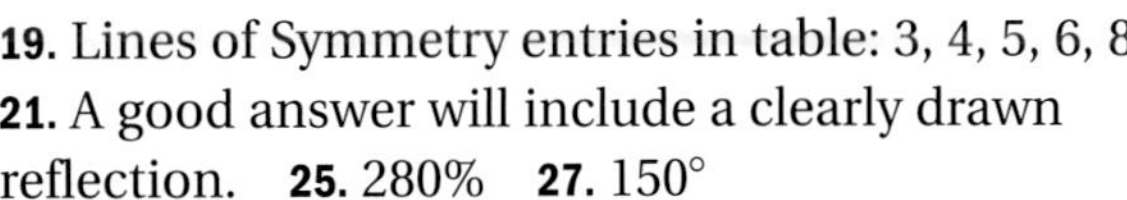

19. Lines of Symmetry entries in table: 3, 4, 5, 6, 8
21. A good answer will include a clearly drawn reflection. **25.** 280% **27.** 150°

8.7 Getting Ready to Practice (p. 411)
1. reflection **3.** rotation

8.7 Practice and Problem Solving (pp. 412–413)
5. reflection **7.** translation **9.** reflection
11. rotation **13.** rotation **15.** $(x + 5, y + 4)$
17. $P'(-5, 0)$, $Q'(-2, 0)$, $R'(0, -2)$
19.

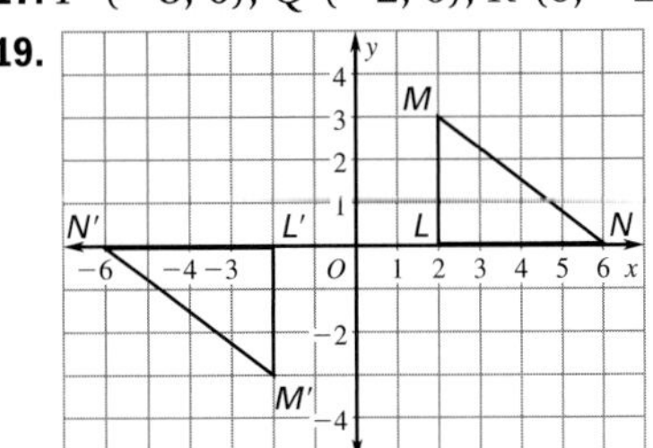

21.

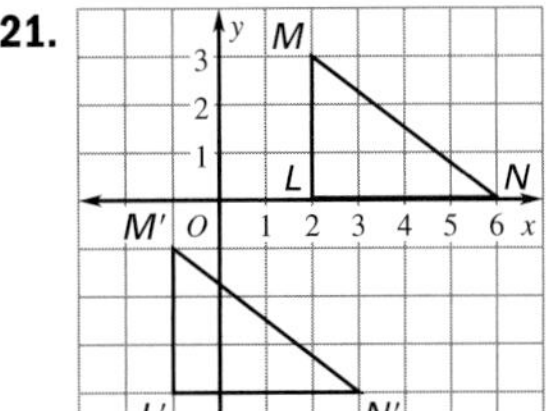

23.

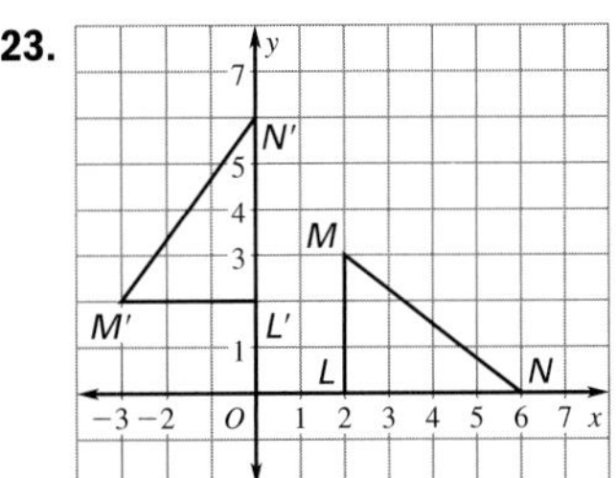

27. *Sample answer:* Reflect in the y-axis and then the x-axis; make two 90° clockwise rotations; make two 90° counterclockwise rotations; reflect in the x-axis and then the y-axis. **29.** 384
31. 49.5; right **33.** 74.8; acute **35.** 110.2, 110, 110

Special Topic Exercises (p. 415) **1.** no **3.** no
5. Check work.
7. *Sample:* translation

Selected Answers

9. A good answer will include a rectangle with a piece cut from one side and slid to another side. The translation of that figure forms a tessellation.
11. *Sample:*

8.8 Getting Ready to Practice (p. 418) **1.** scale factor **3.** $\triangle MNL \sim \triangle PQR$
5. Steps 1, 3:

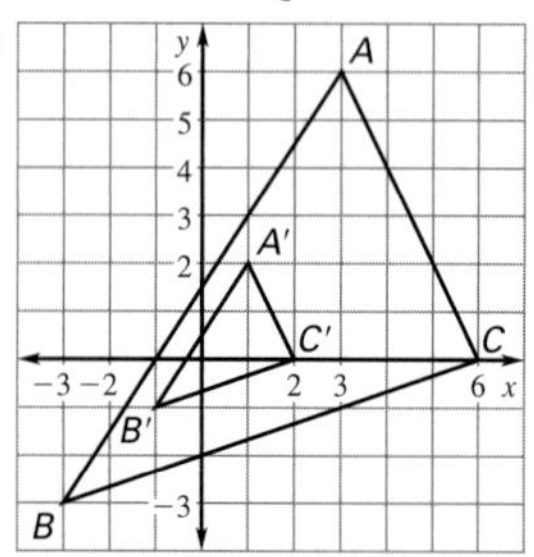

Step 2: $A'(1, 2)$, $B'(-1, -1)$, $C'(2, 0)$

8.8 Practice and Problem Solving (pp. 419–421)
7. $ABCD \sim EDGF$ **9.** 40 **11.** 3 in. **13.** $x = 90$, $y = 6.75$ cm
15.

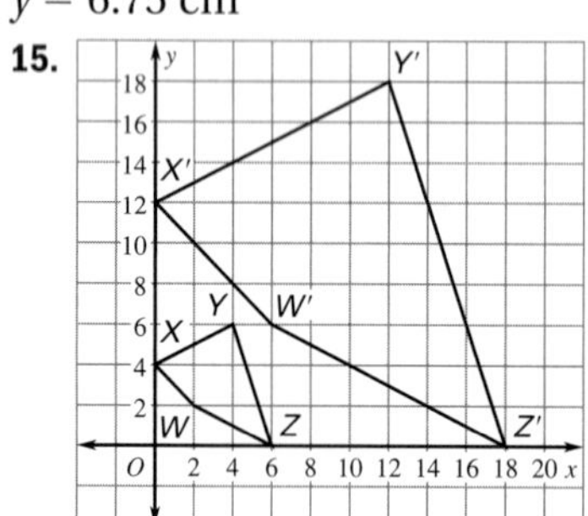

17.

19.

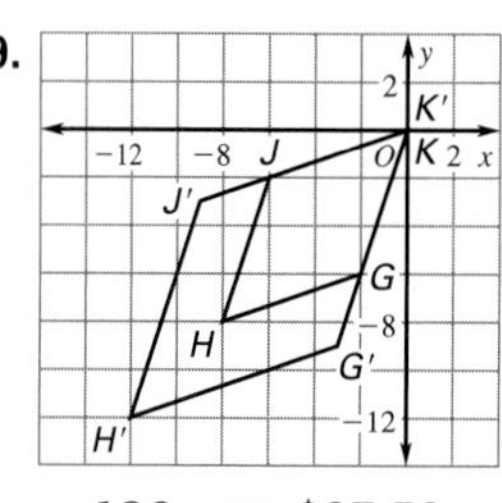

21. 4 in. by 8 in. **23.** $x = 44$, $y = 136$ **27.** $27.50

8.5–8.8 Notebook Review (pp. 422–423)
1. reflection **2.** translation **3.** 3 cm
4.

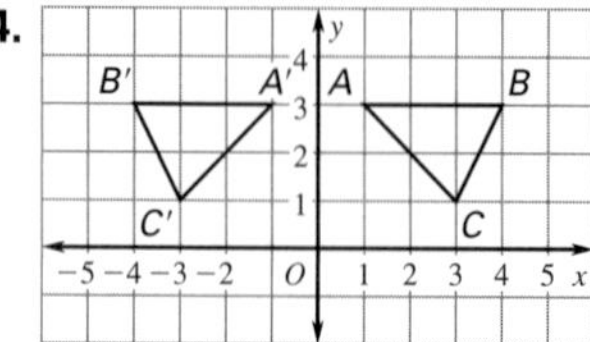

5.

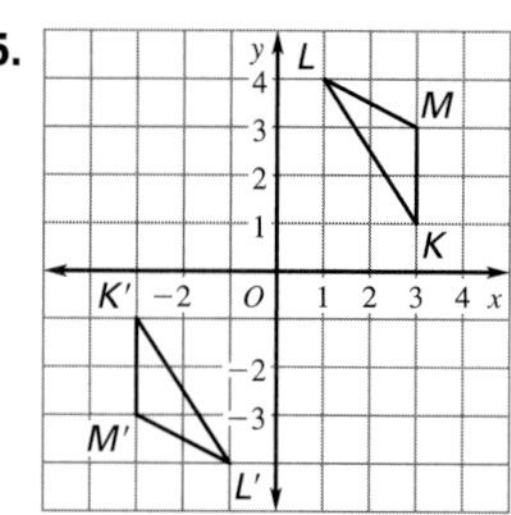

6. 25 m **7.** *Sample answer:* The perimeter of the image is the product of the scale factor and the perimeter of the original figure. **8.** *Sample answer:* A person turning around to face the opposite way

Chapter Review (pp. 424–425) **9.** 109° **11.** 25° **13.** rectangle **15.** 900° **17.** $\angle A \cong \angle P$, $\angle B \cong \angle Q$, $\angle C \cong \angle R$, $\angle D \cong \angle S$, $\angle E \cong \angle T$ **19.** $\triangle ABC \cong \triangle GFH$; two sides and the included angle of one triangle are congruent to two sides and the included angle of the other triangle, so the triangles are congruent by Side-Angle-Side. **21.** no **23.** no
25.

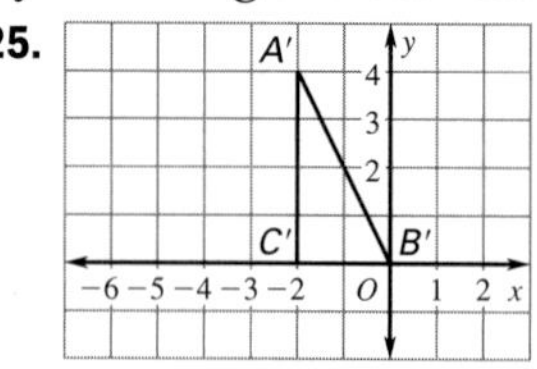

27.

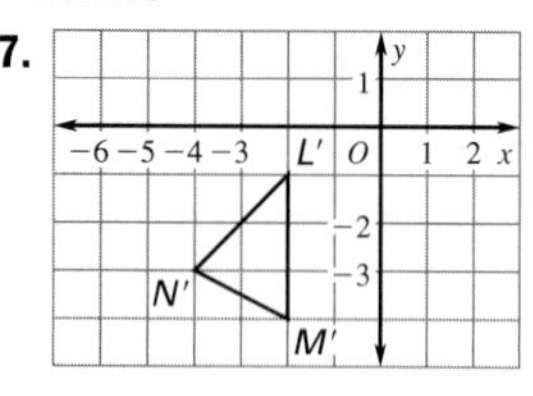

29. $A'(-4, 0)$, $B'(-4, 8)$, $C'(-12, 16)$, $D'(-24, 12)$

Chapter 9

9.1 Getting Ready to Practice (p. 434) **1.** $b^2 = c$ **3.** ± 4 **5.** ± 11 **7.** -22.0 **9.** 49.4 **11.** ± 7 **13.** ± 9

9.1 Practice and Problem Solving (pp. 434–436)
15. -1 **17.** 12 **19.** 6 **21.** 11 **23.** 4.7 **25.** -38.4 **27.** 0 **29.** ± 13 **31.** ± 6 **33.** No. *Sample answer:* There is no real number whose square is a negative number. **35.** ± 6.40 **37.** ± 11.66 **39.** ± 14.14 **41.** 4 **43.** 9 **45.** ± 1.2 **47.** ± 1.4 **49.** No. *Sample answer:* The table measures $\sqrt{34.5} \approx 5.9$ feet on a side. Since 5.9 feet is over 70 inches, the tablecloth is not big enough. **51.** $\frac{1}{2}$ **53.** $\frac{7}{8}$ **55.** $\frac{12}{13}$ **59.** neither **61.** supplementary **63.** 34 ways. *Sample answer:* I used the strategy Draw a Diagram so that I could draw all the ways that 3 stamps can be arranged and still be attached. **65.** $5\frac{7}{20}$ **67.** $-9\frac{1}{20}$

9.2 Getting Ready to Practice (p. 439)
1. irrational **3.** Irrational. *Sample answer:* 5 is not a perfect square. **5.** Rational. *Sample answer:* $\sqrt{\frac{25}{49}} = \frac{5}{7}$ which is a quotient of two integers.

7. 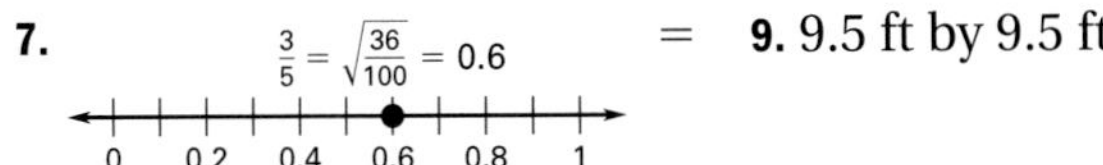

= **9.** 9.5 ft by 9.5 ft

9.3 Practice and Problem Solving (pp. 440–441)
11. Rational. *Sample answer:* $\frac{9}{46}$ is a quotient of two integers. **13.** Irrational. *Sample answer:* neither 3 nor 5 is a perfect square.

15. 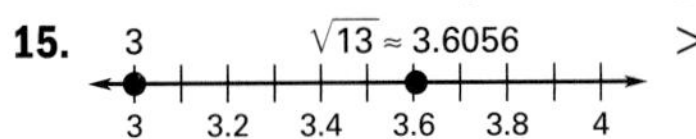

>

17. $-5 = -\sqrt{25}$ =
−5.5 −5.3 −5.1 −4.9 −4.7 −4.5

19. $0.\overline{262}, 0.2\overline{6}, 0.266, 0.\overline{26}$ **21.** $\sqrt{4} = 2$; rational
23. $\sqrt{20}$; irrational

25. 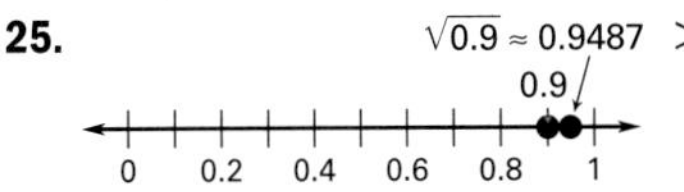

>

27. $\sqrt{2.25} = \frac{3.6}{2.4} = 1.5$ =
1 1.2 1.4 1.6 1.8 2

29. $-4, -3.75, 1.5, \sqrt{8}$ **31.** $-3.5, -\sqrt{12}, -\frac{3}{4}, -\sqrt{\frac{1}{4}}$
33. Yes; too small. *Sample answer:* Because $\sqrt{110} \approx$ 10.5, the piece of carpet should about fit the 10.5 foot dimension, but will be about 0.7 foot too short in the other dimension. **37.** $30a^{11}$ **39.** -5
41. c^4 **43.** $-\frac{2}{3n^4}$ **45.** rotation; $(x, y) \rightarrow (y, -x)$
47. translation; $(x, y) \rightarrow (x - 3, y + 1)$

9.3 Getting Ready to Practice (p. 445)
1. hypotenuse **3.** 15 **5.** 25 **7.** yes **9.** no

9.3 Practice and Problem Solving (pp. 446–447)
11. 34 ft **13.** 19.6 ft **15.** 24.5 in. **17.** no **19.** yes **21.** 8.9 ft **23.** 9 m **25.** 4.24 ft **27.** no **29.** yes **31.** 2 **33.** 5.3 **35.** 3

39. 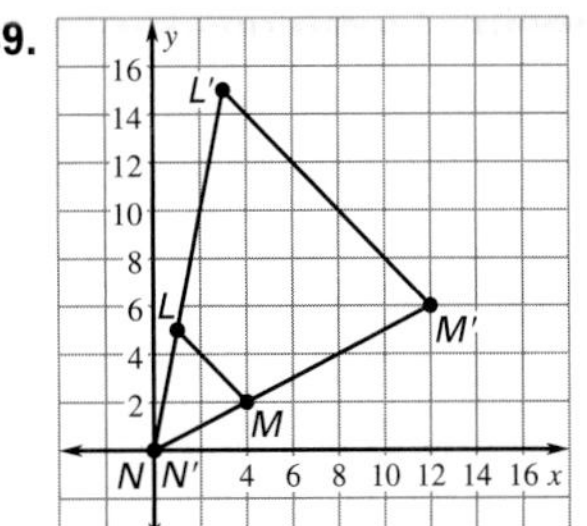

9.4 Problem Solving Strategies (p. 449) **1.** 7.1 m **3.** 37 ft **5.** yes **7.** $140 **9.** 6 possibilities

9.4 Getting Ready to Practice (p. 452)
1. Pythagorean triple **3.** 96 ft
5. Steps 1–2: 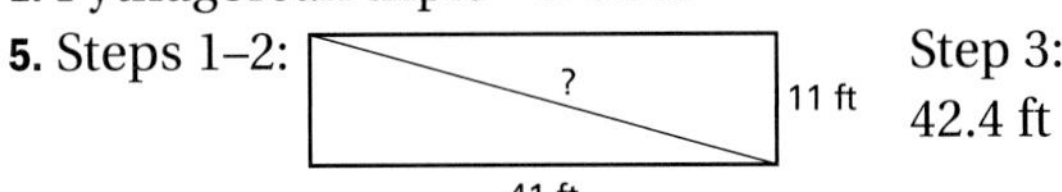

Step 3: 42.4 ft

9.4 Practice and Problem Solving (pp. 452–453)
7. 15 ft; 60 ft^2, 40 ft **9.** 6 in.; 8.64 in.^{2}, 14.4 in. **11.** 44 m; 2574 m^2, 286 m **13.** yes **15.** no **17.** 30 in. **19.** 18 in. **21.** 24 m **23.** 182 cm

25. 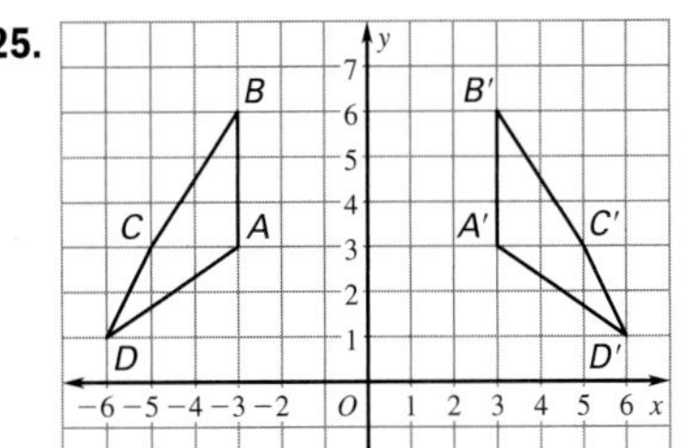

27. -12 **29.** 8.5

9.1–9.4 Notebook Review (pp. 454–455) **1.** real numbers **2.** ± 13 **3.** ± 11 **4.** ± 8

5. 4 $\sqrt{31} \approx 5.5678$ >
4 4.4 4.8 5.2 5.6 6

6. 7 $\sqrt{59} \approx 7.6811$ <
7 7.2 7.4 7.6 7.8 8

7. $-9 = -\sqrt{81}$ =
−9.5 −9.3 −9.1 −8.9 −8.7 −8.5

8. 6.3 $\sqrt{48} \approx 6.9282$ >
6 6.2 6.4 6.6 6.8 7

9. 15 **10.** 32 **11.** 2.5

12. *Sample answer:* The decimal form of a rational number terminates or repeats, while the decimal form of an irrational number does neither. For example, $\frac{3}{4}$ and $\frac{1}{3}$ are rational because $\frac{3}{4} =$ 0.75 (terminates) and $\frac{1}{3} = 0.\overline{3}$ (repeats), but $\pi \approx$ 3.1415926535..., which never terminates or repeats.

9.5 Getting Ready to Practice (p. 458) **1.** The length of the hypotenuse is $\sqrt{2}$ times the length of a leg. **3.** 50 ft **5.** Step 1: $\frac{5\sqrt{3}}{2}$ in.; Step 2: 7.5 in.

9.5 Practice and Problem Solving (pp. 459–460) **7.** 28 cm **9.** $x = 11$ in., $y = 11\sqrt{3}$ in. **11.** $y = 36\sqrt{3}$ m, $z = 72$ m **13.** 115 ft **15.** 10 in. **17.** $x = 8$ m, $y = 8\sqrt{3}$ m **19.** $x = 32\frac{1}{2}$ cm, $y = \frac{65\sqrt{3}}{2}$ cm **21.** $x^2 + (x\sqrt{3})^2 \stackrel{?}{=} (2x)^2$, $x^2 + 3x^2 \stackrel{?}{=} 4x^2$, $4x^2 = 4x^2$. *Sample answer:* $3^2 + (3\sqrt{3})^2 \stackrel{?}{=} 6^2$, $9 + 27 \stackrel{?}{=} 36$, $36 = 36$. **25.** $1\frac{1}{2}$ **27.** $\frac{7 \text{ people}}{1 \text{ team}}$ **29.** $\frac{61 \text{ rotations}}{1 \text{ min}}$ **31.** 10

9.6 Getting Ready to Practice (p. 466)

5. Step 1: [right triangle: angle 42°, base 50 ft, vertical side labeled totem pole] Step 2: $\tan 42° = \frac{x}{50}$; Step 3: 45 ft

9.6 Practice and Problem Solving (pp. 466–468) **7.** $\sin P = \frac{11}{61}$, $\cos P = \frac{60}{61}$, $\tan P = \frac{11}{60}$, $\sin R = \frac{60}{61}$, $\cos R = \frac{11}{61}$, $\tan R = \frac{60}{11}$ **9.** 1.2349 **11.** 0.5878 **13.** 3.440 in. **15.** 20.796 m **19.** The tangent ratio is the length of the opposite side over the length of the adjacent side, not over the length of the hypotenuse. So $\tan 25° = \frac{x}{13}$, and $x \approx 6$ cm. **21.** $m\angle C = 60°$, $AC = 10$ in.; $\sin A = \frac{1}{2}$, $\cos A = \frac{8.7}{10}$, $\tan A = \frac{5}{8.7}$ **23.** $m\angle A = 19.7°$, $BC \approx 17.2$ cm; $\sin A = \frac{17.2}{51}$, $\cos A = \frac{48}{51}$, $\tan A = \frac{17.2}{48}$ **25.** about 1813 m **27.** 84.4 in. **29.** 119 ft

33. 10.73 **35.** Rational. *Sample answer:* 484 is a perfect square, $22^2 = 484$. **37.** Irrational. *Sample answer:* Neither 17 nor 29 is a perfect square. **39.** 3.625 mi/h

9.6 Technology Activity (p. 469) **1.** 14.0° **3.** 42.6° **5.** 87.7° **7.** $\tan^{-1}(32.46)$. *Sample answer:* The greater the tangent of an angle, the larger the angle.

9.5–9.6 Notebook Review (pp. 470–471) **1.** opposite; hypotenuse **2.** $8\sqrt{2}$ in. **3.** 20 cm **4.** $x = 6$ m, $y = 6\sqrt{3}$ m **5.** $\sin A = \frac{3}{5}$, $\cos A = \frac{4}{5}$, $\tan A = \frac{3}{4}$, $\sin B = \frac{4}{5}$, $\cos B = \frac{3}{5}$, $\tan B = \frac{4}{3}$ **6.** $\sin A = \frac{48}{73}$, $\cos A = \frac{55}{73}$, $\tan A = \frac{48}{55}$, $\sin B = \frac{55}{73}$, $\cos B = \frac{48}{73}$, $\tan B = \frac{55}{48}$ **7.** $\sin A = \frac{36}{85}$, $\cos A = \frac{77}{85}$, $\tan A = \frac{36}{77}$, $\sin B = \frac{77}{85}$, $\cos B = \frac{36}{85}$, $\tan B = \frac{77}{36}$ **8.** *Sample answer:* Use the Pythagorean theorem to find that the length of the other leg is 4. Use this fact to find the cosine ratio, $\frac{4}{5}$.

Chapter Review (pp. 472–473) **1.** *Sample answer:* A rational number can be written as a quotient of two integers, while an irrational number cannot. A rational number has a decimal representation that either terminates or repeats, while an irrational number does not. **3.** *Sample answer:* $\sqrt{2}$, π, $\sqrt{7}$ **5.** perfect square **7.** shorter **9.** 9.7 **11.** -46.02 **13.** ± 14 **15.** ± 8 **17.** Rational. *Sample answer:* 100 is a perfect square, since $10^2 = 100$. **19.** Rational. *Sample answer:* $\frac{16}{25}$ is the quotient of two integers. **21.** $0.\overline{181}$, $0.1\overline{8}$, 0.188, $0.1\overline{8}$ **23.** 11 in. **25.** no **27.** yes **29.** 679.23 m **31.** $x = 15\sqrt{3}$ m, $y = 30$ m **33.** $\sin P = \frac{21}{29}$, $\cos P = \frac{20}{29}$, $\tan P = \frac{21}{20}$, $\sin Q = \frac{20}{29}$, $\cos Q = \frac{21}{29}$, $\tan Q = \frac{20}{21}$ **35.** $\sin P = \frac{21}{29}$, $\cos P = \frac{20}{29}$, $\tan P = \frac{21}{20}$, $\sin Q = \frac{20}{29}$, $\cos Q = \frac{21}{29}$, $\tan Q = \frac{20}{21}$ **37.** 0.3346 **39.** 0.8391

Chapter 10

10.1 Getting Ready to Practice (p. 483) **1.** $A = bh$ **3.** $A = \frac{1}{2}(b_1 + b_2)h$ **5.** 56 in.^{2}

7. Step 1:

Step 2: trapezoid: $49\frac{1}{2}$ ft^2; parallelogram: 72 ft^2;

Step 3: $121\frac{1}{2}$ ft^2

10.1 Practice and Problem Solving (pp. 483–485)

9. 126 ft^2 **11.** 35 ft^2 **13.** 70 in.^{2}

15.

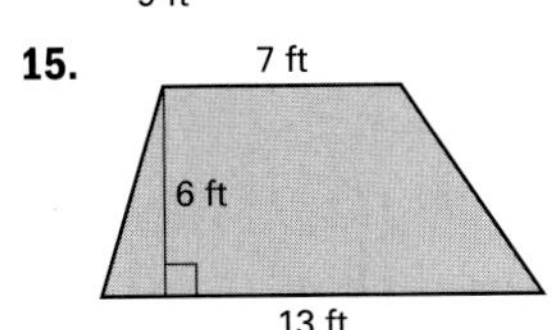

60 ft^2 **17.** 162 in.^{2} **19.** 480 m^2

21.

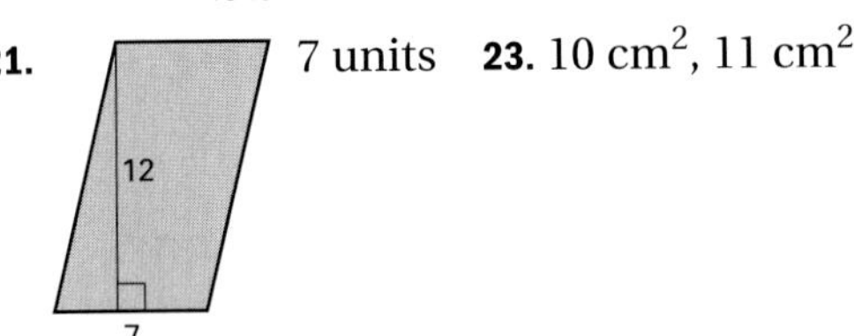

7 units **23.** 10 cm^2, 11 cm^2

25. 90 cm^2, 99 cm^2; the new areas are nine times the original areas. **27.** *Sample answer:* about 112,500 mi^2 **29.** 79.85 in.^{2} **31.** 162 m^2 **33.** 360 ft^2

35.

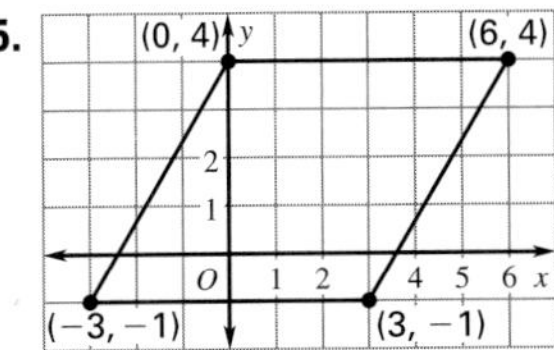

30 units^2

41. $11\frac{2}{3}$ **43.** $\sin P = \frac{8}{17}$, $\cos P = \frac{15}{17}$, $\tan P = \frac{8}{15}$, $\sin R = \frac{15}{17}$, $\cos R = \frac{8}{17}$, $\tan R = \frac{15}{8}$

10.2 Getting Ready to Practice (p. 488) **1.** radius **3.** 314 cm^2 **5.** about 7 m

10.2 Practice and Problem Solving (pp. 488–490)

7. 555 m^2 **9.** 340 cm^2 **11.** 314 ft^2 **13.** 615 mm^2 **15.** 1256 in.^{2} **17.** 1 m **19.** 6 in. **21.** 9 cm **23.** 10 mm; 314 mm^2 **25.** 239 in.^{2} **27.** 5 ft **29.** $18.84 = 2(3.14)r$; 3 ft; 28.3 ft^2 **31.** $37.68 = 2(3.14)r$; 6 cm; 113 cm^2

33. Larger square: 400 mm^2, smaller square: 200 mm^2, estimate: 300 mm^2; actual: 314 mm^2. *Sample answer:* The estimate is close to the actual area of the circle. **37.** no

10.2 Technology Activity (p. 491) **1.** multiplied by 3 **3.** multiplied by 5 **5.** Multiplied by $\sqrt{2}$; multiplied by $\sqrt{3}$. *Sample answer:* If the area of a circle is multiplied by n, then the radius is multiplied by $\sqrt{n}$.

10.3 Getting Ready to Practice (p. 494)

1. cylinder; no **3.** sphere; no

5.

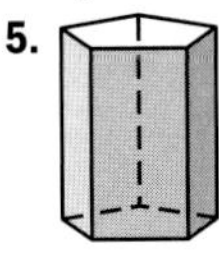

7 faces, 15 edges, 10 vertices

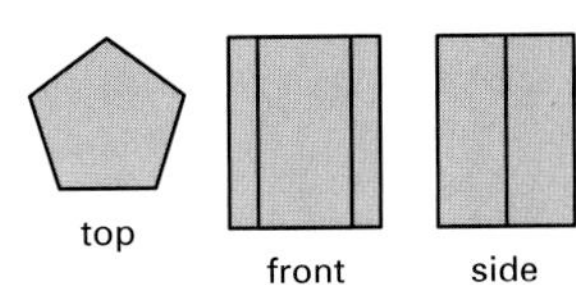

10.3 Practice and Problem Solving (pp. 494–495)

7. sphere; no **9.** cylinder; no

11.

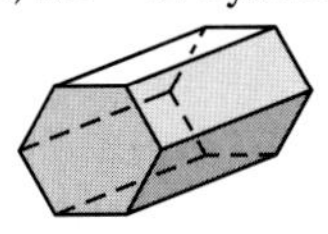

4 faces, 6 edges, 4 vertices

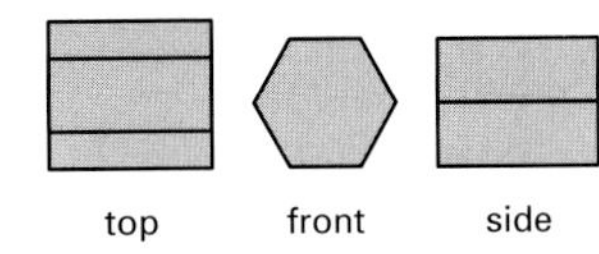

19. pentagonal prisms **21.** cylinder and cone

23.

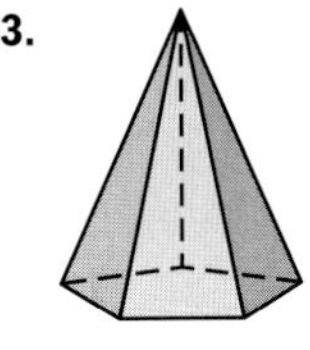

25. 346 in.^{2}

Special Topic Exercises (p. 497)

1. **3.**

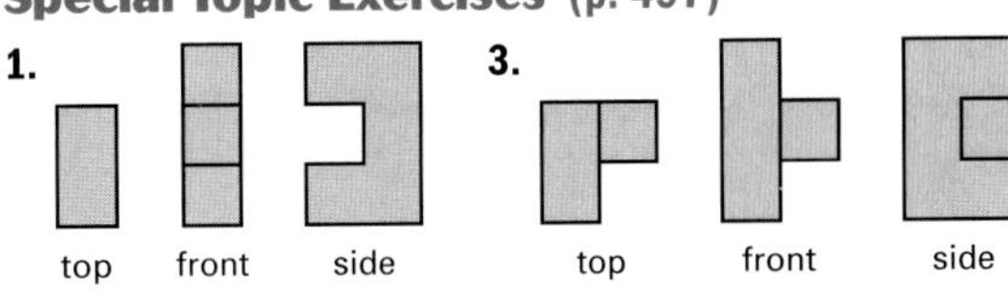

Selected Answers

5. 7.

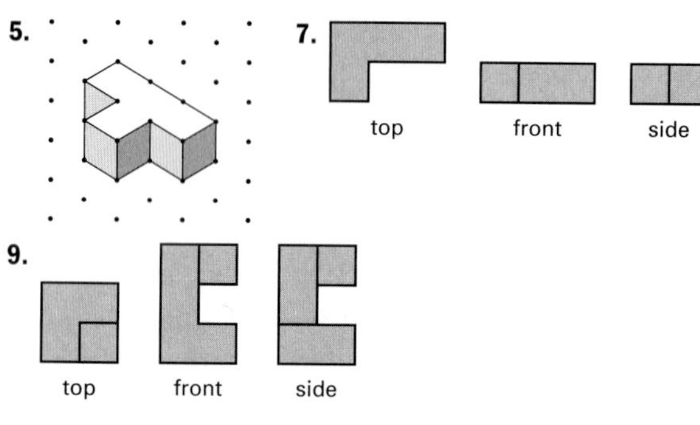

10.1–10.3 Notebook Review (pp. 498–499)

1. polyhedron 2. 160 ft^2 3. 1810 in.^{2} 4. 50.2 mm^2 5. 254 yd^2 6. *Sample:*

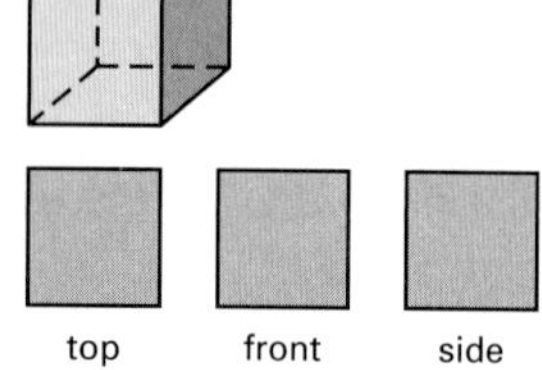

7. *Sample answer:* A cone and a cylinder both have circular bases, but a cone has only one circular base while a cylinder has two. A cross-section of either solid parallel to a base is a circle, but for the cone these circles get smaller toward the vertex, while for the cylinder they are all the same size. A cylinder and a prism both have two parallel bases, but the bases of a cylinder are circles, while the bases of a prism are polygons. 8. No. *Sample answer:* The only vertices of a prism are on its bases. Because the bases are two congruent polygons, the total number of vertices is twice the number on one base, so it is an even number.

10.4 Problem Solving Strategies (p. 501)

1. 396 in.^{2} 3. 11 0's, 21 1's, 20 of each of the digits 2–9 5. 12 sandwiches 7. 4 and 13

10.4 Getting Ready to Practice (p. 505)

1. *Sample answer:* Surface area is the sum of the areas of all the faces and lateral surfaces of a solid. 3. *Sample:* 184 m^2

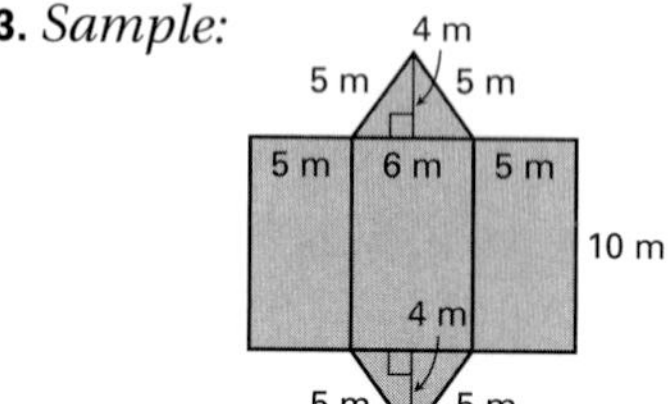

10.4 Practice and Problem Solving (pp. 505–506)

5. 48 in.^{2} 7. 150 yd^2
9. 301.6 m^2

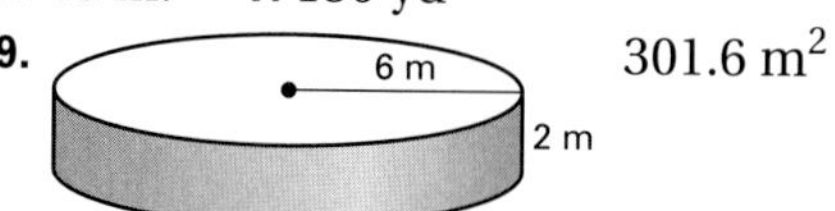

11. 1885.0 cm^2

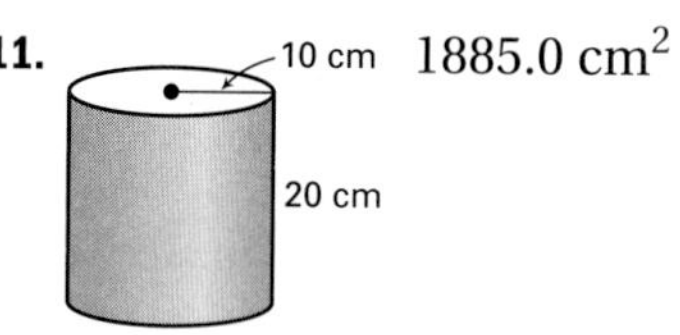

13. triangular prism; 680 in.^{2}
15. *Sample:* 600 in.^{2}

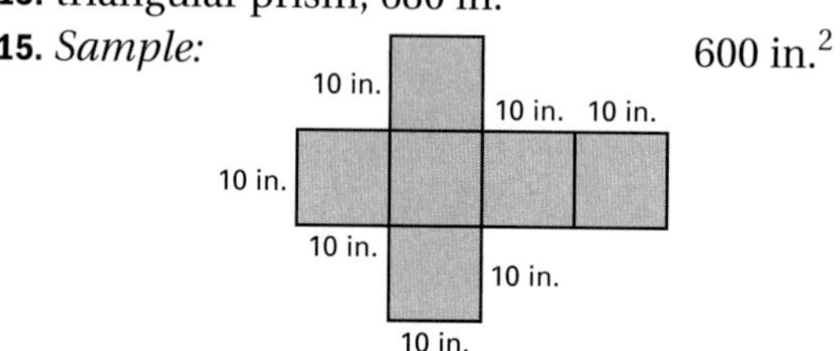

17. *Sample:* 88 m^2

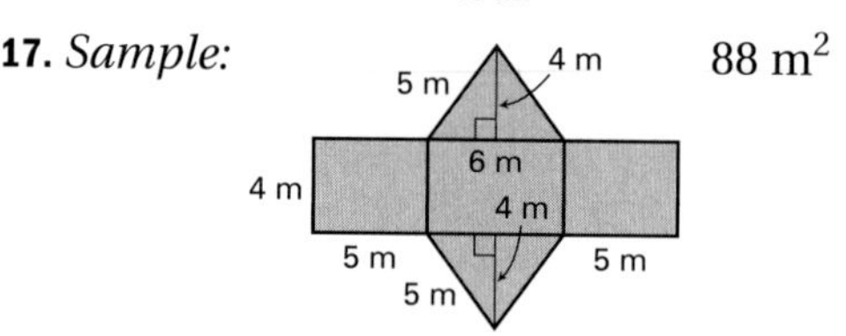

19. 1062 ft^2 21. 76 cm^2
23. *Sample:* 46 in.^{2}

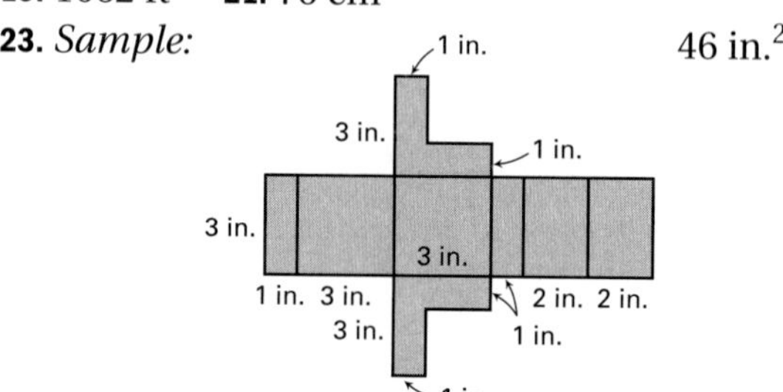

27. yes 29. 0.4245 31. 0.9135 33. 216 in.^{2}

10.5 Getting Ready to Practice (p. 509)

1.

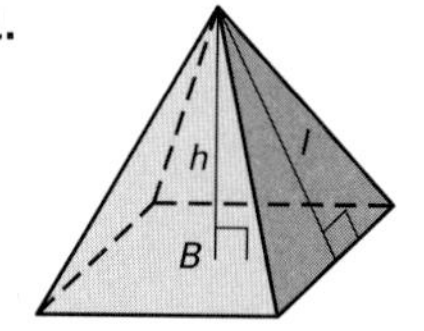

3. *Sample:* 36.9 ft^2

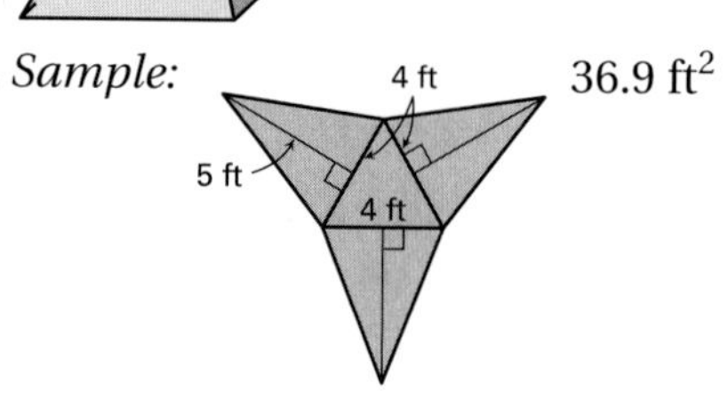

5. Step 1: $(\pi r^2 + \pi rl) - \pi r^2 = \pi rl$; Step 2: $\pi(1)\left(4\frac{1}{4}\right)$; Step 3: 13.4 in.^{2}

10.5 Practice and Problem Solving (pp. 510–511)

7. 144 m^2 **9.** 525 yd^2 **11.** 138.2 in.^{2} **13.** 119.4 mm^2 **15.** *Sample:* 552.9 in.^{2}

8 in.

14 in.

17. 261 in.^{2} **19.** 1508.0 m^2 **21.** 373.8 ft^2 **23.** 243.3 in.^{2} **25.** 6π in.^{2} **27.** 54π in.^{2} **29.** $S = B + \frac{1}{2}Pl = \pi r^2 + \frac{1}{2}(2\pi r)l = \pi r^2 + \pi rl$; the simplified expression is the same as the formula for the surface area of a cone. **33.** rational **35.** irrational

10.6 Getting Ready to Practice (p. 515)

1. *Sample answer:* Area is the measure of the region inside a two-dimensional shape, while volume is the measure of the space inside a solid. **3.** 200 in.^{3} **5.** The area of the base is πr^2, not $2\pi r$; $V = Bh = \pi r^2 h = \pi(4^2)5 \approx 251.3$ m^3.

10.6 Practice and Problem Solving (pp. 516–517)

7. 343 in.^{3} **9.** 120 ft^3 **11.** 254.5 cm^3 **13.** 64 yd^3 **15.** 1260 m^3 **17.** 25,446.9 mm^3 **19.** surface area **21.** volume **23.** 3820.2 cm^3 **25.** 8.6 mm^3 **27.** 336 m^3 **29.** 11 times **31.** They would have the same effect. *Sample answer:* Since $V = lwh$, if any dimension is doubled, the volume is doubled. **33.** 36 **35.** 192 in.^{2} **37.** 75.4 ft^2

10.7 Getting Ready to Practice (p. 521)

5. 96 cm^3 **7.** 3141.6 ft^3

10.7 Practice and Problem Solving (pp. 522–523)

9. 60 ft^3 **11.** 2560 m^3 **13.** 247.5 ft^3 **15.** 144 yd^3 **17.** 3421.2 cm^3 **19.** 5399.6 ft^3 **21.** 506.8 ft^3 **23.** 134.0 m^3 **25.** 70.7 ft^3 **27.** 0.2 cm^3 **29.** Doubling the radius. *Sample answer:* The radius is squared in the volume formula, but the height is not. **31.** Find the volume of the rectangular pyramid and the volume of the rectangular prism and add; $V = \frac{1}{3}lwh_1 + lwh_2$. **33.** 28.8 ft; 36.7 ft **37.** 2770.9 in.^{3}

10.4–10.7 Notebook Review (pp. 524–525)

1. For a regular pyramid, it is the height of a face that is not a base; for a cone, it is the length of any segment joining the edge of the base to the top point of the cone. **2.** 471.24 m^2 **3.** 146 in.^{2} **4.** 105 m^2 **5.** 785.40 ft^2 **6.** 126 m^3 **7.** *Sample answer:* Area is the measure of the region inside a two-dimensional figure, while surface area is the sum of the areas of all faces or surfaces of a solid.

Chapter Review (pp. 526–527)

5. *Sample:*

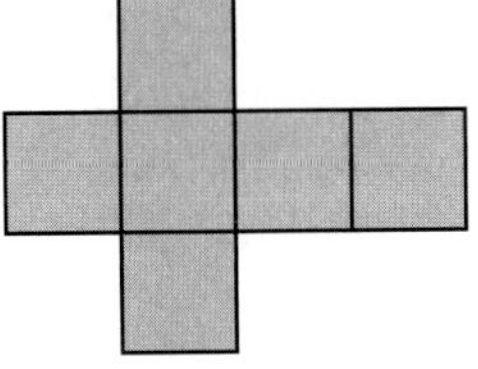

7. $S = 2\pi r^2 + 2\pi rh$; $V = \pi r^2 h$ **9.** $S = B + \frac{1}{2}Pl$; $V = \frac{1}{3}Bh$ **11.** 112 ft^2 **13.** $53\frac{1}{4}$ in.^{2} **15.** 90 yd^2 **17.** 707 yd^2 **19.** 1.77 m^2 **21.** *Sample:*

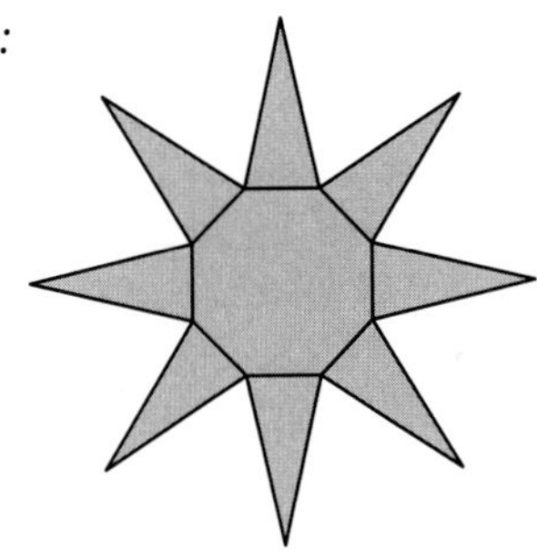

9 faces, 16 edges, 9 vertices

23. 2921.7 yd^2 **25.** 785.4 ft^2 **27.** 144 in.^{2} **29.** 103.8 mm^3 **31.** 20 in.^{3} **33.** 314.2 ft^3 **35.** No. *Sample answer:* The volume of the pyramid is 15 cubic inches, which is greater than the 12 cubic inches of candle wax.

Chapter 11

11.1 Getting Ready to Practice (p. 543)

1. function **3.** yes **5.** 18, 13, 8, 3 **7.** $y = -5x$

11.1 Practice and Problem Solving (pp. 543–544)

9. No; one input, 4, has two output values. **11.** Yes; each input has exactly one output value.

13.

Input x	−2	−1	0	1	2
Output y	−3	−2	−1	0	1

range: −3, −2, −1, 0, 1

15.

Input x	-2	-1	0	1	2
Output y	-10	-5	0	5	10

range: $-10, -5, 0, 5, 10$

17. $y = 5x$ **19.** No; the weight of the cans that Stanley recycles is a function of the amount of money. **21.** $t = 3r - 2$ **23.** Yes; each input has exactly one output value. **25.** 113.5 m^2 **27.** 6670 ft^2

11.2 Getting Ready to Practice (p. 547)

1. scatter plot

11.2 Practice and Problem Solving (pp. 547–548)

3. no relationship **5.** negative relationship

7.

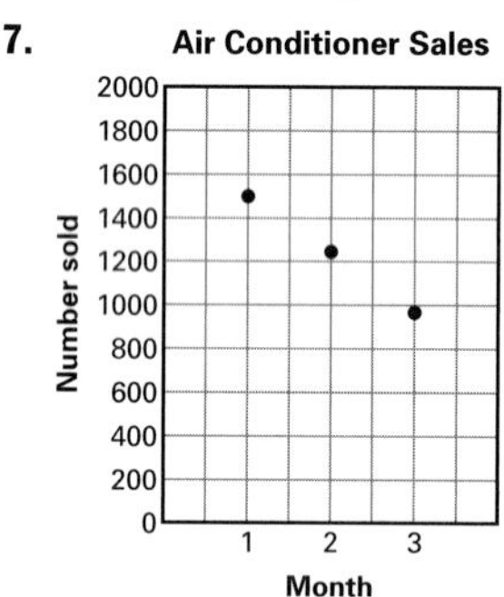

There is a negative relationship. As the summer turns to fall, sales of air conditioners decrease.

9.

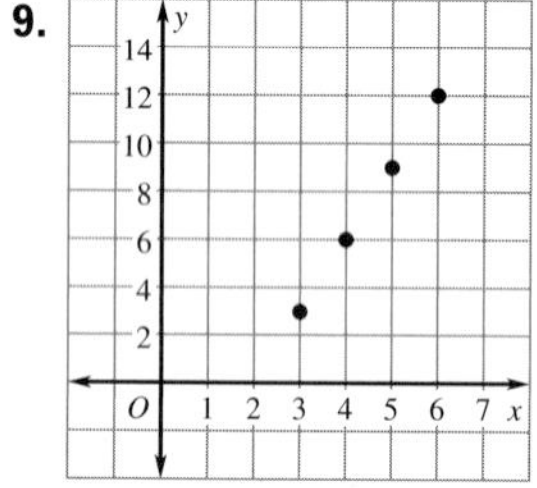

There is a positive relationship, with each increase of 1 in x corresponding to an increase of 3 in y; (7, 15).

11. positive relationship **13.** *Sample answer:* When the weather is nicer, more people will vote; no, because it would be hard to find a single measure that would accurately indicate how "nice" the weather is. **15.** 90 m^2

17.

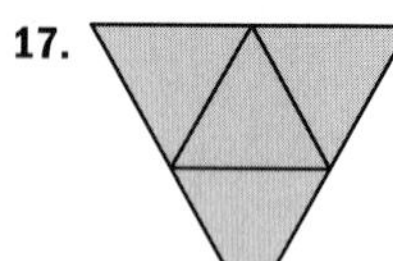

21. 19 **23.** 19

11.3 Getting Ready to Practice (p. 551)

1. solution **3.** $y = 2x + 4$ **5.** The x value was substituted for y and the y value was substituted for x. The second step should be $2(-5) + 3(4) \stackrel{?}{=} -7$, followed by $-10 + 12 \stackrel{?}{=} -7$ and $2 \neq -7$. So, $(-5, 4)$ is not a solution.

11.3 Practice and Problem Solving (pp. 551–553)

7. y values in the table: 3, 8, 13, 18 **9.** y values in the table: $-25, -20, -15, -10$ **11.** no **13.** yes **15.** yes **17.** *Sample answer:* $(-1, -6), (0, -10), (1, -14), (2, -18)$ **19.** no **21.** yes **23–27.** Sample answers are given. **23.** $(-1, -15), (0, -13), (1, -11), (2, -9)$ **25.** $(-1, 8), (0, 3), (1, -2), (2, -7)$ **27.** $(-1, -45), (0, -51), (1, -57), (2, -63)$ **29.** 20 wk **31.** $y = -x + 8$. *Sample answer:* $(-1, 9), (0, 8), (1, 7), (2, 6)$ **33.** $y = 3x + 33$. *Sample answer:* $(-1, 30), (0, 33), (1, 36), (2, 39)$ **35.** $y = 2 - 3x$. *Sample answer:* $(-1, 5), (0, 2), (1, -1), (2, -4)$ **37.** $y = 2x + 4$ **39.** *Sample answer:* $9x = 24$ and $8y \approx -6$, so $9x + 8y \approx 18$, which is greater than 16. **41.** $(2, -1)$ **43.**

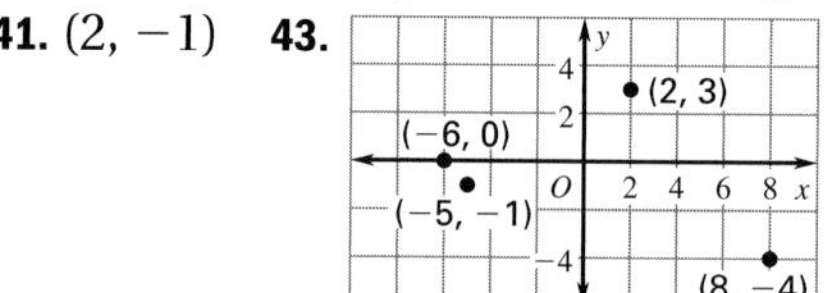

45.

Input x	-2	-1	0	1	2
Output y	3	2.5	2	1.5	1

range: 1, 1.5, 2, 2.5, 3

47.

Input x	-2	-1	0	1	2
Output y	12	10	8	6	4

range: 4, 6, 8, 10, 12 **49.** -8.75

11.4 Problem Solving Strategies (p. 555)

1. 2nd row: 140, 120, 100, 80 **3.** 60 ft **5.** Krystal **7.** 27 rectangles; 81 rectangles **9.** Leslie

11.4 Getting Ready to Practice (p. 558)

1. line **3.** *Sample:*

Input x	-2	-1	0	1	2
Output y	-4	-4	-4	-4	-4

11.4 Practice and Problem Solving (pp. 559–560)

9. yes **11.** *Sample answer:* $(-1, -3), (0, -2), (1, -1)$ **13.** *Sample answer:* $(-1, 6), (0, 6), (1, 6)$

15.

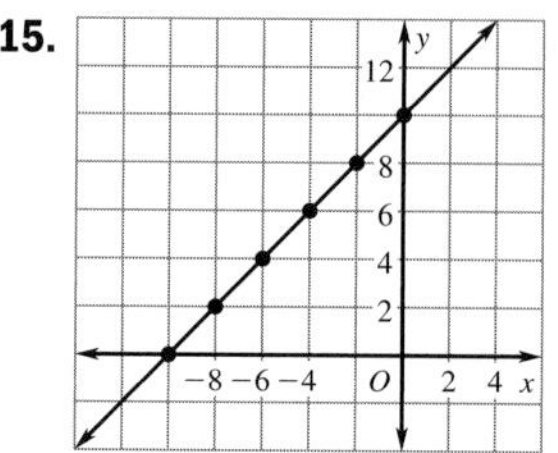

17.

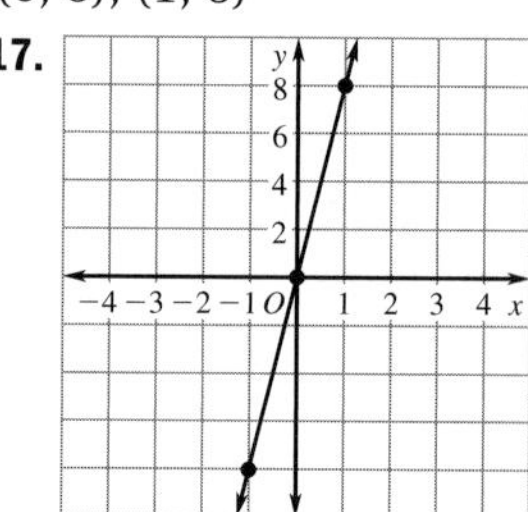

19. 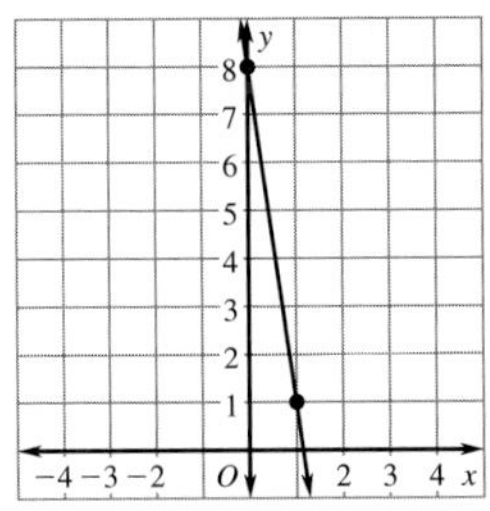

23. 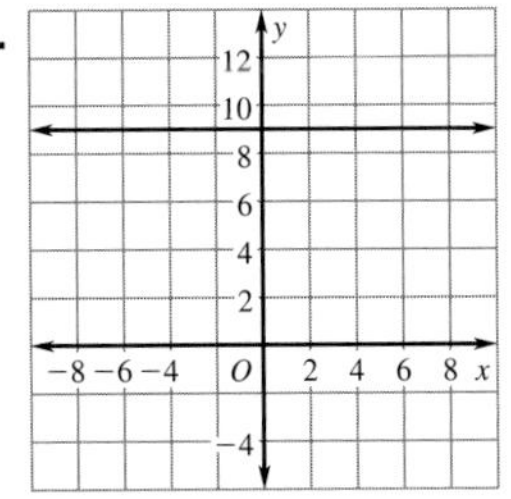

27. $x = 5$

29. 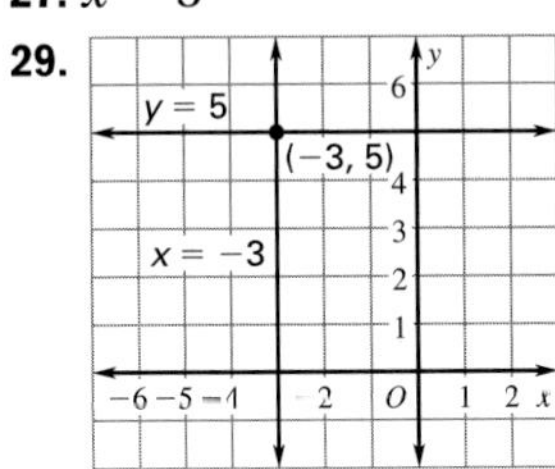

(−3, 5). *Sample answer:* Since $x = -3$ and $y = 5$, (−3, 5) will be the coordinates of the point of intersection.

37. $y = 2$ **39.** *Sample answer:* The line must be horizontal and contain all points with a y-coordinate of −8.6, so the equation of the line is $y = -8.6$. **41.** 140 square units **43.** 1056 square units **45.** y values in table: −14, −8, 1, 4, 13 **47.** −252

11.4 Technology Activity (p. 561)

1. 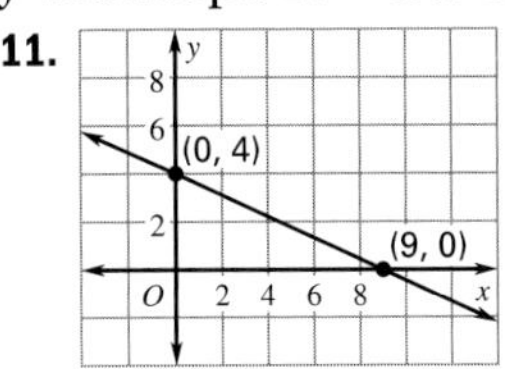 **3.** 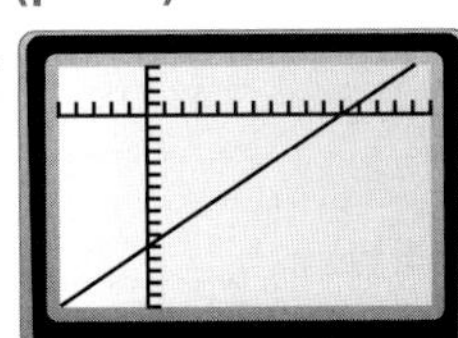

5. yes

11.1–11.4 Notebook Review (pp. 562–563)

1. input-output table **2.** $y = -4x$ **3.** $y = x + 3$

4. 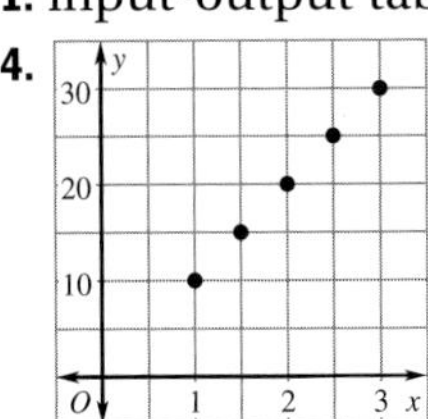

The data have a positive relationship, with every increase of 0.5 in x there is a corresponding increase of 5 in y.

5–7. Sample solutions are given.

5. (0, 5), (1, 3), (2, 1) 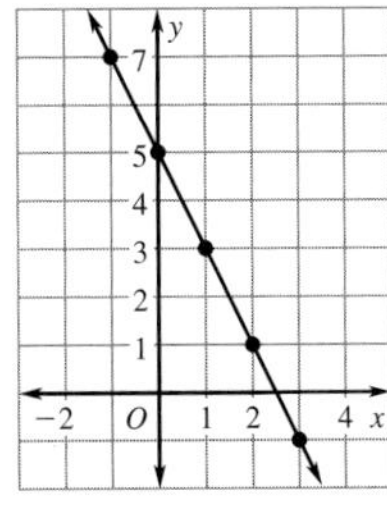

6. (0, −6), (1, −3) (2, 0) 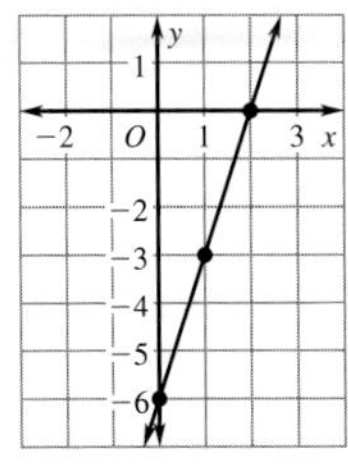

7. (0, 4), (4, 5), (8, 6) 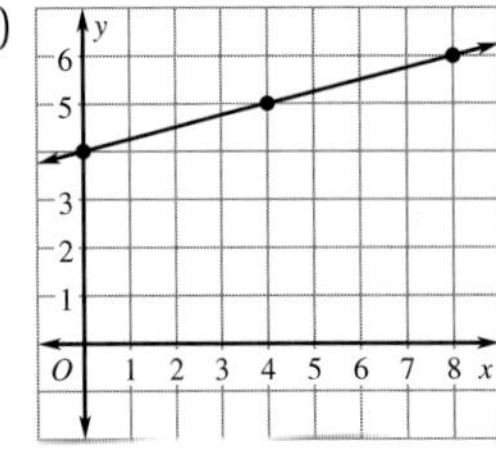

8. *Sample answer:* $4y = -2x + 16$ can be rewritten as $16 = 2x + 4y$, or $8 = x + 2y$, so the equations are equivalent and have the same solutions.

11.5 Getting Ready to Practice (p. 566)

1. y-intercept, x-intercept **3.** x-intercept: 3, y-intercept: −1

11.5 Practice and Problem Solving (pp. 566–567)

5. x-intercept: $\frac{1}{2}$, y-intercept: −3 **7.** x-intercept: −2, y-intercept: 10 **9.** x-intercept: 5, y-intercept: 4

11. 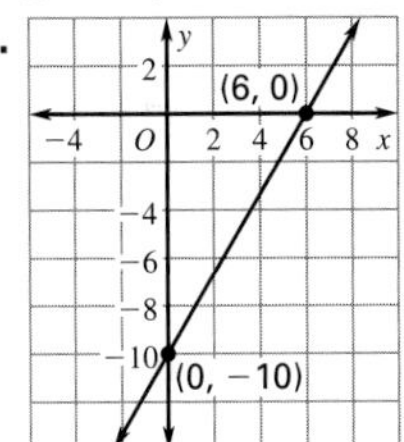

13. 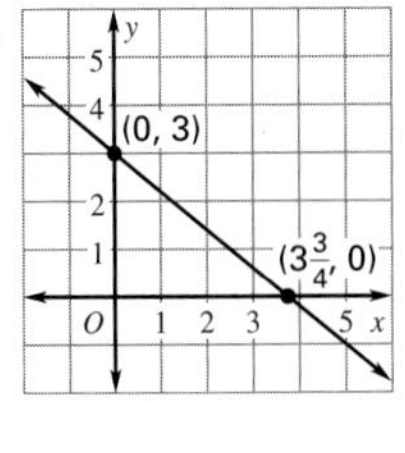

15. Up. *Sample answer:* The x-intercept will be on the positive side of the x-axis and the y-intercept will be on the negative side of the y-axis, so the line will slant up from left to right. **17.** x-intercept: none, y-intercept: 14

19. 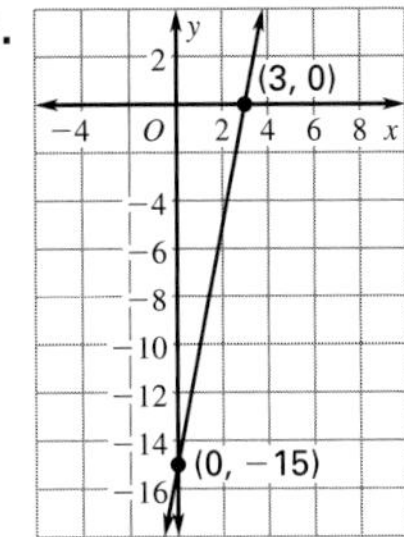

21.

25. x-intercept: 1.71, y-intercept: 3.65
27. x-intercept: −3.64, y-intercept: −15.01

31.

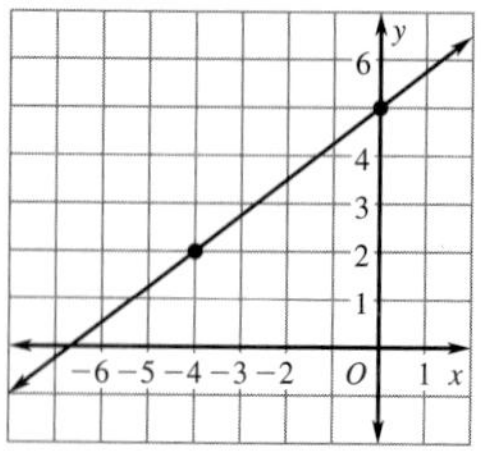

33.

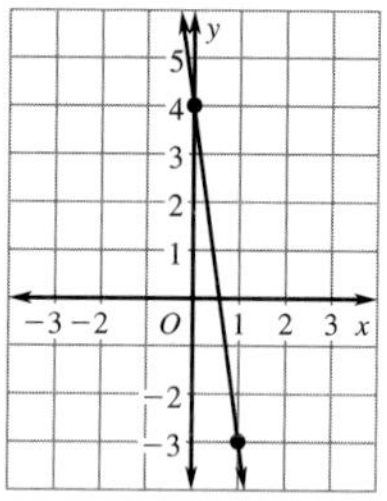

35. 60 km/h

11.6 Getting Ready to Practice (p. 572)

1. rise

3, 5. Sample answers are given.

3.

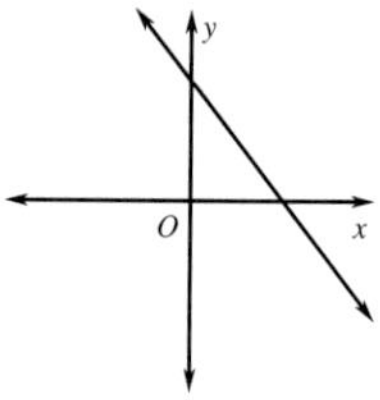

5.

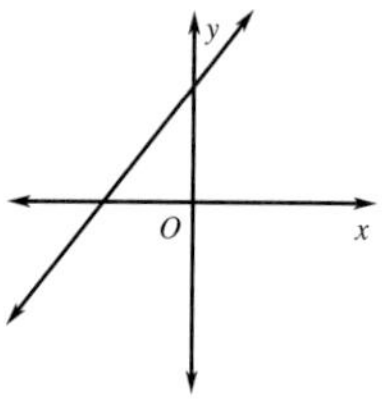

7. 3 **9.** 1

11.6 Practice and Problem Solving (pp. 573–574)

11. (1, 0), (−2, 6); −2 **13.** $-\frac{1}{5}$ **15.** 1 **17.** $\frac{3}{5}$

19. $-\frac{5}{12}$ **21.** $\frac{3}{32}$

23.

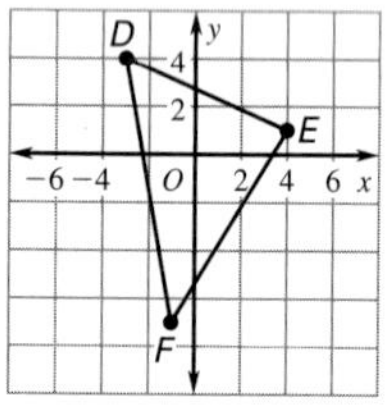

slope of $\overline{DE} = -\frac{3}{7}$, slope of $\overline{EF} = \frac{8}{5}$, slope of $\overline{FD} = -\frac{11}{2}$

25.

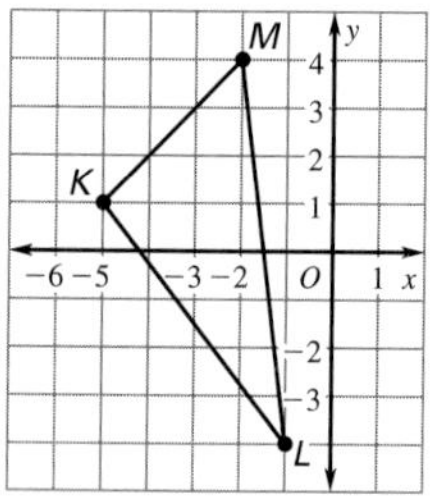

slope of $\overline{KL} = -\frac{5}{4}$, slope of $\overline{LM} = -8$, slope of $\overline{MK} = 1$

27. The line through (1, 1) and (3, 4); the line with the greater slope is steeper; the line with the greater slope has a greater number for the slope.

31. $x = 12$ **33.** $x = 4, y = 3$ **37.** yes **39.** no **41.** 63

11.7 Getting Ready to Practice (p. 579)

1. −5, 7 **3.** $y = 2x - 5$ **5.** 1, 3 **7.** 2, −1

11.7 Practice and Problem Solving (pp. 579–580)

9. 1, −8;

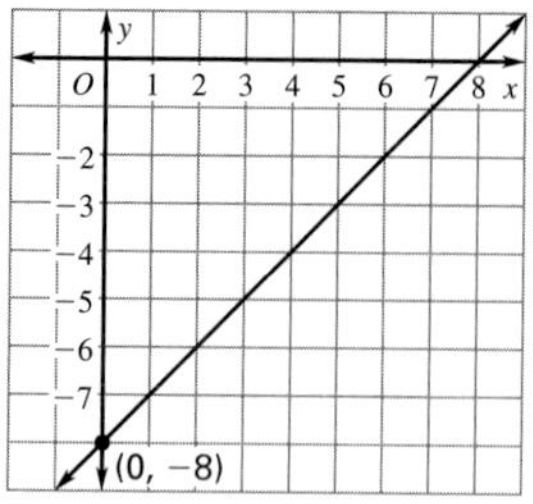

11. −1, 7;

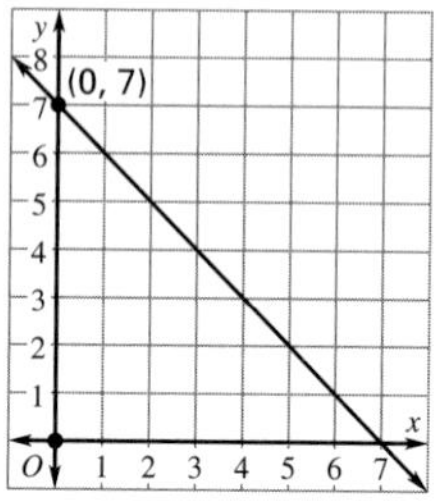

13. $\frac{2}{3}$, −4;

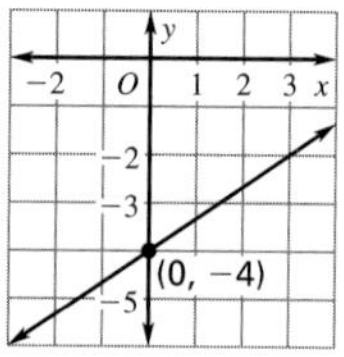

15. $y = -6x + 10$; −6, 10 **17.** $y = \frac{2}{3}x - 3$; $\frac{2}{3}$, −3

19. $y = -12x$; −12, 0

21.

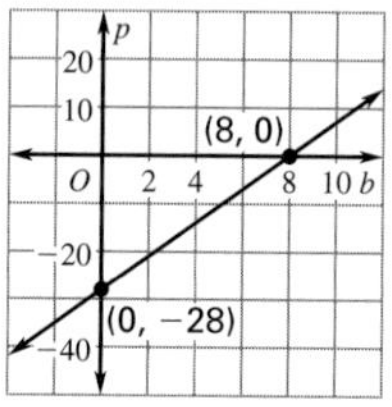

9 bracelets **23.** $y = -\frac{3}{2}x - 3$

25.

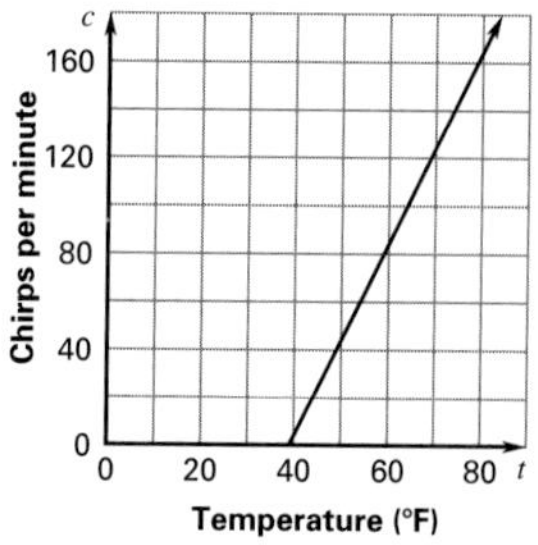

At 39°F, the number of chirps per minute is 0.

27. $y = -\frac{a}{b}x - \frac{c}{b}$ **29.** $5x \geq 35$; $x \geq 7$ **31.** 75 ft^3

33. $t > 6$;

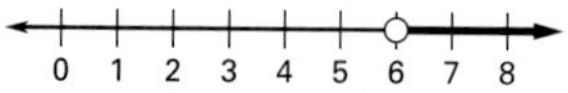

Special Topic Exercises (p. 582)

1. 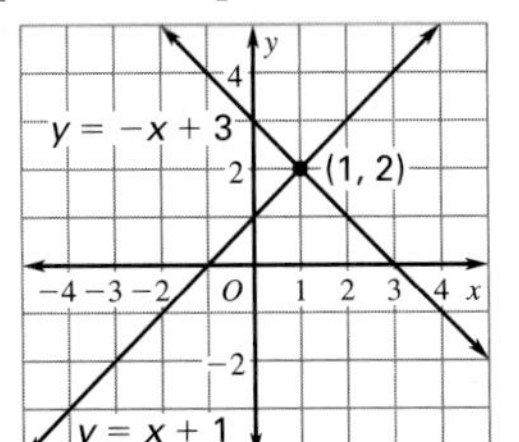

(1, 2)

3. 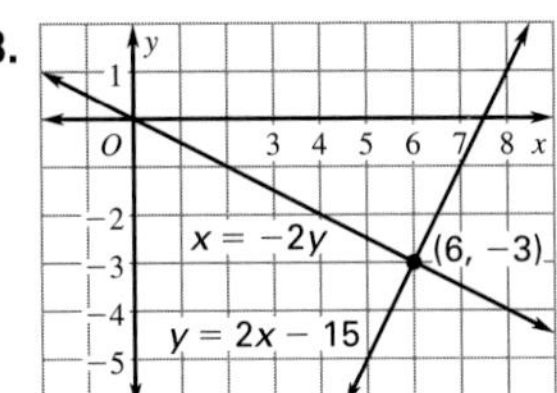

(6, −3) **5.** (−1, 5)

7. 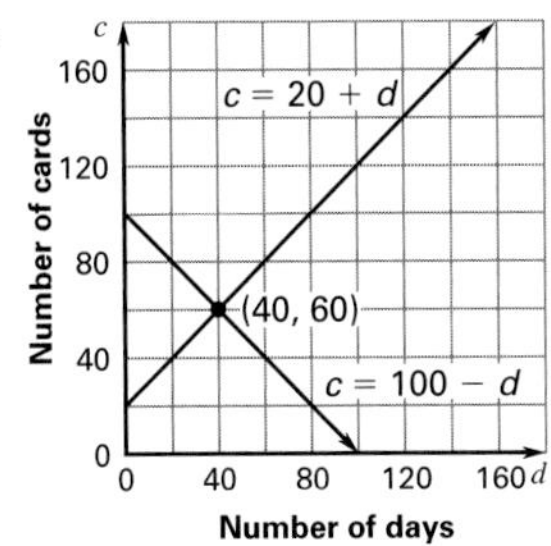

in 40 days

11.8 Getting Ready to Practice (p. 585)

1. half-planes **3.** yes **5.** no

7. 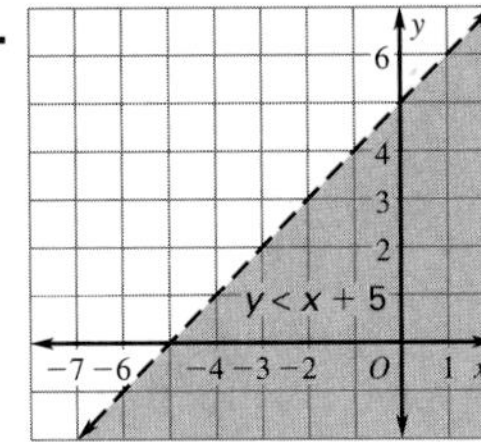

9. 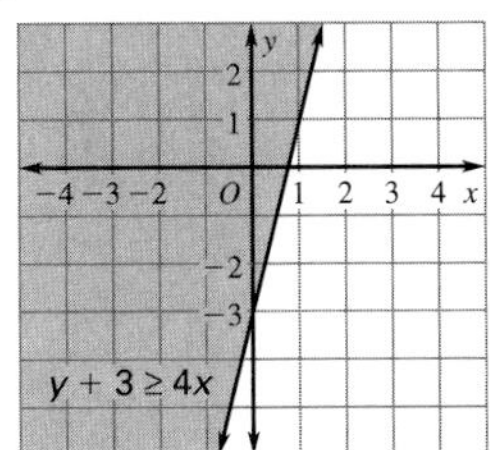

11.8 Practice and Problem Solving (pp. 586–587)

11. yes **13.** no **15.** Use a dashed line when the inequality symbol is < or >. Use a solid line when the inequality symbol is ≤ or ≥.

21. 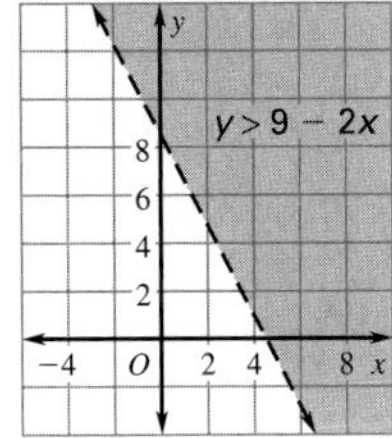

23. 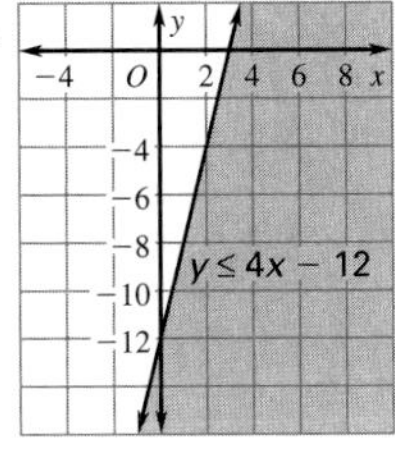

27. 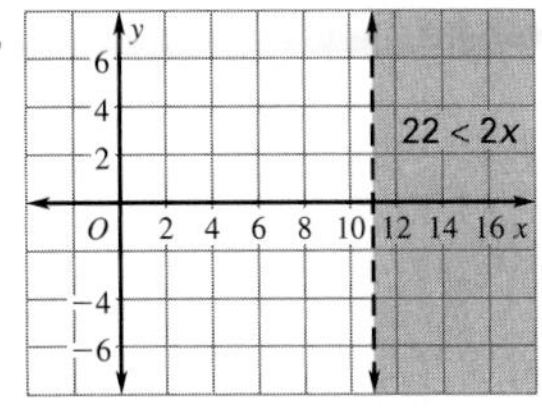

29. 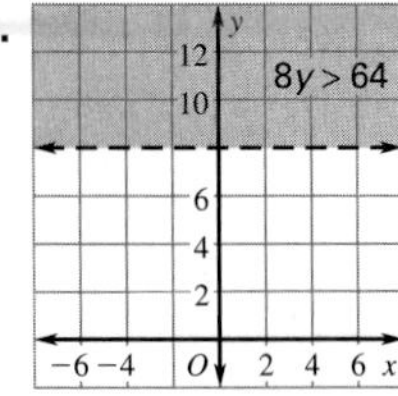

31. 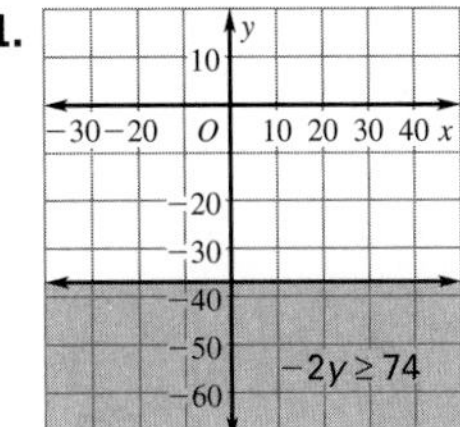

33. 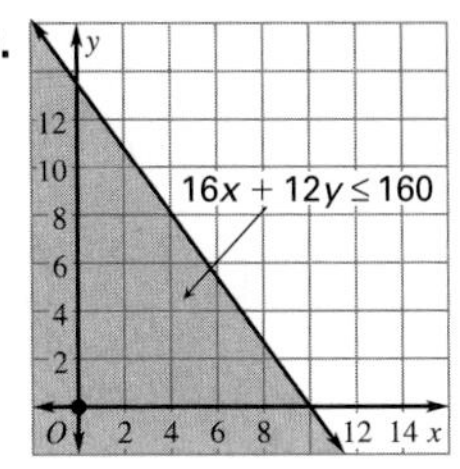

37. $y < -\frac{1}{3}x + 5$; $y > \frac{1}{3}x - 5$; $y > \frac{2}{3}x - 6$; $y < -\frac{2}{3}x + 6$

39. $\frac{6}{5}$ **41.** $3\frac{3}{4}$ **43.** $7\frac{41}{250}$

11.5–11.8 Notebook Review (pp. 588–589)

1. slope; *y*-intercept **2.** $\frac{4}{3}$ **3.** $\frac{2}{5}$ **4.** $-\frac{5}{3}$

5. 5, 20; 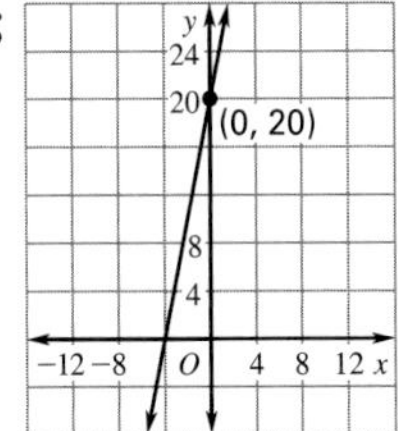

6. $\frac{2}{3}$, 4; 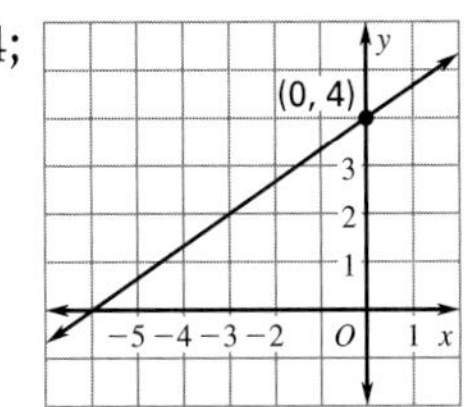

7. $-\frac{1}{4}$, $4\frac{1}{2}$; 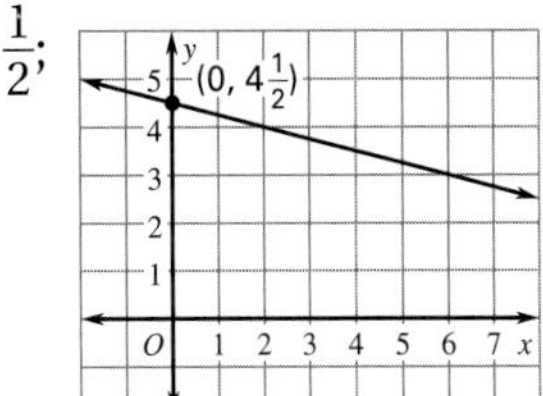

8. 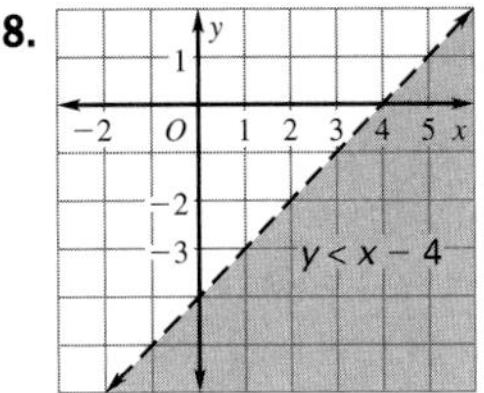

9. 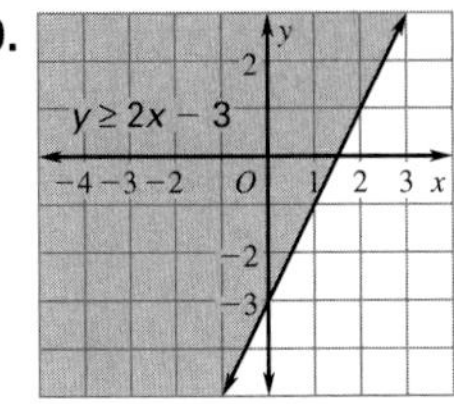

10. 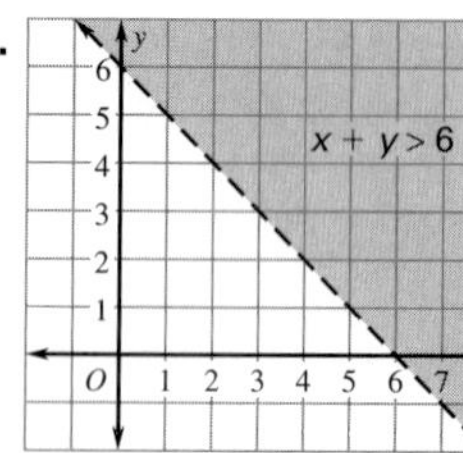

11. 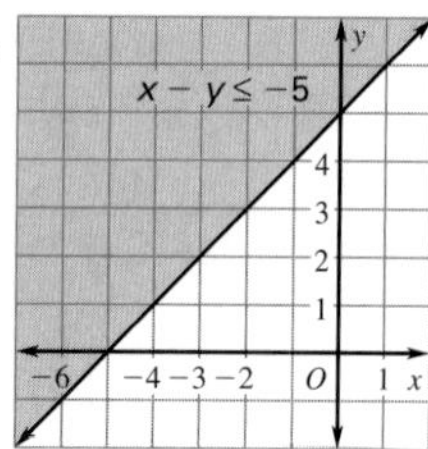

12. 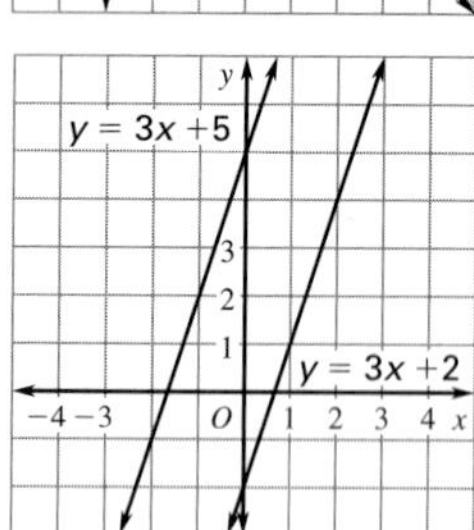

They are parallel.

Chapter Review (pp. 590–591) **1.** half-plane **3.** rise, run **5.** A good answer will include a situation that changes over time, such as time and distance traveled, and an explanation that the slope tells you how quickly something changes. **7.** No; each input has more than one output. **9.** Yes; each input has exactly one output. **11.** \$141

15. 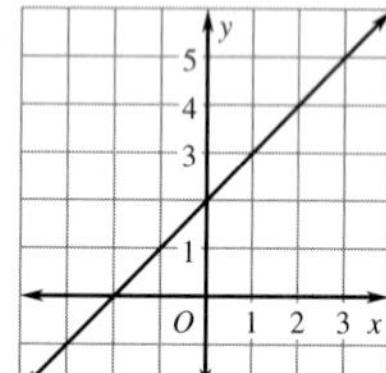

17. 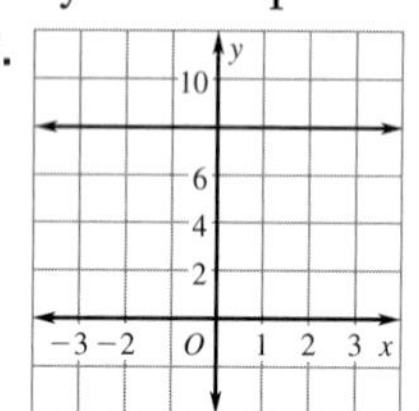

19. *Sample answer:* $(-2, 3)$, $(2, 3)$; 0 **21.** $y = 4x + 10$; 4, 10 **23.** $y = -\frac{3}{7}x - 3$; $-\frac{3}{7}$, -3

25. 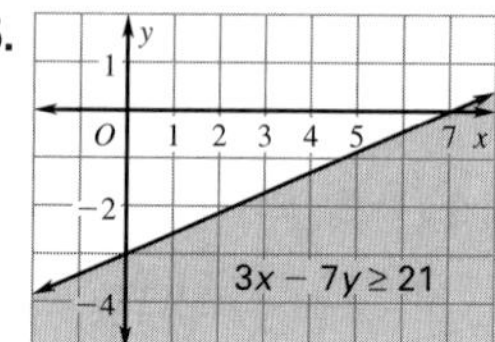

Chapter 12

12.1 Getting Ready to Practice (p. 599) **1.** stem, leaf **3.** 11 | 7; stem: 11, leaf: 7 **5.** 4 | 6; stem: 4, leaf: 6

12.1 Practice and Problem Solving (pp. 599–600)

7. 60–69

Stem	Leaves
4	5 8
5	0
6	3 5 7
7	4
8	2

Key: 5 | 0 = 50

9. 100–109

Stem	Leaves
8	9
9	4 5
10	3 8 9
11	2

Key: 10 | 3 = 103

11. 18.0–18.9

Stem	Leaves
18	1 3 7
19	
20	2
21	
22	5 6

Key: 18 | 1 = 18.1

13. Count the total number of values in the data set. Then count from the first leaf to half the total number of values to find the median value.

15. 53; greater than

Stem	Leaves
4	3 7
5	5 8 9
6	5
7	2 8
8	4 4
9	5 6

Key: 4 | 3 = 43

17.

Set C		Set D
	6	5
7 0	7	
	8	7 8
8 2	9	3 5
2	10	2
8 1	11	5

Key: 2 | 9 | 3 = 92 and 93

19.

Wins		Losses
	0	6 7 7
8	1	0 2 4 5 6
7 4 4 3 0	2	1
	3	
1	4	

Key: 0 | 2 | 1 = 20 and 21

Sample answer: When the Browns scored less than 20 points, they usually lost. When they scored more than 20 points, they usually won.

21. 13.8, 14.2, 14.4, 15.6, 17.1, 18.7, 20.6, 21.4, 21.1, 19.3, 16.4, 13.8 **23.** 3.5, 6, 6 and 14, 42

12.2 Getting Ready to Practice (p. 603)

1. lower quartile; upper quartile

12.2 Practice and Problem Solving (pp. 603–604)

3.

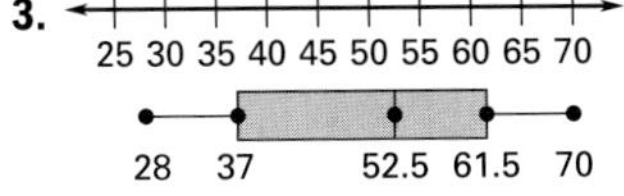

5.

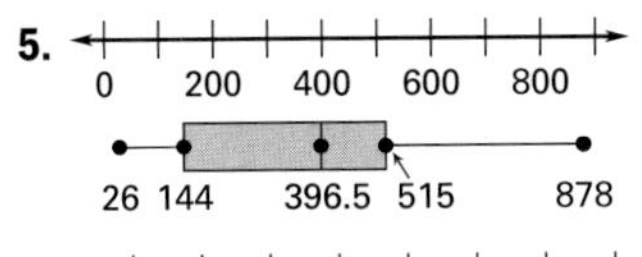

7. 15 in. **9.** 22 in. **11.** 28 in.

13.

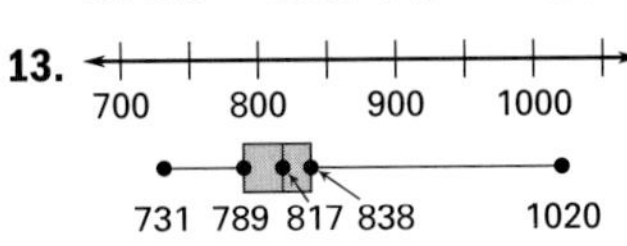

Sample answer: The middle half of the pumpkin weights clustered within about a 50 pound range, from 789 pounds to 838 pounds, but the range was much wider, nearly 300 pounds.

17.

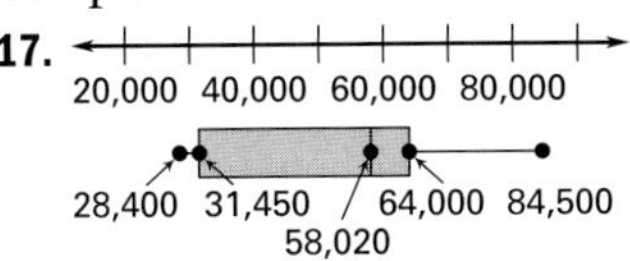

Sample answer: The outlier does not have much of an effect on the quartiles, but it makes a whisker very long and thus greatly increases the range.

19.

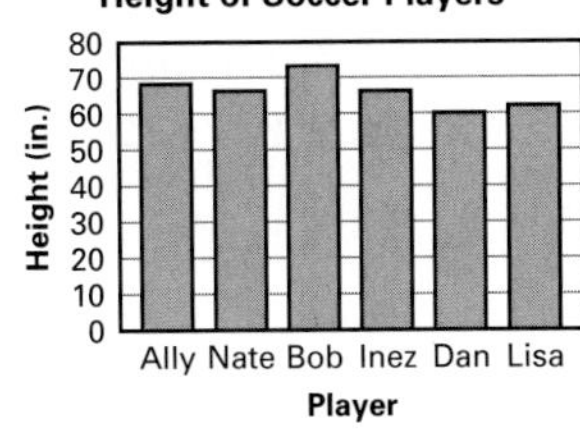

21. x-intercept: 10, y-intercept: -6, slope: $\frac{3}{5}$

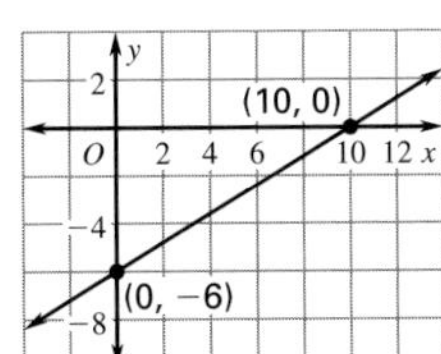

12.3 Getting Ready to Practice (p. 607) **1.** circle graph **3.** 112° **5.** 50° **7.**

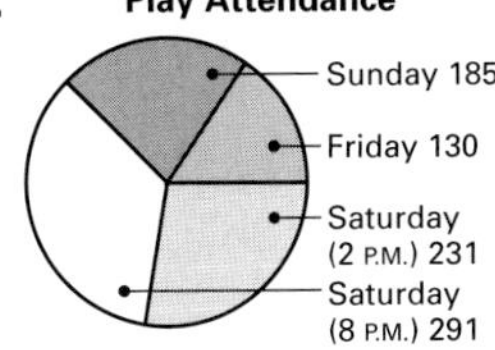

12.3 Practice and Problem Solving (pp. 608–609)

9.

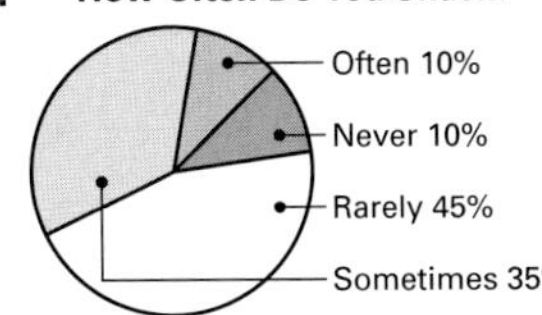

11.

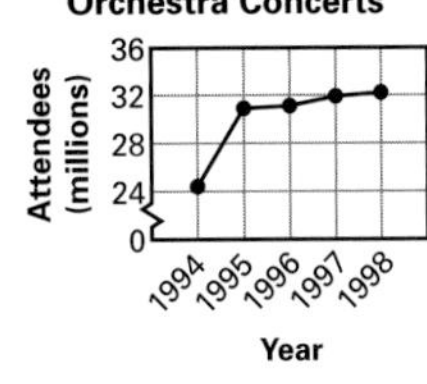

Sample answer: The number of people who attend symphony orchestra concerts increased rapidly from 1994 to 1995, and then at a slower rate from 1995 to 1998.

13.

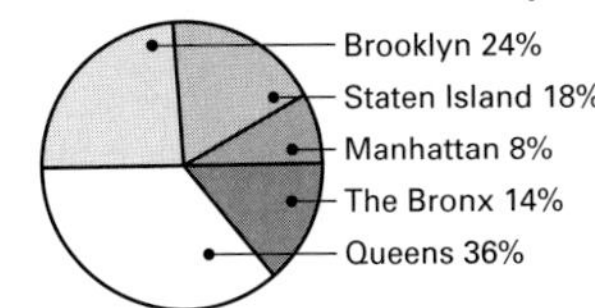

15. *Sample answer:* Line graph; the data is collected over time. **17.** *Sample answer:* Histogram; the data is the frequency of occurrence in equal intervals for a certain range. **19.** red; dark blue **21.** No; it does not show a change in data over time; yes; it shows data in distinct categories.

23.

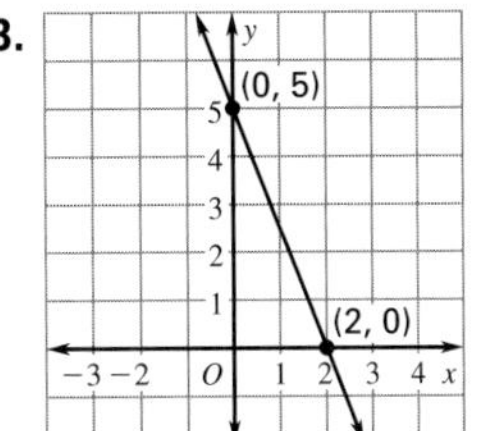

25.

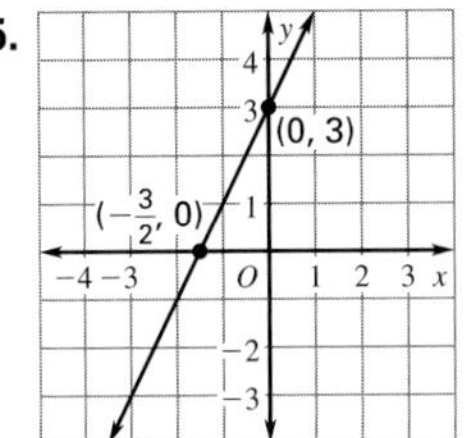

12.3 Technology Activity (pp. 610–611)

1.

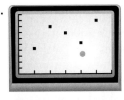

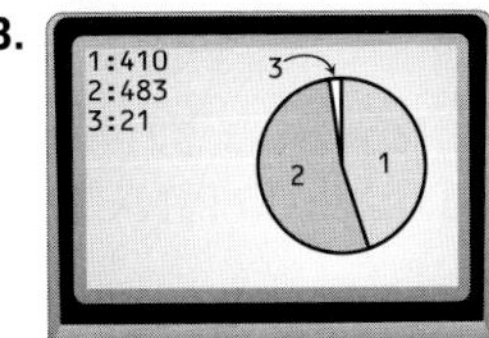

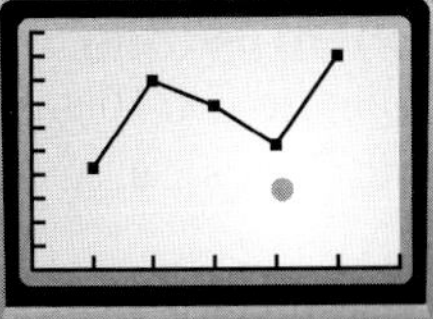

3.

Special Topic Exercises (p. 613)
1. No. *Sample answer:* There is a break in the vertical scale, so the relative change is smaller than it appears.

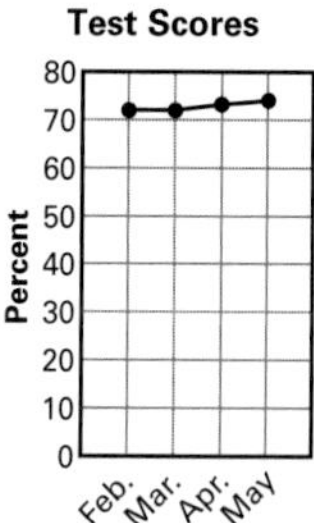

3.

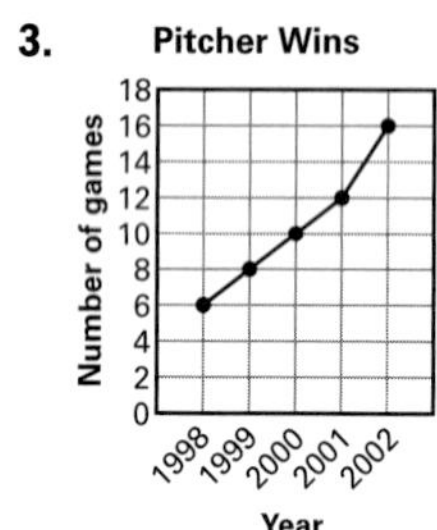

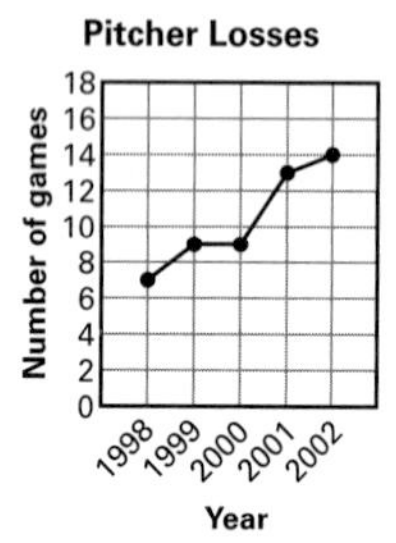

12.1–12.3 Notebook Review (pp. 614–615)
1. lower extreme, upper extreme

2.

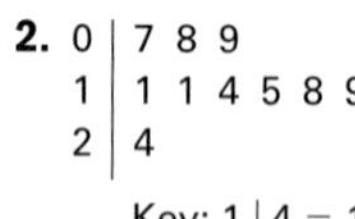

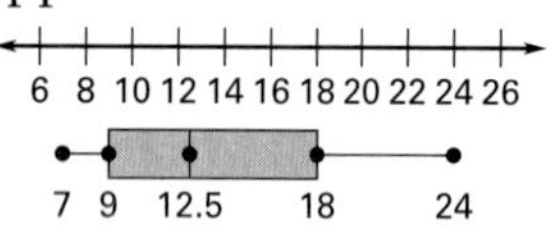

3.

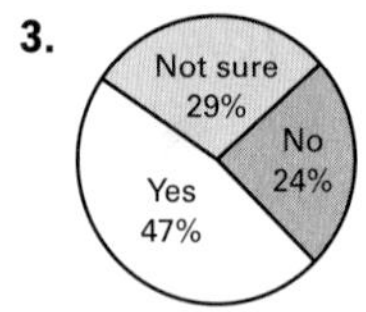

4.

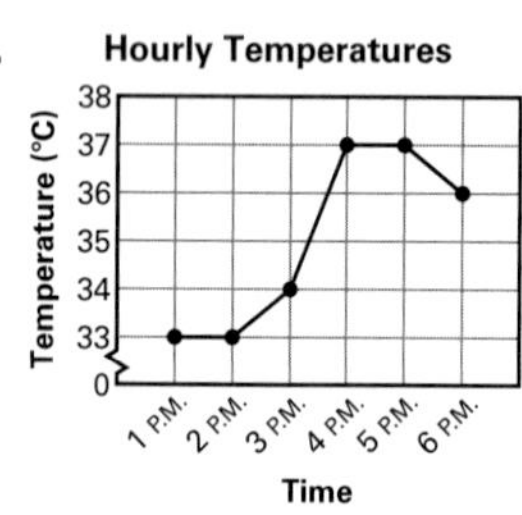

5. *Sample answer:* movie attendance each night for two weeks **6.** No. *Sample answer:* It does not show data that vary over time; bar graph.

12.4 Problem Solving Strategies (p. 617)
1. 60 people; no **3.** 10 games **5.** 2500 **7.** 58 palindromes **9.** 55 squares **11.** Saturday

12.4 Getting Ready to Practice (p. 620) **1.** $m \cdot n$ **3.** 9 choices **5.** 6 choices **7.** $\frac{1}{64}$

12.4 Practice and Problem Solving (pp. 621–622)
9. 24 choices **11.** 16 choices **13.** 26,000 PINs **15.** $\frac{1}{64}$ **21.** 3 desserts **25.** $\frac{1}{2}$

27.

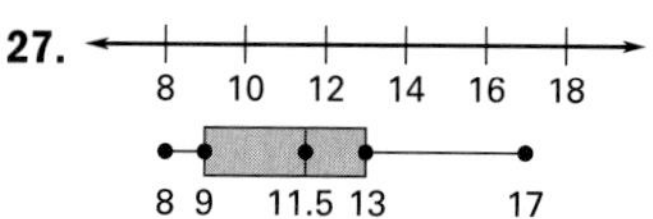

12.5 Getting Ready to Practice (p. 625) **1.** ${}_{15}P_7$ **3.** 1 **5.** 362,880 **7.** 60,480 **9.** 120

12.5 Practice and Problem Solving (pp. 625–626)
11. 24 orders **13.** 20 **15.** 504 **17.** 840 **19.** 6840 **21.** 360,360 ways **23.** yes; $11! = 11 \cdot 10 \cdot 9 \cdot 8 \cdot 7 \cdot 6 \cdot 5 \cdot 4 \cdot 3 \cdot 2 \cdot 1 = 11 \cdot 10!$ **25.** 32,760 ways

29.

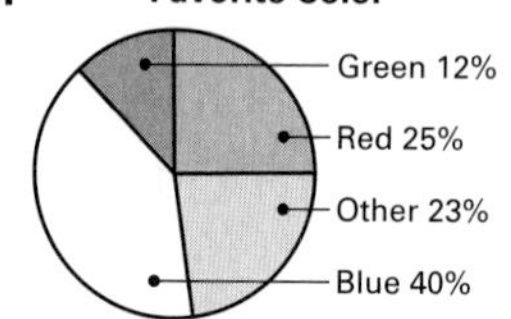

12.6 Getting Ready to Practice (p. 629) **1.** 9; 5 **3.** 4 **5.** 7 **7.** combination; 6 pairs

12.6 Practice and Problem Solving (pp. 630–631)
11. 1 **13.** 70 **15.** 8 **17.** 126 **19.** 78 **21.** 100 **23.** 792 teams **25.** No. *Sample answer:* You cannot choose more items than you have to start with, that is, *r* must be less than or equal to *n*. **27.** combination; 10 sets **29.** permutation; 1,814,400 ways; combination, 45 ways **31.** 4845 **35.** 30,240 **37.** 4896 **39.** $\frac{2}{3}$

12.7 Getting Ready to Practice (p. 634) **1.** odds in favor **3.** $\frac{3}{5}$ **5.** $\frac{1}{10}$ **7.** $\frac{1}{3}$ **9.** $\frac{3}{7}$

12.7 Practice and Problem Solving (pp. 635–636)
11. $\frac{4}{13}$; $\frac{9}{4}$ **13.** $\frac{3}{7}$; $\frac{5}{9}$ **15.** $\frac{5}{1}$ **17.** $\frac{1}{2}$ **21.** $\frac{7}{25}$ **23.** $\frac{4}{1}$ **27.** 0.04 **29.** 51 in. **31.** $-\frac{1}{10}$ **33.** $\frac{7}{15}$ **35.** $\frac{3}{56}$

12.8 Getting Ready to Practice (p. 641)
1. independent **3.** dependent; $\frac{1}{506}$

12.8 Practice and Problem Solving (pp. 642–643)
5. 0.1 **7.** 0.375 **9.** 0.13 **11.** dependent; $\frac{2}{21}$ **13.** $\frac{1}{17{,}018}$

17. 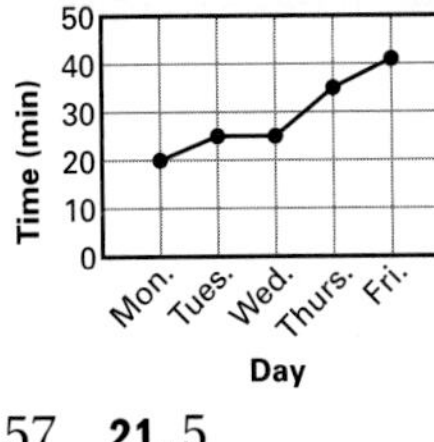

Sample answer: About 46 min; if you extend the graph, it passes through 46 on Saturday.

19. 57 **21.** 5

Special Topic Exercises (p. 645) **1.** Yes; people who call in to a sports talk show are likely to favor sports. **3.** Yes; people who enter a sporting goods store are likely to favor sports. **5.** *Sample answer:* Yes; this question suggests the mall is noisy and crowded. It encourages respondents to favor staying at home. So, the question could lead to biased results. **7.** *Sample answer:* No; this question is straight forward with no suggestions. It is not likely to lead to biased results.

12.4–12.8 Notebook Review (pp. 646–647)
1. permutation **2.** 20 birdhouses **3.** 35 ways **4.** $\frac{3}{11}$ **5.** $\frac{2}{121}$ **6.** *Sample answer:* Ordering toppings on a pizza

Chapter Review (pp. 648–649)

7. 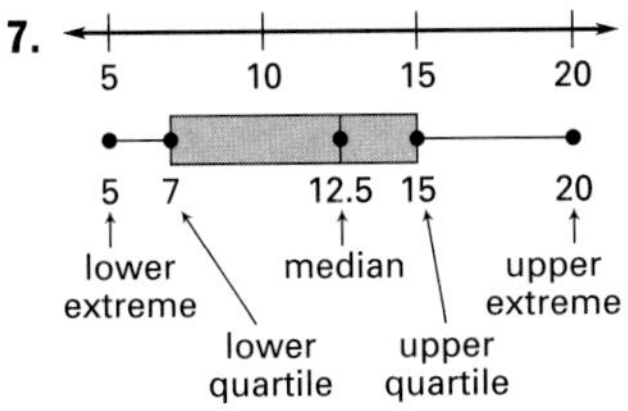

9.

Stem	Leaves
6	7
7	5
8	
9	
10	
11	2 3
12	
13	
14	
15	0 1 7

Key: 7 | 5 = 7.5

15.0–15.9

11. 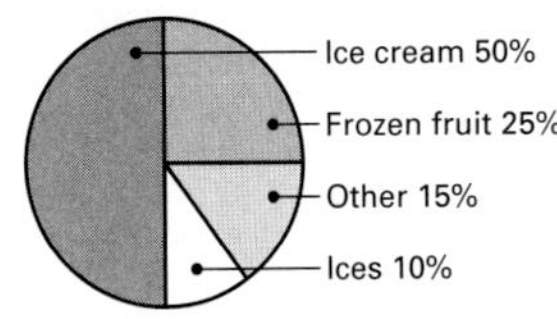

13. 1680 **15.** 36 **17.** 5040 ways **19.** permutation; 120 ways **21.** $\frac{7}{13}$ **23.** $\frac{1}{380}$

Chapter 13

13.1 Getting Ready to Practice (p. 659)
1. trinomial **3.** monomial **5.** $3m + 7$ **7.** $6b^3 + 4b - 4$ **9.** $5y - 1$ **11.** $-3x^2$ and $-20x$ are not like terms and cannot be combined. The expression $-3x^2 - 20x - 4$ cannot be simplified.

13.1 Practice and Problem Solving (pp. 659–660)
13. $4x^{10} - 13x^3$; binomial **15.** $4x - 4$ **17.** $-7q^5 + 3q^3 + 3q$ **19.** $-3b + 17$ **21.** $2(2x + 3) + 4x$; $8x + 6$ **23.** $12m^2 + m - 6$ **25.** $8x^2 - 15x + 30$ **27.** 98 ft **29.** 122 ft **31.** $18t^2 + 12t - 37$ **33.** always **35.** never **41.** $\frac{1}{4}$ **43.**

Stem	Leaves
34	2
35	8
36	2 3 4 6
37	5 6
38	6 6

Key: 35 | 8 = 35.8

45. -21 **47.** 60

13.2 Getting Ready to Practice (p. 663) **1.** like terms **3.** $6x + 12$ **5.** $3p + 8$ **7.** $-a + 6$

13.2 Practice and Problem Solving (pp. 664–665)
9. $5x + 4$ **11.** $7n - 2$ **13.** $6g^2 + g + 3$ **15.** $-10d - 7$ **17.** $-11h^2 + 10h$ **19.** $3r^2 + 2r + 4$ **21.** $(x + 7) + (3x - 2) + (4x - 1)$; $8x + 4$ **23.** $6k^2$ **25.** $6x^3 + 8x^2 - 12x - 3$ **27.** $12n + 3$ **29.** $16r^2 - 4(\pi r^2)$; $3.44r^2$; yes; one coaster needs $3.14r^2$ of clay, which is less than what is left over. **31.** $-7s^2 + 5s - 9$ **33.** $-14t^3 - 10t^2 + 22t$ **35.** $-14v^4 + 15v^3 - 21v^2 + 37$ **39.** b^{10} **41.** m^4n^3 **43.** 10,000 passwords

13.3 Getting Ready to Practice (p. 668)
5. $2x^3 - 2x$ **7.** z^{16}

13.3 Practice and Problem Solving (pp. 669–670)
9. $-20x^4$ **11.** $3x^3$ **13.** b^{11} **15.** $m^2 + 4m$ **17.** $-t^3 + 4t$ **19.** $-2w^3 - w^2$ **21.** $\frac{1}{2}(b - 6)(3b + b)$; $2b^2 - 12b$ **23.** $x^5y^5z^5$ **25.** $-216z^3$ **27.** $9r^2s^2$ **29.** $100{,}000b^5h^5$ **31.** y^4 **33.** x^{20} **35.** x^6y^6 **37.** $8r^9$ **39.** $(2w^2 + 4w)$ in.^{2} **41.** $-3a^{26}b^8c^4$ **43.** $\frac{\pi r^2}{(2r)^2}$; $\frac{\pi}{4}$ **45.** 2.7×10^{13} **47.** 6.25×10^{30} **49.** about 7.36×10^8 km^3 **55.** $\frac{71}{100}$ **57.** $\frac{9}{50}$ **59.** $\frac{1}{36}$

13.1–13.3 Notebook Review (pp. 671–672)
1. monomial **2.** polynomial **3.** $a^2 + 18$ **4.** $2z^2 - 3z + 1$ **5.** $2n^3 + 5n^2 - 2n - 3$ **6.** $-5x^2 + 4x + 4$ **7.** $48x^{10}$ **8.** $36n^6m^2$ **9.** $16a^4b^4$ **10.** $4r^3 - 20r^2$ **11.** *Sample answer:* By the associative property of multiplication, $(2x)(x^2y) = 2(x \cdot x^2)y$. By the product of powers property, $2(x \cdot x^2)y = 2x^3y$. So $(2x)(x^2y) = 2x^3y$. **12.** $24\pi h^2$ or $\frac{8\pi r^2}{3}$

13.4 Getting Ready to Practice (p. 676)
1. binomial **3.** $6m^2 + 2m$ **5.** $y^2 - 3y - 4$ **7.** $z^2 + 2z - 8$

13.4 Practice and Problem Solving (pp. 676–677)
9. $x^2 + 7x - 18$ **11.** $a^2 + 6a - 40$ **13.** $3q^2 - 4q + 1$ **15.** $6r^2 + r - 7$ **17.** $-11x^2 - 43x + 60$ **19.** $x^2 - 16$ **23.** $4\pi(0.6875 + x)^2 = 4\pi(0.4727 + 1.375x + x^2) = 1.8908\pi + 5.5\pi x + 4\pi x^2$ **25.** $3b^2 - 58b + 72$ **27.** $(30 - 2x)(20 - x) = 600 - 70x + 2x^2$; 300 ft^2 **31.** $x + 1$

33.

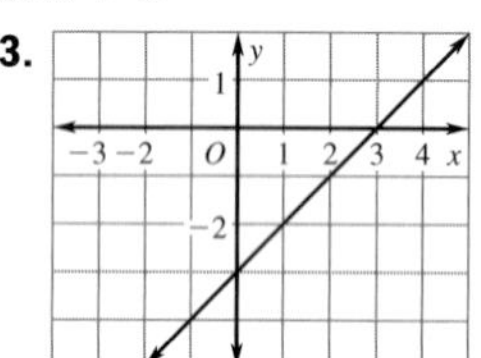

35. $-4r^2 - 24r$ **37.** $15x^2 - 10x$

38–41.

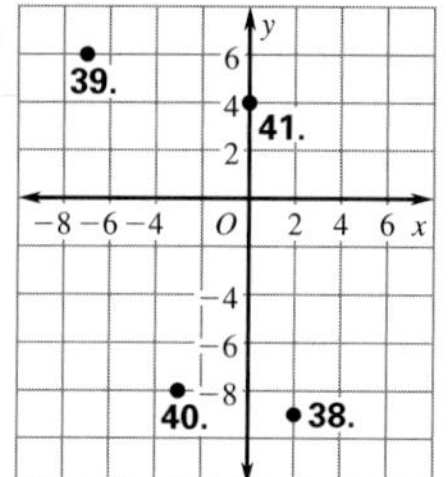

13.5 Problem Solving Strategies (p. 679)
1. 128 e-mails **3.** 10 cuts

5.

Hours	0.5	1	1.5	2
Points	2.5	5	7.5	10

about 9 points

7. 50 squares **9.** 1809.56 cm^3

13.5 Getting Ready to Practice (p. 682) **3.** -1, -5, -1 **5.** yes **7.** yes

13.5 Practice and Problem Solving (pp. 682–684)
9. $f(x) = 2x^2 - x$ **11.** $f(t) = -16t^2 + 4$; -140 ft

13.

x	−3	−2	−1	0	1	2	3
f(x)	17	12	9	8	9	12	17

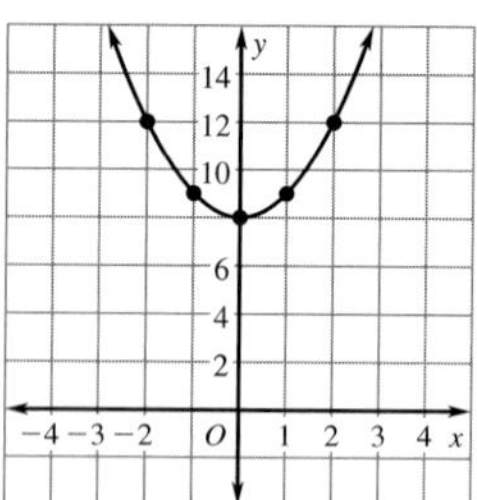

15.

x	−3	−2	−1	0	1	2	3
f(x)	−9	−4	−1	0	−1	−4	−9

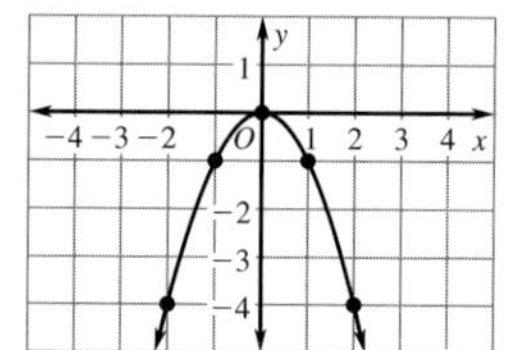

19. yes **21.** $f(x) = 1500x$

23.

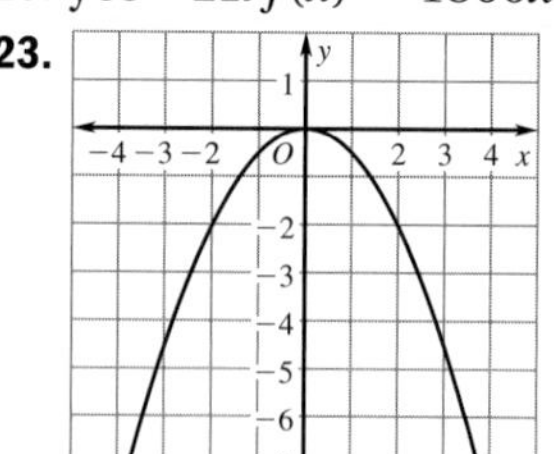

27.

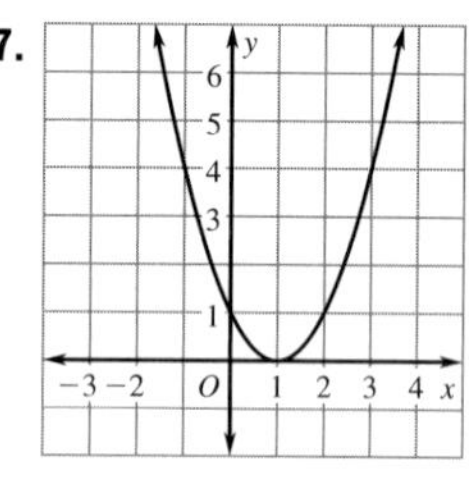

33. $f(x) = x^3$ **35.** $f(t) = (2.8 \times 10^8)(1.008)^t$; about 2.9×10^8 **37.** 4 **39.** $-1\frac{2}{3}$ **41.** 3 **43.** -3 **45.** $x^2 + 4x + 4$ **47.** $5a^2 + 14a - 3$

13.5 Technology Activity (p. 685) **1–4.** *Sample answer:* The graphs are all parabolas with the same shape and with vertices on the y-axis, but the graph moves up or down compared to the graph of $y = x^2$ by the number of units that are added to or subtracted from x^2. The graph moves up if this number is positive and down if this number is negative. **5–8.** *Sample answer:* The graphs are all downward-opening parabolas with vertices at the origin, but opening to different widths. As the absolute value of the coefficient of x^2 gets larger, the parabola becomes narrower (rises more steeply).

13.4–3.5 Notebook Review (pp. 686–687) **1.** function notation **2.** vertical line test **3.** $f(x) = 5x - 12$ **4.** $f(x) = 2x^3 + 8$ **5.** $f(x) = x^3 + 3x^2 - 10$

6.

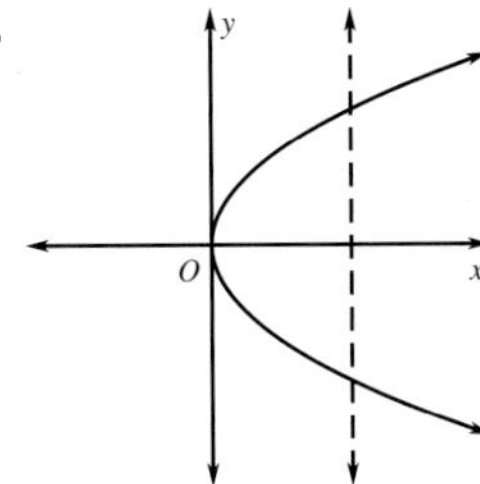

Sample answer: The graph is not that of a function because there are vertical lines that pass through more than one point of the graph.

7. $x^2 + 12x + 35$ **8.** $g^2 + 8g - 20$ **9.** $3y^2 - 13y + 4$

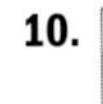

10.

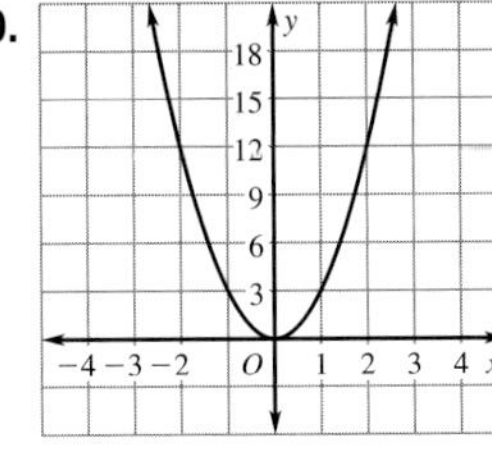

11.

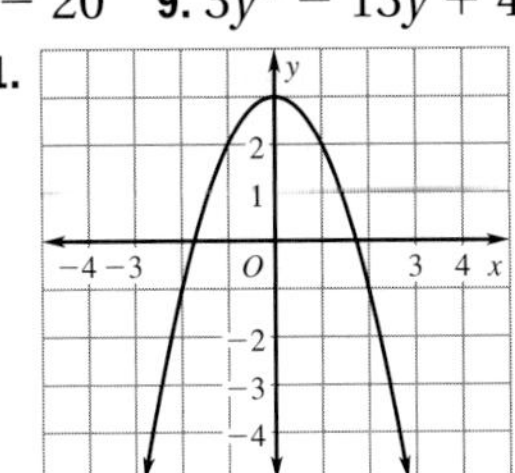

12.

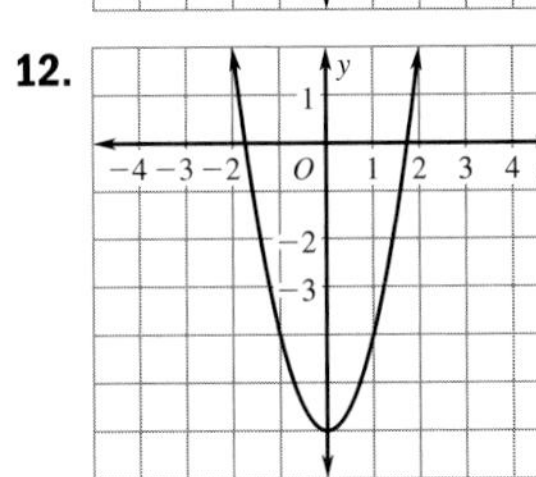

13. *Sample answer:* If there is any vertical line that intersects a graph at more than one point, then the graph does not represent a function. If every vertical line intersects a graph in at most one point, then the graph does represent a function.

Chapter Review (pp. 688–689) **1.** trinomial **3.** vertical line test **5.** monomial **7.** binomial **9.** $-3x^3 + x^2 + 5x - 4$ **11.** $6t^3 - t^2 + 9t + 8$ **13.** $-3n^4 + n^2 + 5n + 25$ **15.** $2w^2 + 3w - 8$ **17.** $-x^2 + 16x + 28$ **19.** $-10y^2 + 20y + 44$ **21.** $-3p^2$ **23.** $8y^2 - 5$ **25.** $-5v^3 - 10v^2 - 2v$ **27.** $8x^3y^3$ **29.** $-216a^6b^{12}$ **31.** $-21{,}609p^8n$ **33.** $-3a^3 + 6a^2$ **35.** $y^5 - 11y^4$ **37.** $-18g^3 - 60g^2$ **39.** $9x^2 + 27x$ **41.** $t^2 - t - 12$ **43.** $q^2 - 16q + 63$ **45.** $3d^2 - 10d - 48$ **47.** $-8k^2 + 34k + 9$ **49.** $2b^2 + 7b - 4$

51.

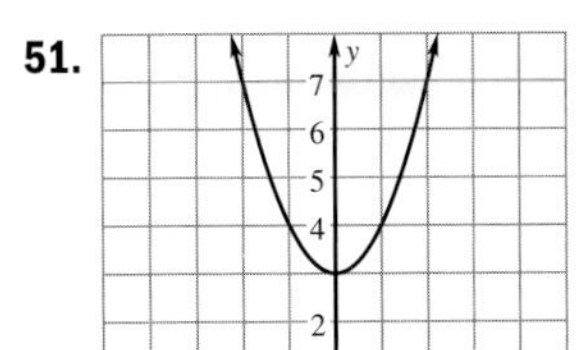

53.

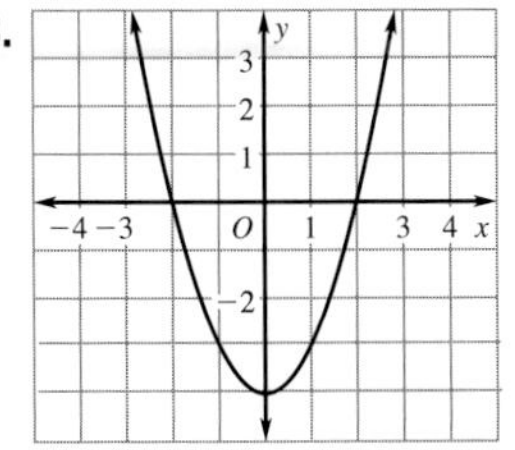

55. yes **57.** yes

Skills Review Handbook

Place Value (p. 704) **1.** $5 \times 10{,}000 + 6 \times 1000 + 8 \times 100 + 9$ **3.** $1 \times 1000 + 2 \times 1 + 3 \times 0.001$ **5.** 500,069.007

Rounding (p. 705) **1.** 1300 **3.** 8.2 **5.** 40,000 **7.** 450 **9.** 62.8 **11.** 164.5 **13.** 52.96 **15.** 3,501,700

Divisibility Tests (p. 706) **1.** 2 **3.** 3, 5 **5.** 2, 3, 4, 6, 9 **7.** 5 **9.** 2, 4

Mixed Numbers and Improper Fractions (p. 707) **1.** 38 **3.** 3 **5.** $\frac{7}{2}$ **7.** $\frac{35}{8}$ **9.** $\frac{43}{4}$ **11.** $7\frac{1}{2}$ **13.** $5\frac{2}{3}$

Ratio and Rate (p. 708) **1.** $\frac{13}{12}$; 13 to 12; 13 : 12 **3.** $\frac{11}{23}$; 11 to 23; 11 : 23 **5.** $\frac{\$24}{8 \text{ pens}} = \frac{\$3}{1 \text{ pen}}$ **7.** $\frac{280 \text{ words}}{5 \text{ min}} = \frac{56 \text{ words}}{1 \text{ min}}$ **9.** $\frac{8 \text{ in.}}{6 \text{ days}} = 1\frac{1}{3}$ in. per day

Adding and Subtracting Decimals (p. 709) **1.** 6.3 **3.** 31.1 **5.** 10.956 **7.** 2.91 **9.** 18.88 **11.** 57.8 **13.** 286.19 **15.** 88.064

Adding and Subtracting Fractions (p. 710) **1.** $\frac{2}{3}$ **3.** $\frac{3}{7}$ **5.** 1 **7.** $\frac{11}{15}$ **9.** $\frac{2}{9}$ **11.** $1\frac{7}{12}$ **13.** $\frac{1}{9}$ **15.** $\frac{9}{14}$ **17.** $\frac{7}{12}$ **19.** $1\frac{4}{7}$

Estimation in Addition and Subtraction (p. 711) **1-5.** Estimates may vary. **1.** 2700 **3.** 20,000 **5.** 2200

Solving Problems Using Addition and Subtraction (p. 712) **1.** \$93 **3.** \$2.01 **5.** 248 min

Multiplying Fractions (p. 713) **1.** $\frac{4}{5}$ **3.** $2\frac{2}{9}$ **5.** $5\frac{1}{4}$ **7.** $2\frac{4}{7}$ **9.** $\frac{8}{15}$ **11.** $\frac{3}{40}$ **13.** $\frac{10}{27}$ **15.** $\frac{25}{72}$

Multiplication of a Decimal by a Whole Number (p. 714) **1.** 225.4 **3.** 671.5 **5.** 35.28 **7.** 644.36 **9.** 1707.2 **11.** 18,663.6 **13.** 15,093.8 **15.** 36,833.5 **17.** 949.992 **19.** 3707.352 **21.** 4998.7 **23.** 1809.665 **25.** 5477.336 **27.** 120,455.25 **29.** 7564.91

Dividing Decimals (p. 715) **1.** 0.45 **3.** 0.85 **5.** 4.57 **7.** 6R2 **9.** 8R604

Estimation in Multiplication and Division (p. 716) **1-19.** Estimates may vary. **1.** 400 and 1000 **3.** 40,000 and 54,000 **5.** 30 and 40 **7.** 200 and 300 **9.** 12,000 and 20,000 **11.** 70,000 and 160,000 **13.** 12,000 and 21,000 **15.** 90 and 100 **17.** 700 and 800 **19.** 10 and 20

Solving Problems Using Multiplication and Division (p. 717) **1.** $9.48 **3.** 576 flowers

Points, Lines, and Planes (p. 718) **5.** *Sample answer:* $\overrightarrow{SR}$ and $\overrightarrow{ST}$ **7.** *Sample answer:* $\overline{SR}$

Angles (p. 719) **5.** $\angle HJK, \angle J, \angle KJH$ **7.** $\angle TUV, \angle U, \angle VUT$ **9.** $\angle FGH, \angle G, \angle HGF$

Using a Ruler (p. 720) **1-7.** Check drawings.

Using a Protractor (p. 721) **1.** 110° **3.** 88°

Using a Compass (p. 722) **1.** A good answer will show a circle with radius 4 centimeters.
3. ____________

Reading and Making Line Plots (p. 723)
1.

3. 19 people
5. 5 people

Reading and Making Bar Graphs (p. 724)
1. 9 students **3.** Vanilla and Rocky Road

Reading and Making Line Graphs (p. 725)
1. Thursday and Friday **3.**

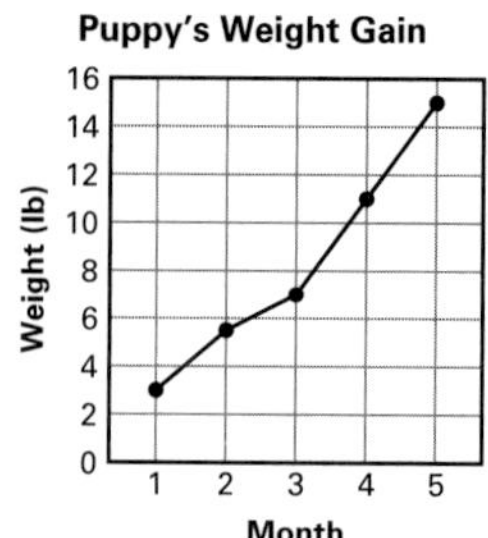

Venn Diagrams and Logical Reasoning (p. 726)
1.

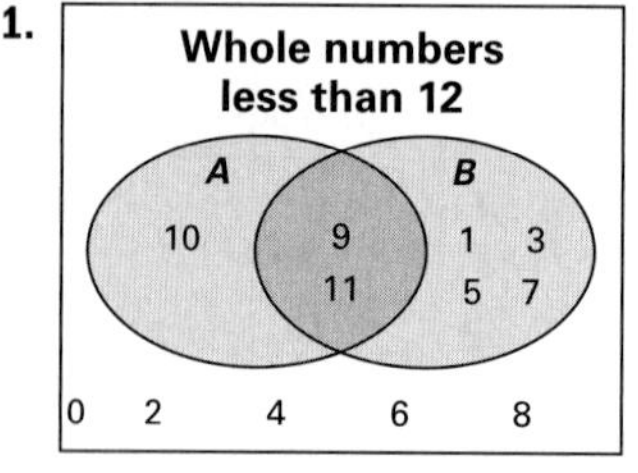

3. false; both 9 and 11 are odd numbers greater than 8 and less than 12

Extra Practice

Chapter 1 (p. 727)
1.

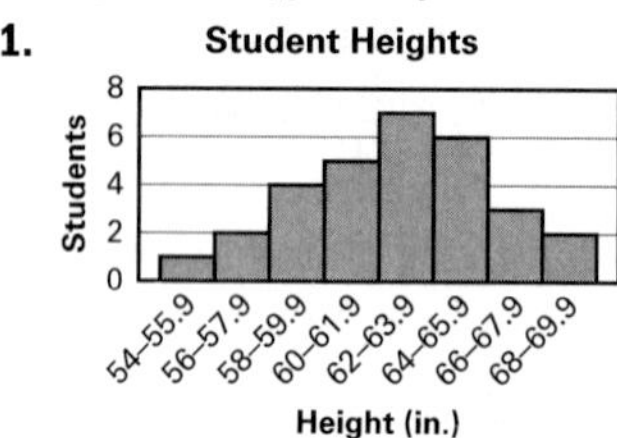

3. Yes; you can add the frequencies for the intervals 60–61.9, 62–63.9, 64–65.9, 66–67.9, and 68–69.9.

5. 7 **7.** 4 **9.** 36 **11.** 8.4 **13.** 11.7 **15.** 27 **17.** 7 **19.** 63 **21.** 8 **23.** 9 **25.** 42 ft; 104 ft^2 **27.** 8 cm

Chapter 2 (p. 728) **1.** $-43, -24, -2, 7, 19, 33$ **3.** 25; 25 **5.** 0; 0 **7.** -409 **9.** 179 **11.** 0 **13.** -16 **15.** 51 **17.** -15 **19.** 68 **21.** 350 **23.** -64 **25.** 0 **27.** 240 **29.** -12 **31.** 0 **33.** -4

35. $7\left(2 \cdot \frac{3}{7}\right)$ [original expression]

$= 7\left(\frac{3}{7} \cdot 2\right)$ [commutative property of multiplication]

$= \left(7 \cdot \frac{3}{7}\right) \cdot 2$ [associative property of multiplication]

$= 3 \cdot 2$ $\left[\text{Multiply 7 and } \frac{3}{7}.\right]$

$= 6$ [Multiply 3 and 2.]

37. $(-5)(-3) + (-5)(8); -25$ **39.** $-4 - 9r$ **41.** $5x - 2y$ **43.** $-a - 10b$

44–47.

45. Quadrant I **47.** Quadrant III

Chapter 3 (p. 729) **1.** 8 **3.** 5 **5.** 64 **7.** 4 **9.** 7 **11.** 7.5 **13.** 20 **15.** -58 **17.** $6n - 5 = 13$; 3 **19.** 1.5 h **21.** 60 in.^{2}; 36 in. **23.** 5 m; 34 m **25.** $j \geq -5$; **27.** $z \leq -2.5$; **29.** $x < -5$; **31.** $s \leq 8$;

Chapter 4 (p. 730) **1.** $2^3 \cdot 3^2$ **3.** $3^2 \cdot 17$ **5.** $5^2 \cdot p \cdot q$ **7.** $2 \cdot 11 \cdot x \cdot y \cdot y$ **9.** 15 **11.** bc **13.** $3m$ **15.** $17w^2z^2$ **17.** $\frac{1}{2}$ **19.** $-\frac{2}{7}$ **21.** $\frac{2}{9y}$ **23.** $-\frac{3a}{2c}$ **25.** 60 **27.** $15ab^2c^2$ **29.** > **31.** > **33.** < **35.** > **37.** z^6 **39.** $(-7)^9$ **41.** 6^4 **43.** $(-v)^3$ **45.** $\frac{6}{k}$ **47.** $\frac{1}{s^7}$ **49.** 1.24×10^8 **51.** 7.91×10^{-5} **53.** 0.0027 **55.** 588,000,000,000

Chapter 5 (p. 731) **1.** $1\frac{1}{2}$ **3.** $-\frac{2m}{3}$ **5.** $\frac{1}{15}$ **7.** $8\frac{1}{8}$ **9.** $\frac{3}{16}$ **11.** $-\frac{10}{27}$ **13.** $\frac{5}{18}$ **15.** $-3\frac{3}{32}$ **17.** -0.384 **19.** $-\frac{7}{25}$ **21.** $\frac{3}{500}$ **23.** 3.875 **25.** $-2.5, -2.43, -2\frac{5}{12}, -2\frac{2}{5}, -\frac{7}{3}$ **27.** $\frac{26}{5}$, 5.21, $5\frac{2}{9}$, 5.3, $5\frac{3}{8}$ **29.** 3.81 **31.** 13.1 **33.** -16.55 **35.** -8.115 **37.** 3.9104 **39.** 1.5 **41.** -31.866 **43.** -8.2 **45.** 43; 39; no mode; 57 **47.** 88; 87; 78 and 95; 22

Chapter 6 (p. 732) **1.** 7 **3.** -9 **5.** 2 **7.** -2 **9.** 5 **11.** -1 **13.** 0.13 **15.** -4 **17.** -4 **19.** 4.5 cm **21.** 7 yd; use $\frac{22}{7}$ for π since 44 is divisible by 22. **23.** $c < 2$; **25.** $s \geq -1$; **27.** $b > 8$; **29.** $\frac{1}{2}n + 12 \leq 8$; $n \leq -8$ **31.** $4n \geq 16$; $n \geq 4$ **33.** at least $1\frac{1}{2}$ h

Chapter 7 (p. 733) **1.** $\frac{3}{1}$, 3 : 1, 3 to 1 **3.** $\frac{2}{3}$, 2 : 3, 2 to 3 **5.** 4 **7.** 225 **9.** 9.3 **11.** 12% **13.** 8.96 **15.** 12.5% **17.** 72% **19.** 0.31; $\frac{31}{100}$ **21.** 1.75; $\frac{7}{4}$ **23.** increase; 12% **25.** decrease; 1% **27.** $22.08 **29.** $83\frac{1}{3}$ **31.** 0.084 **33.** $\frac{1}{6}$

Chapter 8 (p. 734) **1.** $m\angle 1 = 50°$ **3.** $m\angle 5 = 50°$; $m\angle 6 = 50°$; $m\angle 7 = 130°$ **5.** $x = 90$; right **7.** rhombus **9.** trapezoid **11.** 160° **13.** $\angle A \cong \angle P$; $\angle B \cong \angle Q$; $\angle C \cong \angle R$

15.

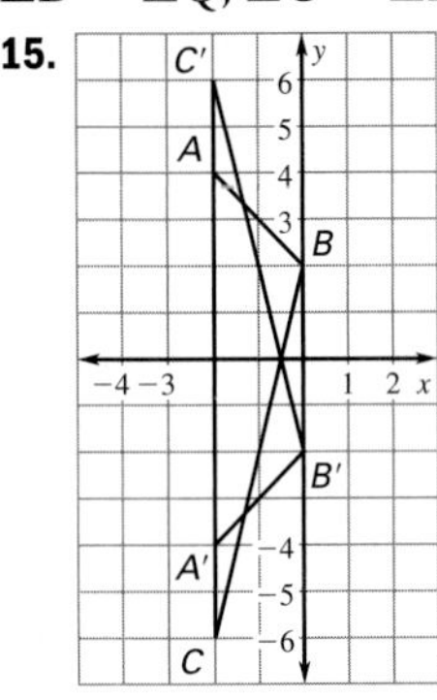

17.

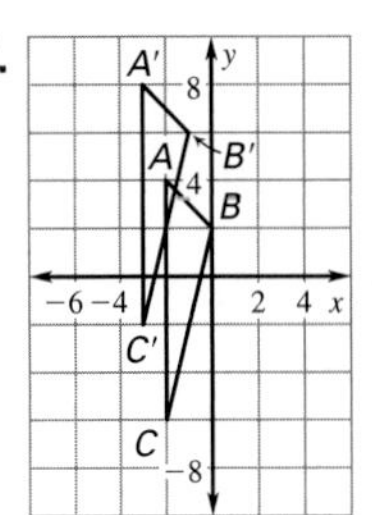

19.

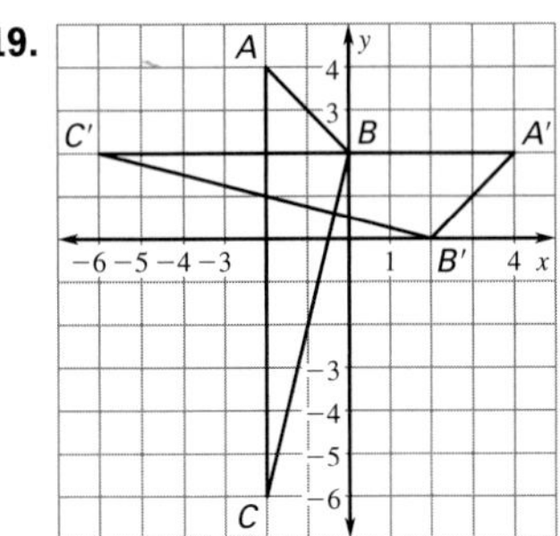

21.

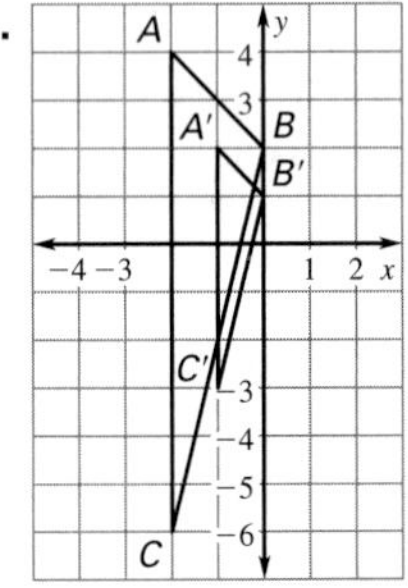

Chapter 9 (p. 735) **1.** 7.2 **3.** -27.2 **5.** 30, -30 **7.** 15, -15 **9.** 9, -9 **11.** 8, -8 **13.** > **15.** > **17.** $0.\overline{1}$, 0.12, $0.\overline{12}$, 0.123, $0.\overline{123}$ **19.** 35 **21.** 33 **23.** 75 **25.** yes **27.** yes **29.** $x = 7\sqrt{2}$; $y = 7$ **31.** $x = 19\sqrt{3}$; $y = 38$ **33.** $\sin A = \frac{36}{85}$; $\cos A = \frac{77}{85}$; $\tan A = \frac{36}{77}$; $\sin B = \frac{77}{85}$; $\cos B = \frac{36}{85}$; $\tan B = \frac{77}{36}$ **35.** $\sin 62° \approx 0.8829$; $\cos 62° \approx 0.4695$; $\tan 62° \approx 1.8807$

Chapter 10 (p. 736) **1.**

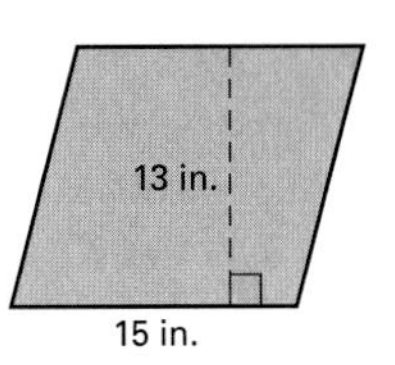

195 in.^{2}

3. $1\frac{1}{5}$ cm, $8\frac{1}{3}$ cm 10 cm^2

5. 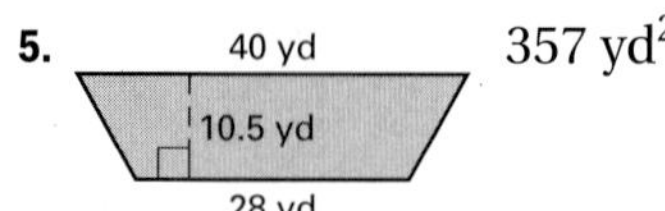

357 yd^2

7. 5020 in.^2 **9.** 26.4 ft^2 **11.** 0.283 cm^2 **13.** 201 mi^2

15. 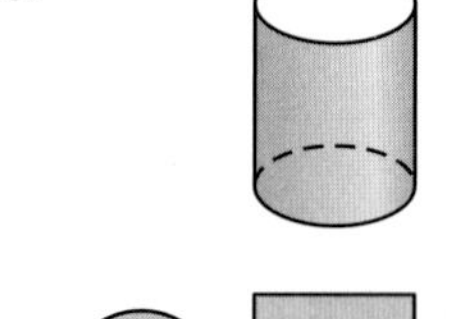

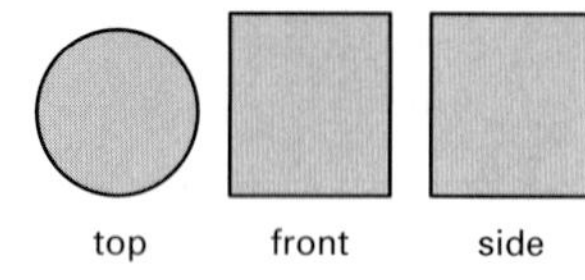

It is not a polyhedron because circles are not polygons.

17. 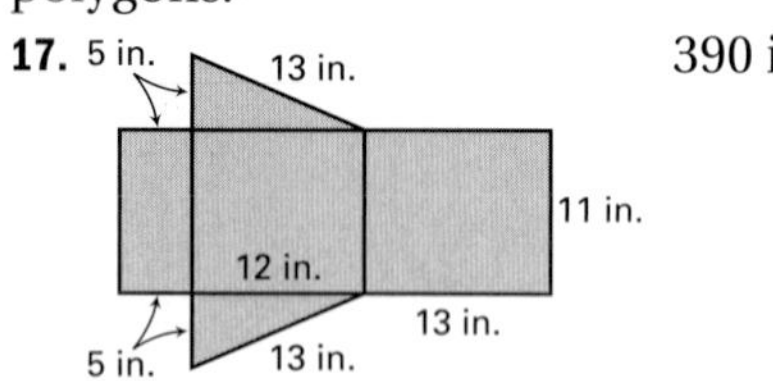

390 in.^2

19. 360 m^2 **21.** 369.9 m^2 **23.** 330 in.^3 **25.** 266.7 ft^3 **27.** 252 cm^3

Chapter 11 (p. 737) **1.** Yes; each input has exactly one output. **3.** $y = x - 1$ **5.** no **7.** yes
9. *Sample answer:* $(-2, 3)$, $(-1, 5)$, $(0, 7)$, $(1, 9)$
11. *Sample answer:* $(-2, 2)$, $(-1, 1)$, $(0, 0)$, $(1, -1)$
13. $(-2, 4)$, $(-1, 1)$, $(0, -2)$, $(1, -5)$ **15.** $(-2, -5)$, $(1, -1)$, $(4, 3)$, $(7, 7)$

17. 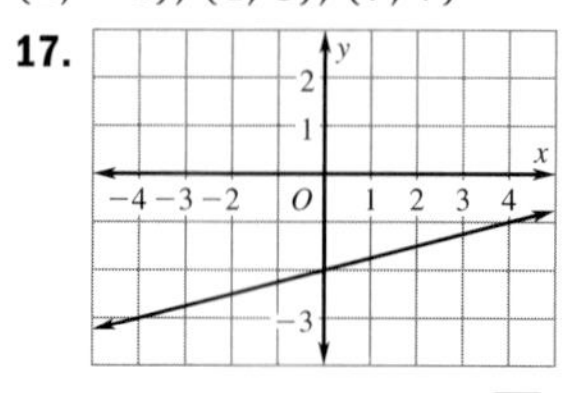

19. 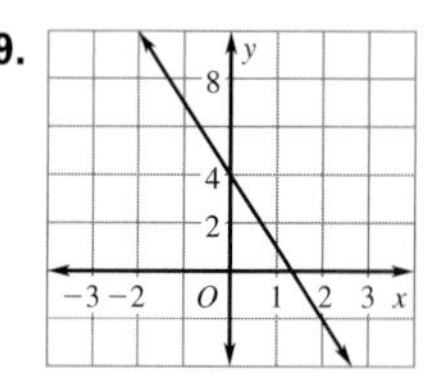

21. x-intercept, $\frac{1}{5}$; y-intercept, -1 **23.** x-intercept, 6; y-intercept, -4

25. 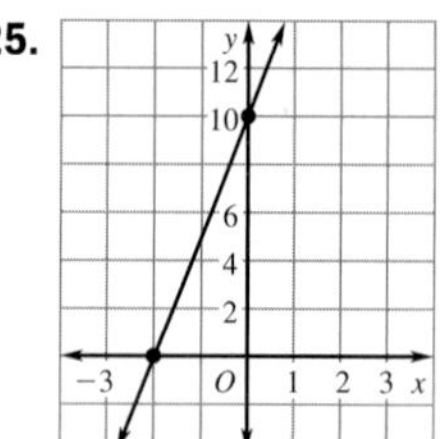

27. undefined **29.** 1 **31.** -1 **33.** $\frac{17}{3}$ **35.** 0; 2 **37.** 2; -8

39. 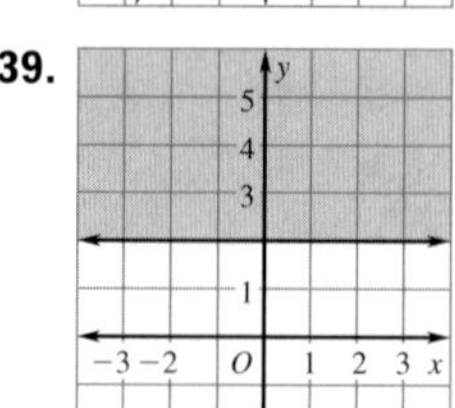

41. 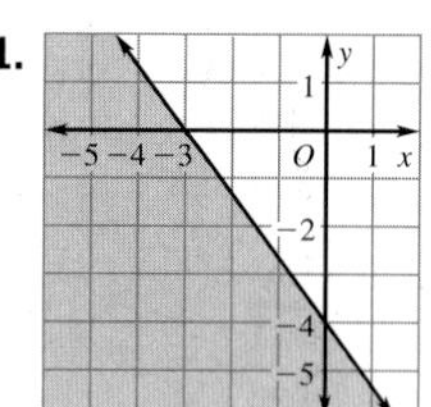

Chapter 12 (p. 738)

1.

9	9
10	0 1 3 5
11	6 7 8
12	7 9
13	0
14	0 0 3

Key: 13 | 0 = 130

100 to 109

3. 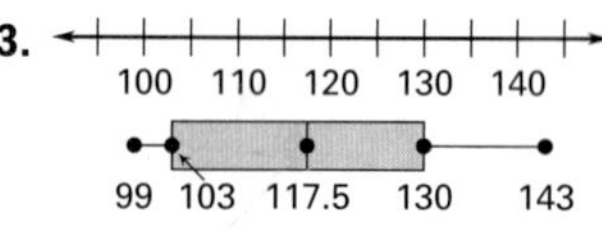

Sample answer: About 50% of the lengths were between 103 inches and 130 inches.

5. Line graph; a line graph is used to represent data that change over time. **7.** 17,576,000 license plates **9.** 11 **11.** 720 **13.** 5 **15.** 20 **17.** 4060 ways **19.** $\frac{3}{4}$ **21.** $\frac{2}{9}$

Chapter 13 (p. 739) **1.** $-x^2 - 2x + 7$ **3.** $-k^2 + 21$ **5.** $-2x^3 + 4x^2 + 14x - 4$ **7.** $3x^3 - 9x^2 + 6x - 3$ **9.** $x^3 - 2x^2 + 9x + 6$ **11.** $-28z^6$ **13.** $-6n^2 + 15n$ **15.** $125a^3b^3$ **17.** p^{24} **19.** $2x^2 - 9x - 5$ **21.** $d^2 + 10d + 24$ **23.** $a^2 - 15a + 56$ **25.** $f(x) = 2x - 5$ **27.** $f(x) = 5x^2 + 1$ **29.** 1; $\frac{1}{4}$; 0; $\frac{1}{4}$; 1 **31.** -16; -5; 0; -1; -8 **33.** -7; -4; -3; -4; -7

35. 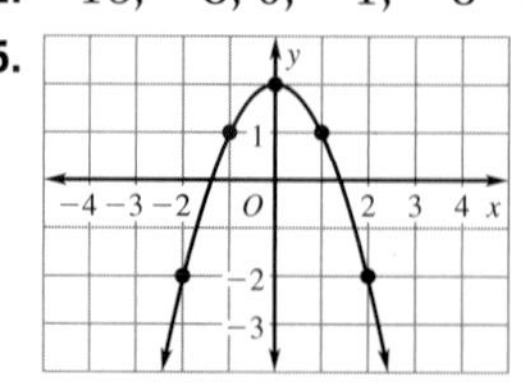

37. no **39.** yes